The Eerdmans Critical Commentary

†David Noel Freedman, *General Editor*

Astrid B. Beck, *Associate Editor*

The Eerdmans Critical Commentary offers the best of contemporary Old and New Testament scholarship, seeking to give modern readers clear insight into the biblical text, including its background, its interpretation, and its application.

Contributors to the ECC series are among the foremost authorities in biblical scholarship worldwide. Representing a broad range of confessional backgrounds, authors are charged to remain sensitive to the original meaning of the text and to bring alive its relevance for today. Each volume includes the author's own translation, critical notes, and commentary on literary, historical, cultural, and theological aspects of the text.

Accessible to serious general readers and scholars alike, these commentaries reflect the contributions of recent textual, philological, literary, historical, and archaeological inquiry, benefiting as well from newer methodological approaches. ECC volumes are "critical" in terms of their detailed, systematic explanation of the biblical text. Although exposition is based on the original and cognate languages, English translations provide complete access to the discussion and interpretation of these primary sources.

ISAIAH 40–66

Translation and Commentary

Shalom M. Paul

WILLIAM B. EERDMANS PUBLISHING COMPANY
GRAND RAPIDS, MICHIGAN / CAMBRIDGE, U.K.

Published 2012 by
Wm. B. Eerdmans Publishing Co.
2140 Oak Industrial Drive N.E., Grand Rapids, Michigan 49505 /
P.O. Box 163, Cambridge CB3 9PU U.K.

Printed in the United States of America

18 17 16 15 14 13 12 7 6 5 4 3 2 1

Library of Congress Cataloging-in-Publication Data

Paul, Shalom M.
Isaiah 40-66: translation and commentary / Shalom M. Paul.
p. cm. — (The Eerdmans critical commentary)
Includes bibliographical references.
ISBN 978-0-8028-2603-9 (pbk.: alk. paper)
1. Bible. O.T. Isaiah XL–LXVI — Commentaries.
I. Bible. O.T. Isaiah XL–LXVI . English. 2011. II. Title.

BS1515.53.P38 2011
224′.1077 — dc23

2011022239

www.eerdmans.com

To my wife Yona

on our Golden Wedding Anniversary

Contents

Preface ix

Abbreviations xi

Introduction 1

1. Deutero-Isaiah 1
2. Trito-Isaiah? 5
3. Historical Survey 12

   Excursus A: Prayer of Nabonidus 14

   Excursus B: Cyrus Cylinder 15
4. *Rishonôt* and *Ḥadashôt* 17
5. Servant Songs 18
6. Attitudes toward Foreigners and Religious Universalism 18
7. Deutero-Isaiah, Polemicist 19
8. Descriptions of Jerusalem 22
9. Descriptions of God, His Attributes, and His Relationship to His People 23
10. Unique Style and Literary Sequence 24
11. Language of the Book: Aramaic and Late Hebrew 43
12. Inner-Biblical Traditions Reflected in Deutero-Isaiah 44

13. Deuteronomic and Deuteronomistic Influences on Deutero-Isaiah 47

14. Influence of First Isaiah on Deutero-Isaiah 50

15. Influence of Jeremiah on Deutero-Isaiah 53

16. Additional Prophetic Influences on Deutero-Isaiah 55

17. Psalmic Influences on Deutero-Isaiah 56

18. Parallels between the Book of Lamentations and Deutero-Isaiah 57

19. Deutero-Isaiah and the Literary Heritage of the Ancient Near East 59

20. Isaiah Scrolls from Qumran and Ancient Translations 63

21. Deutero-Isaiah in Jewish Liturgy 71

Translation **73**

Commentary **127**

Selected Bibliography 633

Index of Authors 657

Index of Subjects 660

Literary Devices 665

Scribal Phenomena 666

Index of Sources 668

Index of Commentaries on Isaiah 711

Preface

For a score or more years, I have been enchanted by the prophecies in Isaiah 40–66, in which the anonymous prophet comforted and encouraged his people during the last years of the Babylonian exile and the early years of their return to Zion.

In this commentary I have not attempted to review all the possible interpretations of modern exegetes or the plethora of secondary literature. Medieval commentators, who are often overlooked or rarely referred to, are cited when their remarks are significant to the understanding of a verse. The reader is also referred to the comprehensive bibliography at the end of the volume that covers all aspects of this prophetic work. What is unique about this commentary is the exegesis of the Hebrew text with its emphasis on the philological, poetic, literary, linguistic, grammatical, historical, archaeological, ideational, and theological aspects of the prophecies, in which every word, phrase, clause, and verse is examined and explicated, and, in addition, aided by both inner-biblical allusions, influences, and parallels, and extrabiblical sources, primarily from Akkadian and Ugaritic literature. The Septuagint, as well as the Isaiah scrolls from Qumran — especially the complete Isaiah scroll, IQIsa[a] — are of paramount significance and are adduced when they shed light on the verses or deviate from the Masoretic text.

It is my pleasant duty to thank Dr. Tzemah Yoreh, who worked assiduously and skillfully to translate the preliminary manuscript, prior to my updating, revising, and expanding the present work, and to Ḥani Davis for her unstinting devotion, professional advice, and acumen in preparing the final version of the manuscript. I happily convey my gratitude to Allen C. Myers, senior editor of Eerdmans Publishing Company, who patiently and understandingly waited several years for my manuscript to reach his hands. The invitation to write the commentary was initiated by my very dear friend and colleague,

Professor David Noel Freedman, of blessed memory, whose wish was for my volume to launch this new series for Eerdmans. Unfortunately, he passed away before he could review and edit it, a personal loss for me since he undoubtedly would have contributed to a further understanding of the manifold issues in these prophecies. It is my hope that this volume will provide an important link in the ongoing chain of commentaries to this profound and inspiring prophetic work.

My commentary is dedicated to my loving wife, Yona, with whom I have been fortunate and blessed to have shared the last fifty years.

I would like to acknowledge the generosity of The Nathan Cummings Foundation, at the recommendation of Stephen Durchslag, Judy Lavin, and Janet and Gary Resnick, who have made this publication possible.

Shalom M. Paul
The Hebrew University of Jerusalem

Abbreviations

AB	Anchor Bible
ABD	*Anchor Bible Dictionary*
AcOr	*Acta Orientalia*
AHw	*Akkadisches Handwörterbuch*
AJSL	*American Journal of Semitic Languages and Literature*
AnBib	Analecta Biblica
ANEP	J. B. Pritchard, ed., *The Ancient Near East in Pictures Relating to the Old Testament,* 2nd ed. (Princeton, 1969)
ANET	J. B. Pritchard, ed., *Ancient Near Eastern Texts Relating to the Old Testament,* 3rd ed. (Princeton, 1969)
AOAT	Alter Orient und Altes Testament
BETL	Bibliotheca Ephemeridum Theologicarum Lovaniesium
Bib	*Biblica*
BibOr	*Biblica et orientalia*
Bijdr	*Bijdragen*
BJRL	*Bulletin of the John Rylands University Library of Manchester*
BKAT	Biblischer Kommentar: Altes Testament
BN	*Biblische Notizen*
BWANT	Beiträge zur Wissenschaft vom Alten und Neuen Testaments
BWL	W. G. Lambert, *Babylonian Wisdom Literature* (Oxford, 1960)
BZ	*Biblische Zeitschrift*
BZAW	Beihefte zur Zeitschrift für die alttestamentliche Wissenschaft
CAD	*The Assyrian Dictionary of the Oriental Institute of the University of Chicago*
CAT	M. Dietrich et al., eds., *The Cuneiform Alphabetic Texts from Ugarit, Ras Ibn Hani and Other Places* (Münster, 1995)
CB	Century Bible

CBC	Cambridge Bible Commentary
CBQ	*Catholic Biblical Quarterly*
CCAR	*Central Conference of American Rabbis: A Reform Jewish Quarterly*
CHANE	Culture and History of the Ancient Near East
COS	W. W. Hallo et al., eds., *The Context of Scripture,* 3 vols. (Leiden, 1997-2002)
CTM	Calwer theologische Monographien
DJD	Discoveries in the Judean Desert
DSSSE	F. García Martínez and E. J. C. Tigchelaar, eds., *The Dead Sea Scrolls Study Edition,* 2 vols. (repr. Grand Rapids, 2000)
EJ	*Encyclopaedia Judaica*
ErIsr	*Eretz Israel*
ETL	*Ephemerides theologicae Lovanienses*
EvQ	*Evangelical Quarterly*
EvT	*Evangelische Theologie*
FAT	Forschungen zum Alten Testament
FRLANT	Forschungen zur Religion und Literatur des Alten und Neuen Testaments
GKC	*Gesenius' Hebrew Grammar,* ed. E. Kautzsch, trans. A. E. Cowley, 2nd ed. (Oxford, 1910)
HAR	*Hebrew Annual Review*
HCOT	Historical Commentary on the Old Testament
HdO	*Handbuch der Orientalistik*
HKAT	Handkommentar zum Alten Testament
HS	*Hebrew Studies*
HSM	Harvard Semitic Monographs
HTR	*Harvard Theological Review*
HUCA	*Hebrew Union College Annual*
ICC	International Critical Commentary
IEJ	*Israel Exploration Journal*
Int	*Interpretation*
IOS	*Israel Oriental Studies*
JANES	*Journal of the Ancient Near Eastern Society*
JAOS	*Journal of the American Oriental Society*
JBL	*Journal of Biblical Literature*
JBQ	*Jewish Bible Quarterly*
JNES	*Journal of Near Eastern Studies*
JQR	*Jewish Quarterly Review*
JSOT	*Journal for the Study of the Old Testament*
JSOTSup	Journal for the Study of the Old Testament Supplement

JSS	*Journal of Semitic Studies*
JTS	*Journal of Theological Studies*
KAI	H. Donner and W. Röllig, *Kanaanäische und aramäische Inschriften*, 3 vols. (Wiesbaden, 1964-68; vol. 1, 5th ed., Wiesbaden, 2002)
KAT	Kommentar zum Alten Testament
LCL	Loeb Classical Library
LD	Lectio divina
Leš	*Lešonenu*
LXX	Septuagint
MT	Masoretic text
OBT	Overtures to Biblical Theology
OTL	Old Testament Library
OtSt	*Oudtestamentische Studiën*
RB	*Revue biblique*
RSR	*Recherches de science religieuse*
SAA	State Archives of Assyria
SBLDS	Society of Biblical Literature Dissertation Series
SBLWAW	Society of Biblical Literature Writings from the Ancient World
SBT	Studies in Biblical Theology
SFSHJ	South Florida Studies in the History of Judaism
SJOT	*Scandinavian Journal of the Old Testament*
SP	Studia Pohl
ST	*Studia Theologica*
STDJ	Studies on the Texts of the Desert of Judah
SThU	*Schweizerische theologische Umschau*
ThR	*Theologische Rundschau*
TZ	*Theologische Zeitschrift*
UF	*Ugarit-Forschungen*
VF	*Verkündigung und Forschung*
VT	*Vetus Testamentum*
VTSup	Vetus Testamentum Supplement
WMANT	Wissenschaftliche Monographien zum Alten und Neuen Testament
ZAW	*Zeitschrift für die alttestamentliche Wissenschaft*
ZTK	*Zeitschrift für Theologie und Kirche*

Introduction

1. DEUTERO-ISAIAH

The Masoretic book of Isaiah is composed of two distinct sections written by two different authors at different times. The first section (chaps. 1–39, with the possible exceptions of chaps. 34 and 35; see below) was composed by Isaiah ben Amoz of Jerusalem (First or Proto-Isaiah), and the second by an anonymous prophet, referred to as Second or Deutero-Isaiah, whose prophecies (encompassing chaps. 40–66) were added to the opus of his predecessor. The melding of these two works into one book is quite ancient, as is evident from Sir 48:24 (composed ca. 190 BCE): "With inspired power he prophesied the future (חזה אחרית) and consoled the mourners in Zion (וינחם אבלי ציון)," which clearly alludes to both Isa 2:1 and 61:2-3. Moreover, in the large Isaiah scroll discovered in Cave 1 of Khirbet Qumran (1QIsa[a]), dated to the mid-second century BCE, there is no sign of a separation between the two sections of the book. The present-day accepted division is based on many distinctive features, for example, differences in language (the second half of the book is characterized by Late Postexilic Hebrew and bears signs of Aramaic influence; see below, §11) and ideology, including his concept of universal monotheism, the incomparability and singularity of God, his fierce polemic against idol worship, the eternal covenant of God with the nation, his religious universalism, the future splendor of Jerusalem, and the sui generis idea of the divine servant (see below, §5). Special attention must also be paid to the different historical background reflected in his prophecies that distinguishes him from First Isaiah.

First Isaiah prophesied in Jerusalem during the second half of the eighth century BCE, at a time when both the northern kingdom of Judah and the southern kingdom of Israel were still in existence, and when the nation was still in possession of its ancestral land (although the north was indeed destroyed in the latter days of his prophetic career). The monarchs referred to in Isaiah's prophecies are Uzziah (1:1; 6:1), Jotham (1:1), Ahaz (1:1; 7:1, 3, 10, 12; 38:8), and Hezekiah (1:1; and frequently in chaps. 36–39) — kings of Judah; Pekah son of Remaliah, king of Israel (7:1, 4, 5, 9; 8:6); and Rezin, king of Aram (7:1, 4, 8; 8:6; 9:10) — all of whom rule within this time frame. The Assyrians are the sole enemy mentioned (e.g., 7:17, 20; 8:4, 7; 10:12 [scholars acknowledge the prophecy against Babylon in chap. 13 to be a late addition]), serving as the rod of the divine wrath (10:5). Three of their kings are noted by name — Sargon (20:1), Sennacherib (36:1; 37:17, 21, 37), and Esarhaddon (37:38) — while the Babylonian monarch, Merodach-baladan, is presented in the positive light of a well-wisher, following Hezekiah's recovery from illness (39:1). The events described in chaps. 1–39 all occurred in this period, for example, the death of Uzziah, king of Judah (chap. 6); the war between Judah and the Syro-Ephraimite alliance (chaps. 7–8); the Assyrian conquest of Ashdod (chap. 20); and, above all, the capture of the Judean cities and the siege against Jerusalem in 701 BCE (chaps. 36–37).

In contrast, Deutero-Isaiah prophesied in the second half of the sixth century BCE, during the final years of the Babylonian exile and the beginning of the return of the exiles to Jerusalem. The kingdom of Israel had ceased to exist many years earlier (720 BCE), and the Judean monarchy had met the same fate in 586 BCE. The cities of Judah, foremost among them Jerusalem, and the Temple were in ruins, while the forlorn Israelites languished in the Babylonian exile. Babylon, itself on the brink of destruction, is depicted as full of sorceries (44:25; 47:9-15), riches (45:3), overweening pride ("I am, and there is none but me"; 47:8, 10), and possessed by an overblown sense of security and self-importance (47:1, 7, 8). The description of the deportation of its two chief deities — Bel (= Marduk, the head of the Babylonian pantheon) and his son, Nebo (= Nabû, the divine scribe; 46:1-2) — alludes to Babylon's imminent downfall. In the latter chapters, the prophet describes the domestic scene prevalent in Jerusalem, where pagan practices prevail and a discernible split is evident within the community itself (e.g., chaps. 65–66).

The only foreign monarch who appears in the prophecies of Deutero-Isaiah is Cyrus, king of Persia (559-530 BCE), who is mentioned by name (44:28; 45:1), alluded to explicitly (41:2-3, 25; 43:14; 45:2-6, 13; 46:11; 48:14-15), and referred to as "My shepherd" (44:28), "His anointed one" (45:1), and "the man of My counsel" (46:11). Cyrus appears on history's stage as a tool of God whose purpose is to free Israel from captivity and perform the divine will of rebuilding the Temple and Jerusalem (44:28). The nation, in turn, is commanded: "Go forth from Babylon! Flee from Chaldea!" (48:20; and cf. 52:11). In contrast to First Isaiah, who predicts the ascension of a Davidic scion in the latter days (11:1-9), Deutero-Isaiah reinterprets these promises of the eternal covenant promised to David as applying to the nation as a whole (55:3-4) — an ideological revolution at odds with most of the historiographical and psalmic literature (e.g., 1 Sam 25:28; 2 Sam 7:4-17; 23:5; 1 Kgs 2:4; 8:23-26; 11:38; Ps 89:25-37; 132:10), as well as the prophetic literature (e.g., Jer 23:5-6; 33:14-18, 19-22, 26; Ezek 34:23-24; 37:24-25; Hag 2:23).

This bipartite division of the canonical book of Isaiah was first alluded to in Abraham Ibn Ezra's commentary (where he also quotes the Spanish sage Moshe ben Shemuel HaKohen ben Jaqtila, who lived in Cordoba at the beginning of the eleventh century CE), where he comments several times that chaps. 40ff. are prophecies of consolation delivered to the Babylonian expatriates, that is, to Deutero-Isaiah's contemporaries:

> The first consolations from the second half of the book refer to the Second Temple, according to Rabbi Moshe Hakohen, may he rest in peace. And according to my opinion, they all refer to our exile. Nevertheless, issues of the Babylonian exile are spoken of in the book, along with mention of Cyrus, who freed the expatriates. At the end of the book, however, there are references to the future . . . and he who is wise shall understand.
>
> (Ibn Ezra, commentary on 40:1)

> Or it is a reference to the Babylonians, and that is correct. . . . Indeed, I have already hinted to you of the secret in the second half of the book. And according to many, the mention of "kings" (in his prophecies) refers, for example, to Cyrus.
>
> (Ibn Ezra on 49:7)

> We have already said regarding this prophecy that it refers to the Babylonian exile.
>
> (Ibn Ezra on 52:1)

See also his remarks on, for example, 41:2, 6, 25; 43:14, 16; 44:25; 45:1; 46:11.

The distinction between the two parts of the book was rediscovered by J. Ch. Döderlein in 1776 in his Latin commentary to Isaiah and popularized by J. G. Eichhorn in 1783, and since then has become part and parcel of all scholarly research. One reason for combining the two sets of prophecies was their linguistic affinity, which was due to the influence of First Isaiah on this prophet (see below, §14) — though, as will be seen, Deutero-Isaiah was influenced just as much, if not more, by Jeremiah (see below, §15). Another likely motive for the combination of the two prophetic works was the desire to append prophecies of consolation and comfort to the impending exile prophesied in chap. 39. After Israel would serve their term of punishment, they would be redeemed. Compare Ibn Ezra's comment on 40:1: "This passage [i.e., chap. 40] comes next, since above [39:6-7] it was prophesied that all the king's treasure and his sons would be exiled to Babylon, and thus there follow prophecies of consolation." A narrative continuity spanning the three great empires of the ancient Near East — Assyria, Babylonia, and Persia — is thereby established.

(A) Isaiah 34–35

According to many commentators, chap. 34 and, in particular, chap. 35 should also be attributed to Deutero-Isaiah. Their claims are based primarily on the linguistic and thematic affinities between these two chapters and the prophecies of Deutero-Isaiah:

(1) Chapter 34

34:1-5; 66:15-16: A general trial against the nations.

34:6-17; 63:1-6: The specific mention of the destruction of Edom.

Common images:

34:6: "The Lord has a sword; it is sated with blood. . . . For the Lord holds a sacrifice in Bozrah, a great slaughter in the land of Edom" — 63:1: "Who is this coming from Edom, in crimsoned garments from Bozrah?"

34:8: "For it is the Lord's day of vengeance, the year of vindication for Zion's cause" — 63:4: "For I had planned a day of vengeance, and My year of redemption arrived"; cf. also 61:2: "And a day of vengeance for our God."

(2) Chapter 35

Ecological reversal — Water in the desert and the flowering of the wilderness: 35:1-2; 41:18-19; 43:19-20; 44:3; 49:10; 51:3. Note too 35:6-7: "For waters shall burst forth in the desert, streams in the wilderness. Torrid earth shall become a pool; parched land, fountains of water" — the term שרב ("torrid earth") appears only here and in 49:10; and the expression: מבועי מים ("fountains of waters") only in this verse and 49:10.

Common images:

The revelation of the Lord's presence: 35:2: "They shall behold the Lord's presence" — 40:5: "The presence of the Lord shall appear, and all flesh, as one, shall behold"; cf. 59:19; 60:1-2, 13; 61:6; 62:2.

The consolation and encouragement of Israel: 35:4: "Say . . . 'Fear not! Behold your God!'" — 40:9: "Fear not! Say . . . 'Behold your God!'"

Revenge on the nations: 35:4: "Vengeance is coming, the recompense of God. He Himself is coming to give you triumph" — 63:4-5: "For I had planned a day of vengeance, and My year of redemption arrived. . . . So My own arm wrought the triumph." For the bringing of God's "recompense" upon the nations, see also 59:18.

The return of the redeemed to Israel on a straight and level highway: 35:8: "And a highway shall appear there" — 40:3: "Clear in the desert a road for the Lord! Level in the wilderness a highway for our God!" (cf. also 57:14; 62:10). This road shall be named "the Sacred Way" (35:8), or, alternatively, "the Lord's Road" (40:3). The image of a path or highway in the desert is reiterated in 42:16; 43:19; 49:9, 11; 57:14; 62:10.

35:10: This verse, "And the ransomed of the Lord shall return and come with shouting to Zion, crowned with joy everlasting. They shall attain joy and gladness, while sorrow and sighing flee," is repeated word for word in 51:11; and the expression שׂמחת עולם ("joy everlasting") appears again in 61:7.

The image of the blind and deaf: 35:5; 42:18-20.

The synonymous pair שׂושׂ/גיל ("to be glad/to rejoice") is found in 35:1; 61:10; 65:18-19; 66:10; and the term גילה ("exultation") appears only in 35:2; 65:18.

The expression "the glory of Lebanon" (כבוד הלבנון) is present only in 35:2; 60:13.

Compare also the terms גאולים ("the redeemed"; 35:9; 51:10), גאולי ה׳ ("the redeemed of the Lord"; 62:12), which appears again only in Ps 107:2.

Although it is not at all certain that chap. 34 was once part of Deutero-Isaiah's opus, it is entirely possible that chap. 35 was, since, as seen above, this chapter shares a fair number of features characteristic of his prophecies. Chapter 35 may have originally preceded chap. 40, prior to the addition of the historical chapters (Isa 36–39).

2. TRITO-ISAIAH?

A major turning point in the study of this book was reached in 1892 with the publication of B. Duhm's commentary on Isaiah and his contention that chaps. 56ff. were the work of a different prophet, called "Trito-Isaiah." (He was preceded by the Dutch scholar Abraham Kuenen, who made similar claims in the

1880s.) Many scholars have accepted his opinion, although there is no basic agreement among them regarding the exact date of composition. Proposed dates range from the first years following the return from Babylonia, from the period of the prophets Haggai and Zechariah (mid–sixth century BCE), from the days of Ezra and Nehemiah (mid–fifth century BCE), and some even date the opus as late as the third century BCE. Commentators also disagree about the unity of these chapters. Some posit that they were composed by one individual, while others claim that they are a disparate collection of prophecies from different periods. The various arguments for the division of chaps. 40–66 into two separate units are presented below, together with their respective refutations.

Beginning with chap. 56, there is an increased emphasis on the prophetic rebuke against the people's present conduct (e.g., 56:9-12; 57:3-13; 58:1-14; 59:1-18; 65:1-15; 66:1-9, 15-17, 24), as opposed to Deutero-Isaiah's concentration on the sins of the past (e.g., 42:18-21; 43:22-28; 50:1). However, there is ample proof of the prophet's calling the people to task also for their iniquities in the present (e.g., 46:8, 12; 48:4-11; 50:11; 51:13).

Some claim that one can deduce from some of the later chapters that both the Temple (56:5, 7; 60:7, 13; 62:9; 66:1, 6, 20, 23; cf. the term הר קדשי, "My holy mountain," 56:7; 57:13; 65:11; 66:20) and the walls of Jerusalem were already rebuilt (49:16; 56:5; 60:10, 18; 62:6). This is cited as evidence of a later period, since the foundation of the Second Temple took place in 515 BCE (Ezra 6:15) and the walls of the city were rebuilt only in 445 BCE. This may be countered, however, by citing Isa 64:10 (properly part of Trito-Isaiah according to this theory), which explicitly states that "our holy temple" was still in ruins, and there is no indication whatsoever in the verses referred to above of the actual completion of the walls. All references are to the future when, for example, "Aliens shall rebuild your walls" (60:10). This is very similar to 44:28: "He shall say of Jerusalem, 'She shall be rebuilt,' and to the Temple, 'You shall be founded again'"; and 49:16: "Your walls are ever before Me," an obvious reference to the future, since none will argue that at the time of Deutero-Isaiah the walls had been rebuilt.

There is a difference in the geographical locus of the prophecies. The claim is made that the prophecies in chaps. 40–55 were delivered in a Babylonian milieu, whereas chaps. 56–66 were composed for a Jerusalem audience, in a different locus and therefore by a different prophet. Some, however, contend that chap. 49 is the turning point, wherein the Jerusalem background can be detected (e.g., 49:14-23; 51:1-3, 17-23; cf., as well, 52:11: "Depart from there," in comparison to 48:20: "Go forth from Babylon! Flee from Chaldea!" — the locus of the latter referring to the Babylonian captivity). The Babylonian setting of the first nine chapters (40–48) is blatantly clear (see especially 43:14; 46:1-2; 47; 48:14, 20). The reason for the shift in focus from Babylon to Jerusalem is not due to the appearance of a different prophet. Rather, it seems very likely that

Deutero-Isaiah practiced as he preached and returned to Jerusalem with his compatriots, where he continued his prophetic career.

After chap. 48 there is no further mention of Cyrus, in contrast to his being previously mentioned specifically by name (44:28; 45:1) and by allusions (41:2-3, 25; 43:14; 45:2-6, 13; 46:11; 48:14-15), which leave no doubt as to his identity. However, this lack of concern regarding Cyrus in chaps. 49ff. does not point to a different author, but rather to the fact that after Cyrus's conquest of Babylon in 539 (see below, §3) the king was no longer of any interest to Deutero-Isaiah, since his importance in the eyes of the prophet was restricted solely to the role he played in helping to bring about the redemption of the nation and in serving as the agent for the Deity's plan for Israel.

Some claim that there is a dissonance between the earlier chapters and the later ones with regard to the redeemer and the redemption. According to chaps. 40–48, the redeemer is Cyrus, who shall put an end to the Babylonian hegemony, and thus redemption is understood in historical terms. Chapters 56–66 indicate, however, that the Lord is the sole redeemer, and that He alone contends on Israel's behalf (e.g., 59:16-20; 63:1-6; 66:16-17), and thus redemption is essentially eschatological. In the earlier chapters, Cyrus indeed stands tall on history's stage. All his actions, however, are initiated by the Deity, and he is no more than the instrument with which God implements His plan to bring about Israel's redemption (regarding the polemic against a foreign king as redeemer see 45:9-13). Thus Cyrus's role does not in any way contradict the assertion that God and God alone is Israel's savior (see 43:1; 44:22, 23; 48:20; 52:3, 9). Nevertheless, his conception of redemption did become eschatological and did become contingent on the nation's conduct (58:1-14). Redemption was shifted to the future since Deutero-Isaiah's earlier prophecies of redemption were not fully realized.

Some argue that the conquest and subjugation of the world by Cyrus (41:2-3; 45:1-6) stands in contrast to an Israelite empire, with Jerusalem as its international capital and locus of tribute (e.g., 60; 61:6; 66:12). This dichotomy, however, does not truly exist, since the subjugation of foreign kings is described also in the earlier chapters (49:7, 22-23). Israel shall conquer nations (54:3) and command peoples: "So you shall summon a nation you did not know, and a nation that did not know you shall come running to you" (55:5).

The motif of repossession of the land by the Lord's servants appears only in chaps. 56–66 (e.g., 57:13; 60:11; 61:7; 65:9). The rationale for this, however, is quite simple. The earlier chapters emphasize the nation's redemption from captivity, and only afterward, when the expatriates have returned, does the prophet emphasize the repossession and inheritance of the land.

In the earlier chapters the prophet's audience is the entire nation: "And all your children shall be disciples of the Lord" (54:13) and are named "the Lord's servant" (in the singular; see below). The later chapters (chaps. 56–66), on the other hand, are characterized by a socioreligious schism dividing the returnees. A struggle ensues between "My servants" (65:8, 9, 13, 14, 15) — who are also called "mourners" (57:18; 61:2; 66:10), "mourners in Zion" (61:3), "all you who love her [Jerusalem]" (66:10), "My chosen ones" (65:9, 15), "those who trust in Me" (57:13), "who is concerned about My word" (66:2), "You who are concerned about His word" (66:5), "My people who seek Me" (65:10), "righteous . . . pious men" (57:1) — and a second group, variously termed "you who forsake the Lord" (65:11), "the wicked" (57:20, 21), "His foes" (66:6, 14), "the men who rebelled against Me" (66:24), "your kinsmen who hate you, who spurn you" (66:5). It follows from 66:3-4 that the priestly caste was among those adverse to Deutero-Isaiah and his teachings (see the commentary on chap. 66). This schism, however, which may reflect a struggle between the returnees and the nonexiled Judeans, emerged only when the two groups came into contact following the return. There is, however, no reason to date this national schism to the days of Ezra and Nehemiah (Ezra 4; Neh 5), since its existence is already apparent from Jer 24; Ezek 33:23-29.

In the earlier chapters, the nation as a whole is called "(the Lord's) servant," almost invariably in the singular (41:8, 9; 42:1, 19; 43:10; 44:1-2, 21, 26; 45:4; 48:20; 49:3, 5-6; 50:10; 52:13; 53:11; the only exception being 54:17). In the later chapters, however, the term always appears in the plural (56:6; 63:17; 65:8-9, 13-15; 66:14). The reason for this difference is, as mentioned above, the national schism that emerged only upon the return, when only those loyal to the Lord were called His servants. Nevertheless, the earlier chapters also remonstrate against the "deaf and blind ones" (42:18-19) who sinned (43:22-25, 27; 44:22; 50:1) and rebelled against Him (46:8; 48:8), and those "stubborn of heart" (46:12) "who swear . . . though not in truth and sincerity" (48:1).

The latter prophecies of Deutero-Isaiah include numerous terms and ideas that originate in his earlier ones. These are presented below in table form:

40:3 קול קורא במדבר פַּנּוּ דרך ה׳ יַשְּׁרוּ בערבה מְסִלה לאלהינו	57:14 ואמר סֹלּוּ סֹלּוּ פַּנּוּ דרך 62:10 פַּנּוּ דרך העם סֹלּוּ סֹלּוּ המְסִלה
40:10 הנה אדֹנָי ה׳ בְּחָזָק יבוא . . . הנה שׂכרו אתו ופעֻלתו לפניו	62:11 הנה ישעֵך בא הנה שׂכרו אתו ופעֻלתו לפניו
41:19 ברוש תדהר ותאשור יחדָּו	60:13 ברוש תדהר ותאשור יחדָּו

42:7 לפקח עינַיִם עִוְרות להוציא מִמסגר אסיר מבית כֶּלֶא יֹשְׁבֵי חֹשֶׁךְ	61:1 לקרֹא לשבוּיִם דרור ולאסורים פְּקַח־קוֹחַ
43:18 אל תִּזכרו רִאשֹׁנות	65:17 ולא תזכרנה הרִאשֹׁנות
46:13 קֵרבתי צִדקתי לא תרחק ותשועתי לא תְאַחֵר	56:1 כי קרובה ישועתי לבוא וצִדקתי להִגָּלות
48:22 אין שלום אמר ה׳ לרשעים	57:21 אין שלום אמר אלֹהי לרשעים
49:12 הנה אלה מרחוק יבֹאו והנה אלה מצפון ומִיָּם ואלה מארץ סינים 49:18 שאי סביב עיניך וראי כֻּלָּם נקבצו באו לך 49:22 והביאו בנַיִךְ בחֹצֶן ובנֹתַיִךְ על כתף תנשאנה	60:4 שאי סביב עיניך וראי כלם נקבצו באו לך בניך מרחוק יבאו ובנֹתיך על צד תֵּאָמַנָה
49:23 והיו מלכים אֹמנַיִךְ ושָׂרותיהם מיניקֹתַיִךְ אַפַּיִם ארץ ישתחוו לך ועפר רגלַיִךְ יְלחכו וידעתְּ כי אני ה׳ אשר לא יֵבֹשׁוּ קֹוָי	60:14 והלכו אלַיִךְ שְׁחוחַ בני מעַנַּיִךְ והשתחוו על כפות רגלַיִךְ כל מנאצָיִךְ 60:16 וידעתְּ כִּי אני ה׳ מושיעֵךְ
49:26 וְיָדעו כל בשר כי אני ה׳ מושיעֵךְ וגֹאֲלֵךְ אֲבִיר יעקב	60:16 וידעתְּ כי אני ה׳ מושיעֵךְ וגֹאלֵךְ אֲבִיר יעקב
50:2 הֲקָצור קצרה ידי מִפדות	59:1 הן לא קָצרה יד ה׳ מֵהושיע
52:12 כי הֹלך לפניכם ה׳ ומְאַסִּפְכֶם אלֹהי ישראל	58:8 והלך לפניך צִדקך כבוד ה׳ יַאַסְפֶךָ

These shared ideas and terminology, however, do not imply plural authorship, since the prophet may very well cite his own words. Compare, for example, the fourfold repetition of a prophecy of Jeremiah in 7:34; 16:9; 25:10; 33:11. Moreover, these citations were often adapted and expanded to fit the changing situation and integrated into their new context.

The prophet's polemic against foreign rituals (57:3-13; 65:3-7, 11; 66:3-4, 17) reflects the situation that emerged in Jerusalem following the return from exile. Conversely, there is no mention of the national sins that prevailed in the days of Ezra and Nehemiah, such as intermarriage (Ezra 10:2, 10, 14, 17, 18, 44; Neh 13:26, 27) or the indenture of children (Neh 5:5).

The prophet's revolutionary egalitarian policy regarding inclusion of foreigners in the national effort to rebuild the walls and their participation in the Temple ministry (56:3, 6-7; 60:6-7, 10; 61:5; 66:21) is to be explained as an adaptation to the new conditions prevailing in Israel after the return from Babylonia.

The distinction between "the word of the Lord" that comes to pass (45:23; 55:10-11), an idea well anchored in Deuteronomistic theology (e.g., Deut 18:21-22; 2 Kgs 17:23; 24:2), and "the word of the Lord" that is said to perform the divine will is not reason in and of itself to divide the opus between two prophets.

The renamings of Jerusalem (Isa 60:14; 62:4, 12), of its walls and gates (60:18), of the land (62:4), and of the loyal followers of the Deity (61:3, 6; 62:12) are part of the prophet's vision of the future and serve as a symbol of rejuvenation.

On the other hand, the following ideas are commonly shared by the two sections:

Consolation of the people, or at least the loyal segment of the people (40:1; 49:13; 51:3, 12, 19; 52:9; 61:2; 66:13)

The expectation of an ingathering (49:17-23; 56:8; 57:14; 60:4, 9; 62:10; 66:20)

Jerusalem referred to as "daughter Zion" (52:2; 62:11), and described, on the one hand, as desolate, bereaved, and forsaken (49:14, 17; 54:1, 6, 7; 60:15; 61:4; 62:4, 12; 64:9), and, on the other hand, as a city that shall be splendidly rebuilt (44:26; 54:11-12; 62:3-4) and shall become the focus of international pilgrimage and tribute (45:14; 60:5-9, 11, 13; 66:12)

An "eternal covenant" (ברית עולם) made between the Lord and His people (55:3; 61:8)

Images of the Lord as a female figure (42:14; 45:10; 49:14-15; 66:13)

An ambivalent attitude toward the nations: they shall transport the Judeans back to Zion (49:22; 60:4; 66:20) and shall be their subjects (45:14; 49:23; 60:14), effectively converting to Yahwism (45:22-24; 56:7). The prophet, however, also warns that they shall perish (49:26; 60:12). (Regarding the prophet's universalism and his attitude toward the nations, see below, §6.)

Shared expressions: כבוד ה' ("the Lord's presence"; 40:5; 58:8; 60:1); כבודו ("His presence"; 60:2); כבודי ("My presence"; 66:18, 19)

לאור גוים ("a light of nations"; 42:6; 49:6); לאור עמים ("for the light of peoples"; 51:4); והלכו גוים לאורך ("and nations shall walk by Your light"; 60:3)

Both parts of the book employ the term הָרִאשֹׁנוֹת (41:22; 42:9; 48:3; 65:17). For the meaning of this term see below, §4 (note that in 65:16 the meaning of this term is different)

In the first part of the book, the Lord is the creator of the heavens and earth (40:26, 28; 42:5; 45:12, 18), and in the second He creates "a new heaven and a new earth" (65:17; 66:22)

The so-called watershed between chaps. 55 and 56, separating Deutero-Isaiah from "Trito-Isaiah," is artificial since, as will be shown in the introduction to chap. 56, there are clear linguistic and thematic links between the two.

It appears, therefore, that there is no conclusive reason to attribute chaps. 56–66 to a distinct and later prophet living in the mid–fifth century (or later). The period reflected in these chapters is no later than the early years following the return. If one draws a line between two sections of the book, the line should be drawn between the prophecies delivered in Babylonia (chaps. 40–48) and those delivered in Jerusalem (chaps. 49–66). One should not speak of two different personalities, but of a change in locus following the prophet's return to Israel.

Both Y. Kaufmann and M. Haran agree that the division between the two sections of this book should be drawn between chaps. 48 and 49. According to Kaufmann, however, the prophet's shift in orientation was due to his disappointment when his vision of the future was not realized and he thus remained in Babylon (*The Babylonian Captivity and Deutero-Isaiah,* trans. C. W. Efroymson [New York, 1970], 67-73). Haran, on the other hand, maintains that the thematic change in the prophecies is a reflection of the prophet's change in residence, since he most likely made the pilgrimage back to Jerusalem along with the early group of returnees (*Between Ri'shonôt [Former Prophecies] and Ḥadashôt [New Prophecies]* [Jerusalem, 1963], 73-96 [Heb.]).

The prophecies in chaps. 40–48 are characterized by a unique ideological tapestry: the declaration of God's singularity (43:11-13; 44:6; 45:21-24; 46:9; 48:2) and incomparability (40:18, 25; 46:5); proof of God's authenticity is drawn from His creative performances in nature (i.e., the cosmogony; 40:12-15, 26, 28; 44:22; 45:7, 11-12, 18; 48:13) and history (i.e., His predictions that came to pass; 41:26; 43:9, 18; 46:9; 48:3; see below, §4); a staged polemical trial against the nations, in which the prophet mocks and derides idolaters and their gods (40:19-20; 41:6-7, 21-24, 29; 42:17; 44:9-20; 45:20-21; 46:1-2, 5-7; see below, §7); Israel as witnesses of the Deity (43:10, 12; 44:8); the proclamation regarding Cyrus's divinely ordained mission and the fall of Babylon (41:2-3, 25; 43:14; 44:28; 45:1-6, 13; 46:11; 47; 48:14-15); and an indictment against Babylon and its gods (47:1-2; 48).

As long as the prophet was in Babylonia, he gave voice to the nation's feelings of distress over the destruction of Jerusalem and the Temple. His tenor was consolatory and comforting, and his emphasis was on the splendor of their future return. Most of his expectation, however, was not realized, although the nation — or at least part of it — did return to Zion. The dismal situation in their homeland, which included internal schisms, the proliferation of foreign cults, and apathetic leaders, disappointed the prophet and were reason enough for the delay of the redemption and the impetus for his harsh chastisement. This being said, he never ceased in expressing his vision of the splendor and centrality of eschatological Jerusalem and of the ultimate redemption of the faithful.

Contemporary scholars tend to divide the book as a whole — chaps. 1–66 — into three parts (chaps. 1–39, 40–55, and 56–66); these were edited, expanded, and combined by a redactor whose purpose was to create a work of unique ideas, images, and language. For more regarding the literary frame encompassing the entire book, see below, the introduction to chaps. 65–66.

Regardless of the arguments presented above, most commentators still divide chaps. 40–66 into two: Deutero-Isaiah and Trito-Isaiah. In contrast, I maintain that chaps. 40–66 are one coherent opus composed by a single prophet.

3. HISTORICAL SURVEY

The sixth century BCE was a tumultuous period in the ancient Near East, and Judah did not escape these upheavals. The Neo-Babylonian Empire collapsed and was replaced by the Persian Empire, under the leadership of Cyrus. Jerusalem and the Temple were destroyed, and the nation was exiled to Babylonia. But the sixth century also witnessed the redemption of the exiles and their return to Jerusalem. All these events left their mark on Deutero-Isaiah and are reflected in his prophecies.

The Neo-Babylonian Empire was established in 626 BCE by Nabopolassar. His son and heir, Nebuchadnezzar II (604-562 BCE), occupied Judah in Jehoiachin's inaugural year (597 BCE), when "he exiled all of Jerusalem: all the commanders and all the warriors — ten thousand exiles — as well as all the craftsmen and smiths. Only the poorest people in the land were left. He deported Jehoiachin to Babylon and the king's mother and wives and officers and the notables of the land were brought as exiles from Jerusalem to Babylon" (2 Kgs 24:14-16; cf. 2 Chr 36:9-10; Jer 24:1; 27:20; 52:28). In 586 BCE the Babylonian army under the command of Nebuzaradan, the chief of the guards, destroyed the Temple and the city and exiled the remaining population (2 Kgs

25:8-11; Jer 39:1-10; 40:1; 52:4-27, 29-30; 2 Chr 36:17-21). Following the death of Nebuchadnezzar, his son Evil-merodach assumed power for two years (561-560 BCE), releasing the exiled King Jehoiachin from his imprisonment in Babylon (2 Kgs 25:27-30; Jer 52:31-34). Next in line was Neriglissar, Nebuchadnezzar's brother-in-law (559-556 BCE), who is mentioned in Jer 39:3, 13, in the account of the siege upon Jerusalem.

After a short period of insurrection led by Labashi-Marduk, the king's son Nabonidus, who had served as Nebuchadnezzar's army general but was unrelated to the royal family, ascended the throne (555-539 BCE). His anomalous personality is reflected not only in his idiosyncratic visions (see A. L. Oppenheim, *The Interpretation of Dreams in the Ancient Near East* [Philadelphia, 1956], 202-5, 250) but more importantly in the cultic reform he initiated. He established Sin, the moon god, as the new chief deity of the Babylonian pantheon, exalting him over Marduk, who ever since the establishment of the Babylonian monarchy had been regarded as the undisputed king of the gods. This cultic reform was initiated during the monarch's sojourn in Teima, a desert oasis in the northwest of the Arabian Peninsula (see below, Excursus A: The Prayer of Nabonidus). His residence in this strategic desert city afforded him control of the trade routes between Babylonia and Arabia, and it has been suggested that during this time he attempted to extend the borders of the empire further south. During the ten years of his absence, Nabonidus appointed his son Belshazzar as co-regent, but the latter was never named king.

Sin's ascension was a great blow to the status of Marduk's priests, fanning their anger to a blazing flame. Their fierce opposition to Nabonidus was made public in a libelous document from that period, which declared: "But he [Nabonidus] mixes up the rites, confuses the (hepatoscopic) oracles, and commands the important ritual observance to cease. He looks at the representations (of the gods) and utters blasphemies." Further on in the inscription, the priests recount that Nabonidus attempted to prove to the priests of Marduk that the Esagila, the central sanctuary of Marduk in Babylon, was in fact a temple honoring Sin: "Is not this the sign [the half moon] (of ownership indicating) for whom the temple was built? If it belongs (really) to Bel [= Marduk], it would have been marked with the spade [i.e., Marduk's symbol]. (Therefore) Sin (himself) has marked (already) his (own) temple with his [half moon]" (*ANET,* 314). The hatred and abhorrence of Nabonidus greatly intensified due to his ten-year sojourn in Teima, since the Babylonian New Year festival, Akitu, which took place at the beginning of the month of Nissan, could not be celebrated. During this holiday, there was a festive procession in which the king would "grasp the hand" of Marduk, and at the end of these rituals, which spanned eleven days, the promise of peace and fertility would be renewed. The cancellation of the holiday was considered to be sacrilegious and came as a blow to the entire nation's morale. Furthermore, the Cyrus Cylinder adds insult to injury: "By his own plan, he [Nabonidus] did away with the worship of Marduk, the king of the gods. He continually did evil against his (Marduk's) city. Daily . . . he [imposed] the corvée upon its inhabitants unrelentingly, ruining them all" (trans. M. Cogan, *COS* 2:315).

While Nabonidus was residing in Teima (he did not return to Babylon until 539 BCE), a new star was rising on the horizon — Cyrus, governor of Anshan (a princedom in Elam) and a vassal of Astyages, king of the Medes (585-550 BCE). In 553 BCE Cyrus rebelled against his overlord and captured him, and in 550 BCE he succeeded in conquering his capital, Ecbatana. In 547 BCE he subdued Sardis and its capital Lud (Lydia) in Asia Minor and overthrew its king, Croesus. Babylon alone now stood between Cyrus and complete control of the entire region. In 540 BCE Cyrus proceeded to wage war against this last stronghold, and on the third of Marheshvan (Oct. 29th) 539 BCE the priests of Marduk opened the gates of Babylon and granted Cyrus a bloodless victory. With this, Babylon's days as the sovereign city of Mesopotamia came to an end and the Persian era dawned. Cyrus was greeted by the Babylonians as the savior who redeemed them from the yoke of Nabonidus's idiosyncrasies. He restored Babylon to its former glory, and Marduk and the deity's priests to their former predominate prestige. Cyrus proceeded to rehabilitate the temples of Babylon and declared himself the rightful king of the Babylonian Empire, which included the land of Israel. His propagandists publicized his exploits in a famous Babylonian inscription referred to as the Cyrus Cylinder (see below, Excursus B).

Cyrus followed a policy of religious tolerance vis-à-vis his subjects throughout his empire. In the first year of his reign he publicized his famous proclamation that granted the Judean expatriates the right to return to their ancestral land, allowing them — and even assisting them in — the rebuilding of their Temple in Jerusalem (Ezra 1:1-4; 6:1-5; 2 Chr 36:22-23; see also Isa 44:28). The actual implementation of this building project, however, took place only during the reign of Darius I in 515 BCE, and the walls were rebuilt during the reign of Artaxerxes I in 444 BCE, at the time of Ezra and Nehemiah.

The historical horizon reflected in Deutero-Isaiah's prophecy can be narrowed down to the final period of the exile and the beginning of the return. Except for the references to Cyrus, no other explicit historical references may be gleaned.

Excursus A: Prayer of Nabonidus

A faint echo of this monarch's residence in Teima was preserved in an Aramaic fragment discovered in Cave 4 at Qumran (4Q242), commonly referred to as "The Prayer of Nabonidus." This fragment recounts that King "Nabni"

(= Nabonidus) was afflicted for seven years with a dire disease while sojourning in Teiman (= Teima), since he offered prayers to graven gods of gold and silver, wood, stone, and clay. His sin was (apparently) forgiven and he was cured of his affliction following his encounter with a Jewish diviner who advised him to pray to "the God Most High":

> The words of the p[ra]yer which Nabonidus, king of [Baby]lon, [the great] king, prayed [when he was smitten] with a bad disease by the decree of G[o]d in Teima. [I, Nabonidus, with a bad disease] was smitten for seven years, and sin[ce] G[od] set [his face on me, he healed me], and as for my sin, he remitted it. A diviner, he was a Jew fr[om among the exiles, came to me and said:] "Pro[clai]m and write to give honour and exal[tatio]n to the name of G[od Most High," and I wrote as follows:] 'I was smitten by a b[ad] disease in Teima [by the decree of the Most High God.] For seven years [I] was praying [to] the gods of silver and gold, [bronze, iron,] wood, stone, clay, since [I thoug]ht that th[ey were] gods.'"

(J. J. Collins, "4QPrayer of Nabonidus," in G. Brooke et al., *Qumran Cave 4.XVII: Parabiblical Texts, Part 3*, DJD 22 (Oxford, 1996), 83-93, pl. VI)

For the latest inscriptions mentioning Nabonidus in Teima, along with an updated bibliography, see A. Livingstone, "'Taima' and Nabonidus: It's a Small World," in P. Bienkowski et al., eds., *Writing and Ancient Near Eastern Society: Papers in Honour of Alan R. Millard* (New York, 2005), 29-39. A similar narrative tradition is found in the book of Daniel (chap. 4), in which the diviner is identified as Daniel, and instead of Nabonidus, the monarch punished for idolatry, the tale substitutes the more famous Babylonian king, Nebuchadnezzar.

Excursus B: Cyrus Cylinder

The cylinder inscription, written in Akkadian and composed by the priests of Babylon, welcomed Cyrus, who returned Marduk's idol to the metropolis and reestablished Babylon as a holy city and as the nation's capital:

> An incompetent person was installed to exercise lordship over his country. [. . .] he imposed upon them. An imitation of Esagila he ma[de?] for Ur and the rest of the sacred centers, improper rituals [ ] daily he recited. Irreverently, he put an end to the regular offerings; he [ ], he established in the sacred centers. By his own plan, he did away with the worship of Marduk, the king of the gods; he continually did evil against his (Marduk's) city.

Daily, [without interruption . . .], he [imposed] the corvée upon its inhabitants unrelentingly, ruining them all.

Upon (hearing) their cries, the lord of the gods became furiously angry [and he left] their borders; and the gods who lived among them forsook their dwellings, angry that he had brought (them) into Babylon. Marduk [ ] turned (?) towards all the habitations that were abandoned and all the people of Sumer and Akkad who had become corpses; [he was recon]ciled and had mercy (upon them). He surveyed and looked throughout all the lands, searching for a righteous king whom he would support. He called out his name: Cyrus, king of Anshan; he pronounced his name to be king over all (the world). He (Marduk) made the land of Gutium and all the Umman-manda bow in submission at his feet. And he (Cyrus) shepherded with justice and righteousness all the black-headed people, over whom he (Marduk) had given him victory. Marduk, the great lord, guardian (?) of his people, looked with gladness upon his good deeds and upright heart. He ordered him to march to his city Babylon. He set him on the road to Babylon and like a companion and friend, he went at his side. His vast army, whose number, like the water of the river, cannot be known, marched at his side fully armed. He made him enter his city Babylon without fighting or battle; he saved Babylon from hardship. He delivered Nabonidus, the king who did not revere him, into his hands. All the people of Babylon, all the land of Sumer and Akkad, princes and governors, bowed to him and kissed his feet. They rejoiced at his kingship and their faces shone. Ruler by whose aid the dead were revived and who had all been redeemed from hardship and difficulty, they greeted him with gladness and praised his name.

I am Cyrus, king of the world, great king, mighty king, king of Babylon, king of Sumer and Akkad, king of the four quarters, son of Cambyses, great king, king of Anshan, grandson of Cyrus, great king, king of Anshan, descendant of Teispes, great king, king of Anshan, (of an) eternal line of kingship, whose rule Bel (i.e., Marduk) and Nabu love, whose kingship they desire for their hearts' pleasure.

When I entered Babylon in a peaceful manner, I took up my lordly reign in the royal palace amidst rejoicing and happiness. Marduk, the great lord, caused the magnanimous people of Babylon [to . . .] me, (and) I daily attended to his worship. My vast army moved about Babylon in peace; I did not permit anyone to frighten (the people of) [Sumer] and Akkad. I sought the welfare of the city of Babylon and all its sacred centers. As for the citizens of Babylon, upon whom he imposed corvée which was not the god's will and not befitting them, I relieved their weariness and freed them from their service (?). Marduk, the great lord, rejoiced over my [good] deeds. He sent gracious blessings upon me, Cyrus, the king who worships him, and upon Cambyses, the son who is [my] offspring, [and upo]n all my army, and in peace, before him, we move [about].

By his exalted [word], all the kings who sit upon thrones throughout the world, from the Upper Sea to the Lower Sea, who live in the dis[tricts far-off], the kings of the West, who dwell in tents, all of them brought their heavy tribute before me and in Babylon they kissed my feet. From [Ninev]eh (?), Ashur and Susa, Agade, Eshnunna, Zamban, Meturnu, Der, as far as the region of Gutium, I returned the (images of) the gods to the sacred centers [on the other side of] the Tigris whose sanctuaries had been abandoned for a long time, and I let them dwell in eternal abodes. I gathered all their inhabitants and returned (to them) their dwellings. In addition, at the command of Marduk, the great lord, I settled in their habitations, in pleasing abodes, the gods of Sumer and Akkad, whom Nabonidus, to the anger of the lord of the gods, had brought into Babylon. May all the gods whom I settled in their sacred centers ask daily of Bel and Nabu that my days be long and may they intercede for my welfare. May they say to Marduk, my lord: "As for Cyrus, the king who reveres you, and Cambyses, his son, [ ] a reign." I settled all the lands in peaceful abodes. . . .

Trans. M. Cogan, *COS* 2:315-16

4. *RISHONÔT* AND *ḤADASHÔT*

The two expressions רִאשֹׁנוֹת and חדשות, and their cognates (listed below), in chaps. 40–48 can have various shades of meaning depending on the context. The רִאשֹׁנוֹת refer to God's deeds in the past, both His involvement in history and the changes He effected in the natural order. They serve as proof and precedent that the חדשות, "the new things," shall come to pass as well. These former occurrences span the period from creation through the exodus and up until Cyrus's victories. Due to some ambiguity in the verses, commentators are divided over the final occurrences that one should include under the term ראשנות, and the first occurrences that should be accounted as חדשות. Thus many exegetes regard Cyrus's first victories in 550-547 BCE as the latest of things "once predicted" (see §3 above), whereas Cyrus's predicted victory over Babylon is considered the first of the "new things." In contrast, Haran maintains that the victory over Babylon should still be considered one of "the former events," and that the "new things" yet to occur refer to the redemption of the exiles and their return to Zion (Haran, *Between Ri'shonôt and Ḥadashôt*, 23-29). Following are the specific terms and their occurrences: (ה)רִאשֹׁנוֹת (41:22; 42:9; 43:18; 46:9; 48:3) and its parallels: מֵרֹאשׁ (40:21; 41:4, 26; 48:16), רֵאשִׁית (46:10),

קַדְמֹנִיּוֹת (43:18), מִקֶּדֶם (45:21; 46:10), מֵאָז (44:8; 45:21; 48:3, 5, 7, 8), מֵעוֹלָם (44:7; see the commentary); מִלְּפָנִים (41:26). חֲדָשׁוֹת (42:9; 48:6) and its parallels: בָּאוֹת (41:22), הָאֹתִיּוֹת (41:23; 44:7), אַחֲרִית (41:22; 46:10), לְאָחוֹר (41:23). The expression רִאשׁוֹן . . . אַחֲרוֹן ("the first . . . the last"; 44:6; 48:12; and cf. also 41:4) refers to the Lord and expresses His eternal immutability.

5. SERVANT SONGS

Commentators are divided as to the identity of the servant in the four prophecies referred to as the "Servant Songs," ever since they were first isolated by Duhm in 1892. According to his division, the first of these prophecies is 42:1-4 (although most exegetes include vv. 5-7 or 5-9); the second is 49:1-4 (here too many commentators extend the prophecy to v. 6 or 9); the third is 50:4-9; and the fourth — 52:13–53:12 — is the most problematic of them all. In the rest of Deutero-Isaiah's early prophecies (41:8, 9; 42:19; 43:10; 44:1-2, 21, 26; 45:4; 48:20; 50:10; 54:17 is the only example in the plural) there is unanimity regarding the identification of the servant as the nation in its entirety. Beginning in chap. 56, however, the plural "My servants" refers only to the Israelite faithful (56:6; 63:17; 65:8-9, 13-15; 66:14). The identification of the servant in the four Servant Songs listed above is, nevertheless, very ambiguous. He has both a national and universal destiny: לברית עם ("a covenant people"; 42:6; 49:8) and לאור גוים ("a light of nations"; 42:6; 49:6). He is described as afflicted (42:2, 3; 49:7; 50:6-7; 52:14; chap. 53) and as a silent sufferer who expiates the sins of others (chap. 53).

There are two main ways of interpreting his identity — as a collective entity or as an individual. According to the former, the servant represents Israel as a whole, or a selected segment of the nation, the chosen ones, idealized and righteous Israel, as opposed to the more realistic Israel who are unfaithful. According to the latter interpretation, the servant is a specific individual for whom various identifications have been proposed, including Moses, Hezekiah, Uzziah, Jehoiachin, Jeremiah, Zerubbabel, the prophet himself, an anonymous individual, or a messianic figure. In the present commentary, I interpret the servant as representative of the Israelite nation. For the problem of suffering on another's behalf, see the discussion in chap. 53.

6. ATTITUDES TOWARD FOREIGNERS AND RELIGIOUS UNIVERSALISM

The role of the nations in Deutero-Isaiah is multifaceted. On the one hand, the prophet initiates mock legal proceedings against the foreign idolaters and their gods (see §7 below), who are viewed as the adversaries of Israel and God, who is destined to punish and utterly subdue them (41:1-3, 11-12; 42:13; 43:14; 45:1-3; 47; 49:26; 51:22-23; 59:17-19; 60:12; 63:1-6; 66:15-16); alternatively, they shall be dominated by Israel (45:14; 49:7, 23; 54:4-5; 60:11, 14). On the other hand, they are charged with transporting the returning expatriates to Zion (49:22; 60:6, 9; 66:20) and shall offer rich tribute to the Temple (45:14; 60:5, 11, 13, 16; 61:6; 66:12). Israel shall "suckle at their breasts" (60:16) or, in less flowery language, shall benefit from the riches of many nations. They, the foreigners, shall be God's ransom, ensuring Israel's deliverance from Babylon (43:3-4); they shall serve Israel and shall rebuild the walls of Jerusalem (60:10). Israel is destined to be a light to the nations (42:6; 49:6) and shall establish a just order for them (42:1, 3); they, in turn, shall yearn for His instruction (42:4).

The most surprising element of Deutero-Isaiah's vision regarding the nations is their ultimate integration into Israel (56:3, 6-7). They will recognize the Lord as the only true God, will worship Him and be redeemed (45:14-15, 22-23; 60:7; 66:23), and will walk by His light (60:3). Moreover, they will participate in the Temple ministry as priests and Levites (66:21), and their survivors will announce God's glory to the rest of the world (60:19). The prophet promises the foreigners "who attach themselves to the Lord": "I will bring them to My sacred mount and let them rejoice in My house of prayer. Their burnt offerings and sacrifices shall be welcome on My altar. For My house shall be called a house of prayer for all peoples" (56:6-7). Herein is to be found the beginning of religious conversion to the worship of the God of Israel.

7. DEUTERO-ISAIAH, POLEMICIST

a. Deutero-Isaiah, while residing in Babylon, polemicized against various beliefs prevalent among the Babylonians, which are reflected in their cosmogonic epic, *Enuma Elish* (= *EE*) (references are to B. R. Foster, *COS* 1:390-402):

According to this epic tale, the head of the Mesopotamian pantheon, Marduk, was born (*EE* I:83ff.). Deutero-Isaiah submits, in contrast, "And understand that I am He. Before Me no god was formed and after Me none shall exist" (43:10).

They believed that Marduk created the heavenly host (*EE* V:1ff.), whereas the prophet maintains that the Lord was the one who created and ruled over this mighty host (40:26).

As opposed to the Babylonian belief that the gods had personal advisors, e.g., the god Mummu is referred to as a *tamlāku* ("counselor") (*EE*

I:47ff.) and the god Ea counseled Marduk (*EE* VI:11ff.), Deutero-Isaiah definitively declares: "Who has plumbed the mind of the Lord? What man could tell Him His plan? Whom did He consult, and who taught Him, guided Him in the way of right? Who guided Him in knowledge and showed Him the path of wisdom?"(40:13-14).

According to the Babylonians it was Marduk who created the heavens and the earth (*EE* IV:136ff.). In contrast, the prophet repeatedly states that it was God, and God alone (see the references in §9 below).

As opposed to the declaration of Marduk's kingship (*EE* V:85ff.), Deutero-Isaiah states unequivocally that the Lord alone is King over all (41:21; 43:15; 44:6; 52:7).

The Babylonians boasted that Marduk was the greatest of all gods and that none compared to him (*EE* VI:95ff.), whereas the prophet declares time and again that the Lord alone is God and that there is none but Him (40:18, 21-23; 43:11; 44:6, 8; 45:6; 46:9, etc.; and see §9 below).

b. The prophet did not restrict his polemics to the Babylonians and often argues against ideas that had taken root in the Israelite nation itself. He takes a decisive stance against four beliefs embedded in P, the priestly account of the creation narratives: the preexistence of darkness, joint participation in the act of creation, a corporeal image of God, and God's fatigue following the six days of creation.

According to Gen 1:2, darkness was primordial, existing before God began His creative acts: "And darkness over the surface of the deep"; only light was created by God (Gen 1:3). In contrast, the prophet decisively declares that the Lord "formed light and created darkness" (45:7). This is the only place in the Bible that attributes the creation of darkness to God.

According to Gen 1:26: "And God said: 'Let us make man in our image and our likeness'" (cf. also 3:22: "And the Lord God said, 'Now that the man has become like one of us'"; 11:7: "Let us, then, go down and confound their speech there"), it may be discerned that God at times did not act alone, but consulted with other divine beings. The prophet refutes this belief with a series of rhetorical questions: "Who has plumbed the mind of the Lord? What man could tell Him His plan? Whom did He consult, and who taught Him, guided Him in the way of right? Who guided Him in knowledge and showed Him the path of wisdom?" (Isa 40:13-14).

The literal meaning of the text, "in our image and our likeness. . . . And God created man in His image, in the image of God He created him" (Gen 1:26-27), implies that God has a corporeal image. Against this concept, the prophet retorts: "To whom, then, can you liken God? What form compare to Him?" (Isa 40:18); "To whom, then, can you liken Me, to whom can I be compared? — says the Holy One" (40:25); "To whom can you compare Me or declare Me similar? To whom can you liken Me, so that we seem comparable?" (46:5).

Following His creative effort, the Lord "ceased from work and was refreshed" (Exod 31:17). The prophet, however, maintains that "He [God] never grows faint or weary" (Isa 40:28). Indeed, "He gives strength to the weary, fresh vigor to the spent" (40:29).

c. According to Num 18, only the priests descended from Aaron are instructed to "discharge the duties connected with the shrine and the altar" (v. 5). And the Levites are commanded "to be attached to you [the priests] and to minister to you . . . before the tent of the pact. They shall discharge their duties to you and to the tent as a whole, but they must not have any contact with the furnishings of the shrine or with the altar" (vv. 2-3). Moreover, "Any foreigner [i.e., any non-Levite] who attempts to minister shall die" (v. 7). In contrast with this ritual hierarchy, which banned the Israelites who were not priests or Levites from approaching the shrine, the prophet proposes a revolutionary reform and declares: "You shall be called 'priests of the Lord,' and termed 'servants of our God'" (Isa 61:6). This means that not only the Levitical priests shall serve in the Temple, but the entire nation of Israel shall minister to the Deity, thus fulfilling the mission of being "a kingdom of priests and a holy nation" (Exod 19:6). Deutero-Isaiah, the most universalistic of all the prophets (see above, §6), also allows for foreign participation in the Israelite cult: "And from them [the nations] likewise I will take some to be Levitical priests, said the Lord" (Isa 66:21), and promises that "their burnt offerings and sacrifices shall be welcome on My altar. For My house shall be called a house of prayer for all peoples" (56:7).

d. Deutero-Isaiah reserves his most virulent and derisive polemic for the idol industry and against idol craftsmen (40:19-20; 41:6-7, 21-24, 28-29; 42:17; 43:9; 44:9-20; 45:16, 20-21; 46:1-2, 6-7). Since idols are unable to declare what happened in the past or predict what is destined to occur, they are patently unreal. Thus neither do they have the power to save their worshipers nor is there any benefit whatsoever in worshiping them. In contrast, the Lord, God of Israel, predicted the course of history, and Israel, as God's witnesses, can testify to the veracity of His pronouncements (43:9-12). In the past, attacks on idol worship were addressed to the errant Israelites, who breached their covenant with God: "You shall have no other gods besides Me. You shall not make for yourself a sculptured image, or any likeness. . . . You shall not bow down to them or serve them" (Exod 20:3-5). Here the attack on idolatry is directed at their very existence and totally denies and refutes any substance whatsoever to idols.

e. Deutero-Isaiah polemicizes against those who would refuse to accept Cyrus as a means to their salvation (Isa 45:9-13).

f. Contrary to the general belief in the future reinstatement of a Davidic scion upon the throne, the prophet unequivocally states that "the enduring loyalty promised to David" shall be transferred to the nation as a whole (55:3-4) and that God alone shall rule over them (41:21; 43:25; 44:6; 52:7).

g. For other polemics and severe rebukes against the nation or parts of the nation, see the comments on the following verses: 40:27 (the nation moans their bitter fate, complaining that they were forgotten by God); 42:18-20, 23-25 (the nation is unaware of the reason for their dire predicament); 43:22-28 (cultic issues); 46:8, 12 (the nation as criminals and individuals of little faith); 48:1-2 (the nation swears by the name of God, but disingenuously); 50:1-3, 11 (the schism dividing the Lord from His people because of their iniquities); 51:12-13 (the people have forgotten God, and their anxiety vis-à-vis their enemies); 56:9–57:2 (the national leadership as indifferent to the people's plight); 57:3-13 (foreign ritual, including harlotry); 57:17-21; 58:1ff.; 59:1-15 (the nation's sin); 65:1-7; 66:3-4, 17 (foreign rituals); 66:1 (the desire to build an earthly residence for the Lord).

8. DESCRIPTIONS OF JERUSALEM

Following its destruction and the first days of the return, Jerusalem in the time of the prophet is described as desolate and unconsoled. Deutero-Isaiah portrays the city as a bereaved and barren widow (e.g., 49:14, 17, 19-21; 54:1, 11; 62:4; 64:9-10). Her days of mourning, however, are now over (60:20), and she shall be rebuilt and resettled as of old (e.g., 44:26; 58:12; 60:10; 65:21). She shall gleam with newfound splendor and be bathed in a shining light (e.g., 52:1; 60:18-19). The city shall be immune to evil (54:14) and all her sons (i.e., inhabitants) shall be righteous (60:21) and disciples of the Lord (54:13). Jerusalem shall be engraved on the Lord's hands, and her walls shall always be present before Him (49:16). The nation shall be consoled therein (66:13), and never again shall cries of woe be heard within the city (65:19), but only shouts of gladness (65:18-19). Her inhabitants shall live to a ripe old age (65:20), and she shall be a glorious diadem in the hands of the Lord (62:3). She shall be renamed "I Delight in Her" (62:4) and "City of the Lord, Zion of the Holy One of Israel" (60:14). The nations, who will transport all of the expatriates back to Jerusalem (49:22; 60:9; 66:20), shall offer rich tribute at her sanctuary (45:14; 60:5-6, 11, 13, 16; 61:6; 66:12). Jerusalem shall be the "Holy City" and shall be sanctified in her entirety (48:2; 52:1). She shall thus be transformed into a focal point of international prayer and pilgrimage (56:7; cf. 66:23). The divine light shall shine upon her with resplendence, and she shall be a light to all nations (60:1-3).

9. DESCRIPTIONS OF GOD, HIS ATTRIBUTES, AND HIS RELATIONSHIP TO HIS PEOPLE

Deutero-Isaiah's prophecies have many and varied descriptions of the Lord and His attributes. First and foremost, the prophet reiterates time and again the Lord's singularity (44:6, 8; 45:5-6, 14, 18, 21, 22; 46:9), His incomparability (40:18, 25; 46:5), and His eternal being (41:4; 43:10; 48:12). The proliferation of divine attributes is concentrated primarily in the first part of his prophecies and is usually connected to his repeated polemics against idols and idolaters. God is referred to variously as "the Mighty One of Jacob" (49:26; 60:16), "the Holy One" (40:25; 43:15; 57:15; 58:13), and especially "the Holy One of Israel" (41:14, 16, 20; 43:3, 14; 45:11; 47:4; 48:17; 49:7; 54:5; 55:5; 60:9, 14). There are many iterations of the "name of the Lord," "My name," "His name" (41:25; 42:8; 43:7; 48:1, 9; 50:10; 51:15; 52:5-6; 54:5; 60:9; 66:5); "His presence" (40:5; 42:8; 43:7; 48:11); "His renown" (42:8; cf. also "honor" in v. 12; "praise," 43:21; "glory," 48:9); and "His glory" (46:13; 60:7, 21); He is Israel's "Savior" (43:3, 11-13; 45:15, 17, 21; 46:13; 49:25-26; 51:5-6, 8; 52:7, 10; 59:1, 16-17; 60:16; 62:1, 11; 63:1, 5, 8-9) and "Redeemer" (41:14; 43:1, 14; 44:6, 22-24; 48:17, 20; 49:7, 26; 52:3, 9; 54:5, 8; 59:20; 60:16; 63:9, 16); Israel are the "redeemed" (51:10), "the redeemed of the Lord" (62:12), whose "year of redemption" (63:4) has arrived. Redemption has both judicial and social connotations. Between the Redeemer (God) and the redeemed (the nation) there exists a familial link, and thus Israel is considered the Lord's personal possession. Just as a redeemer is required to redeem his property or his kin if they are sold to someone outside the family (Lev 25:25, 47-55), so the Lord redeemed His people from the past Egyptian subjugation (e.g., Deut 7-8; 9:26) and shall redeem them from the present Babylonian captivity: "You were sold for no price, and shall be redeemed without money" (Isa 52:3).

The Lord is Israel's "Helper" (41:10, 13-14; 44:2; 49:8; 50:7, 9), their Creator (43:1, 7, 15, 21; 44:2, 21, 24; 45:11; 49:5, 8; 64:7), their Shepherd (40:11; and cf. also 49:9-10), and their King (41:21; 43:15; 44:6; 52:7). He is "as a warrior; like a fighter. . . . He triumphs over His enemies" (42:13), and He exacts His revenge from His adversaries, in the present and in the future (63:1-6; 66:15-16), in a reenactment of days long gone, when He defeated the mythic beasts (51:9-10). He shall contend on Israel's behalf in judgment and in war (49:25; 50:8; 51:22). However, He shall also contend against His people when they are in the wrong (43:26) and even against all of humanity (66:16). The Lord loves His people (49:10, 13; 54:7-8, 10; 55:7; 60:10; 63:7, 15), for His own sake (43:25; 48:11), and for the sake of His name (48:9; 66:5; cf. 45:4; 49:7; 55:5; 62:1; 63:17; 65:8). He is their comforter (40:1; 49:13; 51:3, 12; 52:9; 61:2; 66:13) and provides for the destitute and the downtrodden (41:17; 49:13; 54:11; 66:2). He "foretells reliably and announces what is true" (45:19). The Lord created not only human beings (45:12) and "the smith to fan the charcoal fire . . . [and] the instruments of havoc" (54:16), but also the heavenly host (40:26), the earth (40:28; 45:18), the heavens (42:5; 45:18), and Israel (43:1, 15). His creative efforts have not ended, however, since He will create "a new heaven and a new earth" (65:17; cf. 66:22), and He "shall create Jerusalem as a joy" (65:18). Moreover, He "forms light and creates darkness, makes weal and creates woe" (45:7; cf. also 41:20; 43:7; 65:18).

Deutero-Isaiah also employs several different verbs to indicate God's acts on the broad stage of history and nature: **עשׂי** (e.g., 41:20; 42:16; 43:7, 19; 44:2, 24; 45:7, 12, 18; 51:13); **יצר** (43:1, 7, 21; 44:2, 21, 24; 45:7, 11, 18; 46:11; 49:5, 8); **יסד** (48:13; 51:13, 16; 54:11); **נטי** (40:22; 42:5; 44:24; 45:12; 51:13); **כון** (45:18; 54:14; 62:7); **רקע** (42:5; 44:24); **קרא** (41:4, 9; 43:1; 46:11; 48:12, 15; 51:2).

The Lord chose Israel (41:8-9; 43:10; 44:1-2; 49:7), His "chosen one" (41:8-9; 42:1; 43:20; 44:1-2; 45:4; 65:9, 15), who is named by Him (41:9; 43:1; 48:12). The nation is His servant (41:8-9; 42:1, 19; 43:10; 44:1-2, 21, 26; 45:4; 48:20; 49:3, 5, 6; 50:10; 52:13; 53:11), but at other times only those who are faithful to Him are named thus (54:17; 63:17; 65:8, 9, 13-15; 66:14). Israel is His nation (51:16), formed by His very hands (45:11). They are His children (43:6; 45:11), and He is their Father (63:16; 64:7). The Lord is portrayed as Israel's husband and master (54:5-6; 62:5) and is also depicted in female imagery (42:14; 45:10; 49:15; 66:9, 13). The Lord wipes away Israel's sins (43:25; 44:22) and forgives them (55:7). All of earth's nations shall worship Him (45:14-15) and will be saved (45:22).

"His predictions" (44:26; 46:10), "His desires" (42:21; 44:28; 46:10; 48:14; 53:10; 55:11), and "His word" (40:8; 44:26; 55:11) set the course of history. Just as "the things of old" came to pass (41:22; 42:9; 43:9, 18; 46:9; 48:3), so too shall the "new things" occur (42:9; 43:19; 48:6-7). "His arm rules for Him" (40:10), cares for His people, and brings success and victory to them (40:11; 48:14; 51:5, 9-10; 52:10; 53:1). He establishes an eternal covenant of well-being with His nation (54:10; 59:21; 61:8; cf. also 42:6; 49:8; 56:4, 6) and transforms them into priests and ministers in His sanctuary (61:6). The prophet, moreover, prophesies that they "shall be a glorious crown in the hand of the Lord" (62:3), a nation of prophets, fulfilling the wish of Moses in Num 11:29 (see commentary to 42:6; 44:3), and all of Israel shall be a righteous people (60:21).

10. UNIQUE STYLE AND LITERARY SEQUENCE

A. Unique Style

The prophet's style is lyrical, descriptive, flowery, and replete with pathos and enthusiasm. Examples of some of the more common characteristics follow.

(1) The repetition of words for emphatic purposes: 40:1: **נחמו נחמו**; 43:11,

25; 51:12: אנכי אנכי; 48:11: למעני למעני; 48:15: אני אני; 51:9; 52:1: עורי עורי; 51:17: התעוררי התעוררי; 52:11: סורו סורו; 57:14; 62:10: סֹלּוּ סֹלּוּ; 57:19: שלום שלום; 62:10: עִבְרוּ עִבְרוּ; 65:1: הִנֵּנִי הִנֵּנִי. Additional examples are cited ad loc. in the commentary. His prophecies contain the largest concentration of doubled terms and phrases in the Bible.

(2) Rhetorical questions in polemical contexts: 40:12-14: "Who measured the waters with the hollow of His hand, and gauged the skies with a span, and meted earth's dust with a measure, and weighed the mountains with a scale and the hills with a balance? Who has plumbed the mind of the Lord? What man could tell Him His plan? Whom did He consult and who taught Him, guided Him in the way of right? Who guided Him in knowledge and showed Him the path of wisdom?"; v. 18: "To whom, then, can you liken God, what form compare to Him?"; v. 21: "Do you not know? Have you not heard? Have you not been told from the very first? Have you not discerned from the time the earth was founded?"; v. 25: "'To whom, then, can you liken Me, to whom can I be compared?' says the Holy One"; v. 26: "Who created these?"; v. 28: "Do you not know? Have you not heard? The Lord is the everlasting God, Creator of the earth from end to end. He never grows faint or weary. His understanding cannot be fathomed"; 41:2: "Who has roused a victor from the east, summoned him to His service? Who has delivered up nations to him, and trodden sovereigns down? Who has rendered their swords like dust, their bows like wind-blown straw?"; v. 4: "Who has wrought and achieved this? Who announced the generations from the start?"; v. 26: "Who foretold this from the start, that we may note it; from aforetime, that we might say, 'He is right'?"; 42:19: "Who is so blind as My servant, so deaf as the messenger I send? Who is so blind as the chosen one, so blind as the servant of the Lord?"; v. 24: "Who was it that delivered Jacob over to despoilment and Israel to plunderers?"; 43:13: "When I act, who can reverse it?"; 44:7: "Who like Me can announce, can foretell it — and match Me thereby?"; v. 8: "Have I not from of old predicted to you? . . . Is there any god, then, but Me? There is no other rock; I know none!"; 45:9: "Shall the clay say to the potter, 'What are you doing? Your work has no handles'"; v. 11: "Will you question Me on the destiny of My children? Will you instruct Me about the work of My hands?"; v. 21: "Who announced this aforetime, foretold it of old?"; 46:5: "To whom can you compare Me, or declare Me similar? To whom can you liken Me, so that we seem comparable?"; 48:14: "Who among you foretold these things?"; 49:15: "Can a mother forget her baby, a young woman the child of her womb?"; v. 24: "Can spoil be taken from a warrior, or captives retrieved from a victor?"; 50:1: "Where is the bill of divorce of your mother whom I dismissed? And which of my creditors was it to whom I sold you off?"; v. 2: "Is my arm, then, too short to rescue? Have I not the power to save?"; vv. 8-9: "Who dares contend with me? . . . Who would be my opponent? . . . Who can get a verdict

against me?"; 52:5: "What therefore do I gain here?"; 58:5: "Is such the fast I desire, a day for men to starve their bodies? Is it bowing the head like a bulrush and lying in sackcloth and ashes? Do you call that a fast, a day when the Lord is favorable?"; 66:1: "Where could you build a house for Me? What place could serve as My abode?"; v. 8: "Who ever heard the like? Who ever witnessed such events? Can a land pass through travail in a single day? Or is a nation born all at once?"

(3) The employment of triads for purposes of accentuation: 40:2: "That (כי) her term of service is over, that (כי) her penalty is paid; that (כי) she has received at the hand of the Lord double for all her sins"; v. 24: "Scarcely are (אף בל) they planted; scarcely are (אף בל) they sown; scarcely has (אף בל) their stem taken root in earth"; 41:26: "Not one (אף אין) foretold; not one (אף אין) announced; not one (אף אין) has heard your utterance!"; 43:4: "Because you are precious to Me, and honored, and I love you"; 45:21: "Speak up and compare testimony — let them even take counsel together!"; 46:11: "(אף) I have spoken, so (אף) I will bring it to pass . . .; so (אף) I will complete it"; 48:8: "You had never (גם לא) heard; you had never (גם לא) known; your ears were never (לא . . . גם) opened of old"; 49:12: "Look! These (אלה) are coming from afar, these (אלה) from the north and the west, and these (אלה) from the land of Sinim"; v. 21: "Who bore these (אלה) for me? . . . By whom, then, were these (אלה) reared? . . . And where have these (אלה) been?"; 50:8-9: "Who (מי) dares contend with me? . . . Who (מי) would be my opponent? . . . Who (מי) can get a verdict against me?"; 51:6: "Though the heavens should melt away like (כ) smoke, and the earth wear out like (כ) a garment, and its inhabitants die out as (כמו) well"; 52:7: "Announcing well-being, heralding good news, announcing victory"; 52:13: "My servant shall prosper, be exalted and raised to great heights"; 53:4: "We accounted him plagued, smitten, and afflicted by God"; 54:1: "Shout . . . shout aloud and rejoice!"

(4) The insertion of quotations within the verses: 40:6: "A voice rings out: 'Proclaim!' And I asked, 'What shall I proclaim?' All flesh is grass, all its goodness like flowers of the field"; v. 9: "Ascend a lofty mountain, O herald of joy to Zion! Raise your voice with power, O herald of joy to Jerusalem! Raise it, have no fear! Announce to the cities of Judah, 'Behold your God!'"; v. 27: "Why do you say, O Jacob, why declare, O Israel, 'My way is hid from the Lord, my cause is ignored by my God'?"; 41:13: "For I the Lord am your God, who grasped your right hand, who say to you: 'Have no fear; I will be your help'"; 42:22: "They are given over to plunder, with none to rescue them; to despoilment, with none to say 'Give back!'"; 43:6: "I will say to the north, 'Give back!' And to the south, 'Do not withhold! Bring My sons from afar, and My daughters from the end of the earth'"; v. 9: "All the nations assemble as one, and the peoples gather. Who among them declared this, foretold to us the things that have happened? Let

them produce their witnesses and be vindicated, that men, hearing them, may say, 'It is true!'"; 45:9: "Ah! He who argues with his Maker, a potsherd among earthenware! Shall the clay ask the potter, 'What are you making? Your work has no handles'"; v. 10: "Ah! he who asks his father, 'What are you begetting?' Or his mother, 'What are you bearing?'"; 46:10: "I foretell the end from the beginning, and from the past, things that have not yet occurred. I say: 'My plan shall be fulfilled; I will do all I have purposed'"; 47:7: "You thought, 'I shall always be queen forever.' You did not take these things to heart. You gave no thought to its outcome"; v. 8: "And now hear this, O pampered one, who dwells in security. You say to yourself, 'I am, and there is none but me. I shall not become a widow or know loss of children'"; v. 10: "You said, 'No one can see me.' . . . And you said to yourself, 'I am, and there is none but me'"; 49:14: "Zion says, 'The Lord has forsaken me; my Lord has forgotten me'"; v. 20: "The children you thought you had lost shall yet say in your hearing, 'The place is too crowded for me. Make room for me to settle!'"; v. 21: "And you will say to yourself, 'Who bore these for me, when I was bereaved and barren, exiled and disdained/imprisoned? By whom, then, were these reared? I was left all alone — and where have these been?'"; 52:7: "How lovely on the mountain are the footsteps of the herald, announcing well-being, heralding good news, announcing victory, telling Zion, 'Your God is King!'"; 65:5: "Who say, 'Keep your distance! Don't come closer!'"; 65:8: "As when new wine is present in the cluster, one says, 'Don't destroy it; there is good in it.'"

(5) The prophet also has a proclivity for words, expressions, and phrases containing a series of similar sounding syllables and consonants, creating multiple assonances and alliterations:

40:3
קול קורא

40:4
גֶּיא יִנָּשֵׂא

40:6
(כל) הבשר חציר (וכל) חסדו כציץ השדה

40:9
הר . . . הרימי . . . הרימי

40:9-11
על . . . עֲלי . . . עָלות

40:11
כרֹעֶה עֶדְרוֹ יִרְעֶה בִּזְרֹעוֹ . . . עָלות

40:12
מים ושמים

40:24
זֹרָעוּ . . . שֹׁרָשׁ בארץ גזעם . . . נשף . . . וַיִּבָשׁוּ וסערה כקש תִּשָּׂאֵם

40:26
המוציא במספר צְבאם

40:28-31
(לא) יִיעַף (ולא) יִיגָע . . . לַיָּעֵף . . . וִיעֲפו . . . וִיגָעו . . . (ולא) יִיגָעו . . .
(ולא) יִיעָפו

40:30
כשול יִכָּשֵׁלוּ

41:15-16
כַּמֹּץ תשִׂים. תִּזְרֵם . . . תִּשָּׂאֵם וסערה תפיץ

41:17
מים וָאַיִן

41:18
וארץ צִיָּה למוצאי (מים)

42:7
להוציא ממסגר אסיר

42:14
הֶחֱשֵׁיתי . . . אחריש . . . אֶשֹּׁם ואֶשְׁאַף

45:12
צְבָאָם צִוֵּיתי

46:1
נְשֻׂאֹתיכם עמוסות מַשָּׂא

46:4
(ועד) זקנה . . . ועד שֵׂיבה (ואני) אסבֹּל (אני) עשיתי (ואני) אֶשָּׂא (ואני)
אסבֹּל

46:6
הַזָּלים זהב מִכיס וכסף . . . ישקֹלו ישׂכְּרו צורף ויעשֵׂהו . . . יסגדו . . .
ישתחוו

46:8
זִכרו זאת והתאֹשָׁשו השיבו פושעים (על לב)

47:1
שְׁבי לארץ . . . כסא . . . כשׂדים . . . תוסיפי

47:2
קחי רֵחַיִם וטחני קמח

47:14
כקַשׁ אֵשׁ שֹׂרָפָתַם . . . יצילו (את) נפשם

49:17
מִהרו . . . מְהרסיך ומחרִיביך מִמֵּךְ (יצאו)

49:18 (= 60:4)
שְׂאִי סביב

50:3

וַשַּׂק אשׂים כְּסותם

51:1

צור חֻצבתם . . . מַקֶּבֶת . . . נֻקַּרְתֶּם

51:3

שׂשׂון ושׂמחה יִמָּצֵא . . . זמרה

51:11

ישובון . . . ציון . . . ושמחת (עולם על) ראשם שׂשׂון ושׂמחה יַשׂיגון נָסו

52:1-2

עוּרי . . . עיר . . . ערל . . . התנערי מֵעפר עוּרי

52:7

מבשׂר משמיע שלום מבשׂר . . . משמיע ישועה . . . ציון

52:11

סורו סורו צְאו משם

53:2

מארץ צִיָּה

54:6

כאשה עזובה ועצובת (רוח)

54:8

שֶׁצֶף קֶצֶף

55:10

כאשׁר . . . הגשׁם והשׁלג . . . השׁמים ושׁמה . . . ישׁוב

57:13

בזעקֵך יצילֻךְ קִבּוּצַיִךְ

57:14

הרימו מכשול מִדרך עמי

58:3

(ביום) צֹמְכם תמצאו חֵפֶץ . . . עַצְּבֵיכֶם תִּנְגֹּשׂוּ

58:13

(אם) תשיב מִשַּׁבָּת . . . עֲשׂות חֲפָצֶיךָ . . . קָדשי . . . לַשַּׁבָּת . . . לִקדוש . . .
מֵעֲשׂות . . . מִמְּצוא חֶפְצְךָ

59:7

רגליהם לָרַע יָרֻצוּ

59:13

פָּשֹׂעַ וכַחֵשׁ . . . ונָסוג . . . עֹשֶׁק וסָרָה

61:11

כארץ תוציא צמחהּ . . . תצמיח . . . יצמיח צדקה

62:10

סֹלּו סֹלּו המסִלה סַקלו . . . נֵס

(6) Wordplays:

41:2
כקשׁ . . . קשׁתו
41:5
רָאוּ . . . וַיִּירָאוּ
41:17
העניים . . . אֶעֱנֵם . . . אֶעֶזְבֵם
43:24
קָנִית . . . קָנֶה
48:19
מֵעֶיךָ כִּמְעֹתָיו
54:9
מי נח . . . מי נח
58:12
מְשׁוֹבֵב . . . לָשֶׁבֶת
58:13
תשׁיב מִשַּׁבָּת
61:10
וְכַכַּלָּה . . . כֵלֶיהָ
63:1-2
מֵאֱדוֹם . . . אָדֹם
63:2
ובגדיך . . . בְּגַת
63:9
צָרָתָם . . . צָר
65:8-9
התירוש . . . יורשׁ . . . וִירֵשׁוּהָ
65:11-12
לַמְנִי . . . וּמָנִיתִי
65:25
יִרְעוּ . . . יָרֵעוּ

(7) Phrases expressing and accentuating a leitmotif: "Fear not" (40:9; 41:10, 13-14; 43:1; 44:2; 51:7; 54:4, 14); "I am the first and I am the last" (44:6; 48:12); and cf. 41:4: "I, the Lord, who was first and will be with the last as well"; "I am the Lord and there is none else" (45:5-6, 18, 22; 46:9); and see also 45:14: "Only among you is God. There is no other god at all!"; 45:21-22: "No god exists other than I. . . . I am God, and there is none else."

(8) The repetition of words and expressions in the same or consecutive verses: 40:7-8: "Grass withers, flowers fade" (יבשׁ חציר נבל ציץ); 40:9: "Raise!" (הרימי); 40:10-11: "His arm" (זְרֹעוֹ); the repetition of declined forms of the roots יעף ("to be tired") and יגע ("to be weary"), 40:28-31: "He never tires or

becomes weary . . . to the tired . . . may grow tired and weary . . . and not grow weary . . . and not tire" (לא יִיעַף ולא יִיגָע . . . לַיָּעֵף . . . וְיִעֲפוּ . . . וְיִגָעוּ . . . ולא יִיגָעוּ . . . ולא יִיעָפוּ); 40:31–41:1: the repetition of the expression "shall renew strength" (יחליפו כח); 42:3-4: the repetition of derived forms from the roots רצץ and כהי ("bruised," "dim"): "Bruised . . . dim . . . He shall not grow dim or be bruised" (רצוץ . . . כֵהָה . . . לא יִכְהֶה ולא יָרוּץ); 44:1-2: "My servant . . . whom I have chosen" (עבדי . . . בחרתי בו); 46:1-4: the repetition of derived forms from the root נשׂא: "The things you would carry in procession are now piled as a burden . . . the burden . . . who have been carried . . . I who will carry" (נְשֻׂאֹתֵיכֶם . . . מַשָּׂא . . . מַשָּׂא . . . הַנְּשֻׂאִים . . . אֶשָּׂא); and cf.: "They must carry it" (יִשָּׂאֻהוּ) (v. 7); 46:4: "I will be the bearer" (אֶסְבֹּל . . . אֶסְבֹּל), and cf.: "Transport it" (יִסְבְּלֻהוּ) (v. 7); 47:1: "Sit down" (שְׁבִי); 47:12: "Perhaps" (אולי); 53:6: "all of us" (כֻּלָּנוּ); 53:7: "He did not open his mouth" (ולא יפתח פיו); the repetition of derived forms from the root מוט ("to be shaken") in 54:10: "Be shaken . . . be shaken" (תְּמוּטֶינָה . . . תָמוּט); the repetition of the substantives מחשבות ("plans") and דרכים ("ways") in 55:7-9; the repetition of verbal forms from the root נחם ("to comfort"): "Comforts . . . I will comfort you . . . you shall find comfort" (תְּנַחֲמֶנּוּ . . . אֲנַחֶמְכֶם . . . תְּנֻחָמוּ) in 66:13.

(9) Many different literary genres are represented in Deutero-Isaiah's prophecies: hymns praising God (e.g., 40:22-24, 26, 28-31; 42:5; 44:24; 45:7, 12-13, 18; 48:20-21; 49:13; 52:9); polemics against idols and their creation, and against Israel and their beliefs (see above, §7); a derisive poem (47); prophecies of consolation (e.g., 40:1-2; 52:7-9; 61:1-9; 66:12-14); rebukes and prophecies of revenge (e.g., 42:18-25; 43:22-28; 45:1-11; 57:3-13; 58:1-12; 59:1-15); mock court scenes (41:1-5, 21-29; 43:8-13, 22-28; 44:6-11; 45:20-25; 48:3, 6, 14-16; 50:8-9); eschatological prophecies (e.g., 60; 65:8-25; 66:6-14, 20-24); prophecies relating to Cyrus and the conquest of Babylon (see above, §3); the Servant Songs (see above, §5); prophecies reflecting a national schism (e.g., 66:3-4, 5); prophecies relating to foreigners (56:3-8; 60:10; 61:5; 62:8).

Additional literary characteristics pertaining to synonymous phrases, parallelisms, and idiomatic expressions are found in the commentary.

B. Literary Sequence

The sequence of prophecies of Deutero-Isaiah creates a tightly knit tapestry by employing many of the same phrases, terms, and motifs in consecutive units (be they complex amalgams or single prophecies). These links weave together the entire work from beginning to end, chapter by chapter. In addition, there are also many associative concatenations and natural progressions between individual literary units, which are demonstrated in the introduction to each prophecy.

Isaiah 40–66

The following examples of sample phraseology link consecutive pairs of chapters. Others will be presented in the introductions to the respective chapters.

40:3-4 במדבר . . . בערבה . . . לבִקעה	41:18-19 בְּקָעוֹת . . . מדבר . . . במדבר . . . בערבה
40:4, 12 הר וגבעה . . . הרים וגבעות	41:15 הרים . . . וגבעות
40:5 וראו . . . יַחְדָּו	41:20, 23 למען יראו . . . יַחְדָּו . . . ונראה יַחְדָּו
40:9 מבשׂרת ציון . . . מבשׂרת ירושלם	41:27 לציון . . . ולירושלם מבשׂר אתן
40:9 אל תיראי	41:10, 13, 14 אל תירא
40:12 מי מדד . . . מי תִכֵּן . . . את מי נועָץ	41:2, 4, 26 מי העיר . . . מי פעל . . . מי הגיד
40:14 את מי נועץ	41:28 ואין יועץ
40:15 גוים . . . איים	41:1, 2, 5 איים . . . גוים . . . איים
40:17 כאַין . . . מאֶפֶס ותֹהו	41:11, 12, 24, 29 כאַין . . . כאין וכאפס . . . מאָין . . . אָפַע . . . אָוֶן [= אַין] אֶפֶס . . . ותֹהו
40:19-20 חָרָשׁ . . . צֹרף . . . לא יִמּוֹט	41:7 חָרָשׁ . . . צֹרף . . . לא יִמּוֹט
40:19 נָסַךְ	41:29 נִסכיהם
40:21 תדעו . . . תשמעו . . . הֻגַּד מראש	41:21-23, 26 ויגידו . . . הגידו . . . ונֵדְעָה . . . השמיעֻנו. הגידו . . . ונֵדְעָה . . . מי הגיד מראש ונֵדָעָה . . . אין מגיד . . . אין משמיע . . . אין שֹׁמֵע 41:4 קֹרא . . . מראש

40:24 אף . . . אף . . . אף	41:10, 26 אף . . . אף . . . אף 26 אף
40:24 כקש	41:2 כקש
40:24 וסערה . . . תִשָּׂאֵם	41:16 ורוח תִשָּׂאֵם וסערה
40:27 משפטי	41:1 למשפט (different meaning)
40:28 קצות הארץ	41:5, 9 קצות הארץ . . . מקצות הארץ
40:31 יחליפו כֹח	41:1 יחליפו כֹח

41:25 יקרא	42:6 קראתיך
41:25 בשמי	42:8 שמי
41:26 הגיד . . . מגיד	42:9 מגיד
41:26 צדיק	42:6 בצדק
41:26 משמיע . . . שֹׁמֵעַ	42:2 ישמיע 42:9 אשמיע
41:27 רִאשון (לציון) הנה (הנם)	42:9 הרִאשֹׁנות הנה (באו)
41:27 אתן	42:1 נתתי 42:5 נֹתן

42:1 **רוחי** (different meaning) 42:5 **ורוח** (different meaning)	41:29 **רוח** (different meaning)
46:11 קֹרא ממזרח עיט	45:3 הקורא בשמך 45:4 ואקרא לך בשמך
46:9 אנכי אל ואין עוד	45:5 אני ה׳ ואין עוד
46:9 אנכי . . . אלהים וְאֶפֶס כמוני	45:6 אֶפֶס בלעדי 45:14 אֶפֶס אלהים
46:7 לא יושיענו 46:13 קרבתי צדקתי . . . ותשועתי . . . ונתתי בציון תשועה	45:15 אלהי ישראל מושיע 45:17 ישראל נושע בה׳ תשועת עולמים 45:20 אל לא יושיע 45:21 אל צדיק ומושיע 45:22 וְהִוָּשְׁעוּ
46:3 בית יעקב	45:19 זרע יעקב
46:1 נְשֻׂאֹתֵיכֶם . . . משא 46:2 משא 46:3 הנְשֻׂאִים 46:4 אֶשָּׂא 46:7 יִשָּׂאֻהוּ	45:20 הַנֹּשאים את עץ פסלם
46:10 ומִקדם	45:21 מִקדם

45:22 כל 45:23 כל (twice) 45:24 כל	46:3 כל
45:23 כי לי תכרע כל ברך	46:1 כרע 46:2 כרעו
45:24 צדקות 45:25 יצדקו	46:12 מצדקה 46:13 צדקתי
46:2 לא יכלו מַלֵּט ונפשם . . . בשבי הָלָכה	47:14 לא יצילו את נפשם
46:4 זקנה	47:6 זקן
46:7 מצרתו לא יושיענו	47:13 יעמדו נא ויוֹשִׁיעֻךְ
46:9 כי אנכי אל ואין עוד אלהים ואפס כמוני	47:8, 10 אני ואפסי עוד
46:10 אֹמֵר עצתי תקום 46:11 איש עצתי	47:13 נלאית ברֹב עֲצָתָיִךְ
47:1, 5 יקראו לך	48:1 הנקראים 48:2 נקראו 48:8 קֹרָא לך 48:12 מְקֹרָאִי

47:4 גֹאלנו ה׳ צבאות שמו קדוש ישראל	48:2 ה׳ צבאות שמו 48:17 ה׳ גֹאלך קדוש ישראל
47:6 חִללתי	48:11 יֵחָל
47:7 לא . . . ולא	48:1 לא . . . ולא
47:8 שִׁמעי זאת	48:1 שִׁמעו זאת 48:20 השמיעו זאת
47:11 ותבא עליך פתאֹם	48:3 פתאֹם . . . ותבאנה
47:12 הועיל	48:17 להועיל
47:13 החֹזִים	48:6 חֲזֵה

48:1, 3, 5, 7, 8, 12, 14, 16, 20 שמ״ע	49:1 שִׁמעו
48:1, 12 יעקב/ישראל	49:5, 6 יעקב/ישראל
48:1 הנקראים בשם ישראל 48:8 ופֹשֵׁעַ מבטן קֹרָא לך	49:1 ה׳ מבטן קראני
48:1 ממ(ע)י יהודה יצאו . . . ובאלהי ישראל יזכירו 48:19 צאצאי מעיך כִּמְעֹתָיו	49:1 מִמְּעֵי אמי הזכיר שמי
48:8 מִבֶּטֶן קֹרא לָךְ	49:1 מִבֶּטֶן קְרָאָנִי
48:10 בחרתיך	49:7 ויבחרך (different meaning)

48:16 **מֵעֵת**	49:8 **בְּעֵת**
48:17 **כה אמר ה׳ גֹאלך קדוש ישראל**	49:7 **כה אמר ה׳ גֹאל ישראל קדושו . . . קְדֹשׁ ישראל**
48:17 **מדריכך בדרך תלך**	49:9 **על דרכים** 49:11 **ושמתי כל הָרַי לדרך**
48:18 **לוא הקשבת למצוֹתי**	49:1 **והַקשיבו**
48:20 **צְאוּ מבבל**	49:9 **לאמר לאסורים צֵאוּ**
48:20 **בקול רנה . . . עד קצה הארץ**	49:13 **רָנּוּ שמים וגילי ארץ** 49:6 **עד קצה הארץ**
48:20 **גאל ה׳ עבדו יעקב**	49:3 **עבדי אתה** 49:5 **לְעֶבֶד לו** 49:6 **מהיותך לי עבד** 49:7 **עבד מֹשלים**
48:21 **ולא צמאו**	49:10 **ולא יצמָאו**
48:21 **מים (מצור הזיל למו)**	49:10 **(ועל מבועי) מים (ינהלם)**

49:1 **אמי**	50:1 **אמכם**
49:2 **ידו**	50:11 **מידִי**
49:2 **הסתירני**	50:6 **הסתרתי**

49:3 **עבדי**	50:10 **עבדו**
49:4 **כֹחי**	50:2 **כֹח**
49:4 **משפטי**	50:8 **משפטי**
49:8 **עניתיך**	50:2 **עונֶה**
49:8 **עזרתיך**	50:7, 9 **יעזָר לי**
49:9 **בחֹשך**	50:10 **חֲשֵׁכִים**
49:20 **באזניך**	50:4, 5 **אֹזן**
49:20 **גְשָׁה לי**	50:8 **יִגַּשׁ אלי**
49:23 **לא יֵבֹשׁוּ**	50:7 **לא אֵבושׁ**
49:24 **צדיק**	50:8 **מצדיקִי** (different meaning)
49:25 **את יְרִיבֵךְ אנֹכי אריב**	50:8 **יָרִיב אתי**
49:26 **והאכלתי**	50:9 **יֹאכלֵם**
50:2 **קראתי**	51:2 **קראתיו** 51:19 **קֹרְאֹתיך**
50:2 **אחריב ים**	51:10 **המַחֲרֶבֶת ים** 51:10 **מַעמקי ים** 51:15 **הים**

50:2 **בגערתי**	51:20 **גערת אלהיך**
50:3 **אלביש שמים קדרוּת**	51:6 **כי שמים כעשן נמלָחו** 51:16 **שמים**
50:4 **יעיר**	51:9 **עורי עורי . . . עורי** 17 **התעוררי התעוררי**
50:4 **לשׁמֹע** 50:10 **שֹׁמֵעַ**	51:1 **שְׁמעו אלי** (51:4) (**הַקשיבו אלי . . . האזינו**) 51:7 **שְׁמעו אלי** 51:21 **שְׁמעי**
50:8 **קרוב מצדיקי**	51:1 **רֹדפֵי צדק** 51:5 **קרוב צדקי** (different meaning) 51:6, 8 **צדקתי** 51:7 **יודעי צדק**
50:8 **מי יריב אתי**	51:22 **אלהיך יריב עמו**
50:8 **בעל משפטי**	51:4 **ומשפטי** (different meaning) **לאור עמים** 51:5 **ישפֹטו**
50:9 **הן כֻּלם כבגד יְבלו עש יֹאכלֵם**	51:6 **והארץ כבגד תבלה** 51:8 **כי כבגד יֹאכלֵם עש**

51:4 **אוֹר**	50:11 **אוּר**

58:14 **אז תתענַּג על ה׳**	57:4 **על מי תתענָּגו**
58:13-14 **קדשִׁי . . . ארץ**	57:13 **ארץ . . . קדשִׁי**
58:2 **דְּרָכַי** 58:13 **מֵעֲשׂוֹת דרכיך** (different meaning)	57:14 **פַּנּוּ דרך . . . מדרך עמי** 57:18 **דרכיו**
58:1 **הָרֵם**	57:14 **הָרימו**
58:4, 6 **רֶשַׁע**	57:20-21 **רשעים**
58:4 **במרום**	57:15 **מרום**
58:8 **וַאֲרֻכתך מהרה תִצְמָח**	57:18 **וְאֶרְפָּאֵהוּ** 57:19 **וּרְפָאתִיו**

59:12 **פשעינו . . . וחטאתינו ענתה** 59:13 **פָּשֹׁעַ** 59:20 **ולשָׁבֵי פשע ביעקב**	58:1 **פשעם . . . חטאתם**
59:14 **משפט וצדקה**	58:2 **צדקה . . . ומשפט . . . משפטי צדק**
59:6 **יתכסו**	58:7 **וכִסִּיתוֹ**
59:5 **בִּקְעוּ . . . תִּבָּקַע**	58:8 **יִבָּקַע**

59:9 נקוֶּה לאור והנה חֹשך לִנְגֹהוֹת בָּאֲפֵלוֹת נְהַלֵּךְ 59:10 כָּשַׁלְנוּ בצהרים כנשף	58:8 אז יִבָּקַע כשחר אורֶךָ 58:10 וזרח בחֹשֶׁךְ אורֶךָ ואפלתך כצהרים
59:19 כבודו	58:8 כבוד ה׳
59:4 ודַבֵּר שָׁוְא . . . והולֵיד אָוֶן 59:6 מעשי אָוֶן 59:7 מחשבות אָוֶן	58:9 ודַבֶּר אָוֶן

66:18 ואנכי מעשיהם ומחשבֹתיהם	65:2 אחר מחשבֹתיהם
66:3 זובח השֶׂה 66:17 המתקדשים והמטהרים אל הגַּנות	65:3 זֹבחים בגַּנות
66:3 מעלה מנחה דם חזיר 66:17 אֹכְלֵי בשר החזיר	65:4 הָאֹכְלִים בשר החזיר
66:15 כי הנה ה׳ באש יבוא . . . להשיב בחֵמה אפו וגערתו בלהבי אש 66:16 כי באש ה׳ נשפט 66:24 ואִשָּׁם לא תִכבה	65:5 עשן באפי אש יקדת כל היום
66:6 משלם גמול לאֹיביו	65:6 כי אם שלמתי ושלמתי על חיקם
66:14 עבדיו	65:8, 9, 13, 14 עבדי 65:15 עבדיו

66:22 כן יעמֹד זרעכם	65:9 והוצאתי מיעקב זרע 65:23 זרע ברוכֵי ה׳ המה
66:20 הר קדשי	65:11, 25 הר קדשי
66:16 ובחרבו	65:12 לַחֶרֶב
66:4 יען קראתי ואין עונה דברתי ולא שמֵעו ויעשו הרע בעינַי ובאשר לא חפצתי בחרו (66:3) (גם המה בחרו בדרכיהם ובשקוציהם נפשם חפצה)	65:12 יען קראתי ולא עניתם דברתי ולא שמעתם ותעשו הרע בעינַי ובאשר לא חפצתי בחרתם
66:5 ונראה בשמחתכם והם יֵבֹשו	65:13 הנה עבדי ישמחו ואתם תֵּבֹשו
66:24 תמות	65:15 והֱמיתך
66:22 כן יעמֹד זרעכם ושמכם	65:15 ולעבדיו יקרא שם אחר
66:22 כאשר השמים החדשים והארץ החדשה אשר אני עֹשֶׂה	65:17 כי הנני בורא שמים חדשים וארץ חדשה
66:10 שִׂמְחוּ את ירושלם וגילו בה כל אֹהביה שִׂישׂוּ אִתָּהּ מָשׂוֹשׂ	65:18-19 שִׂישׂוּ וגילו . . . כי הנני בורא את ירושלם גילה ועַמָּהּ מָשׂוֹשׂ. וְגַלְתִּי בירושלם וְשַׂשְׂתִּי בעמי
66:7 בטרם תחיל ילָדה 66:8-9 אם יִוָּלֵד גוי פעם אחת . . . ולא אוליד	65:23 ולא יֵלדו לבהלה
66:7 בטרם	65:24 טרם

11. LANGUAGE OF THE BOOK: ARAMAIC AND LATE HEBREW

The prophecies of Deutero-Isaiah, written in the latter days of the Babylonian exile and in the first years of the return, contain representative examples of Postexilic Hebrew and also evince the influence of Aramaic, which was the lingua franca of the period. For an explication of each of the examples cited below, see the commentary ad loc.

A. Aramaic Influence

See the following terms: the noun **אֹרַח**, "shackle" (41:3); the root **אשׁשׁ**, "stand firm" (46:8); the root **אתי**, "to come" (41:5, 23, 25; 44:7; 45:11; 56:9, 12); the root **בחר**, "to test (metal)" (48:10); the root **גשׁשׁ**, "to grope" (59:10); the root **יצא** in the *hiph'il,* a calque of Aramaic **שֵׁיצִי**, in the *shaphel,* "to destroy" (43:17); the adverb **כאחד**, "together" (65:25), a calque of Aramaic **כַּחֲדָה**; the preposition *lamed* preceding a direct object (53:11); the noun **מִדָּה**, "tribute/tax" (45:14), an Akkadian loanword that came to Hebrew via Aramaic; the noun **מָעוֹת**, "grains of sand" (48:19); the root **נטל** in the *pi'el,* "to raise" (63:9); the root **נשׁי**, "to forget" (44:21); the root **סבל**, "to bear" (46:4, 7; 53:4, 11); the root **סגד**, "to bow down" (44:15, 17, 19; 46:6); the noun **עַיִט** (to be vocalized **עַיָּט**), "advisor" (46:11); the root **צער**, "to afflict" (63:18); the root **שׂלק**, "to kindle" (44:15); the noun **שִׁרְיָן**, the Aramaic form of Heb. **שריון**, "coat of mail" (59:17).

B. Late Biblical Hebrew

The examples appear solely in the exilic and postexilic periods or are only sporadically attested in Classical Hebrew: **בין**, in the *hiph'il* as a transitive verb, "to teach" (40:14); **בלוא כסף ובלוא מחיר** (55:1); **בלוא לשבעה** (55:2); **בן בטן**, "child of the womb" (49:15); **ברר**, "to be purified" (52:11); **גאל**, instead of the earlier **געל**, "to defile" (59:3); **דור ודור** (58:12; 60:15; 61:4) instead of **לדר דר** (Exod 3:15) and **מדר דר** (Exod 17:16); **הלך**, in the *pi'el* stem (59:9); **זיקות**, "firebrands" (50:11); **יְדוּעַ** — a passive *pa'ul* participle (the construct form of **יָדוּעַ**) instead of an active *po'el* participle; **כונֵן**, "to intend" (51:13); **כי**, "just as" (44:3); **כני**, "to give an endearing and honorable name" (44:5; 45:4); **כעס**, in the *hiph'il* stem (65:3); **לאחור**, "what is yet to happen" (41:23; 42:23); **לשון**, "nation" (66:18); **מבועי מים**, "springs of water" (35:7; 49:10); **מלבוש**, "clothing" (63:3); **מני**, "to destine" (65:12); **מסמרים**, "nails" (41:7); **מערב**, "west" (43:5; 45:6; 59:19); **מצץ**, "to suckle" (66:11); **מתח**, "to stretch out" (40:22); **נבח**, "to bark" (56:10);

סגנים, "rulers," an Akkadian loanword via Aramaic (41:25); סמך, "to support" (59:16; 63:5); עולמים and עולמי עד, "everlasting," "for eternity" (45:17); עור, "to rouse up" in the *hiphʿil* stem (41:2), instead of the *hiphʿil* of קים in Classical Hebrew; עיר הקֹּדֶשׁ, "the holy city" (48:2; 52:1); על, "though, despite" (53:9); עמד, instead of earlier קום, "to stand up" (44:11; 47:12; 48:13; 50:8; 59:14; 61:5; 66:22); עמד, "to be ready" (61:5); עָצְמָה, "vigor" (40:29); עשׂי חפץ, "to do what one has purposed" (46:10); פעי, "to scream" (42:14); צאצאים, "offspring" (42:5; 44:3; 48:19; 61:9; 65:23); קצות/מקצות הארץ, "from the ends of the earth" (40:28; 41:5, 9), as opposed to the variant form מקצה הארץ; שרב, "torrid earth/heat" (35:7; 49:10); תחתיות (44:23), instead of the earlier תחתית ("bottom") (Exod 19:17).

Double plurals: בבתי כְלָאִים (42:22), חָרָשֵׁי צירים (45:16), בני שִׁכֻּלָיִךְ (49:20), דֹּרות עולמים (51:9; cf. לדֹרות עולם, Gen 9:12), סְעִפֵי הסלעים (Isa 57:5; cf. סעיף סלע, Judg 15:8, 11).

The pronominal suffix appended to verbal forms, a common indicator of Late Hebrew, is prevalent in this opus, appearing over 300 times! See, for example, Isa 45:11: שאלוני; 45:19: בקשוני; 46:5: תדמיוני; 47:13: ויושיעֻךְ; 57:12: יועילוךְ; 57:13: יצִילֻךְ; 65:10: דְּרשוני. This is in contrast to Classical Hebrew, where the suffix is usually separate from the verb, which is evidenced in Deutero-Isaiah a mere four times (41:6; 42:9; 50:1; 65:12).

Note the appearance of כי as introducing a query with a negative answer (54:6b; appears again only in 2 Kgs 18:34 = Isa 36:19).

There are also a considerable number of substantives, specifically abstractions, that appear in either the feminine or the masculine plural, and that are indicative of Late Hebrew (though not exclusive to this period). For the feminine plurals see 59:9: אֲפֵלות; 63:15: גבורות; 59:18: גְמֻלות; 42:9; 48:6: חדשות; 48:21: חֳרָבות; 50:6: כְּלִמות; 66:4: מְגוּרֹתם; 53:3: מכאֹבות; 59:9: נְגֹהות; 64:2: נוראות; 48:6: נְצֻרות; 46:1: נְשֻׂאֹת; 41:21: עֲצֻמותיכם; 57:16: נשמות; 45:24: צדקות; 58:11: צחצחות; 43:18: קדמוניות; 41:22; 42:9; 43:9; 48:3; 65:17: רִאשֹׁנות; 40:14: תבונות; 60:6; 63:7: תהִלות; 63:13: תהֹמות. For the rarer masculine plural see 40:26, 29: אוֹנִים; 53:3: אישים; 63:4: גאולַי (שנת) (and cf. 51:10; 62:12); 50:10: חֲשֵׁכִים; 57:18: נִחֻמִים; 54:6: נעורים; 54:4: עלומיך; 66:11: תַּנְחֻמֶיהָ; 66:4: תַּעֲלֻלֵיהֶם (cf. 3:4, but with a different meaning).

12. INNER-BIBLICAL TRADITIONS REFLECTED IN DEUTERO-ISAIAH

The prophet was deeply influenced by Israel's epic traditions and often alludes to them, all the while reshaping them to fit his own worldview:

- The prophet used the mythic echoes of God's victory over the primeval dragon and the sea prior to creation as a precedent to demonstrate God's ability to redeem His nation (51:9-11).

- The tradition of the Garden of Eden served as a paradigm for Deutero-Isaiah in his depiction of Zion's rehabilitation and everlasting peace (51:3; 65:25).
- The tradition of the flood and its aftermath formed the basis for God's commitment to remain faithful to His covenant with His people: Just as He promised never again to destroy the world (Gen 8:21-22; 9:11-17), so too will His covenant of well-being with the nation remain immutable (Isa 54:9-10).
- The tradition of Abraham and Sarah as the progenitors of the nation (this is the only time Sarah is mentioned in the Hebrew Bible outside Genesis) (51:1-2; cf. also 41:8: "Abraham, My friend") and the allusion to matriarchal barrenness (54:1) were used as prototypes: Just as Abraham and Sarah were commanded to leave Ur of the Chaldees in Babylonia (Gen 12:1), so too was the nation commanded to leave Babylon (Isa 48:20; 52:11). And just as the former were blessed with progeny and inherited the land (Gen 15:7, 18-21; 22:17; 24:60; 28:14), so too will Israel be blessed with many descendants (Isa 44:4; 48:19; 49:20-21; 54:3) and settle the land (48:19; 49:8; 57:13; 58:14; 60:21; 61:7; 65:9).
- The name "Jacob" is one of Deutero-Isaiah's most common sobriquets in his addresses to Israel (41:8, 14, 21; 42:24; 43:1, 22, 28; 44:1, 2, 5, 21, 23; 45:4, 19; 48:12, 20; 49:5, 6, 26; 58:14; 59:20; 60:16; 65:9).
- The tradition regarding Israel's descent to Egypt appears in 52:3. Note also the allusion to the rotting of the Nile's fish and to the plague of darkness (50:2-3; 60:2; see Exod 7:18, 21; 10:22-23).

Many traditions connected to the Egyptian exodus and the subsequent desert journey were used as models for the contemporary exodus from Babylon:

- Just as the Lord redeemed Israel "with great power and a mighty hand" (Exod 6:6; 13:9; 32:11; Deut 4:34; 5:15; 7:19; 11:2; 26:8), so too will He deliver His nation from Babylonia: "Behold, the Lord God comes in might, and His arm rules for Him" (Isa 40:10). Compare also the description of the splitting and the crossing of the sea (42:15; 44:27; 50:2; 51:10; 63:12; see Exod 14:16, 21-22, 29; 15:19).
- Moses is mentioned here in this very same context (Isa 63:11-12).
- The utter annihilation of Pharaoh's army, including the horses and the chariots (Exod 14:26, 28; 15:1, 4, 19, 21), is alluded to in Isa 43:17, and the hymn of the redeemed (Exod 15) is echoed by a similar composition in Isa 42:10-12.

- God is called a warrior (איש מלחמה/ות) in Exod 15:3 and in the "new hymn" in Isa 42:13. Everywhere else in the Bible this term is relegated to humans.
- A declaration of God's kingship over Israel follows the redemption (Exod 15:18; Isa 43:15; 52:7).
- The guiding of the nation through the desert (Deut 8:2, 15; 29:4; Isa 42:16; 48:21; 63:13-14).
- Supply of potable water sources in the wilderness/the transformation of the desert into rivers (Exod 17:1-7; Num 20:2-11; Isa 41:17-18; 43:20; 48:21; 49:10).

The prophet also speaks of miracles that shall overshadow and eclipse the miracles of the Egyptian exodus:

- During the Egyptian exodus, the Lord's presence was seen exclusively by the nation (Exod 16:7, 10), whereas during the Babylonian exodus His presence shall be universally revealed (Isa 40:5).
- Israel left their Egyptian bondage "in panicky haste" (Deut 16:3; cf. also Exod 12:11). In contrast, when they leave Babylon, it shall not be so (Isa 52:12), but rather, "You shall leave in joy and be led home secure" (55:12).
- When Israel left Egypt the waters of the sea were dried up so as to ensure a passage on dry land (Exod 14:16, 22, 29; 15:19). Conversely, when they leave Babylon all of the Syrian desert shall become lush with water (Isa 41:18; 43:20; 49:10), an abundance of trees shall spring up from the ground (41:19; 55:13), and the path to Zion shall be cleared of all obstacles (40:3-4; 42:16; 43:19; 49:11; 57:14; 62:10).
- During their first desert journey, an angel accompanied and guided them (Exod 14:19; 23:20, 23), or, alternatively, a pillar of cloud or fire (Exod 13:21-22; 14:19-20; Num 14:14), i.e., the Lord's messengers shepherded the nation through the desert. In contrast, when they leave Babylonia, the Lord Himself, in His full glory, shall guide them: "For the Lord is marching before you. The God of Israel is your rear guard" (Isa 52:12; cf. also 58:8; 63:9, and see the commentary there).
- Two additional contrastive elements may be noted: When Israel left Egypt they took with them "objects of silver and gold, and clothing" (Exod 12:35); whereas when they leave Babylon they shall take only the Temple vessels that were confiscated as booty by the Babylonians (Isa 52:11). Moreover, in contrast to Moses, the dominant figure in the Babylonian exodus shall be a foreign monarch, Cyrus (44:28; 45:1). This was a point of serious contention, and echoes of the ensuing polemic are heard in 45:9-13.

13. DEUTERONOMIC AND DEUTERONOMISTIC INFLUENCE ON DEUTERO-ISAIAH

The influence of Deuteronomy and Deuteronomistic literature on the prophecies of Deutero-Isaiah is manifold, encompassing language, style, and ideology:

First and foremost one can cite the idea of divine exclusivity, patently pronounced in many verses, e.g., Deut 4:35: "It has been clearly demonstrated to you that the Lord alone is God. There is none beside Him"; cf. also 2 Sam 7:22 = 1 Chr 17:20: "You are great indeed, O Lord God. There is none like You, and there is no other God but You"; 1 Kgs 8:60: "To the end that all the peoples of the earth may know that the Lord alone is God. There is no other." This, in turn, is echoed by Deutero-Isaiah, e.g., Isa 45:5: "I am the Lord and there is none else. Beside Me, there is no god"; v. 21: "No god exists beside Me." For the expression **אין עוד** ("none else") see 43:10, 11; 44:6; 45:5-6, 14, 18, 21, 22; 46:9.

Negation of corporeality and likeness: "The Lord spoke to you out of the fire. You heard the sound of words but perceived no shape — nothing but a voice" (Deut 4:12; cf. vv. 3, 36). Compare also Isa 40:18: "To whom, then, can you liken God? What form compare to Him?" (cf. 40:25; 46:5).

The doublet **אני אני** ("I, I alone"), with the Deity as the subject, occurs only in Deut 32:39 (cf. Hos 5:14) and in Isa 48:15. Note also the appearance of **אני הוא** ("I am He") in both literatures (Deut 32:39; Isa 41:4; 43:10, 13; 46:4; 48:12; 52:6; as well as in 1 Chr 21:17). Isa 43:13, "I am He; none can deliver from My hand" (**אני הוא ואין מידי מציל**), is a direct quote from Deut 32:39: "See, then, that I, I am He . . . none can deliver from My hand (**כי אני אני הוא . . . ואין מידי מציל**)."

The expression **האל הנאמן** ("the steadfast God"; Deut 7:9) is echoed in Isa 49:7: **ה׳ אשר נאמן**.

Israel is referred to often as **עם קדוש** ("a holy people") in Deuteronomy (Deut 7:6; 14:2, 21; 26:19; 28:9); cf. Deutero-Isaiah: **עם הקֹדֶשׁ** (62:12) and **עם קדשך** (63:18; again only in Dan 12:7).

The expression **כּוּר ברזל** ("iron blast furnace"), which is an allusion to the Egyptian subjugation (Deut 4:20; 1 Kgs 8:51; Jer 11:4), is echoed in Isa 48:10: **בְּכוּר עֹנִי** ("furnace of affliction").

For the expression **ספר כריתות** ("bill of divorcement"; 50:1) see Deut 24:1; Jer 3:8.

The idea of the "chosenness" (**בחר**) of Israel is first expressed in Deuteronomy and Deuteronomistic literature, but is absent from the prophetic literature prior to Deutero-Isaiah. See Deut 4:37; 7:6-7; 10:15;

14:2; Jer 33:24; and Isa 41:8-9; 42:1; 43:10, 20; 44:1-2; 45:4; 49:7; 65:9, 15. For the joint appearance of the verbs בחר and אהב ("to choose," "to love"), see Deut 4:37; 7:8, 13; 10:15; Isa 41:8; for the root אהב on its own see Deut 7:8, 13; 23:6; 1 Kgs 10:9 and Isa 43:4; 63:9 — all the above references describe the relationship between God and His people. For אהב as delineating the relationship of God and Cyrus, see Isa 48:14.

The motif of the redemption from Egypt is emphasized in Deut 7:8; 9:26; 13:6; 15:15; 21:8; 24:18; 2 Sam 7:23 (note that all the above references use the root פדי ["to redeem/ransom"]), and in Isa 41:14; 43:1, 14; 44:22-23; 48:20; 51:10; 52:3, 9; 62:12; 63:9, 16 (which all employ the root גאל [a synonym of פדי]; but cf. also 35:10; 51:11, where the root פדי appears.

The absence of angels in both the exodus from Egypt and from Babylonia (as opposed to the traditions reflected in Exod 14:19; 23:20-23; 32:34; 33:2; Num 20:16). God and God alone frees the nation and leads them through the desert: Deut 4:37: "He Himself, in His great might, led you out of Egypt"; and see the commentary on Isa 63:8-9 based on the reading in the LXX.

"A mighty hand and an outstretched arm": Deut 4:34; 5:15; 7:19; 11:2; 26:8; 1 Kgs 8:42; Jer 21:5; 32:21; cf. also Isa 40:10.

The insistence on remembering the past (especially regarding the exodus and the desert journey): Deut 5:15; 7:18; 8:2; 9:7; 15:15; 16:3, 12; 24:9, 18, 22; 25:17; and Isa 44:21; 46:8-9 (cf. also 43:18).

The constant reiteration of the Lord's name (Isa 41:25; 42:8; 43:7; 48:1, 9; 50:10; 51:15; 52:5-6; 54:5; 56:6; 59:19; 60:9; 66:5) is influenced by the "Name" (שֵׁם) ideology in Deuteronomy and Deuteronomistic literature, e.g., the oft-repeated expressions: "where My/His name might abide" (1 Kgs 3:2; 5:17, 19; 8:16-20, 29, 44, 48; 9:3; 2 Kgs 23:27); "to build a house for My name" (2 Sam 7:13; 1 Kgs 3:2; 5:17, 19); "where the Lord God will choose to establish His name" (Deut 12:11; 14:23); "to establish His name there" (Deut 12:5, 21; 14:24; and a great number of additional references in the books of Deuteronomy and Kings).

God's granting of the land of Israel as a hereditary possession (Deut 15:4; 16:20; 25:19; 26:1; 1 Kgs 8:36; Isa 57:13; 60:21; 61:7; 65:9).

Heaven as the divine abode (as opposed to the Temple): Deut 26:15; 1 Kgs 8:30, 39, 43, 49; Isa 57:15; 66:1; cf. also 40:22. Instead of Solomon's proclamation: "I have now built for You a stately (זְבֻל) house, a place where You may dwell forever" (1 Kgs 8:13), the prophet states: "Look down from heaven and see, from Your holy and glorious height (זְבֻל)" (Isa 63:15).

According to Deutero-Isaiah and Deuteronomistic literature, the function of the Temple is to be the locus and focus of national (1 Kgs 8:29-35, 38-39, 44-45, 47-49) and international (1 Kgs 8:41-43) prayer. Thus in Deutero-Isaiah: "As for the foreigners who attach themselves to the Lord to minister to Him and to love the name of the Lord, to be His servants, all who keep the Sabbath and do not profane it, and who hold fast to My covenant. I will bring them [the foreigners] to My sacred mount and let them rejoice in My house of prayer. Their burnt offerings and sacrifices shall be welcome on My altar. For My house shall be called a house of prayer for all peoples" (56:6-7). Compare also 66:21: "And from them [the nations] likewise I will take some to be Levitical priests, said the Lord."

The expression נקרא שם על, referring to Israel being called by the Lord's name: Deut 28:10; Jer 14:9; 15:16; Isa 63:19.

The expression השיב על/אל לב: Deut 4:39; 30:1; 1 Kgs 8:47; Isa 44:19; 46:8.

The expression הכעיס את ה׳: Deut 4:25; 9:18; 31:29; 32:16, 21; and many additional references throughout Deuteronomy and Jeremiah; see also Isa 65:3.

The expression האריך ימים, e.g., Deut 4:26, 40; 5:16, 33; 6:2; 11:9; 22:7; 25:15; 30:18; 32:47; Josh 24:31; Judg 2:7; 1 Kgs 3:14; Isa 53:10.

The expression שפך דם נקי: Deut 19:10; 21:7; 2 Kgs 21:16; 24:4; Jer 7:6; 22:3, 17; Isa 59:7.

The expression שׂימת/נתתי דברי ה׳ בפה: Deut 18:18; Jer 1:9; Isa 59:21.

The simile of "groping like a blind man in the dark": Deut 28:29; Isa 59:9-10.

For the connection between Deut 32:9-13 and Isa 58:11-14 see the commentary. Compare especially the unique expressions in Deut 32:13: ירכיבֵהו על במתי ארץ ויאכל, and Isa 58:14: והרכבתיך על במתי ארץ והאכלתיך.

For the connection between Deut 33:26-29 and Isa 45:14-19 see the commentary. Compare especially the singular expressions in Deut 33:29: ישראל . . . נושע בה׳, and Isa 45:17: ישראל נושע בה׳.

The unusual sobriquet of Israel, יְשֻׁרוּן, is found only in Deut 32:15; 33:5, 26; and Isa 44:2.

The expression ספר כריתות and the verb שלח in the *piʿel,* signifying the divorce of a woman, appear together in Deut 24:1, 3; Jer 3:1, 8; Isa 50:1.

The use of the term עבד/עבדים when referring to the chosen nation (e.g., 1 Kgs 8:23, 32, 36) appears thirty times throughout Deutero-Isaiah.

Derisive terms in reference to idols: תֹּהוּ (1 Sam 12:21; Isa 40:17; 41:29; 44:9), תועבה (Deut 7:25, 26; 27:15; 32:16; 2 Kgs 23:13; Isa 41:24; 44:19), שקוץ/שקוצים (Deut 29:16; 1 Kgs 11:5, 7; 2 Kgs 23:13, 24; Jer 4:1; 7:30; 13:27; 16:18; 32:34; Isa 66:3).

The multiple use of the term פֶּסֶל ("idol") (e.g., Deut 4:16, 23, 25; 5:8; 7:5, 25; 12:3; 27:15; Isa 40:19-20; 42:8, 17; 44:9-10, 15, 17; 45:20; 48:5). Compare the expressions פסל ומַסֵּכָה (e.g., Deut 27:15; Judg 17:3-4; 18:14, 17), הפסל נסך (Isa 40:19), and ופסלי ונסכי (Isa 48:5); note that the parallel term אליל (e.g., Isa 10:10; Hab 2:18) appears neither in Deuteronomy nor in Deutero-Isaiah.

An idol crafted by a woodworker/smith (Deut 13:2; 27:15; Jer 10:3, 9, 14; 51:17; cf. Isa 40:19-20; 41:7; 44:12-13; 46:6; cf. 45:16).

The expression לא/בל/בלא יועיל (1 Sam 12:21; Jer 2:8, 11; Isa 44:9, 10; 57:12).

Idol worship "under every verdant tree" (Deut 12:2; 1 Kgs 14:23; 2 Kgs 16:4; 17:10; Jer 2:20; 3:6, 13; 17:2; Isa 57:5).

Offering sacrifices or incense to foreign idols (e.g., 1 Kgs 22:44; 2 Kgs 18:4; Jer 11:13, 17; 44:3, 5, 8; Isa 65:3, 7).

Further parallels: the verbal sequence of דרשׁ/בקש . . . מצא . . . שׁוב . . . רחם (Deut 4:29-31; Isa 55:6-7); the expression שׁוב אל ה׳ (Deut 30:10; 1 Kgs 8:48; 2 Kgs 23:25; Jer 4:1; Isa 55:7); the expression עלי על לב (2 Kgs 12:5; Jer 3:16; 7:31; 19:5; 32:35; Isa 65:17); the expression קדח אש (Deut 32:22; Jer 15:14; 17:4; Isa 50:11; 64:1); the expression צבא השמים (Deut 4:19; 17:3; 1 Kgs 22:19; 2 Kgs 17:16; 21:3, 5; 23:4-5; Jer 8:2; 19:13; 33:22; cf. Isa 48:2); "bringing water forth from flinty rock" (Deut 8:15; Isa 48:21); צור ("Rock") as a divine sobriquet (Deut 32:4, 15, 18, 30, 37; 1 Sam 2:2; 2 Sam 22:3, 32, 47; 23:3; Isa 44:8); the command "Fear not . . . and be not dismayed" (Deut 1:21; 31:8; Josh 8:1; 10:25; Jer 23:4; 30:10; 46:27; Isa 51:7).

See now, in detail, S. M. Paul, "Deuteronom(ist)ic Influences on Deutero-Isaiah," in N. S. Fox et al., eds., *Mishneh Todah: Studies in Deuteronomy and Its Cultural Environment in Honor of Jeffrey H. Tigay* (Winona Lake, IN, 2009), 219-27.

14. INFLUENCE OF FIRST ISAIAH ON DEUTERO-ISAIAH

The two independent sections of Isaiah were combined into one book in a relatively early period (see above, §1). One of the primary reasons for this is the linguistic affinity between the two prophets. In some places there is little doubt that Deutero-Isaiah used earlier Isaianic expressions, but in other instances this relationship is more difficult to prove. The cumulative evidence of common terms and idioms is, however, very impressive.

Most obvious is the use of the divine appellation קדוש ישראל by both prophets (1:4; 5:19, 24; 10:20; 12:6; 29:19; 30:11-12, 15; 31:1; 37:23; 41:14, 16,

20; 43:3, 14; 45:11; 47:4; 48:17; 49:7; 54:5; 55:5; 60:9, 14) and the use of the term קדוש without further specificity (5:16; 6:3; 10:17; 43:15; 58:13).

The people of Israel are depicted as blind and deaf in both (29:18 [and cf. 6:9-10; 32:3]; 35:5; 42:16, 18-20; 43:8).

The image of raising an ensign to the nations for the return of Israel to their ancestral land (11:12; 49:22; 62:10).

Utopic depictions of the latter days (2:2-4; 51:4-5; 60:2; and especially 11:6-9; 65:25).

The expression יאמר ה׳ (instead of אמר ה׳) in the middle of the verse (1:11, 18; 33:10; 41:21; 66:9), referring to a direct quote, occurs again only in Ps 12:6.

The expression כי פי ה׳ דִּבֵּר (1:20; 40:5; 58:14) is found only once more in the Hebrew Bible (Mic 4:4).

The expression רם וְנִשָּׂא appears in 6:1 (describing the heavenly throne) and 57:15 (as a divine appellation).

The image of a potter crafting clay (29:16; 45:9; 64:7).

The expression נִדחי ישראל (11:12; 56:8) occurs again only in Ps 147:2.

The depiction of the Lord as "dwelling on high" (33:5, 16; 57:15).

The expression חֵיל גוים/עמים, "the wealth of nations/peoples" (10:14; 60:5, 11; 61:6), appears again only in Zech 14:14.

The expression יִבְלֵי מים, "watercourses" (Isa 30:25; 44:4), appears only here.

The expression סְעִפֵּי הסלעים, "crevices in the cliffs" (2:21; 57:5), occurs only twice more, in the singular (Judg 15:8, 11).

A fair number of terms are common to both books: אגמון, "reed" (Isa 9:13; 19:15; 58:5), again only in Job (40:26; 41:12); אוּר, "fire" (Isa 31:9; 44:16; 47:14; 50:11), again only in Ezek 5:2; אֶפְעֶה, "viper" (Isa 30:6; 59:5), again only in Job 20:16; גֶּזַע, "stump" (Isa 11:1; 40:24), again only in Job 14:8; לִמֻּדִים/לִמֻּדֵי, "disciples" (Isa 8:16; 50:4); נעצוץ, "briar" (7:19; 55:13); נֵצֶר, "twig, tender branch" (11:1; 14:19 [with a different meaning]; 60:21), again only in Dan 11:7, which was influenced by Isa 11:1; the root נשת, "to be dry" (19:5; 41:17), again only in Jer 51:30, as a metaphor; צאצאים, signifying progeny of flora and fauna as well as of humans (Isa 22:24; 42:5; 44:3; 48:19; 61:9; 65:23), again only in Job 5:25; 21:8; 27:14; 31:8; תעלולים, "babes," "mockery" (Isa 3:4; 66:4, but note that in each case the term means something different). See also the redactional frame encompassing both books in the introduction to chaps. 65–66.

Since chaps. 34–35 may have originally been part of Deutero-Isaiah (see above), the terms and expressions these chapters have in common with the rest of Deutero-Isaiah are not listed here.

For the connections between chaps. 47 and 10, see the introduction to chap. 47, and for the connections between chaps. 65 and 1:12, 15, see the commentary to 65:1-3. Below are some additional comparisons:

49:19 כי חָרְבֹתיך ושֹׁמְמֹתיך וארץ הֲרִסֻתֵךְ כי עתה תֵּצְרִי מִיּוֹשב וְרָחֲקוּ מְבלעיך	6:11-12 וַיֹּאמֶר עד אשר אם שָׁאוּ ערים מֵאֵין יושב. . . . ורִחַק ה׳ את האדם
51:4-5 כי תורה מאִתי תצא ומשפטי לאור עמים. . . . וזרֹעַי עמים ישפֹּטו	2:2-4 ונהרו אליו כל הגוים. . . כי מציון תצא תורה. . . . ושָׁפַט בין הגוים והוכיח לעמים רבים
59:1-3 ולא כבדה אזנו מִשמוע. . . . הִסתירו פנים מכם מִשמוע. . . . כי כפיכם נְגֹאֲלו בדם	1:15 ובְפָרִשְׂכם כפיכם אעלים עינַי מכם גם כי תרבו תפִלה אינני שֹׁמע ידיכם דמים מלֵאו
59:20 ובא לציון גואל ולשָׁבֵי פשע ביעקב	1:27 ציון במשפט תִּפָּדֶה ושָׁבֶיהָ בצדקה
60:3 והלכו גוים לְאוֹרֵךְ 5 אז תראי ונהרת	2:2-3 ונהרו אליו כל הגוים. . . . והלכו עמים רבים
60:14 ציון קְדוש ישראל	12:6 ציון . . . קְדוש ישראל
65:25a-c זאב וטָלֶה יִרעו כאחד ואריה כַּבָּקָר יֹאכל תבן ונחש עפר לחמוֹ	11:6-8 וגר זאב עם כבשׂ ונמר עם גדי ירבץ. . . . ופרה ודֹב תרעֶינה יחדָּו . . . ואריה כַּבָּקָר יֹאכל תבן ושעשע יונק על חֻר פָּתֶן ועל מאורת צפעוני
65:25d-e לא יָרֵעו ולא ישחיתו בכל הר קדשי	11:9 לא יָרֵעו ולא ישחיתו בכל הר קדשי
66:10 שִׂישׂו אִתָּהּ מָשׂושׂ	8:6-7a ומְשׂושׂ את. . . . הנה אדֹנָי . . . מֵי הנהר
66:12 הנני נֹטֶה אליה כנהר . . . שוטף כְּבוד גוים	8:7b-8 ואת כל כבודו. . . . שטף . . . מֻטּוֹת

15. INFLUENCE OF JEREMIAH ON DEUTERO-ISAIAH

This long list of cross-references exemplifies the multiple linguistic and ideological influences of Jeremiah on Deutero-Isaiah:

Jeremiah	**Isaiah**
16:18 וְשִׁלַּמְתִּי רִאשׁוֹנָה מִשְׁנֵה עֲוֹנָם וחטָּאתם	40:2 כי לקחה מיד ה׳ כִּפְלַיִם בכל חטֹאתיה 61:7 תחת בָּשְׁתְּכֶם מִשְׁנֶה... לכן בארצם מִשְׁנֶה יִירָשׁוּ
31:16 כי יש שָׂכָר לפעֻלתך	40:10 = 62:11 הנה שְׂכרו אתו ופעֻלתו לפניו
1:5 בטרם אֶצָּרְךָ בבטן ידעתיך ובטרם תצא מרחם הִקדשתיך נביא לגוים נתתיךָ	42:6 וְאֶצָּרך ואתנך לברית עם לאור גוים 49:6 ונתתיך לאור גוים 49:8 וְאֶצָּרך ואתנך לברית עם
27:5 אנכי עשיתי את הארץ את האדם ... ובזרועי הנטויה ונתתיה לאשר ישר בעינָי	45:12-13 אנכי עשיתי ארץ ואדם עליה בראתי אני ידַי נטו שמַים... וכל דרכיו אֲיַשֵּׁר
33:3 ואגידה לך גדֹלות ובצֻרות לא ידעתָּם	48:6 השמעתיך חדשות מעתה ונצֻרות ולא ידעתָּם
9:6 הנני צוֹרְפָם ובחנתים כי איך אעשה	48:10-11 הנה צרפתיך ולא בכסף בחרתיך בכוּר עֹני למעני למעני אעשה
31:9-10 אובילם... אל נחלי מים בדרך ישר לא יִכָּשלו בה... וּשְׁמָרוֹ כרעה עדרו	49:9-11 יִרעו... מרעיתם.... ועל מבועי מים יְנהלם.... ושמתי כל הרַי לדָרך
2:32 התשכח בתולה עֶדְיָהּ כַּלָּה קִשֻּׁרֶיהָ ועמי שכחוני ימים אין מספר	49:14 ותאמר ציון עזבני ה׳ ואדֹנָי שכחני 49:15 התשכח אשה עולָהּ מֵרַחֵם בן בטנהּ גם אלה תשכחנה ואנכי לא אשכחֵך 49:18 כי כֻלם כעדִי תלבשי וּתְקַשְּׁרִים כַּכַּלָּה

50:1 אי זה ספר כריתות אִמכם אשר שִׁלחתיה	3:8 שִׁלחתיהָ ואתן את ספר כריתֻתֶיהָ אליה
51:3 ששון ושמחה יִמָּצא בה תודה וקול זמרה	33:11 קול ששון וקול שמחה . . . אֹמרים הודו את ה׳ צבאות . . . מבִאים תודה בית ה׳
51:7 שִׁמעו אלַי ידעֵי צדק עַם תורתי בלבם	31:33 נתתי את תורתי בקרבם ועל לבם אכתבנה 32:40 ואת יראתי אתן בלבבם
51:11 (= 35:10) וּפְדוּיֵי ה׳ ישובון ובאו ציון ברִנה ושמחת עולם על רֹאשם ששון ושמחה ישיגון נסו יגון ואנחה	31:11-13 כי פדה ה׳ את יעקב. . . . ובאו ורִנְּנו במרום ציון. . . . והפכתי אֶבלם לששון ונחמתים ושמחתים מיגונם
51:13-14 וַתְּפַחֵד תמיד כל היום מפני חמת המציק כאשר כונֵן להשחית. . . . מִהַר צֹעֶה לְהִפָּתֵחַ ולא ימות לשחת ולא יחסר לחמוֹ	11:19 נשחיתה עץ בלחמו ונכרתנו מארץ חיים ושמו לא יִזָּכֵר עוד
51:15 ואנכי ה׳ אלהיך רֹגַע הים וַיֶּהֱמוּ גליו ה׳ צבאות שמו	31:35 רֹגַע הים וַיֶּהֱמוּ גליו ה׳ צבאות שמו
51:16 ואשים דברַי בפיך . . . לנטֹע שמים וליסֹד ארץ 59:21 ודברַי אשר שמתי בפיך	1:9-10 הנה נתתי דברַי בפיך. . . . ולנטוע
53:7 כַּשֶּׂה לַטֶּבַח יובל	11:19 ואני כְּכֶבֶשׂ אלוף יובל לטבוח
54:1-2 רָנִּי עקרה לא יָלָדָה פִּצחי רנה וצהֲלי לא חלה כי רבים בנֵי שוממה מבני בעולה אמר ה׳. הרחיבי מקום אהלך ויריעות משכנותיך יטו אַל תחשׂכי האריכי מיתריך ויתדתיך חַזֵּקִי	10:20 אָהֳלִי שֻׁדָּד וכל מיתרַי נִתָּקוּ בנַי יְצָאֻנִי ואינם אין נֹטה עוד אהלי ומקים יריעותָי 4:20 שֶׁבֶר על שֶׁבֶר נקרא כי שֻׁדְּדָה כל הארץ פתאֹם שֻׁדְּדוּ אֹהָלַי רגע יריעֹתָי

32:40 וכרתי להם ברית עולם 50:5 ברית עולם לא תִשָּׁכֵחַ	55:3 ואכרתה לכם ברית עולם 61:8 וברית עולם אכרות להם

Jer 29:10-14: See commentary below on Isa 55:6-13

31:9 בבכי יבֹאו ובתחנונים אובילֵם	55:12 כי בשמחה תצֵאו ובשלום תוּבָלון
12:9 לכו אִספו כל חית השדה הֵתָיוּ לאכלה 12:10 רֹעים רבים שִׁחֲתוּ כרמי	56:9 כל חַיתו שׂדי אֵתָיוּ לאכֹל כל חַיתו ביער 56:11 והמה רֹעים לא ידעו הָבין כֻּלם לדרכם פָּנו

Jer 2:20-28: See commentary below on Isa 57:3-13

2:23 ראי דרכך בגַּיְא 2:25 ותאמרי נואש	57:10 ברֹב דרכך יגעת לֹא אמרת נואש
6:13 = 8:10 כֻּלּוֹ בוצע בָּצַע 6:14 = 8:11 וירפאו את שבר עמי על נקלה לאמר שלום שלום ואין שלום	57:17 בַּעֲוֹן בִּצְעוֹ קצפתי 57:18 דרכיו ראיתי וְאֶרפאֵהו 57:19 שלום שלום . . . ורפאתיו 57:21 אין שלום

All the verses listed above are dealt with in the commentary.

16. ADDITIONAL PROPHETIC INFLUENCES ON DEUTERO-ISAIAH

From time to time, additional sporadic influences and/or similarities are discernible from other prophetic books.

The motif of the "desecration of God's name," as in Isa 48:11: "For My sake, My own sake, do I act — lest My name be dishonored," is very common in Ezekiel; see 20:9: "But I acted for the sake of My name, that it might not be profaned in the sight of the nations among whom they were"; cf. also vv. 22, 39; 36:21-23.

For a comparison between Isa 54 and Hos 2 see the introduction to chap. 54. For a comparison between Isa 58:1-2 and Hos 8:1-2 see the introduction to 58:1-2.

Compare Mic 3:8: "To declare to Jacob his transgressions and to Israel his sin"; Isa 58:1: "Declare to My people their transgression, to the house of Jacob their sin."

Nah 2:1: "Behold on the hills the footsteps of a herald announcing good fortune. . . . Never again shall scoundrels invade you," is divided into two separate verses: Isa 52:1: "For the uncircumcised and the unclean shall never enter you again"; v. 7: "How welcome on the mountain are the footsteps of the herald announcing happiness, heralding good fortune" — see the commentary there for the contextual change.

The prophecy in Zeph 2:15: "Is this the gay city that dwelt secure, that thought in her heart, 'I am, and there is none but me'?" (which relates to Nineveh), is quoted in Isa 47:8: "And now hear this, O pampered one — who dwells in security, who thinks to yourself, 'I am, and there is none but me'" — see the commentary there for the contextual change.

17. PSALMIC INFLUENCE ON DEUTERO-ISAIAH

The psalmic literature left a clear impression on Deutero-Isaiah's prophecy:

Isaiah	**Psalms**
40:6-8 כל הבשר חציר וכל חסדו כציץ השדה. יבש חציר נָבֵל ציץ כי רוח ה׳ נשבה בו אכן חציר העם. יבש חציר נָבֵל ציץ ודבר אלהינו יקום לעולם	103:15-20 אנוש כחציר ימיו כציץ השדה כן יציץ. כי רוח עברה בו ואיננו ולא יַכִּירֶנּוּ עוד מקומו. וחסד ה׳ מעולם ועד עולם על יְרֵאָיו. . . . עֹשֵׂי דְבָרו . . . בקול דְבָרו
40:26 המוציא במספר צְבאם לְכֻלָּם בשם יקרא מֵרֹב אונים ואמיץ כֹּח איש לא נעדר.	147:4-5 מונה מספר לכוכבים לְכֻלָּם שמות יקרא. גדול אדונינו ורב כֹּח לתבונתו אין מספר
41:18 אשים מדבר לאגם מים וארץ צִיָּה למוצאי מים	107:35 יָשֵׂם מדבר לאגם מים וארץ צִיָּה לְמֹצאי מים

96:1 שירו לה׳ שיר חדש 98:1 שירו לה׳ שיר חדש 98:3 ראו כל אפסי ארץ	42:10 שירו לה׳ שיר חדש תהִלתו מִקצה הארץ
96:11-12 ירעם הים ומלֹאו.... אז ירננו כל עצי יער 98:7 ירעם הים ומלֹאו תבל ויֹשבי בהּ 98:8 יחד הרים ירנֵּנו	42:10 יורדי הים ומלֹאו איים ויֹשביהם 42:11 ישאו מדבר ועריו... ירֹנו יֹשבי סלע מראש הרים יצוָחו
96:7-8 הבו לה׳ כבוד.... הבו לה׳ כבוד שמו	42:12 ישימו לה׳ כבוד
51:3-6 מְחֵה פשעָי.... ומֵחַטָּאתִי.... למען תצדק בְּדָבְרֶךָ תִּזְכֶּה בְשָׁפְטֶךָ	43:25-26 אנכי אנכי הוא מֹחה פשעיך.... וחטֹאתיך.... נִשָּׁפטה יחד... למען תצדק
107:16 כי שִׁבַּר דלתות נחֹשת ובריחי ברזל גִּדֵּעַ	45:2 דלתות נחושה אֲשַׁבֵּר ובריחי ברזל אֲגַדֵּעַ
22:24-32 יראי ה׳ הללוהו כל זרע יעקב... כל זרע ישראל.... מאתך תהִלתי.... כל אפסי ארץ וישתחוו ... יכרעו.... צדקתו	45:22-25 וְהִוָּשְׁעוּ כל אפסי ארץ.... תִּכרע.... בה׳ יצדקו ויתהללו כל זרע ישראל

For an analysis of these parallels see the commentary ad loc.

18. PARALLELS BETWEEN THE BOOK OF LAMENTATIONS AND DEUTERO-ISAIAH

Deutero-Isaiah contrasted the depressing present condition of Jerusalem and the nation with the prospects for a splendid and resplendent future. In this he was influenced by the book of Lamentations, whose authors contrasted the dismal present with memories of a glorious past. Both the language and ideas in the laments of the latter book influenced Deutero-Isaiah. In addition to the examples offered in the introduction to chap. 54, cf. the common motifs and expressions listed below, which are dealt with more fully in the commentary.

The motif of mourning and mourners (57:18; 60:20; 61:2, 3; 66:10 — Lam 1:4; 2:8; 5:15).

The term מָשׂוֹשׂ ("joy") in connection with the nation and with Jerusalem (60:15; 65:18; 66:10 — Lam 2:15).

The motif of reprisal against enemies (59:18; 66:6 — Lam 3:64).

The term עטרת ("crown") in the depiction of Jerusalem (62:3 — Lam 5:16).

The image of God trampling grapes at a winepress (63:2 — Lam 1:15).

Edom as Israel's declared and definitive enemy (63:1 — Lam 4:21, 22).

God as the adversary vis-à-vis His nation (63:1 — Lam 2:4).

God's excessive wrath, as in 64:8: "Do not be extremely angry, O Lord" (אל תקצף ה׳ עד מאד) — Lam 5:22: "You have been extremely angry with us" (קצפת עלינו עד מאד); and His concomitant abundant mercy: 63:7: "According to His mercy and His great kindness" (כרחמיו וכרֹב חסדיו) — Lam 3:32: "And He has mercy according to His great kindness."

The devastation of "all that is precious" within the city (64:10 — Lam 1:7, 10, 11; 2:4).

The sordid description of Zion's desperate straits: 51:19-20: "famine. . . . Your sons lie in a faint at every street corner" — Lam 2:19: "Who faint for hunger at every street corner."

"Turn! Turn away! Depart from there! Touch nothing unclean!" (52:11) — "'Turn away! Unclean!'" people shouted at them, 'Turn away! Turn away! Touch not!'" (Lam 4:15).

Compare also the expressions:

להוריד לארץ, "to hurl to the ground" (63:6 — Lam 2:10).

נְגֹאֲלוּ בדם, "defiled with blood" (59:3 — Lam 4:14) — only here.

עֲנִיִּים מרודים, "wretched poor" (58:7) — עָנְיָהּ וּמְרוּדֶיהָ, "her woe and sorrow" (Lam 1:7); עָנְיִי ומרודי, "my woe and sorrow" (Lam 3:19); the expression appears only in these two books.

הֲדֹם רגלי, "My footstool" (66:1), as a reference to the entirety of the earth in a polemic against the Temple as God's earthly abode — in Lam 2:1 the Temple is said to be the divine footstool. (The term is also found with this meaning in Ps 99:5; 110:1; 132:7; 1 Chr 28:2.)

The image of Zion as a bereaved widow, symbolizing the nation's suffering, is borrowed directly from Lamentations; cf. Lam 1:11; Isa 54:4.

Deutero-Isaiah reverses the motif of lack of consolation in the laments — Lam 1:2: "There is none to comfort her"; 1:9, 17: "With none to comfort her"; 1:16: "Far from me is any comforter"; 1:21: "There was none to comfort me"; 2:13: "What can I match with you to comfort you" — and emphasizes from the very first verse of the first chapter (Isa 40:1): "Comfort, comfort, My people!" — a theme that reverberates throughout his prophecies until the very last chapter (66:13; for the references see the commentary).

Compare also the dirge sung by the walls of Jerusalem in Lam 2:18 and the prophecy in Isa 62:6-7, which reverses the lament and replaces it with a joyful hymn.

For further influences see the introductions to Isa 50:4-9 (Lam 3); Isa 54 (Lam 4–5); 63:7–64:11 (Lam 1–3).

19. DEUTERO-ISAIAH AND THE LITERARY HERITAGE OF THE ANCIENT NEAR EAST

A. Influence of Ugaritic Literature

The Ugaritic influence is found in word-pair parallelisms, literary images, and descriptions. The specific references to Ugaritic are cited in the respective commentaries to each of the verses listed below:

(1) Word-pair parallelisms:

אדם/לְאֹם = Ugar. *adm/lim* ("man [collective]/people"); see 43:4: "I give men in exchange for you and peoples in your stead."

אֹהֶל/מִשְׁכְּנוֹת = Ugar. *ahl/mšknt* ("tent/dwelling"); see 54:2: " Enlarge the site of your tent, extend the size of your dwelling."

יד/ימין = Ugar. *yd/ymn* ("hand/right hand"); see 48:13: "My own hand founded the earth. My right hand spread out the skies."

ים/נהר = Ugar. *ym/nhr* ("sea/river"); see 50:2: "By My rebuke I dried up the sea and turned rivers into desert."

ים/תהום = Ugar. *ym/thm* ("sea/great deep"); see 51:10: "It was you that dried up the sea, the waters of the great deep."

ירא/שׁתע = Ugar. *yr'/ṯtʿ* ("to fear/to be frightened"); see 41:10: "Fear not . . . be not frightened!"

כוס/קֻבַּעַת = Ugar. *ks/qbʿt* ("cup/goblet"); see 51:17: "You who from the Lord's hand have drunk the cup of His wrath . . . the goblet, the cup of reeling!"; 51:22: "Herewith I take from your hand the cup of reeling, the bowl, the goblet of My wrath."

עולם/דור ודור = Ugar. *ʿlm/dr dr* ("forever/perpetuity"); see 51:8: "But My triumph shall endure forever, My salvation in perpetuity"; 60:15: "I will make you a pride everlasting, a joy for perpetuity"; see also 58:12.

עפר/ארץ = Ugar. *ʿpr/arṣ* ("dust/ground"); see 47:1: "Get down and sit in the dust! . . . Sit on the ground dethroned!"

שער/חומה = Ugar. *ḥmt/ṯǵr* ("wall/gate"); see 60:10-11: "Aliens shall rebuild your walls. . . . Your gates shall always stay open."

תנין/ים = Ugar. *tnn/ym* ("Dragon/Sea"); see 51:9-10: "It was you . . . who pierced the sea serpent. It was You who dried up the sea."

The expression נשׂא עינים וראי (lit. "to raise one's eyes and see"); 60:4: "Raise your eyes and see," is exceedingly common in Ugaritic literature: *nšʾ ʿn wyʿn/wphm.*

The expression להעיר אֹזֶן ("to rouse the ear") is unique to Deutero-Isaiah (50:4) and Ugaritic literature: *yqǵ udn.*

(2) Literary descriptions:

El (the head of the Canaanite pantheon), while mourning for Baal, is described as follows: "He descended *(yrd)* from his chair *(lksi)* and sat *(yṯb)* on the footstool, and from the footstool he sits *(yṯb)* on the ground *(larṣ)*" (*CAT* 1.5.VI:12-14). Compare 47:1: "Get down (רדי)! Sit (שבי) in the dust! . . . Sit (שבי) on the ground (לארץ) dethroned (כסא)!"

Regarding the son's duties vis-à-vis his father, it is stated in the epic of Aqhat that the son is obliged "to grasp his [father's] arm *(aḥd ydh)* when he is drunk *(bškrn),* carry him when he is inebriated" (*CAT* 1.17:I:30-31). Compare 51:17-21 (at a time when Zion the mother is drunk [שְׁכֻרַת, v. 21] from sorrow): "She has none to guide her of all the sons she bore. None takes her by the hand (מחזיק יד), of all the sons she reared" (v. 18).

Compare the following Hebrew metaphorical adaptation from the Kirta epic: "He will suck on the milk *(ynq ḥlb)* of Ashtarte, be suckled from the breast *(mṣṣ ṯd)* of Maiden Anat" (*CAT* 1.15.II:26-27) — 60:16: "You shall suck the milk (וינקתְּ חלב) of the nations, suckle at royal breasts (ושֹד מלכים תינָקי)"; 66:11: "That you may suck from her breast (ותינקו . . . משֹד) consolation to the full, that you may suckle (תָּמֹצּוּ) from her bosom glory to your delight."

Deutero-Isaiah transfers the epic struggle between Anat (the consort of Baal) and Yam *(ym),* the god of the sea, the dragon *(tnn),* and their various cohorts, to a battle between Israel's Deity and these primordial maritime creatures. See 50:2: "With a mere rebuke I dried up the sea (ים) and turned rivers into desert"; 51:9-10: "It was you who hacked Rahab in pieces (המחצבת), who pierced the sea serpent (תנין). It was you who dried up the sea (ים), the waters of the great deep."

The rare verb חצב ("to hew, hack"), appearing in the epic struggle of God versus the sea monsters mentioned above (51:9, and only once more in Hos 6:5), is found in a description of Anat's battle against her adversaries in the Baal epic (*CAT* 1.3.II:5-7).

(3) The coordination of gender parallels:

For male figures a masculine noun was used in Ugaritic, and for the corresponding female figures a feminine noun was used: "He provided the gods with rams [masc.] and the goddesses with ewes [fem.]. He provided the gods with bulls [masc.] and the goddesses with cows [fem.]. He provided the gods with chairs [masc.] and the goddesses with couches [fem.]. He provided the gods with jars of wine [masc.] and the goddesses with jars of wine [fem.]" (*CAT* 1.4.VI:47-54). Compare 49:22: "And they shall bring your sons in their bosoms [חֹצֶן, masc.], and carry your daughters on their backs [כתף, fem.]"; 49:23: "Kings shall be your foster fathers and their queens your nurses."

B. Influence of Mesopotamian Traditions on Deutero-Isaiah

The influence of Mesopotamian traditions on Deutero-Isaiah is especially apparent when one compares his prophecies to the Mesopotamian royal inscriptions. For the initial research in this field of study and for the examples cited below, see the commentary to the respective verses; and Paul, "Deutero-Isaiah and Cuneiform Royal Inscriptions," *Divrei Shalom,* 11-22.

Compare the following selection of metaphors, ideas, and expressions between the royal inscriptions and Deutero-Isaiah's prophecies, the earlier ones having been delivered while the prophet was still in Babylonia. The Mesopotamian analogues are spelled out in detail ad loc.

In the royal inscriptions of Mesopotamia, the "calling of the monarch by name" signifies his divine election and selection. Compare this to God's choice of Israel in Deutero-Isaiah: 43:1: "I have singled you out by name"; 49:1: "He designated my name"; and the election of Cyrus: 45:3: "Who call you by name"; 45:4: "I call you by name."

Occasionally it is written in these inscriptions that the god selected the monarch "duly, truly" *(kīniš)*, which signifies divine legitimization of the king, similar to the Hebrew cognate term found in 42:6: "I, the Lord, have duly (בצדק) called you."

From the twelfth century BCE onward, including the royal inscriptions of Nabonidus, the last king of Babylon and a contemporary of Deutero-Isaiah, there appears the motif of prenatal divine predestination and selection of the king while still *in utero*. In Isa 49:1 this idea of chosenness is applied to the servant: "The Lord called me before I was born. He designated my name while I was yet in my mother's womb"; 49:5: "He who formed me in the womb to be His servant" (cf. also Jer 1:5).

The king is also designated the "favorite" and "beloved" of the deity, to which one can compare Isa 43:4: "And I love you" (see also 41:8), regarding Israel; 48:14: "He whom the Lord loves," regarding Cyrus.

Mesopotamian royal inscriptions employ the expression "I grasped his arm" to describe divine support of the king. Compare likewise 42:6: "And I have grasped you by the hand" (cf. 41:9, 13; 42:1; 45:1), in connection with the Lord's support of Israel; and 45:1: "Whose right hand I have grasped," pertaining to the Lord's support of Cyrus.

Following the god's choice of the monarch, it is often stated that he extends him his assistance. Compare similarly the help offered to Israel by God (41:10, 13, 14; 44:2).

The king, chosen by the deity, is then given a task to fulfill. A similar sequence is found in 42:6-7, when the servant, after being selected and designated to fulfill a twofold mission, is bidden "to open blind eyes, to liberate prisoners from confinement, dwellers in darkness from prison." The expression "to open blind eyes" is a metaphor for releasing the imprisoned and is corroborated by a similar Akkadian expression (see ad loc.). Note also the hapax legomenon פְּקַח-קוֹחַ (61:1), a duplication of the root פקח referring to the "opening of the eyes," which is parallel to דרור ("liberation").

The three trees, ברוש תדהר ותאשור (60:13; and in the same order in 44:14), which the nations shall bring to Jerusalem to adorn the Temple, are identical to the three trees enumerated in Mesopotamian inscriptions pertaining to the building of temples and sanctuaries (see ad loc.).

The conclusion of the passage recounting the nations returning the dispersed to Jerusalem also notes that they shall come "on horses, in chariots and wagons [צַבִּים, a loanword from Akk. *ṣumbu*], on mules and כִּרְכָּרוֹת" (66:20). This hapax legomenon can now be identified in light of the identical word-for-word sequence in Akkadian royal inscriptions that conclude with the mention of "camels."

The description just cited regarding the transportation of the expatriates to Zion as a tribute was influenced by an abundance of Sumerian hymns and royal documents, in which the capital city and sanctuary are described as the focus of international pilgrimage and tribute. Thus, for example, in a hymn to Enlil, the god of Nippur, it is stated: "All lands bow to it [Nippur]. . . . All the lords and all the princes bring there holy meal offerings, and they offer sacrifices and prayers to you." (See M. Weinfeld, *From Joshua to Josiah* [Jerusalem, 1992], 124 [Heb.].) Likewise in the hymn to the sanctuary Ningirsu in the city of Lagash: "Foreigners from all corners of the heavens flock to his name. The people of Magan and Meluhha come there from their distant land" (ibid., 125).

20. ISAIAH SCROLLS FROM QUMRAN AND ANCIENT TRANSLATIONS

A. Qumran Scrolls and Pesher Literature

In caves 1, 4, and 5 at Qumran, as well as in Wadi Murabbaʿat, 22 manuscripts of Isaiah were discovered. They are dated from the late Hasmonean or Herodian period (first century BCE) up until the first century CE; all, except for the famous Isaiah scroll (1QIsa^{a}), are fragmentary. (The sigla for the manuscripts are: 1QIsa^{a}, 1QIsa^{b}, 4QIsa^{a}, 4QIsa^{b} 4QIsa^{c}, 4QIsa^{d}, 4QIsa^{e}, 4QIsa^{f}, 4QIsa^{g}, 4QIsa^{h}, 4QIsa^{i}, 4QIsa^{j}, 4QIsa^{k}, 4QIsa^{l}, 4QIsa^{m}, 4QIsa^{n}, 4QIsa^{o}, 4QIsa^{p}, 4QIsa^{q}, 4QIsa^{r}, 5QIsa, Mur Isa.) These manuscripts predate the Leningrad Codex (the earliest complete manuscript of the MT) by more than one thousand years. 1QIsa^{a} is an important exemplar of the spelling, vocalization, syntax, verbal forms, lexicon, proper names, phonetics, and phonology of the period. The scroll reflects Late Hebrew from the Second Temple period as well as Rabbinic Hebrew and contemporary Aramaic, as the following eclectic list exemplifies (many more examples are cited in the commentary to the specific verses):

(1) The substitution of a common form in place of a rare form:
  - 42:11: The hapax legomenon יִצְוָחוּ (the substantive צְוָחָה is found four times in the Bible) was replaced by the equivalent יצרחו, which appears again in v. 13 and Zeph 1:14.
  - 47:2: The hapax legomenon שֹׁבֶל was replaced by the more familiar synonym שוליך, e.g., Isa 6:1; Jer 13:26.
  - 47:9: The hapax legomenon אַלְמֹן, which rhymes with the preceding שְׁכוֹל, was replaced by the familiar אלמנה, also influenced by the appearance of the latter in the preceding verse.

49:7: The anomalous form בְּזֹה נפש was replaced by בזוי נפש; see Jer 49:15; Obad 2; Ps 22:7.

51:9: המחצבת was replaced by המוחצת, a verb found fifteen times in the Bible, e.g., Job 26:12, in the same context describing God defeating the sea monster.

56:9: (שָׂדָי) חַיְתוֹ is an archaic poetic form that was replaced by חיות (שָׂדָי).

62:1: אֶחֱשֶׁה, from the root חשי, appearing fifteen times throughout the Bible, was replaced by the synonymous verb אחריש, which is much more frequent (47 times in the Bible) and is also found in Rabbinic Hebrew.

(2) The substitution of more common verbal paradigms instead of rarer forms:

49:25: יֻקָּח, an archaic *qal* passive, was replaced by ילקח, the standard *niph'al* passive.

65:14: יָרֹנּוּ, a *qal* form derived from רנן, which appears five more times in the Bible, was replaced by the more common ירננו, which appears twenty-eight times throughout the Bible.

(3) Additions to the MT reflecting variant readings (see the commentary):

52:8: At the end of the verse, the scroll has ברחמים.

52:12: At the end of the verse, the scroll adds the phrase: אלהי כל הארץ יקרא; cf. 54:5.

53:11: The word אור appears between the verbs יראה and ישׂבע. This variant is corroborated by 1QIsa[b], partially by 4QIsa[d], and by the LXX.

58:7: Following וְכִסִּיתוֹ, the scroll adds בגד.

60:19: The scroll appends the word בלילה to the phrase לא יאיר לך, and is corroborated by the LXX and Targum, בְּלֵילְיָא.

60:21: Instead of מטעי (Qere) and מטעו (Ketib), the scroll has מטעי ה׳.

62:10: סקלו אבן — 1QIsa[b] has the additional word הנגף, also found in the Targum, תַּקְלָא.

(4) Selected additional variant readings (see the commentary):

43:19: נתיבות instead of נהרות, parallel to דרך in the previous hemistich.

43:23: לעולה instead of עֹלֹתֶיךָ, corroborated by the Targum, לַעֲלָא.

44:4: כבין instead of בבין, corroborated by the Targum and LXX.

44:8: תיראו instead of the hapax legomenon תִּרְהוּ.

44:11: חובריו instead of חֲבֵרָיו.

44:16: ויאכל ועל גחליו ישב ויחם instead of יאכל יצלה צלי וישׂבע אף יָחֹם.

45:2: וההררים instead of the hapax legomenon וההדורים; so too the LXX.
45:8: (ישע) ויפרח instead of (ישע) ויפרו.
45:9: הוי האומר instead of הַ‏יאמר. This reading harmonizes with הוי רב at the beginning of the verse.
45:20: ואתיו replaces יחדו and parallels ובאו in the previous hemistich.
47:3: אמר instead of אדם.
47:10: ורעתך instead of ודעתך, which was influenced by the preceding ברעתך.
47:13: חוברי שמים instead of the hapax legomenon הֹברי שמים; see v. 9.
49:5: עזרי instead of עֻזִּי (cf. the alternative forms for the Judean monarch, Uzziah/Azariah, 2 Kgs 15:1, 13, 30, 32, 34), corroborated by the Targum, בְּסַעֲדִי.
49:25: ריבך instead of יריבך, a rare form found only twice more in the Bible (Jer 18:19; Ps 35:1), whereas ריב is very common, as is the phrase here, רִב ריב, a reading corroborated by the LXX.
51:19: מי ינחמך instead of מי אנחמך, which is in harmony with the previous מי ינוד לך; so too in the Targum, LXX, Vulgate, and Peshitta.
52:5: והוללו, from the root הלל, instead of יהילילו, from ילל.
53:8: נגוע instead of נֶגַע.
53:9: במתו instead of בְּמֹתָיו.
53:10: ויחללהו instead of the anomalous הֶחֱלִי.
54:11: ויסודותיך instead of וִיסַדְתִּיךְ; so too the LXX.
56:12: ונקחה, instead of אקחה, which harmonizes with the later ונסבאה; so too the LXX, Vulgate, and Peshitta.
60:3: לנגד instead of לְנֹגַהּ; cf. likewise the Targum, לָקֳבֵיל.
63:5: תומך instead of the synonymous סומך.
63:11: המעלה instead of המעלֵם.
64:6: ותמגדנו instead of וַתְּמוּגֵנוּ.
65:5: תגע instead of תִּגַּשׁ.
66:16: (כי באש ה׳) יבוא instead of (כי באש ה׳) נשפט.

For clarification of most of these readings, see ad loc.

(5) Tendentious omissions and emendations:
56:6: (ובני נכר הנלוים על ה׳) לשרתו, the infinitive לשרתו is omitted. Moreover, instead of the next phrase, (את שם ה׳) ולאהבה, the scroll has (את שם ה׳) ולברך, since according to the Qumran sect, identified with the priestly house of Zadok, it was forbidden to permit the participation of non-Levites, let alone non-Israelites, in the cult. This ideology is explicitly expressed in the *Florilegium* (4Q174 3-4): "That is the house [the sanctuary] where there shall never more enter . . . the

Ammonite and the Moabite and the bastard and alien and sojourner for ever, for my holy ones are there" (J. M. Allegro, *Qumrân Cave 4.I (4Q158-4Q186),* DJD 5 [Oxford, 1968], 53-54).

63:3: (פורה דרכתי לבדי) ומעמים (אין איש אתי), instead of ומעמים the scroll has ומעמי, since it is obvious that none of the foreign nations would come to God's aid.

For an in-depth analysis see E. Y. Kutscher, *The Language and Linguistic Background of the Isaiah Scroll (1QIsa[a]),* STDJ 6 (Leiden, 1974). All variants reflected in this scroll and others are recorded in M. H. Goshen-Gottstein, ed., *The Book of Isaiah,* Hebrew University Bible Project (Jerusalem, 1995).

Of the six very fragmented manuscripts of the pesher to Isaiah, which are dated to the first century BCE, only two have excerpts from Deutero-Isaiah: 4QpIsa[d] (4Q164) quotes 54:11-12 and relates to the community of Qumran. The only variance from the MT is the *plene* spelling of שמשותיך. 4QpIsa[e] (4Q165) quotes 40:12, the only difference being the omission of the *waw* preceding the verb ושקל. The manuscript, however, is so fragmentary that it is not clear how this verse was understood. (See Allegro, DJD 5, 27-29.)

B. Ancient Translations

(1) Septuagint

The Greek translation (LXX) of Deutero-Isaiah, which was most likely written in the mid–second century BCE, reflects many divergent readings from the MT. Below are some representative examples, while many others will be cited in the commentary to the relevant verses.

(a) Additions and divergent readings:

40:1-2: "Comfort, O comfort, My people!" — the LXX adds that this call is addressed to the "priests."

42:1: "This is My servant . . . My chosen one" — the Greek translator adds "Jacob" and "Israel," respectively, to each hemistich, thus identifying the servant as the nation in its entirety (cf. also 41:8; 44:1).

44:2: יְשֻׁרוּן is translated: "Israel, the cherished one."

49:17: Instead of "your sons" (בָּנַיִךְ), the LXX renders "your builders" (בֹּנַיִךְ); see ad loc.

49:25: יריבך ("your adversaries") is translated ריבך ("your legal case"); so too 1QIsa[a].

51:9: "Awake, awake!" — the LXX adds "Jerusalem" as the subject of the two imperatives (see 51:7).

52:1: עורי עורי — the LXX adds "Zion" as the subject of the two imperatives.

53:11: יראה the LXX adds the word אור ("light"); so too 1QIsa[a], 1QIsa[b], 4QIsa[d].

60:19: לא יאיר לך — the LXX adds "by night"; so too the Targum, בְּלֵילְיָא.

66:16: באש ה׳ נשפט — the LXX adds: "with the whole land."

(b) Omissions:

41:14: "Fear not, O worm Jacob" — the word תולעת ("worm") was omitted so as not to deride Israel.

59:10: the hapax legomenon אַשְׁמַנִּים was omitted since it was not understood.

(c) Misunderstandings of the Hebrew *Vorlage*:

41:1: הַחֲרִישׁוּ ("Be silent!") was translated התחדשו ("be renewed!") — a graphic substitution of the *dalet* and *resh,* together with a transposition of letters. The same substitution appears in 45:16: חָרָשֵׁי צירים, where the LXX translates התחדשו and adds the phrase "to Me, nations," on the basis of 41:1.

42:19: מלאכי ("My messenger") was translated as being derived from מלך ("ruler").

48:9: (אפי) אאריך ("I control [My wrath]") is translated: "I shall show you [My wrath]" ([אפי] אראך).

(d) Avoidance of anthropomorphization:

40:5: פי ה׳ דבר (lit. "The Lord's mouth has spoken") is replaced by "The Lord has spoken."

(e) Updating:

43:3: סְבָא ("Seba") is transcribed as the Egyptian "Syene"; see Ezek 29:10.

46:1: נְבוֹ ("Nabu") was replaced by "Dagon," a deity with whom the translator was familiar.

49:12: ארץ סינים ("the land of Sinim") was translated "the land of the Persians."

(f) Aramaic influence:

53:10: וה׳ חפץ דַּכְּאוֹ, "But the Lord chose to crush him"; דַּכְּאוֹ was translated as being derived from the Aramaic root דכי, "to purify" (cf. Targum).

(g) Variant readings:

46:12: אֹבְדֵי לב ("those who have lost heart") instead of אבירי לב ("stubborn of heart") — note again the graphic substitution of the *dalet* for the *resh*.

51:12: מנחמך ("He who comforts you [singular]") instead of מנחמכם ("He who comforts you [plural]"), to correspond with the adjacent second-person feminine singular.

51:19: מי ינחמך ("Who shall comfort you?") instead of מי אנחמך ("How shall I comfort you?"), as in 1QIsa[a], Targum, Vulgate, and Peshitta.

53:8: לַמָּוֶת ("to death") instead of למו ("to them"); this variant seems preferable; see ad loc.

54:11: ויסודותיך ("and your foundations") instead of וִיסַדְתִּיךְ ("I shall make your foundations"); so too 1QIsa[a].

56:11: רָעִים ("evil ones") instead of רֹעים ("shepherds"), corroborated by the Targum and Peshitta.

56:12: ונקחה ("Let us take") instead of אקחה ("I will take"), which is in harmony with the adjacent ונסבאה ("Let us swill"), corroborated by 1QIsa[a], Targum, Vulgate, and Peshitta.

63:9: צִר ("messenger") instead of צָר ("He was troubled"); see ad loc. for verse division.

63:14: תַּנְחֵנוּ (from the root נחי, "to guide"), "guided them," instead of תְּנִיחֶנּוּ (from the root נוח, " to give rest"), "gave them rest," corroborated by the Targum, Vulgate, and Peshitta.

(h) A sample of other variations:

50:11: באוֹר ("by light") instead of באוּר ("by fire"); cf. the Vulgate.

56:6: There are signs that the LXX was reticent regarding the prophet's enthusiastic universalism. The verb לשרתו ("to minister to Him") was translated by a verb denoting "work," which in Greek is not restricted to cultic ministration and is not the usual translation of the root שׁרת.

59:2: פניו ("His face") instead of פנים (simply "face"); thus in the Vulgate and Targum.

63:7: גְּמָלָנוּ ("He bestowed on us") instead of גְּמָלָם ("He bestowed on them"); the form גְּמָלָנוּ appears earlier in the verse.

63:18: הר קדשך ("Your holy mountain") instead of עם קדשך ("Your holy people").

63:19: בנו ("us") instead of בם ("them").

For all the variations between the LXX and the MT, see Goshen-Gottstein, *Book of Isaiah,* passim.

(2) Aramaic Targum

In addition to being a free translation with a penchant against anthropomorphization, the Aramaic Targum is also characterized by a definite theological agenda. Selective examples in several categories follow.

(a) Theological interpretations:

46:13: ישועה (ונתתי בציון) ("[I will grant] triumph [in Zion]") is translated: פָּרִיק (וְאֶתֵּין בציון) ("[I will grant] a redeemer [to Zion]").

52:13: Adds מְשִׁיחָא ("the anointed one") to "this is My servant."

57:16: כי רוח מלפני יעטוף — this difficult colon is translated: אֲרֵי רוּחֵי מִיתַיָא אֲנָא עֲתִיד לְאָתָבָא ("For I am destined to restore the spirit of the dead").

57:18: דרכיו ("His paths") is translated: אוֹרַח תְּיוּבַתְהוֹן ("the path of their repentance").

57:19: שלום שלום לרחוק ולקרוב ("It shall be well, well, with the far and the near") is translated: שְׁלָמָא יִתְעֲבֵיד לְצַדִּיקַיָא דִּנְטַרוּ אוֹרָיְתִי מִלְקַדְמִין וּשְׁלָמָא יִתְעֲבֵד לְתָבַיָא דְּתָבוּ לְאוֹרָיְתִי קָרִיב ("Well-being shall be brought about to the righteous, who have observed My Torah since the days of old, and well-being shall be brought about to the returnees who returned to My Torah recently").

58:11: ועצמֹתיך יחליץ is translated: וְגוּפָךְ יֵיחֵי בְּחַיֵּי עָלְמָא ("And your body shall live life everlasting").

58:12: מְשֹׁבֵב נתיבות לָשָׁבֶת is translated: מְתִיב רַשִׁיעַיָא לְאוֹרָיְתָא ("He who leads the wicked back to the Torah").

62:6: על חוֹמֹתיך is translated: הָא עוּבָדֵי אֲבָהָתַךְ צַדִּיקַיָא ("These are the deeds of your righteous fathers").

65:5: אֵלֶּה עָשָׁן באפי is translated: אִלֵין רֻגְזְהוֹן כְּתַנְנָא קֳדָמַי פּוּרְעָנוּתְהוֹן בְּגֵיהִנָם ("Their anger is like smoke before Me; their punishment is in Gehenna").

(b) Explanatory additions:

60:19: יאיר לך ("to shine for you") — the term בְּלֵילְיָא ("at night") was added; so too 1QIsa[a] and LXX.

62:10: סקלו מאבן ("Remove the rocks") — the word תַּקְלָא ("obstacle") was appended; similarly, הנגף in 1QIsa[a].

(c) Variants:

40:10: בְּתְקוֹף ("in strength") instead of בְּחָזָק ("as a mighty one"); so too 1QIsa[a], LXX, Vulgate, and Peshitta.

41:29: לְמָא ("in vain") instead of אָוֶן ("iniquity"); so too 1QIsa[a] and Peshitta.

42:24: דְּחָבוּ ("they who sinned") instead of חטאנו ("we have sinned"); so too the LXX.

42:25: חֲמַת רוּגְזֵיהּ ("the anger of His wrath"), construct state instead of absolute, חֵמָה אפו; so too 1QIsa[a], LXX, and Peshitta.

43:23: לַעֲלָא ("for a burnt offering") instead of עֹלֹתֶיךָ ("your burnt offerings"), corroborated by 1QIsa[a], לעולה.

44:4: כְּלַבְלָבֵי עֲסַב ("like plant blossoms") instead of the hapax legomenon בְּבֵין, corroborated by 1QIsa[a] and LXX; see the commentary.

44:7: לָנָא ("to us") instead of לָמוֹ ("to them"); cf. the LXX.

56:11: רֹעִים ("shepherds") is translated מַבְאֲשִׁין (= רָעִים, "evil ones"); so too in the LXX.

56:12: וְנִסְבֵּי ("Let us take") instead of אקחה ("I will take"), which conforms with the adjacent plural form נסבאה ("Let us swill"); cf. 1QIsa[a], LXX, Vulgate, and Peshitta.

63:14: תניחנו ("gave them rest") is translated דַּבְּרִינוּן ("shall guide them"), which supposes Heb. תַּנחנו; similar to the LXX, Vulgate, and Peshitta.

(d) Aramaic influences:

53:10: דַּכְּאוֹ ("to crush him") is translated לְמִצְרַף ("to purify, cleanse"), based on the Aramaic root דכי.

For complete documentation of the variances between the Aramaic translation and the MT, see Goshen-Gottstein, *Book of Isaiah,* passim.

(3) Vulgate and Peshitta

The Latin translation of Isaiah, the Vulgate, is very close to the MT, the most important difference between the two being the occasional christological exegeses reflected in the translation. Allusions to Jesus, for example, appear in 45:5; 51:5; 62:1, 2, 11. This is apparent in the translation of צדק and ישע as *iustus* ("the righteous one") and המושיע as *salvator;* note the expression רוח קדשו ("His holy spirit") in 63:10, which is translated as "the holy spirit" (רוח הקודש). The Syriac translation, the Peshitta, is also very close to the MT.

For a fuller documentation of the variations between the Latin and Syriac translations and the MT, see Goshen-Gottstein, *Book of Isaiah,* passim.

21. DEUTERO-ISAIAH IN JEWISH LITURGY

"Comfort, comfort, My people!" — the opening of the first prophecy (40:1) is also the first of the prophetic sections recited in the synagogue on the seven Sabbaths between the ninth of Ab and the New Year (referred to as שִׁבַע דְנֶחָמָתָא, "the seven [Sabbaths] of Comfort"). This Sabbath is also called *Shabbat Naḥamu* ("the Sabbath of Comfort"), relating to these very first words.

On the second of these Sabbaths, the prophetic portion is from 49:14–51:3. The section beginning with the words "Afflicted, storm-tossed one" (54:11–55:5) is read on the third Sabbath. 51:12–52:12 is the prophetic portion on the fourth of the seven Sabbaths. On the fifth of the seven Sabbaths, the prophetic portion begins with 54:1. Sephardic congregations conclude with 54:10; Ashkenazic congregations, with 55:5 (so as to emphasize the message of comfort); and Yemenite congregations, with 55:3. Chapter 60 opens the prophetic section of the sixth of the seven Sabbaths. 61:10–63:9 is the seventh and final reading of the Sabbaths of Comfort. In some congregations this is also the prophetic reading for a wedding celebration.

Other prophetic portions from Deutero-Isaiah that are recited in the synagogue:

55:6–56:8, which begins with the injunction "Seek God when He is near," is read in the afternoon service on the fast of the ninth of Ab as well as on other fast days, since the section deals with repentance.

57:14–58:14 is the prophetic portion recited during the morning service on the Day of Atonement. According to the Tannaitic passage in *b. Meg.* 31a, the actual recitation begins with v. 15. Some congregations add a short excerpt from chap. 59 (vv. 20-21), following the recitation of the portion.

On Sabbaths that coincide with the beginning of the lunar month, chap. 66 is recited, primarily because of v. 23 (the penultimate verse): "And new moon after new moon, and Sabbath after Sabbath, all flesh shall come to worship Me — said the Lord." So as not to end the book on a negative note (v. 24: "They shall go out and gaze on the corpses of the men who rebelled against Me. Their worms shall not die, nor their fire be quenched. They shall be a horror to all flesh"), v. 23 is repeated. The next to the last verse is also repeated in three other books that end on a negative note — Malachi, Lamentations, and Ecclesiastes.

The first verse of the prophecy beginning in 42:5: "Thus said God the Lord, who created the heavens and stretched them out, who spread out the earth and what it brings forth, who gave breath to the people upon it and life to those who walk thereon," and its affinity with the cosmogony described in Gen 1, marked it and the verses that follow as the prophetic section recited on the first Sabbath of the New Year. Yemenite congregations read vv. 1-16, Sephardic congregations end with v. 21, and Ashkenazic congregations continue until 43:10.

On the third Sabbath of the year, when the story of Abraham's travels and travails is recounted (Gen 12:1ff.), Isa 40:27–41:16 is read since, according to Jewish tradition, Abraham is the one alluded to in 41:2: "Who has roused a victor from the east?"

On the Sabbath when the beginning of the third book of the Torah is read (Lev 1:1ff.), Isa 43:20–44:23 is recited since this section deals with sacrifices.

Many other verses in Deutero-Isaiah have also entered Jewish prayer and liturgy.

Translation

40 1 "Comfort, comfort My people!"
Says your God.
2 "Speak tenderly to Jerusalem!
And proclaim to her
That her term of service is over,
That her punishment has been expiated!
For she has received at the hand of the Lord
Double for all her sins."
3 A voice rings out:
"Clear in the desert a road for the Lord!
Level in the wilderness a highway for our God!
4 Let every valley be raised
And every hill and mount be made low.
Let the rugged ground become a plain
And the mountain ranges become a valley.
5 The Presence of the Lord shall be revealed,
And all humanity, as one, shall see it."
For the mouth of the Lord has spoken.
6 A voice rings out: "Proclaim!"
And I asked, "What shall I proclaim?"
"All flesh is grass,
All its goodness like flowers of the field.
7 Grass withers, flowers fade
When the breath of the Lord blows on them.
Indeed, people are but grass.
8 Grass withers, flowers fade,
But the word of our God endures forever."

9 Ascend a lofty mountain, O herald of joy to Zion!
Raise your voice with power, O herald of joy to Jerusalem!
Raise it! Have no fear!
Announce to the cities of Judah:
"Behold your God!"
10 Behold, the Lord God is coming in might
And His arm is ruling for Him.
See, His reward is with Him,
And His recompense before Him.
11 Like a shepherd He pastures His flock:
He gathers the lambs in His arms
And carries them in His bosom;
Gently He leads the ewes.
12 Who measured the waters with the hollow of His hand,
And who gauged the skies with a span,
And meted the earth's dust with a measure,
And weighed the mountains with a scale,
And the hills with a balance?
13 Who has measured the mind of the Lord?
What man could tell Him His plan?/Who is His counselor, who instructs Him?
14 Whom did He consult
And who gave Him understanding?
Taught Him in the path of justice
And showed Him the path of understanding?
15 Indeed, the nations weigh but a speck on the scales,
Reckoned as dust on a balance.
The very coastlands weigh no more than fine dust.
16 Lebanon is not fuel enough,
Nor its beasts enough for sacrifice.
17 All nations are as nothing in His sight,
They are accounted as nil and naught.
18 To whom, then, can you liken God?
What form can you compare to Him?
19 The woodworker shapes the idol
And a smith overlays it with gold,
Forging ornaments of silver.
20 The mulberry wood (as a gift?),
A wood that will not rot he chooses.
Then he seeks a skillful woodworker
To make a firm idol that will not topple.

21 Do you not know? Have you not heard?
Have you not been told from the very first?
Have you not discerned from the foundation/s of the earth?
22 It is He who sits enthroned on the vault of the earth
So that its inhabitants seem as grasshoppers,
Who spread out the skies like gauze,
And stretched them out like a tent to dwell in.
23 He brings potentates to naught,
Makes rulers of the earth as nothing.
24 Scarcely are they planted,
Scarcely are they sown,
Scarcely has their stem taken root in the earth,
When He blows on them and they dry up,
And a whirlwind bears them off like chaff.
25 "To whom, then, can you liken Me?
To whom can I be compared?" —
Says the Holy One.
26 Lift up your eyes to the heaven and see:
Who created these?
It is He who leads out their host by number,
Who calls them each by name.
Because of His great might and vast power
Not one is missing.
27 Why do you say, O Jacob,
And why declare, O Israel:
"My way is hidden from the Lord
And my cause is ignored by my God"?
28 Do you not know?
Have you not heard?
The Lord is the everlasting God,
Creator of the earth from end to end.
He never grows faint or weary,
His understanding cannot be fathomed.
29 He gives strength to the weary,
Fresh vigor to the exhausted.
30 Youths may grow faint and weary,
And young men may totter;
31 But those who trust in the Lord shall renew their strength:
They will grow pinions like eagles,
They shall run and not grow weary,
They shall march and not grow faint.

41 1 Stand silent before Me, coastlands!
And let the peoples renew their strength.
Let them approach to state their case.
Let us come forward together for trial.
2 Who has roused a victor/victory from the east,
Summoned him to His service,
Has delivered up nations to him,
And has trodden down sovereigns?
His sword has rendered them like dust,
His bow like windblown chaff.
3 He pursues them, passing on unscathed.
No fetter is placed on his feet.
4 Who has planned and achieved this?
Who announced the generations from the start?
It is I, the Lord, who was the first,
And I am He with the last as well.
5 The coastlands look on in fear,
The ends of the earth tremble.
They draw near and come.
6 Each one helps the other,
Saying to his fellow, "Be strong!"
7 The woodworker encourages the goldsmith.
He who smooths with the hammer [encourages] him who pounds the anvil.
He says of the soldering, "It is good!"
And he fixes it with nails, that it may not topple.
8 But you, Israel, My servant,
Jacob, whom I have chosen,
Offspring of Abraham, whom I love,
9 You, whom I drew from the ends of the earth
And called from its far corners,
To whom I have said: "You are My servant.
I have chosen you and have not rejected you,"
10 Fear not, for I am with you!
Be not frightened, for I am your God!
I strengthen you and I help you,
I uphold you with My victorious right hand.
11 Frustrated and chagrined shall be all who contend with you.
They who strive with you shall become as naught and shall perish.
12 You will look for those who struggle with you
But shall not find them.

As nothing and as naught shall be the men who battle against you.
13 For I the Lord am your God
Who grasps your right hand,
Who says to you: "Have no fear!
I will be your help."
14 Fear not, O worm Jacob,
O men of Israel!
I will help you — declares the Lord,
Your Redeemer, the Holy One of Israel.
15 I will make you a threshing board,
A new thresher, with many spikes.
You shall thresh mountains to dust
And make hills like chaff.
16 You shall winnow them,
And the wind shall carry them off.
The whirlwind shall scatter them.
Then you shall rejoice in the Lord
And exult in the Holy One of Israel.
17 The afflicted and the needy seek water
But there is none.
Their tongue is parched with thirst.
I the Lord will respond to them,
I the God of Israel will not forsake them.
18 I will open up streams on the bare heights/sand dunes
And fountains amid the valleys.
I will turn the desert into pools
And the arid land into springs of water.
19 I will plant in the wilderness cedars,
Acacias and myrtles and oleasters.
I will set in the desert junipers, box trees, and cypresses as well.
20 That men may see and know,
Take note and discern
That the Lord's hand has done this,
That the Holy One of Israel has wrought it.
21 "Submit your case!" says the Lord;
"Bring forward your plea!" says the King of Jacob.
22 Let them approach and tell us what will happen
Or announce to us what has occurred!
Tell us and we will take note of it,
That we may know their outcome.
23 Foretell what is yet to happen,

That we may know that you are gods!
Do anything, good or bad,
That we may be totally awed and afraid!
24 Behold, you are nothing
And your works are nullity!
One who chooses you is an abomination.
25 I have roused him from the north, and he has come;
From the east, one who invokes My name.
And he has trampled rulers like mud,
Like a potter treading clay.
26 Who foretold this from the start, that we may note it,
From aforetime, that we might say, "He is right"?
Not one foretold, not one announced,
Not one has heard your utterance.
27 The things once predicted to Zion,
Behold, here they are!
And for Jerusalem I am providing a herald.
28 But I looked and there is no one.
Not one of them is an advocate,
Nor can any respond when I question them.
29 See, they are all nothingness;
Their works are nullity,
Their effigies are naught and nil.

42 1 This is My servant, whom I uphold,
My chosen one, with whom I am pleased.
I have put My spirit upon him,
He shall promulgate justice to the nations.
2 He shall not cry out
Or raise his voice,
Or make his voice heard in the streets.
3 He shall not break even a splintered reed
Or snuff out even a dimly burning wick.
He shall promulgate in truth/justice to the nations.
4 He shall not grow dim or be crushed
Till he has established justice on earth,
And the coastlands shall await His teaching.
5 Thus said God the Lord,
Who created the heavens and stretched them out,
Who spread out the earth and what it brings forth,
Who gave breath to the people on it

And life to those who walk thereon:
6 "I, the Lord, have duly called you
And have grasped you by the hand.
I created you and appointed you
A covenant people, a light of nations,
7 To open eyes that are blind,
To rescue prisoners from confinement,
From the dungeon, those who dwell in darkness.
8 I am the Lord, that is My name.
I will not yield My Presence to another
Nor My renown to idols.
9 See, the things once predicted have come to pass,
And now I foretell new things.
I announce to you ere they sprout up."
10 Sing to the Lord a new song,
His praise from the ends of the earth!
Let the sea roar and all the creatures in it,
You coastlands and their inhabitants.
11 Let the desert and its towns cry aloud,
The villages where Kedar dwells.
Let the inhabitants of Sela shout for joy,
Cry out from the peaks of mountains.
12 Let them ascribe honor to the Lord
And recite His glory in the coastlands.
13 The Lord goes forth as a warrior,
Like a fighter He rouses up His frenzy.
He shouts a battle cry, He roars aloud,
He triumphs over His enemies.
14 "I have been idle far too long,
Kept still and restrained Myself.
Now I will scream like a woman in labor,
I will pant and I will gasp.
15 I will lay waste mountains and hills,
And cause all their herbage to wither.
I will turn rivers into deserts
And dry up the ponds.
16 I will lead the blind
On a road they do not know,
And I will make them walk
On paths they do not know.
I will turn darkness before them to light

And twisting paths into level ground.
All these I will do
And not forsake them."
17 Turned back and utterly disappointed
Shall be those who trust in an image,
Who say to the idols, "You are our gods."
18 Listen, you who are deaf!
And you blind ones, look and see!
19 Who is so blind but My servant,
Who so deaf as the messenger I send?
Who is so deaf as the one whom I commission,
So blind as the servant of the Lord?
20 Seeing many things but giving no heed,
With ears wide open but hearing nothing.
21 The Lord desires his/His vindication,
So that He may magnify and glorify [His] teaching.
22 Yet it is a people plundered and despoiled.
All of them are ensnared in holes,
Imprisoned in dungeons.
They are given over to plunder, with none to rescue them,
To despoilment, with none to say, "Give back!"
23 If only you would listen to this,
Attend and give heed from now on!
24 Who was it who gave Jacob over to despoilment
And Israel to plunderers?
Surely, the Lord against whom they sinned,
In whose ways they would not walk
And whose teaching they would not obey.
25 So He poured out His wrathful anger on them,
And the fury of war.
It blazed upon them all about but they remained unaware,
It burned among them but they gave it no thought.

43 1 But now thus said the Lord,
Who created you, O Jacob,
Who formed you, O Israel:
"Fear not, for I will redeem you!
I have called you by name;
You are mine.
2 When you pass through water,
I will be with you;

And through streams,
They shall not drown you.
When you walk through fire,
You shall not be scorched;
And through flame,
It shall not burn you.
3 For I the Lord am your God,
The Holy One of Israel, your Savior.
I give Egypt as a ransom for you,
Nubia and Seba in exchange for you.
4 Because you are precious to Me
And honored, and I love you,
I give people in exchange for you
And nations in your stead.
5 Fear not, for I am with you!
I will bring your folk from the east
And gather you from the west.
6 I will say to the north, 'Give back!'
And to the south, 'Do not withhold!'
Bring My sons from afar
And My daughters from the ends of the earth!
7 All who are called by My name,
Whom I created, formed, and made for My glory."
8 Free this people, blind though it has eyes
And deaf though it has ears!
9 All the nations are gathered together
And the peoples assemble.
Who among them predicted this,
Foretold to us the things that have happened?
Let them produce their witnesses and be vindicated,
So that people, when hearing it, will say, "It is true!"
10 "My witnesses are you," says the Lord,
"My servant, whom I have chosen.
So that you may take thought and believe in Me,
And understand that I am He.
Before Me no god was formed
And after Me none shall exist.
11 I, I Myself, am the Lord.
Besides Me, none can grant triumph.
12 I alone foretold, delivered, and announced it,
And no foreign god was among you.

So you are My witnesses," declares the Lord,
"And I am God.
13 From this very day, I am He.
None can deliver from My hand.
When I act, who can reverse it?"
14 Thus said the Lord, your Redeemer,
The Holy One of Israel:
"For your sake I have sent to Babylon;
I will destroy all [her] bars/boats
And the Chaldeans in their ships of joy.
15 I am the Lord, your Holy One,
The Creator of Israel, your King."
16 Thus said the Lord,
Who made a road through the sea
And a path through mighty waters,
17 Who destroyed chariots and horses
And all the mighty infantry host;
They lay down to rise no more,
They were extinguished, snuffed out like a wick:
18 "Do not recall what happened of old!
Neither ponder what happened of yore!
19 I am about to do something new.
Right now it shall come to sprout.
Can you not perceive it?
I will make a road through the wilderness
And paths in the desert.
20 The wild beasts shall honor Me,
Jackals and ostriches,
For I will provide water in the wilderness,
Rivers in the desert,
To give drink to My chosen people.
21 The people whom I formed for Myself
Shall proclaim My praise.
22 But Me you have not worshiped, O Jacob.
Nevertheless you are weary of Me, O Israel.
23 You have not brought Me your sheep for burnt offerings,
Nor honored Me with your sacrifices.
I have not burdened you with meal offerings,
Nor wearied you about frankincense.
24 You have not bought Me fragrant cane with money,
Nor sated Me with the fat of your sacrifices.

Instead you have burdened Me with your sins,
You have wearied Me with your iniquities.
25 It is I, I who — for My own sake —
Wipe your transgressions away
And remember your sins no more.
26 Remind Me!
Let us join in argument!
Tell your version, that you may be vindicated!
27 Your first father sinned
And your spokesmen rebelled against Me.
28 So I profaned the holy princes/My holy name.
And I delivered Jacob to proscription
And Israel to mockery."

44 1 But hear now, O Jacob, My servant,
Israel, whom I have chosen!
2 Thus said the Lord, your Maker,
Your Creator from the womb,
Who has helped you:
"Fear not, My servant Jacob,
Jeshurun, whom I have chosen!
3 Even as I pour water on thirsty soil
And streams on dry ground,
So will I pour My spirit on your offspring
And My blessing on your posterity.
4 And they shall sprout like a green tamarisk,
Like willows by watercourses.
5 One shall say, 'I am the Lord's.'
Another shall be called by the name 'Jacob.'
Yet another shall mark his hand 'of the Lord'
And be entitled 'Israel.'"
6 Thus said the Lord, the King of Israel,
His Redeemer, the Lord of Hosts:
"I am the first and I am the last,
And there is no god but Me.
7 Who is like Me that can announce?
Let him foretell it and match Me/state his case,
Announcing the future from the very beginning.
Let him foretell coming events to us.
8 Do not be frightened! And do not be shaken!
Have I not from old announced to you and foretold?

And you are My witnesses.
Is there any god, then, but Me?
Or any other rock? I know none!"
9 The makers of idols are all worthless,
And their cherished images can do no good,
And they are their very own witnesses.
They neither see nor know,
So they shall be confounded.
10 Who would fashion a god or cast a statue
That can do no good?
11 Lo, all its votaries shall be frustrated.
They are craftsmen, merely mortal.
Let them all assemble and stand up!
They shall cower, totally dismayed.
12 The blacksmith, with his cutting tool,
Works it over charcoal
And fashions it with hammers,
Working with the strength of his arm.
When hungry, his strength ebbs.
Should he drink no water, he grows faint.
13 The woodworker stretches a plumb line
And traces its outline with a stylus.
He forms it with scraping tools,
Outlining it with a compass.
He fashions it like a human figure,
The beauty of a man to dwell in a shrine.
14 For his use he cuts down cedars;
He selects a plane tree or an oak,
Or chooses among the trees of the forest,
Or plants a cedar, and the rain makes it grow.
15 It becomes fuel for man:
He takes some of it to warm himself
And he also kindles a fire and bakes bread.
He also makes a god of it and worships it!
Fashions an idol and bows down to it!
16 One half he burns in the fire:
On that half he roasts meat, eats, and is sated.
He also warms himself
And exclaims, "Ah! I'm warm!
I'm enjoying the heat!"

17 And out of the rest he makes a god, his effigy!
He bows down to it and worships it,
And he prays to it, saying, "Save me, for you are my god!"
18 They do not realize or understand.
Their eyes are besmeared and they see not,
Their minds — unable to think.
19 He does not give thought,
He lacks the wit and sense to say:
"Half of it I burned in a fire.
I even baked bread on its coals,
I roasted meat and ate it.
And the rest of it I turned into an abomination,
And I bow down to a block of wood!"
20 He pursues ashes.
A deluded mind has led him astray
And he cannot save himself.
Nor can he say to himself:
"The thing in my hand is a sham!"
21 Remember these things, Jacob,
For you, Israel, are My servant.
I fashioned you, you are My servant.
Israel, you shall not be forgotten by Me.
22 I have wiped away your sins like a cloud
And your transgressions like a mist.
Come back to Me,
For I redeemed you!
23 Exult, O heavens, for the Lord has acted!
Shout aloud, O lowest depths of the earth!
Break into songs of joy, O mountains,
Forests, with all your trees!
For the Lord has redeemed Jacob
And has glorified Himself through Israel.
24 Thus said the Lord, your Redeemer,
Who formed you in the womb:
"It is I, the Lord, who made everything,
Who alone stretched out the heavens,
Unaided spread out the earth;
25 Who annuls the omens of the diviners
And makes fools of the augurs;
Who nullifies the sages
And makes nonsense of their knowledge;

26 But confirms the word of His servant
And fulfills the design of His messengers;
Who says of Jerusalem, 'She shall be inhabited,'
And of the towns of Judah, 'They shall be rebuilt';
And I will restore her ruined places.
27 I, who said to the deep, 'Be dry!'
Shall dry up your streams.
28 I am the One who says of Cyrus, 'He is My shepherd;
He shall fulfill all My purposes,'
Saying to Jerusalem, 'She shall be rebuilt,'
And to the Temple: 'You shall be founded again.'"

45 1 Thus said the Lord to His anointed one, to Cyrus,
Whose right hand I have grasped,
To subdue nations before him
And ungird the loins of kings,
To open doors before him
And letting none of the gates stay shut:
2 "I will go before you
And I will level the hills.
I will shatter doors of bronze and hew iron bars.
3 I will give you treasures concealed in the dark
And secret hoards,
So that you may know that it is I the Lord, the God of Israel,
Who calls you by your name.
4 For the sake of My servant Jacob
And Israel, My chosen one,
I call you by your name.
I hail you by title, though you have not known Me.
5 I am the Lord and there is none else.
Besides Me there is no god.
I gird you, though you have not known Me.
6 So that they may know, from the rising of the sun to its setting,
That there is none but Me.
I am the Lord and there is none else.
7 I form light and create darkness,
I make weal and create woe.
I the Lord do all these things."
8 Trickle, O heavens, from above!
Let the heavens rain down victory!
Let the earth open up,

So that triumph will sprout
And vindication spring up!
I, the Lord, have created it.
9 Ho! He who contends with his Maker,
A potsherd among earthenware.
Shall the clay ask the potter, "What are you making?
Your work has no handles"?
10 Ho! He who says to [his] father, "What are you begetting?"
Or to [his] mother, "What are you bearing?"
11 Thus said the Lord, Israel's Holy One and his Maker:
"Will you question Me?
Will you instruct Me
Concerning My children and the work of My hands?"
12 It was I who made the earth
And created humankind upon it.
My own hands stretched out the heavens,
And I commanded all their host.
13 It was I who roused him for victory,
And I will make level all roads for him.
He shall rebuild My city
And let My exiled people go free,
Without price and without payment" —
Said the Lord of Hosts.
14 Thus said the Lord:
"Egypt's wealth and Nubia's gains
And Sabeans bearing tribute
Shall pass over to you and be yours.
They will follow you and pass by in fetters.
They shall bow down to you,
And they shall pray to your God.
'Only among you is God,
And there is no other god at all!
15 Truly you are a God who protects,
O God of Israel, the Deliverer.'"
16 All of them are confounded and put to shame.
To a man they slink away in disgrace,
Those who fabricate idols.
17 But Israel is saved by the Lord, salvation everlasting.
You shall not be confounded or put to shame for all ages to come.
18 Yea, thus said the Lord,
The creator of the heavens, He who is God,

Who formed the earth and made it,
Who fixed it firmly,
Who did not create it a wasteland,
But formed it to be inhabited:
"I am the Lord, and there is none else.
19 I did not speak in secrecy
At a site in a land of darkness.
I did not say to the offspring of Jacob,
'Seek Me out in a wasteland/in vain.'
I, the Lord, foretell reliably,
Announce what is true."
20 Assemble yourselves and come,
Approach together,
You survivors of the nations,
Who have no awareness,
Who carry their wooden idols
And pray to a god who cannot save!
21 Speak up! Present your case!
Let them even take counsel together!
Who announced this aforetime,
Foretold it of old?
No god exists other than Me,
Who is triumphant and able to save.
22 Turn to Me and be saved,
All the ends of the earth!
For I am God, and there is none else!
23 By Myself have I sworn,
From My mouth has issued truth,
A word that shall not be revoked:
"To Me every knee shall bend,
Every tongue shall swear loyalty,
24 Saying: 'Only in the Lord are victory and might.'
To Him will come and be ashamed
All those who are incensed against Him,
25 But it is in the Lord that all the offspring of Israel
Shall have victory and glory."

46 1 Bel has crouched down,
Nabu has stooped low.
Their images are consigned to beasts and cattle.
The things you would carry [in procession]

Are loaded as a burden on tired animals.
2 They stoop low, totally crouched down.
They are unable to rescue the burden,
And they themselves go into captivity.
3 Listen to Me, O house of Jacob
And the entire remnant of the house of Israel,
Who have been carried since birth,
Supported since leaving the womb:
4 "Till you grow old, I am He.
Till you turn gray, it is I who will continue to carry you.
I was the Creator and I will be the Bearer,
And I will carry and rescue [you]."
5 To whom can you liken Me or declare Me similar?
To whom can you liken Me so that we are comparable?
6 Those who squander gold from the purse
And weigh out silver on the balance,
They hire a goldsmith to make it into a god
To which they bow down and prostrate themselves.
7 They must hoist it on their shoulders and carry it.
When they put it down it stands,
It does not budge from its place.
If one cries out to it, it does not answer.
It cannot save him from his distress.
8 Remember this and be firm!
Take it to heart, you rebels!
9 Remember what happened long ago!
For I am God and there is none else.
I am God and there is none like Me.
10 I foretell the outcome from the beginning,
And from the past, things that have not yet occurred.
I say: "My plan shall be fulfilled,
I will do all I have purposed.
11 I summoned a bird of prey/counselor from the east,
From a distant land, the man of My counsel.
I have spoken, so I will bring it to pass;
I have designed it, so I will complete it."
12 Listen to Me, you obstinate of heart
Who are far from victory:
13 "I am bringing My victory near.
It shall not be far off
And My triumph shall not be delayed.

I will grant salvation in Zion,
To Israel, in whom I glory."

47 1 "Get down and sit in the dust,
Fair maiden Babylon!
Sit on the ground dethroned,
Daughter of the Chaldeans!
Nevermore shall they call you the tender and dainty one.
2 Grasp the hand mill and grind meal!
Remove your veil!
Strip off your train!
Bare your thighs!
Wade through rivers!
3 Your nakedness shall be uncovered,
And your very shame shall be exposed.
I will take vengeance,
And I shall not be entreated."
4 [Says] our Redeemer — Lord of Hosts is His name —
the Holy One of Israel.
5 "Sit in silence!
Enter into darkness,
Daughter of the Chaldeans!
Nevermore shall they call you
'Queen of Kingdoms.'
6 I was angry at My people,
I profaned My heritage.
I delivered them into your hands,
But you showed them no mercy.
Even upon the aged
You made your yoke exceedingly heavy.
7 You thought, 'I shall always be queen forever.'
You did not take these things to heart,
You gave no thought to its outcome."
8 And now hear this,
O lover of luxury,
Who dwells in security,
Who thinks to herself:
"I am, and there is none but me.
I shall neither become a widow
Nor experience the loss of children."
9 Yet these two things shall come upon you

In a moment, in a single day:
Loss of children and widowhood
Shall come upon you in full measure,
Despite your many enchantments
And despite your countless spells/enchanters.
10 You were secure in your wickedness.
You thought: "No one can see me."
It was your very skill and your science that led you astray.
And you thought to yourself: "I am and there is none but me."
11 Evil is coming upon you,
Which you will not know how to bribe/charm away.
Disaster is falling on you,
Which you will not be able to propitiate.
Coming upon you suddenly is disaster,
Of which you are unaware.
12 Persist in your many spells and your many enchantments
On which you labored from your youth!
Perhaps you will be able to avail,
Perhaps you will find strength/you will inspire terror.
13 You are helpless, despite all your art.
Let the astrologers stand up and save you,
The stargazers who foretell, month by month,
Whatever will come upon you.
14 See, they are like stubble,
Fire consumes them.
They cannot save themselves from the flames.
This is no coal for warming themselves,
No fire to sit in front of!
15 Such are they for you, your sorcerers,
With whom you have toilsomely dealt since your youth.
Each has wandered off his own way;
There is none to save you.

48 1 Listen to this, O house of Jacob,
Who are called by the name of Israel
And have issued from the womb of Judah,
Who swear by the name of the Lord
And invoke the God of Israel,
Though not in truth and sincerity,
2 Even though you are named after the Holy City
And lean for support on the God of Israel,

Whose name is the Lord of Hosts.
3 Long ago I foretold things that would happen.
From My mouth they issued, and I announced them.
Suddenly I acted, and they came to pass.
4 Because I know how stubborn you are:
Your neck is like an iron sinew
And your forehead bronze.
5 Therefore I told you long beforehand,
Announced things to you ere they happened,
So that you could not say, "My idol caused them,
My carved and molten images ordained them."
6 You have heard all of this;
Must you not acknowledge it?
As of now I announce to you new things,
Secret things that you did not know.
7 Only now they are created, and not of old.
Before today you had not heard of them,
Lest you say, "I knew them already."
8 You have not heard, nor have you known,
Your ears were not opened of old.
For I know that you are treacherous
And that you were called a rebel from birth.
9 For the sake of My name I control My wrath,
(For the sake of) My own glory I hold Myself in check,
Not to destroy you.
10 See, I refined you, but not as silver;
I tested you in the furnace of affliction.
11 For My sake, My own sake, do I act,
Lest (My name) be dishonored!
And I will not give My glory to another.
12 Listen to Me, O Jacob,
And Israel whom I have called!
"I am He, I am the first,
And I am the last as well.
13 My own hand founded the earth,
And My right hand spread out the skies.
I call to them, 'Let them stand up together'!"
14 Assemble, all of you, and listen!
Who among you foretold these things?
"He whom the Lord loves
Shall work His will against Babylon

And with His might against Chaldea.
15 I, I predicted, and I called him.
I have brought him,
And he shall succeed in his mission.
16 Draw near to Me and hear this!
From the beginning I did not speak in secret,
From the time anything existed I was there.
And now the Lord God has sent me with His spirit."
17 Thus said the Lord your Redeemer,
The Holy One of Israel:
"I the Lord am your God,
Instructing you for your own benefit,
Guiding you in the way you should go.
18 If only you would heed My commands!
Then your prosperity would be like a river,
Your triumph like the waves of the sea,
19 Your offspring would be as many as the sand,
And your posterity as many as its grains.
Their name would never be cut off
Or obliterated from before Me."
20 Go forth from Babylon!
Hasten away from Chaldea!
Declare with shouts of joy!
Announce this!
Proclaim it to the ends of the earth!
Say: "The Lord has redeemed His servant Jacob!"
21 They have known no thirst,
Though He led through parched places.
He made water flow for them from the rock,
He cleaved the rock and water gushed forth.
22 "There is no safety — said the Lord — for the wicked."

49 1 Listen to me, O coastlands!
And give heed, O nations far away!
The Lord called me from birth,
He named me while I was in my mother's womb.
2 He made my mouth like a sharpened dagger,
He hid me in the shadow of His hand.
He made me like a polished arrow,
He concealed me in His quiver.
3 He said to me: "You are My servant,

Israel, in whom I glory."
4 I thought, "I have labored in vain;
I have spent my strength for nothing, for empty breath.
Yet in truth my case is with the Lord,
And my recompense is with my God.
5 And now the Lord — who formed me in the womb to be His servant —
Has resolved to bring back Jacob to Himself,
That Israel may be gathered to Him.
And I have been honored in the sight of the Lord
And my God has been my strength."
6 For He has said:
"It is too slight (a task) that you should be My servant
To restore the tribes of Jacob
And to bring back the survivors of Israel.
I will also make you a light to nations,
That My salvation may reach the ends of the earth."
7 Thus says the Lord, the Redeemer of Israel, his Holy One,
To the one whose very self is despised,
To the abhorred of nations/Whose body is detested,
To the slave of rulers:
"Kings shall see and stand up,
Princes, and they shall prostrate themselves —
For the sake of the Lord who is faithful,
For the Holy One of Israel who chose you."
8 Thus said the Lord:
"In a favorable moment I answer you
And on a day of salvation I help you.
I created you and appointed you a covenant people,
Restoring the land,
Allotting anew the desolate holdings,
9 Saying to the prisoners, 'Go free!'
To those who are in darkness, 'Reveal yourselves!'"
They shall pasture along the roads,
On every bare height shall be their pasture.
10 They shall neither hunger nor thirst,
Burning heat and sun shall not strike them.
For He who loves them will lead them,
He will guide them to springs of water.
11 I will make all My mountains a road,
And My highways shall be built up.
12 Look! These are coming from far away.

Look! These from the north and the west,
And these from the land of Syene.
13 Shout, O heavens! And rejoice, O earth!
Break into shouting, O hills!
For the Lord has comforted His people
And has taken back His afflicted ones in love.
14 Zion says:
"The Lord has forsaken me,
My God has forgotten me."
15 Can a mother forget her baby?
Or a young woman the child of her womb?
Though they might forget,
Yet I never will forget you.
16 See, I have engraved you on the palms of My hands,
Your walls are ever before Me.
17 Swiftly your children are coming,
Those who ravaged and ruined you shall leave you.
18 Look up all around you and see!
They are all assembled, are come to you.
As I live — declares the Lord —
You shall don them all like jewels
And adorn yourself with them like a bride.
19 As for your ruins and desolate places and your land laid waste,
You shall soon be too constrained for your inhabitants,
While those who destroyed you remain far from you.
20 The children born in your bereavement
Shall yet say in your hearing:
"The place is too cramped for me;
Make room for me to live in!"
21 And you will say to yourself:
"Who bore these for me
When I was bereaved and barren,
Exiled and spurned/imprisoned?
By whom, then, were these reared?
I was left all alone,
And where have these been?"
22 Thus said the Lord God:
"I will raise My hand to the nations
And lift up My ensign to the peoples.
And they shall bring your sons in their bosoms,
And your daughters shall be carried on their shoulders.

23 Kings shall be your foster fathers,
Their queens shall be your nursemaids.
They shall bow to you, face to the ground,
And lick the dust of your feet.
And you shall know that I am the Lord;
Those who trust in Me shall not be disappointed."
24 Can booty be taken from a warrior?
Or captives rescued from a victor?
25 Yet thus said the Lord:
"Captives shall be taken from a warrior
And booty shall be rescued from one who is ruthless.
For I will contend with your adversaries,
And I will save your children.
26 I will make your oppressors eat their own flesh.
They shall be drunk with their own blood as with fresh wine,
And all humankind shall know that I the Lord am your Savior,
The Mighty One of Jacob, your Redeemer."

50 1 Thus said the Lord: "Where is the bill of divorce of your mother
Whom I have sent away?
And which of My creditors was it to whom I sold you?
Indeed, you were sold for your sins,
And your mother was sent away for your crimes.
2 Why, when I came, was no one there?
Why, when I called, did no one respond?
Is My arm, then, too short to redeem?
Have I not the power to save?
Lo, with a mere rebuke I dried up the sea
And turned rivers into desert.
Their fish stank from lack of water
And died of thirst.
3 I clothe the skies in darkness/mourning
And make their raiment sackcloth."
4 The Lord God has given me a skilled tongue,
To know how to speak timely words to the weary.
Morning by morning He rouses,
He rouses my ear to give heed like disciples.
5 The Lord God opened my ears,
And I did not disobey,
I did not turn myself away.
6 I offered my back to the floggers

And my cheeks to those who tore out my hair.
I did not hide my face from insults and spittle.
7 But the Lord God will help me;
Therefore I am not humiliated.
Therefore I have set my face like flint,
And I know I shall not be shamed.
8 My Vindicator is at hand;
Who dares contend with me?
Let us stand up together!
Who would be my opponent?
Let him approach me!
9 Lo, the Lord God will help me.
Who can get a verdict against me?
They shall all wear out like a garment,
The moth shall consume them.
10 Who among you reveres the Lord
And heeds the voice of His servant?
Though he walks in darkness
And has no light,
Let him trust in the name of the Lord
And rely on his God.
11 But you are all kindlers of fire,
Setting ablaze firebrands.
Walk in the flame of your fire,
In the firebrands that you have lit!
This has come to you from My hand:
You shall lie down/die in pain.

51 1 Listen to Me, you who pursue justice,
You who seek the Lord!
Look to the rock from which you were hewn,
To the quarry from which you were dug!
2 Look back to Abraham your father
And to Sarah who brought you forth!
For he was only one when I called him,
But I blessed him and made him many.
3 Truly the Lord has comforted Zion,
Comforted all her ruins.
He will make her wilderness like Eden,
Her desert like the garden of the Lord.
Joy and gladness shall be found in her,

Thanksgiving and the sound of music.
4 Hearken to Me, My people!
And give ear to Me, O My nation!
For teaching shall go/shine forth from Me,
And My justice for the light of peoples.
In a moment I will bring it.
5 My triumph is near,
My salvation has gone forth/shone.
My arms shall rule the peoples,
The coastlands shall look eagerly for Me,
They shall wait hopefully for My arm.
6 Raise your eyes to the heavens!
And look at the earth beneath!
Though the heavens should dissipate like smoke,
And the earth wear out like a garment,
And its inhabitants die out as well,
Yet My salvation is forever,
My triumph shall remain unbroken.
7 Listen to Me, you who care for justice,
O people who lay My instruction to heart!
Fear not the insults of humans!
And be not dismayed at their jeers!
8 For the moth shall eat them up like a garment,
The moth shall eat them up like wool.
Yet My triumph shall endure forever,
My salvation through all the ages.
9 Awake, awake!
Clothe yourself with strength, O arm of the Lord!
Awake as in days of old, as in former ages!
It was You who hacked Rahab in pieces,
Who pierced the sea serpent.
10 It was You who dried up the sea,
The waters of the great deep,
Who made the depths of the sea
A road the redeemed might walk.
11 So let the ransomed of the Lord return
And come with joyful cries to Zion,
Crowned with joy everlasting.
Let them attain joy and gladness
While sorrow and sighing flee.
12 I, I am He who comforts you!

What ails you that you fear a human, who must die,
A mortal, who fares like grass?
13 You have forgotten the Lord your Maker
Who stretched out the skies and founded the earth.
And you live all day in constant dread
Because of the rage of the oppressor
Who is aiming to cut [you] down.
Yet where is the rage of an oppressor?
14 Quickly the tree blooms;
It is not cut down and slain
And its fruit will not fail.
15 For I, the Lord your God,
Who stirs up the sea into roaring waves,
Whose name is Lord of Hosts —
16 I have put My words in your mouth
And sheltered you with My hand.
I, who planted the skies and made firm the earth,
Have said to Zion: "You are My people!"
17 Rouse, rouse yourself! Arise, O Jerusalem!
You, who from the Lord's hand
Have drunk the cup of His poison,
You, who have drained to the dregs
The goblet, the cup of reeling.
18 She has none to guide her
Of all the sons she bore,
And none of all the sons she reared
Takes her by the hand.
19 These two things have befallen you —
Who can console you?
Wrack and ruin, famine and sword,
How shall I comfort you?
20 Your sons lie in a faint at every street corner
Like an antelope caught in a net,
Full of the poison of the Lord,
With the rebuke of your God.
21 Therefore, listen to this, afflicted one,
Drunk, but not with wine!
22 Thus said the Lord, your Lord,
Your God, who contends for His people:
"Herewith I take from your hand the cup of reeling,
The goblet, the cup of My wrath.

You shall never drink it again.
23 I will put it in the hands of your tormentors
Who have commanded you,
'Bend down, that we may walk over you!'
So you made your back like the ground,
Like a street for passers-by."

52 1 Awake, awake!
Clothe yourself in your strength/splendor, O Zion!
Put on your robes of beauty, Jerusalem, holy city!
For the uncircumcised and the unclean
Shall never enter you again.
2 Shake off the dust from yourself!
Arise! Sit up/Captive Jerusalem!
Loose the bonds from your neck,
O captive daughter Zion!
3 For thus said the Lord: "You were sold for no price
And shall be redeemed without payment."
4 For thus said the Lord God:
"At first My people went down to Egypt to sojourn there,
But Assyria oppressed them for no reason/in the end.
5 What am I doing here? — declares the Lord.
For My people have been carried off without cause,
Their mockers howl/their rulers boast — declares the Lord —
And constantly, unceasingly, My name is reviled.
6 Assuredly, My people shall know My name,
Assuredly, they shall know on that day
That I, the One who promised, am now at hand."
7 How lovely on the mountain
Are the footsteps of the herald,
Announcing well-being, heralding good news, announcing victory,
Telling Zion, "Your God is King!"
8 Hark!
Your watchmen raise their voices,
As one they shout for joy.
For their eyes shall behold clearly
The Lord's return to Zion.
9 Break forth together in joyful shouts,
O ruins of Jerusalem!
For the Lord has comforted His people,
Has redeemed Jerusalem.

10 The Lord has bared His holy arm
In the sight of all the nations,
And the very ends of the earth
Shall see the salvation of our God.
11 Turn! Turn away!
Depart from there!
Touch nothing unclean!
Go forth from there!
Keep yourselves pure,
You who bear the vessels of the Lord!
12 But you will not depart in urgent haste,
Nor will you leave in flight.
For the Lord is marching before you,
The God of Israel is your rear guard.

13 Indeed, My servant shall prosper,
He shall be exalted, elevated, and uplifted.
14 Just as the many were appalled at you/him,
So marred was his appearance, unlike that of a man,
His form, beyond human semblance,
15 Just so he shall startle many nations.
Kings shall be silenced because of him,
For they shall see what has not been told them,
Shall behold what they never have heard.
53 1 Who can believe what we have heard?
Upon whom has the arm of the Lord been revealed?
2 For he has grown, by His favor, like a sapling,
Like a tree trunk out of arid ground.
He had no form or beauty, that we should look at him,
No appearance, that we should take delight in him.
3 He was despised, shunned by men,
A man of suffering, familiar with disease.
As one who hid his face from us,
He was despised, and we held him of no account.
4 Yet it was our sickness that he was bearing,
Our suffering that he bore.
We accounted him plagued, smitten, and afflicted by God.
5 But he was wounded because of our sins,
Crushed because of our iniquities.
He bore the chastisement that made us safe and secure,
And by his bruises we were healed.

6 We all went astray like sheep,
Each going his own way,
But the Lord visited on him the punishment of all of us.
7 He was maltreated, yet submissive,
And he did not protest.
Like a sheep being led to slaughter,
Like a ewe, dumb before those who shear her,
He did not open his mouth.
8 By oppressive judgment he was taken away.
Who gave a thought to his fate?
For he was cut off from the land of the living,
Because of the sin of My people,
He was brought/struck to death.
9 His grave was set among the wicked
And with the rich/evildoers, his burial place,
Though he had done no injustice
And had spoken no deceit.
10 But the Lord chose to crush him with sickness.
If he makes himself an offering for guilt,
He shall see offspring and have long life,
And through him the Lord's purpose will prosper.
11 Because of his anguish he shall be sated and saturated with light.
Through his devotion My righteous servant shall vindicate the many,
And it is their punishment that he bears.
12 Assuredly, I will give him the many as his portion/allot him a portion with the many.
He shall receive the multitude as his spoils/shall share the spoils with the multitude.
Because he exposed himself/poured out his life to death
And was numbered among the sinners,
Because he bore the guilt of the many
And made intercession for sinners.

54 1 Sing aloud, O barren one,
You who bore no child!
Break into cries of joy,
You who did not travail!
For the children of the wife desolate
Shall outnumber those of the espoused — said the Lord.
2 Enlarge the site of your tent!
Spread out the curtains of your dwelling!

Do not stint!
Lengthen the ropes!
And drive the pegs firm!
3 For you shall spread out to the north and the south.
Your offspring shall dispossess nations
And shall inhabit the desolate cities.
4 Fear not, you shall not be shamed!
Do not cringe, you shall not be disgraced!
For you shall forget the shame of your youth
And remember no more the disgrace of your widowhood.
5 For He who created you will espouse you,
His name is "Lord of Hosts."
The Holy One of Israel is your Redeemer;
He is called "God of all the earth."
6 For the Lord has called you back,
As a wife once deserted and despondent.
Can one reject the wife of his youth? — said your God.
7 In a fit of rage I deserted you,
But with vast love I will gather you back.
8 In an outpouring of anger, for a moment,
I hid My face from you.
But with devotion everlasting
I will take you back in love —
Said the Lord your Redeemer.
9 For this to Me is like the waters/days of Noah:
As I swore that the waters of Noah never again would pour over the earth,
So I swear that I will not be angry with you or rebuke you.
10 For the mountains may move
And the hills totter,
But My loyalty shall never move from you,
Nor My covenant of friendship be shaken —
Said the Lord, who takes you back in love.
11 Afflicted, storm-tossed one, uncomforted,
I will lay carbuncles as your building stones
And make your foundations of lapis lazuli.
12 I will make your battlements of rubies,
Your gates of firestones,
Your whole encircling territory/boundary stones of desirable gems.
13 And all your children shall be disciples of the Lord
And great shall be the welfare of your children.

14 You shall be established through righteousness.
You shall have no fear of oppression, as it shall be far off,
Of terror, and it shall not come near you.
15 Surely no harm can be done without My consent.
Whoever would harm you shall fall because of you.
16 It is I who created the smith
To fan the charcoal fire
And produce weapons, each for its own purpose;
So it is I who create the destroyer to lay waste.
17 No weapon formed against you shall succeed,
And every tongue that contends with you at law you shall defeat.
Such is the lot of the servants of the Lord,
Such their triumph through Me — declares the Lord.

55 1 Ho! All who are thirsty,
Come for water!
Even if you have no money.
Come! Buy food! And eat!
Come! Buy food without money,
Wine and milk without cost!
2 Why do you spend money for what is not bread?
Your earnings for what does not satisfy?
Give heed to Me!
And you shall eat choice food
And enjoy the richest viands!
3 Incline your ear! And come to Me!
Hearken! And you shall be revived.
And I will make with you an everlasting covenant,
The enduring loyalty promised to David.
4 As I appointed him a leader of peoples,
A prince and commander of peoples,
5 So you shall summon nations you did not know,
And nations that did not know you shall come running to you.
For the sake of the Lord your God,
The Holy One of Israel who has glorified you.
6 Seek the Lord while He can be found!
Call to Him while He is near!
7 Let the wicked give up his way,
The sinful man his plans.
Let him return to the Lord,
And He will have compassion on him,

To our God, for He freely forgives.
8 For My plans are not your plans,
Nor are My ways your ways — declares the Lord.
9 But as the heavens are high above the earth,
So are My ways high above your ways
And My plans above your plans.
10 For as the rain or snow drops from heaven
And returns not there,
But soaks the earth and makes it bring forth vegetation,
Yielding seed for he who sows and bread for he who eats,
11 So is the word that issues from My mouth:
It does not come back to Me unfulfilled,
But performs what I purpose
And succeeds in what I sent it to do.
12 You shall indeed leave in joy
And be led forth safely.
Before you, mountains and hills shall shout aloud,
And all the trees of the field shall clap their hands.
13 Instead of the briar, a cypress shall grow;
And instead of the nettle, a myrtle shall grow.
These shall stand as a monument to the Lord,
As an everlasting memorial that shall not perish.

56 1 Thus said the Lord:
"Observe what is right and do what is just,
For soon My salvation shall come,
And My deliverance be revealed.
2 Happy is the man who does this
And the man who holds fast to it:
Who keeps the Sabbath and does not profane it,
And stays his hand from doing any evil.
3 Let not the foreigner who has attached himself to the Lord say:
'The Lord will surely keep me apart from His people.'
And let not the eunuch say: 'I am a withered tree.'"
4 For thus said the Lord:
"As for the eunuchs who keep My Sabbath,
Who have chosen what I desire
And hold fast to My covenant,
5 I will give them in My house and within My walls
A monument and a name
Better than sons or daughters.

I will give them an everlasting name that shall not perish.
6 As for the foreigners who attach themselves to the Lord,
To minister to Him,
And to love the name of the Lord,
To be His servants —
All who keep the Sabbath and do not profane it
And who hold fast to My covenant,
7 I will bring them to My sacred mount,
And I will give them joy in My House of prayer.
Their burnt offerings and sacrifices shall be acceptable on My altar,
For My House shall be called a House of prayer for all peoples."
8 Thus declares the Lord God,
Who gathers the dispersed of Israel:
"I will gather still more to those already gathered."
9 All you wild beasts of the plain, come and devour,
All you beasts of the forest!
10 The watchmen are blind, all of them;
They are unaware.
They are all dumb dogs
That cannot bark.
Stretched out they babble/drowse,
They love to drowse.
11 And the dogs have a lusty appetite,
They never know satiety.
And as for the shepherds,
They know not what it is to give heed.
Everyone has turned his own way,
Every last one seeks his own advantage.
12 "Come!
I will fetch some wine, and let us swill liquor.
And tomorrow will be just the same
Or even much grander!"

57 1 The righteous man perishes,
And no one takes it to heart.
Pious men are swept away,
And no one gives a thought
That because of evil the righteous are swept away.
2 Yet he shall come to peace.
They shall have rest on their couches
Who walk straightforward.

3 But as for you, come forward,
You sons of a soothsayer,
You offspring of an adulterer and a harlot!
4 Of whom do you make sport?
At whom do you gloat
And stick out your tongue?
You are indeed children of iniquity,
Offspring of treachery,
5 Inflaming yourselves among the terebinths,
Under every verdant tree;
Slaughtering children in the wadis,
Among the clefts of the rocks.
6 With the smooth stones of the stream is your portion.
They, they are your allotment.
Even to them you have poured out libations,
Presented offerings.
Should I relent in the face of this?
7 On a high and lofty hill you have set your couch.
There too you have gone up to perform sacrifices.
8 Behind the door and doorpost
You have stationed your phallic images.
Abandoning Me,
You have gone up/you have stripped and lain down
On the couch you made so wide.
You have made a covenant with them;
You have loved bedding with them;
You have seen their genitalia/chosen lust.
9 You have traveled to the king with oil,
You have multiplied your perfumes,
And you have sent your envoys afar,
Even down to the netherworld.
10 Though wearied by much travel,
You never said, "I give up!"
You found gratification for your lust
And so you never cared.
11 Whom do you dread and fear
That you should be false?
But you gave no thought to Me,
You paid no heed.
It is because I have stood idly by so long and heedless
That you have no fear of Me.

12 I hereby pronounce your punishment,
Your deeds shall not avail you.
13 When you cry out,
Let your assembly of idols save you!
They shall all be borne off by the wind,
Snatched away by a puff of air.
But those who seek refuge in Me
Shall inherit the land
And possess My sacred mount.
14 [The Lord] says:
"Build up, build up a highway!
Clear a road!
Remove all obstacles from the road of My people!"
15 For thus said the High and Exalted One
Who forever dwells,
Whose name is "Holy":
"I dwell on high, in holiness,
Yet with the broken and the lowly in spirit,
Reviving the spirits of the lowly,
Reviving the hearts of the crushed.
16 For I will not always contend,
I will not be angry forever.
Nay, I who make spirits flag
Also create the breath of life.
17 For his sinful greed I was angry.
I struck him and in My wrath I stayed hidden,
But he waywardly follows the way of his heart.
18 Then I noted his ways and I healed him.
And I guided/granted him relief,
And meted out solace to him,
And to his mourners,
19 Creating fruit of the lips/heartening words:
It shall be well, well, with the far and the near,"
Said the Lord, "and I will heal them.
20 But the wicked are like the troubled sea
That cannot rest,
Whose waters toss up mire and mud.
21 But it shall not be well" — said my God — "for the wicked."

58 1 Call with a full throat!
Without restraint!

Raise your voice like a ram's horn!
Declare to My people their transgression,
To the house of Jacob — their sins!
2 Me they seek daily,
Eager to learn My ways.
Like a nation that does what is right,
That has not abandoned the law of its God.
They ask Me for righteous laws,
They are eager for the nearness of God:
3 "Why, when we fasted, do You not see?
When we mortify ourselves, do You pay no heed?"
Because on your fast day you attend to your business
And oppress all your laborers.
4 You fast in strife and contention,
And you strike with a wicked fist.
Your fasting now is not such as to make your voice heard on high.
5 Is such the fast I desire,
A day for humans to mortify themselves?
Is it bowing the head like a bulrush
And lying in sackcloth and ashes?
Do you call that a fast,
A favorable day to the Lord?
6 Is this not the fast I desire:
To unlock fetters of wickedness
And untie the cords of the yoke,
To let the oppressed go free
And snap every yoke?
7 It is to share your bread with the hungry
And to take the homeless poor into your home.
When you see the naked, to clothe him,
And not to ignore your own kin.
8 Then shall your light burst through like the dawn
And your healing spring up quickly.
Your Vindicator shall be your vanguard,
The Presence of the Lord shall be your rear guard.
9 Then, when you call, the Lord will answer;
When you cry out, He will say: "Here I am."
If you banish perversion from your midst,
The pointing finger and evil speech,
10 And you offer your sustenance to the hungry
And satisfy the famished creature —

Then shall your light shine in darkness
And your gloom shall be like noonday.
11 The Lord will guide you always.
He will slake your thirst in withering heat/in parched places
And invigorate/strengthen your bones.
You shall be like a well-watered garden,
Like a spring whose waters do not fail.
12 Men from your midst shall rebuild the ancient ruins;
You shall restore foundations laid long ago.
And you shall be called:
"Repairer of breached walls,
Restorer of lanes for habitation."
13 If you refrain from trampling the Sabbath underfoot,
From pursuing your affairs on My holy day;
If you call the Sabbath "Delight,"
The Lord's holy day "Honored,"
And if you honor it by not engaging in your business
Nor looking to your affairs, nor striking bargains —
14 Then you shall find your delight in the Lord.
I will set you astride the heights of the earth,
And I will let you enjoy the heritage of your father Jacob.
The mouth of the Lord has truly spoken.

59 1 Indeed, the Lord's arm is not too short to save,
Nor His ear too dull to hear.
2 But it is your iniquities that have been a barrier
Between you and your God.
Your sins have made Him turn His face away
And refuse to hear you.
3 For your hands are defiled with blood
And your fingers with iniquity.
Your lips speak lies,
Your tongue utters treachery.
4 No one sues justly
Or pleads honestly.
They rely on emptiness
And speak falsehood,
Conceiving wrong
And begetting mischief.
5 They hatch adder's eggs
And weave spiderwebs.

He who eats of their eggs will die,
And if one is crushed it hatches out a viper.
6 Their webs will not serve as a garment;
What they make cannot serve as clothing.
Their deeds are deeds of mischief,
Their hands commit lawless acts.
7 Their feet run after evil,
They hasten to shed the blood of the innocent.
Their schemes are schemes of mischief;
Destructiveness and injury are on their roads.
8 They do not care for the way of integrity;
There is no justice on their paths.
They make their courses crooked for themselves;
No one who walks in it cares for integrity.
9 "That is why redress is far from us
And vindication does not reach us.
We hope for light, but lo! there is darkness;
For a gleam, but we must walk in gloom.
10 We grope like blind men along a wall,
Like those without eyes we grope.
We stumble at noon as if at twilight,
At daytime we are like the dead.
11 We all growl like bears
And moan like doves.
We hope for redress, but there is none,
For deliverance, but it is far from us.
12 For our many transgressions are before You,
Our guilt testifies against us.
We are well aware of our sins,
And we know well our iniquities:
13 Rebellion, faithlessness to the Lord,
And turning away from our God,
Planning fraud and treachery,
Conceiving lies and uttering them with the throat.
14 And so redress is turned back
And vindication stands afar.
Indeed, honesty stumbles in the public square
And uprightness cannot enter.
15 Honesty has been lacking;
He who turns away from evil is thought a fool/madman/is despoiled."
The Lord saw and was displeased that there was no redress.

16 He saw that there was no one;
He was appalled that no one interceded.
Then His own arm won Him triumph,
His victorious right hand supported Him.
17 He donned victory like a coat of mail,
With a helmet of triumph on His head.
He clothed Himself with garments of vengeance
And wrapped Himself in zeal as in a robe.
18 According to their deserts, so shall He repay/The Lord of retribution shall deal out retribution:
Fury to His foes, retribution to His enemies;
He deals retribution to the coastlands.
19 From the west they shall revere/behold the name of the Lord,
And from the east, His Presence.
For He shall come like a hemmed-in stream,
Which the wind of the Lord drives on.
20 He shall come as redeemer to Zion,
To those in Jacob who turn back from sin —
Declares the Lord.
21 And this shall be My covenant with them, said the Lord:
"My spirit that is upon you
And the words that I have placed in your mouth
Shall never depart from your mouth, nor from the mouth of your children, nor from the mouth of your children's children" — said the Lord —
"From now on, for all time."

60 1 Arise! Shine!
For your light has dawned.
The Presence of the Lord has shone on you.
2 For though darkness shall cover the earth,
And thick clouds, the peoples,
Yet on you the Lord will shine
And His Presence be seen over you.
3 And nations shall walk by your light,
Kings, by your shining radiance.
4 Raise your eyes and look about!
All of them have gathered together and come to you.
Your sons shall come from afar,
And your daughters shall be carried on hips.
5 Then, as you behold, you will glow;

Your heart will throb and thrill.
For the wealth of the sea shall pass on to you,
The riches of nations shall come/be brought to you.
6 Dust clouds of camels shall cover you,
Dromedaries of Midian and Ephah.
They all shall come from Sheba.
They shall bear gold and frankincense,
And shall herald the praises of the Lord.
7 All the flocks of Kedar shall be assembled for you,
The rams of Nebaioth shall serve your needs.
They shall be welcome offerings on My altar,
And I will add glory to My glorious House.
8 Who are these that float like a cloud,
Like doves to their cotes?
9 The vessels of the coastlands shall assemble,
With ships of Tarshish in the lead,
To bring your sons from afar;
Their silver and gold with them,
For the name of the Lord your God,
For the Holy One of Israel, who has glorified you.
10 Foreigners shall rebuild your walls,
Their kings shall wait on you.
For though in My anger I struck you down,
In favor I take you back in love.
11 Your gates shall always stay open,
Day and night they shall never be shut,
To bring to you the riches of the nations,
With their kings in procession.
12 For the nation or the kingdom that does not serve you shall perish.
Such nations shall be utterly destroyed.
13 The majesty of Lebanon shall come to you,
Junipers, box trees, and cypresses all together,
To bring glory to the site of My sanctuary.
I will honor the place where My feet rest.
14 The sons of all those who tormented you
Shall come to you bending low;
And all who reviled you
Shall prostrate at the soles of your feet.
And they shall call you, "City of the Lord,
Zion of the Holy One of Israel."
15 Whereas you have been forsaken, rejected, with none passing through,

I will make you a pride everlasting,
A joy for age after age.
16 You shall suck the milk of the nations,
Suckle at royal breasts.
And you shall know that I the Lord am your Savior,
I, the Mighty One of Jacob, am your Redeemer.
17 Instead of copper I will bring gold;
Instead of iron I will bring silver;
Instead of wood, copper;
And instead of stone, iron.
And I will appoint well-being as your government,
Prosperity as your rulers.
18 The cry "Violence!"
Shall no more be heard in your land,
Nor "Wrack and Ruin!"
Within your borders.
But you shall name your walls "Salvation"
And your gates "Praise."
19 The sun shall no longer be your light by day,
Nor the shining of the moon for radiance [by night],
For the Lord shall be your light everlasting
And your God shall be your glory.
20 Your sun shall set no more,
Your moon no more withdraw,
For the Lord shall be a light to you forever,
And the days of your mourning shall be ended.
21 And your people, all of them righteous,
Shall possess the land for all time.
A shoot of My own planting,
My handiwork in which I glory.
22 The smallest shall become a clan,
The least, a mighty nation.
I, the Lord, will speed it in due time.

61 1 The spirit of the Lord God is upon me
Because the Lord has anointed me.
He has sent me as a herald to the humble,
To bind up the brokenhearted,
To proclaim release to the captives,
Liberation to the imprisoned;
2 To proclaim a year of the Lord's favor

And a day of vengeance for our God;
To comfort all who mourn,
3 To provide for the mourners in Zion,
To give them a turban instead of ashes,
Oil of gladness instead of mourning,
A robe of splendor/radiance instead of a faint spirit.
They shall be called "Terebinths of Victory"
Planted by the Lord for His glory.
4 And they shall build the ancient ruins,
Raise up the desolations of old,
And renew the ruined cities,
The desolations of many ages.
5 Strangers shall be ready to pasture your flocks,
Foreigners shall be your plowmen and vine trimmers,
6 While you shall be called "Priests of the Lord"
And termed "Ministers of our God."
You shall enjoy the riches of nations
And revel in/be provided abundantly with their wealth.
7 Instead of your shame that was double,
And instead of the disgrace that they inherited as their portion/they will exult in their portion.
Assuredly, they shall have a double share in their land,
Joy shall be theirs evermore.
8 For I the Lord love justice;
I hate robbery and/with injustice.
I will pay them their wages faithfully
And make an everlasting covenant with them.
9 Their offspring shall be known among the nations,
Their descendants in the midst of the peoples.
All who see them shall acknowledge
That they are a stock the Lord has blessed.
10 I greatly rejoice in the Lord;
Let my whole being exult in my God.
For He has clothed me with garments of triumph,
Wrapped me in a robe of victory,
Like a bridegroom adorned with a priestly turban,
Like a bride bedecked with her jewelry.
11 For as the earth sprouts forth its growth,
And as a garden makes its seeds shoot up,
So the Lord God will make victory and glory
Shoot up in the presence of all the nations.

62 1 For the sake of Zion I will not remain silent,
And for the sake of Jerusalem I will not be still,
Till her victory shines forth resplendent
And her triumph burns like a flaming torch.
2 Nations shall see your victory
And all the kings your glory,
And you shall be called by a new name
That the Lord Himself shall bestow.
3 You shall be a glorious crown in the hand of the Lord
And a royal diadem in the palm of your God.
4 Nevermore shall you be called "Forsaken,"
Nor shall your land be called "Desolate."
But you shall be called "I Delight in Her"
And your land "Espoused,"
For the Lord takes delight in you,
And your land shall be espoused.
5 As a youth espouses a young woman,
So shall your sons/builders espouse you.
And as a bridegroom rejoices over his bride,
So shall your God rejoice over you.
6 On your walls, O Jerusalem,
I have posted watchmen,
Who shall never remain silent by day or by night.
You, who invoke the Lord,
Take no rest!
7 And give no rest to Him!
Until He establishes Jerusalem
And makes her renowned on earth.
8 The Lord has sworn by His right hand,
By His mighty arm:
"Nevermore will I give your grain
To your enemies for food,
Nor shall foreigners drink the new wine
For which you have labored.
9 But those who harvest it shall eat it
And give praise to the Lord.
And those who gather it shall drink it
In My sacred courts."
10 Pass through! Pass through the gates!
Clear the road for the people!
Build up! Build up the highway! Remove the rocks!

Raise an ensign over the peoples!
11 Lo, the Lord has proclaimed to the end of the earth:
"Announce to daughter Zion,
Behold, your Deliverer is coming!
See, His reward is with Him
And His recompense before Him."
12 And they will call them "The Holy People,
The Redeemed of the Lord,"
And you shall be called "Sought Out,
A City Not Forsaken."

63 1 Who is this coming from Edom,
In crimsoned garments from Bozrah?
Majestic in attire,
Pressing forward in His great might?
"It is I, proclaiming victory,
Powerful to give triumph/Who contends in order to save."
2 "Why is your clothing so red,
Your garments like one who treads grapes in a press?"
3 "I trod out a winepress alone,
No one from the peoples was with Me.
I trod them down in My anger,
Trampled them in My rage.
Their lifeblood bespattered My garments,
And all My clothing was stained.
4 For I had planned a day of vengeance,
And My year of redemption has arrived.
5 Then I looked, but there was none to help;
I was appalled, but there was none to aid.
So My own arm brought Me victory
And My own rage was My aid.
6 I trampled peoples in My anger,
I made them drunk with My rage/poison,
I shall cause their lifeblood to flow to the ground/netherworld."
7 I will recount the Lord's acts of love,
The praises of the Lord,
For all that the Lord has done for us,
His bountiful goodness to the house of Israel
That He bestowed on them/us,
According to His mercy and His great love.
8 He thought, "Surely they are My people,

Children who will not play false."
So He was their deliverer
9 In all their troubles.
No emissary or angel — He Himself delivered them.
In His love and compassion He Himself redeemed them,
Raised them and sustained them all the days of old.
10 But they rebelled and grieved His holy spirit.
Then He changed into their enemy,
And He Himself made war against them.
11 Then they remembered the days of old —
Him, who drew out His people:
"Where is He who brought them up from the sea
Along with the shepherd of His flock?
Where is He who put within him His holy spirit,
12 Who made His mighty arm
March at the right hand of Moses,
Who divided the waters before them
To make for Himself a name everlasting?
13 Who led them through the watery depths,
Like a horse in a desert without stumbling,
14 Like cattle descending into the plain?"
The spirit of the Lord gave them rest/guided them.
Thus did You shepherd Your people
To win for Yourself a glorious name.
15 Look down from heaven!
And see from Your holy and glorious height!
Where is Your zeal, Your power,
Your yearning, and Your love?
Let (them) not be restrained!/Do not restrain Yourself!
16 Surely You are our Father.
Though Abraham does not know us
And Israel does not recognize us,
You, O Lord, are our Father;
From of old, Your name is "Our Redeemer."
17 Why, Lord, do You make us stray from Your ways
And turn our hearts away from revering You?
Relent for the sake of Your servants,
The tribes that are Your very own possession!
18 Why have evildoers afflicted Your holy people,
Our foes trampled Your Sanctuary?
19 We have become as though You never ruled us,

As though Your name was never attached to us.
If You would but rend the heavens and come down,
So that mountains would quake before You —

64 1 As when fire kindles brushwood,
And as fire makes water boil,
To make Your name known to Your adversaries,
So that nations will tremble before You.
2 When You did awesome deeds we dared not hope for,
You came down and mountains quaked before You.
3 Such things had never been heard or noted.
No eye has seen any god but You,
Who acts for those who trust in Him.
4 Yet you have struck him who would gladly do justice,
Who remembers You in Your ways.
It is because You are angry
That we have sinned.
Because when You have hidden Yourself,
We have acted wickedly/rebelled.
5 We have all become like an unclean thing,
And all our virtues like a soiled rag.
We are all withering like leaves,
And our iniquities, like a wind, carry us off.
6 Yet no one invokes Your name
Or rouses himself to cling to You.
For You have hidden Your face from us
And delivered us (to our enemies) because of our iniquities.
7 But now, O Lord, You are our Father.
We are the clay, and You are the Potter.
We are all the work of Your hands.
8 Be not implacably angry, O Lord,
Do not remember iniquity forever.
Look, we are Your people, all of us!
9 Your holy cities have become a desert:
Zion has become a desert,
Jerusalem, a desolation.
10 Our holy Temple, our glory,
Where our fathers praised You,
Has been consumed by fire;
And all that was dear to us is ruined.

11 At such things will You restrain Yourself, O Lord?
Will You stand idly by and torment us implacably?

65 1 I was there to be sought
By those who did not ask for Me,
I was to be found
By those who did not seek Me.
I said, "Here I am, here I am,"
To a nation that did not invoke My name.
2 I constantly spread out My hands
To a disloyal people
Who walk the way that is not good,
Following their own designs,
3 The people who provoke My anger continually to My very face,
Offering sacrifices in gardens,
Burning incense on brick altars,
4 Sitting inside tombs,
And passing the night in between the rocks,
Eating the flesh of swine,
With broth of unclean things in their bowls.
5 Who say, "Keep your distance!
Don't come close to me!
For I am too sacred for you."
Such things make My anger smoke,
A fire blazing all day long.
6 See, this is recorded before Me;
I will not stand idly by but will repay,
Repay into their bosom
7 Your sins and the sins of your fathers as well — said the Lord;
For they made burnt sacrifices on the mountains
And affronted Me on the hills.
I will pay back their recompense in full, into their bosom.
8 Thus said the Lord:
"As when the grape/new wine is present in the cluster,
One says, 'Don't destroy it;
There is a blessing in it.'
So will I do for the sake of My servants
And not destroy everything.
9 I will bring forth offspring from Jacob,
And from Judah heirs to My mountains.
My chosen ones shall possess it,

My servants shall dwell there.
10 Sharon shall become a pasture for flocks
And the Valley of Achor a place for cattle to lie down,
For My people who seek Me.
11 But as for you who forsake the Lord,
Who ignore My holy mountain,
Who set a table for Gad,
And fill a mixing bowl for Meni,
12 I will destine you for the sword.
You will all kneel down to be slaughtered,
Because I called, but you did not answer,
I spoke, but you did not listen.
You did what was wrong in My eyes
And chose what I do not want."
13 "Assuredly," thus said the Lord God:
"My servants shall eat, but you shall starve;
My servants shall drink, but you shall thirst;
My servants shall rejoice, but you shall be shamed;
14 My servants shall exalt in the gladness of their hearts,
But you shall cry out in the anguish of your heart,
Howling with a broken spirit.
15 You shall leave behind your name
By which My chosen ones shall curse:
'So may the Lord God slay you!'
But My servants shall be called by another name.
16 For whoever blesses himself in the land
Shall bless himself by the true God;
And whoever swears in the land
Shall swear by the true God.
The former troubles are forgotten
And are hidden from My sight.
17 For behold! I am creating new heavens and a new earth.
The former things shall not be remembered,
And they shall never come to mind.
18 But rather be glad and rejoice forever
In what I am creating!
For I shall create Jerusalem as a delight
And her people as a joy,
19 And I will rejoice in Jerusalem
And delight in My people.
Never again shall be heard in her

Cries of weeping and cries for help.
20 No more shall there be there an infant or old man
Who does not live out his days.
He who dies at the age of one hundred
Shall be considered a youth;
And he who falls short of a hundred
Shall be reckoned accursed.
21 They shall build houses and dwell in them,
They shall plant vineyards and eat their fruit.
22 They shall not build for others to dwell in,
Nor plant for others to enjoy.
For the days of My people shall be as long as the days of a tree.
My chosen ones shall enjoy the work of their hands.
23 They shall not toil to no purpose,
They shall not bear children in vain.
For they are an offspring blessed by the Lord
And their descendants with them.
24 Before they call, I will answer;
While they are still speaking, I will hearken.
25 The wolf and the lamb shall graze together,
And the lion shall eat straw like the ox,
And the serpent's food shall be earth.
They shall not hurt or destroy in all My holy mountain" —
Said the Lord.

66 1 Thus said the Lord:
"The heaven is My throne
And the earth is My footstool.
Where will you build a House for Me?
Where will My resting place be?
2 All these were made by My hand,
And thus they all came into being" — declares the Lord.
"Yet to such a one I look:
To the oppressed and brokenhearted,
And he who trembles at My word.
3 He who slaughters an ox, slays a man;
He who sacrifices sheep, breaks the neck of a dog;
He who makes a grain offering, offers the blood of swine;
He who makes a memorial offering with frankincense, blesses idols.
Just as they have chosen their ways
And take pleasure in their abominations,

4 So will I, for My part, choose to mock them,
And I will bring on them the very thing they dread.
For I called but none responded,
I spoke but none paid heed.
They did what was evil in My sight
And chose what I do not want.
5 Hear the word of the Lord,
You who tremble at His word!
Your kinsmen who hate you, who spurn you because of My name, are saying:
'Let the Lord manifest His Presence,
So that we may look upon your joy!'
But they shall be put to shame."
6 Hark, tumult from the city!
Thunder from the Temple!
It is the thunder of the Lord
As He deals retribution to His foes.
7 Before she labored, she gave birth;
Before her birth pangs came, she bore a son.
8 Who ever heard the likes of this?
Who ever witnessed such things?
Can a land pass through travail in a single day?
Or is a nation born all at once?
Yet Zion travailed
And at once bore her children!
9 "Shall I who bring to the point of birth not deliver?" — says the Lord.
"Shall I who cause birth shut the womb?" — said your God.
10 Rejoice with Jerusalem and be glad for her,
All you who love her!
Join in her jubilation,
All you who mourned for her!
11 So that you may suckle from her breast consolation to the full,
So that you may suck from her overflowing bosom to your delight.
12 For thus said the Lord:
"I will extend to her prosperity like a stream,
The wealth of nations like a wadi in flood
You shall suck.
And you shall be carried on hips
And dandled on knees.
13 As a mother comforts her son,
So I will comfort you;

And you shall find comfort in Jerusalem.
14 You shall see and your heart shall rejoice;
Your limbs shall flourish like spring grass.
The power of the Lord shall be revealed for His servants;
But He shall rage/His rage against His foes.
15 Lo, the Lord is coming with fire;
His chariots are like a whirlwind,
To vent His anger in fury,
His rebuke in blazing fire.
16 With fire will the Lord surely contend,
And with His sword against all humanity,
And many shall be the slain of the Lord.
17 Those who sanctify and purify themselves (to enter) the gardens,
One after another into the center,
Eating the flesh of the swine, detestable things/the reptile, and the mouse,
Shall one and all come to an end" — declares the Lord.
18 "For I [know] their deeds and designs.
[The time] has come/I am coming
To gather all the nations and peoples;
They shall come and behold My Presence.
19 I will set a sign among them
And send from them survivors to the nations:
To Tarshish, Pul, and Lud, that draw the bow/Meshech;
To Tubal, Javan, the distant coasts
That have never heard My fame
Nor beheld My Presence.
They shall declare My Presence among these nations,
20 And they shall bring all your brothers from all the nations
As an offering-tribute to the Lord,
On horses, in chariots and wagons, on mules and dromedaries,
To Jerusalem, My holy mountain" —
Said the Lord —
"Just as the Israelites bring an offering in a pure vessel to the house of the Lord.
21 And from them likewise I will take some to be Levitical priests" — said the Lord.
22 "For as the new heaven and the new earth
That I will create shall endure by My will" — declares the Lord,
"So shall your seed and your name endure.
23 And new moon after new moon,

And Sabbath after Sabbath,
All humankind shall come to bow down before Me" — said the Lord.
24 "They shall go out and gaze on the corpses of the men who rebelled against Me.
Their worms shall not die,
Nor their fire be quenched.
They shall be a horror to all humankind."

Chapter 40

[1-11] The initial literary pericope of chap. 40 is composed of four distinct units: vv. 1-2, 3-5, 6-8, 9-11. In his first prophecy, which begins, "Comfort, comfort My people!" Deutero-Isaiah conveys words of consolation and encouragement to his oppressed compatriots in Babylon and promises them salvation and redemption from their captors. The four and one half decades of exile are about to end since they have "served their sentence." The two devastating blows they had suffered because they had violated their covenant with God — the destruction of the Temple by the Babylonians and their subsequent exile (586 BCE) — shook the foundations of their belief in the eternity and inviolability of Jerusalem, the Temple, and the Davidic dynasty. By commencing his oracle with the words "My people" (עמי) and "your God" (אלהיכם), terms that echo the well-known covenant formula (e.g., Jer 7:23: "I am your God and you are My people"; cf. Exod 6:7; Lev 26:12; Jer 11:4; 31:33), the prophet is declaring that the covenant between God and Israel, which they thought had been broken because of their iniquities, was still intact.

Commentators differ in their explanations as to whom the double imperative, "Comfort, comfort My people!" is addressed: to the prophets (Targum, Rashi, Ibn Ezra, Kimchi); to the priests (LXX); or "to all the nations and peoples, the world and all its inhabitants" (Luzzatto). Most likely, however, is that this call for consolation here and in the ensuing verses, "Speak tenderly . . . and declare to her!" (v. 2); "A voice rings out" (v. 3); "A voice rings out: 'Proclaim!'" (v. 6), are actually directed toward members of the heavenly council, who function as God's heralds to the people. This council appears in 1 Kgs 22:19ff.; Isa 6; Jer 23:18, 22; Ps 82:1; 89:7; Job 1:6ff., and elsewhere. (See F. M. Cross, "The Council of Yahweh in Second Isaiah," *JNES* 12 [1953]: 274-77.) There is an intertextual connection between this introductory unit and Isaiah's prophecies in the first part of the book. The imminent destruction that God announced to His people in the presence of His divine council (chap. 6) had come to pass, and now the time had arrived to announce words of consolation (cf. 12:1, "Although You were wroth toward me, Your wrath has turned back and You comfort me"). In both chap. 40 and chap. 6 members of God's council "call out" (קרא; 40:3; 6:3, 4) and "speak" (אמר; 40:6; 6:8); both prophets have an apprehensive response to God's call (6:5; 40:6); the expiation of "sin" is mentioned (in 6:7 the prophet's sin, and in 40:2 the people's sin); and God's "presence" (כבוד) is revealed (6:3; 40:5). (For additional references see the introduction, §14.)

One can discern in these first four units a chiastic literary structure that is created by alternating the names ה׳ and אלהים: v. 1: אלהיכם; v. 2: ה׳; v. 3: ה׳, לאלהינו; v. 5: ה׳ (twice); v. 7: ה׳; v. 8: אלהינו; v. 9: אלהיכם; v. 10: אדני אלהיכם. (Regarding the structure of the first eleven verses, see D. N. Freedman, "The Structure of Isaiah 40:1-11," in E. N. Conrad and E. G. Newing, eds., *Perspectives in Language and Text: Essays and Poems in Honor of Francis I. Andersen's Sixtieth Birthday, July 28, 1985* [Winona Lake, Ind., 1987], 167-93.) Chapter 40 is the first of "the seven [prophecies] of consolation," which are read in synagogues on the seven Sabbaths following the ninth of Ab (a fast day commemorating the destruction of the First and Second Temples). This first Sabbath is known as "the Sabbath of comfort" (שַׁבָּת נַחֲמוּ), an expression based on the first two words of the chapter.

[1] *"Comfort, comfort My people!"* — Reiteration for emphasis is a recurrent and unique stylistic feature in Deutero-Isaiah, appearing more than in any other book of the Bible (cf., e.g., 43:11; 51:9, 17; 52:1; and see the introduction, §10). The transitive verb נַחֲמוּ is a plural imperative of the *pi'el* stem. The recurrent use of this verb (49:13; 51:3, 12; 52:9; 61:2; 66:13 [twice]), along with the consolatory words of the prophet, which are meant to encourage the people and the city in their plight following the destruction of the Temple and the subsequent exile (cf. 51:19; 54:11; Lam 1:2: "There is none to comfort her"; see there vv. 9, 16, 17, 21), have earned Deutero-Isaiah the title "Isaiah the comforter." "My people," an endearing expression of God's fondness for His people, serves as the direct object of the verb. Even though they have sinned and were punished, they are still His people. See Isa 51:16: "You are My people."

Says your God — The declaration in the imperfect (יאמר) denotes frequency. For the same form in similar grammatical contexts, see below, v. 25; 41:21; 66:9. It is found again only in the prophecies of First Isaiah; see 1:11, 18; 33:10; see the introduction, §14.

[2] The time of calamity has passed and God has finally forgiven His people. The context does not imply repentance on the part of the nation, nor reprieve for the sake of their forefathers, but rather that God, who was responsible for the people's sentencing, has decided that the time for reconciliation is at hand. For similar decisions connected entirely to God's will, see 44:22; 48:9-11.

"Speak tenderly to Jerusalem!" — These words of reconciliation parallel the previous words of comfort. The two also appear in tandem in Gen 50:21: "Thus he comforted them (וַיְנַחֵם) and spoke kindly to them (וידבר על לִבָּם)"; Ruth 2:13: "You have comforted me (נחמתני) and spoken kindly (ודברת על לב) to your maidservant." Anthropomorphized Jerusalem represents here the people of Israel; see Isa 52:9: "For the Lord will comfort His people, will redeem Jerusalem."

"And proclaim to her!" — Compare similarly Jonah 3:2: "Go at once to Nineveh, that great city, and proclaim to it (וּקְרָא אליהָ) what I tell you!"; Zech 1:4.

"That her term of service is over" — The term set by God for the people's exile has come to its end. For צבא, "term of service," see Job 7:1: "Truly man has a term of service (צבא) on earth"; Job 14:14: "All the time of my service (צבאי) [i.e., my life] I wait until my replacement comes." For the verb מלא, "to reach completion" within a time frame, see Lev 8:33: "You shall not go outside the entrance of the tent of meeting for seven days, until the day that your period of ordination is completed (מְלֹאת)"; see also Gen 25:24; Lam 4:18. Compare the Akkadian etymological and semantic equivalent, *malû*, "to reach fullness (said of time)" (*CAD* M/1:180-81). The relative pronoun כי is repeated in this and the two following clauses for emphasis. (For threefold repetitions, see the introduction, §10.)

"That her punishment has been expiated!" — The root רצי signifies "to be accepted"; see Lev 26:41: "And they accept (יִרְצוּ) their punishment; cf. v. 34; Job 14:6. For עָוֹן, "punishment," see Gen 4:13: "Cain said to the Lord: 'My punishment (עֲוֹנִי) is too great to bear.'"

"For she has received at the hand of the Lord double for all her sins" — She has been punished twice as much as she has deserved. This raises a difficult theological question: Why did God inflict on the Israelites more than they justly deserved? According to Luzzatto this mode of expression is hyperbolic: "The custom of consolers is to exaggerate the plight of the stricken individual in order to show that they sympathize with him, because if they do not do this, he will close his ears to their words of consolation." The significance of these words, however, is dependent on the prophecies of Jeremiah and their influence on Deutero-Isaiah. In light of Jeremiah's admonitory prophecy, God threatened the people of Israel by saying: "I will pay them in full — nay, doubly for their iniquity and sins" (Jer 16:18), i.e., the nation will indeed receive double the punishment for their sins. Thus according to Deutero-Isaiah this threat actually materialized, and now the people have finally completed serving their double portion of punishment. The motif appears again in Isa 61:7: "Because your shame was double . . . assuredly they shall possess a double share in their land" — measure for measure: having suffered twofold for its iniquities, Jerusalem

will be doubly rewarded; cf. also 65:6-7. (See the introduction, §15.) The noun כִּפְלַיִם, "double," is found only once more in the Bible, in Job 11:6; and for the causative ב in בכל, cf., e.g., Deut 24:16: "A person shall be put to death only for his own crime (בְּחֶטְאוֹ)."

"For she has received at the hand of the Lord" — For the verbal expression לקח מיד, "to receive, accept," see Gen 33:10: "No, I pray; if you would do me this favor, accept from me (ולקחת . . . מידי) this gift;" Num 5:25: "Then the priest shall take from the woman's hand (ולקח . . . מיד) the meal offering of jealousy." It also appears in the eighth-century BCE Aramaic inscription of King Panamuwa: "They [the gods] accepted from my hands (יקחו מנ ידי)" (*KAI* 214:12).

[3-5] A divine voice rings out commanding the construction of a level highway in the desert, free of all obstacles, on which God will lead the redeemed from Babylonia to Israel, thereby revealing the glory of God.

[3] *A voice rings out* — The identical first syllable of these two words (קו) creates a reverberating echo, declaring:

"Clear in the desert a road for the Lord!" — The Masoretic division (attaching במדבר to the second clause) is preferable to the reading reflected in the LXX, Vulgate, and Peshitta, as well as in the Gospels: Matt 3:3; Mark 1:3; Luke 3:4; and in Qumran (1QS 8:14) (D. W. Parry and E. Tov, *The Dead Sea Scrolls Reader,* 1: *Texts Concerned with Religious Law* [Leiden, 2004] 32, line 14): "A voice rings out in the desert, 'Clear a road for the Lord!'" (where במדבר is attached to the first clause). This is supported by the obvious parallelism here: "Clear in the desert" = "Level in the wilderness" (במדבר = בערבה), "A road for the Lord" = "A highway for our God" (דרך ה׳ = מְסִלָּה לאלהינו). The verb פני denotes the removal of obstacles from the path; see also 57:14: "Build up, build up a highway! Clear a road!"; 62:10: "Clear the road for the people!" For other examples of the parallel pair מסלה/דרך, see 49:11; 59:7-8; 62:10; cf. 57:14. The "desert" referred to here is the Syrian Desert stretching between Babylonia and Israel. Just as God led Israel through the desert after their exodus from Egypt, He will now lead them through yet another desert, from Babylonia to Israel. For other references to this "road," also known as "the road for My people" (57:14; 62:10), i.e., the road on which God will lead the redeemed on their return journey to Israel, see 42:16: "I will lead the blind by a road they did not know, and I will make them walk by paths they never knew"; 43:19: "I will make a road through the wilderness"; Jer 31:8-9: "I will bring them in from the northland . . . the blind and the lame among them, those with child and those in labor . . . I will lead them . . . by a level road where they will not stumble." (See the introduction, §15.) The "Lord's Road" may actually be the very name of this road, since in Mesopotamia roads were occasionally named after the gods; see, e.g., *ḫarrān* ^{d}mar•tu, "The road of (the god) Amurru" (*CAD* Ḫ:108).

"Level in the wilderness a highway for our God!" — "Leveling (יַשְּׁרוּ) a road" refers to making it smooth and straight and keeping it in good order, similar to its Akkadian etymological and semantic cognate, *šūšuru/šutēšuru* (the *shaph'el* of *ešēru,* "to straighten") (*CAD* E:357, 359-60). For the parallel pair ערבה/מדבר see 41:19; 51:3. Also worthy of note is the mention of a straight and leveled road in honor of Cyrus, 45:2: "I will march before you and level the hills that loom up"; 45:13: "It was I who roused him for victory and who level all roads for him" — a description that was probably influenced by the majestic roads of Babylonia, which were built to accommodate the grand processions of the Babylonian gods (*CAD* M/1:362-63).

[4] *"Let every valley be raised"* — The vocalization גֶּיא (in the construct state), instead of גַּיְא (the absolute state; see Num 21:20), creates an alliterative assonance with the verb יִנָּשֵׂא. The juxtaposition of גיא with הרים וגבעות (immediately following) is also found in Ezek 6:3.

"And every hill and mount be made low" — The repetition of כל (in the first and last hemistichs) emphasizes the wondrous miracle of the preparation of the straight and level highway. For further examples of the synonymous pair "hill and mount," see Isa 55:12; Jer 16:16; 50:6. The pair is also found in Ugaritic, *ġr — gbʿ* (*CAT* 1.4.V:31-32, 38-39).

"Let the rugged ground become a plain" — The substantive מישור, which contains the same root, ישר, found in the previous verse, serves as the antonym of עָקֹב here, and of מעקשים, "twisted, crooked," in Isa 42:16. Compare similarly Judg 5:6: "And wayfarers went by roundabout (עקלקלות) paths." The terms may be an allusive wordplay based on the names of the founding father, יעקב and ישראל (Deut 32:15; 33:5, 26).

"And the mountain ranges become a valley" — The hapax legomenon רכסים serves here as the antonym of בִּקְעָה, "valley."

[5] *"The Presence of the Lord shall be revealed"* — The "presence" (כבוד) of God refers, as it does in Akkadian, to a supernatural awe-inspiring sheen that envelops the deity at the moment of revelation. (For the phenomenon in Akkadian sources see especially the entries *melammu* and *puluḫtu* in *CAD* M/1:9-12; P:505-9. See also M. Weinfeld, "God the Creator in Genesis 1 and in Second Isaiah," *Tarbiz* 37 [1968]: 131-32 [Heb.].) For additional occurrences of "the presence of the Lord," see, e.g., 42:8, 12; 43:7; 48:11. For the verbal sequence ראי . . . גלי ("to be revealed . . . to appear"), see 47:3.

"And all humanity, as one, shall see it" — Everyone will witness the universal revelation of the Lord; see 66:18: "[The time] has come to gather all nations and tongues. They shall come and behold My glory"; Ps 97:6: "The heavens proclaim His righteousness and all peoples see His glory." Since the destruction of the Temple was followed by the departure of God's presence from the Temple and from Jerusalem (see Ezek 10:18-19; 11:23) — a phenomenon that the nations

understood as the severing of God's connection with His people — the prophet emphasizes that at the time of redemption God's presence will appear to all the nations; see Isa 52:10: "The Lord will bare His holy arm in the sight of all nations, and the very ends of earth shall see the salvation of our God." (The LXX, influenced by this latter verse, added the phrase "the salvation of our God" to the end of the present verse.) For the return of God's presence to the Temple see Ezek 43:2ff. For כל בשׂר, "all flesh," referring to all humanity, see Isa 49:26; Gen 6:12. This expression, which marks the conclusion of the first unit of this chapter, also appears in the last two verses of the final chapter, 66:23, 24, and creates a literary frame to the entire book. God's international recognition is also a recurrent motif of Ezekiel's prophecies; see Ezek 21:10: "And all flesh shall know that I the Lord have drawn My sword from its sheath"; cf. 25:11, 17; 26:6; 28:23. For the expression כל . . . יַחְדָּו, see Isa 43:9; 45:16. The term יַחְדָּו, which appears frequently in these prophecies, indicates the conclusion of a series of nouns or verbs (see, e.g., 41:1, 19, 20).

"For the mouth of the Lord has spoken" — The conjunction כי serves here as a conclusion to the prophecy and emphasizes its inevitability, leaving no doubt that it will come to pass; see also, e.g., 1:20: "But if you refuse and disobey, you will be devoured by the sword — for the mouth of the Lord has spoken"; 58:14: "I will set you astride the heights of the earth and let you enjoy the heritage of your father Jacob — for the mouth of the Lord has spoken."

[6-8] This short literary unit is similar to the prior one and is connected to it poetically, structurally, and thematically. Poetically — through word combinations such as קול קורא (v. 3) — קול . . . קרא (v. 6); כל בשר (vv. 5, 6); דִּבֶּר ה׳ (v. 5) — דְּבַר אלהינו (v. 8). Structurally — the first verse of each unit opens with an imperative, followed by a statement in the indicative (vv. 3 and 6). Thematically — once again a heavenly voice is heard. Here, however, the prophecies diverge: whereas the first heavenly voice addressed the divine council, the second heavenly voice presents a direct command to the prophet. This is followed by a short discourse in which he is commanded to proclaim the finiteness of humans in comparison to God. In order to emphasize human transience, the word "grass" is repeated four times, "flowers" three times, and the verbs "wither" and "fade" twice each. There are also thematic and literary sequences that appear both here and in Ps 103:15-17, which indicate that Deutero-Isaiah was influenced by this particular psalm:

Ps 103:15: "Man, his days are like grass (כחציר). He blossoms like the flowers of the field (כציץ השדה)" — v. 6: "All flesh is grass (חציר). All its goodness is like flowers of the field (כציץ השדה)."

Ps 103:16: "A wind passes by and he is no more (כי רוח עברה בו ואיננו)" — v. 7: "When the breath of the Lord blows on them (כי רוח ה׳ נשבה בו)."

Ps 103:17: "But the Lord's steadfast love (חסד) is for all of eternity (מעולם ועד עולם)" — v. 6: "his goodness (חסדו)"; v. 8: "but the word of our God endures forever (לעולם)."

Ps 103:20: "who fulfill His word . . . (עֹשֵׂי דְבָרוֹ)" — v. 8: "the word of our God (דבר אלהינו)."

This pericope, in turn, influenced the Qumranic author of the sapiential work 4Q185 9-11: "For behold like grass it springs from its earth and bears fruit; like a blossom is His mercy. His wind blows and . . . dries up, and the wind whisks its blossom away into oblivion" (J. M. Allegro, *Qumrân Cave 4.I (4Q158-4Q186)*, DJD 5 [Oxford, 1968], 85). For a survey of the Psalter's influence on Isaianic prophecy, see M. Zeidel, "Parallelisms in Isaiah and the Psalms," in *Mincha leDavid: Rabbi David Yellin's Jubilee Volume* [Jerusalem, 1935], 23-47 (Heb.); and see the introduction, §17.

[6] *A voice rings out: "Proclaim!"* — A heavenly voice calls on the prophet to deliver God's message; cf. Zech 1:14: "Then the angel who talked with me said to me: 'Proclaim!' (ויאמר . . . קְרָא)."

And I asked, "What shall I proclaim?" — The Masoretic vocalization of the verb וְאָמַר ("and [another] asks") indicates that it was understood to be part of a dialogue between members of the heavenly council; cf. Isa 6:3: "And one would call to the other, 'Holy, holy holy!'" However, the LXX reading of this verb as a first-person singular imperfect, וָאֹמַר, is preferable; cf. the Vulgate and 1QIsa[a], ואומרה. According to this vocalization, it is the prophet who responds to the heavenly call querulously.

"All flesh is grass" — This simile highlights humanity's transitory existence; see Isa 51:12: "Why fear man who must die, mortals who fare like grass?"; Ps 37:2: "For they soon wither like grass, like verdure fade away"; cf. 90:4-6; 129:6. The כי particle of comparison, "as," in the second hemistich, כציץ ("like flowers"), does double-duty and applies to this hemistich as well: "All flesh is as grass."

"All its goodness like flowers of the field" — For another example of the parallel pair חציר/ציץ, see Ps 103:15 quoted above. The Lord's steadfast love (חסדו), which stands eternal (Ps. 103:17), is in stark contrast to humans, whose "goodness" (חסדו) is as transient as "grass . . . and flowers of the field." For additional similes of this nature, see Ps 90:5-6: "At daybreak they are like grass that springs up and renews itself; by dusk it withers and dries up"; Job 14:2: "He blossoms like a flower and withers. He vanishes like a shadow and does not endure." Note the assonance of the sibilants in the second half of v. 6: כל הבשר חציר וכל חסדו כציץ השדה.

[7] *"Grass withers, flowers fade"* — For the verb נבל, "to wither, fade," see Isa 28:1: "Ah, the proud crowns of the drunkards of Ephraim whose glorious

beauty is but wilted flowers (צִיץ נֹבֵל)"; 28:4: "The wilted flowers (ציצת נֹבֵל) on the heads of men bloated with rich food"; 34:4: "All their host shall wither (יִבּוֹל) like a leaf withering (כִּנְבֹל) on the vine or like shriveled fruit (וּכְנֹבֶלֶת) on a fig tree." For a similar image see Ps 37:2: "For they soon wither like grass, like verdure fade away."

"When the breath of the Lord blows on them" — When God's wind blows, everything withers and fades. רוח ה׳ refers here to the searing east winds. Compare likewise Ps 103:15-16, cited above; Hos 13:15: "For though he flourish among reeds, a blast, a wind of the Lord, shall come blowing up from the wilderness. His fountain shall be parched, his spring dried up"; Ezek 19:12: "The east wind withered her branches. They broke apart and dried up"; cf. Ezek 17:10. For God's breath as a blowing wind, see Ps 147:18: "He blows with His wind (יַשֵּׁב רוחו), and the waters flow."

"Indeed" — The word אכן always introduces that which is unexpected. See Rashbam's commentary on Gen 28:6: "This place seemed ordinary and profane, but it is apparent that it is a holy place. This is the meaning of every אכן in the Bible — אך כן — indeed it is thus, and not as I expected"; cf. Exod 2:14: "Moses was frightened, and thought: 'Then (אכן) the matter is known!'," contra his expectations that the murder he committed was not known; see Isa 49:4; 53:4; Jer 3:20; Zeph 3:7.

"People are but grass" — The fate of humankind is identical to the fate of all blades of grass — ultimately everything withers and fades away. "Life is a terminal disease." For עם denoting people in general, humankind, see 42:5: "Who gave breath to the people (עם) on it."

[8] *"Grass withers, flowers fade"* — Repetition for the sake of emphasis.

"But the word of our God endures forever" — But (contrastive *waw*) "the word of our God" is fulfilled now and forever. For the unique power of the "Lord's word" see 45:23: "By myself I have sworn, from My mouth has issued truth, a word that shall not turn back"; 55:11: "So is the word that issues from My mouth. It does not come back to Me unfulfilled, but performs what I purpose, achieves what I sent it to do." For the "Lord's word" as consistent and unalterable, see Jer 4:28: "For this the earth mourns, and skies are dark above — because I have spoken, I have planned, and I will not relent or turn back from it"; Ezek 12:25: "But whenever I the Lord speak, what I speak, that word shall be fulfilled without any delay"; see also Isa 45:11. The motif of a deity's word as unalterable and everlasting is also found in other ancient Near Eastern texts. For the root קום as denoting the fulfillment of a word or vow, see Num 30:5: "All her vows shall be valid (יקום)"; Deut 19:15: "A case can be established (יקום) only on the testimony of two witnesses or more"; Isa 8:10: "Make plans, but they shall not succeed (יקום)."

[9-11] The message of redemption. This prophecy is thematically connected to the second unit of the chapter, specifically to v. 3, which alludes to the forthcoming liberation from exile. Other links to the previous units are the words קול (vv. 3, 6, 9) and the homonymous roots בשׂר (vv. 5, 6, 9). Again a heavenly herald (a female one this time) is called upon. Her mission is to ascend "a lofty mountain" and address the city of Jerusalem, informing the nation that the Lord is coming to redeem them from Babylonia and return them to Israel. Jeremiah's prophecy of consolation (31:15-16) left its thematic and linguistic mark on this passage: "Thus said the Lord: 'A cry is heard in Ramah — wailing, bitter weeping — Rachel weeping for her children.' . . ." Thus said the Lord: 'Restrain your voice from weeping . . . for there is reward for your labor (שָׂכָר לִפְעֻלָּתֵךְ). They shall return from the enemy's land.'" Deutero-Isaiah adopted Jeremiah's expression, שָׂכָר לִפְעֻלָּתֵךְ, split it into two, and created a parallel couplet: "His reward (שְׂכָרוֹ) is with Him; His recompense (פְּעֻלָּתוֹ) before him." (For a similar division of a Jeremian expression, see 65:6-7.) Jeremiah's imagery also reverberates in other verses of this unit: "Like a shepherd He pastures His flock (כְּרֹעֶה עֶדְרוֹ). He gathers (יְקַבֵּץ) the lambs in His arms" (v. 11) — Jer 31:10: "He who scattered Israel will gather them (יְקַבְּצֶנּוּ) and will guard them as a shepherd his flock (כְּרֹעֶה עֶדְרוֹ)." A further allusion to Jeremiah's prophecy may possibly explain the rare reference to a female herald, which may have been influenced by his image of mother Rachel, quoted above in Jer 31:15-16 (See Paul, *Divrei Shalom,* 401-2.) The threefold repetition of הנה in v. 9 (once) and v. 10 (twice) emphasizes that God's redemption is nigh.

[9] *Ascend a lofty mountain, O herald of joy to Zion!* — The prophetic herald is bidden to ascend a mountaintop so that her voice may be heard all the way to Zion; see also 41:27: "The things once predicted to Zion — behold, here they are! And again I send a herald to Jerusalem"; 52:7: "How welcome on the mountain are the footsteps of the herald!" — and there too the herald (מבשׂר) addresses Zion: ". . . telling Zion, 'Your God is king.'" This reflects the common practice of sending messengers from the battlefield to report the results of combat; cf., e.g., 1 Sam 4:16-17: "The man said to Eli, 'I am the one who has just arrived from the battlefield.' . . . The bearer of news (המבשׂר) replied . . ."; 2 Sam 18:19: "Ahimaaz the son of Zadok said, 'Let me run and report (ואבשׂרה) to the king that the Lord has vindicated him against his enemies.'" For female heralds see also Ps 68:12: "The Lord gives a command. The women who bring the news (המבשׂרות) are a great host." (For "heralds," *mubassiru,* in Mesopotamian literature, see *CAD* M/2:158-59.) For the imperative expression עלי לך (in the masculine), see Josh 17:15, and compare similarly constructed expressions, such as לך לך (Gen 12:1) and דְּמֵה לך (Cant 2:17). One should also note the repetition of the letters הר three times in this verse: הָר . . . הָרימי . . . הָרימי. For other proclamations delivered on the top of mountains, see Deut 27:12-13; Judg 9:7; 1 Sam 26:13-14.

Raise your voice with power, O herald of joy to Jerusalem! — The herald must shout aloud in order to be heard from Babylonia all the way to Jerusalem. For the same image see Dan 3:4: "The herald proclaimed loudly (בְּחָיִל)." Heralds in Mesopotamia were also commanded likewise: "Let the heralds make a proclamation with a loud voice in the country" (*CAD* N/1:117). The verbal expression הרים קול ("raise one's voice") is also found in Ugaritic, *ql trm* (*CAT* 1.16.II:33-34).

Zion . . . Jerusalem — For this parallel pair, see Isa 41:27; 52:1 (for the reverse order, see 52:2).

Raise it! Have no fear! — The command is reiterated to emphasize its urgency. The herald must raise her voice fearlessly and without hesitation; cf. 58:1: "Shout with a full throat, without restraint."

Announce to the cities of Judah — Announce not only to Jerusalem but to all the ruined and desolate cities of Judah from which the Israelites had been exiled (see 54:3; 61:4; 64:9). (The prophet speaks of Judean cities as opposed to Israelite cities, since the latter were destroyed by the Assyrians already in 720 BCE.) For the pair "Jerusalem/cities of Judah," see Jer 1:15; 4:16.

"Behold your God!" — God is about to appear and return His people to their homes in Judah. For this expression, see also Isa 35:4.

[10] *Behold, the Lord God is coming in might* — A reiteration of the previous clause for emphasis, now citing the particular name of the God of Israel. Hebrew בחזק, if vocalized בְּחֹזֶק (as in LXX, Vulgate, Targum, and 1QIsa[a], בחוזק), means "in might, with power." According to the Masoretic vocalization בְּחָזָק, the *beth* functions as a *beth essentiae,* hence "as a mighty one" (cf. Exod 6:1; Deut 26:8). Either way, בחזק along with וזרעו in the following clause echoes a recurrent motif taken from the tradition of the exodus from Egypt, when God redeemed the Israelites with a "mighty arm" (בזרוע חזקה) (Jer 21:5). This is an example of the breakup of a stereotype expression.

And His arm is ruling for Him — Compare Isa 59:16; 63:5. The "strong arm" image also appears in Akkadian tablets from Tell el-Amarna (287:27): "The [str]ong arm [of the king] (*qāt/zuruḫ dannu*) gave it [the city of Jerusalem] to me" (cf. W. L. Moran, *The Amarna Letters* [Baltimore, 1987], 328). See also 286:12 (p. 326); 288:14, 34 (p. 331).

See, His reward is with Him, His recompense before Him — God is accompanied by "His reward" and "His recompense" (see also 62:11), i.e., His redeemed nation, the Israelites. The word פְּעֻלָּה in Biblical Hebrew may refer to the fruits of one's labor; cf. Lev 19:13: "You shall not keep back the wages (פְּעֻלָּה) of a laborer until the next morning." For other examples of this pair of nouns see Ezek 29:19-20: "He [Nebuchadnezzar] shall carry off her [Egypt's] wealth and take her spoil and seize her booty; and she shall be the reward (שָׂכָר) of his army. As the wage (פְּעֻלָּתוֹ) for which he labored, for what they did for Me, I give him the land of Egypt"; see also Prov 11:18; 2 Chr 15:7. For the breakup of this stereotype expression taken from Jeremiah, see the introduction, §15. For reward or recompense in the context of shepherding (the following verse), see Gen 30:28, 32, 33; 31:8.

[11] God is described as a shepherd who steadfastly and diligently guards His flock and cares for each and every individual ewe and lamb; cf. Ps 80:2: "Give ear, O shepherd of Israel, who leads Joseph like a flock!" God's "arm," which was manifest in all its "strength" (v. 10), will now tend to His flock with heightened protection and tenderness at the time of the redemption. For Israel as God's flock, see also Jer 13:17: "My eyes must stream and flow with copious tears because the flock of the Lord is taken captive."

Like a shepherd He pastures His flock — As in the bygone days of Egypt, God will lead His returning flock through the desert to Israel; cf. Isa 49:9-10; Ezek 34:12: "As a shepherd seeks out his flock when his flock is dispersed, so I will seek out My flock"; Ps 78:52: "He set His people moving like sheep and drove them like a flock in the wilderness." "Flock" (עֵדֶר) is a general term comprising "lambs" (טְלָאִים) and "ewes" (עָלוֹת) (see below). The term "shepherd" (רועה) is one of the oldest attributes of deities, documented already in the earliest Sumerian *(sipa)* and Akkadian *(rēʾû)* records (*CAD* R:309-10).

He gathers the lambs in His arms — For טָלֶה (written only here with an *aleph*), see Isa 65:25: "The wolf and the lamb (טלה) shall graze together"; 1 Sam 7:9: "Thereupon Samuel took a suckling lamb (טלה) and sacrificed it as a whole burnt offering to the Lord." For images of the gathering of the scattered populace at the time of the redemption, frequently with the verb קבץ, see Isa 43:5; 49:18; 54:7; 56:8; 60:4; Jer 31:10: "He who scattered Israel shall gather them (יְקַבְּצֶנּוּ) and watch over them as a shepherd watches his sheep"; Ezek 34:13: "I will take them out from the peoples and gather them (וקִבַּצְתִּים) from the countries." The same image of gathering a scattered populace by a "shepherd" is also found in the Mesopotamian royal inscriptions; cf., e.g., "The shepherd who gathers the dispersed (people)" (*CAD* R:311).

And carries them in His bosom — an image of loving and tender individualized care; cf. Num 11:12: "Did I conceive these people? Did I bear them, that you should say to me, 'Carry them in your bosom (בחיקך) as a nurse carries an infant'?"; 2 Sam 12:3: "But the poor man had only one little ewe-lamb that he had bought. . . . It used to share his morsel of bread, drink from his cup, and nestle in his bosom (בחיקו)." The Akkadian semantic and etymological equivalent of Heb. נשׂא, *našû,* also refers to the care and nurture of animals (*CAD* N/2:95-96). In an Assyrian prophecy the goddess Ishtar offers words of encouragement to King Esarhaddon in similar terms: "Do not fear Esarhaddon! I will place you between my arm and my forearm" (S. A. Parpola, *Assyrian Prophecies* = SAA IX [Helsinki, 1997], 18, lines 30ff.). For the bosom as a place of shelter and protection, compare the epilogue to Hammurabi's laws (XLVII:49-52): "I held the people of the lands of Sumer and Akkad safely on my lap" (M. T. Roth, *Law Collections from Mesopotamia and Asia Minor,* SBLWAW 6 [Atlanta, 1995], 133).

Gently He leads the ewes — Hebrew עָלוֹת from the root עול, "to give suck," appears four other times in the Bible (Gen 33:13; 1 Sam 6:7, 10; Ps 78:71) and refers to lactating animals; cf. also the words for a "suckling child": עול (Isa 49:15; 65:20), עוֹלֵל (1 Sam 15:3; Jer 44:7), עוֹלָל (Joel 2:16), and עֲוִיל (Job 19:18) (so too their cognates in Ugaritic, Phoenician, Syriac, and Arabic). The verb נהל, "to lead," is especially connected to the guiding to watering places; see Isa 49:10: "He will guide them (יְנַהֲלֵם) to springs of water"; Ps 23:2: "He leads me (יְנַהֲלֵנִי) to water in places of repose." In Isa 7:19 the substantive נַהֲלֹלִים refers to "waterholes." Compare also Arab. *nahila,* "to take a drink of water," and Akk. *na'ālu,* "to water, to make wet" (*CAD* N/1:6).

[12-17] This unit is characterized by a series of rhetorical questions that contrast with the imperative forms of the previous verses. The prophet begins with a triad of מי ("who") questions (vv. 12, 13, 14; see below vv. 18, 25, 26), the purpose of which is to emphasize the Israelite God's total control over creation and the shaping of history. The rhetorical questions here serve as a prelude to a scathing polemic against nonmonotheistic beliefs and concepts. As will be seen below, the prophet argues against the idea that God sought the advice of the heavenly council before creating man (Gen 1:26) (see Weinfeld, "God the Creator," 120-26). In contrast to the previous units, which concluded with the motif of redemption, this unit begins with the act of creation, representing the two poles of God's handiwork: the beginning — creation, and the end — redemption.

[12] This verse features four verbs drawn from the terminology of measurement: מדד, תכן, כל, and שקל, all of which refer to God's handiwork in creation — the water, the sky, the earth, the mountains, and hills. For another example of God's creation preceded by rhetorical מי questions, describing cosmology in terms of "engineering," see Job 38:5-6: "Do you know who (מי) fixed its dimensions? . . . Or who (מי) measured it with a line? . . . Who (מי) set its cornerstone in place?" The same motif is found in the Mesopotamian creation epic, *Enuma Elish* (IV:143): "The lord [Marduk] measured the construction of Apsu" (Foster, *COS* 1:398). For other descriptions of creation preceded by rhetorical מי questions, see Prov 30:4: "Who has ascended to heaven and come down? Who has gathered up the wind in the hollow of His hand? Who has wrapped the waters in His garment? Who has established all the extremities of the earth?"; Sir 1:3: "Who knows the height of the sky, the width of the earth, or the depth of the abyss?" All these queries have of course only one answer — God. The first three hemistichs as well as the last two form chiasms.

Who measured the waters with the hollow of His hand — For שֹׁעַל see Ezek 13:19: "You have profaned My name among My people in return for handfuls (בְּשַׁעֲלֵי) of barley and morsels of bread"; cf. also 1 Kgs 20:10. The reading of 1QIsa[a], מי ים, "the waters of the sea" (instead of MT מים, "waters"), since it is similar to the construct in the following clause, "the earth's dust," has led many commentators to explain the MT as a result of haplography, i.e., one of the letters, *yod,* having been erroneously deleted. In further support of the Qumran version is 4Q511 (4QShir[b]), frag. 30:4, which quotes this verse with the variant reading, מי רבה (M. Baillet, *Qumrân Grotte 4.III (4Q482-4Q520),* DJD 7 [Oxford, 1982], 236). The reading of the MT, however, which also refers to the collective bodies of water, is preferable since: (1) this verse is part of a polemic against the first chapter of Genesis (Gen 1:1-2), which features מים, שמים, and ארץ (all mentioned here), but not מי ים; (2) the present reading, מים, creates a rhyme pair with שמים; cf. above, v. 4; (3) the MT is supported by Aquila, LXX, and Peshitta; (4) the Qumranic version is secondary and is the result of a dittography, the *yod* having been written twice instead of once.

One must also consider the possibility of a covert polemic here against the Babylonian belief that it was Marduk "who measures the water of the sea" *(mādidi mê tâmti)* (the text continues to relate that it was he "who crosses the sky, who heaps up the earth" [*CAD* T:151]), i.e., the same cosmologic triad (water, sky, and earth), which the Babylonians attributed to Marduk, is here attributed to the God of Israel.

And who gauged the skies with a span — Hebrew זֶרֶת is a unit of measurement whose "span" is from the tip of the little finger to the tip of the thumb of a fully splayed hand. According to *t. Kelim, B. Metzia* 6:12, it is half a cubit. The term in 1QIsa[a], בזרתו, harmonizes with the parallel בשעלו of the previous hemistich. The verb תִּכֵּן (in the *pi'el*) is also found in Job 28:25: "When He fixed the weight of the winds, set the measure (תִּכֵּן) of the waters"; cf. also (in the *qal*) Prov 16:2; 21:2; 24:12: תֹּכֵן רוחות/לִבּוֹת ה׳, "God measures the spirits/hearts." And for the *niph'al,* see 1 Sam 2:3: "For the Lord is an all-knowing God. By Him actions are measured (נִתְכְּנוּ)." Substantives derived from the same root are תֹּכֶן (Exod 5:18), מַתְכֹּנֶת (Exod 5:8), תכנית (Ezek 43:10), תכונה (Ezek 43:11), "measurement"; and in Qumran, in a variant form, תכון, 4Q298, frag. 3-4 i 6 (S. J. Pfann and M. Kister, "Words of the Maskil to All Sons of Dawn," in T. Elgvin et al., *Qumran Cave 4.XV: Sapiential Texts, Part 1,* DJD 20 [Oxford, 1997], 24) and 4Q418, frag. 127 6 (J. Strugnell et al., *Qumran Cave 4.XXIV: Sapiential Texts, Part 2, 4QInstruction: 4Q415ff.,* DJD 34 [Oxford, 1999], 357).

And meted the earth's dust with a measure — The expression "the earth's dust" (עפר הארץ) indicates a number beyond all measure; see Gen 13:16: "I will make your offspring as the dust of the earth, so that if one can count the dust of the earth, then your offspring can be counted." The verb כָּל (third-person masculine singular *qal,* from the root כול), "to measure," is a hapax legomenon in Biblical Hebrew. The noun appears in the Hebrew Gezer Calendar (tenth century BCE): "His month is harvest and measuring (וכל)" (*KAI* 182:5). (Some also interpret the verbal forms ויכל, כל, and כלת, which appear in the Hebrew ostracon from Meṣad Ḥashavyahu [= Yavneh-Yam] from the last quarter of the seventh century BCE, as derivatives of the same verb; but others claim that the verbs derive from the root כלי, "to finish" [*KAI* 200:5, 6, 8].) The verb is found in Aramaic; see, e.g., Exod 16:18: וַיָּמֹדּוּ, which Targum Onqelos translates as וּכְלוֹ, and Pseudo-Jonathan as וְאָכִילוּ; Onqelos to Lev 19:35 translates Heb. וּבַמְּשׂוּרָה by וּבְמְכִילְתָא (this is also the origin of the title of the earliest Midrash Halakah to Exodus, מְכִילְתָא, "the measures" [by which the Torah is elucidated]). The phrase וכל בשליש עפר הארץ is found in an abbreviated form in 4Q511, frag. 30:5 (quoted above): כול עפר הארץ (Baillet, DJD 7, 236).

Hebrew שליש, "third," is a receptacle that measures volume. Some say it refers to a third of an ephah (a grain measure); others understand it to be a third of a seah (which equals one third of an ephah). The term is also found in Ps 80:6: "You have . . . made them drink tears of threefold (שליש)." (ה)ארץ reappears in the following verses (21, 22, 23, 24, 28) as a key word.

And weighed the mountains with a scale — The word פֶּלֶס appears only once more in the Bible, again parallel to מֹאזְנַיִם (see the following clause), in Prov 16:11: "Honest scales and balances (פלס ומאזני משפט) are the Lord's." Some commentators suggest that this term denotes a vertical rather than a horizontal scale. (For pictures of various types of scales, see E. L. Sukenik et al., eds., *Encyclopaedia Biblica* 4 [Jerusalem, 1962], 539-42 [Heb.].) For God as a creator of mountains, see Amos 4:13; Ps 65:7; Prov 8:25.

And the hills with a balance? — "Mountains" and "hills" are a very common parallel pair; see above, v. 4.

[13-14] Further rhetorical questions. Just as no one is able to imitate God's creations, so too no one can ponder and hope to divine God's spirit or serve as His advisor. The inner-biblical polemic is thus expanded, and the prophet now speaks out against the view that God sought the advice of the heavenly council, as stated in Gen 1:26: "And God said: 'Let us make man in our image, after our likeness'"; 11:7: "Let us, then, go down and confound their speech, so that they shall not understand one another's speech"; cf. 3:22. There may also be here a covert polemic against *Enuma Elish* (the Mesopotamian creation epic), wherein the chief god, Marduk, seeks the advice of Ea just as he is about to create the first man (VI:1-16; Foster, *COS* 1:400). For the Mesopotamian concept that there are deities, male *(māliku)* and female *(māliktu),* who serve as advisors, see *CAD* M/1:164. Verses 13-14 are characterized by "wisdom" vocabulary: יעץ, בין, ידע; see below. For a series of similar expressions cf. Isa 11:2: "The spirit of the Lord shall alight upon him: A spirit of wisdom and insight (ובינה), a spirit of counsel (עצה) and valor, a spirit of knowledge (דעת) and reverence for the Lord."

[13] *Who has measured the mind of the Lord?* — Who has plumbed the depth of God's thoughts? Indeed, only the Lord Himself has the measure of all hearts/spirits (Prov 16:2). The expression רוח ה׳ is yet another allusion to the creation narrative; see Gen 1:2, where the similar expression רוח אלוהים appears. For theological reasons the Masoretes divided the rhetorical question into a question and an answer: Q. "Who has measured (one's) mind?" A. "The Lord."

What man could tell Him His plan?/Who is His counselor, who instructs Him? — The prophet denies the existence of a heavenly council from whom God seeks advice. The rhetorical מי found at the beginning of the verse applies here as well. For עֵצָה, "plan," see 46:10: "I say: 'My plan (עצתי) shall be fulfilled.'" There are two alternate traditions concerning the accentuation of איש עצתו. According to one there is a pausal accentuation between the two words and thus the first translation above. According to the other this is a construct phrase and thus the second translation (cf. 46:11; Ps 119:24). The feminine suffix in 1QIsa[a], יודיענה, refers back to the feminine noun עצה, contra the masculine suffix in the MT (יודיעֶנּוּ). The verb ידע recurs a number of times in the latter half of the chapter: vv. 14 (twice), 21.

[14] This verse contains a fourfold assonance created by the verbal suffix -*û*.

Whom did He consult and who gave Him understanding — For the *niph'al* of the verb יעץ ("to counsel"), see 1 Kgs 12:6: "King Rehoboam took counsel (וַיִּוָּעַץ) with the elders who had served his father Solomon during his lifetime. He asked: 'What answer do you advise [me] (נועצים) to give to this people?'"; and cf. there v. 8. For the verb בין in the *hiph'il,* "to cause another to understand, to teach," see Isa 28:9: "To whom would he give instruction? To whom expound (יבין) a message?"; 1 Chr 25:8: "They cast lots for shifts on the principle of small and great alike, like teacher (מבין), like apprentice."

Taught Him in the path of justice? — For this expression, see Prov 2:8: "Guarding the paths of justice (ארחות משפט), protecting the way of those loyal to Him"; and cf. Prov 8:20: "I walk on the path of justice (בארח צדקה)." For the phrase ללמד ארח/דרך, see Ps 25:4: "Teach me your way (ארחתיך לַמְּדֵנִי)"; Ps 25:9: "He teaches the lowly His way (וִילַמֵּד . . . דרכו)." (For synonymous Akkadian phrases, *ḫarrān/uruḫ kitti,* "path/way of justice," see *CAD* Ḫ:109. For the Akkadian equivalent of "teaching the true path," see Hammurabi's law collection, V:17-18; Roth, *Law Collections,* 80.)

And showed Him the path of understanding? — No one, since God's wisdom is unfathomable (v. 28, below). For תבונות (an abstract plural noun) see Prov 11:12: "A man of understanding (תבונות) holds his peace." For the parallel pairs הודיע/למד and אֹרַח/דרך, see Ps 25:4: "Let me know (הודיעני) Your paths (דרכיך), O Lord! Teach me (למדני) Your ways (אֹרחותיך)!" For additional occurrences of להודיע דרך, see Exod 33:13; Ps 103:7; 143:8.

[15] God is the only one in control of creation as well as of history; see also Isa 45:12-13. In God's eyes the nations of the world are no more than miniscule grains of sand on a balance.

Indeed, the nations weigh but a speck on the scales — Both the terms מַר and דְּלִי are hapax legomena whose meanings can be determined contextually by comparing the three parallel hemistichs of this verse: כְּמַר is parallel to כְּשַׁחַק ("dust") and to כַּדַּק ("fine dust"). Thus מַר must also refer to something miniscule and insignificant, and is to be compared to its Arabic cognate, *mûr,* "dust blown in the wind." The prevalent understanding of this word, "drop," i.e., "a drop in the bucket" (cf. the ancient translations), is based on the erroneous translation of דלי as "a bucket." All other nominal occurrences of דלי derivatives make clear, however, that its meaning is "bough" or "branch"; see Num 24:7: "Their boughs (דָּלְיָו) drip with moisture; their roots have abundant water"; Jer 11:16: "He has set it on fire and its boughs (דָּלִיּוֹתָיו) are broken" (see also Ezek 17:6). On the basis of the subsequent imagery, which refers to scales and weighing — "reckoned as dust on a balance, the very coastlands weighed like fine dust" — it is most likely that this substantive also refers to weight or measurement, as does its Arabic and Ethiopic cognate *dalawa.* The proper vocalization, then, should be מַדְלֵי, not מִדְּלִי (cf. Deut 7:15: מַדְוֵי מצרים, which is a derivative of דוי), and it is a synonym of מֹאזנים. For הן as a prelude to a conclusion based on the previous statement, see Isa 41:24, 29. (See D. Winton Thomas, "'A Drop of a Bucket'? Some Observations on the Hebrew Text of Isaiah 40:15," in M. Black and G. Fohrer, eds., *Memoriam Paul Kahle,* BZAW 103 [Berlin, 1968], 214-21.)

Reckoned as dust on a balance — שחק ("dust") is also a hapax legomenon, derived from the verbal form meaning "to beat fine, pulverize"; see Exod 30:36: "Beat (ושחקת) some of it into powder." See also Sir 42:1-4: "Be not ashamed . . . of the small dust of the scales (שחקי מֹזנים)," i.e., do not hesitate to demand dust-free scales while making a purchase, so as not to pay for the extra poundage (Y. Yadin, *The Ben Sira Scroll from Masada* [Jerusalem, 1965], 43; cf. 22-23). For additional references to the verbal expression נחשב כ-, see Isa 5:28; 29:16.

The very coastlands weigh no more than fine dust — The repetition of הן is for emphasis. The noun דַּק, yet another hapax legomenon, refers to "fine dust"; cf. 29:5: "And like fine dust (אבק דק) shall be the multitude of your strangers." The verb נטל here serves as a synonym of שׁקל ("to weigh"); cf. Zeph 1:11: "All who weigh silver (נטילי כסף) are wiped out"; Prov 27:3: "A stone is heavy, sand a weight (נֵטֶל), but a fool's vexation outweighs them both," and should be vocalized יִטּוֹלוּ (intransitive, *niph'al,* third-person masculine plural), with

Aquila, Theodotion, Symmachus, LXX, and Peshitta. The final letter *waw* was omitted by haplography from the beginning of the next word. The prophecy continues in v. 17 (see below). In Deutero-Isaiah the word **אִיִּים** is parallel to a number of different words/expressions: **קְצוֹת הארץ** ("the ends of the earth," 41:5), **לְאֻמִּים** ("peoples," 41:1), **עמים** ("nations," 51:5), and **גוים** ("nations," here and 62:2; 66:19).

[16] This verse, which interrupts the continuity of vv. 15 and 17, is secondary and may have been interpolated here since it expands on the motif of everything being insignificant in the eyes of God — including plant and animal life.

Lebanon is not fuel enough — All the densely wooded forests of Lebanon cannot yield enough fuel for sacrifices in honor of the Deity. For "Lebanon" referring to the trees of Lebanon, see Isa 10:34: "The thickets of the forest shall be hacked away with an axe, and the Lebanon [i.e., the trees of Lebanon] shall fall in their majesty." For the substantive **בָּעֵר**, "fuel" (in this case, firewood), see 44:15: "All this serves man for fuel (**לְבָעֵר**)." For **דֵּי** (a construct form), "enough for, sufficient for," see Lev 5:7; 12:8.

Nor its beasts enough for sacrifice — Even if all the animals were sacrificed to God, it still would not be sufficient. **חַיָּתוֹ** ("beasts") is a poetic form that preserves the original nominal case ending; cf. Isa 56:9: "All the beasts (**חיתו**) of the forest." For the idea that nature is utterly inconsequential vis-à-vis God, cf. Ps 50:10-12: "For mine is every animal of the forest, the beasts on a thousand mountains. . . . Were I hungry I would not tell you, for Mine is the world and all it holds." The negative **אין** is found twice in this verse and continues as a key word in vv. 17, 23, 28, 29.

[17] The direct continuation of v. 15. The utter insignificance of all nations is described in a pair of parallel clauses highlighted by a series of terms indicating nullity.

All nations are as nothing in His sight — For the term **נֶגְדּוֹ**, "in front of, in the sight of," see 1:7: "Before your eyes (**לנגדכם**) the yield of your soil is consumed by strangers." For the parallel pair **אין/אפס**, see 41:12; 45:6, 14.

They are accounted as nil and naught — The Masoretic reading **מֵאֶפֶס** should be emended here to **כאפס**, "as nil"; cf. LXX, Vulgate, and 1QIsa[a]. For **תֹּהוּ**, "naught, nothingness," see 49:4: "I have spent my strength for nothing (**לתהו**), to no purpose"; 1 Sam 12:21: "False gods that can neither profit nor save, but are nothingness (**תֹּהוּ**)." The same sentiment appears in Isa 41:29: "See, they are all nothingness. Their works are nullity (**אפס**)." For **אין** and **תהו** as a parallel pair, see v. 23 below. These descriptions elaborate on the previous similes in v. 15: "as grains of dust," "as fine dust," "as specks." Both here and in v. 15, all things "are considered" (**נחשבו**) as naught in the eyes of God. For the verbal expression **נחשב ל-** ("considered as"), see Gen 31:15: "Surely, he regards us (**נחשבנו לו**) as outsiders."

[18-25] The prophet now proceeds to mock and deride idol craftsmanship in a scathing satire. This polemic, which is also found in Isa 41:6-7; 44:9-20; and 46:5-7, opens with a rhetorical מי question (see above, vv. 12, 13, 14, and below, v. 26; 41:2, 4; 46:5). On the one hand, the prophet sharply derides the craftsmen for creating deaf-and-dumb images that are of no use to anyone. This is contrasted, on the other hand, by God's uniqueness, His great deeds throughout history, and His magnificent creations. Here, moreover, the prophet also continues his polemic against Gen 1:26 and the idea of a heavenly council. The unit has a literary frame opening and concluding with the motif of God's incomparability (vv. 18, 25) (see Weinfeld, "God the Creator," 105-25).

[18] *To whom, then, can you liken God?* — The *waw* appended to the first word (וְאֶל) indicates that this is the logical conclusion of that stated above. For the verbal expression דמי אל, see below, v. 25.

What form can you compare to Him? — The term דמות ("form") denotes an entity with a discernible shape; see 2 Kgs 16:10: "King Ahaz sent . . . a sketch (דמות) of the altar and a detailed plan of its construction"; 2 Chr 4:3: "Beneath were figures (דמות) of oxen set all around it." It also appears in the bilingual Aramaic-Akkadian inscription from the third quarter of the ninth century BCE found at Tell Fekherye in southeastern Syria near the source of the Habor River. In lines 1 and 15 of the inscription, the Aramaic דמותא and its Akkadian equivalent *ṣalmu* refer to the "statue" of the king who erected the commemorative pillar. (See J. C. Greenfield and A. Shaffer, "Notes on the Akkadian-Aramaic Bilingual Statue from Tell Fekherye," *Iraq* 45 [1983]: 109-16.) For the verbal expression ערך ל- ("to compare to"), see Ps 89:7: "For who in the sky is comparable to the Lord (יערך לה'), can compare (ידמה) with the Lord among divine beings?" (note the parallel between ערך and דמי, as here). The reading in 1QIsa[a], לי ("to Me"), instead of MT לו ("to Him"), was probably influenced by v. 25: "To whom then can you liken Me?"; and by 46:5: "To whom can you compare Me?"

[19-20] The following two verses consist of a stinging mockery against the crafting of images and their adornment. The prophet reverses the natural order of the manufacturing craft and begins with the finishing touches — the coating of the idol by an expert "goldsmith" (v. 19). He then proceeds to describe the beginning of the process — the careful choosing of the wood and its shaping by a "woodworker" (v. 20). Contra most commentators, shifting and rearranging the verses is not justified, since this reverse order of work appears again in 44:12-14 and is characteristic of Deutero-Isaiah's biting satires against idolaters and their objects of worship. It is interesting to note that in Mesopotamian cultic tablets describing the ritual of *mīs pî* (lit. "the washing of the mouth"), whereby the god is said to enter the idol (thus becoming the deity's earthly manifestation), one also finds a reverse process beginning with the last adornments and only subsequently the description of the initial stages of the workmanship. According to the Mesopotamian belief the creation of idols — shaped by woodworkers and adorned by smithies — is an act attributed in particular to Ea, the god of the subterranean freshwaters, wisdom, and magic. Though the idol is the deity's representation, the deity himself/herself remains, nevertheless, above and beyond his/her earthly manifestation. Thus the destruction of the idol does not entail the demise of the god, whose "existence" is independent of his/her earthly image. Their fates are unconnected. (See T. Jacobsen, "The Graven Image," in P. D. Miller Jr. et al., eds., *Ancient Israelite Religion: Essays in Honor of Frank Moore Cross* [Philadelphia, 1987], 15-32; A. Horowitz, "How to Make an Idol," *Beth Miqra* 143 [1995]: 337-47 [Heb.].) It is very likely, therefore, that the prophet who lived in Babylonia was aware of this process (even if he did not understand its full significance), and that it underlies the source of his mocking description. (For further studies on idols and their construction see G. Roeder, *Aegyptische Bronzenfiguren* [Berlin, 1956]; O. Negbi, *Canaanite Gods in Metal: An Archeological Study of Ancient Syro-Palestinian Figures* [Tel Aviv, 1976]; A. Spycket, *Les statues de culte dans les textes mésopotamiens des origines à la 1re dynastie de Babylone* [Paris, 1968]; idem, *La statuaire de Proche-Orient ancien* [Leiden, 1981]; W. W. Hallo, "Cult, Statue and Divine Image: A Preliminary Study," in W. W. Hallo et al., eds., *Scripture in Context, 2: More Essays on the Comparative Method* [Winona Lake, Ind., 1983], 1-18; K. Holter, *Second Isaiah's Idol-Fabrication Passages* [Frankfurt am Main, 1995]; A. Berlejung, *Die Theologie der Bilder: Herstellung und Einweihung von Kultbildern in Mesopotamien und die alttestamentliche Bilderpolemik* [Göttingen, 1998]; C. Walker and M. B. Dick, "The Induction of the Cult Image in Ancient Mesopotamia: The Mesopotamian *mīs pî* Ritual," in M. B. Dick, ed., *Born in Heaven, Made on Earth: The Making of the Cult Image in the Ancient Near East* [Winona Lake, Ind., 1999], 55-121; M. B. Dick, "Prophetic Parodies of Making the Cult Image," in *Born in Heaven*, 1-53.)

There is a great similarity between Jer 10 and these verses: "The idol (הפסל), a woodworker (חרש) shaped it (נסך), and a goldsmith (צֹרֵף) overlaid it with gold" (v. 19) — "Every goldsmith (צֹרֵף) is put to shame because of the idol (מִפָּסֶל), for his molten image (נִסְכּוֹ) is a deceit" (Jer 10:14); "overlaid" (יְרַקְּעֶנּוּ) (v. 19) — "silver beaten flat (מְרֻקָּע)" (Jer 10:9); "and a smith (וצֹרֵף) . . . with gold (בזהב) . . . silver (כסף)" (v. 19) — "with silver and gold" (בכסף ובזהב) (Jer 10:4); "and gold (וזהב) . . . the work of a craftsman (חָרָשׁ) and the goldsmith's (צורף) hands" (Jer 10:9); "to make a firm idol, that will not topple (לא יִמּוֹט)" (v. 20); (cf. Isa 41:7: "And he fixes it with nails, that it may not topple" — "He fastens it with nails (במסמרות . . . יְחזקום) and hammer, so that it does not totter (ולוא יפיק)" (Jer 10:4); "a skillful woodworker (חָרָשׁ חכם)" (v. 20) — "For it is the work of a craftsman's (חרש) hands" (Jer 10:3), "The work of a craftsman (חרש) . . . the work of skilled men (חכמים)" (Jer 10:9); and cf. also the craftsman's utensils: "nails" (מסמרים) (Isa 41:7) — "nails" (מסמרות) (Jer 10:4); "hammers" (מקבות) (Isa 44:12; Jer 10:4); and a "cutting tool" (מעצד) (Isa 44:12; Jer 10:3). (See the introduction, §15.)

[19] *The woodworker shapes the idol* — Some commentators and ancient translations interpret the *heh* of the first word as an interrogative (cf. LXX, Vulgate). For the anomalous vocalization of this interrogative הַ (the usual punctuation is הֲ), see הַלְּבֶן (Gen 17:17); הַיִּיטַב (Lev 10:19). If so, then the clause should be understood as a question and answer: "The idol? The woodworker shaped it." It is preferable, however, to interpret this *heh* as the definite article and הפסל as the direct object of the verb. For the woodworker's role in the crafting of idols, see Deut 27:15; Hos 8:6; 13:2; Jer 10:3. For the verb נסך, "to fashion, shape," in connection with the act of creation, see Prov 8:23: "In the distant past I was fashioned (נִסַּכְתִּי), at the beginning, at the origin of earth" (echoing the previous v. 22: "The Lord created me at the very beginning"). The sequence הפסל נסך brings to mind the parallel pair פסל/מַסֵּכָה ("idol/graven image"); see 42:17; 48:5. The vast majority of idols (10-30 cm. in height) were made of wood (and thus were combustible; cf. Exod 32:20, the golden calf), and some were plated with silver or gold; cf. Deut 7:25: "You shall consign the images of their gods to the fire. You shall not covet the silver and gold on them and keep it for yourselves." For the prophet's attack against the construction of idols and the absolute negation of their existence, without mention of the nations who worship these idols, see A. Wilson, *The Nations in Deutero-Isaiah* (Lewiston, N.Y., 1986), 181-92.

And a smith overlays it with gold — After the woodworker shapes the idol, the goldsmith plates it with thin sheets of gold. For רקע, "to beat out, plate," see Num 17:4: "And they were hammered into plating (וַיְרַקְּעוּם) for the altar"; and for a similar construction process see Jer 10:9: "Silver beaten flat (מְרֻקָּע) that is brought from Tarshish, and gold from Uphaz, the work of a craftsman and a goldsmith's hands." For the cooperative effort of goldsmiths and woodworkers in the construction of the image, see Isa 41:7; and for the goldsmith fashioning the idol, see 46:6. Mesopotamian inscriptions also describe smiths and metalworkers who overlay wooden idols with gold and silver (*CAD* K:609). For pictures of gold-plated statuettes, see *ANEP*, nos. 481, 483, 484, 497. For an "instruction manual" on how one "finishes" an idol whose face is already overlaid with precious metals but whose body and legs are not, see S. Parpola, *Letters from the Assyrian and Babylonian Scholars*, SAA XIII (Helsinki, 1993), text 476, p. 284. Perhaps by choosing the verb רקע the prophet is providing yet another veiled contrast: the smith overlaid (רקע) his idol with gold; God, however, stretched out (רקע) the heavens (42:5; 44:24). One should also note that this clause and the clause that follows are chiastically parallel.

Forging ornaments of silver — צורף here is not a substantive as in the previous clause but a verb. The same smith now forges רְתֻקוֹת of silver for his precious image. This term is usually understood to mean "chains" (see 1 Kgs 6:21; Ezek 7:23; and for the verb, "to bind, chain," see Nah 3:10: "And all her nobles were bound (רֻתְּקוּ) in chains"). This is then interpreted to mean that the idol is so unstable that the smith must forge chains to stabilize it in order to prevent its collapse. However, since this idea is mentioned below in v. 20: "To make a firm idol that will not topple," here I suggest that the term denotes chain-like adornments or jewelry; cf. the Targum: "The smith overlays it with silver links," and Vulgate: "silver plates"; see also Ibn Balaam: "rings" (M. Goshen-Gottstein, ed., *Ibn Balaam's Commentary on Isaiah* [Ramat Gan, 1992], 177 [Heb.]). This interpretation accords well with the very common ancient Near Eastern practice of adorning idols with silver and golden decorations. For a description of these adornments see, e.g., King Esarhaddon's inscription: "I adorned their [the gods' images] necks and covered their breasts with magnificent ornaments, precious jewelry, splendidly suited to their majesty" (*CAD* T:422). For pictures of idols decorated with all manner of adorments, see S. Schroer, *In Israel gab es Bilder: Nachrichten von darstellender Kunst im Alten Testament* (Göttingen 1987), photos 80, 81; *ANEP*, nos. 464, 482, 507, 508, 512, 516, 552.

[20] *The mulberry wood* — This hapax legomenon, a loanword from Akk. *musukkannu* (*CAD* M/2:237-39), is the name of a tree *(Dallergia sissoo)* that grows in northwest India, Afghanistan, and Nepal, whose wood was used for the decorations of buildings, furniture, and door leaves, and was employed, as well, for ceremonial and ritual purposes (see I. Ephal, "Isa 40:19-20: The Question of Isaiah's Cultural and Linguistic Background," *Shnaton* 10 [1989]: 31-35 [Heb.]). One should note that in Deutero-Isaiah, more than in any other book, names of trees abound; see 44:4, 14; 60:13.

As a gift — One can hardly interpret תרומה in its usual sense, i.e., the section of the harvest set apart for priests or Levites, since the wooden idol is not an offering, but rather a figurine designated for worship. Some commentators suggest that this term is an erroneous gloss inserted into the text for the purpose of clarifying the hapax legomenon מְסֻכָּן, and read תְּמוֹרָה ("date palm"), the middle letters being inverted by metathesis. Others prefer the LXX, which translates: "he who sets up (המכונן) a likeness (תמונה)"; cf. Exod 20:4: "You shall not make for yourself a sculpted image or any likeness (תמונה)." Others suggest that the term refers to a pedestal for the idol, and such a pedestal crafted from the *musukkannu* tree is mentioned in an Assyrian inscription of King Esarhaddon (see A. Fitzgerald, "The Technology of Isaiah 40:19-20," *CBQ* 51 [1989]: 426-46). Other exegetes understand this word as the Hebrew equivalent of Akk. *tarīmtu*, "present" (*CAD* T:231). Nevertheless, despite all attempts to explain this word, its meaning remains unclear.

A wood that will not rot he chooses — The *musukkannu* wood is frequently cited in Akkadian sources as *iṣu dārû,* "everlasting wood" (*CAD* D:118), or, in Deutero-Isaiah's terms, "a wood that does not rot." There is a hidden irony here: God "chooses" His people (41:8, 9), while, in pitiful contrast, idolaters can only "choose" the type of wood they prefer for the construction of their god. For **עץ**, "wood," as a derogatory term denoting "idols," see 44:19; 45:20; Jer 10:3; Hos 4:12; Hab 2:19.

Then he seeks a skillful woodworker — After choosing the wood, the aspiring idolater invites a skilled artisan to sculpt his idol. For similar scenarios recorded in Mesopotamian documents see, for example, King Esarhaddon's statement: "I brought in and set to work carpenters, goldsmiths, . . . expert craftsmen, (to make statues of the gods and jewelry for them)" (*CAD* G:138). Another Assyrian king, Sargon, brags: "I had images of these great gods made skillfully" (*CAD* N/1:187). For skilled artisans, *mudû,* in Akkadian sources, see also *CAD* M/2:165. For the verbal expression **בקשׁ ל-**, see Ps 122:9; Lam 1:19.

To make a firm idol that will not topple — For this verb ("to make firm and stable"), see Isa 45:18: "Who formed the earth and made it, who fixed it fast (**כוֹנְנָהּ**)"; 2 Sam 7:12: "I will establish firmly (**וַהֲכִינֹתִי**) his kingship." (For the Akkadian etymological and semantic equivalent, *kunnu,* also in contexts of "setting up" an idol, see *CAD* K:163-64.) This stinging mockery is repeated below in 41:7: "And he fixes it with nails, that it may not topple"; Jer 10:4: "He fastens it with nails and hammers so that it does not totter." For an idol that "was not fastened well enough" and fell to the ground, see 1 Sam 5:3-5; and for a Mesopotamian account of the collapse of an idol and its subsequent shattering, see *CAD* D:81. This very blatant satire juxtaposing idol craft and God's creation (immediately following) reverberates throughout Deutero-Isaiah.

[**21**] *Do you not know? Have you not heard?* — These rhetorical questions introduced by **הֲלוֹא**, which is repeated four times for the sake of emphasis, are intended to convince all listeners of the greatness of God's creation. Note that these four hemistichs are constructed in an escalating fashion. For other instances of the pair of verbs **שמע** and **ידע**, see below, v. 28; 48:8; and for the triad **הֲלֹא**, **ידע**, and **שמע**, see 44:8.

Have you not been told from the very first? — For **מֵרֹאשׁ**, "the days of yore," see 41:4: "He who announced the generations from the start (**מראש**)"; 41:26: "Who foretold this from the start (**מראש**), that we may note it"; 48:16: "From the beginning (**מראש**), I did not speak in secret." For the verbs **נגד** and **שׁמע** in conjunction, see 41:22, 26; 42:9.

Have you not discerned from the foundation/s of the earth? — There are two ways in which the expression **מוסדות ארץ** can be interpreted. When one reads the verse in light of the prior hemistich and vocalizes **מִיסֻּדַת הארץ**, "from the foundation of the earth," it creates a parallelism with **מראש** ("from the very first"). For the rare substantive יְסוּדָה, "foundation," see Ps 87:1: "His [God's] foundation (יסודתו) on the holy mountains." For a similar idea couched in different terms, see Prov 8:23: "In the distant past I was fashioned, at the beginning, at the origin of earth." If, on the other hand, one maintains the Masoretic vocalization, then the reference is to "the foundations of the earth," similar to מוסדות השמים, "the foundations of the sky" (2 Sam 22:8; Akk. *išid šamê;* cf. *CAD* I:240); מוסדות תבל, "the foundations of the world" (2 Sam 22:16); and מוסדי ארץ, "the foundations of earth" (Ps 82:5). (Cf. also the Ugaritic etymological and semantic equivalent, *msdt arṣ* (*CAT* 1.4.I:40.) For the verbal sequence בין-ידע, see 43:10; 44:18. הארץ is a key word, repeated three more times in vv. 22-24.

[22-24] In a series of three clauses, each beginning with a *qal* participle preceded by the definite article, this hymn of praise juxtaposes God's creation of the world with His involvement in historical processes, i.e., His total control over monarchs. For these motifs in close proximity, see also vv. 15, 17; 44:24-25.

[22] The verb ישב, which is found three times here, also creates a literary *inclusio* to the entire verse.

It is He who sits enthroned on the vault of the earth — The reference here is to God enthroned in the heavens; see Ps 2:4: "He who is enthroned (יושב) in heaven laughs." (The Ugaritic etymological and semantic equivalent *yṯb* [*HdO* 2:995] and Akk. *wašābu* [*CAD* A/2:430] also share this meaning with Heb. ישב.) God is described here as a monarch who sits on the horizon of the sky, which forms a circle around the earth. The Mesopotamians also thought that the heavens were circular and referred to them as *kippat šamê/burūmê,* "the circle of heaven/the sky" (*CAD* K:397-99), which is most likely the Akkadian equivalent of חוג הארץ here. Compare similarly Prov 8:27: "He fixed the horizon (חוג) upon the deep"; Job 22:14: "As he moves about the circuit of heaven (חוג השמים)"; cf. Job 26:10. (See W. Horowitz, *Mesopotamian Cosmic Geography* [Winona Lake, Ind., 1998], 264-65.) The statement that God sits "enthroned on the vault of the earth" and not in an earthly temple is akin to the Deuteronomistic conception of the Deity; cf. 1 Kgs 8:39: "O hear in Your heavenly abode"; cf. vv. 30, 43, and 49); and see Isa 66:1: "Thus said the Lord: 'The heaven is My throne.'" (See the introduction, §13.)

So that its inhabitants seem as grasshoppers — A wordplay: in the eyes of God, who sits enthroned (יושב) in heaven, all people who dwell (יֹשְׁבֶיהָ) on earth are as grasshoppers, an image of insignificance; cf. Num 13:33: "And we looked like grasshoppers to ourselves." For a similar simile, see the commentary to Isa 51:6: "And its inhabitants die out as gnats (כן)."

Who spread out the skies like gauze — For another image of God's spreading out the skies, see Ps 104:2: "You spread the skies like a tent"; and cf. Isa 42:5: "Thus said God the Lord, who created the heavens and stretched them out"; 44:24: "It is I, the Lord, who made everything, who alone stretched out the heavens and unaided spread out the earth"; see also 45:12; 51:13; Zech 12:1; Job 9:8: "Who by himself spread out the heavens." The term דֹּק is a hapax legomenon, which associatively links with v. 15, דַּק, another hapax legomenon. In Mesopotamian literature the skies are also described as being "stretched out": "Wherever the earth is laid, and the heavens are stretched out" (see *BWL*, 58-59, line 37).

And stretched them out like a tent to dwell in — See Ps 104:2, cited above; cf. Ps 19:5: "He places in them [in the sky] a tent for the sun." The root מתח (common in Rabbinic Hebrew) is another hapax legomenon (see the introduction, §11).

[23] *He brings potentates to naught* — God has total control over earthly monarchs. The term רוזנים (elsewhere parallel to מלכים, "kings"; see Judg 5:3; Hab 1:10; Ps 2:2; Prov 8:15; 31:4) is found in the Phoenician inscription of King Azitawada, from the end of the eighth century BCE: "If a king among kings and a potentate among potentates (ורזן ברזנים)" (*KAI* 26A III:12); and as verb is documented in Neo-Punic (*KAI* 145 I:5). For God's control of the kings of the world, see also Job 12:18; Dan 2:21. For the verbal expression נתן ל-, see below, v. 29.

Makes rulers of the earth as nothing — This hemistich creates a chiastic parallel with the preceding one. For the root שׁפט, "to govern," see 1 Sam 8:5: "Therefore appoint a king for us to govern us (לשפטנו)"; 2 Kgs 15:5: "While Jotham, the king's son, was in charge of the palace and governed (שֹׁפֵט) the people of the land"; Prov 8:15-16, where the terms "kings" (מלכים), "potentates" (רוזנים), "princes" (שָׂרִים), and "rulers of the earth" (שופטי ארץ), appear as parallel terms; Ps 148:11: "All the kings of the earth . . . princes and all the rulers of the earth (שֹׁפטי ארץ)." (For the etymological and semantic equivalent in Akkadian, *šāpitu*, see *CAD* Š/1:459.) For אַיִן and תֹהוּ as synonyms, see v. 17 above.

[24] By means of a metaphor drawn from the planting of trees, the prophet describes how God "brings these potentates to naught." In order to enhance the potency of his words he repeats the unique expression אף בל, "scarcely," three times in the same verse. For a similar series of אף, see 41:10 (twice); 41:26 (three times); 44:15 (twice); 46:11 (three times).

Scarcely are they planted — almost at the very moment of their planting. נִטָּעוּ is the sole example of the verb נטע in the *niph'al*, and, as is common in verbs beginning with a *nun*, the first letter of the radical was assimilated.

Scarcely are they sown — Almost at the very same time as they are sown. The verb זֹרָעוּ is an archaic *qal* passive of the root זרע (it too appears only here).

Scarcely has their stem taken root in the earth — almost at the very same time that their stem takes root. For an opposite image, see Jer 12:2: "You have planted them, and they have taken root (שֹׁרָשׁוּ)" (both verses employ the *pu'al* form). For the parallel pair שרש/גזע, see Isa 11:1: "But a shoot shall grow out of the stump (גזע) of Jesse. A twig shall sprout from his stock (שרשיו)"; Job 14:8: "If its roots (שרשו) are old in the earth, and its stump (גזעו) dies in the ground."

When He blows on them and they dry up — And suddenly when God blows upon them, they shrivel up and wither away. For a similar image, see above, v. 7. The root נשׁף, "to blow," appears only once more, in Exod 15:10: "You blew (נשפת) with Your wind; the sea covered them." For the etymological and semantic equivalent in Akkadian, *našāpu*, see the following hemistich.

And a whirlwind bears them off like chaff — A storm wind carries them off and scatters them as if they were mere chaff; cf. Isa 41:16: "And the wind shall carry them off; the whirlwind (סערה) shall scatter them." The term קַשׁ ("chaff") denotes something weightless and easily carried off by the wind; see Jer 13:24: "So I will scatter you like chaff that flies before the desert wind"; Ps 83:14: "Like chaff driven by the wind." For the same image in Akkadian literature, expressed by *našāpu* (= נשף, "to blow") and *pû* (= קש, "chaff"), see *CAD* N/2:56-57; P:472. One should note the accretion of sibilants in these three words: וסערה כקש תִּשָּׂאֵם.

[25] *"To whom, then, can you liken Me? To whom can I be compared?"* — So then (the *waw* of ואל indicates result) who is My equal? See also 46:5: "To whom can you compare Me or declare Me similar? To whom can you liken Me so that we seem comparable?" This is the closing verse of the literary frame that opened with v. 18.

Says the Holy One — The "Holy One" (קדוש) is one of God's proper names; see 57:15: "Whose name is 'Holy'"; Hab 3:3: "God is coming from Teman, the Holy One from Mount Paran." Compare also "the Holy One of Israel" (קדוש ישראל), 41:14, 16, 20; 43:14; 45:11; 47:4; 48:17; 49:7; 54:5; 60:9. Similarly in Ugaritic, *qdš*, "the Holy One," serves as an epithet of the chief god El; cf. too *bn qdš*, "sons of the Holy One" (*HdO* 2:696). The semantic equivalents in Akkadian, *ellu*, and in Sumerian, kù, "holy," are also prevalent in descriptions of deities in Mesopotamian literature beginning in the third millennium BCE (see *CAD* E:105; K. Tallqvist, *Akkadische Götterepitheta* [Helsinki, 1938], 20).

[26] This is a hymn of praise to the power of the God of Israel who rules the heavenly legions and is described here as a military commander who checks the formations of His "star" soldiers. This short doxology has a clear affinity with Ps 147:4-5:

Ps 147	**Isa 40:26**
v. 4: He reckoned the number (מספר) of the stars. To each He gave its name (לְכֻלָּם שמות יקרא). v. 5: Mighty is our God and great His power (ורב כֹּחַ).	He who sends out their host by count (במספר), who calls them all by their names (לְכֻלָּם בשם יקרא) through His great might and power (מרב . . . כֹּחַ).

(For other connections between this psalm (v. 5) and our chapter, see below, v. 28; and the introduction, §17.) One should also compare the conclusion of the previous verse (25): "says the Holy One (קדוש)," and the beginning of this verse: "Lift high (מרום) your eyes," to 57:15: ". . . whose name is the Holy One (קדוש). . . . I dwell in a high (מרום) and holy (קדוש) place." The rhetorical מי question in this verse, which links it with the immediately preceding one, also serves as part of the prophet's polemic against Babylonian beliefs, according to which Marduk, king of the gods, was the creator of the stars, as is recounted in the Babylonian epic of creation, *Enuma Elish*: "He established (in) constellations the stars" (V:2; Foster, *COS* 1:399).

Lift up your eyes to the heaven and see — מרום, "height," refers to the height of heaven; see Isa 33:5; 57:15; Jer 25:30; Mic 6:6; Ps 93:4; 102:20. For the same idea, employing the term שמים, see Isa 51:6: "Raise your eyes to the heavens and look." The expression "to lift one's eyes and see" (see also 49:18) is common in Ugaritic: *yšu ʿnh wyʿn* (*HdO* 1:167). So too is the phrase *šmm rmm,* "(Lady, i.e., the goddess Anat) of the sublime heavens" (*CAT* 1.108:7). Compare also the Phoenician inscription of King Bodashtart from the fifth century BCE, which also refers to שממ רממ, "high heavens" (*KAI* 15:1).

Who created these? — the stars. Another rhetorical-polemical מי question. The root ברא, which always refers to divine creation, is found some fifty times in the prophecies of Deutero-Isaiah, accounting for about half of all its occurrences in the entire Bible.

It is He who leads out their host by number — The Israelite deity is described here as an army commander-in-chief leading out His army, the entire host of heaven, i.e., the stars, by number; see 24:21: "In that day the Lord will punish the host of heaven in heaven." (For the terminology, cf. the census of the Israelites taken in the desert: "Take a census of the whole Israelite community . . . listing by number [במספר] the names of every male, head by head" [Num 1:2; cf. 18:20].) Needless to say, this is a feat that no one else can ever perform; cf. Gen 15:5: "Look toward heaven and count the stars — if you are able to count them." The verb יצא in the *hiphʿil* has a military connotation, "to lead out an army, to deploy." For a similar image, applied to David, see 2 Sam 5:2. For this verb in other "stellar" contexts, see Job 38:32: "Can you lead out (התוציא) Mazzaroth [i.e., a certain constellation of stars] in its season?" One should note the assonance of the successive sequence of sibilants: המוציא במספר צְבאם.

Who calls them each by name — Not only is God able to count the stars in heaven, He even knows the name of each and every one of them. (For a similar use of בשם קרא, cf. Esth 2:14.) This is another proof of God's unparalleled uniqueness, since according to the Aramaic Proverbs of Ahiqar from the fifth century BCE: "The stars (in the sky) are so numerous (that) no one knows their names" (J. Lindenberger, *The Aramaic Proverbs of Ahiqar* [Baltimore, 1983], 104, line 116). For a similar image, cf. the inscriptions of several Assyrian kings: "The people who, like the stars in the sky, bear no counting" (*CAD* K:48; M/2:99). This clause is chiastically parallel to the preceding one.

Because of His great might and vast power — No star is left out of God's census. The *mem* in מֵרֹב, which applies also to the next couplet as well, is causative. For אוֹנִים, "strength," see below, v. 29; and for the parallel pair כֹּחַ/אוֹנִים, see Gen 49:3: "My might (כֹּחִי) and the firstfruits of my vigor (אוֹנִי)." For the phrase אַמִּיץ כֹּחַ as a description of the Deity's power, see Job 9:4: "Wise of heart and mighty in power (אמיץ כח)"; v. 19: "If a trial of strength (לכח), He is the strong one (אמיץ)." Compare the similar expression "in His great might" (ברב כח[ו]), Isa 63:1; Job 23:6.

Not one is missing — Not one of the stars fails to appear. For the same turn of phrase, see Isa 34:16: "Not one of these shall be absent (לא נעדרה)." For איש as referring to inanimate objects, cf. 1 Kgs 7:30, 36.

[27-31] The Israelites' plight and weariness in the Babylonian exile reverberate here. They see themselves as being abandoned by God and feel there is no hope of salvation. (For the motif of divine abandonment in Sumerian laments, see F. W. Dobbs-Allsopp, *Weep, O Daughter of Zion: A Study of the City-Lament Genre in the Hebrew Bible,* BibOr 44 [Rome, 1993], 45-51.) Prophets often quote the people's complaints in order to properly address their grievances, and then condemn, refute, or comfort, depending on the issue at hand. In this section the prophet addresses the people's disillusionment and insecurity and offers them consolation. He describes God's great power and promises that those who believe in God shall renew their strength and be reinvigorated. This literary unit is connected to the former one by several terms and expressions: דרך and משפט (vv. 14, 27 — with different meanings); תבונות/תבונתו (vv. 14, 28); הֲלֹא תדעו הֲלֹא תשמעו — הֲלֹא ידעת אמלא שמעת (vv. 21, 28); כֹּחַ (vv. 26, 29, 31). The creation motif as proof of God's greatness and uniqueness (vv. 21-23, 26) is found here as well (v. 28). In v. 29 a number of the terms that appear at the end of the previous unit (v. 26), i.e., מרב, אונים, and כח, are repeated, and instead of אמיץ the equivalent term, עצמה, appears.

[27] The people complain that God ignores their plight and that He has forgotten them; cf. Ps 44:25: "Why do you hide your face, ignoring our affliction and distress?"; Ps 89:47: "How long, O Lord, will you forever hide Your face?"

Why do you say, O Jacob, and why declare, O Israel — The prophet turns his attention directly to the people (the "Jacob/Israel" parallel pair is found 17 times in Deutero-Isaiah up to and including chap. 49, and then it is replaced by the "Jerusalem/Zion" pair) and addresses their continual complaints (the verbs are in the imperfect, denoting frequency) regarding their extended stay in exile. "Why" (למה) is a query common to public lamentations; see Ps 74:11; 79:10; 80:13.

"My way is hidden from the Lord" — Cf. Isa 49:14: "Zion says, 'The Lord has forsaken me. My Lord has forgotten me,'" a complaint substantiated by God's words: "For a little while I forsook you . . . I hid My face from you" (54:7-8). For דרך, "way," denoting one's lot in life, cf. Jer 12:1: "Why does the way (דרך) of the wicked prosper?"

"And my cause is ignored by my God?" — My plight is "passed over" by God. For משפט referring to one's "cause" see Isa 49:4. (The Akkadian semantic equivalent of Heb. עבר, *etēqu,* also means "to avoid, disregard" in legal contexts; see *CAD* E:309.)

[28] The prophet's response to the people's repeated complaints, in which he describes God's unparalleled power, is reflected in His eternal existence, His creation of the cosmos, that He never tires, and His wisdom, which knows no bounds. Since God's wisdom is infinite, there is no reason for them to claim that their cause has been overlooked. The prophet repeats the negative particle (ה)ל(ו)א four times for the sake of emphasis.

Do you not know? Have you not heard? — For an identical verbal sequence, serving a rhetorical ploy to highlight an argument, see above, v. 21.

The Lord is the everlasting God — Cf. Gen 21:33: "And he invoked there the name of the Lord, the everlasting God (אל עולם)"; Dan 12:7: "the ever-living One (חֵי עולם)"; see also Dan 4:31. For other imagery referring to God's eternal existence, see Ps 102:28: "But You are the same and Your years never end"; Job 36:26: "The number of His years cannot be counted." Somewhat similarly, El, the head of the Ugaritic pantheon, is described as "the father of years" *(ab šnm)* (*CAT* 1.6.I:36). The title *ʾl ḏ ʿlm* ("eternal god") also appears in a Proto-Canaanite inscription from Serabit el-Khadim in the Sinai Desert from the fifteenth century BCE (W. F. Albright, *The Proto-Sinaitic Inscriptions and Their Decipherment* [Cambridge, 1966], 24).

Creator of the earth from end to end — For קְצוֹת הארץ, "the ends of the earth," see Isa 41:5, 9; and for its by-form, (מ)קצה הארץ, see 42:10; 48:20. The cosmology motif is once more brought as proof of God's uniqueness, and it links this unit with the previous one (v. 26).

He never grows faint or weary — For the pair of synonyms יגע and עיף/יעף, see Deut 25:18; Jer 51:58; Hab 2:13. The prophet is polemicizing against the belief that God had to rest when He finished creating the world; cf., e.g., Exod 20:11: "And He rested on the seventh day"; Exod 31:17: "And on the seventh day He ceased from work and was refreshed" (see Weinfeld, "God as Creator," 105-25). Moreover, there is another covert polemic here: Though God never becomes weary, this is not true of the idol craftsman: "Should he drink no water, he would grow faint (וַיִּעָף)" (44:12). The root יעף (which is synonymous with עיף) recurs four times in this unit and the verb יגע three times. For similar descriptions of gods who never tire in Mesopotamian literature, see *CAD* A/2:121.

For the contrast between "youths . . . and young men," who "may grow faint and weary" (v. 30), and God who "never grows faint and weary," cf. the Mesopotamian inscription: "Human virility becomes exhausted, but the goddess Ishtar never grows weary" (*CAD* A/2:102).

His understanding cannot be fathomed — There is no quantifying God's infinite wisdom. For a similar motif, see Ps 145:3: "His greatness cannot be fathomed (אֵין חֵקֶר)"; Job 5:9; 9:10: "Who performs great deeds that cannot be fathomed (ואין חקר)." This hemistich, too, was influenced by Ps 147:5, where the same expression appears (see above in the introduction to v. 26). Perhaps the hidden polemic against idol craftsmen continues even here: God's wisdom may be unfathomable, but "they neither know nor understand" (Isa 44:18).

[29] *He gives strength to the weary, fresh vigor to the exhausted* — God in "His great might and vast power" (v. 26) not only does not grow weary, but He has an infinite reserve of strength for people at the end of their tether. For other examples of complete reversals of the status quo, see above, v. 23; 49:7, 24-26. This chiastic clause is constructed as a negative parallelism: יָעֵף/אין אוֹנִים. For a similar construction, cf. Amos 5:18: "It shall be darkness, not light" (הוּא חֹשֶׁךְ ולא אור). For the substantive עָצְמָה, see 47:9, and note the wordplay אין אונים.

[30] *Youths may grow faint and weary* — Regardless of youth's great endurance, there comes a point where their strength fades and their vigor is exhausted.

And young men may totter — An infinitive absolute followed by a finite verbal form of the same root (כָּשׁוֹל יִכָּשֵׁלוּ) serves to emphasize their fatigue. Even the young and the vigorous (see Prov 20:29: "The glory of youths [בחורים] is their strength") become weak and stumble. See also Lam 5:13: "Youths stagger (כשלו) under loads of wood." For the root כשל denoting "failing strength" (Luzzatto), see Ps 31:11: "My strength fails (כשל) because of my iniquity"; Neh 4:4: "The strength of the basket carrier has failed (כשל)"; and it is synonymous with the root עיף: "In its ranks, none is weary (עָיֵף), nor exhausted (כושל)" (Isa 5:27).

[31] *But those who trust in the Lord shall renew their strength* — However (the *waw* of וְקוֹיֵ indicates contrast), contrary to the young, those who place their trust in the Lord will ever renew their strength; cf. 49:23: "And you shall know that I am the Lord — those who trust in me (קֹוָי) shall not be disappointed"; Ps 37:9: "Those who trust in (קֹוֵי) the Lord — they shall inherit the land." (This too is the meaning of the Akkadian etymological and semantic cognate *qu'û; CAD* Q:330-31.) For the root חלף, "to renew," see Ps 90:6: "At daybreak it flourishes anew (וחלף); by dusk it withers and dries up"; Job 14:7: "There is hope for a tree: If it is cut down, it will renew itself (יחליף). Its shoots will not cease"; and in a metaphoric context: "My vigor refreshed; my bow ever new (תחליף) in my hand" (Job 29:20) This is also the verb's meaning in Rabbinic Hebrew; see, e.g., *b. B. Bat.* 80b: "Their trunk does not renew itself (מחליף)." The Tetragrammaton is emphasized yet a third time; see above, vv. 27, 28.

They will grow pinions like eagles — They shall grow new wings like eagles, i.e., they shall once more become rejuvenated and vigorous. For the root עלי indicating "growth," see Isa 5:6: "And it shall be overgrown (ועלה) with briars and thistles"; Amos 7:1: "At the time when the late-sown crops were beginning to sprout (עֲלוֹת)." For the collective noun אֵבֶר, "wings," see Ezek 17:3: "The great eagle with the great wings and the long pinions (האבר)"; Ps 55:7: "O that I had the wings (אבר) of a dove! I would fly away and find rest." (For the singular form, אֶבְרָה, see Deut 32:11; Job 39:26.) An echo of folk belief is preserved here similar to the fable of the phoenix. The eagle, according to popular belief, periodically regrows its wings and is rejuvenated; see also Ps 103:5: "So that your youth is renewed like the eagle's." Compare the remarks of Kimchi, who quotes Saadyah Gaon: "Once every ten years, the eagle soars high in the sky and comes close to the searing heat of the fire. He then dives into the sea because of the great heat, sheds (his feathers) and regrows them. He then soars once more, reinvigorated. This he does every ten years to one hundred years. At that time he soars high in the sky, as his wont, but then falls into the sea and dies." The image of an eagle is also reminiscent of the exodus when God "bore the Israelites on eagles' wings"; Deut 32:11: "Like an eagle who rouses his nestlings, gliding down to his young, so did He spread His wings and take him, bear him along on His pinions."

They shall run and not grow weary, they shall march and not grow faint — God grants those who trust in Him great endurance and vigor so that they (unlike the youths of the previous verse) will never tire in their endeavors. For a similar motif see Prov 4:12: "You will walk without breaking stride. When you run, you will not grow faint."

Chapter 41

[1-7] The first pericope of chap. 41 begins with a trial scene: God invites the nations of the world to a legal contest and contends that He alone determines the fate of nations and that He is the sole weaver of history. God's evidence for this lies in the fact that He alone foretold Cyrus's sequential victories and victorious ascension (vv. 1-5). The prophet proceeds with a mocking description of graven images and their craftsmen (vv. 6-7), which supplements his derisive account above (40:19-20). This unit is associatively connected to the former one by several shared expressions: **יחליפו כֹחַ** (40:31; 41:1); **משפט** (40:27; 41:1); **קְצוֹת הארץ** (40:28; 41:5); **יעבור** (40:27; 41:3); the rhetorical-polemical question, **מי** (40:12, 13, 14, 18, 25, 26; 41:2); cf. also the shared imagery of **קש**, "straw" (40:24; 41:2). The same rhetorical sequence recurs in both chapters: first the **מי** queries (40:18; 41:2), followed by a description of idol craft (40:19-20; 41:6-7). For a similar sequence, see 44:7ff.; 46:5-7.

[1] *Stand silent before Me, coastlands*! — God, the prosecutor at this trial, addresses the "coastlands" (**איים**, this term is paired here and in 49:1 with **לְאֻמִּים**, and in 40:15 with **גוים**) and commands their silence so that He may present His accusations against them. For this terminology in other legal contexts, see Job 13:13: "Be silent (**הַחֲרִישׁוּ**)! I will have my say"; also v. 19; 33:31, 33.

And let the peoples renew their strength — The term **לְאֻמִּים**, "peoples," appears in Deutero-Isaiah's prophecies only in the plural, e.g., 43:9: "All the nations assemble as one, the peoples (**לאמים**) gather" (also in a legal context). The word is also found in Ugaritic, *lim* (singular), *limm* (plural), "people(s), clan(s)" (*HdO* 2:487-88), and in Mari Akkadian, *līmum,* "family, clan" (a West Semitic loanword) (*CAD* L:198). (See A. Malamat, "A Recently Discovered Word for 'Clan' in Mari and Its Hebrew Cognate," in Z. Zevit, S. Gitin, and M. Sokoloff, eds., *Solving Riddles and Untying Knots: Biblical, Epigraphic, and Semitic Studies in Honor of Jonas C. Greenfield* [Winona Lake, Ind., 1995], 177-79.) The expression יחליפו כח, which denotes "reinvigoration," links this verse directly with the last verse in the former chapter, 40:31. For a similar image applied in the confrontation of God and Job, see Job 38:3.

Let them approach to state their case — The nations are "subpoenaed" to present their case. Both verbs, יִגְּשׁוּ (from the root נגשׁ) and ידברו (from the root דבר), appear frequently in the context of trials. For the former, see vv. 21, 22; 45:20, 21; 50:8; Deut 25:1. (The Akkadian semantic equivalent *sanāqu* ["to draw near"] appears in similar contexts, i.e., approaching the authorities with a complaint, to proceed legally against another [*CAD* S:137-38].) And for the latter verb relating to the presenting of legal arguments, see Isa 32:7; Job 33:31-33. (So too in Akkadian, its semantic cognate *dabābu*, "to speak," also has legal connotations [*CAD* D:3].) For the adverb אז prior to an imperfect verb, indicating a logical sequence, see Job 3:13: "I would be asleep, then (אז) I would be at rest."

Let us come forward together for trial — the two parties, God and the peoples, in order to present their respective cases. For the verb קרב, with legal connotations, see vv. 5, 21; Mal 3:5. (The Akkadian semantic and etymological equivalent *qerēbu* also appears in similar legal contexts [*CAD* Q:228ff., 239], as does another semantic equivalent *kašādu*, lit. "to come forward and state one's case before the authorities" [*CAD* K:276].) For the verbal sequence "approach . . . come forward," see v. 21.

[2-4] God's claim that He is unique is based on the fact that He alone foretold the coming of Cyrus, and He alone aided the Persian king to conquer and subjugate a multitude of nations. To both those who believed that it was Marduk, the head of the Babylonian pantheon, who anointed Cyrus as his chosen one and accompanied him on his conquests (*ANET,* 315), and the Israelite nation who doubted God's power since they — His chosen people — still languished in exile, the prophet announces that God alone weaves the tapestry of history from the first threads to the finishing touches. For rhetorical מי questions as introducing polemics, see the introduction to the unit.

[2] *Who has roused a victor/victory from the east* — Who roused Cyrus, the overlord of Persia? The *hiphʿil* of עור in Late Biblical Hebrew denotes stirring up to perform a specific activity and appears again in connection with Cyrus in v. 25: "I have roused (העירותי) him from the north"; 45:13: "It is I who roused him (הַעִירֹתִהוּ) for victory." See also Ezra 1:1: "The Lord roused (העיר) the spirit of Cyrus," which is elucidated in the following verse: "The Lord God of heaven has given me all the kingdoms of the earth and has charged me with building Him a house in Jerusalem, which is in Judah." (In Classical or First Temple Hebrew, the verbal root קום expressed this same meaning.) For Cyrus's "arousal" in Babylonian sources, see the Sippar Cylinder inscription of Nabonidus (the last Babylonian king before the ascension of Cyrus and a con-

temporary of Deutero-Isaiah): "At the beginning of the third year they [the gods] roused Cyrus the king of Anshan" (trans. P.-A. Beaulieu, *COS* 2:311). (The verb employed here is the Akkadian semantic equivalent, *šutbû,* "to rise up against, mobilize," the *shaph'el* of *tebû,* "to rise;" *CAD* T:319-20.) For other allusions to Cyrus and his mission, see v. 25; 43:14; 44:28; 45:1-7; 46:11; 48:14-16.

From the east — This is a reference to Cyrus, who came from Persia and Media, east and southeast, respectively, from Babylonia proper; see also 46:11, which once again mentions that God summoned him from the east.

Victory/victor — **צדק** denotes "victory"; see v. 10: "My victorious (**צדקי**) right hand"; 46:13: "I am bringing My victory (**צדקתי**) close. It shall not be far, and My triumph shall not be delayed"; 51:5: "My triumph (**צדקי**) is near. My salvation has gone forth." According to the Masoretic vocalization (supported by 1QIsa[a], which adds a consecutive *waw* to the next verb, **ויקראהו**, "and summoned him"), **צדק** is connected with the first clause of the verse: "Who has roused victory from the east?" It has also been suggested to vocalize this word as **צדיק**, "victor," rather than **צדק**, "victory." For this meaning see 49:24: "Can spoil be taken from a warrior or captives retrieved from a victor (**צדיק**)?" Some commentators, however, prefer this alternative division and attach the word to the second clause; see immediately below.

Summoned him to His service — The verb **יִקְרָאֵהוּ** has been interpreted in two different ways. Some commentators prefer to derive it from **קרי**, "to befall, encounter," comparing 51:19: "These two things have befallen you (**קֹרְאֹתַיִךְ**)"; Gen 42:4: "Lest disaster befall him (**יִקְרָאֶנּוּ**)" (cf. Gen 42:38); and by attaching **צדק** to this clause, translate, "Wherever he goes [**לרגל**, lit. "at every step"] victory greets him." If, however, one derives the verb from **קרא**, without attaching **צדק** to this clause, the meaning is: "God summoned Cyrus to follow Him in His footsteps." For this meaning, see 1 Sam 25:42: "And with five of her maids in her attendance (**לְרַגְלָהּ**)"; Hab 3:5: "And plague comes forth at His footsteps (**לרגליו**)." For other instances of Cyrus being "summoned" by God, see Isa 45:3, 4; 46:11; 48:15. Both the LXX and 1QIsa[a] read **לרגליו** (plural), which conforms with the plural of this same term in the next verse here.

Has delivered up nations to him — For the verbal expression **נתן לפני**, see Deut 28:7: "The Lord will deliver up to you (**יתן . . . לפניך**) the enemies who attack you"; cf. Deut 1:8; Josh 10:12; 11:6.

And has trodden down sovereigns? — According to the Masoretic vocalization, the verb **יַרְדְּ** is understood to be an apocopated imperfect from the root **רדי** ("to rule over"; cf. **וַיַּשְׁקְ**, "he watered" [Gen 29:10; Exod 2:17], from the root **שׁקי**). This verb, however, is always followed by the particle *beth,* e.g., Gen 1:28: "And rule over (**וּרְדוּ ב-**) the fish of the sea." For this reason some commentators prefer the reading of 1QIsa[a]: **יוריד** ("to bring down"), i.e., Cyrus will topple kings; see, e.g., 2 Sam 22:48: "And subdued (**ומֹרִיד**) peoples under me" (cf. Ps

56:8; 59:12). The correct vocalization, however, should be יָרֹד, from the root רדד, "to beat down, subdue"; see Ps 144:2: "Who makes peoples subject (הָרֹדֵד) to me." This verb is found again in Isa 45:1, לרד, where it should be vocalized לָרֹד. (For this vocalization of roots with doubled radicals, cf. לָרֹס ["to moisten"] [Ezek 46:14], from רסס; and יָסֹב ["to circle"] [1 Sam 5:8], from סבב). God is the one responsible for Cyrus's trampling over his enemies. Treading upon defeated enemies is often illustrated in ancient Near Eastern iconography; see, e.g., *ANEP*, nos. 300, 390; Y. Yadin, *The Art of Warfare in Biblical Lands*, trans. M. Pearlman, 2 vols. (New York, 1963), 1:150. For the pair גוים/מלכים ("kings/nations"), see Isa 45:1; 52:15.

His sword has rendered them like dust — Some commentators prefer to read יַתְּנֵם, instead of יתן, i.e., Cyrus's potent sword cuts up his enemies and renders them like dust. Others understand "like dust" as referring to the enemies' swords (reading חַרְבָּם instead of חַרְבּוֹ) rather than to the enemies themselves: "He has rendered their swords like dust." In light of the common biblical image of subdued enemies ground to dust (cf., e.g., 2 Kgs 13:7: "For the king of Aram had trampled them like dust under his feet"; Zeph 1:17: "Their blood shall be spilled like dust"; Ps 18:43: "I ground them fine as windswept dust"), the first interpretation seems preferable.

His bow like windblown chaff — There are, once more, two ways of understanding this image. The first interpretation is similar to the first one in the prior clause: Cyrus's lethal bow (קשתו) renders his enemies as windblown chaff. The other option is that Cyrus renders their bows (קשתם) like windblown chaff. Again, the first seems preferable. For a similar image, see Ps 83:14: "Make them like thistledown, like chaff driven by the wind." Take note of the wordplay: קַשׁ . . . קשׁתו.

[3] *He pursues them, passing on unscathed* — Cyrus, while in pursuit of his enemies, passes through their territories unscathed. The two consecutive verbs יעבור ירדפם, without the *waw* prefix on the second verb, indicate expeditiously performed actions. The Akkadian cognate equivalent, *šalmiš etēqu* ("to pass safely"), appears in the same military context (*CAD* Š/1:255).

No fetter is placed on his feet — He is not bogged down by any hindrance whatsoever. The hapax legomenon אֹרַח, "fetter, hobble," appears in the Aramaic proverbs of Ahiqar in the context of child rearing: "The son who is instructed and restrained, and on whose foot the fetter (ארחא) is placed. . . ." (See Lindenberger, *Aramaic Proverbs of Ahiqar*, 46, line 80. This rare term is etymologically related to Aram. אֲרִיחָא, אַרְחָא, "half-brick, bar," and Akk. *arḫu*, "a half-brick"; *CAD* A/2:64; Lindenberger, *Aramaic Proverbs of Ahiqar*, 48, 224.) For shackling someone's feet as an image of impeding that individual, see Job 13:27: "You place my feet in stocks."

[4] *Who has planned and achieved this?* — The polemical מי question is

repeated once more (see v. 2): Who was it that planned and executed Cyrus's triumphant arrival? For the verb פעל, denoting "planning, designing," see Mic 2:1: "Ah, those who plan iniquity and design (וּפֹעֲלֵי) evil on their beds"; Ps 58:3: "In your minds you plan (תפעלון) wrongdoing in the land." The verb עשי in this context denotes execution of the act. For substantives derived from the roots עשי and פעל, as parallel terms, see Ps 28:4, 5; 64:10; for the two verbs in conjunction, see Isa 44:15.

Who announced the generations from the start? — Some commentators suggest that this is the answer to the polemical question posed in the first hemistich of the verse: the "director" of all these events is none other than "He, who has announced the generations from the very beginning" (cf. v. 26: "predicted from the very start"). Others prefer to understand this hemistich as the continuation of the rhetorical מי question from the previous hemistich, which is answered only in the subsequent hemistich. The plural substantive הַדֹּרוֹת indicates the time and event cycles of each generation.

It is I, the Lord, who was the first, and I am He with the last as well — I am the eternal Lord: I was first, and I will continue to be He until the last beings expire; see 44:6: "I am the first and I am the last"; 48:12: "I am the first and I am the last as well." "First and last" are the two extremes, composing a temporal merism. The proclamation אני הוא appears frequently in these prophecies; see 43:10, 13; 46:4; 48:12; 52:6, and is first found in Deut 32:39: "See, then, that I, I am He (אני הוא)." It serves as a surrogate name for the God of Israel, and is similar to the refrain chanted by the people at the Feast of Tabernacles while marching around the altar: "God (אני והו), save us!" (*m. Suk.* 4:5).

[5] The nations, fearful and trembling, "approach the bench" and prepare themselves for the "legal" confrontation.

The coastlands look on in fear — For other wordplays combining the verbs ראי and ירא, see Zech 9:5; Ps 40:4; Job 6:21. For איים "(inhabitants of) coastlands," see v. 1.

The ends of the earth tremble — When the earth hears the Lord's portentous proclamation, it trembles from one end to the other. For the construct קְצוֹת הארץ, see Isa 40:28; and for the verbal pair חרד/ירא, see Judg 7:3; 1 Sam 28:5. For the root חרד, "to tremble," see Exod 19:16: "And all the people who were in the camp trembled (וַיֶּחֱרַד)"; Exod 19:18: "And the whole mountain trembled (וַיֶּחֱרַד) violently." For the three verbs ירא, ראה, and חרד in conjunction, see 1 Sam 28:5. The reading of 1QIsa[a], יחדו, "together" (cf. LXX), as against MT יחרדו, may have been influenced by its appearance in v. 1.

They draw near and come — They, the nations, draw near to participate in the upcoming legal battle; see v. 1: "Let us come forward (נקרבה) together for argument"; v. 21: "Submit (קָרְבוּ) your case!" For the Aramaic verb אתי, "to come" (here in the *qal*, with the archaic *nun* suffix added to verbs in the third-person masculine plural; see, e.g., Exod 15:14, ירגזון), see v. 23, the plural substantive: הָאֹתִיּוֹת ("the upcoming events"); v. 25: "I have roused him from the north, and he has come (וַיַּאת)." (For the Aramaic influence on Deutero-Isaiah's prophecies, see the introduction, §11.) The verb is used here in a legal sense similar to its semantic parallel in Hebrew, בוא; cf., e.g., Ps 143:2: "Do not enter (תבוא) into judgment with your servant"; Job 9:32: "That we can go (נבוא) to trial together." Some commentators suggest transferring this clause to the end of v. 1 — God's "subpoena" of the nations and their reaction.

[**6**-7] The prophet intensifies his diatribe against idol craft. Since this description is similar to the satiric speech of 40:19-20, some commentators suggest that these verses were originally part of that prophecy. There is good reason, however, to leave these verses in place, since the fellowship of the idol craftsmen and their maintenance of the idols are juxtaposed here with God's consolation of His people and His ever-"helping hand" (vv. 8ff.). Below are some of the poignant points of contrast:

1. As against each one of the craftsmen "helping" the other (v. 6), God declares three times that He will "help" (עזר) Israel (vv. 10, 13, 14).
2. As against each of the craftsmen "strengthening" the other (vv. 6-7), God reiterates that He will "strengthen" (חזק) Israel (vv. 9, 13).
3. Contrary to the idol craftsman "saying" to his fellow worker: "Be strong!" (v. 6), and "It is good!" (i.e., the riveting) (v. 7), God "says" (אמר) to Israel, "You are My servant."
4. The connection between the two units is also evident in the nations' frightened reaction to the prophetic announcement (וְיִירָאוּ, v. 5), as opposed to the threefold repetition of God's emphatic message to His people, "Do not fear (אל תירא)!" (v. 10); "Have no fear (אל תירא)!" (v. 13); "Fear not (אל תירא)!" (v. 14).
5. See also the recurring terms: צדק (vv. 2, 10); קְצוֹת הארץ (vv. 5, 9).
6. As opposed to the idol, which the craftsmen declare "good" (טוב הוא), God simply "is" (אני הוא).

[**6**] *Each one helps the other* — Each one lends a helping hand in the construction of the precious images. For the sequence איש . . . רֵעֵהוּ, "each other," see Isa 13:8; 19:2.

Saying to his fellow, "Be strong!" — And each craftsman encourages his fellow to take courage. For the sequence איש . . . אח, which denotes mutuality, see 2 Kgs 7:6; Zech 8:17.

[7] *The woodworker encourages the goldsmith* — The woodworker (חָרָשׁ), who sculpts the wooden idol, urges on the gilder (צֹרֵף), who coats the idol with gold. (For the collaboration between the two in the construction of the

idol, see Isa 40:19-20; and cf. a similar satirical pronouncement in Jer 10:9: "The product of a woodworker and the goldsmith's hands".) For the root חזק denoting "encouragement," see 1 Sam 23:16-17: "And [Jonathan] encouraged (ויחזק) him [David] in the name of God. He said to him, 'Do not be afraid!'"; Jer 23:14: "They encourage (וחזקו) evildoers, so that no one turns back from his wickedness."

He who smooths with the hammer [encourages] *him who pounds the anvil* — The two master craftsmen, identified by the tools of their trade, offer each other words of encouragement as they work. The first artisan pounds with his hammer (see Jer 23:29: "And like a hammer [פטיש] that shatters rock"), "to smooth" (חלק; cf. Arab. *ḫalaqa,* "to make smooth") the metal prior to the coating of the idol, while the second artisan smites the "anvil" (פעם, a hapax legomenon) to flatten the metal. For the verb הלם, "to strike, hammer," see Prov 23:35: "They struck me . . . they beat me (הלמוני), but I was unaware"; and for the substantive הַלְמוּת ("hammer"), see Judg 5:26: "Her right hand (reached) for the workmen's hammer (הלמות)." The receded penultimate syllable of הולם is stressed (instead of the ultimate, as expected), due to the following word, פעם, which also has a penultimate stress. The verb פעם appears in Judg 13:25: "The spirit of the Lord first moved him (לפעמו)"; cf. Gen 41:8; Ps 77:5; Dan 2:1, 3.

He says of the soldering, "It is good!" — The artisan declares the soldering to be very sound. The assessment of the craftsman, who surveys his work following its completion and deems it worthy, is similar to God's appraisal ("It was good") at the conclusion of every day of the creation (except for the second day), and finally, on the sixth day, "It was very good" (Gen 1:31).

And he fixes it with nails, that it may not topple — The prophet concludes his diatribe with a final stinging piece of mockery: In order to prevent the possible collapse of the precious graven image (cf. 40:20), the artisan bolsters it by "fixing it with nails"; see also Jer 10:4: "He fastens it with nails and hammer, so that it does not totter."

[8-13] For the associative connection between this unit and the one immediately before it by means of key words and phrases that juxtapose God's relationship to His people and the idolaters' construction of idols, see the introduction to vv. 6-7. God gives His people a boost of morale by emphasizing His continual support and by promising that all those "who contend" with His chosen people "shall come to naught and shall perish." These heartening words reverberate in the minds of the listeners by means of the constant repetition of the second-person masculine pronominal suffix, ךָ‍ִי (9 times), which emphasizes the special connection between God and Israel. This pericope shares many motifs with the Neo-Assyrian prophecies of the seventh century BCE, which contain messages from the goddess Ishtar to the Assyrian kings Esarhaddon and Ashurbanipal, in which the goddess first introduces herself and then offers the kings words of encouragement in times of crisis. She tells them that they need not fear, since she, Ishtar, chose them and loves them. She also promises to extend a helping hand to ensure their success in thwarting the enemy's plans (see Parpola, *Assyrian Prophecies,* LXVI; and v. 10 here). Despite the similarities, there is one very important difference: Ishtar's words are directed solely to the monarch, whereas God directs His pronouncements to the whole nation of Israel.

[8] This verse is very similar to the Deuteronomic pronouncement: "And because He loved your fathers, He chose their heirs after them" (Deut 4:37); and to the promise to Isaac: "Fear not! . . . and I will bless you and increase your offspring for the sake of My servant Abraham" (Gen 26:24). For an additional example of the theme "Abraham," the substantive "servant," and the verb **בחר** ("to choose") in conjunction, see Ps 105:42-43: "Mindful of . . . His servant Abraham, He led His people out in gladness, His chosen ones with joyous song." Note the triad of references here to "Israel–Jacob–seed of Abraham."

But you, Israel, My servant — But you (the *waw* is contrastive), as opposed to those mentioned above, "are My servant" and therefore have nothing to fear. The term **עבדי** appears frequently in Deutero-Isaiah (cf., e.g., v. 9; 42:19; 43:10; 44:1, 2, 21; 45:4; 48:20; 54:17. Abraham [Gen 26:24], Moses [Deut 34:5], and David [Ps 89:4]) were also referred to as servants of God) and is an indication of the close relationship between God and His people. (For the semantic equivalent in Akkadian, *wardu,* indicating the ties between a devotee and his God, see *CAD* A/2:250-51; and for the etymological cognate in Ugaritic, *'bd,* see *HdO* 1:140-41.) One should note that the appearance of Israel before Jacob in the parallel stich here is a deviation from the prophet's norm (see Isa 40:27; 44:1, 5).

Jacob, whom I have chosen — from among the nations. God's choice, indicated by the verb **בחר**, is emphasized many times in Deutero-Isaiah's prophecies (see v. 9; 42:1; 43:10, 20; 44:1, 2; 45:4; 49:7; 65:9, 15, 22), and was influenced by the ideology of the book of Deuteronomy, where it appears for the first time; see Deut 7:6; 14:2: "Of all the peoples on earth the Lord God chose you to be His treasured people" (cf. 4:37; 10:15). (See the introduction, §13.) In many of the verses in which the prophet expresses this theology of "chosenness" he also appends the term **עבד**, "servant." Compare also Ps 105:6: "O offspring of Abraham, His servant. O descendants of Jacob, His chosen ones"; 1 Chr 16:13: "O offspring of Israel, His servant. O descendants of Jacob, His chosen ones." God's choice of Israel is in direct contrast to the idolatrous nations that chose "wood that does not rot" (Isa 40:20) or "an abomination" (41:24). In Mesopotamian royal inscriptions the king is referred to as the one chosen by the gods, a thought expressed by the verbs *nasāqu* (*CAD* N/2:22) and *atû* (*CAD* A/2:519-20). Here, however, the whole nation, not just the king, is chosen by God.

Offspring of Abraham — You are the descendants of the progenitor Abraham (see also Jer 33:26; Ps 105:6). For similar sobriquets, cf. "the offspring of Jacob" (Isa 45:19); "the offspring of Israel" (45:25); "an offspring the Lord has blessed" (61:9); "an offspring blessed by the Lord" (65:23). Compare also Akkadian literature, where individuals (but not nations) are known as the *zerû*, "descendant," of their father (*CAD* Z:95-96). Abraham (who is referred to only infrequently in prophetic literature; see Isa 29:22; Jer 33:26; Ezek 33:24; Mic 7:20) is mentioned again in Isa 51:2: "Look back to Abraham, your father"; 63:16: "Though Abraham regard us not."

Whom I love — For the verb אהב depicting God's relationship with Israel, see 43:4; Deut 4:37; 2 Chr 20:7 (where the same expression, אברהם אֹהַבְךָ, appears); and with regard to Cyrus, Isa 43:4; 48:14. It is also intimately connected to the establishment of alliances and indicates the ties of loyalty between the two sides; cf., e.g., 1 Kgs 5:15. The king as the gods' cherished and loved one *(migru, namaddu, narāmu)* appears frequently in Mesopotamian royal inscriptions. (See M.-J. Seux, *Épithètes royales akkadiennes et sumériennes* [Paris, 1967], 162-68, 184, 189-97.)

[9] *You whom I drew from the ends of the earth* — The verb חזק and the expression החזיק ביד/בימין denote support and choice (Luzzatto; Ehrlich, *Randglossen zur hebräischen Bibel,* 4 [Leipzig, 1912], 149-50); see 41:13; 42:6 (in connection with Israel); 45:1 (pertaining to Cyrus). The singling out of Israel (lit. "grasping [the hand]") "from the ends of the earth" is similar to Marduk's elevation of Cyrus in the Cyrus Cylinder: "[Marduk] surveyed and looked throughout all the lands, searching for a righteous ruler whom he would support [lit. 'take by his hand']. He called out his name: 'Cyrus, king of Anshan'" (M. Cogan, *COS* 2:315). This motif is also found in Mesopotamian sources. Compare the Sumerian king Uruinimgina's (Urukagina's) inscription in which the king maintains that his god, Ningirsu, "drew him forth [lit. 'grasped his hand'] from the multitude [lit. 'from among 36,000 people']." (See H. Stiebel, *Die altsumerische Bau- und Weihenschriften,* 1 [Wiesbaden, 1982], 299, col. 7, lines 18-19 = col. 8, lines 5-6.) So too in the Sumerian inscription of King Enmetena (Entemena), it is written that the god Ningirsu "drew him forth [lit. 'grasped his hand'] from among 3600 people" (ibid., 248, lines 2-3). Moreover, by employing the verb חזק, the prophet juxtaposes God's actions with those of the idol craftsmen; see vv. 6-7. In Akkadian, as well, the verbal expression *qātam aḫāzu/ṣabātu,* "to grasp by the hand," means "to assist" (*CAD* A/1:179; Ṣ:31-32). Compare also the semantic parallel in Ugaritic: "She takes the hungry by the hand. She takes the thirsty by the hand [= supports; *yd mṯkt*]" (*CAT* 1.15.I:1-2).

From the ends of the earth — From the farthest reaches of the world (see v. 2). Other commentators compare this expression to that found in Gen 47:2: מקצה אחיו; Judg 18:2: מקצותם; and 1 Kgs 12:31: מקצות העם, which they interpret to mean "from the elite, most worthy") (see A. B. Ehrlich, *Mikrâ ki-Pheshuṭo,* 3 [New York, 1969], 125 [Heb.]; on the verse here see also Kimchi).

And called from its far corners — I chose you and brought you forth from the remotest corners of the earth, which parallels the first interpretation given in the preceding hemistich. On the other hand, based on the expression אצילי בני ישראל, "the leaders of Israel" (Exod 24:11), the term here would parallel the second interpretation offered above (Rashi; Ibn Ezra; Ehrlich, *Randglossen,* 4:150).

To whom I have said: "You are My servant — Contra the statements above concerning the craftsmen and their idols — "Saying to his fellow, 'Take courage!'" (v. 6); "He says of the soldering: 'It is good!'" — God "says" to Israel: "You are My servant."

I have chosen you and have not rejected you" — A positive statement followed by a negative parallel is common in biblical poetry and accentuates the idea expressed. For this same pair of contrasting verbs, see Isa 7:15-16: "Reject (מָאֹס) the bad and choose (וּבָחוֹר) the good"; and in the context of a covenant violation, Jer 33:24: "The two families that the Lord chose (בחר) have now been rejected by Him (וַיִּמְאָסֵם)." The feeling of being "rejected" is poignantly stated in Isa 54:6: "Can one reject (תִמָּאֵס) the wife of his youth?"; Lam 5:22: "You have utterly rejected us (מָאֹס מְאסתנו)." The Akkadian cognate *mēšu* also means "to despise, disregard," and is employed in reference to gods and their rites, allegiance to kings, oaths, and commands (*CAD* M/2:41-42).

[10] Two parallel clauses followed by a triad of morale-inducing pronouncements: "I strengthen you . . . I help you . . . I uphold you."

Fear not, for I am with you! — Contrary to the quaking fear of the coastlands (see v. 5), Israel has nothing to be afraid of since God is with them. This promise and these words of encouragement, which are repeated once again below, were first delivered to the progenitors, Abraham, Isaac, and Jacob. To Abraham (also referred to in v. 8), see Gen 15:1: "Fear not, Abraham, I am a shield for you!"; to Isaac, Gen 26:24: "Fear not, for I am with you!"; and to Jacob, Gen 46:3: "Fear not to go down to Egypt!"; cf. also Jer 30:10-11. This literary-theological motif is also characteristic of Ishtar's prophecies to Esarhaddon and Ashurbanipal (kings of Assyria) from the seventh century BCE, which all begin with the same exhortation: "Do not fear *(la tapallaḫ)*!"; cf. "Esarhaddon, king of the lands, Fear not! . . . Fear not! . . . I am the Great Lady, I am Ishtar of Arbela, who has thrown your enemies under your feet. . . . King of Assyria, Fear not! . . . Fear not! I will deliver up the enemy of the Assyrian king for slaughter" (see Parpola, *Assyrian Prophecies,* 4-5). For the Aramaic semantic equivalent: אל תזחל ("Fear not!"), followed by a statement of the god's support, see the inscription of Zakkur, king of Hamath, from the first quarter of the eighth century BCE. The king, under siege, cornered by sixteen kings under the leadership of Bar-Hadad, king of Aram, pleads with his god, Baalshamayn, who answers him through prophetic seers: "Fear not, for I was the one who made you ki[ng, and I shall sta]nd with you and I shall save you [from all these kings]!" (*KAI* 202 II:12-14). (One should note that Aram. אנה אקם עמך, "I shall stand with you," is the semantic equivalent of Heb. כי עמך אני, "I am with you.") This expression also appears in an Ugaritic document, in which the king of Ugarit exhorts his mother not to be afraid: "And you, my mother, fear not *(al tdḥln)*!" (*CAT* 2.30:20-21). As mentioned above, however, this motif was extended and adapted to include the whole of Israel.

Be not frightened — The rare verb תשתע (from the root שׁתע), "to be afraid," parallel to תירא in the first hemistich and once again in v. 23, is also found in Ugaritic: "Mighty Baal feared *(yraun),* the Rider of the Clouds was frightened *(ṯtʿ)*" (*CAT* 1.5.II:6-7) — note that here too there is a parallel between *yrʾ* (= ירא) and *ṯtʿ* (= שתע); in Phoenician (in King Azitawada's inscription from the end of the eighth century BCE): "Even in places that formerly were feared (נשתעם), where a man feared (ישתע) to walk the road . . ." (*KAI* 26A II:3-5); and in Ammonite, on a broken gravestone from Rabbath-Ammon, dated to 825/775 BCE: תשתע (see S. Aḥituv, *Ha-Ketav veha-Miḵtav,* 2nd ed. [Jerusalem, 2005], 329, line 6 [Heb.]).

For I am your God! — Thus there is no reason to fear; see also Isa 43:3: "For I the Lord am your God . . . your Savior." For further reiteration the prophet now employs a series of three verbs that emphasize God's absolute support of His nation.

I strengthen you — For the verb אמץ, "to strengthen," see Amos 2:14: "The strong shall find no strength (יאמץ)"; Job 4:4: "You have strengthened (תאמץ) failing hands." The root also appears in Ugaritic, as an adjective: "(May) your hand (be) strong *(amṣ)*" (*HdO* 1:74).

And I help you — אף is an emphatic particle found 25 times in the prophecies of Deutero-Isaiah (cf., e.g., the threefold repetition in 40:24, and in 41:26). God's succor of Israel is in opposition to the idol craftsmen who can only aid and support one another (v. 6). The helping-hand motif, which appears again in vv. 13 and 14 (and see 44:2), is also found in the Neo-Assyrian prophecies; and the Akkadian semantic equivalent, *tukkulu,* referring to a deity "encouraging" the king, is well documented in Mesopotamian royal inscriptions (*CAD* T:66).

I uphold you — אף is repeated for emphasis. For the verb תמך, "to grasp, support, uphold," see 42:1: "This is my servant whom I uphold (אתמך)." Compare also Marduk's support of Cyrus, which is described in the Cyrus Cylinder as "grasping" (*tamāḫu* = תמך) Cyrus's hand (Cogan, *COS* 2:315). The Aramaic etymological and semantic cognate appears in the Phoenician (the dialect was influenced by Aramaic) inscription of King Kilamuwa from the second half of the ninth century BCE: "And I took . . . by the hand (תמכת . . . ליד)" (*KAI* 24:13), which is very similar to the expression here (see the following clause) and to Ps 63:9: "Your right hand supports me (בי תמכה)."

With My victorious right hand — For the root צדק, denoting victory and salvation, see v. 2. Compare also the similar image in Ps 20:7: "Now I know that the Lord will give victory to His anointed . . . with the mighty victories of His right hand (ימינו)." For the right hand as a symbol of strength and valor, see also Exod 15:6: "Your right hand, O Lord, glorious in power, Your right hand, O Lord, shatters the foe." The expression ימין צדקי, "My victorious right hand," occurs only here.

[11-12] Following the boost of morale and strength conferred by God upon His chosen people, the prophet delineates in four parallel stichs the devastation He will wreak upon Israel's enemies.

[11] *Frustrated and chagrined shall be all who contend with you* — For הַנֶּחֱרִים, "to contend," a *niph'al* participle from the root חרי, "to burn, be incensed against," see also 45:24. The pair of synonymous verbs (כלם/בוש) often appear in conjunction; cf., e.g., 45:16. God's enemies will be disillusioned and frustrated, but "those who trust in me shall not be disappointed (יֵבֹשׁוּ)" (49:23); see also 45:17; 50:7; 54:4. For the Akkadian etymological cognate *ba'āšu* (*CAD* B:5-6), see the promise conferred upon King Esarhaddon of Assyria by the goddess Ishtar: "Have no fear, my King! . . . I will not let you come to shame" (Parpola, *Assyrian Prophecies,* p. 7, 1.4.IV:2); and, similar to the verse here: "Those who hate (Assyria) have come to shame" (*CAD* B:5). For other instances of the adverb הן preceding conclusions based on prior arguments in the text, see vv. 24, 29.

They who strive with you shall become as naught and shall perish — For ריב, "strife, dispute, legal controversy," see Jer 15:10: "A man of conflict and strife (ריב)"; Job 31:35: "My accuser (ריבי)"; and for the verb ריב in a legal context, see 50:8: "My Vindicator is at hand. Who dares contend (יריב) with me?" The legal terminology in this stich refers back to the trial scene at the beginning of the chapter (v. 1) and is taken up again in vv. 21ff. The terms אַיִן and אֶפֶס, both expressing nonexistence (vv. 11, 12, 17, 24, 29), reiterate the utter insignificance of those who contend against Israel. For another example of the verbal pair חרי/ריב, see Gen 31:36.

[12] *You will look for those who struggle with you, but shall not find them* — The term מַצֻּתֶךָ (derived from מַצֻּת, a by-form of מַצָּה, from the root נצי, "to struggle," and for which it has been suggested to vocalize מַצָּתֶךָ; see Luzzatto; Ehrlich, *Randglossen,* 4:150) is polysemous, creating a Janus parallelism. On the one hand, it denotes strife, specifically legal strife, and thus is parallel to אנשי ריבך in the previous verse; see 58:4, where the two appear in conjunction: "Because you fast in strife and contention (לריב ומַצָּה)." On the other hand, it also refers to physical struggle and warfare; see Exod 2:13: "Two Hebrew men fighting (נִצִּים)," and thus is parallel to the following stich: "The men who battle with you (אנשי מלחמתך)." (See Paul, *Divrei Shalom,* 457-76,

477-83.) One should also note the wordplay between מצתך and תמצאם. In Akkadian as well, the very verbs denoting physical confrontations can also denote legal battles; cf., e.g., the expressions *bēl gēri* and *bēl ṣalti* ("adversary"), derivatives of the verbs *ṣâlu* and *gēru*, which, among other things, mean "to wage war, fight" (*CAD* G:63; Ṣ:88-89). The verbal pair מצא/בקש is very common; cf., e.g., Cant 3:1, 2.

As nothing and as naught shall be the men who battle against you — For the parallel pair אֶפֶס/אַיִן, see vv. 24, 29; 40:17; and for further examples of ריב (at the end of v. 11) and לחם in conjunction, see Ps 35:1: "O Lord, strive (ריבה) with my adversaries (יריבי)! Give battle (לְחַם) to my foes (לֹחֲמָי)!"

[13] *For I the Lord am your God, who grasps your right hand* — Israel should not fear its enemies since God is at their side actively helping them (see vv. 9, 10). This is in contrast to the idol worshipers, who have only one another to rely on: "Each one helps the other, saying to his fellow, 'Take courage' (חזק)!" (v. 6); "The woodworker encourages (ויחזק) the smith" (v. 7). God's "victorious right hand" (v. 10), which brings with it salvation, is now grasping Israel's right hand. His support of Cyrus is described in the same way: "Whom I grasped by his right hand" (45:1). For Akkadian parallels, see v. 9. Compare also the declaration of the Hittite king, Hattushili III: "Since my Lady, the goddess [= Arinna], held my hand and did not abandon me" (E. H. Sturtevant and G. Bechtel, *Hittite Chrestomathy* [Philadelphia, 1935], 65, line 21). For illustrations of gods grasping their chosen one's hand, see the references in 42:6. The introductory formula, "I the Lord am your God," also occurs in 43:3; 48:17; 51:15.

Who says to you: "Have no fear! I will be your help" — The prophet continues his morale-boosting message (see v. 10: "Fear not! . . . I help you"). God "says" (אמר) these words, which contrast with the idol craftsmen's statements (also introduced by the verb אמר): "Saying to his fellow 'Take courage!'" (v. 6); "He says of the soldering, 'It is good!'" (v. 7).

[14-16] More morale-inducing words to the Israelite community. This time the prophet borrows images from agriculture — images that emphasize the drastic change soon to occur in the life of the nation. God's people shall emerge from the depths of despair to a new reality in which they shall utterly defeat their enemies. This unit — connected to previous verses by the phrases: "Fear not (אל תירא)!" "I help you (אני עזרתיך)" (v. 14 and vv. 10, 13), and the parallel pair יעקב/ישראל — has a literary frame beginning (in v. 14) and ending (in v. 16) with the expression קדוש ישראל; see too the conclusion of the following unit (v. 20).

[14] *Fear not, O worm Jacob* — Israel, likened to a worm wallowing in exile, is commanded by God not to fear. For the worm as an image of a destitute and pitiful human being, see Ps 22:7: "But I am a worm (תולעת), not a man;

scorned by men, despised by people"; Job 25:6: "How much less man, a maggot, the son of man, a worm (תולעה)."

O men of Israel! — The term מְתִים, "men," which appears only in the plural (e.g., Deut 2:34; Isa 5:13, except for its occurrence in proper names: מְתוּשָׁאֵל, Gen 4:18; מְתוּשֶׁלַח, Gen 5:22), is also documented in Ugar. *mt* (*HdO* 2:598-99), and Akk. *mutu* (*CAD* M/2:316). The translation of Aquila, Theodotion, and the Vulgate: "the dead of Israel," was based incorrectly on the vocalization מֵתֵי (Isa 22:2; Ps 143:3), instead of MT מְתֵי. It has also been suggested to read רִמָּה ("maggot") for מתי, in light of the parallel תולעה/רמה in Isa 14:11; Job 25:6.

I will help you — declares the Lord — God addresses His downtrodden people and promises them His unwavering support. The verb plus the pronominal suffix, עזרתיך, is repeated here for the third time (see vv. 10, 13). This time the statement is "authenticated" by the formula נאם ה׳.

Your Redeemer — God, the deliverer, is preparing to redeem His chosen people from their captivity in Babylonia. This image, common to the prophecies of Deutero-Isaiah (43:1, 14; 44:6, 22, 23; 47:4; 48:17, 20; 49:7, 26; 51:10; 52:3, 9; 54:5, 8), is drawn from family law. If a destitute man sells his ancestral plot or himself to pay off a debt, his relatives are obliged to redeem him and his property (Lev 25:33-55). Furthermore, if a man is murdered in cold blood, his relatives are duty-bound to avenge him (Deut 19:6). Portraying God as a "redeemer" is also connected to the covenant between God and His people, which, in turn, was influenced by the clauses in treaties between kings in the ancient Near East. These pacts usually stipulate that the king (here God) must guard his vassals (here Israel) and aid them in times of need. (See the introduction, §9.)

The Holy One of Israel — This appellation is also frequent in the prophecies of Deutero-Isaiah and is usually found in the contexts of salvation/redemption (see vv. 16, 20). For its appearance along with the image of "redeemer" (in the prior clause), see 43:14; 47:4; 48:17; 49:7; 54:5. (See the introduction, §9.) The expression קדוש ישראל is another indication of the influence of First Isaiah on Deutero-Isaiah (see the introduction, §14). In Akkadian literature male and female deities are also referred to as *ellu/elētu,* "holy" (*CAD* E:105). Compare Ugar. *qdš,* "the Holy One," one of El's sobriquets (*HdO* 2:696); see 40:25.

[15] *I will make you a threshing board* — מוֹרַג is a threshing sledge harnessed to an ass or a bull, on whose lower board sharpened metal spikes or shards of flint were attached to shred the grain. (The tool is mentioned again in 2 Sam 24:22; 1 Chr 21:23.) For the verbal expression שׂים ל-, which signifies the alteration from one state into another, see v. 18; 42:15, 16; 60:15; and cf. the Akkadian semantic equivalent: *ana . . . šakānu* (*CAD* Š/1:148). The root שׂים reappears as a key root in vv. 18, 19, 20, 22.

A new thresher — Since חָרוּץ and מורג are synonymous terms (Isa 28:27;

Amos 1:3; Job 41:22) (cf. Akk. *ḫarāṣu,* "to cut a furrow"; *CAD* Ḫ:94), it is possible that a doublet was preserved in the text. If this is not the case, then חרוץ should probably be understood as an adjective meaning "sharp," and would then be the first in a series of three descriptive terms: חרוץ, חדש, and בעל פיפיות.

With many spikes — The poetic plural פיפיות ("spikes"), formed by doubling the singular פי/פה and adding the feminine plural suffix, is also used to describe a sharp sword (Judg 3:16; Ps 149:6; cf. Prov 5:4). The Akkadian etymological and semantic cognate *pû* also denotes the "blade of a dagger" (*CAD* P:470); cf. also the expression: לְפִי חרב (Josh 10:35; 1 Sam 22:19).

You shall thresh mountains to dust — The act of threshing involves stomping and pounding the ears of grain in order to extract the kernels. This agricultural imagery, "threshing grain," now becomes "threshing enemies like grain"; see Amos 1:3: "Because they threshed (דוּשָׁם) Gilead with threshing boards (בַּחֲרֻצוֹת) of iron"; Hab 3:12: "You trample (תדוש) nations in fury." This also holds true for the Akkadian semantic and etymological cognate *dāšu,* "to thresh," and metaphorically "to thresh one's enemies" (*CAD* D:121). For the verb תָּדֹק, from the root דקק, "to grind very finely, pulverize," see Exod 30:36; 32:20. These same two verbs, דקק and דוש, appear together also in Isa 28:28; Mic 4:3 (in a military context); Dan 7:23.

And make hills like chaff — מֹץ is the chaff from the outer layer of the kernel that falls away during the winnowing process and serves as an image for ephemera; cf., e.g., Ps 1:4: "They are like chaff that the wind blows away"; Ps 35:5: "Let them be as chaff in the wind." Compare also the expressions: כמץ הרים ("chaff on the hills"; Isa 17:13); וכמץ עֹבֵר ("and like flying chaff"; 29:5). For the parallel terms הרים/גבעות, see 40:4. One should also note the verse's literary frame, created by the root שׂים at the beginning and end of the verse.

[16] *You shall winnow them and the wind shall carry them off* — The agricultural imagery is further expanded to include the next stage in grain production. After the threshing comes the winnowing of the grain by means of "shovel and fan" (Isa 30:24), and the byproduct, chaff, then gets carried away in the wind; cf., e.g., Jer 49:36: "And I shall scatter them (וְזֵרִתִים) to all those winds"; Ezek 5:2: "And scatter (תִּזְרֶה) a third to the wind." Compare the Akkadian verbs *dāšu* and *zarû* ("to thresh" and "to winnow"), which denote the same consecutive stages of grain production (*CAD* Z:71).

The whirlwind shall scatter them — Finally a gale shall scatter Israel's enemies every which way; cf. Isa 40:24: "And the storm (וסערה) bears them off like straw." For similar imagery, cf. Jer 13:24: "So I will scatter them (ואפיצֵם) like straw that flies before the desert wind"; Ezek 36:19: "I scattered (ואפיץ) them among the nations, and they were dispersed through the countries"; Hos 13:3: "Like chaff whirled away (יְסֹעֵר) from the threshing floor." For the expression רוח סערה, a construct consisting of two synonyms (רוח appears in the previous clause), see Ezek 1:4; Ps 107:25. Note the series of sibilants in vv. 15-16: כמץ, תפיץ, סערה, תִּשָּׂאֵם, תְּזָרֵם, תשׂים.

Then you shall rejoice in the Lord — As a result of the dispersal of your enemies, you, Israel, shall rejoice; see Isa 61:10: "I greatly rejoice (תָּגֵל) in the Lord"; Ps 35:9: "Then shall I rejoice (תגיל) in the Lord."

And exult in the Holy One of Israel — This hemistich is chiastically parallel to the former one. The expression התהלל ב- is commonly understood to mean "to praise, boast, glory in"; see Isa 45:25: "It is through the Lord that all the offspring of Israel have vindication and glory (בה׳ יצדקו ויתהללו)." In light of the similar parallelism in Ps 63:12, where שׂמח ב- is paired with התהלל ב-, "But the king shall rejoice in God. All who swear by Him shall exult" (see too Ps 34:3; 64:11; 105:3; 106:5), however, some have suggested that in these contexts the meaning is "to rejoice, be jubilant" (see Y. Ibn Ganaḥ, *Sefer ha-Shorashim* [Jerusalem, 1966], 119 [Heb.]). For the sobriquet קדוש ישראל and the chiastic frame of this unit, see the introduction to the pericope; and cf. v. 20, where קדוש ישראל concludes the following literary unit as well.

[17-20] The complete reversal of the people's fortunes — from a forlorn exile to a joyous present and future in Jerusalem — is portrayed as the quenching of a desperate thirst in a dry land and as the planting of a large variety of trees in the desert (see also 43:20; 49:10). God will quench parched tongues in the Syrian Desert between Babylonia and Israel, just as He did for the nation's forefathers in the Sinai Desert. For a desert journey replete with miracles, see 40:3-4; 42:15-16; 43:19-20; 49:9-11. The root בקשׁ and the substantive אין (v. 17) link this unit with the previous one (vv. 11, 12). For the influence of the exodus motif and the miracles in the desert on Deutero-Isaiah's prophecies, see B. W. Anderson, "Exodus Typology in Second Isaiah," in B. W. Anderson and W. Harrelson, eds., *Israel's Prophetic Heritage: Essays in Honor of James Muilenberg* (New York, 1963), 177-95; idem, "Exodus and Covenant in Second Isaiah and Prophetic Tradition," in F. M. Cross, W. E. Lemke, and P. D. Miller Jr., eds., *Magnalia Dei: The Mighty Acts of God: Essays on the Bible and Archaeology in Memory of G. Ernest Wright* (Garden City, N.Y., 1976), 339-60.

[17] *The afflicted and the needy seek water, but there is none* — The utterly destitute refugees march across the Syrian Desert on their way to Israel and seek water to quench their desperate thirst. For other instances of the Israelites described as עֲנִיִּים, see 49:13; 51:21; 54:11; 66:2. For the parallel terms עניים/אביונים in contexts of lamentation, see Ps 40:18; 86:1; 109:16. The juxtaposition of מַיִם and אַיִן creates a rhyme. For other examples, see Isa 40:4: כל גֶּיא יִנָּשֵׂא; 40:12: מַיִם וְשָׁמַיִם. Note also the series of four consecutive words ending in ־ִים. For אין מים, see also Deut 8:15.

Their tongue is parched with thirst — The root נשׁת (found only twice more, in Isa 19:5; Jer 51:30) means "to be dry, parched." For a similar image, see

Lam 4:4: "The tongue of the suckling cleaves to its palate for thirst." The penultimate accent on נָשָׁתָּה is due to its being the final word in the clause and having a pausal ending. For the substantive צָמָא, "thirst," see also Isa 50:2.

I the Lord will respond to them — I, the Lord God, will provide for them in their time of need. The Deity is always ready to "answer" Israel's need; cf., e.g., 58:9: "Then when you call, the Lord will answer. When you cry, He will say: 'Here I am'"; 65:24: "Before they pray, I will answer." For the pair of verbs ענ׳ and עזר (in the following hemistich), see 49:8: "In an hour of favor I answered you (עניתיך), and on a day of salvation I helped you (עזרתיך)." God's willingness and propensity to help are contrasted to the idols, which are incapable of responding to the desperate cries of their worshipers: "If they cry out to it, it does not answer. It cannot save them from their distress" (46:7). The verb אֶעֱנֵם creates a wordplay with the beginning of the verse — העניים. For further examples of אני ה׳, see, e.g., v. 4, 42:6; 43:10; 45:8.

I the God of Israel will not forsake them — I shall not abandon them nor ever cease from aiding them; cf. 42:16: "These are the promises — I will keep them without fail (ולא עזבתים)." For the literary device of a positive expression followed by the same idea couched in the negative, see v. 9, and also note the assonance: אֶעֱ[נֵ]ם . . . אֶעֱ[זְ]בֵם.

[18-19] These verses elaborate on God's general promise by specifying the miracles He will perform in the desert.

[18] *I will open up streams on the bare heights/sand dunes* — The miracle of water in the desert: God will open up streams on the dry sand dunes in the desert. (The Akkadian verb *petû* appears in similar contexts of the "opening up" of rivers, canals, streams, and springs; *CAD* P:346-47.) Compare also 43:20: "For I provide water in the wilderness, rivers in the desert." The term שְׁפָיִים occurs once more in 49:9 and six times in Jeremiah (3:2, 21; 4:11; 7:29; 12:12; 14:6), several of which are in the context of the desert or wilderness. Here it serves as the antonym of "valleys," and thus is understood to denote "hills/heights" by most of the ancient translations and medieval commentators. The word also appears in the Ugaritic poem, "The Birth of the Beautiful and Pleasant Gods," in the context of the desert: *bmdbr špm,* "in the desert, on the heights/dunes" (*CAT* 1.23:4).

And fountains amid the valleys — I shall cause water sources to spring forth in the desert valleys.

I will turn the desert into pools — I will turn the desert into a reservoir of spring water; see Ps 107:35: "He turns the wilderness into pools, parched land into springs of water." (This verse in Psalms left its impression on the prophet, since he brings an additional excerpt from the same psalm [v. 16] in 45:2; see below, and the introduction, §17.) For the verbal expression שׂים ל-, which denotes transformation, see v. 15; and for a similar image with the verb הפך, see Ps

114:8: “Who turned the rock into a pool of water.” The two verbs are synonymous in Aramaic as well; see the Sefire inscription, I C: 19-20: “I shall upset (אהפך) the relations, and turn (ואשם) (them) [to evil]” (J. A. Fitzmyer, *The Aramaic Inscriptions of Sefîre,* BibOr 19 [Rome, 1967], 20). (The verb שׂים appears twice more in this chapter, in vv. 19, 20.) For further instances of the lush desert motif, see 43:20: “For I provide water in the wilderness, rivers in the desert to give drink to My chosen people”; 48:21: “They have known no thirst, though He led them through parched places. He made water flow for them from the rock”; 49:10: “They shall not hunger or thirst . . . He will guide them to springs of water.” These images are influenced by the descriptions of the desert wandering following the Israelite exodus from Egypt (see the introduction, §12). For the opposite motif, see 42:15.

And the arid land into springs of water — For the expression מוצא(י) מים, see 58:11; 2 Kgs 2:21; and Ps 107:35, quoted in the commentary to the previous hemistich. For similar images see Ps 114:8: “Who turned the rock into a pool of water, the flinty rock into a fountain.” צִיָּה and ארץ צִיָּה (“arid land”) are poetic terms for the desert; see Isa 35:1: “The arid desert shall be glad, the wilderness shall rejoice”; Hos 2:5: “And I will make her like a wilderness, render her like desert land.” Take note of the repetitive sibilant צ in the first three words of this clause.

[19] Deutero-Isaiah has a penchant for referring to a variety of trees. No less than seven types of trees are named here (though not all can be identified with certainty), trees that will transform the wilderness into a lush forest and provide shade for the emancipated on their journey to Israel. For another description of the transformation of the desert into a verdant garden, see Isa 55:13.

I will plant in the wilderness . . . I will set in the desert — For the pair ערבה and מדבר, see Jer 2:6: “Who led us through the wilderness (במדבר), a land of desert (ערבה) and pits, a land of drought (צִיָּה) and darkness”; note that the term ציה is also found here, as in the previous clause. For the verbs נתן and שׂים in parallelism, see Isa 43:19-20; 61:3.

Cedars — The reference is to the Lebanese cedar *(Cedrus lebani),* mentioned again in 44:14 as one of the trees whose wood is used in the construction of idols and also referred to as the “majesty of Lebanon” (60:13). It is described in ample detail in Ezek 31:3-7.

Acacias — The name of the tree is of Egyptian derivation: *šnḏt,* and is a loanword in Akkadian: *šamṭu* (*CAD* Š/1:339), and in Arabic: *sanṭ.* This tree is common to Israel and the Sinai Desert.

And myrtles — *Myrtus communis,* which grows in the wild on the Carmel, in the Upper Galilean mountains, and adjacent to the streams and springs in the Golan, is a ground-hugging fragrant bush with triangular leaves.

And oleasters — This tree, *Elaeagnus hortensis,* is usually identified with the Jerusalem pine or the silver oleaster. In the days of Nehemiah its leaves and olive branches were used as roofs of the holiday tabernacles (Neh 8:15). In 1 Kgs 6 the two cherubs in the inner sanctum (v. 23), the two doors (v. 32), and the doorposts of the "great hall" (v. 33) were all constructed with the wood of the oleaster. The three following trees appear together also in Isa 60:13 along with the cedar.

Junipers — This tree, *Juniperus oxycedrus,* is common to Lebanon and was used in the construction and decoration of the First Temple (see 1 Kgs 5:22, 24; 6:15, 34; 9:11), as its Akkadian etymological and semantic cognate, *burāšu,* was used in the building of palaces and temples in Mesopotamia (*CAD* B:326-27).

Box trees — In spite of the different opinions as to its exact identification ("box," "juniper"), this is one of two trees (see immediately following) frequently mentioned in Mesopotamian royal inscriptions together with the "juniper" *(burāšu)* in connection with construction projects. The first is Akk. *duprānu* (*CAD* D:189-90), Ugar. *dprn* (*HdO* 1:277), a variety of the juniper, *Juniperus drupacea.* (See Paul, *Divrei Shalom,* 16-17.)

And cypresses — In light of the above, this tree should be identified with the other Mesopotamian tree, *šurmēnu* (*CAD* Š/3:349-53), which appears together with the previous two, *Cyperus sempervirens* (cf. Talmudic שׁוּרְבִּינָא [*b. Rosh Hash.* 23a; *B. Bat.* 80b]; Saadyah Gaon's translation into Judeo-Arabic, *'lšrbyn;* Syr. *šrwwyn', šrbyn*), and Ugar. *tišr* (*HdO* 2:855-56). This tree is mentioned once again, in Ezek 27:6, in a description of a Tyrian ship. The MT, however, erroneously divided the term there into two separate words. It grows in the Lebanese foothills, in the Bashan, and in the mountains of Cyprus. (See Paul, *Divrei Shalom,* 15-17.)

As well — יחדו is often used as a concluding stamp following a series of substantives or verbs, and signifies "all together, as one"; see vv. 20, 23; 45:21.

[20] The prophet explains the purpose of all the desert miracles in two verbal couplets.

That men may see and know, take note and discern — יָשִׂימוּ is elliptical for ישימו לב ("consider"); see v. 22. Either due to this unusual shortened form, or perhaps influenced by 44:18, where the verbal root בין follows ידע, 1QIsa[a] has the variant reading ויבינו. However, the scribe subsequently corrected this by writing וישימו above the line, and then recanted and added a dot before and after the word to indicate erasure. The verb יַשְׂכִּיל appears in 44:18, also in conjunction with other verbs of comprehension: "They neither know nor understand . . . their minds cannot discern (מֵהַשְׂכִּיל)." For another example of the combination of these last two verbs, see Neh 8:8: וְשׂוֹם שֶׂכֶל. As opposed to the Masoretic division, one should combine these two verbs instead of separating them. Just as in the previous verse, יַחְדָּו functions as the concluding signature of a series, this time a verbal one.

That the Lord's hand has done this — They will then realize that it was God who brought about all these miracles; see also Isa 66:2: "All this was made by My hand"; Ps 109:27: "That men may know that it is Your hand, that You, O Lord, have done it"; Job 12:9: "Who among all these does not know that the hand of the Lord has done this?" The expression, יד ה׳, "the Lord's hand," symbolizes God's power and is very frequent in Deutero-Isaiah's prophecies; see, e.g., Isa 40:2; 43:13; 48:13; 49:2.

That the Holy One of Israel has wrought it — For other examples of the parallel couplet ברא/עשׂה, see 43:7; 45:7, 18. The sobriquet קדוש ישראל is frequent in Deutero-Isaiah's prophecies more than in any other biblical composition (e.g., vv. 14, 16; 43:3, 14; 45:11; 47:4) and functions as the conclusion of the literary unit, as above (v. 16).

[21-29] The final literary unit of this chapter shares with the introductory unit the trial motif, as well as the idea that Cyrus was summoned by God to perform His master plan, thereby creating a literary frame for the entire chapter. The two units share much common phraseology: יִגְּשׁוּ (v. 1) — הגישו (v. 21), יגישו (v. 22); מי (vv. 2, 4, 26); קרב (vv. 1, 5, 21); העיר ממזרח (v. 2) — העירותי ממזרח (שמש) (v. 25); קרא (vv. 2, 4, 25); צדק (vv. 2, 26); נתן (vv. 2, 27); פעל (vv. 4, 24); מרֹאש ... רִאשון (v. 4) — הרִאשֹׁנוֹת (v. 22), רִאשון (v. 27); אתי (vv. 5, 23, 25). In this final unit, however, instead of subpoenaing the idolatrous nations, God invites these nations' gods to a free-for-all legal battle to determine which of them is responsible for both the earlier determining events in history (הרִאשֹׁנוֹת), i.e., the emergence of Cyrus and the destruction of Babylon, and the latter (הָאֹתִיּוֹת/הַבָּאוֹת), i.e., the Israelite liberation from exile and return to Israel. Verses 21-29 constitute a two-part unit. In vv. 21-24 — the first scene — God challenges the pagan deities to submit their case and thus prove that they are authentic. Their inability to have recalled past events or predicted future ones, and their silence prove that these gods are nonentities. In vv. 25-29 — the second scene — God presents His case: the Holy One of Israel is the one who summoned Cyrus and made him victorious, so that His plan for the nations of the world would come to pass. To this the gods do not and cannot respond. The verbal root נגד is repeated five times throughout this unit as a sort of mantra: in v. 22 (twice), in v. 23, and in v. 26 (twice). Verses 22-24 also form a symmetry with vv. 26 and 29: הגיד ... ונדעה ... הן ... אָוֶן — הגידו ... ונדעה ... הן ... מֵאַיִן ... מֵאָפַע, and both sections conclude with the exclamatory הן (vv. 24, 29), followed by the conclusion that all gods are null and void. Only the God of Israel is in control. He alone determines the fate of the nations, predicts events, and then brings them to pass.

[21] *"Submit your case!" says the Lord* — קָרְבוּ (second-person masculine *piʿel* imperative; see vv. 1, 5, in the *qal*), like its Akkadian cognate, *qerēbu* (*CAD* Q:239), has legal connotations (see also Num 27:5; Deut 1:17). The term

ריב is also part of the juristic jargon; see Deut 25:1: "When there is a dispute (ריב) between men, and they go to law, and a decision is rendered"; Jer 11:20: "O Lord of Hosts, O just judge . . . for I have committed my case (ריבי) to You"; cf. also v. 11. In order to prove their existence, the gods must bring forth concrete evidence of their ability to foretell the future accurately.

"Bring forward your plea!" — For the only other example of the rare substantive עֲצֻמָה, see Prov 18:18: "Casting the lot puts an end to strife, and separates those locked in dispute (עצומים)." The root עצם is also documented in Rabbinic Hebrew in a similar context; see *b. Sanh.* 31b: "Two partners locked in legal dispute (שנתעצמו)"; cf. Syr. *ʿṣm,* which also denotes strife and contention. For further examples of the verb נגש in legal contexts, see vv. 1, 22; 45:20, 21.

Says the King of Jacob — a unique expression. For other examples of God as King, see 43:15: "Your King, the Creator of Israel"; 44:6: "Thus said the Lord, the King of Israel"; cf. 52:7: "Telling Zion, 'Your God is King'!" This sobriquet may have been chosen here because of the present legal context, since one of the king's duties in the ancient Near East was to arbitrate in legal disputes; cf. 2 Sam 15:2: "And whenever a man had a case that was to come before the king for judgment." (See the introduction, §9.)

[22] The gods are asked to prove their ability to predict the future.

Let them approach and tell us — This clause repeats the previous verse's summons (הגישו/יגישו), and then goes on to explain what the gods must prove. The vocalization of the verb (יַגִּישׁוּ) as a *hiphʿil* was perhaps influenced by v. 21, הגישו, and the following verb יגידו, also in the *hiphʿil;* note the rhyming syllables, יַגִּ, common to the two verbs. Alternatively, one may vocalize יִגְּשׁוּ in the *qal* (cf. LXX, Peshitta, Vulgate, and Targum, יִתְקָרְבוּן), which refers to "approaching the bench"; see 50:8: "Who would be my opponent? Let him approach (יִגַּשׁ) me!"; cf. Exod 24:14. For the same root in the *niphʿal,* see Deut 25:1; and in the *hithpaʿel,* 45:20. The verb נגד in the *hiphʿil* functions here as a derisive refrain. It is repeated twice in this verse, and then once again in vv. 23 and 26, emphasizing and reiterating that the pagan gods have no ability to predict or influence future events. For the two verbs in conjunction, see 45:21.

What will happen — future events.

Or announce to us what has occurred! — Or tell us what has happened (הָרִאשֹׁנוֹת), i.e., the past events up to and including the ascension of Cyrus and the destruction of Babylon. For הֵנָּה, the third-person feminine plural pronoun, see also Gen 21:29.

Tell us and we will take note of it — Provide definite proof of an accurate prediction and it will be taken note of as evidence of your genuineness. The lengthened imperfect verbal forms, נשימה and ונדעה (directly following), express the cohortative.

That we may know their outcome — This phrase should be shifted to the end of the next hemistich: or announce to us what will occur, that we may know their outcome. If you are unable to provide evidence of accurate prediction of past events, then "announce to us what will occur (הַבָּאוֹת)," so that when they come to pass we will have definite proof of your existence; see v. 23: "Foretell what is yet to happen." For another instance of אחרית, see 46:10: "I foretell the end (אחרית) from the beginning." (1QIsa[a] אחרונות was likely influenced by the antonym רִאשֹׁנות, directly above.) The terms הָרִאשֹׁנות, "what has occurred," and הבאות, "what will occur," which appear in conjunction here, are together all-inclusive, i.e., they denote every event, past, present, and future. God describes himself in similar terms, e.g., "I am the first (רִאשון) and I am the last (אחרון)" (44:6); see also 48:12. This is also an allusion to Deutero-Isaiah's ongoing polemic against the Mesopotamian gods, who, according to the Assyrians, also were omniscient, e.g., "You [the god Ashur] know (everything) from beginning *(maḫrâti)* to end *(arkâti)*"; "I [the god] Nabu (am able) to announce (both) the past and the future" (*CAD* A/2:282).

[23] *Foretell what is yet to happen* — foretell future events. The prophet continues his cutting diatribe with a third repetition of the verb הִגידו. The word הָאֹתִיּוֹת (from the Aramaic root אתי, a feminine plural participle; for similar forms cf. הומיה, צופיה, בוכיה) is the equivalent of Heb. הבאות (v. 22); cf. 44:7, where both roots appear together. (For the Aramaic influence on Deutero-Isaiah, see the introduction, §11.) The word לְאָחוֹר denotes "the future" (see 42:23) and serves as an alternate term for אחריתן in v. 22.

That we may know that you are gods! — And thus we shall "know" (נדעה, another cohortative, repeated from the previous verse) that you are truly gods! Cf. Ps 82:6: "I thought you were gods (אלהים)."

Do anything, good or bad — אף is an emphatic conjunction (see v. 10; 40:24). The prophet inserts words of mockery and demands that they, the gods, do anything at all to prove their existence, since knowledge of both good and bad is a trait of divine beings (Gen 3:5). For the verbal merism תיטיבו ותָרֵעוּ cf. Lev 5:4: "Or when a person utters an oath to a bad (לְהָרַע) or good purpose (להיטיב)" (i.e., any oath); Zeph 1:12: "Who say to themselves, 'The Lord will do nothing, good (יֵיטִיב) or bad (יָרֵעַ)'"; and in a similar context pertaining to the construction of idols, Jer 10:5: "For they can do no harm (יָרֵעוּ); nor is it in them to do any good (היטיב)."

That we may be totally awed and afraid! — The prophet derides them: If indeed you succeed in doing something, anything, we will be totally awestruck. For the verb שתע ("to be awed"), see v. 10; the form here, נִשְׁתָּעָה, is an imperfect cohortative *qal* with a pausal ending. Both the Ketib (ונרא) and the Qere (ונראה) of the second verb derive from the root ראי ("to see"), and thus the scribe at Qumran (1QIsa[a]) "corrected" the previous verb and substituted ונשמעה ("to hear"). One should, however, vocalize וְנִרָא, from the root ירא ("to fear"), which is synonymous with שׁתע, similar to v. 10: "Fear not (תירא) . . . Be not frightened (תשתע)!" Once again, יַחְדָּו concludes a series of verbs; see v. 20.

[24] The prophet's scathing polemic now reaches its apogee.

Behold, you are nothing — הן serves as a prelude to the conclusion of the prophet's derisive remarks (see vv. 11 and 29). Since the gods do not answer the prophet, thus proving their impotence and their inability to predict what is to come, the obvious conclusion is that they are less than nothing; in other words, they are nonexistent. One must consider, however, the possibility of a dittographic error, i.e., the doubling of the *mem* from the last letter of the previous word, ם(את), and read, אַיִן, "nothing," instead of מֵאַיִן; cf. vv. 11, 12; 40:17.

And your works are nullity! — Your deeds amount to nothing (for פעל, see 45:9, 11). This phrase is diametrically opposed to the God of Israel, who is described as having "wrought and achieved" (מי פעל ועשה). מֵאָפַע is a hapax legomenon, the meaning of which may be deduced from the parallel term אַיִן. It too is most likely a result of dittography, the doubling of the *mem* from the last letter of the previous word, and the repetition of the *peh* and *ʿayin* of פָּעָלְכֶם. One must note, however, that the word was incorporated into later Hebrew as אפעה, in the *Hodayot Scroll* from Qumran, alongside other words for "wickedness" (1QH[a] 10:30; see also 11:13, 18, 19. (See H. Stegemann, E. Schuller, and C. Newsom, *Qumran Cave 1.III: 1QHodayot*[a], DJD 40 [Oxford, 2009], 133, 144-45.) For the parallel pair אַיִן/אפס (here too some commentators correct אפע to אפס), characteristic of the prophet's derisive attitudes toward the idolatrous nations, see vv. 12, 29; 40:17; 45:14.

One who chooses you is an abomination — Whoever "chooses" you is as abominable as you, contrary to Israel, whom God "chose" from the far corners of the universe (vv. 8-9). For תועבה as a derisive reference to idols, see 44:19: "And the rest of it I will make an abomination (לתועבה)"; Ezek 7:20: "They made their images and their detestable abominations (תועבֹתם)."

[25-29] The chapter ends in the same way it began: with allusions to Cyrus, who was anointed by God to perform His will (vv. 2-3). This historical fact is God's ultimate proof in His trial against the idols. He alone was responsible for Cyrus's ascension and victories. Since they did not predict Cyrus's triumphant arrival on the world stage and were of no help to him, it follows that they are all nullity. Cyrus is presented as God's servant in the first verses of Ezra: "The Lord roused the spirit of King Cyrus of Persia. . . . Thus said King Cyrus of Persia: 'The Lord God of Heaven has given me all the kingdoms of the earth and has charged me with building Him a house in Jerusalem, which is in Judah'" (Ezra 1:1-2). A similar ideology — against which the prophet is polemicizing — is found in Mesopotamian sources. In the Cyrus Cylinder, a Babylonian inscription describing Babylon's downfall, Cyrus, the king of Persia, attributes his success to the head of the Babylonian pantheon, Marduk: "He

[Marduk] surveyed and looked throughout all the lands, searching for a righteous king whom he would support. He called out his name: 'Cyrus, king of Anshan.' He pronounced his name to be king . . . I am Cyrus, king of the world, great king, mighty king, king of Babylon, king of Sumer and Akkad, king of the four quarters . . . whose rule Bel (i.e., Marduk) and Nabu [Marduk's son] love, whose kingship they deserve for their hearts' pleasure. . . . Marduk, the great lord, rejoiced over my [good] deeds. He sent gracious blessings upon me, Cyrus, the king, who worships him" (M. Cogan, *COS* 2:315; see also the introduction, excursus B). In yet another Babylonian inscription, Cyrus is described as the moon god Sin's messenger: "Sin, the light of heaven and earth, has granted me in an auspicious sign (sovereignty) . . . over the four corners of the earth." (See H. Tadmor, "The Historical Background of Cyrus' Declaration," in Y. Kaufmann et al., eds., *Oz Le-David: Dedicated to David Ben Gurion on His Seventy-seventh Birthday* [Jerusalem, 1964], 470 [Heb.]). The final section of this chapter is connected to the unit immediately preceding it by many linguistic connections: the roots **אתי** (vv. 23, 25), **בוא** (vv. 22, 25), **נגד** (in the *hiphʿil*, vv. 22, 23, 26), **שמע** (vv. 22, 26), **ראש** (vv. 22, 26, 27), **אָוֶן/אַיִן** (vv. 24, 29), **אפס** (**אפע**, vv. 24, 29; cf. also **וּפָעָלְכֶם** [v. 24] and **מעשיהם** [v. 29], both referring to the "works" of the idols).

[25] *I have roused him from the north, and he has come* — I was the one who selected and designated Cyrus (see v. 2; 45:13). Cyrus reached Babylon after conquering both Media and its king, Astyages, in 550 BCE, and Croesus, king of Lydia in Asia Minor, north of Babylonia, in 547 BCE. One should also note that, according to Jeremiah, there was a tradition whereby Babylon's nemesis would rise from the north (see Jer 50:3, 9, 41; 51:48). For the *hiphʿil* of the verb **עור**, "to rouse, stir up," in this and similar contexts, see v. 2; Jer 50:9; 51, 1, 11. The word **וַיַּאת**, from the root **אתי**, is an apocopated imperfect for **וַיֶּאֱתֶה**.

From the east, one who invokes My name — literally "from the sunrise." Persia and Media are east of Babylonia. See v. 2: "Who has roused a victor from the east?" He who "invokes" God's name is His faithful servant, e.g., Gen 4:26: "It was then that men began to invoke the Lord by name (**לקרא בשם**)" (i.e., it was then that men began to worship the Lord). 1QIsa[a] has **ויקרא בשמו** ("And He invoked his name"), i.e., God designated Cyrus to be His loyal messenger; see Isa 45:3: "So that you know that it is I the Lord, the God of Israel, who call you by name." Compare the interdialectal Akkadian equivalent, *šumam nabû*, "to invoke (a deity)" (*CAD* N/1:35).

And he has trampled rulers like mud — One should redivide the letters of the first two words and read: **וַיָּבֹס סגנים**. The error could have occurred scribally by haplography, in which one of the two consecutive *samek*s was deleted; or it could have been an aural error, whereby the reader did not pause between the two words, and one *samek* was elided into the other and thus miscopied by the scribe. Another reason, perhaps, for this error is the presence of the Aramaic verb ויאת at the beginning of the verse, which may have caused the scribe to write its Hebrew parallel, ויבא, in this hemistich. Cyrus is described as having trampled the kings he opposed like "mud" (חֹמֶר). For this term, which refers to "cement, mortar, clay," used for holding building stones together and as the material for manufacturing vessels, see 45:9; 64:7; Nah 3:14. For the verb בוס, "to tread down, trample," see Isa 63:6: "I trampled (ואבוס) people in My anger"; 63:18: "Our foes have trampled (בוססו) Your sanctuary"; and cf. the parallel image in 63:3: "I trod them down in My anger, trampled them in My rage." (For pictures of enemies trampled by the chariots of the Egyptian ruler, see *ANEP*, nos. 315, 345.) The Akkadian loanword סְגָנִים, which denotes prefects, military commanders, and other high officials (*CAD* Š/1:180ff.), is found only in the plural and only in exilic and postexilic works (Jer 51:23, 57, in reference to Babylon; Jer 51:28 — Media; Ezek 23:6 — Assyria; Ezra 9:2; Neh 2:16 — Israel), which is evidence that it entered into Hebrew only at a late date. (See the introduction, §11.) It is also found in a variant form in Isa 22:15 (סוכן); in Ugaritic, *s/škm* (*HdO* 2:757-59); in Phoenician, in Ahiram's inscription (*KAI* 1:2); and in an Aramaic inscription from Tel Ḥama (*KAI* 203:1).

Like a potter treading clay — For טִיט, an Akkadian loanword *(ṭīṭu)*, see also Nah 3:14: "Tread the clay (טיט)! Trample (רמסי) the mud (חֹמֶר)!" This graphic description of enemy subjugation is reminiscent of v. 2 here and 63:3.

[26] This verse is a rhetorical-polemical question (see vv. 2, 4) followed by a derisive answer that highlights the idols' impotence by the threefold repetition of אף אין ("not one"; cf. 40:24, the sequence of three clauses, each beginning with אף בל; on sequences of three, see the introduction, §10). For other rhetorical questions followed by a triad of answers, see 42:24; 45:21.

Who foretold this from the start, that we may note it — Who from among the pagan gods foretold Cyrus's ascension and his conquests, before they actually happened? For מראש ("from the beginning"), see v. 4; 40:21.

From aforetime, that we might say, "He is right"? — Which god was able to predict beforehand the triumphs of Cyrus? If there is such a one, we will readily admit, "He is right." For צדיק with legal connotations, see Deut 25:1; and for the verb, see 43:9. מִלְּפָנִים is a hapax legomenon, a by-form of the more common לפנים, "formerly"; see 1 Sam 9:9: "For the prophet of today was formerly (לפנים) called a seer."

Not one foretold, not one announced — Not one of them prophesied, or, for that matter, said anything at all. For the same two verbs in a similar context, see v. 22.

Not one has heard your utterance — For the use of the term אִמְרֵיכֶם (the plural of אֹמֶר) in another dispute, see Job 32:14: "Nor shall I use your reasons (ובאמריכם) to reply to Him." For the same sequence of verbs in a legal context, see 43:9: "Who among them declared this, foretold to us the things that have happened? Let them produce their witnesses and be vindicated, that men, hearing them, may say, 'It is true!'" In Akkadian the nouns *amatu* and *dibbu*, both meaning "word" (similar to **אמריכם** here), are also employed in legal contexts, especially in conjunction with the verb *šemû* (= **שמע** here) (*CAD* A/2:38-39; D:133-34; Š/2:282-83).

[27] *The things once predicted to Zion, behold, here they are!* — a difficult clause. Some exegetes explain that **רִאשׁוֹן** refers to God (see v. 4; 44:6; 48:12) and thus translate: "I, God, was the first to tell Zion what was to happen, and behold it is happening now." Others suggest that **רִאשׁוֹן** is short for **הָרִאשֹׁנוֹת**, "former events," i.e., "The things [I] once predicted" are now occurring. Yet others accept the reading of 1QIsa[a]: **הנומה** (from the root **נום**), rather than MT **הִנֵּם**, which in Rabbinic Hebrew means "to speak" (e.g., *t. Ohal.* 4:14; *m. Yebam.* 16:7) and explain **הַנּוֹמֶה** as parallel to **מְבַשֵּׂר** in the second stich: "God was the first speaker to proclaim to Zion what would come to pass." The common denominator of the above explanations is that it is God alone, and not the deaf and dumb idols, who proclaims future events. God is thereby vindicated and the pagan gods are found guilty of impotence. Note, however, Luzzatto's alternative explanation: "The phrase's last hemistich must be read before the first hemistich: I will send first a herald to Jerusalem, who will say, 'Behold, here they are.'" **ראשון** is a forerunner who arrives in Zion before the returning exiles and proclaims, 'Here are your children, they are coming now.'" It is possible that **הנה** functions here as the introduction to the proclamation; see 40:9: "Behold (**הנה**) your God!" The final syllables of the expression **ראשון לציון** rhyme.

And for Jerusalem I am providing a herald — For heralds, see 40:9; 52:7; 61:1 (in which the prophet himself functions as the herald).

[28] *But I looked and there is no one* — But (the *waw* denotes contrast) when I looked (**וְאֵרֶא** should be vocalized **וָאֵרֶא**, past tense; cf. Vulgate, Peshitta, and 1QIsa[a]: **ואראה**) among the pagan gods, I saw that there was none among them who was able to debate with Me. For the expression **אין איש**, see 50:2; 57:1; 59:16.

Not one of them is an advocate — Not one of them can advocate on their behalf or speak in their defense. For the root **יעץ** in legal contexts, see 45:21: "Speak up, present your case! Let them even take counsel (**יִוָּעֲצוּ**) together!" For the connection between this verb and the verbal expression **השיב דבר** in the following hemistich, see 1 Kgs 12:6: "What answer do you advise [me] (**נועצים להשיב . . . דבר**) to give this people?" The negative **אין** is repeated here for the sake of emphasis.

Nor can any respond when I question them — The negative **אין** from the preceding clause is assumed here as well: Not one of them can respond when I ask: "Who among you foretold this from the start?" (v. 26). For **שאל** denoting legal inquiry or interrogation, see Deut 13:15: "You shall investigate and inquire and interrogate (ושאלת) thoroughly." The Akkadian semantic and etymological equivalent, *šâlu,* also signifies legal investigation by judges (*CAD* Š/1:276-77). The expression דבר להשיב ("to respond") is pan-Semitic, e.g., Aram. התב פתגם (Ezra 5:11), Akk. *awatum turru* (*CAD* T:271), Ugar. *ṯb rgm* (*HdO* 2:734).

[29] *See, they are all nothingness. Their works are nullity* — הן introduces the logical conclusion based on the gods' lack of response (see v. 24). Some exegetes understand אָוֶן as a derogatory term for idols; cf. 66:3; Hos 10:8; Amos 5:5. In light of the parallel pair אין/אפס (see v. 12), however, the LXX's reading אַיִן is preferable (cf. 1QIsa[a] and Targum, לְמָא, "naught"). This phrase repeats the same idea as found in v. 24. For the term מעשיהם in connection with idol worship, see also Ezek 6:6: "Thus your altars shall be laid waste and bear their punishment. Your fetishes shall be smashed and annihilated. Your incense stands cut down, and your handiworks (מעשיכם) wiped out."

Their effigies are naught and nil — Their idols have no substance; they are in essence nothing. רוח ותֹהו ("naught and nil") are parallel to אָוֶן ואפס of the previous hemistich. For רוח, "wind, naught," see Jer 5:13: "The prophets shall prove mere wind (לרוח)"; Eccl 1:14: "And I found all is futile and a pursuit of wind (רוח)." (Cf. Akk. *šāru,* "wind," which can also signify nullity and nothingness [*CAD* Š/2:139].) For תֹּהו ("emptiness, nothingness"), see Isa 40:17; 44:9, also referring to idols. For נֶסֶךְ ("a molten image"), see, e.g., 48:5: "That you might not say, 'My idol caused them. My carved and molten images (וְנִסְכִּי) ordained them'"; Jer 10:14: "Every goldsmith is put to shame because of his idol, for his molten image (נִסְכּוֹ) is deceit." It is also found in a Neo-Punic inscription from the first century CE: "The idol (הנסכת) of the god Augustus" (*KAI* 122:1). The term may also have a double entendre here in light of Isa 30:1: "Making plans against My wishes, weaving schemes (לִנְסֹךְ מַסֵּכָה) against My will." In that case, נִסְכֵּיהֶם would be parallel to מעשיהם in the preceding clause: "Their schemes are naught and nil."

Chapter 42

[1-9] The first Servant Song. For the history of exegesis, as well as the varying opinions regarding the servant's identity, see the introduction, §5. The servant (= the Israelite nation) is portrayed here as God's chosen one (cf., e.g., 41:8, 9; 42:19; 44:1, 21), upon whom God has conferred His spirit. Although his plight is great, he will yet fulfill a twofold mission: national, to be a covenant people, and universal, to be a light to the nations. This prophecy is connected to the last literary unit of chap. 41 by a plethora of similar expressions and words: ראשון . . . הנה הִנָּם (41:27) — הָרִאשֹׁנוֹת הנה . . . (42:9); שֵׁם (41:25; 42:8); הגיד — מגיד (41:26; 42:9); רוח (41:29; 42:1, with two different meanings); נתן (41:27; 42:1, 5); קרא (41:25; 42:6); צדק (41:26; 42:6); שמע (41:26; 42:2, 9); בחר (41:24; 42:1); and both units mention graven images (41:29; 42:8).

[1] *Behold, this is My servant, whom I uphold* — Hebrew הן functions here as a demonstrative. The verbal expression תמך ב- denotes "support" (see Exod 17:12: "Aaron and Hur, one on each side, supported his [= Moses'] hands [תמכו בידיו]") as well as being singled out and chosen, as is shown by the parallel hemistich: "My chosen one." For God's support of His servant see 41:10: "I strengthen you, I help you, I uphold you (תמכתיך) with My victorious right hand." "My servant" (עבדי) is the most common expression of God's special relationship with His nation and often appears in conjunction with the root בחר, "to choose"; see 41:8, 9; 43:10; 44:1, 2; 45:4. The LXX adds the word "Israel" after "My servant," and "Jacob" after "My chosen one"; cf. 41:8. (See the introduction, §20.B.)

My chosen one, with whom I am pleased — Israel is God's chosen nation, God's favored people; cf., e.g., "You are My servant. I chose you. I have not rejected you" (41:9); "For the sake of My servant Jacob, Israel, My chosen one" (45:4); see also 41:8; 43:10, 20; 44:1, 2; 45:4; 49:7. For the connection between "to choose" and "to be pleased with," see 1 Chr 28:4: "The Lord God of Israel chose

(ויבחר) me . . . for He chose (בחר) Judah . . . He preferred (רצה) me." These manifold allusions to God's choice and preference find their parallel in Akkadian royal inscriptions that single out the king as the gods' "beloved one" *(narām ilī)* and "favored one" *(migir ilī);* cf. likewise Isa 41:8: אֹהֲבִי ("the one whom I love"). (See Seux, *Épithètes royales,* 162-68, 189-97.)

I have put My spirit upon him — God's bestowal of His spirit upon His chosen one refers to the special charisma He confers on those who are designated by Him to fulfill a specific mission; cf., e.g., 48:16: "And now the Lord God has sent me, endowed with His spirit (ורוחו)"; 59:21: "And this shall be My covenant with them, said the Lord: My spirit that is upon you, and the words that I have placed in your mouth"; 61:1: "The spirit (רוח) of the Lord God is upon me." This "spirit" is equivalent at times to the prophetic spirit; cf., e.g., Num 11:25: "He drew on the spirit that was upon him [Moses] and put it upon the seventy elders"; Num 11:29: "But Moses said to him, 'Are you wrought up on my account? Would that all the Lord's people were prophets, that the Lord put His spirit upon them!'" This gifted charisma is also conferred on the nation's leaders, such as judges and kings; see Judg 6:34; 14:6; 15:14; 1 Sam 11:6; and is also the fortunate lot of Israel's descendants forevermore (Isa 44:3).

He shall promulgate justice to the nations — The servant's mission is universal: He is chosen and enveloped by the spirit of God in order to bring forth truth and justice to the nations. For the verb יצא in the *hiph'il* with the connotation of "promulgating, bringing forth," see 48:20: "Declare this with loud shouting, announce this, promulgate (הוציאוּהָ) the word to the ends of the earth"; and cf. Ps 37:6: "He will cause your vindication to shine forth (והוציא) like the light, and the justice of your case like the noonday sun." The word משפט should be understood here as in v. 4, where it parallels תורתו ("His teaching"); see also Isa 51:4: "For My teaching (תורתי) shall go forth from Me, and My justice (ומשפטי) for the light of peoples;" Hab 1:4: "That is why teaching (תורה) fails and justice (משפט) never emerges." 1QIsa[a] has משפטו, "His justice," and the Targum has דיני, "My justice." The word משפט appears three times in this unit, accentuating the importance of this part of the servant's mission.

[2] In a triad of verbs the prophet emphasizes the quiescent, frail, and weak state of God's servant.

He shall not cry out — The root צעק expresses the cry of an oppressed individual in need of help, who lifts his voice against his oppressor, e.g., Exod 22:22: "If you do mistreat him, I will heed his outcry (צעקתו) as soon as they cry out (צָעֹק יצעק) to me"; 2 Kgs 6:26: "A woman cried (צעקה) out to him: 'Help, my lord king!'"

Or raise his voice — The direct object קול is supplied from the end of the adjacent clause. Compare similarly Num 14:1. For the Ugaritic interdialectal semantic equivalent of the complementary Hebrew terms נשׂא קול and צעק, *nś' gh* ("to raise one's voice") and *ṣḥ* ("to shout"), see *HdO* 1:781.

Or make his voice heard in the streets — For חוּץ, "streets," see Prov 1:20: "Wisdom cries aloud in the streets (בחוץ), raises her voice in the squares."

[3] The first two hemistichs of this verse are unclear. Some commentators explain that the images refer directly to the oppressed servant, while others maintain that the prophet is describing the servant's weak and frail state.

He shall not break even a splintered reed — A hollow reed, which splinters under the slightest pressure, denotes someone or something unreliable; see Isa 36:6: "You are relying on Egypt, that splintered reed (הַקָּנֶה הרצוץ) of a staff"; Ezek 29:6-7: "Because you were a staff of reed (קנה) to the house of Israel. When they grasped you with the hand, you would splinter (תֵּרוֹץ) . . . and when they leaned on you, you would break." There are those who explain this to mean that the servant is so weak that he is unable to break even the most fragile reed. Akkadian employs similar imagery with reference to *qanû* (= קָנֶה): "You broke the people in it (the city) like reeds *(qanî)*" (*CAD* Q:88). Others, however, explain that the verse is referring to the servant: Though he is a "splintered reed," nevertheless, he will not break (vocalizing in the *niph'al*, יִשָּׁבֵר).

Or snuff out even a dimly burning wick — The servant cannot even muster enough strength to extinguish a smoldering wick. As in the previous hemistich, some commentators explain that this "dim wick" is the servant himself who, although on the point of total collapse, will nevertheless not be extinguished (vocalizing in the *niph'al*, יִכָּבֶה; cf. 1QIsa[a], LXX, Vulgate, Peshitta, and Targum — all versions without the pronominal suffix (יכבה). For the imagery, see 43:17: "They were crushed, snuffed out like a wick (כפשתה כבו)." The word פשתה (lit. "flax," *linum usitalissimum*) is a plant with blue flowers and edible seeds. One of the months of the Gezer Calendar is named after this plant: "The month of chopping flax (פשת)" (*KAI* 182:3).

He shall promulgate in truth/justice to the nations — Despite his great weakness, the servant will succeed in promulgating "justice" (see v. 1, here in a chiastic parallelism). Some vocalize לְאֻמֹּת ("to the nations"), rather than the MT לֶאֱמֶת; and cf. the parallel גוים in v. 1 (see Gen 25:16; Num 25:15).

[4] The prophet elaborates on the images from the previous verse but reverses chiastically the order of expressions: רצוץ . . . כֵהָה — יִכְהֶה . . . ירוץ.

He shall not grow dim — Despite his weakness, the servant's light shall not grow dim; cf. Deut 34:7: "His [Moses'] eyes were undimmed (לא כָהֲתָה)"; Ezek 21:12: "Every spirit shall grow faint (וְכִהֲתָה)."

Or be crushed — The verb יָרוּץ (from the root רוץ, a by-form of רצץ) denotes "shattering, bruising"; see Eccl 12:6: "And the jug is shattered (וְנָרֹץ) at the cistern." Some commentators prefer to vocalize יֵרוֹץ; see Ezek 29:7: "When they grasped you with the hand, you would be crushed (תֵּרוֹץ)."

Till he has established justice on earth — עד should be understood here as referring to the completion of the task at hand. In the end the servant will bring about the "justice" of God on earth. For this use of עד, cf. Isa 62:1: "For the sake of Zion I will not be silent. For the sake of Jerusalem I will not be still, till (עד) her victory emerge resplendent and her triumph like a flaming torch"; 62:7: "And give no rest to Him until (עד) He establishes Jerusalem and makes her renowned on earth"; Ps 71:18: "And even in hoary old age do not forsake me, God, until (עד) I proclaim Your strength to the next generation"; Ps 110:1: "The Lord said to my lord, 'Sit at My right hand while (עד) I make your enemies your footstool under your feet.'"

The expression שׂים בארץ משפט (see Josh 24:25) is a calque on the Akkadian phrase *kittam u mīšaram ina mātim šakānum,* "to establish truth and justice in the land" (*CAD* M/2:117), which appears in contexts of acts of social justice ordered by the king following his inauguration and sporadically thereafter (these acts include the freeing of prisoners, see v. 7; cf. 61:1). (See M. Weinfeld, *Social Justice in Ancient Israel and in the Ancient Near East* [Jerusalem, 1995], 11-13, 141.)

And the coastlands shall await His teaching — The word איים here, along with ארץ in the first hemistich, make up a merism indicating that the world in its entirety will await God's instruction. For the root יחל ("to wait for"), see 51:5: "For me the coastlands shall hope, and wait for (יְיַחֵלוּן) My arm." For other examples of the pair משפט and תורה, see 51:4; Num 15:16.

[5] In this hymn of praise, characterized by a series of participles, God proclaims His great deeds from the dim and dark past, i.e., the creation of the earth, the sky, plants, animals, and people. This verse was very much influenced by the description of God's creation in Genesis: "God . . . who created the heavens (האל ה׳ בּוֹרֵא השמים) . . . who spread out the earth (רֹקַע הארץ)" — "When God began to create the heavens and earth (בראשית ברא אלהים את השמים ואת הארץ)" (Gen 1:1); and cf. also here נשמה ("breath") and נשמת חיים ("the breath of life") (Gen 2:6).

Thus said God the Lord — The title האל ה׳ (1QIsa[a], האל האלהים) is found only here and in Ps 85:9.

Who created the heavens and stretched them out — This poetic description of the creation begins with the heavens; see also Isa 44:24: "Who alone stretched (נֹטֶה) the heavens and unaided stretched out (רֹקַע) the earth"; 45:18: "For thus said the Lord, the creator of the heavens, who alone is God, who formed the earth and made it, who alone established it." For the "stretching out" of the heavens (similar to the pitching of a tent; see Gen 12:8), see Isa 40:22: "Who stretched out (הנוטה) the skies like gauze, spread them out like a tent to dwell in"; cf. also 45:12; 51:13. The *yod* in נוטיהם is part of the root (נטי) and does not denote plurality; cf., e.g., Gen 41:21: מראיהן ("their appearance"); Num 5:3: מחניהם ("their camp").

Who spread out the earth — Cf. Ps 136:6: "Who spread (לְרוֹקַע) the earth over the water." For another instance of the pair of verbs רקע and נטה, see Isa 44:24. For a similar description of creation, cf. the Mesopotamian composition *Ludlul bēl nēmeqi:* "Wherever the earth is established *(šaknat),* and the heavens spread out *(ritpašu)*" (*BWL,* 58-59, line 37; *CAD* Š/1:343; R:382).

And what it brings forth — "The plants on the earth['s surface]" (Ibn Ezra); see Isa 34:1: "Let the earth and those in it hear; the world and what it brings forth (צאצאיה)"; and cf. Job 31:8: "May I sow and another reap, may the produce (וצאצאי) of my field be uprooted." The verb רקע accords with the first object (הארץ) but not with the second (צאצאיה) — a literary device called *zeugma.*

Who gave breath to the people on it — God blew the breath of life into every living being; see Gen 2:7: "He blew into his nostrils the breath of life (נשמת חיים), and man became a living being." For עם as a general term for all of humanity, see Isa 40:7.

And life to those who walk thereon — For רוח, "breath of life," see Ps 104:29-30: "When you take away their breath (רוחם), they perish. . . . When you send back Your breath (רוחך), they are created." For the parallel terms נשמה/רוח, see Isa 57:16; Job 32:8: "But truly it is the spirit (רוח) in men, the breath (נשמת) of Shaddai, that gives them understanding"; Job 33:4: "The spirit (רוח) of God formed me; the breath (ונשמת) of Shaddai sustains me."

[6] Once again, the juxtaposition of cosmology and history (see Isa 40:22-23): God, who created the universe, chose His earthly servant to be His emissary.

"I, the Lord, have duly called you" — For God's "calling," which denotes election, see also 41:9. Divine selection of the king, which in Mesopotamia is often recorded with the addition of the Akkadian adverb *kiniš* (*CAD* K:385), indicating favor and legitimation, is reflected here in the Hebrew interdialectal semantic equivalent, בצדק. (See Paul, *Divrei Shalom,* 12.)

"And have grasped you by the hand" — The firm grasp of God's hand denotes support; see 41:9, 10, 13 (God's support of Israel); 45:1 (God's support of Cyrus). This imagery is also documented in Mesopotamian royal inscriptions, beginning in the Sumerian period. In the Akkadian Cyrus Cylinder, Marduk, the king of the gods, tells of his long search for a worthy monarch: "He reached for a righteous king whom he would support [lit. 'grasp by the hand']" (M. Cogan, *COS* 2:315; see also the introduction, excursus B). (For further Akkadian parallels, see 41:9 and Paul, *Divrei Shalom,* 12-13.) For illustrations of the deity extending his supportive hand to his chosen monarch, see O. Keel, *The Symbolism of the Biblical World* (New York, 1978), figs. 272-73, 346, 414.

"I created you and appointed you" — The first verb, וְאֶצָּרְךָ, may derive ei-

ther from the root נצר (in which case one would translate, "I have safeguarded you"), or from יצר ("I created you"), which is preferable; see 44:2: "Thus said the Lord, your Maker, who has created you (וְיֹצֶרְךָ) from birth"; 44:21: "The people that I have created (יצרתי) for Myself"; 49:5: "He who has created me (יֹצְרִי) in the womb"; cf. also 43:1. For the second verb, וְאֶתֶּנְךָ, "And I appointed you," see Num 8:16: "For they are formally appointed (נְתֻנִים נְתֻנִים) to Me from among the Israelites"; Num 18:6: "They are appointed (נְתֻנִים) to you in dedication to the Lord, to do the work of the tent of meeting." The servant was designated for this special task from the moment of his creation; see Isa 49:1, 5. The motif of being appointed prior to birth to carry out a special task is very common in Mesopotamian royal inscriptions. For example, cf. the gods' choice of Nabonidus, the last Babylonian king before Cyrus's conquest (and contemporary of Deutero-Isaiah): "I, Nabonidus, who was raised by [the god] Sin and [the goddess] Ningal, was chosen for this destiny while still in my mother's womb." (For this example as well as many others, see Paul, *Divrei Shalom,* 18-20.) The choice of these two verbs, אצרך and אתנך, was influenced by the verse in Jeremiah, which pertains to his prenatal appointment and dedication (Jer 1:5). (See ibid., 20-21, 405-6, and introduction, §15).

"A covenant people" — The expression ברית עם is a reversed construct and should be understood as עם ברית ("a people of the covenant"); cf. מֶלַח ברית (Lev 2:13) and ברית מֶלַח (Num 18:19); בְּשָׂמִים ראש (Exod 30:23) and ראשי בְּשָׂמִים (Cant 4:14). (See Y. Avishur, "The Reversed Construct Structure in the Bible, Qumran Scrolls, and Early Jewish Literature," *Leš* 57 [1993]: 278-86 [Heb.].) The servant was chosen by God for a dual task. The first mission is a national one, to be a "covenant people"; see also Isa 49:8: "I created you and appointed you a covenant people." For the 1QIsa[a] variant לברית עולם, "an everlasting covenant" (documented also in a number of medieval Hebrew manuscripts), see 55:3: "And I will make with you an everlasting covenant"; 61:8: "I will make an everlasting covenant with them," which, in turn, was influenced by God's eternal covenant with the Davidic lineage, "He made an everlasting covenant with me" (2 Sam 23:5).

"A light of nations" — The second mission is a universal one; see also Isa 49:6: "I will make you a light of nations (לאור גוים), that My salvation may reach the ends of the earth." The servant was chosen by God to be a spiritual beacon of light for all people, a role model through which God will spread His holy word; cf. 51:4: "For teaching shall go forth from Me, My justice for the light of the peoples (לאור עמים)." This mission is reminiscent of Tiglath-pileser's and Esarhaddon's royal titles (Assyrian kings from the eighth century BCE): *nūr kiššat nišē* ("the light of all humankind"); *nūr kibrāti* ("the light of the world") (Seux, *Épithètes royales,* 209). Similar titles are conferred on the Babylonian gods Sin and Marduk (*CAD* N/2:349). This motif is elaborated on in 60:1-3:

"Arise, shine, for your light has dawned! The presence of the Lord has shone upon you! Behold! Darkness shall cover the earth, and thick clouds the peoples; but upon you the Lord will shine, and His presence be seen over you. And nations shall walk by your light (גוים לאורך), kings by your shining radiance."

[7] Bringing light to the blind and to the prisoners in their dim and dark cells denotes their release from captivity, i.e., the Babylonian exile, and is similar in meaning to its Akkadian interdialectal semantic equivalents: *nūram amāru* (lit. "to see light") and *nūram kullumu* ("to show light"). (See *CAD* N/2:349; Paul, *Divrei Shalom,* 14.) For the combination of "opening the eyes of the blind" and the "releasing of prisoners," see Ps 146:7-8.

"To open eyes that are blind" — A metaphor for freeing captives; see the commentary to 61:1.

"To rescue prisoners from confinement" — The *hiph'il* verbal expression הוציא מ-, similar to its Akkadian etymological cognate *šūṣû,* the *shaph'el* of the verb *waṣû,* "to leave" (*CAD* A/2:373ff.), denotes "setting free." God, who freed His nation from under the Egyptian yoke, will now release His loyal subjects from their servitude in Babylonia. For אסיר/אסור, "bound, imprisoned," see 49:9; 61:1. מַסְגֵּר is literally "a place of confinement," i.e., a prison; see 24:22: "They shall be gathered in a dungeon as captives (אסיר) are gathered, and shall be locked up in a prison (מסגר)"; Ps 142:8: "Free me from prison (ממסגר) that I may praise your name." It appears also on a Judean seal: "To Azaryahu, the warden of the prison (המסגר)" (see R. Deutsch and M. Heltzer, *Forty New Ancient West Semitic Inscriptions* [Tel Aviv, 1994], 41); and a variant, מסגרת, is found in the Aramaic inscription of King Panamuwa from the second half of the eighth century BCE (*KAI* 215:4, 8). Note the series of similar sounding sibilants in this clause.

"From the dungeon, those who dwell in darkness" — The prisoners trapped in deep, dark dungeons will see God's light, i.e., will be liberated; cf. v. 22, "hidden in dungeons." (Cf. its Akkadian etymological cognate *bīt kīli* (*CAD* K:360-61.) For similar imagery, see 49:9: "Saying to the prisoners, 'Go free!'; to those in darkness, 'Show yourselves!'"; Ps 107:14: "He brought them out of deepest darkness." For an additional example of אסיר and ישב בחשך in parallel hemistichs, see Ps 107:10: "Some dwelled in deepest darkness, bound in cruel irons." (The Akkadian interdialectal equivalent of this expression, *āšib ikletim* ["he who dwells in darkness"], refers to an embryo [*CAD* I:61].)

[8-9] Once again the motif of the Deity's uniqueness is reiterated. Only the Lord God foretold the events that were once predicted and brought them to pass, i.e., Cyrus's victories and Babylon's downfall. Now He is predicting events "yet to come," i.e., the salvation of the nation and their return to Israel. God's accurate and reliable prediction of past events lends credence to His future promises.

[8] *"I am the Lord, that is My name"* — God introduces himself in a festive manner. For this emphasis on God's name in Deutero-Isaiah, cf. 43:7; 47:4; 48:1, 2, 9; 50:10; 51:15; 52:5, 6; 54:5.

"I will not yield My Presence to another" — See also 48:11. For אחר, "another," referring to pagan gods, see Exod 20:3: "You shall have no other gods beside Me"; Exod 34:14: "You must not worship any other god."

"Nor My renown to idols" — The negative in the previous clause applies here as well. For the parallel pair כבוד ("glory") and תְּהִלָּה ("renown"), see v. 12; Ps 66:2. For the divine "presence" and its manifestations, see v. 10; 43:21; 48:9. This is the sole occurrence in Deutero-Isaiah of the word פסילים; see Jer 50:38: "For it is a land of idols (פסילים)," also referring to Babylonia.

[9] The logic of these verses, i.e., God's accurate prediction of past events, which provides assurance and certainty to future prophecies, is also found in an Assyrian prophetic text referring to the goddess Ishtar's promise to King Esarhaddon: "Could you not rely on the precious utterance which I spoke to you? Now you can rely on this later one too." (See Parpola, *Assyrian Prophecies,* p. 10, lines 7-12; and LXVI for other examples.)

"See, the things once predicted have come to pass" — The motif of prophecy and fulfillment reverberates throughout Deutero-Isaiah's prophecies, e.g., 48:3: "Long ago I foretold what happened. From My mouth they issued, and I announced them. Suddenly I acted, and they came to pass"; cf. 41:22; 44:7; 45:21; 46:10; 48:3.

"And now I foretell new things" — Just as the "things once predicted" (הָרִאשֹׁנוֹת) have come to pass, so too will God's new prophecies (חדשות) prove to be accurate. The triumphant *eisodos* to Zion that God promised will soon become a glorious reality. For other examples of חדשה/חדשות, see 43:19; 48:6.

"I announce to you ere they sprout up" — I now announce future events before their actual occurrence. The "announcement" motif appears also in 48:6: "As of now, I announce to you new things." For the root צמח ("to sprout") signifying an immediate forthcoming event, see 43:19: "I am about to do something new; even now it shall sprout forth (תצמח)"; 45:8: "Let the earth open up and triumph spring forth (תצמיח)."

[10-13] An ode to God for the imminent salvation from the Babylonian exile. Just as Israel sang to God when He parted the Reed Sea (Exod 15), so too they will sing as God leads them through the Syrian Desert to the promised land, and this time the mountains, the oceans, and the desert — all of nature, in fact — will join Israel in their joyous hymn of thanksgiving. The first three verses of the ode reverberate with imagery from Psalms 96 and 98 (see the introduction, §17):

Isaiah 42:10-12	**Psalms 96 and 98**
v. 10: שירו לה׳ שיר חדש	96:1; 98:1: שירו לה׳ שיר חדש
מִקְצֵה הארץ	98:3: אפסי ארץ
ירעם [יורדי MT] הים וּמְלֹאוֹ	96:11; 98:7: ירעם הים וּמְלֹאוֹ
וְיֹשְׁבֵיהֶם	98:7: תֵּבֵל וישבי בה
v. 11: יִשְׂאוּ	96:8: שְׂאוּ
חֲצֵרִים	96:8: לְחַצְרוֹתָיו
יָרֹנּוּ	96:12: ירנְּנו
הרים יִצְוָחוּ	98:8: הרים ירנֵּנו
v. 12: ישימו כבוד לה׳	96:7: הבו לה׳ כבוד 96:8: הבו לה׳ כבוד שמו

This hymn is linked to the previous unit by many common words and expressions: ישׂא, [קול] ישׂאו (vv. 2, 11); איים (vv. 4, 10, 12); ארץ (vv. 4, 5, 10); ישׂים, ישׂימו (vv. 4, 12); יֹשְׁבֵי, יֹשְׁבֵיהֶם, תשב, (vv. 7, 10, 11); תְהִלָּתִי (v. 8), תְהִלָּתוֹ (vv. 10, 12); כבודי, כבוד (vv. 8, 12); חדשות, חדש (vv. 9, 10); יגידו, מגיד (vv. 9, 12). For other doxologies in Deutero-Isaiah, see 44:23; 49:13.

[10] *Sing to the Lord a new song* — This hemistich also introduces Ps 149:1: "Sing to the Lord a new song, His praise. . . ." The difference here is that this hymn has the whole world as its audience (cf. Ps 96 and 98), whereas Ps 149 is restricted to Israel (see also Ps 33:3).

His praise from the ends of the earth! — From one end of the earth to the other a call goes forth to sing an ode to God; cf. Ps 40:4: "He put a new song (שיר חדש) into my mouth, a praise (תְהִלָּה) to our God"; Ps 106:12: "They sang His praises" (ישירו תהלתו). The expression מִקְצֵה הארץ (see Isa 43:6; 48:20; 49:6) and its variant, מִקְצוֹת הארץ (40:28; 41:9), appear also in Ugaritic, *lqṣm arṣ* (*CAT* 1.16.III:3).

Let the sea roar and all the creatures in it — Although the expression יורדי הים can refer to sailors, as in Ps 107:23: "Those who go down to the sea (יורדי הים) in ships," in light of the multiple cross-references between Ps 96 and Ps 98 and this section (see above), one should probably read יִרְעַם instead of יורדי, as in 96:11 and 98:7 (see also 1 Chr 16:32). The word מְלֹאוֹ (lit. "that which fills it") is an allusion to marine life.

You coastlands and their inhabitants — Not only Israel but the inhabitants of the coastlands are also bidden to sing a hymn to God. The root ישב is repeated here and in v. 11.

[11] *Let the desert and its towns cry aloud* — The Vulgate, Peshitta, Targum (יִשַּׁבַּח), and 1QIsa[a] (ישא) all read the verb in the singular. Note that the expected object, קול, is absent here; see v. 2. The biblical term עיר may refer to cities or towns; cf. Josh 15:21; 1 Kings 15:8.

The villages where Kedar dwells — Also the unfortified villages (חֲצֵרִים), in which the desert nomads of Kedar dwell, are commanded to raise their voices in praise of God. The term חצרים often appears in conjunction with עיר or ערים, e.g., Josh 13:28: "Those towns with their villages (הערים וחצריהם)." For the tribe of Kedar (one of Ishmael's sons, Gen 25:13), who dwelled in tents, see Jer 49:28-29: "Arise, march against Kedar and ravage the Kedemites [or 'people of the east']! They will take up their tents and their flocks"; Ps 120:5: "Woe is me . . . that I dwell among the clans of Kedar"; Cant 1:5: "Like the tents of Kedar."

Let the inhabitants of Sela shout for joy — The verb רנן denotes here a ringing cry of joy and exultation (Isa 44:23; 49:13) and appears together with נשא קול in 24:14. The term סֶלַע is polysemous and creates a Janus parallelism with the two adjacent hemistichs. On the one hand, similar to the previous clause (קֵדָר), it denotes the proper name of a settlement (cf. Judg 1:36; 2 Kgs 14:7); on the other, as in the following clause (הרים), it indicates a mountainous terrain; cf. Amos 6:12: "Can horses gallop on a rock (סלע)?"; Prov 30:26: "Badgers are a folk without strength, yet they make their home among the rocks (בסלע)." (*Selaʿ* should not be identified with modern-day Petra, which did not exist in the sixth century BCE.)

Cry out from the peaks of mountains — The root צוח denotes raising one's voice, either in joy (only here) or in sorrow (Jer 46:12), and appears also in Ugaritic (see v. 2), Akkadian, Syriac, and Arabic. 1QIsa[a] has the variant verb יצרחו (see also v. 13) instead of MT יִצְוָחוּ; see Zeph 1:14, where צֹרֵחַ is translated by the Targum as צָוַח. For the inclusion of mountains in celebrating Israel's deliverance, see also Isa 44:23; 49:13.

[12] *Let them ascribe honor to the Lord* — All of the above are bidden to honor God (ישימו כבוד), as in Ps 66:2: "Make glorious His praise" (שימו כבוד תהלתו). (The construct, כבוד תהלתו, is divided into its two components and parceled out between the two hemistichs of the verse here.) Compare also Ps 151:5 from Qumran: ואשימה לה׳ כבוד (J. A. Sanders, *The Psalms Scroll of Qumrân Cave 11 (11QPs[a])*, DJD 4 [Oxford, 1965], 49). Compare also the Akkadian semantic equivalents: *kabtam/kubātam šakānu* ("to confer honor on") (*CAD* K:27, 482), and (for the following clause): *tanattu šakānu* ("to give praise, glory") (*CAD* T:169).

And recite His glory in the coastlands — This hemistich forms a chiastic parallel with the immediately preceding clause and repeats two words from the opening verse of this hymn: תְּהִלָּתוֹ and איים (v. 10).

[13] The reason for glorifying God is now spelled out. God, in a warrior's guise (cf. Ps 24:8), takes on His Babylonian enemies, just as in the past He fought the Egyptians as the Israelites were fleeing Egypt; see also Isa 59:16-18.

The Lord goes forth as a warrior — The verb יצא has military connotations in this context and denotes deployment on a battlefront; cf., e.g., Judg 20:28: "Shall we again march out (לצאת) to battle?"; Amos 5:3: "The town that marches out (הַיֹּצֵאת) a thousand strong"; cf. Isa 40:26; and its etymological and semantic cognates in Ugaritic: *yṣu* (*HdO* 2:985), and Akkadian: *waṣû* (*CAD* A/2:356ff.). For God described as a גבור, see Deut 10:17; Isa 9:5; 10:21; Jer 32:18; Neh 9:32.

Like a fighter He rouses up His frenzy — As in the Song on the Sea praising God the "warrior" (איש מלחמה; Exod 15:3) for routing the Egyptian taskmasters, the Deity prepares to combat zealously His Babylonian enemies. For איש מלחמה and גִּבּוֹר as parallel expressions, see Samuel's description of David, 1 Sam 16:18: "He is a stalwart fellow and a warrior" (וגבור חַיִל ואיש מלחמה); and cf. Isa 3:2; Ezek 39:20; Joel 2:7; 4:9. For other instances of איש מלחמות, see 2 Sam 8:10; 1 Chr 18:10; 28:3. For God's zeal (קנאה) in battle for His people, combined with His mighty valor (גבורה), see Isa 63:15; and cf. יעיר קנאה with the expression: ולא יעיר כל חמתו, "He did not rouse up His full fury" (Ps 78:38).

He shouts a battle cry, He roars aloud — God raises His thunderous alarm of battle, putting fear into the hearts of His enemies. For the "roar of war" (Jer 4:19; 49:2) as a prelude to the actual battle engagement, cf. Joshua's command to the Israelites just before the invasion of Jericho, Josh 6:16: "Joshua commanded the people, 'Shout (הריעו)! For the Lord has given you the city'"; 1 Sam 17:52: "The men of Israel and Judah rose up with a war cry (ויריעו) and pursued the Philistines." Compare likewise the employment of Akk. *rigmu*, "noise" (*CAD* R:331), referring to the war cries as one side engages the other in combat, and especially *irnittu*, which expresses the concept of divine anger that results in an annihilating outburst and a cry of triumph over an enemy (*CAD* I:178-79).

The verb צרח, "to roar" (in battle), appears again only in Zeph 1:14: "Hark, the day of the Lord! It is bitter. There a warrior shrieks (צֹרֵחַ)" (and see v. 11 for this variant reading in 1QIsa[a]). The word אף may be polysemous, functioning as a pivot in a Janus parallelism. On the one hand, it adds intensity to the verb יצריח (cf. Isa 41:10); on the other, it is parallel to יעיר קנאה in the prior hemistich: "He shouts (in) rage." For אף and קנאה as parallel terms, see Deut 29:19: "Then the Lord's anger (אף) and His passion (קִנְאָתוֹ) will rage against that man"; Ezek 35:11: "I will act with the same anger (באפך) and passion (ובקנאתך) you acted with." On the basis of this parallelism, some have suggested altering the Masoretic division of the verse: "Like a fighter he is aroused. He shouts in rage (קנאה יריע). He roars aloud in anger (אף יצריח)." For the root עיר as an intransitive *hiph'il* denoting the arousal of one's self, see Ps 35:23. (See D. N. Freedman, "Isaiah 42, 13," *CBQ* 30 [1968]: 225-26.)

He triumphs over His enemies — The verse begins and ends with the root גבר, creating a literary *inclusio*. For another example of this verb in the *hithpa'el*, see Job 15:25.

[14-15] God's bellicose outburst is in complete contrast to His restrained behavior in the past. Throughout the years of the Babylonian exile the Deity suppressed His wrath; now He goes on a vengeful rampage in order to expedite the greatly anticipated liberation of Israel from Babylonia. His self-restraint is emphasized in a series of three verbs, immediately followed by a triad of verbs that accentuate His wrath. Deutero-Isaiah paints a bold picture of God as a woman in labor whose fearsome shouts cause everyone to shudder. Unlike other birthing imagery, which emphasizes the travails and pain the woman is going through (with the notable exception of Isa 66:7-8), the outcries here relate to God's destructive power. These shrieking cries create a link with the above unit describing God's shouting fury. For an Akkadian example of a woman in labor being compared to a warrior, see *CAD* Q:143: "She [the woman in childbirth] lies in her own blood like a fighting warrior." For other metaphors that accentuate God's feminine aspects, unique to Deutero-Isaiah, see 45:10; 46:3-4; 49:15; 66:9, 13. (See M. I. Gruber, "The Motherhood of God in Second Isaiah," in *The Motherhood of God and Other Studies,* SFSHJ 57 [Atlanta, 1992], 3-15; K. P. Darr, "Like Warrior, Like Woman: Destruction and Deliverance in Isaiah 42:10-17," *CBQ* 49 [1987]: 560-71.) Other ancient Near Eastern gods are described in similar feminine terms. In Ugaritic the male deity Athtar is referred to as *'ṯtr um,* "Athtar is the mother" (see also *'ṯtr ab,* "Athtar is the father"). Compare also the proper name *adanu-ummu,* "the master is our mother." (See F. Gröndahl, *Die Personennamen der Texte aus Ugarit,* SP 1 [Rome, 1967], 46 §75; p. 83 §141.) In the ninth-century BCE Phoenician inscription of King Kilamuwa, it is written: "But I was to some a father and to some a mother" (*KAI* 24:10). In another Phoenician inscription (the Azitawada inscription from the eighth century BCE), the king states: "Baal made me a father and a mother to the Danunians" (*KAI* 26:3). One also finds the opposite imagery, that of goddesses addressed as fathers. In a Sumerian prayer from the third millennium, Gudea, king of Lagash, addresses the goddess of the city, saying: "I have no mother — you are my mother, I have no father — you are my father, you implanted in the womb the germ of me. You gave birth to me from out the vulva" (Cylinder A, iii:5-7; see T. Jacobsen, *The Harps That Once . . . : Sumerian Poetry in Translation* [New Haven, 1987], 391); and in the Hittite hymn to Istanu, the male sun god, the scribe writes: "You, Istanu, are father and mother of the destitute, the lonely and the bereaved." (See H. Güterbock, "The Composition of Hittite Prayers to the Sun," *JAOS* 78 [1958]: 240.)

[14] *"I have been idle far too long"* — For the verb חשי, "to be idle, inactive," see 64:11: "At such things will You restrain Yourself, O Lord? Will you stand idly by (תֶּחֱשֶׁה) and let us suffer so heavily?"; 65:6: "I will not stand idly by (אֶחֱשֶׁה) but will repay, deliver their sins into their bosom"; Judg 18:9: "For we have found that the land was very good, and you are sitting idle (מַחְשִׁים). Don't delay! Go and invade the land and take possession of it!"; 1 Kgs 22:3: "You know that Ramoth-Gilead belongs to us, and yet we do nothing (מחשים) to recover it from the hands of the king of Aram." For other occurrences of מעולם, see Isa 46:9; 63:16, 19; 64:3.

"Kept still" — The verb חרש can also denote "inactivity" (Luzzatto); see 2 Sam 19:11: "But Absalom, whom we anointed over us, has died in battle. Why then do you sit idle (מַחֲרִשִׁים) instead of escorting the king back?"

"And restrained Myself" — See also Esth 5:9-10: "Haman was filled with rage at Mordechai. Nevertheless, he controlled himself (ויתאפק)." For the verbal pair חשי/אפק, see Isa 64:11: "At such things will You restrain Yourself (תתאפק), O Lord? Will You stand idly by (תֶּחֱשֶׁה)?"

"Now I will scream like a woman in labor" — But God's silence and inactivity have now come to an end, and His screams will reverberate like a woman in the midst of childbirth. For similar imagery, see 13:8: "And overcome by terror, they shall be seized by pangs and throes, writhe like a woman in travail (כיולֵדה)"; 21:3: "I am gripped by pangs like a woman in travail (יולֵדה)"; Ps 48:7: "They were seized there with a trembling, like a woman in the throes of labor (כיולֵדה)." The root פעי, "to cry out," is a hapax legomenon in Biblical Hebrew, but is common in Rabbinic Hebrew; see *Lev. Rab.* 27:7 (ed. M. Margaliot [New York, 1993], 638): "The one hundred screams (פְּעִיות) a woman screams (פועה) when she is enduring the throes of labor." A similar image appears in the Gilgamesh Epic (XI:116), when Ishtar witnesses the annihilation of the universe: "She cried out like a woman giving birth" (Akk. *ālittu* = יולֵדה).

"I will pant and I will gasp" — Note the assonance of the two verbs אֶשֹּׁם and וְאֶשְׁאַף, which are antonyms. The first, a hapax legomenon from the root נשם, denotes the exhaling of breath, panting; and the second signifies inhalation, gasping; cf., e.g., Jer 14:6: "And the wild asses . . . snuffing (שאפו) the air like jackals"; Ps 119:131: "I open my mouth wide, I pant (וָאֶשְׁאָפָה)." Panting and gasping, exhaling and inhaling in rapid succession, reminiscent of the woman in travail, continue the imagery of the prior hemistich. For יחד, which concludes and summarizes a series of substantives or verbs, see, e.g., Isa 44:11.

[15] The result of these intense inhalations and exhalations is devastating, effecting all of nature. This verse is arranged in an ABCB construction: אחריב . . . אוביש . . . ושמתי . . . אוביש. For another example of this literary pattern, see 45:7. For God's destructive power vis-à-vis nature, see S. E. Loewenstamm, "The Trembling of Nature during the Theophany," in *Comparative*

Studies in Biblical and Ancient Oriental Literatures, AOAT 204 (Neukirchen-Vluyn, 1980), 173-89.

"I will lay waste mountains and hills" — For the verb חרב, see 49:17. For the substantives הרים and גבעות in parallel clauses, see 40:4; 41:15.

"And cause all their herbage to wither" — All the plant life on these mountains and hills will shrivel up and die. For God's desiccating wind, see 40:24: "When He blows on them, they wither away (וַיִּבָשׁוּ)." The first two clauses of this verse create a chiastic parallelism. For the parallel pair of verbs הוביש and החריב, see Nah 1:4: "He rebukes the sea and dries it up (וַיַּבְּשֵׁהוּ), and He makes all the rivers fail (החריב)."

"I will turn rivers into deserts" — In light of the motif of dryness and aridity, which is repeated four times in this verse, and in light of the opposite image in Isa 41:18: "I will turn the desert into ponds, the arid land into springs of water," some have suggested substituting לָצִיִּים or לָצִיּוֹת (the plural of צִיָּה, "desert") for MT לָאִיִּים; see Ps 105:41: "It flowed as a stream in a parched land (בַּצִּיּוֹת)."

"And dry up the ponds" — For אגמים, see Exod 7:19; 8:1.

[16] The exodus tradition, which began in the previous verse with the drying up of bodies of water, continues here with the motif of God's leading the people on their way back to the land of Israel.

"I will lead the blind on a road they do not know" — God will now lead His newly emancipated people, who are "blind" from their forced sojourn in the Babylonian exile (see v. 7), upon paths heretofore unknown. The emphasis in this verse is on the "road they did not know," "since blind men are accustomed to walking on known paths" (Luzzatto). For the verb להוליך in connection with God's leading the people in the desert, see Deut 8:15; Jer 2:6; Ps 136:16.

"And I will make them walk on paths they do not know" — This clause forms a chiastic parallelism with the previous one. For the parallel substantives דרך/נתיב(ות), see Isa 43:16; 59:8; and for the expression הדריך בנתיב, see Ps 119:35: "Lead me in the paths (הַדְרִכֵנִי בנתיב) of Your commandments."

"I will turn darkness before them to light" — For מַחְשָׁךְ, "dark place," see Isa 29:15: "Who do their work in dark places (במחשך)."

"And twisting paths into level ground" — God will level the road so that no one will stumble or fall. The hapax legomenon substantive מַעֲקַשִּׁים, from the root עקש, denotes twisted and crooked places; see 59:8: "They make their courses crooked (עִקְּשׁוּ)"; Prov 2:15: "Men whose paths are crooked (עִקְּשִׁים) and who are devious in their course."

"All these I will do" — For the presentation of deeds yet to be performed as deeds performed in the past (עֲשִׂיתִם), cf. Gen 23:13: "I shall pay (נתתי) the price of the land."

"And not forsake them" — I will not show any neglect or forgetfulness when it comes to fulfilling My promises; cf. Isa 41:17: "I, the God of Israel, will

not forsake them (לֹא אֶעֶזְבֵם)." This statement is aimed at countering the complaint of the Israelites: "The Lord has forsaken me" (עזבני ה'; 49:14). For the negative parallelism עשׂה/לא עזב, see 58:2.

[17] This verse does not fit into the context of the adjacent verses and was most likely part of a polemic against graven images and their worshipers, which was mistakenly inserted into this unit devoted to God's power and promises. Perhaps the expression יֵבֹשׁוּ בֹשֶׁת, which is phonetically very similar to אוביש (v. 15), was the reason for this erroneous insertion.

Turned back — Cf. 50:5: "And I did not disobey. I did not turn back (אחור לא נְסוּגֹתִי)"; cf. Ps 35:4; 40:15; 129:5; and 70:3, where the verb בושׁ also appears, as here, in the next hemistich.

And utterly disappointed shall be those who trust in an image — Those idolaters who put all their stock in images shall be gravely disappointed when their trusted gods prove ineffective (see also Isa 44:9, 11; 45:16; Ps 97:7). The verb בושׁ signifies not only deep shame but also frustration, disappointment, and disillusionment; cf., e.g., Jer 2:26: "Like a thief frustrated (כְּבֹשֶׁת) when he is caught, so is the house of Israel frustrated (הֹבִישׁוּ)"; Ps 119:116: "Do not disappoint (תְּבִישֵׁנִי) my expectation." The unique cognate accusative, יֵבֹשׁוּ בֹשֶׁת, is a variant of the similar expression ילבשו בֹּשֶׁת (Ps 35:26; Job 8:22). For other examples of the pair בושׁ/נסג אחור, see Ps 35:4; 40:15; 70:3; 129:5; and for the verbal expression בטח ב-, see Isa 50:10.

Who say to the idols, "You are our gods" — For this motif of disillusionment, see Jer 2:26-27: "Like a thief disappointed when he is caught, so is the house of Israel disappointed. . . . They who say to wood, 'You are my father,' to stone, 'You gave birth to me'"; cf. Isa 44:18; 30:22; Hab 2:19. For the tendency of the prophets to quote the people's words back at them in order to implicate them, see Isa 41:7; 44:20. For the parallel terms פֶּסֶל/מַסֵּכָה, see Deut 27:15; Judg 17:3; Isa 30:22.

[18-25] The prophet reproaches Israel, structuring his critique around a typical series of three rhetorical-polemical מי questions (vv. 19, 23, 24; cf. 40:12, 13, 14, 25; 41:2, 4, 26). God's servant, Israel, is both blind and deaf to the reasons of his lengthy and demeaning captivity in Babylonia. This metaphor of a blind and deaf people was most likely influenced by First Isaiah's Temple vision, and particularly by God's command: "Dull that people's mind! Stop its ears! And seal its eyes, lest, seeing with its eyes and hearing with its ears, and grasping with its mind, it repent and be healed" (6:10). The prophet then asks: "How long, my Lord?" and God replies: "Till towns lie waste without inhabitants and houses without people, and the ground lies waste and desolate" (6:11). According to Deutero-Isaiah, this prophecy came to pass. The people were indeed blinded, and the desolation indeed occurred. (See the introduction, §14.) For this idea of ignorance with regard to history and events, described in the same terms, see also Deut 29:1-3: "You have seen all that the Lord did before your very eyes in the land of Egypt. . . . Yet to this day the Lord has not given you a mind to understand or eyes to see or ears to hear"; Jer 5:21: "Hear this, O foolish people, devoid of intelligence, that have eyes but cannot see, that have ears but cannot hear." Thus the deaf-and-dumb Israelites resemble the pagan idols that "have eyes but cannot see, have ears but cannot hear" (Ps 115:5-6). The motif of "blindness" links this unit to the two units preceding it (vv. 7, 16). Other links are the root חרש (vv. 14, 18, 19), דרך (vv. 16-24), and אחור (vv. 17, 23, with a different meaning). The first scene of this unit, vv. 18-20, is arranged chiastically, alternating between "deaf" and "blind": v. 18: הַחֵרְשִׁים . . . הַעִוְרִים; v. 19: עִוֵּר . . . חֵרֵשׁ . . . עִוֵּר . . . חֵרֵשׁ (read חֵרֵשׁ instead of MT עִוֵּר in the third clause of v. 19; see below); v. 20: "Seeing many things but giving no heed" (= blind) — "With ears open but hearing nothing" (= deaf). Note also the logical rhetorical development in these verses: The prophet first addresses the deaf and the blind (v. 18), and the obvious question is, to whom is he referring? He proceeds to identify the deaf and the blind as his people (v. 19), and then goes on to explain why they are so incapacitated (v. 20).

[18] *Listen, you who are deaf! And you blind ones, look and see!* — For the combination of the two verbs הביט and ראה, see Ps 142:5; Job 35:5.

[19] *Who is so blind but My servant* — Israel.

Who so deaf as the messenger I send? — Hebrew מלאך is derived from the root לאך, which in Ugaritic means "to send." For the parallel pair עבד/מלאך, see Isa 44:26: "But confirm the word of His servant (עבדו) and fulfill the prediction of His messengers (מלאכיו)."

Who is so deaf as the one whom I commission — In light of the chiastic structure of the previous hemistichs, in which עִוֵּר and חֵרֵשׁ ("blind" and "deaf") alternate, and in light of the fact that עִוֵּר appears twice in this hemistich without its complement חֵרֵשׁ, it seems most likely that עִוֵּר was mistakenly repeated from the adjacent clause and the original clause had חֵרֵשׁ instead of עִוֵּר. One should note that even some medieval commentators went so far as to emend עִוֵּר in the last clause to חֵרֵשׁ. Ibn Ganaḥ comments that this is an example of substitution since "all handicaps are grouped together" (*Sefer ha-Riqmah,* ed. Walensky [Jerusalem, 1964], II, §28 [27], 300, lines 14-15). Compare also Ibn Balaam (ed. Goshen-Gottstein, 183): "חֵרֵשׁ was meant, but וְעִוֵּר was written in its stead because the two are the same degree of handicap." The substitution suggested here, however, to replace עִוֵּר by חֵרֵשׁ in this hemistich, is preferable since it preserves the chiastic structure. The hapax legomenon מְשֻׁלָּם remains ambiguous. Some suggest to derive it from the Arabic root *salama,* which denotes acquiescence (cf. "Islam," lit. "those who surrender their will to God"). Others suggest emending the text to כִּמְשֻׁלָּח[י], parallel to the third clause, כמלאכי אשלח ("as the messenger I send"). But perhaps no emendation is necessary, if one compares 44:26, which, in addition to the עבד/מלאך parallel, also features the verb ישלים. Thus מְשֻׁלָּם may be the sobriquet for he who is destined to "fulfill" God's word.

So blind as the servant of the Lord? — The verse begins and ends in the same manner, forming a literary *inclusio.* The expression עבד ה׳ ("servant of the Lord") is also applied to Moses (Deut 34:5; Josh 1:1), Joshua (Josh 24:29; Judg 2:8), and David (Ps 18:1; 36:1), and is found on a Hebrew seal from the beginning/middle of the eighth century BCE: "Miqneyaw, servant of Yahweh (עבד ה׳)." (See N. Avigad and B. Sass, *Corpus of West Semitic Stamp Seals* [Jerusalem, 1997], 59, no. 27.)

[20] *Seeing many things but giving no heed* — God proceeds to explain that He accuses His servant of blindness and deafness because he has paid no attention to the reasons for the events that have occurred. The MT preserves two versions: the Qere רָאוֹת, an infinitive absolute that functions here as a participle and accords with the adjacent clause, פָּקוֹחַ, and the Ketib ראית, second-person masculine singular, in line with the other verb, תשמר, also in the second-person singular (so too Symmachus, Vulgate, and 1QIsa[a], ראיתה). (For the form רָאוֹת [as against רָאֹה, Exod 3:7; Isa 6:9], cf. שָׁתֹה [1 Sam 1:9], שָׁתוֹ [Isa 22:13; Jer 49:12], and שָׁתוֹת [Isa 22:13].) (For other variant readings, cf. Targum חֲזֵיתוֹן and LXX "you saw" [plural]. The Peshitta, on the other hand, translates the verbs as first-person singulars.) For the verb שמר ("giving heed, take to heart"), see Gen 37:11: "And his father kept the matter in mind (שמר)"; Ps 107:43: "Let the wise man take these things to heart (ישמר)."

With ears wide open but hearing nothing — The servant is not literally deaf, he just does not draw the proper conclusions from what he hears. Since the verb פקח is used elsewhere in connection with eyes (Isa 42:7; 2 Chr 6:40; 7:15), and not ears, for which the verb is פתח (50:5), it is not surprising that 1QIsa[a] has the reading פתחו instead of פקוח. Nevertheless, one should take into account both the evidence from Lachish ostracon 3:4-5, where the verb פקח is employed along with "ears": "Open the ear (הפקח . . . אזן) of your servant" (Aḥituv, *Ha-Ketav veha-Miktav,* 58), and Rabbinic Hebrew, e.g., *m. Yebam.* 14:1: "If a deaf mute married [a woman] who could hear (פִּקַּחַת), or one who could hear (פִּקֵּחַ) married [a woman] who was a deaf mute." The idea of open eyes and ears with the inability to see and hear appears in Akkadian literature as well: "My eyes stare, but do not see. My ears are open, but do not hear" (*BWL,* 42-43, lines 73-74; see also Lambert's note on these lines on p. 293, in which he cites another example from Sumerian literature.)

[21] God's desire to glorify and magnify His teaching.

The Lord desires his/His vindication — The meaning of this hemistich is not entirely clear, since the pronominal suffix in צִדְקוֹ may refer to the servant; see, e.g., Targum: "for the sake of Israel's vindication (לְזַכָּאוּתֵיהּ)"; Metzudat Zion; Ehrlich, *Randglossen,* 4:155. Others explain that the referent is God (e.g.,

Rashi, Ibn Ezra, Kimchi, Luzzatto). Moreover, the exact meaning of צדקוֹ is also contested: "his/His vindication," or, "his/His salvation"? Y. Kaufmann (*Babylonian Captivity and Deutero-Isaiah,* 222-23, n. 58), on the other hand, suggests a metathesis and reads: . . . ה׳ חפץ צדקו למען, "The Lord delights in his [Israel's] righteousness in order that . . . ," since Israel's salvation will be the magnification and glorification of God's teaching. (For the expression חפץ צדק, see Ps 35:27.)

So that He may magnify and glorify [His] teaching — The verb אדר ("glorify"), which appears only three times in the Bible (here in the *hiph'il,* and twice in the *niph'al,* Exod 15:6, 11), also occurs in the Phoenician inscriptions of King Azitawada (*KAI* 26A III:10) and Eshmunazor (*KAI* 14:16, 17). The feminine suffix *heh* in 1QIsa[a], ויאדרהה, refers to God's "teaching" (תורה).

[22-25] The second scene commences with a *waw* (v. 22), which contrasts the present tortuous situation of Israel in Babylonia with the ideal euphoric future expressed in the previous verse.

[22] *Yet it is a people plundered and despoiled* — For בזז and שׂסי ("to plunder" and "to despoil") in parallel hemistichs, see Jer 30:16: "Assuredly, all those who despoiled you (שֹׁאסַיִךְ) shall be despoiled. All those who plundered you (בֹּזְזַיִךְ) shall go into captivity."

All of them are ensnared in holes — הָפֵחַ (an infinitive absolute in the *hiph'il*) is a denominative verb derived from the substantive פח ("trap"). For Heb. חוּר, "hole" (a variant spelling of חוֹר), see also Isa 11:8: "A babe shall play over a viper's hole (חֹר)"; and cf. the Akkadian etymological cognate, *ḫurru* (*CAD* Ḫ:252-53). The initial *beth* of בַּחוּרִים is not part of the root (בחר, "to choose"), but rather is the preposition *beth,* "in."

Imprisoned in dungeons — The nation is "hidden away" (הָחְבָּאוּ, *hoph'al* of the root חבא) in jails (cf. the Akkadian etymological and semantic equivalent *bīt kīli* [*CAD* K:360-61]). Israel's exile is akin to imprisonment; cf. the imagery in v. 7. The plural form of both components of the construct form בָּתֵּי כְלָאִים is characteristic of Second Temple Biblical Hebrew. Compare שָׂרֵי חַיִל (2 Sam 24:4) to שׂרי הַחֲיָלִים (Jer 40:7); גבורי החיל (Josh 1:14) to גבורי חֲיָלִים (1 Chr 7:5); חָרָשֵׁי עֵץ (2 Sam 5:11) to וְחָרָשֵׁי עֵצִים (1 Chr 14:1); and Rabbinic Hebrew: ערבי שבתות, ערבי פסחים, בתי מדרשות, בתי כנסיות. (See the introduction, §11.)

They are given over to plunder, with none to rescue them — Marauders pillage and plunder God's nation, and there is none they can depend on for rescue; see also Ps 7:3; 71:11; Job 5:4; 10:7.

To despoilment, with none to say, "Give back!" — Israel's enemies despoil them, and there is no one to whom they can turn to retrieve what was plundered. For the term מְשִׁסָּה, "plunder, spoil," from the root שׁסס, parallel to בז in the previous hemistich, see also 2 Kgs 21:14: "They shall be plunder (לְבַז) and spoil (וְלִמְשִׁסָּה) to all their enemies." הָשַׁב ("give back") is a pausal *hiphʿil* imperative. The preposition ל in 1QIsa[a] (למשוסה) and the Targum (לְבִזָּא) may have been deleted from the MT as the result of a haplography from the final letter of the previous word (מציל). But since the *lamed* appended to לבז in the previous clause does double-duty and refers to משסה as well, a common phenomenon in biblical poetry, it was most likely added to clarify the meaning.

[23] The prophet reiterates and emphasizes his point through a triad of synonymous verbs; see also Isa 28:23: "Give diligent ear (הַאזינו) to My words, attend carefully (הַקשיבו ושִׁמעו) to what I say!"

If only you would listen to this — This phraseology (מי בכם) is an expression of wistfulness; see Mal 1:10: "If only you (מי . . . בכם) would lock My doors." Contrary to the majority of instances, where the usual order of the parallel verbs is הקשיב/שמע . . . האזין, the reverse order here may be due to the following זאת, which together with יאזין creates a sibilant assonance (יאזין זאת).

Attend and give heed from now on! — לְאָחוֹר refers to the future, e.g., Isa 41:23: "Foretell what will happen hereafter (לאחור)." For the verbal pair שמע/הקשיב see, e.g., 49:1 (in the reverse order); 28:23; Jer 8:6; for the האזין/שמע parallel see Deut 32:1.

[24] God explains the זאת ("this") of the previous verse, i.e., what Israel is supposed to heed. For other questions followed by a threefold answer, see Isa 41:26; 45:21.

Who was it who gave Jacob over to despoilment — Who was it that handed Jacob over (for נתן ל- cf. 34:2) to plunderers?

And Israel to plunderers? — This hemistich is chiastically parallel to the previous one, and together the two hemistichs form a chiasm with the preceding verse.

Surely, the Lord against whom they sinned — The answer to the above question is obvious: "Surely" (הֲלוא, for emphasis) the reason for Israel's desperate plight is the magnitude of their iniquity. For the relative pronoun זו in biblical poetry, see 43:21; Exod 15:13; Ps 62:12. Instead of MT חטאנו (first-person plural), the LXX and Targum (דְּחָבוּ) translate the verb as a third-person plural (חטאו), which is a preferable reading. Compare also the final clauses of this verse: "They would not walk . . . they would not obey."

In whose ways they would not walk — For the infinitive absolute הָלוֹךְ, see Num 22:14; and for the expression הלך בדרך, see Isa 48:17. For the verb אבי, "to consent to the will of another," see 1:19. It is likely that this clause, as well as the following one, were influenced by 30:9: "Children who refused to heed (אבו שמוע) the instruction of the Lord (תורת ה׳)." For the verbal pair אבה/שמע, see Deut 13:9: "Do not assent (תֹאבֶה) or give heed (תשמע) to him"; see also Ps 81:12.

And whose teaching they would not obey — For the expression שמע ב-, "to obey," see, e.g., Gen 22:18: "Because you have obeyed (שמעת בקולי) My command"; and for שמע תורה, see Zech 7:12; Prov 28:9; Neh 13:3. The plural reading of the LXX, "teachings," accords with the previous clause, "ways."

[25] *So He poured out His wrathful anger on them* — Since they refused to follow God's precepts, He inflicted His anger upon them. For the construction חֵמָה אַפּוֹ, which appears again in Isa 66:15 (for the two synonymous terms, see 63:6: "I trampled people in My anger (באפי). I made them drunk with My rage [בחמתי]"), rather than the expected חֲמַת אפו, in the construct state, as is found in 1QIsa[a], LXX, Peshitta, Targum (חֲמַת רוּגְזֵיהּ), and a number of medieval Hebrew manuscripts; see similarly Ps 60:5: יַיִן תַּרְעֵלָה, and the verses cited by Kimchi: Isa 24:22; Ruth 2:17. For further examples, see GKC §131a-h. Others suggest transferring אפו from this clause to the following: "So he poured out [His] wrath upon them, His anger and fury of war." For the "pouring out of wrath," see Jer 10:25 (= Ps 79:6): "Pour out Your wrath (שְׁפֹךְ חמתך) on the nations who have not heeded You"; Lam 2:4: "He poured out His wrath (חמתו . . . שָׁפַךְ) like fire in the tent of Zion"; and for the "pouring of anger," see Lam 4:11: "He poured out His blazing wrath (שָׁפַךְ . . . אפו)."

And the fury of war — God declared war on His people and poured out His full fury on them. The word עֱזוּז (see also Ps 145:6) is a by-form of עֹז (similar to Akk. *ezzu* [*CAD* E:432-34]); cf. Ezra 8:22: "His fierce anger (וְעֻזּוֹ) is against all who forsake Him." The image of a king who engages his enemies in fierce battle is also found in Akkadian inscriptions: "Fearing the fierceness of my battle [*uzzi* (= *ezzi*) *qablia* = עזוז מלחמה], they submitted to me" (*CAD* Q:12). For similar imagery, see Ps 24:8: "The Lord, mighty (עִזּוּז) and valiant, the Lord, valiant in battle."

It blazed upon them all about but they remained unaware — God's fury (חֵמָה, "heat, rage") blazed (וַתְּלַהֲטֵהוּ, *pi'el* from the root להט) on every side, but Israel remained totally unaware of the lethal environment. For the same image, see Ps 97:3: "Fire is His vanguard, burning His foes on every side (תְלַהֵט סביב)." For לא ידע, "to be unaware," see Hos 7:9: "Strangers have consumed his strength, yet he is unaware (לא ידע). Mold is also scattered over him, but he remains unaware (לא ידע)"; Job 9:5: "He who moves mountains without their being aware (ולא ידעו)." This also is the meaning of its Akkadian semantic and etymological equivalent, *la idû*. (See Paul, *Divrei Shalom*, 7-8.)

It burned among them but they gave it no thought — Even as the fire burned at the core of their being, they did not lay it to heart. For another image of fiery anger, see Jer 4:4 (= 21:12): "Lest My wrath break forth like fire and burn, with none to quench it." For the expression לא שׂם על לב, "to pay no heed," see Isa 47:7; 57:11; and for its semantic equivalent in Akkadian, see 41:22. For the synonymous pair להט and בער, see Ps 83:15: "As a fire burns (תִּבְעַר) a forest, as flames scorch (תְּלַהֵט) the hills"; Ps 106:18: "A fire raged (וַתִּבְעַר) among their party, a flame that blazed up (תלהט) against the wicked."

Chapter 43

[1-8] The prophet announces that salvation and repatriation are imminent. The release of the Israelites from their Babylonian exile is nigh. Israel is so precious to God that He is willing to grant Cyrus dominion over all of Africa in return for His people's redemption. The first unit of chap. 43 (plus v. 9) has a lot in common with Jer 31:3-10:

Isaiah 43:1-8 (+ 9)	**Jeremiah 31:3-10**
v. 3: Your Savior (מושיעך)	v. 7: Save (הוֹשַׁע)
v. 4: And I love you (ואני אהבתיך)	v. 3: And I love you with an eternal love (ואהבת עולם אהבתיך)
v. 5: I will bring (אביא); v. 6: Bring (הביאי)	v. 8: I will bring (מביא)
v. 5: I will gather you (אקבצך)	v. 8: I will gather them (וקבצתים)
v. 6: North (צפון)	v. 8: From the north land (מארץ צפון)
v. 6: From the end of the earth (מקצה הארץ)	v. 8: From the ends of the earth (מירכתי ארץ)
v. 8: That people, blind (עם עִוֵּר)	v. 8: The blind among them (בם עִוֵּר)
v. 9: Declare (יגיד)	v. 10: Declare (הַגידו)

Note also the similarity between the first verse of the next unit (43:9): . . . הגוים ישמיעֻנו, and Jer 31:7: הגוים הַשמיעו, as well as Jer 31:10: גוים . . . שִׁמעו. For further Jeremian influence on these verses, cf. Jer 30:10-11: "But you, have no fear, My servant Jacob — declares the Lord! Be not dismayed, O Israel! I will deliver you from far away, your folk from their land of captivity. . . . For I am with you to deliver you — declares the Lord." (See the introduction, §15.)

Linguistic links connect this prophecy of redemption and the plight of the exile with the last pericope of chap. 42: לא תבער בך (v. 2) — ותבער בו (42:25); אמר (v. 6) — (אין) אֹמֵר (42:22); (אל) תִּכְלָאִי (v. 6) — (בתי) כְלָאִים (42:22); עִוֵּר . . . חֵרְשִׁים (v. 8) — הַעִוְרִים . . . הַחֵרְשִׁים (42:18). Many exegetes maintain that the unit ends in 43:7. If so, the first and last verses form a literary frame that begins with the words: "The Lord who created you (בֹּרַאֲךָ), O Jacob, who formed (וְיֹצֶרְךָ) you, O Israel. I have called you by name (קראתי בשמך)" (v. 1), and concludes: "All who are called by My name (הנקרא בשמי), whom I have created (בראתיו), formed (יצרתיו)" (v. 7). Note also possible allusions to the Israelite patriarch Jacob (v. 1: "who created you, O Jacob"), who received a boost of morale from God as he was about to return from his exile in Aram: "Return to the land of your fathers where you were born, and I will be with you!" (Gen 31:3). Jacob, too, crossed a river, the Jabbok (Gen 32:23; cf. v. 2 here). See below, v. 8, for further discussion regarding the division of units.

[1] *But now thus said the Lord* — The beginning of a new prophecy (cf. 44:1; 47:8; 49:5).

Who created you, O Jacob, who formed you, O Israel — For the verbal pair ברא/יצר, see below, v. 7. For other joint appearances of Jacob and Israel (e.g., vv. 22, 28), see 40:27; 44:1. The creator of the universe (40:12ff.; 42:5) is also He who fashioned the nation (see vv. 7, 15, 21; 44:2, 21, 24; 45:11).

"Fear not" — A formula of encouragement that appears frequently in Deutero-Isaiah's early prophecies; see v. 5; 41:10, 13, 14; 44:1. For its ancient Near Eastern parallels, see 41:10.

"For I will redeem you!" — Salvation is imminent: "The image is one of a relative redeeming his kin from indenture, and thus he states below: 'I will give as a ransom'" (v. 3) (Luzzatto). God as Redeemer is a very common motif in these prophecies; see, e.g., v. 14; 41:14; 44:6; 47:4. (See the introduction, §9.) For the juxtaposition of God as the creator of Israel and the nation's redeemer, see 44:24. He who created Israel is also He who will redeem them, and thus Israel has nothing to fear: "Fear not! . . . [I am] your Redeemer" (41:14).

"I have called you by name" — God declares that Israel is His, and only His. To "call by name" (קרא בשם) denotes choosing, singling out an individual, e.g., "It is I the Lord, the God of Israel, who call you [Cyrus] by name." In Akkadian the semantic cognate *šumam nabû/zakāru* also denotes choice (*CAD* N/1:36-37; Z:18; Paul, *Divrei Shalom*, 12). The Targum, LXX, Vulgate, and Peshitta all add the second-person masculine pronominal suffix ךָ to the verb קראתי; cf. 41:9.

"You are mine" — For this formula, which denotes personal ownership, cf. Gen 48:5, where Jacob declares that Ephraim and Manasseh are his (לי הם).

[2] To emphasize the absolute protection God will confer upon them on their return journey to Israel, a metaphorical merism is employed (to express all possible dangers that they may encounter): God will be with them in water and fire and will allow no harm to come to them; cf. Ps 66:12: "We have gone through fire and water, but You have brought us through to relief."

"When you pass through water, I will be with you" — I shall save you from drowning, since you are Mine and I will protect you. This formula is a variant of כי עמך אני; see Isa 41:10 and the references there to ancient Near Eastern parallels. For the verb עבר, referring to passing through water, see 47:2.

"And through streams, they shall not drown you" — For the pair מים/נהרות, see below, v. 20; and for the imagery cf. Cant 8:7: "Many waters (מים) cannot quench love, nor rivers (ונהרות) drown it." Hebrew נְהָרוֹת may also be an illusion to the canals (Akk. *nāru*) (*CAD* N/1:386ff.) that they would have to cross in their departure from Babylon.

"When you walk through fire, you shall not be scorched" — The verb כוי appears only once more in the Bible, in Prov 6:28: "Can a man walk on live coals without scorching (תִּכָּוֶינָה) his feet?" The substantive כְּוִיָּה appears only in Exod 21:25: כויה תחת כויה, "burn for burn." For בְּמוֹ, an elongated poetic form of the preposition ב, see Isa 44:16, 19.

"And through flame, it shall not burn you" — For the parallel pair אש/לֶהָבָה, see 47:14; Num 21:28.

[3] Up until now there was no one who listened, "None to say, 'Give back!'" (42:22). But now God, Israel's redeemer, is ready to redeem His nation, and for their ransom He will surrender all of Africa to Cyrus.

"For I the Lord am your God" — This self-introductory declaration is reminiscent of the opening phrase of the Ten Commandments, Exod 20:2: "I the Lord am your God (אנכי ה׳ אלהיך)," which comes to encourage Israel; see Isa 41:13: "For I the Lord am your God, who grasped your right hand, who says to you, 'Have no fear!'"

"The Holy One of Israel, your Savior" — It is I, the Holy One of Israel (cf. vv. 14, 15), who shall save you. God is Israel's sole defender: "I, I Myself, the Lord. Besides Me, none can save" (v. 11). Instead of מושיעך, "your Savior," the scribe of 1QIsa[a] inserted above the line גואלך ("your Redeemer"), which is probably a variant. Compare the compound expression מושיעך וגאלך in 49:26; 60:16. For the theme of redemption coupled with the divine title קדוש ישראל ("the Holy One of Israel"), see v. 14; 48:17; 49:7. The verb ישע, as well as the substantives ישעי, תשועה, and ישועה, reverberate throughout Deutero-Isaiah's prophecy (for the verb see vv. 11, 12; 45:15, 17, 21; 49:6, 8; 51:5, 6, 8; 52:7, 10; and for the substantive forms see 45:8, 17; 46:13; 49:6, 8; 51:5, 6, 8; 52:7, 10) — all

of which contrast with the gods of the nations who are unable to save themselves or their worshipers (see 46:7; 47:13, 15).

"I give Egypt as a ransom for you" — Since God is Israel's redeemer, He is responsible for releasing them from their indenture to their Babylonian overlords. The verb נתן (lit. "to give"), similar to its Akkadian semantic and etymological equivalent *nadānu* (*CAD* N/1:45), denotes payment; cf. Gen 23:13: "Let me pay (נתתי) the price of the land"; Exod 30:12: "Each shall pay the Lord a ransom (ונתנו . . . כֹּפֶר) for himself." For the substantive כֹּפֶר, "ransom," see also Exod 21:30; Num 35:31, 32; and cf. Prov 21:18: "The wicked are the ransom (כֹּפֶר) of the righteous; the traitor comes in place (תחת) of the upright."

"Nubia and Seba in exchange for you" — For תחת, "instead of," "in exchange for," see v. 4 (twice); Gen 44:33: "Therefore, please let your servant remain as a slave to my lord instead (תחת) of the lad"; Exod 21:23-25: "Life for (תחת) life, eye for (תחת) eye," etc. For another instance of the parallel pair כֹּפֶר/תחת, see Prov 21:18, quoted above. Nubia (כּוּשׁ) refers to the land south of Egypt, and in the genealogy of Ham in Gen 10 Kush is listed as Ham's firstborn, followed by Egypt (Gen 10:6). For other joint appearances of these countries, see Isa 20:3-5; Ezek 30:4, 9; Nah 3:9; Ps 68:32. Seba (סְבָא), Kush's firstborn in the same genealogical list, is not to be identified with Sheba (שְׁבָא) in southern Arabia (see Ps 72:10: "Kings of Sheba and Seba offer gifts"), but rather is the name of another African country. The three countries, Egypt, Nubia, and Seba, are grouped together in Isa 45:14. In the eyes of the prophet they constitute the whole of Africa. God is willing to pay a very high price to free His people.

[4] In a triad of parallel clauses, God explains why He is willing to pay such a high price for Israel's freedom. (For Deutero-Isaianic triads see the introduction, §10.A.3.)

"Because you are precious to Me and honored" — The substantive בעיני (lit. "in My eyes") relates to both of the verbs of this clause. On the one hand, according to the Masoretic punctuation, it refers to נכבדת ("honored"); see also 49:5: "And I have been honored in sight of the Lord" (ואכבדה בעיני ה׳). On the other hand, it also is combined with the verb יקר; see 1 Sam 26:21: "Since you have held my life precious (יקרה . . . בעיניך)"; 2 Kgs 1:14: "Let my life be precious in your eyes (תיקר . . . בעיניך)." The latter expression is also found in Akkadian: *ina īni aqāru* ("precious in my eyes"; *CAD* A/2:205-6). For מֵאֲשֶׁר, "because," see also Num 6:11.

"And I love you" — God has a deep emotional connection to His people; cf. Isa 41:8: "Seed of Abraham whom I love (אֹהֲבִי)"; Deut 23:6: "For the Lord your God loves you (אֲהֵבְךָ)." Whereas in the Mesopotamian royal inscriptions the gods express their love for the monarch, here God proclaims His love for the entire nation. Moreover, in the legalese of pacts and treaties in the ancient Near East, the various verbs expressing "to love" denote mutual loyalty between

the monarch and his vassals and between them and their sovereign. So too in Israel; cf. Deut 6:5: "You shall love [ואהבת, i.e., you shall be loyal to] the Lord your God with all your heart and with all your soul and with all your might." The God of Israel also expresses His love for Cyrus: "He whom the Lord loves (אֲהֵבוֹ) shall work His will against Babylon" (Isa 48:14).

"I give people in exchange for you and nations in your stead" — This is a reference to v. 3 and to the lands God will grant Cyrus in return for Israel's redemption. For אדם, "people, humankind," see Jer 32:20: "You displayed signs and marvels in the land of Egypt . . . and won renown in Israel and among humankind (אדם)"; Job 36:28: "The skies rain; they pour down on all humankind (אדם)." In the Baal and Anat epic from Ugarit, the substantives *lim* (= לְאֻמִּים) and *adm* (= אדם) are also parallel to one another: "She [the goddess Anat] smites the peoples *(lim)* on the west [lit. 'seashore'], destroys humans *(adm)* on the east" (*CAT* 1.3.II:7-8).

[5-6] The repatriation of all Israelites is imminent, for God is about to bring back His scattered nation from the four corners of the earth. At the time of this prophecy, the Israelites were widely dispersed in Assyria, Babylonia, Egypt (cf. Jer 43), and Elephantine (49:12). Compare also Ps 107:3: "Whom He gathered in from the lands, from east and west, from the north and from the sea."

[5] *"Fear not, for I am with you!"* — This boost of morale repeats and emphasizes the above statements (vv. 1-2). For ancient Near Eastern parallels, see Isa 41:3.

"I will bring your folk from the east and gather you from the west" — I shall gather and regroup all the exiles from the east and from the west. For this geographical merism, see 45:6; 59:19; and for parallel constructions in cognate languages, see 45:6. For the term זרע, parallel to בנים (v. 6), see 57:3. The terms also appear together in the Phoenician inscription of Eshmunazor: "Let him have no son (בן) or offspring (זרע)" (*KAI* 14:8); in an Aramaic document: "I myself, my son (בני), and my progeny (וזרעי)" (see B. Porten and A. Yardeni, eds., *A Textbook of Aramaic Documents from Ancient Egypt,* 2: *Contracts* [Winona Lake, Ind., 1989], 34, B2.7:8); and in Akkadian: *šumu-zēru,* "son-progeny" (*CAD* Z:94-95). The term may also be polysemous, referring here also to Israel's diaspora; cf. Zech 10:9: "I dispersed them (וָאֶזְרָעֵם; lit. 'I scattered them like seed') among the nations" (Ehrlich, *Randglossen,* 4:156). For the root קבץ, denoting "gathering, assembling," see Isa 40:11; 49:18; 54:7; 56:8; 60:4; and cf. the Akkadian semantic equivalent *puḫḫuru,* which also refers to the "gathering" of dispersed peoples (*CAD* P:30). For the verbal pair קבץ and בוא/הביא, see 49:18; 60:4; Zeph 3:20. One should note that מערב ("west") is a late biblical term and, aside from the verses cited above, is found only in Daniel and Chronicles. (See the introduction, §11.)

[6] *"I will say to the north, 'Give back!' and to the south, 'Do not withhold!'"* — "The feminine is used here for north and south, since the referent is רוח, which is usually feminine" (Ehrlich, *Randglossen,* 4:96). God will command the north and south (תימן; see Josh 15:1) winds to deliver His people to their promised land. For the anthropomorphization of these two winds, see also Cant 4:16: "Awake, O north wind (צפון)! Come, O south wind (תימן)!" For the gathering of people from the farthest reaches of the world, see Isa 49:12: "Look! These are coming from afar: These from the north and the west, and these from the land of Syene [= Aswan]"; Ps 107:3: "Whom he gathered in from the lands, from east and west, from the north and from the sea."

"Bring My sons from afar, and My daughters from the ends of the earth!" — Each one of the winds is commanded to bring back the members of God's nation even from the farthest reaches of the world. (For the expression מקצה הארץ, see Isa 42:10; and for מקצות הארץ, see 41:9.) God is described in this verse as Israel's concerned Father, who looks out for His sons and daughters; cf. 63:16: "Surely You are our Father"; 64:7: "But now, O Lord, You are our Father." For a similar divine injunction, this time directed toward the nations of the world, see 49:22: "I will raise My hand to nations and lift up My ensign to peoples. And they shall bring your sons in their bosoms and carry your daughters on their shoulders." The plural verb in 1QIsa[a], הביאו, refers to both the north and south winds together. This reading (rather than the MT feminine singular) is also found in the Targum, *Yalqut Shimoni* (§452), and in some medieval Hebrew manuscripts. 1QIsa[b] has בניך . . . ובנותיך, "your sons and daughters," also attested in *Yalqut Shimoni* (§452), a reading that may very well have been influenced by 49:22 (quoted above).

[7] This verse, which is in apposition to the previous one, is similar to v. 1; both have the common verbal elements: יצר, ברא, קרא בשם.

"All who are called by My name" — For the expression נקרא (ב)שם, see 48:1; 63:19.

"Whom I created, formed, and made for My glory" — This triad of synonymous verbs reiterates and emphasizes that Israel was created for the sole purpose of glorifying God's name. (For triads as a stylistic marker see the introduction, §10.A.3.) For these three verbs of creation in conjunction, see also 45:7; 45:18. For the nominal pair שֵׁם/כבוד, found here and in 59:19, cf. also כבוד שמו (Ps 29:2) and השם הנכבד (Deut 28:58). Compare also their Akkadian etymological and semantic cognate: *šumu kabtu* (*CAD* K:27). This כבוד is mutual: Here God maintains that Israel was made for His "glory," and above, in v. 4, Israel is "glorified" in God's eyes.

[8] This verse is the direct continuation of v. 6. God commands that His people be set free. Nevertheless, His nation is deaf and blind, because although they have eyes and ears, they do not fully comprehend the significance of the historical events that have occurred. Thus they resemble idols that "[have] eyes but cannot see . . . [have] ears but cannot hear" (Ps 115:6). Compare also Ezek 12:2: "O mortal, you dwell among the rebellious breed. They have eyes to see, but see not, ears to hear, but hear not; for they are a rebellious breed."

Free this people, blind though it has eyes — The verb יצא in the *hiph'il* denotes release from bondage, e.g., Exod 12:51: "The Lord freed (הוציא) the Israelites from the land of Egypt"; Exod 13:3: "The Lord freed (הוציא) you from it [Egypt] with a mighty hand." The form here, third-person masculine singular, is, however, somewhat problematic. Some suggest vocalizing the verb as an imperative, either in the feminine singular, הוֹצִיאִ, or in the plural, הוציאו (1QIsa[a]), referring to the wind(s) in v. 6, while others prefer here an infinitive absolute, הוֹצֵיא, serving as an imperative. 1QIsa[b], on the other hand, has אוציא ("I will free"). For יש as an emphatic, see 1 Sam 21:5: "I have no ordinary bread on hand; there is only (יש) consecrated bread."

And deaf though it has ears! — For the poetic form לָמוֹ, see, e.g., Deut 33:2; Ps 119:165.

[9-10] The prophet returns to the motif of the trial scene, to which he has summoned the pagan gods and their worshipers. Once again, Deutero-Isaiah reiterates that only the God of Israel is able to predict future events, and His witnesses are Israel. In the previous unit the prophet announced an ingathering of the Israelites; now he gathers the nations for their trial.

[9] *All the nations are gathered together* — for the express purpose of conducting a trial. For the verb קבץ with the connotation of assembling for judicial proceedings, see Isa 45:20: "Come, gather together (הִקָּבְצוּ)!"; 48:14: "Assemble (הִקָּבְצוּ), all of you, and listen!" The Akkadian semantic equivalent *puḫḫuru*, "to assemble," is also used in juristic contexts (*CAD* P:28).

And the peoples assemble — This hemistich forms a chiastic parallel with the previous one. For the parallel verbal pair קבץ/אסף, see 62:9; 11:12; Ezek 11:17; 39:17; Joel 2:16; and for the parallel nouns גוים/לְאֻמִּים, see Isa 34:1.

Who among them predicted this, foretold to us the things that have happened? — Who among you so-called gods can say that they accurately predicted the twists and turns of history? For the declaring/foretelling motif, see 41:22-23: "Let them approach and tell us what will happen. Tell us what has occurred and we will take note of it. Or announce to us what will occur, that we may know the outcome. Foretell what is yet to happen"; 44:8: "Have I not of old predicted to you? I foretold, and you are My witnesses"; 45:21: "Speak up . . . Who announced this aforetime, foretold it of old?" 1QIsa[a] has a slightly different reading: יגידו and ישמיעו. Compare also the variant in the LXX, "foretold to you" (plural). For a similar polemical context, see 48:14: "Assemble, all of you, and listen! Who among you foretold these things?" For רִאשֹׁנוֹת, see 41:22; 42:9; 43:18; 46:9; 48:3. (See the introduction, §4.)

Let them produce their witnesses and be vindicated — The prophet derisively demands that they produce their witnesses, so that they can testify to their gods' oracular abilities and thus be vindicated. The so-called witnesses, however, "neither see nor know" (44:9) and thus cannot even serve as witnesses (see Lev 5:1). For **צדק**, "to be cleared of all charges, vindicated," see v. 26 below: "Tell your version, that you may be vindicated (**תצדק**)!"; 50:8: "My Vindicator (**מַצדיקי**) is at hand — who dares contend with me?"; cf. also 41:26.

So that people when hearing it will say, "It is true!" — Let all hear the truth of the matter, that they are supposedly able to predict and foretell events. 1QIsa[a] **וישמיעו** *(hiph'il),* contra MT **וישמעו** *(qal),* is identical to its previous variant reading in the previous clause. For **אמת** in a judicial context, see Deut 22:20: "But if the charge proves true (**אמת**), the girl was found not to have been a virgin."

[10] *"My witnesses are you," says the Lord* — As opposed to the heathen gods, who cannot furnish reliable witnesses because, as the prophet accuses, they are indeed unable to predict future events, Israel can testify to God's ever true oracular prowess. The motif of Israel bearing testimony on behalf of God appears again immediately below in v. 12, and see 44:8: "Have I not from of old predicted to you? I foretold, and you are My witnesses."

"My servant, whom I have chosen" — You, the people of Israel, are "My servant"; see also 41:8: "But you, Israel, My servant, Jacob, whom I have chosen"; and cf. 44:1-2; 45:4. The word **עבדי**, in the singular, functions here as a collective noun.

"So that you may take thought and believe in Me, and understand" — I chose you so that you would know and put your faith in Me. For the Ugaritic interdialectal etymological and semantic parallel to **בין/ידע**, see *CAT* 1.3.III:27: *td'/tbn.*

"That I am He" — For Heb. **אני הוא**, an emphatic formula stressing God's uniqueness, see v. 13; 41:4; 46:4; 48:12; 52:6; Deut 32:39. In all these verses the term **הוא**, "He," refers to the Deity Himself. Compare the celebratory cry on the Feast of Tabernacles, when those assembled around the altar cry out: "**אני והו**, save us!" (*m. Sukkah* 4:5).

"Before Me no god was formed, and after Me none shall exist" — God alone is everlasting: no god existed before Him and none shall exist after Him; see Isa 44:6; 48:12: "I am first and I am last"; and cf. 41:4.

[11-13] God's uniqueness is further elaborated upon (note the threefold repetition of **אין** and the fivefold repetition of **אני/אנכי** in vv. 11, 12, 13), as well as His role as Israel's sole protector. This pericope is linked to the preceding one by the motif of Israel being God's witnesses (vv. 9, 10, 12) and by the combination of verbs to "foretell" and "announce" (vv. 9, 12); cf. also **אֵל** (vv. 10, 12); **אני הוא** (vv. 10, 13); and the play on words, **עֵדַי** (v. 10) and **מִבַּלְעָדַי** (v. 11).

[11] *"I, I myself, am the Lord"* — Emphatic doubling is a hallmark of

Deutero-Isaiah's style. For a similar repetition, see v. 25; 48:15; 51:12. (See the introduction, §10.A.1.)

"Besides Me, none can grant triumph" — God alone is Israel's savior. The two motifs — God's uniqueness (see 44:6: "I am the first and I am the last, and there is no god but Me"; 44:8: "Is there any god, then, but Me? There is no other rock; I know none!"; 45:6: "That there is none but Me"; 45:21: "Was it not I the Lord? Then there is no god beside Me") and His uncontested and irrefutable ability to redeem His nation (see 45:15: "O God of Israel, who brings victory"; 49:26: "That I am the Lord, your Savior") — are central to Deutero-Isaiah's prophecy. The progression of ideas here — God's self-presentation, followed by the theme of salvation — may have been indirectly influenced by the introduction to the Decalogue, "I, the Lord, am your God who brought you out of the land of Egypt" (Exod 20:2).

[12] This verse echoes the Sinaitic revelation and most likely was influenced by Ps 81:9-11: "Hear (שְׁמַע), My people, and I will admonish (ואעידה) you. Israel, if you would but listen (תשמע) to Me! You shall have no foreign god (אל זר) . . . I the Lord (אנכי ה׳) am your God who brought you out of the land of Egypt." (See the introduction, §17.) The rabbis based a very daring midrash on this verse: "When you are My witnesses, I am God. When you are not My witnesses, it is as if I am not God" (*Sifre Deuteronomy* 144 [ed. Finkelstein], 403-4).

"I alone foretold, delivered, and announced it" — The triad of verbs emphasizes and confirms God's claim that only He foretold future events, brought them to pass, and then triumphantly redeemed His nation from Babylon. The repetition of אנכי (twice in v. 11), together with the verb "to save" (also v. 11), reiterates that God alone is His nation's salvation. The position of the verb והושעתי, sandwiched between הגדתי and והשמעתי (for the latter two paired together, see v. 9), is problematic since it would fit better in the final position, i.e., after God has foretold and announced He delivered His people. Accordingly, some commentators explain that the verb is a corrupt dittography of the subsequent והשמעתי, while others emend to והודעתי, which is synonymous with the two other verbs in the series.

"And no foreign god was among you" — Commentators are divided regarding the reference of the term זָר in the present context. Some understand that Deutero-Isaiah is declaring that not a single Israelite is ignorant of God's oracular powers, and thus each and every one of them is able to testify on God's behalf. It is, however, preferable to interpret it as an elliptical form of the expression אל זר ("foreign god"). For other examples, see Deut 32:16: "They roused His jealousy with foreign gods (זרים)"; Jer 2:25: "No, I love foreign gods (זרים), and after them I must go"; Jer 3:13: "And you scattered your favors among foreign gods (זרים) under every leafy tree."

"So you are My witnesses," declares the Lord — For this reason all of you are My very own witnesses.

"And I am God" — You are my witnesses that I am the one and only God; cf. Isa 45:22: "For I am God, and there is none else."

[13] The first two hemistichs of this verse were influenced by the formula in Deut 32:39: "See, then, that I, I am He; there is no God beside Me . . . none can deliver from My hand." (See introduction, §13.)

"From this very day, I am He" — מִיּוֹם has been understood by some as denoting the beginning of time; cf. LXX, Vulgate, Peshitta, Targum (מֵעַלְמָא, "from the beginning"), and the majority of medieval commentators. Luzzatto, however, explains that it refers to the future, basing his interpretation on Ezek 48:35: "And the name of the city from that day on (מיום) shall be 'The Lord Is There.'" This explanation is indeed preferable, since the particle גם indicates that this state is in addition to a previous state. Compare similarly the cognate expressions: Akk. *ištu ūmi annî* (*CAD* U/W:404), and Ugar. *l ym hnd* (*HdO* 2:964), which both mean "from this day forth" (cf. Hag 2:15, 19). For אני הוא as referring to God, see v. 10 above.

"None can deliver from My hand" — The expression הציל מיד denotes seizing an object forcibly from someone who does not wish to relinquish it, e.g., Isa 47:14: "They cannot save themselves from (יצילו . . . מיד) the flames"; Exod 3:8: "I have come down to rescue them from (להצילו מיד) the Egyptians." Compare likewise the Akkadian semantic cognate: *ina/ištu qāti eṭēru/šūzubu* ("to save or deliver from someone's hand") (*CAD* E:403, 424).

"When I act, who can reverse it?" — No one! For להשיב, "to reverse, revoke," see Isa 14:27: "For the Lord of Hosts has planned, who then can frustrate it? It is His arm that is poised, and who can turn it back (יְשִׁיבֶנָּה)?"; Amos 1:3: "For three transgressions of Damascus, for four, I will not revoke it (אשיבנו)"; Esth 8:8: "For an edict that has been written in the king's name and sealed with the king's signet may not be revoked (להשיב)." The third-person feminine singular pronominal suffix -נָּה expresses a neuter object or, alternatively, refers to יד in the previous hemistich (see Ps 74:11).

[14-15] A description of Babylon's downfall (Babylon is named here for the first time in Deutero-Isaiah's prophecies; see also 47:1; 48:14, 20) and a declaration of God's kingship. Although the Deity's messenger is not mentioned here by name, it is clear from earlier prophecies that Cyrus is God's "rod of wrath" (cf. 44:28; 45:1). This small unit begins with קדוש ישראל and ends with קדושכם . . . ישראל, creating a literary frame. The redemption and creation motifs appear once again in these verses: "Your Redeemer" (v. 14); "Creator of Israel" (v. 15).

[14] *Thus said the Lord, your Redeemer, the Holy One of Israel* — For

גֹּאַלְכֶם and קדוש ישראל in conjunction, see 41:14; 48:17; 49:7; 54:5. (See the introduction, §9.)

"For your sake I have sent to Babylon" — "Cyrus was dispatched to Babylon on your behalf, to expedite your departure and the return to your land" (Kimchi). Since the object of the verb is missing, some commentators emend to שלחתיו, "I have sent him." It is also possible that a preposition ב was omitted from בָבֶלָה by haplography, בבבלה (or, preferably, בבבל, 1QIsa[a]), with the meaning "to send against, attack" (שׁלח ב-); cf. Joel 2:25; Amos 4:10; Isa 10:6: "I send him against an ungodly nation." The MT may have been influenced by Jer 29:20: "But you, the whole exile community which I have sent from Jerusalem to Babylon (שלחתי . . . בבלה), hear the word of the Lord!"

"I will destroy all [her] bars/boats" — This hemistich is very ambiguous and has been resolved in a variety of ways. First of all, there is disagreement on whether the *waw* appended to the verb והורדתי should be understood as a *waw* conversive, with the stress on the final syllable (thus according to MT): "I will destroy"; or whether the verb should be stressed on the penultimate syllable, rendering the *waw* a *waw* consecutive: "I have destroyed." According to the first interpretation Babylon has not yet fallen, and according to the second Babylon's fall has already occurred (539 BCE).

Another difficulty is the term בריחים. Some commentators explain it as referring to the bars that keep the city gates locked (Vulgate, Ibn Ezra, Abravanel, Luzzatto; see Isa 45:2; Lam 2:9: "He has smashed her bars [בְּרִיחֶיהָ] to bits"). Others (including LXX, Peshitta [ערוקא], Kimchi) interpret it from the verb ברח, "to flee," i.e., to those who are fleeing before the attack of Cyrus (cf. Isa 15:5: "Those who have fled [בְּרִיחֶהָ] as far as Zoar"). Yet others relate the word to Ugar. *br,* "a type of barge" (*HdO* 1:236), which would create a parallel with "ships" (אֳנִיּוֹת) in the next clause (so too in Ugaritic, where *anyt,* "ships," appears alongside *br* [*CAT* 4.81:1-2; 4.421:2-3]), and thus they emend to בָּרֵיהֶם, "their barges." On the other hand, some see no reason to resort to emendation, since the prefix ב could be interpreted as a preposition, and not as an integral part of the root. Thus, according to Ehrlich (*Miqra ki-Pheshuṭo,* 3:98), ריחים is the plural form of רִיחַ [a derivative of רוּחַ, "wind"], which denotes a sailboat having no oars or a boat not dependent solely on oars; see also Yellin, *Ḥiqrei Miqra,* 49; and Metzudat Zion, "boats propelled by the wind." According to this interpretation, God declares that He will sink the Babylonian ships and thereby drown the Babylonians. Another possibility is to divide בריחים into two separate words: ברוח ים, "I shall destroy Babylon by means of an ocean wind." For the verb ירד in the *hiph'il,* "to destroy," see Ps 56:8: "Destroy (הוֹרֵד) nations in Your anger, O God!"

"And the Chaldeans in their ships of joy" — And I shall destroy (the verb in the first clause does double-duty and applies here as well) the Babylonians in

the boats on which they sing in joy. Some maintain that רִנָּתָם denotes "lamentation"; cf. Lam 2:19: "Arise, cry out (רוני) in the night!" (e.g., Kimchi). Yet others interpret אֳנִיּוֹת not as the plural of אֳנִיָּה, but as a homonym that appears solely in the expression "mourning and moaning" (Isa 29:2; Lam 2:5), and translate: "I shall transform the Babylonians' cries of joy into wails of lamentation" (Luzzatto). The first explanation is preferable, however, since אֲנִיָּה ("mourning") does not appear in the Bible in the plural, and its only two occurrences are, as just mentioned, in conjunction with תַּאֲנִיָּה. The Chaldeans, who are mentioned here for the first time in Deutero-Isaiah's prophecies (see also 47:1, 5; 48:14, 20), were originally an Aramaic tribe from southern Mesopotamia whose name became synonymous with Babylon and the Babylonians; see 48:20: "Go forth from Babylon! Hasten away from Chaldea! Declare with sounds of joy!" The latter verse, in addition to the mention of Chaldea, also contains other similar elements to the verse here: בריחים-בִּרְחוּ and רִנה-רִנתם.

[15] *"I am the Lord, your Holy One"* — The unit ends in the same way it began in v. 14, creating a literary *inclusio.* For this divine title, see also 41:14, 16, 20; 45:11; 47:4; 48:17; 49:7; 54:5; 60:9, 14.

"The Creator of Israel, your King" — The root ברא links this verse with vv. 1, 7. For God as King, see 41:21; 44:6; 52:7. (See the introduction, §9.)

[16-21] The imminent redemption brings to mind the miracles of yesteryear, especially the splitting of the Reed Sea and the drowning of the Egyptians (cf. 51:10; 63:11-13). Moreover, this time the miracles will be even more spectacular, and God will literally turn nature upside down. Instead of "making a road through the sea," He will make a "road through the desert," providing both a pathway for the returning Israelites and an abundant water supply.

[16] *Thus said the Lord, who made a road through the sea* — A clear allusion to the parting of the Reed Sea (Exod 14:21-22, 29); see also Isa 51:10. The participle הנותן indicates here a past action. For the verbal expression נתן ב-, see 41:19.

And a path through mighty waters — parallels the previous hemistich. For further examples of the pair ים/מים, see Exod 15:10; and for דרך/נתיבה, see Isa 42:16; 59:8. Similar imagery appears in Ps 77:20: "Your way was through the sea; Your path, through mighty waters." The expression מים עזים ("mighty waters"), which appears once more in a similar context (Neh 9:11), is a variant of מים אדירים (Exod 15:10). Its cognate equivalent in Akkadian, *ezzu,* also describes floodwaters (*CAD* E:434); so too *mû dannūtu* and *mû ašṭūtu,* "mighty waters," "stormy waters" (*CAD* A/2:475, in the lexical list).

[17] *Who destroyed chariots and horses and all the mighty infantry host* — Although the verb הוציא, "to free" (lit. "to take out"), is fairly common in descriptions of the exodus, its referent is always the Israelite nation, e.g., Exod 12:51: "The Lord freed (הוציא) the Israelites from the land of Egypt," but never the Egyptian army. Here, therefore, it should be interpreted as the cognate Hebrew *hiph'il* of the Aramaic verb שֵׁיצִי (*shaph'el*, from the root יצא), meaning "to destroy." Compare, e.g., Targum Onqelos to Gen 18:23: "Will you sweep away (תִּסְפֶּה) the innocent along with the guilty?" where the verb is translated תְּשֵׁיצֵי; and Gen 34:30: "I will be destroyed (ונשמדתי)," which is translated, וְאֶשְׁתֵּיצֵי. The pair רכב וסוס ("chariots and horses"; see Ps 76:7) is an allusion to Pharaoh's host; see Exod 14:23: "The Egyptians came in pursuit after them into the sea, all of Pharaoh's horses (סוס), chariots (רכבו), and horsemen"; see also Exod 15:21. The phrase חַיִל וְעִזּוּז refers to the elite infantry units of the Egyptian army; cf. Exod 14:9: "The Egyptians, all the chariot horses of Pharaoh, his cavalry, and his infantry (חֵילוֹ), pursued them" (see also Exod 14:17, 28). (For חַיִל as an infantry force as opposed to cavalry, see 1 Kgs 20:1; 2 Kgs 6:14; Ezra 8:22.) The adjective עִזּוּז ("mighty, powerful") denotes a mighty warrior in Ps 24:8: "The Lord is strong (עזוז) and mighty," and is related to the substantive עֱזוּז ("strength, might"); see Ps 78:4: "Telling the coming generation the praise of the Lord and His might (וֶעֱזוּזוֹ) and the wonders He performed"; Ps 145:6: "Men shall talk of the might (ועזוז) of Your awesome deeds"; cf. also Isa 42:25: "The fierceness (עזוז) of battle." This term creates a wordplay with the preceding verse's עזים ("mighty"). One should transfer the Masoretic pausal accentuation, *atnach,* from עזוז to יחדו, which is commonly used at the close of a series of substantives or verbs; see, e.g., 41:19, 20.

They lay down to rise no more — The entire army, whose intent was to destroy the Israelite nation, was itself destroyed as it sank in watery graves, never to rise again. The expression בל יקומו ("to rise no more"), which is the corresponding negative parallel to ישכבו, denotes total demise; see 26:14: "The dead will not live again; they never shall rise (בל יקומו)." This also is the meaning of the verb שׁכב; cf. Ps 41:9: "He has lain down (שכב), never to rise again (לא יוסיף לָקוּם)"; Job 14:12: "So man lies down (שכב), never to rise (ולא יקום)."

They were extinguished, snuffed out like a wick — For דעך, "to be extinguished," see Prov 13:9: "The lamp of the wicked is extinguished (ידעך)"; Job 18:5: "Indeed, the light of the wicked goes out (ידעך)." Pharaoh's army was extinguished like the flickers of a dying candlewick. For כבי ("to be snuffed out, extinguished"), see 1 Sam 3:3, and for a similar image, cf. Isa 42:3: "Or snuff out even a dim wick (פִּשְׁתָּה . . . יְכַבֶּנָּה)."

[18] *"Do not recall what happened of old!"* — Forget the days gone by, for they will pale in comparison to what is about to take place; cf. 65:17. For רִאשֹׁנוֹת, see 41:22; 42:9; 43:9; 46:9; 48:3; and the introduction, §4.

"Neither ponder what happened of yore!" — There is no need to brood or to bring to mind any of the feats of days already past (cf. Lam 2:17). The roots קדם and ראשׁ are synonymous and both denote past occurrences; see Prov 8:22: "The Lord created me at the beginning (רֵאשִׁית) of His course, as the first

(קדם) of His works of old." For the substantive קַדְמֹנִיּוֹת, see Mal 3:4: "As in the days of yore and in the years of old (קדמׂניות)," as well as 4Q298, frags. 3-4 ii 9-10: "in order that you may give heed to the end of the ages and that you may look upon former things (קדמוניות) in order to know" (Pfann and Kister, DJD 20, 25-28). For the *hithpolel* form of the root בין, see also Jer 23:20; Ps 107:43. The two hemistichs of this verse form a chiastic parallel.

[19] The general statement of v. 19 is now explained: The miracle that is about to come to pass will be more wondrous than anything that has happened before. The miraculous journey across the Syrian Desert will overshadow all the feats performed by God in the Sinai Desert. For a similar declaration, see Jer 23:7-8: "Assuredly, a time is coming — declares the Lord — when it shall no more be said, 'As the Lord lives, who brought the Israelites out of the land of Egypt,' but rather, 'As the Lord lives, who brought out and led the offspring of the house of Israel from the northland and from all the lands to which I have banished them.' And they shall dwell on their own soil."

"I am about to do something new" — God is about to perform a new wonder (i.e., the exodus from Babylon). The substantive חדשה (Jer 31:22) is the singular of חדשות (Isa 42:9; 48:6).

"Right now it shall come to sprout" — "As a plant sprouts forth from the earth, it shall suddenly come to pass" (Luzzatto). The verb צמח denotes here the sudden sprouting of the predicted events; cf. 42:9: "And now I foretell new things (חדשות), announce to you ere they sprout up (תצמחנה)"; 58:8: "And your healing shall spring up (תצמח) quickly."

"Can you not perceive it?" — A rhetorical question whose purpose is to emphasize that which is being expressed: There is no doubt you shall perceive it (that which shall come to pass).

"I will make a road through the wilderness" — God's "new miracle" (accentuated by אף at the beginning of the clause; cf. v. 7; 40:24) will be the road from Babylon to Israel, which will span the Syrian Desert and on which the Judeans will travel. See 40:3-4; 49:11; 35:8: "And a highway shall appear there, which shall be called the 'Sacred Way.'"

"And paths in the desert" — Though water in the desert is another frequently recurring theme in Deutero-Isaiah's prophecies of redemption (see 41:18; 49:10), the reading in 1QIsa[a], נתיבות ("paths"), is preferable to MT נהרות ("rivers"), since v. 20 features the water motif in the exact same words and in a chiastic parallel. (For the parallel pair נתיבות/דרך, see 42:16; Jer 18:15.) This verse, therefore, describes only the path, while v. 20 describes the provision of water in the wilderness. For the synonyms ישימון and מדבר, see Deut 32:10: "He found him in a desert (מדבר) in an empty howling wasteland (יְשִׁמֹן)"; Ps 78:40: "How often did they rebel against Him in the wilderness (במדבר), did they grieve Him in the wasteland (בישימון)!"

[20] The path on which the Israelites will travel will be provided with abundant water sources that will quench the thirst of all living things in the desert, including the animals. For the same sequence of motifs (the desert journey and the abundance of water), see Isa 48:20-21; 49:9-10.

"The wild beasts shall honor Me" — The desert animals will honor God for providing them with water, since when there is an absence of this vital resource, "The very cattle of the field crave for You, for the watercourses are dried up, and fire has consumed the pastures in the wilderness" (Joel 1:20). For the expression חַיַּת השדה, see Isa 43:20; Exod 23:11; Hos 2:14; Job 5:23; and for its poetic variant חַיְתוֹ שָׂדָי, see Isa 56:9.

"Jackals and ostriches" — two additional examples of desert denizens (animal and bird) who will honor God for providing them with water. For these two coupled together, see Isa 34:13; Mic 1:8; Job 30:29.

"For I will provide water in the wilderness, rivers in the desert" — The parallel pair מדבר/ישימון are chiastically parallel to the same two in the previous verse. For the opposite imagery, see Ps 107:33: "He turns rivers into a wilderness, springs of water into thirsty land."

"To give drink to My chosen people" — The beasts of the field will give thanks to God and will be grateful for the water resources, but the primary reason behind the sudden abundance of water is to supply Israel with water throughout their long trek from Babylonia to Israel. For the quenching of the thirst of the Israelites and the animals in the desert, see Num 20:8. For Israel as God's "chosen" people see, e.g., Isa 42:1; 45:4.

[21] *"The people whom I formed for Myself"* — Hebrew זוּ is a relative pronoun found elsewhere in poetic passages, e.g., 42:24: "The Lord against whom (זוּ) they sinned"; Exod 15:13: "The people whom (זוּ) You have redeemed"; Exod 15:16: "Your people whom (זוּ) You have ransomed."

"Shall proclaim My praise" — I formed Israel so that they would declare My praise, since "I will not yield My glory to another, nor My praise (תְהִלָּתִי) to idols" (42:8); cf. also Ps 79:13: "Then we, Your people, the flock You shepherd, shall glorify You forever. For all time we shall tell Your praises." The variant in 1QIsa[a], יאמרו, has the same meaning as the MT יְסַפֵּרוּ.

[22-28] In the following section the prophet castigates the nation for their cultic practices. Since, in the days of Deutero-Isaiah, the Temple had already been destroyed, it is obvious that his admonishment is directed against First Temple practices, as was the wont of earlier prophets who criticized Israel for performing abundant sacrifices while continuing to act in a morally reprehensible manner (cf. Isa 1:11-15; Jer 6:20; 7:18, 21-31; Hos 6:6; Amos 4:4ff.). According to these prophets, an individual's sacrifice is not accepted if his conduct is unacceptable; morality overrides cultic practice. God has no need for sacrifices, as stated in Ps 50:9-10: "I take no young bull from your estate, no he-goats from your pens. For Mine is every animal of the forest" (cf. Isa 40:16). Yet Deutero-Isaiah's castigation differs from his predecessors. First, he does not emphasize the moral dimension, as opposed to cult; second, the prophet does not reprimand the nation that their sacrifices per se are unacceptable. His rebuke is that they are not dedicated to God, but are self-serving: God has not "burdened" them by demanding offerings, but they have "burdened" Him with their transgressions. There may be an indirect polemic here against the people who claim that God does not respond favorably to them despite their sacrifices.

This unit is linked to vv. 18-21 by the root כבד: The beasts of the field honor God with their praise (תכבדני; v. 20), but Israel, God's chosen nation, does not (לא כבדתני; v. 23; cf. 1:3: "An ox knows its owner, and an ass its master's crib, but Israel, My own people, does not know." Compare also the contradiction between Israel's mission: "That they might declare My praise" (v. 21), and their behavior in practice: "But you have not worshiped Me, O Jacob. . . . Instead you have burdened Me with your sins." Other links are the verbs ספר (vv. 21, 26) and זכר (vv. 18, 25, 26). This unit is framed by the references to Jacob and Israel (vv. 22, 28), reverberates with God's weariness (יגע, vv. 22, 23, 24), and contains a sevenfold repetition of the negative לא. For similar themes and imagery, cf. Ps 51.

[22] *"But Me you have not worshiped, O Jacob"* — The initial *waw* indicates contrast to the above, and the positioning of the direct object אתי ("Me") at the beginning of the hemistich is for emphasis. For the expression קרא אתי with this connotation, see Jer 29:12: "When you call Me (וקראתם אתי) and come and pray to Me, I will take heed of you." For the parallelism Jacob/Israel, see, e.g., Isa 43:1.

"Nevertheless you are weary of Me, O Israel" — a difficult clause. When כי follows a negative statement, it usually qualifies it (see Gen 17:15: "As for your wife Sarai, you shall not (לא) call her Sarai, but (כי) her name shall be Sarah"; Gen 45:8: "So it was not (לא) you who sent me here, but (כי) God." The meaning would then be, "You have not worshiped Me, but nevertheless you are weary of Me." Some commentators, however, explain the כי conjunction as an emphatic and apply the negative לא to this clause as well: "But you have not worshiped Me, O Jacob. You have not wearied yourself for Me, O Israel" (parallel hemistichs). Another possibility is understanding the clause as a question, the response to which is always negative: "Are you indeed tired of Me, Israel?" For this syntactical option, frequent in rabbinic sources, cf., e.g., *b. Shabb.* 4a: "Could you possibly (וכי) say to a person . . . ?", and sporadically in the Bible, cf. Isa 36:19: "And did [וכי] they save Samaria from Me?" The expression: יגע ב- denotes wearying toil for something or on the behalf of someone, as in 57:10: "Though wearied by much travel (ברב . . . יגעת), you never said, 'I give up!'"; 62:8: "For which you have toiled (יגעת בו)"; see also Josh 24:13; Jer 45:3.

[23] For the same series of sacrifices, in the same order, see Jer 17:26: "Bringing burnt offerings and sacrifices, meal offerings, and frankincense."

"You have not brought Me your sheep for burnt offerings" — The לי is emphatic: You have not brought to *Me* your offerings, rather they were for yourself. (For שֶׂה as one of a flock of sheep or goats, see Gen 30:32: "Every dark colored animal [שֶׂה] among the sheep and every spotted and speckled one among the goats.") For the verb בוא in the *hiph'il,* "to bring a sacrifice," see Gen 4:4: "Abel, for his part, brought (הביא) the choicest of the firstlings of his flock"; Num 15:25; Deut 12:6. An עולה is an offering that is totally immolated at the time of sacrifice. 1QIsa[a], LXX, and Targum all read לעולה, instead of MT עֹלֹתֶיךָ; cf. Gen 22:7: "But where is the sheep for the burnt offering (לְעֹלָה)?"

"Nor honored Me with your sacrifices" — זבחים, a general term for sacrifices, was one in which the blood was dashed on the altar, the fat placed on the altar, and the flesh eaten by the owner of the animal (see Lev 7:1ff.). 1QIsa[a] (ובזבחיכה), Peshitta (בדבחיך), as well as LXX and Vulgate, all conform to the subsequent series of substantives preceded by the preposition *beth* (vv. 23-24).

"I have not burdened you with meal offerings" — As for Me, I did not burden you by requiring that you bring Me meal offerings (מנחה), which is a gift of produce from either the wheat or barley crop (see Lev 2:1ff.).

"Nor wearied you about frankincense" — Nor did I overburden you with demands for frankincense (לבונה). The name לבונה is derived from the shining white sap that Boswellia trees secrete. It was one of the important ingredients of the holy incense (Exod 30:34: "And the Lord said to Moses: 'Take the herbs stacte, onycha, and galbanum — these herbs together with pure frankincense. Let there be an equal part of each'") and was placed upon the meal offering; see Lev 2:1: "When a person presents an offering of meal to the Lord . . . lay frankincense upon it." Frankincense (which has a cognate in Akkadian, *labanatu* [*CAD* L:8], and is a loanword in Greek, *libanatos*) was imported from Sheba (Jer 6:20: "What need have I of frankincense that comes from Sheba"; Isa 60:6: "They shall all come from Sheba. They shall bear gold and frankincense"), was very expensive, and was kept in the Temple (1 Chr 9:29). For the root יגע in the *hiph'il,* see Mal 2:17: "You have wearied (הוֹגַעְתֶּם) the Lord with your talk. But you ask, 'By what have we wearied (הוֹגָעְנוּ) [Him]?'"

[24] *"You have not bought Me fragrant cane with money"* — The indirect object לי is again emphatic: You did not buy for *Me* aromatic cane *(Calamus aromaticus)* — also known as the קְנֵה בֹּשֶׂם, which was an important ingredient of the sacred oil of anointment (Exod 30:23); see Jer 6:20: "What need have I of frankincense that comes from Sheba, or fragrant cane from a distant land?" For this expensive import, see also Ezek 27:19; Cant 4:14. The Akkadian cognate, *qanû,* was also used in the cult (*CAD* Q:88-89).

"Nor sated Me with the fat of your sacrifices" — For the verb רוי, "to be sat-

urated," see Lam 3:15: "He has filled me with bitterness, sated me (הִרְוַנִי) with wormwood." This hemistich forms a chiasm with the previous clause. For other instances of the expression חֵלֶב זְבָחִים, see Lev 4:26; Deut 32:38; and several times in Phoenician inscriptions: עַל חֵלֵב וְעַל זֵבַח (*KAI* 69.14; 74:10).

"Instead you have burdened Me with your sins" — On the contrary, "I have not burdened you (הֶעֱבַדְתִּיךָ) with meal offerings" (v. 23), but "you have burdened Me (הֶעֱבַדְתַּנִי) with your sins." For אַךְ as an emphatic, see Isa 45:14, 24; 63:8.

"You have wearied Me with your iniquities" — For the expression יָגַע בְּ- in the *hiph'il*, see v. 22. For the parallel pair חטא/עון, see 40:2.

[25-28] There is a distinct resemblance between this short passage and Ps 51:3-4, 6: "In the fullness of Your compassion, blot (מְחֵה) out my transgressions (פְּשָׁעַי) . . . and cleanse me from my sin (וּמֵחַטָּאתִי)! You are just (לְמַעַן תִּצְדַּק) in Your sentence and right in Your judgment (בְשָׁפְטֶךָ)"; see also Ps 51:11: "Blot out all my iniquities!"; and perhaps the verb וַאֲחַלֵּל (Isa 43:28) is a play on words with חוֹלַלְתִּי (Ps 51:7). Compare Isa 43:25: "It is I, I who — for My own sake (לְמַעֲנִי) — wipe your transgressions away (מֹחֶה פְשָׁעֶיךָ) and remember your sins (וְחַטֹּאתֶיךָ) no more"; 43:26: "Let us join in argument (נִשָּׁפְטָה) . . . that you may be vindicated (לְמַעַן תִּצְדָּק)." (See the introduction, §17.)

[25] A sudden reversal: Without any prior indication and without the nation expressing any sincere regret or mending of their ways, God declares that He is going to wipe away all of Israel's sins — not for their sake, but rather for His very own sake, as in 48:9: "For the sake of My name I control My wrath"; 48:11: "For My sake, My own sake, do I act — lest My name be dishonored." This outpouring of mercy is one of God's chief attributes: "Forgiving iniquity, transgression, and sin" (Exod 34:7; the same three types of sins appear in this latter verse as in vv. 24-25 here).

"It is I, I who — for My own sake — wipe your transgressions away" — The repetition is emphatic (see above, v. 11, and the introduction, §10.A.1), accentuating the munificence of God's act of mercy. The root מחי denotes wiping the slate clean; cf. 44:22: "I wipe away (מָחִיתִי) your sins like a cloud, your transgressions like mist" (see also Jer 18:23; Ps 51:3, 11; Neh 3:37). This imagery reflects the common belief that all sins are recorded in a heavenly book; see Exod 32:32-33: "Erase me (מְחֵנִי) from the record that You have written. But the Lord said to Moses, 'He who has sinned against Me, him only will I erase (אֶמְחֶנּוּ) from My record'"; Ps 69:29: "May they be erased (יִמָּחוּ) from the book of life." (See Paul, *Divrei Shalom*, 345-53.) For the emphatic predicate use of the third-person singular pronoun הוּא, see also vv. 10, 13; 46:4; 48:12.

"And remember your sins no more" — Not only is the nation granted a clean slate, but God promises them that He will not hold their previous sins against them; cf. 64:8: "Do not remember iniquity forever"; Jer 31:34: "For I will forgive

their iniquities and remember their sins no more"; Ps 25:7: "Be not mindful of my youthful sins and transgressions." Note the negative parallelism: "wipe away" (מֹחֶה) and "remember no more" (לא אזכר), which appears also (albeit in reverse order) in Ps 109:14: "May the sin of his father be remembered (יִזָּכֵר) by God, and may the sin of his mother never be wiped out (תִּמָּח)." The reading עוד at the end of this clause in 1QIsa[a] is almost identical to the verse in Jer 31:34: "For I will forgive their iniquities and remember their sins no more (עוד)."

[**26**] *"Remind Me!"* — The verb (הַזְכִּירֵנִי) links up with the end of v. 25 (לא אזכר). In God's legal polemic against His nation, He urges them to remind Him of any possible reasons for their vindication. For the *hiph'il* of זכר in other legal contexts, see *m. Sanh.* 5:5: "If the [judges] were in error, the court's two scribes remind them (מזכירין) [of their errors]" (Ehrlich, *Randglossen,* 4:159); *b. Ber.* 60a: "Miracles must not be cited as evidence [מזכירין, lit. 'recalled']." The Aramaic equivalent, דכר, appears in judicial contexts as well; see *b. Ketub.* 20a: "One (witness) may recall (מַדְכַּר) (the circumstances) to the other."

"Let us join in argument!" — Let us submit our arguments together at a trial, I and you, God and Israel; cf. Isa 41:1: "Let us come forward together for argument." The longer form of the verb נִשָּׁפְטָה (cf. 41:1: נִקְרָבָה) indicates a cohortative, expressing encouragement.

"Tell your version, that you may be vindicated!" — The nation under trial is given precedence and requested to relate their side of the case, so that they may ultimately be vindicated. The verb ספר here is similar to נגד, which is frequently used in legal contexts, e.g., 58:1: "Declare (וְהַגֵּד) to My people their transgression!"; Ezek 23:36: "And charge (וְהַגֵּד) them with their abominations!" The verb צדק is also part of the legal jargon; see above, v. 9; 41:26; Ps 51:6: "So You are just (תצדק) in Your sentence and right in Your judgment"; Job 9:20: "Though I were innocent (אצדק), my mouth would condemn me." The people are now bidden to proclaim (סַפֵּר) their innocence in court, as opposed to proclaiming (יְסַפֵּרוּ) God's praise to the world (v. 21).

[**27**] They, however, remain speechless, and "silence," as the popular adage states, "is tantamount to confession" (*b. Yebam.* 87b). Since the advocate has nothing to say for himself, the prosecutor (God) can now level His accusations against the nation for all the injustices they have perpetrated from the very beginning of their history; cf. Isa 48:8: "You were called a rebel from birth." Compare similarly Ezek 20:5ff., which is an extended passage listing Israel's sins from their sojourn in Egypt onward.

"Your first father sinned" — Although there is disagreement as to the identity of the one referred to here, the prophet is most likely referring to Jacob; see Isa 58:14: "The heritage of your father Jacob." Jacob's sins are recounted in detail in Genesis; see also Hos 12:3-5. The verbs חטא and פשעו form a chiastic parallelism with their substantive forms in v. 25.

"And your spokesmen rebelled against Me" — For the expression פשע ב-, "to rebel against," see 1 Kgs 12:19: "Thus Israel revolted against the house of David"; 2 Kgs 3:7: "The king of Moab has rebelled against me." The term מליציך, however, is ambiguous. Some commentators suggest that this is a reference to the nation's leaders, either their statesmen, their religious leaders, or their spiritual leaders. Although it is impossible to decide for certain, on the basis of the word's other occurrences — Gen 42:23: "They did not know that Joseph understood, for there was an interpreter (המליץ) between him and them"; Job 16:20: "O my advocates (מליצי), my fellows"; Job 33:23: "If he has a representative, one mediator (מליץ) against a thousand to declare a person's uprightness"; 2 Chr 32:31: "So too in the matter of the ambassadors (במליצי) of the princes of Babylon" — the term denotes spokesmen or intermediaries. Thus the prophet accentuates the continuation of sinfulness from Jacob, up and through the nation's "spokesmen." (The term המלץ, "interpreter, translator," is the title of an individual in a Phoenician inscription discovered at the Osiris temple in Abydos, in Upper Egypt, from the third century BCE [*KAI* 49:17].)

[28] On account of their sins, God defiled the nation's religious leaders and committed the people to destruction; cf. Lam 2:2: "He desecrated (חִלֵּל) the kingdom and its leaders."

"So I profaned the holy princes/My holy name" — Therefore I profaned Israel's religious leaders. (The MT vocalizes the verb as a *waw* consecutive [וְ], future tense. In light of the context, however, it should be vocalized as a *waw* conversive [וָ], past tense.) The title שָׂרֵי קֹדֶשׁ appears also in 1 Chr 24:5, where it refers to the priests, sons of Eleazar and Ithamar, who were the hereditary leaders of the "priestly divisions." See also three Phoenician inscriptions where the term in the singular refers to the deity Ashman (*KAI* 14:17; 15:1; 16:1), and at Qumran in 4Q401, frag. 6 4 (C. Newsom, *"Shirot 'Olat HaShabbat,"* in E. Eshel et al., *Qumran Cave 4.VI: Poetical and Liturgical Texts, Part I,* DJD 11 [Oxford, 1998], 203), where it apparently refers to angels. (For שָׂרֵי הַכֹּהֲנִים, "chiefs of the priests," see Ezra 8:24, 29; 10:5.) It is still unclear why priests would be singled out here, and thus it has been suggested to emend the MT to שֵׁם קָדְשִׁי ואחלל, "So I profaned My holy name," and the clause would be interpreted as an allusion to the destruction of the Temple and to the exile that profaned God's name; see Isa 48:8-11: "For the sake of My name . . . lest [My name] be dishonored (יֵחָל)." This idea is reiterated time and again in Ezekiel's prophecies; see, e.g., Ezek 36:20: "But when they came to those nations, they caused My holy name to be profaned (ויחללו), in that it was said of them, 'These are the people of the Lord, yet they had to leave His land'" (see also vv. 21-22). On the other hand, one should note the LXX (and Peshitta): "Your princes profaned My sanctuary (ויחללו שריך קדשי)"; and cf. Zeph 3:4: "Her priests profane the sanctuary."

"And I delivered Jacob to proscription" — Once again, the *waw* should be vocalized as a *waw* conversive (וַ), past tense. For the concept of חרם, "proscription, extinction," see Josh 6:18: "You will cause the camp of Israel to be proscribed (חרם)"; Mal 3:24: "So that, when I come, I do not strike the whole land with utter destruction (חרם)." (For the verbal expression נתן ל-, "to hand over, assign," see Josh 17:13 and its Akkadian semantic equivalent: *nadānu ana* (*CAD* N/1:46). In light of the chiastic parallel with the following clause, some suggest emending the text from לַחֵרֶם, "to proscription," to לַחֶרְפָּה, "to taunts," thus creating a parallel with the following גִּדּוּפִים, "jeers, revilings," as in Isa 51:7: "Fear not taunts (חרפת) of men, and be not dismayed at their jeers (וּמִגִּדֻּפֹתָם)"; Zeph 2:8: "I have the heard the taunts (חרפת) of Moab and the jeers (גִּדּוּפֵי) of the Ammonites"; and see also Isa 37:23: "Whom have you blasphemed (חֵרַפְתָּ) and reviled (גִּדַּפְתָּ)?"; Ps 44:17: "At the sound of taunting revilers (מְחָרֵף וּמְגַדֵּף)."

"And Israel to mockery" — For this term, see the above references. Israel's enemies reveled in their misfortune, and mocked and cursed them. The chapter ends in the same way it began (in v. 1) — with the two national sobriquets, "Israel" and "Jacob."

Chapter 44

[1-5] God blesses His chosen people, still residing in the Babylonian exile, with a dual blessing: spiritual — He will confer His spirit upon them; and physical — He will grant them multiple posterity. As a consequence, the nations of the world will want to join the Israelite nation and will participate in the worship of the Lord. For the first time in Deutero-Isaiah's prophecy there are intimations of the universal monotheistic religion he envisions, a sentiment expressed even more clearly in 45:23: "To Me every knee shall bend, every tongue shall swear loyalty"; 56:7: "For My house shall be called a house of prayer for all peoples." This pericope is part of a larger literary *inclusio* that encompasses the chapter as a whole: the two names, Jacob and Israel, appear in v. 1, linking this chapter to the previous one, and in vv. 21, 23. Compare also the other key words: **עבדו/עבדי** (vv. 1, 21, 26), **עשׂי** (vv. 2, 23, 24), **יצר** (vv. 21, 24). This chapter begins, like chap. 43, with the words **ועתה** (43:1; 44:1) and **וְיֹצֶרְךָ . . . אל תירא** (43:1; 44:2).

[1] *But hear now, O Jacob, My servant* — For the term "My servant," which denotes divine endearment, see also 41:8, 9; 42:1, 19; 43:10; 45:4.

Israel, whom I have chosen! — Despite the fact that you are still in exile, you remain My chosen people. For other instances of the term **עבדי** followed by **בחר**, see below, v. 2; 41:8, 9; 43:10; 45:4. The idea that Israel is God's chosen people appears already in Deut 4:37: "And because He loved your fathers, and chose their children after them"; cf. Deut 7:6; 14:2. (See the introduction, §13.)

[2] *Thus said the Lord, your Maker, your Creator from the womb* — For the concept of Israel being chosen from the womb, see v. 24; 49:1, 5. The motif of prenatal choice appears also in the Samson narrative, Judg 13:3-5, and in Jeremiah's appointment, Jer 1:5: "Before I created you in the womb I selected you. Before you were born I consecrated you. I appointed you a prophet to the nations" (the last verse also influenced Isa 42:6). The same idea is frequent in

royal inscriptions from Mesopotamia. Compare, for example, Nabonidus's claim (the last king of the Neo-Babylonian Empire, who reigned 556-539 BCE and who was Deutero-Isaiah's contemporary): "Nabonidus, whose fate Sin [the moon god] and Ningal [his consort] (while yet) in the womb of his mother had destined for dominion." (See Paul, *Divrei Shalom,* 18-20, for this and many more examples.) Note also that Sin is called *bānîka,* "your creator" (*CAD* B:94). As noted above, the prophet maintains that the entire nation of Israel was chosen from the very outset as God's special servant. The verb יצר is a key word, repeated in vv. 9, 10, 12, 21, 24. For God as the "Maker" (עֹשִׂי) of Israel, see 51:13; 54:5.

Who has helped you — The imperfect tense of the verb implies frequency: I have aided you many times in the past and will continue to do so in the present and future. 1QIsa[a] has ועוזרכה, a participle, "your Helper" (cf. Vulgate and Peshitta), which is in line with the above pair, "your Maker" and "your Creator," both participles with a second-person masculine singular pronominal suffix. The word מִבֶּטֶן, which according to the Masoretic accentuation is attached to the previous hemistich, applies here as well: "Who has helped you from the womb."

"Fear not, My servant Jacob" — This encouraging message appears also, word for word, in Jer 30:10; 46:27, 28. For the "Fear not" motif, see Isa 41:10, 13; 43:1, 5; and for extrabiblical parallels, see above on 41:10. This verse may very well be a type of midrash on Gen 46:2-4: "Jacob, Jacob. . . . Fear not! . . . I . . . am with you."

"Jeshurun, whom I have chosen!" — Israel's special status as God's chosen is reiterated yet again (see the conclusion to v. 1). The name יְשֻׁרוּן ("upright one") is a poetic term for Israel that appears elsewhere only in early biblical poetry: once in Deut 32:15: "So Jeshurun grew fat and kicked"; and twice in Moses' final blessing, Deut 33:5: "Then He became king in Jeshurun"; v. 26: "O Jeshurun, there is none like God." Its derivation is from the root ישר ("straight"), which contrasts with יעקב (from עקב, "crooked"), and is perhaps somehow related to ישראל. In form it resembles other personal names, such as זבולון and ידותון.

[3] The spiritual blessing: God will pour His spirit on Israel.

"Even as I pour water on thirsty soil" — Even as I cause the clouds to rain on "thirsty soil (צָמֵא)." Compare also צָמָא, Ezek 19:13: "Now she is planted in the desert, in ground that is arid and thirsty (צָמָא)"; and צִמָּאוֹן, Deut 8:15: "Who led you through the great and terrible wilderness . . . a thirsty land (צמאון) with no water in it"; Isa 35:7: "Torrid earth shall become a pool, and thirsty land (צמאון) fountains of water." The word צמאון may also have been the original reading here too, with the final two letters having been deleted as a result of haplography, since the first two letters of the following word are also ונ (ונוזלים; cf. Ehrlich, *Mikrâ ki-Pheschuṭô,* 3:99). (In Akkadian as well, the sub-

stantives *ṣumāmītu, ṣumāmu, ṣummû, ṣūmu* [*CAD* Ṣ:243-44, 246-48], derived from the verb *ṣamû*, "to be thirsty," are used in descriptions of the desert.) For the כי particle with the meaning "even as," see 55:9: "But even as (כי) the heavens are high above the earth"; 62:5: "Even as (כי) a youth espouses a maiden." It also is prevalent in Rabbinic Hebrew for the introduction of similes; cf., e.g., *b. Taʿan.* 9b: "Even as (כי) the Babylonians deceive, so also do their rains deceive them."

"And streams on dry ground" — For the parallel pair נוזלים/מים, see Prov 5:15: "Drink water (מים) from your own cistern, running water (נוזלים) from your own well"; Cant 4:15: "[You are] a garden spring, a well of fresh water (מים), a rill (ונזלים) of Lebanon." For the verb נזל, see Isa 45:8; 48:21.

"So will I pour My spirit on your offspring" — The word כן ("so"), added above the line in 1QIsa[a] (cf. Targum), facilitates the reading of the text: "So shall I pour [אֶצֹּק, from the root יצק, "to pour from one receptacle to another," means here "to confer upon"] My spirit on the entire nation." For the correlates כ(י) . . . כן, see 54:9; 55:9; 61:11; 63:14; 66:13. This blessing is none other than the fulfillment and actualization of Moses' wish: "Would that all the Lord's people were prophets, that the Lord put His spirit upon them!" (Num 11:29). For the same motif, cf. Ezek 39:29; Joel 3:1; Zech 12:10 (in these last verses the root שפך ["to pour"] appears instead of יצק). (For a similar image of "pouring out," see *CAD* T:5, Akk. *tabāku,* referring to joy, terror, splendor, etc.)

"And My blessing on your posterity" — For other examples of the parallel pair צאצאים/זרע, see Isa 48:19: "Your offspring (זרעך) would be as many as the sand, and your posterity (צֶאֱצָאֵי) as many as its grains"; 61:9: "Their offspring (זרעם) shall be known among the nations, and their posterity (וְצֶאֱצָאֵיהֶם) in the midst of the peoples"; 65:23: "For they shall be an offspring (זֶרַע) blessed by the Lord, and their posterity (וצאצאיהם) shall remain with them." The term צאצאיך, which serves also as a general term for flora (see 42:5), may have influenced the imagery in the following verse. Another possible link between these two verses is the term ברכה ("blessing"), which in Ezek 34:26 relates to the beneficial fall of rain: "I will send down the rain in its season, rains that bring blessing (ברכה)."

[4] The physical blessing: an abundance of progeny.

"And they shall sprout like a green tamarisk" — Many commentators explain the anomalous בְּבֵין as a preposition, similar to the term בתוך, "in the midst of." This interpretation is unlikely, however, since the image of Israel sprouting amid the grass is extremely bland. In light of the parallel term, כַּעֲרָבִים, one should read כְּבֵין (as in 1QIsa[a], LXX, and Targum, כְּלַבְלַבֵּי עֲסַב, "as flowers of the grass"; and cf. Luzzatto: "In some manuscripts we find כבין," but he rejects the reading). Hebrew בין means "tamarisk," with cognates in Akk. *bīnu* (*CAD* B:239-42), Aram. בינא/Syr. *byn'*, and Arab. *bān*. For חציר (or

חצור) with the meaning "greenery," cf. Arab. *ḫaḍira* ("to be green") and *ḫuḍrat* ("vegetable"). Deutero-Isaiah has more references to different types of trees than anywhere else in the Bible. See v. 14: "cedars, plane trees, oaks, firs"; 41:19: "cedars, acacias, myrtles, oleasters, cypresses, box trees, elms." For the verb **צמח** ("to sprout") see 42:9; 43:19; 45:8.

"Like willows by watercourses" — Further plant imagery: The people shall abundantly spring up like willows by flowing streams; cf. Ps 137:1-2: "By the rivers of Babylon . . . there on the willow trees (עֲרָבִים)." For ערבי נחל, "willows of the brook," see Lev 23:40; Job 40:22. For יִבְלֵי מים, or according to the reading of 1QIsa[a], יובלי מים, see Jer 17:8: "Sending forth its roots by a stream (יוּבַל)"; Isa 30:25: "There shall appear brooks and watercourses (יבלי מים)." For the lush imagery of willows, cf. Esarhaddon's inscription: "The willows grew profusely (in Babylon) and threw out many offshoots" (*CAD* Ṣ:108).

[5] These prolific blessings will induce individuals from other nationalities to want to worship the God of Israel and thereby become, in effect, part of the Israelite nation. Compare *Abot R. Nat.*, Version A, 36: "These are the proselytes from among the nations." (See S. Lieberman, *Greek in Jewish Palestine* [New York, 1942], 83-84.) One must note, however, that Deutero-Isaiah is not yet predicting a mass conversion of the nations, but rather the conversion of a select few, as the threefold repetition of זה ("one, another") indicates; cf. 1 Kgs 22:20: "Then one (זה) said thus and another (וזה) said thus"; Job 1:17: "This one (זה) was still speaking when another (זה) came."

"One shall say, 'I am the Lord's'" — I belong to the God of Israel. For the *lamed* indicating "belonging to," see immediately below. Compare the *lamelek* inscriptions on many shards of pottery and seals discovered in Israel. (See Aḥituv, *Ha-Ketav veha-Miktav,* 69, 149, 215, 216, 220, 222.)

"Another shall be called by the name 'Jacob'" — It is preferable to vocalize the verb as a *niph'al,* יִקָּרֵא (Symmachus). For the expression see, e.g., 43:7; 48:1.

"Yet another shall mark his hand, 'of the Lord'" — Another shall engrave on his hand, לה׳: "Belonging to the Lord" (again, the *lamed* denoting "belonging to"), i.e., he shall be counted as a worshiper of the Israelite God. The tattooing of the hand, arm, or other body parts to indicate ownership was common throughout the ancient world (cf. Ezek 9:4), and in Mesopotamia slaves especially were marked in this way. (See the entry *qātu,* "hand," *CAD* Q:186.) Compare also an Aramaic inscription from Elephantine from the fifth century BCE, which states that a certain male slave had the name of his owner branded on his hand. (See B. Porten and A. Yardeni, eds., *Textbook of Aramaic Documents,* 2: *Contracts* [Winona Lake, Ind., 1989], 48, B2.11:4, 6.) The prophet was likely influenced by the extant Babylonian practice of marking the symbol of one's god on the hand as a sign of identification and an indication of commitment to the deity. Ishtar's priestesses, for example, inscribed the symbol of the goddess, a

star-shaped brand, on the back of their hands (*CAD* K:45). Compare also the picturesque image of the Deity Himself with the walls of Jerusalem engraved on the palm of His hand (49:16).

"And be entitled, 'Israel.'" — Yet another will be given the epithet "Israel" (as above, the verb should be vocalized as a passive *puʿal,* יְכֻנֶּה); cf. all the ancient translations, except for LXX). The verb is cognate to Akk. *kinûtu,* "nickname" (*CAD* K:396); Arab. *kunja,* denoting an honorary title; and Rabbinic Hebrew כינוי, "byname, surname." For the parallel pair כני/קרא, see also 45:4; Sir 36:12; and 4Q246 1:9: "He will be called (יתקרא) The Great and will be designated (יתכנה) by his name." (See G. Brooke et al., *Qumran Cave 4.XVII: Parabiblical Texts, III,* DJD 22 [Oxford, 1996], 169.)

[6-8] An emphatic declaration of God's uniqueness: God is the One and Only. He, and He alone, can predict the future with accuracy, and His nation, Israel, serves as witness to His ongoing polemic with the Babylonian idol worshipers. God's sui generis qualities are stated for the first time in Deut 4:35: "It has been clearly demonstrated to you that the Lord alone is God. There is none beside Him"; Deut 4:39: "The Lord alone is God in heaven above and on earth below. There is no other"; Deut 32:39: "See, then, that I, I am He. There is no god beside Me." (See the introduction, §13.) The unit is framed chiastically by the phrases ומבלעדי אין אלהים (v. 6) and היש אלוה מבלעדי (v. 8).

[6] *Thus said the Lord, the King of Israel, his Redeemer, the Lord of Hosts* — The opening of a new prophecy in which the name of God is accompanied by three specific epithets: King of Israel, Redeemer, and Lord of Hosts. The first, which emphasizes God's sovereignty, appears in 41:21: "The King of Jacob" (also in the context of a polemic against heathen gods); 43:15: "your King"; 52:7: "your God is King." The second emphasizes God's unique relationship with Israel. He is bound to Israel and is responsible for their redemption, just as a next-of-kin has the duty of redemption for his destitute kinsman (Lev 25:25ff.). For גאל, see vv. 22, 23; 41:14; 43:14. The third and final title, "Lord of Hosts," makes its first appearance here in Deutero-Isaiah's prophecies (see also 45:13; 47:4; 48:2; 51:15; 54:5) and expresses God's omnipotence; He controls even the heavenly host. 1QIsa[a] appends שמו to the end of the verse: "The Lord of Hosts is His name"; cf. likewise 47:4; 48:2; 51:15; 54:5. (See the introduction, §9.)

"I am the first and I am the last" — The polarity emphasizes totality: I am first and I am last, thus I am, was, and will be always present, as in 41:4: "I am the Lord, who was first and will be with the last as well." (The first hemistich in 41:4 is also similar to the first hemistich in the next verse here, v. 7.) Compare 48:12: "I am He — I am the first and I am the last as well." These verses left their mark on New Testament texts; cf. Rev 1:8: "I am the *alpha* and the *omega*" (the first and last letters of the Greek alphabet); see also Rev 1:17; 21:6; 22:13.

"And there is no god but Me" — See likewise Isa 43:11; 45:6, 14, 18, 21; 46:9.

[7] The polemic against the idols and idolaters continues. God's oracular powers are brought as evidence of His uniqueness, and God's nation is presented as a corroborating witness; cf. 41:1ff., 21-29; 43:9-13.

"Who is like Me that can announce?" — Which other god predicted or announced the future as I have? The prophet employs this rhetorical question, "Who is like Me?" (see also Jer 49:19; 50:44), and others (cf. Isa 40:18, 25; 46:5) as a literary device to emphasize God's uniqueness. This sentiment is expressed in personal names such as מיכאל ("Who is like God?" Dan 10:13), מיכיהו ("Who is like Yahu?" Neh 12:35, 41; 2 Chr 18:23); and cf. similar Akkadian names: *mannu kīma/(a)kî Sin/Šamaš/Ištar,* "Who is like Sin/Shamash/Ishtar?). (See J. J. Stamm, *Die akkadische Namengebung* [Leipzig, 1939], 237ff., 303; K. L. Tallqvist, *Assyrian Personal Names* [Helsingfirs, 1914], 124a.) The Akkadian names, however, emphasize only the god's preeminence within the pantheon; they do not signify the god's uniqueness or sui generis qualities. (See C. J. Labuschagne, *The Incomparability of Yahweh in the Old Testament* [Leiden, 1966], 31-63.) Announcing and proclaiming events before they happen characterize the Israelite God and no other, and thus are God's most potent arguments in His polemic against idol worshipers; see Isa 41:4: "Who has wrought and achieved this? He who announced the generations from the beginning"; 41:22: "Let them approach and tell us what will happen"; 43:9: "Who among them predicted this?" The LXX and Peshitta add here an additional verb: "Who is like Me? Let him stand up (in trial) (and announce)"; cf. v. 11; 47:13; 50:8.

"Let him foretell it and match Me/state his case" — This clause is the direct continuation of the above. For the expression ערך ל-, "to match, resemble," see 40:18: "To whom, then, can you liken God? What form compare to Him (תערכו לו)?"; Ps 89:7: "For who in the skies can equal the Lord (יערך לה׳)?" The verb ערך, moreover, is polysemous and refers not only to matching God, but also has a legal meaning, "to present a case," i.e., "Let him present his case to Me"; cf. Ps 50:21: "So I censure you and confront you with charges (ואערכה)"; Job 13:18: "See now, I have prepared (ערכתי) a case"; 23:4: "I would set out (אערכה) my case before Him"; see also 32:14; 33:5. The longer imperfect forms, יַגִּידֶהָ, יַעְרְכֶהָ, imply expeditiousness, i.e., a call to foretell and match as soon as possible; cf. Isa 5:19: "Let Him hasten (יחישה)." (Some scholars vocalize יגידָהּ, יערכָהּ, with a *mappiq* in the ה, with the same meaning.)

"Announcing the future from the very beginning" — The Masoretic division of the words is erroneous, and one should read: משמיע מעולם אֹתִיּוֹת; "(Who like Me) has announced the future from the very outset?" אֹתִיּוֹת (a present participle from the Aramaic verb אתי, "to come") denotes "things to come," future events; cf. 41:23: "Foretell what is yet to happen (האתיות)." (The MT עם עולם, "an ancient people," was adapted in later literature as a sobriquet

for Israel. The expression appears also in Ezek 26:20, but there it denotes the "ancient dead," similar to מתי עולם, "long dead"; see also Ps 143:3; Lam 3:6.)

"Let him foretell coming events to us" — Contra the MT, one should read the verb in the singular (יגיד), and instead of לָמוֹ (a poetic archaic form, meaning "to them"), one should follow the Targum לָנָא and read לנו ("to us").

[8] *"Do not be frightened! And do not be shaken!"* — A message of reassurance to Israel that they should not fear the upcoming trial. The verb תִּרְהוּ is a hapax legomenon, which according to the context is parallel in meaning to תפחדו ("be frightened"). Although some commentators suggest emending the text to תראו ("to be afraid"), based on 1QIsa[a], תיראו, this substitution is incorrect (Ibn Ezra), since the Qumranic scribe was simply substituting a more common verb in order to facilitate the understanding of the text. The verb is derived from the root ירי, which according to the cognate root in Arabic *(wariha)* denotes frozen with fear and should be punctuated with a *metheg*, תִּרְֽהוּ. For the idea of fear and trembling at the time of a trial, see Isa 41:5: "The coastlands look on in fear; the ends of the earth tremble." One should note that later Hebrew poets employed this verb in their poems in similar contexts ("fear and petrification"). (See M. Wallenstein, *Some Unpublished Piyyutim from the Cairo Genizah* [Manchester, 1956], 26.) For the parallel pair ירי/ירא, see Saadyah Gaon's *siddur* (ed. Y. Davidson, S. Asaf, and Y. Yoel [Jerusalem, 1931], 417 line 21): מיראיהם ומרהיהם ("Those who frighten them and those who scare them").

"Have I not from old announced to you and foretold?" — הֲלֹא introduces an emphatic question whose implied response is always positive; cf. 40:21 (where the same two verbs appear): "Have you not heard? Have you not been told from of old?" You have nothing to fear since I informed you a long time ago what the future holds. For announcing and foretelling in conjunction with אז ("from old"), in order to emphasize the truth of the predictions that have come to pass, see 45:21: "Who announced (השמיע) this aforetime, foretold it of old (מאז הגידה)?"; 48:3: "Long ago (מאז) I foretold (הגדתי) things that would happen. From My mouth they issued, and I announced them (ואשמיעם)"; 48:5: "Therefore I told you (ואגיד) long beforehand (מאז), announced things to you (השמעתיך) ere they happened." The expression מאז השמעתיך is parallel to the emended text משמיע מעולם in v. 7; see also 48:7.

"And you are My witnesses" — You can corroborate that the prophecies indeed came to pass. For Israel as God's witnesses, see also 43:10, 12.

"Is there any god, then, but Me?" — As stated above, this prophetic unit begins and ends with similar phrases: v. 8: "Is there any god, then, but Me?" — v. 6: "And there is no God but Me." This time, moreover, the prophet articulates the sentiment by framing it in a rhetorical double question. אֱלוֹהַּ, the poetic singular of אלהים, appears twice in the Pentateuch (Deut 32:15, 17), three times

in the Prophets (2 Sam 22:32; Hab 1:11; 3:3), and is very frequent in the Writings (52 times). For the theme of God's exclusiveness, see also Isa 45:21: "No god exists other than I, who is triumphant and able to save."

"Or any other rock? I know none!" — **ואין** opens the second half of the two-pronged rhetorical question. **צור** ("rock"), an image of steadfast and constant strength, appears in parallel with **אלוה** also in Deut 32:15: "He forsook the God (**אלוה**) who made him and spurned the Rock (**צור**) of his support" (and see there vv. 4, 18, 31, 37); Ps 18:32: "Truly, who is a god (**אלוה**) except the Lord? Who is a Rock (**צור**) but our God?" For **צור**, see also Ps 89:27; 95:1. The expression **בל ידעתי** is a play on words with the previous hemistich, **מִבַּלְעָדַי**. The poetic negation **בל** (see also Isa 40:24, three times in the space of one verse) appears in Akkadian, Ugaritic, Phoenician, and Aramaic.

[9-20] Following the description of God's uniqueness, the prophet launches into the most derisive and extensive polemic against idol craftsmanship in the entire Bible. (For other polemics, see 40:19-20; 41:6-7, 29; 42:17; 45:20-22; 46:1-7; 48:5; and see the introduction, §7.) Deutero-Isaiah describes with stinging sarcasm and precise details the zeal of the craftsmen and the way they wholeheartedly and devotedly engage themselves in their work. The entire sculpting process itself, however, is presented in an ironic reverse order, for which see also 40:19-20. (For idol sculpting in Mesopotamia, see A. Berlejung, "Washing the Mouth: The Consecration of Divine Images in Mesopotamia," in K. van der Toorn, ed., *The Image and the Book* [Leuven, 1997], 45-72; C. Walker and M. B. Dick, "The Induction of the Cult Image in Ancient Mesopotamia: The Mesopotamian *mīs pî* Ritual," in M. B. Dick, ed., *Born in Heaven, Made on Earth: The Making of the Cult Image in the Ancient Near East* [Winona Lake, Ind., 1999], 55-121; M. B. Dick, "Prophetic Parodies of Making the Cult Image," in *Born in Heaven,* 1-53. For the same ritual in Egyptian sources, see R. B. Finnestad, "The Meaning and Purpose of Opening the Mouth in Mortuary Contexts," *Numen* 25 [1978]: 118-34.) The prophet does not mince words and delivers a scathing tirade against the craftsmen's total lack of understanding. He points out that the wood used for mundane purposes such as heating and cooking, and the wood used for constructing the image, are one and the same. How, the prophet asks derisively, could an image constructed and shaped by human hands (**יצר** — vv. 9, 10, 12; **פעל** — vv. 12, 15; **עשׂי** — v. 13 [twice], 15, 17, 19) be considered divine?

The section begins with an accusation in the plural (vv. 9-11), continues with a description of the idol construction in the singular (vv. 12-17), and concludes, as it began, with a tirade of accusations in the singular and plural. Note also the repetition of the following key phrases and words: **בל ידעו** (v. 9), **לא ידעו** (v. 18), **לא דעת** (v. 19); **יֵבֹשׁוּ** (vv. 9, 11 [twice]); and the negation **לא**, which appears seven times in vv. 18-20 (including **הלוא**, v. 20). The negatives **בל**

(three times in v. 9) and בלתי (v. 10) connect these verses with the previous pericope: בל and בלעדי in vv. 6, 8 (note the wordplay, and see v. 8). For other links between the two units, cf. מי (vv. 7, 10); עֵדָי (v. 8) — ועדיהם (v. 9); אל תפחדו (v. 8) — יפחדו (v. 11); and the wordplay צור — (פסל) יֹצְרֵי (v. 9) — all of which emphasize the juxtaposition between God and Israel, on the one hand, and the idolaters and their images, on the other. Note also other key terms that emphasize the difference between God and the heathen images: (פסל) יֹצְרֵי (v. 9), (אל) יצר (v. 10), יִצְּרֵהוּ (v. 12), as opposed to וְיֹצֶרְךָ (v. 2, and cf. v. 24); יפחדו (v. 11) contra אל תפחדו (v. 8); the verb עשׂי (in contexts of idol craftsmanship, vv. 13, 15, 17, 19), contra (כה אמר ה׳) עֹשֶׂךָ (v. 2); (אנכי ה׳) עֹשֶׂה (כל) (v. 24); בל ידעו (v. 9); לא ידעו ,לא דעת (v. 19), contra בל ידעתי (v. 8); (ויעשהו) . . . כתפארת (אדם) (v. 13), contra (ובישראל) יתפאר (v. 23). The idol was fashioned from the "trees of the forest" (v. 14) and is nothing more than a "stump of wood" (v. 19); but the trees themselves were created by God and thus: "Shout . . . O forests with all your trees!" (v. 23). The idolaters proclaim, "You are my god," whereas God proclaims, "You are My servant" (v. 21). For another satire against idol construction, see Wisdom of Solomon, ch. 13.

[9] For a similar derisive statement, see Hab 2:18: "What has a carved image availed, that he who fashioned it has carved it for an image, and a false oracle — that he who fashioned his product has trusted in it, making dumb idols?"

The makers of idols are all worthless — Or alternatively, "Their idols are all of no worth." For תֹּהוּ as parallel to אַיִן and אפס, see Isa 40:17; 41:29; and cf. 40:23; 45:18, 19; 49:4.

And their cherished images can do no good — The idols that these craftsmen so treasure are all for naught. For similar phraseology in reference to idols, cf. v. 10: "That can do no good (לבלתי הועיל)"; Jer 2:8: "And the prophets prophesied by Baal and followed what can do no good (לא יועילו)"; Jer 2:11: "But My people has exchanged its glory for what can do no good (בלוא יועיל)." This, of course, is in contrast with the one and only true God who "instructs you for your own benefit (להועיל)" (Isa 48:17). For the parallel תֹּהוּ/לא יועיל in the same context, see 1 Sam 12:21: "Which can neither profit (לא יועילו) nor save, but are worthless (תהו)."

And they are their very own witnesses — The pronoun המה emphasizes the substantive עֵדֵיהֶם, i.e., the craftsmen's testimony is self-incriminating and proves the worthlessness of their handiwork. This contrasts with Israel, God's true witnesses (v. 8; 43:9). This phrase may also refer to the idols themselves. המה is one of the fifteen words in the Bible marked with dots (above the word) according to the Masoretic tradition — a scribal practice known from ancient Greece indicating that their authenticity was questionable and were supposed to be deleted. See *Abot R. Nat.*, Version A, 34 (ed. Schechter [New York, 1945],

51a); Version B, 37 (49a-b): "And why are all these letters marked? Thus said Ezra: 'If Elijah shall come and ask me: "Why did you include [these words/letters]?" I shall answer "I have marked them (for deletion)," and if he shall tell me: "It is good and well (that these words/letters) were included," I shall erase the marks [I made].'" One should note that in 1QIsa[a] the word המה was written above the line and was likely added by a later scribe. The word, if not original, is a product of dittography (עדיהם המה).

They neither see nor know — The idol sculptors do not qualify as witnesses since, according to Lev 5:1, one can testify only if one has seen (ראה) or known (ידע) about the matter. Others maintain that this phrase refers to the idols themselves, who cannot see or know anything; cf. Ps 115:5 (= 135:16): "They have eyes but cannot see"; cf. also Deut 4:28: "There you will serve manmade gods of wood and stone that cannot see or hear or eat or smell." For other references to the blindness of idolaters, see v. 18.

So they shall be confounded — In the end, after the futility of their worship becomes self-evident, the idolaters shall be confounded. The word למען here indicates result rather than purpose, as in Jer 7:18: "The children gather sticks, the fathers build the fire, and the mothers knead dough, to make cakes for the Queen of Heaven [= the goddess Ishtar] . . . thus (למען) vexing Me" — the end result being that they provoke God. The root בוש, which appears here again in v. 11 (twice), denotes frustration and disappointment (see also Isa 42:17; 45:16, 24), as in Jer 2:36: "You shall be disappointed (תֵּבֹשִׁי) by Egypt, just as you were frustrated (בֹּשְׁתְּ) by Assyria." This is in complete contrast with Israel, who shall never be disappointed or frustrated by God; see Isa 45:17; 49:23; 54:4.

[10] *Who would fashion a god or cast a statue that can do no good?* — This ironical-polemical question (see, e.g., 40:12, 13, 14; 41:26) is phrased chiastically: יצר אל — פסל נסך. For the parallel pair אל ("god") and פסל ("statue"), see below, vv. 15, 17; 45:20. So too in the initial stages of the idol-making ceremony in Mesopotamia, called *mīs pî* ("mouth washing"), the "idol," *ṣalmu* (= צלם), is called a "god," *ilu* (= אל). The expression לבלתי הועיל (v. 10) is equivalent to בל יועילו (v. 9). Israel, however, was fashioned by God Himself (vv. 2, 21, 24). The expression פסל נסך echoes the paired combination פסל ומסֵכה (Deut 27:15).

[11] *Lo, all its votaries shall be frustrated* — The term הן (1QIsa[a] הנה) introduces the verdict against those who adhere to idols (see also Isa 41:11, 24, 29). They are all destined to be bitterly confounded. The verb יֵבֹשׁוּ, appearing at the beginning of the verse and at its end (cf. v. 9), creates an *inclusio* framework for the entire verse. For the root חבר in the context of idol worship, see Hos 4:17: "Ephraim is addicted (חֲבוּר) to images." The term חֲבֵרָיו is also polysemous. According to the Masoretic punctuation, חֲבֵרָיו, it refers to those who attach themselves to idols; but if one vocalizes the substantive חֲבָרָיו or חֹבְרָיו (1QIsa[a]

חובריו), it would refer to one who casts magical spells, as in Deut 18:10-11: "An augur, a soothsayer, a diviner, a sorcerer, one who casts spells (וְחֹבֵר חָבֶר)"; Ps 58:6: "So as not to hear the voice of charmers or the expert mutterer of spells (חובר חֲבָרִים)." The term appears again in Isa 47:9: "Despite your many enchantments and all your countless spells (חֲבָרַיִךְ)"; 47:12: "Stand up, with your spells (בַּחֲבָרַיִךְ) and your many enchantments!"; and is part of the rabbinic lexicon as well: cf. חַבָּר (*b. Sanh.* 56b); חובר (*Lam. Rab.* 1:5); חַבּוּרֵי חֲבוּרָא (Targum Jonathan to Deut 18:11), "sorcerers, charmers."

They are craftsmen, merely mortal — There may be a double entendre here as well. On the one hand, חָרָשִׁים, according to the Masoretic vocalization, denotes the craftsmen or sculptors of the idol, as in v. 12, "the craftsman (חרש) in iron"; and v. 13: "the craftsman (חרש) in wood." On the other hand, however, if one vocalizes חֲרָשִׁים, the reference is to sorcerers, as in Isa 3:3: "Skilled sorcerer (חֲרָשִׁים) and expert enchanter." See also the Targum to 47:9, 12, which translates Heb. כשפיך by חַרְשַׁךְ. In the cognate languages, Ugaritic, Rabbinic Aramaic, Syriac, and Ethiopic, this root is also connected to magical spells and magicians. Many commentators explain the end of the ambiguous verse as the proclamation of the prophet that these craftsmen/sorcerers are merely human (and how could they possibly presume that it is within their power to construct a god!). It then would be intended as a barb against the Mesopotamian "mouth-washing" ritual, where the craftsmen swear that the image they have fashioned is, in fact, the work of the gods. For אדם as a key word in this section, see vv. 13, 15.

Let them all assemble and stand up! — in preparation for the legal proceedings. For the root קבץ in legal contexts, see 43:9; 45:20; 48:14; and for the verb עמד in the context of a trial, see 47:13; 50:8. Its Akkadian semantic equivalent, *uzzuzu* ("to stand"), is also employed in legal parlance with the same meaning (*CAD* U/W:378-79).

They shall cower, totally dismayed — When they assemble for the trial, they shall all be frightened (the Israelites, however, are urged not to fear; v. 8), dismayed, and shamed (as opposed to Israel, who shall never be confounded; see also 45:17; 49:23; 50:7; 54:4). The word יחד, like its variant יַחְדָּו (1QIsa[a]), appears at the end of a series of verbs or nouns; cf., e.g., 42:14.

[12-20] The prophet now begins a mocking prose description of the idol's construction, all in reverse order (see 40:19-20). The roots חרשׁ and יצר in v. 12 link these verses with the above section; see יצר in v. 10 and חרשים in v. 11.

[12] Compare the stark contrast of 40:28-31: "He never grows faint or weary. . . . He gives strength to the weary. . . . But those who trust in the Lord shall renew their strength," with the end of the verse here: "When hungry, his strength ebbs. Should he drink no water, he grows faint."

The blacksmith, with his cutting tool — This is a difficult clause on two counts: First, it lacks a verb; second, the term מַעֲצָד, which is linked here to "the craftsman in iron," actually refers to a type of ax with which one chops wood; see Jer 10:3: "For it [the carved image] is the work of a (wood) craftsman's hands. He cuts down a tree in the forest with an ax (במעצד)"; Isa 10:33: "Lo! The Sovereign Lord of Hosts will hew off the tree crowns with His ax." (MT במערצה is a scribal error for בְּמַעֲצָדֹה, caused by the graphic similarities of the letters ר and ד.) The term *mʿṣd,* "an agricultural cutting tool," also appears in Ugaritic (*HdO* 2:523) (along with *mqb,* "hammer" [*HdO* 2:567], which is also found in this verse), Arabic, and Rabbinic Hebrew (*m. Kelim* 13:4). The root עצד (= Akk. *eṣēdu,* "to harvest"; *CAD* E:338-41) appears in the Gezer Calendar, line 3: "His month is chopping (עצד) flax" (*KAI* 182), and in the bilingual inscription (Akkadian-Aramaic) from Tell Faḫariyeh, line 31: "May he sow but not reap" (יחצד = יעצד) (*KAI* 309).

In order to solve these problems, some commentators suggest following the LXX and Peshitta, which do not have the word מעצד but read יָחֵד (from the root חדד, "to sharpen"; see Prov 27:17: "As iron sharpens [read: יָחֵד] iron") and translate the verse: "the craftsman sharpens his ax." This word, according to those who accept this reading, was lost as a result of haplography caused by the last word of v. 11, יָחַד. The rest of the verse, however, deals with the sculpting of the idol itself and does not relate to the preparation of the tools. Others suggested emendations are: "The blacksmith fashions (מְעַצֵּב) his work (פעלו) with charcoal"; "The blacksmith works with the ax (במעצד יפעל)" — both of which combine words from the next hemistich. For חרש ברזל ("blacksmith"), see Gen 4:22.

Works it over charcoal — He sculpts his idol (or according to others, his ax) by smelting the metal over hot charcoal; cf. Isa 54:16: "It is I who created the smith to fan the charcoal (פֶּחָם) fire and produce the tools for his work." Contrast the use of the verb פעל here, the "work" of the blacksmith, with its use when applied to God (41:4; 43:13).

And fashions it with hammers — The craftsman continues to work by shaping it with מַקָּבוֹת, "hammers" (elsewhere found only in Judg 4:21). The *yod* of the verb יְצֻּרֵהוּ (a *qal* imperfect from the root יצר) is assimilated into the צ, with its subsequent doubling. Compare similarly יַצִּתוּ, from the root יצת ("to set on fire"; Isa 33:12). This hemistich forms a chiasm with the previous clause.

Working with the strength of his arm — In order to make the metal behave as he wants, the craftsman must use the strength of his arm.

When hungry, his strength ebbs — The prophet continues mocking the craftsman. Although he possesses great strength, he is but human, and when he gets hungry, his strength fails.

Should he drink no water, he grows faint — God, however, "never wearies," but rather "gives strength to the weary" (40:28-29). For the root יעף and its metathetic variant, עיף, both of which denote "faint from thirst," see 2 Sam 16:2: "And the wine is to be drunk by any who are faint (היעף) in the wilderness"; Isa 29:8: "And like one who is thirsty and dreams he is drinking, but wakes to find himself faint (עיף)." 1QIsa[a] reads the present participle שותה, instead of the MT past tense שתה.

[13] *The woodworker stretches a plumb line* — The prophet goes on to describe the carpenter's part in fashioning the idol (cf. 2 Sam 5:11 = 1 Chr 14:1). He first measures with a plumb line (קו) to determine the size of the wood that he will use for the image. In 1QIsa[a] נטהו conforms to the other four verbs in the verse, which are all third-person singular masculine imperfect, with a third-person pronominal suffix. For the figurative use of the expression נטה קו, see Isa 34:11; Lam 2:8; Job 38:5.

And traces its outline with a stylus — The second stage of the construction: the carpenter outlines the contours of the idol with a שֶׂרֶד ("stylus"), a hapax legomenon related to the root שׂרט, "to incise" (Lev 19:28; 21:5), and Arab. *sirād/sarīd*, a tool with which one punches holes. For the denominative verb תאר (from תֹּאַר, "outline, form"), "to trace out" (boundaries), see Josh 15:9, 11; 18:14, 17.

He forms it with scraping tools — The third stage: he continues his work with "scraping tools" (בַּמַּקְצֻעוֹת), a hapax legomenon. For the verbal root, see Lev 14:41: "The house shall be scraped (יקציע) inside all around." Some commentators suggest that instead of the MT יַעֲשֵׂהוּ, one should read יְשַׁעֲהוּ (a metathesis), from the verb שׁעע, "to smooth" (cf. Isa 6:10; 29:9; and common in Rabbinic Hebrew and Aramaic), i.e., "he makes the work smooth by planing the wood" (I. Eitan, "A Contribution to Isaiah Exegesis," *HUCA* 12-13 [1937-38]: 78; N. H. Tur-Sinai, *Peshuṭo shel Miqra*, III/1 [Jerusalem, 1967], 119 [Heb.]).

Outlining it with a compass — The fourth stage: the craftsman of the idol uses a compass (מחוגה, a hapax legomenon from the verb חוג, "to draw around") to sketch the outline of the idol.

He fashions it like a human figure, the beauty of a man — The finishing touches: he shapes it into the figure of a man, comely as the human form. This is yet another derisive statement against the images. If they are shaped like humans, how then can they be gods?! For תבנית, "figure, image," see Deut 4:16: "The figure (תבנית) of a man or a woman"; Ps 106:20: "They exchanged their glory for the image (בתבנית) of a bull that feeds on grass." For תפארת, "beauty," see Ezek 16:39: "And take away your beautiful (תפארתך) jewels." The idols may be the "beauty of man" (תפארת אדם); Israel, however, is God's "glory" (תפארתי); see v. 23; 46:13; 49:3; 55:5.

To dwell in a shrine — All the effort the craftsmen have expended in the construction of the image is for a single purpose — to set the idol up motionless in a shrine. The cognate Akkadian expression, *wāšib bītim*, is also employed for gods residing in their temples (*CAD* A/2:396-97). The placing of the idol in a sanctuary is also the final stage of the "mouth-washing" ritual.

[**14**] Following this detailed description of idol making, the prophet resumes his ever-escalating mockery, this time concentrating on the initial stages of this industry — the planting of the tree, the choice of wood, and the monumental effort the craftsman puts into his work. Deutero-Isaiah, as is his wont, mentions the various trees available to the craftsman (cf. 41:19; 60:13). As was explained earlier (40:19-20), this reverse description of the construction process, from the end to the beginning, is parallel to the Mesopotamian *mīs-pî* ("mouth-washing") instruction manual for the crafting of an idol. Deutero-Isaiah, who lived in Babylon, obviously had this common ritual in mind in his manifold tirades against idol worship and construction. (See the introduction, §19.B.)

For his use he cuts down cedars — Cf. Jer 10:3: "He cuts down (כְּרָתוֹ) a tree in the forest." The infinitive construct at the beginning of this verse (לִכְרָת) is anomalous (one would expect either the imperfect, past tense, or participle), and some commentators suggest that this may be an example of the emphatic ל; cf., e.g., Isa 32:1 (see Eitan, "Contribution to Isaiah Exegesis," 78). This rare syntactic construction, however, can be compared to Job 5:9-11, where, after an extended series of finite verbs, the description is followed by an infinitive construct, לָשׂוּם. Another suggestion is that the verb הלך was originally written at the beginning of the verse but was subsequently omitted by a partial haplography caused by the repetition of the letters לכ.

He selects a plane tree or an oak — He may also choose a תִּרְזָה — a hapax legomenon that has been variously translated as a plane tree or ilex, and that, according to Saadyah Gaon, Ibn Ganah (*Sefer ha-Shorashim,* 549), and Kimchi, corresponds to Arab. *sinabr,* a type of fir that grows in mountainous regions. (For other possible identifications see Y. Felix, *Flora and Fauna in the Bible* [Jerusalem, 1964], 90-91 [Heb.].) Or he may select an "oak" (אלון) (see, e.g., Hos 4:13; Amos 2:9). For the verb לקח ("to select"), see, e.g., 1 Kgs 11:37.

Or chooses among the trees of the forest — The master craftsman may choose any other tree of the forest. For the verbal expression אמץ ל-, see Ps 80:16: "The stock planted by Your right hand, the stem you have chosen as Your own (אִמַּצְתָּה לָּךְ)" (this verse also has an arboreal context); 80:18: "Grant Your help to the man at Your right hand, the one You have chosen as Your own (אִמַּצְתָּ לָּךְ)."

Or plants a cedar, and the rain makes it grow — The last tree the prophet lists is the אֹרֶן (a hapax legomenon, and note that in the MT the final *nun* is miniscule), whose Akkadian cognate is *erēnu,* "cedar." (For Akkadian texts describing figurines made out of cedar wood, see *CAD* E:276.) For the verb גדל in the context of tree cultivation, see Ezek 31:4; Jonah 4:10; and cf. the Akkadian semantic equivalent, *rubbu,* "to grow" (*CAD* R:47-48).

[15-16] The prophet continues to deride the idolater-craftsman and lists all the other ways he uses the wood with which he constructed the idol; the list includes fuel, heating, baking, and roasting. This derisive tone left its impression on the author of the pseudepigraphic book Wisdom of Solomon (13:11-16): "For granting some skilled woodworker has sawn a ready tree, skillfully scraped off all the bark, and with cunning art shaped a vessel for everyday use, while the castings of his manufacture he used for the preparation of his food and had his fill. But taking one of these useless castings, a crooked piece of wood streaked with knots, he diligently carved it in his spare moments, fashioned it with leisurely skill, and made it into the likeness of a human image. . . . Then making for it a worthy shrine, he fixed it in a wall and secured it with iron, thus taking precautions that it might not fall, in the knowledge that it is powerless to fend for itself, for it is an image and in need of help." For a similar satire, see Horace: "I was once the stump of a fig tree, useless wood, until a carpenter who was agonizing whether to make a footstool or a statue of the garden god, decided that I would become a god" (Horace, *Satires* 1.8.1-3).

[15] *It becomes fuel for man* — The same wood he uses to construct the effigy serves the craftsman for fuel. For בער, see Isa 40:16: "Lebanon is not fuel (בָּעֵר) enough."

He takes some of it to warm himself — some of the wood he previously used to construct the idol. The intransitive verb וַיָּחָם, from the root חמם, recurs twice more in v. 16.

And he also kindles a fire and bakes bread — This multipurpose wood is good even for baking bread. The Aramaic verb ישיק (here in the *hiphʿil*) from the root שלק, "to kindle, burn," appears only twice more in the Bible: Ezek 39:9: "And light their fires (והשיקו) with the weapons — shields and bucklers"; Ps 78:21: "Fire blazed up (נִשְּׂקָה) against Jacob"; but is very common in Rabbinic Hebrew and Aramaic (with a *samekh* rather than a *sin*); see, e.g., *b. Pesaḥ.* 27b, 30b. Note the assonance created by the repetition of אַף (three times in vv. 15-16) and the verb אָפָה ("bakes").

He also makes a god of it and worships it! — This is the height of irony: from the wood left over from stoking the stove and baking the bread he makes an idol that he then worships. The verb פעל is repeated twice more in v. 12 and contrasts with God's master creations that none can reverse (43:13). Here too אף is repeated in order to sharpen the prophet's sting.

Fashions an idol and bows down to it! — parallel to the previous hemistich. For the Aramaic root סגד ("to bow down"), see vv. 17, 19; 46:6; Dan 3:5: "You shall fall down and worship (ותסגדון)"; and Targum Onqelos to Gen 22:5; 24:52; 33:3. (At the time of the prophet, Aramaic was the lingua franca in the ancient Near East and had begun to penetrate into Hebrew as well. For further examples of Aramaic and Aramaisms in Deutero-Isaiah's prophecy, see the introduction, §11.) For the poetic form לָמוֹ, which usually refers to the plural, "to them," but here denotes the singular, "to it," cf. עָלֵימוֹ: "Can a man be of use to God, a wise man benefit Him (עלימו)?" (Job 22:2); "It claps its hands at him (עלימו) and whistles at him from its place" (Job 27:23). See GKC §103g n. 3. For the parallel pair "idol/god," see vv. 10, 17; 45:20.

[16] *One half he burns in the fire* — half of the tree he uses for firewood. בְּמוֹ is a poetic expansion of the preposition ב; see v. 19; 43:2: "When you walk through (במו) fire, you shall not be scorched"; and note the rhyming pair לָמוֹ (end of v. 15)/בְּמוֹ.

On that half he roasts meat, eats, and is sated — As many commentators have noted, one should reverse the order of the verbs in this clause: יאכל ("he eats") should come after יצלה ("he roasts"), as in the LXX and Peshitta; and see v. 19: "I roasted meat and ate it". For a similar sequence, see Exod 12:8-9: "They shall eat the flesh that same night. They shall eat it roasted over the fire. . . . Do not eat any of it now . . . but roasted . . . over the fire." 1QIsa[a] has a variant reading: ויאכל על גחליו ישב ויחם, "He shall eat and sit by the coals and be warmed." The words "by the coals" are also found in the Peshitta, *ʿl gwmrwhy.*

He also warms himself — By the light of the same wood fire the craftsman "warms himself." יָחֹם, an intransitive verb from the root חמם, appears again later in this verse (חַמּוֹתִי), as well as in v. 15 (וַיָּחָם), forming an emphatic triad, along with the threefold repetition of אף, here and twice in v. 15; the verb פעל, in v. 12 (twice) and v. 15; and the pair אל/פסל in vv. 10, 15, 17.

And exclaims, "Ah! I'm warm!" — The craftsman cries out in joy: הֶאָח, while enjoying the warmth of the fire. This exclamation of joy, which always appear in conjunction with the verb אמר, generally expresses satisfaction over the misfortune of an enemy or rival (Ezek 25:3; Ps 35:21, 25) and metaphorically stands for the neighing of a war horse in battle (Job 39:25). For other exclamations of idol craftsmen and worshipers, see vv. 17, 19. The intransitive verb (from the root חמם) is accented on the final syllable; cf. שַׁנּוֹתִי (Deut 32:41), from the root שנן, and דַּלּוֹתִי (Ps 116:6) from דלל.

"I'm enjoying the heat!" — The reading in 1QIsa[a], חמותי נגד אור ("I warm myself by the fire"), was perhaps influenced by Isa 47:14. For אוּר, "flame, fire," see 50:11.

[17] *And out of the rest he makes a god, his effigy!* — From what is left of the wood, after roasting the meat and using it as fuel, the craftsman constructs an idol. For the פסל/אל parallel, see above, vv. 10, 15; 45:20.

He bows down to it and worships it — For Aram. סגד, see vv. 15, 19; 46:6.

And he prays to it, saying, "Save me, for you are my god!" — Cf. Jer 2:27: "They say to the wood. . . . But in their hour of calamity they cry, 'Arise and save us!'" For the cry הצילני, "Save me!" (note the wordplay: צָלִי — הַצִּילֵנִי [vv. 16, 17]) in times of distress, cf., e.g., Ps 31:3, 16; 39:9; and for the declaration אלי

אתה, "You are my god," see Ps 140:7: "I said to the Lord: 'You are my God'"; and relating to idols, Isa 42:17: "Those who say to idols, 'You are our gods!'" For other pleas directed to idols, see 30:22; Jer 2:27-28; Hab 2:19.

[18-20] The worshipers of graven images are incapable of reaching the logical conclusion regarding their senseless modes of worship. Beginning with v. 18 and ending in v. 20, **לא** is repeated no less than seven times and **לב** three times. For the same idea — clouded vision and plugged ears that inhibit understanding — cf. Isa 6:9-10: "Hear, indeed, but do not understand! See, indeed, but do not grasp! Dull that people's mind . . . and seal its eyes!"

[18] *They do not realize or understand* — For the same phrase, see Ps 82:5. Cf. also v. 9.

Their eyes are besmeared and they see not — The **כי** particle is emphatic. The verb **טח** (with a *pataḥ*), "besmeared, plastered over," is a hapax legomenon intransitive verb from the root **טחח**. Their eyes are figuratively plastered over and thus they cannot see the obvious. (For the transitive by-form **טוח**, see Lev 14:42; Ezek 13:10; Rabbinic Hebrew, and the Ugaritic Aqhat epic: "He plasters [*ṭḫ*] his roof" [*CAT* 1.17.I:32].) Instead of the MT's singular verb, the Targum, LXX, and Vulgate all substituted a plural, which accords with the plural **עיניהם** ("their eyes"). In Biblical Hebrew, however, when the verb precedes the subject of the sentence, there is not always a one-for-one agreement between the verb and subject's gender and number.

Their minds, unable to think — Their minds are impervious to rational thought. For the anomalous plural form **לִבֹּת**, see also Ps 125:4. For **מֵהַשְׂכִּיל** (= **מלהשכיל**), an infinitive construct, cf. Exod 3:6: "And Moses hid his face, for he was afraid to look (**מֵהַבִּיט**) at God." The word **לב** appears twice more (in vv. 19, 20), creating another of Deutero-Isaiah's emphatic triads. For the pair **עינים**/**לב(ב)**, "eyes/mind," see Ps 73:7; 101:5; Prov 4:21; 21:4; 23:33; and for the verb **השׂכיל**, see Isa 41:20.

[19] This verse and v. 18 form a chiasm.

He does not give thought — The expression **להשיב אל לב**, a variant of **להשיב על לב** (cf. 46:8), denotes the cognitive process; see 1 Kgs 8:47; Lam 3:21. The word **לא** appears three times in this verse for emphasis.

He lacks the wit and sense to say — He lacks the basic common sense to come to the logical conclusion regarding his idol's impotence (cf. v. 18). "To say . . ." — once again the prophet quotes the idol craftsman and his ridiculous statements; cf. vv. 16, 17.

"Half of it I burned in a fire" — See the first clause of v. 16.

"I even baked bread on its coals" — See above, the middle clause of v. 15. For the **אף** (an emphatic conjunction) — **אפיתי** wordplay, see v. 15. For cakes baked on embers, cf. Akk. *akal tumri* (*CAD* T:472) and Rabbinic Hebrew **חֲרָרָה** (*m. Shab.* 1:10). For the pair **גחלים/אש** ("fire/coals"), see 2 Sam 22:9 (= Ps 18:9):

"From His mouth came devouring fire (אש). Live coals (גֶּחלים) blazed forth from Him."

"I roasted meat and ate it" — See the middle clause of v. 16.

"And the rest of it I turned into an abomination" — It is obvious that the idol worshiper or craftsman would not refer to his handiwork in such pejorative terms. This, rather, is the prophet putting the mocking words into his mouth. For תועבה ("abomination") as a derogatory term for idols, see 2 Kgs 23:13: "And for Milcom, the abomination (תועבת) of the Ammonites"; Ezek 7:20: "They made their images and their detestable abominations (תועֵבֹתם)." The word יִתְרוֹ ("the rest") appears here instead of שאריתו in v. 17.

"And I bow down to a block of wood!" — The mocking jest continues: "How in the world could I 'stoop so low' as to bow down [סגד is repeated here yet a third time; see vv. 15, 17] to an inanimate stump of wood?" The substantive בול ("block"), a hapax legomenon, is a loanword from Akk. *bulû*, "dry firewood" (*CAD* B:312-13).

[20] The prophet summarizes his remarks on idolatry.

He pursues ashes — The root רעי here denotes pursuit and association with; cf. Prov 15:14: "The mind of a prudent man seeks knowledge, but the mouth of a dullard pursues (ירעה) folly"; Prov 29:3: "But he who keeps company (וְרֹעֶה) with harlots will lose his wealth"; and see also Hos 12:2: "Ephraim chases (רֹעֶה) the wind and pursues the gale"; and from here evolved the expressions רְעוּת רוח ("pursuit of the wind"; Eccl 1:14; 2:11) and רַעְיוֹן רוח ("chasing the wind"; 1:17; 4:16). He who fashions the idol is compared to one who pursues ashes, a figure of worthlessness and insignificance; cf. Gen 18:27; "I am but dust and ashes (אֵפֶר)." Here, moreover, it is very apt, for after using the wood for the purpose of cooking and heating, what is left is literally "ashes." Note also the possible wordplay on Hos 12:2 cited above: <u>אפר</u>ים רעה (רוח).

A deluded mind has led him astray — His deluded mind has led him to the worship of idols. This is what happens when one "does not give thought" (v. 19). הוּתַל is a *huph'al* adjective from the root תלל, which denotes "deception, delusion"; see Judg 16:10: "You have deceived (הֵתַלְתָּ) me! You lied to me!"; Jer 9:4: "One man deludes (יְהָתֵלּוּ) the other. . . . They have trained their tongues to lies." Note the third (and last) appearance here of לב; cf. vv. 18, 19.

And he cannot save himself — Since his deluded mind has led him to worship worthless pieces of wood that do not answer him in his time of need (cf. v. 17), he is unable to save himself.

Nor can he say to himself: "The thing in my hand is a sham!" — The idol craftsman is incapable of realizing that the idol he has fashioned and now holds in his hand is but a sham. (הֲלוא, which implies certainty, is the last of the seven לא words in vv. 18-20.) Note, moreover, the double entendre, since שקר is also one of the many derogatory terms for an idol, e.g., Jer 10:14 (= 51:17): "For his molten image is a deception (שקר)"; Jer 16:19: "Our fathers inherited utter delusions (שקר), things that are futile and worthless." The word שקר also denotes naught and nothingness, as in 1 Sam 25:21: "Now David had been saying, 'It was all for nothing (לשקר) that I protected that fellow's possessions in the wilderness'"; Jer 3:23: "Surely, futility (לשקר) comes from the hills." The word בימיני ("in my right hand") is an allusion to v. 12: "Working with the strength of his arm (בזרוֹעַ)." The prophet concludes with yet another of the craftsman's statements or, more accurately, what he should have said had he not been led astray (cf. vv. 16, 17).

[21-23] God wipes away all of Israel's sins and commands the universe, as a whole, to share in the joy of Israel's redemption. The unit begins and ends with the two national sobriquets, Jacob and Israel, and forms a literary *inclusio.* The verbal root יצר is one of the many links between these verses and the preceding unit (vv. 9, 10, 21). Additional links, which contrast God's actions with those of the idolaters, are found in the terms עץ (vv. 13, 14, 23) and פאר (vv. 13, 23). The idolater cries out to his image: "Save me, for you are my god!"; and God tells His people, "You are My servant — I fashioned you. You are My servant" (v. 21). The first verse of this unit (v. 21) also echoes vv. 1-2: "Jacob," "Israel," "My servant," and the root יצר ("to fashion").

[21] *Remember these things, Jacob, for you, Israel, are My servant* — God addresses His servant Israel and instructs him to pay close attention. For the frequent "Jacob/Israel" parallelism, see vv. 1 and 23. The key words "Israel" and "My servant" are repeated twice in this verse for emphasis. Cf. 46:8-9 for the command to "remember" following a polemic against idolatry.

I fashioned you, you are My servant — I created you to be My servant. For the connection between the creation of Israel and being God's servant, see v. 2; 49:5. The repeated proclamation, "You are My servant," contrasts with the idolater's statement, "You are my god" (v. 17).

Israel, you shall not be forgotten by Me — The verb תִּנָּשֵׁנִי is a *niph'al* imperfect of the root נשי ("to forget"); cf. Gen 41:51: "God has made me forget (נַשַּׁנִי) completely my hardship"; Lam 3:17: "My life was bereft of peace. I forgot (נשיתי) what happiness was." Though the people complain that God had forgotten them (Isa 49:14; Lam 5:20), He declares that this will never happen. Due to the rarity of *niph'al* forms followed by a pronominal suffix (cf. Ps 109:3: "They attack me [וַיִּלָּחֲמוּנִי] without cause"), Kutscher comments that this form is an Aramaism: "The root נשה is to be found in Palestinian Aram.: in Gal Aram., and Samar., as well as in the Targ., in the *ethp'el* (which = the Hebr. *Niph'al*!) with a transitive connotation + pronominal suffix! — i.e. the usage here is exactly parallel to it. . . . It is still evident that there is no call to emend the text" (*Language and Linguistic Background,* 267); cf. also the remarks of Luzzatto. Alternatively, one may revocalize the verb as a *qal* (תִּנְשֵׁנִי), "You shall (not) forget Me," comparable to the similar negative parallelism in Deut 9:7:

"Remember, never forget!" (זְכֹר אַל תשכח). Compare also Isa 54:4: "For you shall forget . . . and remember no more." For the equivalent parallelism in Akkadian, *ḫasāsu//la/ul/ay mašû*, see *CAD* M/1:398-99.

[**22**] God announces a general pardoning of all sins and transgressions, followed by an earnest plea to return to Him. In later prophecies, however, after returning to the promised land, the nation slid back into their morally and cultically reprehensible ways, and there was again a need to demand that they return to God (see 55:6-7; 59:20; and cf. 56:1-2; 59:9-13).

I have wiped away your sins like a cloud and your transgressions like a mist — For the motif of a wholesale pardoning of transgressions, see also 43:25: "It is I, I who — for My own sake — wipe (מֹחֶה) your transgressions away." There will remain absolutely no trace of Israel's iniquities, which will disappear like the ephemeral clouds. For similar images, see Hos 6:4: "Your loyalty is like morning clouds (ענן), like dew that vanishes so early" (cf. Hos 13:3); Job 7:9: "As a cloud (ענן) fades away"; Job 30:15: "And my dignity vanishes like a cloud (וכעב)." For the parallel pair ענן-עב, see also Job 26:8; 37:11; and cf. the construct form, בעב הענן ("a thick cloud"; Exod 19:9).

Come back to Me — Since God has forgiven them, there is no reason why they should not return to Him. The form שובה is a lengthened imperative.

For I redeemed you! — from the Babylonian exile. For the recurring motif of God as Redeemer, see, e.g., Isa 41:14; 43:1, 14; 44:6; 47:4; 54:8; and the introduction, §9.

[**23**] A passionate call to the entire universe — the heavens, the depths of the earth, the mountains, and the forests — to participate in the joy of Israel's redemption. For similar calls, see 42:10-12; 49:13; 52:9; 54:1; 55:10.

Exult, O heavens, for the Lord has acted! — רָנּוּ is the *qal* imperative of the root רנן ("to shout"). The heavens themselves are commanded to shout in joy, for God has finally acted: He has redeemed Jacob. Although it is unusual for the verb עשי not to be followed by an object, there are a few examples, e.g., 46:4; 48:3, 11. Nevertheless, one commentator has interpreted the verb on the basis of the Arabic cognate *ǵāṯa* ("to rescue, save"), forming a parallel to גאל ("to redeem") in the final hemistich of the verse (see Eitan, "Contribution to Isaiah Exegesis," 79).

Shout aloud, O lowest depths of the earth! — The very bowels of the earth (see Ps 63:10) are called upon to cry aloud in joy. For תחתיות/תחתית, "lower, lowest part," see Exod 19:17: "They took their places at the lower part (בתחתית) of the mountain"; Ezek 26:20: "in the netherworld (תחתיות)." For the parallel pair הריע/רנן, see Zeph 3:14: "Shout for joy (רָנִּי), Fair Zion! Cry aloud (הָרִיעוּ), O Israel!"; Ps 95:1: "Come, let us sing joyously (נרננה) to the Lord, raise a shout (נריעה) to our Rock and Deliverer."

Break into songs of joy, O mountains — After commanding the heavens and the earth, the prophet urges the mountains to join in as well. For the expression **פצח רִנָּה**, see Isa 49:13; 52:9; 54:1; 55:12.

Forests, with all your trees! — In contrast with the trees enumerated above, which were used to construct idols (v. 14), here the trees of the forests are commanded to break into songs of joy as they witness the redemption of the nation; cf. 55:12: "You shall indeed leave in joy. . . . Mountains and hills shall shout aloud, and all the trees of the field shall clap their hands"; Ps 96:11-12: "Let the heaven rejoice and the earth exult. . . . Then shall all the trees of the forest shout for joy."

For the Lord has redeemed Jacob — reiterates the previous verse, "For I redeemed you."

And has glorified Himself through Israel — For similar phraseology, see Isa 46:13: "To Israel, in whom I glory (**תפארתי**)"; 49:3: "Israel in whom I glory (**אתפאר**)"; 60:21: "My handiwork in which I glory (**להתפאר**)." God reveals His glory to the world through Israel, as opposed to the idol craftsmen who construct deaf-and-dumb idols in the form of "the beauty (**תפארת**) of a man."

[24-28] A hymn of praise to God for the creation of the cosmos and for making fools of the Babylonian magicians and augurs. God also commands Jerusalem and all the cities of Judah to be rebuilt and appoints Cyrus to oversee these plans and carry them out. One should note that Israelite prophets prior to Deutero-Isaiah explained the ascension and appointment of foreign kings by God as a means of punishing the nations of the world, including Israel. Cf., e.g., Assyria: "Ah! Assyria, rod of My anger . . . I charge him against a people that provokes Me" (Isa 10:5-6); and Babylon: "I herewith deliver all these lands to My servant, King Nebuchadnezzar of Babylon" (Jer 27:6). Deutero-Isaiah, however, declares that Cyrus the Persian was chosen by God to redeem the nation and to return them to Israel so that they may rebuild Jerusalem and the Temple. These verses are connected to the previous section by the motifs of redemption (**גאל**, vv. 22, 23, 24); God, the Creator of Israel and of the cosmos (**יצר**, vv. 21, 24); Israel as God's servant (**עבד**, vv. 21, 26). Other key words/roots appearing throughout the chapter are: **אמר** (v. 24 — vv. 2, 16, 17, 19, 20), **עשׂי** (v. 24 — vv. 13, 15, 17, 23), **יצר** (vv. 21, 24 — vv. 2, 9, 10, 12), **דעת** (v. 25 — v. 19), **שׁוב** (v. 25 — v. 19), **ישב** (v. 26 — v. 13), **רעה** (v. 28 — v. 20). The words **כל** (vv. 24, 28) and **ישל[י]ם** (vv. 26, 28) are also repeated in this section.

[24] *Thus said the Lord, your Redeemer* — For a similar introductory formula, see v. 6; 43:1, 14; 48:17; 49:7. God is preparing to redeem His nation from the Babylonian exile. This verse forms a chiasm with the previous one: v. 23: **עשה ה׳ . . . גאל ה׳**; v. 24: **גֹּאַלְךָ ה׳ . . . ה׳ עשה**.

Who formed you in the womb — For the motif of formation of Israel while yet in the womb, see v. 2; 49:5. God's providence began at the nation's very inception and conception.

"It is I, the Lord, who made everything" — As the following verses will claim, God is He who created the cosmos and all in it, and it is He alone who controls history; cf. 45:7: "I, the Lord, made all these things"; Jer 10:16 (= 51:19): "For it is He who formed all things . . . Lord of Hosts is His name."

"Who alone stretched out the heavens" — Cf. Isa 40:22; 51:13, 16. For לבדי ("alone"), see 49:21; 63:3.

"Unaided spread out the earth" — For the spreading out of the earth, i.e., hammering it out (רקע), see 42:5; Ps 136:6. According to the Qere, מֵאִתִּי (one word), the meaning is, "on My own, unaided" (cf. Peshitta); according to the Ketib, מי אתי (two words), "Who was with Me [when I created the earth]?" (a rhetorical question); cf. Aquila, LXX, Vulgate, 1QIsa[a,b]. Both forms express the same sentiment: God, and God alone, was responsible for the creation of the universe. "Heaven and earth" are a merism emphasizing totality.

[25] God's greatness manifests itself also in His ability to annul the powers of the Babylonian magicians and diviners. The prophet polemicizes against the all-pervasive practice of divining in Mesopotamia, whereby the diviner was able to understand what the gods had in mind by applying traditional and tested rules of observation to a variety of phenomena. Each hemistich here forms a separate chiasm.

"Who annuls the omens of the diviners" — Instead of בַּדִּים (possibly influenced by לְבַדִּי in v. 24), one should read here (and in Jer 50:36 — also a prophecy against Babylon): בָּרִים, i.e., the *bārû* diviners (*CAD* B:121-26), who were the experts in interpreting "omens," אֹתוֹת (also a technical term from Akk. *ittu; CAD* I-J:305), which appeared in the liver and other viscera of sacrificed sheep and lambs, and through which they were able to explicate the will of the gods; cf. Ezek 21:26. The omnipotent God of Israel annuls the power of these Babylonian diviners. For the verb מֵפֵר, from the root פרר, "to frustrate, make ineffectual," see 2 Sam 17:14: "It was the Lord's purpose to frustrate (להפר) Ahitophel's good advice"; Job 5:12: "Who thwarts (מפר) the designs of the crafty." For other scribal errors as a result of the confusion between the graphically similar ד and ר, see Num 24:17: (וקרקר (כל בני שֵׁת — Jer 48:45: (וקדקד (כל בני שאון; 2 Sam 22:43: אֲדִקֵּם (כטיט חוצות) — Ps 18:43: אֲרִיקֵם (כטיט חוצות).

"And makes fools of the augurs" — God make the diviners look like imbeciles by annulling their omens. For the verb יְהוֹלֵל, here in the *polel* stem from the root הלל ("to make a fool of, to cause to go mad"), see Job 12:17: "And causes judges to go mad (יהולל)"; Eccl 7:7: "For cheating drives a wise man crazy (יהולל)." For קֹסְמִים, see also Deut 18:14; Zech 10:2.

"Who nullifies the sages" — God invalidates, literally "turns back," the wisdom of the Babylonian sages. For the expression השיב אחור ("turn back"), see Ps 44:11; Lam 1:13; 2:3. See also the Akkadian semantic equivalent *kutallu târu* (lit. "to turn back," "to make invalid" (*CAD* K:605-6).

"And makes nonsense of their knowledge" — For סכל with the meaning "to make foolish," see 1 Sam 13:13; 1 Chr 21:8; and "to annul," see 2 Sam 15:31. For the synonymous pair שׂ/סכל and הלל (in the first hemistich), see Eccl 1:17.

[**26**] One finds the same motifs detailed below — the resettlement of cities and the rebuilding of ruins — in Mesopotamian royal inscriptions and prophecies (*CAD* A/1:67-68; A/2:407-8; K:284-85).

"But who confirms the word of His servant" — God makes fools of the augurs and diviners, but the word of God's servant is always validated. For the expression הקים דבר, denoting the fulfillment of a promise or a prophecy, see 1 Sam 15:11; 1 Kgs 2:4. For דבר meaning "prophecy," cf. 2 Kgs 24:2; Jer 28:6. Whereas the MT has "His servant" (singular), the LXX Codex Alexandrinus and Targum have "His servants," conforming with the plural "His messengers" in the following hemistich.

"And fulfills the design of His messengers" — In contrast with the *bārû* diviners, whose omens God invalidates and annuls, God fulfills His plans in history through His messengers, i.e., His prophets (see Hag 1:13). For עֵצָה, "plan, design," see Isa 46:10, 11; cf. 5:19; 19:17. For the pair דבר/עצה, see 8:10: "Make your designs (עצה), but they shall be foiled. Propose your plans (דבר), but they shall not succeed"; and for the pair עבד/מלאך, see 42:19: "Who is so blind as My servant (עבדי), so deaf as My messenger (מלאכי) that I send?" The imperfect tense of the verb ישלים ("fulfill") indicates frequency: I have and will continue to fulfill the designs of My messengers (see also v. 28). Compare the Akkadian etymological and semantic cognate *šullumu* (the *shaphʿel* of *šalāmu*), which also denotes the fulfillment and execution of commands (*CAD* Š/1:223-24). The first two hemistichs form a poetic chiasm.

"Who says of Jerusalem, 'She shall be inhabited'" — God now specifies what is about to come to pass, introducing each of the elements with the verb הָאֹמֵר ("who says"), which is repeated four times in vv. 26-28. He first announces that Jerusalem shall be repopulated (תּוּשָׁב); cf. 54:3: "And they shall repeople (יושיבו) desolate towns." In Akkadian the verb *(w)ašābu* ("to sit, to dwell") in the *shaphʿel, šūšubu,* also denotes the (re)settling of people in cities and countries (*CAD* A/2:407-8). For the *huphʿal* stem of the verb ישב, see also 5:8; Ezek 35:9. Note the wordplay created by the juxtaposition of the letters י, מ, ל, שׁ in ירושלם and the verb ישלים in the preceding hemistich; and see v. 28: יַשְׁלִם . . . ירושלם.

"And of the towns of Judah, 'They shall be rebuilt'" — God then announces that the cities of Judah shall be rebuilt; see v. 28: "He shall say of Jerusalem, 'She shall be rebuilt (תִּבָּנֶה)'"; 45:13: "He shall rebuild (יבנה) My city." For the motif of the repopulation and restoration of Jerusalem expressed in similar terms, see Ps 69:36: "For God will deliver Zion and rebuild (ויבנה) the cities of Judah. They shall live (וישבו) there and inherit it." For the pair "Jerusalem/Zion" and

"the towns of Judah," see Isa 40:9; Jer 4:16. In Akkadian the cognate verb *banû* also denotes the building or rebuilding of cities (*CAD* B:85).

"And I will restore her ruined places" — I shall restore and refurbish the present ruins of Jerusalem and her environs; cf. Isa 52:9: "Raise a shout together, O ruins (חָרְבוֹת) of Jerusalem!"; 58:12: "Men from your midst shall rebuild ancient ruins (חָרְבוֹת)"; cf. 49:19; 51:3. For the repopulating and rebuilding of ruins, see Ezek 36:33: "I will repeople (והושבתי) your cities, and the ruined places (הֶחֳרָבוֹת) shall be rebuilt." The verb אקוֹמֵם, a *polel* form from the root קום, denotes restoration and rebuilding what was once ruined, as in Isa 58:12: "You shall restore (תקוֹמֵם) foundations laid long ago"; 61:4: "Restore (יקוֹמֵמוּ) the desolations of old." Note that the verse, as a whole, begins and ends with the root קום, creating a literary *inclusio*.

[27] The drying up of the Reed Sea at the time of the exodus serves as a portent of God's future redemption.

"I, who said to the deep, 'Be dry'!" — I commanded the deep (צוּלָה, a hapax legomenon variant of מצולה, "the depths of the sea") to be dry. This verse alludes to the early traditions regarding the transformation of the Reed Sea into dry land; see Exod 14:21: "And He turned the sea into dry ground (לֶחָרָבָה)"; see also Josh 3:17: "While all of Israel crossed over on dry land (בֶּחָרָבָה)." The verb חֳרָבִי (a pausal form of the second-person feminine *qal* imperative), "to be dry" (see Isa 50:2: "With a mere rebuke I dry up [אחריב] the sea"; Ps 106:9: "He sent His blast against the Sea of Reeds; it became dry [וַיֶּחֱרַב]") and חרבותיה in v. 26 are juxtaposed for wordplay. (See the introduction, §12.)

"Shall dry up your streams" — The motif of the drying up the mighty currents of water (cf. Ps 74:15: "You made the mighty rivers dry [הובשת נהרות]"), which appears in the Reed Sea traditions (cf. Exod 15:19: "But the Israelites marched on dry ground [וביבשה] in the midst of the sea"; Neh 9:11: "They passed through the sea on dry land [וביבשה], but You threw their pursuers into the depths"), may also be an allusion here to the "rivers of Babylon" (נהרות בבל; Ps 137:1), which God will dry up upon Israel's exodus from Babylon. For the verbal pair חרב/יבש, in the same context, see Nah 1:4: "He rebukes the sea and dries it up (וַיַּבְּשֵׁהוּ) and desiccated (החריב) all the rivers"; Job 14:11: "And the river dries up (יֶחֱרַב) and is desiccated (וְיָבֵשׁ)"; cf. Isa 42:15.

[28] Israel's redemption is tied to the ascension of Cyrus, God's appointee, whose mission it is to fulfill all of the Deity's purposes (see also 45:1, 13). The literary connection between the victory over the waters and the building of the Temple was borrowed from the Ugaritic and Mesopotamian epics where, after Baal's/Marduk's victory over the sea god Yam/Tiamat, a temple/palace was built as an abode for the triumphant god. (For a translation of *Enuma Elish*, see Foster, *COS* 1:390-402; and for the Baal epic, D. Pardee, ibid., 240-74.) (See the introduction, §19.)

"I am the One who says of Cyrus, 'He is My shepherd'" — With the third and final repetition of האֹמֵר ל-, the prophecy reaches its climax. For the first time Cyrus is specifically mentioned by name. (כורש is the Hebrew transcription of the Old Persian *Kurûs*, the founder of the Persian Empire, who reigned from 559 to 530 BCE). He is named by God as "My shepherd" (רֹעִי), the most prevalent of the royal titles in Mesopotamia, beginning with the Sumerian kings in the third millennium BCE (called "sipa" in Sumerian) and continuing afterward with the Babylonian and Assyrian kings, who were hailed as *rēʾû* (Akkadian; see Seux, *Épithètes royales*, 244-50, 441-46). Shepherding, i.e., protecting and providing for the people, was seen as one of the monarch's main responsibilities. The Israelite kings were also seen as shepherds; see Jer 3:15: "And I will give you shepherds (רֹעִים) after My own heart, who will pasture you with knowledge and skill." This verse poignantly polemicizes against the idea that a Davidic king is the only true "shepherd," as in Ezek 34:23: "Then I will appoint a single shepherd over them to tend them — My servant David. He shall tend them; he shall be a shepherd (לְרֹעֶה) to them"; 37:24: "My servant David shall be king over them. There shall be one shepherd (רועה) for all of them"; cf. 2 Sam 5:2; Jer 23:3-5; Ps 78:70-72. And he, the Davidic king, will rebuild the Temple; see Ps 132:2-5: "How he [David] swore to the Lord . . . 'I will not give sleep to my eyes . . . until I find a sanctuary for the Lord, an abode for the Mighty One of Jacob.'" Deutero-Isaiah declares that Cyrus, not a scion from the house of David, will be responsible to see that the Temple will be rebuilt. The term רֹעִי also creates a contrastive wordplay with the expression רֹעֶה (אפר) (v. 20).

"He shall fulfill all My purposes" — Cyrus is destined to "fulfill" (יַשְׁלִם) (see v. 26) God's master plan, which is immediately spelled out in the following hemistichs. The substantive חֵפֶץ appears twice more in the context of Cyrus's carrying out God's purpose: 46:10: "I say, 'My plan shall be fulfilled. I will do all I have purposed (חפצי)'" (God's call to Cyrus appears in the subsequent verse); 48:14: "[Cyrus] shall work His [God's] plan [חפצו] against Babylon."

"Saying to Jerusalem, 'She shall be rebuilt'" — The *waw* appended to ולאמר is explanatory and is best understood as "i.e." *(id est)*. The stated purpose of Cyrus, God's messenger, is to see that Jerusalem will be rebuilt. For the ישלם-ירושלם wordplay, see v. 26.

"And to the Temple: 'You shall be founded again'" — Cyrus's mission is also to see that the Temple's foundations will be laid once again (the ל preposition, appended to לירושלם in the prior hemistich, applies here as well to the Temple [היכל]). Since Heb. היכל, "Temple" (see Ezra 4:1: "The exiles were building a Temple [היכל] to the Lord God of Israel"), is always in the masculine, the verb תִּוָּסֵד is to be understood as a second-person masculine *niphʿal* from the root יסד. This verse alludes to Cyrus's famous proclamation recorded in Ezra 1:2 (= 2 Chr 36:23): "Thus said King Cyrus of Persia: 'The Lord God of Heaven has

given me all the kingdoms of the earth and has charged me to build Him a house in Jerusalem, which is in Judah'" (cf. Ezra 6:3). The idea expressed in these verses is very common among Mesopotamian monarchs, who frequently claimed that their god had commanded them to build him or her a shrine. Compare also Cyrus's proclamation in which he recounts how the idols were returned to their rightful owners and temples were built in Babylonian cities (*ANET,* 315-16). One should note that here, 66:1 (which contrasts with this verse), and 66:6 are the only places Deutero-Isaiah mentions the Temple. For the verbal pair יסד־בני in a similar context, see Ps 78:69: "He built (וַיִּבֶן) His sanctuary like the heavens, like the earth that He established (יְסָדָהּ) forever."

Chapter 45

[1-7] God chose Cyrus, the king of Persia, to overwhelm kings, subdue nations, and free Israel from their Babylonian oppressors. (On October 29, 539 BCE, the priests of Marduk opened the gates of Babylon to the conqueror, and the city capitulated without raising a weapon.) Moreover, God's objectives for selecting Cyrus are threefold: personal — that he will come to know the God of Israel; national — for the sake of Israel; and universal — to be the means whereby the entire world will acknowledge God's uniqueness (emphasized by the fourfold repetition of the formula: "I am the Lord" — vv. 3, 5, 6, 7, and repeated again in the next pericope, vv. 8, 18, 19, 21, 22). This literary unit is linked to the final verses of the previous chapter in that in only these two sections is Cyrus mentioned specifically by name (44:28; 45:1). For additional connections between the two chapters, cf. 44:24: "It is I, the Lord, who made everything" — 45:7: "I, the Lord, do all these things"; 44:26-28: -אמר ל (three times); and 45:1. The motifs in these verses — the "naming" of the king, the "grasping of his hand," and his multiple conquests — all appear in the Cyrus Cylinder as well (*ANET,* 315-16). For the concept of nations acknowledging God, see Ezek 38:23.

[1] *Thus said the Lord to His anointed one, to Cyrus* — a common introductory formula; cf., e.g., Gen 32:4: "Thus shall you say, 'To my lord, to Esau.'" Cyrus is referred to as God's "anointed one," i.e., he whom God appointed to carry out His historic mission. The origin of the term משיח is rooted in the Israelite custom of anointing important personages at the time of their appointment, such as the high priest (Lev 4:3, 5, 16), kings (1 Sam 12:3, 5; 24:6; 26:9 — Saul; 1 Kgs 19:15ff. — Hazael), prophets (Isa 61:1), and patriarchs (Ps 105:15). This is just one of the several designations employed to express God's selection of Cyrus. Compare also: "My shepherd" (Isa 44:28); "the man of My purpose" (46:11); and "He whom the Lord loves" (48:14). Cyrus was chosen to be God's instrument to execute the Deity's master plan, similar to the selection of As-

syria in First Isaiah: "The rod of My wrath" (Isa 10:5), and Nebuchadnezzar in the prophecies of Jeremiah: "My servant" (Jer 25:9; 27:6). This prophecy most likely came as an utter shock to the exiled Judeans since they certainly did not expect that their salvation would be facilitated by a foreign king. In the past, Moses was God's agent for redeeming Israel from Egypt. If anyone would deliver them from their present exile, they would naturally expect that he would be a descendant of the house of David. This ambivalent attitude toward Cyrus is documented in the Talmud (*b. Meg.* 12a): "What is the meaning of this [biblical verse]? Was Cyrus truly God's anointed?! Rather God, Blessed be He, said to His anointed one: 'I adjure you to inform Cyrus. . . .'" According to this midrashic interpretation, God's anointed one is none other than the prophet, and לכורש is understood not as "to Cyrus," but rather "regarding Cyrus." Compare similarly the Masoretic accentuation of this clause, which attempted to avoid the theological implications of the verse. By placing a partial pause between the two words, they parsed the text "to His anointed one [accented with the pausal *zarqa*], regarding Cyrus" (למשיחו, לכורש) (cf. Rashi, and see S. Kogut, *Correlations Between Biblical Accentuation and Traditional Jewish Exegesis* [Jerusalem, 1994], 52 [Heb.]).

Whose right hand I have grasped — thereby supporting and assisting him. Compare in regard to Israel, 41:13: "For I the Lord am your God, who grasped your right hand"; and, as here, regarding Cyrus, 42:6: "I have grasped you by the hand." Compare also the Akkadian semantic equivalents *qātam aḫāzu/ṣabātu,* "to grasp by the hand," which also denote aid (divine or otherwise) (*CAD* A/1:179; Ṣ:31-32). For God holding the hand of his chosen one, see also the references cited in 42:6.

To subdue nations before him — Hebrew לרד should be vocalized as a *qal* infinitive construct (from the root רדד), לָרֹד, which denotes subduing, as in 41:2: "And he shall subdue sovereigns" (there too vocalized יָרֹד); Ps 144:2: "Who subdues (הרודד) nations under my feet." Note that in Exod 39:3 Targum Onqelos translates וַיְרַקְּעוּ as וְרַדִּידוּ, "And they beat out." God aids Cyrus in his quest to subjugate nations, and this support is emphasized by the threefold repetition of לפניו/ך: "Subduing nations before him . . . opening doors before him. . . . I will march before you" (vv. 1-2).

And ungird the loins of kings — "Ungirding of loins" is a metaphor for subduing or weakening an individual by divesting him of his weapons. The antonym, אזר, in turn, denotes the girding of one loins in preparation for battle and often conveys the idea of "steeling oneself," e.g., Jer 1:17: "So you, gird up (תאזר) your loins." Compare their semantic parallels in Akkadian: *rakāsu* ("to gird") and *paṭāru* ("to ungird"), both employed with *qablu* ("loins"), also in contexts of war (*CAD* P:289; Q:11). For a similar series of an infinitive construct followed by a finite verb (לָרֹד . . . אפתח), see Isa 49:5: "To bring back Jacob to

Himself (לשובב), that Israel may be restored to Him (יֵאָסֵף)." For the pair "kings/nations," see 41:2; 52:15; 60:3, 11, 16; 62:2.

To open doors before him — The verb פתח (*qal* as opposed to the *pi'el* in the previous clause) alludes to breaking through the gates, which is the first stage of the conquest of a city. Compare the Akkadian: "I opened the city gates and let in the enemy" (*CAD* B:21). The dual דְּלָתַיִם refers to the two doors at the city's entrance, which were shut and locked by a bar that was inserted across them, and hence the expression, "doors and bars" (Deut 3:5; 1 Sam 23:7); see also Neh 3:14: "And he set its doors in place with their locks and bars." The Qumran scribe of 1QIsa[a] substituted דלתות, the plural of דלת (as in v. 2, below), for the dual דלתים, a form that had become obsolete at the time the scroll was copied.

And letting none of the gates stay shut: — This clause, together with the above hemistich, forms a complementary parallelism (the first of the two elements is expressed positively, "to open," and the second negatively, "none stay shut." Compare, similarly, Isa 60:11: "Your gates shall always stay open — day and night; they shall never be shut."

[2] *"I will go before you"* — The prophet switches from the third person to the first person and addresses Cyrus directly. God declares that He Himself will march before Cyrus as his vanguard and will aid him in his conquests. Compare, likewise, Deut 1:30: "The Lord your God, who goes before you, will fight for you." Deutero-Isaiah makes a similar declaration in 52:12, when referring to God's leading Israel: "For the Lord is marching before you." For similar promises of "military aid," cf. Deut 31:8 (Joshua); Judg 4:14 (Barak, the son of Abinoam); and 2 Sam 5:24 (David). The god(s) marching before the king (*ina pani*, or *ina maḫri*) or at his side *(ina idi)*, so as to ensure his success, is a common theme in Mesopotamian royal inscriptions (*CAD* A/1:317-20). Compare also Ishtar's morale-boosting message to King Esarhaddon: "I am Ishtar of Arbella. I will go before you and behind you. Fear not!" (Parpola, *Assyrian Prophecies*, 5, lines 20-24). Note also the Cyrus Cylinder (line 15), which states that Marduk led Cyrus to Babylon, "going at his side like a real friend" (*ANET*, 315).

"And I will level the hills" — הדורים is a hapax legomenon, and attempts to explain this ambiguous term are numerous. Many commentators, following LXX and 1QIsa[a], suggest that the ד of הדורים is a graphic corruption of ר, and that the word should be read הררים, "mountains." (The reading of 1QIsa[b], הרורים, is a conflated version incorporating both 1QIsa[a], הררים, and MT הדורים.) See also Ibn Ezra's second commentary, where he explains that הדורים are, in fact, הרים. For other images of leveling mountains, see 40:4; 49:11. Other commentators prefer to emend the MT to והדרכים or דרכיך ("the roads," or "your roads"), based on parallel terminology in v. 13, "And I shall level all roads for him." Yet others prefer to leave the text as is and interpret הדורים as a deriv-

ative of the Aramaic root הדר ("to go around"). According to this interpretation, God is promising Cyrus to level all the winding paths and twisted roads (Ibn Balaam; Ibn Ganaḥ, *Sefer ha-Shorashim*, 117; Rashi; Kimchi; Luzzatto). Another suggestion is based on the same root in Arabic, which denotes cragginess or bumpiness; cf. 40:4: "Let the rugged ground become level." Finally, there are those who retain the MT consonants but alter the pointing, reading הַדּוּרִים instead of הֲדוּרִים, deriving the word from Akk. *dūru*, "city wall, fortification" (*CAD* D:192-96), which God will raze before Cyrus. Cf. also Targum, שׁוּרַיָּא, "walls." (See C. H. Southwood, "The Problematic *hadûrîm* of Isaiah XLV 2," *VT* 25 [1975]: 801-2.) This last explanation fits well with the images of "doors of bronze and iron bars" immediately following. Whatever the correct meaning, it is clear that God is promising Cyrus to remove every obstacle from his path to facilitate his onslaught. The leveling of paths for kings also appears in Mesopotamian literature (see *CAD* E:360, for the citations for *šutēšuru* [*shaph'el* of *ešēru*] = Heb. ליישר). Compare likewise Ps 5:9: "Make Your way straight [הושר, Ketib; הַיְשַׁר, Qere] before me." The Ketib, הושר, in this example, as in the verse here, is in the *hiph'il*. (For a similar form of the primal weak radical *yod*, see Isa 13:12: אוקיר, from the root יקר.) The Qere, אֲיַשֵּׁר, is in the *pi'el*, which would denote intensification and multiplication: God will level many הדורים for Cyrus.

"I will shatter doors of bronze and hew iron bars" — The same motif and terminology appear almost exactly in Ps 107:16: "For He has shattered doors of bronze. He has hewed down iron bars." (See introduction, §17.) "Doors" and "bars" are the two components of city gates and often appear as a pair (see v. 1). Compare, likewise, the Akkadian epic text, "Ishtar's Descent to the Netherworld": "If you do not open the gate, so that I can enter, I shall smash the door and shatter the bar" (*ANET*, 107, lines 16-17). For נחושה ("bronze"), a poetic byform of נחושת, see Isa 48:4; Lev 26:19. The verb אֲשַׁבֵּר ("to shatter") in the *pi'el* (parallel to אֲגַדֵּעַ, "to hew," also a *pi'el* form) rhymes with the Qere of the verb in the previous clause, אֲיַשֵּׁר. (1QIsa[a], on the other hand, has אשבור, in the *qal*.) The phrase "doors of bronze" recalls the Mesopotamian custom of coating the city doors with bronze (Akk. *siparru; CAD* D:54; S:298) and is corroborated by the Greek historian Herodotus: "There are a hundred gates in the circuit of the wall [of Babylon], all of bronze, with posts and lintels of the same" (Herodotus, *Histories* 1.179, trans. A. D. Godley, LCL [repr. Cambridge, 1975], 223). See also the illustrations of the bronze gates of the city of Balawat in Iraq, against which Shalmaneser III, king of Assyria, laid siege (*ANEP*, nos. 357-65).

[3] *"I will give you treasures concealed in the dark and secret hoards"* — After the conquest of the city God promises to reveal to Cyrus the treasure hoards stored in the hidden places of the cities. מַטְמֹן is a variant of מַטְמוֹן, "treasures" (Gen 43:23; Jer 41:8). (Cf., similarly, the dual forms חר [2 Kgs 12:10]

and, חוּר/חֻר [Isa 11:8; 42:22].) This is an allusion to both the treasures of Croesus, king of Lydia, who was renowned in the ancient world for his vast wealth, and to the vast treasures of Babylon; see Jer 50:37: "A sword against its treasures, and they shall be pillaged"; Jer 51:13: "Vast treasures"; and cf. Hab 2:8. The fame of Babylon's wealth left its imprint in classic literature as well. In a dialogue between Cyrus and Croesus, as reported by the Greek historian Xenophon, the Persian king brags that he conquered Lydia, the second wealthiest kingdom in Asia (Babylon was the wealthiest) (Xenophon, *Cyropaedia* 7.2.11, trans. W. Miller, 2 vols., LCL [1914; repr. Cambridge, 1968], 2:235). Cf. also Pliny the Elder, *Natural History* 33.15.51-52, trans. H. Rackham, LCL [Cambridge, 1958], 9:43).

"So that you may know that it is I the Lord, the God of Israel, who calls you by your name" — By calling Cyrus by name, God thereby chooses him to fulfill His mission and purpose, so that he will realize that it is the "God of Israel" who is responsible for his unbroken chain of conquests (Isa 41:17; 48:1; 52:12), and not Marduk, as recorded in his cylinder: "He [Marduk] scanned and looked (through) all the countries, searching for a righteous ruler willing to lead him (i.e. Marduk) (in the annual procession). (Then) he pronounced the name of Cyrus, . . . declared him . . . to be(come) the ruler of all the world" (*ANET,* 315). For the expression "to call by name," see 42:6; 43:1; and Exod 31:2: "See, I have singled out by name Bezalel." For the cognate equivalent expressions in Akkadian, *šumam nabû/zakāru* ("to single out by name"), see Paul, *Divrei Shalom,* 12-13.

[4] *"For the sake of My servant Jacob and Israel, My chosen one"* — Another reason for Cyrus's anointing is "for the sake" of Israel. For the paired terms בחיר/עבד ("servant/chosen one"), see Isa 42:1, and cf. 41:8, 9; 43:10; 44:1, 2.

"I call you by your name" — I single you out and choose you; a reiteration of the "name" motif (v. 3). The LXX reads בשמי ("by My name"), and 1QIsa[a] has בשם ("by name," without the pronominal suffix).

"I hail you by title, though you have not known Me" — I have given you a "title of honor" (אֲכַנְּךָ), even though you heretofore have not recognized or worshiped Me as your God. For the paired terms קרא בשם/כני, see 44:5. The verb כני is the etymological and semantic cognate of Arab. *kana, kunyat.* Compare also Akk. *kanûtu,* "worshiped, honored, beloved" (*CAD* K:171-72) and Ugar. *knyt,* "glorious, of noble ancestry" (*HdO* 1:451-52).

[5] For the motifs of this verse, cf. Ps 18:32-33: "Truly, who is a God except the Lord? Who is a rock but (זולתי) our God? The God who girds me (המאזרני) with strength."

"I am the Lord and there is none else" — This monotheistic declaration reverberates throughout the chapter (see vv. 6, 14, 18, 21, 22).

"Besides Me there is no god" — זולתי is not the poetic construct form with

an archaic suffixal ending, as in Deut 4:12: "But perceived no shape — nothing (זולתי) but a voice," but rather the preposition (זולת) with the personal pronoun referring back to the speaker; see v. 21: "No god exists other than Me (זולתי)"; Hos 13:4: "You have never known a god but Me (זולתי)."

"I gird you" — I am He who aids and strengthens you (lit. "I am He who girds" your loins for battle); see Jer 1:17; Job 38:3. This metaphor is diametrically opposed to v. 1, where the enemies' impotence is described as the "ungirding of loins." The verb אזר is denominative, derived from the substantive אֵזוֹר, "waistcloth."

"Though you have not known Me" — The conclusion of v. 4 is reiterated. God is the sole cause of Cyrus's victories, yet Cyrus remains unaware of His existence.

[6] The third reason God chose Cyrus is universal: by means of his victories Cyrus will spread God's renown throughout the world. For the subjugation of enemies, which a deity cites to substantiate that he is the undisputed power broker and king of the gods, cf. the Neo-Assyrian prophecy in which the god Assur brags: "I slaughtered your [Esarhaddon] enemies and filled the river with their blood. Let them see (it) and praise me, (knowing) that I am Assur, lord of the gods" (Parpola, *Assyrian Prophecies,* 24, lines 22-25).

"So that they may know, from the rising of the sun to its setting" — The two geographical opposites denote a totality, from one end of the world to the other; cf. Isa 43:5: "I will bring your folk from the east and gather you from the west"; 59:19: "From the west they shall revere the name of the Lord, and from the east, His presence." מזרח ("east") is the direction from which the sun "rises," and מערב ("west") is where the sun "sets." For מערב, derived from the root meaning "to enter," cf. its cognate equivalents in Ugaritic, *ʿrb špš* and *mʿrab špš* (*CAT* 1.15.V:18-20; 1.19.IV:48-49). These polar opposites also appear in Phoenician inscriptions, e.g., לממצא שמש ועד מבואי ("From the place where the sun rises till the place where the suns sets") (*KAI* 26A I:4-5; II:2-3); in Punic, מצא שמש ... מבא שמש (*KAI* 78:5-6); in Aramaic, מן מוקא שמש ועד מערב ("From the place where the sun rises to where it sets") (*KAI* 215:13); and in Akkadian, *ultu ṣīt šamši adi erēb šamši* ("From where the sun departs to where it sets") (*CAD* Ṣ:217). The ה (suffixed to וּמִמַּעֲרָבָה) is unvocalized (i.e., without a *mappiq*) and is not pronominal (i.e., it does not refer to the sun) since in all the parallel expressions the word "sun" is treated as masculine, e.g., Mal 1:11: "From where the sun rises to where it sets (מבואו)"; and cf. Ps 113:3. For a similar form, see Deut 4:41, מזרחה שמש.

"That there is none but Me" — there is no deity other than Myself; see v. 5. For אפס, see v. 14; 40:17; 41:12, 29; 45:6, 14; 46:9; 47:8, 10; and for בלעדי, see v. 21; 43:11; 44:6, 8.

"I am the Lord and there is none else" — a parallel repetition of the last

clause. The final clauses of this verse form a chiasm with the beginning of v. 5. For a similar declaration, see Deut 4:35: "It has been clearly demonstrated to you that the Lord alone is God. There is none beside Him." (For the influence of Deuteronomy on Second Isaiah, see the introduction, §13.)

[7] Many exegetes attribute this verse to a polemic that the prophet is supposedly waging against Zoroastrianism, the Persian religion that believed in a binary universe, where Ahuramazda, the deity of light and good, and Ahriman, the deity of darkness and evil, were in constant combat. Accordingly, when the prophet declares that the God of Israel, He and He alone, created both light and darkness, weal and woe, he is polemicizing against this belief. Compare already Saadyah Gaon, quoted by Kimchi: "Our teacher Saadyah, of blessed memory, wrote [in his philosophical work, *Emunot veDe'ot*, 57-58]: 'He [the prophet] attributed the creation of both good and evil to God, contrary to those who believed in two deities, one good and one evil, and therefore [the prophet] said, 'I the Lord do all these things.'" This explanation, accepted until today by most commentators, however, does not stand up to the test of scrutiny, since there is no definitive indication that Cyrus was a Zoroastrian or that he believed in such a duality. Moreover, nowhere in the Bible is this religion alluded to, and no mention is ever made of any Persian deity. Thus one must concur with Weinfeld that this verse reflects an internal biblical polemic against Gen 1:3, which states that God created light but not darkness, with the assumption being that darkness already existed and was not part of God's creation. (For three other mythic ideas reflected in Gen 1–2, against which the prophet polemicizes, see M. Weinfeld, "God the Creator in Gen 1 and in the Prophecy of Second Isaiah," *Tarbiz* 37 [1968]: 105-32, esp. 120-26 [Heb.]; see also the introduction, §7.) For the three verbs for creation that appear here, **ברא**, **עשי**, and **יצר**, see also v. 18; 43:7.

"I form light and create darkness" — The prophet emphasizes here God's omnipotence and total control over nature. "Light and darkness" are a merism encompassing a totality. This hemistich is linked associatively with v. 6, which speaks of the "rising" (light) and "setting" (darkness) of the sun (see Yellin, *Hiqrei Miqra*, 56). The verb **יצר** is repeated five times throughout these verses (vv. 7, 9, 11, 18 [twice]) and creates the leitmotif of God's absolute creative power.

"I make weal and create woe" — These two polar opposites also constitute a merism: God is the one and only Creator of all that happens on earth. The word **שלום** is polysemous, denoting peace, prosperity, blessing. **רע**, on the other hand, does not indicate moral judgment in this context, but rather serves as the antonym of **שלום**. See Jer 18:11: "I am devising disaster (**רעה**) for you"; Amos 3:6: "Can misfortune (**רעה**) come to a town if the Lord has not caused it?" Since in later times **שלום** came to mean primarily peace (as opposed to war), however, the scribe of 1QIsa[a] replaced it with **טוב**, which is the usual ant-

onym of רע, "evil"; cf. Isa 52:7; 5:20; Ps 34:15; Job 30:26. The Rabbis in the Talmud who were hesitant to attribute evil to God emended this formula in the liturgy (in the first blessing before the morning *Shema* prayer) to: "He who forms light and creates darkness, makes peace and creates everything (הַכֹּל)" (*b. Ber.* 11a). (Perhaps this reading was also influenced by the subsequent clause: "I the Lord do all these things.") The verse, as a whole, follows an *abcb* paradigm (forms-creates-makes-creates).

"I the Lord do all these things" — "All these things" is an all-encompassing expression denoting God's absolute sovereignty over everything created; cf. 44:24: "It is I, the Lord, who made everything"; Jer 14:22: "For only You made all these things"; Jer 10:16: "For it is He who formed all things"; Sir 51:24: "Praise Him who created everything, for His goodness is eternal."

[8] A lyric interlude associatively linked to v. 7 by the root ברא and the expression אני ה׳. The verse begins with a plural imperative and continues in the jussive. The roots צדק (8 times) and ישׁע (7 times) are key words throughout the rest of the chapter. Several of the motifs here also appear in Jer 33:15-16. (See the introduction, §15.)

Trickle, O heavens, from above! — For Heb. מִמַּעַל ("from above") serving as an adverb, see Exod 20:4: "Or any likeness of what is in the heavens above (ממעל)"; Job 31:28: "For I would have denied God above (ממעל)." The root רעף, here in the *hiphʿil,* is a metathetic variant of ערף, "to trickle, drip." Compare in the *qal* Prov. 3:20: "And the skies dripped (ירעפו) dew"; Ps 65:12. Since the root רעף does not carry this meaning in later Hebrew and thus was apparently not understood, the scribe of 1QIsa[a] substituted הריעו ("shout aloud"), which is similar graphically to הרעיפו and perhaps also was influenced by Isa 44:23: "Shout aloud (הָרִיעוּ), O lowest depths of the earth!" (cf. LXX and Peshitta).

Let the heavens rain down victory! — יִזְּלוּ is a third-person masculine plural jussive of the root נזל, whose basic meaning is "to flow, drip." The parallelism between נזל and רעף also appears in Job 36:28: "The skies rain (יִזְּלוּ); they trickle down (ירעפו) on all humankind." For שחקים in parallelism with שמים (in the preceding colon), see Deut 33:26; Jer 51:9. The word צדק denotes vindication and victory, as do the following parallel nouns, ישע and צדקה. The singular verb in 1QIsa[a], ויזל, is based on an erroneous division of the verse, according to which צדק functions as the subject and שחקים as the second object of the verb הרעיפו.

Let the earth open up — Another jussive verb whereby God commands the earth to open up so as to receive the rain of victory from above. The midrash expresses this imagery very poignantly: "As a woman opens up for a man [the fertile earth will open up and receive victory from above, so that] vindication shall spring up and be fruitful and multiply" (*Gen. Rab.* 13:13 [ed.

Theodore-Albeck, 122, lines 5-6]). The verb פתח in the *qal* at times functions as a reflexive; see, e.g., Ps 106:17: "The earth opened up (תפתח) and swallowed Dathan." The LXX and Vulgate translate the verb as a *niphʿal,* "will be opened." For the image of the sky impregnating the earth, which then gives birth to the grass, see Isa 55:10; and cf. a Late Babylonian inscription: "As the sky inseminated the earth (so that) vegetation became abundant" (*CAD* E:309). The Akkadian verb *petû,* similar to Heb. פתח, is also used in sexual contexts (*CAD* P:346), as well as in agricultural ones (ibid., 349-50).

So that triumph will sprout — From these fruitful rains, salvation shall spring forth. The *qal* third-person plural וְיִפְרוּ, from the root פרי, here means "to sprout"; cf. Deut 29:17: "Sprouting (פֹּרֶה) poison weed and wormwood"; Isa 11:1: "A twig shall sprout (יפרה) from his stock." The plural form ויפרו, nevertheless, is somewhat difficult in this context since the referent is singular, but according to Kimchi: "Although ישע is accentuated with a *zaqef* [a pausal accent] [in our MT it has a *reviʿi* — also pausal], it is linked to צדקה, and thus [the verb] ויפרו is plural." 1QIsa[a] solved this apparent inconsistency by substituting the verb ויפרח in the singular; cf. likewise some LXX manuscripts, Vulgate, and Peshitta, which also have a singular verb.

And vindication spring up — further agricultural imagery that creates a parallel to the preceding clause. (Some ancient translations read תצמח, *qal,* for MT תצמיח, *hiphʿil.*) For the imagery, see 61:11: "So the Lord God will make victory and renown shoot up (יצמיח)"; Ps 85:12: "Truth shoots up (תצמח) from the earth"; Jer 33:15: צֶמַח צדיק. (For this expression see also a Phoenician inscription from Lapethos dated to the third century BCE; *KAI* 43:11.) If (contra the MT division) one connects וצדקה to the preceding clause and reads: ויפרו ישע וצדקה ("Let triumph and vindication sprout"), then ותצמיח יחד functions as a conclusion to the fertility images. For יחד used as a conclusion for a series of verbs, see Isa 42:14; 44:11.

I, the Lord, have created it — Compare the conclusion of the previous unit: "I, the Lord, do all these things" (v. 7). The masculine suffix in בראתיו, "it," refers to that which was previously described. Although neuter in Hebrew is usually indicated by a feminine pronominal suffix (see 43:13: "Who can reverse it [יְשִׁיבֶנָּה]?"; 44:7: "Let him announce it and provide its evidence [וְיַגִּידֶהָ וְיַעְרְכֶהָ]"), there are exceptions to this generalization, e.g., Amos 1:3: "I will not revoke it (אשיבנו)." According to the Targum (בְּרֵיתִינוּן), as well as the Peshitta and LXX, the pronominal suffix is plural (perhaps they read בראתין instead of MT בראתיו). The verb ברא, which serves as a link between this verse and the preceding unit, also appears in vv. 12, 18 (twice).

[9-13] The prophet polemicizes against those among his nation who find it incomprehensible to believe that Cyrus, a foreign king, is really their long-hoped-for salvation. They were expecting a homegrown "Mosaic" deliverer, who would lead them out of Babylon and into the promised land. The prophet castigates them for their doubtful thoughts and reprimands them for daring to question God's design, and he emphasizes this reprimand by the threefold repetition of "I" in vv. 12-13. How can God's creatures dare to disagree with or doubt their Creator? The metaphor and the phraseology are reminiscent of yet another polemic, 29:15-16, which very likely left its mark on Deutero-Isaiah: "Ho! . . . Should the potter be accounted as the clay? Should what is made say of its Maker, 'He did not make me'? And should what is formed say of Him who formed it, 'He did not understand'?" (Also note that both 45:9-13 and 29:15-16 begin with the polemical interjection הוי [and this is the only place in Deutero-Isaiah's prophecies that this word appears]; see the introduction, §14.) For a similar polemical-ironic question, see 10:15: "Does an ax boast over him who hews with it, or a saw magnify itself above him who wields it?" And cf. the following Aramaic proverb of Ahiqar: "Why does wood argue with the fire, meat with the meat cleaver, or a man with a king?" (See Lindenberger, *Aramaic Proverbs of Ahiqar,* 87.)

This unit is linked associatively to the above by the roots יצר (vv. 7, 9, 11), ברא (vv. 7, 12, 18), צדק (vv. 8, 13), and ישר (vv. 2, 13).

[9] *Ho! He who contends with his Maker* — The prophet rebukes those of the exiles who dare to undermine and question God's choice of Cyrus as His agent to liberate Israel from exile. The word יֹצְרוֹ is polysemous, referring to God as both Israel's Creator/Maker (see 43:1; 44:2, 24) and its "potter" (see 41:25; 64:7), as becomes apparent as the verse progresses. For the meaning "potter," see also Ugar. *yṣr* (*HdO* 2:987-88), Eblaite Akk. *wāṣirum* (G. Pettinato, *Materiali epigrafici di Ebla* [Naples, 1980], 23, 31, no. 1012), and Punic יצר (C. R. Krahmalkov, *Phoenician-Punic Dictionary* [Leuven, 2000], 214). Some exegetes suggest reading הֲיָרִיב instead of MT הוי רב. For רָב, *qal* participle of ריב, "to contend," see 41:11, 21.

A potsherd among earthenware — For חֶרֶשׂ, "earthen vessel, potsherd," see Jer 19:1: "Go buy an earthenware jar"; Ps 22:16: "My vigor dries up like a shard." Luzzatto suggests, on the other hand, to revocalize MT חַרְשֵׂי to חָרָשֵׁי, explaining the expression as "crafters of clay," similar to חרשי עץ וחרשי אבן ("carpenters and stonemasons"; 2 Sam 5:11); לחרשי ברזל ונחֹשת ("craftsmen in iron and bronze"; 2 Chr 24:12). The LXX also interprets the word as being pointed with a שׁ rather than with a שׂ, but translated it from the homonymous root, חרשׁ, "ploughers of the earth"; cf. also 1QIsa[a], חורשי האדמה.

Shall the clay ask the potter, "What are you making?" — another rhetorical question, the negative response to which is clearly understood: How can "clay" (חֹמֶר, 41:25) level any complaints against the one who molds it? For similar imagery, see 64:7: "We are the clay and You are the Potter"; Jer 18:6: "Just like clay in the hands of the potter, so are you in My hands." For an Egyptian parallel, cf.

Amenemope's proverb (chap. 25, 24:13-14): "Man is clay and straw, the god is his builder" (M. Lichtheim, "Instruction of Amenemope," *COS* 1:121). For the interrogatory **מה**, "what" (which appears twice in v. 10 as well, and forms a triad of rhetorical questions), as an accusation, see Gen 3:13: "And the Lord God said to the woman, 'What (**מה**) is this you have done?'"; Gen 4:10: "Then He said, 'What (**מה**) have you done?'"; Judg 18:18: "The priest said to them, 'What (**מה**) are you doing?'" See also Job 9:12; Eccl 8:4. 1QIsa[a] has **הוי האומר [לי] צרו** (without the word for "clay"), repeating the interjection from the beginning of this verse and the next one, and thereby creating a triad of **הוי** exclamations.

"Your work has no handles"? — Can clay criticize the potter for shoddy craftsmanship or for constructing an object without handles? Hebrew **ידים** has the meaning "handles" only here. The singular appears in Mishnaic Hebrew, e.g., "the handle (**יד**) of the adze" (*m. Kelim* 29:4). (The Akkadian term for "hand," *qātu,* which also denotes handles of dishes and other receptacles, was borrowed into Rabbinic Hebrew [**קֶנֶת**] and Aramaic [**קַתָּא**].) For the root **פעל**, see Isa 41:4; 43:13. Instead of the MT **ופעלך אין ידים לו**, the LXX and Peshitta render: "For you are not acting, and you have no hands." According to this reading, some have suggested to understand the final clause of this verse on the basis of the Arabic idiom *la yaday lahu,* i.e., "it is above and beyond his power." (See F. Delitzsch, *Jesaia* [Leipzig, 1889], 462.) In light of 1QIsa[a] **ופועלכה**, others suggest that the vocalization be emended from **פָּעָלְךָ** ("your work") to **פֹּעַלְךָ** ("your craftsman").

[10] The polemic continues. The prophet questions the people's stubborn persistence in their doubts. For other metaphors comparing God to a woman (here a woman in labor), see 42:14; 46:3-4; 49:15; 66:9, 13. (See Gruber, "Motherhood of God in Second Isaiah.")

Ho! He who says to [his] father, "What are you begetting?" — Woe to him who dares ask his father such an impudent and impertinent question.

Or to [his] mother, "What are you bearing?" — And woe to him who questions his mother, "Why did you give birth?" (For **אשה** with the meaning "mother," see 49:15.) The verb **חיל** denotes "labor pangs," e.g., 13:8; "They shall be seized by pangs and throes, writhe like a woman in travail (**יחילון**)"; and "birth," as in 51:2: "Sarah who gave birth to you (**תחוללכם**)." The verb appears here in the second-person feminine imperfect of the *qal* stem, with poetic nunation. For the parallel verbs **ילד/חיל**, see 23:4; 26:17, 18; 54:1; 66:8. Compare too Deut 32:18: "You neglected the Rock that begot you (**יְלָדְךָ**), forgot the God who brought you to birth (**מְחֹלְלֶךָ**)."

[11-13] As an answer and rebuttal to the legions of doubters, the prophet responds in turn with the same and similar words as those that appear in their complaints: **ויוצרו** (v. 11) — **ל׳צרו** (v. 9); **פֹּעַל ידי** (v. 11) — **ופעלך . . . ידים** (v. 9); **עשיתי** (v. 12) — **תעשה** (v. 9); **בראתי** (v. 12) — **תוליד, תחילין** (v. 10); **ידי** (v. 12)

— ידים (v. 9). Just as parents and craftsmen create and beget, so too God creates the world and controls its destiny.

[11] *Thus said the Lord, Israel's Holy One and his Maker* — In this opening line of the response, two of God's titles are emphasized: קדוש ישראל ("the Holy One of Israel"; see 41:14; 43:3, 14; 47:4; 48:17; 49:7; 54:5; 60:9, 14) and יוצרו ("his Maker"; see 43:1, 7, 21; 44:2, 21, 24; 49:5, 8, and also note 64:7: "But now, O Lord, You are our Father. We are the clay, and You are the Potter, and we are all the work of Your hands." Compare similarly 43:15: "I am the Lord your Holy One, the Creator of Israel, your King"). (See the introduction, §9.)

"Will you question Me?" — Many commentators interpret this clause as the prophet's castigation of the people for their queries regarding what is yet to occur (understanding אותיות as "future events," a derivative of the Aramaic root אתי, "to come." For the verb שאל as inquiring of God regarding the future, see 1 Sam 28:6; and cf. Isa 7:11: "Ask for a sign [שְׁאַל ... אות] from the Lord your God"). It is preferable, however, to accept Ehrlich's proposal (*Miqra ki-Pheshuṭo,* 3:107) to divide the words differently and read: הַאֹתִי תשאלוני, "Will you ask Me?" (or, as others propose, הַאֹתִי תשאלון): "Since the scribe erred and left out a ת at the beginning of the word [שאלוני], and instead inserted it at the end of the previous word." For another example of אֹתִי, along with a finite verb having a pronominal suffix, see Gen 30:20: "God has given me my reward (זְבָדַנִי אלהים אֹתִי)." The position of this word before the verb is for the purpose of emphasis. Perhaps 1QIsa[a], האותות ("omens"; cf. likewise Peshitta, אתותא), was influenced by Isa 44:25: "Who annuls the omens (אותות) of diviners"; and cf. the commentary on that verse.

"Will you instruct Me concerning My children and the work of My hands?" — Do you dare instruct Me how to treat My children, the children of Israel, the work of My hands? For the expression פֹּעַל ידים, see also Deut 33:11. For Israel as God's "handiwork," see Isa 60:21; 64:7. (The Akkadian semantic equivalent *binût qāti* also denotes an act of creation, applying to gods, humans, and animals [*CAD* B:244].) For Israel as God's "children," see 43:6; and for the expression צוי על, see 1 Kgs 2:43; 1 Chr 22:12.

[12-13] From whence the temerity to question My decision to appoint Cyrus as the executor of My plans? Did I not create the world and all on it, and do I not determine the course of history? For similar self-proclamations describing God as creator of nature and director of history, see Isa 42:5; 44:24-25. Note the connections between this hymn in the context of God's selection of Cyrus and Jer 27:5-6 — a prophecy regarding Nebuchadnezzar: "It is I who made the earth and humankind . . . by My great might and My outstretched arm . . . and I give it to whomever I deem proper." Both prophets then link God's creation of the universe and His choice of the two kings, Nebuchadnezzar and Cyrus: "I now deliver all these lands to My servant Nebuchadnezzar, king

of Babylon" (Jer 27:6) = "It was I who roused him [Cyrus] for victory." This being said, there is still an important difference in these kings' missions: According to Jeremiah, Nebuchadnezzar's mission is to sow destruction and exile Israel to Babylon, whereas Cyrus's mission is more benevolent. He is instructed to free Israel from their long indenture and allow them to return and rebuild Jerusalem. (See the introduction, §15.)

[12] *It was I who made the earth* — The position of the pronoun **אנכי** at the beginning of this verse and v. 13 is emphatic, and for further reiteration **אני** appears at the beginning of the second half of the verse. God's assertion: "It was I who made (**עשיתי**) the earth," is a rebuttal of the people's impertinent question: "What are you doing (**תעשה**)?" (v. 9). For this sequence of creation (earth-heavens), see Gen 2:4. The opposite order, however, is the rule in Deutero-Isaianic prophecy; see above, v. 8; 42:5; 44:23, 24.

And created humankind upon it — Cf. Gen 1:26; Deut 4:32; Jer 27:5.

My own hands stretched out the heavens — Note the pronoun's position at the beginning of the verse, for emphasis, as in the previous clause. It was I, and I alone, who stretched out the heavens; cf. Isa 40:22; 42:5; 51:13. Since the heavens are compared to a tent (see 40:22: "Who spread out the skies like gauze, and stretched them out like a tent to dwell in"), they also are described as being stretched out, e.g., Gen 12:8; 26:25. The emphasis on "My hands" (**ידי**) is a response to v. 9, "Your work has no handles (**ידים**)."

And I commanded all their host — The verb **צוי** in the context of cosmogony appears also in Ps 33:9: "He commanded (**צוה**), and it stood firm"; 148:5: "For it was He who commanded (**וצוה**) that they be created." Note the assonance between **צויתי** and **צבאם**. For the use of **צבא** with reference to the stars, see Isa 40:26: "He who leads out their host [**צבאם**, the host of stars] by count." The verb **צויתי** contrasts with v. 11, **תְּצַוֻּנִי**.

[13] *It was I who roused him for victory* — For the third and last time the personal pronoun "I" is placed at the beginning of the verse: It was I, and I alone, who was responsible for bringing Cyrus; cf. 41:2: "Who has roused (**העיר**) a victor from the east?"; 41:25: "I have roused him (**העירותי**) from the north." **בצדק** is polysemous: on the one hand, it denotes victory and vindication, as in v. 8 and 41:2; and on the other, as in 42:6, it is equivalent to Akk. *kīnu* ("right"), *kīnis* ("by right"), which verifies the divine legitimization and confirmation of Mesopotamian kings. (See Paul, *Divrei Shalom,* 13.) Compare the name of the Assyrian king, Sargon, which is a transcription of Akk. *šarru kīn,* the semantic equivalent of **מלכיצדק** (Gen 14:18; Ps 110:4), literally "the rightful/legitimate king."

And I will make level all roads for him — For the motif of "leveling of paths," see v. 2; 40:3, 4.

He shall rebuild My city — Cyrus is destined to rebuild Jerusalem; see

44:28: עירי ("My city") refers to Jerusalem, as do עיר ה׳ ("the city of the Lord"; 60:14; Ps 101:8), עיר הקודש ("the holy city"; Isa 48:2; 52:1), and עיר אלהינו ("the city of our God"; Ps 46:5; 48:2, 9).

And let My exiled people go free — גָּלוּת refers to the exiled community, as in Isa 20:4: "So shall the king of Assyria drive off the captives of Egypt and the exiles (גלות) of Nubia"; Jer 28:4: "And all the Judean exiles (גלות) who went to Babylon." The LXX and Targum added עמי ("My [exiled] nation") as an explanatory gloss. For the verb שלח in the *pi'el,* meaning "liberate, go free," see Exod 10:4.

Without price and without payment — Cyrus will not be reimbursed for freeing Israel; see Isa 52:3: "For thus said the Lord: 'You were sold for no price, and shall be redeemed without payment.'" For the parallel pair שֹׁחַד/מחיר, see (in reverse order) Mic 3:11: "Her rulers judge for gifts (בשחד), and her priests give rulings for a fee (במחיר), and her prophets divine for pay." For the expression לא במחיר, see Jer 15:13.

Said the Lord of Hosts — The prophecy concludes with God's military title, ה׳ צבאות. Note the link to v. 12: "I commanded all their hosts (צבאות)" (= the host of stars). For the formulaic signature אמר ה׳, see Isa 50:1; and for ה׳ צבאות ("Lord of Hosts"), see 44:6; 47:4; 48:2; 51:15; 54:5.

[14-17] The three nations of Africa (listed in the same order in 43:3) will bring all their wealth to Israel, will acknowledge and accept God's supremacy and uniqueness, and Israel shall be vindicated forevermore. (The root ישע appears three times in this section, vv. 15, 17 [twice].) Not only will Cyrus free Israel without demanding payment, Egypt and Nubia will shower them with gifts upon their return. The themes of this pericope recur in vv. 21-24.

[14] The theme of the nations of the world coming to Jerusalem also appears in 60:5-7, 9, 11-12. And for their indenture to Israel, see 60:14; 49:23. The same motifs are in evidence in psalmic literature vis-à-vis the king of Israel; cf. Ps 72:10-11: "Let the kings of Tarshish and the islands pay tribute, the kings of Sheba and Seba offer gifts. Let all kings bow to him and all nations serve him." Compare also the pilgrimage of "many peoples" to Jerusalem, described in Isa 2:2-4 as the supreme court, from whence God will mete out judgment to all the nations of the world. For similar ideas in Mesopotamian literature, see M. Weinfeld, *From Joshua to Josiah* (Jerusalem, 1992), 114-30 (Heb.). For an illustration of Jehu, king of Israel, paying tribute to Shalmaneser III, king of Assyria, see *ANEP,* no. 355.

Thus said the Lord — the opening words of a new prophecy.

"Egypt's wealth" — יגיע denotes hard-earned wealth (derived from the root יגע, "to toil/be weary"), e.g., Jer 20:5: "And I will deliver all the wealth, all the riches (יגיעה), and all the prized possessions of this city, and I will also deliver all the treasures of the kings of Judah into the hands of their enemies"; Ps

109:11: "May strangers plunder his wealth (יְגִיעוֹ)." For the parallel terms יגיע/כסף ("wealth/money"), see Isa 55:2: "Why do you spend money (כסף) for what is not bread, your earnings (ויגיעכם) for what does not satisfy?"

"And Nubia's gains" — Nubia's gains from commerce as in 23:3: "From the trade (סחר) of nations"; cf. 23:18. For כּוּשׁ (Ham's oldest son [Gen 10:6]), i.e., Nubia, a land south of Egypt, see Ezek 29:10: "And I will reduce the land of Egypt to utter ruin and desolation, from Migdol to Syene, all the way to the border of Nubia (כוש)." The reading in both the LXX and Peshitta, "the merchants of Kush," is based on the reading סוחרי כוש.

"And Sabeans bearing tribute" — a third African nation, from the line of Ham and Kush (Gen 10:7); cf. Ps 72:10: "Kings of Sheba and Seba shall pay tribute." אנשי מִדָּה is usually understood as "giant in stature," e.g., אנשי מִדות (Num 13:32), in reference to the Canaanites; 1 Chr 11:23: "He also killed an Egyptian, a giant of a man (איש מִדה)"; cf. also 1 Chr 20:6. This explanation, however, does not fit the present context. The term מִדָּה here is actually a loanword from Akk. *mandattu/maddattu* ("tribute") via Aram. מִדָּה/מִנְדָּה; see Ezra 4:20: "And tribute (ומדה), poll tax, and land tax"; Ezra 7:24: "tribute (ומנדה), poll tax, or land tax"; Neh 5:4: "We have borrowed money . . . to pay the king's tax (לְמִדת המלך)"; and cf. Ezra 6:8. One should also transpose the letters of אנשי and read נֹשְׂאֵי מִדָּה, which is the interdialectal cognate of Akk. *nāš maddattu* ("bearers of tribute") (*CAD* M/1:14; N/2:92). (For the cognate Hebrew expression, see 2 Sam 8:2: "And the Moabites became tributary vassals [נֹשְׂאֵי מנחה] of David.") The scribe clearly did not understand the loanword מִדה, thus leading to the textual corruption of the MT; see also Tur-Sinai, *Peshuṭo shel Miqra,* III/1:121.

"Shall pass over to you and be yours" — The three African nations will parade their tribute before you, as was the custom of vassals. Compare Sennacherib's royal inscription, which uses the Akkadian interdialectal cognate of Heb. עבר, *etēqu,* meaning to "march in review, parade": "The king sits on his throne and the wealth of Lachish is paraded before him" (*CAD* E:386).

"They will follow you" — They shall be loyal to you. This diplomatic expression, which is common in the Bible (cf. Deut 13:5; 1 Kgs 14:8) and in Akkadian, *ina arki alāku,* denotes national and religious loyalty (*CAD* A/1:320).

"And pass by in fetters" — The nations of the world will march before Israel in prisoner queues. For אֲזִקִּים/זִקִּים, "fetters," see Jer 40:1, 4; Nah 3:10; Ps 149:8. It is an Akkadian loanword, *iṣ qātī* (*iṣ,* "wood"; *qātī,* "of the hands"), signifying a wooden manacle (*CAD* I-J:205-6). For depictions of chained prisoners marching in line, see Yadin, *Art of Warfare,* 1:132-33, 151; 2:342-43, 462; *ANEP,* nos. 7-10.

"They shall bow down to you" — as vassals before their sovereign. For this expression, see Ps 5:8; 138:2: "I bow toward (אשתחוה אל) Your holy temple." In both these latter verses, however, אל denotes direction — they shall bow in the

direction of the Temple rather than to the Temple itself. Thus it is very probable that אליך is a scribal error, influenced by the repetition of the letters אל throughout the verse, and one should read here לך, the preposition that most commonly follows the verb השתחוה.

"And they shall pray to your God" — Luzzatto understood this clause correctly: "Praying is only to God. Therefore, all the commentators who understand התפללו אליך at face value were in error. Clearly [the prophet] meant to say . . . that they will pray to your God." Thus one should emend the MT and read: ואל אלהיך יתפללו. The word אלהיך was lost as the result of haplography (note the א and the ל that appear in both ואל and ואלהיך) (cf. also Ehrlich, *Randglossen,* 4:166).

"'Only among you is God'" — For the conjunction אך as emphatic, see v. 24; 63:8.

"'And there is no other god at all!'" — See v. 6: "That there is none but Me. I am the Lord and there is none else"; 46:9: "For I am God and there is none else. I am God and there is none like Me." For similar declarations cf. below, vv. 18, 21, 22.

[15] The nations continue their hymnal confession.

"'Truly you are a God who protects'" — אכן in Biblical Hebrew denotes cognizance of an unexpected and surprising reality contrary to expectations, e.g., Gen 28:16: "Truly (אכן) the Lord is present in this place and I did not know it!" (See the commentary of Rashbam on that verse, where he explains that only after Jacob awoke did he realize that he was sleeping in a holy place: "This is the meaning of every אכן in the Bible — אך כן — 'indeed it is thus,' and not as I expected"; cf. Exod 2:14: "Moses was frightened, and thought, 'Now (אכן) the matter is known'!" [contrary to Moses' expectations that the murder he committed was unknown to anyone; *The Commentary of Rashbam on the Torah* (New York, 1949), 35, 82].) Compare also Ps 31:23: "Alarmed, I had thought, 'I am thrust out of Your sight.' Nevertheless (אכן), You listened to my cry for mercy when I called out to You"; cf. also Isa 49:4; 53:4. The nations confess that, contrary to their previous understanding, the God of Israel is a God מסתתר. Although most commentators explain this term as meaning God who conceals Himself (see 54:8), in light of the clause immediately following: "O God of Israel, the Deliverer," it is more likely that the nations are referring to God as a protector, as one who gives shelter to His followers; cf. Deut 32:38: "Let them rise up to your help, and let them be a shield (סִתְרָה) unto you!"; Isa 4:6: "As a shelter for protection (מִסְתּוֹר) against drenching rain"; 16:4: "Be a shelter (סֵתֶר) for them against the despoiler" (see Ehrlich, *Randglossen,* 4:166, and his suggestion that the Masoretic version was the result of an erroneous dittography from אל מסתיר). Hebrew אתה אל contrasts with the nations' declarations to their deities: "You are our/my god" (42:17; 44:17).

"'O God of Israel, the Deliverer'" — The God of Israel alone brings victory; see v. 21: "No god exists beside Me who foretells truly and grants salvation (ומושיע)"; 43:11: "Besides Me, none can grant triumph (מושיע)" (cf. 43:3; 49:26; 60:16). From this point forth the root ישע serves as a refrain; see vv. 17 (twice), 20, 21, 22.

[16-17] After the nations' confession, the prophet juxtaposes their disappointment in their idols with the eternal salvation granted by God to Israel.

[16] *All of them are confounded and put to shame* — The nations shall be frustrated and shamed when they finally realize that their idols are totally impotent. For this motif, expressed by the root בוש, see vv. 17, 24; 41:11; 42:17; 44:9, 11. The pausal accentuation, *atnach*, should be transferred from כֻּלָּם to יַחְדָּו (cf. LXX, Vulgate, and Peshitta), which appears as a summary of a series of verbs (or substantives); see v. 21; 41:19, 20, 23; 52:9. For the construction of כֻּלָּם together with יַחְדָּו, see Isa 31:3; cf. also Ps 14:4 = 53:4; Isa 40:5. The juxtaposition of the roots בוש and כלם here serves as emphasis; cf. v. 17; Ps 35:26: "Let them be clad in frustration (בֹּשֶׁת) and shame (וּכְלִמָּה)"; and see Isa 41:11.

To a man they slink away in disgrace — This expression, which reiterates the prior clause, is unique. For הלך ב-, see v. 14.

Those who fabricate idols — The Targum (צַלְמַיָא) and many of the medieval commentators translate צירים correctly as "idols." This hapax legomenon is related to Akk. *uṣurtu,* which denotes "design" and also refers to idols (*CAD* U-W: 292). (Cf. Heb. צורה, "design," which appears four times in Ezek 43:11 in connection with the Temple. For צורה as referring to idols in Rabbinic Hebrew, see *m. ʿAbod. Zar.* 3:3 and the discussion in *b. ʿAbod. Zar.* 42b.) Moreover, צירים in the present context is polysemous, since it can also denote "travail"; see Isa 13:8: "They shall be seized by pains (צירים) and throes, writhe like a woman in travail" (Kimchi; Ibn Balaam; Ibn Ganaḥ, *Sefer ha-Shorashim,* 429; and Luzzatto).

[17] *But Israel is saved by the Lord, salvation everlasting* — Unlike the utter shame that will befall "those who fabricate idols," Israel's triumph shall be everlasting, since "the God of Israel is the Deliverer" (v. 15). For the expression נושע בה׳, see Deut 33:29: "O happy Israel! Who is like you, a people delivered by the Lord (נושע בה׳)!" According to Luzzatto, נושע is a present participle and should be vocalized with a *qametz,* נוֹשָׁע, rather than a *pataḥ,* נוֹשַׁע (past tense), as it appears in the MT (cf. Zech 9:9). For the plural עולמים, "everlasting," see Isa 51:9; Ps 145:13.

You shall not be confounded or put to shame for all ages to come — as opposed to the nations, who "are all confounded and put to shame" (v. 16); cf. Joel 2:26, 27: "My people shall be shamed (יֵבֹשׁוּ) no more." The same sentiment appears in a Neo-Assyrian prophecy to King Esarhaddon, in which Ishtar promises the monarch: "I shall help you. I shall not shame you" (IV:1-2;

Parpola, *Assyrian Prophecies,* 7; for Akk. *ba'āšu* ["to be ashamed"], see *CAD* B:5-6). The unique expression עד עולמי עד, "for all ages to come" (a variant of the common עד עולם, e.g., Ps 9:6; 21:5, and עדי עד, e.g., Isa 65:18; 26:4), is a clever play on words — the first עד functions as a preposition, the second as a substantive.

[18-25] A trial scene in which the God of Israel once again takes the idolatrous nations to task (cf. 41:1ff., 21-24). God claims that He alone is able to foretell the future. He alone is the Lord and there is no other savior. The Deity then appeals to the nations to turn to Him so that they too will be saved. Finally, He takes an oath that in the future all peoples will bow before Him and swear allegiance to Him. This prophecy is linked to the preceding unit by a series of common motifs and expressions: אני ה׳ ואין עוד (v. 18; cf. v. 21) — אך בך אל ואין עוד (v. 14); בַּסֵּתֶר (v. 19) — מסתתר (v. 15); ומתפללים אֶל אֵל (v. 20) — ואליך יתפללו (v. 14); מושיע (v. 21), וְהִוָּשְׁעוּ (v. 22) — מושיע (v. 15), נושע בה׳ תשועת [עולמים] (v. 17); וְיֵבֹשׁוּ (v. 24) — בּוֹשׁוּ (v. 16), תֵבֹשׁוּ (v. 17). The key root צדק appears five times throughout this unit: vv. 19, 21, 23, 24, 25. Compare likewise the reiteration of the root ישע in vv. 15, 17, 20, 21, 22. The declaration אני ה׳ is also repeated in vv. 18, 19, 21; and cf. the variant אני אל in v. 22.

[18] This doxology lauds God as the sole creator of the universe. The series of verbs, ברא, יצר, עשה, appears in a similar hymn (v. 7; see also 43:7). For a similar sequence of the verbs ברא, יצר, and כון, see Jer 33:2.

Yea, thus said the Lord — the beginning of a new prophecy, which is introduced by an emphatic כי.

The creator of the heavens, He who is God — The third-person masculine pronoun הוא is emphatic; cf. Isa 43:25: "It is I, I who (הוא) wipe your transgressions away"; Gen 42:6: "Now Joseph was (הוא) the vizier of the land. It was he (הוא) who dispensed rations to all the people of the land." For the pronouncement הוא האלהים ("He is God"), see 1 Kgs 8:60; 18:24, 39; 2 Kgs 19:15.

Who formed the earth and made it — It was God who formed the earth from start to finish. The verb עשׂי (lit. "to make") denotes here the finishing touches of the creation process; cf. Isa 41:4: "Who has planned and achieved (ועשה) this?" For the verbs יצר and עשה in sequence, see v. 7; 46:11: "I have designed it (יצרתי), so I will complete it (אֶעֱשֶׂנָּה)." For the pair ארץ/שמים, see 40:12; 42:5; 44:24; 51:13. For עשׂי ארץ ("to create the earth"), see v. 12 above. For the parallel verbs יצר/ברא, see also v. 7.

Who fixed it firmly — The root כון (here in the *polel*) denotes the creating of a firm and stable base, as in 54:14: "You shall be firmly established (תִּכּוֹנָנִי) in triumph"; 62:7: "Until He firmly establishes (יְכוֹנֵן) Jerusalem"; Ps 119:90: "You have firmly established (כוננת) the earth and it stands." See also 2 Sam 7:13: "And I will establish (וכֹנַנְתִּי) his royal throne firmly forever." For the same motif and terms that appear in this verse, cf. Jer 33:2: "Thus said the Lord who made it (עָשָׂהּ), the Lord who formed (יוצר) it and firmly established it (להכינהּ), whose name is the Lord." For עשׂי and כון as parallels, see Jer 10:12: "He made (עשה) the earth by His might, firmly established (מֵכִין) the world by His wisdom." This is also the meaning of its cognates, Akk. *kânu*/*kunnu* (*CAD* K:159ff.) and Ugar. *kn* (*HdO* 1:447-48).

Who did not create it a wasteland — God did not create the earth to be an uninhabitable wasteland. For תֹּהוּ ("wasteland"), see Deut 32:10: "He found him in a desert region, in an empty howling wasteland (ובתהו)"; Jer 4:23: "I looked at the earth, and it was an unformed wasteland" (i.e., the earth had returned to its precosmogonic state). (The word also appears in Ugaritic, *thw*, with the meaning "desert" [*CAT* 1.5.I:15].) 1QIsa[a] has לתהו (the MT has לא תהו), which agrees with the Targum, לָא לְרֵיקָנוּ, and LXX. Note the possibility of a hidden polemic against Gen 1:2, where תהו existed before the cosmos was created.

But formed it to be inhabited — The earth was formed (note the repetition of the verb יצר) for human habitation. Compare *m. Giṭ.* 4:5: "The earth was created only for procreation, as is said [Isa 45:18] 'He did not create it a wasteland.'"

"I am the Lord, and there is none else" — The Deity once again declares His uniqueness; see vv. 5, 21, 22.

[19] God does not reveal His plans in hidden places or in ambiguous terms, as was the common practice among the foreign deities, but instead informs His people directly of what will come to pass.

"I did not speak in secrecy" — Deutero-Isaiah is referring here to God's promises concerning Cyrus and the return of the exiles to Zion; cf. 48:16: "From the very beginning I did not speak in secret (בַּסֵּתֶר)." For idol worship in secret, see Deut 13:7; 27:15.

"At a site in a land of darkness" — God did not reveal His promises and predictions in a realm of darkness, an allusion to the desert, as in Jer 2:6: "Who led us through the wilderness . . . a land of drought and deep darkness"; Jer 2:31: "Have I been like a desert to Israel, or like a land of deep darkness?" For the parallel terms חֹשֶׁךְ/סֵתֶר, see v. 3: "I will give you treasures concealed in the dark (חשך) and secret (מסתרים) hoards"; and note the chiastic order between the two.

"I did not say to the offspring of Jacob, 'Seek Me out in a wasteland/in vain'" — I never commanded Israel to seek Me in out-of-the-way places. For תֹּהוּ, "desolate place, a desert devoid of habitation," see v. 18; cf. Job 12:24: "And He makes them wander in a trackless wasteland (בתהו)." The preposition ב appended to בסתר and במקום in the previous clauses applies here as well, i.e., (ב)תהו; or its omission was caused by haplography due to the previous word (יעקב), which ends with a ב. There may be a double entendre intended here since תֹּהוּ can also mean "in vain" (Rashi); cf. Isa 40:17, 23; 41:29; 44:9; 59:4. The sobriquet זרע יעקב ("the offspring of Jacob") appears twice more in the Bible (Jer 33:26; Ps 22:24); cf. also v. 25: זרע ישראל ("offspring of Israel"). For seeking

God (בקש ה׳), see, e.g., Exod 33:7: "And whoever sought the Lord (מבקשי ה׳) would go out to the tent of meeting that was outside the camp."

"I, the Lord, foretell reliably, announce what is true" — I declare what is yet to occur with complete reliability (cf. v. 21; 41:22, 26; 42:9; 43:9, 12; 44:7, 8; 46:10; 48:3, 4) — "the reference being to the above prophecies" (Ibn Ezra), i.e., concerning Cyrus and the liberation of Israel from bondage. **צדק/ה** and **מישרים/מישור** are parallel terms in biblical poetry (see 11:4; 33:15; Ps 9:9); in Ugaritic: *ṣdq/yšr* (*CAT* 1.14.I:12-13); in Phoenician (the inscription of Yeḥawmilk): **כמלך צדק ומלך ישר** (*KAI* 4:6-7); and cf. the Akkadian cognates: *kittu u mišāru* (*CAD* K:470).

[**20**] *Assemble yourselves and come, approach together* — In a triad of verbs drawn from juridical terminology, the prophet commands the nations of the world to stand in judgment. For the verb **בוא** in the legal sense, meaning to come to trial, cf. 2 Sam 15:2, 6; and for **נגש** ("approach") (the *hithpaʿel* imperative, **התנגשו**, is a hapax legomenon), see v. 21; Exod 24:14: "Let anyone who has a legal matter approach (**יִגַּשׁ**) them"; Deut 25:1: "When there is a dispute between men and they approach (**וְנִגְּשׁוּ**) for judgment, and they shall be tried." For the trial motif, see Isa 41:1; 43:9; 48:13-14; 50:8. Instead of MT **יַחְדָּו** (which often comes at the end of a series of verbs or substantives, e.g., v. 16; 41:1; 43:9), 1QIsa[a] has an additional verb, **ואתיו** ("and come"). (For the Aramaic root **אתי**, see 41:5.) According to this version, there are two parallel pairs: **הקבצו ובאו** and **התנגשו ואתיו**, rather than a triad of synonyms as in the MT. (See the introduction, §10.A.)

You survivors of the nations — you, the remnants of the nations who escaped Cyrus's onslaught. Compare also "survivors (**פליטי**) of the sword," Jer 44:28; Ezek 6:8.

Who have no awareness, who carry their wooden idols — This derisive comment is addressed to the idolaters, who carry their wooden idols in procession during holidays or, according to another, less likely, interpretation, as they flee Cyrus's sword (see Isa 46:1-2). They are completely unaware of the reasons for these historical events. For the motif of the idolater's ignorance, see 44:9, 18, 19. For wooden images, see 40:20; 44:19.

And pray to a god who cannot save! — Unlike the "God of Israel, the Deliverer!" (v. 15); "But Israel is saved by the Lord, salvation everlasting" (v. 17); "No God exists other than Me, who is . . . able to save" (v. 21); "Turn to Me and be saved" (v. 22). Compare Jer 11:12: "'They will go and cry out to the gods to whom they sacrifice; but they will not be able to save them in their time of disaster." For prayer and supplication to the images, see Isa 44:17: "Save me, for you are my god!"

[**21**] *Speak up, present your case! Let them even take counsel together!* — another series of three imperatives addressed to the idolaters to stand trial and

present their case. Cf. 41:21: "Present (הגישו) your pleas!"; 41:22: "Let them approach (יגישו) and tell us!" They are ironically urged to take counsel together in order to come up with their most persuasive arguments. The prophet switches here from the second-person masculine imperative to the third-person masculine jussive, as in 41:1: "Stand silent (הַחרישו) . . . let nations renew (יחליפו) their strength!"; 41:21-22: "Present yourselves (הגישו) . . . approach (יגישו)!" For the emphatic **אף**, see 40:24 (three times); 41:10 (twice), 23, 26 (three times). For another instance of the root **יעץ** ("to take counsel") in a legal context, see 41:28. Once more, **יַחְדָּו** concludes and accentuates a series of verbs.

Who announced this aforetime — Who among the nations' gods foretold Cyrus's coming or Babylon's downfall before it actually happened? Cf. 43:9; 48:14; and see 41:22, 26. For **מִקֶּדֶם** ("from the remote past"), see 46:10: "I foretell the outcome from the beginning, and from the past (מקדם), things that have not yet occurred."

Foretold it of old? — Who, in fact, did predict these events? Cf. 44:8: "Have I not from of old (מֵאָז) predicted and foretold to you?"; 48:3: "Long ago (מאז), I foretold things that happened"; 48:5: "Therefore I told you long beforehand (מאז)." For the parallel pair **אז/קֶדֶם**, see Prov 8:22: "The Lord created me at the beginning of His course, as the first of His works of old (קדם . . . מאז)."

Was it not I, the Lord? There is no god but Me — The interrogative **הלוא** introduces a question, the answer to which is positive; see 40:28; 42:24; 44:8. Since I, the Lord, am the only God with oracular powers, in truth there is no other god. For God as sui generis, see vv. 6, 14, 18, 22; 43:11; 44:6, 8; and cf. 1 Sam 2:2: "There is no holy one like the Lord. Truly there is none beside You. There is no rock like our God"; Ps 18:32: "Truly, who is a God except the Lord." For **אין עוד** ("there is none other"), see vv. 5, 14, 22. (See the introduction, §9.)

No god exists other than Me, who is triumphant and able to save — Cf. Hos 13:4: "You have never had one who can save other than Me." For the root **צדק**, meaning victory and vindication, see v. 8; 41:2. For **אין זולתי**, see v. 5. For the parallel pair **זולתי/מבלעדי**, see Ps 18:32.

[22-25] An emotional appeal to the nations to recognize the God of Israel and be saved. The motif and vocabulary are very similar to Ps 22 and may have been influenced by the latter: Ps 22:24: "You who fear the Lord, praise Him (הללוהו)! All you offspring of Jacob, honor Him! And stand in awe of Him, all you offspring of Israel"; v. 26: "Because of You I offer my praise (תְהִלתי) in the great congregation"; v. 28: "Let all the ends of the earth (כל אפסי ארץ) pay heed and turn to the Lord, and let the families of all the nations prostrate (ישתחוו) themselves before You"; v. 30: "All shall bend the knee (יכרעו) before Him"; v. 32: "They shall come and tell of His beneficence (צדקתו)." (See the introduction, §17.) The pericope here in Deutero-Isaiah is characterized by a fivefold repetition of the word **כל**, vv. 22, 23 (twice), 24, 25.

[22] *Turn to Me and be saved* — The *waw* at the beginning of the verb וְהִוָּשְׁעוּ (*niph'al*, from the root ישע) indicates the reason for God's passionate appeal: "Turn to Me" in order to "be saved" since I, and only I, am a God who grants salvation (v. 21). (For a similar instance of the *waw* indicating purpose, see Amos 5:6: "Seek the Lord, that you will live [וִחְיוּ].")

All the ends of the earth! — Cf. Isa 52:10: "And the very ends of the earth (אפסי ארץ) shall see the salvation of our God." In Ugaritic the cognate *aps* also denotes "extremity, edge, end" (*HdO* 1:91).

For I am God, and there is none else! — The verse ends in the same way it began, with a reiteration of God's uniqueness; see vv. 14, 21.

[23] God's irrevocable oath that all the peoples of the earth will worship Him. For this universalistic theme, cf. 56:7: "For My house shall be called a house of prayer for all peoples." (See the introduction, §6.)

By Myself have I sworn — an emphatic oath: God swears by His very Self; see also Gen 22:16. For other formulas of a divine oath, see Isa 62:8: "The Lord has sworn by His right hand (בִּימִינוֹ)"; Amos 6:8: "My Lord God swears by Himself (בנפשו)." For oaths preceding divine declarations, see 1 Sam 3:14; Jer 22:5.

From My mouth has issued truth — a truthful declaration (Ibn Ezra). For צדק or צדקה with the meaning "truth," "right," "reliably," see v. 19: "Who foretells reliably (צדק)"; 41:26: "Who foretold this from the start, the very beginning, that we may note it; from aforetime, that we might say, 'He is right (צדיק)'?" The expression יצא מִפֶּה ("to issue from one's mouth") (cf. 48:3; 55:11) is related to oath taking; cf., e.g., Num 30:3: "If a man makes a vow to the Lord or takes an oath imposing an obligation on himself . . . he must carry out all that has issued forth from his mouth (הַיֹּצֵא מפיו)." In Biblical Hebrew, when the verb (here, masculine, יצא) precedes the noun (here, feminine, צדקה) it does not always conform to the gender.

A word that shall not be revoked — an oath that shall never be taken back. For the root שׁוב, meaning "to revoke, annul," see Isa 43:13: "When I act, who can revoke it (ישיבֶנה)?"; Amos 1:3: "For three transgressions . . . for four I will not revoke it (אשיבנו)"; Ps 132:11: "The Lord swore to David a firm oath that He will not renounce (יָשׁוּב)." In Mesopotamian literature as well, a word "that issues from a god's mouth" (Akk. *ṣīt pî*) is irrevocable; see *CAD* Ṣ:219.

"To Me every knee shall bend" — Hebrew לי is positioned at the beginning of the clause for emphasis: Everyone will worship Me. For the expression כרע ברך ("to bend the knee"), see 1 Kgs 19:18. Genuflection to the gods is common in Mesopotamian literature, e.g., "All human beings kneel before you [Shamash]" (*CAD* K:119).

"Every tongue shall swear loyalty" — The expression הִשבע ל- (which echoes בי נשבעתי, above) denotes a pledge of allegiance: Every human being

shall swear an oath of loyalty to God, as in Isa 19:18: "In that day, there shall be five cities in the land of Egypt . . . swearing loyalty to the Lord (נשבעות לה׳) of Hosts"; Ezek 16:8: "Then I pledged My loyalty to you (וָאֶשָּׁבַע לָךְ) and entered into a covenant with you"; 2 Chr 15:14: "So they pledge allegiance to the Lord ('וַיִּשָּׁבְעוּ לה׳') in a loud voice."

[24] *"Saying: 'Only in the Lord are victory and might'"* — The construction לי אמר is unclear. Though there have been different attempts to explain it as a quotation formula inserted within the verse (see, e.g., 49:3), the preferable way to understand it is to follow the LXX (cf. also Peshitta), which reads לאמר and places it at the beginning of the verse, thus linking v. 23 to v. 24: "Every tongue shall swear loyalty, saying, 'Only in the Lord are victory and might.'" For צדקות, "victories," see Judg 5:11: "There they chant the gracious victories (צדקות) of the Lord"; 1 Sam 12:7: "All the victories (צדקות) that the Lord has won for you and your fathers"; Mic 6:5: "So that you may know victories (צדקות) of the Lord." The root צדק functions as a leitmotif in this section; cf. vv. 19, 21, 23. For עֹז, see 49:5: "My God has been my strength (עֻזִּי)."

"To Him will come and be ashamed all those who are incensed against Him" — All who are incensed against God (נֶחֱרִים is the *niphʿal* participle of the verb חרי; see above, 41:11) shall come (reading the plural יבואו, with 1QIsa[a], LXX, Vulgate, and Peshitta — the *waw* was omitted as a result of a haplography) to Him and be abashed in His presence. For the expression בוא עד, see Ps 65:3: "All humankind comes to You (עָדֶיךָ . . . יבואו), You who hear prayer"; Job 6:20: "They are disappointed in their hopes. When they come to (באו עָדֶיהָ) the place, they are confounded." Perhaps, however, one should reverse two letters of ויבשו to read וישבו ("they shall return [to Him]").

[25] *"But it is in the Lord that all the offspring of Israel shall have victory and glory"* — Only through God (Peshitta reads בי, "in Me") will the Israelite stock (cf. the parallel זרע יעקב, v. 19) achieve their glorious and victorious destiny. This verse complements v. 24: בה׳ — אך בה׳; יצדקו — צדקות. For the expression להתהלל ב-, see 41:16; Ps 97:7. For a further instance of the roots צדק and הלל in conjunction, see Isa 61:11: "So the Lord God will make victory and glory (צדקה ותהִלה) shoot up in the presence of all the nations."

Chapter 46

[1-7] A satirical description of the shameful collapse of the Babylonian gods who are hastily thrown on beasts of burden while fleeing the Persian conquerors. The practice described in these verses mirrors the removal of the city's idols on the eve of an invasion so as to prevent their falling into the hands of the pillaging conquerors, who often would carry off the idols from their temples and display them in their native lands. Compare the propagandistic vitriolic attack in the Cyrus Cylinder against Nabonidus (555-539 BCE), the last Babylonian monarch before the Persian invasion (and Deutero-Isaiah's contemporary), for removing idols from the Babylonian cities and the praise for Cyrus for restoring the idols to their rightful abodes: "Furthermore, I resettled upon the command of Marduk, the great lord, all the gods of Sumer and Akkad whom Nabonidus had brought into Babylon . . . to the anger of the lord of the gods [Marduk], unharmed, in their (former) chapels, the places which make them happy" (*ANET,* 316). One should note that Marduk's idol itself was captured several times throughout the centuries. The Assyrian king Tukulti-Ninurta I (1244-1208 BCE) removed the idol from Babylon following his invasion. The Babylonian king Nebuchadnezzar I (1126-1103 BCE) retrieved Marduk's idol from the Elamites, who carried it off in 1189 BCE. And Sennacherib (705-681 BCE) brought the statue to Assyria in 689 BCE. For further instances of idols fleeing their cities or of their removal by conquerors, cf. Jer 48:7; 49:3; Hos 10:5-6; Amos 5:26; Dan 11:8. (See also *CAD* I-J:274; *ANET,* 283, 300, 306, 309; *ANEP,* no. 538; M. Cogan, *Imperialism and Religion: Assyria, Judah, and Israel in the Eighth and Seventh Centuries B.C.E.,* Society of Biblical Literature Monograph Series 19 [Missoula, Mont., 1974], 21-44; W. W. Hallo, "Cult Statue and Divine Image: A Preliminary Study," in W. W. Hallo et al,. eds., *Scripture in Context, 2: More Essays on the Comparative Method* [Winona Lake, Ind., 1983], 13-14.)

The two deities mentioned here, Bel and Nabu, stood at the head of the Babylonian pantheon in the Neo-Babylonian period and are referred to in tandem in the Cyrus Cylinder (*ANET*, 315-16, lines 22, 35). The first, Bel (= Akk. *bēlu*, "lord"), is none other than Marduk, who is mentioned in Jer 50:2: "Declare: Babylon is captured, Bel is shamed, Marduk is dismayed"; see also 51:44. .The origin of his name is Sumerian: amar.uda.ak (interpreted as "bull calf/son of the sun," or, "bull calf of the storm"). It appears in the names of the Babylonian kings "Merodach-baladan" (Isa 39:1; cf. 2 Kgs 20:12); "Evil-merodach" (2 Kgs 25:27); and is also the source of the name "Mordechai" in the book of Esther. Marduk's prestige took a severe blow in the twilight years of the Neo-Babylonian dynasty, when, under Nabonidus's patronage, the moon god, Sin, was declared Babylon's new king of the gods. Cyrus, who captured Babylon in 539 BCE, reinstated Marduk as the head of the Babylonian pantheon, thus restoring Marduk's lost glory. The second deity, Nabu (or Nebo; Akk. *nabû*), serves as the theophoric element in the names of three Neo-Babylonian kings: Nabopolassar, his son Nebuchadnezzar, and finally, the last king, Nabonidus; cf. also the names of two of Nebuchadnezzar's ministers (2 Kgs 25:8; Jer 39:9), Nebuzaradan and Nebushazban (Jer 39:13). Nabu, whose cultic center was in the city Borsippa (a few kilometers south of Babylon), was the patron god of writing and during this period was worshiped as Marduk's son. During the *Akitu* (the Babylonian New Year) ceremonies, which were celebrated between the second and eleventh of Nisan, Marduk and Nabu were paraded around as part of the festivities. For more on the Babylonian New Year, see J. A. Black, "The New Year Ceremonies in Ancient Babylonia: 'Taking Bel by the Hand' and a Cultic Picnic," *Religion* 11 (1981): 39-59; B. Leisten-Pongratz, *Ina Šulmi Îrub: Die kultspographische und ideologische Programmatik der Akîtu-Prozession in Babylonien und Assyrien im 1. Jahrtausend v. Chr.* (Mainz am Rhein, 1994). For the cultic vessels and paraphernalia connected with this holiday, see T. W. Mann, *Divine Presence and Guidance in Israelite Traditions: The Typology of Exaltation* (Baltimore, 1977), 76-79. For pictures of the idols carried on beasts of burden, see *ANEP*, no. 537.

This chapter is linked to chap. 45 by a string of words and phrases: 45:3: **הקורא (בשמך)**, 4: **ואקרא (לך בשמך)** — 46:11: **קֹרֵא (ממזרח עיט)**; 45:5: **אני ה׳ ואין עוד** — 46:9: **אנכי אל ואין עוד**; 45:6: **אפס בלעדי**, 14: **אפס אלהים** — 46:9 **אנכי . . . אלהים ואפס כמוני**; 45:15: **אלהי ישראל מושיע**, 17: **ישראל נושע בה׳ תשועת עולמים**, 20: **אל לא יושיע**, 21: **אל (צדיק) ומושיע**, 22: **וְהִוָּשְׁעוּ** — 46:7: **לא יושיענו**, 13: **קרבתי צדקתי . . . ותשועתי . . . ונתתי בציון תשועה**; 45:19: **זרע יעקב** — 46:3: **בית יעקב**; 45:20: **הנשאים את עץ פסלם** — 46:1: **נְשֻׂאֹתֵיכֶם . . . מַשָּׂא**, 2: **מַשָּׂא**; 3: **הנשֻׂאים**, 4: **אֶשָּׂא**, 7: **יִשָּׂאֻהוּ**; 45:21: **מִקֶּדֶם** — 46:10: **וּמִקֶּדֶם**; 45:23: **כי לי תכרע כל ברך** — 46:1: **כרע**, 2: **כרעו**; 45:21: **צדיק**, 24: **צדקות**, 25: **יצדקו** — 46:12: **מצדקה**, 13: **צדקתי**; and **כל**, which appears in 45:22, 23 (twice), 24; 46:3;

and cf. also 45:21–46:13. There are also a number of thematic links between this chapter and chap. 45. The first verses of chap. 45 deal with Cyrus's conquests, and chap. 46 describes the removal of the idols from Babylon as it falls to Cyrus's armies.

Verses 1-4 of this chapter are characterized by many repetitions of key roots: **נשׂא** appears five times in the space of four verses (vv. 1 [twice], 2, 3, 4); **סבל** appears twice (v. 4); **עמס** appears twice as well (vv. 1, 3), as does **מלט** (vv. 2, 4). The chapter is also replete with imperative forms: **שִׁמְעוּ** (vv. 3, 12), **זִכְרוּ** (vv. 8, 9), **הִתְאֹשָׁשׁוּ** (v. 8), **הָשִׁיבוּ** (v. 8). (The two imperatives **שמעו** and **זכרו** form a chiastic parallel: vv. 3, 8, and vv. 9, 12.)

[1] The midrash takes its cue from this verse and prohibits all mockery or satire except when it comes to idolatry (*b. Meg.* 25b; *Sanh.* 63b). For another prophetic attack on Babylon and its idols, see Isa 21:9: "Fallen, fallen is Babylon, and all images of her gods lie shattered to the ground." This verse, which mentions Bel and Nabu, may also be a clever allusion to the downfall of both *Nabo*nidus and his son *Bel*shazar, who ruled Babylon as co-regent during his father's extended stay in Teima (located in what is now Saudi Arabia).

Bel has crouched down — Bel (Marduk), the head of the Babylonian pantheon, has collapsed as his city was invaded. Aside from Jer 50:2, quoted in the introduction to this section, the god Bel is satirically mocked in a double wordplay in Jer 51:44: "And I will punish Bel (**בל**) in Babylon (**בבבל**) and make him disgorge what he has swallowed (**בִּלְעוֹ**)." The Hebrew verb **כרע** is related to Akk. *kurītu,* which denotes the area between the knee and the fetlock of animals (*CAD* K:560); see Exod 12:9; Lev 9:14.

Nabu has stooped low — Nabu cowers. Nabu was number two in the Babylonian hierarchy of deities and according to the Babylonian belief at this time period was Marduk's son. The verb **קרס**, a hapax legomenon related to the substantive **קרסים**, "hooks" (Exod 26:11, 33) and **קַרְסֹל**, "ankle" (2 Sam 22:37 = Ps 18:37), is cognate to Akk. *kursinnu,* "the lower leg of animals and humans" (*CAD* K:566). The verb, vocalized as a present participle in the MT, is translated as a past tense by all the ancient translations and 1QIsa[a], thus harmonizing with and creating a chiastic parallelism with the first two words of the verse.

Their images are consigned to beasts and cattle — The Babylonians loaded their idols onto beasts of burden as they prepared to flee the triumphant armies of Persia. The plural substantive **עֲצַבִּים**, "images of idols" (see 2 Sam 5:21, in connection with the Philistines; Isa 10:11, the images of Jerusalem; Jer 50:2, Babylonian idols; Hos 14:9, Ephraimite images; Ps 115:4, a general term referring to all idols), is derived from the root **עצב**, "to fashion." But its homonym, **עֶצֶב**, denotes "pain" and "suffering" (Gen 3:16; Prov 10:22), and thus the prophet's implication (through a subtle wordplay) is that these images are the very cause of the Babylonians' travails. For the same double entendre, see Isa 48:5. According to common belief, the idols were the embodiment of the gods themselves, and thus their removal and exile implied that the gods themselves were being deported from the city; see 40:19-20. For the expression היה ל-, see 45:14.

The things you would carry [in procession] are loaded as a burden on tired animals — The prophet, after his third-person description of the idols being led off, now addresses his audience directly in the second-person. The clause, however, is ambiguous. Though many different suggestions have been offered in light of the prophet's subsequent rhetoric, which juxtaposes the idol's impotence with God's omnipotence, it seems best to vocalize נֹשְׂאֵיכֶם (Luzzatto, second comment; cf. Tur Sinai, *Peshuṭo shel Miqra,* III/1:122, who reads נֹשְׂאֵיהֶם; Ehrlich, *Mikrâ ki-Pheshuṭo,* 3:109), with the meaning: Your gods, which by all rights should be carrying you, cannot even carry themselves, for they are loaded on cattle and (other) beasts of burden. One could, however, maintain the Masoretic vocalization and interpret נְשֻׂאֹתֵיכֶם (with Yellin, *Ḥiqrei Miqra,* 57) as a *po'el* participle (on the paradigm of יָקוּשׁ, "hunter" [Ps 91:3; Prov 6:5]; cf. Rabbinic רָכוּב, "mounted"; שָׁתוּי, "drunken"; נָשׂוּי, "married"). If so, it would still have the same meaning and would also rhyme alliteratively with the next word, עֲמוּסוֹת. (See also J. Blau, "The *Pa'ul* Form as an Active," *Leš* 18 [1952-53]: 67-81 [Heb.].) For the verb עמס, "to carry a load," see Gen 44:13: "Each reloaded (ויעמֹס) his pack animal"; Neh 13:15: "Bringing heaps of grain and loading (ועֹמסים) them onto asses." Compare also the substantive מַעֲמָסָה ("a heavy load") in Zech 12:3. The word מַשָּׂא refers to a "load" carried by asses (Exod 23:5), mules (2 Kgs 5:17), camels (2 Kgs 8:9), and also humans (2 Sam 15:33). Compare its Akkadian semantic equivalent, *biltu,* "burden," from the verb *wabālu,* "to carry," which also refers to burdens loaded upon beasts of burden (*CAD* B:230). The two verbs עמס and נשא are parallel in three separate instances in the Phoenician inscription of Eshmunazor, king of Sidon: "And do not carry away (ישא) the coffin of my resting place and move me (יעמסן) from this resting place" (*KAI* 14:5-6, and see lines 7 and 21). Compare likewise in Ugaritic: "Load me *('ms),* please, Mighty Baal . . . She [the goddess Shupshu] placed him [*tšth* — the verb is derived from *nš'* = נשא] on Anat's shoulders" (*CAT* 1.6.I:12, 14-15). The first three words in this hemistich are all alliterative, created by the repetition of the sibilants *shin* and *samekh.* For the form of the Hebrew hapax legomenon עֲיֵפָה, "weary (animal)," cf. יְרֵשָׁה, "possession" (Num 24:18), צְנֵפָה, "winding" (Isa 22:18). In contrast to the idols that must be carried on beasts, the Lord "carries Israel in His bosom" (40:11).

[2] *They stoop low, totally crouched down* — The verbs form a chiastic parallel to the previous verse with the addition of יחדו, indicating a total collapse. There is some controversy as to the subjects of the verbs: either the beasts of burden (cf. Gen 49:9: "He crouches [כרע] . . . like a lion") or the idols. A third option is that they refer both to the beasts and the images that bow and cower.

In light of the following hemistich, however, the second option (the idols) is preferable.

They are unable to rescue the burden — Bel and Nabu are unable to rescue their burden (מַשָּׂא, "burden," is repeated in this verse for emphasis), i.e., their worshipers. The Targum (נָטְלֵיהוֹן) and Peshitta *(ṭ'wnyhwn)* read מַשָּׂאָם, "their burden," with the plural pronominal suffix. For the verb מלט, "to deliver, save" (here vocalized as an infinitive absolute), see Isa 49:24, 25.

And they themselves go into captivity — Not only are these idle idols unable to save their pleading penitents, they cannot even save themselves from being captured. For the expression הלך בשבי ("to go into captivity"), see Deut 28:41; Amos 9:4. 1QIsa[a] has here a plural verb, הלכו, instead of the MT third-person feminine singular.

[3-4] In contrast to the Babylonian gods, who are utterly impotent, unable to save their own people, and must be carried on the backs of beasts of burden, God carries Israel in His bosom (40:11) and is perennially present as Israel's protector and redeemer, expressed metaphorically by the pair מִנִּי, "since" (v. 3, twice) and עד, "till" (v. 4, twice). For מן . . . עד, see Gen 46:34: From our youth until now"; Ps 71:17-18: "From my youth . . . until old age." The Israelite God shelters His people from day one on. For a similar idea, cf. Ps 71:6: "From birth (מבטן) I depended on You" (similar to v. 3 here: "Who have been carried since birth [בטן]"); and Ps 71:18: "And even until hoary old age do not forsake me, God" (similar to v. 4 here: "Till you grow old . . . till you turn gray, it is I who will continue to carry you"). For female imagery applied to God, cf. also Isa 42:14; 45:10; 49:15; 66:9, 13; and see Gruber, "Motherhood of God in Second Isaiah."

[3] *Listen to Me, O house of Jacob and the entire remnant of the house of Israel* — The prophet addresses the people in the second-person plural. For the parallelism ישראל/יעקב, see 40:27; 41:14; 43:1; 48:1. For שארית as a surviving "remnant" (after the purges of conquest and exile), see 37:32; Jer 23:3. For the expression שִׁמְעוּ אלי, see v. 12 here; 48:12; 51:1, 7; 55:2.

Who have been carried since birth — In contrast to the impotent gods of vv. 1-2, the God of Israel has been carrying and caring for Israel from the very day of their birth, i.e., from the time they became a nation.

Supported since leaving the womb — The verb נשׂא denotes carrying, supporting, providing basic necessities; cf. 63:9: "He raised them and carried them (וַיְנַשְּׂאֵם) all the days of old"; Deut 1:31: "And in the wilderness, where you saw how the Lord your God carried you (נְשָׂאֲךָ), as a man carries his son." The Akkadian interdialectal and semantic equivalent, *našû,* also refers to supporting a fellow human being; cf. Hammurabi's law collection, §148: "He shall continue to support her [i.e., his divorced wife] all the days of her life" (for additional examples, see *CAD* N/2:95-96). From the moment God chose Israel as

His people, He guarded them and provided them with all their needs; see Isa 44:2: "Your Creator from the womb, who has helped you"; cf. 44:24; 49:1, 5. For further instances of the parallelism רחם/בטן ("womb/birth"), see Ps 22:11: "I became Your charge at birth (מרחם); from my mother's womb (מבטן) You have been my God"; see also Jer 1:5; Ps 58:4; Job 3:11; 31:15; and cf. Isa 49:1: "Before I was born . . . while I was in my mother's womb." For the poetic-archaic preposition מִנִּי, see Ps 78:2; Job 20:4.

[4] God's constant vigil is reiterated by the fivefold repetition of the personal pronoun אני. God fulfills the role reserved for a parent. But whereas a mother/father cares for their child from birth until adolescence, God watches over the nation from birth until hoary old age. Note the accretion of sibilants in this verse: זקנה, שׂיבה, אסבול, עשׂיתי, אשׂא, אסבל. The verse functions as an encouraging response to the people's plea in Ps 71:18: "And even until hoary age do not forsake me, God!"

"Till you grow old, I am He" — Till the nation reaches senescence, i.e., throughout all future time, I am He who shall continue to support you. For the expression אני הוא, referring to God, see Isa 41:4; 43:10, 13; 48:12; 52:6. For the synonymous pair שֵׂיבה/זקנה (next clause), see Ps 71:18, quoted above; 1 Sam 12:2: "I have grown old and gray (זקנתי ושַׂבְתִּי)"; see also Lev 19:32; and cf. Prov 20:29.

"Till you turn gray, it is I who will continue to carry you" — God will faithfully shoulder His burden and carry Israel till they are old and gray. Aramaic סבל is the cognate equivalent of Heb. נשׂא; see, e.g., v. 7: "They must bear it (יִשָּׂאֻהוּ) on their shoulders and carry it (יִסְבְּלֻהוּ)"; 53:4: "Yet it was our sickness that he bore (נשׂא), our suffering that he endured (סְבָלָם)"; and cf. 53:11. For its occurrence in Aramaic texts with the meaning "to provide, support," see saying 106 in the Aramaic proverbs of Ahiqar: "One [day a man said] to the wild ass, ['Let me ride] on you and I will provide for you (אסבלנך).' [The wild ass answered: 'Keep] your support (סבוליך) and fodder to yourself!'" (See Lindenberger, *Aramaic Proverbs of Ahiqar,* 203, lines 204-5.) Compare likewise the following Aramaic text from Elephantine: "I, Anani, gave it [my house] to Jehoishma my daughter, at my death in affection because she supported me (סבלתני) when I was old of days (ימין סב)." (See Porten and Yardeni, *Textbook of Aramaic Documents,* 2:86, 89, B3.10:16-17; and note the connection between ימין סב ["old of days"] here and in Deutero-Isaiah.) Compare also: "And Tapamet and Jeh(o)ishma her daughter said: 'We shall serve you, as a son or daughter supports (יסבל) his father, in your lifetime. And at your death we shall support Zaccur your son, like a son who supports (יסבל) his father'" (ibid., 72, 73, B3.6:11-12). For further appearances of the verb סבל, see vv. 4, 7. The verbal pair נשׂא/סבל is also attested in Ahiqar (saying 10): "The ass abandons his load and will not carry it (יסבלנה). He will be shamed by his fellow

and will carry (וינשא) a burden which is not his own" (Lindenberger, *Aramaic Proverbs of Ahiqar,* 62, lines 90-91).

"I was the Creator" — I, the Lord, molded Israel into a people. For עשי, "to create," see Isa 43:7; 44:2; 45:7, 18; 51:13. For the alliterative verbal pair עשה and נשא (following colon), see Exod 19:4: "You have seen what I did (עשיתי) to the Egyptians, how I bore (ואשא) you on eagles' wings and brought you to Me."

"And I will be the Bearer" — I shall continue to be your support and provider, as I have been in the past.

"And I will carry and rescue [you]" — as opposed to the heathen gods, who cannot save their own worshipers (v. 2). The verb מלט ("to rescue") also carries an additional nuance, "to give birth"; see Isa 66:7: "Before she labored, she was delivered. Before her birth pangs, she bore (והמליטה) a son"; 34:15: "There the arrow snake shall nest and lay eggs (וַתְּמַלֵּט)" — a nuance that follows well v. 3 and its imagery.

[5-7] For the prophet's claim that God cannot be compared to anything or anybody in the context of a polemic against idols and idolatry, see 40:18, 25 (which also begins with the same rhetorical question: "To whom can you compare Me?"). For his scathing satire against idol craftsmanship, see 40:18-20; 41:6-7; 44:9-19. There is a structural and thematic link between this unit and the next one (vv. 8ff.) and 44:8ff. In both sections following the polemic against the fashioning of images (44:9-20), there is an exhortation to remember: "Remember these things!" (44:21) — "Remember this!" (46:8). This unit (46:5-7) is linked thematically to the prior one by the derisive tone the prophet employs against the idols and by the verbs נשא, vv. 1 (twice), 2, 3, 4, 7; סבל, vv. 4, 7; and עשי, vv. 1, 7.

[5] *To whom can you liken Me or declare Me similar?* — The verse begins and ends with the verb דמי, forming a literary *inclusio.* The first-person pronominal suffix affixed to the first verb, תְדַמְּיוּנִי, is implied in the second as well. Is there any god in any pantheon who can be compared to Me? For the same sequence of verbs, see 40:25: "To whom, then, can you liken Me (תדמיוני)? To whom can I be compared (וְאֶשְׁוֶה)?" Lam 2:13: "To what can I compare (אֲדַמֶּה) you, Zion, to what can I liken (אַשְׁוֶה) you?" The two verbs, however, carry slightly different nuances, according to Ehrlich (*Miqra ki-Pheshuṭo,* 3:110): "He who likens (דמי) two things, one to another, and says that this is like that, may be right or may be mistaken. But he who declares two things equal (שוי) is making an apt comparison, and the two things are truly similar." According to this distinction, the bipartite rhetorical question should be interpreted: "To whom can you compare Me, so that the comparison is indeed apt?"

To whom can you liken Me so that we are comparable? — Although the root משל does appear in the *qal* (Ezek 17:2), *niphʿal* (Isa 14:10; Ps 28:1), and *hithpaʿel* (Job 30:19) with the meaning "to be likened or compared" to another, this is the only time the verb appears in the *hiph'il* in such a context. For Mesopotamian gods who are sui generis, see the references under *mašālu/muššulu,* "to be similar, equal" (the Akkadian semantic and etymological cognate of משל; *CAD* M/1:355-57), and *šanānu,* "to become equal" (another semantic equivalent; *CAD* Š/1:367-69). 1QIsa[a] reads ואדמה in the singular. The Masoretic plural conforms to the three previous verbs, which are all in the plural.

[6] More devastatingly derisive words leveled against the idolaters. This time they are satirized for the vast amount of gold and silver they lavish on their idol craft. (For gold and silver as coating and adornment for idols, see Isa 40:19.) The prophet's sarcastic mockery is accentuated by an extended series of sibilants: הזלים, זהב, מכיס, וכסף, ישקלו, יִשְׂכְּרוּ, צורף, וְיַעֲשֵׂהוּ, יִסְגְּדוּ, ישתחוו. For a similar taunting tirade, see 44:9-19.

Those who squander gold from the purse — Commentators disagree regarding the exact meaning of the hapax legomenon verb זלים. Some explain it as deriving from נזל, "to flow" (cf. Menaḥem ben Saruq, *Sefer ha-Maḥberet* [Wadenburg, 1854], 79; Saadyah Gaon; Rashi), i.e., their money flows like water when it comes to providing the material means for the construction of idols. Others take their cue from Rabbinic Hebrew, where זול means "to be of little value, cheap," and translate זלים as "to squander" (Luzzatto; cf. Kimchi, *Sefer ha-Shorashim,* 86). Yet others base their understanding of the root on the Arabic cognate *zāla,* which denotes "removing/taking from," i.e., they remove the gold from their purses (Ibn Balaam [ed. Goshen-Gottstein], 191; Ibn Ganah, *Sefer ha-Shorashim,* 128). Nevertheless, the basic meaning of this clause, commonly accepted by all, is that the idolaters squander vast amounts of gold and silver taken from leather "bags" (כיס), which usually hold gold weights and silver (Deut 25:13; Mic 6:11; Prov 1:14). Compare its Akkadian etymological and semantic equivalent, *kīsu* (*CAD* K:431-32). 1QIsa[a] בכיס is influenced by בַּקָּנֶה in the next clause.

And weigh out silver on the balance — Hebrew קָנֶה, "stalk, reed," refers (only) here to the beam of a scale, and by extension to the scales themselves. It is possible that the prophet selected this specific term to differentiate between a regular scale and a steel yard, on which one weighs particularly heavy objects by means of an iron slab attached to a beam. The first two clauses are chiastically parallel.

They hire a goldsmith to make it into a god — Cf. Isa 44:15: "He makes a god of it." The use of the verb עשׂי in these verses stands in contrast to v. 4, where God is the "Maker" (עָשִׂיתִי) par excellence. The LXX, Peshitta, Vulgate, and 1QIsa[a] all read ויעשה without the pronominal suffix. According to these versions, the gold and the silver are the payment to the goldsmith for making the idol. For the goldsmith's participation in the fashioning of idols, see 40:19; 41:7.

To which they bow down and prostrate themselves — To this idol of wood and precious metal, they then do obeisance. For the parallel verbs סגד (an Aramaism) and השתחוה, both of which denote prostration, see 44:15, 17. For the emphatic conjunction אף (which is repeated in v. 7 and once again in v. 11), see 40:24 (three times); 44:15.

[7] More derision, which is emphasized this time by a threefold repetition of לא, accentuating the utter impotence of these supposed gods.

They must hoist it on their shoulders and carry it — The idol worshipers have to carry the heavy weight of their idols on their backs and shoulders; cf. above, v. 1; 45:20: "They who carry their wooden images"; Jer 10:5: "They have to be carried, for they cannot walk." According to Luzzatto, the vocalization of the first three verbs in the plural was influenced by the previous verse, and they should all be vocalized as singulars, so as to agree with the final hemistichs of the verse: "He cries out to it. . . . It cannot save him from his distress." This is yet another jab at the idols' impotence: They must be carried, whereas God bears Israel tirelessly (above, v. 4). Another irony is that these idolaters, who carry their idols on their shoulders, will, in the not too distant future, "carry your daughters on their shoulders" (49:22). For "shouldering burdens," see also Num 7:9.

When they put it down it stands — When they set the idol down, it remains there motionless. תַּחְתָּיו refers to the place in which it stands; cf. Exod 10:23: "No one could get up from where he was (מתחתיו)"; Exod 16:29: "Let everyone remain where he is (תחתיו). Let no one leave his place on the seventh day." According to Ehrlich (*Randglossen,* 4:170), the *waw* of תחתיו was repeated by dittography and appended mistakenly to the verb ויעמד, and he suggests, similar to LXX, that one should read וְיַנִּחֻהוּ תחתיו יעמד, i.e., once the idol is put in place, it remains standing in that very place. This would also correspond with the Masoretic trope division connecting תחתיו with the following verb. For the intransitive verb עמד ("to stand without moving"), see Josh 10:13: "And the sun stood still and the moon halted (עמד)." For immobile idols, see Ps 115:7: "They have feet but cannot walk."

It does not budge from its place — The idol remains immobile. ממקומו ("from its place") is parallel to מתחתיו, as in Exod 16:29, quoted above. For the root מוש (ימיש in MT; ימוש in 1QIsa[a]), "to leave one's place," see Exod 33:11: "But his attendant, Joshua son of Nun, a youth, never moved out (ימיש) of the tent."

If one cries out to it, it does not answer — If the idolater cries out to his god: "Save me, for you are my god!" (Isa 44:17), there is no sign of an answer. This, of course, is in stark contrast to the God of Israel, who, "in an hour of favor" answers (49:8), and answers His people even before they call to Him (65:24). Hebrew אף is emphatic; cf. v. 6, 11 (three times). For the verb צעק, which almost always denotes a cry in times of distress, see, e.g., 42:2; Exod

22:22; 2 Kgs 8:3. For another example of the sequence of the verbs צעק and ענה, see Job 19:7: "I cry (אצעק) 'Violence,' but am not answered (אֵעָנֶה)."

It cannot save him from his distress — The idol cannot save his worshiper in his time of greatest need; cf. Isa 45:20: "And they pray to a god who cannot save." Israel, however, "has been saved by the Lord, saved for eternity" (45:17); "There is no god but Me, victorious and able to save" (45:21).

[8-11] Once more the prophet proclaims God's omnipotence and uniqueness attested to by His foretelling the end from the beginning; cf. 42:9. For the structural connection between this unit, which begins with the imperative "Remember!" reiterated again in v. 8, and the polemic against idol craft in 44:9-20, see the introduction to the previous unit.

[8] *Remember this and be firm!* — What they are supposed to keep in mind ("this") is clarified in the next verse, i.e., the "things that happened long ago." The exact meaning of the verb הִתְאֹשָׁשׁוּ is the subject of controversy. Some interpret it as a denominative hapax legomenon derived from the substantive איש, comparing 1 Sam 4:9: "Brace yourselves and be men (לאנשים)" (see Kimchi's first commentary). It is preferable, however, to derive it from Aram. אשש, "to make firm"; cf. Ezra 4:12: אֻשַּׁיָּא, "foundations," and thus render, "be firm" (cf. Targum וְאִיתַּקְפוּ ["strong"]; Rashi; and Ibn Ezra's first commentary). This meaning is also attested in Rabbinic Hebrew: "Well-founded (הַמְאוּשָּׁשׁוֹת) regulations" (*Midr. Song Rab.* 2:5). This is another example of the Aramaic influence on Hebrew at the time of Deutero-Isaiah. (See the introduction, §11.A.)

Take it to heart, you rebels! — In the Hebrew text the vocative address, "you rebels," intervenes within the expression "take to heart," and thereby intensifies the rebuke against exiled Israel and their grave doubts regarding their imminent salvation. For פשע denoting rebellion, see Isa 48:8: "For I knew you are treacherous, and that you were called a rebel (וּפֹשֵׁעַ) from birth"; 2 Kgs 1:1: "Moab rebelled (ויפשע) against Israel." See also Isa 43:25, 27.

[9] *Remember what happened long ago!* — "Remember" (repeated from the former verse) all the predicted events of the past that have been fulfilled. For ראשׁנות, see 41:22; 42:9; 43:9, 18; 48:3; and the introduction, §4. For מעולם, "long ago," see 42:14; 63:16, 19; 64:3.

For I am God and there is none else — The conjunction כי emphasizes the validity of the declaration. For the recurring emphasis on God's uniqueness, see 44:6, 8; 45:5-6, 21-22. This pronouncement ("I am God") contrasts with v. 6: "And they make it into a god." For similar formulae, see 43:12; 45:22. For אין עוד ("there is none else"), see 45:5, 6, 14, 18, 21; and for the two formulae in conjunction, see 45:22.

I am God and there is none like Me — Cf. 45:6: "There is none (אפס) but Me"; 45:14: "Only among you is God, and there is no other god at all (אפס)."

[10-11] God's authenticity is attested to by His accurate prediction of future events and is proof that His present plan will also bear fruit, i.e., the victory of Cyrus and Israel's salvation will indeed come to pass. The verb עשי is repeated three times in the space of these two verses, so as to accentuate and magnify God's wondrous deeds. For added emphasis the conjunction אף is repeated three times in v. 11.

[10] *I foretell the outcome from the beginning* — It is I, God, the Lord of Israel, who predicts the end from the very outset. For אחרית, "future," see 41:22; 47:7. The two temporal extremes imply the totality of time.

And from the past, things that have not yet occurred — It is I, God, who announces forthcoming events from the dim and dark past. For קֶדֶם ("past"), see 45:21; and for the expression כימי קדם ("like in the days of yore"), see 51:9. For the parallel pair קדם and ראשית, see Prov 8:22: "The Lord created Me at the beginning (ראשית) of His course, as the first (קדם) of His works of old."

I say: "My plan shall be fulfilled" — For the very same combination of "plan" (עצה) being "fulfilled" (תקום), see Isa 14:24: "What I have planned, that shall come to pass"; Prov 19:21: "Many designs are in man's mind, but it is the Lord's plan that will prevail." For עצה ("plan, purpose"), see also v. 11; 44:26.

"I will do all I have purposed" — I shall accomplish everything I set out to do (referring to God's plans for Cyrus in the next verse). For the same expression, "to fulfill" (עשׂה) a "purpose" (חפץ), in connection with God's plans for Cyrus, see 48:14: "He whom the Lord loves shall fulfill His purpose (יעשׂה חפצו) against Babylon"; 55:11: "But performs what I purpose (עשׂה . . . חפצתי)"; cf. similarly 44:28; 53:10. (The Akkadian semantic equivalent *ṣibûtam epēšu* also denotes the execution of a plan [*CAD* Ṣ:169].) For an image of God's omnipotence couched in identical terms, see Ps 115:3: "And our God is in heaven. All that He wills He accomplishes"; Ps 135:6: "Whatever the Lord desires He does in heaven and earth." (For this originally juristic expression, also attested in postexilic literature and in Aramaic and Nabatean sources, see A. Hurvitz, "The History of a Legal Formula," *VT* 32 [1982]: 257-67.) 1QIsa[a] reads עשׂה in the third-person and corresponds with the Ketib of v. 11: איש עצתו, "the man of His purpose"; and see 48:14: "He shall execute His purpose against Babylon." One should note, however, that the final verb in v. 11 is also in the first-person singular, אֶעֱשֶׂנָּה.

[11] *"I summoned a bird of prey/counselor from the east"* — God summoned Cyrus, who comes from the east to conquer Babylon. Compare also 48:14-15. The geographical reference "from the east" (see also 41:2) refers to Cyrus's origin as king of Persia and Media, both of which are east of Babylon. Most commentators interpret עַיִט, "bird of prey" (see Gen 15:11; Job 28:7), as a metaphor for Cyrus, who comes from afar to swoop down on his victims, and relate it to Deut 28:49: "The Lord will bring a nation against you from afar, from the end of the earth, which will swoop down like the vulture"; Jer 48:40: "See, he

soars like a vulture and spreads out his wings against Moab"; Hab 1:6-8: "For lo, I am raising up the Chaldeans. . . . They come flying from afar like vultures rushing to devour." In light of the fact that in all these other instances the bird of prey that is specified is the "vulture" (נֶשֶׁר), however, it is possible that the prophet selected the word עַיִט intentionally in order to create a deft double entendre with the parallel clause, אִישׁ עֲצָתִי ("man of my purpose"), based on the Aramaic root that means "counsel." See Dan 2:14: "He responded with counsel (עֵטָא)"; Dan 6:8: "They took counsel (אִתְיָעַטוּ)"; Ezra 7:14: "His seven counselors (יָעֲטוֹהִי)" (see Menahem ben Saruq, *Sefer ha-Maḥberet,* 132; Rashi; Kimchi, *Sefer ha-Shorashim,* 262; Yellin, *Ḥiqrei Miqra,* 58; Ehrlich, *Randglossen,* 4:171). Ehrlich also suggests that the vocalization be emended to עַיָּט ("counselor"). (For other parallel terms, one in Aramaic and the other in Hebrew, see Isa 44:15, סגד/השתחווה; 46:4: נשׂא/סבל; for Aramaic influence on the prophet, see the introduction, §11.A.)

"From a distant land, the man of My counsel" — Cyrus is identified here as "the man of God's counsel," i.e., the one whom God has chosen to execute His plan to conquer Babylon and to redeem the Israelites from exile. (For the same expression in a polemical context, see 40:13.) The Ketib, איש עצתו ("the man of His counsel"), is attested in 1QIsa[a] and 4QIsa[d]. The Qere, איש עצתי (in LXX, Vulgate, Peshitta, and Targum), fits well with the first-person forms in v. 10 ("My plan," "I have purposed," "I will do"). For God's intention to bring Cyrus and rebuild Jerusalem and the Temple, see 44:26, 28; and for God's summoning from afar, see 13:3-5: "I have summoned My fighting men to execute My wrath. . . . They are coming from a distant land (מארץ מרחק), from the end of the horizon"; Jer 5:15: "Lo, I am bringing against you, O house of Israel, a nation from afar (ממרחק)"; cf. also Isa 13:5; Jer 4:16.

"I have spoken, so I will bring it to pass. I have designed it, so I will complete it" — The threefold repetition of the conjunction אף (see vv. 6, 7; 40:24; 41:26 [also repeated three times]), and the series of four verbs in the first-person singular, emphasize the decisiveness and definitiveness of God's design in history. For the paired verbs יצר and עשׂי, see 37:26 (= 2 Kgs 19:25): "Have you not heard? Of old I planned it (עשיתי). I designed it (ויצרתיהָ) long ago." For יצר with the meaning to "design, devise," see Jer 18:11: "I am devising (יוצר) disaster for you and laying plans against you." (In most other places, e.g., Isa 43:7; 45:18, the pair of verbs refers to acts of creation.) Just as the verbs אֲבִיאֶנָּה ("I will bring it to pass") and אֶעֱשֶׂנָּה ("I will complete it") are parallel, so too are the verbs דברתי and יצרתי — both of which indicate the creative power of God's words. 1QIsa[a] has יצרתיהָ (third-person feminine singular suffix), which harmonizes with the suffixal endings of the other verbs, אביאנה and אעשנה.

[12-13] In this short pericope the prophet castigates once again the disbelieving Israelites. In the previous unit he called them "rebels" (v. 8), and here, "obstinate of heart," but he nevertheless proclaims again that salvation is imminent. The substantives צדקה and תשועה are twice repeated here. The root רחק (vv. 12, 13) and לב (v. 12) link this unit with the preceding verses: for the former see v. 11; for the latter, see v. 8.

[12] *Listen to Me, you obstinate of heart* — those Israelites whose hearts are stubborn, who doubt the imminence of God's salvation. For similar expressions denoting stubbornness, see Ezek 2:4: חִזְקֵי לב; Ezek 3:7: וּקְשֵׁי לב. (In another context, Ps 76:6, the same expression [אבירי לב] refers to the powerful and mighty.) The LXX translates, "those whose heart fails," reading אֹבְדֵי לב, instead of אבירי לב (the common ד-ר graphic error); see Jer 4:9: "The heart of the king and the hearts of the nobles shall fail (יאבד לב)."

Who are far from victory! — For the root צדק, "victory," see the following verse and 59:17; 61:10, 11; 63:1. For the same idea, see 59:11: "We hope for redress, and there is none; for victory, and it is far from us."

[13] *"I am bringing My victory near. It shall not be far off"* — God declares that His salvation is just around the corner — truly it is not far away. (For the literary construct of a positive expression followed by a negative one [negative parallelism] see 54:14: "You shall be safe from oppression . . . and it shall not come near you.") This hemistich, together with the final one of the previous verse, are chiastically parallel. 1QIsa[a] קרובה (so too Targum קָרִיבָא) is similar to 51:5: "My victory is near (קרוב). My deliverance has gone forth"; and cf. also 56:1: "For soon (קרובה) My salvation shall come." In 4QIsa[c] the verb is in the *hiphʿil* first person, הקרבתי, instead of MT *qal.*

"And My triumph shall not be delayed" — This is to be contrasted with v. 7, where the prophet declares that the gods of Babylon cannot save them. Compare also 47:15: "There is none to save you." For the parallel pair צדק/צדקה and ישע/ישועה/תשועה ("victory," "triumph"), see 51:5, 6, 8; 56:1; Ps 71:15. For the expression לא תאחר, see also Exod 22:28; Deut 23:22; Eccl 5:3.

"I will grant salvation in Zion" — The beneficiaries of God's deliverance are now mentioned — both Zion and Israel (next clause).

"To Israel, in whom I glory" — Some commentators explain תפארתי, "My glory," as the second object of the verb "I will grant" in the previous clause. (Cf. Ibn Ezra's first comment: "[The verb] נתתי takes an additional [object], and thus [one should read]: 'I will grant My glory to Israel'"; and cf. Vulgate, Peshitta, 1QIsa[a], and 4QIsa[c], which read ולישראל.) The preferable understanding, however, is "I shall grant My salvation to Israel, in whom I find glory" (cf. ibn Ezra's second comment, where he adds: "And this is the correct [understanding]," and then quotes Isa 49:3: "Israel in whom I glory [אתפאר].") Compare also 44:23: "He has glorified Himself (יתפאר) through Israel"; and see 49:3; 55:5; 60:21; 61:3. (It should be noted that one medieval Hebrew manuscript reads here [in 46:13] ובישראל, parallel to בציון in the previous stich.)

Chapter 47

The entire chapter is dedicated to a lament over "fair Babylon's" fate and describes the decline and fall of this once powerful nation. Chapter 47 is divided into two pericopes that complement one another. The first (vv. 1-7) details Babylon's humiliation in a series of degrading scenes usually reserved for prostitutes and slave women. Babylon now stands stripped of her splendor and self-confidence. She is accused of extremely cruel behavior toward Israel and of excessive hubris. Her accelerated decline and her shameful degradation are accentuated by an extended series of stinging imperatives: "Get down! Sit! [שבי appears twice in v. 1 and once again in v. 5] Grasp! Grind! Remove! [גלי appears twice in v. 2, and once in v. 3, תִּגָּל] Strip! Bare! Wade!" In the second unit (vv. 8-15), her overwhelming pride is emphasized by the megalomaniacal declaration of her divinity: "I am, and there is none but me!" — which is grounded in her wisdom and expertise in sorcery and magic. Babylon was renowned for its magicians and diviners, so much so that in the Greek period the general term for stargazers was "Chaldeans." These professional skills will, however, be of no use to her, for her downfall will be sudden and there will be no hope of reversal or succor. The revenge God wreaks upon Babylon certainly provided some consolation to the downtrodden Judeans, who had suffered greatly under Babylonian tyranny. This chapter echoes Isa 10: in both, the enemy (here, Babylon; there, Assyria) is sent by God to punish His wayward nation, Israel (47:6; 10:5-6); but the enemy, who attributes his success to his own prowess (47:7-8, 10; 10:7-15), will be punished by God (47:11ff.; 10:16ff.). The literary genre of this chapter can be compared to the oracles against foreign nations, e.g., Isa 13ff.; Jer 46ff.; Ezek 25ff.

This chapter, which describes Babylon's ultimate demise, is connected to chap. 46, in which the prophet heaps ridicule upon Babylon's chief gods, who cannot save her from devastation. Here as well, the diviners, soothsayers, and astrologers all stand helpless, unable to prevent the arrogant empire's imminent downfall. The linguistic and thematic links between the two chapters are abundant: 46:2: לא יכלו מַלֵּט . . . ונפשם בשבי הלכה — 47:14: לא יצילו את נפשם; 46:4: זִקנה — 47:6: זקן; 46:7: יושיענו — 47:13: ויושיעך; 46:9: כי אנכי אל ואין עוד אלהים ואפס כמוני — 47:8, 10: אני ואפסי עוד; 46:10: עצתי, 46:11: [Qere עצתי] איש עצתו — 47:13: עֲצָתָיִךְ.

[1] The anthropomorphization of Babylon as a queen mourning the fate of her city. For other cities designated as "queens," cf. the two Assyrian names [f]*Ninua-šarrat* ("[The city of] Nineveh is queen"); [f]*Arabailu-šarrat* ("[The city of] Arbela is queen") (*CAD* Š/2:73). For this literary motif of abasement as an expression of mourning, specifically the descent from the throne into dust/ashes, see Jonah 3:6: "He rose from his throne, took off his robe, put on sackcloth, and sat in ashes." Compare also El's reaction at hearing of Baal's death in the Ugaritic Baal epic: "El descends from the throne, sits on the footstool, [and] from the footstool, he sits on the ground. He pours dirt of mourning on his head, dust of humiliation on his cranium" (*CAT* 1.5.VI:12-15). So too in a lamentation in memory of Niqmadu III, king of Ugarit: "Descend to the 'earth' [= netherworld]! Descend to the ground! Plunge yourself into the 'dust'!" (*CAT* 1.61:21-22). The prophetic description is similar to Mesopotamian laments, in which the state deity cries and keens at the destruction of his/her city and temple. (See Dobbs-Allsopp, *Weep, O Daughter of Zion;* idem, "The Syntagma of *bat* Followed by a Geographical Name in the Hebrew Bible: A Reconstruction of Its Meaning and Grammar," *CBQ* 57 [1995]: 451-70; A. Fitzgerald, "*BTWLT* and *BT* as Titles for Capital Cities," *CBQ* 37 [1975]: 167-83.) Compare also the "Lament over the Destruction of Ur and Sumer," in which the goddess's throne is pushed to the ground and she sits in the dust, lamenting the destruction of her city and temple. (See M. Michalowski, *The Lament over the Destruction of Sumer and Ur* [Winona Lake, Ind., 1989], 62-63, lines 408-10.)

"Get down and sit in the dust" — Babylon is commanded to descend from her throne and sit on the ground, abasing herself as a mourner. Cf. Jer 13:18: "Say to the king and the queen mother, 'Sit in a lowly spot!'"; Jer 48:18: "Descend from honor and sit on the thirsty ground, O inhabitant of fair Dibon!"; Ezek 26:16: "All the rulers of the sea shall descend from their thrones . . . and shall sit on the ground"; Lam 2:10: "The elders of fair Zion sit silent on the ground. They have strewn dust on their heads and girded themselves with sackcloth. The maidens of Jerusalem have bowed their heads to the ground." For the contrasting image, see Isa 52:2: "Arise, shake off the dust, captive Jerusalem!" עפר, "dust," and ארץ, "earth, ground," are frequently parallel (e.g., 49:23; 29:4; Mic 7:17; Ps 44:26), as too in Ugaritic: *arṣ/ʿpr* (*CAT* 1.2.IV:5; 1.17.I:27-28). Compare also the devastation of Moab, whose walls sink all the way into the ground: "The Lord has leveled them [the walls] to the earth (לארץ), to the dust (עפר)"

(Isa 25:12). The verb ישב ("to sit") (here and in vv. 5, 8, and 14) is a key word throughout the unit.

"Fair maiden Babylon!" — This appellation (בתולת בת) is also employed to refer to Zion (2 Kgs 19:21 = Isa 37:22; Lam 2:13), Judah (Lam 1:15; cf. Jer 14:17), Sidon (Isa 23:12), Egypt (Jer 46:11), and Israel (Amos 5:2; Jer 18:13). For בת as a description of the Chaldeans, see v. 5 here; of Zion, see 52:2; 62:11; of Jerusalem, see 2 Kgs 19:21 = Isa 37:22. In all these examples the dual title serves as a female personification of a city or country on the brink of imminent destruction. Compare also the Akkadian semantic cognate *martu*, "daughter," which occurs in Mesopotamian lamentation literature (*mārat Bābili*, "Maiden Babylon"; *mārat Akkadi*, "Maiden Akkad"). (See W. G. Lambert, "A Neo-Babylonian Tammuz Lament," in J. M. Sasson, ed., *Studies in Literature from the Ancient Near East Dedicated to Samuel Noah Kramer* [New Haven, 1983], 211-15; and cf. also Tallqvist, *Akkadische Götterepitheta*, 124-26; Dobbs-Allsopp, "Syntagma of *bat*.")

"Sit on the ground dethroned, daughter of the Chaldeans!" — The construction ישב ל- ("to sit on"), which is similar to ישב על- (see 1QIsa[a]), also appears in contexts of death and mourning, e.g., Job 2:13: "They sat with him on the ground"; Lam 2:10: "Silent sit on the ground." (For sitting on the ground [*ina qaqqari*] as a sign of mourning in Akkadian literature, see *CAD* N/1:271-72; Q:114.) Similar to Akk. *kussu* (*CAD* K:590-92) and Ugar. *ks'* (*HdO* 1:460-61), Heb. כסא designates a "throne." The term כַּשְׂדִּים refers both to the Babylonian nation and to Babylon the city. For the former, see Jer 21:4: "Those who are besieging you — the king of Babylon and the Chaldeans"; Hab 1:6: "I am raising up the Chaldeans, that fierce, impetuous nation"; and for the latter, see Isa 48:20 (also parallel to בבל): "Go forth from Babylon! Flee from Chaldea!"; cf. 43:14; 48:20. Note the series of sibilants in this clause: לארץ . . . כסא . . . כשדים.

"Nevermore shall they call you the tender and dainty one" — The particle כי is emphatic. This pair of terms denotes the height of spoiled luxury, as in Deut 28:56: "And she who is most tender (הָרַכָּה) and dainty (והענֻגה) among you, so tender and dainty that she would never venture to set a foot on the ground, shall begrudge the husband of her bosom, and her son and her daughter." See also Deut 28:54 (in the masculine), and cf. Jer 6:2: "Fair Zion, the lovely and delicate (והמענֻגה)." For the rare syntactical construction here (repeated in v. 5): לא תוסיפי יקראו לך, similar to 52:1: כי לא יוסיף יבא בך; Hos 1:6: כי לא אוסיף עוד ארחם, see GKC §102b. According to Luzzatto, this construction is a conflation of two expressions: לא תוסיפי להיקרא ("You [feminine] shall nevermore be called") and לא יוסיפו לקרוא לך ("They shall never again call you"), or, alternatively, the phrase is elliptical and one should understand it to mean, "You shall never again be in a situation where they shall call you by that name." (For the latter explanation of this clause see Ehrlich, *Mikrâ ki-Pheshuṭo*, 3:112.)

[2] A series of six imperatives emphasize Babylon's shame and disgrace. For the motif of degradation, see L. M. Bechtel, "Shame as a Sanction of Social Control in Biblical Israel: Judicial, Political, and Social Shaming," *JSOT* 49 (1991): 47-76.

"Grasp the hand mill and grind meal!" — The grinding of wheat at the hand mill, onomatopoeically emphasized by the fourfold repetition of the letter ח, was considered the most menial of jobs, fit only for the lowliest slaves, as in Exod 11:5: "And every firstborn in the land of Egypt shall die, from the firstborn of Pharaoh who sits on his throne to the firstborn of the slave girl who is behind the millstones, and all the firstborn of the cattle"; and prisoners, as in Judg 16:21: "And [they] shackled him [Samson] in bronze fetters, and he became a mill slave in prison" (see also Job 31:10; Lam 5:13); and cf. also the Egyptian proverbs of Ptahhotep (*ANET,* 412, lines 58-59). The dual form רֵחַיִם ("hand mill") refers to two stones, the bottom stone (which is also the larger of the two) called שֶׁכֶב, and the top stone, רֶכֶב (see Deut 24:6), which "rides" on the lower one.

"Remove your veil!" — The veil, an upper-class garment, was worn by a noblewoman when she left her house. Evidence of this custom is found in the Middle Assyrian Law collection (A:40), which states that married women (lines 42-57), concubines, and temple prostitutes, accompanied by their mistresses (lines 58-60), are obligated to cover themselves with veils while in the public domain. Conversely, unmarried temple personnel (lines 61-63), prostitutes (lines 66-67), and female slaves (lines 88-93) were strictly forbidden to wear a veil, i.e., they were required to remain unveiled and uncovered as a sign of their lower status. If they were caught covering themselves, they were punished with the utmost severity: they were stripped and whipped fifty lashes, and tar was poured on their heads (a symbolic "mirror" punishment — since they covered themselves illegally, they were "covered" in turn). If a slave woman wore a veil, her ears were cut off and her clothes confiscated. (See Roth, *Law Collections,* 167-69.) The intent of the prophet is that fair Babylon must strip herself from her noble accouterments, including the veil, and be degraded to the status of a prostitute. For Heb. צַמָּה, "veil," see Cant 4:1: "Ah, you are fair, my darling, ah you are fair. Your eyes are like doves behind your veil (צַמָּתֵךְ)"; see also 4:3; 6:7. The verb גלי appears again in the next hemistich and in the following verse.

"Strip off your train! Bare your thighs! Wade through rivers!" — further humiliation. Instead of sailing in a pleasure boat, as befits a queen, she is commanded to cross the river on foot, and to do so she must bare her legs to the thigh, revealing her nakedness to all. This vulgar and shameful state is illustrated on the bronze gates of the Assyrian city of Balawat, where a procession of women from Dabigi are portrayed hiking up their dresses as they are being led away into exile by Shalmaneser III. (See A. Jeremias, *The Old Testament in the Light of the Ancient East,* trans. C. L. Beaumont, ed. C. H. W. Johns, 2 vols. [New

York, 1911], 2:277.) Thus Babylon is destined to be exposed, from top to bottom. For the stripping of captives before they are led off in exile, see Isa 20:4: "So shall the king of Assyria drive off the captives of Egypt and the exiles of Nubia, young and old, naked and barefoot and with bared buttocks — to the shame of Egypt." For the verb עבר in the context of a river crossing, see 43:2; Gen 31:21; so too its Akkadian etymological and semantic interdialectal equivalent, *ebēru* (*CAD* E:10-12).

"Strip off your train!" — שֹׁבֶל is a hapax legomenon, which denotes a "flowing skirt, train," and is a by-form of שׁוּל (1QIsa[a] שוליך; see Isa 6:1; Nah 3:5. For the interchange of the letters ב and ו, see also שבט and שוט). For the verb חשׂף ("to strip") parallel to גלי ("to uncover"), see Jer 13:26: "I myself have stripped (חשׂפתי) your skirts over your face," and v. 22: "Your skirts are uncovered (נִגלו)"; Nah 3:5: "I will uncover (וגִליתי) your skirts over your face." These degradations are also characteristic of the punishments meted out to adulteresses and prostitutes (see v. 3). For the anomalous vocalization חֶשְׂפִּי, see GKC §46d.

[3] Babylon is to be punished as if she were an adulteress or a common whore.

"Your nakedness shall be uncovered, and your very shame shall be exposed" — As she lifts her skirts above her thighs, her nakedness and shame (עֶרְוָה, "sexual organs") are exposed (גם is added for emphasis) — here symbolic of her national disgrace. For חֶרְפָּה as sexual degradation, see 2 Sam 13:13; Ezek 16:57. The verb תִּגָּל (the third occurrence of this verb) is a third-person *niphʿal* form. For the shame and public humiliation of adulteresses and whores, see Ezek 16:35-37; Hos 2:12, in addition to the verses quoted above in v. 2. The expression גלי עֶרְוָה, "the uncovering of nakedness" (Lev 18:6, 10, 17-18; 20:11), is comparable to ראי עֶרְוָה, "seeing one's nakedness" (Lam 1:8). For this expression in the context of the public degradation of adulteresses, see Ezek 16:37; 23:10, 29.

"I will take vengeance" — I will exact My revenge on Babylon for their cruel treatment of My people. The expression לקח נקם occurs only once more, when Jeremiah's enemies who plot to kill him say: "And we shall take our vengeance (ונקחָה נקמתֵנו) on him" (Jer 20:10). Perhaps this rare usage is a play on words in v. 2. There Babylon is commanded to "take" (קחי) the hand mill, and here God is going to "take" (אקח) vengeance. For God as avenger, see Deut 32:35: "To be My vengeance (נקם) and recompense"; Mic 5:14: "In anger and wrath will I wreak vengeance (נקם) on the nations." Only here and in v. 6 does God speak in the first person.

"And I shall not be entreated" — One should vocalize ולא אֶפָּגַע (first-person *niphʿal,* from the root פגע) and transfer the following word to the beginning of v. 4 (see there). God states that He shall not acquiesce or accede to any pleas on Babylon's behalf, but shall wreak His vengeance on them. For פגע

meaning intercession and prayer, see Isa 53:12; Jer 7:16: "As for you, do not pray for this people! Do not raise a cry of prayer on their behalf! Do not plead (תפגע) with Me!"; cf. also Jer 15:11. Intercession and vengeance are also linked together in Isa 59:16-17: "He gazed long, but no one intervened (מפגיע) . . . He clothed Himself with garments of vengeance (נקם)." 4QIsa[d] also has here the *hiph'il*: **אפגיע**.

[4] A declaration in God's name that He is prepared to wreak vengeance on Babylon on behalf of His nation, as is stated in the previous verse.

[Says] our Redeemer — Lord of Hosts is His name — the Holy One of Israel — Hebrew **אדם** at the end of v. 3 should be transferred here to the beginning of the verse and read **אמר** (as in LXX Codex Alexandrinus). This textual error was caused by the graphic similarity of *resh* and *dalet* along with a metathesis. For the attributes **גואל** and **קדוש ישראל** in tandem, see 41:14; 43:14; 48:17; 49:7; and for all three together (including **ה׳ צבאות**), see 54:5. The appellation "Lord of Hosts" (see also 48:2; 51:15) emphasizes God's military aspect, here as the avenger of His people. (See the introduction, §9.) For the same context, cf. 63:4. (Perhaps God as the commander-in-chief of the "heavenly host" is a discrete polemic against the Babylonian "scanners of heaven, the stargazers," who think they can announce "month by month, whatever will come" [v. 13].)

[5] The verse repeats some of the expressions and phrases found in v. 1 and thus functions as a literary frame. Compare: "Sit in the dust . . . sit dethroned, Daughter of the Chaldeans! Nevermore shall they call you" — "Sit silent . . . daughter of the Chaldeans! Nevermore shall they call you."

"Sit in silence!" — As mourners do. The adverbial accusative **דוּמָה** (from the root **דום**, "to be silent" (see also Hab 2:19; Lam 3:26) describes a situation or state; cf. **ריקם**, "empty." Babylon is commanded to maintain a state of silence. 1QIsa[a] **דממה**, from the root **דמם**, also means "to be silent, still." (Cf. Ugar. *dm*, "to remain still" [*CAT* 1.14.III:10].) But it should be noted that its homonym, **דמם**, denotes "groaning, wailing, lamenting," and this too describes the state of a mourner. See Ezek 24:17: "Groan lamentably (**דֹּם**)" Compare its cognates, Akk. *damāmu*, "to mourn" (*CAD* D:59-61), *dimmu*, "mourning" (ibid., 144), *dumāmu*, "moaning" (ibid., 179); Ugar. *dmm*, "to wail, moan, lament" (*HdO* 1:274). The Akkadian etymological and semantic cognate of Heb. **ישב**, *(w)ašābu*, can also denote sitting in mourning (*CAD* A/2:390).

"Enter into darkness, daughter of the Chaldeans!" — another metaphor for death and mourning. Perhaps this is also an allusion to the darkness of imprisonment, as in 42:7: "Rescuing prisoners from confinement, from the dungeon those who sit in darkness"; 49:9: "Saying to the prisoners, 'Go free!' To those in darkness, 'Show yourselves!'"

"Nevermore shall they call you 'Queen of Kingdoms'" — since she has now

undergone a complete reversal, i.e., instead of being a queen she has become one of the lowest of the ruled, a shamed handmaiden among nations. The term גְּבֶרֶת is repeated below in v. 7, and is a by-form of גבירה, which denotes both a "queen" (1 Kgs 2:19) and a "queen mother" (2 Kgs 10:13; Jer 13:18; 29:2). For similar epithets, cf. Akk. *šarratu* ("queen"), employed as a descriptive term for goddesses, e.g., *Ištar šarrati kullat dadmē,* "Ishtar, queen of all the inhabited world"; *Tašmētu šarrat kibrāti,* "Tashmētu, queen of the four corners of the world" (*CAD* Š/2:75). Compare also *bēltu,* "lady, mistress," of the "inhabited world," "of the "nations" (*CAD* B:189-90; Tallqvist, *Akkadische Götterepitheta,* 58, 61, 235.)

[6] God, out of anger with His people, handed them over to the Babylonians. They, however, took too many liberties with Israel and punished them excessively. Compare the same motif in Isa 10:5-15; Zech 1:15. The motif of divine anger, which causes the destruction of cities and nations, is very common in Mesopotamian lamentations as well.

"I was angry at My people" — Cf. Isa 54:8: "In an outpouring of anger (קצף), for a moment, I hid My face from you"; 54:9: "So I swear that I will not be angry (מִקְּצֹף) with you or rebuke you"; Lam 5:22: "You have . . . bitterly raged against (קצפת) us."

"I profaned My heritage" — Hebrew חלל ("to defile, to profane") is the antonym of קדש ("to make holy"), as in Isa 43:28: "So I profaned (וַאֲחלל) the holy princes (קֹדֶשׁ)"; Ezek 22:26: "They have profaned (ויחללו) what is sacred to Me (קָדָשַׁי). They have not distinguished between the sacred (קֹדֶשׁ) and the profane (לחֹל)." The word נחלתי ("My heritage") may refer to Israel as God's holy land, as in Jer 2:7: "But you came and defiled My land. You made My possession (נחלתי) abhorrent"; Jer 16:18: "Because they have defiled My land with the corpses of their abominations and have filled My possession (נחלתי) with their abhorrent things"; or to the nation itself, as in Deut 9:29: "Yet they are Your people, Your own possession (נחלתך), whom You freed with Your great might and Your outstretched arm." In light of the parallel terms נחלתי/עמי (see also Joel 2:17; Mic 7:14; Ps 28:9), however, in the adjacent clause: "I delivered them into your hands," the latter explanation, which is based on Deut 32:9: "For the Lord's portion is His people, Jacob His own allotment (נחלתו)," is preferable. For Israel as the Lord's portion or allotment, see also Isa 63:17: "Relent for the sake of Your servants, the tribes that are Your very own possession (נחלתך)!" The LXX has the second-person feminine singular, attributing the profanation to the Babylonians. For the profanation of Israel by the Babylonians, see Ezek 7:21-22.

"I delivered them into your hands" — Babylon was the means and executor, but God was the orchestrator; cf. Isa 10:5 (where Assyria is the executor of God's will): "Ha! Assyria, rod of My wrath." The expression נתן ביד, like its Akkadian cognate *ana qāti nadānu* (*CAD* N/1:46-47), denotes delivery of men

and cities into enemy hands; cf. Josh 6:2 (Jericho); 8:1 (the king of Ai). For the sequential occurrence of the verbs חלל and נתן, see Isa 43:28.

"But you showed them no mercy" — the first clause in God's indictment of Babylon: You were cruel and unmerciful, and pitied no one. The unique expression שׂים רחמים ("show mercy") is the Hebrew interdialectal equivalent of Akk. *ana rēmi šakānu* ("to show mercy to an individual") (*CAD* R:262; Š/1:149, 6.g.10'). (Cf. also the more common Hebrew expression נתן רחמים, e.g,. Jer 42:12.) Assyria — God's "rod of wrath" — also overstepped its boundaries and continued to wantonly destroy: "For he means to destroy, to wipe out nations, not a few" (Isa 10:7).

"Even upon the aged you made your yoke exceedingly heavy" — The prophet indicts the Babylonians on another count of excessive cruelty: they showed no mercy toward the elderly, but made their yoke weigh heavily upon them. For the suffering of the aged during the exile and conquest, see Lam 4:16: "They showed no favor to elders"; 5:12: "No respect has been shown to elders"; 5:14: "The old men are gone from the gate" (cf. also 1:19; 2:21). Moses' prophecy of doom was thus fulfilled: "A ruthless nation that will show the old no regard and the young no mercy" (Deut 28:50). Overburdening subject nations (see 1 Kgs 12:10, 14; and cf. Neh 5:15) is well documented in Mesopotamian sources as well. Compare, for example, Esarhaddon's statement: "I put the full weight of my sovereign yoke upon them" (*CAD* N/2:263). For the use of מְאֹד to further intensify what is described, see also v. 9.

[7] *"You thought, 'I shall always be queen forever'"* — This hemistich should conclude with עד, contra the Masoretic division, since the final עד is the second half of the word pair לעולם ועד. (See D. N. Freedman, "Mistress Forever: A Note on Isaiah 47:7," *Bib* 51 [1970]: 538.) This expression may be a veiled innuendo against the contemporary (and last) king of Babylon, Nabonidus, who bore the title *šarru dārû*, "the eternal king" (see Seux, *Épithètes royales*, 297). 1QIsa[a] עוד ("yet") is based on the traditional division of the verse (which placed עד at the beginning of the next clause). For the expression היי לעולם ("to always be"), see Isa 51:6, 8.

"You did not take these things to heart" — Your overbearing egotism caused you to ignore the obvious, and you did not think there would be any consequences when you acted with such unrelenting cruelty. The substantive לב ("heart") reverberates throughout this unit (vv. 7, 8, 10). For the parallel expressions לא שמת לבך על and ולא זכרת (next hemistich), see 57:11. For the expression שׂים לב, see 42:25; 57:1; and for the semantic equivalent in Akkadian see 41:22. For אלה in similar contexts, see 44:21.

"You gave no thought to its outcome" — You remained blissfully unaware of the consequences of your cruelty. For the same expression, see Lam 1:9: "She gave no thought to her future (אחריתהּ)." (The pronominal feminine suffix in

אחריתה represents the neuter.) This substantive, similar to its etymological and semantic equivalent in Akkadian, *aḫrâtu* (*CAD* A/1:193-94), refers to all that will take place in the future. In Hebrew, however, it usually has negative connotations (cf. Jer 5:31; Amos 8:10). For Heb. זכר, "bear in mind" (lit. "remember") something in the future, see Eccl 11:8: "But let him remember how many the days of darkness are going to be."

[8-15] A scathing satire against Babylon's self-deification and its dependence on magical arts. The unit begins with the prophet's call to heed his warnings of impending doom and has a lot in common with the first verse of the previous unit: In v. 1 Babylon is personified as "tender and dainty," and here as "pampered"; in v. 1 "fair maiden Babylon" is commanded twice to "sit," and here she says she is "sitting" complacently, unaware of the looming disaster; in v. 7 she brags that she shall be "queen forever," and here she claims that she is sui generis ("I am, and there is none but me"). Verse 8 is a direct borrowing from Zeph 2:15, referring to Nineveh: "The gay city that dwelt secure, that thought in her heart, 'I am, and there is none but me.'" The sobriquet עדינה ("pampered") is substituted here for Zephaniah's עליזה ("gay"), since in v. 1 Babylon is called "tender and dainty." (See the introduction, §16.) Her trust in her magical prowess, however, will not prevent her fall.

[8] *And now hear this, O lover of luxury* — For the root עדן (the adjective appears only here), meaning "delight, luxuriate," see Ps 36:9; Lam 4:5; Neh 9:25. It appears in Ugaritic as part of a description of Baal's life-giving rains (*CAT* 1.4.V:6-7) and is also documented in Aramaic in the bilingual (Akkadian-Aramaic) inscription from Tell Faḫariyah (from the end of the second millennium BCE), line 7: "He who confers a rich bounty (מעדן) on the whole world." (See J. C. Greenfield and A. Shaffer, "Notes on the Akkadian-Aramaic Bilingual Statue from Tell Fekherye," *Iraq* 45 [1983]: 109-16.)

Who dwells in security — you, who sit on the throne (v. 1) in total complacency, blissfully unaware of your impending doom. Compare Jer 49:31: "Rise up and attack a tranquil nation that dwells secure (יושב לבטח), says the Lord!"; cf. also Lev 25:18; Judg 18:7.

Who thinks to herself — who, in her megalomaniacal self-delusion, aspires to godhood. For similar examples of self-apotheosis, cf. Isa 14:13; Dan 11:35-36. For the expression אמר בלב ("to think in one's heart, to say to oneself"), see v. 10; Gen 17:17; Zeph 1:12; 2:15. The semantic equivalent in Akkadian is *ina libbi qabû* (*CAD* Q:26). The prophet is once again quoting Babylon's self-incriminating statements; see v. 7.

"I am, and there is none but me" — This egotistical proclamation of self-exaltation, repeated again in v. 10, is drawn directly from Zeph 2:15 (see above). Despite the similarity to v. 7: "I shall always be queen forever," this time around she goes one step further and arrogantly proclaims her self-deification in terms

reserved for God, and God alone; see Isa 45:6: "That there is none but Me"; 45:14: "Only among you is God, there is no other god at all"; 46:9: "For I am God and there is none else. I am God and there is none like Me"; and see 45:5, 18, 21, 22. The word **אפסי** is an archaic poetic form; the *yod* suffix is not pronominal.

"I shall neither become a widow" — For the expression **ישב אלמנה**, which denotes the state of widowhood, see Gen 38:11: "Then Judah said to his daughter-in-law Tamar, 'Remain as a widow (**שבי אלמנה**) in your father's house'"; and cf. the Akkadian interdialectal equivalent *almattu (ina bīti) (w)ašābu* ("to remain as a widow [at home]"; *CAD* A/2:402). The image of a city or nation as a widow (see Isa 54:4: "And remember no more the shame of your widowhood"; Lam 1:1: "She that was great among the nations has become like a widow") conveys a loss of independence. A nation that was once mighty is forced into subjugation to another nation like a widow who is dependent on the goodwill of others. (See Ch. Cohen, "The 'Widowed' City," *JANES* 5 [= D. Marcus, ed., *The Gaster Festschrift;* New York, 1973]: 75-81; Dobbs-Allsopp, *Weep, O Daughter of Zion*, 178-79.) The same motif appears in the Egyptian King Merneptah's victory stele: "Hurru [the land of greater Palestine] has become widowed" (*ANET*, 378). For the verb **ישב**, meaning to remain in a certain state, see Lev 12:4: "She shall remain (**תשב**) in a state of blood purification for thirty-three days"; 1 Sam 1:23: "Remain (**שבי**) at home until you have weaned him." Compare also in Rabbinic Hebrew: "Whoever remains inactive (**הַיֹּשֵׁב**) and does not transgress" (*m. Mak.* 3:15).

"Nor experience the loss of children" — Compare 49:21 (in regard to Israel): "Who bore these for me when I was bereaved (**שְׁכוּלָה**) and barren?" For the loss of children and widowhood striking at the same time, see Jer 18:21: "Let their wives be bereaved of children and husbands." (The same pair appears in Ugaritic literature as the names of the two staffs the god Mot holds in his hands: the "staff of bereavement *(ṯkl)*" and the "staff of widowhood *(ulmn)*" (*CAT* 1.23:8-9). 1QIsa[a] **ואראה**, instead of MT **אדע**, has the same meaning, "to experience." The verb **ידע** is repeated once more in v. 10 and twice more in v. 11.

[9] *Yet these two things shall come upon you* — As punishment for your arrogant thoughts, these two calamities (the loss of your children and widowhood) shall befall you; cf. Isa 51:19: "These two things have befallen you."

In a moment, in a single day — The calamities shall be very sudden, without any prior warning. **רֶגַע** ("suddenly," "in a moment") is usually associated with sudden calamity, as in 54:7: "For a moment I forsook you"; Lam 4:6: "Sodom, which was overthrown in a moment." For **ביום אחד** ("in a single day"), also in calamitous contexts, see Isa 9:13; 10:17.

Loss of children and widowhood — The order that the calamities are mentioned are in chiastic parallelism with v. 8. For the hapax legomenon abstract noun **אַלְמֹן**, "widowhood" (cf. Jer 51:5: "For Israel and Judah were not bereft [**אַלְמָן**] of their God"), 1QIsa[a] substituted the familiar **אלמנה**, "widow." The anomalous MT form was selected in order to rhyme with the adjacent שְׁכוֹל. (For the form itself, see Kutscher, *Language and Linguistic Background,* 366.)

Shall come upon you in full measure — Widowhood and bereavement shall be your fate, which you shall experience in full effect. For תֹּם, "in full," "in full measure," see Job 21:23. Tur-Sinai (*Peshuto shel Miqra,* III/1:123), however, suggested that the *aleph* was elided in MT כְּתֻמָּם and should be read כִּתְאֹמִים ("like twins"), i.e., "twin punishments of bereavement and widowhood."

Despite your many enchantments — which will be of no avail in attempting to thwart or avert the bereavement and widowhood that shall descend upon you suddenly. The *beth* prefix appended to בְּרֹב ("many") indicates contrast; cf., e.g., "And how long will they have no faith in Me despite all (בכל) the signs that I have performed in their midst?" (Num 14:11); "Yet for all that (ובדבר) you have no faith in the Lord your God" (Deut 1:32). (For multiple references to sorcery *(kišpu)* practiced in Babylon, see *CAD* K:454-56; and for a study of this topic, see A. L. Oppenheim, *Ancient Mesopotamia* [Chicago, 1964], 206-27.)

And despite your countless spells/enchanters — This clause, which parallels the previous one, is further intensified by the addition of מאד (see also v. 6): All your charms, spells, and magical practices will not prevent your eventual downfall. For the synonymous terms עצום/רב, see Exod 1:9; Isa 31:1. For עָצְמָה ("countless"), see Nah 3:9: "Countless (עצמה) Nubia and teeming Egypt." Some, however, interpret עָצְמָה as "power" or "potency"; cf. 40:29. Hebrew חֲבָרַיִךְ denotes "spells." But if vocalized חֹבְרַיִךְ (cf. 1QIsa^a חובריך), it would refer to those who cast the spells, "enchanters," as in Deut 18:11: "One who casts spells" (חוֹבֵר חָבֶר); Ps 58:6: "So as not to hear the voice of charmers or the expert mutterer of spells (חוֹבֵר חֲבָרִים)." Etymologically and semantically, the pair חבר/כשף are cognate to Akk. *kuššupu/ubburu* (the latter denoting "to bind magically"). (See M. Held, "Studies in Biblical Lexicography in the Light of Akkadian," *ErIsr* 16 [= B. A. Levine and A. Malamat, eds., *Festschrift in Honor of Harry M. Orlinsky;* Jerusalem, 1982]: 78-79 [Heb.].) For the same pair in Ugaritic, *ḥbrm-kšpm,* see *CAT* 1.169:9-10.

Note the linguistic, thematic, and structural affinity between vv. 8-9 and 10-11:

Verses 8-9	**Verses 10-11**
היושבת לבטח	ותבטחי ברעתך
האֹמרה בלבבה	אמרת
אני ואפסי עוד	אני ואפסי עוד
ולא אדע שְׁכול	לא תדעי שַׁחְרָהּ
ותבֹאנה לך שתי אלה	ותפל עליך הֹוָה
רגע ביום אחד	ותבא עליך פתאם
שְׁכול ואלמן	שואה לא תדעי

[10] Babylon's blasphemy.

You were secure in your wickedness — "The verse does not imply that you (Babylon) put your trust in your wickedness . . . but, rather, you persisted in your evil ways in total security. You continued to transgress without any fear [of retribution]" (Luzzatto). For the expression בטח ב-, see Hos 10:13; Amos 6:1. 1QIsa[a] has the variant reading בדעתך ("in your knowledge"), which may have been influenced by the same word occurring in this verse or caused by a graphic similarity of the *dalet* and *resh*.

You thought: "No one can see me" — The prophet quotes Babylon once more: You were under the impression that no one was looking or holding you accountable for your evil ways — even God Himself was supposedly not paying attention. And since there were no eyewitnesses, no punishment would be forthcoming (cf. Exod 22:9: "There being no eyewitnesses"). For similar statements, cf. Ezek 8:12: "For they say, 'The Lord does not see us'"; Ezek 9:9: "For they say . . . 'And the Lord does not see.'" Compare also Ps 10:11: "He thinks, 'God is not mindful; He hides His face; He never looks'"; Ps 94:7: "Thinking, 'The Lord does not see it'"; see also Isa 29:15; Ps 64:6. רֹאָנִי is a pausal form; cf. the nonpausal רֹאֵנוּ (Isa 29:15); so too pausal יִרְאָנִי (Exod 33:20) and nonpausal וַיִּרְאֵנִי (2 Sam 1:7).

It was your very skill and your science that led you astray — Your command of the occult sciences (היא serves here as an emphatic in the singular since "skill and science" function as a hendiadys) is what caused you to become wayward (שובב). For the verb שׁוֹבְבָתֶךְ, a third-person feminine singular *polel* stem (from the root שׁוב) with a pronominal suffix, see Isa 57:17; Jer 50:6: "My people were lost sheep. Their shepherds caused them to wander about. They led them astray (שׁוֹבְבָם) on the mountains."

And you thought to yourself: "I am and there is none but me" — A verbatim repetition from v. 8 of the egomaniacal statement of self-deification.

[11] A three-pronged devastation is about to fall on hapless Babylon, with no hope of succor. The negative לא appears thrice in this verse, as does עליך. The prophet's threat of doom is meant to counter the well-known Babylonian apotropaic *namburbû* ritual for warding off portended evil (see *CAD* N/1:224-25). (For a study of this ritual, see E. Reiner, *Astral Magic in Babylonia* [Philadelphia, 1995], 81-96.)

Evil is coming upon you — Despite all your magical skills and prowess, your demise is imminent. You felt secure in your wickedness (ברעתך, v. 10), and now ultimate disaster (רעה) shall befall you — tit for tat. For רעה, "calamity," "disaster," see Jonah 3:10: "And God renounced the disaster He had planned to bring upon them." This intended disaster (רעה) was also in response to Nineveh's רעה — 1:2: "For their wickedness (רעתם) has come before me." (1QIsa[a] באה, third-person feminine, corresponds to the feminine noun רעה. In

Biblical Hebrew, however, when the predicate precedes the subject, there is not necessarily agreement between the two.)

Which you will not know how to bribe/charm away — Once more tit for tat: Babylon claimed that she would never know (לא אדע) bereavement (v. 8) because of her vaunted skills (דעתך) (v. 10); nevertheless, calamity will befall her from which she will not know (תדעי) how to extricate herself. The verb שַׁחְרָהּ is a *pi'el* infinitive construct with a feminine pronominal suffix referring to the רעה in the first hemistich and should be vocalized שַׁחֲרָהּ. Some commentators connect this rare verb to Arab. *saḥara,* "to enchant" (cf. also Akk. *saḫāru,* "to encircle, said of magic or sorcery" [*CAD* S:46]; see v. 15), and interpret it as a privative *pi'el* (cf. לְשָׁרֵשׁ, "to uproot" [Ps 52:7]; לְסָעֵף, "to remove the סעיפים, branches" [Isa 10:33]). However, in light of the following hemistich, "[Disaster is falling on you], which you will not be able to propitiate (כַּפְּרָהּ)," and the parallelism between כֹּפֶר and שֹׁחַד in Prov 6:35: "He will not have regard for any ransom (כפר), He will refuse your bribe (שחד), however great," it is preferable to emend שחרה to שַׁחֲדָהּ (the common graphic similarity between *dalet* and *resh*): "Evil is coming upon you that you will not be able stave off by bribes." (For the Akkadian and Arabic cognates cited above, see v. 15.)

Disaster is falling on you — See Ezek 7:26: "Disaster (הֹוָה) shall follow disaster (הֹוָה)." For the verbal expression נפל על, with other similar substantives, cf. Ps 105:38 ("fear" — פחד); Josh 2:9 ("dread" — אֵימָה); Dan 10:7 ("terror" — חֲרָדָה). Compare also the Akkadian semantic cognate *eli . . . maqātu,* "to fall upon" (*CAD* M/1:247-48).

Which you will not be able to propitiate — Cf. Gen 32:21, "I shall propitiate (אֲכַפְּרָה) him with presents in advance"; Prov 16:14: "The king's wrath is a messenger of death, but a wise man can appease it (יְכַפְּרֶנָּה)." In light of the comments to the previous clause, however, one can also interpret this hemistich as polysemous, since the Akkadian etymological and semantic equivalent, *kuppuru,* can also denote purification by magical means (*CAD* K:179).

Coming upon you suddenly is disaster, of which you are unaware — See Isa 10:3: "Disaster (שׁוֹאָה) that comes from afar"; Ps 35:8: "Let disaster (שואה) overtake them unaware" (which is the exact same Hebrew expression as here). This disaster will strike suddenly without warning. The word פִּתְאֹם, "suddenly," similar to רֶגַע (v. 9), usually appears in contexts of calamity, e.g., Isa 30:13, "Whose crash comes suddenly (פִּתְאֹם) and swiftly"; Jer 4:20: "Suddenly (פִּתְאֹם) my tents have been ravaged, in a moment (רגע), my tent cloths"; Prov 3:25: "You will not fear sudden (פִּתְאֹם) terror or the disaster that comes upon the wicked." The addition of this term here accentuates the terror. Although the phrase לא תדעי is repeated from the first hemistich, here it denotes lack of foreknowledge: disaster will come of which you are totally unaware; for this meaning, see Hos 7:9; Job 9:2. For the expression "to come upon suddenly," see Isa 48:3.

[12] *Persist in your many spells and your many enchantments* — The prophet ridicules "fair Babylon" and calls on her to attempt to stave off destruction by resorting to her sorceries and enchantments — if she can. For the expression עמד ב-, "to persist, withstand," see Josh 10:8: "Not one of them shall withstand you"; Ezek 13:5: "That they might persist in battle on the day of the Lord." The order of the two substantives חבריך and כשפיך creates a chiastic parallelism with v. 9. As in v. 9, 1QIsa[a] has חובריך, "enchanters."

On which you labored from your youth! — The phrase alludes to the sorcerous skills Babylon was famous for and had spent many years mastering. 1QIsa[a] adds ועד היום ("up until today"); cf. 1 Sam 12:2: "From my youth until this day"; Jer 3:25: "From our youth to this day." For the verbal expression יגע ב-, see Isa 43:22; 62:8.

Perhaps you will be able to avail — The prophet continues to deride Babylon and mockingly suggests that her spells and enchantments may yet aid and abet her. For the verb להועיל, used negatively against idol worshipers, see 44:9: "And the things they treasure are to no avail"; 44:10: "Or cast a statue that has no avail"; 57:12: "Your assorted [idols] shall not avail you." Compare, however, 48:17: "I the Lord am your God, instructing you for your own benefit (להועיל)."

Perhaps you will find strength/you will inspire terror — תַּעֲרוֹצִי is explained by some as an intransitive verb denoting strength and potency (Kimchi; see also Ibn Balaam [ed. Goshen-Gottstein, 193]; ibn Ezra; note also the parallelism between גבור and עריץ in 49:25). Others interpret it as meaning "to terrify"; see 2:19: "Before the terror of the Lord . . . when he comes forth to overawe (לערץ) the earth"; Job 13:25: "Will you terrify (תערוץ) a driven leaf?" Another suggestion is to emend the verb by metathesis and read תעצורי, "to stop or halt": "Perhaps you will stop" [the disaster in its tracks] (Yellin, *Ḥiqrei Miqra,* 60; Tur-Sinai, *Peshuṭo shel Miqra,* III/1:123); or explain the verb to mean "ability to persevere"; cf. 2 Chr 20:37: "The ships were wrecked and unable (עצרו) to go to Tarshish" (Eitan, "Contribution to Isaiah Exegesis," 80).

[13] In v. 12 the prophet mocked the Babylonian proclivity toward magic. In this verse his derision is directed against their professional sorcerers.

You are helpless, despite all your art — Despite (for *beth* as indicating a negative contrast, see v. 9) your sorcery, you remain helpless to avert the forthcoming calamity. For the root לאי, "to be unable," see Exod 7:18: "The Egyptians shall be unable (ונִלאו) to drink the water of the Nile," which is explicated in v. 21: "The Egyptians could not (לא יכלו) drink the water from the Nile"; cf. Jer 20:9: "I was unable (נִלאיתי) to hold it in; I was helpless." The word עֵצָה, "counsel" (see Isa 28:29: "His counsel is unfathomable"; Job 12:13: "He has counsel and understanding"), is used here as an all-embracing term for the sorcerous arts. The prophet's declaration that Babylon's עצה will be to no avail contrasts with God's עצה; see 44:26: "He [Cyrus] shall fulfill the counsel (עצה)

of My messengers"; 46:10: "My plan (עצתי) shall be fulfilled." The vocalization עֲצָתַ֫יִךְ is anomalous since it conflates both the singular, עֲצָתֵךְ, and plural, עֲצוֹתַ֫יִךְ, forms. 1QIsa[a] עצתך and Targum מִלְּכֵךְ render in the singular, while LXX, Vulgate, and Peshitta translate in the plural.

Let the astrologers stand up and save you — Cf. Jer 2:28: "And where are those gods you made for yourself? Let them arise and save you, if they can." Although the unique expression הֹבְרֵי שמים refers to astrologers, commentators disagree as to the origin of the term. Some claim that it derives from Arab. *habara,* "to cut" (cf. Kimchi in his commentary, as well as in his *Sefer ha-Shorashim,* 76-77), i.e., they divide the sky into different sectors and astrological signs, and through their observations of the heavens predict future events. This explanation has been soundly rejected by Blau, however, who suggests that the word is derived from the Ugar. *hbr,* "to bow" (*HdO* 1:333), i.e., those who bow down to, worship the heavens (J. Blau, "HOBRE ŠAMAJIM" (Jes XLVII 12) = *Himmelsanbeter?*" *VT* 7 [1957]: 183-84). Yet others maintain that the MT is corrupt, and that originally the text read בָּרֵי שמים, derived from Akk. *bārû;* see 44:25 and comments there. The problem with this suggestion is that the *bārû*'s expertise was to scan animal innards and not the skies (*CAD* B:121-25). Finally, others propose to substitute a ח for the initial ה, reading חֹבְרֵי (see Ibn Ganaḥ, *Sefer ha-Shorashim,* 161, 141; and cf. Judah Ibn Karish quoted in Menaḥem Ben Saruq, *Sefer ha-Maḥberet,* 12-13), and cf. vv. 9, 12, חבריך ("enchantments/enchanters"); note too 1QIsa[a] חוברי השמים. Whatever the origin of the term may be, the art of predicting by the stars was very developed in Babylon, beginning with the second millennium BCE (see Reiner, *Astral Magic*). Note the derisive יעמדו נא and cf. v. 12, עִמְדִי נא.

The stargazers — who examine the night sky in order to predict the future. This phrase may refer to another set of astrologers or may function as an explanatory gloss to the previous unique expression. For the expression חזה ב-, see Job 36:25. In Akkadian as well, the verbs *amāru* and *dagālu* ("to see," "to behold") also refer to stargazing (*CAD* A/2:14; D:21). Compare, for example, King Esarhaddon's letter regarding "two astrologers who gaze day and night at the stars." (See S. Parpola, "A Letter from Šamaš-šumu-ukin to Esarhaddon," *Iraq* 34 [1972]: 22, 24-25.) For the substantive pair כוכבים/שמים, see Isa 14:13: "Once you thought in your heart, 'I will climb to the sky (השמים); higher than the stars (לכוכבי) of God I will set my throne.'" For the same parallelism in Ugaritic, see the Baal epic: "Dew that the skies *(šmm)* poured upon her [Anat], drizzle that the stars *(kbkbm)* pour upon her" (*CAT* 1.3.II:40-41), and the Aqhat epic: "He made his offering of perfumes (?) go up to the sky *(šmym),* an offering of perfumes (?) . . . to the stars *(kbkbm)*" (*CAT* 1.19.IV:30-31).

Who foretell, month by month, whatever will come upon you — Each month, when they scan the heavens, the astrologers announce your monthly "horoscope." For the *lamed* denoting continuity, "every month, month by month," see also Ezek 47:12: "They shall bear early fruit every month (לחדשים)." Compare similarly לבקרים, "day by day, daily" (Job 7:18; Lam 3:23). (For monthly portents in Mesopotamia [*arḫišam*], see *CAD* A/2:258.) Note too Nabonidus's supplication to Sin, the moon god: "Let me always see your [Sin's] favorable sign when you renew yourself at the beginning of each month" (*CAD* S:56). Some commentators explain מֵאשר (which occurs elsewhere in the Bible only in Exod 29:27 — but with a different meaning) to mean "about" or "which." Others suggest that the initial מ is a dittography (the final ם of לחדשים being mistakenly appended to this word), and one should read אשר. The third-person masculine plural suffix in 1QIsa[a], עליהמה, is in accord with the other masculine plurals in v. 14: שְׂרָפָתַם, נפשם, לַחְמָם. 1QIsa[a], LXX, Peshitta, and Targum all read יבוא, third-person singular, instead of the MT plural יָבֹאוּ.

[14] A fiery devastation is announced (cf. 66:24), reinforced by four synonyms: אש, להבה, גחלת, אוּר. The imagery here has much in common with the prophet's derisive polemic against idol craftsmanship in 44:16, 19.

See, they are like stubble, fire consumes them — All the astrologers and stargazers will be consumed like stubble (קַשׁ) before the fiery rage; cf. 5:24: "As stubble is consumed by a tongue of fire." For הנה as introducing a legal verdict, see 41:11, 21, 29; 50:9. Note the successive series of similar sounding sibilants, כקש אש שׂרפתם, which vividly simulate the hissing and burning of the fire.

They cannot save themselves from the flames — Not only are they powerless to help their own people (cf. v. 13), these astrologers cannot even save their very selves from their fiery fate. Compare Bel and Nabu's predicament in 46:2: "They could not rescue the burden, and they themselves went into captivity"; and the idolater's fate, 44:20: "And he cannot save himself." For the synonymous pair לֶהָבָה/אש, see 43:2; and for the expression הציל מיד, "to save from," see Gen 37:22; Exod 3:8. 1QIsa[a] הצילו harmonizes with the past tense of the verb in the previous clause, היו.

This is no coal for warming themselves — The prophet declares that this conflagration, which is about to consume them, is not mere "coals" (Isa 44:19) for warming themselves. For the anomalous form לַחְמָם, see GKC §§28b, 67cc). 1QIsa[a] reads לחוממה.

No fire to sit in front of! — The negative אין in the prior clause is to be understood here as well, i.e., this fire is not a bonfire to sit by and enjoy. For אוּר, "flame, heat," see 44:16: "I am warm; I can feel the heat (אוּר)"; 50:11: "Walk by the blaze (באוּר) of your fire." For נגד, "in front of," see 40:17.

[15] *Such are they for you, your sorcerers, with whom you have toilsomely dealt since your youth* — סֹחֲרַיִךְ is a general term for all types of sorcerers and enchanters and is the etymological and semantic interdialectal equivalent of Arab. *saḥiru,* "to enchant," and Akk. *sāḫiru,* an adjective "designating a sor-

cerer" (*CAD* S:60); cf. *sāḫāru*, "to encircle, said of magic or sorcery" (ibid., 46). (See Held, "Studies in Biblical Lexicography," 79.) The beginning of this verse, **כן היו**, is similar to the beginning of the previous verse: **הנה היו**.

Each has wandered off his own way — They, the sorcerers, have all stumbled off in all different directions. The root **תעי** denotes wandering astray, walking unstably, at times as a result of inebriation, as in Isa 19:14: "As a vomiting drunkard goes astray." Compare also 53:6: "We all went astray like sheep each going his own way." For **עֵבֶר**, "side," see 1 Sam 14:40.

There is none to save you — since "I, I myself, am the Lord, and none besides Me can save" (43:11); cf. also 45:21, 22. This chapter, which was devoted entirely to a polemic against Babylon, concludes with a sentiment that mirrors the previous chapter: "There is none to save you"; but "I will grant salvation in Zion, to Israel, in whom I glory" (46:13).

Chapter 48

The tripartite division of the chapter (vv. 1-11, 12-19, 20-21) and its (secondary) appendix (v. 22) contain a significant number of key words common to all the units: **שמע**, vv. 1, 3, 5, 6 (twice), 7, 8, 12, 14, 16, 20 (the verb in the imperative opens each of the chapter's three units, and in each of these three verses the name "Jacob" appears as well); **ידע**, vv. 4, 6, 7, 8 (twice); **קרא**, vv. 1, 2, 8, 12, 13, 15; **נגד**, vv. 3 (and note **גיד**, "neck" [v. 4], and the resultant wordplay), 5, 6, 14, 20; **שֵׁם**, vv. 1 (twice), 2, 9, 19; **יצא**, vv. 1, 3, 20 (twice), and **צאצאי** (v. 19); **צדקה**, vv. 1, 18; **מאז**, vv. 3, 5, 7, 8; **עשׂי**, vv. 3, 5, 11, 14; **ראש**, vv. 3, 12, 16; **כרת**, vv. 9, 19; **אני**, vv. 12 (thrice), 13, 15 (twice), 16, 17. Note also the relative abundance of imperative forms: v. 1: **שִׁמְעוּ**; v. 6: **חֲזֵה**; v. 12: **שְׁמַע**; v. 14: **הִקָּבְצוּ, וְשִׁמְעוּ**; v. 16: **שִׁמְעוּ, קִרְבוּ**; and especially v. 20: **אִמְרוּ, הוֹצִיאוּהָ, הַשְׁמִיעוּ, הַגִּידוּ, בִּרְחוּ, צְאוּ**.

The first unit, in which the prophet juxtaposes **רִאשֹׁנוֹת** with **חדשות** (see below), contains a scathing rebuke against the nation of Israel (cf. 42:18ff.; 45:9ff.; 46:9ff.), whom God will redeem for the sake of His name, in spite of their traitorous ways, and is characterized by a large number of negatives: **לא**, vv. 1 (twice), 6 (and cf. also **הלוא** in that verse), 7 (twice), 8 (three times), 10, 11. The unit is also symmetrical in form:

v. 3b: "Suddenly I acted and they came to pass" — v. 7a: "Only now are they created."
v. 4a: "Because I know" — v. 8b: "For I know."
v. 5b: "That you could not say" — v. 7b: "You cannot say."
v. 6a: "You have heard" — v. 7a: "You had not heard of them"; v. 8a: "You had never heard."

This chapter is linked to the preceding one by a number of common phrases: 47:1, 5: **יקראו לך** — 48:1: **הנקראים**, 2: **נקראו**, 8: **קֹרָא לך**, 12: **מְקֹרָאִי**;

47:4: גֹאלנו ה׳ צבאות שמו קדוש ישראל — 48:2: ה׳ צבאות שמו, 17: ה׳ גֹאלך קדוש ישראל; 47:8: שִׁמְעִי זאת — 48:1: שִׁמְעוּ זאת, 20: הַשמיעו זאת; 47:6: חללתי — 48:11: יֵחָל; 47:7: לא . . . לא — 48:1: לא . . . לא; 47:11: ותבא עליך פתאם — 48:3: פִּתְאֹם . . . ותבאנה; 47:12: הועיל — 48:17: להועיל; 47:13: הַחֹזִים — 48:6: חֲזֵה.

[1-2] In the opening lines of the rebuke, the prophet addresses himself to the "house of Jacob" (see 46:3), "Israel" (for the "Jacob/Israel" parallelism, see, e.g., 40:27; 41:8; 43:1; 44:1), and "Judah" (for the "Jacob/Judah" parallelism, see 65:9). Note the similar phraseology in vv. 1 and 2, and the partial chiastic structure:

Verse 1	**Verse 2**
Who *are called* by the name Israel	For you *are called* after the Holy City
Who swear by the name of the *Lord*	And you lean on the *God of Israel*
And invoke *the God of Israel*	Whose name is the *Lord* of Hosts

[1] *Listen to this, O house of Jacob* — Listen to the following chastisement. For the same sequence of verbs as here, שמע . . . קרא . . . זכר, see 49:1.

Who are called by the name of Israel — For the expression קרא בשם, see 43:1.

And have issued from the womb of Judah — Some compare the expression "the waters of Judah" (מֵי יהודה) to other aquatic sobriquets, such as עֵין יעקב ("Jacob's fountain"; Deut 33:28) and מקור ישראל ("the fountain of Israel"; Ps 68:27), and interpret it as a poetic reference to Israel's progeny (see also Targum וּמִזַּרְעֲיַת, "from the seed, family"; Ibn Ezra and Kimchi: זרע). Since the expression "issuing forth from water" is unparalleled, however, it is preferable to accept the proposal to emend to וּמִמֵּעֵי יהודה יצאו (the elision of the *ayin* and the transfer of the *tzereh* vowel to the *mem*). For the expression יצא מִמֵּעַיִם, which refers to procreation (issuing forth from the inner organs), see Gen 15:4; 2 Sam 7:12; 16:11. It thus creates a chiastic literary frame encompassing the first two literary units: ממעי . . . יָצָאוּ — וצאצאי מעיך (v. 19). For another (possible) example of a similar occurrence of the elision of the *ayin* in this expression, see Isa 39:7: מבניך אשר יֵצְאוּ ממך, where 1QIsa[a] has the reading ממעיכה.

Who swear by the name of the Lord — Cf. Deut 6:13: "Revere only the Lord your God and worship Him alone, and swear only by His name"; see also Deut 10:20; Jer 12:16.

And invoke the God of Israel — you who invoke the "name" (Heb. בשם of the prior hemistich does double-duty) of "the God of Israel"; cf. Josh 23:7: "Do not invoke (תזכירו) the names of their gods nor swear (תשבעו) by them," where the same two verbs appear in conjunction as here. For the expression להזכיר בשם ה׳, see Amos 6:10 and, similarly, the mid-eighth-century BCE

Hadad inscription in Aramaic: ויזכר אשם הדד ("He invokes the name of the god Hadad") (*KAI* 214:16). In Akkadian the interdialectal etymological and semantic equivalent *šumam zakāru* also denotes the invocation of the deity in oaths and vows (*CAD* Z:15-17). Compare also the synonymous pair זֵכֶר/שֵׁם, Exod 3:15: "This shall be My name (שמי) forever, this My appellation (זכרי) for all eternity," which appears also in Phoenician: סכר ושם (*KAI* 18:6); in Aramaic: שם-זכר (*KAI* 202 C:2); and in Akkadian: *šumšu u zikrišu,* e.g., in the epilogue of Hammurabi's law collection, §49:80. (See M. T. Roth, *Law Collections from Mesopotamia and Asia Minor,* SBLWAW 6 [Atlanta, 1995], 137; cf. *ANET,* 179, rev. 26:79-80.)

Though not in truth and sincerity — You pay lip service to My name, but when you invoke it there is no honesty or sincerity behind your words. For the pair of nouns אמת and צדקה in connection with swearing an oath, see Jer 4:2: "And you swear, 'As the Lord lives,' in truth (אמת), justice, and sincerity (בצדקה)"; and in other contexts, see 1 Kgs 3:6; Zech 8:8.

[2] *Even though you are named after the Holy City* — The expression נקרא מ- appears only here and remains unclear. Most likely the clause is connected to v. 1: Although you are named (נקראו, the *niphʿal* is reflexive here) after Jerusalem, the Holy City, there is no truth or sincerity behind your words. Jerusalem's celebrated sobriquet, "Holy City" (עִיר הַקֹּדֶשׁ), was most likely coined by Deutero-Isaiah; see also 52:1; Joel 4:17; Dan 9:24; Neh 11:1, 18. The city's holiness derives from the Temple in its midst, and thus it is "the city of the Temple" (עיר המקדש). (See M. Broshi and E. Eshel, "248: 4QHistorical Text A," in S. J. Pfann et al., *Qumrân Cave 4.XXVI: Cryptic Texts and Miscellanea, Part I,* DJD 36 [Oxford, 2000], 193, 195, on line 7; J. M. Baumgarten, *Qumrân Cave 4.XIII: The Damascus Document (4Q266-273),* DJD 18 [Oxford, 1996], 181-82, 4Q271, frag. 5 i 17. For the *Temple Scroll,* in which the expression is documented no less than 36 times, see Y. Yadin, *The Temple Scroll,* 3 vols. in 4 [Jerusalem, 1977-83], 1:278-85; J. Milgrom, "The City of the Temple," *JQR* 85 [1994]: 125-28.) Ugaritic *qdš* denotes a "sanctuary" (*HdO* 2:696-97); and cf. Akk. *qašdu* and *quddušu,* "holy" (*CAD* Q:146-47, 294). The concept of a "holy city" appears occasionally in Mesopotamian literature as well: "[My] city, Babylon, the holy." (See A. D. Kilmer, "An Oration on Babylon," *Altorientalische Forschungen* 18 [1991]: 9-22, line 1.) Compare also *āl elli,* "the holy city," which appears in Sennacherib's inscription referring to the freedom granted to the city of Ša-uṣur-adad by the Assyrian ruler. (See C. B. F. Walker and S. N. Kramer, "Cuneiform Tablets in the Collection of Lord Bining," *Iraq* 44 [1982]: 71-76; M. Weinfeld, *Social Justice in Ancient Israel and in the Ancient Near East* [Minneapolis, 1995], 110.) Perhaps this is also meant to be a subtle polemical hint that Babylon is not the "holy city" — only Jerusalem deserves this distinguished title. For the innovation in this term, see Isa 52:1.

And lean for support on the God of Israel — You depend on the God of Israel for your security; cf. Ps 71:6: "While yet in the womb, I leaned for support (נסמכתי) on You." The title אלהי ישראל, which appears in v. 1, is repeated here.

Whose name is the Lord of Hosts — For this appellation, see also Isa 44:6; 45:13; 47:4; 51:15; 54:5. Hebrew שם appears here for the third time (in v. 1 it is repeated twice).

[3-5] The fulfillment of earlier prophecies serves as a precedent that the future prophecies will also come to pass, specifically the promise of redemption. Here, however, instead of using this claim of authenticity in his usual polemic against idolaters and their gods, comparing their impotence with God's omnipotence and omniscience (e.g., 41:21-24; 42:8-9; 43:9-10; 46:9-11), Deutero-Isaiah castigates the people's disbelief and their propensity to attribute the events to their idols. For a similar theme in a Neo-Assyrian prophecy, see Ishtar's prophecy to King Esarhaddon: "[Esarhaddon] . . . you [saw] you could trust my previous statement *(dababu pānīu)* to you. Now you can rely on this latter one *(urkīu)* as well" (Parpola, *Assyrian Prophecies,* 10, lines 3-12). So too in an oracle addressed to King Esarhaddon, the prophetess encourages the king by declaring: *urkīute lu kî pānīute,* "The future ones shall be like the past ones" (ibid., 6, line 37').

[3] *Long ago I foretold things that would happen* — For מאז ("long ago") (repeated three more times throughout this unit, vv. 5, 7, 8), see 44:8; 45:21; cf. Ps 93:2: "Your throne stands firm from long ago (מאז)." For the verbal construction הגיד רִאשֹׁנות, see Isa 41:22; and for the term (ה)ראשֹׁנות, see 41:22; 42:9; 43:9, 18; 46:9; 65:17; and the introduction, §4.)

From My mouth they issued, and I announced them — Vocalize וָאשמיעם in the past tense, parallel to הגדתי in the prior hemistich. For the expression יצא מפה ("to issue from one's mouth"), which signifies a binding and irrevocable proclamation, see 45:23: "From My mouth has issued truth, a word that shall not turn back"; 55:11: "So is the word that issues from My mouth. It does not come back to Me unfulfilled, but performs what I purpose"; cf. Judg 11:36; Jer 44:17. The Akkadian etymological and semantic equivalent, *ṣīt pî,* can also denote an (irrevocable) declaration of a deity (*CAD* P:459; Ṣ:219).

Suddenly I acted, and they came to pass — Cf. Isa 42:9: "See, the things once predicted have come to pass." For the expression בוא פתאֹם ("to come about suddenly") in the context of Babylon's destruction, see 47:11: "Coming upon you suddenly is ruin of which you know nothing"; cf. also, e.g., 30:13; Jer 4:20; 6:26. For the verb עשי ("to act") without an object, see Isa 41:4; 46:4.

[4-5] In a triad of condemnations (v. 4) that emphasizes the absolute obduracy of the Israelite nation, God clarifies that He foretold events so that the people would not attribute their occurrence to their idols. For the connection between stubbornness and idol craftsmanship, see Deut 9:6: "For you are a stiff-

necked people," and immediately following: "They have made themselves a molten image" (v. 16); see also 2 Kgs 17:14-16: "They stiffened their necks . . . they made molten idols for themselves"; Neh 9:17-18: "They stiffened their necks . . . they made themselves a molten calf."

[4] *Because I know how stubborn you are* — God is well aware of the extent of Israel's stubbornness (Exod 32:9; 33:3, 5; Deut 31:27: "Well I know how defiant and stiff-necked you are"; see also Jer 7:26) and their hardness of heart (Ezek 3:7). For the causal *mem* appended to an infinitive construct (מִדַּעְתִּי), cf. Deut 7:8: "It was because the Lord loved you (מֵאַהֲבַת) and kept (וּמִשָּׁמְרוֹ) the oath He made to your fathers." (Although 1QIsa[a] has the variant reading מאשר ידעתי [cf. 43:4: מאשר יקרת בעיני, "Because you are precious to Me"], instead of MT מדעתי, the dots above and below the letters *shin, resh,* and *yod* in the words מאשר ידעתי indicate that the scribe wished to correct what had been written.) For Heb. קשה, "hard, stubborn," cf. also Akk. *dannu,* which shares these same two meanings (*CAD* D:93, 97).

Your neck is like an iron sinew — and since I know that your neck is as stiff and hard as iron. For Heb. גיד ("sinew"), see Gen 32:33; Ezek 37:6, 8. The two words that make up the common biblical metaphor for stubbornness, קְשֵׁה עֹרֶף ("stiff-necked"), were divided here between the two first hemistichs. Note the wordplay between גיד, הגדתי (v. 3), and ואגיד (v. 5).

And your forehead bronze — and because I know that your forehead is as hard as bronze (נחושה, a by-form of נחושת; see, e.g., 45:2). For similar imagery connected with "forehead," see Jer 3:3: "You had the brazenness (מֵצַח) of a harlot"; Ezek 3:7: "Brazen of forehead (מֵצַח)." For the two terms נחושה and מֵצַח ברזל, see Isa 45:2; Job 20:24; 40:18. This clause is chiastically parallel to the previous one.

[5] The first two clauses of this verse (which also form a chiasm) are parallel to v. 3. In his diatribe against Israel, the prophet employs three different terms to refer to the nation's idols.

Therefore I told you long beforehand — For this reason I informed you long ago (מאז) of what was going to happen; cf. Isa 44:8: "Have I not from old (מאז) predicted to you?" For מאז, which functions as a key word in this unit, see also vv. 3, 7, 8.

Announced things to you ere they happened — The subject of the verb תבוא is neutral; such neutral subjects are often expressed in Biblical Hebrew by a feminine singular; cf. Ezek 12:25: "But whenever I the Lord speak what I speak, it shall be fulfilled without any delay (תִּמָּשֵׁךְ)"; Ezek 33:33: "But when it comes (בְּבֹאָהּ) — and come it will (באה)." For the combination of the verbs נגד and שמע, both in the *hiph'il* in consecutive hemistichs, see vv. 6, 20; 41:26; 43:9, 12; 44:7, 8; 45:21.

So that you could not say, "My idol caused them" — So that you might not be able to claim: "My idol brought these events to pass," and not You. The term עָצְבִּי is bivalent and derogatory. On the one hand, the form derived from עֹצֶב, with the meaning of a "crafted image," is a hapax legomenon with the tendentious vocalization בֹּשֶׁת ("shame"), a cacophonous term for an idol. On the other hand, it denotes "pain," as in 1 Chr 4:9: "I bore him in pain (בְּעֹצֶב)"; see also Isa 14:3.

"My carved and molten images ordained them" — For the pair of synonyms פסל and נסך/מסכה, see Deut 27:15: "Cursed be anyone who makes a sculptured or molten image (פסל ומַסֵּכָה)"; Jer 10:14: "Every goldsmith is put to shame, because of his idol (פסל), for his molten image (נִסְכּוֹ) is a deceit." Instead of MT צִוָּם ("ordained them"), both LXX and Peshitta translated "ordained me" (i.e., צִוָּנִי), resulting from the graphic error of dividing the final *mem* into a *nun* and *yod.* (See R. Weiss, *Studies in the Text and Language of the Bible* [Jerusalem, 1981], 13-14 [Heb.].)

[6] It is possible that Jer 33:3: "And I will tell you wondrous things, secrets you have not known (וּבְצֻרוֹת לא יְדַעְתָּם)" left its imprint on the way this verse is phrased.

You have heard all of this — a very difficult clause. Some explain it to mean: You have already heard everything I have announced, now see how it all comes to pass. Luzzatto, however, suggested reversing the order of the words in this clause to interpret it as a question: חזה שמעת כלה, "See, have you not heard all this? Haven't I told you the details of what is to come beforehand?" Ehrlich, on the other hand, was of the opinion that there was a graphic error: The ח in חזה should be read as a ה, and should then be attached to the preceding word: שמעתה זֶה כלה, "You have heard all of this" (Ehrlich, *Randglossen,* 4:175).

Must you not acknowledge it? — Hebrew הלוא often introduces and accentuates rhetorical questions that invite an affirmative answer (see, e.g., Isa 40:28; 44:8, 20; 45:21): "Must you not admit the truth of what I say?" For the verb נגד as indicating acknowledgment or confession, see 3:9: "They avow (והגידו) their sins like Sodom; they do not conceal them"; Ps 38:19: "I acknowledge (אגיד) my iniquity."

As of now I announce to you new things — In addition to the things that I told you long beforehand, which did materialize, I now announce to you new things that have yet to occur, i.e., the prophecies concerning Cyrus, his conquest of Babylon, and the return to Zion. (For רִאשֹׁנוֹת, "past occurrences," and חדשות, "future occurrences," see Isa 42:9; 43:18-19 [חדשה, singular]; and the introduction, §4.)

Secret things that you did not know — I am now going to reveal to you well-guarded secrets of the future, "since there is no way you could know them before they come to pass" (Luzzatto). For the root נצר ("secret, guarded"), see

65:4: "Who sit inside tombs and pass the night in secret places (נצורים)"; Prov 7:10: "Secret minded" (נְצֻרַת לֵב). Some suggest vocalizing as נֹצָרוֹת, the *niph'al* participle of יצר, thus interpreting the verse: I shall announce to you things that have yet to be created (cf. Ehrlich, *Randglossen,* 4:175; Tur-Sinai, *Peshuṭo shel Miqra,* III/1:124; the creation motif is also apparent in the LXX). The verbal sequence שמע . . . ידע appears also in vv. 7 and 8. 1QIsa[a] ידעתן (feminine plural suffix), instead of יְדַעְתָּם (masculine plural), is in accord with the feminine plurals חדשות and נְצֻרוֹת.

[7] *Only now they are created, and not of old* — The adverb עתה (appearing in the preceding verse as well) emphasizes the imminence and suddenness of the events: These events are being conceived now, not in the far past. The verb ברא in Biblical Hebrew always denotes a wondrous creation of the Deity.

Before today you had not heard of them — The momentous events are occurring at this very moment. Some commentators suggest that the text should be emended to וְלְפָנִים, "beforehand" (instead of the anomalous ולפני יום), i.e., previously you had not heard of these momentous occurrences; see 41:26.

Lest you say, "I knew them already" — God did not inform His wayward people of these events until moments before their occurrence, so that they would be unable to say that they already knew they were coming.

[8] Three short hemistichs — all beginning with גם לא (גם serves here as an emphatic particle; cf. the threefold repetition of אף ["even"] in 40:24; 41:26) — utterly reject any pretensions that Israel may have known of the upcoming events and serve as an introduction to the prophet's forthcoming denouncement: "You were called a rebel from birth." This is a complete reversal of their other "callings" by God (vv. 1, 12) and of their being selected and elected "from birth" to fulfill God's mission (e.g., 49:1). Could this be a vague allusion to Jacob, who "in the womb (בבטן) tried to supplant his brother" (Hos 12:4; Yellin, *Ḥiqrei Miqra,* 61)? This castigation is very much akin to other accusations and condemnations; cf., e.g., "Take this to heart, you sinners" (Isa 46:8); "Listen to Me, you stubborn of heart" (46:12). The idea that Israel sinned from their very inception features prominently in Ezek 20:6-36. In light of the motif of divine restraint in v. 9, it is likely that these verses were influenced in one way or another by the prophecy in Ezekiel. (See the introduction, §16.)

You have not heard, nor have you known — these prophecies before I informed you of them. Thus you cannot say: "I knew them already" (v. 7). For the combination of the verbs שמע and ידע, see vv. 6, 7.

Your ears were not opened of old — For "the opening of ears," see 50:5: "The Lord God has opened my ears" (and see the Akkadian cognate there). For another example of the verb פתח in the *pi'el* with a passive force, see 60:11: "Your gates shall always stay open (וּפִתְּחוּ)"; Cant 7:13: "If its blossoms have opened (פִּתַּח)." 1QIsa[a]'s reading of a second-person *qal* singular, פתחת, is a harmonistic simplification and conforms to the previous verbs, שמעת and ידעת. Compare likewise the Targum: לָא אַרְכֵּינְתָּא אוּדְנָךְ, "You did not bend your ear." The LXX translates the verb as a first-person singular, "I have not opened your ears of old," which conforms to the next clause: "For I know that you are treacherous."

For I know that you are treacherous — You were not privy to this information, since I knew that you would capriciously attribute the events to your idols (v. 5) or claim that you knew all along. The infinitive absolute בָּגוֹד preceding the finite verb תבגוד emphasizes the depth of their betrayal and the strength of the rebuke. For the verb בגד signifying the breach of a pact or covenant, see Jer 5:11; Hos 6:7.

And that you were called a rebel from birth — Since you emerged from the womb, i.e., became a nation, you were rebellious; cf. Ps 58:4: "The wicked are defiant from birth. The liars go astray from the womb." For the repeated theme of the nation's sins, see Isa 43:25; 44:22; 53:5, 8, 12; and cf. 46:8: "Take this to heart, you sinners." For the verb פשע signifying rebellion, see 2 Kgs 1:1; 3:7. For קֹרָא, a *qal* archaic passive, see also Isa 58:12; 61:3; 62:2.

[9-11] Instead of punishing His wayward nation, God delivers a shocker and announces that, for His name's sake, He will show restraint and not annihilate them. This abundant mercy is one of God's renowned attributes that is manifest throughout the Bible; see Exod 34:6: "The Lord! The Lord! A God compassionate and gracious, slow to anger, abounding in kindness and faithfulness"; and cf. Num 14:18; Jonah 4:2; Nah 1:3; Ps 86:15; 103:8; 145:8; Neh 9:17. God's forgiving nature is for His name's sake, which is defiled by the nation's protracted exile. See Ezek 20:13-14: "Then I thought to pour out My fury upon them in the wilderness and to make an end of them. But I acted for the sake of My name, that it might not be profaned in the sight of the nations" (see also vv. 8-9, 21-22; 36:22, 26). As noted above, it is highly probable that Deutero-Isaiah was influenced here by Ezekiel. (See the introduction, §16.)

[9] *For the sake of My name I control My wrath* — I am patient and show restraint. For a similar theme, see Isa 43:25: "It is I, I who — for My own sake — wipe your transgressions away." The preposition למען is repeated twice more in v. 11, forming an emphatic triad. For "God's name," see 52:5, 6. The verbal expression האריך אף ("to control one's wrath") appears only once more in the Bible, in Prov 19:11. However, the nominal expression אֶרֶךְ אף is found in Jer 15:15, and ארך אַפַּיִם appears multiple times, e.g., Exod 34:6; Ps 86:15; Neh 9:17.

(For the sake of) My own glory I hold Myself in check — "For the sake of" is drawn from the first hemistich (Ibn Ezra). The Akkadian interdialectal etymological cognate of the hapax legomenon Hebrew verb חטם, *ḫaṭāmu,* refers to "muzzling" the mouth of an individual (*CAD* Ḫ:152; cf. the noun *ḫuṭṭimu,* "muzzle" (ibid., 265), which also appears in Arabic, *ḫiṭām.* Note the possible

bivalency, moreover, since the root חטם can also be related to later Rabbinic Hebrew חֹטֶם, "nose" (thus Rashi, Ibn Ezra, Kimchi), and thus would be synonymous with אף ("nose") in the expression אאריך אפי in the prior hemistich. For the synonymous pair תְהִלָּה/שם, see Ps 102:22; 106:47; and cf. Isa 42:8.

Not to destroy you — so that I will not annihilate you.

[10-11] For the image of refining a nation, see Isa 1:25: "And I will smelt out (ואצרף) your dross as with lye and remove all your slag"; Jer 6:29-30: "The bellows puff; the lead is consumed by fire. Yet the refiner smelts (צָרַף צָרוֹף) to no purpose — the dross is not separated out. They are called 'rejected silver,' for the Lord has rejected them"; Ezek 22:22: "As silver is melted in a crucible, so shall you be melted in it"; Zech 13:9: "And I will refine them as one refines (וצרפתיך כִּצְרֹף) silver and test them as one tests gold"; cf. also Mal 3:2-3. The most striking parallel, however, is Jer 9:6: "Lo, I shall refine (צורפם) and assay them (ובחנתים) — for what else can I do (איך אעשה) because of My people?", which very likely influenced the phraseology of this verse. This threat, according to Deutero-Isaiah, was carried out: the nation was indeed melted and smelted in the crucible of exile and destruction. Deutero-Isaiah contends, however (contra Jeremiah), that this rigorous smelting was done for the sake of God's name. (See the introduction, §15.)

[10] *See, I refined you, but not as silver* — which is put through fire to eliminate the dross; cf. Isa 1:25: "And I will smelt out (ואצרף) your dross" (quoted above). For the prefixed preposition *beth,* meaning "as," see Num 18:10: "You shall partake of them as most sacred donations (בַּקֹּדֶשׁ)." Some commentators suggest that כּוּר, "furnace," in the next clause, is implied here as well, and thus translate: "See, I refined you, but not [in a furnace in which one refines] silver"; cf. Prov 17:3; 27:21: "For silver — the crucible; for gold the furnace." The Akkadian etymological and semantic equivalent, *ṣarāpu,* also denotes the smelting of metals (*CAD* Ṣ:102), and the noun *ṣarpu* means "silver" (ibid., 113-14).

I tested you in the furnace of affliction — The furnace in which you were "refined" is metaphorical: You suffered the destruction of Jerusalem and languished in exile for many years. For a "furnace" as an image for affliction and hardship, see Deut 4:20: "But you the Lord took and brought out of Egypt, that iron blast furnace"; cf. 1 Kgs 8:51; Jer 11:4. For the Aramaic verb בחר, which denotes refining and testing, see Job 36:21: "Because of that you have been tried (בחרת) by affliction"; cf. also Targum Jonathan to Gen 42:15: "By this you shall be put to test," where Heb. תִּבָּחֵנוּ is translated תִּתְבָּחֲרוּן; and Targum Jonathan to Zech 13:9: "And test them as one tests gold," where ובחנתים is translated וְאֶבְחֲרִינוּן. Perhaps the prophet chose this verb (בחר) in order to create a wordplay with בְּכוּר. (For other instances of Aramaic influence on Deutero-Isaiah's language, see the introduction, §11.A.) The substitution of the Hebrew verb בחנתיכה in 1QIsa[a] for Aram. בחרתיך creates a parallelism between בחן

and צרף, as in Zech 13:9; see also Ps 66:10: "You have tried us (בחנתנו), O God, refining us (צרפתנו) as one refines silver." The prophet's choice of the term עֳנִי ("affliction") refers to the hardships the nation suffered at the time of their exile; see Lam 1:7, 9; 3:1, 19.

[11] This first literary unit concludes with a poignant declaration that the Deity will spare the nation so that His name will not be dishonored. As noted above, these verses and this theme were likely influenced by similar ideas in Ezekiel: "But I acted for the sake of My name, that it might not be profaned in the sight of the nations" (Ezek 20:9, 14, 22); and cf. Ezek 36:22.

For My sake, My own sake, do I act — an emphatic reiteration of למעני (for other examples see v. 15; 40:1; 43:11, 25; 51:12, 17; 52:1, 11), which, together with למען שמי ("for the sake of My name") in v. 9, creates a triad (cf. also the threefold repetition of למען in 45:3, 4, 6). God assertively and resolutely declares that He is not sparing the nation for their sake, nor for the sake of their fathers, but rather that He is acting only because it is imperative for Him that His name not be defiled. For other instances of the verb עשׂי ("to act") without an object, see v. 3; 41:4; 44:23.

Lest (My name) be dishonored! — I will not tolerate My name being defiled in the eyes of the nations (cf. Ezek 20:9, 14, 22; 36:21-23). יֵחָל is the pausal form of the third-person masculine singular imperfect *niph'al,* from the root חלל; cf. Ezek 22:26: "I am profaned (וָאֵחַל) in their midst." The LXX adds "My name" to the elliptical MT, as does one medieval Hebrew manuscript. 1QIsa[a], 4QIsa[c], and 4QIsa[d] all read איחל, the *plene* writing of the first-person masculine *niph'al,* "Lest I be defiled." For the defilement of God's name, see Isa 52:5.

And I will not give My glory to another — I shall not share My glory with another god. Cf. 42:8: "I am the Lord, that is My name. I will not yield My glory (כבודי) to another, nor My renown to idols." God's "glory" is His name and renown; see v. 9.

[12-19] The second literary unit, like the first (v. 1), begins with the divine imperative, "Listen!" with Israel as the subject. This same imperative is directed toward the nations in v. 14, and in v. 16 to both Israel and the nations; cf. also v. 20. Other links between the first two units are the terms צדקה (v. 1) and צדקתך (v. 18); the roots קרא (vv. 1, 2, 8, 12, 13, 15) and כרת (vv. 9, 19); the conjunction אף (vv. 12, 13, 15; but note the divergent usages); the adverb [מ]עתה (vv. 6, 7, 16); the substantives רִאשֹׁנוֹת (v. 3), ראשון (v. 12), and מראש (v. 16); and cf. also ממ(ע)י (יהודה) (v. 1) and מֵעֶיךָ (v. 19). This pericope is also characterized by an emphasis on the first-person pronoun אני, repeated eight times: vv. 12 (three times), 13, 15 (twice), 16, 17. In this literary unit the eternal God (v. 12), creator of all (v. 13), declares that He called on Cyrus to work His will against Babylon (vv. 14-16). The unit concludes with a divine blessing on Israel's posterity if they would only heed His commandments (vv. 17-19).

[12] *Listen to Me, O Jacob, and Israel whom I have called!* — מְקֹרָאִי is an archaic *qal* passive participle: He whom I have called by name, i.e., whom I have chosen; see vv. 1, 2; 41:9: "I called you . . . I chose you"; and cf. the Akkadian cognate *nibīt ili* ("He whom god has called," i.e., "has chosen") (Seux, *Épithètes royales*, 205-6). The reading in 1QIsa[a], אלה ("[Listen] to these"), contra MT אלי ("to Me"), accords with v. 14: "Who among you foretold these things (אלה)?"

"I am He" — See 41:4; 43:10, 13; 46:4; 52:6; in each the pronoun "He" refers to God.

"I am the first and I am the last as well" — For this merism emphasizing the eternality of God, see also 41:4: "I, the Lord, who was the first, and I am He with the last as well"; 44:6: "I am the first and I am the last." For אף as an emphatic, see, e.g., vv. 13, 15; 40:24 (three times); 41:10 (twice), 23, 26 (three times); 42:13.

[13] *"My own hand founded the earth"* — The emphatic אף is again repeated: I alone established the foundations of the earth with My very own hand; see 40:21; 51:13, 16. 1QIsa[a] יסדו (plural) indicates that the scribe understood Heb. ידי to be in the plural.

"And My right hand spread out the skies" — The hapax legomenon denominative verb טִפְּחָה (derived from טֶפַח/טֹפַח, "handbreadth"; see Exod 25:25; 1 Kgs 7:26) is a technical architectural term, which Luzzatto correctly interpreted: "It appears to me that it [the verb] is akin to 'from foundation to coping' (ממסד עד הטפחות) (1 Kgs 7:9), since here he [the prophet] used 'founded' (יסדה) when he referred to the earth, which is at the base like a foundation, and 'spread' (טפחה) when he referred to the sky, which is like a ceiling above." (There is no connection between this verb and its homonym in Lam 2:22.) For other architecturally inspired descriptions of the cosmogony, see Amos 9:6: "Who built His chambers in heaven and founded His vault on the earth"; Ps 24:2: "For He founded it upon the ocean, set it on the nether streams"; and especially Job 38:4-6. The other verbs employed in connection with the sky are: נטי ("to spread"; Isa 40:22; 42:5; 44:24; 45:12; 51:13), מתח ("to stretch"; 40:22), and נטע ("to plant"; 51:16). The nominal pair שמים/ארץ, usually appearing in the opposite order, ארץ/שמים (42:5; 44:24; 45:18; 51:13, 16), is another merism expressing totality. For the parallelism ימין/יד, found also in Ugaritic: *yd . . . ymn* (e.g., *CAT* 1.15.II:17-18), see Judg 5:26: "Her hand (ידה) reached for the tent pin, her right hand (וימינה) for the workman's hammer"; Ps 89:14: "Your hand (ידך) is strong, your right hand (ימינך), exalted."

"I call to them, 'Let them stand up together'!" — The verb עמד in this context has legal connotations, as does its Akkadian semantic equivalent, *uzzuzu* (*CAD*, U/W: 378-79); e.g., 44:11: "Let them all assemble and stand up (יעמדו)"; 50:8: "Who dares contend with me? Let us stand up (ונעמדה) together." God calls on the sky and the earth to bear witness in the proceedings against Israel; cf. Deut 32:1; Isa 1:2; and Ps 50:4: "He summons the heavens above, and the

earth, for the trial of His people." If this clause, however, functions as an introduction to the following verse, then the call to "them" is a reference to the nations of v. 14 (and not to the sky and the earth) to stand trial. (The verb עמד replaces קום in Late Biblical Hebrew. See the introduction, §11.B.)

[14] *Assemble, all of you, and listen!* — The trial commences: God calls on the nations to heed His claims. For "assembling" (here in the *niph'al*) in a legal context, see 43:9: "All the nations assemble (נקבצו) as one"; 44:11: "Let them all assemble (יתקבצו) and stand up" (note the עמד-קבץ sequence, also in vv. 13-14); 45:20: "Come, gather together (הִקָּבְצוּ), draw nigh." (The Akkadian semantic cognate, *paḫāru*, "to gather, to assemble," also appears in legal contexts [*CAD* P:24, 28].) 1QIsa[a] יקבצו כולם וישמעו (third-person masculine plural imperfect, instead of MT second-person masculine imperatives; cf. LXX) accords with the final clause of v. 13: "Let them stand up!" and with the following clause in this verse: "Who among you?" (however, see below).

Who among you foretold these things? — a rhetorical, polemical question implying a negative answer (cf. 40:12, 13, 14): Who among the gods foretold Cyrus's ascent and his conquest of Babylon? The Peshitta and many medieval Hebrew manuscripts read בכם (the second-person masculine plural suffix) contra MT בהם (third-person masculine plural suffix), which conforms better with the beginning of the verse: כלכם ("all of you"). However, some commentators accept the abrupt transition from the second-person masculine to the third-person masculine since it is attested in other passages, e.g., 1 Kgs 22:28 (= Mic 1:2 = 2 Chr 18:27): "Listen [שִׁמְעוּ — second-person plural imperative], nations, all of them [כלם, third-person masculine plural]."

"He whom the Lord loves" — an asyndetic relative clause, with which the prophet begins to foretell the future events. The expression referring to Cyrus indicates divine choice, and its semantic analogues are well documented in royal Mesopotamian inscriptions, the most common being *narām ili,* "the beloved of god" (Seux, *Épithètes royales,* 189-96). The choice of this terminology was very likely irksome to the people since the subjects of God's love (אהב) heretofore were Abraham (Isa 41:8), Israel (43:4), and Solomon (2 Sam 12:24), all members of the Israelite nation, while here, according to Deutero-Isaiah, God is conferring His love on a foreign king. 1QIsa[a] reads אוהבי ("My beloved"); cf. Isa 41:8. (See Paul, *Divrei Shalom,* 12.)

"Shall work His will against Babylon" — Cyrus shall do as God has planned and will conquer Babylon; cf. 44:28: "I who say of Cyrus, 'He is My shepherd. He shall fulfill all My purposes!'" The expression עשׂי חֵפֶץ ("to fulfill a purpose") is also found in 46:10; 55:11; its Akkadian semantic equivalent, *ṣibûtam epēšu,* also denotes executing a mission (*CAD* Ṣ:169). 1QIsa[a] reads חפצי ("My will"), which accords with its other reading, אוהבי, in the previous hemistich.

"And with His might against Chaldea" — The preposition *beth* of the preceding clause, בבבל, is implied here as well. God shall bring "His arm" (i.e., His might; see 40:10; 51:5, 9; 52:10) to bear against the Babylonians. For other examples of the parallelism "Babylon/Chaldea," see v. 20; 43:14. The LXX translates "His seed" (זַרְעוֹ) instead of זְרֹעוֹ ("His arm" = might), meaning that Cyrus shall do God's bidding against the Chaldean seed. This reading would then contrast the fate of the Chaldean seed and the fate of the Israelite seed, which, according to v. 19, "would be as many as the sand."

[15] God answers His own rhetorical questions with overwhelming vigor. The personal pronoun אני is repeated twice and is followed by a series of four verbs, all in the first person: the first three refer to Cyrus's mission, and the fourth to its successful execution. This is the final allusion to Cyrus in the prophecies of Deutero-Isaiah.

"I, I predicted, and I called him" — an emphatic repetition of the first-person pronoun (see v. 11 and the introduction, §10.A.1), further accentuated by the conjunction אף (see also vv. 12, 13): I and I alone predicted Cyrus's coming; see 46:11: "I summoned that swooping bird from the east . . . I have spoken, so I will bring it to pass." (Note in this last verse that the same three verbs appear as they do here and in the following clauses: קרא, דבר, הביא.)

"I have brought him and he shall succeed in his mission" — For the expression הצליח דרך ("to bring a mission to a successful conclusion"), see Gen 24:21, 40, 42, 56; Deut 28:29 (in the negative). The LXX, Peshitta, and Targum all read here the first-person singular, "I shall make successful," which complements the first three verbs, also in the first person.

[16] *"Draw near to Me and hear this!"* — The drama continues and God calls on Israel and the nations to draw near and pay close attention to His claims. For the legal connotations of the verb קרב, see Isa 41:1, 5, 21. For the repetition of the verb שמע in the imperative throughout the chapter, see the introduction to the chapter.

"From the beginning I did not speak in secret" — Transpose the negative לא to follow מֵרֹאשׁ; cf. 45:19: "I did not speak in secret." For מֵרֹאשׁ see 40:21; 41:4, 26.

"From the time anything existed I was there" — The referent of the feminine pronominal suffix attached to the infinitive construct (הֱיוֹתָהּ) is unspecified and difficult to ascertain. It has been interpreted as "from when it first began"; hence "from the time anything existed" My presence was manifest; cf. Prov 8:27: "I was there (שם אני) when He set the heavens into place."

"And now the Lord God has sent me with His spirit" — This is one of the very few verses where the prophet speaks in the first person. See, e.g., 61:1: "The spirit of the Lord God is upon me. . . . He has sent me as a herald to the humble." For a similar statement of the prophetic mission, see Zech 7:12: "They hardened

their hearts like adamant against heeding the instruction and admonition that the Lord of Hosts sent (שלח) to them by His spirit (ברוחו) through the earlier prophets." Some commentators suggest emending ורוחו (lit. "and His spirit") to ברוחו (as it appears in Zechariah). (See already Ibn Balaam [ed. Goshen-Gottstein], 198; Saadyah, 109; Ibn Ganaḥ, *Sefer ha-Riqmah,* 71.) For רוח referring to the prophetic spirit, see Isa 42:1; Num 11:17, 25, 26; and for the appellation אֲדֹנָי ה׳, see Isa 40:10; 50:4, 5, 7, 9; 52:4; 61:1.

[17] *Thus said the Lord your Redeemer, the Holy One of Israel* — For the divine attributes גואל and קדוש ישראל in conjunction, see 41:14; 43:14; 47:4; 49:7; 54:5. (See the introduction, §9.)

"I the Lord am your God instructing you for your own benefit" — For the verb להועיל, albeit in a negative context, referring to the lack of benefit idols confer on their most ardent worshipers, see 44:9, 10; 47:12; 57:12.

"Guiding you in the way you should go" — The root דרך appears here both as a verb and as a substantive. For this expression, see also Ps 107:7; cf. above, Isa 42:16. For the synonymous verbal pair למד (in the previous hemistich)/הדריך, see Ps 25:5, 9. For the connection between this clause and the beginning of the next verse, see below.

[18-19] Israel's prosperity is dependent on their fulfillment of the divine commandments. This is the first time that the message of contingency is found in his prophecies.

[18] This verse, together with the last clause of v. 17, is very similar to Ps 81:14: "If only (לוּ) My people would listen to Me; if Israel would follow My paths."

"If only you would heed My commands!" — לוּא introduces a conditional clause, expressing a wish, sometimes referring to the past or the present; cf. Num 14:2: "If only (לוּ) we had died in the land of Egypt; or if only (לוּ) we might die in this wilderness!"; Num 20:3: "If only (ולוּ) we had perished when our brothers perished at the instance of the Lord!" See also Isa 63:19; Ps 81:14 (cited above). This is the only time God's "commands" are mentioned in this prophetic corpus.

"Then your prosperity would be like a river" — For the image of God's blessing as ever-flowing water, see Isa 66:12: "I will extend to her prosperity like a stream, the wealth of nations like a wadi in flood." For the parallelism שלום/צדק(ה) (צדקה appears in the adjacent hemistich), see 54:13-14; 60:17; Ps 72:3; 85:11.

"Your triumph like the waves of the sea" — Your success shall be like the never-ending waves of the ocean. This hemistich is chiastically parallel to the preceding one. For the parallelism ים/נהר (common in Ugaritic: *ym/nhr;* see, e.g., *CAT* 1.2.III:16), see Isa 19:5; Ps 24:2.

[19] For the blessing of abundant progeny, see Isa 44:3-4; 54:1. The emendation suggested above, וממ[ע]י יהודה יצאו (v. 1), and מֵעֶיךָ (v. 19), along with בשם (v. 1) and שמו (v. 19), בצדקה (v. 1) and צדקתך (v. 18), create a literary frame that encompasses the first two units of the chapter.

"Your offspring would be as many as the sand" — The verb ויהי, repeated from the former verse, introduces an additional blessing (that of multiple progeny) in language very much akin to the patriarchal promises. Cf. Gen 22:17: "I will bestow My blessing on you and make your descendants as numerous as the stars of heaven and the sands on the seashore"; Gen 32:12: "I will deal bountifully with you and make your offspring as the sands of the sea, which are too numerous to count"; Hos 2:1: "The number of the people of Israel shall be like that of the sands of the sea, which cannot be measured or counted."

"And your posterity as many as its grains" — literally, "the issue of your loins" (see Gen 15:4; 2 Sam 7:12; 16:11) shall be as infinite as the motes of sand on the beach. The hapax legomenon מְעֹתָיו (from מָעָה, "grain," which creates a play on words with the immediately preceding מעיך, "your inner organs") is an Aramaic loanword, which in Targumic Aramaic translates various biblical currencies and weights, e.g., גֵּרָה (Exod 30:13), אגורה (1 Sam 2:36), and קְשִׂיטָה (Job 42:11). Here it denotes minuscule grains of sand. (For the Aramaic influence on Deutero-Isaiah's prophecy, see the introduction, §11.A.) For זרע and צאצאים as parallel terms (here forming a chiastic parallelism) in the context of divine blessings, see Isa 44:3: "Even as I pour water on thirsty soil and rain upon dry ground, so I will pour My spirit on your offspring (זרעך), My blessing on your posterity (צאצאיך)"; cf. 61:9; 65:23.

"Their name would never be cut off or obliterated from before Me" — Israel would then exist for eternity. Hebrew שֵׁם here has the same connotation as זרע ("offspring") in the first hemistich. For the two together, see 66:22; זרעכם ושמכם. So too in Akkadian, where the etymological and semantic cognate *šumu* also denotes "offspring" and is coupled with *zēru*, "progeny" (*CAD* Š/3:295). The two are also coupled together (זרע/שם) in Aramaic inscriptions (*KAI* 225:10-11; 228 A:14, 22). For the nonobliteration of a name as a metaphor for eternity, see 56:5: "I will give them an everlasting name that shall not perish (יִכָּרֵת)." For the verbal pair השמיד/כרת ("to cut off/to obliterate") in a similar context of posterity, see 1 Sam 24:22: "So swear to me by the Lord that you will not destroy (תכרית) my descendants or wipe out (תשמיד) my name from my father's house." The LXX reads the second-person masculine singular pronominal suffix, שמך, in lieu of MT שמו (the third-person masculine singular suffix), which accords with the other substantives in this verse. For the verbal construction כרת מִלְּפָנַי ("to be obliterated before Me"), see Lev 22:3; 1 Kgs 8:25; Jer 33:18; and for the similar שמד מִפָּנַי ("to be cut off before Me"), see Deut 2:12.

[20-21] The final pericope of this chapter (which is also the last unit of the first section in Deutero-Isaiah) begins with an emotional exhortation (consisting of six imperatives) directed at Israel, commanding them to leave Babylon posthaste and to announce with joyous shouts their salvation to the rest of the world. (For the victory song of the people as they go forth from Babylon, see 42:9-10, and cf. also Exod 15, the Song of the Sea.) The desert miracles, which helped sustain the nation following the exodus from Egypt, will now be repeated on their trek through the Syrian Desert. (For other links between the Babylonian exodus [v. 20] and the Egyptian exodus [v. 21], cf. 43:16-20 and the introduction, §12.) The motif of water creates a literary link with the previous unit, where water served as a simile for success and prosperity (v. 18). God as Israel's "Redeemer" is another theme both units share: "Thus said the Lord your Redeemer" (v. 17); "The Lord has redeemed His servant Jacob" (v. 20). Note also the linguistic connections between this unit and Deut 32:1-4: **הַשמִיעו** (v. 20) — **ותשמע** (Deut 32:1); **הִזִּיל** (v. 21) — **תִּזַּל** (Deut 32:2); **צור/מְצוּר** (v. 21) — **הצור** (Deut 32:4).

[20] *Go forth from Babylon! Hasten away from Chaldea!* — This is not a fearful escape, as it was from Egypt, but rather a proud and joyous departure. The verb **ברח** here does not denote "fleeing," but rather refers to leaving swiftly. This was already seen by Kimchi, quoting his father, who referred to Jonah 1:3, 10, to which can also be added Amos 7:12; Cant 8:14. This specific verb, moreover, was chosen in order to allude to Israel's exodus from Egypt: "When the king of Egypt was told that the people had fled (**ברח**)" (Exod 14:5). Compare this urgent call to other commands to flee Babylon: Isa 52:11: "Turn, turn away! Depart from there! Go forth from its midst!"; Jer 50:8: "Flee from Babylon! Leave the land of the Chaldeans!"; Jer 51:6: "Flee from the midst of Babylon and save your lives, each of you!" (cf. also v. 45 in the same chapter). For the parallelism "Babylon/Chaldea," see v. 14.

Declare with shouts of joy! Announce this! Proclaim it to the ends of the earth! — In a vibrant series of three imperatives, the nation is commanded to declare "this" (their salvation) to the entire world. For the *hiph'il* of the verb **יצא** with the meaning "announce, proclaim," see 42:1, 3; Neh 6:19. Note the wordplay here between **הוציאוּהָ . . . צְאו**. The imperative expressions become progressively longer in length: **הַגידו**, **הַשמִיעו זאת**, **הוציאוּהָ עד קצה הארץ** (note the alliteration of sibilants), and finally (in the next hemistich), **אִמרו גאל ה׳ עבדו יעקב**. For this same stylistic principle, see Isa 49:19. The expression **קול רִנָּה** ("joyous shouts") appears several times in the Psalms, e.g., Ps 42:5; 47:2; 118:15; and for the verbal expression **קול רנן**, see Isa 52:8: "Hark! Your watchmen raise their voices, as one they shout for joy"; 24:14: "They shall lift up their voices joyously." For the combination of imperatives, **הַגידו**, **הַשמִיעו**, and **אִמרו** (next hemistich), see also Jer 4:5; 5:20; 46:14; 50:2.

Say: "The Lord has redeemed His servant Jacob!" — Following the three imperatives of the previous hemistich, God, with a final, fourth, imperative, reveals the gist of His celebratory announcement, the redemption of Israel (see Isa 41:8; 44:1, 21). The LXX translates "His nation" (**עמו**), contra MT **עבדו** ("His servant"); cf. Ps 78:71. For other appearances of salvation and joy in tandem, see Isa 44:23; 52:9.

[21] *They have known no thirst, though He led through parched places* — The Israelites were never in need of potable water, despite their forced trek through the arid desert, since divine providence was never lacking. This motif (which also appears in 41:17-18; 43:20; 49:10) reflects, of course, the Egyptian exodus (see below). Note that בֶּחֳרָבוֹת is not to be derived from חָרְבָּה/חֳרָבוֹת, "ruins" (see 44:26; 49:19; 52:9), but rather from חֹרֶב/חָרָבָה, "dryness, dry ground," and should be vocalized בֶּחָרָבוֹת; cf. Exod 14:21: "And turned the sea into dry ground (לֶחָרָבָה)"; Josh 3:17: "While all Israel crossed over on dry land (בֶּחָרָבָה)"; Ezek 30:12: "I will turn channels into dry ground (חָרָבָה)." Could the use of the term in this specific context also be a veiled allusion to the miracle in the desert? "I will be standing there before you on the rock at Horeb (חֹרֵב). Strike the rock and water will issue from it and the people will drink!" (Exod 17:6). For *beth* denoting "although," see Isa 47:9, 13; Num 14:11; Deut 1:32.

He made water flow for them from the rock — God caused water to spring from a dry rock. (The term צור appears in similar contexts in Exod 17:6; Ps 78:15, 20; 105:41; 114:8. According to a variant tradition, the water gushed forth from a סלע ["rock"]; see Num 20:8, 10, 11; Ps 78:16; Neh 9:15.) 1QIsa[a] reads הזיב (from the root זוב, "to flow, gush," the only occurrence of this verb in the *hiph'il;* for the *qal* see the verses cited in the following hemistich), in lieu of MT הִזִּיל (the *hiph'il* of נזל ["to flow, trickle"] which also appears only here; for the *qal* see Isa 45:8: "Let the heavens trickle [יִזְּלוּ] down victory"). The scroll's version was no doubt influenced by the adjacent clause, where the verb וַיָּזֻבוּ occurs, since both clauses also share two other terms, מים and צור. למו is the poetic form of the preposition *lamed,* plus the third-person masculine plural pronominal suffix; cf. 43:8. Note the alliterative mimation in this clause: מים מצור הזיל למו.

He cleaved the rock and water gushed forth — Cf. Ps 78:15-20: "He split rocks (יְבַקַּע צֻרִים) in the wilderness. . . . He brought forth streams from a rock. . . . He struck the rock (צור) and waters flowed (וַיָּזֻבוּ מים)"; 105:41: "He opened a rock (צור), so the water gushed forth (וַיָּזֻבוּ מים)." This clause is chiastically parallel to the preceding one.

[22] *There is no safety — said the Lord — for the wicked* — An editorial conclusion to the chapter (copied word for word from Isa 57:21; see the comments there for the influence of Jeremiah), which marks this unit as the final segment of the first of the three large sections in this prophetic book. The verse (when secondarily interpreted as part of the unit) is a threat against the wicked among the expatriates, those who willfully refuse to heed the prophet's call to leave Babylon. They shall have no "safety" (שלום). For those who observe God's laws, however, their שלום shall be "like a river" (v. 18). For the expression אין שלום, see Jer 6:14; 8:11; 12:12; Ezek 7:25; 13:10.

Chapter 49

From chap. 49 onward the prophecies are set within Jerusalem and reflect the situation of the nation after the return from Babylon. The motifs of the first section of prophecies, which were delivered while the prophet was still in Babylonia, are absent from chaps. 49–66, i.e., there is no mention of the exclusiveness and unity of the Deity, no polemic against idolatry and their worshipers, no mention of judicial proceedings against the nations, and no arguments for God's omniscience and omnipotence as proven by His work in history and nature. Moreover, there is no reference to either Babylon or Cyrus as God's agent in bringing about the deliverance of Israel. Furthermore the two names, "Jacob and Israel," oft-repeated in chaps. 40–48, do not feature here at all, except for 49:5, 6.

Despite the controversy regarding the number of literary units in this chapter, three separate pericopes are recognizable: vv. 1-13, 14-23, 24-26. The first two units are linked to each other by a shared terminology: **מִבטן** (v. 1) — **בטנהּ** (v. 15); **מְרחמם** (v. 10), **ירחם** (v. 13) — **מֵרחם** (v. 15); **גוים** (v. 6) — **גוים** (v. 22); **שׂרים, מלכים, ישתחוו** (v. 7) — **מלכים, שׂרותיהם, וישתחוו** (v. 23); **שֹׁמֵמוֹת** (v. 8) — **וְשֹׁמְמֹתַיִךְ** (v. 19); **לאסורים** (v. 9) — **סורה** (=**אסורה**) (v. 21); **צֵאוּ** (v. 9) — **יֵצֵאוּ** (v. 17); **אלה** (v. 12) — **אלה** (v. 21), both thrice repeated and referring to the returning expatriates. The first unit begins with a description of the appointment of the Deity's servant (= Israel) and concludes with the motif of return (vv. 12-13); the second unit features natal imagery (v. 15) and also ends with repatriation (vv. 22-23). In both pericopes the people's complaint regarding their frustration (vv. 4a, 14) is followed by a message of encouragement (vv. 4b, 15), and in both a sudden reversal is described in which the tyrants who ruled the downtrodden nation will bow down prostrate (vv. 7, 23); finally, both speak of an exodus — Israel's departure from Babylonia (v. 9) and an exodus of their enemies from Zion (v. 17). Several terms are repeated more than once in this first unit: מרחוק (vv. 1, 12), להקים (vv. 6, 8), ישועה/ישועתי (vv. 6, 8). For a discussion regarding the final unit see vv. 24-26.

The initial pericope is connected to the previous chapter by many thematic and linguistic links: the root שמע (48:1, 3, 5, 8, 12, 14, 16, 20; 49:1); the parallelism "Jacob/Israel" (48:1, 12; 49:5, 6); הנקראים בשם ישראל (48:1), ופֹשֵׁעַ
מבטן קֹרָא לך (48:8) — ה׳ מִבטן קראני (49:1); ובאלהי ... ממ(ע)י יהודה יצאו
ישראל יזכירו (48:1), צאצאי מֵעיך (48:19) — מִמעי אמי הזכיר שמי (49:1);
מבטן קֹרָא לך (48:8) — מבטן קראני (49:1); בחרתיך (48:10) — ויבחרך (49:7;
two different meanings); מעת (48:16) — בעת (49:8); כה אמר ה׳ גֹּאַלְךָ קדוש
ישראל (48:17) — קְדֹשׁ ישראל ... כה אמר ה׳ גֹּאֵל ישראל קדושו (49:7);
מדריכך בדרך תלך (48:17) — על דרכים (49:9), ושׂמתי כל הרי לדרך (49:11);
לוא הקשבת למצותי (48:18) — והקשיבו (49:1); מֵעֶיךָ כִּמְעֹוֹתָיו (48:19) — מִמְּעֵי
(49:1); צאו מבבל (48:20) — לאמר לאסורים צְאו (49:9); עד קצה ... בקול רנה
הארץ (48:20) — רָנו שמים וגילי ארץ (49:13), עד קצה הארץ (49:6); עבדו יעקב
(48:20) — עבדי אתה (49:3), לעֶבֶד לו (49:5), מהיותך לי עבד (49:6), עבד
מֹשלים (49:7); ולא צמאו (48:21) — ולא יצמאו (49:10); מים מצור הזיל למו
(48:21) — ועל מבועי מים ינהלֵם (49:10).

This chapter is reminiscent of the prophecy of doom in Jer 13:18ff., which features many of the same images and phraseology (e.g., the imminent arrival of the enemy, the people's subjugation, and the exile), but which Deutero-Isaiah reverses into a prophecy of restoration and rehabilitation:

Isaiah 49	**Jeremiah 13**
vv. 9-10: God is described as a shepherd leading His flock back to Zion	v. 20: Imagery of a flock
v. 18: Raise your eyes all around you and see! They are all assembled, coming back to you — the return of Israel	v. 20: Raise your eyes and see those who are coming from the north! — the arrival of the enemy
v. 21: And you will say to yourself — Zion's astonishment at the return of her children	v. 22: And when you say to yourself — the shock at the destruction of Jerusalem
vv. 20-21: Zion, who was bereaved and desolate, is bemused at the number of her children returning: "Who raised them?" she asks	v. 21: Shall not pangs seize you like a woman in labor — the disaster and desolation are compared to the suffering of a woman in the throes of childbirth
v. 21: Astonishment of exiled Zion	v. 19: Judah is exiled completely, all of it is exiled

Isaiah 49	**Jeremiah 13**
v. 23: Kings shall tend your children. Their princesses shall serve you as nurses. They shall bow to you, face to the ground, and lick the dust of your feet	v. 18: Say to the king and the queen mother, "Sit in a lowly spot!"

(See P. T. Willey, *Remember the Former Things: The Recollection of Previous Texts in Second Isaiah,* SBLDS 161 [Atlanta, 1997], 203-4; and the introduction, §15.)

The first part of the initial pericope is usually referred to as the second Servant Song. (See the introduction, §5.) The servant (vv. 3, 5, 6, 7), identified explicitly as the nation (v. 3), is the speaker, whereas in the first Servant Song God addresses His devoted servant in the third person (42:1ff.). For the motif of the prenatal selection and election of the servant (vv. 1, 5, 8; 42:6; 43:1; 44:2, 24; 46:3), cf. also the Samson birth narrative (esp. Judg 13:7) and Samuel's prenatal appointment as a nazirite (as attested to by the LXX and the Samuel scroll from Qumran — 4Q51 2:3 = v. 22) (see F. M. Cross et al., eds., *Qumran Cave 4.XII: 1-2 Samuel,* DJD 17 [Oxford, 2005], 31). The most striking parallel, however, is found in Jeremiah: "Before I created you in the womb, I selected you. Before you were born, I consecrated you. I appointed you a prophet to the nations" (Jer 1:5). (See Paul, *Divrei Shalom,* 399-416.) This concept of appointment and mission is very common in the royal inscriptions of Mesopotamia, which often state that the king was selected to rule even before he was born. Compare, e.g., the inscription of Nabonidus, the last king of Babylon and Deutero-Isaiah's contemporary: "The gods ordained his rule while still in the womb of his mother." (For multiple examples, see: Paul, *Divrei Shalom,* 18-22. For the same motif in Egyptian documents, see Hellmut Brunner, "Egyptian Texts," in W. Beyerlin, ed., *Near Eastern Religious Texts Relating to the Old Testament,* trans. J. Bowden, OTL [Philadelphia, 1978], 27-30.) Despite the literary and thematic similarities between Jeremiah, the Mesopotamian kings, and the servant, there are two major differences: As opposed to Jeremiah, who was an individual chosen as "a prophet to the nations," Israel was chosen to be a prophet-nation; and as opposed to the Babylonian and Assyrian kings, who were preordained to rule the nations of the world, Israel was chosen for a spiritual destiny, to be "a light unto the nations."

[1] *Listen to me, O coastlands! And give heed, O nations far away!* — a call to the distant coastlands to heed the message of the servant (cf. 66:19: "the distant coastlands"). For the parallel pair לאֻמים/איים, see 41:1; and for the synonyms הקשיבו/שמעו, see 28:23. For the term מרחוק, see v. 12; 43:6.

The Lord called me from birth — literally "while in (my mother's) belly";

see v. 5; 44:2, 24. Compare the Assyrian monarch Ashurbanipal's claim to the throne: "I Ashurbanipal . . . whom Assur and Sin . . . had called by name in the distant past for ruling, and who had created him in his mother's womb for the shepherding of Assyria" (see Paul, *Divrei Shalom,* 19). For other "calls" that are de facto appointments, see 41:9; 42:6; 43:1.

He named me while I was in my mother's womb — The expression הזכיר שם ("to name") is the interdialectal etymological and semantic equivalent of Akk. *šumam zakāru,* which appears in these royal inscriptions describing the divine preordination of kings. For the parallel synonyms מְעֵי אמי/בטן, both of which signify "womb," see Gen 25:23: "Two nations are in your belly (בבטנך). Two peoples shall issue from your womb (ממעיך)"; Ps 71:6: "From birth (מבטן) I depended on You. In the womb (ממעי) of my mother You were my support." For the same sequence of verbs, זכר . . . קרא . . . שמע, see 48:1.

[2] The servant (i.e., the nation), armed with his potent message, is protected and shielded by God. For the two weapons, חרב ("sword, dagger") used for close contact, and חץ ("arrow"), a projectile weapon, see Deut 32:42: "I will make My arrows (חצי) drunk with blood. My sword (חרבי) shall devour flesh." Both weapons are also used as metaphors for sharp rhetoric, as in Ps 57:5: "Whose teeth are spears and arrows, whose tongue is a sharp sword"; cf. also Jer 9:7; Ps 64:4. For placing the Deity's message in the prophet's mouth, see Isa 51:16; Jer 1:9.

He made my mouth like a sharpened dagger — חרב refers here to a knife that can be concealed in the palm of one's hand; cf. Josh 5:3: "Flint knives (חרבות)"; and Ehud ben Gera's dagger, which he hid beneath his clothing (Judg 3:16, 22). This image is also a play on words, since the expression פי חרב (cf. Deut 13:16) denotes the blade of a dagger (cf. the Akkadian etymological and semantic equivalent, *pû* [*CAD* P:470]). And here that which issues from the prophet's "mouth" is likened to a sharp dagger. The adjective חדה ("sharp") appears in three other places in the Bible (Ezek 5:1; Ps 57:5; Prov 5:4), and in each it is used to describe a sword. For the same image in Akkadian, *patru šēlu,* "a sharp dagger," see *BWL,* 146, line 52. The metaphor of a sword appears also in the Gilgamesh Epic, when Gilgamesh mourns the death of his loyal companion Enkidu, whom he describes as "the sword in my belt, the shield in front of me" (VIII.ii:5; *CAD* N/1:246).

He hid me in the shadow of His hand — God hid and protected me as one who conceals a knife in the palm of one's hand. The same motif appears in Isa 51:16: "I have put My words in your mouth and have sheltered you in the shadow (ובצל) of My hand." For צֵל (lit. "shadow" or "shade") denoting shelter and protection, see Ps 17:8: "Hide me in the shadow of Your wings"; Ps 91:1: "You abide in the protection of Shaddai." This is also the meaning of the Akkadian semantic and etymological equivalent *ṣillu* (*CAD* Ṣ:190-92).

He made me like a polished arrow — "so that I could project the message to the nations" (Kimchi). For the root ברר ("to polish"), see also Jer 51:11: "Polish (הָבֵרּוּ) the arrows!" 1QIsa[a] כחץ ("like an arrow"; cf. Targum and some medieval Hebrew manuscripts), as against MT לְחֵץ, conforms with the first clause, כחרב. (The expression שִׂים ל-, like its semantic equivalent in Akkadian, *ana šakānu* [*CAD* Š/1:148], can denote "to turn into"; see v. 11; 41:15, 18.) For the use of "polished arrows" *(šēlu)* in the Assyrian king Shalmaneser's inscriptions, see *CAD* Š/2:275.

He concealed me in His quiver — For אשפה ("quiver"), cognate of Ugar. *uṯpt* (*HdO* 1:126), appearing together with *ḥẓm* ("arrows"), see *CAT* 4.204:1, 2, 4; and Akk. *išpatu* (*CAD* I-J:257-58), see Jer 5:16: "His quivers (אשפתו) are like a wide opened grave"; Ps 127:5: "Happy is the man who fills his quiver (אשפתו) with them" (i.e., sons).

[3] *He said to me: "You are My servant"* — For Israel as the Lord's servant, see vv. 5, 6; 41:8, 9; 42:1, 19; 43:10; 44:1, 2, 21, 26; 45:4.

"Israel in whom I glory" — For Israel as God's "glory," see also 44:23: "He has glorified Himself through Israel"; 46:13: "To Israel in whom I glory"; 55:5 and 60:9: "The Holy One of Israel who has glorified you"; 60:21: "My handiwork in which I glory"; 61:3: "Planted by the Lord for His glory."

[4] A psychological reversal from depression and disbelief to recovery and security, as in Ps 31:23 (an ideological and structural parallel): "Alarmed, I had thought, 'I am thrust out from Your sight.' Yet You listened to my plea for mercy when I cried out to You."

I thought, "I have labored in vain" — two statements juxtaposed: God may have "said to me" that I was His servant (v. 3), but I thought (lit. "I said"; the pronoun אני was added for emphasis) that all my striving was in vain. For the expression יגע לריק ("to labor in vain"), see 65:23.

"I have spent my strength for nothing, for empty breath" — I thought that I had wasted my strength and labored to no purpose. For the expression כלי כֹּחַ, see Ps 71:9: "When my strength fails (כִּכְלוֹת כֹּחִי), do not forsake me." The pair of words תהו (Isa 40:17) and הבל (57:13), along with לריק in the first colon, form a triad describing desperate and utter despair. 1QIsa[a] ולהבל (instead of MT והבל) harmonizes with the preceding לְתֹהוּ. A similar phenomenon is apparent in 58:4, where 1QIsa[a] has לריב ולמצה instead of the elliptical MT לריב ומצה.

"Yet in truth my case is with the Lord" — Rashbam, on Gen 28:16, interpreted the first word of this clause correctly: "This is the meaning of every אכן in the Bible — אך כן — indeed it is thus, and not as I expected"; see Isa 40:7; 53:4. Its meaning here is: "Though I thought that God was inattentive to my dire plight, actually my case rests with Him." The word את is prepositional and denotes "with." For the literary paradigm אני/אנכי אמרתי . . . אכן ("I said/thought . . . but"), see Jer 3:19-20; Ps 31:23; and cf. Zeph 3:7.

"And my recompense is with my God" — For פעולה, "recompense, reward," see Isa 40:10; 61:8; 62:11; 65:7. Once again, את denotes "with."

[5] *"And now the Lord — who formed me in the womb to be His servant"* — The words "who formed me in the womb" are parenthetical, and the subsequent לשובב in the following clause states God's resolve, i.e., God, who created me in my mother's womb to be His loyal servant, has resolved to restore Jacob back to Himself. 1QIsa[a] has יוצרך, "your Creator," instead of MT יוצרי, as in 44:2: "Your Creator from the womb, who has helped you"; 43:1: "who formed you, O Israel." The adverb כה ("thus") precedes the verb אמר in 1QIsa[b], LXX, and Peshitta.

"Has resolved to bring back Jacob to Himself" — To recover Israel and restore them to His protection. For לשובב ("to bring back"), a *polel* form, see 58:12; Jer 50:19.

"That Israel may be gathered to Him" — According to the Ketib, לא (followed by Symmachus, Theodotion, Vulgate, and 4QIsa[d]), the clause should be translated: "So that Israel shall not perish." For the root אסף, "to perish," see Isa 57:1: "The righteous man perishes (אבד), and no one takes it to heart. Pious men are perishing (נאספים), and no one gives thought that because of evil the righteous are expiring (נאסף)"; cf. also Hos 4:3; Zeph 1:2; Ps 26:9. In Ugaritic as well, *'sp* denotes "taking away, to be removed": "A fifth (wife), Resheph (the god of pestilence), gathered to himself" *(yitsp),*" i.e., killed (*CAT* 1.14.I:18-19). In light of the chiastic parallel with the previous clause, however, it is preferable to follow the Qere, לו (so too Aquila, Targum, and 1QIsa[a]): Israel, scattered among the nations, will be gathered together to the Lord. For the *niph'al* of אסף, see Isa 43:9. For the pair "Jacob/Israel," see 44:1 and many other examples. For a similar variation in the Ketib and Qere versions (לא/לו), see 63:9.

"And I have been honored in the sight of the Lord" — I was found worthy of honor in God's eyes; cf. 43:4. For the *niph'al* of כבד, see Lev 10:3.

"And my God has been my strength" — contrary to v. 4, where Israel thought that it had exhausted its strength in vain. 1QIsa[a] reads here עזרי ("my help"; cf. Targum בְּסַעֲדִי) instead of MT עֻזִּי. For the scroll's version, which conforms with עזרתיך in v. 8, cf. the interchange of these two roots in the name of the Judean monarch, עֻזיה/ו and עזריה/ו, Uzziyahu (Uzziah) and Azaryahu (Azariah; Isa 1:1; Hos 1:1; 2 Kgs 15:1, 8).

[6] *For He has said: "It is too slight (a task) that you should be My servant"* — Acting as My servant is a facile mission. The verb נָקֵל (the *niph'al* of קלל) precedes an a fortiori claim, as in 1 Kgs 16:31: "Not content (הֲנָקֵל) to follow the sins of Jeroboam son of Nebat, he took as wife Jezebel"; Ezek 8:17: "Is it not enough (הֲנָקֵל) for the house of Judah to practice the abominations that they have committed here, that they must fill the country with lawlessness and provoke Me still further?" As in both these verses, 1QIsa[a] also reads here הנקל,

instead of MT נקל. The *mem* that prefixes the infinitive construct מִהיותך denotes "more than."

"To restore the tribes of Jacob" — It is too easy for Me just to restore the tribes of Jacob.

"And to bring back the survivors of Israel" — If one follows the Qere (נְצוּרֵי), the clause refers to the survivors of Israel who will be brought back to their native land. For the root נצר ("to be protected, be rescued"), see Ezek 6:12: "And he who survives and is preserved (והנצור) shall die of famine." According to the Ketib (נצירי), which is the reading in 1QIsa[a], the word derives from נֵצֶר, meaning a tender shoot; cf. Isa 60:21: "They are the shoot (נצר) that I planted"; 11:1: "And a shoot (ונצר) shall sprout from his stock," and would refer to the offshoots of Israel. The plural construct נצירי is morphologically identical with פסילי (Deut 7:25).

"I will also make you a light to nations" — This is God's ultimate purpose: Israel is destined to be a light unto the nations, as in Isa 42:6. The noun אור is a metaphor for salvation (see the following clause); cf. 60:3: "And nations shall walk by your light." For the expression נתן ל-, see 40:23.

"That My salvation may reach the ends of the earth" — For this expression of universalism, see also 48:20; cf. 42:10; 43:6.

[7] Despite the promise for such a resplendent future, Israel is still "the slave of nations," downtrodden and despised, a metaphoric triad emphasizing their dire and desperate state. A reversal is on its way, however, and soon the very kings who enslaved them will prostrate themselves before the nation. For the sovereign rule of Israel over the nations, see v. 23; 60:2-7, 11, 14; 61:6. The verse is partially framed by the chiastic repetition of the divine sobriquet: ישראל קְדֹשׁוֹ . . . קְדֹשׁ ישראל.

Thus says the Lord, the Redeemer of Israel, his Holy One — For a similar introductory formula, see 48:17. For the conjunctions of the two appellations, גֹּאֵל ("Redeemer") and קדוש ישראל ("the Holy One of Israel"), see 41:14; 43:14; 48:17; 54:5. Both the LXX and 1QIsa[a] read גואלכה ("your Redeemer") instead of MT גֹּאֵל (without the pronominal suffix); cf. v. 26; 47:4; 48:17; 54:5, 8. (See the introduction, §9.)

To the one whose very self is despised — Luzzatto suggests emending the vocalization to לִבְזֶה instead of MT לִבְזֹה, explaining it as an Aramaic passive participle, like בְּנֵה (Ezra 5:11), שְׁרֵא (Dan 2:22), and חֲזֵה (Dan 3:19). Others interpret it as a *qal* infinitive construct or as an adjective (Ibn Balaam [ed. Goshen-Gottstein], 199; Ibn Ganaḥ, *Sefer ha-Riqmah* [ed. Walensky], 324). One should note, however, the reading of 1QIsa[a], 4QIsa[d], לבזוי נפש, a passive participle. See also Jer 49:15: "Most despised (בזוי) among men"; Obad 2: "You shall be most despised (בזוי)." The servant is also described as "despised" (נבזה) in

Isa 53:3 (twice in the same verse). For נפש indicating one's own person, one's self, see 47:14.

To the abhorred of nations/Whose body is detested — One should emend the Masoretic vocalization to לִמְתֹעַב גוי (a *puʿal* participle in the construct state) (Saadyah; Ibn Balaam [ed. Goshen Gottstein], 199; Ibn Ganaḥ, *Sefer ha-Riqmah* [ed. Walensky], 325). Hebrew גוי in this hemistich serves as a double entendre, creating a Janus parallelism. On the one hand, it parallels the following clause, "the slave of rulers," since גוי is a political term synonymous with ממלכה (Exod 19:6) and parallel to לְאֻמִּים ("nations"; Ps 149:7) and מלכים ("kings"; Gen 35:11). On the other hand, when vocalized גֵּ(י)ו (with the *waw* and *yod* transposed), meaning "back of a body" (see 1 Kgs 14:9; Ezek 23:35), it parallels the preceding clause (for the two words together, see Isa 51:23) and thus may be translated, "whose body is detested" (see Tur-Sinai, *Peshuṭo shel Miqra,* III/1:126; Paul, *Divrei Shalom,* 477-78).

To the slave of rulers — subjugated to kings; cf. 52:5.

"Kings shall see and stand up" — The reversal is now imminent: The tyrants and monarchs who ruled you shall now show you respect and honor and will rise in your presence. For rising from one's place as a sign of respect, see Lev 19:32: "You shall rise before the aged"; Job 29:8: "Young men saw me and hid, elders rose and stood"; cf. Judg 3:20.

"Princes, and they shall prostrate themselves" — Nobles shall do obeisance before you; cf. v. 23. For the nominal pair שׂרים/מלך, see Hos 3:4; 7:3; 8:4; 13:10.

"For the sake of the Lord, who is faithful" — They shall show you such honor and respect for the sake of (למען) your God, who is always steadfast and true to His word; cf. Deut 7:9: "Know, therefore, that only the Lord your God is God, the faithful God (האל הנאמן)."

"For the Holy One of Israel who chose you" — For the sake of (למען does double-duty) the Holy One who singled you out as His, as in Isa 41:9-10: "My servant, Jacob, whom I have chosen . . . to whom I said: 'You are My servant'"; 43:10: "My servant whom I have chosen"; cf. 44:1, 2; 45:4. For the sobriquet קדוש ישראל, see 41:14, 16, 20; 43:3, 14; 45:11; 47:4; 48:17; 54:5; 55:5; 60:9, 14.

[8] In light of shared terminology it is possible that Ps 69:14: "As for me, may my prayer come to You, O Lord, at a favorable moment (עת רצון). O God, in Your abundant faithfulness, answer me (ענני) with Your sure deliverance (ישעך)," influenced the composition of this verse. (See the introduction, §17.)

Thus said the Lord: "In a favorable moment I answer you" — Cf. Isa 58:5: "A day favorable (יום רצון) to the Lord"; 61:2: "A year of the Lord's favor (שנת רצון)." 1QIsa[a] reads here אענכה in the imperfect, and אעזרכה in the adjacent clause, instead of the perfect forms in the MT.

"And on a day of salvation I help you" — For the servant (i.e., Israel) as the recipient of divine aid, see 41:10, 13, 14; 44:2; 50:7, 9.

"I created you and appointed you a covenant people" — One should vocalize וָאצרך וָאתנך (cf. LXX Codex Vaticanus, Vulgate, and Peshitta) in the past tense, and understand the clause as parenthetical. For the combination of these two verbs and the connection with Jer 1:5, see Isa 42:6.

"Restoring the land" — The subject of the verb לְהָקִים ("to restore") is the Deity, who is the subject of the sentence at the beginning of the verse. God shall rebuild the land and restore its ruins, just as He will rehabilitate "the tribes of Jacob" (v. 6). For the anomalous syntactical construction, see v. 6, and cf. 51:16: "I have put My words in your mouth and sheltered you with My hand. I, who planted the heavens and made firm the earth, have said to Zion: 'You are My people!'" where the subject of the infinitive constructs (לנטע, ליסד) is also the Deity.

"Allotting anew the desolate holdings" — God shall resettle the returning Israelites on their forefathers' holdings, which remained desolate since the time of the destruction of Jerusalem. For Israel as deserted and uninhabited, see v. 19; 61:4; 62:4; 64:9.

[9-13] The description of the redemption was influenced both thematically and linguistically by Jer 31:7-10:

Jeremiah 31	**Isaiah 49**
v. 7: Cry out (רָנּוּ)	v. 13: Cry out (רָנּוּ)
v. 8: I will bring them in from the northland (צפון)	v. 12: These from the north (מצפון)
v. 9: I will lead them to streams of water (מים)	v. 10: He will guide them to springs of water (מים)
v. 10: And will guard them as a shepherd (כְּרֹעֶה) (guards) his flock	v. 9: They shall pasture . . . their pasture (יִרְעוּ . . . מרעיתם)

Another similarity worthy of note is that, according to Jeremiah (v. 9), Israel shall return "on a level road, on which they will not stumble," and according to Deutero-Isaiah (v. 11): "I will make all My mountains a road and My highways shall be built up," so as to provide an obstacle-free highway. (See the introduction, §15.)

[9] *"Saying to the prisoners, 'Go free!'"* — God commands Israel, who have been languishing in the metaphoric prison of Babylonia, to free themselves and return to their land; cf. 48:20; "Go forth from Babylon!"

"To those who are in darkness, 'Reveal yourselves!'" — God, who is Israel's redeemer (v. 7), addresses those imprisoned in dark places (another metaphor

for the exile; cf. 42:7: "Rescuing prisoners from confinement, from the dungeon those who sit in darkness"), "Reveal yourselves!" i.e., "Be free!" (For the reverse, see 47:5: "Retire into darkness.") The LXX, Vulgate, Peshitta (and cf. 1QIsa[a]), as well as several midrashic texts (*Pesiqta Rabbati* 31 [ed. Friedman, 147a]; *Num. Rab.* 16:25; *Yalqut Shimoni, Numbers,* §459), read ולאשר, adding a *waw* to MT. The Masoretic reading may have been due to haplography, caused by the final *waw* of the preceding verb, צאו.

They shall pasture along the roads — Following their emancipation, the nation shall return to Israel along lush green paths, and the Lord will provide their food in abundance. For the image of Israel as sheep and God as their shepherd (40:11), see Ezek 34:31: "For you are My flock, the flock that I shepherd"; Ps 79:13: "Then we, Your people, the flock that You shepherd." The reading כול ("all [your roads]") in the LXX and 1QIsa[a] is a harmonistic addition, conforming with the next clause, ובכל שְׁפָיִים. 1QIsa[a] has הרים ("mountains") instead of MT דרכים ("roads").

On every bare height shall be their pasture — The pastoral imagery continues: All the "bare hillocks" (for שְׁפָיִים, see Isa 41:18) shall be their grazing grounds.

[10] Isa 35:7: "Torrid earth (השרב) shall become a pool; parched land (צִמָּאוֹן), fountains of water (למבועי מים)," left its imprint on this verse. Note the threefold emphatic use of the negative לא.

They shall neither hunger nor thirst — The redeemed shall experience neither hunger nor thirst while traversing through the desert, as in 48:21: "They have known no thirst, though He led them through parched places." Note the wordplay: "They shall pasture (יִרְעוּ)" (v. 9) and "they shall not hunger (ולא יִרְעָבוּ)."

Burning heat and sun shall not strike them — They shall not be affected by the scorching heat of the desert. The term שרב appears only once more in the Bible, in 35:7 (see above), where it refers to "parched earth." For other instances of "sunstroke," see Jonah 4:8: "The sun beat down on Jonah's head"; Ps 121:6: "By day the sun will not strike you."

For He who loves them will lead them — since God, who is deeply enamored of His people, will lead them through the desert as a shepherd leads his flock to the finest pasture; cf. Ps 78:52: "He set His people moving like sheep, leading them (וַיְנַהֲגֵם) like a flock in the wilderness"; Ps 80:2: "O Shepherd of Israel, who leads (נֹהֵג) Joseph like a flock." The root רחם here means "to love" (see Ps 18:2: "He said: 'I love you [אֶרְחָמְךָ], Lord, my strength,'" similar to its cognates, Aram., רְחֵם and Akk. *râmu* (*CAD* R:137-45); cf. v. 13; 54:8, 10; 55:7; and the substantive רחמים ("love") in 54:7.

He will guide them to springs of water — He shall direct them to waterbanks (cf. 41:18; 43:20). For the verb נהל in connection with leading one to water reserves, see Ps 23:2: "He leads me (ינהלני) to water in places of repose"; cf. also the Akkadian interdialectal etymological and semantic equivalent *na'ālu*, "to water," "to make damp" (*CAD* N/1:6). The reading ינחלם in 1QIsa[a], instead of MT ינהלם (exchange of gutturals), may have been influenced by v. 8: להנחיל נחלות. (The scribe made a similar error in 51:18, where he wrote מנחל instead of MT מנהל.)

[11] *I will make all My mountains a road* — I shall transform (-שׂים ל; see 41:18) all the hills and mountains in your path into a well-paved thoroughfare; cf. 40:4. Both Peshitta and Targum translate טוּרַיָא ("the mountains") without the pronominal suffix ("My"), and the LXX has the singular ("mountain"). According to Luzzatto, the *yod* suffix in הָרַי is not pronominal, but rather represents the Aramaic definite suffix (הריא) with the deletion of the final *aleph*.

And My highways shall be built up — The verb רום in this phrase denotes the construction and erection of the said highways. For this meaning, see Prov 11:11: "A city is built up (תרום) by the blessing of the upright, but is torn down by the speech of the wicked." Compare also Sir 49:12: "They built (בנו) a house, constructed (וירימו) a holy temple." (See also Rashi, ad loc.; Yellin, *Ḥikrei Miqra,* 63; idem, "Lost Connotations," *Leš* 1 [1929]: 22 [Heb.]). The same synonymous pair also features in the Ugaritic Baal epic: "Quickly build *(tbnn)* the house! Quickly erect *(rmmn)* the palace!" (*CAT* 1.4.V:53-54). The form יְרֻמוּן is a third-person masculine plural *qal,* with an archaic *nun* suffix. For the synonymous parallelism מסלה/דרך, see Isa 40:3; 62:10; and cf. also 57:14.

[12] The prophet issues a festive announcement, emphasized by a threefold repetition of אלה, together with a doubled הנה: Behold, Israel is now returning from the four corners of the earth to Israel. For this motif, see 43:5-6, and cf. Ps 107:3: "Whom He gathered in from the lands, from east and west, from north and from south."

Look! These are coming from far away — Israel is coming back to its ancestral home from distant lands; cf. Isa 43:6: "Bring My sons from afar (מרחוק)"; 60:4: "Your sons shall be brought from afar (מֵרָחוֹק)"; see also 60:9. Here, in light of the ensuing three directions mentioned in the next two hemistichs, מֵרָחוֹק refers to the "east"; cf. also the parallelism in 46:11. The word also provides a link to the beginning of the chapter: "And give heed, O nations far away (מֵרָחוֹק)."

Look! These from the north and the west — The children of Israel are returning from the northern and western lands. For ים (lit. "ocean") as "west," see Gen 12:8: "With Bethel on the west (מִיָּם), and the Ai on the east"; Josh 11:3: "To the Canaanites in the east and in the west (מִיָּם)."

And these from the land of Syene — Hebrew סינים refers to Syene, modern-day Aswan, located on the southernmost tip of Upper Egypt, opposite the island of Elephantine. This city, mentioned also in Ezek 29:10; 30:6 (סְוֵנֵה),

15, 16 (סְוֵן), is referred to in the Elephantine documents as סְוֵן בִּירְתָא ("the fortress Syene"). (See, e.g., Porten and Yardeni, *Textbook of Aramaic Documents,* 1:68, 71, A4.7 recto 7.)

[13] The unit concludes with a triad of imperative forms calling on the sky, earth, and mountains, i.e., the entire natural world, to participate in Israel's redemption. Cf. Isa 42:11; 44:23; 52:9; 55:12.

Shout, O heavens! And rejoice, O earth! — Burst into joyous song; see 48:20 and the verses cited above.

Break into shouting, O hills! — According to the Ketib, יפצחו, the verb is a third-person masculine future, and according to the Qere, ופצחו (which is the reading of the Targum, Vulgate, Peshitta, and 1QIsa[a]), it is a second-person masculine imperative. For the verbal expression פצח רנה, see 44:23; 52:9; 54:1; 55:12. For the imagery of mountains breaking out in song, see Ps 98:8: "The mountains sing joyously together."

For the Lord has comforted His people — Cf., e.g., Isa 40:1; 51:3, 12; 52:9; 66:13. Divine consolation signifies the nation's redemption and return to their homeland. Instead of MT נִחַם (past tense), 1QIsa[a] has the participle מנחם.

And has taken back His afflicted ones in love — God "who loves them" (v. 10) is about to return His downtrodden people back to their native land. For עני as "afflicted," "downtrodden," see 41:17; 54:11; 66:2. For the parallel between עמך and עֲנִיֶּיךָ, see Ps 72:2.

[14-21] The pericope opens with a bitter accusation in which Zion, anthropomorphized as a bereaved mother (see Isa 50:1; 54:1ff.), laments her bitter lot and her desolate state, since all her children have departed and her "husband" has left her. This complaint reflects the dire state of the nation upon their return, their feelings of abandonment vis-à-vis God (the root שכח is repeated four times in vv. 14-15), and their feelings of isolation (v. 21). Did the Lord not promise them: "I the Lord will respond to them. I, the God of Israel, will not forsake them" (41:17)? In response to these despondent feelings, God promises Zion that He will expel her enemies and that her children shall return in droves to rebuild her ruins. For similar promises of population increase, see 43:5-6; 44:4; 48:19; and for the restoration of the city, see 44:26, 28; 45:13. In this pericope the influence of Jeremiah is manifest, and once again Deutero-Isaiah reverses Jeremiah's prophecies of adversity. Jeremiah bemoaned: "Can a maiden forget (הֲתִשְׁכַּח) her jewels (עֶדְיָהּ), a bride (כלה) her adornments (קִשֻּׁרֶיהָ)? Yet My people have forgotten Me (שכחוני), days without number" (Jer 2:32). To which Deutero-Isaiah pointedly responds: "Can a woman forget (הֲתִשְׁכַּח) her baby or a young mother the child of her womb? Though they might forget (תשכחנה), yet I never will forget you (אשכחך)" (Isa 49:15); "You shall don them all like jewels (כַּעֲדִי), and adorn yourself with them like a bride (וּתְקַשְּׁרִים כַּכַּלָּה)" (49:18). Both prophecies begin with the rhetorical query התשכח (feminine), "Can one forget?" and proceed to describe a young woman who is even able to forget the things most precious to her — her bridal jewelry and her children. But God's favor is not dependent on the nation's conduct or on His regard for their forefathers. The people's rehabilitation is dependent solely on God's initiative and goodwill. (See the introduction, §15.)

In this and the following literary units, the prophet contrasts the bitter lot of Babylon to that of restored Israel: Whereas Babylon is commanded: "Get down! Sit in the dust! Fair Maiden Babylon" (47:1), the nations shall now "lick the dust" off Israel's feet (49:23). Babylon, who in her pride claimed that she would never know bereavement (47:8), will experience both bereavement and widowhood (47:9), while Zion, although bereaved (49:21), shall be blessed and consoled with numerous progeny (49:20, 21). No one shall be able to rescue Babylon from her imminent disaster (47:11-15), whereas Zion and her children shall be saved by God Himself (49:25-26).

For connections between this and the prior literary unit, see the introduction to the chapter.

[14] For the marriage/divorce imagery of God and His people, see 50:1; 54:5-6. Perhaps the compound title **ה' אדני** was divided here between two hemistichs in order to allude to the additional meaning of **אדון**, "husband," which is the image the prophet is conveying; see Gen 18:12; Amos 4:1.

Zion says: "The Lord has forsaken me, my God has forgotten me" — Jerusalem is inconsolable and accuses God of forsaking her as a husband who deserts his wife, a recurrent image in Deutero-Isaiah's prophecy, e.g., 54:6: "As a wife forsaken (**עזובה**) and forlorn"; 54:7: "For a little while I forsook you (**עזבתיך**)"; 60:15: "Whereas you have been forsaken (**עזובה**), rejected"; 62:4: "Nevermore shall you be called 'Forsaken' (**עזובה**)"; 62:12: "And you shall be called 'Sought Out, A City Not Forsaken (**נעזבה**).'" Compare also Ps 22:2: "My God, my God, why have you abandoned me (**עזבתני**)?" In Akkadian as well, the verb *ezēbu* (cognate of **עזב**) denotes the abandonment of a wife or even her divorce (*CAD* E:416, 422). For the synonymous pair **שכח/עזב** ("to forsake/to forget"), see Isa 65:11: "But as for you who forsake (**עֹזְבֵי**) the Lord, who forget (**השְּׁכֵחִים**) My holy mountain"; Lam 5:20: "Why have You forgotten us (**תשכחנו**) utterly, forsaken us (**תעזבנו**) for all time?" For a similar accusation, cf. Isa 40:27: "Why do you complain, O Jacob, why declare, O Israel, 'My cause is hidden from the Lord; my cause is ignored by my God'?" For Zion (parallel to Jerusalem), see, e.g., 40:9; 41:27; 52:1, 2.

[15] God's poignant response is conveyed by a two-part rhetorical question, which describes an almost implausible scenario: There may be cases (however unlikely) in which mothers might forget the babies they birthed, but God will never forsake His nation. The connection between God and His people supersedes even that of a mother's regard for her children. For other feminine images of the deity (birth, motherhood), see 42:14; 45:10; 46:3-4; 66:9, 13. (See Gruber, "Motherhood of God in Second Isaiah.")

Can a mother forget her baby? — Is it conceivable that a mother could ever forget her infant child? For אשה referring to a "mother" (thus LXX), see 45:10. The word עול (see also 65:20) and its variants, עוֹלֵל (1 Sam 15:3; Jer 44:7) and עוֹלָל (Jer 6:11; Lam 4:4), all denote "suckling infants" (as in Syriac). Compare likewise Ugar. *'l:* "I shall smite my brother's slayer, finish off him who finished off my mother's child *('l)*" (*CAT* 1.19.IV:34-35). And for the verb *'l,* "to suck," "He sucked *(y'l)* his navel" (*CAT* 1.10.III:25).

Or a young woman the child of her womb? — The second part of the two-part query: Is it at all plausible that a woman would be capable of neglecting the child she bore? Some commentators propose emending the text to אם רחם instead of מרחם, so that the hemistich would conform to the familiar הֲ . . . אם structure of a two-part rhetorical question. However, in light of the alternative formula, without אם, as in Jer 13:23: "Can the Ethiopian change (הֲיַהֲפֹךְ) his skin, or the leopard his spots?", there is no need for the emendation. The verb מרחם should not be understood as a *pi'el* preceded by the negative particle *mem,* but rather as a substantive, "young woman," which parallels אשה in the previous hemistich. Corroborating evidence that the verse refers to two similar terms is the employment of the plural אלה ("these") in the following hemistich, which refers both to אשה and to מרחם. This rare poetic substantive appears in Judg 5:30: "A damsel or two (רַחַם רַחֲמָתַיִם) for each man"; and in Amos 1:13: "And ravaged his women (רחמיו)," where רחמיו is polysemous and can also be translated: "And he repressed all his pity." Compare also רחמת in the Moabite Mesha Stele (*KAI* 181:17); Ugar. *rḥm,* "damsel," an appellative of the goddess Anat (*CAT* 1.6.II:14, 27); and the eighth-century BCE Balaam ben Beor inscription, written in a local Transjordanian dialect akin to Hebrew, found at Deir 'Alla in the Transjordanian Valley of Sukkoth (combination II, line 13): "Death shall take the young woman's infant (על רחם)," which, like the verse here, features both עול and רחם (see J. A. Hackett, *The Balaam Text from Deir 'Alla,* HSM 31 [Chico, Calif., 1980], 28, 70). This verse left its imprint on the *Hodayot Scroll,* 1QH[a] 17:35-36: "You [God] rejoice over them as a loving mother (מרחמת) over her nursing child (עולה)" (see Stegemann et al., DJD 40, 227, 233). The term מרחם also creates an associative link with the previous unit's homonym, רחם (vv. 10, 13).

Though they might forget — Nevertheless, there are unlikely cases that they might forget their child. For גם as an oppositional conjunction, see v. 25; Ps 23:4: "Though (גם) I walk through a valley of deepest darkness, I fear no harm, for You are with me." This conjunction was chosen since it occasionally follows compound rhetorical questions. See Jer 13:23 (quoted above): "Can the Ethiopian change his skin, or the leopard his spots? Just as much (גם) can you do good, who are schooled in evil!" (For the abandonment of children, see Ezek 16:5.)

Yet I never will forget you — Even though a woman could potentially forget her nursing babe, however implausible the scenario, I cannot and will not ever forget you, Zion. Cf. Deut 4:31: "For the Lord your God is a compassionate God. He will not fail you nor will He let you perish. He will not forget the covenant that He guaranteed on oath with your forefathers."

[16] The reason God will never forsake Zion is that she is deeply ingrained in His memory, like a tattoo, forever seared into the skin. For tattoos on hands, see Isa 44:5.

See, I have engraved you on the palms of My hands — Behold (the emphatic adverb הן), I have carved your form, O Jerusalem, on the palms of My hands. (For the engraving of Jerusalem on a brick, see Ezek 4:1: "And you, O mortal, take a brick and put it in front of you, and incise [וְחַקּוֹתָ] on it a city, Jerusalem." For the use of the verb חקק for inscribing words on a tablet, see Isa 30:8.) The LXX, Vulgate, and Peshitta translate כפי ("My hands") with the pronominal suffix, instead of MT כפים. The *mem* at the end of the word may serve as an enclitic suffix, or, conversely, may have been added to mitigate the potent anthropomorphic image of an engraving on God's hands.

Your walls are ever before Me — The walls of Jerusalem, which surround and symbolize the city, stand eternal in God's mind. These same walls were commanded to mourn the destruction of the city: "O wall of fair Zion, shed tears like a torrent day and night! Give yourself no respite!" (Lam 2:18). As compensation for this cruel fate, God now tells the walls of Jerusalem: "Upon your walls, O Jerusalem, I have set watchmen, who shall never be inactive by day or by night" (Isa 62:6). For the preposition נגד meaning "in front of," see 40:17; 47:14.

[17] God is about to fulfill His promise and expel Zion's enemies, and, at the same time, repopulate her with her long-lost children. Note the repetition of the letters *mem* and *resh* in this verse: מהרו . . . מהרסיך ומחריביך ממך.

Swiftly your children are coming — This clause is the pivot of a two-sided Janus parallelism, the bivalency centering around the word בניך. On the one hand, according to the Masoretic vocalization (also Symmachus, Peshitta, and one targumic version), בָּנָיִךְ ("your children") accords with the images of children at the beginning of the pericope, v. 15: "Can a mother forget her baby?"; and below: "The children you thought you had lost" (v. 20); "Who bore these for me?" (v. 21); "And they shall bring your sons in their bosoms" (v. 22); cf. also v. 23 — thus: "Your children are coming posthaste." On the other hand, according to another tradition (found in Theodotion, Vulgate, Targum: יִבְנוֹן, and 1QIsa[a], בוניך [cf. LXX [תבני], and supported by Saadyah Gaon's translation, 111], and Shmuel Ben Ḥofni's and Ibn Balaam's commentaries [ed. Goshen-

Gottstein, 200]), בניך (vocalized בֹּנָיִךְ) derives from בני ("to build") and thus creates a polar contrast between "your builders" and the following: "those who ravaged and ruined you." For the pair of verbal antonyms, הרס/בנה ("to build/to ruin"), see Jer 24:6; and cf. Jer 1:10; Ezek 36:36; Mal 1:4. The oft-quoted excerpt from *b. Ber.* 64a: "Read not בָּנָיִךְ, but בּוֹנָיִךְ," was not made in connection with this verse, but rather as a comment on Isa 54:13 (see there). For a similar midrashic interpretation, cf. *Exod. Rab.* on Cant 1:5: "'I am dark and lovely, daughters of Jerusalem': Our rabbis said: 'Read not בנות ירושלים ("daughters of Jerusalem"), but rather בונות ירושלים ("builders of Jerusalem")." (See Paul, *Divrei Shalom,* 479-81; H. Yalon, *Pirqe Lashon* [Jerusalem, 1971], 123-24 [Heb.].)

Those who ravaged and ruined you shall leave you — As your children/builders speedily arrive, those who destroyed and despoiled you shall depart. The *pi'el* participle of both verbs (as opposed to the *qal*) denotes here the plurality of the destroyers. Instead of MT מְהָרְסַיִךְ, the LXX (along with 1QIsa[a]) reads מהורסיך, with the *mem* prefix serving as a comparative, i.e., "your children/builders are swifter than your despoilers." (See Kutscher, *Language and Linguistic Background,* 496, who explains this as an *a-o* shift influenced by *resh* in a closed syllable [assimilation].) The two synonymous roots חרב and הרס are repeated in v. 19: "As for your ruins (חָרְבֹתַיִךְ) . . . and your land laid waste (הֲרִסֻתֵךְ)."

[18] Zion shall adorn herself with her returning children as a bride is bedecked in all her finery. For bridal jewels, see Isa 61:10. The first two clauses are repeated almost word for word in 60:4, and the final clauses are clearly influenced by Jer 2:32: "Can a maid forget her jewels, a bride her adornments?": עֶדְיָהּ ("her jewels") — כַּעֲדִי ("like jewels"); כַּלָּה קִשֻּׁרֶיהָ ("a bride her adornments") — וּתְקַשְּׁרִים כַּכַּלָּה ("Adorn yourself with them like a bride"). (See Paul, *Divrei Shalom,* 399-416.)

Look up all around you and see! — The words שׂאי סביב are alliterative. The expression נשא עינים וראי (lit. "raise one's eyes and see"; see Isa 40:26) is part of the biblical literary heritage from Ugaritic epic poetry, e.g., *bnši 'nh wtphn:* "When she raises her eyes and sees" (*CAT* 1.4.II:12), and denotes beholding a new object/person (cf. Gen 18:2; 24:63). The semantic parallel appears in Akkadian as well: *matāḫu īnu . . . amāru* ("to raise one's eyes and see"; *CAD* M/1:404).

They are all assembled, are come to you — All your returning children/builders are gathering and converging on you, Zion; cf. Isa 40:11; 43:5; 54:7; 56:8; 60:4; 62:9. The absence of a conjunctive *waw* between the two verbs indicates alacrity: They are coming and assembling with maximum speed. For the verbal pair קבץ — הביא/בוא ("to assemble–to come/bring") in the context of Israel's ingathering, see 43:5; 60:4; Zeph 3:20. For the expression בוא לך, see Isa 47:9; 60:5.

As I live — declares the Lord — a formulaic oath in which God promises and guarantees fulfillment by putting His own name, so to speak, on the line. The same formula recurs in Jer 46:18: "As I live (חי אני) — declares the King whose name is the Lord of Hosts." For other oath formulae of the deity, see Isa 45:23: "By Myself (בי) I have sworn"; 62:8: "The Lord has sworn by His right hand (בימינו), by His mighty arm (וּבִזְרוֹעַ)." The divine oath and, similarly, the royal oath precede only the most significant and momentous promises or decisions (see 14:24; Jer 22:5).

You shall don them all like jewels — This is My promise (introduced by the emphatic כי): Your sons, who shall return from exile, shall be as the jewelry with which a bride adorns herself. The term כֻּלָּם, which is repeated in this verse, emphasizes the totality of the return. For the donning of jewels (עדי), see Jer 4:30; 31:4; Ezek 16:11; 23:40; and for the verbal form עדי, see Isa 61:10.

And adorn yourself with them like a bride — The imagery and phraseology are a direct borrowing from Jer 2:32 (see above). The verb תְּקַשְּׁרִים is a denominative, derived from קִשֻּׁרִים ("jewelry"; see Isa 3:20). Compare also 61:10: "Like a bride bedecked in her jewels." Note here the wordplay: כלם . . . כלה.

[19] The desolation and ruin of the land (see v. 8; 44:26; 61:4; 62:4; 64:9) are conveyed through a series of three substantives, each lengthier than the next: the first, חָרְבֹתַיִךְ, is four syllables long; the second, (ו)שֹׁמְמֹתַיִךְ, is five syllables long; and the third, ארץ הֲרִסֻתֵךְ, consists of two words and is six syllables long (for a similar syllabic progression, see 48:20). Isa 6:11-12 left its imprint on this verse: "I asked, 'How long, my Lord?' And He replied: 'Until towns lie waste without inhabitants (מֵאֵין יושב), and houses without people, and the land lies waste and desolate (שממה). For the Lord will banish (וְרִחַק) the population, and deserted sites are many in the midst of the land (הארץ).'" The calamity predicted by Isaiah did indeed occur; but now Deutero-Isaiah announces a reversal: The land that was "without inhabitants" (מֵאֵין יושב), and which "was waste" (שממה), its wasteland (שֹׁמְמֹתַיִךְ) shall become "crowded with settlers" (תֵּצְרִי מִיּוֹשֵׁב); and the "banishment" (רחק) of the native population announced by First Isaiah shall now be executed (וְרָחֲקוּ) against the land's destroyers and ravagers. (See the introduction, §14.)

As for your ruins and desolate places and your land laid waste — an elliptical verse (without a verb) with an emphatic triad: in place of (תחת) the uninhabited ruins and deserted, barren land destroyed by marauders (cf. Ezek 36:35: "The cities, once ruined [החרבות], desolate [והנשמות]"). The pair חָרְבֹתַיִךְ . . . הֲרִסֻתֵךְ ("your ruins . . . and your land laid waste") mirrors chiastically v. 17: מהרסיך ומחריביך ("those who ravaged and ruined you"). For the ruins (חרבות) of Judah and Jerusalem, see Isa 44:26; 51:3; 52:9. The word הֲרִסֻתֵךְ (an abstract noun that occurs only here, similar in form to ילדות, שחרות) is a variant of וַהֲרִסֹתָיו (the feminine plural of הריסה) (Amos 9:11), which also is a hapax legomenon. The scribe of 1QIsa[a] wrote instead הרוסתך, for which cf. 1 Kgs 18:30: "He repaired the damaged (הֶהָרוּס) altar of the Lord."

You shall soon be too constrained for your inhabitants — Instead of the present desolation described in the preceding clause, you shall soon be swarming with inhabitants, and there will not even be enough room for all the returning expatriates. For the verb תֵּצְרִי (a *qal* from the root צרר, "to be narrow, cramped"), cf. Prov 4:12; Job 18:7. For the repopulation of Jerusalem and the subsequent need for its expansion, see Isa 54:1-2.

While those who destroyed you remain far from you — Those who laid you waste (מְבַלְּעָיִךְ, a *pi'el* participle indicating a great number; cf. the synonymous מהרסיך, v. 17) shall remain far from your vicinity, as in v. 17. For the root בלע signifying "destruction," see 2 Sam 20:20: "Far be it from me to destroy (אֲבַלַּע) or to ruin"; Lam 2:5: "He destroyed (בִּלַּע) all her citadels"; cf. Lam 2:2, 16.

[20] As the exiles return (cf. Isa 44:4; 54:1), the population boom shall result in overcrowding, which is expressed in the same terms as v. 19: "The place is too cramped for me . . . to live in (צר לי המקום . . . וְאֵשֵׁבָה)" — "You shall soon be too constrained for your inhabitants (תֵּצְרִי מִיּוֹשֵׁב)."

20 *The children born in your bereavement shall yet say in your hearing* — Your progeny, once given up for dead (שִׁכֻּלָיִךְ — an abstract hapax legomenon), shall give voice to their complaint. For the expression אמר בְּאֹזֶן (lit. "to say in one's ear"), see Judg 17:2; Job 33:8. For the root שׁכל, which denotes the loss of one's children, see v. 21; Gen 43:14; 1 Sam 15:33.

"The place is too cramped for me" — Since Zion shall be blessed with many children, she shall become jam-packed with people, who will claim claustrophobia, as in 2 Kgs 6:1: "See, the place where we live under your direction is too cramped (צר) for us."

"Make room for me to live in!" — One shall say to another: גְּשָׁה לִּי, "Move to one side for my sake" (Rashi), so that I will have room to settle in; cf. Gen 19:9: "But they said: 'Move (גֶּשׁ) away!'" The lengthened *qal* imperative גְּשָׁה expresses a desire, as in Gen 27:21: "Come closer (גְּשָׁה) that I may feel you, my son"; v. 26: "Come close (גשה) and kiss me, my son." One should note the alliteration of the letter *shin* in the three verses just quoted: גְּשָׁה . . . ואשבה; גְּשָׁה . . . וַאֲמֻשְׁךָ; גְּשָׁה . . . וּשְׁקָה.

[21] Zion's bemused response to these astonishing developments is conveyed in a typical rhetorical triad. Each one of the three questions is accompanied by the pronoun אלה, which refers to her long-lost children and is reminiscent of the threefold repetition of this term in v. 12. For a similar anthropomorphic image of desolate Zion, see Isa 54:1: "Shout, O barren one! You who bore no child. . . . For the children of the wife forlorn shall outnumber those of the espoused — said the Lord"; cf. 54:6.

And you will say to yourself: "Who bore these for me" — And you, completely bewildered, shall ask, "Who gave birth to all these children on my behalf?" This exclamation contrasts with v. 20: "The children you thought you had lost shall yet say in your hearing. . . ." For the Akkadian semantic equivalent of אמר בלב ("to say to oneself," see 47:8, 10; Zeph 1:12; 2:15), *ina libbi qabû*, see *CAD* Q:26. For the expression ילד ל-, see Gen 6:4; 30:1.

"When I was bereaved and barren" — Compare v. 20: "The children born in your bereavement (בני שִׁכֻּלָיִךְ)." For the adjective גלמוד ("barren") to describe people, see Job 15:34: "For the company of the impious is barren (גלמוד)"; and for its use metaphorically to depict the night, see Job 3:7: "Let that night be desolate (גלמוד)." The Arabic cognate *ǧulmūd* refers to a "stone, impregnable rock, stony infertile soil." The form שְׁכוּלָה is a unique variant of שַׁכֻּלָה (see Jer 18:21; Cant 4:2; 6:6).

"Exiled and spurned/imprisoned?" — Hebrew גֹּלָה is a *qal* feminine passive participle from the root גלי ("to exile"); cf. also 2 Sam 15:19; 2 Kgs 24:14. For Heb. סורה, also a feminine passive participle from the root סור ("to turn aside, away"), see Jer 17:13. However, it is possible that the *aleph* was elided and one should read ואסורה ("and bound/imprisoned"); cf. Symmachus and Vulgate. For another example of the elision of an *aleph,* see Eccl 4:14, where בית הסורים = בית האסורים ("prison").

"By whom, then, were these reared?" — Someone must have reared these children because I was not aware of their existence. For the verbal pair גִּדֵּל/ילד, see Isa 1:2; 51:18.

"I was left all alone" — At the time of my exile I was completely solitary; cf. Gen 42:38: "He alone (לבדו) is left"; Dan 10:8: "I was left alone (לבדי)." The sentiment is reminiscent of the mourners' lament: "Alas! Lonely sits the city, once great with people" (Lam 1:1).

"And where have these been?" — If this was the case and I was all by myself, whence all these children?

[22-23] The Lord, as supreme commander of the army, shall raise His arm as a sign to the nations to bring back the sons and daughters of Israel, portrayed here as young children. The rulers of the nations shall serve as nursemaids and guardians of Israel and shall prostrate themselves before them. Then it shall be known that those who put their trust in God shall never be disappointed. For other similar images, see Isa 11:12: "He will raise a signal to the nations and assemble the driven out of Israel, and gather the dispersed of Judah from the four corners of the earth"; 13:2: "Raise a standard upon a bare hill! Cry aloud to them! Wave a hand! And let them enter the gates of the nobles!" For murals depicting captive children being carried on the backs of their parents, see M. Haran, *Ezekiel,* in G. Brin, ed., *The Encyclopedia of the Biblical World* 12 (Jerusalem, 1984), 85 (Heb.); O. Keel, "Kanaänische Sühneriten auf ägyptischen Tempelreliefs," *VT* 25 (1975): 448, nos. 16, 17; *ANEP,* no. 10.

[**22**] This verse features an excellent example of gender parallelism: The sons are carried in the nations' bosoms (חֹצֶן), a masculine noun; and the daughters are placed on their backs (כָּתֵף), a feminine noun. For similar examples, see Jer 48:46: "Woe to you, O Moab! The people of Chemosh are undone, for your sons are carried off into captivity (שֶׁבִי) and your daughters led away captive (שִׁבְיָה)"; Nah 2:13: "And [the lion] filled his lairs with prey (טֶרֶף חֹרָיו) and his dens with mangled prey (וּמְעֹנֹתָיו טְרֵפָה)." This literary device was borrowed from Ugaritic, which employs a feminine synonym when the subject is female and a masculine form when the subject is male. Compare: "He provides the gods with rams [masculine]. He provides the goddesses with ewes [feminine]. He provides the gods with bulls [masculine], the goddesses with cows [feminine]. He provides the gods with thrones [masculine]. He provides the goddesses with chairs [feminine]. He provides the gods with jars [masculine] of wine. He provides the goddesses with barrels [feminine] of (wine)" (*CAT* 1.4.VI:47-54). (See W. G. E. Watson, *Classical Hebrew Poetry: A Guide to Its Techniques,* rev. ed., JSOTSup 26 [1986; repr. Sheffield, 2005], 123.) For God raising an ensign to the nations, see Isa 5:26. There, however, God signals the nations to come and punish Israel; here the context is one of salvation, as in 11:12. For transporting Israel back to Jerusalem, see 43:6; 60:4; 66:20.

Thus said the Lord God — For this compound title at the beginning of a pericope, see v. 14.

"I will raise My hand to the nations" — "God acts as a human monarch or general, who assembles his army by waving his arm or lifting his flag" (Luzzatto).

"And lift up My ensign to the peoples" — I will hoist My flag so that all the nations shall gather; cf. 62:10: "Raise an ensign (נֵס) to the peoples."

"And they shall bring your sons in their bosoms" — And the nations shall carry your sons as one clasps a babe to the bosom; cf. Num 11:12: "Carry them in your bosom as a nurse carries an infant." חֹצֶן ("bosom") appears twice more in the Bible: Ps 129:7: "(Like grass) with which a reaper fills not his hand, nor a binder of sheaves, his bosom (חִצְנוֹ)"; Neh 5:13: "I also shook out the bosom (חָצְנִי) of my garment." It has a similar meaning both in Arabic and Syriac, while in Akkadian *ḫiṣnu* signifies "protection" (*CAD* Ḫ:203) and the verb *ḫaṣānu,* "to shelter" (*CAD* Ḫ:129-30).

"And your daughters shall be carried on their shoulders" — Your daughters shall ride on their shoulders (כָּתֵף), as though they were small children; cf. Isa 60:4: "Your daughters like babes on shoulders (צד)"; 66:12: "You shall be carried on (their) hips." The verse concludes with the same verb with which it began (אֶשָּׂא . . . תִּנָּשֶׂאנָה), thus forming a literary *inclusio.* The same image of being carried on someone's shoulders appears in the Ugaritic Baal epic, when Anat mourns her dead brother Baal: "She hoists mighty Baal and places him on

Anat's shoulders *(ktp)*" (*CAT* 1.6.I:14-15). Compare also Ishtar's prophecy to King Ashurbanipal: "My shoulders are alert and always ready to carry you" (Parpola, *Assyrian Prophecies,* 41, lines 18-19).

[23] Zion's new status is apparent in the way the kings and queens shall treat her children. They shall function as nursemaids and guardians and shepherd them to Zion, where they will prostrate themselves and submit to Israel's rule. This description is very much akin to Ps 72:9, 11: "Let desert dwellers kneel before him, and his enemies lick the dust. . . . Let all kings bow to him." Both sets of verses describe the tribute that the nations shall bring: Ps 72:10: "Let kings of Tarshish and the islands bring gifts, kings of Sheba and Seba present tribute"; and here the tribute is the transportation of Israel itself in a royal entourage. This verse features the same gender parallelism delineated above in v. 21: the kings are Israel's "foster fathers," whereas their queens are the nation's "nursemaids." For the show of abject submission and its semantic parallels in Akkadian and Ugaritic, see M. I. Gruber, *Aspects of Nonverbal Communication in the Ancient Near East,* 2 vols., SP 12 (Rome, 1980), 1:182-291.

"Kings shall be your foster fathers" — Cf. Num 11:12: "Did I conceive all these people, did I bear them, that you should say to me, 'Carry them in your bosom as a nurse (הָאֹמֵן) carries an infant'?" For אֹמֵן ("foster father"), see also 2 Kgs 10:1, 5; Esth 2:7; and for אומנת ("foster mother"), see 2 Sam 4:4; Ruth 4:16.

"Their queens shall be your nursemaids" — The king's consorts shall care for your children as if they were their nurses. For שָׂרוֹת ("royal consorts"), see 1 Kgs 11:3: "He had seven hundred royal wives (שָׂרוֹת) and three hundred concubines." This is also the meaning of the Akkadian interdialectal etymological and semantic equivalent, *šarratu* (*CAD* Š/2:72-75). For מֵינֶקֶת ("nurse"), see Gen 35:8; Exod 2:7; and for the Akkadian cognate *mušēniqtu,* see *CAD* M/2:265-66.

"They shall bow to you, face to the ground" — They shall prostrate themselves before you in deference and submission; see Gen 19:1: "Bowing low with his face to the ground (אַפַּיִם ארצה)"; cf. Isa 60:14: "Prostrate at the soles of your feet shall be all those who reviled you." For similar Akkadian idioms, cf. *qadādu* ("to bow"), in conjunction with *appu* ("face," "nose"; *CAD* Q:44-45); *napalsuḫu* with *ina qaqqari* ("to throw oneself to the ground [in supplication]") (*CAD* N/1:271-72); *labānu* in the expression *labān appi* ("to beg humbly"), which denotes complete submission (*CAD* L:10-12). For capitulation to Israel's rule, see 45:14. Compare also the Assyrian king Shalmaneser III's stele, which depicts him receiving tribute from the representatives of many nations, among them "Jehu the son of Omri," who is shown kissing his feet (*ANEP,* nos. 351, 355).

"And lick the dust of your feet" — as a sign of total subjection; cf. Ps 72:9 (quoted above): "Let desert dwellers kneel before him, and his enemies lick the dust (עפר יְלַחֵכוּ)." The same expressions of abasement: *kamāsu* ("to kneel in

submission"; *CAD* K:117-20) and *šukênu* ("to prostrate oneself"; Š/3:214-18), and the kissing of a ruler's feet, *šēpam našāqu,* or the ground before the ruler, *qaqqaram našāqu* (*CAD* N/2:58-59), appear in Mesopotamian royal inscriptions. The expression "the dust of one's feet" (עפר רגלים = Akk. *epri šēpē*) is also found in contexts of submission and humiliation (*CAD* E:186-87). For the synonymous pair עפר/ארץ ("ground/dust"), in Hebrew and in Ugaritic, see 47:1.

"And you shall know that I am the Lord; those who trust in Me shall not be disappointed" — You shall then realize that "those who trust in the Lord" (קֹוֵי ה׳; see 40:31) shall never be disappointed; cf. Ps 25:3: "O let none who trust in You (קֹוֶיךָ) be disappointed (יֵבֹשׁוּ)"; Lam 3:25: "The Lord is good to those who trust in Him (לְקֹוָו)"; Ps 37:9: "But those who trust in (וקֹוֵי) the Lord — they shall inherit the land." For the same motif in Mesopotamian literature, cf. the Neo-Assyrian colophons: "Those who trust in you, Nabu, shall not be shamed" (*CAD* B:6), where the verb, *ba'āšu,* is the cognate of Heb. בוש.

[24-26] The final pericope of this chapter begins (like the previous unit) with a compound rhetorical question, commencing with the הֲ interrogative, followed by אם, and concluding with the emphatic גם, which, as in v. 15, introduces an unexpected conclusion. This unit is connected to the preceding one in several ways: by the motif of redemption, the nation is once again referred to as children (vv. 15, 17, 20, 22, 25), and the purpose of the redemption is the same — so that "You shall know that I am the Lord" (v. 23), "And all humankind shall know that I the Lord am your Savior" (v. 26).

[24] *Can booty be taken from a warrior?* — Is it at all likely that the spoils of war can be taken away from a conqueror? The term מַלְקוֹחַ ("booty") appears here and in the following verse, and again only in Num 31 (where it appears five times); cf. Num 31:26: "The booty that was captured, man and beast." Hebrew יֻקַּח is an archaic *qal* passive; see Gen 18:4.

Or captives rescued from a victor? — The second part of the rhetorical parallelism forms a chiasm with the first part: Or is it possible that שְׁבִי (a generic term for "captives") can be rescued from a conqueror? For צדיק ("victor"), see Isa 41:2; 45:21. The reading of 1QIsa[a], עריץ, "ruthless" (reflected in LXX, Vulgate, and Peshitta), conforms with the next verse, in which this term appears. For the verb מלט ("to be saved"), see 46:2, 4.

[25] The long-awaited redemption. This verse is in chiastic parallelism with the preceding one: "Can booty be taken from a warrior, or captives rescued from a victor?" — "Captives shall be taken from a warrior, and booty rescued from a ruthless tyrant," with עריץ replacing צדיק. For שְׁבִי and מַלְקוֹחַ, see Num 31:12, 26.

Yet thus said the Lord: "Captives shall be taken from a warrior" — However unlikely, it is occasionally possible to retrieve prisoners from a conqueror. (For גם as an introduction to the statement following a compound rhetorical question, see v. 15.) The scribe of 1QIsa[a] substituted ילקח *(niph'al)* for the archaic *qal* passive יֻקַּח, and then transposed שבי ("captives") and מלקוח ("spoil") — the former in the second hemistich and the latter in the first hemistich (cf. also Peshitta), so as to create a one-for-one parallelism with the previous verse (as opposed to the chiastic parallelism in the MT).

"And booty shall be rescued from one who is ruthless" — It is implausible, but on occasion booty can be retrieved from a tyrant. For the combination of עריץ and גבור, see Jer 20:11: "But the Lord is with me, strong and ruthless (כגבור עריץ)." In the Ugaritic epic literature the god Athtar is known as *'rẓ*, "terrible" (*CAT* 1.6.I:54-56).

"For I will contend with your adversaries" — The unlikely scenarios depicted above are possible since "I" (the pronoun אנכי is added for emphasis) shall be your deliverer and contend with your foes; cf. Ps 35:1: "O Lord, contend (ריבה) with my adversaries (יריבי). Fight against those who battle against me"; Jer 18:19: "Hear what my adversaries (יריבי) say." Instead of MT יריבך ("your adversaries"), the LXX, Targum, Peshitta, and 1QIsa[a] (the original reading before a *yod* was added) all read ריבך ("your cause"); cf. Lam 3:58: "You championed my cause (ריבי), O Lord. You have redeemed my life." The verbal expression רב ריב ("to champion a cause") is a legal idiom that appears some sixty times throughout the Bible. For the expression רב את ("to contend with"), which appears here, see Isa 45:9; 50:8.

"And I will save your children" — from their adversaries.

[26] The motif of cannibalism (see Jer 19:9: "And I will cause them to eat the flesh of their sons"; cf. also Lev 26:29; Ezek 5:10; 39:18; Zech 11:9; Lam 2:20; 4:10; and metaphorically, Ps 27:2; Eccl 4:5), as well as the drinking of human blood, appear in other ancient Near Eastern documents. For examples in Akkadian, see *CAD* A/1:250; D:75, 76; in Ugaritic (in an incantation against the evil eye): "It [the evil eye] eats his flesh without a knife. It drank his blood without a cup" (*CAT* 1.96:3-5; for this incantation, as well as many additional ancient Near Eastern parallels, see J. N. Ford, "'Ninety-Nine by the Evil Eye and One from Natural Causes': Epigraphic and Philological Notes to *CAT* 1.96," *UF* 30 [1998]: 201-78, esp. 230-36); and on a bowl written in Mandaic: "They eat human flesh and are sated, and drink their fill of [human] blood" (see J. Naveh, "Another Mandaic Lead Roll," *IOS* 5 [1975]: 48, lines 18-20). Self-cannibalism, as here, however, is rarely documented. According to the MT of Isa 9:19, "Each devoured the flesh of his own arm (זְרֹעוֹ)"; however, the LXX and many citations from midrashic literature read זַרְעוֹ ("his progeny").

"I will make your oppressors eat their own flesh" — Those who oppressed you shall be forced to resort to self-cannibalism. The word מוניך is a *hiph'il* participle from the root ינ׳ ("to oppress"); see Exod 22:20; Jer 46:16; Zeph 3:1.

"They shall be drunk with their own blood as with fresh wine" — Your op-

pressors shall become inebriated by drinking their own blood. The only other place in the Bible where the drinking of blood is described is in the LXX of Zech 9:15: "They shall drink their blood (דָּמָם) like wine," whereas the MT has: "They shall drink, rage (הָמוּ) as with wine." For a metaphoric expansion of becoming drunk from blood, see Deut 32:42: "I will make My arrows drunk (אַשְׁכִּיר) with blood." In the first stages of the grape's fermentation, the liquid is called עסיס; see Joel 1:5: "Wake up, you drunkards, and weep! Wail, all you swillers of wine, for the new wine (עסיס) that is denied you!"; cf. Amos 9:13; Cant 8:2.

"And all humankind shall know that I the Lord am your Savior" — The same expression appears word for word in Ezek 21:10. Note the dual meanings of בשׂר in this verse: in the previous clause it denotes "flesh," and here, "(all) humankind" (for the latter, see also Isa 40:5, 6; 66:16, 23, 24). The redemption of the nation as proof of God's omnipotence is a recurring motif throughout Deutero-Isaiah's prophecies (cf. 52:10: "The Lord will bare His holy arm in the sight of all the nations, and the very ends of earth shall see the victory of our God"), since when Israel is saved, God's name is defiled no more. The substantive מושיעך ("your Savior") accentuates the previous verse, "I will save" (אנכי אושיע).

"The Mighty One of Jacob, your Redeemer" — The final two clauses of this verse are repeated almost word for word in 60:16: "And you shall know that I the Lord am your Savior. I, the Mighty One of Jacob, am your Redeemer." The word אֲבִיר, which denotes "the Mighty One," is an ancient title of the Deity (see Gen 49:24; Isa 1:24; Ps 132:2, 5; and cf. Akk. *abāru*, "strength"; *CAD* A/1:38). Many commentators explain that the anomalous vocalization אֲבִיר was deliberate, since אַבִּיר, "bull" (Isa 34:7; Ps 50:13), was the symbol of many Near Eastern deities.

Chapter 50

The chapter is composed of three short and distinct pericopes: vv. 1-3, 4-9, 10-11. The first unit continues the metaphor of the last chapter, which describes Zion as the mother, God as the father, and Israel, the nation, as their children (49:14, 21). God advises Israel that the rift between Zion and Himself did not originate with the writ of divorce by which Zion was supposedly dismissed, but rather their wholesale abrogation of God's commandments was the ultimate catalyst. The second unit consists of the "third Servant Song" (see the introduction, §5). In the last section God encourages the righteous among the nation to take heart and derides and threatens the "kindlers of fire." The chapter as a whole shares many linguistic features with chap. 49:

Chapter 49	**Chapter 50**
v. 1: אמי	v. 1: אמכם
v. 8: עניתיך	v. 2: עונה
v. 4: כחי	v. 2: כח
v. 20: באזניך	vv. 4, 5: אֹזן
v. 2: הסתירני	v. 6: הסתרתי
v. 23: לא יֵבֹשׁוּ	v. 7: לא אבוש
v. 8: עזרתיך	vv. 7, 9: יעזר לי
v. 24: צדיק	v. 8: מצדיקי
v. 25: את יריבך אנכי אריב	v. 8: יריב אתי
v. 4: משפטי	v. 8: (בעל) משפטי
v. 20: גשה לי	v. 8: יגש אלי
v. 26: והאכלתי	v. 9: יאכלם
v. 3: עבדי	v. 10: עבדו
v. 9: בחשך	v. 10: חֲשֵׁכִים
v. 2: ידו	v. 11: מידי

The two chapters also contain rhetorical questions: 49:15, 24 (a two-part question); 50:2 (a three-part question).

[1] The covenant between the Lord and His nation is described in terms of a marriage contract that ends with a bill of divorce and with the "dismissal" of the wife from the husband's house. The prophet's metaphor is based on the verses in Deuteronomy that delineate the divorce process: Deut 24:1: "When a man takes a wife and possesses her, but she fails to please him because he finds something obnoxious about her, and he writes her a bill of divorce (ספר כריתות), hands it to her, and sends her away (וְשִׁלְּחָהּ) from his house" (cf. also v. 3); and Jer 3:8: "Since rebel Israel had committed adultery, I cast her off (וְשִׁלַּחְתִּיהָ) and handed her a bill of divorce (ספר כְּרִיתֻתֶיהָ)." For the covenant between God and Israel as a marriage covenant — sometimes abrogated — see Jer 2:2: "I accounted to your favor the devotion of your youth, your love as a bride"; Hos 2:4: "Rebuke your mother, rebuke her — for she is not My wife and I am not her husband"; Hos 2:9: "Then she shall say, 'I will go and return to my first husband'"; and cf. also Mal 2:14-16. God addresses the people (Zion represents the estranged wife, and her children — the nation) and rebukes them by declaring that He did not dismiss their mother as a husband divorces his wife, but rather it was their sins that were the cause of their predicament. For another image depicting God as husband and Zion/Israel as estranged or reconciled wife, see Isa 62:3-5. For similar female metaphors of Zion, see 49:15; 54:1; 60:4; 66:7. (See the introduction, §8.) This first verse is framed chiastically: "Your mother whom I dismissed . . . I sold — You were sold . . . your mother dismissed."

Thus said the Lord: "Where is the bill of divorce of your mother" — Where is the evidence that I delivered a bill of divorcement to your mother (Zion)? This is a rhetorical question, since the marriage between God and Zion had never been annulled. The expression ספר כריתות appears only here, in the Deuteronomic divorce laws (Deut 24:1, 3), and in Jer 3:8 (both quoted above). For the query איזה ("where"), which is a combination of the interrogative adverb אֵי, a shortened form of אַיֵּה (see Gen 4:9: "Where [אֵי] is your brother Abel?"; Deut 32:37: "Where [אֵי] are their gods"; cf. too Ugar. *iy* [*HdO* 1:133] and Akk. *aj* [*CAD* A/1:220]), and the demonstrative pronoun זה, which in this case serves as an emphatic (cf. Gen 18:13); see Isa 66:1: "Thus said the Lord: 'The heaven is My throne and the earth is My footstool. Where (איזה) could you build a house for Me? Where (איזה) shall My resting place be?'"; 1 Sam 9:18: "Where (אי זה) is the house of the seer?"

"Whom I have sent away?" — For the *pi'el* form of the verb שלח signifying divorce and estrangement, see the verses quoted in the introduction to the unit, as well as Deut 22:19, 29: "He shall not have the right to divorce her (לְשַׁלְּחָהּ) all his life long"; Jer 3:1: "If a man divorces (יְשַׁלַּח) his wife"; Mal 2:16: "For I detest divorce (שַׁלַּח) — said the Lord God of Israel."

"And which of My creditors was it to whom I sold you?" — Do you really think I sold you to pay for My debts? For the interrogative מי that introduces an accusation, see Judg 6:29: "They said to one another: 'Who (מי) did this thing?'"; Job 9:24: "If it is not He, then who (מי)?" For the practice of selling children to pay debts, see 2 Kgs 4:1: "A certain woman, the wife of one of the disciples of the prophets, cried out to Elisha: 'Your servant my husband is dead, and you know how your servant revered the Lord. And now a creditor (נֹשֶׁה) is coming to seize my two children as slaves.'" See also Deut 24:11. The indenture of children to cover their parents' debts was also very common in Mesopotamia. For Israel being sold to their enemies, see Isa 52:3; Deut 32:30; Judg 2:14; 3:8; Ps 44:13.

"Indeed, you were sold for your sins" — "Indeed" (הן) is emphatic and introduces the logical conclusion immediately following a rhetorical question; see Isa 40:12-15; 44:10-11. You were sold to your enemies, not for any debt, but rather because of your sins and iniquities. The prepositional *beth* here and in the adjacent clause indicates cause. For the verbal construction מכר ב-, see Ps 44:13; Nah 3:4.

"And your mother was sent away for your crimes" — Your mother was dismissed because of her crimes against Me. For the synonymous pair פשע/עָוֹן, see Num 14:18. Note the chiasm with the first hemistich.

[2] Divine shock and displeasure are expressed here. According to Luzzatto, God is addressing the expatriate Judeans and chastising the majority of them for remaining in Babylon despite their ability to return. The verse is constructed according to the well-known paradigm of a tripartite rhetorical question, but in reverse. In other texts the series begins with הֲ-, is followed by אם, and concludes with מדוע (Jer 2:14, 31; 8:4-5, 19, 22); whereas here the series begins with the interrogative מדוע, continues with הֲ-, and concludes with אם. For the same sequence of motifs see Isa 59:1-2: "No, the Lord's arm is not too short (קצרה ידי) to save. . . . But your iniquities have been a barrier between you and your God." Two of the Egyptian plagues are alluded to in verses 2-3: the plague of blood, by which God smote the Nile and caused all the fish to die, and the plague of darkness. (See the introduction, §12.) The negative אין is repeated four times in the space of this single verse.

"Why, when I came, was no one there?" — Cf. 41:28: "But I looked and there was no one there (ואין איש)"; 59:16: "He saw that there was no one there (אין איש)." For a similar futile search, see Ezek 22:30: "And I sought a man among them to repair the wall and to stand in the breach before Me in behalf of this land, that I might not destroy it; but I found none."

"Why, when I called, did no one respond?" — Cf. Isa 65:12: "Because when I called, you did not respond." The Lord, however, acts in a different manner: "Then, when you call, the Lord will answer" (58:9); "Before they pray, I will answer" (65:24).

"Is My arm, then, too short to redeem?" — The syntactical construction of an infinitive absolute followed by a finite verb of the same root serves to emphasize: Did you think that I did not have enough strength to rescue you from your enemies? For a parallel image, see Num 11:23: "And the Lord answered Moses, 'Is there a limit to the Lord's power' (היד ה׳ תקצר)?" The Masoretes vocalized מִפְּדוּת as an abstract substantive, whereas the LXX, Vulgate, and Targum (מִלְמִפְרַק) all read here an infinitive construct: מִפְּדוֹת; cf. 59:1: "No, the Lord's arm is not too short to save (מהושיע)." For the substantive פְּדוּת ("redemption"), see Ps 111:9; 130:7.

"Have I not the power to save?" — For the synonymous pair להציל/לפדות, see Jer 15:21: "I will save you (והצלתיך) from the hands of the wicked and rescue you (ופדיתיך) from the clutches of the violent."

"Lo, with a mere rebuke I dried up the sea" — הן is emphatic (see above, v. 1). My power is so vast that with no more than a mere blast, rebuke, I dried up the waters of the sea; cf. Nah 1:4: "He rebukes the sea and dries it up, and He makes all rivers fail" (note the shared terminology in both verses: ים, נהרות, גער, החריב); Ps 104:7: "They [the waters] fled at Your blast (גערתך)"; Ps 106:9: "He sent His blast (ויגער) against the Sea of Reeds; it became dry." For oceans drying up, see Isa 44:27: "I, who said to the deep, 'Be dry!' shall dry up your streams"; 51:10: "It was You [the arm of the Lord] who dried up the sea." These verses reflect the Israelite version of the rebellion of the sea god and the forces of chaos against the god of heaven, which appears in the Mesopotamian *Enuma Elish* (Tiamat wages war against Marduk) (see B. R. Foster, *COS* 1:390-402), and in the Ugaritic Baal epic (Yam versus Baal) (see D. Pardee, "The Baʿlu Myth," *COS* 1:241-74). In all three of these theomachies, the god of heaven defeats the rebellious sea monsters. The myth still reverberates in rabbinic literature: *b. Ḥag.* 12a: "Until the Holy One Blessed be He rebuked him [the sea monster] and he dried up"; *Yalqut Shimoni, Genesis,* §8: "Until the Holy One Blessed be He rebuked them, conquered them, and forced them under His feet." For more on this myth and its influence on biblical literature, see U. Cassuto, "The Israelite Epic," in *Biblical and Oriental Studies,* 2: *Bible and Ancient Oriental Texts,* trans. I. Abrahams (Jerusalem, 1975), 69-109.

"And turned rivers into desert" — I transformed vigorous streams into an arid wilderness; see 44:27: "I will dry up your rivers"; Ps 107:33 (the exact same wording as here): "He turns rivers into a desert." For the reverse miracle, see Isa 43:20: "For I provide water in the wilderness, rivers in the desert." For the synonymous pair ים and נהרים/נהרות, see 43:2, 20; Ezek 31:15; Nah 1:4; Hab 3:8; Cant 8:7; and Ugar. *ym/nhr* (which serve as parallel names for the sea god; see *CAT* 1.2.II:30).

"Their fish stank from lack of water" — As a result of the aridity and lack of a water source, the fish died and their stench filled the air; see Exod 7:21:

"And the fish in the Nile died. The Nile stank (וַיִּבְאַשׁ)" (cf. Exod 7:18; Ps 105:29). דָּגָה is the collective term for "fish," as in Gen 1:26: "They shall rule the fish (בדגת) of the sea"; Deut 4:18: "The form of any fish (דגה) that is in the waters below the earth." Both the LXX and 1QIsa[a] have תִּיבָשׁ ("dried up"), rather than תִּבְאַשׁ, most likely an aural error. The *mem* prefix appended to the negative אין denotes cause, as in Exod 14:11: "Was it for want of (הֲמִבְּלִי) graves in Egypt that you brought us to die in the wilderness?"

"And died of thirst" — For צָמָא, "thirst," see Isa 41:17: "Their tongue is parched with thirst (בצמא)." There are those who suggest vocalizing בצָמֵא, "on parched and arid land," as in 44:3: "Even as I pour water on thirsty soil (צָמֵא)"; i.e., when there was no more water the fish were left on dry land and died.

[3] God is in control not only of the sea, but of the heavens as well. This polarity indicates that God exercises His power over the entire world. In vv. 2-3 the prophet juxtaposes the first plague — the plague of blood (Exod 7:19ff.), and the ninth plague — the plague of darkness (Exod 10:21ff.; Ps 105:28). There may be an additional nuance at work here: "In the same way the Lord can dry up everything, He can also clothe the skies with heavy rain clouds . . . alluding to the abundance of water within them" (Yellin, *Ḥikrei Miqra,* 65). The black raiment of the sky recurs frequently as a metaphorical portent of the day of judgment; see Joel 2:2, 10; Amos 8:9; Zeph 1:15; Ezek 32:7-8; for the darkening of the sun, see Amos 8:9.

"I clothe the skies in darkness/mourning" — I cover the sky with black clouds. The same image appears in Mesopotamian literature, where the cognate expression *nalbaš šamê* (lit. "garb of the sky") denotes "clouds" (*CAD* N/1:200) and as a result of this cloud cover the sky darkens (*CAD* Š/1:346). For קַדְרוּת, a hapax legomenon abstract noun from the root קדר, "to be dark" (so too Ugar. *qdr;* see *HdO* 2:695), see 1 Kgs 18:45: "Meanwhile the sky grew dark (והתקדרו) with clouds"; Joel 2:10; 4:15: "Sun and moon are darkened (קָדָרוּ)." Moreover, in light of the next hemistich, one can also interpret the root קדר as referring to "mourning," as in Ezek 31:15: "I put Lebanon in mourning (וָאַקְדִּר) for him"; Ps 35:14: "I was bowed with gloom, like one mourning (קֹדֵר) for his mother."

"And make their raiment sackcloth" — I clothe the skies in the blackness of sackcloth, a coarse fabric worn as a sign of bereavement — once again, a two-pronged allusion to cloudiness and morbidity. For donning a sackcloth in mourning, see Gen 37:34: "He put sackcloth on his loins"; 1 Kgs 21:27: "And he put sackcloth on his body"; 2 Kgs 19:1: "And he covered himself with sackcloth." For the same mourning custom in Mesopotamia, see *CAD* B:137; S:169. For the parallel pair of substantives, כְּסוּת/לְבוּשׁ, see Job 24:7; 31:19. Note the string of alliterative sibilants in these three consecutive words.

[4-9] The third Servant Song describes the servant's obedience and responsiveness to God despite his travails and abasement (see the introduction,

§5). In this unit the expression אדני ה׳ is repeated four times (vv. 4, 5, 7, 9) and the indirect pronoun לי appears five times (vv. 4 [twice], 5, 7, 9). The description of the servant's suffering here has much in common with the trials and travails depicted in Lam 3:

Isaiah 50	**Lamentations 3**
v. 4: בבקר בבקר	v. 23: לבקרים
v. 5: ואנכי לא מריתי	v. 42: מרינו
v. 6: גֵּוִי נתתי למכים וּלְחָיַי לְמֹרְטִים	v. 30: יתן למכהו לֶחִי
v. 8: מי יריב אתי	v. 58: רַבְתָּ אדני ריבֵי נפשי
v. 8: מי בעל משפטי	v. 59: שָׁפְטָה משפטי
v. 10: אשר הלך חֲשֵׁכִים	v. 2: אותי נהג וַיֹּלַךְ חֹשֶׁךְ ולא אור

(See the introduction, §18.) The stylistic links between this unit and the preceding one are the interrogative מי, "who" (vv. 1, 8 [twice]), followed by a conclusion introduced by the emphatic הן (vv. 2, 9 [twice]).

[4] The repetition of לִמּוּדִים (with a different meaning each time) may very well be an allusion to 8:16: "Bind up the message! Seal the instruction with My disciples (בְּלִמֻּדָי)!", i.e., by the use of this term the divine servant is establishing a relationship with the disciples of Isaiah son of Amoz. For other linguistic allusions linking this unit with Isa 8, cf. "I did not hide my face" (פני לא הסתרתי; 50:6) — "Who is hiding His face" (המסתיר פניו; 8:17); "The Lord God has given me" (אדני ה׳ נתן לי; 50:4) — "The Lord has given me" (נתן לי ה׳; 8:18). (See the introduction, §14.)

The Lord God has given me a skilled tongue — The dual divine appellation is for emphasis; see 49:22. For the adjective לִמּוּדִים, "skilled, accustomed to," see Jer 2:24: "Or like a wild ass used to (לִמֻּד) the desert"; Jer 13:23: "Who are skilled in doing evil (לִמֻּדֵי הָרֵעַ)"; cf. also the Akkadian cognate equivalents *lummudu, limdu, lamdu* (*CAD* L:67, 191, 246). The servant's strength lies in his tongue. Compare the second Servant Song, Isa 49:2: "He made my mouth like a sharpened blade."

To know how to speak timely words to the weary — The meaning of this clause is obfuscated by the hapax legomenon infinitive לָעוּת. Some have emended it to לענות, "to answer," as in 36:21: "And [they] did not answer him with a single word (ענו . . . דבר)." Others, who accept the MT, derive the verb from the substantive עת ("time"): "to speak timely" (cf. LXX: "in season"). Another possibility is to relate it to an Arabic root meaning "to aid, sustain" (cf. Vulgate), i.e., God has blessed me with a tongue skilled to offer succor to the weary of heart (see also Yalon, *Pirqe Lashon*, 326-28). Further support for this interpretation may be found in the *Hodayot Scroll* from Qumran (1QH[a] 16:37), where this verb parallels לְחַיּוֹת: "To give life (לחיות) to the spirit of those who stagger, and to support (לעות) the fatigued with a word" (Stegemann et al., DJD 40, 217). Yet others base themselves on the Targum's translation, לְאַלָּפָא ("to teach"), i.e., the servant is skilled at teaching even the weary. Despite all these suggestions, it is still difficult to understand to whom the prophet was referring when he spoke of the "weary." For an indefinite substantive יָעֵף following the accusative marker את, see 41:7.

Morning by morning He rouses, He rouses my ear — Each and every morning, God makes my ear receptive to hear His message. The doubling of the substantive denotes constancy; see Exod 16:21: "So they gathered it every morning (בבקר בבקר)"; Isa 28:19; Zeph 3:5. The Ugaritic semantic equivalent of the unique expression "to rouse, awaken the ear," appears in the Kirta epic: "Listen and let your ear be alert *(tqġ udn)*" (*CAT* 1.16.VI:30, 42). The Ugaritic verb *yqġ* is the etymological cognate of Heb. יקץ ("to awaken"). For God's message delivered early in the morning, see Ezek 12:8.

To give heed like disciples — to listen to the divine message as a student would listen to his teacher; cf. Isa 54:13: "And all your children shall be disciples of the Lord (לִמֻּדֵי ה׳)." Note the dual meaning of לִמֻּדִים here and above.

[5] *The Lord God opened my ears* — For this expression, see 48:8: "Your ears were not opened (פִּתְּחָה אזנך) of old" (and cf. the MT of 42:20: פקוח אזנים, with the reading in 1QIsa[a]: פתחו אזנים). The expression is a metaphor for lucidity: The Lord opened my ears so I could understand. So too the Akkadian etymological and semantic cognate *uznam petû/puttû* (*CAD* P:346, 356). For the opposite expression, אטם אזן ("to close an ear"), see Ps 58:5.

And I did not disobey — The first-person pronoun אנכי opening the clause is emphatic. I never showed disobedience no matter what the mission was. The root מרי signifies rebellious behavior; cf. Hos 14:1: "Samaria must bear her guilt, for she has rebelled (מרתה) against her God"; Jer 4:17: "For she has rebelled (מרתה) against Me — declares the Lord"; see also Isa 63:10.

I did not turn myself away — I did not shy away from my duty; cf. 42:17; 59:13, 14; as well as 2 Sam 1:22: "The bow of Jonathan never turned back (נשׂוג אחור)." The verb נְסוּגֹתִי is a *niph'al* past tense from the root סוג. (For the form, cf. the morphologically similar נְבֻנוֹתִי, from the root בין, in Isa 10:13.) Its cognate Akkadian expression is *arkatu suḫḫuru,* "to turn away, turn back" (*CAD* S:47-48).

[6] For the servant's suffering and humiliation at the hands of his enemies, cf. Isa 53 and similar descriptions in Ps 22; 31; 35; Lam 3:30. One should note that the first two items on this list of travails — flogging and tearing of the hair — appear in the same order in the Assyrian Law Code (MAL A.44, 59) as punishments of debasement (see G. R. Driver and J. C. Miles, *The Assyrian Laws* [1935; repr. Aalen, 1975], 412, line 44; 425, lines 60-61; and their notes on 289, 484); see also Neh 13:25 (cited below).

I offered my back to the floggers — For גֵּו, see Isa 38:17; 51:23.

And my cheeks to those who tore out my hair — For the verb מרט, see Ezra 9:3: "I tore hair out (וָאֶמְרְטָה) of my head and beard, and I sat desolate"; Neh 13:25: "I flogged them, tore out (וָאֶמְרְטֵם) their hair" (note again the same sequence of punishments as here). Tearing out one's hair or slapping one's face is a humiliating act, as is shaving one's beard (2 Sam 10:4). For the slapping of one's cheek, see 1 Kgs 22:24 = 2 Chr 18:23; Mic 4:14. Compare also the semantic equivalents in Akkadian: *lētam maḫāṣu* (*CAD* L:149; M/1:74-75) and *lētam ṭerû* (*CAD* L:150).

I did not hide my face from insults and spittle — further debasing acts; cf. Job 30:10: "They abhor me . . . they do not withhold spittle (רֹק) from my face"; Deut 25:9: "She shall spit (וְיָרְקָה) in his face" (the ritual humiliation of one who is unwilling to marry his brother's widow by levirate marriage). For the connection between spitting and shame, see Num 12:14: "If her father spat (יָרֹק) in her face, would she not bear her shame for seven days?" Note also the connection between the face and humiliation, as in Jer 51:51: "We were shamed; we heard taunts. Humiliation (כְּלִמָּה) covered our faces"; Ps 69:8: "Shame (כְּלִמָּה) covers my face." The LXX, Peshitta, and 1QIsa[a] read הסירותי (*hiphʿil* of סור): "I [did not] remove," instead of MT הסתרתי, a reading that was likely influenced by the fact that the expression "hiding of the face" is usually a sign of divine anger; see Isa 54:8; 59:2; 64:6. Compare, however, 53:3 and Exod 3:6 for a human hiding his face.

[7-9] Despite the shame and abasement of the servant, his feelings of security are in no way diminished, since he believes that God will come to his rescue (cf. also Isa 49:4). Verses 7 and 9, both of which open with "But the Lord God will help me," emphasize the servant's steadfast belief in divine succor. The language and imagery of these verses are drawn from the legal world. With God as his advocate, none dares challenge him. This confidence is expressed by his thrice-repeated query: "Who dares contend with me? Who would be my opponent? Who can get a verdict against me?" Thus the servant's enemies are doomed to perdition.

[7] *But the Lord God will help me* — The *waw* indicates contrast: I am unshaken in my belief that God will stand by me in my hour of tribulation; cf. 41:10, 13, 14; 44:2; 49:8.

Therefore I am not humiliated — despite the debasing and disparaging treatment I experience.

Therefore I have set my face like flint — I strengthen myself by making my face as hard as flint (an especially hard stone) in the face of my tormentors; cf. Ezek 3:8-9: "But I will make your face as hard as theirs, and your forehead as brazen as theirs. I will make your forehead like adamant, harder than flint." For a similar image of obstinacy, see Jer 5:3: "They made their faces harder than rock." The repetition of the expression על כן in the two adjacent clauses serves for added emphasis.

And I know I shall not be shamed — since those who trust in the Lord are never put to shame; see Isa 45:17: "But Israel has won through the Lord salvation everlasting. You shall not be shamed or disgraced in all the ages to come!"; 49:23: "And you shall know that I am the Lord — those who trust in Me shall not be shamed"; cf. also 54:4.

[8] *My Vindicator is at hand* — "My advocate, He who makes the righteousness of my cause shine forth is none other than God" (Luzzatto), and He is close by my side. For the judicial meaning of the verb הצדיק, "to vindicate, acquit," see Deut 25:1: "When there is a dispute between men and they go to law, and a decision is rendered acquitting (והצדיקו) the innocent and condemning the guilty"; 1 Kgs 8:32: "Hear in heaven and take action to judge Your servants, condemning him who is guilty and bringing down the punishment of his conduct on his head, and vindicating (ולהצדיק) him who is innocent by rewarding him according to his innocence." Compare also Isa 43:9: "Let them produce their witnesses and be vindicated (ויִצְדָּקוּ)"; 43:26: "Tell your version, that you may be vindicated (תצדק)."

Who dares contend with me? — Who dares enter into a court and accuse me? Cf. Job 13:18-19: "See now, I have prepared my case. I know that I will win it (וצדקתי). For who is it that would contend (יריב) with me?" The accusers or contenders in a trial are called אנשי ריב (Isa 41:11); cf. Job 31:35: "My accuser (איש ריבי)." For the verbal construction ריב את ("to contend with"), see Isa 45:9; 49:25.

Let us stand up together! — and face the judge. For the verb עמד in legal contexts, see 44:11: "Let them all assemble and stand up (יעמדו)"; 48:13: "I call to them, let them stand up together (יעמדו יַחְדָּו)." Compare also Num 27:2: "They [the daughters of Zelophehad] stood (ותעמֹדנה) before Moses [to state their case]"; Num 35:12: "So that the manslayer may not die unless he has stood (עָמְדוֹ) trial before the assembly." (The Akkadian semantic equivalent *uzzuzu*, "to stand," has similar legal connotations [*CAD*, U/W: 378-79].) For approaching the judge to stand trial before him, see Isa 41:1; 43:26; 45:20. For the *dagesh* (the doubling of the initial *yod* of יחד), see GKC §20f.

Who would be my opponent? — Who would dare dispute my cause, with God as my vindicator? בעל משפט ("legal adversary") is a unique expression, similar to בעל דברים in Exod 24:14: 'Let anyone who has a legal matter (בעל דברים) approach them" (cf. the semantic equivalent in Akk. *bēl dabābi* [*CAD* D:3-4] and Rabbinic Hebrew בעל דבב; as well as Akk. *bēl dīni* [*CAD* D:155-56] and בעל דין in Rabbinic Hebrew).

Let him approach me! — Let him approach the bench and present his case. The root נגשׁ is legalese for initiating legal action, as in Isa 41:1: " Let them approach (יגשו) to state their case"; 41:21: "Submit (הַגִּישׁוּ) your case!"; 41:22: "Let them approach (יגשו) and tell us what will happen"; 45:20: "Come, gather together, draw nigh (התנגשו)!"; 45:21: "Come forward and present your case (וְהַגִּישׁוּ)! Let them even take counsel together!" Compare similarly the verb קרב, 41:21; Num 27:1.

[9] *Lo, the Lord God will help me* — A word-for-word repetition of the opening clause of v. 7, which emphasizes the servant's feelings of security; cf. Ps 118:7: "With the Lord on my side as my helper (בְּעֹזְרָי), I will see the downfall of my foes." For the emphatic הן preceding a legal conclusion, see Isa 41:11, 24, 29.

Who can get a verdict against me? — Who, therefore, can find me culpable? The verb הרשיע ("to pronounce a guilty verdict") is the antonym of הצדיק ("to vindicate, declare innocent"; see above, v. 8); cf. 54:17: "And every tongue that contends with you at law you shall defeat (תרשיעי)"; Exod 22:8: "He whom God declares guilty (יַרְשִׁיעֻן) shall pay double to the other."

They shall all wear out like a garment — All your opponents, your contenders in the legal arena, shall be worn out to the seams. For the identical simile, see Isa 51:6; Ps 102:27.

The moth shall consume them — For this figure of speech, see Isa 51:8; Job 13:28. The Akkadian etymological equivalent *ašašu* appears in a bilingual lexical list (Sumerian-Akkadian) immediately following *sāsu* (Heb. סס, 51:8; *CAD* A/2:422). For clothing ruined by moths in Mesopotamian literature, see *CAD* S:196-97.

[10-11] This short literary unit distinguishes between those who revere and trust in the Lord, despite their hardships, and the "kindlers of fire," who are vilified and threatened. The exact meaning of the chastisement is obfuscated by the difficult metaphors and terminology and our lack of knowledge regarding the referents. A clear divide is apparent, however, between the faithful and those who refuse to rely on the Lord. For the connection between this section and the preceding one, compare the terms מי (vv. 8, 9, 10), הן (vv. 9, 11), שמע (vv. 4, 11), כֻּלָּם (v. 9)/כֻּלְּכֶם (v. 11).

[10] *Who among you reveres the Lord* — Compare similarly phrased queries in 42:23; 48:14. 1QIsa[a] (יראי ה׳) and Targum read in the plural instead of the MT singular.

And heeds the voice of His servant? — Who among you hearkens to the voice of the Lord's servant? Both the LXX and Peshitta translate ישמע, an imperfect, in lieu of שֹׁמֵעַ (a participle), which fits better with the adjacent יבטח and יִשָּׁעֵן. For the expressions ירא ה׳ and שמע בקול, see Deut 13:5; 1 Sam 12:14.

Though he walks in the darkness — Although in dire straits, he nevertheless obeys the voice of the Lord. For the expression הלך חֲשֵׁכִים ("to walk in darkness"; a unique plural form of חֲשֵׁכָה) as a metaphor for hardship, see Isa 9:1: "The people that walked in darkness (ההלכים בחשך) have seen a brilliant light"; Ps 82:5: "They go about in darkness (בחשכה יִתְהַלָּכוּ)"; Lam 3:2: "Me He drove on and on in darkness (וַיֹּלַךְ חשך) without light," cf. also Isa 59:9: "We must walk in gloom (באפֵלות נְהַלֵּךְ)."

And has no light — He nevertheless remains steadfast. For the combination of "darkness/no light" (negative parallelism), see also Amos 5:18, 20: "Why do you long for the day of the Lord? It shall be darkness, not light. . . . The day of the Lord shall be not light, but darkness"; and see Isa 59:9: "We hope for light, and lo! There is darkness. For a gleam, but we must walk in gloom." The same expression appears in the Balaam inscription discovered in Tell Deir ʿAlla, located in the Valley of Sukkoth east of the Jordan Valley, dated to the second quarter of the eighth century BCE: "Darkness (חשך) exists there, not brilliance (ואל נגה)" (B. A. Levine, *COS* 2:143, combination I, lines 6-7). Compare also the Akkadian equivalent in the Gilgamesh Epic IX:163, 167 (and elsewhere): "The darkness is dense; there is no light."

Let him trust in the name of the Lord — Let him put his faith in the Lord's name (a reference to the Deity Himself), as in 48:1; 56:6; 59:19; 60:9. Compare also Ps 33:21: "For in His holy name we trust."

And rely on his God — This is the only time that the verb appears together with the preposition *beth* (all the other occurrences are with על, ל, or תחת), and was probably influenced by the use of this preposition in the previous expression, יבטח בשם ה׳. For the pair of synonymous verbs שען *(niphʿal)* and בטח, see Isa 30:12; 31:1. For the same idea expressed by the verb סמך, see 48:2: "And lean for support on the God of Israel."

[11] *But you are all kindlers of fire* — For the expression קדח אש, "to kindle fire," see 64:1; Jer 17:4. (The root קדח appears also in Ugaritic, Phoenician, Arabic, and Syriac.) In the *Damascus Document* discovered in the Cairo Genizah (CD A, 5:13), this hemistich appears with the reading כלם ("all of them") instead of MT כלכם, "all of you" (*DSSSE* 1:558).

Setting ablaze firebrands — Read מאירי instead of MT מאזרי, parallel to the prior hemistich, and cf. the *Damascus Document* (just cited): מבעירי, with the same meaning. For the *hiphʿil* of אור ("to light up, ignite"), see Isa 27:11: "Women come and light their fires (מאירות) with them"; Mal 1:10: "And do not ignite a fire (תאירו) on My altar." The term "firebrands" appears only once more, in Prov 26:18: "Like a madman shooting deadly firebrands (זִקִּים)." It also is documented in various forms: זיק, זיקות, זיקים, זיקוקים, in Sirach (43:13), Rabbinic Hebrew, and Aramaic. See, for example, *b. B. Metzia* 85b: דנורא זקוקין, "brands of fire." Compare also the etymological and semantic equivalent in Akkadian, *zīqtu/zīqu*, "torches" (*CAD* Z:133-34), and especially the expression *zīqāte ušanmaru*, "they light the torches" (*CAD* Z:133; N/1:217), which is the exact equivalent of the emended reading in this colon.

Walk in the flame of your fire — a derisive statement. The prophet commands the unbelievers to walk in the flames of the fire that they themselves have lit! For אוּר ("flame, fire"), see Isa 44:16; 47:14. On the basis of the LXX and Vulgate, some exegetes suggest vocalizing בְּאוֹר אשכם ("by the light of your fire"), comparing it with Ps 78:14: "He led them with a cloud by day, and throughout the night by the light of fire (באוֹר אש)." The phrase may also reflect a deliberate play on words, based in part on Isa 2:5: "Come let us walk by the light of the Lord (באור ה׳)" — for those who trust in the Lord it shall be a light; for the unbelievers it shall be a blazing inferno.

In the firebrands that you have lit! — measure for measure: punishing "fire for fire."

This has come to you from My hand: — Hebrew זאת is anticipatory: this shall be your fate (explicated in the next clause).

You shall lie down/die in pain — Hebrew מַעֲצֵבָה is a hapax legomenon derived from עֶצֶב ("pain, hurt"). If the verb שכב is a euphemism here for "to die" (as in 14:18: "All the kings of nations lie [שכבו], every one, in honor, each in his own tomb"; Job 7:21: "For soon I shall lie down [אשכב] in dust"; and see Isa 43:17), then the phrase should be understood as: "You shall die in misery" (Ibn Ezra). This euphemism is also manifest in the Tel Dan stele (from the eighth century BCE), line 3: "Then my father lay down (וישכב) and went to his fathers." (See A. Biran and J. Naveh, "An Aramaic Stele Fragment from Dan," *IEJ* 43 [1993]: 81-98.) The Akkadian equivalent, *sakāpu,* "to lie down," also serves as a euphemism for death (*CAD* S:74), as does *ṣalālu,* "to lie down, to die" (*CAD* Ṣ:67-70). For משכב ("tomb" or "grave" in Hebrew and cognate languages), see the comments on שכב ל- at 57:2; and cf. Job 7:21; Lam 2:21.

Chapter 51

The chapter is composed of six short independent literary units, each (except for the fifth unit, vv. 12-16) preceded by the anaphoric imperatives "Listen!" (v. 1); "Hearken!" (v. 4); "Listen!" (v. 7); "Awake, awake! Clothe yourself with strength!" (v. 9); "Rouse, rouse yourself!" (v. 17). In the first unit, vv. 1-3, those who seek the Lord are promised that, although few in number, they shall be fruitful and multiply like their progenitors, Abraham and Sarah, and that Zion shall be rehabilitated and transformed into a veritable Garden of Eden, where joy and happiness shall reign. In the second unit, vv. 4-6, God declares that His salvation will encompass the world in its entirety and shall outlast even the heavens and the earth. In the third unit, vv. 7-8, the prophet offers encouragement to those who care for justice and urges them not to fear contempt and derision, since God's victory and salvation shall be everlasting. In the fourth unit, vv. 9-10, the Lord's holy arm is addressed and is requested to repeat the miracles of yore, the creation of heaven and the parting of the sea, so as to facilitate Israel's triumphant return to their homeland. In the fifth unit, vv. 12-16, God comforts His people once again and reassures them that they should not fear the rage of the oppressor, since the oppressor shall be cut off, and they shall be rescued. In the sixth and final unit, vv. 17-23, the Lord promises that He shall retrieve "His cup of reeling," since His nation has drunk their fill, and pass it to their enemies and oppressors.

This chapter shares many linguistic and thematic links with chap. 50: **קראתי** (50:2) — **קראתיו** (51:2), **קְרָאתַיִךְ** (51:19); **אחריב ים** (50:2) — **המחרבת ים**
(51:10), **ים** (51:10 [twice], 15; 50:2); **בגערתי** (50:2) — **גערת אלהיך** (51:20); **שמים**
(50:3; 51:6, 16); **יעיר** (50:4) — **עורי . . . עורי עורי** (51:9), **התעוררי התעוררי**
(51:17); **לשמע** (50:4), **שְׁמַע** (50:10) — **שמעו אלי** (51:1, 7; cf. v. 4: **הקשיבו אלי**,
האזינו), **שמעי** (51:21); **מצדיקי קרוב** (50:8) — **רדפי צדק** (51:1), **צדקי קרוב** (51:5),
צדקתי (51:6, 8), **ידעי צדק** (51:7); **מי יריב אתי** (50:8) — **אלהיך יריב עמו** (51:22);

הן כלם כבגד יבלו עש יאכלם (51:5); ישפטו (51:4), ומשפטי — (50:8) משפטי (50:9) — והארץ כבגד תבלה (51:6), כי כבגד יאכלם עש (51:8); אור (50:11) — אור (light; 51:4). Compare also 50:10: ירא ה׳; and 51:1: מבקשי ה׳.

[1-3] The first three verses are a prophecy of consolation addressed to Zion, formulated as an allegory and followed by a promise of posterity and the rehabilitation of the land. For the idea of a future population boom, see 44:4; 49:19-21; and cf. Jer 3:16; 30:19; Ezek 36:10-11. The prophet forges a typological link between the first progenitor and the nation of his day based on the literary model positing that the deeds of the forefathers will be repeated by their progeny. Just as Abraham left Mesopotamia and journeyed to Canaan, so too shall Israel depart from Babylonia and return to the land of Israel; and just as Abraham was blessed with progeny like grains of sand (Gen 12:1-3; 22:16-17), so too shall the nation now proliferate and propagate. The stylistic formulation of the allegory was influenced by the Ugaritic literary convention of gender conformity: the males are described in masculine terms ("rock" [צור] = "Abraham"), and the females in feminine terms ("quarry" [מַקֶּבֶת בור] = "Sarah"). Compare also Isa 49:22-23 and the Ugaritic parallels quoted there. (See the introduction, §19.A.) One should note the phonetic harmony of the two pairs: צור חֻצַּבְתֶּם and מקבת . . . נֻקַּרְתֶּם.

[1] *Listen to Me, you who pursue justice, You who seek the Lord!* — For the first expression, רֹדפי צדק, see Deut 16:20: "Justice, justice shall you pursue" (cf. also Prov 15:9; 21:21). For the second, מבקשי ה׳, see Zeph 2:3: "Seek the Lord . . . seek righteousness" (cf. also Ps 105:3 = 1 Chr 16:10; Prov 28:5). For the synonymous pair בקש/רדף ("to pursue, seek"), see Ps 34:15. The root צדק functions as a key word in the first three units of the chapter: vv. 1, 5, 6, 7, 8. For the imperative address, "Listen to Me!", see 46:3, 12; 48:12; 49:1.

Look to the rock from which you were hewn — The allegory is explained in the following verse: "The rock from which you were hewn" refers to their ancestor, Abraham. The phrases are somewhat elliptical and both omit ממנו ("from which"). (See Ibn Balaam [ed. Goshen-Gottstein], 206; Saadyah Gaon, 114; Ibn Ganaḥ, *Sefer ha-Riqmah,* 287; Ibn Ezra; Kimchi.) For the expression חצב אבן, see 2 Kgs 12:13; and for the verb חצב, see Isa 5:2; 22:16. (The root here in the archaic *qal* passive is sui generis.) It also appears in the first line of a Hebrew burial inscription: ברך חצבך, "Bless those who hewed you" (see R. Deutsch and M. Heltzer, *Forty New Ancient West Semitic Inscriptions* [Tel Aviv, 1994], 27, no. 7a, line 1) and in the Siloam Tunnel Inscription, החצבם, "the excavators" (*KAI* 189:4, 6; and see the following hemistich).

To the quarry from which you were dug! — i.e., Sarah, your progenitress. The word בור is most likely an explanatory gloss added to the hapax legomenon מַקֶּבֶת ("quarry"), which is derived from the root נקב ("to bore"); see 2 Kgs 12:10: "He bored (וַיִּקֹּב) a hole in its lid." A variant of this term appears in the Siloam Inscription (see above), written in archaic Hebrew script in the eighth century BCE and found in Jerusalem's Siloam tunnel in 1880. The inscription describes the poignant meeting between the two groups of stonemasons who were hewing the rock from opposite ends in order to bring the waters of the Gihon Spring into Jerusalem: "This is the record of how the tunnel (הנקבה) . . . was breached. . . . While there was yet three cubits to be hewn, a voice was heard, each man calling to his coworker. . . . So on the day of the breach (הנקבה), the excavators (החצבם) struck, each man to meet his coworker, pickax against pickax." This impressive architectural project was undertaken for the purpose of ensuring a water supply during Sennacherib's siege in 701 BCE (2 Kgs 20:20; 2 Chr 32:30). For the root נקר in the context of rock or stone, see Exod 33:22: "In a crevice (נִקְרַת) in the rock" (cf. also the Akkadian etymological and semantic equivalent *naqāru* [*CAD* N/1:331]). For other allegorical usages of בור ("cistern") as representing the female, see Prov 5:15: "Drink water from your own cistern"; cf. also Cant 4:15. It is quite likely that in an incantation against infertility the Ugaritic cognate *bir* is also used as a euphemism for genitalia: "For the woman is closed; the 'cistern' covered" (see J. C. de Moor, "An Incantation against Infertility [KTU^2 1.13]," *UF* 12 [1980]: 306, lines 24-25; 309-10, notes to lines 24-25.) The Sumerian cognate pu_3 is polysemous as well, denoting both a waterhole and female genitalia.

[2] A subtle polemic is being waged here against the Judeans who remained in the land while the rest of the nation was led into exile; cf. Ezek 33:24: "O mortal, those who live in these ruins in the land of Israel argue: 'Abraham was but one man (אחד היה אברהם), yet he was granted possession of the land. We are many; surely, the land has been given as a possession to us.'" The prophet reassures the expatriates that, although they are the minority and although the remaining Judeans claim priority over Zion, they (those who return) shall repossess the land and repopulate it, similar to Abraham who was only one but was blessed and his progeny many. (See the introduction, §16.)

Look back to Abraham your father — The explanation of the metaphor repeats the imperative of v. 1, הַבִּיטוּ (and is repeated yet a third time in v. 6): Observe your ancestor Abraham, the rock from which you were hewn. Abraham, the progenitor of the nation, is mentioned also in Isa 41:8; 63:16.

And to Sarah who brought you forth! — For the root חיל ("to writhe," "to give birth") in the *polel* stem, חולל, see Deut 32:18: "You neglected the Rock that begot you, forgot the God who brought you to birth (מְחֹלְלֶךָ)"; see also Prov 25:23; and cf. Isa 45:10: "Shame on him who asks his father, 'What are you begetting?' Or a woman, 'What are you bearing (תחילין)'?" Compare likewise the Phoenician incantation: חל ולד (*KAI* 27:27); Ugar. *ḫl ld*, "writhe (with birth pangs) (and) give birth," (*CAT* 1.12.I:25); and Akk. *ḫâlu* (*CAD* Ḫ:55; cf. also *ḫajjāltu*, "a woman in travail" [ibid., 32], and *ḫilū*, "labor pains" [ibid., 189]; the

Akkadian root, however, may be an Aramaic loan). For the pair of synonymous verbs חיל/ילד, see Deut 32:18; Ps 90:2; Job 39:1. This verb is a homonym of מחוללת, "pierced" (v. 9). This is the only place outside Genesis where the founding mother of the nation is mentioned, and is but one example of the many allusions the prophet makes to Israelite traditions. (See the introduction, §12.)

For he was only one when I called him — A message of encouragement to the nation: When I called upon Abraham to leave his native land (also the present locus of the Judean exile) and to embark on the journey to Canaan, he was but one solitary individual. For אחד with the meaning of a lone individual, see 1 Chr 29:1: "God has chosen my son Solomon alone (אחד)."

But I blessed him and made him many — The two *waws* that prefix the verbs should be vocalized with a *qamatz,* indicating the past tense (cf. the Targum; Ibn Balaam [ed. Goshen-Gottstein], 206; Saadyah Gaon, 114; Kimchi): I, however (the *waw* denotes contrast), blessed him and multiplied his progeny, and he became a large nation; cf. Gen 22:15-17: "The angel of the Lord called to Abraham . . . 'I will bestow My blessing on you (אברכך) and make your descendants as numerous (וְהַרְבָּה אַרְבֶּה) as the stars of heaven.'" The prophet's intention is clear: He wishes to draw an analogy between Abraham and Sarah's promised progeneration, and the nation's proliferation, as promised in Gen 22:17 (quoted above; and cf. also Deut 7:13). The synonymous pair פרי/רבי ("to be fruitful/to multiply"), which is exceedingly common throughout the Bible (e.g., Gen 1:28), influenced the scribe of the Isaiah Scroll, 1QIsa[a], who substituted ואפרהו ("I made him fruitful") for MT וָאֲבָרְכֵהוּ ("I blessed him"); cf. Gen 48:4: "I will make you fertile and numerous." For the conjunction of the three verbs ברך, פרי, and רבי, see Gen 17:20: "As for Ishmael, I have heeded you. I hereby bless him (ברכתי). I will make him fertile (והפריתי) and exceedingly numerous (והרביתי)." The LXX's addition, "And I loved him," between the two verbs ואברכהו וארבהו was most likely influenced by Isa 41:8: "Seed of Abraham whom I loved," and by a similar triad of verbs in Deut 7:13: "He will love you and bless you and multiply you."

[3] In the same way that God transformed Abraham from a lone individual into a large nation (implying that the present nation shall grow accordingly), so too will there be a reversal in Zion's lot: Today she is in ruins; tomorrow she shall be like the Garden of Eden. The concrete expression of God's comfort is the rebuilding and rehabilitation of Zion. In light of the striking parallels in phraseology, it seems quite likely that Jer 33:11 left its impression on the second part of this verse: "Yet in this place shall be heard once again the sound (קול) of joy (שׂשׂון) and the sound (קול) of gladness (שׂמחה) . . . the sound (קול) of those who shout, 'Give thanks to the Lord of Hosts' . . . as they bring thanksgiving offerings (תודה) to the house of the Lord" — all this in the

context of Zion's complete restoration: "For I will restore the fortunes of the land as of old — said the Lord." For another verse that perhaps influenced this verse in Deutero-Isaiah, see Jer 31:13: "I will turn their mourning to joy (לְשָׂשׂוֹן). I will comfort them (ונחמתים) and cheer them (וְשִׂמַּחְתִּים) in their grief." (See the introduction, §15.) Compare also the heartening words of Ezek 36:33-35: "The ruined places shall be rebuilt . . . and men shall say: 'That land, once desolate, has become like the Garden of Eden. And the cities, once ruined, desolate, and ravaged, are now populated and fortified.'" The future of the nation shall be as it was at the very beginning of creation — a veritable Garden of Eden (Gen 2:8, 15).

Truly the Lord has comforted Zion — The כי particle introducing the phrase is emphatic. Divine comfort and reassurance to the nation (Isa 40:1; 49:13; 52:9; 66:13) are adapted and applied to Zion; cf. Zech 1:17: "For the Lord will yet comfort Zion." The root נחם is a key word in the following units as well; see vv. 12, 19.

Comforted all her ruins — The Lord consoles all the sites that were ruined and left in desolation following the exile (see Isa 44:26; 49:19); cf. 52:9: "Raise a shout together, O ruins (חרבות) of Jerusalem! For the Lord will comfort His people, will redeem Jerusalem." For the reiteration of the verb נחם, see 40:1.

He will make her wilderness like Eden — God shall transform Zion, which has lain desolate since the exile (cf. 64:9: "Your holy cities have become a desert. Zion has become a desert, Jerusalem a desolation") into a veritable Eden. For this total reverse turnabout, see Joel 2:3: "Before them [the locusts], the land was like the Garden of Eden, behind them, a desolate waste." For the expression שׂים כ- ("to make like"), see Isa 49:2; 50:7.

Her desert like the garden of the Lord — God shall transform the wilderness of Zion into a lush garden blessed by the Lord. For the synonymous pair ערבה/מדבר, see 40:3; and for the expression עדן גן ה'/אלהים ("Eden, garden of the Lord/of God"), see Ezek 28:13; 31:9. For גן ה', see Gen 13:10.

Joy and gladness shall be found in her — Since "joy and gladness" constitute a hendiadys, the verb appears in the singular, as opposed to the plural form in the LXX and 1QIsa[a], ימצאו, which corresponds with v. 11: ששׂון ושׂמחה ישׂיגון ("Let them attain joy and gladness"). For ששון ושמחה, see also Isa 22:13; 35:10. Note the alliteration of sibilants in the first three words of this clause.

Thanksgiving and the sound of music — תודה is elliptical for "[hymns of] thanksgiving"; cf. Jer 30:19: "From them shall issue thanksgiving (תודה) and the sound (וקול) of merrymakers"; cf. also Ps 26:7; 42:5; 1QIsa[a] appends here: נסו יגון ואנחה ("sorrow and sighing shall flee"), thus conforming to v. 11, as well as Isa 35:10. The expression קול זִמְרָה appears once more, in Ps 98:5 and, as here, denotes song accompanied by musical instruments; cf. Amos 5:23: "And let Me not hear the song of (זִמְרַת) your lutes."

[4-6] The themes and language of Isa 2:2-4 are manifest in the first two verses of this unit:

Isaiah 2		**Isaiah 51**	
v. 2:	"And all nations shall gaze on it with joy" ונהרו אליו כל הגוים	v. 4:	"For the light of peoples" לאור עמים
v. 3	"Peoples" עמים	v. 4:	"My people," "peoples," עמים ,עמי
	"For teaching shall come forth from Zion" כי מציון תצא תורה		"For teaching shall go forth from Me" כי תורה מֵאִתִּי תצא
v. 4:	"Thus He will judge among nations" ושפט בין עמים	v. 4: v. 5:	"My way for the light of peoples" ומשפטי לאור עמים "Shall judge the peoples" עמים ישפֹּטו

The linguistic connection between the expression לאור עמים ("for the light of peoples") and נהרו . . . הגוים ("nations . . . shall gaze") is manifest when one understands the root נהר to mean "to shine, be radiant as a light-filled gaze" (see 60:5; Jer 31:12; Ps 34:6). Moreover, the universality of God's rule and תורה ("teaching") appears in both units. There is, however, one important difference: The source of God's instruction does not stem from Zion (i.e., it does not emanate from a specific locale, as in First Isaiah's prophecy), but rather derives directly from God, who is not restricted to a single place (cf. Isa 66:1). (See the introduction, §14.) This unit is linked to the preceding unit by the root צדק: v. 1, צדק; v. 5, צדקי; v. 6, צדקתי; and the repetition of the imperative: הַביטו (vv. 1, 2, 6).

[4] *Hearken to Me, My people!* — This unit begins in much the same way as the first unit: "Listen to Me!" (v. 1). The Peshitta and many medieval Hebrew manuscripts read here עמים (plural) instead of MT עמי (singular), which accords well with the end of this verse and the beginning of the next one (both of which read עמים).

And give ear to Me, O My nation! — mirrors the first hemistich. The plural variant ולאומים instead of MT ולאומי (singular) appears in the midrashic collection *Yalqut Hamachiri on Tehillim* 23:1 (S. Buber, *Yalqut Hamachiri on Tehillim* [Jerusalem, 1964], 1:78 [Heb.]); cf. 49:1. For the pair of verbal synonyms האזין/הקשיב, see 42:23; Ps 17:1. The Ugaritic cognate of the denominative verb האזין ("to give ear"), derived from אֹזן ("ear"), appears in line 8 of an incantation against sorcery: *ltudn,* "Do not give ear" (D. Pardee, "A Ugaritic Incantation against Serpents and Sorcerers [1.100]," *COS* 1:328). Compare, too, in Akkadian, the hapax legomenon *uzzunu* (*CAD,* U/W: 396).

For teaching shall go/shine forth from Me — The כי particle may also be emphatic here. In light of the following hemistich it is very probable that the verb תצא is polysemous. On the one hand, it denotes "coming forth, emerging," as in Isa 42:1: "He shall make justice emerge (יוציא) to the nations"; Hab 1:4: "That is why decision fails and justice never emerges (יֵצֵא)." On the other hand, it also signifies "shining forth," as in Isa 62:1: "Till her victory shine (יֵצֵא) resplendent and her triumph like a flaming torch"; Ps 37:6: "He will cause your vindication to shine forth (והוציא) like the light." For the play on words between תורה ("teaching") and אור ("light") (in the adjacent hemistich), see also Isa 42:4, 6: "His teaching . . . a light of nations"; Prov 6:23: "For the commandment is a lamp, the teaching is a light."

And My justice for the light of peoples, in a moment I will bring it — ארגיע is usually understood as a denominative verb derived from the substantive רֶגַע, "suddenly, in the blink of an eye" (Ibn Balaam [ed. Goshen-Gottstein, 206]), i.e., I shall bring it momentarily; cf. Prov 12:19: "Truthful speech abides forever, a lying tongue for but a moment (ארגיע)". Ibn Ganaḥ interprets likewise and further explicates that the א prefix is "an addition of no consequence to the speaker," i.e., ארגיע is a variant of the substantive רגע, as in the case of זרוע/אזרוע, in which the א is prosthetic; thus the א of ארגיע does not indicate the first person imperfect (see *Sefer ha-Shorashim,* 469; *Sefer ha-Riqmah* [ed. Walensky], 155). This explanation accords well with the following verse: "My victory is near." For רגע as "immediately," see Isa 47:9; Jer 4:20 (parallel to פתאום, "suddenly"); Ps 6:11; Job 34:20. (Some have suggested to derive this verb from Arab. *raʿaga* [transposition of final letters], meaning "to flash, glow," which would parallel one of the meanings of תצא in the previous hemistich.) For the expression לאור עמים, cf. Isa 42:6; 49:6: לאור גוים ("a light of nations"). For the parallel between the synonyms תורה and משפט, see 42:4; Hab 1:4 (quoted above). For the metaphor, cf. Zeph 3:5: "He issues judgment every morning, as unfailing as the light."

[5] There is a repetition here of the previous verse's phraseology, יצא — תצא; עמים . . . ומשפטי — עמים ישפֹטו; ארגיע — קרוב; the universal dimension also continues in this verse. The root ישע functions as a key word in vv. 5, 6, and 8.

My triumph is near. My salvation has gone forth/shone — Cf. Isa 56:1: "For soon My salvation shall come, and My triumph be revealed." For the parallel pair ישע/צדק in a similar context, see 46:13: "I am bringing My victory close; it shall not be far. And My triumph shall not be delayed"; and cf. 45:8. In lieu of MT קרוב, the LXX translates: "I shall bring near (אקריב)."

My arms shall rule the peoples — The plural זְרֹעַי is anomalous, since in every other place in the Bible the expression זרוע ה׳ ("the Lord's arm") appears in the singular (except for Deut 33:27, where the meaning is enigmatic), and thus the LXX translates the word as a singular; cf. v. 9; 52:10; 53:1. This may be the reason that prompted the scribe of 1QIsa[a] to substitute זרועו, "His arm." For "arms" symbolizing strength of arms, might, see Ezek 30:24: "I will strengthen the arms of the king of Babylon . . . and I will break the arms of Pharaoh"; and for "arms" as armies, cf. Dan 11:15, 22, 31. For the verb שפט meaning "to rule," see 1 Sam 8:5: "Therefore appoint a king for us, to rule us (לשפטנו) like all other nations." This is also the meaning of the Akkadian cognate *šapāṭu* (*CAD* Š/1:450-51). For the expression לשפוט עמים, see also Ps 67:5; 98:9.

The coastlands shall look eagerly for Me — איים, which corresponds here to עמים in the preceding stich (cf. Ezek 27:3), is also found in parallel with גוים (Isa 40:15), לְאֻמִּים (41:1; 49:1), and קְצוֹת הארץ (41:5).

They shall wait hopefully for My arm — The verb יְיַחֵלוּן is the third-person masculine plural of the root יחל, with the archaic nunation. In 1QIsa[a] the scribe substituted the *hiph'il* form יוחילון (with the same meaning). For the verbal pair יחל/קוי, see Mic 5:6; Ps 130:5; cf. also Ps 39:8.

[6] Even though heavens and earth (a merism indicating totality) may fade away, depicted by the prophet in a triad of similes, the Lord's salvation and redemption shall be everlasting. For the same idea, see Ps 102:26-27: "Of old You established the earth (הארץ). The heavens (השמים) are the work of Your hands. They shall perish, but You shall endure. They shall all wear out like a garment (כבגד יִבְלוּ)." For the opposite motif, that of the renewal of the heavens and earth, see Isa 65:17; 66:22.

Raise your eyes to the heavens! — Cf. 40:26: "Lift your eyes to the heavens and see: Who created these?"

And look at the earth beneath! — The imperative הַביטו connects this unit with the initial unit, vv. 1, 2. 1QIsa[a] both deletes and adds: It adds the phrase ראו מי ברא את אלה ("Behold, who created these," influenced by 40:26); and the next two hemistichs are absent from the scroll. For the phrase ארץ מתחת, see Exod 20:4.

Though the heavens should dissipate like smoke — Some interpret the hapax legomenon verb נמלחו as a denominative from מֶלַח ("salt") and translate "grow murky," while others derive it from the expression (בְּלוֹיֵ) מְלָחִים, "(worn-out) rags" (Jer 38:11), with the meaning "wear away," "being diffused," comparing the image to Ps 68:3: "Disperse them as smoke is dispersed." For the image of "dissipating like smoke" in Akkadian, see *CAD* B:73; Q:327.

And the earth wear out like a garment — Cf. Isa 50:9: "They shall wear out like a garment."

And its inhabitants die out as well — The Targum translates אַף אִינוּן הָכֵין

("they too likewise"), thus bringing about the demise of all of the earth's inhabitants. In light of the two previous similes, "like smoke," "like a garment," some commentators interpret כן as the singular of כִּנִּים, "lice" (see Exod 8:13, 14; and cf. possibly Num 13:33: "And we looked like grasshoppers to ourselves, and as lice [וְכֵן] in their eyes"). Others suggest that the original reading was כִּנִּים, but due to haplography caused by the following verb, ימותון, the plural suffix of the noun כִּנִּים was erroneously deleted. According to these last two interpretations, the population shall die away as if they were short-lived lice. Luzzatto offers a novel interpretation, suggesting that the expression כמו כן means "momentarily," in the time it takes to say the monosyllabic word כן.

Yet My salvation is forever — The *waw* denotes contrast to what was just stated, i.e., the transience of both nature and human beings. See v. 8: "My salvation [shall endure] through all ages."

My triumph shall remain unbroken — lit. "My triumph shall not be shattered," i.e., shall not be abolished; cf. v. 8: "My triumph shall endure forever." For the root חתת (here in the *qal*) denoting shattering or breaking, see Isa 9:3; Jer 51:56. For its meaning "to be dismayed," see v. 7. The LXX, on the other hand, translates "shall not cease," and the Targum לָא תִתְעַכַּב, "shall not be delayed." Note the chiastic order of the words ישועתי and צדקתי in this verse, as compared to צדקי and ישעי in the preceding one.

[7-8] This pericope is linked to the above verses by common phraseology: צדק (vv. 5, 7, 8); ישע (vv. 5, 6, 8); תורה (vv. 4, 7); עמי/עמים/עם (vv. 4, 5, 7); לא תֵחָת (v. 6) — אל תֵּחָתּו (v. 7). Compare also the simile of the cosmos dissipating together with all its inhabitants (vv. 6, 8), juxtaposed by the eternity of the Lord's victory: "My salvation is forever, My triumph shall remain unbroken" (v. 6) — "But My triumph shall endure forever, My salvation through all the ages" (v. 8; note also the chiastic structure). The introductory formula to this unit, "Listen to Me, you who care for justice!" is very much akin to the opening words of the chapter, "Listen to Me, you who pursue justice!"

[7] The motif of the Lord's teaching inscribed on Israel's heart also appears in Jer 31:33: "I will put My teaching into their inmost being and inscribe it on their hearts."

Listen to Me, you who care for justice — The expression יודעי צדק, unique in the Bible, appears twice in the *Damascus Document* from Qumran Cave 4: 4Q268 2 i, frag. 1, 9; 4Q270, frag. ii 2, 19 (J. M. Baumgarten, *Qumran Cave 4.XIII: The Damascus Document (4Q266-273),* DJD 18 [Oxford, 1996], 119, 145).

O people who lay My instruction to heart! — a nation that heeds instruction; cf. Ps 37:31: "The teaching of his God is in his heart"; Ps 40:9: "Your teaching is in my inmost parts"; cf. Jer 32:40: "And I will put into their hearts reverence for Me."

Fear not the insults of men! — You, My nation, should not cringe at the abuse leveled at you by mere mortals.

And be not dismayed at their jeers! — Neither is there reason for you to take their derision to heart. For גִּדּוּפִים ("jeers") see Isa 43:28. For the parallel pair חרפה — גִּדֻּפִים/גדופה ("insults" — "jeer/jeers"), see Ezek 5:15: "You shall be a mockery (חרפה) and a derision (וגדופה)"; Zeph 2:8: "I have heard the insults (חרפת) of Moab and the jeers (גִּדֻּפֵי) of the Ammonites"; Ps 44:17: "At the sound of taunting revilers (מחרף ומגדף)." For the parallel verbs חתת/ירא ("to fear"/ "to be dismayed"), see Deut 1:21; 31:8; Jer 30:10; 46:27. The final hemistichs of this verse form a chiasm.

[8] *For the moth shall eat them up like a garment* — There is no reason to fear their ridicule, since they shall be consumed like moth-eaten clothes; see also Isa 50:9: "They shall all wear out like a garment; the moth shall consume them"; Job 13:28: "Like a garment eaten by moths." The Akkadian etymological and semantic cognate of Heb. עשׁ, *ašāšu,* appears in a lexical list followed (as here) by *sāsu* (see *CAD* A/2:422).

The moth shall eat them up like wool — A parallel simile portraying extinction. For צֶמֶר ("a woolen garment"), see Lev 13:47; and cf. Ezek 44:17. The hapax legomenon סס, parallel to עשׁ in the first hemistich, also appears in Akkadian, *sāsu,* in connection with the consumption of clothing: "If a moth should eat a person's garments" (*CAD* S:196-97; and see the reference on the previous clause). And in the Aramaic Sefire inscription it appears in a list of rodents and predators (I.A:31; see Fitzmyer, *Aramaic Inscriptions of Sefîre,* 15). For the repetition of the same verb in two sequential clauses (יאכְלֵם), see v. 3 in connection with נחם.

Yet My triumph shall endure forever — The *waw* indicates contrast. The two substantives צדקתי and ישועתי are ordered in such a way as to form a chiasm with v. 6.

My salvation through all the ages — forever and ever (לדור דורים), an emphatic repetition. For the synonyms דור(ו)דור and לעולם, see Exod 3:15: "This shall be My name forever (לעולם), this My appellation for all eternity (לדור דֹר)"; cf. also Isa 58:12; 60:15; 61:4. For the parallel in Aramaic, see Dan 3:33: "His kingdom is an everlasting (עָלַם) kingdom, and His dominion endures throughout the generations (דָּר וְדָר)"; in Ugaritic: "Assume your eternal *(ʿlmk)* kingship, your everlasting *(drdrk)* dominion" (*CAT* 1.2.IV:10); and cf. Akk. *dār dūr* and *dūr dār* (*CAD* D:108). The expression דור דורים appears again only in Ps 72:5; 102:25. For the connection between the latter psalm and the imagery in these verses, see the introduction to v. 6.

[9-11] A number of ancient Near Eastern epics narrate the rebellion of the sea (in Mesopotamia, Tiamat and her henchmen; in Ugarit, Yam and his allies) against the god of the heavens (in Mesopotamia, Marduk; in Ugarit, Baal), a battle that ends with the capitulation and demise of the instigators. This tradition reverberates throughout many of the biblical genres (wisdom literature, psalms, and prophecy) explicitly and implicitly, through expressions and idioms (see U. Cassuto, *The Goddess Anath: Canaanite Epics of the Patriarchal Age*, trans. I. Abrahams [Jerusalem, 1971], 71-75; idem, *Biblical and Oriental Studies*, 2: *Bible and Ancient Oriental Texts*, trans. I. Abrahams [Jerusalem, 1975], 83-155). The prophet, in an effort to arouse the Lord and fan the flames of His wrath, recalls His antediluvian exploits and the miracle at the sea at the time of the exodus from Egypt. The prophet implores God to deliver His people just as He subdued the monsters of the deep. In three sequential verses the prophet juxtaposes the mythic past (v. 9), historical events (v. 10 — the parting of the Reed Sea), and the long-aspired hopes for future redemption (v. 11). Verses 9-11 are connected to the first unit by the expressions **שׂשׂוֹן ושׂמחה** (vv. 3, 11); **וָאַרְבֵּהוּ** (v. 2) — **רַבָּה** (v. 10); **וַיָּשֶׂם** (v. 3) — **הַשָּׂמָה** (v. 10); **ציון** (vv. 3, 11); and by the homonymic plays on the roots **חרב**: **חָרבותיה** ("her ruins," v. 3), **המחרבת** ("who dried up," v. 10); **חיל**: **תחוללכם** ("who brought you forth," v. 2) — **מחוללת** ("pierced," v. 9); and **חצב**: **חֻצַּבְתֶּם** ("you were hewn from," v. 1) — **המחצבת** ("who hacked in pieces," v. 9). For its connections to the preceding unit, cf. the metaphor of the divine arm (**זרוע ה׳**, vv. 5, 9) and **דֹרות עולמים** (v. 9) — **לעולם . . . לדור דורים** (v. 8). There are also thematic and linguistic connections between this unit and psalms of lament and hymns glorifying divine strength, e.g., Ps 44, 74, 77, 93. (See the introduction, §17.)

[9] Compare the similarities between Ps 89:11, 14, 22, and this verse: "You crushed Rahab; he was like a corpse. With Your powerful arm You scattered Your enemies" (v. 11); "Your arm is endowed with might" (v. 14); "My arm" (v. 22).

Awake, awake! — a double imperative for emphasis (see vv. 12, 17; 52:1, 11; and in the introduction, §10.A.1), repeated yet a third time in the following hemistich. The first two times the accent is on the ultimate syllable of the verb, whereas the third time the accent is penultimate, as in Judg 5:12. The verb **עור** denotes, on the one hand, preparedness for battle, similar to the Akkadian semantic cognate *tebû* (*CAD* T:313-15); and, on the other, it is a call to God to rise and take charge, as in Ps 44:24: "Rouse (**עורה**) Yourself! Why do You sleep, O Lord? Awaken, do not reject us forever!"; Ps 59:5: "Rouse (**עורה**) Yourself on my behalf and look!"

Clothe yourself with strength, O arm of the Lord! — The prophet addresses himself to the Lord's arm in allegorical language (see v. 5; cf. 40:10; 52:10; 53:1), to gird itself for battle. Hebrew **עֹז** denotes "strength"; see v. 5; Ps 89:11: "With Your powerful arm (**בזרוע עֻזְּךָ**) You scattered Your enemies" (cf. also Ps 66:3; 77:13); and "splendor" (see Isa 52:1, where **עֻזֵּךְ** is parallel to **תפארתך**). In Mesopotamian literature as well the gods are depicted as being girded in majesty and splendor as they prepare to wage battle (*CAD* E:434 [*ezzu* = עֹז]; Ḫ:36; L:18; N/2:86). For the Deity clothed in the metaphoric garb of a warrior, see 59:17: "He donned victory like a coat of mail, with a helmet of triumph on His head. He clothed Himself with garments of retribution, wrapped Himself in zeal as in a robe"; cf. also Ps 104:1: "You are clothed in glory and majesty." The Israelite tradition attributes God's victory over the rebellious waters to the prowess of His mighty arm; see also Exod 15:6, 12.

Awake as in days of old, as in former ages! — This third reiteration of the imperative עורי stresses the need for action: Rouse yourself, O mighty arm, and act against your enemies, as in days of yore when you smote the sea monsters, and as in the days of the exodus, when you annihilated the Egyptian army at the sea. For the parallel synonyms קֶדֶם/עולמים, see Ps 77:6: "My thoughts turn to days of old (מִקֶּדֶם), to years long past (עולמים)"; and cf. the similar parallelism above in v. 8 (דור דורים/עולם). For the expression כימי קדם ("as in days of old"), see Jer 46:26; cf. also מימי קדם (Isa 23:7; Mic 7:20) and בימי קדם (Ps 44:2). The plural in both components of the construction of דרות עולמים is characteristic of postexilic Hebrew. (See the introduction, §11.B.)

It was You who hacked Rahab in pieces — It was the Lord's arm that hewed Rahab, the monster of the sea, according to the Israelite epic tradition; see also Ps 89:11: "You crushed Rahab; he was like a corpse"; Job 9:13: "Under Him Rahab's helpers sink down"; Job 26:12: "By His skill He struck down Rahab." This substantive never appears with the definite article ה and thus designates a proper name. It is derived from the Akkadian verb *ra'ābu,* which means both "fury" and "trembling" (*CAD* R:1-3). The verb המחצבת is a *hiph'il* participle from the root חצב, which appears only once more in the Bible with this meaning, in Hos 6:5: "That is why I have hewn down (חצבתי) the prophets. I have slain them with words of My mouth." It appears in the same bellicose context in the Ugaritic Baal epic describing the slaughter of the sea god Yam's allies: "And behold, Anat fights in the valley, battles *(tḫtṣb)* between the two cities, and kills the people *(lim)* on the seacoast [the west], slays the inhabitants *(adm)* of the sun's source [the east])" (*CAT* 1.3.II:5-8). (For the Hebrew interdialectal etymological and semantic equivalents אדם/לְאֻמִּים of the Ugaritic pair *adm/lim* ["nation/people"], see Isa 43:4.) Note also the wordplay with the homonym חֲצַבְתֶּם in v. 1. The scribe of 1QIsa[a] substituted the more common verb המוחצת for the rare המחצבת; cf. Job 26:12: "By His skill He struck down (מחץ) Rahab." Furthermore, the name רהב serves as a poetic sobriquet for Egypt in Ps 87:4: "I mention Rahab and Babylon among those who acknowledge Me" (cf. also Isa 30:7). It, along with תנין (immediately following), serve as literary markers for the subsequent allusion to the splitting of the Reed Sea. For the exclamatory הלוא, see, e.g., 40:21 (three times), 28; 58:6; and for the parallel masculine expression הלוא אתה הוא, see Jer 14:22.

Who pierced the sea serpent — The verb מחוללת is a *polel* stem from the root חלל, which denotes piercing or killing. Compare (in the same context of the epic battle between God and Yam's minion) Job 26:13: "His hand pierced (חֹלְלָה) the fleeing serpent." For תנין, another of the maritime sea serpents involved in the epic struggle between God and the rebellious waters, see Isa 27:1: "In that day the Lord will punish with His great, cruel, and mighty sword Leviathan, the fleeing serpent (נחש בריח), Leviathan, the winding serpent (נחש עֲקַלָּתוֹן). He will slay the serpent (התנין) of the sea"; Job 7:12: "Am I Yam or the sea serpent?" (two primordial allies in the Baal epic). Compare similarly the names of the other conspirators against Baal in the Ugaritic epic: *tnn . . . bṯn ʿqltn,* "the dragon . . . the winding serpent" (*CAT* 1.3.III:40-41); *bṯn brḥ . . . bṯn ʿqltn,* "the fleeing serpent . . . the winding serpent" (*CAT* 1.5.I:1-2). For the names *ym* and *tnn* (Yam and the dragon), see *CAT* 1.3.III:39-40.

As with חצב above, note the homonymic wordplay formed by מחוללת ("pierced") and תחוללכם ("who brought you forth") (v. 2). As mentioned above, תנין is also a sobriquet for Pharaoh, king of Egypt (as is Rahab), e.g., Ezek 29:3: "I am going to deal with you, O Pharaoh king of Egypt, mighty monster (התנים [=התנין]), sprawling in your channels, who said, 'My Nile is my own; I made it for myself'" (cf. also Ezek 32:2); and it creates a literary bridge to the next verse, which describes the drying up of the Reed Sea at the time of the exodus. (Note also that this term [תנין] appears in Jer 51:34, in a description of how Nebuchadnezzar king of Babylon will be swallowed up.)

[10] *It was You who dried up the sea* — The prophet combines the mythic description above with the historical tradition regarding the exodus from Egypt. On the one hand, ים is the proper name of the deity Yam, who features prominently in the Ugaritic Baal epic (*CAT* 1.2.I:7, 9; II:17, 22; 1.3.III:38) and parallels Rahab and the dragon of the previous verse (cf. Job 7:12, where ים and תנין appear together). According to one recension of the Israelite epic, the Lord defeated the sea by drying up its waters, e.g., Isa 50:2: "With a mere rebuke I dry up the sea"; Nah 1:4: "He rebukes the sea and dries it up." On the other hand, ים serves as a reference to the waters of the Sea of Reeds, which God dried up so that Israel could pass through; see Exod 14:21: "And turned the sea into dry ground (לחרבה). The waters were split"; Ps 106:9: "He sent His blast against the Sea of Reeds; it became dry (וַיֶּחֱרָב)." Thus Deutero-Isaiah is engaged in a quasi-historicization of the theomachian myth.

The waters of the great deep — yet another of the sea god's appellations, as well as an allusion to primordial days, e.g., Gen 7:11: "All the fountains of the great deep (תהום רבה) burst apart." The adjective רבה is commonly attached to תהום ("the deep") (see Amos 7:4; Ps 36:7; 78:15), referring to deep subterranean waters, as in Jonah 2:6: "The waters closed in over me, the deep engulfed me." The word תהום appears primarily with a feminine adjective or verb, e.g.,

Gen 49:25; Ezek 31:4, and is none other than the Hebraic counterpart of Tiamat, the goddess of the salty water, who, according to the Babylonian epic *Enuma Elish,* was defeated by Marduk. The substantives *thm* ("the god Ocean") and *thmt* ("primordial ocean") often also appear in Ugaritic epic poetry (*HdO* 2:864). The two components of the construction מֵי תהום appear as parallels in Ezek 31:4, quoted above, but the composite construction מי תהום רבה is unique. For the parallel תהום/ים ("the sea/the deep"), see Job 28:14; 38:16.

Who made the depths of the sea a road the redeemed might walk — You, God's puissant arm, transformed (for שׂים ל- ["to turn into"], see, e.g., Isa 41:15) the depths of the sea into a highway for Israel to cross as they fled from Egypt. The prophet's intent is clear: Just as the Lord redeemed Israel from their Egyptian exile, so too will He rescue them from Babylon. (The statements here contrast with 47:1-2, in which the "fair maiden Babylon" is commanded to cross rivers as she is marched into captivity.) The penultimate accent on הַשָּׂמָה (the participle's referent is the Lord's arm) marks it as a past tense (see Gen 15:17; 29:9), since the reference is to the exodus. Some, however, suggest putting the stress on the final syllable, marking it as a feminine participle, corresponding with the two previous participles. The definite article prefixing the verb functions as a relative pronoun, as in Gen 21:3: "Abraham named his son, who was born (הנולד) to him"; Ruth 1:22: "Naomi, who returned (הַשָּׁבָה) from the land of Moab." 1QIsa[a], Peshitta, and several medieval Hebrew manuscripts read במעמקי ים ("in the depths of the sea") instead of MT מעמקי ים (which is sui generis; but cf. מעמקי מים, Ezek 27:34; Ps 69:3, 15), since the verbal expression שׂים ל- does not usually take two direct objects. (For the *dagesh* in the ק of מעמקי, see GKC §93pp.) For the motif of the highway through the sea, see Isa 43:16: "Thus said the Lord, who made a road through the sea and a path through mighty waters"; cf. also Ps 78:13; 106:9; 136:13-14; and it also appears in the description of the crossing of the Jordan River in Joshua's days (Josh 4:23). For the verb עבר in contexts of crossing the Sea of Reeds, see Exod 15:16 (twice); and in the *hiph'il,* see Ps 78:13; 136:14. For the "redeemed," see Isa 62:12; 63:4.

[11] The mythical-historical background of the previous two verses serves as a prelude to the prophet's true aim — the return to Zion, i.e., just as the Lord defeated His enemies of yore and rescued the Israelites from Egypt, so too will He expedite Israel's redemption from Babylon. This verse is a word-for-word repetition of Isa 35:10, which also features a path and highway (v. 8) in a similar context. Moreover, this motif and the accompanying phraseology appear in Jer 31:11-13, which left its mark on this verse: Jer 31:11: "For the Lord will ransom (פדה) Jacob, redeem him (וּגְאָלוֹ)" = Isa 51:10-11: "The redeemed (גאולים) ... the ransomed of the Lord (פדויי ה׳)"; Jer 31:13: "To joy (לשׂשׂון) ... and cheer them in their grief (ושׂמחתים מיגונם)" = Isa 51:11: "With joy (שׂמחת)

everlasting. . . . Let them attain joy and gladness (שׂשׂוֹן ושׂמחה), while grief (יגון) and sighing flee." The sequence of ideas in both Jeremiah and Deutero-Isaiah is similar: redemption followed by a joyous return, which is followed, in turn, by happiness and gladness. (See the introduction, §15.) Note also the concentration of sibilants in this verse: ישובון . . . ציון . . . ושמחת . . . ראשם שׂשׂון ושׂמחה ישׂיגון נסו.

So let the ransomed of the Lord return — the prophet's ultimate wish, the redemption of His people and their return to Zion. For the parallel synonyms גאל (at the end of the previous verse) and פדה, see Hos 13:14. 1QIsa[a] has the variant ופזורי ה׳ ("those whom the Lord scattered") instead of MT ופדויי ה׳. For the verb פזר in the context of the Israelite Diaspora, see Jer 50:17: "Israel are scattered (פזורה) sheep"; Joel 4:2: "For they have scattered (פִּזְּרוּ) My very own people, Israel, among the nations."

And come with joyful cries to Zion — The ransomed ones shall return "to Zion" (לציון, according to the ancient translations: LXX, Vulgate, Peshitta, Targum, and a number of medieval Hebrew manuscripts, contra MT ציון) with shouts of joy. For רִנָּה, see Isa 44:23; 48:20; 49:13; 54:1; 55:12.

Crowned with joy everlasting — allegorical phraseology: They shall be surrounded by unending happiness, as in 61:7: "Everlasting joy (שׂמחת עולם) shall be theirs." For a similar allegory, cf. the expression ראש שׂמחתי in Ps 137:6, with שׂמחת (עולם על) ראשם.

Let them attain joy and gladness — See v. 3: "Gladness and joy shall abide there." Note the alliterative sequence of sibilants in this hemistich (mentioned in the introduction to this verse).

While sorrow and sighing flee — The grief with which Israel was afflicted in Babylonia shall be no more; cf. Lam 1:4, 8, 11, 22. For the parallel terms יגון/אנחה ("sorrow/sighing"), cf. Ps 31:11: "My life is spent in sorrow (ביגון), my years in groaning (באנחה)." The two antonymous pairs, שׂשׂון ושׂמחה and יגון ואנחה, form a rhyming couplet: שׂשׂוֹן/יגוֹן, שׂמחה/אנחה; in both, the masculine form precedes the feminine. 1QIsa[a] reads here, as in Isa 35:10, ונס in the singular.

[12-16] This unit, which intervenes between the two prophecies — "Awake, awake!" (vv. 9-11) and "Rouse, rouse yourself!" (vv. 17-23) — is a message of consolation to Israel, who, living in constant fear, are told not to worry since the Lord will not allow their enemies to overcome them. This statement contrasts with the feelings of helplessness following the destruction of their Temple and homeland; see Lam 1:16: "Far from me is any comforter who might revive my spirit. My children are forlorn, for the foe has prevailed." The prophecy is connected to the preceding unit by the motif of the sea (v. 15) and the call to Zion (vv. 11, 16), as well as by the comfort motif (v. 12), which is also manifest in the first unit (v. 3).

[12] *I, I am He who comforts you!* — an emphatic doubling: I, and I alone (see also vv. 9, 17; 52:1). The pronoun אנכי is repeated for a third time in v. 15; cf. the threefold repetition of עורי in v. 9. (See the introduction, §10.A.1.) For the syntax of the first three words, cf. 43:25: "It is I, I who — for My own sake — wipe your transgressions away." In light of the following, the LXX reading, מנחמך ("who comforts you [feminine singular]"), is to be preferred over MT מנחמכם ("who comforts you [masculine plural]"), which is most likely the result of dittography (מנחמכם מי) or possibly an example of an enclitic *mem*. For the oft-repeated consolatory message, see, e.g., v. 3; 40:1; 49:13; 52:9. In light of the Targum, מִמַן ("from whom"), some commentators transfer the final מ of מנחמכם to the next word and read ממי.

What ails you that you fear a human, who must die — For what reason do you fear a human, who is mortal? Compare v. 7: "Fear not the insults of humans." The *waw* of the verb ותיראי functions as a relative pronoun. For the verbal expression ירא מ- ("to fear something"), see Lev 19:14; 25:17; Jer 1:8; for מי אַתְּ with a different connotation, cf. Ruth 3:16.

A mortal who fares like grass? — Why should you cringe before a mere mortal, whose lifespan is as short-lived as grass (cf. Targum: דִכְעִסְבָּה חֲשִׁיב, "who is reckoned as grass")? See Isa 40:6: "All flesh is grass"; Ps 103:15: "Man, his days are like those of grass." For the verb נתן meaning "similar to, like," see Ezek 28:2: "Though you likened (ותתן) your mind equal to a god's"; Hos 11:8: "How can I make you (אֶתֶּנְךָ) like Admah?" (one of the cities destroyed along with Sodom and Gomorrah); cf. Deut 29:22. For the synonymous pair בן אדם/אנוש, see Ps 8:5: "What is man (אנוש) that You are mindful of him, mortal man (ובן אדם) that You take note of him?"; Job 25:6: "How much less man (אנוש), a worm, the son of man (ובן אדם), a maggot."

[13] Israel lives in a state of constant fear, since they have forgotten the Lord their Maker, creator of heaven and earth. For these two motifs (God as the creator of Israel, and God as the creator of the universe), see Isa 44:24; 45:12.

You have forgotten the Lord your Maker — You have failed to remember the Lord, who created you. For the verb עשׂי with the meaning "to create," see 44:2; 54:5. For Israel forgetful of their Deity, their "Maker," see Deut 32:18; cf. Jer 2:32; 3:21.

Who stretched out the skies and founded the earth — a merism (see also v. 16): God is the creator of the entire cosmos. He spread (נטי) the sky like a tent (see Isa 40:22; 42:5; 44:24; 45:12) and established (יסד) the earth on firm foundations (see 48:13).

And you live all day in constant dread because of the rage of the oppressor — You cringe constantly and consistently before the fury of the tormentors and tyrants who oppress you. (For the root צוק, "to constrain, bring into straits," see Deut 28:53: "Because of the desperate straits [ובמצוק] to which your enemy shall constrain [יציק] you.") The verb פחד in the *pi'el,* stressing intensification, appears only once more in the Bible, in Prov 28:14: "Happy is the man who is in great dread always," and there as well it is in conjunction with the adverb תמיד, which emphasizes the extent of the trepidation. For this emphasis on constancy, in which תמיד and כל היום are combined, see also Isa 52:5; Ps 72:15. (The same linguistic emphasis has a parallel in Akkadian. Compare, for example, a royal inscription from the Old Baylonian period that describes the constancy and regularity of the daily offerings: *ūmišam . . . ana dāriš ūmī,* "Daily . . . regularly every day" [*CAD* D:114].). The LXX divides the words differently and attaches the *kaph* of כאשר to the last letter of the previous word, reading: . . . המציקך אשר, "He who oppresses you who. . . ."

Who is aiming to cut [you] *down* — The root כון denotes here, as in Rabbinic Hebrew, intent and preparedness (Ehrlich, *Mikrâ ki-Pheshuṭo,* 3:123). As will be made clear in the following verse, the verb להשחית denotes cutting down trees; see Deut 20:19: "You must not cut down (תשחית) its trees" (and cf. also v. 20). With Rashi and Luzzatto (in accord with LXX [see above], Vulgate, Peshitta, and many medieval MT manuscripts), many commentators read אשר instead of MT כאשר (see also the comment of Minḥat Shai).

Yet where is the rage of an oppressor? — The prophet asks derisively: Where is this so-called oppressor before whom you tremble?

[14] This verse is clarified in light of the metaphor in Jer 11:19-21, which describes the plot of the inhabitants of Anathoth (Jeremiah's village) to murder the prophet, who is compared to a tree, and thus prevent him from delivering his prophecies: "I did not realize that it was against me they fashioned their plots: 'Let us destroy (נשחיתה) the tree [i.e., Jeremiah] with its fruit (בלחמו) [i.e., his prophecies]. Let us cut him off from the land of the living, that his name be remembered no more! . . . You must not prophesy any more in the name of the Lord, or you will die by our hand.'" The danger Jeremiah faced is representative of the dangers facing Israel as a whole: the oppressors there (the inhabitants of Anathoth) and the oppressors here (the Babylonians) both seek to uproot the tree (= Jeremiah, Israel). Instead of being destroyed, however, it shall persevere and bloom anew. Its fruit, once in danger of extinction, shall be abundant (ולא יֶחסר לחמו). (See the introduction, §15.) For the analogy of trees and humans when a city is being besieged, see Deut 20:19.

Quickly the tree blooms — One should transpose the order of the letters and read העץ ("the tree") in lieu of MT צעה (H. L. Ginsberg, oral communication). Despite the oppressor's plot to cut down the tree, it blooms unimpeded and quickly. For the root פתח, "to open," denoting "to bloom," see Cant 7:13. For the expression מהר ל-, "quickly," see Isa 59:7.

It is not cut down and slain — It [i.e., the tree = the people] shall not be cut down or slain. The word שַׁחַת is polysemous here: On the one hand, it is connected to the cutting down of the tree, as explained above. On the other, it is a reference to the grave or Sheol; see Ezek 28:8; Jonah 2:7; Ps 16:10. This is also the meaning of the etymological and semantic cognate in Akkadian (with the transposition of the letters): *ḫaštu* (*CAD* Ḫ:143).

And its fruit will not fail — It shall continue to be bursting with fruit.

[15] In order to prove that His prowess is adequate to rescue Israel from all its enemies, God refers to His victory over Yam (see vv. 9-10). This verse appears word-for-word in Jer 31:35 and was likely borrowed from there. (See the introduction, §15.)

For I the Lord your God who stirs up the sea — There are two possible explanations of the verb **רגע**, both of which may find support in the epic struggle between Marduk and Tiamat, the salty water sea monster. First, some understand it to mean "to calm" or "to still," as in Jer 31:35 (mentioned above) and Job 26:12: "By His power He stilled (**רגע**) Yam [= the sea serpent]" (cf., e.g., Ibn Ezra, who compares it to Heb. **מרגוע**, "rest" [Jer 6:16]). For the same idea, though expressed by a different verb, see Ps 89:10: "You rule the swelling of the sea. When its waves surge, You still them"; Ps 107:29: "He reduced the storm to a whisper; the waves were stilled." Compare also the account of the defeat of Tiamat in the cosmogonic epic *Enuma Elish*, where Marduk "shot off the arrow, pierced her [Tiamat's] abdomen, sliced her innards, smashed her heart. He subdued her and snuffed out her life. He flung down her carcass; he took his stand on it" (IV:101-4; B. R. Foster, *COS* 1:398). Second, others explain **רגע** as the exact opposite, i.e., "to stir up" (cf. LXX, Vulgate; Ibn Balaam [ed. Goshen-Gottstein, 208]; Ibn Ganaḥ, *Sefer ha-Shorashim*, 469). This explanation is also in accord with the Babylonian epic, in which Marduk "causes a wave to roil Tiamat. Tiamat was roiled, churning day and night" (I:109-10; *COS* 1:392). Compare also Ps 77:17: "The waters saw You, O God. The waters saw You and were convulsed; the very deep quaked as well." The vocalization of **רֹגַע** with a *pataḥ* instead of a *ṣere* is due to the following guttural, **ע**, as in Isa 42:5: **רֹקַע הארץ**.

Into roaring waves — As a result of the stirring of the sea, the waves roar, heave, and toss. For the identical expression, see Jer 5:22; 51:55.

Whose name is Lord of Hosts — For this same expression as a proof of God's puissance, see Isa 47:4; 48:2.

[16] The motif of putting the Lord's words into an individual's mouth appears once more in Deutero-Isaiah, in 59:21, and its source is most likely the opening prophecy of the book of Jeremiah (who, in turn, was influenced by Deuteronomy; see Deut 18:18; 31:19), in which Jeremiah is consecrated as the Lord's prophet: "The Lord put out His hand and touched my mouth, and the Lord said to me: 'Herewith I put My words into your mouth'" (Jer. 1:9). The links between this prophecy and the verse here are readily apparent. Moreover, the verb לנטוע ("to plant"), which appears in the following verse in Jeremiah, also left its mark on this prophecy, since instead of the more common expression שמים נטי ("to stretch out the sky"; see v. 13), the verse has נטע שמים ("to plant the sky"), which is unique (see the commentary below). However, in contrast to Jeremiah, who was but a sole prophet (Jer 1:5), Deutero-Isaiah submits that Israel, as a whole, is to be consecrated a prophetic nation. (See the introduction, §15.) This designation comes in conjunction with the cosmogony motif. Both motifs, the Lord's creation of the universe and His control of history, are dual evidence of His power and uniqueness.

I have put My words in your mouth — I have conferred on the people, as a whole, a spirit of prophecy; see Isa 50:4; 59:21: "And the words that I have placed in your mouth"; Deut 18:18: "I will put my words in his mouth"; Deut 31:19: "Teach it to the people of Israel! Put it in their mouths!" (cf. also Num 22:38; 23:5, 12, 16). The LXX, Vulgate, and 1QIsa[a] read אשים without the *waw* conjunction, thus connecting this clause to the beginning of the previous verse: "And I, the Lord your God, . . . have put."

And sheltered you with My hand — I have provided you with My protection; cf. Isa 49:2: "He hid me in the shadow of His hand." For a similar expression, "in the shadow of Your wings," conveying shelter offered by God, see Ps 17:8; 36:8; 57:2; 63:8.

I, who planted the skies and made firm the earth — This hemistich, which describes the creation of the world by the Lord, is linked to the previous verse: "I am the Lord your God," and parallel to v. 13: "Who stretched out (נוטה) the skies and made firm the earth." Here, however, the root נטע replaces נטי (see also Isa 40:22; 42:5; 44:24; 45:12). This verb's meaning is not restricted to planting, since it can also denote establishing, placing on firm ground, as in 2 Sam 7:10: "I will establish a home for My people Israel and will plant them firmly (ונטעתיו)"; Amos 9:15: "And I will plant them firmly (ונטעתים) on their soil"; Dan 11:45: "He will pitch (ויטע) his royal pavilion." This graphic portrayal was chosen for a number of reasons: the influence of the tree imagery in v. 14, and the influence of Jeremiah's inaugural prophecy, as explained in the introduction to the verse. Moreover, in light of the appearance of the verb נטע in the context of planting tents, as in Dan 11:45, it can be applied to the sky as well, which is compared to a tent in Isa 40:22: "He stretched them [the heavens] out like a tent to dwell in."

Have said to Zion: "You are My people!" — Cf. 63:8: "Surely they are My people." Moreover, by using the expression "You are My people!" (which is naturally linked to the statement in v. 15: "I am the Lord your God"), one overhears an echo of the traditional covenant formula between God and Israel. This unit, which begins in v. 12: "I, I am He who comforts you (מנחמכם)," and ends: "My people (עמי)," is reminiscent of the first prophecy (40:1): "Comfort, comfort My people (נחמו נחמו עמי)!"

[17-23] Jerusalem is depicted as a mother in dire straits, but her children, who are duty bound to come to the aid of their parent, are unable to lend her a helping hand, since they too have drunk from the dregs of God's poison and lie in a stupor on the thoroughfares. A son's obligation to aid an inebriated father is mentioned twice in the epic literature of Ugarit: In the Aqhat epic, in a list of commands regarding the respect due to one's father, the son is obligated "to hold his hand when he is drunk, to support him when he is sated with wine" (*CAT* 1.17.I:30-31); and in "El's Divine Feast" when "El drinks wine until sated, vintage till inebriated . . . [his sons] carry him" (*CAT* 1.114:16-18).

This desperate description of Jerusalem shares a number features with Lam 4: Lam 4:1: בראׁש כל חוצות — Isa 51:20: ראׁש כל חוצות; Lam 4:9: חרב . . . רעב — Isa 51:19: והרעב והחרב; Lam 4:10: שֶׁבֶר — Isa 51:19: והשֶׁבֶר; Lam 4:10: ילדיהן — Isa 51:18: יָלָדָה; Lam 4:11: חֲמָתוֹ — Isa 51:17: חֲמָתוֹ; 51:20: חמת ה׳; 51:22: חמתי. Compare also the transfer of the "cup of reeling" from Israel to its enemies: Lam 4:21: "To you [Edom] too the cup shall pass. You shall get drunk and expose your nakedness" — Isa 51:21-23: "Who are drunk but not with wine. . . . Herewith I take from your hand the cup of reeling, the bowl, the cup of My wrath. . . . I will put it in the hands of your tormentors." (See the introduction, §18.) For the motif of a cup, which symbolizes a doomed destiny, see also Jer 25:15-16; 49:12; 51:7; Ezek 23:32-34; Hab 2:16; Ps 75:9; Lam 4:21. For the allegory of a cup full of poison, cf. the Neo-Assyrian prophecy that portrays King Esarhaddon as a "cupful *(kāsu)* of lye," i.e., Esarhaddon shall avenge his father and kill his assassins (see Parpola, *Assyrian Prophecies,* 8, line 12).

This pericope is connected to the unit preceding it by a number of common words and expressions: חֵמָה (vv. 13, 17, 20, 22); עמי (v. 16) — עמו (v. 22); ידי (v. 16) — יד ה׳ (v. 17); cf. also בְּיָדָהּ (v. 18); מיד (v. 22), and ביד (v. 23); and in lieu of אנכי אנכי הוא מנחמכם (v. 12), the prophet laments, מי אנחמך (v. 19). This final section is also linked to the unit before the last by the double imperative calling for wakefulness: התעוררי התעוררי (v. 17) and עורי עורי ("Awake, awake!") (v. 9) (cf. also the following unit that begins with the same call, עורי עורי, "Awake, awake!"; 52:1). There is, however, a significant difference between the unit beginning in v. 9 and the two units that follow, since in v. 9 the prophet calls on the Lord's mighty arm to awake, and in the latter units Jerusalem is commanded to rouse itself.

[17] *Rouse, rouse yourself! Arise, O Jerusalem!* — a double imperative for emphasis (see vv. 9, 12; 52:1, 11, and in the introduction, §10.A.1). Jerusalem, portrayed as an inebriated woman, is now commanded to sober up — "to rouse herself" (התעוררי — a reflexive *hithpaʿel*). For the employment of another verb for "to awaken" to express the arousal from the effects of alcohol, cf. קיץ, Joel 1:5: "Wake up (הָקִיצוּ), you drunkards!"; and יקץ: Gen 9:24: "When Noah woke up (וַיִּיקֶץ) from his wine." For individuals so saturated with wine that they lack the ability to rise from their stupor, see Jer 25:27: "Drink and get drunk and vomit! Fall and never rise again!" For similar words of consolation to Jerusalem, cf. Isa 52:2.

You, who from the Lord's hand have drunk the cup of His poison — Hebrew חֵמָה (emphasized three times in vv. 17, 20, 22) denotes, in addition to wrath, "venom," as in Deut 32:24: "With venomous (חמת) creepers in the dust"; Deut 32:33: "Their wine is the venom (חמת) of asps, the pitiless poison of vipers"; Ps 58:5: "Their venom (חמת) is like that of a snake." For similar imagery, see Job 21:20: "And let him drink the poison (וּמֵחֲמַת) of Shaddai." Note that the etymological Akkadian cognate *imtu* also shares these two meanings (*CAD* I-J:139-40); whereas in Ugaritic *ḥmt* refers only to "poison" (*HdO* 1:365). For the cup as a symbol of one's fate and destiny, see Ps 16:5: "The Lord is my allotted share and my cup (כוסי)."

You, who have drained to the dregs the goblet, the cup of reeling — One verb follows the other without the conjunction *waw,* and together they denote imbibing to the very last drop; see also Ezek 23:34: "You shall drink and drain it (וְשָׁתִית אותה וּמָצִית)" (the phrase in Ezekiel appears in a similar context of drinking and drunkenness; see vv. 32-33); Ps 75:9: "There is a cup in the Lord's hand with foaming wine fully mixed . . . draining it to the very dregs (יִמְצוּ ישתו)." The anomalous vocalization מָצִית (according to the "weak" ל״י paradigm), in lieu of מָצֹּת (the expected form, since the root is מצץ), creates a rhyming assonance with the preceding verb, שָׁתִית. For a similar revocalization for alliterative rhyming purposes, cf. Cant 3:11: צְאֶינָה וּרְאֶינָה, instead of צְאנָה (from the root יצא) and וּרְאֶינָה (from the root ראי).

The goblet — Hebrew כוס is added here and in v. 22 as a gloss on קֻבַּעַת, which appears only in these two verses. In the Ugaritic Aqhat epic, the two serve as poetic parallels: "Take the cup *(ks)* from my hand, the goblet *(qbʿt)* from my right hand" (*CAT* 1.19.IV:53-54; cf. also lines 55-56). It also is cognate with Phoenician *qbʿ,* Syr. *qubʿā,* Arab. *qubʿat,* Egyptian *qbḥw,* and Akk. *qabūtu* (*CAD* Q:43-44).

Reeling — For Heb. רעל and Syr. *rʿl,* "to quiver, shake, reel" (thus Saadyah Gaon; Ibn Ezra; Kimchi; Ibn Ganaḥ, *Sefer ha-Shorashim,* 483; Luzzatto), see also Zech 12:2: "Behold, I will make Jerusalem a bowl of reeling (רעל) for all the peoples around her"; Ps 60:5: "You have given us wine that makes us reel (יַיִן תַּרְעֵלָה)."

[18] For a description of Jerusalem's misery, the prophet switches from a direct address in the second-person feminine to an indirect lament in the first-person feminine. For the distinction between Jerusalem, the city and the mother, and her children, see Isa 50:1.

She has none to guide her of all the sons she bore — None of her sons is able to perform even the most basic duty a son has vis-à-vis his mother — they cannot even accompany her home (see the introduction to the unit). The root נהל denotes carefully guiding and leading (see 40:11; 49:10; and cf. Gen 33:14; Ps 23:2). Symmachus, LXX, Vulgate, Peshitta, and Targum read לֵית דִּמְנַחֵים לַהּ ("She has no one to comfort her") instead of MT אין מנהל לה. The variant reading was probably influenced by the same phrase in Lam 1:9, 17.

And none of all the sons she reared takes her by the hand — None of the sons (the negative אין is repeated from the prior hemistich for added emphasis) whom she cared for and helped raise is able to take hold of her hand and lead her home safely. For the synonyms גדל/ילד ("to bear/to rear"), see Isa 49:21; and for the expression החזיק ביד (lit. "took by the hand"), meaning "to help and support," see 41:13; 42:6; 45:1; cf. Job 8:20: "Surely God does not despise the blameless. He gives no support (יחזיק ביד) to evildoers." (For the Akkadian semantic cognate *qātam ṣabātu* ["to grasp by the hand"], see *CAD* Ṣ:30-32.)

[19] The prophet returns to speak in the second-person singular, reminiscent of Jeremiah's prophecy of doom (15:2-5): "Those destined for the sword (לחרב), to the sword (לחרב); those destined for famine (לרעב), to famine (לרעב). . . . But who will pity you, O Jerusalem? Who will console you (מי ינוד לך)?" Compare also Nahum's prophecy regarding Nineveh (3:7): "Who will console her (מי ינוד לה)? Where shall I look for anyone to comfort (מנחמים) you?"

These two things have befallen you — You were the victim of "double disasters, two at a time" (Rashi). For "two" (שתים) denoting two pairs, cf. Prov 30:7-8: "Two things I ask of you. Do not deny them to me before I die: Keep lies and false words far from me. Give me neither poverty nor riches, but provide me with my daily bread." Babylon was also dealt a double blow: "These two things shall come upon you, suddenly, in one day: Loss of children and widowhood" (Isa 47:9). For the root קרא, a by-form of קרי ("to befall, occur"), see Gen 42:4: "Lest he might meet (יִקְרָאֶנּוּ) with disaster"; Exod 1:10: "If in the event (תִקְרֶאנָה) of war." And perhaps the "two things that befell her" serves also as an indirect allusion to 40:2: "For she has received at the hand of the Lord double for all her sins." Note the wordplay שתים/שתית with v. 17.

Who can console you? — Who shall wring his head in sorrow when he hears of your fate? Cf. Jer 15:4 and Nah 3:7 cited above. The answer to these rhetorical questions is obvious.

Wrack and ruin, famine and sword — These two pairs of substantives describe the predicament of the land and the people following the exile and the destruction of the land. For the first set (שֹׁד וָשֶׁבֶר), see Isa 59:7: "Wrack and ruin are on their roads"; 60:18: "The cry, 'Violence!' shall no more be heard in your land, nor 'Wrack and Ruin!' within your borders." For the "ruin" (שבר) of devastated Jerusalem, see Lam 2:11, 13; 3:47, 48; 4:10. For the second pair (רעב וחרב), see Jer 14:12, 13, 15, 16, 18; Ezek 14:21; and cf. especially the situation within Jerusalem following the conquest, Lam 4:9; 5:9. These same disasters are also found in curse lists from Mesopotamia.

How shall I comfort you? — In light of the previous query: "Who can console you?" many commentators prefer reading here the third-person masculine singular ינחמך, "Who can comfort you?" (Ibn Balaam [ed. Goshen-Gottstein, 210]; Saadyah Gaon, 116; cf. Symmachus, LXX, Vulgate, Peshitta, Targum: דִּינַחֲמִנִיךְ; 1QIsa[a]: ינחמך, as well as one medieval MT manuscript). For other א-י variations, see 2 Sam 14:19: אִשׁ instead of יֵשׁ; Isa 10:12: אפקד instead of יפקד. Others opine "that a ב was omitted (by haplography from the last letter of the previous word, ב[והחר]), and one should read: במי אנחמך, 'By whom shall I comfort you?'" (Ibn Ezra; cf. also Rashi: "Whom shall I bring to comfort you, and say to you, 'No other nation has suffered as you have suffered'?"). Another possibility is that the interrogative מי should be interpreted as "How" rather than "Who," as in Amos 7:2, 5: "How (מי) will Jacob survive?"; cf. Ruth 3:16. For the parallel pair נחם/נוד ("to console/to comfort"), see Nah 3:7; Ps 69:21; Job 2:11; 42:11. The same inability to console and soothe Jerusalem reverberates in Lam 2:13: "What can I take as witness or liken to you, daughter Jerusalem? To what can I compare you to comfort you (ואנחמך), maiden Zion? For your ruin (שִׁבְרֵךְ) is vast as the sea."

[20] The reason for the children's inability to come to their mother's aid is now clarified.

Your sons lie in a faint at every street corner — Your children have all fainted and lie prostrate in the streets and thus are unable to offer you any help. The root עלף ("to faint, swoon"), similar to עטף, "denotes loss of consciousness and dizziness" (Ibn Balaam [ed. Goshen-Gottstein, 210]) due to the lack of food: "Lift up your hands to Him for the life of your infants, who faint (העטופים) with hunger at every street corner (בראֹש כל חוצות)" (Lam 2:19); from lack of water: "In that day, the beautiful maidens and the young men shall faint (תתעלפנה) with thirst" (Amos 8:13); or from excessive heat: "The sun beat down on Jonah's head, and he became faint (ויתעלף)" (Jonah 4:8). Here, as will be seen, the cause for their faintness is the draught of poison. חוצות in Biblical Hebrew refers to "streets"; for the expression ראֹש כל חוצות, see Nah 3:10; Lam 2:19 (cited above); 4:1.

Like an antelope caught in a net — This depiction evokes the image of a trapped animal futilely attempting to escape until it has lost all of its strength to resist. Hebrew תְּאוֹ (written here, תוֹא) is listed among the clean animals in Deut 14:5. For Heb. מִכְמָר see also מִכְמֹרֶת (Isa 19:8), מכמרתו (Hab 1:15, 16), and מכמריו (Ps 141:10), all of which denote net(s). (Cf. also the Akkadian cognate *kamāru*, "trap"; *CAD* K:111.)

Full of the poison of the Lord — The sons are in a stupor since they too have drunk their fill of the Lord's venom. The expression חמת ה׳ is polysemous: On the one hand, as explained in v. 17, it denotes poison. On the other hand, in light of v. 13 and the parallel below: "The rebuke of your God," it can also mean "anger," i.e., the Lord's wrath.

With the rebuke of your God — For גערה, see also 66:15.

[21] The turning point: Jerusalem's consolation.

Therefore, listen to this, afflicted one — Cf. 54:11: "Afflicted (עֲנִיָּה), storm-tossed one, uncomforted!"; 66:2: "To the afflicted (עָנִי) and brokenhearted"; 41:17; 49:13.

Drunk, but not with wine! — but from the Lord's venom. For this expression, see Isa 29:9: "They are drunk, but not from wine." (For intoxication as the result of excessive drink, see Jer 51:7; Lam 4:21; and cf. Jer 25:15-16.) The ת suffix of שְׁכֻרַת ("drunk") does not designate the construct state, but rather is the archaic feminine ending (Ibn Balaam [ed. Goshen-Gottstein, 211]; Saadyah, 116; Ibn Ganaḥ, *Sefer ha-Riqmah* [ed. Walensky, 78, 112]). For additional examples, see, e.g., חכמת (Isa 33:6); גילת (35:2).

[22] This verse, a reversal of v. 17, concludes with the annulment of the calamitous prophecy of the cup.

Thus said the Lord, your Lord — For a similar introductory formula, see 49:22.

Your God, who contends for His people — God, who is the nation's advocate and who pleads their cause, has decided that Israel has been punished enough; cf. 49:25: "For I will contend (אריב) with your adversaries"; Isa 1:17: "Plead the cause (ריבו) of the widow."

"Herewith I take from your hand the cup of reeling" — The cup of tremors, which the Lord gave you to drink, will now be taken back, and your fate shall be ameliorated. The perfect, לקחתי, is used to convey the definitiveness of this act, as though the act has already been accomplished; cf. Gen 23:11: "I give you (נתתי) the field"; Gen 23:13: "Let me pay (נתתי) the price of the land."

"The goblet, the cup of My wrath" — See v. 17.

"You shall never drink it again" — The Lord declares that the people's trials and travails are over. As in Isa 54:9, the message is driven home by the adverb עוד ("again"): "For this to Me is like the waters of Noah: As I swore that the waters of Noah never again (עוד) would pour over the earth."

[23] For the transfer of the cup of venom, i.e., the destiny of doom, to the nations, see also Jer 25:15: "For thus said the Lord, the God of Israel, to me: 'Take from My hand this cup of wine — of wrath — and make all the nations to whom I send you drink of it.'" The nations, who tormented, oppressed, and trampled on Israel, shall now get their just desert. For the image of lying prostrate as a symbol of Israel's subjugation, see Lam 2:21: "Prostrate in the streets lie both young and old." The two roots שים and עבר appear twice in this verse.

"I will put it in the hands of your tormentors" — I shall pass the cup of poi-

son from you to your abusers, who caused you so much sorrow and anguish. For the combination of drunkenness and sorrow, cf. Ezek 23:33: "You shall be filled with drunkenness and woe. The cup of desolation and horror, the cup of your sister Samaria. . . ." The *hiph'il* participle מוֹגַיִךְ derives from the root יגי, "to cause grief, sorrow"; cf. Job 19:2: "How long will you grieve (תּוֹגְיוּן) my spirit?"; Lam 1:5: "Because the Lord has afflicted her (הוֹגָהּ) for her many transgressions"; see also Lam 1:12; 3:32. The LXX and 1QIsa[a] add the synonym ומעניך ("your oppressors") after מוגיך (likely influenced by Isa 60:14: "The children of those who oppressed you [מעניך]"). For the pair of verbs עני/יגי ("to torment/ to oppress"), see Lam 3:33: "For He does not willfully bring grief (עִנָּה) or affliction (וַיַּגֶּה) to anyone." For the expression שׂים ב-, see v. 16.

"Who have commanded you, 'Bend down, that we may walk over you!'" — Lie prostrate so that we may trample on your body; cf. Ps 44:26: "We lie prostrate (שחה . . . נפשנו) in the dust; our body clings to the ground." שְׁחִי is a second-person feminine singular *qal* imperative from the verb שׁחי, a by-form of the verb שׁחח, "to be bowed down, prostrated"; see Isa 2:9; 5:15. For the expression אמר ל-, "to command," see 43:6.

"So you made your back like the ground" — You lowered your back to the ground so that you could be stomped on. For the pair גֵּו/נפש ("back, body"), see the commentary on 49:7. For the verbal expression שׂים ל-, see 41:15; 49:2; 50:7; 51:3.

"Like a street for passers-by" — You became like a sidewalk on which pedestrians walk. For treading on a cowed and subdued enemy, see Deut 33:29; Josh 10:24; Ps 110:1. Similar images are depicted in murals from Egypt and Mesopotamia. (See M. Avi-Yonah and A. Malamat, eds., *The Face of the Biblical World* [Jerusalem, 1958], 1:297 [Heb.] — a picture from the friezes of Habbu, which depicts Rameses III crushing the bodies of the defeated inhabitants of the coast; G. Galil and H. Reviv, *Ezra and Nehemiah*, in *The Encyclopedia of the Biblical World* 17 [Jerusalem, 1986], 18 [Heb.] — a picture drawn on a rock in Behistun, which depicts a procession of eight trussed captives led by neck chains and handcuffs, while Darius, king of Persia, stands with his left leg on the insurgent Gaumata. For stepping on a prisoner's midriff, see the Sumerian fresco in Y. Hoffman, *Isaiah*, in *The Encyclopedia of the Biblical World* 10 [Jerusalem, 1986], 184 [Heb.]; cf. also *ANEP*, no. 300 — the Eannatum stele; no. 97 — the Ur Standard; and no. 309 — the Naram-Sin stele.) For the pair ארץ/חוצות ("the ground/the streets"), see Lam 2:21; Job 5:10.

Chapter 52

This chapter is linked to chap. 51 through a number of thematic and stylistic motifs: Zion, debased and humbled, trampled by those who pass through her (51:23), is commanded to shake off the dust on which she lies. Instead of: "Get down, that we may walk over you!" God commands her: "Arise and sit up!" (52:2). The motif of comforting Israel, which refers to her ultimate redemption, is manifest in both chapters (51:11, 12, 19; 52:8-9). As in the preceding chapter (51:9, 12, 17), here there are sets of double imperatives (52:1, 11): The first of the two (52:1), "Awake, awake, O Zion! Clothe yourself in strength!" is parallel to 51:9: "Awake, awake! Clothe yourself with strength, O arm of the Lord!"; and 51:17: "Rouse, rouse yourself! Arise, O Jerusalem!" is echoed in 52:2: "Shake off the dust from yourself! Arise!" (The imperative **קומי** is repeated in both, and **התעוררי** sounds similar to **התנערי**. The first two verses of the chapter feature seven imperatives.) Other common motifs are God's mighty arm: "My arms shall provide for the peoples" (51:5); "Clothe yourself with strength, O arm of the Lord!" (51:9) — "The Lord will bare His holy arm in the sight of all the nations" (52:10); and God's salvation: "The salvation I grant is near" (51:5); "My salvation shall stand forever" (51:6); "My salvation through all the ages" (51:8) — "And the very ends of the earth shall see the salvation of our God" (52:10). Compare also: "You shall never drink it again" (51:22); and "They shall never enter you again" (52:1). The chapter may be divided into four units: vv. 1-6, 7-10, 11-12, 13-15; the final unit is a prelude to the fourth Servant Song (see below).

[1-6] Nah 2:1 left its indelible impression on the first verse of this and the following pericope (v. 7): "Behold on the mountains the footsteps of a herald announcing well-being! . . . Never again shall scoundrels invade you. They are totally destroyed"; and here, in reverse order: "For the uncircumcised and the unclean shall never enter you again (v. 1). . . . How lovely on the mountain are the footsteps of the herald!" (v. 7). Compare also the expression **שב ה׳** (Nah

2:3), and here: בשוב ה׳ (v. 8). Both prophets prophesied the fall of a great power, a power that had brought much devastation and hardship to Judah and Israel (Nahum: Assyria; Deutero-Isaiah: Babylonia); and both of them spoke of the footsteps of the metaphorical herald who from the mountaintop delivers his message of redemption to Israel. Nonetheless, there is a very important difference between the two: Nahum couched his prophecies in moral terms ("scoundrel," which is very much akin to Nebuchadnezzar's injunction: "No wicked or unjust person is allowed to walk in it [the palace]" [*CAD* I-J:226]), whereas Deutero-Isaiah expresses himself in phrases borrowed from the cultic milieu: "uncircumcised and unclean," since Jerusalem was the "holy city" (see 48:2), sacrosanct by merit of the Temple within. (See the introduction, §16.) This cultic undertone is absent also from Joel 4:17: "And Jerusalem shall be holy. Nevermore shall strangers pass through it"; Lam 1:10: "She has seen her sanctuary invaded by nations that you have denied admission into your community"; cf. also Ps 101:8: "Each morning I will destroy all the wicked of the land, to rid the city of the Lord of all evildoers." However, one should note a similarity with Isa 35:8: "And a highway shall appear there, which shall be called the 'Sacred Way.' No one unclean (טמא) shall pass along it." The "Sacred Way," however, is not Jerusalem. The idea of forbidding the wicked and the unclean from entrance to a temple city is very ancient and is already documented in the Sumerian inscription from the days of Gudea, king of Lagash (twenty-third century BCE), at the dedication of the temple to his god Ningirsu, up until the time of Nebuchadnezzar (sixth century BCE), and is also found in an Egyptian injunction to the gatekeepers of Isis's temple from the Ptolemaic period, which forbade the uncircumcised and the foreigner from entering the temple perimeter. (See M. Weinfeld, *Social Justice in Ancient Israel and in the Ancient Near East* [Minneapolis, 1995], 98-100.)

The prophet introduces a revolutionary theological innovation in this chapter: The holy area, which until this time was restricted to the Temple itself, is now expanded to include the entire city. Jerusalem becomes a temple city, and thus strict guidelines to insure its holiness must be introduced; cf. 60:14: "And you shall be called 'City of the Lord, Zion of the Holy One of Israel.'" (For this revolutionary concept, cf. also Zech 14:21: "Indeed, every metal pot in Jerusalem and in Judah shall be holy to the Lord of Hosts. . . . In that day there shall be no more traders in the house of the Lord of Hosts.") This prophecy complements another one that predicts that all of Israel shall become priests in the Lord's service: "And you shall be called 'Priests of the Lord,' and termed 'Servants of our God'" (Isa 61:6); cf. 62:12: "And they shall be called 'The Holy People.'" This innovation is none other than a fulfillment of the promise in Exod 19:6: "But you shall be to Me a kingdom of priests and a holy nation." This idea, that all of Jerusalem would be considered out of bounds for the unclean, was adopted by the sectarians at Qumran. According to their rulings in the *Temple Scroll,* which were more stringent than the Pharisaic halakah, no one unclean and nothing unclean was allowed into the city: "And the city which I will sanctify to make dwell My name and [My] Temp[le within it] shall be holy and pure from every impurity which they may be defiled by. . . . Everything that there is in it shall be pure and everything that goes into it shall be pure . . . , and they shall not defile the city within which I make dwell My name and My Temple" (11Q19 47:3-11; *DSSSE* 2:1265, 1267). "If a man lies with his wife carnally, he shall not enter the whole city of the Temple in which I will cause My name to dwell for a period of three days. . . . And they shall not defile the city in whose midst I dwell" (11Q19 45:11-14). Compare also the injunction in the *Damascus Document* against copulation: "[Let no] man lie with a woman in the city of the sanctuary, to defile the [city of the sanctuary with their pollution]" (4Q271:17-18; Baumgarten, DJD 18, 181-82.)

[1-6] This unit is characterized by the repetition of many terms and phrases: "Zion" and "Jerusalem" appear in vv. 1 and 2 and form a chiasm; **עורי עורי** (v. 1); **חִנָּם** (vv. 3 and 5 — used differently each time); **עמי** (vv. 4, 5, 6); **שמי** (vv. 5, 6); **שבי . . . שִׁבְיָה** (v. 2; a wordplay); **נְאֻם ה׳** (v. 5; twice in the same verse); **לכן** (v. 6; twice); **היום/ביום** (vv. 5-6).

[1] The prophet begins with a poignant call to Jerusalem to arise from her dormant state and free herself from her abasement in exile. The donning of "beautiful robes" symbolizes the city's rehabilitation and contrasts with the shameful stripping of these same garments in Ezek 23:26: "They shall strip you of your clothing and take away your dazzling jewels." This prophecy, in its entirety, contrasts with the calamitous events in store for Babylon. Compare Isa 47:1: "Get down! Sit in the dust, fair maiden Babylon!" with 52:2: "Rise up! Shake off the dust, Jerusalem!" Babylon is described as a captive led into exile, whereas Jerusalem is now free of those same fetters (52:2). The former (Babylon) reveals her nakedness (47:1-2), while the latter (Israel) is commanded to dress herself in robes of majesty (52:1). Note the repetition of the letters **ע** and **ר** in the first two verses of this chapter: **עורי עורי . . . עיר . . . עָרֵל . . . התנערי מעפר**.

The motif of a majestic city that houses a temple appears already in Sumerian literature, in the Enmerkar and the Lord of Aratta epic: "The city . . . robed in splendor and majesty." (See S. Cohen, "Enmerkar and the Lord of Aratta," Ph.D. diss. [University of Pennsylvania, 1973], 65, 112, line 1.) The city of Nippur is described in a hymn to the god Enlil as "filled with awe and splendor . . . exploitation and despicable acts . . . shall have no place in it." And in a hymn in honor of Ningirsu's temple in the days of King Gudea, it is written: "Its splendor and majesty reach to the sky." (See M. Weinfeld, *From Joshua to Josiah* [Jerusalem, 1992], 124-25 [Heb.].)

Awake, awake! Clothe yourself in your strength/splendor, O Zion! — An emphatic repetition of the imperative עורי; cf. "Awake, awake (עורי עורי)!" (51:9). (Here and in 51:9, as well as in Judg 5:12: "Awake, awake, Deborah!" the accent on the two verbs is on the final syllable.) The language in Isa 51:9 is also metaphoric, the subject of the verb being the divine arm: "Clothe yourself in strength, arm of the Lord (זרוע ה׳)"; and here: "Clothe yourself in your splendor, O Zion!" (One should note that here 1QIsa[a] reads עוז, similar to 51:9, instead of MT עזך.) For other examples of this imagery, see Ps 93:1: "The Lord is King, He is robed in grandeur. The Lord is robed, He is girded with strength"; and cf. the depiction of the majestically robed gods in Mesopotamian literature (*CAD* L:18; N/2:86). For the dual meaning of עֹז, see Isa 51:9.

Put on your robes of beauty, Jerusalem, — Instead of your garments of widowhood and bereavement, don (לבשי — the imperative is repeated again for emphasis) beautiful and lovely garments (cf. 61:3). The noun תפארת, in addition to its meaning of "beauty" and "glory" (cf. 44:13; 62:3), also connotes "strength" and "might"; see 46:13; and for its combination with עֹז, as here, see Ps 78:61; 89:9, 18; 96:6. For the parallel appellations "Jerusalem/Zion," see Isa 40:9: "Herald of joy to Zion . . . herald of joy to Jerusalem."

Holy city! — One of Jerusalem's unique sobriquets, occurring also in 48:2 (see there) and Neh 11:1, 18. Compare also Joel 4:17: "And you shall know that I the Lord your God dwell in Zion, My holy mount, and Jerusalem shall be holy"; Zech 2:16: "The Lord will take Judah to Himself as His portion in the Holy Land, and He will choose Jerusalem once more." The word קֹדֶשׁ is a reference to a place of holiness, i.e., the Temple or the sanctuary; see Lev 16:2: "He must not enter the sanctuary (הַקֹּדֶשׁ) at will"; 1 Kgs 8:10: "When the priests came out of the sanctuary"; Ps 63:3: "I shall behold you in the sanctuary." Here, however, the reference is to the entire city. Holiness blanketing the whole of Jerusalem is already alluded to in Jer 3:17: "At that time they shall call Jerusalem, 'Throne of the Lord,'" i.e., Jerusalem as a whole will replace the ark, which was commonly understood to serve as the divine throne located in the Temple; see Ps 47:9; 99:1.

For the uncircumcised and the unclean shall never enter you again — since they defile the city by their presence. For the injunction against the participation of the uncircumcised (עָרֵל) in the cult, see Exod 12:48: "But no uncircumcised person may eat of it" (of the paschal lamb). All non-Israelites are de facto considered to be uncircumcised, as in Ezek 44:7-9: "You have brought aliens, uncircumcised of spirit and uncircumcised of flesh, to be in My sanctuary and profane My very Temple. . . . Thus said the Lord God: 'Let no alien, uncircumcised in spirit and flesh, enter My sanctuary — no alien whatsoever among the people of Israel.'" A similar injunction exists against those who are unclean or impure (טמא), specifically the leper, those who suffer from discharges, and those who have had a recent death in the family; see Num 5:1-4, and cf. 2 Chr 23:19: "He stationed the gatekeepers at the gates of the house of the Lord to prevent the entry of anyone unclean for any reason." All the heathen nations were considered impure as well; see Ps 79:1: "O God, heathens have entered Your domain, defiled Your holy Temple"; Lam 1:10: "She [Jerusalem] has seen her sanctuary invaded by nations that You have denied admission into Your community." For the syntactical construction לא יוסיף יבא, see also 47:1, 5: כי לא תוסיפי יקראו לך; Hos 1:6: כי לא אוסיף עוד ארחם. For the verbal expression -בוא ב ("enter"), see Judg 11:18; 1 Sam 9:5.

[2] A series of four imperatives underscore the immediacy of the reversal in the city's fate. Jerusalem, of whom it was said in Isa 51:23: "So that you made your back like the ground, like a street for passers-by," is now commanded to elevate herself from the dust of abasement. "Jerusalem" and "Zion" appear in this verse in a chiastic order with v. 1.

Shake off the dust from yourself! — From your vestments (התנערי is a reflexive *hithpaʿel*). For the root נער, see also Job 38:13; Neh 5:13. This contrasts with the prophet's command to "fair maiden Babylon," who is commanded to sit in the dust (47:1, and cf. 47:5). Jerusalem, who made her back like the ground so that people could pass over her, is now instructed to arise from her prostration and to stop wallowing in the dust.

Arise! Sit up/Captive Jerusalem! — Commentators disagree about the meaning of the second word in this clause. Many follow the Masoretic punctuation שבי (from the root ישב), "Sit!" (Saadyah Gaon, Rashi, Ibn Ezra, as well as 1QIsa[a], which adds a *waw* to the second imperative, קומי ושבי). According to Kimchi, however, שבי should not be understood as an imperative, but rather as the identically spelled masculine substantive signifying "captivity"; see 46:2; 49:24, 25. According to this explanation, שבי ירושלם ("Captive Jerusalem") is parallel to שְׁבִיָּה בת ציון ("captive daughter Zion") at the end of the verse. The word therefore serves as a pivot in a bivalent Janus parallelism. On the one hand, as a verbal imperative it complements the previous קומי as a hendiadys, similar to Gen 27:19: "Please sit up" (קום נא שְׁבָה). On the other hand, as a substantive, it is similar to Jer 48:46: "Your sons are carried off into captivity (בשבי), your daughters into exile (בשביה)." (See Paul, *Divrei Shalom,* 465; S. Kogut, *The Bible: Punctuation and Exegesis* [Jerusalem, 1994], 233-35 [Heb.].) For the *dagesh* of the initial שּׁ of שּׁבי, see GKC §20c, g.

Loose the bonds from your neck — According to the Ketib התפתחו (third-person plural; so too Targum and 1QIsa[a]), the expression מוסרי צַוָּארֵךְ functions as the subject, i.e., "The bonds of your neck were loosed," while according to the Qere, התפתחי (second-person feminine imperative), the subject is Jerusalem, which fits well with the other commands directed toward the city throughout the verse (cf. LXX, Vulgate, and Peshitta). The phrase מוסרי צוארך in this case would serve as the direct object: "Loose the bonds from your neck!"

For מוֹסֵר ("bonds") (from the root אסר), see Jer 27:2: "Make for yourself bonds (מוֹסֵרוֹת) and bars of a yoke, and put them on your neck"; Ps 116:16: "You have undone the bonds (לְמוֹסֵרָי) that bound me"; Job 39:5: "Who loosens the bonds (וּמֹסְרוֹת) of the onager." For a *hithpa'el* stem followed by a direct object, see Exod 32:3: "And all the people took off (ויתפרקו) the gold rings that were in their ears"; Exod 33:6: "So the Israelites stripped off (ויתנצלו) their vestments"; 1 Sam 18:4: "Jonathan took off (ויתפשט) the cloak and tunic he was wearing." For illustrations depicting a train of captives being led in neck chains, see *ANEP,* nos. 7, 8, 9, 325, 326.

O captive daughter Zion! — שְׁבִיָּה, "a captive female," is a hapax legomenon and creates a wordplay on שבי above. The pair ירושלם-בת ציון chiastically mirrors ציון-ירושלם in v. 1. For the appellation בת ציון, see 62:11, which stands in contrast to בת בבל in 47:1, 5.

[3-6] The prophet embarks on a brief prose survey of the exiles in Israel's history, beginning with their sojourn in Egypt. Since Israel's exile results in the defiling of the Lord's name, the Deity swears to fulfill His promise to redeem His people. The term עמי ("My nation") is reiterated here so as to further accentuate the indissoluble bond between God and His nation.

[3] *For thus said the Lord: "You were sold for no price"* — For this introductory formula, see Jer 6:6; Hag 2:7; Zech 2:12. For similar imagery, see Ps 44:13: "You have sold Your people for no fortune. You set no high price on them"; cf. also Isa 50:1: "You were only sold off for your sins." (For the repetition of חִנָּם in another context, see v. 5.)

"And shall be redeemed without payment" — Cf. 45:13: "And he shall let My exiled people go without price and without payment." The *beth* prefix attached to במחיר is the *beth pretii:* I shall redeem you without having to pay any ransom money. For the negative parallelism לא בכסף/חנם, see Exod 21:11: "She shall go free (חִנָּם) without payment (אין כסף)." For the Lord as the redeemer of His people, see Isa 41:14; 44:6, 24; 48:17; 59:20; and the introduction, §9.

[4] *For thus said the Lord God* — Parallel to the introductory formula at the beginning of the previous verse, with the additional title, "Lord."

"At first My people went down to Egypt" — In the very beginning of My nation's history they descended into Egypt. For בָּרִאשֹׁנָה ("in the beginning, at first, of old"), see Gen 13:4: "The site of the altar that he had built there at first"; Isa 1:26: "I will restore your magistrates as of old." The journey to Egypt is usually described as a "descent"; cf. Gen 43:15: "They went down (וירדו) to Egypt."

"To sojourn there" — as sojourners and strangers, not as permanent residents; see Deut 26:5: "He went down (וירד) to Egypt and sojourned (ויגר) there"; Gen 12:10: "There was a famine in the land, and Abram went down (וירד) to Egypt to sojourn (לגור) there." Compare also Ps 105:23: "Then Israel came to Egypt, Jacob sojourned (גר) in the land of Ham." The continuation of

this idea is understood, but not stated explicitly — the nation was put under Egypt's yoke and eventually redeemed by God.

"But Assyria oppressed them for no reason/in the end" — At a later point in the people's history they were made to serve the Assyrians, "for naught" (בְּאֶפֶס), i.e., "For no justifiable reason or cause . . . and Assyria was mentioned, since it was the first to exile Israel from their land, and [the verse] includes Babylon as well" (Luzzatto). See also Kimchi, "An allusion to two exiles, the Egyptian exile and the Babylonian exile, since the king of Assyria is also the king of Babylon." For "Assyria" as a generic name for Mesopotamia, see Ezra 6:22. Perhaps Assyria was mentioned in lieu of Babylon because of the frequent parallels between it and Egypt, e.g., Isa 27:13: "And the strayed who are in the land of Assyria and the expelled who are in the land of Egypt shall come." For the verb עשק conveying the trials and travails of Israel as a subject nation, see Jer 50:33: "The people of Israel are oppressed (עשוקים), and so too the people of Judah. All their captors held them, they refused to let them go." Saadyah, however, translates אפס by Arab. אכׄירה, "in the end" (as in אפסי ארץ, "the ends of the earth"; but here used temporally). This interpretation would then correlate with the previous hemistich's בראשׁנה, "at first" (Saadyah Gaon, 117; and see also D. Leibel, "Variant Readings," *Beth Miqra* 8 [1964]: 193 [Heb.]), who does not include a reference to Saadyah in his discussion).

[5] God, who up until this point has restrained from acting and has not redeemed His people, is impatient and worries about the besmirching of His name vis-à-vis the nations.

What am I doing here? — declares the Lord — For what reason (מה לי) do I remain in Babylon? Cf. Judg 18:3: "What is your business (מה לך) here?"; 1 Kgs 19:9: "Why are you (מה לך) here, Elijah?" For the syntactical construction מה ל- כי . . . , see Isa 22:16: "What have you (מה לך) here . . . that (כי) you have hewn out a tomb for yourself here?"; Ps 114:5: "What alarmed you (מה לך), O Sea, that (כי) you fled?" The idea of the Deity's presence in exile together with His nation is reflected in the rabbinic aphorism: "In every one of Israel's exiles, God's presence accompanied them" (*Mekilta de-Rabbi Ishmael, Bo,* 14, ed. H. S. Horowitz and I. A. Rabin [1930; repr. Jerusalem, 1960], 51-52).

For My people have been carried off without cause — My nation was led off into exile for no reason (חִנָּם); cf. 1 Sam 19:5: "Why then should you incur the guilt of shedding the blood of an innocent man, killing David without cause (חנם)?"; Ps 35:7: "For without cause (חנם) they hid a net to trap me. Without cause (חנם) they dug a pit for me." (Note the play on words with חנם here in v. 3.) For לֻקַּח, an archaic *qal* passive, see Isa 53:8; Gen 2:23; and for its connoting the taking of captives, see Jer 48:46: "Your sons are carried off (לֻקְּחוּ) into captivity"; see too 1 Sam 4:11: "The ark of God was captured (נלקח)"; cf. the Akkadian etymological and semantic cognate *lequ* (*CAD* L:143-44).

Their mockers howl/their rulers boast — declares the Lord — Commentators disagree on the exact meaning of the subject מֹשְׁלָו and the predicate יהילילו. Some derive the verb from the root ילל, which appears only in the *hiph'il* (see Isa 13:6, Jer 25:34; Amos 8:3; and for the preservation of the ה in other *hiph'il* forms, see, e.g., 1 Sam 17:47: יהושיע) and signifies "howling" (an intransitive verb), or, alternatively, "causing the shrieking and howling" of the people (a transitive verb). Others prefer a derivation from the root הלל, "to boast" (see Ps 10:3; Targum, מִשְׁתַּבְּחִין), or, according to 1QIsa[a], והוללו, which denotes "making one into a fool" (see Isa 44:25: "And makes fools [יְהוֹלֵל] of augurs"; Jer 25:16: "Let them drink and retch and act crazy [וְהִתְהֹלָלוּ]"; Eccl 7:7: "For oppression makes the wise man like a fool [יְהוֹלֵל]"). These explanations support the bivalency of מֹשְׁלָו, which, on the one hand, may refer to those who "rule" the people; and, on the other, to those who ridicule others in derisive terms (משל); see Deut 28:37: "You shall be a byword (למשל)" cf. 1 Kgs 9:7; Jer 24:9. The repetition of the formula נאם ה' twice in the same verse is worthy of note.

And constantly, unceasingly, My name is reviled — See Ps 74:10: "Will the enemy forever revile (יְנָאֵץ) Your name?" (cf. also Ps 74:18). (Cf. the interdialectal cognates, Akk. *nâṣu*, "scorn, contempt" [*CAD* N/2:53], and Ugar. *n'ṣ*, "despise, insult" [*HdO* 2:612].) Israel's absence from their land and their long sojourn in exile resulted in the desecration of the divine name; cf. Ezek 36:20: "But when they came to those nations, they caused My holy name to be profaned, in that it was said of them: 'These are the people of the Lord, yet they had to leave His land.'" The verb מִנֹּאָץ is a hybrid form, created by the conflation of מְנָּאֵץ (= מתנאץ, a *hithpa'el,* or, alternatively, a *hithpo'al* stem in which the ת was assimilated into the נ; cf. Num 7:89: מְדַּבֵּר = מתדבר) and מְנֹאָץ, a *pu'al* participle. For the phrase תמיד כל היום, which emphasizes the frequency of the act, see Isa 51:13. For the defilement of the divine name, see 48:11.

[6] *Assuredly, My people shall know My name* — in the future, when the redemption shall come to pass, unlike today, when My name is being constantly reviled (v. 5). For the expression ידע שם, see Ps 91:14. Those "who know God's name" (Ps 9:11) are the worshipers and devotees of the Lord.

Assuredly, they shall know on that day — The repetition of the conjunction לכן (absent from LXX, Vulgate, Peshitta, and 1QIsa[a]) is for emphasis: Indeed, at the time of the redemption My people shall know (Targum, תִּידְעוּן) My name.

That I, the One who promised, am now at hand — I, who pledged to redeem you, am present (הנני) and ready to make good on My promise. The Deity is as good as His word; cf. Isa 48:15: "I, I predicted, and I called him. I have brought him and he shall succeed in his mission." God's word is a stamp of authenticity, as in Ezek 5:13: "And when I vent all My fury upon them, they shall know that I the Lord have spoken in My passion." For the expression אני הוא

("I, the One"), which is a divine title, see Isa 41:4; 43:10, 13; 46:4; 48:12. Other than this verse, 58:9, and 65:1, all subjects of הנני (e.g., Gen 22:1, 11; Exod 3:4) are human beings.

[7-10] The Lord returns to Zion as the reigning king. The herald, who comes from afar, and the watchmen, who stand on the walls of Jerusalem, announce to one another the coming redemption that each will experience personally: "Every eye shall behold it clearly (עין בעין)" and all nations shall witness it as well. The practice of sending a fleet-footed runner to deliver messages of salvation and victory is also found in 2 Sam 18:19: "Ahimaaz son of Zadok said: 'Let me run and report to the king that the Lord has vindicated him against His enemies.'" The first to see the runner is the watchman standing on the battlements: "The watchman on the roof of the gate walked over to the city wall. He looked up and saw a man running alone" (2 Sam 18:24). For a runner who announces defeat, see 1 Sam 4:17. The motif of redemption ("He will redeem Jerusalem" [v. 9]), links up with that of the previous unit: "You shall be redeemed without money" (v. 3). Compare also the expression עיר הקֹדֶשׁ, "the holy city" (v. 1), and זרוע קָדְשׁוֹ, "His holy arm" (v. 10), and the appearance of both "Zion" and "Jerusalem" (vv. 1-2, 8-9).

The literary unit is framed by the term ישועה and references to God (אלהיך, v. 7; אלהינו, v. 10), and is characterized by the reverberation of joyful voices (vv. 7, 8, 9). The connections between this unit and Ps 98 are unambiguous, and the psalm clearly left its distinctive imprint on the prophet: Ps 98:1-8: "His right hand and His holy arm (זרוע קָדְשׁוֹ) [this expression appears only here and in Deutero-Isaiah] have won Him victory (הושיע).... He has displayed His triumph (ישועתו) in the sight of the nations (לעיני הגוים).... All the ends of the earth shall see the victory of God (וראו כל אפסי ארץ את ישועת ה׳). Break forth in joyful shouts (פִּצְחוּ וְרַנֵּנוּ) . . . before the Lord, the King (המלך ה׳)! . . . Sing joyously together (יחד . . . יְרַנֵּנוּ)! — Isa 52:7-10: "Your God is King (מלך אלהיך). . . . Sing joyously together (יחד . . . יְרַנֵּנוּ)! . . . Break forth in joyful shouts (פִּצְחוּ וְרַנְּנוּ)! . . . The Lord will bare His holy arm (זרוע קָדְשׁוֹ) in the sight of all the nations (לעיני כל הגוים). And all the ends of the earth shall see the victory of God (וראו כל אפסי ארץ את ישועת ה׳)." (See H. L. Ginsberg, "A Strand in the Cord of Hebraic Hymnody," *Eretz Israel* 9 = *W. F. Albright Festschrift Volume,* ed. A. Malamat [Jerusalem, 1969]: 47-48); and the introduction, §17.) The inversion of the verses is typical in the Bible when a later source is influenced by an earlier one (see M. Seidel, *Ḥiqrei Miqra* [Jerusalem, 1978], 2 [Heb.]).

Repetitions abound in this unit: מְבַשֵּׂר (v. 7 twice — once as a noun, "herald," the second time as a verb, "heralding"), ישועה (vv. 7, 10), משמיע (v. 7 twice), אלהים (vv. 7, 10), קול (v. 8 twice), רנן (vv. 8, 9), יַחְדָּו (vv. 8, 9), עין (v. 8 twice), ירושלם (v. 9 twice), ראי (vv. 8, 10), כל (v. 10 twice).

[7] The prophet, as he beholds the imaginary herald ascending the mountains on the way to Jerusalem, is overwhelmed with joy. This verse repeats the two synonyms מבשׂר and משמיע, and there is an accumulated emphasis on sibilants: ציון ,ישועה ,משמיע ,מבשׂר ,שלום ,משמיע ,מבשׂר. For the influence of Nahum on this verse (Nah 1:15), see the introduction to the chapter.

How lovely on the mountain are the footsteps of the herald! — For מה as an introduction to an exclamatory statement, see Num 24:5: "How (מה) fair are your tents, O Jacob, Your dwellings, O Israel!"; Ps 8:2, 10: "O Lord, our Lord, how (מה) majestic is Your name throughout the earth!"; Cant 7:2: "How (מה) lovely are your feet in sandals, O daughter of nobles!" The verb נָאווּ is a hybrid form, composed of the *qal* perfect of the root נאי ("to be comely"; נָאֲוּ), the *niph'al* perfect of אוי ("to desire"; נַאֲווּ), and the *qal* perfect of the root נוי ("to beautify"; נָוּו; the א in this form would function as a *mater lectionis*); cf. also Cant 1:10: "Your cheeks are lovely (נָאווּ) with plaited wreaths." For the mention of heralds elsewhere in Deutero-Isaiah, see 40:9 (note that there too the female herald is commanded to ascend a lofty mountain); 41:27.

Announcing well-being, heralding good news, announcing victory — A triad of fortuitous announcements. Perhaps these three terms, שלום, טוב, ישועה, along with מלך אלהיך at the end of the verse, are to be understood as direct exclamations: "Well-being!" "Good news!" "Victory!" For the expression משמיע שלום (1QIsa[a] reads מבשׂר שלום), see Lachish ostracon (sixth century BCE) 2, lines 1-3: "May the Lord deliver . . . a message of well-being (. . . ישמע שמעת שלם) to my master" (Aḥituv, *Ha-Ketav veha-Miktav,* 53-54). For the Akkadian cognate *šulmu qabû,* see *CAD* Š/3:251. For מבשר טוב (1QIsa[a] reads משמיע טוב), cf. the expressions in 2 Sam 18:27: "He is a good man, and he comes with good news (בשׂורה טובה)"; 1 Kgs 1:42: "You are a worthy man, and you surely bring good news (וטוב תבשׂר)." In Akkadian as well, the verb *bussuru* ("to herald"), and the substantive *bussurtu* ("announcement"), in conjunction with the terms *dumqu* and *ḫadû* ("good," "joyous") function similarly (*CAD* B:346-48); and heralds are referred to as *mubassiru* (*CAD* M/2:158-59). For the occurrence of שלום and טוב as synonyms, see Deut 23:7: "You shall never seek their welfare or benefit (שלֹמם וטֹבתם)"; for the terms in a negative parallelism, see Jer 14:19: "Why do we hope for happiness (שלום), and find no good (טוב)?"; and in a conjunctive construction, Jer 33:9: "They will thrill and quiver because of all the good fortune (הטובה) and all the prosperity (השלום)." Compare also Esth 10:3: "He [Mordecai] sought the good (טוב) of his people and interceded for the welfare (שלום) of all his kindred." Compare also Lachish ostracon 3, lines 2-4, where the same combination of these first two expressions appears (ישמע . . . שמעת שלם ושמעת טב) (Aḥituv, *Ha-Ketav veha-Miktav,* 58). The expression טב ושלם is found in Aramaic as well. (See J. Hoftijzer and K. Jongeling, *Dictionary of the North-West Semitic Inscriptions,* 2 vols. [Leiden,

1995], 2:1150-51; and cf. the Akkadian interdialectal etymological and semantic cognates *ṭubbātu* and *salīmu* ["goodwill, friendliness," and "peace, concord"; *CAD* Ṭ:114; S:100, 102.) For ישועה ("salvation," "victory"), see v. 10; 59:11; 60:18.

Telling Zion, "Your God is King!" — The herald proclaims God's sovereignty. For similar announcements that characterize hymns celebrating God's coronation as King, see Ps 93:1; 96:10; 97:1; 99:1; and cf. 2 Sam 15:10: "Announce that Absalom has become king in Hebron!" For the title "King" as referring to the Lord, see Isa 41:21; 43:15; 44:6. God, not a scion from the house of David (55:3), is the King of Israel.

[8-9] For the ululations and cries of joy following the king's coronation ceremony, see 1 Kgs 1:40.

[8] The watchmen standing guard on the city's walls (see the introduction to v. 7) see the herald and convey the message as well.

Hark! — Contrary to the Masoretic accents that connect the first two words, קוֹל צֹפַיִךְ, one should interpret קוֹל as an independent exclamatory utterance, "Hark!" Cf. Gen 4:10: "Hark! Your brother's blood cries out to Me from the ground!"; Isa 13:4: "Hark! A tumult on the mountains — Hark! An uproar of kingdoms"; Cant 5:2: "Hark! My beloved knocks"; cf. also Isa 40:3, 6.

Your watchmen raise their voices — There is no pronominal suffix in the MT, but 1QIsa[a] reads קולם, "their voices," and the Targum likewise, קָלְהוֹן. The expression נשׂא קול ("to raise one's voice") is a common biblical expression borrowed from Ugaritic poetry, e.g., *yšu gh* ("he raises his voice"; *CAT* 1.4.IV:30). For צופיו (Qere) ("its watchmen"), see 56:10.

As one they shout for joy — They all cheer together as they hear the fortuitous news. For the combination נשא קול and רנן ("to raise one's voice" and "to shout for joy"), see 42:11; 24:14. For יַחְדָּו signifying unanimity (here and in the following verse), see 40:5; 41:20; 42:14; 43:17.

For their eyes shall behold clearly — They exult joyously since they shall witness with their very own eyes the return of the Lord to Zion. For the expression עין בעין, see also Num 14:14; Jer 32:4; and cf. Jer 34:3. Compare also the Akkadian expression *ina īnī amāru*, "to see with one's own eyes" (*CAD* A/2:8-9). For a similar metaphor, see Exod 33:11: "face to face" (פנים אל פנים).

The Lord's return to Zion — The LXX and 1QIsa[a] add ברחמים ("with compassion") at the end of the clause (a reading that entered the daily Jewish liturgy as part of the *Shemoneh Esreh* [Eighteen Blessings]). For this motif, see Zech 1:16: "Assuredly, thus said the Lord: 'I return to Jerusalem with compassion (ברחמים)'"; and cf. Deut 30:3. For the return of the Lord to Zion, cf. also Zech 8:3.

[9] Following the series of heraldic announcements, the prophet invites the ruined city (desolate since the destruction of the Temple) to join the joyful chorus celebrating salvation. For the song of the redeemed, see Isa 42:10-11.

Break forth together in joyful shouts, O ruins of Jerusalem! — The "ruins of Jerusalem," about which the prophet announced: "Truly the Lord has comforted Zion, comforted all her ruins (חָרְבֹתֶיהָ)" (51:3; cf. 44:26; 49:19), are now told to raise their voice in shouts of triumph. For the verbal expression פצח רנה, see 44:23; 49:13; 54:1; 55:12. 1QIsa[a] substitutes the noun רונה (= רִנָּה) for the verb רַנְּנוּ in the MT. The expression רננו יחדו creates a chiastic parallelism with יחדו ירננו in the preceding verse.

For the Lord has comforted His people, has redeemed Jerusalem — God's comfort of His people is their redemption. For the recurring motif of "comfort," see 40:1; 49:13 (where God's "comforting His people" also appears in conjunction with "raising voices in song"); 51:3, 12, 19. For the motif of redemption, see v. 3.

[10] The Lord's arm, which was called upon to rescue the people (51:9), shall be revealed to all the nations so that God's name, reviled and defiled during the exile, shall never again be desecrated. This universal motif is reiterated throughout the prophecies of Deutero-Isaiah, beginning with 40:5. The centrality of the concept "in the sight of all nations" is manifest in Ezekiel as well, and there too it refers to the redemption of the people so that God's name shall never again be violated: "But I acted for the sake of My name, that it might not be profaned in the sight of the nations among whom they were" (Ezek 20:9; and see also vv. 14, 22, 41). (See the introduction, §6.)

The Lord has bared His holy arm in the sight of all the nations — God has revealed His arm, i.e., His might, to all the world, and they shall witness the salvation wrought by the Lord for His people. For the expression חשׂף זרוע ("to bare one's arm"), see Ezek 4:7: "Then, with bared arm, set your face toward besieged Jerusalem." For the "Lord's arm," see Isa 51:5, 9; 53:1; 59:16; 62:8; 63:5, 12.

And the very ends of the earth shall see the salvation of our God — All the nations from one end of the earth to the other shall behold God's deliverance, as the herald proclaimed in v. 7. For the expression אפסי ארץ ("the very ends of the earth") signifying the entirety of the universe, see 45:22. For the emphasis on universality, see also 40:5; 41:20; 45:22; 49:26: "And all humankind shall know that I the Lord am your Deliverer." The term כל is repeated twice in this hemistich for emphasis.

[11-12] This pericope, which is linked to the initial unit by the motif of uncleanness (vv. 1, 11), features the threefold repetition of the root יצא, emphasizing the exodus from Babylon (cf. 48:20). The entire nation is to remain pure as they carry the vessels of the Lord back to Jerusalem, since according to Deutero-Isaiah: "You shall be called 'Priests of the Lord' and termed 'Servants of our God'" (61:6), which is none other than the fulfillment of Exod 19:6: "You shall be to Me a kingdom of priests and a holy nation." This concept of the holiness of the entire nation is connected to another innovative idea, that of the holiness of Jerusalem as a whole (v. 1). Thus the holy nation returns to the holy city. The prophet's interest in the return of the sacred vessels to Jerusalem and the renewal of cultic activity is also found in 44:28; 56:7; 60:7. This return to Jerusalem from Babylon marks the fulfillment of Jeremiah's prophecy: "For thus said the Lord of Hosts, the God of Israel, concerning the vessels remaining in the house of the Lord. . . . 'They shall be brought to Babylon, and there they shall remain, until I take note of them — declares the Lord of Hosts — and bring them up and restore them to this place'" (Jer 27:21-22). Compare also Jer 28:6: "The prophet Jeremiah said: 'May the Lord do so! May the Lord fulfill what you have prophesied and bring back from Babylon to this place the vessels of the house of the Lord and all the exiles!'" The authorization to do just that was given eventually by Cyrus, king of Persia (Ezra 1:7-11; 5:14-15). (See the introduction, §15.)

[11] This verse was influenced by the negative imperatives in Lam 4:15: "'Away! Unclean!' people shouted at them. 'Away! Away! Touch not!'" In both verses there appears the dual imperative **סורו**, and both feature the words **טמא** ("unclean") and **נגע** ("to touch"). The injunctions are, however, diametrically different: In Lamentations Israel is deemed unclean by the Babylonians, whereas here they are warned to "touch nothing unclean" as they depart Babylon. (See the introduction, §18.)

Turn! Turn away! Depart from there! — an emphatic doubling of the imperative (**סורו**); cf. v. 1; 51:9, 12, 17. (See the introduction, §10.a.) The expatriates in Babylon are commanded in a triad of imperatives to depart Babylon posthaste. Note the sequence of sibilants in the first four words of this verse: **סורו סורו צאו משם**.

Touch nothing unclean! — Touch no unclean objects or people. The prophet instructs the returning Judeans to keep entirely pure in order to enter the Holy City, since entrance is forbidden to those who are unclean (v. 1). 1QIsa[a] reads **בטמא** (cf. Peshitta and Targum, **בִּמְסָאַב**), adding a preposition to the MT **טמא**, since the verb **נגע** is almost always followed by the preposition *beth* (except here; Gen 26:29; Ruth 2:9). For the expression "Turn away! . . . Touch not!", see Num 16:26.

Go forth from there! — Yet another imperative (a repetition of **צאו**), further highlighting the urgency of the command. For a similar command to flee Babylon, see Jer 51:45: "Depart from there, O My people! Save your lives, each of you, from the furious anger of the Lord!"

Keep yourselves pure — The verb **הִבָּרוּ** is a *niph'al* imperative from the root **ברר**, which denotes purification; see Dan 11:35: "That they may be refined and purified (**ולברר**) and whitened"; Dan 12:10: "Many will be purified (**יתבררו**) and purged and refined." It is a mark of late Biblical Hebrew. (See the introduction, §11.B.)

You who bear the vessels of the Lord! — They are the vessels of the Temple taken at the time of the conquest of Jerusalem (2 Kgs 24:13; 25:14-15; Dan 5:2; Ezra 1:7; 6:5). In every other occurrence they are referred to either as "the vessels of the Lord's/of God's house" (Jer 27:16; Dan 1:2; 1 Chr 22:19; 2 Chr 24:14); "the Sanctuary's vessels" (Exod 27:19); "the vessels of the Tent of Meeting" (Num 3:8); "the holy vessels" (Num 4:15; 18:3) or "the Temple's vessels" (Neh 10:40). The bearers of these sacred implements are not just the priests or Levites (as in Num 1:50; 3:8; 4:15), according to the prophet, but rather all of Israel (Ibn Ezra, Kimchi). Some commentators note the possible allusion to the Egyptian exodus and the precious (but not holy) vessels that Israel had procured prior to their departure: "The Israelites had done Moses' bidding and borrowed from the Egyptians objects of silver and gold, and clothing" (Exod 12:35), just after Pharaoh had instructed Moses and Aaron: "Up, depart from my people!" (Exod 12:31).

[12] The redemption from Babylon shall eclipse the wonders of the Egyptian exodus. (See the introduction, §12.) Regarding the departure from Egypt it is written: "For you departed from Egypt in hasty alarm (בחִפזון)" (Deut 16:3; see also Exod 12:11), whereas here the prophet declares: "For you will not depart in hasty alarm (בחִפזון)." Moreover, according to the various traditions preserved in Scripture, the Israelites were led and protected by divine emissaries — be it the pillar of cloud or the pillar of fire (Exod 13:21; 14:20; Num 10:34; 14:14; Deut 1:33; Ps 78:14; Neh 9:12), an angel (Exod 14:19; 23:20, 23; 32:34), or the Ark of the Covenant (Num 10:33). Now, however, the Lord Himself will lead them; see also Isa 63:8-9: "So He was their deliverer in all their troubles; no angel or messenger — He Himself [lit. 'His presence'] delivered them. In His love and compassion He Himself redeemed them" (thus, according to the division and vocalization in the LXX; see there and cf. Exod 33:14-15). God shall protect His people by functioning as both their vanguard and rearguard (the merism implies the totality of God's protection); see similarly Josh 6:9: "The vanguard marched in front of the priests who were blowing the horns, and the rearguard marched behind the ark"; cf. Josh 6:13. For a similar metaphor see Isa 58:8: "Your Vindicator shall march before you, the Presence of the Lord shall be your rear guard." The same motif appears in a Sumerian tablet: "If only the goddess Inanna were my vanguard. If only my [personal] god were in my aid. If only he walked in back of me" (see W. W. Hallo, "Back to the Big House: Colloquial Sumerian, Continued," *Orientalia* 54 [1985]: 59, lines 11-13; N. Veldhuis, "Entering the Netherworld," *Cuneiform Digital Library Bulletin* 6 [2003]: 1, 4 [http://cdli.ucla.edu/pubs/cdlb/2003/cdlb2003_006.html, May 2009]) and is found in an Assyrian prophecy whose subject is Esarhaddon, the king of Assyria: "I am Ishtar of Arbela. I shall walk before you *(ina panâtukka)* and behind you *(ina kutallika)*" (see Parpola, *Assyrian Prophecies,* 5, 1:20′-24′).

But you will not depart in urgent haste — But you shall not leave Babylon with the same trepidation with which you fled Egypt (Deut 16:3). For the verb **חפז** denoting haste and trepidation, see Deut 20:3; Ps 48:6. The verb **יצא** is repeated for the third time for added emphasis (see v. 11).

Nor will you leave in flight — Nor (**לא**, reiterated to highlight the encouragement) will you flee from Chaldea as you did from Egypt; see Exod 14:5: "The king of Egypt was told that the people had fled." The reason for this will be immediately clarified. For the parallelism between **נוס** and **חפז**, see Ps 104:7: "They fled (**ינוסון**) at Your blast, rushed away in alarm (**יֵחָפֵזוּן**) at the sound of Your thunder"; cf. 2 Sam 4:4: "As she was fleeing in haste (**בְּחָפְזָהּ**)." The *nun* suffix of the verb **תלכון** is the archaic suffix of the second-person masculine plural. For the pair **הלך/יצא**, see Jer 6:25; Hab 3:5.

For the Lord is marching before you — since (**כי** — an emphatic conjunction) the Lord Himself shall be your vanguard; cf. Isa 45:2: "I will march before you [Cyrus]"; Deut 1:30: "None other than the Lord your God, who goes before you." For the motif of (the) god(s) marching before the king as he prepares for battle, see *CAD* A/1:317; and for the vanguard that precedes the army, see *CAD* A/2:418.

The God of Israel is your rear guard — And He shall be your rear guard as well (see also Isa 41:17; 45:3, 15), who protects you from all sides. For **מְאַסֵּף** ("rear guard"), see also Num 10:25. 1QIsa[a] adds an entire clause following the final words of the Masoretic verse: **אלוהי כל הארץ יקרא**, which is identical to 54:5: "He is called 'God of all the earth.'"

52:13–53:12

This prophecy, usually called the fourth Servant Song (for the first three, see 42:1-9; 49:1-9; 50:4-9; and the introduction, §5), is framed at both ends by a divine declaration (52:13; 53:11), by the expression עבדי ("My servant"), and by the verbal root נשא (52:13; 53:12). It may be subdivided into four scenes: (1) 52:13-15: God relates the astonishment of the nations at the servant's future success despite his disfigurement "beyond human semblance"; (2) 53:1-6: the nations respond in the first-person with incredulity at the servant who is "despised and shunned," confessing that he is the bearer of their sins and through his endured suffering their misdeeds are forgiven; (3) 53:7-9: a further depiction of the blameless servant who is sick and at death's door due to the people's iniquities; and (4) 53:10-12: the Lord's promise that, in spite of the harrowing treatment to which His servant was subject, he shall be fruitful and multiply and shall live a long life. He shall vindicate the multitude, act as their intercessor, and be recompensed in full. For the problem of the servant's identity — whether an individual (a contemporary of Deutero-Isaiah, the prophet himself, a historical figure from the past such as Moses, Jeremiah, or a messianic figure) or a collective polity (the nation Israel, a particular Israelite group, the ideal Israel [as opposed to the real Israel], or a righteous minority — all these various and divergent possibilities have been proposed by commentators due to the ambiguity shrouding the figure. Others have maintained that the servant's identity is amorphous: sometimes he is the prophet, and at other times he represents the nation of Israel. The identity of the "many" is also in contention, alluding either to the nations or to Israel. Yet others distinguish between the multitude in 52:13-15, who are the nations, and the multitude in chap. 53, which refers to the vast majority of the Israelite nation. For the multitude of opinions, see C. R. North, *The Suffering Servant in Deutero-Isaiah,* 2nd ed. (Oxford, 1956); D. J. C. Clines, *I, He, We and They: A Literary Approach to Isaiah 53,* JSOTSup 51 (Sheffield,

1976) — both with extensive bibliographies; H. M. Orlinsky, "The Lord's Servant," in E. L. Sukenik et al., eds., *Encyclopaedia Biblica,* 6 (Jerusalem, 1972), 15-22 (Heb.); Kaufmann, *Babylonian Captivity and Deutero-Isaiah,* 128-46. For traditional Jewish exegesis on the subject, see A. D. Neubauer, *The Fifty-Third Chapter of Isaiah,* 1: *Texts;* 2: *Translations,* ed. S. R. Driver and A. D. Neubauer (New York, 1969). (For additional bibliographical references, see the introduction, §5.) The servant is identified here as the steadfastly righteous minority; the multitude in 52:13-15 as the nations, whereas the multitude in chap. 53 represents the Israelite majority.

This section is permeated by an impressive array of key words and roots: **נשׂא**, 52:13; 53:4, 12 (note the literary frame mentioned above); **עבדי**, 52:13; 53:11; **רבים**, 52:14, 15; 53:11, 12 (twice); **מַראה(ו)**, 52:14; 53:2; **תֹאר(ו)**, 52:14; 53:2; **איש(ים)**, 52:14; 53:3 (twice), 6; **על**, 52:14, 15; 53:1, 5, 9; **פה**, 52:15; 53:7 (twice), 9; **שמע**, 52:15; 53:1; **ראי**, 52:15; 53:2 (twice), 10, 11 (note the different meaning); **מי**, 53:1 (twice), 8; **לפני**, 53:2, 7 (and 53:3 — **פנים**); **נִבזה**, 53:3 (twice); **כאב**, 53:3, 4; **חֲשַׁבְנֻהוּ**, 53:3, 4 (note the different meaning); **חלי**, 53:3, 4, 10; **ידע**, 53:3, 11; **נגע**, 53:4, 8; **סבל**, 53:4, 11; **עני**, 53:4, 7 (with a different meaning); **פשע**, 53:5, 8, 12 (twice); **דכא**, 53:5, 10; **עָוֹן**, 53:5, 6, 11 (in the last two occurrences **עָוֹן** is understood as "punishment"); **כֻּלָּנוּ**, 53:6 (twice); **הפגיע**, 53:6, 12 (with different meanings); **חפץ**, 53:10 (twice); **נפשו**, 53:10, 11, 12; **צדק**, 53:11 (twice); **חלק**, 53:12 (twice). A number of terms link the beginning of the first verses with 52:10: **גוים** (52:15), **זרוע** (53:1), **ראי** (52:14, 15; 53:2 [twice]).

What makes this servant song sui generis is the idea of suffering for another. The servant bears the sins of the many, and because of his afflictions the multitude is forgiven — an idea that became axiomatic to Christianity, which interpreted these verses as referring to the death and resurrection of Jesus. The roots of this belief that one can be held culpable for the sin of another, however, appear in a number of places throughout the Hebrew Bible. Compare, for example, the oft-repeated, "Guilt of the parents [visited] on the children, on the third and on the fourth generations" (Exod 20:5; 34:7; Num 14:18; Deut 5:9); Num 14:33: "Your children shall roam the wilderness for forty years, suffering for your faithlessness, until the last of your carcasses is down in the wilderness"; Num 25:4: "The Lord said to Moses, 'Take all the nation's leaders and have them publicly impaled before the Lord, so that the Lord's wrath may turn away from Israel'"; cf. also v. 11; Ezek 4:4-6: "Then lie on your left side, and let it bear the punishment of the house of Israel. . . . You shall bear their punishment. . . . And so you shall bear the punishment for the house of Israel . . . and bear the punishment of the house of Judah"; Lam 5:7: "Our fathers sinned and are no more; and we must bear their guilt." For a sacrifice in lieu of a human being, compare the binding of Isaac narrative, in which Abraham sacrifices a ram in place of his son (Gen 22:13); the sacrifice of a sheep instead of a firstborn human (Exod

13:13; 34:20); cf. also Lev 4:13-21. One should also make special note of the ceremony of expiation, in which Aaron sends off a goat that carries on its back all the sins and iniquities of the community (Lev 16:22), and thus the sins are forgiven. In this chapter as well, the slate shall be wiped clean and all the nation's misdemeanors will be forgotten if the servant sacrifices himself in the people's place. For further examples of this "bearing of the cross" for another's sake, note the case of accidental manslaughter, in which the murderer must reside in a chosen city of refuge until the death of the high priest, and only "after the death of the high priest may the manslayer return to his landholding" (Num 35:28), as well as the annulment of a wife's vows *post facto* by her husband: "But if he annuls them some time after he has heard them, he shall bear her guilt" (Num 30:16). The prophet confronts the issue of theodicy and offers his interpretation of the people's suffering. For the linguistic impact of this piece on the final chapters of Daniel, especially chap. 12, see H. L. Ginsberg, "The Oldest Interpretation of the Suffering Servant," *VT* 3 (1953): 400-404.

[52:13] The future ascendance of the servant.

Indeed, My servant shall prosper — The prophecy begins with the same two words as the first Servant Song, הֵן עבדי (42:1), and with the assurance that the Lord's servant shall ultimately have success. For שׂכל with this meaning, see Josh 1:8: "Only then will you prosper in your undertakings and only then will you be successful (תשׂכיל)"; 1 Sam 18:5: "David was successful (ישׂכיל) in every mission on which Saul sent him"; cf. 1 Sam 18:14; 1 Kgs 2:3 (Solomon); 2 Kgs 18:7 (Hezekiah).

He shall be exalted, elevated, and uplifted — a triad of synonyms (רום, נשׂא, גבה) followed by the adverb מאד, which emphasizes the servant's overwhelming future success (in contrast with the threefold emphasis on his present abject dejectedness, Isa 53:2, 4). For these three parallel descriptions, see 2:14-15: "Against all the high (הרמים) mountains and all the lofty (הנִּשָּׂאות) hills; against every soaring (גְבֹהָה) tower." For the parallelism of נשׂא and רם, see 57:15; 2:12; 6:1; 33:10; Prov 30:13; Dan 11:12.

[14-15] The astonishment of the nations regarding the future ascension of the servant, since in the present his form is "beyond human semblance." The section begins in the second-person and continues in the third. For this stylistic phenomenon, see Isa 45:8, 21; for the syntactic paradigm כאשר . . . כן (vv. 14-15), see 55:10-11; 65:8; 66:22.

[14] *Just as the many were appalled at you* — just as the multitude of nations were horrified at your appearance in the past. For the verb שמם, see Lev 26:32: "So that your enemies who settle in it [your land] shall be appalled (ושממו) by it"; Ezek 27:35: "All the inhabitants of the coastlands are appalled (ושממו) over you [Tyre]"; cf. also Ezek 26:16; 32:10; Job 18:20. For the "many" or "multitude" (רבים) denoting a prodigious number of peoples, see v. 15; 53:11, 12;

Dan 11:33, 34; 12:3, 10. The Targum, Theodotion, Peshitta, and a number of medieval Hebrew manuscripts read עָלָיו ("at him") instead of עָלֶיךָ ("at you"), which conforms to the following third-person forms.

So marred was his appearance, unlike that of a man — This is a parenthetical clause that clarifies the reason for the multitude's repugnance: the servant was "marred" beyond recognition. Vocalize מָשְׁחַת, a *hophʿal* participle (similarly Mal 1:14; Prov 25:26, and see Peshitta; Ibn Ganaḥ, *Sefer ha-Shorashim*, 508; idem, *Sefer ha-Riqmah*, 117, line 5; Luzzatto; Ehrlich, *Randglossen*, 4:190), instead of MT מִשְׁחַת, a hybrid form combining the vocalization of the third-person perfect masculine singular *niphʿal*, נִשְׁחַת, and the consonants of the *hophʿal* participle, מָשְׁחַת — a form corroborated by a number of medieval Hebrew manuscripts. (For other hybrid verbal forms, see Isa 59:3; 63:3.) It is possible, however, that the vocalization מִשְׁחַת was tendentious and that the Masoretes wished to obfuscate the negative terminology by vocalizing the substantive as if were a reference to the sacred anointing oil: שֶׁמֶן מִשְׁחַת קֹדֶשׁ (Exod 30:25, 31). For the negative *mem* prefix (מֵאִישׁ), see Isa 17:1. The word כֵן was erroneously repeated here from the opening of the following hemistich, likely influenced by the common syntactical construction: כַּאֲשֶׁר . . . כֵן; one should read כִּי or אָכֵן instead. Others interpret כֵן as emphatic, as in Josh 2:4: "It is true (כֵּן), the men did come to me"; Jer 14:10: "Truly (כֵּן), they love to stray"; Ps 63:3: "Indeed (כֵּן), I shall behold You in the sanctuary."

His form, beyond human semblance — This clause forms a chiastic parallelism with the immediately preceding one: he is disfigured beyond all recognition. For the synonymous pair תֹּאַר/מַרְאֶה, see Gen 29:17; cf. Gen 39:6. For the vocalization תֹּאֲרוֹ (from תֹּאַר) instead of תָּאֳרוֹ (1 Sam 28:14), cf. Jer 22:13: וּפֹעֲלוֹ (from פֹּעַל), and פָּעֳלוֹ (Deut 32:4). For the parallel pair בְּנֵי אָדָם/אִישׁ, see Mic 5:6.

[15] *Just so he shall startle many nations* — כֵן here introduces the final clause of the preceding verse, which began with כַּאֲשֶׁר. The meaning of the verb יַזֶּה (the *hiphʿil* of the root נזי) is unclear. Some relate it to Arab. *nazâ*, which signifies jumping or leaping, i.e., the servant shall cause the nations to jump up in surprise. Others, deriving it from the same root, prefer emending the vocalization to יִזּוּ *(qal)*: "They shall spring up in astonishment" (see G. R. Driver, "Isaiah 52:13–53:12: The Servant of the Lord," in M. Black and G. Fohrer, eds., *In Memoriam Paul Kahle,* BZAW 103 [Berlin, 1968], 92). The prophet may have chosen this term to create a double entendre with יְקַפְּצוּ in the following stich (which can also mean "to jump, leap" [Cant 2:8], but in the present context has another meaning; see Luzzatto; Yellin, *Ḥiqrei Miqra,* 2:72). Another possibility — assuming the MT is corrupt — is to read יְ[רג]זוּ, "to be agitated, excited." For the expression גּוֹיִם רַבִּים ("many nations"), see Deut 7:1; Jer 22:8; Ezek 26:3.

Kings shall be silenced because of him — When the leaders of the multitude shall be faced with the servant, disfigured beyond human semblance, they shall be shocked into silence (lit. "shut their mouths"). For the verb קפץ, "to close, shut," see Deut 15:7. "Do not shut (תקפץ) your hand against your needy kinsman"; and especially Job 5:16 and Ps 107:42: "The mouth of wrongdoing is closed," where, as here, it is employed with the substantive פה. (For the homonym קפץ, "to jump," see above.) For shocking individuals or groups into silence, cf. Job 21:5: "Look at me and be appalled, and clap your hand to your mouth!"; Job 29:9: "Nobles held back their words. They clapped their hands to their mouths." For the pair מלכים/גוים, see Isa 41:2; 45:1; 60:3, 16.

For they shall see what has not been told them — For they shall witness unforgettable wonders. For the *puʿal* form of the verb ספר in a similar context, see Hab 1:5: "For a work is being wrought in your days that you would not believe if it were told (יְסֻפָּר)." The Hebrew phrase כי אשר alliterates with כאשר in the previous verse.

Shall behold what they never have heard — parallel to the preceding clause. They shall become privy to things they would never have imagined. For the synonymous pair התבונן/ראה, see Jer 2:10.

[53:1-6] Commentators disagree about the identity of the speakers in the first verses of this chapter. In light of the parallel features noted above, however, it would appear that the speakers are none other than the nations mentioned in the final verses of chap. 52. Others, however, identify them as Israel. I tend to agree with the view that the speakers are the majority of the Israelite nation, as opposed to the servant who represents the chosen minority.

[1] *Who can believe what we have heard?* — The pronominal suffix of שְׁמֻעָתֵנוּ is accusative, i.e., "the report that we have heard." For שמועה ("report"), see 1 Sam 2:24; Isa 28:9, 19; and for the expression האמין ל-, see Gen 45:26; 1 Kgs 10:7.

Upon whom has the arm of the Lord been revealed? — an extension of the above query: How is it possible that the Lord's potent arm was revealed to such a lowly and despised figure? For the recurring motif of "God's arm" in Deutero-Isaiah's prophecies, see 52:10, which creates an associative link with this chapter; 48:14; 51:5, 9; 59:16; 62:8; 63:5, 12. Instead of על מי ("upon whom"; the combination of the *niphʿal* of the verb with the preposition על occurs again only in Exod 20:26), the LXX, Vulgate, Peshitta, 1QIsa[a], and 1QIsa[b] all read אל מי ("to whom"), which is the more common construction.

[2] The servant is described in arboreal terms, as a sapling in the waterless wilderness, where one would expect all growth to wither and die; cf. Job 18:16. The sequence of three negatives, "no form," "no beauty," and "no appearance," emphasizes the servant's lack of human features. (Cf. v. 4, and the tripartite depiction of the servant's future glory in 52:13.)

For he has grown, by His favor, like a sapling — He has sprung from the ground like a tender shoot in the wilderness (the locale, implied here, is mentioned specifically in the next colon) "before Him" (לפניו), figuratively, "with His approbation," or, "with His help" (Luzzatto). For the preposition לפני referring to the divine will, see Gen 17:18: "O that Ishmael might live by your favor (לפניך)!"; Gen 27:7: "That I may bless you with the Lord's approval (לפני) before I die"; cf. also Num 32:21-23 (Ehrlich, *Randglossen,* 4:191). However, in light of the second-person masculine form of the previous verse, שְׁמֻעָתֵנוּ, and the following ונראֵהו and וְנֶחְמְדֵהוּ, some commentators suggest that the text should be emended to לפנינו ("before us"), assuming a haplography of one of the *nuns*. This is the only occurrence of the term יונק with the meaning "young plant, sapling." The more common feminine form, יונקת ("young shoot, twig"), appears six times in the Hebrew Bible, e.g., Ezek 17:22; Job 15:30. For the verb עלי ("to grow"), see Gen 40:10; 41:22.

Like a tree trunk out of arid ground — For שֹׁרֶשׁ denoting the bottom part of a tree, see Isa 11:1. For the alliterative expression ארץ צִיָּה, parallel here to מדבר, see 41:18; Jer 2:6; 51:43; Ezek 19:13.

He had no form or beauty, that we should look at him — The verb וְנִרְאֵהוּ should be attached to this clause rather than to the next, contrary to the MT division (which most likely attempted to tone down the derision leveled against the servant). (See M. B. Cohen, "The Masoretic Accents as a Biblical Commentary," *JANES* 4 [1972]: 9-11.) Though this unfavorable description refers to the servant (see also 52:14) rather than to the tree, the choice of the substantives תֹּאַר and הדר is nevertheless very apt since they both appear in arboreal contexts as well. For תֹּאַר as the "form" of a tree, see the Phoenician inscription of King Eshmunazor (first half of the fifth century BCE), which contains, as here, the word שרש: "Let him have no root (שרש) below, or fruit above, or form (תֹּאַר) among the living under the sun" (*KAI* 14:11-12); see too Jer 11:16. For the term הדר in the context of trees, see Lev 23:40: "The fruit of goodly (הדר) trees." For the pair תֹּאַר/הדר in an entirely different context, see Sir 43:9: "A form (תאר) like the sky and the beauty (והדר) of a star."

No appearance, that we should take delight in him — For the root חמד in the context of trees, see Gen 2:9: "Every tree that was pleasing (נחמד) to the sight (למראה)" (note there, as here, the appearance of נחמד and מראֶה in tandem; cf. Josh 7:21); Gen 3:6: "And that the tree was desirable (ונחמד) as a source of wisdom." The sequence תאר . . . מראה (see also Gen 29:17; 39:6) forms a chiastic parallel with the above, מַרְאֵהוּ . . . ותֹאֲרו (52:14).

[3] The servant, reviled by all, was tortured by sickness. Compare Ps 22:7: "But I am a worm, not a man, scorned by men, despised by people."

He was despised, shunned by men — For the root בזי ("despised"), see, e.g., Isa 49:7; Jer 49:15: "Most despised among men" (בָּזוּי באדם); Ps 22:7 quoted above; 119:141. The expression חֲדַל אִישִׁים may be interpreted in various ways: a despised individual with whom people have stopped associating (for this meaning of חדל, see Isa 2:22; Job 19:14); "so despised that he is not considered even human" (Ibn Ezra); "he is the least of men," as in Ps 39:5 (Kimchi, second commentary; cf. Luzzatto); or "he shrank from the sight of men." The poetic plural, אישים, which recurs only twice more in the Hebrew Bible (Ps 141:4; Prov 8:4), appears also in the Phoenician Azitawada inscription from the eighth century BCE: אשם רעם, "evil men" (*KAI* 26A I:15). Its use here (instead of אנשים) was perhaps influenced by the appearance of the following word, איש.

A man of suffering — an individual who suffered from infirmity and pain. The feminine plural מַכְאֹבוֹת is a hapax legomenon. For the masculine form, see v. 4; Exod 3:7; Lam 1:12, 18; and 1QIsa[a] here. The people's protracted exile is also depicted as torturous in Lam 1:12: "Look about and see: Is there any agony (מכאוב) like mine that was dealt out to me?" For the syntactical construction איש מכאֹבות, cf. Prov 29:1: איש תוֹכָחות ("one oft reproved").

Familiar with disease — cf. v. 10; and for the substantive חֳלִי ("disease"), see Jer 10:19; Eccl 6:2. For the verb ידע, which, like its Akkadian cognate *idû* ("to know"; *CAD* I-J:27), denotes familiarity and experience, see Deut 1:13, 15: "Wise, discerning, and experienced (וִידֻעִים)." The usually passive *pa'ul* participle יְדוּעַ (the construct form of יָדוּעַ) has here an active connotation, a relatively rare phenomenon in Biblical Hebrew (cf. Isa 26:3: "It trusts [בָּטוּחַ] in You"; Ps 103:14: "He is mindful [זָכוּר] that we are dust"; Cant 3:8: "Each with a sword ready [אֲחוּזֵי] at his side"), but common in later Rabbinic Hebrew, e.g., רָכוּב ("riding"); סָבוּר ("thinking"). Another suggestion is to derive the verb ידע from the cognate Arabic root *wada'u,* "to humble" (cf. Judg 8:16: "He humbled [וַיֹּדַע] the people of Sukkoth with them"), and translate: "He was humbled by suffering." (See D. Winton Thomas, "The Root *yd'* in Hebrew," *JTS* 35 [1934]: 298-306.)

As one who hid his face from us — This clause may be understood in two different ways: (1) The servant is accustomed to concealing his visage "from us" (ממנו, as in Isa 64:6: "You have hidden your face from us [ממנו]"; cf. Lev 13:45, concerning the leper who "covers over [יַעְטֶה] his upper lip"). This explanation accords well with the understanding of חֲדַל אישים as referring to one who ceased interacting with others. Moreover, it is most likely that the text read פניו and that the final *mem* of פנים is a dittography from the following first letter of ממנו. (2) Otherwise ממנו can be understood as a third-person masculine singular, as in Gen 48:19: "Yet his younger brother shall be greater than he (ממנו)," and then the clause is interpreted to refer to the people who wish to dissociate themselves from the servant: "We did not want to behold him because he was so repellent to us" (Kimchi; Saadyah Gaon, 118; Rashi; Ibn Ezra; Luzzatto; Ehrlich, *Randglossen,* 4:191). According to this interpretation, the hemistich fits well with the first explanation of חדל אישים, i.e., one with whom people stopped associating. In this case it is also possible that פנים is an error caused by a ligature, and one should read פנינו (i.e., the *nun* and *waw* were combined into a *mem*); see the comments to Isa 63:7, 14; and cf. Josh 5:1: עברנו (Ketib), עברם (Qere); 2 Kgs 22:4: וְיַתֵּם (את הכסף), compared to 2 Chr 34:9: ויתנו (את הכסף). (See R. Weiss, *Studies in the Text and Language of the Bible* [Jerusalem, 1987], 3-19 [Heb.]). The word מַסְתֵּר can be understood either as the construct form of the *hiph'il* participle מסתיר (as is suggested by the appearance of the fuller form in 1QIsa[a]); as an infinitive, as in Num 10:2: "To summon (לְמִקְרָא) the community and to set the division in motion (וּלְמַסַּע)"; or as a hybrid conflation of the *niph'al* participle נִסְתָּר and the *hiph'il* participle מַסְתִּיר; cf. מִשְׁחַת, Isa 52:14. The *kaph* particle is emphatic, emphasizing the act of concealment. This verse, 50:6, and Exod 3:6 are the only references to a human concealing his visage. All the other occurrences refer to the Deity.

He was despised, and we held him of no account — He was of no importance to us, as in Isa 13:17: "who do not value (יחשבו) silver." Some commentators (e.g., Ehrlich, *Randglossen,* 4:191) emend the MT from נבזה ("despised") to נִבְזֵהוּ ("we despised him"), assuming that the *waw* suffix was omitted as a result of a haplography from the beginning of the next word, ולא. Compare the Peshitta and 1QIsa[a], ונבוזהו (derived from the etymologically related root בוז), which accords well with חשבנֻהו, but may be the result of verbal harmonization. The recurrence of נבזהו/נבזה serves to emphasize his abject despised state.

[4-6] The multitude's realization that the servant bears the burden of their sins and that his suffering atones for their iniquity.

[4] The terms חֳלָיֵנוּ . . . ומכאבינו form a chiastic parallelism with those in the previous verse, מכאבות . . . חלי.

Yet it was our sickness that he was bearing — We were totally taken by surprise when we realized that his maladies were actually in atonement for our own wrongdoings, for he (הוא — the pronoun is emphatic) was, in effect, bearing the sickness that we should have suffered. For the exclamatory and contradictory אכן, see 49:4 and Rashbam's commentary to Gen 28:16: "This is the meaning of every אכן in the Bible — אך כן — indeed it is thus, and not as I expected." For the expression נשׂא חלי ("to bear sickness"), see Jer 10:19: "This is but a sickness and I must bear it."

Our suffering that he bore — parallel to the previous clause. For the root סבל, "to bear," the Aramaic equivalent of Heb. נשׂא, see Isa 46:4-7; Neh 4:4.

We accounted him plagued, smitten, and afflicted by God — His desperate state is depicted in a triad of graphic nouns, contrasted to the tripartite description of the servant's future glory (52:13). We perceived him (אנחנו חשבנֻהו versus לא חשבנֻהו, above) to be an individual bearing a private cross, since he was "plagued," נגוע, as in Ps 73:14: "For all day long I am plagued (נגוע)"; cf. Gen 12:17: "But the Lord afflicted Pharaoh and his household with mighty plagues (נְגָעִים)." Since the noun נגע appears in connection with a leper (Lev 13:45), some have assumed that the servant was afflicted with leprosy; but this is not the meaning of the text here. He also is described as מֻכֵּה אלהים, "smitten by God." (For a similar syntactical construction, see Jer 18:21: "smitten by the sword [מֻכֵּי חרב].") The Akkadian semantic equivalent *maḫāṣu* ("to smite") also appears in contexts of divinely inflicted maladies (*CAD* M/1:75-76). For וּמְעֻנֶּה ("afflicted"), see Ps 119:71: "It was good for me that I was humbled (עֻנֵּיתִי)." For other examples of widespread national affliction caused by God, see Isa 64:11: "At such things will You restrain Yourself, O Lord? Will You stand idly by and let us be afflicted (וּתְעַנֵּנוּ) so heavily?"; Ps 90:15: "For as long as You have afflicted us (עִניתנו), for the years we have suffered misfortune." Although the terms נָגוּעַ and מְעֻנֶּה are vocalized as absolutes, together with the sole construct of the triad, מֻכֵּה, they are all subordinate to אלהים.

[5] Since the servant was their whipping boy and suffered in their stead, they remained hale and healthy.

But he was wounded because of our sins — He ("he," as opposed to "us"; the contrast is expressed by the *waw* prefix), however, was wounded (lit. "pierced," מְחֹלָל) because of our transgressions. The *mem* particle prefixing מִפְּשָׁעֵינוּ is causal, as in Exod 6:9: "Because of their impatience and because of hard labor (מקֹּצר רוח ומעבודה קשה)"; Lam 4:13: "It was for the sins (מֵחַטֹּאת) of her prophets." For other occurrences of פשע referring to the sins of the people, see Isa 43:25, 27; 44:22; 46:8; 48:8; 50:1. For the root חלל (here a *huphʿal* participle, מְחֹלָל) signifying the puncturing of a body with a sharp implement, see 51:9: "That pierced (מחללת) the dragon"; and for a nonlethal injury, see Ps 109:22: "And my heart is pierced (חָלַל) within me."

Crushed because of our iniquities — Once again, in this parallel hemistich, the *mem* in מֵעֲוֹנֹתֵינוּ denotes causation. For another example of both דכא and חלל, see Ps 89:11.

He bore the chastisement that made us safe and secure — the "chastisement" (מוּסַר) meant for us (see Jer 30:14: "With cruel chastisement [מוסר]"), he bore in our stead, thereby guaranteeing our welfare. Hebrew עליו has the connotation here of "to his detriment"; cf. Gen 30:28: "Name your wages you want from me (עלי), and I will pay"; Gen 34:12: "Ask of me a bride-price ever so high (עלי), as well as gifts." Some commentators vocalize שִׁלּוּמֵנוּ ("our retribution/requital") instead of MT שְׁלוֹמֵנוּ; cf. Isa 34:8; Hos 9:7.

And by his bruises we were healed — and his bruises (חֲבֻרָתוֹ) served as a balm for us. (In every other occurrence [Gen 4:23; Exod 21:25; Isa 1:6; Ps 38:6; Prov 20:30], the letter *beth* has a *dagesh* in this word, חַבּוּרָה. Perhaps the

Masoretes omitted it in order to interpret the word as "his company," thereby tempering the gravity of the servant's condition [cf. v. 3; 52:14].) The plural substantive ובחברותיו, which appears in 1QIsa[a], is in harmony with the other plural forms throughout the verse. For the expression רפא ל- ("to heal"), see Isa 6:10; Hos 5:13.

[6] *We all went astray like sheep* — We wandered aimlessly (תעי); cf. Ps 119:176: "I have strayed (תעיתי) like a lost sheep"; cf. Isa 47:15: "Each has wandered off (תעו) his own way," and the verses quoted there.

Each going his own way — The expression לדרך פנה recurs only once more, in 56:11, and denotes sybaritic pleasure seeking (Ehrlich, *Randglossen,* 4:191).

But the Lord visited on him the punishment of all of us — Nevertheless — the *waw* is contrastive — the Lord exacted payment from the servant for our iniquitous ways. For עָוֹן meaning "punishment," see v. 11; Gen 15:16: "For the punishment of the Amorite is not yet complete"; Lam 4:6: "The punishment of my people exceeded the penalty of Sodom, which was overthrown in a moment." Note the employment of the same verb (הפגיע) again, in v. 12, but there with the meaning of intercession. The verse has an *inclusio* framework beginning and concluding with כֻּלָּנוּ.

[7-9] The servant, even on the verge of death, accepts his torturous maltreatment with equanimity. The depiction of the servant in these terms was influenced by Jer 11:19: "For I was like a docile lamb led to the slaughter. . . . 'Let us cut him off from the land of the living.'" Jeremiah, however, is referring to his lack of awareness regarding the nefarious plots to kill him, while here the text speaks of unflinchingly enduring torture. (See the introduction, §15.) Verses 8-9 feature a long series of passive verbs by which the servant's lack of resistance is emphasized.

[7] *He was maltreated* — The verb נִגַּשׂ (here in the *niphʿal*) denotes being treated harshly; cf. 1 Sam 14:24: "The men of Israel were hard-pressed (נִגַּשׂ) that day." It also appears in Job 39:7 in connection with a "wild ass," similar to the animal similes here and in the previous verse.

Yet submissive — A circumstantial clause introduced by והוא; cf. Gen 48:14: "But Israel stretched out his right hand and laid it on Ephraim's head, though he (והוא) was the younger." In spite of the abuse, he faced the injustice with total equanimity. For this meaning of the verb עני, cf. Rabbinic Hebrew: נעניתי לך, "I submit to you" (*b. Ber.* 28a; *Ketub.* 67b). Note the repetition of this root in v. 4, with the meaning "to be afflicted."

And he did not protest — literally "he did not open his mouth," i.e., he did not protest the injustice, but awaited his fate in total silence, as in Isa 42:2 (the first Servant Song): "He shall not cry out, or shout aloud, or make his voice heard in the streets." The imperfect (יפתח) indicates frequency of an action, in this case the continuity of his silence. The Akkadian etymological and semantic parallel to this expression, *pû petû,* also means "to protest" (*CAD* P:352).

Like a sheep being led to slaughter — He did not struggle, but was like a docile sheep about to be sacrificed (an elaboration of the simile in v. 6). Both 1QIsa[a] and 1QIsa[b] read לטבוח instead of MT לַטֶּבַח, similar to Jer 11:19. For the same imagery, see Ps 44:23: "It is for Your sake that we are slain all day long, that we are regarded as sheep to be slaughtered." For the same description in Mesopotamian literature, "to be slaughtered, *ṭabāḫu,* like sheep, *ṣēnu* [and synonyms]," see *CAD* Ṭ:3.

Like a ewe, dumb before those who shear her — The servant's sheeplike docility is emphasized once more. This time the simile is to a ewe (רחל), who yields her wool to the shearers without a protest. (For the shearing of sheep herds, see Gen 38:12; 1 Sam 25:2; 2 Sam 13:23.) The word נֶאֱלָמָה is a pausal form of the feminine *niphʿal* participle.

He did not open his mouth — an emphatic repetition of the previous clause: the servant is unflinching in his total silence. This clause forms a negative parallelism with the preceding נאלמה, "dumb." The servant's state is first described in "positive" terms and then couched in an equivalent negative terminology, as in Ps 38:14: "But I am like a deaf man, unhearing"; Ps 39:10: "I am dumb, I do not speak up." For the opposite image, see Ezek 33:22: "Thus my mouth was opened and I was no longer speechless."

[8] The first two hemistichs and the final hemistich are ambiguous and very difficult to explicate.

By oppressive judgment he was taken away — The meaning of the first two words of this clause is hard to clarify. The first term, עֹצֶר, has been interpreted as "rule" and "sovereignty," as in 1 Sam 9:17: "This is the man that I told you would rule (יַעְצֹר) My people" (cf. also Judg 18:7); as "coercion" (Targum מְיִסּוּרִין, "by suffering"; cf. also LXX and Vulgate), as in Ps 107:39: "After they had been few and crushed by coercion (מֵעֹצֶר), misery, and sorrow"; or as "incarceration," as in 2 Kgs 17:4: "And the king of Assyria arrested him (ויעצרֵהו) and put him in prison"; Jer 33:1: "While he was still imprisoned (עצור) in the court of the guardhouse" (and cf. Jer 39:15). Depending on the commentator's understanding of עֹצֶר, the second term, משפט, has been variously translated as "justice," "verdict," "righteousness," "punishment," "affliction," "doom," or "castigation." There is also little agreement regarding the function of the *mem* prefix (מֵעֹצֶר). Some interpret it is a negation, i.e., he was taken without עצר ומשפט; or, alternatively, he was taken from עצר ומשפט. There is even disagreement regarding the archaic *qal* passive, לֻקָּח (cf. Isa 49:25; 52:5). Some translate it as "rescued and escaped," or "taken forcibly," while others suggest that it is a euphemism for the servant being killed, as in Prov 24:11: "Save those taken off (לְקֻחִים) to death"; cf. Jer 15:15; Ezek 33:4; Ps 31:14). The hemistich remains enigmatic.

Who gave a thought to his fate? — Though several alternate suggestions have been offered to explain the meaning of דּוֹרוֹ here, the most probable is "his fate," based on Arab. *dāʾirat,* which signifies a momentous change in fate. For the verb יְשׂוֹחֵחַ (from the root שׂיח), "to muse, consider," see also Ps 143:5.

For he was cut off from the land of the living — In light of the verb נגזר, "to be cut off," there are those who maintain that this is a reference to the servant's death or murder; cf. Ps 88:6: "Abandoned among the dead, like bodies lying in the grave, of whom You are mindful no more, and who are cut off (נגזרו) from Your care." For similar imagery, see Jer 11:19: "Let us cut him off from the land of the living"; Ps 52:7: "And root you out of the land of the living." However, it is possible that the death and demise of the servant are not literal, but serve as a metaphor for his highly precarious state, as in Ezek 37:11: "And He said to me, 'O mortal, these bones are the whole house of Israel.' They say, 'Our bones are dried up, our hope is gone; we are doomed (נגזרנו)'"; Lam 3:54: "Waters flowed over my head, I said: 'I am done! (נגזרתי).'" For the expression "the land of [the] living" (ארץ [ה]חיים), in addition to the verses cited above, see also Isa 38:11: "I thought, I shall never see Yah, Yah in the land of the living"; Ps 27:13: "Had I not the assurance that I would enjoy the goodness of the Lord in the land of the living." Compare also the Akkadian semantic cognate expression *qaqqar balāṭi* ("the land of the living"; *CAD* B:50; Q:118).

Because of the sin of My people, he was brought/struck to death — The prefix *mem* (מִפֶּשַׁע) indicates causation, as in v. 5: because of the sin of "my people" (עמי); or, according to 1QIsa[a], "his people"; or perhaps one should read מפשעמו/מפשעם ("because of their sin") or מפשענו ("because of our sin"), assuming a dittography of the *ʿayin;* cf. LXX, Vulgate, and Peshitta. According to these readings, לָמוֹ is a poetic form of the indirect third-person pronoun לו, as in Isa 44:15: "He fashions an idol and bows down to it (למו)" (see GKC 302 n. 3). For the people as iniquitous, cf. v. 5; 46:8: "Take this to heart, you sinners (פושעים)!"; 48:8: "That you were called a rebel (ופֹשֵׁעַ) from birth." More probable, however, is the reading of the Vulgate and Peshitta: נֻגַּע (1QIsa[a], נוגע), combined with the LXX reading, לַמָּוֶת (corroborated by one medieval Hebrew manuscript), i.e., he was brought to the very brink of death; cf. Ps 88:4: "My life has reached (הגיעו) the brink of Sheol"; or, alternatively, he was "struck to death," meaning beaten to within an inch of his life.

[9] Since he was thought to be a sinner, the servant's burial site was chosen with this in mind despite his utter blamelessness. This is not to indicate that the servant actually perished; rather, it is a rhetorical device similar to the one found in the Babylonian poem *Ludlul bēl nēmeqi,* "I Shall Praise the Lord of Wisdom": "My grave was waiting, and my funerary paraphernalia ready. Before I had died lamentation for me was finished" (II:114-15; *BWL,* 46).

His grave was set among the wicked — Read וַיֻּתַּן (the archaic *qal* passive of the verb נתן), or וַיִּתְּנוּ, "they set" (indefinite plural, as in LXX, Peshitta, and 1QIsa[a]: ויתנו). His burial plot was set in an area designated for evildoers. For the expression נתן קבר ("to assign a grave"), see Ezek 32:23: "Her graves are set (נִתְּנוּ קִבְרֹתֶיהָ) in the farthest recesses of the Pit"; Ezek 39:11: "On that day I will assign to Gog a burial site (אתן . . . קבר) there in Israel." Here Heb. את denotes "with."

And with the rich, his burial place — The verb of the first colon does double duty and is implied here as well. The problem, however, is the mention of "the rich" (עשיר) (or, according to 1QIsa[a], עשירים, plural; cf. רשעים, "the wicked" [plural], above). Since, however, financial advantage or disadvantage is not pertinent here (although in other contexts "the rich find it difficult to enter the kingdom of heaven" and are, at times, identified with the wicked [cf. Mic 6:12; Jer 17:11]), some commentators have suggested emending the text to עֹשֵׂי רע ("evildoers"); עֹשֵׂי רִב ("contentious individuals," assuming a haplography with the first letter, ב, of the following word); or רשעים ("the wicked"), a metathesis). Compare Ibn Ganaḥ's comment on this verse: "And know that עשיר is not connected to this entry [i.e., עשיר, "the wealthy"]; rather, it is related to רשעים ("the wicked"), which is mentioned directly above" (*Sefer ha-Shorashim,* 389). G. R. Driver has suggested that עשיר is related to Arab. *ġuṭrun,* which denotes "rabble, refuse of mankind" ("Isaiah 52:13–53:12," 95). Furthermore, the plural בְּמֹתָיו is anomalous, since the reference here is to the singular servant and there is no plural of the substantive מָוֶת ("death") in the Bible. Its meaning is, rather, "a grave marker, parallel to קברו, 'his grave site'" (ibn Ezra; and cf. Luzzatto) and should be vocalized בָּמָתוֹ; cf. 1QIsa[a] בומתו (see Kutscher, *Language and Linguistic Background,* 225, 368). One should note that the LXX translates בָּמוֹת as "stele" in Lev 26:30; Num 21:28; 22:41; 33:52; and in Arabic the etymological equivalent, *buhmat,* denotes "a rock slab," "a grave." Compare also במה in Ezek 43:7: "And by the corpses of their kings stand their steles (בָּמוֹתָם)."

Though he had done no injustice — This fate awaits the servant regardless of his blameless conduct; cf. Job 16:17: "For no injustice on my part." For על as a conjunction indicating opposition, see Ezra 10:2: "But there is hope for Israel despite (על) this."

And had spoken no deceit — i.e., he is pure and innocent in both speech and in conduct. For a deceitful mouth, cf. Ps 36:4: "His words are evil and deceitful" (מִרְמָה); Ps 109:2: "For the wicked and the deceitful (מִרְמָה) open their mouth against me." For the pair of synonymous terms מִרְמָה/חמס ("injustice/falsehood"), see Zeph 1:9.

[10a] The servant's suffering, inflicted upon him by God, expiates all the nation's sins. For sacrificial expiation, see, e.g., Lev 5:6, 7, 15, 19.

But the Lord chose to crush him with sickness — This clause, which begins with a *waw* conjunction indicating contrast, is variously explained. Some commentators suggest that, despite the servant's blamelessness, God has chosen (חפץ; for other occurrences of the use of חפץ for divine choice, see 44:28) to inflict disease and sickness on him. According to this explanation, דַּכְּאוֹ is interpreted as an infinitive with a third-person suffixal object. Others vocalize it as a substantive, דַּכָּאוֹ, "the crushed one" (Luzzatto); cf. 57:15: "Yet with the contrite (דַּכָּא) and lowly of spirit." According to both of these interpretations, one should read הֶחֱלִיא (instead of MT הֶחֱלִי, a haplography caused by the omission of one of the two adjacent *aleph*s: החליא אם). For the verb חלא, "to be sick," a rare by-form of חלי, see 2 Chr 16:12: "Asa fell sick (ויחלא). . . . But ill as he was, he still did not turn to the Lord but to physicians"; and cf. the substantive תַּחֲלֻאִים (Jer 16:4; Deut 29:21). For the omission of the final *aleph* in a verb, see 2 Kgs 13:6: "However, they did not depart from the sins that the house of Jeroboam had caused Israel to commit (הֶחֱטִי)." (In this case as well, the probability of haplography is quite likely, since the following word also begins with an *aleph*.) Other commentators suggest combining the first part of the adjacent clause to this one and transposing the letters of אם — adding the *mem* to החלי and the *aleph* to the following *tav*, reading הֶחֱלִים את שׁם אָשָׁם נפשו, "[The Lord desires] to restore His contrite one to health, the one who offered himself in lieu of a sacrifice." For the verb חלם, see Isa 38:16: "You have restored me to health (וְתַחֲלִימֵנִי) and revived me"; Job 39:4: "Their young are healthy (יַחְלְמוּ); they grow up in the open." It is interesting to note that the LXX translated דכאו as "to make him clean and pure," understanding the root as though derived from Aram. דכי/דכא, which is cognate to Heb. זכי (cf. Targum's translation: לְמִצְרַף וּלְדַכָּאָה). In contrast to the above explanations, 1QIsa[a] ויחללהו has been explained in one of two ways: either as a harmonizing reading with the above (v. 5): מחלל . . . ומדכא, or as being derived from the homonym חלל, with the meaning "to pollute, defile." (See Kutscher, *Language and Linguistic Background*, 236-37.)

If he makes himself an offering for guilt — The initial conjunction (אם) may be understood as the beginning of a protasis of condition, "if," or as "when" (cf. Num 36:4: "And even when [ואם] the Israelites observe the Jubilee"), i.e., if/when he puts himself forward in lieu of a guilt offering . . . (lit. "his life [see v. 12] shall be a sacrifice of expiation"). Some suggest vocalizing the verb as a passive, תֻּשַּׂם, which is corroborated by the Peshitta, אתתסים. For the אָשָׁם, "guilt offering," which is an atoning sacrifice, see, in addition to the verses quoted above, Lev 19:22: "With the ram of guilt offering (אשם) the priest shall make expiation for him before the Lord for the sin that he committed. And the sin that he committed will be forgiven him." For an alternative understanding of this clause, see the comments to the preceding colon. For the expression שׂים נפש ("to make oneself"), see 1 Kgs 19:2: "I have not made you (אשים את נפשך) like one of them."

The term נפשו (lit. "his life") is repeated also in vv. 11 and 12, thus forming a triad.

[10b] The blessed lot of the servant in the future.

He shall see offspring and have long life — He will then be blessed with progeny and longevity. These twin blessings (this is the only place where they appear in conjunction) are common to the Bible and ancient Near Eastern literature. For "seeing" one's progeny, see Gen 50:23: "Joseph lived to see children of the third generation of Ephraim"; Ps 128:6: "And live to see your children's children"; Job 42:16: "Afterward, Job lived one hundred and forty years to see four generations of sons and grandsons." Compare the proud but true boast of the mother of Nabonidus (the last king of Babylon and contemporary of Deutero-Isaiah), Adad-guppi, who lived to the ripe old age of 104: "I have seen my great-great-grandchildren . . . unto the fourth generation" (C. J. Gadd, "The Harran Inscriptions of Nabonidus," *Anatolian Studies* 8 [1958]: 48-49, line 28; 50-51, line 34). For a long life, lit. "length of days" (ארך ימים), see Exod 20:12: "That you may live long"; Prov 3:2: "For they will bestow on you length of days, years of life and well-being." Compare the Akkadian blessing: *ūmū arāku/urruku* ("to have long-lasting days"), which, similar to here, is at times combined with the blessing of abundant "progeny" (Akk. *zēru*; see *CAD* A/2:223-24; Z:94). The Phoenician inscription of King Azitawada (eighth century BCE) contains the blessing: "length of days (ארך ימם) and multitude of years" (*KAI* 26A III:5-6), and the same blessing appears in King Yehawmilk's Phoenician inscription (fifth-fourth century BCE): "May the Mistress of Byblos prolong the days (ימו תארך) of Yehawmilk and his years over Byblos" (*KAI* 10:8-9). For the occurrence of "long days" in conjunction with the root שׂבע ("to be sated, satisfied"; the root appears at the beginning of the following verse), see Ps 91:16: "I will sate him with length of days," i.e., "I will let him live to a ripe old age."

And through him the Lord's purpose will prosper — Through the servant's personal sacrifice, the Lord's will shall be done; cf. Isa 55:11 concerning God's word: "But performs what I purpose, achieves what I sent it to do." Note the dual occurrence of the root חפץ in this verse, first as a verb and here as a noun, with the meaning "purpose"; and also its chiastic parallelism with ה' in the first hemistich; see also 44:28; 46:10; 48:14. For the term ביד, which denotes "by the agency or instrumentality of," see Exod 4:13: "Send with whom (ביד) you will." Compare also the Akkadian semantic equivalent: *ina qāti* (*CAD* Q:193).

[11-12] The Lord promises the servant a reward for bearing the sins of the multitude. He will vindicate the many and intercede for the sinners.

[11] *Because of his anguish he shall be sated and saturated with light* — The *mem* particle in מֵעֲמַל is causative. For עָמָל ("anguish"), see Gen 41:51; Judg 10:16. Since the two verbs of this clause, יראה and ישׂבע, both lack objects, some commentators suggest appending the object of יראה in v. 10, "offspring," to יראה in this verse as well (Eliezer of Beaugency, Abravanel, Luzzatto). Others suggest adding טוב (cf. Ibn Ezra, Kimchi; for the expression ראי טוב, see Ps 27:13; Job 7:7; Eccl 3:13). Preferable, however, is the reading found in the LXX, 1QIsa[a], 1QIsa[b]: אור, "light"; see Ps 36:10. (For an objection to this reading, see I. L. Seeligman, "ΔΕΙΞΑΙ ΑΥΤΩΙ ΦΩΣ," in A. Hurvitz, S. Japhet, and E. Tov, eds., *Studies in Biblical Literature* [Jerusalem, 1992], 411-26 [Heb.].) The assumed object of the second verb, יִשְׂבָּע, is often thought to be יָמִים, as in the previous verse. For the expression שְׂבַע יָמִים, see Gen 35:29. More to the point, however, is the conjunction of these two parallel verbs, where the root ראי serves as a variant for רוי, "to be saturated"; cf. Ps 91:16: "I shall sate him (אַשְׂבִּיעֵהוּ) with long life and saturate him (וְאַרְוֵהוּ = וְאַרְאֵהוּ) with My salvation"; Job 10:15: "So sated (שְׂבַע) am I with shame and saturated (וּרְוֵה = וּרְאֵה) with my misery"; cf. also Ps 63:6 (Ehrlich, *Randglossen,* 4:192; Yellin, *Ḥiqrei Miqra,* 2:74; Tur-Sinai, *Peshuṭo shel Miqra,* III/1:132). The meaning of the elliptical phrase, then, is: "He shall be sated and saturated with light." On the other hand, some commentators, contra the Masoretic division of clauses, append the first word of the adjacent clause to this one: "And he shall be saturated with knowledge (בדעתו)." For the expression שבע ב-, "to be sated with, to be filled with," see Jer 50:19; Ps 65:5; 88:4; Lam 3:30.

Through his devotion My righteous servant shall vindicate the many — "My servant" (1QIsa[a] עבדו, with the third-person masculine singular pronominal suffix, is in accord with the other third-person masculine forms: הוא יסבל, נפשו, דעתו). For the expression מצדיקי הרבים, see Dan 12:3; and for "the many," see v. 12 here; 52:14. The precise meaning of בדעתו (1QIsa[a] ובדעתו) is a subject of controversy. A number of commentators explain it as "his devotion," as in Isa 11:2: "A spirit of devotion (דעת) and reverence for the Lord"; 11:9: "For the land shall be filled with devotion (דעה) for the Lord." Some emend the text to ברעתו ("through his misery"; for the graphic substitution of the letters *dalet* and *resh,* cf. 2 Sam 22:43, אֲדִקֵּם, and the parallel אֲרִיקֵם in Ps 18:43; Jer 2:20: אעבור [Ketib אעבד]) and interpret it as parallel to עמל נפשו ("anguish") in the previous hemistich, i.e., through the servant's misery, the multitude will be exonerated (e.g., Ehrlich, *Randglossen,* 4:192). Others relate בדעתו to the Arabic cognate (see v. 3) meaning "abjection." The anomalous syntactical construction, עבדי צדיק, has led many commentators to delete צדיק from the text on the grounds that it is dittography caused by the repetition of the first four letters of the adjacent verb, יצדיק (צדיק is notably absent from a number of medieval MT manuscripts). The *lamed* prefixed to לרבים is generally understood here as an indicator of the direct object, as in 2 Sam 3:30: "Now Joab and his brother Abishai had killed (הרגו ל-) Abner."

And it is their punishment that he bears — since he is evidently blameless. For עָוֺן ("punishment"), see v. 6; Gen 4:13: "My punishment (עֲוֺנִי) is too great to bear." The semantic cognates in Akkadian, *arnu* (*CAD* A/2:294-99) and *ḫīṭu* (= חטא; *CAD* Ḫ:210-12), also denote both "sin" and "punishment" and are often the objects of the verb *našû* (= נשׂא, as here; *CAD* N/2:103-4). For the Aramaic verb סבל, which is parallel to Heb. נשׂא, see v. 4; 46:4, 7.

[12] *Assuredly, I will give him the many as his portion/allot him a portion with the many* — There are two ways of understanding this clause: I shall grant him the multitude as his portion of the spoil (שלל appears in the adjacent clause and is understood here as well) (Ibn Ezra). For the expression חלק ב- ("to give as one's share"), see Job 39:17: "He gave her no share of (חלק ב-) understanding." Or: "I will allot him a share among the many" (Rashi, Luzzatto); see also Num 26:53: "Among these shall the land be apportioned as shares (תֵּחָלֵק ב-)."

He shall receive the multitude as his spoils/shall share the spoils with the multitude — As in the preceding clause, it is possible to understand this clause in one of two ways as well: his share of the spoils shall include the multitude; or, he shall share the spoils with the multitude (note that the first option reads את as the indicator of the direct object, whereas the latter option interprets את as "with"). For the latter interpretation of the division of spoils, see Josh 22:8: "Share the spoils . . . with (חִלְקוּ . . . עם) your kinsmen"; Prov 16:19: "Better to be humble and among the lowly than to share spoils with (מְחַלֵּק את) the proud." For the repetition of the same verb (here חלק) in two adjacent clauses, see Isa 55:1, where there is a threefold repetition of לכו and a twofold שִׁבְרוּ. For the synonymous pair עצומים/רבים, see Ps 135:10: "He struck down many (רבים) nations and slew numerous (עצומים) kings"; Prov 7:26: "For many (רבים) are those she has struck dead, and numerous (ועצומים) are her victims"; cf. also Isa 47:9.

Because he exposed himself/poured out his life to death — For the verb ערי in the *hiphʿil* ("to expose"), see Lev 20:18: "She has exposed (הֶעֱרָה) her blood flow"; and for the *piʿel* see Isa 3:17: "The Lord will expose (יְעָרֶה) their genitalia." Others explain הֶעֱרָה as "to pour out": "He poured out his life to death" (Ibn Ezra, Kimchi); cf. Gen 24:20: "She emptied (וַתְּעַר) her jar"; Isa 32:15: "Till a spirit from on high is poured (יֵעָרֶה) out on us"; 2 Chr 24:11: "And they saw that it contained much money . . . and emptied (וִיעָרוּ) out the chest." For ערי and נפש in conjunction, see Ps 141:8: "My eyes are fixed upon You, O God my Lord; I seek refuge in You. Do not put me in jeopardy [אל תְּעַר נפשי, lit. 'Do not pour my life out']." For analogous imagery with נפש and the verb שפך ("to pour out"), see 1 Sam 1:15; Ps 42:5. For this euphemism for death, see also the Akkadian semantic equivalent, *napištam tabāku* (lit. "the pouring out of life") (*CAD* N/2:299). According to both the possibilities submitted here, the construction תחת אשר should be translated "because"; e.g., Num 25:13: "Because he took impassioned action for his God"; Deut 21:14: "Because you had your will with her"; Deut 28:47: "Because you would not serve the Lord your God in joy and gladness." This is the last of the three occurrences of the term נפשו in this section (see vv. 10, 11).

And was numbered among the sinners — Despite his virtue, he was counted among (את) the transgressors; cf. v. 9: "And his grave was set among (את) the wicked." For the root מני in the *niph'al*, see 1 Kgs 3:8.

Because he bore the guilt of the many — Compare v. 4: "Yet it was our sickness he was bearing"; v. 6: "And the Lord visited on him the guilt of all of us"; v. 11: "It is their punishment that he bears." For the expression נשׂא חטא ("to bear guilt"), see the comments to v. 11. All the ancient translations and three of the Qumran Isaiah scrolls (1QIsa[a], 1QIsa[b], and 4QIsa[d]) have the plural חטאי רבים.

And made intercession for sinners — He advocated and interceded on behalf of the multitudinous sinners. For the verb פגע in the *hiph'il*, meaning "to intercede" (note the wordplay with v. 6), see 59:16: "He gazed long, but no one interceded (מפגיע)"; and in the *qal* (note 1QIsa[a] here has יפגע instead of MT *hiph'il*), see Jer 7:16: "Do not pray for this people . . . do not intercede (תפגע) with Me." (For this verb in the *niph'al*, see the commentary to 47:3.) Instead of MT פֹּשְׁעִים ("sinners"), the LXX, 1QIsa[a] and 1QIsa[b] [ולפשעיהמ(ה)], and 4QIsa[d] [ולפשעיה(   )] read "their sins," i.e., the servant shall intercede and pray to God to forgive the multitude's sins. This version parallels the above plural, רבים חטאי ("the transgressions of the many"), which also diverges from the MT (see above). For the synonymous roots פשע and חטא, see 43:27: "Your earliest ancestor sinned (חטאו) and your spokesmen transgressed (פשעו) against Me."

Chapter 54

This chapter consists of three distinct literary units: vv. 1-8, 9-10, and 11-17. In the first pericope, God comforts Jerusalem, described as a "barren women" who never experienced travail and who was left forlorn and deserted. The Lord (her spouse) now promises her abundant progeny and ample dwelling space for this influx. Zion shall forget her days of widowhood, for although her Lord had left her in a burst of anger, they shall be reconciled with great love and everlasting kindness. In the second unit, God swears an irrevocable and sacred oath: just as He swore never again to bring a flood upon the earth in Noah's days, so too His eternal covenant now with Jerusalem shall never be breached. The first two units of this chapter are connected to the previous Servant Song (52:13–53:12) by common phraseology: 52:14: **כאשר שממו עליך רבים** — 54:1: **כי רבים בני שוֹמֵמָה** (cf. also the recurrence of the term **רבים**, 52:15; 53:11, 12); **גוים**: 52:15; 54:3; 53:3: **וכמַסְתֵּר פנים ממנו** — 54:8: **הסתרתי פני רגע ממך**; 53:10: **זרע** — 54:3: **זרעך**. For additional linguistic features linking this chapter with 52:13–53:12, cf. 53:5: **שלומנו**; 54:10: **שלומי**; 54:13: **שלום**; 53:11: **יצדיק צדיק**; 54:14: **בצדקה**; and 54:17: **וצדקתם**. The third unit emphasizes God's promise to rebuild Jerusalem with precious stones as building blocks and to rehabilitate it as a center of righteousness, in which all who reside shall be disciples of the Lord. The city shall never again experience the tribulations of enemies since the Lord shall place insurmountable obstacles in their paths.

The anthropomorphization of Zion as a barren and widowed woman is related to the Mesopotamian literary image of a female deity crying for her recently razed city. See W. A. M. Beuken, "Isaiah LIV: The Multiple Identity of the Person Addressed," in J. Barr et al., eds., *Language and Meaning: Studies in the Hebrew Language and Biblical Exegesis, OtSt* 19 (Leiden, 1974), 29-70; M. E. Biddle, "The Figure of Lady Jerusalem: Identification, Deification and Personification of Cities in the Ancient Near East," in K. L. Younger Jr., W. W. Hallo, and B. F. Batto, eds., *The Biblical Canon in Comparative Perspective: Scripture in Context*, 4 (Lewiston, 1991), 179-94; K. Jeppesen, "Mother Zion, Father Servant," in H. A. McKay and D. J. C. Clines, eds., *Prophets' Visions and the Wisdom of Sages: Essays in Honour of R. Norman Whybray on His Seventieth Birthday*, JSOTSup 162 (Sheffield, 1993), 109-25; and especially Dobbs-Allsopp, *Weep, O Daughter of Zion.*

This chapter shares many motifs and linguistic features with Lamentations, Hosea, and Ps 89. The depiction in Lamentations of the city's destruction and the decimation of the children are here reversed, as Zion is rehabilitated and rebuilt in a grandiose fashion. Cf. Lam 4:1: "The sacred stones (אבני) are spilled" — Isa 54:11: "I will lay carbuncles as your building stones (אבניך)"; Lam 4:2: "The precious children (בני) of Zion. . . . Alas, they are accounted as earthen pots" — Isa 54:1: "For the children (בני) of the deserted wife shall outnumber those of the espoused"; 54:13: "And great shall be the happiness of your children (בניך)"; Lam 4:7: "Their bodies were lapis lazuli (ספיר)" — Isa 54:11: "And I shall set your foundations in lapis lazuli (בספירים)"; Lam 4:11: "It [God's anger] consumed her foundations (יְסֹדֹתֶיהָ)" — Isa 54:11: "And I shall set your foundations (וִיסַדְתִּיךְ)"; Lam 4:12: "the gates of (שערי) Jerusalem" — Isa 54:12: "And your gates (ושעריך) of precious stones"; Lam 5:1: "Remember (זכֹר), O Lord, what has befallen us. Behold, and see our disgrace (חֶרְפָּתֵנוּ)!" — Isa 54:4: "And remember (תזכרי) no more the disgrace of (חרפת) your widowhood"; Lam 5:2: "Our heritage (נחלתנו) has passed to aliens" — Isa 54:17: "Such is the lot (נחלת) of the servants of the Lord"; Lam 5:20: "Why have You forgotten us (תשכחנו) utterly, forsaken us (ותעזבנו) for all time?" — Isa 54:4: "For you shall forget (תשכחי) the reproach of your youth," 54:6: "As a wife forsaken (עזובה)"; Lam 5:22: "For truly, You have rejected us (מָאֹס מְאַסְתָּנוּ), bitterly raged (קצפת) against us" — Isa 54:6: "Can one reject (תִּמָּאֵס) the wife of his youth?"; 54:9: "So I swear that I will not be angry (מִקְּצֹף) with you." (See the introduction, §18.)

The connection to Hosea is apparent in the motif of the married woman (Zion) who was abandoned by her husband (the Lord) and is to be reconciled: Hos 1:6: "She conceived again and bore a daughter. And He said to him, 'Name her Lo-ruhamah ["Unloved," לֹא רֻחָמָה], for I will never again love (אֲרחם) the house of Israel.'" In the future, however, Hos 2:21: "And I will espouse you . . . with goodness and love (ובחסד וברחמים)"; Hos 2:25: "And I will take Lo-ruhamah back in love (ורחמתי את לא רֻחָמָה)" — Isa 54:7: "But with vast love (וברחמים) I will bring you back"; 54:8: "But with kindness (חסד) everlasting I will take you back in love (רחמתיך)"; 54:10: "But My loyalty (חסדי) shall never move from you . . . said the Lord, who takes you back in love (מְרחמך)." (The symbolic name לֹא רֻחָמָה in Hosea may also have influenced Deutero-Isaiah's phraseology; see לֹא נֻחָמָה in 54:11); Hos 2:20: "In that day, I will make a covenant (ברית) for them" — Isa 54:10: "Nor My covenant (ברית) of friendship be shaken"; Hos 2:18: "And no more will you call Me, 'My Baal (בעלי)'" — Isa 54:5: "For He who made you will espouse you (בֹּעֲלַיִךְ)." (One must note, however, that in Hosea the marriage is depicted as a relationship between the Lord and His people, whereas in Deutero-Isaiah the marriage is between the Lord and Zion.) (See the introduction, §16.)

The connection to Ps 89 is in the actual implementation of the relationship between the Lord and the Davidic dynasty (depicted in Ps 89 as a covenant-based relationship), or, as in Isa 54, between the Lord and Zion: Ps 89:4: "I have made a covenant with My chosen one. I have sworn to My servant David"; 89:25: "My faithfulness and steadfast love shall be with him"; 89:29: "I will maintain My steadfast love for him always. My covenant with him shall endure"; 89:34: "I will not betray my faithfulness"; 89:35: "I will not violate My covenant"; 89:36: "I have sworn by My holiness, once and for all, I will not be false to David"; 89:40: "You have repudiated the covenant with Your servant"; 89:50: "O, Lord, where is Your steadfast love of old that You swore to David in Your faithfulness?" — Isa 54:8: "But with kindness everlasting I will take you back in love"; 54:10: "But my loyalty shall never move from you, nor My covenant of friendship be shaken." The shame and humiliation described in the psalm are now attributed to Zion: Ps 89:42: "He has become the reproach (חֶרפה) of his neighbors"; 89:46: "You have covered him with shame (בושה)"; 89:52: "How Your enemies, O Lord, have flung abuse (חֵרְפוּ), abuse (חֵרְפוּ) at Your anointed at every step" — Isa 54:4: "For you shall forget the reproach (בֹּשֶׁת) of your youth (עלומיך), and remember no more the shame of (חרפת) your widowhood" (cf. Ps 89:46: "You have cut short the days of his youth [עלומיו]"). Compare also Ps 89:47: "How long, O Lord, will You forever hide Yourself (תִּסָּתֵר)?" — Isa 54:8: "In slight anger, for a moment, I hid (הסתרתי) My face from you." And contrast Ps 89:41: "You have breached (פרצת) all his walls, laid his strongholds in ruin (מְחִתָּה)," with Isa 54:3: "For you shall spread out (תִּפְרֹצִי) to the right and the left" (note the wordplay); and 54:14: "From ruin (וּמִמְּחִתָּה), and it shall not come near you."

[1] In a series of three imperatives (רָנִּי . . . פצחי רִנָּה . . . צהלי), God (the espouser) commands barren Zion to shout for joy since her exiled children are preparing to return. The image of barenness brings to mind the barren matriarchs, Sarah (Gen 11:30), Rebekah (Gen 25:21), and Rachel (Gen 29:31), as well as Manoah's wife (Judg 13:2) and Hannah (1 Sam 2:5). For other depictions of the exile as a period of estrangement between the husband (God) and the wife (Zion), cf. Isa 62:4: "Nevermore shall you be called 'Forsaken,' nor shall your land be called 'Desolate.' But you shall be called 'I delight in her' *(Ḥephzi-bah)* and your land 'Espoused' *(Beulah)*, for the Lord takes delight in you, and your land shall be espoused."

Sing aloud, O barren one, you who bore no child! — The term עֲקָרָה ("barren one") is addressed to Zion: "In the days of the exile, Zion was like a barren woman, and was as if she had never given birth" (Luzzatto). The *qal* imperative רָנִּי, from the root רנן, signifies raising one's voice in song; see 44:23; 49:13: רנו; 52:9: רננו; Zech 2:14: "Shout (רני) for joy, fair Zion!" The feminine substantive עקרה, followed by the phrase לא ילדה (the etymological and semantic equivalent of Akk. *la ālittu; CAD* A/1:350), is an example of a common literary construction of negative parallelism, i.e., a positive term or phrase immediately followed by an equivalent negative one. Similarly, Judg 13:2: "His wife was barren and had borne no children" (see also v. 3 there); Job 24:21: "May he consort with a barren woman who bears no child"; and cf. Gen 11:30: "Now Sarai was barren, she had no child." For other descriptions of forlornness, see Isa 49:21: שְׁכולה וגלמודה ("bereaved and barren").

Break into cries of joy, you who did not travail! — "You who did not travail" (לא חלה) is another designation for Zion, who is being addressed here: Be happy and celebrate, O unfertile Jerusalem! For the tandem appearance of רִנָּה/רנן and פצח, see also Isa 44:23; 49:13; 52:9; 55:12; for the צהל/רנן parallelism, see 12:6; 24:14; Jer 31:7. For the verb חלי ("to be in labor"), parallel to ילד, see also Isa 45:10; 66:8. For the same series of verbs in Ugaritic and Akkadian, see the references in the comments to 45:10.

For the children of the wife desolate shall outnumber those of the espoused — said the Lord — The reason for the joyous cry is that the sheer number of returning expatriates shall eclipse the number of inhabitants prior to the exile, i.e., the sons of "desolate" (שׁוֹמֵמָה) mother Zion (see Lam 1:13: "He has left me forlorn [שֹׁמֵמָה], in constant sorrow"; 2 Sam 13:20: "And Tamar remained in her brother Absalom's house, desolate [שֹׁמֵמָה]"; cf. Lam 1:13). For the root בעל, see Isa 54:5; 62:4, 5; Jer 3:14; 31:32. For the motif of proliferation, see Isa 44:3-4; 49:17-21; 66:7-9. For the expression רבים מ- ("shall outnumber"), see Josh 10:11.

[2-3] In order to find living space for this population explosion following Israel's repatriation, Jerusalem's borders shall have to be extended. Thus, in a series of imperatives, the prophet commands Jerusalem to enlarge and extend her "tent" to include a much broader area. This portrayal, which symbolizes the building of "new Jerusalem," is diametrically opposed to Jeremiah's dirge-like prophecy, which equates the ruin of the city with the collapse of a tent: Jer 10:20-22: "My tent is ravaged, all my tent cords are broken. My children have gone forth from me and are no more. No one is left to pitch my tent and hang my tent cloths . . . to make the towns of Judah a desolation (שְׁמָמָה)." Not only will the expatriates return, but it will be necessary to spread the tent over a much greater area in order to fit the teeming population. For another simile comparing Jerusalem to a ravaged tent, see Jer 4:20; and for the opposite simile of Jerusalem as a stable and immutable pergola, see Isa 33:20: "When you gaze upon Zion, our city of assembly, your eyes shall behold Jerusalem as a secure

homestead, a tent not to be transported, whose pegs shall never be pulled up, and none of whose ropes shall be severed." Compare also Jer 30:18: "Thus said the Lord: 'I will restore the fortunes of Jacob's tents and have compassion upon his dwellings.'" (See the introduction, §15.)

[2] *Enlarge the site of your tent!* — The tent metaphor is reminiscent of Israel's patriarchal period. The first two hemistichs form a chiastic parallel.

Spread out the curtains of your dwelling! — Spread wide the tent curtains to encompass a greater space! For the verb **נטי** in connection with pitching a tent, see Gen 12:8, and for spreading out tent curtains, see Ps 104:2. Since the heavens are compared to a tent (Isa 40:22), they too can be pitched. (For another reference to tent curtains, see Exod 26:13.) The plural verb in the MT, **יַטּוּ**, may either refer to the sons of the forlorn wife (v. 1) or is elliptical for an indeterminate subject. The LXX, Vulgate, Peshitta, and Targum, however, translate the verb as a feminine imperative, **הַטִּי**, which is in accord with the other feminine imperative forms in proximity: **הרחיבי, אל תחשׂכי, האריכי, חזקי**; cf. also v. 1: **רני ... פצחי ... וצהלי**. The reading in 1QIsa[a], **יטי**, conflates these two forms (**יטו** and **הטי**). For the parallel pair **יריעות/אהל**, see Hab 3:7: Cant 1:5; and cf. Jer 4:20; 10:20. For the **משכנות/מקום** parallelism, see Ps 132:5; and for **אהל/משכנות** see Num 24:5; Jer 30:18; this last pair also appears in tandem in Ugaritic literature: "The gods go home to their tents *(lahlhm),* the circle of El to their dwellings *(lmšknthm)*" (*CAT* 1.15.III:18-19); "Kothar left for his tent *(lahlh),* Hayyin [another name for this deity] left for his dwelling *(lmšknth)*" (*CAT* 1.17.V:31-33).

Do not stint! — Do not be stingy with space! Stretch your tent cloths to their fullest! For the same expression that denotes acting unreservedly, see Isa 58:1: "Shout with full throat, without restraint (**אל תחשׂך**)!"

Lengthen the ropes! — Make the ropes that tie the tent to its supporting pegs longer, since an expansive tent requires long ropes in order to bolster it sufficiently against the elements. For **מיתרים** ("tent ropes"), see the references quoted in the comments to the following phrase.

And drive the pegs firm! — The pegs must be driven deeply into the ground for stability. For the ropes and pegs that anchor the tent to the ground, see Exod 35:18; 39:40; Num 3:37; 4:32. The final clauses of the verse form a chiasm.

[3] *For you shall spread out to the north and the south* — The reason for this revamping of the tent is now made clear: When the expatriates return in droves, they shall expand in all directions. The polar opposites, north and south, constitute a merism in all geographical directions. This phraseology is reminiscent of the divine blessing to Jacob in Gen 28:14: "Your descendants shall be as the dust of the earth. You shall spread (**ופרצת**) out to the west and to the east, to the north and to the south." For other examples of this geographical merism, see Gen 13:9; Num 22:26. For **ימין**, "south" (lit. "right," since when one

faces the rising sun in the east, the south is to the right), see Ps 89:13: "North and south (ימין), You created them." For שׂמאל ("north"), see Ezek 16:46: "Your elder sister was Samaria, who lived with her daughters to the north of you (שׂמאלך). Your younger sister was Sodom, who lived with her daughters to the south of you (מימינך)." For the verb פרץ ("to spread out"), cf. also Gen 30:30; Exod 1:12; Job 1:10; 1 Chr 4:38.

Your offspring shall dispossess nations — Your progeny shall expel the foreign settlers who inhabited the land during your long exile (see 2 Kgs 17:24) and shall repossess it. For ירש ("dispossess"), see Gen 24:60; Deut 11:23. The plural verb in 1QIsa[a], יירשו, accords with the plural יושיבו in the adjacent clause.

And shall inhabit the desolate cities — They shall repopulate the towns and cities that had been destroyed and abandoned in the long years of the exile; see Isa 44:26: "It is I who say of Jerusalem, 'It shall be inhabited (תושב)'"; Ezek 36:33: "I will repeople (הושבתי) your settlements, and the ruined places shall be rebuilt." The feminine plural נְשַׁמּוֹת is the *niph'al* participle of the root שמם, which denotes desolation; see Amos 9:14: "They shall rebuild ruined cities and inhabit them (נשמות וְיָשָׁבוּ)"; Ezek 36:35: "And the cities, once ruined, desolate, are now populated (וְהַנְּשַׁמּוֹת . . . יָשָׁבוּ); and cf. Isa 49:8. For the identical motif in Mesopotamian literature, "to repopulate deserted cities" *(šūbšubu nidûtu),* see *CAD* N/2:212.

[4-8] The metaphor shifts. Jerusalem is no longer portrayed as a tent, but rather as a once-married woman. The prophet comforts Jerusalem and assures her that the Lord will fulfill His obligations toward her.

[4] The rehabilitation of the relationship between the Lord and Zion is depicted by an emphatic series of negative expressions: "Fear not . . . you shall not be shamed! . . . Do not cringe, you shall not be disgraced . . . and remember no more!" This verse is directly opposed to the dire straits depicted in Jer 3:25: "Let us lie down in our shame (בְּבָשְׁתֵּנוּ). Let our disgrace (כְּלִמָּתֵנוּ) cover us," since now the Lord is reinstituting His covenant with the nation. The theological outlook of this section, moreover, is radically different from the prophecies of Ezekiel. In contrast to Deutero-Isaiah's call to forget the shame and disgrace of the preexilic era, Ezekiel predicts that even in the postexilic future, after God's reconciliation with His people and their return to Zion: "There you will recall your ways and all the acts by which you defiled yourselves; and you will loathe yourselves for all the evils that you committed" (Ezek 20:43; see also 16:61-63; 36:31; 39:26; 43:1-11; 44:12-14). In other words, their past conduct shall haunt them forever. There are two examples in this verse of a nominally enhanced repetition consisting of a verb and a construct state: תֵּבוֹשִׁי — בֹּשֶׁת עֲלוּמַיִךְ ("You shall not be shamed — the shame of your youth"); תחפירי — וְחֶרפת אַלְמְנוּתַיִךְ ("You shall not be disgraced — the disgrace of your widowhood").

Fear not, you shall not be shamed! — since the divine promises shall be fulfilled. For the root בוש denoting shame and disappointment, see Isa 49:23; 50:7; and for the encouraging promise, "Fear not!" (אל תירא/אל תיראי), see 40:9; 41:10, 13, 14; 43:1, 5; 44:2.

Do not cringe, you shall not be disgraced! — parallel to the previous clause. For the synonyms כלם and בוש, see 41:11; 45:16, 17; 50:7. The root חפר, another synonym of בוש (see 1:29; 24:23), is the metathesized equivalent of חרף; note the wordplay with חֶרפת below. For the triad of synonyms, see also Ps 40:15: "Let th[em] . . . be frustrated (יֵבֹשׁוּ) and disgraced (ויחפרו). Let th[em] . . . be shamed (ויִכָּלמו)"; and cf. Jer 31:19: "I am ashamed (בֹּשְׁתִּי) and humiliated (ונכלמתי), for I bear the disgrace (חֶרפת) of my youth."

For you shall forget the shame of your youth — For (כי is causative and emphatic) you shall never again recall the ignominy of your youth, i.e., the sins you committed prior to the exile; cf. Jer 3:25: "Let us lie down in our shame. Let our disgrace cover us, for we have sinned against the Lord our God, we and our fathers from our youth to this day, and we have not heeded the Lord our God." The abstract plural noun עֲלוּמִים ("youth") appears also in Ps 89:46; Job 20:11; 33:25.

And remember no more the disgrace of your widowhood — You shall put the past humiliations of exile and destruction, depicted as widowhood (see Lam 1:1: "She has become like a widow [כאלמנה]"), out of your mind. (For the meaning of "widowhood" in this simile, see C. Cohen, "The Widowed City," in *The Gaster Festschrift,* ed. D. Marcus = *JANES* 5 [1973]: 75-81.) The unique form אַלְמְנוּתַיִךְ, instead of אַלְמְנוּתֵךְ (see 2 Sam 20:3), rhymes with the preceding עֲלוּמַיִךְ. (For a similar rhyming pair see v. 5: בֹעֲלַיִךְ עֹשַׂיִךְ.) For the positive formulation תשכחי ("you shall forget") followed by the negative formulation לא תזכרי ("you shall remember no more"), a negative parallelism, see Ps 137:5-6: "If I forget you (אֶשְׁכָּחֵךְ), O Jerusalem. . . . If I cease to think of you (אֶזְכְּרֵכִי)"; and in the reverse order: "Yet the chief cupbearer did not remember (זכר) Joseph. He forgot him (וישכחֵהו)" (Gen 40:23). For the expression לא . . . עוד, see Isa 51:22; 60:18, 19, 20; 62:4 (twice), 8; 65:19, 20. For the synonymous pair חרפה/בֹּשֶׁת, see 30:5. Compare also the similar expression in Jer 31:19, חֶרפת נעורי ("the disgrace of my youth"). For additional divine promises not to bear the people's sins in mind, see Jer 31:34: "And I shall remember their sins no more"; and for similar phraseology, cf. Hos 2:19.

[5] The reinstitution of the marital ties between God and His people.

For He who created you will espouse you — There is no reason for you to remain in a state of ignominy, since the Lord "who made you (עֹשַׂיִךְ)" (see Isa 44:2: "Thus said the Lord, your Maker [עֹשֶׂךָ], your Creator who has helped you since birth"; cf. also 43:7; 45:7; 51:13) "shall once again take you back as His wife"; cf. 54:1; 62:4, 5; Jer 3:14; 31:31. עֹשַׂיִךְ is a *qal* participle with a second-person feminine singular suffix; cf. Isa 22:11: "But you gave no thought to Him who planned it (עֹשֶׂיהָ)"; Ps 149:2: "Let Israel rejoice in its Maker (בְּעֹשָׂיו)." The *po'el* participle בֹּעֲלַיִךְ (note the phonetic similarity between it and עֹשַׂיִךְ) denotes "one who bonds in a spousal relationship." The plural forms are explained as referring to "the plurality of the Godhead" (Ibn Balaam, ed. Goshen-Gottstein, 217); or, according to Ibn Ganaḥ, "in order to glorify and exalt" (*Sefer ha-Riqmah*, 295, line 18); but see also GKC §124k. Note the variant reading of 1QIsa[a]: בעלכי ("your Husband") (as in LXX, Peshitta, and Targum: מָרִיךְ) and עושך ("your Maker" [singular]); the י is written, however, above the line: עוש֯ךְ. For the espousal image, see v. 1; and for the verb בעל in similar contexts, see 62:5; Deut 21:13; 24:1; Mal 2:11. There may be a deliberate wordplay here as well, since the word בעליך may be phonetically divided into two: ב(א) עליך ("He who comes unto you"), in the sexual sense; cf. 2 Sam 12:24.

His name is "Lord of Hosts" — a divine sobriquet emphasizing the Deity's power and potency; see Isa 44:6; 45:13; 47:4; 48:2.

The Holy One of Israel is your Redeemer — For the two titles, "Redeemer" (גואל) and "the Holy One of Israel" (קדוש ישראל), in tandem, see 41:14; 43:14; 47:4 (where they appear in the same sequence: "Our Redeemer — Lord of Hosts is His name — the Holy One of Israel"); 48:17; 49:7. For similar divine epithets in Mesopotamian literature, see *CAD* D:19-20. (See the introduction, §9.)

He is called "God of all the earth" — For similar expressions, cf. "Sovereign of all the earth" (אדון כל הארץ; Josh 3:11, 13; Zech 4:14; 6:5; Ps 97:5); "King over all the earth" (מלך כל הארץ; Zech 14:9; Ps 47:8); "God of the earth" (אלהי הארץ; Gen 24:3; 2 Kgs 17:26 [twice], 27).

[6] The reconciliation between God, the espouser, and Zion, the espoused.

For the Lord has called you back, as a wife once deserted and despondent — The כי particle is emphatic. For Zion having been deserted (עזובה), cf. Isa 49:14: "My Lord has deserted me (עזבני ה׳)"; 60:15: "Whereas you have been forsaken, rejected (עזובה)"; 62:4: "Nevermore shall you be called 'Forsaken (עזובה).'" Consequently, Zion is in a state of despondency (עצובת רוח); see Prov 15:13: "A despondent heart" (ובעַצבת לב)"; and cf. Isa 63:10; 1 Kgs 1:6. But now the Lord, who is called "God of all the earth" (v. 5), calls her back once more or, in other words, renews His marriage vows with her. In Akkadian the etymological and semantic cognate of Heb. עזב, *ezēbu*, also means "to abandon, desert, disregard," and even "to divorce" (*CAD* E:416ff.). The pair עזובה and עצובה create a rhyming couplet. For the form קְרָאָךְ, cf. פֵּאֲרָךְ (60:9).

Can one reject the wife of his youth? — said your God — A rhetorical question that conveys the unlikelihood of a man spurning (מאס) the wife of his youth. This statement contrasts with the nation's complaint following the destruction of the Temple and the subsequent exile: Lam 5:22; "For truly, You have rejected us (מָאֹס מְאַסְתָּנוּ)." For the conjunction כי introducing a rhetorical question, see 2 Kgs 18:34 (= Isa 36:19): "Did (כי) they save Samaria from me?" This usage is especially common in Rabbinic Hebrew; cf., e.g., *b. Rosh Hash.* 9a: "Does (וכי) one actually fast on the ninth [day]? Indubitably, it is the tenth [day] on which one fasts." (Cf. also הֲכִי in Gen 27:36; Job 6:22.) For the expression "the wife of one's youth" (אשת נעורים), see Mal 2:14-15: "Because the Lord is a witness between you and the wife of your youth . . . and let no one break faith with the wife of his youth"; Prov 5:18: "Find joy in the wife of your youth." For the love between the Lord and His nation in their days of youth, see Hos 2:17. The Akkadian interdialectal etymological and semantic cognate is *mêšu*, "to despise, have contempt for," e.g., "And even if you treat me with contempt, I will love you" (*CAD* M/2:42).

[7-8] God's return to Zion (the return of a husband to a wife), after His period of estrangement, is depicted similarly in Hos 2:21: "And I will espouse you forever (לעולם) . . . with goodness and with love (בחסד וברחמים)."

[7] This verse is echoed in 60:10: "For in anger (בקִצפי) I struck you down, but in favor I take you back in love (רִחמתיך)." One should note that the Lord's rapprochement with Israel is based not on their regret but on His love.

In a fit of rage I deserted you — Indeed, I deserted you (עזבתיך) (and thus the term עזובה, "the deserted one," in v. 6). However, רֶגַע here does not denote a measure of time, as in other places throughout the Bible, but rather is the antonym of רחמים ("love") in the following hemistich, and thus should be translated as "wrath" or "rage" (cf. Targum בִּרְגַז, and Peshitta *brwgz'*). For another example of רגע indicating "wrath," see Ps 30:6.

But with vast love I will gather you back — God will gather Israel back (cf. Isa 43:5: "I will gather you [אֲקבצך] out of the west"; 56:8: "Who gathers [מקבץ] the dispersed of Israel"), since He does not hold an everlasting grudge (see Jer 3:5, 12; Ps 103:9; Lam 3:31-32: "For the Lord does not reject forever. . . . He pardons in His abundant kindness"). For the motif of divine devotion and love (רחמים), see v. 8 here: "I will take you back with love (רִחמתיך)"; v. 10: "Who takes you back in love (מְרחמך)"; and cf. Zech 1:16: "Assuredly, thus said the Lord: 'I graciously return to Jerusalem with love (ברחמים).'" For the root רחם, "love, affection," see also Ps 18:2.

[8] The initial hemistichs of this verse are parallel to the final two hemistichs of the preceding verse. Hebrew רֶגַע here, however, denotes (as it does elsewhere), a short period of time, since it is contrasted here with "everlasting" (עולם) in the verse's second hemistich.

In an outpouring of anger, for a moment, I hid My face from you — The hapax legomenon שֶׁצֶף is a variant spelling of שטף ("flood"), written so as to rhyme with the following קֶצֶף; see vv. 4, 5, and 6 for other examples. God's anger is depicted as a raging flood, as in Nah 1:8: "And with a sweeping flood (שֶׁטֶף) He makes an end of her." In His fit of anger, the Lord fulfilled His threat of Deut 31:17: "Then My anger will flare up against them, and I will abandon them and hide My face from them." (Cf. the psalmist's plea: "Do not hide Your face from me! Do not thrust aside Your servant in anger! . . . Do not forsake me!" [Ps 27:9].) The concealment of the divine countenance is a metaphor for the Lord's disregard and estrangement from Israel; cf. Isa 59:2; 64:6. The term קֶצֶף is polysemous: on the one hand, it denotes "anger" (this is the primary meaning of the word); on the other, it signifies the froth and foam of raging waves, as in Hos 10:7: "Like foam (קצף) on water," thereby creating a prefatory associative connection with the next pericope pertaining to the deluge.

But with devotion everlasting I will take you back in love — But since I am committed to an everlasting covenant (and not because of your remorse, or by virtue of God's love for Israel's ancestors), I take you back in love. The term חסד ("devotion, loyalty") in this verse signifies the pact of eternal loyalty between God and the people, as in Deut 7:9: "The steadfast God who keeps His covenant and devotion (והחסד) to the thousandth generation of those who love Him"; or between the nation and God, as in Jer 2:2: "I accounted to your favor the devotion (חסד) of your youth, your love as a bride." The expression חסד עולם denotes, therefore, a perpetual and immutable pact, comparable to ברית עולם (Isa 55:3); cf. v. 10: "But My devotion (חסדי) shall never move from you, nor My covenant (וברית) of friendship be shaken"; 55:3: "The enduring loyalty (חסדֵי) promised to David"; cf. also Ps 89:2; 107:43; Lam 3:22. For the connection between the terms חסד and רחמים, see Isa 63:7; Jer 16:5: Hos 2:21-22; Ps 25:6.

Said the Lord your Redeemer — the Lord, who is the Redeemer of Israel (see v. 5, and the references quoted).

[9-10] The metaphor of water, "waters of Noah," connects this unit with the preceding one: שֶׁצֶף ("flood") and קֶצֶף (with the meaning "foam"). Compare also קצף ("anger") with מִקְּצֹף ("I will not be angry"); ובחסד עולם ("everlasting devotion") with וחסדִי מֵאִתֵּךְ לֹא יָמוּשׁ ("But My devotion shall never move from you"); and וברחמים ("and in love") with מְרחמך ("who takes you back in love"). The prophet draws an analogy between the primordial deluge that destroyed all of creation in Noah's day and the exile and destruction in 586 BCE. Just as the former expression of divine wrath was a one-time fit of rage — which concluded with the solemn oath of Gen 8:21: "Never again will I doom the earth . . . nor will I ever again destroy every living being, as I have done"; Gen 9:15: "So that the waters shall never again become a flood to destroy all flesh"; an oath accompanied (as was the custom in the ancient Near East) by the formalizing of a pact, referred to in the diluvian narrative as ברית עולם ("an everlasting pact") — so too Jerusalem's disaster, a product of God's fury, will conclude with an immutable covenant of friendship (v. 10), in which the Lord swears that "as the waters of Noah never again would flood the earth, so I swear that I will not be angry with you or rebuke you" (v. 9). And in the same way that the Lord's promise not to flood the earth with a second deluge was upheld, so too shall His promise to preserve the nation be sacrosanct. (See the introduction, §12.) The Lord's decision to forgive and forget is not based on any human regret, as was said in the introduction to v. 7. His resolve is a product of His own munificent and overflowing kindness. For similarly phrased promises and oaths, see 51:22: "You shall never drink it [the draught of divine wrath] again (עוד);" 52:1: "For the uncircumcised and the unclean shall never enter you again (עוד)"; 54:4: "For you shall forget the reproach of your youth, and remember no more (עוד) the shame of your widowhood"; 60:18-20: "The cry 'Violence!' shall no more (עוד) be heard in your land. . . . No longer (עוד) shall you need the sun. . . . Your sun shall set no more (עוד)"; 65:19-20: "Never again (עוד) shall be heard there the sounds of weeping and wailing. No more (עוד) shall there be an infant or graybeard who does not live out his days." In Mesopotamian literature, as well, there is a direct connection between Marduk's anger and the advent of the deluge. Compare the Erra epic: "I [Marduk] got angry long ago. I arose from my seat and brought on the flood" (see L. Cagni, *The Poem of Erra* [Malibu, 1977], 32, line 132).

[9] *For this to Me is like the waters/days of Noah* — This clause may be read in one of two ways: either as כִּי מֵי, "as the waters" of Noah (cf. LXX; Gen 9:11: מי המבול, "the waters of the flood"), or as כִּימֵי, the plural construct of ימים, "as the days of Noah" (thus Aquila, Symmachus, Theodotion, Targum, Vulgate, Peshitta, 1QIsa[a], many midrashim, and medieval Hebrew manuscripts). For the syntactical construction כי . . . כן ("for . . . so"), see 55:9; 61:11.

As I swore that the waters of Noah never again would pour over the earth — For the conjunction אשר with the meaning "as," see Exod 34:18: "You shall observe the Feast of Unleavened Bread — eating unleavened bread for seven days, as (אשר) I have commanded you — at the set time of the month of Abib"; Ps 106:34: "They did not destroy the nations as (אשר) the Lord had commanded them." This verse also alludes to Gen 9:11: "I will maintain My covenant with you. Never again (עוד) shall all flesh be cut off by the waters of a flood, and never again (עוד) shall there be a flood to destroy the earth" (see also the introduction to this unit). For the expression על הארץ ("over the earth") in the context of the flood epic, see Gen 6:12, 17; 7:4, 6, 10, 12; and for the verb עבר in connection with water and rivers, see Isa 43:2; 47:2.

So I swear that I will not be angry with you or rebuke you — I shall never again castigate you, and you shall never again (עוד — this adverb is added in the LXX and 1QIsa[a], following the expression מִקְּצֹף עליך, probably as a result of the term's appearance in the previous verse) be the target of My fury and reproach. The expression מִקְּצֹף (prefixed by a negative *mem;* cf. Gen 44:17) is polyvalent: On the one hand, it means, "I shall be wrathful no more"; and, on the other, "I shall never again raise the foam and froth of the raging flood." The infinitive construct מִגְּעָר, in addition to its basic meaning, "rebuke," in its present context also alludes to God's epic rebuking of the sea, as in Isa 50:2: "With My blast (בגערתי) I dried up the sea"; Ps 104:7: "They ['the waters' of v. 6] fled at Your blast (גערתך)"; Ps 106:9: "He roared (ויגער) at the Sea of Reeds, and it became dry." (For the Ugaritic etymological and semantic cognate *gʿr,* meaning "to reproach" and "to roar," see *HdO* 1:280-91.) For the syntactical construction כאשר followed by כן in the protasis, see Isa 52:14-15; 55:10-11.

[10] For the immutability and eternity of the Lord's covenant, see 59:21; and for the expression ברית עולם, see 55:3; 61:8. For the perpetuity of the Lord's promise to save and redeem His people, as contrasted to the heavens and earth that will eventually erode and disappear, see 51:6.

For the mountains may move — For even in the unlikely event of the mountain's mutability (an image chosen for its durability), My covenant will remain immutable. For כי ("even if"), see Hos 13:15; Prov 6:35. For the verb מוש in connection with the movement of mountains, see Zech 14:4: "And one part of the mountain shall move (ומש) to the north." In Mesopotamian literature as well, the mountains are often portrayed as images of permanency (see *CAD* Š/1:56-57).

And the hills totter — and even though the hills may be shaken out of place. For another example of the verb מוט in connection with mountains, see Ps 46:3: "Though mountains topple (במוט) into the sea" (or, in contrast, Ps 125:1: "Like Mount Zion that cannot be shaken (יִמּוֹט), enduring forever"). The MT's *qal* feminine plural, תְּמוּטֶינָה, is replaced in 1QIsa[a] by תתמוטינה, a *hithpoʿel* feminine, as in Isa 24:19: "The earth is tottering, tottering (מוט התמוטטה)." Compare likewise תתמוטטנה, a *hithpaʿel* from the cognate root מטט, which appears in a Qumran fragment: 4Q176, frag. 8/11, line 12 (see J. M. Allegro, *Qumrân Cave 4.I (4Q158-4Q186),* DJD 5 [Oxford, 1968], 62). For the hapax legomenon נוט, a variant of מוט, with an identical meaning, see Ps 99:1: "The Lord, enthroned on cherubim, is King. Peoples tremble, the earth quakes (תנוט)." Compare similarly its Ugaritic etymological and semantic equivalent, *nṭṭ:* "The heights of the earth shook *(tṭṭn)*" (*CAT* 1.4.vii:35). For the synonymous pair גבעות/הרים, see Isa 40:4, 12; 41:15; 42:15.

But My loyalty shall never move from you — But (the *waw* denotes contrast) the pact that guarantees My fidelity (חסד עולם, v. 8) is immovable; see also 59:21: "And this shall be My covenant with them, said the Lord: My spirit that is upon you, and the words that I have placed in your mouth, shall not depart (ימושו) from your mouth . . . from now on, for all time." For the anomalous vocalization מֵאִתֵּךְ, instead of מֵאִתָּךְ (cf. 1 Kgs 2:20; Prov 30:7), cf. Isa 14:29: "Rejoice not, all (כֻּלֵּךְ) Philistia!" — as opposed to Cant 4:7: "Every part of you (כֻּלָּךְ) is fair, my darling." For חסד parallel to ברית, see Deut 7:9; Ps 89:29; cf. also Isa 55:3. The last verse refers, however, to the covenantal relationship between the Lord and David, whereas here the pact is between the Lord and His nation. Cf. also 1 Kgs 8:23; Dan 9:4; Neh 9:32. For the expression מוֹשׁ מ-, see Isa 46:7.

Nor My covenant of friendship be shaken — The covenant of friendship and peace that I shall establish with you shall endure forever. For the expression ברית שלום, see also Num 25:12; Ezek 34:25; 37:26. Just as the narrative recounting the deluge ends in a solemn promise between God and humanity (see Gen 9:8-17), so too will the nation's and the city's misery and destitution end with an oath that they shall suffer no more. The term שלום is also part of the vocabulary pertaining to pacts and treaties; see Josh 9:15; Ps 55:21. This is also the meaning of the cognate terms in Akkadian: *salāmu* (a verb), *salāmu* (a noun), and *salīmu* (a noun) (*CAD* S:89, 101-3); and the Akkadian expression *riksu u s/šalāmu* is equivalent to Heb. ברית שלום, "covenant of friendship" (*CAD* S:89). For an immutable and everlasting covenant with the nation, see Isa 55:3; 59:21; 61:8.

Said the Lord, who takes you back in love — The conclusion of the pericope repeats the key theme of loving redemption (מְרחמך); see v. 7: "With vast love" (ברחמים גדֹלים), and v. 8: "I will take you back in love (רחמתיך)." For the connection between the terms חסד and רחם, see v. 8.

[11-17] Just as the first section began with a threefold call that conveyed Zion's misery, so too this unit opens with a triad conveying Zion's dejected state: "Afflicted, storm-tossed one, uncomforted." Moreover, just as in the first unit there are many promises to rebuild, rehabilitate, and repopulate Jerusalem (vv. 1-3), so too this pericope assures Jerusalem of a wondrous future rebuilding (vv. 11-12) and promises that all of Zion's sons shall be "disciples of the Lord," enjoying peace and prosperity (v. 13). The first and last units repeat the common reassurance: "Fear not!" (vv. 4, 14) and the promise of שלום (vv. 10, 13). For the rebuilding and refurbishing of Jerusalem, see also 44:26, 28; 45:13. The sequence of five precious stones that shall decorate the newly refurbished city (vv. 11-12) is reminiscent of the gems in "Eden, the garden of God," in Ezek 28:13-14, which are, in turn, an echo of the magical gem-studded garden described at the end of the ninth tablet of the Gilgamesh Epic. Compare also the following dazzling depictions of palaces and temples in Mesopotamia that were decorated with precious stones: "I made (Esagil) [the main temple of Babylon] shine like the sun. I decked the house in lapis lazuli. . . . I made the gates shine like the sun. . . . I studded (the palaces) all around entirely with knobbed nails glazed in gold, silver, and bronze (color) and thus made their facade resplendent. . . . I made its (the temple's) facade gleam with (white and black) gypsum and asphalt" (*CAD* N/1:23). The description here of a transformed Jerusalem influenced Tobit 13:16: "The gates of Jerusalem will be built with sapphire and emerald, and all your walls with precious stones. The towers of Jerusalem will be built with gold and their battlements with pure gold. The streets of Jerusalem will be paved with ruby and with stones of Ophir."

[11] *Afflicted, storm-tossed one, uncomforted* — a triad of descriptive titles depicting Jerusalem's distress and despondency in the days of exile and destruction: (1) Jerusalem is wracked by misery and affliction (עֲנִיָּה) since she was "refine[d] . . . in a furnace of affliction (עֹנִי)" (Isa 48:10); see also 51:21: "Therefore, listen to this, afflicted one (עֲנִיָּה)"; 49:13: "And He has taken back His afflicted ones (עֲנִיָּו) in love"; 66:2: "Yet to such a one I look: to the afflicted (עָנִי) and brokenhearted"; cf. 41:17; Lam 1:3, 7, 9. (2) סֹעֲרָה denotes the tossing to and fro by the wind of storms, as in Jonah 1:13: "For the sea was growing more and more stormy (סֹעֵר) about them" (cf. Jonah 1:11). Here in Isa 54 this verse is associatively linked to the stormy waters of the deluge alluded to in vv. 8 and 9 (and perhaps the expression עֲנִיָּה סערה also contains a phonetic allusion to the flood since it calls to mind אֳנִיָּה סערה, a "storm-tossed ship"). For the stormy metaphor describing the Diaspora, see Zech 7:14: "I tossed them (אֲסָעֲרֵם) among all those nations that they had not known." (3) For לֹא נֻחָמָה ("the uncomforted one"), cf. the image of the desolate city in Isa 51:19; Lam 1:2, 9, 17, 21. Perhaps this description of Zion was influenced by the symbolic name that the prophet Hosea conferred on his daughter, לֹא רֻחָמָה ("the unloved one").

I will lay carbuncles as your building stones — The identification of the precious gem, פּוּךְ, is still debated, but it may refer here to stones of a brilliant hue of antimony, for which see 1 Chr 29:2: אבני פוך; and for its use as eye paint, see 2 Kgs 9:30; Jer 4:30; Job 42:14. Some exegetes identify פוך with another precious stone, נֹפֶךְ ("turquoise"), which was one of the gems on the high priest's breastplate (Exod 28:18; 39:11), next to the lapis lazuli (ספיר), mentioned here in the following hemistich; cf. also the description of the mythical garden in Ezek 28:13. Others interpret פוך as mortar and translate: "I will set your stones in the finest mortar." The architectural term רבץ in this connection is a hapax legomenon.

And make your foundations of lapis lazuli — The city shall be constructed on a foundation of ספירים, another of the gems in the high priest's breastplate, identified as lapis lazuli. For the *pi'el* of the root יסד denoting the setting of building material, see 1 Kgs 5:31: "The king ordered huge blocks of choice stone to be quarried, so that the foundations of the house might be laid (לְיַסֵּד) with hewn stones." Some commentators prefer vocalizing the word as a noun rather than as a verb: וִיסֹדֹתַיִךְ ("your foundations"), as in LXX and 1QIsa[a], creating a chiastic parallel between this and the previous clause. The Ugaritic Baal epic also features a house built with the "purest lapis lazuli" *(ṭhrm iqnim)* (*CAT* 1.4.V:19); and in an Akkadian prophecy regarding the city of Uruk, it is said (line 14) that the king "will build the gates of Uruk with lapis lazuli *(uqnû)*" (see

H. Hunger and S. Kaufman, "A New Akkadian Prophecy Text," *JAOS* 95 [1975]: 371-75). For the expression -יסד ב, see Josh 6:26.

[12] *I will make your battlements of rubies* — The hapax legomenon שִׁמְשֹׁתַיִךְ is an architectural term, the meaning of which is subject to debate. Some scholars suggest that it signifies the battlements through which the sun (שמש) filters through. Others interpret the term as tower turrets or as sun-shaped shields that were hung on the walls (see Ezek 27:10; Cant 4:4 [for the shields on the wall of Lachish, see *ANEP*, nos. 372-73]). Another precious stone, כַּדְכֹּד (exact identity unknown), is mentioned in Ezek 27:16 in conjunction with Aramean (or, according to the ancient translations, Edomite) merchandise exported to Tyre. Note the variant reading of 4QpIsa[d] (= 4Q164, Isaiah's *pesher*): כול שמשותיך (Allegro, DJD 5, 28).

Your gates of firestones — The gates of Jerusalem shall be built of the precious gem אקדח, a hapax legomenon from the root קדח, "to kindle," i.e., gems that shine like fire (see Isa 50:11). The first two hemistichs form a chiastic parallelism.

Your whole encircling territory/boundary stones of desirable gems — All the environs of Zion shall be constructed of "desirable" gemstones. For the expression אבני חפץ, see Sir 45:11; 50:9; and 1QM *(War Scroll)* 5:6, 9, 14; 12:11-12 (Y. Yadin, *The Scroll of the War of the Sons of Light against the Sons of Darkness* [London, 1962], 280-81, 282-83, 318-19). The term גְּבוּל may signify boundary stones or markers; see Deut 19:14: "You shall not move your countryman's landmarks (גבול) set up by previous generations"; Deut 27:17: "Cursed be he who moves his fellow countryman's landmark (גבול)"; or may refer to the extent of a geographical territory or city limits; see Num 35:27: "boundaries of the city"; Deut 19:3: "The territory of your country"; Judg 1:18: "And Judah captured Gaza and its territory, Ashkelon and its territory, and Ekron and its territory." Similarly, the Akkadian semantic equivalent *kudurru* can also denote borders, boundaries, and the territory encompassed (*CAD* K:495-96); so too *miṣru* (*CAD* M/2:113-15) and *taḫūmu* (*CAD* T:56-57) signify both the border and the territory. The 1QIsa[a] plural variant, גבוליך (as in Vulgate and Peshitta), is in accord with the other plural substantives of v. 12. For the pair שערים/גבול in tandem, see Ps 147:13-14: "For He made the bars of your gates (שעריך) strong. . . . He endows your territory (גבולך) with well-being."

[13] In sync with the miraculous rebuilding of Jerusalem, there shall be a spiritual renewal among Jerusalem's inhabitants, as in Isa 59:21: "And this shall be My covenant with them, said the Lord: My spirit that is upon you, and the words that I have placed in your mouth, shall not be absent from your mouth, nor from the mouth of your children, nor from the mouth of your children's children — said the Lord — from now on, for all time." Verse 13 begins and ends with the word בניך, forming a literary *inclusio.*

And all your children shall be disciples of the Lord — See 50:4: "The Lord God gave me a skilled tongue. . . . He rouses my ear to give heed like disciples (כַּלִּמּוּדִים)"; 8:16: "Bind up the message. Seal the instruction with My disciples (בְּלִמֻּדָי)."

And great shall be the welfare of your children — For the expression רב שלום, see also Ps 37:11; 72:7; and in reverse order, 119:165: שלום רב. Cf. Isa 49:17, where the term בניך is polysemous. According to the Masoretic vocalization, it denotes "your children," thus forming a chiastic parallel with the prior hemistich. However, if vocalized בֹּנָיִךְ, as in 1QIsa[a], בוניכי, it means, "your builders," a version that accords nicely with the building motif in vv. 11-12 and parallels the following verb, תִּכּוֹנָנִי, in v. 14, which also relates to building construction (see the comments there). Compare this observation regarding the double entendre with *b. Ber.* 64a: "Rabbi Eleazar said in the name of Rabbi Ḥanina: 'The disciples of the sages proliferate peace in the world', as it is said: [and this verse is cited here]. Do not read, 'your children (בניך),' but 'your builders (בוניך).'" (See Paul, *Divrei Shalom,* 479-81.)

[14] This verse can be compared to Mesopotamian "eschatological" prophecies, which also feature the motif of a secure abode. (See M. Weinfeld, "The Latter-Day Prophecies of Mesopotamia," *Shnaton* 3 [1978]: 263-76 [Heb.].) For the idea of establishing a city in righteousness and of distancing all evils from it, cf. also the hymn to Enlil regarding the city of Nippur: "Distortion, abuse, malice, unseemliness, insolence, enmity, oppression. . . . (All these) evils the city does not tolerate. . . . Nippur, . . . where righteousness (and) justice are perpetuated" (*ANET,* 573-74).

You shall be established through righteousness — You shall be rebuilt on a solid foundation of justice. This hemistich complements the previous verse, and indeed a better division of the verses would have v. 13 ending with this clause. As mentioned above in passing, the verb תִּכּוֹנָנִי (a *hithpaʿel* of the root כון, in which the *tav* of the paradigm was assimilated into the initial letter of the root) also refers to building construction and parallels the verb בני ("to build"); see Num 21:27: "Firmly built and well founded (תִּבָּנֶה וְתִכּוֹנֵן) is Sihon's city"; Hab 2:12: "Ah, you who have built (בֹּנֶה) a town with crime, and established (וכוֹנֵן) a city with infamy"; Prov 24:3: "A house is built (יִבָּנֶה) by wisdom, and is established (יִתְכּוֹנָן) by understanding." Thus here too the verb would serve as a parallel to בוֹנַיִךְ ("your builders"), according to the variant reading of v. 13 in 1QIsa[a]. The Akkadian verb *kânu/kunnu* also means "to be firmly established" (*CAD* K:160-61) and refers to the "founding of a building or a city" (*CAD* K:164-65). Just as בוניך and תכונני are parallel, so too are צדקה and שלום (v. 13); cf. Isa 48:18; 60:17; Ps 85:11. For the expression כון בצדק/ה, see Prov 16:12; 25:5.

You shall have no fear of oppression, as it shall be far off — The translation is based on reversing the order of the Hebrew to facilitate comprehension. The object of the verb לא תִירָאִי is מֵעֹשֶׁק, and the reason your fears will be alleviated is כי רָחֲקִי (since it — the oppression — "shall be far [from you]"). For עֹשֶׁק ("oppression"), see Isa 59:13; Jer 6:6; Ezek 18:18.

Of terror, and it shall not come near you — For מְחִתָּה, from the root חתת ("to be shattered"), meaning "terror," see Jer 17:17, "Do not become a terror to me." For the verbal parallelism ירא/חתת, see Deut 1:21; 31:8; Josh 1:9. The parallel terms רחקי/לא תקרב form a negative parallelism; see also Isa 46:13: "I am bringing My victory near (קרבתי). It shall not be far off (לא תרחק)."

[15] *Surely no harm can be done without My consent* — The verse as a whole defies a coherent interpretation since each one of the words can be explained in many different ways; the above translation is only one possibility. The initial interjection, הֵן, may be understood either as a variant of הנה or as the opening of the protasis, as in Hag 2:12: "If (הֵן) a man is carrying sacrificial flesh in a fold of his garment . . ."; or as an interrogative, "Is it possible?"; cf. Jer 2:10: "Has (הֵן) anything like this ever happened?" The emphatic phrase גּוֹר יָגוּר has been understood as referring to the plotting of hostilities or as assembling for battle in light of the following verses, which concern themselves with war and enmity (cf. Targum אִתְכַּנָשָׁא יִתְכַּנְשׁוּן; Ibn Ganaḥ, *Sefer ha-Shorashim,* 88-89; Rashi [first explanation]; Ibn Ezra; Kimchi; Ehrlich); cf. Ps 59:4: "For see, they lie in wait for me; fierce men lie in ambush (יגורו) against me"; Ps 140:3: "Whose minds are full of evil schemes, who plot (יגורו) war every day"; and cf. the Akkadian cognate *gerû* ("to be hostile," "to make war"; *CAD* G:61-63). Thus, "Should any attack you, it will not be My will." אפס can also be explained as either a negation (the equivalent of לא) or as "only," "nothing but"; cf. Num 22:35: "But the angel of the Lord said to Balaam, 'Go with the men. But (אפס) you must say nothing except what I tell you.'" מאותי (the form is unique) can be understood as either "from me" or "as I will," e.g., "Let every man return to his home, for this thing is My will (מֵאִתִּי)" (1 Kgs 12:24). The wealth of possibilities makes it extremely difficult to determine what the text actually means.

Whoever would harm you shall fall because of you — Yet another enigmatic hemistich: Anybody who provokes you, assembles against you, or plots hostilities against you shall capitulate. For the expression נפל על denoting "capitulation," cf. Jer 21:9: "But whoever goes out and surrenders to (ונפל על) the Chaldeans"; and denoting "defeat" see Ezek 39:4: "You shall fall on (על . . . תפול) the mountains of Israel." The semantic Akkadian cognate *maqātu* also means "to fall in battle" and "to suffer a defeat" (*CAD* M/1:243.)

[16] The Lord created the metal craftsman who shapes his tools and weapons by the heat of the fire. The Deity also created the wreakers of havoc who put these weapons to use. For similar imagery, see Ezek 21:36: "I will pour out My indignation upon you. I will blow upon you with the fire of My wrath, and I will deliver you into the hands of barbarians, craftsmen of destruction (חָרָשֵׁי מַשְׁחִית)"; Ezek 22:20-21: "As silver, copper, iron, lead, and tin are gathered into a crucible to blow the fire on them, so as to melt them. . . . I will blow on you the fire of My fury, and you shall be melted in it."

It is I who created the smith — Indeed, it is I (the first person, אנכי, is for emphasis) who created the craftsman. 1QIsa[a] הנה is identical with the MT Qere (the Ketib is הן).

To fan the charcoal fire — To blow on the smoldering coals so as to cause the fire to flare, thus smelting the metal; cf. Isa 44:12: "The blacksmith . . . works it over charcoal (בַּפֶּחָם)." For the fanning of the fire, see also Ezek 22:20 quoted above: "To blow (לָפַחַת) the fire on them, so as to melt them." Compare also the Neo-Assyrian inscription: "I scattered charcoal (*pēnte* = פֶּחָם); then I kindled the fire [the Akkadian verb *napāḫu* is the etymological and semantic equivalent of נפח]. I kindled the glowing charcoal" (*CAD* N/1:264).

And produce weapons, each for its own purpose — The pronominal suffix of לְמַעֲשֵׂהוּ refers to כלי, which is a collective noun referring to weapons in general; see Gen 27:3; 1 Sam 20:40; 21:9.

So it is I who create the destroyer to lay waste — The first words of this clause, ואנכי בראתי, are a repetition of the beginning of the verse. Together they emphasize that God created both the instruments and the wreakers of havoc, as in Jer 22:7: "I will appoint destroyers against you (מַשְׁחִתִים), each with his tools (וְכֵלָיו)"; Ezek 9:1: "Each bearing his weapons of destruction (כלי משחית)." For the root חבל, which denotes destroying, laying waste, see Isa 13:5: "They come from a distant land, from the end of the sky. The Lord with the weapons (כלי) of His wrath to ravage (לְחַבֵּל) all the earth." The root also appears in Biblical Aramaic; see Ezra 6:12: "To destroy (לְחַבָּלָה) that house of God in Jerusalem" (cf. the Targum to Gen 19:13: Heb. משחתים = Aram. מְחַבְּלִין); and in Akkadian, *ḫabālu/ḫubbulu* (*CAD* Ḫ:5). The noun משחית in military jargon denotes a unit whose task is to raid and attack the enemy; see 1 Sam 13:17: "The raiders (המשחית) came out of the Philistine camp in three columns"; 1 Sam 14:15: "The outposts and the raiders (והמשחית) were also terrified"; and cf. Jer 22:7 quoted above. For the demon-destroyer (משחית) who wreaked havoc upon the Egyptians at the time of the exodus, see Exod 12:13, 23.

[17] As in v. 16, the text first refers to the weapons that might be wielded against Israel, and then to the humans who might contend against her. Jerusalem shall be protected from both. This total immunity is the lot the Lord vouchsafes His servants.

No weapon formed against you shall succeed — All weapons formed with malicious intent against you shall not prevail. For the verb צלח, see 53:10; 55:11. This is the sole occurrence of the verb יצר in the *huph*ʿ*al.*

And every tongue that contends with you at law you shall defeat — And all those who contend with you in a court of law shall be found guilty; cf. 50:9: "Lo, the Lord God will help me. Who then can find me guilty (יַרְשִׁיעֵנִי)?"; Job 40:8: "Would you condemn Me (תַּרְשִׁיעֵנִי) that you may be right?" For the term לשון ("tongue"), a synecdoche for a scheming individual, see Ps 31:21: "You shelter them in Your pavilion from contentious tongues (לְשֹׁנוֹת)." For the root קום in legal contexts, see Deut 19:15; Paul, *Divrei Shalom*, 105-6.

Such is the lot of the servants of the Lord, such their triumph through Me — declares the Lord — Such (referring to the description in the verses above) is the destiny of the "servants of the Lord." For נחלה with the meaning "lot, portion, share," see Job 31:2: "What fate is decreed by God above? What lot (נחלה) by Shaddai in the heights?"; cf. Job 20:29; 27:13. This is also the servants' ultimate victory (צִדְקָתָם), salvation, and vindication (see Deut 25:1) in court and the defeat of those who contend against them. This is the first time in Deutero-Isaiah that the epithet "servant" appears in the plural; and from here on it is used in the descriptions of the Lord's devotees and chosen ones, as opposed to the nation's miscreants and evildoers; see Isa 63:17; 65:8, 9, 13 (three times), 14, 15; 66:14.

Chapter 55

This short chapter is composed of two literary units: vv. 1-5 and 6-13. The first unit begins with an exhortation by the prophet to consume food and drink without cost (v. 1). The prophet's call is similar in form to invitations to "eat and drink" at the behest of Wisdom: Prov 9:5: "Come, eat my food and drink the wine that I have spiced!"; Sir 24:19-21: "Gather near, those who desire me, and be sated by what I produce, for my remembrance is sweeter than honey, and my inheritance than the honeycomb. Those who eat from me shall hunger for more and those who drink from me will thirst for more." The consumption of sustenance refers here, as it does in the wisdom passages cited above, to taking heed of God. As the reward for inclining their ear to the Lord, the prophet promises the people that the covenant, which in the past existed between God and the house of David, shall be renewed; but now the nation as a whole shall be the beneficiaries (vv. 3-5). With the exception of these verses, there are no other allusions to David or his dynasty in Deutero-Isaiah's prophecies of Israel's future, since according to this prophet God is the sole sovereign (see below). This outlook is in contrast with other exilic and postexilic prophets who look forward to the renewal of the Davidic kingship (e.g., Jer 23:5-6; 33:14-26; Ezek 34:23-24; 37:15-24; Hag 2:23; Zech 3:8; 4:6-10; 6:9-15).

These verses constitute a unique ideological innovation: The former Davidic covenant is now extended to the entire nation, and the divine reassurance is formulated using the same terms of the promise to David: "But I will never withdraw My favor from him. . . . Your house and your kingship shall ever be secure before you. Your throne shall be established forever" (2 Sam 7:15-16). Compare especially Ps 89: "I have made a covenant with My chosen one. I have sworn to My servant David; I will establish your offspring forever" (vv. 4-5); "My faithfulness and steadfast love shall be with him" (v. 25); "I will maintain My steadfast love for him always. My covenant with him shall endure. I will establish his line forever, his throne, as long as the heavens last" (vv. 29-30); "But I will not take away My steadfast love from him; I will not betray My faithfulness. I will not violate My covenant. . . . I have sworn by My holiness, once and for all. I will not be false to David. His line shall continue forever, his throne, as the sun before Me, as the moon, established forever, an enduring witness in the sky" (vv. 34-38). The psalm's terminology, "My chosen one," "My servant," "your servant," which refers to David (vv. 4, 21, 40), are in Deutero-Isaiah's prophecy transferred to Israel as a whole (e.g., 41:8, 9; 43:20; 44:1, 2), and David's exclusive messianic title, משיח ("the anointed one," Ps 89:39, 52), is conferred only upon the Persian king Cyrus (Isa 45:1). Moreover, the plural substantive "kings" in his prophecies refers only to heathen monarchs (41:2; 45:1; 49:7, 23; 52:15; 60:3, 16; 62:2), whereas the singular "king" or the verb מָלַךְ is applied solely to the Lord (41:21; 43:15; 52:7) — since He alone is sovereign. What is more, Deutero-Isaiah promises Israel that they shall rule over a vast empire of nations, replacing the empire of David, now lost. (See O. Eissfeldt, "The Promises of Grace to David in Isaiah 55:1-5," in B. W. Anderson and W. Harrelson, eds., *Israel's Prophetic Heritage: Essays in Honor of James Muilenburg* [New York, 1962], 196-207; M. Sweeney, "The Reconceptualization of the Davidic Covenant in Isaiah," in J. van Ruiten and M. Vervenne, eds., *Studies in the Book of Isaiah: Festschrift Willem A. M. Beuken,* BETL 132 [Leuven, 1997], 41-61; and for the relatively minor role David plays in the Dead Sea Scrolls, in rabbinic literature, and in the liturgy, see R. Kimelman, "The Messiah of the ʿAmidah: A Study in Comparative Messianism," *JBL* 116 [1997]: 313-24.) The democratization of the political ideal is connected to similar cultic innovations, which will be elaborated on in the following chapter. (See the introduction, §17.)

The first pericope (vv. 1-5) is characterized by twelve imperatives. Note also the following words that are emphasized: לְכוּ (three times in v. 1, and once in v. 3), בלוא (v. 1 [twice], v. 2 [twice]), כסף (v. 1 [twice], v. 2), the verb שמע (v. 2 [twice], v. 3), שִׁבְרוּ (v. 1 [twice]), אִכְלוּ (vv. 1, 2), נפשכם (vv. 2, 3), אֵלַי (vv. 2, 3), לא(ו)מים (v. 4 [twice]), גוי (v. 5 [twice]), ידע (v. 5 [twice]), הן (vv. 4, 5). These verses are connected to the previous chapter by the following terms: חסד, עולם, ברית; cf. וחסדי מֵאִתֵּךְ לא ימוש וברית שלומי לא (54:8); ובחסד עולם רִחמתיך תָמוּט (54:10) — ואכרתה לכם ברית עולם חסדי דוד הנאמנים (55:3). The divine title "the Holy One of Israel" (קדוש ישראל; 54:5; 55:5) and the exclamatory הן (54:15; 55:4, 5) also appear in both chapters.

[1-2] An invitation for all who hunger and thirst to come forth to eat and drink without having to pay. (For the reverse description during the exile, cf. Lam 5:4: "We must pay to drink our own water.") The Lord's word, which is compared to sustenance, is addressed to the nation, which is desirous of salvation. He exhorts them repeatedly, "Come!" (לְכוּ; three times in the first verse, and the fourth time in v. 3) and "Take heed!" (שִׁמְעוּ, שִׁמְעוּ שָׁמוֹעַ; vv. 2, 3). Similar nonmetaphorical invitations appear in Ugaritic literature: "Eat or drink! Eat some bread at the tables! Drink some wine from the goblets!" (El's invitation to his consort Asherah, in the Baal epic; *CAT* 1.4.IV:35-37); "[For ea]ting, for drinking, I have summoned you" (an invitation of King Kirta's wife to the nobles to share in the repast, in the Kirta epic; *CAT* 1.15.IV:27; V:10; VI:4-5); "Eat of every food! Drink of every vintage wine!" ("Birth of the Gracious Gods"; *CAT* 1.23:6). Compare also Prov 9:5; Sir 24:19-21, quoted above in the introduction. For an image of thirst and hunger for God's word, see Amos 8:11.

[1] *Ho! All who are thirsty, come for water!* — "Ho" (הוי), says the prophet enthusiastically and calls on all who thirst to come and drink water. For the exclamatory הוי, see Isa 1:24; Jer 47:6; Zech 2:10, 11.

Even if you have no money — Even those of you who are unable to pay for potable water. The Masoretes, who marked the division of the clauses, attached this phrase to the previous colon.

Come! Buy food! And eat! — The denominative verb שבר (Gen 43:20; Deut 2:6) is derived from the substantive שֶׁבֶר, which denotes produce, grain (Gen 42:1, 2; Amos 8:5). The LXX translates "and drink" in lieu of the MT "and eat," since the first part of the verse speaks of water but does not mention solids.

Come! Buy food without money — procure sustenance without paying; cf. Gen 44:2: "Together with his money for the rations (כסף שִׁבְרוֹ)"; Gen 47:14: "Joseph gathered in all the money (כסף) . . . as payment for the rations (בַּשֶּׁבֶר) that were being procured (שֹׁבְרִים)." For the grammatical construction בלוא כסף ("without money"), found mostly in later books, see Job 8:11: בלא בִצָּה; Job 15:32: בלא יומו; Eccl 10:11: בלוא לחש; and the following clause here: ובלוא מחיר; v. 2: בלוא לְשָׂבְעָה. The LXX, 1QIsa[a], and a number of medieval Hebrew manuscripts omit this series of verbs (ואכלו לכו שברו), most likely because the scribe's eye skipped from the first שִׁבְרוּ to the second; cf. also the Peshitta.

Wine and milk without cost! — and obtain drink without paying the vendor. For the term מחיר denoting cost or payment, see 2 Sam 24:24: "But the king replied to Araunah, 'No, I will buy them from you at a price'"; 1 Kgs 21:2: "I will pay you the price in money." For another example of the parallelism כסף/מחיר ("money/cost"), see Lam 5:4. For the nominal pair חלב/יין ("wine/milk"), see Gen 49:12; Cant 5:1; cf. also Joel 4:18.

[2] There is little reason to buy the essentials, since you could all partake in luxuries if only you would listen to My word.

Why do you spend money for what is not bread? — Why do you squander your capital (lit. "weigh silver") without receiving your just dues? For payment in weighed units of silver, see Gen 23:16: "Abraham weighed out the money to Ephron (וישקל . . . הכסף)." (Coinage was invented by the Lydians in the seventh century BCE.)

Your earnings for what does not satisfy? — Why give away your hard-earned money and still go unsatisfied? לְשָׂבְעָה is a feminine gerund; cf. Isa 56:6: ולאהבה. For the substantive יגיע ("the fruits of one's labor"), see Deut 28:33; Ps 109:11.

Give heed to Me! And you shall eat choice food — The imperative שִׁמְעוּ, followed by the infinitive absolute שָׁמוֹעַ, adds additional emphasis (see also Job 13:17; 21:2). Those who hearken to God's word shall benefit from the choicest delicacies. For another example of the substantive טוֹב with the verb אכל, see Prov 13:2. Compare Akk. *akūla ṭābu šitâ dašpa,* "Eat good food! Drink sweet (beer)!" (*CAD* A/1:246). For the similar motif of giving heed to God, which leads to eating one's fill, see Deut 11:13-15: "If, then, you obey the commandments that I enjoin upon you, . . . you shall eat your fill."

And enjoy the richest viands! — and pleasure yourselves (or, your "appetites"; for נפש meaning "appetite," see Prov 23:2; Eccl 6:2, 3) by consuming the richest and fattest victuals (דשן); cf. Ps 36:9: "They feast on the rich fair (מִדֶּשֶׁן) of Your house"; Ps 63:6: "I am sated as with a rich feast (וָדֶשֶׁן)"; and cf. Deut 31:20: "And they eat their fill and grow fat (וְדָשֵׁן)." For the synonymous pair דשן/טוב, see Jer 31:14; Ps 65:12. For the *hithpaʿel* of the verb ענג, which denotes enjoyment of eating and drinking one's fill, see Isa 66:11; cf. also 58:14.

[3-5] As their reward for heeding the Lord, the nation is told that the covenant promised to David shall now apply to all of them. And just as David was "the leader of peoples," so too shall Israel reign sovereign over the nations of the world.

[3] *Incline your ear! And come to Me!* — In v. 1 the people are commanded: "Come for water!" and now the water allegory is made clear — the nation "must incline its ears, and come to the Lord." For the verbal pair הט אֹזֶן/שמע (in the following clause), see Prov 5:13; cf. also Jer 7:24; Prov 22:17; Ps 17:6; 45:11; Dan 9:18.

Hearken! And you shall be revived — Compare the invitation in Prov 9:5: "Come, eat my food and drink the wine that I have spiced!" which features the same promised result: "You shall be revived" (וּתְחִי נפשכם, v. 3). For the expression הַחֲיָה נפש ("to revive"), see Gen 12:13; 19:19, 20; and for its semantic cognate in Akkadian, *balāṭ/bulluṭ napištam,* see *CAD* B:46ff.; N/1:300.

And I will make with you an everlasting covenant — God shall establish a covenant with Israel that shall never be broken; see Isa 61:8: "And I shall make a covenant with them for all time (וברית עולם)"; cf. also 54:10 (ברית שלומי); 59:21 (בריתי). For the expression "an everlasting covenant," see also Gen 9:16; 17:7, 13, 19; Exod 31:16; Jer 32:40; 50:5; Ezek 16:60; Ps 105:10. This promise replaces God's assurance to the Davidic dynasty: 2 Sam 7:16: "Your house and your kingship shall ever be secure before you. Your throne shall be established forever"; 2 Sam 23:5: "He has granted me an eternal pact"; Ps 89:4-5: "I have made a covenant with My chosen one. I have sworn to My servant David: 'I will establish your offspring forever'" (and see above, the introduction to this chapter). For the expression כרת ל- ("to make [a covenant] with"), see also Ezek 34:25: "And I will grant them (וכרתי להם) a covenant of friendship"; Ps 89:4: "I have made a covenant with My chosen one (כרתי . . . לבחירי) [David]."

The enduring loyalty promised to David — חסדֵי דוד are the oaths, assurances, and steadfast love that the Lord vouchsafed him, which shall endure forevermore; cf. Ps 89:25: "My faithfulness and steadfast love (ואמונתי וחסדי) shall be with him"; 89:29: "I will maintain My steadfast love (חסד) for him always. My covenant with him shall endure (ובריתי נאמנת)"; 89:50: "O Lord, where is Your steadfast love (חסדך) of old that You swore to David in Your faithfulness (באמונתך)?" In all these verses, as here, the root אמן describes the promised חסד (lit. "loyalty"), which is a synonym of ברית ("covenant"); cf. Isa 54:10: "But my loyalty (חסדי) shall never move from you, nor My covenant (וברית) of friendship be shaken"; Ps 89:29: "I will maintain My steadfast love (חסד) for him always. My covenant (ובריתי) with him shall endure"; and cf. Deut 7:9: "The steadfast (נאמן) God who keeps His covenant faithfully (הברית והחסד)." (See the introduction, §17.) The same expression, חסדֵי דוד, appears in 2 Chr 6:42: "Remember the loyalty of Your servant David." But there David is the subject of these bonds of loyalty, whereas here God is the subject of the bonds and David is the object. This same steadfast loyalty is, as already mentioned, now conferred on the nation as a whole.

[4-5] The verses are reminiscent of Ps 18:44 (= 2 Sam 22:44): "You appointed me [David] to be a ruler of nations. A people I knew not shall serve me." (See the introduction, §17.)

[4] A triad of titles relating to David — "Leader" (עֵד), "Prince" (נגיד), and "Commander of peoples" (מצוה לְאֻמִּים) — connected to his sovereignty over the nations (cf. 2 Sam 22:44-45 = Ps 18:44-45) is now transferred to the nation of Israel. Israel, who in the past was a subject nation, shall now subjugate nations, who shall do its bidding. The verse is framed by the term לְאֻמִּים ("nations"; the first time written *plene*, לאומים).

As I appointed him a leader of peoples — Note the syllogism between הן in this verse and הן in the next one: Just as I appointed David as a sovereign over the nations, so too shall you summon nations you did not know. The term עֵד, understood according to the context to mean a leader, is the *nomen regens* of לאומים, plural of לְאֹם, "people"; see Isa 41:1; 43:4, 9; 49:1; 51:4. Others derive the noun from אֻמָּה ("nation"), preceded by the prepositional particle לְ, as in Ps 117:1: "Praise the Lord, all you nations (כל הָאֻמִּים)!" (According to one lexical list, the Akkadian homonym *adû* signifies "leader" [*CAD* A/1:136].) For the verb נתן ("to appoint, to consecrate for a special mission"), see Isa 49:6; Jer 1:5; 1 Kgs 14:7; 16:2. Instead of the Masoretic נתתיו ("I appointed him"), the Peshitta, *Yalqut Hamachiri* 40, 7 (ed. Buber, 238), and one medieval Hebrew manuscript read נתתיך ("I have appointed you").

A prince and commander of peoples — The archaic title נגיד ("prince"), denoting a ruler, was borne by kings Saul (1 Sam 9:16; 13:14), David (1 Sam 13:14; 25:30; 2 Sam 5:2; 6:21; 7:8), Solomon (1 Kgs 1:35), and Hezekiah (2 Kgs 20:5). Compare also regarding Jeroboam and Baasha: "And I have appointed you a נגיד over My people Israel" (1 Kgs 14:7; 16:2). The Masoretic vocalization מְצַוֵּה in the construct state means "a commander of peoples." If it is punctuated מְצַוֶּה, in the absolute state, however, it would mean, "a commander to the peoples" (ומצוה לאמים [= לְאֻמִּים]), as in Ps 117:1, quoted above. For the expression צוי ל-, see, e.g., Isa 13:3. A paraphrastic form of this clause appears in the Qumran *Psalms Scroll* (11QPs[a]) 151:11-12: וישׂמיני נגיד לעמו ומושל בבני בריתו, "And He made me a prince (נגיד) of His people and a ruler over the sons of His covenant" (J. A. Sanders, *The Psalms Scroll of Qumrân Cave 11,* DJD 4 [Oxford, 1965], 49).

[5] The people are addressed directly.

So you shall summon nations you did not know — Just as (הן) David was a commander of nations (v. 4), so too (הן) shall you (i.e., the nation in its entirety) be appointed over nations (גוי is a collective term for all the nations) you never knew. For the expression, cf. Deut 28:33: "A people you do not know shall eat up the produce of your soil and all your gains." The LXX, Vulgate, and Peshitta all read, here and in the following clause, the plural גוים, which conforms to the phrase לאומים in the preceding verse.

And nations that did not know you shall come running to you — in order to pay homage to you; cf. Ps 18:44 = 2 Sam 22:44: "You have set me at the head of nations. Peoples I knew not shall serve me."

For the sake of the Lord your God, the Holy One of Israel who has glorified you — The image of a pilgrimage of the nations to Jerusalem for the sake of the Lord, who has favored His nation, is also found in Isa 60:9: "The vessels of the coastlands are assembled, with ships of Tarshish in the lead, to bring your sons from afar, and their silver and gold as well — for the name of the Lord your God, for the Holy One of Israel, who has glorified you." For the motif of the Deity acting for His sake alone, see 43:25: "It is I, I who — for My own sake — wipe your transgressions away"; 48:11: "For My sake, My own sake, do I act"; and cf. 49:7, which features the same sequence of ideas: "Kings shall see and stand up; nobles, and they shall prostrate themselves — to the honor of the Lord who is faithful, to the Holy One of Israel who chose you." In the syntactical construction (למען . . . ל(קדוש, the ל denotes "for the sake of," e.g., Ezek 36:22: "Thus said the Lord God: 'Not for your sake (למענכם) will I act, O House of Israel, but for the sake of My holy name (לשם קדשי), which you have caused to be profaned among the nations to which you have come.'" The verb פאר appears in contexts of the Lord glorifying His Temple (Isa 60:7, 13) and His people (here; 44:23; 49:3; 60:9, 21; 61:3); cf. also the substantive תִּפארת ("splendor") (44:13; 46:13; 52:1; 60:7, 19; 62:3; 63:12, 15; 64:10). For the divine sobriquet קדוש ישראל, see 41:14, 16, 20; 43:3, 14; 45:11; 48:17; 49:7; 54:5; 60:9, 14. (See the introduction, §9.)

[6-13] This pericope features a number of interlocking motifs: the advent of the time when the Lord may be sought (v. 6); a call to the wicked to cease their evil ways and return to the Lord, who is merciful (v. 7); the Lord's plans as opposed to those of mere humans are always fulfilled (vv. 8-11) — the Lord's plan being the redemption of His people, which shall be praised by all of nature and celebrated by the flowering of greenery on Israel's desert path (vv. 12-13). The unit begins (vv. 6-7) and concludes (vv. 12-13) with the prophet's words (the intervening verses have God speaking in the first-person). The verb קרא links the final verse of the preceding unit (תקרא, v. 5) with the initial verse of this unit (קְרָאֻהוּ, v. 6), and both the word לחם and the root אכל appear in both sections (vv. 2, 10). Compare also the play on the two meanings of the verb כרת: "And I will make (ואכרתה) with you an everlasting covenant" (v. 3), and "An everlasting sign that shall not perish (יִכָּרֵת)" (v. 13).

It is important to note Jeremiah's influence, specifically Jer 29:10-14, which left a thematic and linguistic imprint on this prophecy: In both, the exhortation to seek the Deity concludes with the promise of redemption, and both feature the verbs קרא, דרש, and מצא (in the *niphʿal*) in identical contexts: "When you call (וקראתם) Me . . . You will seek Me (תדרשֻׁני) and find (ומצאתם) Me . . . I will be at hand (ונמצאתי) for you" (Jer 29:12-14) — "Seek (דִּרְשׁוּ) the Lord while He can be found (בְּהִמָּצְאוֹ)! Call to Him (קְרָאֻהוּ) while He is near!" (Isa 55:6). Compare also Jer 29:11: "For I am mindful of the plans I have made concerning you — declares the Lord — plans for your welfare, not for disaster, to give you a hopeful future" — "For My plans are not your plans . . . so are My ways high above your ways and My plans above your plans" (Isa 55:8-9). And this is connected to the realization of the divine plan, specifically His promise to redeem His people: "I will take note of you, and I will fulfill to you My promise of favor, to bring you back to this place" (Jer 29:10) — "So is the word that issues from My mouth . . . but performs what I purpose, achieves what I sent it to do. Yea, you shall leave in joy, and be led home secure" (Isa 55:11-12). Both prophecies themselves are anchored in the Deuteronomic promise in Deut 4:7, 29: "For what great nation is there that has a god so close at hand as is the Lord our God whenever we call upon Him? . . . But if you search there for the Lord your God, you will find Him, if only you seek Him with all your heart and soul." Thus, according to Deutero-Isaiah, the time Jeremiah (and before him, the book of Deuteronomy) spoke of is at hand, and one should seek the Lord at this opportune time since redemption is imminent. (See the introduction, §15.)

[6-9] The motifs expressed here by the verbs דרש, מצא, שוב, and רחם reflect Deuteronomistic theology; see Deut 4:29-31. (See W. Brueggemann, "Isaiah 55 and Deuteronomic Theology," *ZAW* 80 [1968]: 191-203.)

[6] A message of encouragement to the expatriates, that the Lord has not left them and that He is now near at hand.

Seek the Lord while He can be found! — Seek out the Lord at a time in which He lets Himself be found. The initial ב particle of בְּהִמָּצְאוֹ can be understood as either temporal (Ibn Ganaḥ, *Sefer ha-Riqmah* [ed. Walensky, 83, lines 15ff.]; cf. Ps 114:1: "When Israel went forth (בְּצֵאת)from Egypt"); causative (Abravanel), as in Gen 19:16: "Because of the Lord's mercy (בְּחֶמְלַת) on him"; or tolerative, "When He lets Himself to be found," as in Isa 65:1: "I let Myself be sought by those who did not ask. I let Myself be found (נִמְצֵאתִי) by those who did not seek Me." For the same motif, see Deut 4:29: "But if you seek from there the Lord your God, you will find Him. If only you seek Him with all your heart and soul"; Jer 29:13-14: "You will search for Me and find Me, if only you seek Me wholeheartedly. I will be at hand for you — declares the Lord." For seeking the Lord or for neglecting to seek Him, see Isa 58:2; 65:1, 10.

Call to Him while He is near! — and ready to grant your wishes; cf. Ps 145:18: "The Lord is near to all who call Him, to all who call Him with sincerity"; cf. also Deut 4:7, quoted above.

[7-9] For the motifs featured in these verses, see Ps 103:8-11. Compare especially v. 11: "For as the heavens are high above the earth"; and here v. 9: "But as the heavens are high above the earth."

[7] *Let the wicked give up his way, the sinful man his plans* — The time has come for the evildoer to abandon his ways, and for the "sinful man" (אִישׁ אָוֶן — an expression that recurs in the singular only in Prov 6:12, and in the plural only in Job 34:36), i.e., the man who carries out evil deeds (אָוֶן), to give up his reprehensible schemes; cf. Isa 59:7: "Their plans are plans of mischief (מחשבות אָוֶן)"; Jer 11:19: "I did not realize that it was against me they fashioned their plots (מחשבות)." For דרך ("way," denoting "conduct"), see Gen 6:12. For דרך and מחשבות in conjunction, see 65:2: "To a disloyal people, who walk the way (הדרך) that is not good, following their own designs (מחשבותיהם)."

Let him return to the Lord, and He will have compassion on him — The root שוב ("return") is a key term here, repeated in vv. 10, 11. For the root רחם ("have compassion"), which recurs frequently in Deutero-Isaiah's prophecies, see 49:10, 13; 54:7, 8, 10; 60:10; 63:7, 15.

To our God, for He freely forgives — the sinners. In the Bible the act of forgiveness, סלח, i.e., the total erasure of all one's sins, is attributed to God alone; see Jer 31:34; 33:8; Ps 130:4. Humans may pardon, but only God can wipe the slate clean. For the connection between the roots רחם and סלח relating to God, see Dan 9:9: "To the Lord our God belong mercy (הרחמים) and forgiveness (והסליחות)"; Neh 9:17: "But You, being a forgiving (סליחות) God, gracious and compassionate (ורחום)." For the division of the two elements of the divine name, ה׳ אלהינו, in separate hemistichs, see also Isa 40:3; 52:10.

[8] Together with vv. 9-11, this verse emphasizes and demonstrates how dissimilar the Deity and humans are. One should note the literary structure of the following verses, which, starting with v. 8, all begin with either כי or כן: v. 8: כי; v. 9: כן ... כי; v. 10: כי ... כי אם; v. 11: כן ... כי אם; v. 12: כי.

For My plans are not your plans, nor are My ways your ways — declares the Lord — (It is possible that the כי at the beginning of the verse is emphatic.) According to the fragmentary scroll 1QIsa[b], כם מחשבתי[ ], the order of words accords with the following clause: דרכיכם דְּרָכָי. According to the MT, the two verses form a chiastic parallel. For the "Lord's plans" parallel to "His counsel," see Mic 4:12.

[9] *But as the heavens are high above the earth, so are My ways high above your ways and My plans above your plans* — The כי-כן syntactical construction is characteristic of a syllogism (see also below, vv. 10-11; 54:9; 66:22): Just as the sky towers over the earth, so too do My plans exceed your own. It is possible that 1QIsa[a] כגובה ("as the height of"), in lieu of the finite verb גבהו — supported by the majority of the ancient translations — was influenced by Ps 103:11: "For as the heavens are high (כי כְגְבֹהַּ שמים) above the earth"; cf. Job 22:12: גֹבַהּ שמים. For כי ("as"), see Isa 44:3: "As (כי) I pour water on thirsty soil"; 62:5: "As (כי) a youth espouses a maiden." For the expression גבה מ- ("high above") in a similar context, see Job 35:5: "Look at the skies high above you (גבהו ממך)."

[10-11] The Lord's word is compared to precipitation, which soaks through the earth and makes it bloom. Just as rain and snow do not return to the sky until they quench the earth's thirst, i.e., function as a catalyst for a positive chain reaction, so too the Lord's promise to redeem Israel shall come to pass. (See A. Rofé, "How Is the Word Fulfilled? Isaiah 55.6-11 within the Theological Debate of Its Time," in G. M. Tucker, D. L. Petersen, and R. R. Wilson, eds., *Canon, Theology, and Old Testament Interpretation: Essays in Honor of Brevard S. Childs* [Philadelphia, 1988], 246-61.) The Lord offers proof of His prowess through the portents of nature: Just as His power resonates throughout the natural world, so too does it resonate through history; and the results, though not immediate, form part of an inexorable process. For imagery comparing the word of the Lord to rain and other forms of precipitation, see Deut 32:2: "May My discourse come down as the rain, My speech distill as the dew." For rainfall representing the Lord's munificence, see Isa 44:3-4; 45:8. Verses 10-11 form another syllogism (as in v. 9): כי/כאשר ("just as," v. 10) — כן ("so", v. 11); see also 52:13-15. Note the multiple occurrences of the sibilant *shin* in the first two clauses of v. 10.

[10] *For as the rain or snow drops from heaven* — just as precipitation is a constant phenomenon (the imperfect יֵרֵד implies frequency). When the predicate (ירד, singular) precedes the subject (הגשם והשלג, plural), the gender and number do not always correspond; cf. Exod 15:1: "Then Moses and the Israelites [plural] sang" (ישיר — singular). For the verb ירד in connection with rain, see Ezek 34:26: "I will send down (והורדתי) the rain in its season, rains that bring blessing." For the שלג־גשם ("rain snow") sequence, see Job 37:6.

And returns not there — to the sky (note the wordplay: שמה־שמים). Compare the similar description in Mesopotamian literature: "Just as rain does not return to its source" (*CAD* Š/1:346).

But soaks the earth and makes it bring forth vegetation — The rainwater does not return to the sky until it accomplishes its task of causing the earth's vegetation to grow and sprout (והצמיחה); cf. Isa 61:11: "And as a garden makes the seed shoot up (תצמיח)"; Ps 147:8: "He makes mountains put forth (המצמיח) grass." For the verb ילד in the *hiph'il* denoting procreation, see Job 38:28: "Who begot (הוליד) the dewdrops." The triad of verbs also allude to sexual activity; and the image of rain as the inseminator of the fertile earth, which gives birth to all manner of greenery, appears also in Job 38:26-27: "To rain down on uninhabited land. . . . To saturate the desolate wasteland and make the crop of grass sprout forth." For the reproductive image of the rain in talmudic thought, see *b. Ta'an.* 6b, which explains the rabbinic term for "rainfall" (רביעה) as that which "fructifies the earth." For rain as quenching the soil, cf. Ps 65:11. For כי אם ("but"), see v. 11.

Yielding seed for he who sows and bread for he who eats — The formative result of this chain of events is food production; cf. Lev. 26:4: "So that the earth shall yield (ונתנה) its produce." The reading in 1QIsa[a], לאכול ("to eat"; so too LXX), instead of MT לָאֹכֵל, was perhaps influenced by Gen 28:20: לחם לֶאֱכֹל. For the expression נתן לחם, see Ps 147:9.

[11] The apodosis of the syllogism, in which the anthropomorphized word of the Lord is appointed as a messenger responsible for the fulfillment of the divine will. For the Lord's word as His emissary, see Ps 147:15: "He sends forth His word to the earth. His command runs swiftly." The phraseology in this verse is reminiscent of Isa 48:14-15: "He shall work His will against Babylon. . . . I, I predicted . . . and he shall succeed in his mission." Instead of Cyrus, however, "the word of the Lord" shall execute God's will. The idea that God's word is irrevocable, immutable, and comes to pass once uttered is found in Mesopotamian thought as well; see the references in the next paragraph.

So is the word that issues from My mouth — so (just as the rain and snow, etc.) is (יהיה — the imperfect is used here to indicate frequency) My delivered message. For the expression יצא מפי, see 45:23; 48:3; Esth 7:8. Compare also the cognate expression in Akkadian, *ṣīt pî* ("utterance, command"), referring to the unalterable utterance of a deity: "Marduk the great lord whose utterance no god can alter"; "Nanâ, whose command cannot be altered, whose order cannot be changed" (*CAD* Ṣ:219).

It does not come back to Me unfulfilled — It shall not return to Me without achieving its mission. For ריקם, see 2 Sam 1:22: "The sword of Saul never returned empty (ריקם)"; cf. also Jer 14:3. For the expression . . . עֲשׂתוֹ לא ישוב עד ("It shall not return . . . until achieving"), see Jer 23:20; 30:24.

But performs what I purpose — My intended mission. This phraseology recurs in similar contexts in Isa 44:28: "He [Cyrus] shall fulfill all My purposes"; 46:10: "I will do all I have purposed"; 48:14: "He shall work his will against Babylon"; and cf. 53:10: "And that through him the Lord's purpose might prosper." Compare also the Akkadian cognates *ṣibûtam epēšu/kašādu* (*CAD* E:218; Ṣ:169-70). For the expression כי אם ("but"), see v. 10.

And succeeds in what I sent it to do — cf. 48:15: "I have brought him and he shall succeed (והצליח) in his mission"; 53:10: "And that through him the Lord's purpose might succeed (יצלח)." For the verbs הצליח and עשה in tandem, see Ps 1:3.

[12-13] The metaphor is now made clear: The word of the Lord that shall presently be fulfilled refers to His promise to redeem His people from the Babylonian exile and to return them to Zion. Just as the Lord's word "issued from His mouth," so too shall Israel issue forth from Babylon. On their return journey, all of nature shall rejoice with them and the desert shall bloom. For similar imagery, see Isa 41:18-19; 43:19-20; 44:23; 49:9-11, 13.

[12] *You shall indeed leave in joy* — The כי is emphatic: You shall depart from Babylon joyously, not in panicky haste as you did from Egypt (Exod 12:11, 33; Deut 16:3); see Isa 52:12: "For you will not depart in haste (בחִפזון)." For God's command to depart from Babylonia, see 48:20; 52:11. Note the repetition of the verb יצא found in the previous verse.

And be led forth safely — You shall be guided with all necessary precaution and you shall be safeguarded from the dangers of the road (cf. 41:3: "He [Cyrus] goes on safely [שלום]"). For the use of the verb יבל ("to be led") in a similar context, see Jer 31:9: "And with compassion will I lead them (אוביל͏ֵם)." But whereas Jeremiah says in that same verse: "they shall come weeping," Deutero-Isaiah proclaims that "they shall leave in joy" and security. The same idiom occurs in Akkadian as well: *šalmiš wabālu* ("to lead in safety"; *CAD* Š/1:255). 1QIsa[a] תלכו ("you shall walk"; cf. Peshitta *t'zlwn*), instead of MT תובלון, was likely influenced by the preceding verb, תצאו. For the same Akkadian expression cited above, but with the verb *alāku*, see also *CAD* Š/1:255.

Before you, mountains and hills shall shout aloud — For the participation of the mountains and hills in the joy of Israel's redemption, see Isa 44:23: "Shout, O heavens, for the Lord has acted! Shout aloud, O depths of the earth! Shout for joy, O mountains, O forests with all your trees! For the Lord has redeemed Jacob, has glorified Himself through Israel"; 49:13: "Shout, O heavens, and rejoice, O earth! Break into shouting, O hills! For the Lord has comforted

His people, and has taken back His afflicted ones in love." For the image of the hills and valleys rejoicing in the exodus of the Israelites from Egypt, see Ps 114:4: "Mountains skipped like rams, hills like sheep."

And all the trees of the field shall clap their hands — when the redeemed come forth. For the image of nature applauding, see Ps 98:8: "Let the rivers clap their hands (ימחֲאו כף), the mountains sing joyously together." It is possible that כף in this arboreal context may also allude to "branches" (probably palm branches), as in Lev 23:40: "Branches (כַּפֹּת) of palm trees"; Job 15:32: "His boughs (כִּפָּתוֹ) never having flourished"; and cf. the expression כִּפָּה ואגמון ("palm branch and reed"; Isa 9:13; 19:15). (This is also one of the meanings of the Akkadian cognate *kappu* [*CAD* K:187].) It is apparent, therefore, that the image the prophet wishes to convey is of a tree swaying its branches in applause. The root מחא ("to clap") literally means "to strike," as do its cognates in Akkadian *(maḫāṣu)*, Ugaritic *(mḫṣ)*, and Aramaic (מחא). For the expression עצי השדה, see Ezek 17:24; 31:4, 5; Joel 1:12, 19.

[13] The metamorphosis of the desert into a blooming garden shall vouchsafe that the miracle of the return shall be remembered forevermore. For the briars and thistles that blanketed the land of Israel in the days of destruction and desolation, see Isa 5:6; 7:23-25; 32:13; and cf. Gen 3:18.

Instead of the briar, a cypress shall grow — Instead of thorn thickets, stately cypresses shall flourish (see Isa 41:19). For the verb עלי ("to grow"), see 53:2; and in a "prickly" context cf. 5:6: "And it shall be overgrown (ועלה) with briars and thistles"; 34:13: "Thorns shall grow up (ועלתה) in its palaces, nettles and briars in its strongholds." This specific thorn, נעצוץ, appears only once more, in 7:19. For תחת ("instead of"), see 60:15, 17; 61:3, 7.

And instead of the nettle, a myrtle shall grow — In place of the thorny nettle bush (סִרפד is a hapax legomenon) a myrtle, renowned for its exquisite fragrance, shall burst forth. For the two trees, ברוש (preceding colon) and הדס ("myrtle"), mentioned together, see 41:19: "I will plant cedars in the wilderness, acacias and myrtles and oleasters. I will set cypresses in the desert, box trees and elms as well." The Qere ותחת is supported by Symmachus, LXX, Vulgate, Targum, and both 1QIsa[a] and 1QIsa[b].

These shall stand as a monument to the Lord — In all likelihood this phrase is polysemous. On the one hand, שֵׁם denotes "fame," as in Jer 33:9, i.e., all this will ensure great fame for the Lord. On the other, it can also be interpreted as a "testimonial," i.e., the new verdant blossoming state of the wilderness shall constitute a monument to the Lord commemorating the nation's redemption. For שֵׁם, "victory stela," see 2 Sam 8:13: "David erected a stela (שם) when he returned from defeating Edom in the Valley of Salt"; and for שם, "memorial," see the commentary to 56:5. In 1QIsa[a] the words לשם and לאות are found in the reverse order. Perhaps the expression שם עולם ("an everlasting name," 56:5) influenced this switching of the nouns. Another possible reason is the appearance of שם in conjunction with the verb כרת ("to be cut off") in a number of places throughout Scripture (see Ruth 4:10 and the verses cited in the next paragraph), but not once in the same context with אות. For similar reversals of the sequence of nouns in 1QIsa[a], see 49:25; 52:7.

As an everlasting memorial that shall not perish — And this verdant desert shall be an everlasting monument that shall be imperishable; cf. 48:19: "Its name (שמו) shall never be cut off (יִכָּרֵת) or obliterated from before Me"; 56:5: "I will give them an everlasting name (שם עולם) that shall not perish (יִכָּרֵת)." For אות ("memorial"), see Josh 4:6: "This [the twelve stones that the Israelites carried as they crossed the Jordan] shall serve as a memorial (אות) among you"; see also v. 7. Compare also Isa 19:19-20: "In that day there shall be an altar to the Lord inside the land of Egypt and a pillar to the Lord at its border. They shall serve as a memorial (אות) and reminder of the Lord of Hosts in the land of Egypt." In the same way that the ancient Near Eastern monarchs warned potential saboteurs from harming their monuments, so too God promises that this desert memorial shall be preserved as a national garden for all of eternity. Note also the possible bivalence: The physical elements of the monument shall also not perish, i.e., the trees and the plants shall not be "cut down" (כרת). For the expression לאות עולם, see Exod 31:17 regarding the Sabbath.

Chapter 56

This chapter consists of two literary units: vv. 1-8 and 9-12. In the first pericope Israel, the foreigners who have "attached themselves to the Lord," and the faithful eunuchs are promised that the Lord's salvation is imminent on condition that they abide by the Lord's commandments. For the first time in Deutero-Isaiah's prophecies, salvation is made conditional upon acting justly toward one's fellows ("Observe what is right and do justice") and observing divine precepts ("Who keeps the Sabbath and does not profane it"). For another example of divine salvation that is conditional upon the observance of the Sabbath, see 58:13-14. Sabbath observance emerged as a cardinal component in the life of Israel during the Babylonian exile and the beginning of the Second Temple period since, being independent of any geographical locus, it was possible to observe the Sabbath in exile even after the destruction of the Temple. For emphasis on Sabbath observance during this period, see also Jer 17:19-27; Ezek 20:12-24; 22:8, 26; 23:38; 44:24; 45:17; 46:1, 3, 4, 12; Neh 9:14; 10:32-34; 13:15-22. (For the importance and the spread of Sabbath observance in later periods, see Josephus, *Against Apion* 2.282, trans. H. St. J. Thackeray, LCL [1926; repr. Cambridge, 1961], 1:405-7: "There is not one Greek or barbarian city, nor is there any nation among whom our custom of refraining from work on the seventh day has not spread.") An extraordinary prophecy regarding universal monotheism also appears in this pericope: "For My house shall be called a house of prayer for all peoples" (v. 7). For other prophecies emphasizing this universal theme, see 44:5: "One shall say, 'I am the Lord's.' Another shall use the name of 'Jacob,' and yet another shall mark his arm 'of the Lord' and adopt the name of 'Israel'"; 45:14: "They [the nations] shall bow low to you and reverently address you: 'Only among you is God. There is no other god at all!'"; 45:23: "To Me every knee shall bend, every tongue swear loyalty." (See the introduction, §6.)

In the prophet's address to "the foreigners who have attached themselves to the Lord" (v. 6), he refers to a new socioreligious phenomenon that emerged in the Babylonian-Persian period, that of groups made up of foreigners desiring to join the Israelite religious community. Cf. Isa 14:1 (a late verse): "And strangers shall join them (וְנִלְוָה) and shall cleave to the house of Jacob"; Zech 2:15: "In that day many nations will attach themselves (ונִלְוו) to the Lord and become His people"; Zech 8:23: "Thus said the Lord of Hosts: In those days ten men from nations of every tongue will take hold — they will take hold of every Jew by a corner of his cloak and say, 'Let us go with you, for we have heard that God is with you'"; Esth 9:27: "The Jews undertook and irrevocably obligated themselves, and their descendants, and all who joined (הַנִּלְוִים) them." A scathing polemic against the Judean isolationists reverberates in Deutero-Isaiah's words. This group, which had a considerable following, preached vigilantly against allowing foreigners to join Israel, let alone participate in Temple worship. A reflection of this exclusivist ethnocultic worldview is found in Zerubbabel's explicit remark against the participation of the "adversaries of Judah and Benjamin" in the rebuilding of the Jerusalem Temple: "It is not for you and us to build a house to our God, but we alone [i.e., the returning expatriates] will build it for the Lord God of Israel" (Ezra 4:3). These separatists went as far as extending the prohibition of Deut 23:4: "No Ammonite or Moabite shall be admitted into the congregation of the Lord. None of their descendants, even to the tenth generation, shall ever be admitted into the congregation of the Lord." They aimed to keep the race pure of outside influences and thus castigated those who intermarried; see Ezra 9:1-2: "The people of Israel and the priests and Levites have not kept themselves apart from the peoples of the land. . . . They have taken their daughters as wives for themselves and for their sons so that the holy seed has become intermingled with the peoples of the land"; Ezra 9:12: "Now then, do not give your daughters in marriage to their sons or let their daughters marry your sons. Never seek their well-being or advantage." Thus Ezra himself urges those who married the indigenous population to divorce their wives: "Separate yourselves from the peoples of the land and from the foreign women" (Ezra 10:11). Compare also Neh 9:2: "Those of the stock of Israel separated themselves from all foreigners"; Neh 13:3: "They separated all the alien admixture from Israel."

Deutero-Isaiah objected to this particularism and instead preached inclusion and integration of foreigners in the community: 56:8: "I will gather still more to those already gathered." He even advocates their participation in the cult, v. 7: "I will bring them to My sacred mount and let them rejoice in My house of prayer. Their burnt offerings and sacrifices shall be acceptable on My altar." Compare also 60:10: "Aliens shall rebuild your walls"; 61:5: "Strangers shall stand and pasture your flocks. Aliens shall be your plowmen and vine trimmers." Inclusion in the community, according to Deutero-Isaiah, is not determined merely by ethnicity, but also by willingness to observe God's commandments. For the first time in Israelite history the idea of religious conversion begins to emerge. The prophet takes matters even further and makes a bold and unprecedented promise to the new converts. He assures them that they shall be included in Temple service, as servants of the Lord: "As for the foreigners who attach themselves to the Lord, to minister (ולשרתו) to Him" (v. 6). The verb שרת ("to minister") is a cultic term denoting the performance of sacred duties in the Temple, previously out of bounds to anyone but the Levites; see Num 18:2; Deut 10:8; 18:7.

The prophet's diatribe against the isolationists' exclusionary policies — especially regarding participation in the Temple service — is further emphasized when compared, for example, with Ezek 44:6-9: "Thus said the Lord God: Too long, O Israel, have you committed all your abominations, admitting aliens, uncircumcised of spirit and uncircumcised of flesh, to be in My Sanctuary and profane My very Temple . . . but you have appointed them to discharge the duties of My Sanctuary for you. . . . Let no alien . . . enter My Sanctuary." According to Ezekiel, only priests, sons of Zadok, are permitted to discharge the holy duties. The Levites serve as aides, and non-Israelites are completely barred from the Temple. In contrast, according to Deutero-Isaiah these same non-Israelites will serve as priests: "And from them likewise I will take some to be Levitical priests, said the Lord" (Isa 66:21).

Deutero-Isaiah's polemic also relates to the status of eunuchs. In contrast with the exclusionary policy in Deut 23:2: "No one whose testes are crushed or whose member is cut off shall be admitted into the congregation of the Lord" (note that this injunction appears in the same unit as the prohibition against the inclusion of Moabites, Ammonites, and bastards in the Israelite congregation), as well as in Lev 21:21: "No man among the offspring of Aaron the priest who has a defect shall be qualified to offer the Lord's offering by fire," Deutero-Isaiah promises the eunuchs: "I will give them in My house and within My walls, a monument and a name" (v. 5). The prophet thus boldly revokes the pentateuchal injunction excluding these physically handicapped people from the congregation.

As indicated, there were two parties among the Judeans at that time. One, the "universalists," advocated inclusion of all who wished to worship the Lord. The other, the pietistic and exclusionary, advocated purity of stock. The latter worldview is apparent in the 1QIsa[a], which introduces a deliberate change into the text: The term לשרתו (v. 6), which denotes performing Temple duties — the prerogative of the Levites and no one else (Deut 17:12; 18:7; Jer 33:21-22; Ezek 40:46), is deleted from the text, and instead of the MT ולאהבה את שם ה׳ ("and to love the name of the Lord"), the Scroll has: ולברך את שם ה׳ ("and to bless the Lord's name"). Accordingly, foreigners are not permitted to minister to the

Lord. At the very most, they would be allowed to glorify His name. Since the Yahad sect of Qumran identified itself with the Zadokite priests, it comes as no surprise that they would not allow foreigners to participate in the Temple cult. Compare in particular 4Q174 *(Florilegium)* 1-2, I 3-4: "The sanctuary . . . is the house [= Temple] 'where there shall never more enter' . . . 'the Ammonite and the Moabite,' and 'bastard' and 'alien' and sojourner 'for ever'" (Allegro, DJD 5, 53-54). A similar attitude is evident in the LXX, which translates **לשרתו** by a Greek verb meaning "to serve" that is nowhere else used as a translation of the root **שׁרת**, referring to ritual service. (See M. Weinfeld, "The Universalist and Exclusionary Trends in the Period of the Return to Zion," *Tarbiz* 33 [1974]: 228-42 [Heb.]; M. Greenberg, "Is the Return of the Nations to the Lord in the End of Days Dependent on Israelite Mediation?" in M. Garsiel et al., eds., *Biblical and Exegetical Studies, 5: Tributes to Uriel Simon in Friendship and Esteem* [Ramat Gan, 2000], 93-102 [Heb.]).

The first pericope of this chapter and the preceding one share the following terms and phrases: **ברית עולם** (55:3) — **(ומחזיקים) בבריתי . . . (שם) עולם** (56:4, 5); **(קְרָאֻהוּ בהיותו) קרוב** (55:6) — **קרובה (ישועתי לבוא)** (56:1); **(עשה את) אשר חפצתי** (55:11) — **(בחרו) באשר חפצתי** (56:4); **בשמחה** (55:12) — **וְשִׂמַּחְתִּים** (56:7); **(והיה לה׳) לְשֵׁם (לאות) עולם לא יִכָּרֵת** (55:13) — **שֵׁם עולם (אתן לו אשר) לא יִכָּרֵת** (56:5); **לה׳ לשם** (55:13) — **שֵׁם ה׳** (56:6). Both this unit and chap. 55 end with the theme of the ingathering of nations (55:12-13; 56:8). This pericope also features a series of verbs emphasizing observation and action: **שִׁמְרוּ . . . וַעֲשׂוּ** (v. 1); **יעשה . . . שֹׁמֵר . . . וְשֹׁמֵר . . . מֵעֲשׂוֹת** (v. 2); **ישמרו** (v. 4); the expressions **החזיק ב-** (vv. 2, 4, 6) and **שֵׁם** (vv. 5 [twice], 6) are repeated three times each.

[1-2] A call to observe the Lord's commandments and act justly so as to hasten divine salvation. This call is addressed not only to Israel but to all people, as is evident by the choice of terms **בן אדם** and **אֱנוֹשׁ**. The two verses are framed by verbs calling for observation of the divine precepts: **שִׁמְרוּ . . . וַעֲשׂוּ** (v. 1); **וְשֹׁמֵר . . . מֵעֲשׂוֹת** (v. 2).

[1] Despite the common terminology between the second half of this verse and 46:13: "I am bringing My victory close. It shall not be far; and My triumph shall not be delayed," the context is different. The latter verse is directed to the "stubborn of heart who are far from victory" (46:12) but without a demand for better behavior, whereas here the prophet refers to the people's responsibility to act justly so as to expedite the arrival of the Lord's salvation.

Thus said the Lord: "Observe what is right and do what is just" — The pair **שִׁמְרוּ** and **וַעֲשׂוּ** indicate the strict observance of commandments; cf. Gen 18:19: "To keep faithfully the way of the Lord by doing (**ושמרו . . . לעשות**) what is just and right"; Deut 19:9: "If you faithfully observe (**תשמר . . . לַעֲשֹׂתָהּ**) all this instruction that I enjoin upon you this day"; Ezek 20:19: "Follow My laws and be careful to observe (שִׁמְרוּ וַעֲשׂוּ) My rules." The nation is thus commanded to adhere to the path of righteousness and rectitude (משפט . . . צדקה), a hendiadys denoting social justice, which is the collective responsibility of the entire nation. See Isa 58:2: "Like a nation that does what is right (צדקה), that has not abandoned the laws (משפט) of its God, they ask Me for righteous laws (משפטי צדק). They are eager for the nearness of God"; and cf. Amos 5:24: "But let justice (משפט) well up like water, righteousness (צדקה) like an unfailing stream"; Ps 106:3: "Happy are those who act justly (משפט), who do right (צדקה) at all times." Cf. also Gen 18:19; Ezek 18:5. For the sociojuristic significance of this concept and its Akkadian *(kittum u mīšarum)* and Phoenician (צדק ומשר) equivalents, see M. Weinfeld, *Social Justice in Ancient Israel and in the Ancient Near East* (Minneapolis, 1995).

"For soon My salvation shall come" — Keep these commandments because My salvation is imminent; cf. Isa 51:5: "My triumph is near. My salvation has gone forth." For the expression קרב לבוא, see Isa 13:22; Jer 48:16; Ezek 36:8.

"And My deliverance be revealed" — In contrast with צדקה in the first hemistich, which denotes acts of righteousness performed by human beings, here the subject of צדקה is the Lord and it is parallel to ישועתי, as in Isa 46:13: "I am bringing My victory close. It shall not be far, and My triumph shall not be delayed"; 51:6: "My victory shall stand forever. My triumph shall remain unbroken"; see also 51:8; 59:17. God's צדקה ("deliverance") is the reward for the people's צדקה ("just/upright conduct").

[2] *"Happy is the man who does this"* — "This" (זאת) refers to the precepts mentioned at the end of this verse.

"And the man who holds fast to it" — Synonymous with the above clause, "it" (בָּהּ) refers to the following injunctions. For the verbal expression החזיק ב-, "to hold fast to" (note its repetition in vv. 4, 6), as "adhering to a position," cf. Job 2:3: "He still holds fast (מחזיק ב-) to his integrity"; Job 27:6: "I hold fast to (ב . . . החזקתי) my righteousness and will not yield." The pair of synonyms בן אדם/אנוש refers to human beings in general, purposely excluding any defining characteristic of ethnicity. The prophet's message is thus universal; see Isa 51:12; Ps 8:5; 144:3.

"Who keeps the Sabbath and does not profane it" — The *mem* prefix of מֵחַלְּלוֹ indicates negation; cf. Isa 54:9: "As I swore that the waters of Noah never again would flood (מֵעֲבֹר) the earth, so I swear that I will not be angry (מִקְּצֹף) with you or rebuke you (וּמִגְּעָר)." For שבת as a masculine noun, see v. 6 here; 58:13. This refers to the cultic precept that they are to observe. For the expression שמר שבת, see Exod 31:16; Lev 19:30; 26:2; and for חלל שבת, see Ezek 20:13, 16, 24.

"And stays his hand from doing any evil" — and concomitantly refrains from (note the *mem* prefix again indicating negation, מֵעֲשׂוֹת) wronging his

neighbor. The expression מעשות רע is the opposite of וַעֲשׂוּ צדקה in v. 1. The expression וְשֹׁמֵר ידו, "to stay one's hand" (which appears only here), is the third repetition of this verb in the first two verses. The LXX, Vulgate, Peshitta, Targum (יְדוֹהִי), and 1QIsa[a] all read here ידיו (plural), in lieu of MT ידו. This refers to the socioethical precept that they are commanded to follow.

[3] For the new socioreligious phenomenon beginning in the Persian period regarding foreigners wishing to join the Israelite community, see the introduction to the chapter. This verse expresses the group's apprehension regarding possible exclusion from the community because of the prevailing separatist trends. The eunuchs were most likely Jews who were castrated while serving in the Babylonian and Persian courts; cf. Isaiah's admonishment (39:7 = 2 Kgs 20:18), following the initiation of ties between King Hezekiah and Merodach-baladan, king of Babylon: "And some of your sons, your own issue, whom you will have fathered, will be taken to serve as eunuchs in the palace of the king of Babylon." These eunuchs feared they would be excluded from the community because of their physical blemish (see above, in the introduction).

"Let not the foreigner who has attached himself to the Lord say" — The foreigners, wishing to become part of the community, should not say thus (see the following statement). (For בני נכר ["foreigners"], see Isa 60:10; 61:5; 62:8.) הַנִּלְוָה is in the past tense (although some prefer vocalizing as a participle, הַנִּלְוֶה), and the *heh* prefix serves as an introduction to a relative clause, as in 51:10: "It was You who dried up (המחרבת) the sea, the waters of the great deep . . . who made (השָּׂמָה) the abysses of the sea a road the redeemed might walk." The expression נלוה אל denotes attachment and allegiance; see Gen 29:34: "And she [Leah] declared, 'This time my husband will become attached to me (יִלָּוֶה אלי), for I have borne him three sons'" (cf. Jer 50:5; Zech 2:15); cf. also נלוה על (see v. 6; Isa 14:1; Esth 9:27; Dan 11:34; and 1QIsa[b] here).

"'The Lord will surely keep me apart from His people'" — The Lord will exclude me and prevent me from joining His people. Note the use of the third-person masculine pronominal suffix עמו ("His people") rather than עמי ("My people"), since this group was not native born. This distinction or separation is a term usually reserved for cultic contexts; cf. Lev 10:10: "For you must make a distinction (ולהבדיל) between the sacred and the profane"; Lev 11:47: "For making a distinction (להבדיל) between the clean and the unclean"; 1 Kgs 8:53: "For You, O Lord God, have set them apart (הבדלתָּם) for Yourself from all the peoples of the earth." The infinitive absolute הַבְדֵּל, followed by the finite verb יבדילני, is an emphatic construction. For the vocalization יַבְדִּילַנִי (with a *pataḥ* instead of a *ṣere*), cf. Gen 19:19: "Lest the disaster overtake me [תִּדְבָּקַנִי]"; Gen 29:32: "Now my husband will love me [יֶאֱהָבַנִי אישי]").

"And let not the eunuch say: 'I am a withered tree'" — The eunuch should not despair and say: "Since I am unable to procreate, I am like a barren tree

without fruit." Hebrew סריס is a loanword from the Akkadian expression *ša rēši* ("of the head"), which is the title of high-level functionaries in the royal court, some of whom, but not all, were castrated.

[4-5] The first part of the consolation is addressed to the eunuchs, who were mentioned last. They shall be permitted to join the congregation, and their name shall be perpetuated, by "a monument better than sons or daughters," on condition that they adhere to the Lord's commandments. The prophet thus overturns and abolishes the restrictions of Deut 23:2-9.

[4] *For thus said the Lord: "As for the eunuchs who keep My Sabbath"* — לסריסים = "regarding the eunuchs." For this use of the *lamed* prefix, see also Gen 20:13: "Say there regarding me (לי): 'He is my brother.'" They, as those referred to in v. 2, are commanded to observe the Sabbath; cf. Lev 19:3: "And keep My Sabbaths: I the Lord am your God." According to Ehrlich, however, the *lamed* prefix here indicates emphasis (*Mikrâ ki-Pheshuṭo,* 3:132). For an emphatic *lamed,* see Eccl 9:4. It also appears in Ugaritic (*HdO* 2:484-85), Akkadian (*CAD* L:225-26), and Arabic.

"Who have chosen what I desire" — For the opposite statement, see Isa 65:12: "And chose what I do not desire"; see also 66:4.

"And hold fast to My covenant" — and who adhere to My covenant. For the expression החזיק ב-, see v. 2. Note the possible double entendre. On the one hand, the prophet is referring to the general covenant between God and His people. On the other hand, the Sabbath specifically was called a covenant, as in Exod 31:16: "The Israelite people shall keep the Sabbath, observing the Sabbath throughout the ages as a covenant (ברית) for all time." Furthermore, "to hold fast to a covenant" is a legal expression, as is exemplified by the equivalent semantic expressions הגביר ברית (Dan 9:27); Aram. לְתַקָּפָה אֱסָר (Dan 6:8); Akk. *ṭuppam dunnunu* (*CAD* D:85); all of which denote the ratification and authentication of a contract. (See Paul, *Divrei Shalom,* 139-44, 189-90, 287-88.)

[5] Note the chiastic frame: The verse begins: "I will give them . . . a name" (ונתתי להם שֵׁם), and concludes: "An everlasting name I will give them (שֵׁם עולם אתן לו)."

"I will give them in My house and within My walls" — Note that the term "walls" is also found in connection with foreigners in Isa 60:10: "Aliens shall rebuild your walls."

"A monument and a name" — The two substantives joined together by a *waw* compose a hendiadys, denoting a memorial, in this case in lieu of progeny. For יד as a "monument" erected for a man lacking male heirs, see 2 Sam 18:18: "Now Absalom, in his lifetime, had taken the pillar which is in the King's Valley and set it up for himself, for he said, 'I have no son to keep my name alive.' He had named the pillar after himself, and it has been called Absalom's Monument

(יד) to this day." For יד as a victory monument, see 1 Chr 18:3: "David defeated Hadadezer, king of Zobah-hamath, who was on his way to set up his victory monument (ידו) at the Euphrates River" (cf. the parallel variant in 2 Sam 8:3). שֵׁם too may refer to a victory stela, as in 2 Sam 8:13: "David built a monument (שֵׁם) when he returned from defeating Edom in the Valley of Salt, 18,000 in all"; and cf. Isa 55:13: "These shall stand as a testimony (שֵׁם) to the Lord, as an everlasting sign that shall not perish," where שֵׁם ("testimony") is parallel to אות ("sign"). Moreover, this pair (יד ושֵׁם) may very likely have been chosen for the multiple meanings of each one of its individual components. The noun שֵׁם may be interpreted as "offspring," as in 66:22 "So shall your seed and your name [שִׁמכם = offspring] endure." Compare likewise the Akkadian cognate *šumu*, which also denotes "progeny" (*CAD* Š/3:295-96). And the term יד can serve as a euphemism for the phallus (see the comments to 57:8, and the Ugaritic cognate *yd;* note, in particular, the connection to the predicate יִכָּרֵת [lit. "to be cut off"] and to the addressees who are castrated). It may, moreover, refer to a "place," as in Num 2:17: "As they camp, so they shall march, each in its place (ידו), by their standards," as well as a "share, portion," as in "Benjamin's portion was five times (ידות) that of anyone else" (Gen 43:34); cf. 2 Sam 19:44; Dan 1:20; and the phrase שתי ידות ("a double portion") in Rabbinic Hebrew (*Tosefta Menaḥot* 9:10). Compare also the semantic equivalent in Akkadian, *qātu* (*CAD* Q:195-97), as well as the Ugaritic cognate *yd,* e.g., *šbʿ ydty,* "seven portions" (*CAT* 1.5.I:20-21). For the manifold interpretations of this expression, see S. Talmon, "*Yād Wāšēm:* An Idiomatic Phrase in Biblical Literature and Its Variations," *HS* 25 (1984): 8-17; S. Japhet, "יד ושם (Isa 56:5): A Different Proposal," *Maarav* 8 (1992): 68-80; D. W. van Winkle, "The Meaning of *yad washem* in Isaiah LVI 5," *VT* 47 (1997): 378-85; M. Kister, "Some Blessing and Curse Formulae in the Bible, Northwest Semitic Inscriptions, Post-Biblical Literature and Late Antiquity," in M. F. J. Baasten and W. Th. van Peursen, eds., *Hamlet on a Hill: Semitic and Greek Studies Presented to Professor T. Muraoka on the Occasion of His Sixty-fifth Birthday* (Dudley, Mass., 2003), 314-17.

"Better than sons or daughters" — This commemoration shall be superior to offspring.

"I will give them an everlasting name that shall not perish" — Thus the memory and name of the eunuch shall be remembered forevermore; cf. Isa 55:13: "These shall stand as a testimony to the Lord, as an everlasting sign that shall not perish (לא יִכָּרֵת)." For the endurance and perpetuity of one's offspring, see 48:19: "Your offspring shall be as many as the sand, their issue as many as its grains. Their name shall never be cut off (לא יִכָּרֵת) or obliterated from before Me"; cf. 14:22. (For the contrary statement, see Josh 7:9: "And wipe out our very name from the earth.") Note the possible wordplay: The eunuch, who is also referred to as one "who is cut off" (כרות) and is forbidden entry into the Temple

(see Lev 22:24: "You shall not offer to the Lord anything with its testes bruised or crushed or torn or cut [כָּרוּת]"; Deut 23:2: "No one whose testes are crushed or whose member is cut off [כָּרוּת] shall be admitted into the congregation of the Lord"), is promised "an everlasting name that shall not be cut off (לֹא יִכָּרֵת)." The LXX, Vulgate, Peshitta, Targum (לְהוֹן), and 1QIsa[a] (להמה) all have a third-person plural, in accord with להם at the beginning of the verse, instead of the MT's singular לו. Compare Eliezer of Beaugency's comment on this verse: "I bear witness that in all the books of our kingdom, אתן לו is written as the Ketib, whereas אתן להם is the Qere. ([The reading] לו in any case would refer to each one individually." So too Kimchi: "לו is written despite להם above, and [the singular] is employed since [the address] is to each one of the eunuchs individually.") It is possible, moreover, that לו is employed here since it rhymes with the negative לא that immediately follows. For the Akkadian interdialectal equivalent of שם עולם ("an everlasting name"), *šumu dārû,* see *CAD* D:116. For the connection between observing (or defiling) the Sabbath and the punishment of כָּרֵת ("to be cut off"), see Exod 31:14.

[6] The prophet now returns to the first of those addressed above, the foreigners, and promises them that they shall minister to the Lord in His Temple, which was until the time of its destruction under the sole jurisdiction of the Levites: "You shall also associate with yourself your kinsmen the tribe of Levi, your ancestral tribe, to be attached to you and to minister to you" (Num 18:2; see also Deut 10:8; 18:7; Jer 33:21-22; Ezek 40:46) — thereby further exacerbating the polemic raging between the isolationists and the universalists (see the introduction to this chapter).

"As for the foreigners who attach themselves to the Lord to minister to Him" — in the Temple. For the verb שרת denoting Temple service, see Exod 29:30: "He among his sons who becomes priest in his stead, who enters the tent of meeting to officiate (לשרת) within the sanctuary, shall wear them [the sacral vestments] seven days"; and Isa 61:6: "While you shall be called 'Priests of the Lord' and termed 'Ministers (משרתי) of our God.'" For foreigners in the capacity of Levitical priests, see 66:21. For the conjunction of the verbs לוי and שרת in tandem, see Num 18:2: "You shall also associate with yourself your kinsmen the tribe of Levi, your ancestral tribe, to be attached (וְיִלָּווּ) to you and to minister to you (וִישָׁרְתוּךָ)." For בני נכר ("foreigners"), see also Isa 60:10; 61:5; 62:8.

"And to love the name of the Lord, to be His servants" — לאהבה is a feminine form of the infinitive construct (cf. similarly לְיִרְאָה). The motif of love and worship of God also appears in Deut 10:12: "And now, O Israel, what does the Lord your God demand of you? Only this: To revere the Lord your God, to walk only in His paths, to love (לאהבה) Him and to serve (ולעבד) the Lord your God with all your heart and soul"; see also Deut 11:13. For the expression שם ה׳, instead of ה׳ alone, see Isa 48:1; 50:10; 59:9; 60:9; and for the expression

אהבי שמו/שמך, see Ps 5:12; 69:37; 119:132. For the joint appearance of the roots שרת ("to minister") and עבד ("to serve"), see Num 3:31: "And the sacred vessels that were used (ישרתו) with them, and the screen — all the service (עֲבֹדתו) connected with these"; Num 16:9: "To perform the duties (לַעֲבֹד את עֲבֹדת) of the Lord's Tabernacle and to minister to the community and serve them (לשרתם)."

"All who keep the Sabbath and do not profane it" — See v. 2 regarding the covenant between Israel and God and the observance of the Sabbath.

"And who hold fast to My covenant" — See v. 4 regarding the castrated. 1QIsa[a] offers a variant reading of this verse: ובני הנכר הנלויים אל ה׳ להיות לו לעבדים ולברך את שם ה׳ ושומרים את השבת מחללה ומחזיקים בבריתי ("As for the foreigners who attached themselves to the Lord to be His servants, to praise the Lord's name, and who keep the Sabbath and do not profane it, and who hold fast to My covenant"). For the reason that the scribe omitted לשרתו, see the introduction to this chapter. He also altered the phrase "to love the name of the Lord" to "to praise the Lord's name." Perhaps the relative frequency of the latter expression, which appears (with some variation) ten times in the Bible (e.g., Ps 113:2; Job 1:21; Neh 9:5), as opposed to the former expression אהב + שם, which appears only twice more (Ps 5:12; 69:37), was the reason for the alteration.

[7] The personal tone is sounded here, as in the previous verse ("My covenant"), by a fourfold repetition of the first-person pronominal suffix: "My sacred mount," "My House of prayer" (twice), "My altar." In outright defiance of the isolationists who were against the inclusion of foreigners in the Temple service, the prophet reaches a new crescendo in his advocacy of universal monotheism: "For My House shall be called a house of prayer for all peoples." For the idea that the Temple is the locus of universal prayer (Israelites and foreigners alike), see 1 Kgs 8:27-53.

"I will bring them to My sacred mount" — Those who observe My commandments shall be brought to My sacred mount to serve there; cf. Isa 27:13: "They shall come and worship the Lord on the holy mount (בהר הקֹדש), in Jerusalem"; see also 57:13; 65:11; 66:20.

"And I will give them joy in My house of prayer" — And they shall celebrate in My Temple, which is "My house of prayer" (בית תְּפִלָּתִי), a hapax legomenon.

"Their burnt offerings and sacrifices shall be acceptable on My altar" — 1QIsa[a] adds the verb יעלו ("shall be offered"). Compare also the Targum, יִתַּסְקוּן; and Isa 60:7: "They shall be acceptable offerings on My altar," where the verb יעלו appears. The expression לעלות ל/על רצון denotes the desirability of such offerings before the Lord.

"For My House shall be called a House of prayer for all peoples" — For the

Temple as a universal cultic center for foreigners, see 1 Kgs 8:41-43: "When he [the foreigner] comes to pray toward this house, hear in Your heavenly abode and grant all that the foreigner asks You for. Thus all the peoples of the earth will know Your name and revere You, as does Your people Israel. And they will recognize that Your name is attached to this House that I have built."

[8] The root קבץ ("to gather") is reiterated here three times: not only shall the Lord gather His dispersed flock (see 43:5; 49:18; 54:7; 60:4), but He shall also gather all the nations of the world and bring them to Jerusalem — yet another revolutionary idea advocated by Deutero-Isaiah. (For the Akkadian semantic equivalent *puḫḫuru* ["to gather"], which is also said in connection with dispersed peoples, see *CAD* P:30.)

Thus declares the Lord God, who gathers the dispersed of Israel — the conclusion of the prophecy: the Lord proclaims that He will assemble the Israelite Diaspora and bring them back to their ancestral homeland. For the expression קבץ נִדָּחִים, see Deut 30:4: "Even if your dispersed (נִדָּחֲךָ) are at the ends of the world, from there the Lord your God will gather you (יְקַבֶּצְךָ), from there He will fetch you"; Isa 11:12: "He will assemble the dispersed (נדחי) of Israel and gather (יקבץ) the scattered of Judah from the four corners of the earth."

"I will gather still more to those already gathered" — In addition to the Israelite Diaspora, the Lord will assemble an additional group, the foreigners (Luzzatto; see also Ibn Ezra; Ehrlich, *Mikrâ ki-Pheshuṭo,* 3:132). For the expression נקבץ על, see 2 Chr 13:7.

[56:9–57:2] The second pericope extends beyond the present chapter division until 57:2; or according to some, even until 57:13 (Luzzatto; Ehrlich, *Mikrâ ki-Pheshuṭo,* 3:133). The section begins with an allegory: An abandoned herd is overwhelmed by predators since its shepherds and keepers (whose task it is to keep watch) are blind and immersed in their own sybaritic pleasures, and even the sheepdogs, who are responsible for the welfare of the herd, are mute and unable to bark their warning. Of course, the shepherds and their dogs represent the nation's leaders (be they political and/or religious), who are indifferent to the people's fate. And, as is often the case when there is no worthy leader at the helm, the nation is vulnerable to attacks. One of the key words in this unit is כל, which links this unit with the former one (vv. 6, 7, 9 [twice], 10 [twice], 11). Other terms that appear more than once in this unit are חַיְתוֹ (v. 9), כְּלבים (vv. 10, 11), and the expression לא ידעו (vv. 10, 11 [twice]).

[9] A call to Israel's enemies (depicted as wild beasts) to devour the hapless nation, portrayed as sheep. The verse was influenced by Jeremiah's similar call: "Go, gather all the wild beasts, bring them to devour!" (12:9); and cf. also Jer 12:10: "Many shepherds have destroyed my vineyard," comparable to the shepherds of v. 11 here. Compare other similar expressions in the subsequent verses of Jeremiah: מִקָּצֵהוּ (v. 11) — מקצה (הארץ ועד) קצה (הארץ) (Jer 12:12);

ואין איש שם על לב (57:1) — כי אין איש שם על לב (Jer 12:11); שלום (57:2) — אין שלום (Jer 12:12). (See the introduction, §15.) Compare also Ezek 39:17: "Say . . . and to all the wild beasts . . . 'Assemble! Come and gather! . . . and eat flesh!'"; 34:8; 39:4. For similar threats appended to national treaties in the ancient Near East, compare the Aramaic Sefire pact: "May the gods send every sort of devourer against Arpad and against its people! [May the mo]uth of a snake [eat], the mouth of a bear, the mouth of a panther! And may a moth and a louse. . . !" (I.A.30-32; Fitzmyer, *Aramaic Inscriptions of Sefîre,* 14-15). See also the treaty between the Assyrian king Esarhaddon and his vassals: "May dogs and pigs eat your flesh! . . . May dogs and pigs drag your carcasses throughout the squares of Ashur! . . . May your burial place be in the bellies of dogs and pigs!" (D. J. Wiseman, *The Vassal-Treaties of Esarhaddon* [London, 1958], 63-64, 65-66, lines 451, 483-84); see also Deut 28:26.

All you wild beasts of the plain, come and devour — Carnivorous predators are commanded to consume the hapless herd of sheep. The expression חַיְתוֹ שָׂדָי (see also Ps 104:11) is a poetic archaism and preserves the original case ending (see GKC §90k). אֵתָיוּ is the second-person masculine plural imperative of the Aramaic verb אתי ("to come"); see v. 12 here; 21:12: "Come (אֵתָיוּ) back again!" For other instances of this verb, see 41:5: "They draw near and come (וַיֶּאֱתָיוּן)"; 41:25: "I have roused him from the north, and he has come (וַיַּאת)." My translation does not follow the Masoretic parsing of the verse, which places a major pause under שָׂדָי.

All you beasts of the forest! — The two verbs in the former colon, "come and devour," apply here as well. As above, the poetic expression חַיְתוֹ ביער (see too Ps 50:10; 104:20) preserves the archaic case ending. Here, however, the preposition *beth* interrupts the two elements of the construction, as in 2 Sam 1:21: הָרֵי בַגִּלְבֹּעַ; Isa 28:9: גמולי מֵחלב עתיקי מִשָּׁדָיִם. It is possible, however, that this repetitive phrase is simply a textual variant doublet.

[10] A scathing rebuke against the watchmen's obtuseness.

The watchmen are blind, all of them — All of Israel's guardians, responsible for perceiving any threats (wild beasts), are blind. For the negligent "watchman" (צוֹפֶה; a term for a prophet as well; see 52:8; Jer 6:17; Ezek 3:17; 33:7), see Ezek 33:6: "But if the watchman sees the sword advancing and does not blow the horn, so that the people are not warned, and the sword comes and destroys one of them, that person was destroyed for his own sins. However, I will demand a reckoning for his blood from the watchman." 1QIsa[a] reads צופיו in the plural, in accordance with the Qere. (For the Ugaritic cognate *ṣp* ("to look, glance"), see *CAT* 1.14.III:45; and for Akk. *ṣubbû (ṣuppû),* "to look from afar," see *CAD* Ṣ:226.) For the motif of blindness, see Isa 42:7, 16, 18, 19; 43:8; 59:10.

They are unaware — They are totally incognizant of the impending danger. For the expression לא ידע ("to be unaware, not to realize"), see Hos 7:9.

They are all dumb dogs — For sheepdogs, see Job 30:1. For the motif of deafness, see Isa 42:18, 19; 43:8.

That cannot bark — They cannot bay their warning to the sheep and the shepherds. This hemistich forms a negative parallelism with the prior one; cf. Amos 5:18: "It shall be darkness, not light." The hapax legomenon verb נבח ("to bark") appears in Rabbinic Hebrew, and it has an Akkadian cognate, *nabāḫu* (*CAD* N/1:8).

Stretched out they babble/drowse — The root הזי appears only here and its meaning is debated. There are those who connect it to Syr. *hdy* and Arab. *hadā*ʾ, which denotes babbling or mumbling unintelligibly. Ibn Balaam (ed. Goshen-Gottstein, 220) comments: "In Arabic הזהז is the sound a dog makes, lower in volume, however, than a normal bark." Others explain that it refers to somnolence (Targum נָיְמִין; Dunash ben Labrat, quoted by Rashi, Ibn Balaam [in his second comment]; Ibn Ganaḥ, *Sefer ha-Shorashim,* 118; Ibn Ezra; Kimchi). According to this explanation, the hemistich is parallel to the following one: "They love to drowse." 1QIsa[a], however, has המה חוזים, "they are watchmen" (cf. Symmachus, Vulgate, Peshitta [*ḥzyn*], and many medieval MT manuscripts), which would then be parallel to the first hemistich.

They love to drowse — Those responsible for Israel's safety are asleep on the job, whereas: "See, the guardian of Israel neither slumbers nor sleeps!" (Ps 121:4). For a prepositional particle interrupting a construct (אֹהֲבֵי לנום), see above.

[11] *And the dogs have a lusty appetite* — These so-called dumb dogs are also possessed of a voracious appetite. For נפש ("appetite"), see Prov 23:1-2: "When you sit down to dine with a ruler, . . . thrust a knife into your gullet if you have a large appetite (נפש)!"

They never know satiety — They are never satisfied with what they have; they always want more. For the expression, see also Isa 55:2.

And as for the shepherds, they know not what it is to give heed — The nation's leaders are heedless, similar to v. 10: "The watchmen . . . are unaware." Read והמה הרעים, with 1QIsa[a]; the initial *heh* of הרֹעים was omitted in the MT as the result of haplography. For רֹעִים (lit. "shepherds") as a reference to national leaders, see Jer 2:8; 10:21; 22:22; 23:1-4; Ezek 34:1-10. Symmachus, LXX, Peshitta, and Targum (מַבְאֲשִׁין) read רָעִים ("the evil ones"), instead of MT רֹעִים. This is the third time לא ידעו appears in vv. 10-11.

Everyone has turned his own way — "They all look each after their own affairs, and neglect their shepherds" (Yellin, *Ḥiqrei Miqra,* 78); cf. 53:6: "Each going his own way (איש לדרכו פנו)."

Every last one seeks his own advantage — Each and every one of them is concerned solely with his own profits and proceeds while ignoring the common good. The term מִקָּצֵהוּ is an ellipsis for the expression מקצהו עד קצהו

("from one end to the other," "each and every one"); cf. Gen 19:4: "The men of Sodom, young and old — all the people to the last man (מִקָּצֶה) — surrounded the house" (Yellin, *Ḥikrei Miqra,* 78; see also Rashi; Ehrlich, *Mikrâ ki-Pheshuṭo,* 3:134). For similar expressions, see Jer 51:31; Ezek 25:9.

[12] An excerpt from a ribald party song, which begins with the same rare imperative, אֵתָיוּ ("Come!"), as in v. 9. Instead of governing the people, the politicos invite their compatriots to imbibe with them, and the next day they promise more of the same, if not better. For the boastful claims of drunkards, see Isa 22:13.

"Come!" — Invitation follows invitation: in v. 9 the wild beasts of the field were summoned to attack a hapless herd, which was abandoned by its absent shepherds. Here the leaders of the nation invite others to participate in their drunken celebration.

"I will fetch some wine, and let us swill liquor" — Instead of MT's singular אקחה, Symmachus, some versions of the LXX, Vulgate, Peshitta, Targum (נִסְבֵּי), and 1QIsa[a] have the plural ונקח, which agrees with the following verb, נסבאה. The elongated future form of both verbs refers to invitation and inducement. The verb סבא denotes the swilling of strong drink until the onset of intoxication; cf. Prov 23:20: "Do not be of those who guzzle (סֹבְאֵי) wine." For the pair שֵׁכָר/יין ("wine/liquor"), see Isa 5:11: "Ah, those who chase liquor (שֵׁכָר) from early in the morning, and till late in the evening are inflamed by wine (יין)!"; 29:9: "They are drunk, but not from wine (מיין). They stagger, but not from liquor (שֵׁכָר)."

"And tomorrow will be just the same" — Tomorrow we shall continue our bacchanalia. 1QIsa[a] has היום ומחר ("today and tomorrow") instead of MT יום מחר; cf. Exod 19:10; 2 Sam 11:12; see also Gen 30:33; Prov 27:1; and note the appearance of the equivalent Canaanitism in the Amarna documents: *ūmi maḫari* (*CAD* M/1:50).

"Or even much grander!" — Tomorrow's earthly pleasures will be "on a grander scale than today's drink and delicacies" (Ibn Ezra). For the employment of יֶתֶר as an adverb, see Dan 8:9.

Chapter 57

Except for the first two verses (see below), the remainder of the chapter comprises two literary units: vv. 3-13 and 14-21. In the first, the prophet castigates foreign cultic practices connected with licentious behavior that reflects the situation in Jerusalem after the return from the Babylonian exile. For additional descriptions of foreign customs, see 65:3-4; 66:3, 17. The prophecy ends with a promise that those who trust in the Lord shall possess the land. (For the second unit, see below.) The chapter in its entirety is associatively linked to chap. 56 by common words and phrases, several of which are homonyms with entirely different meanings: **צדקתי** (56:1) — **צדקתך** (57:12); **להִגָּלוֹת** (56:1) — **גִּלִּית** (57:8); **יד** (56:5) — **יד** (57:8); **לא יִכָּרֵת** (56:5) — **וַתִּכְרָת** (57:8); **עולם** (56:5) — **ומעולם** (57:11; but see the commentary on that verse); **אל הר קדשי** (56:7) — **הר קדשי** (57:13); **אקבץ . . . מקבץ** (56:8) — **קִבּוּצַיִךְ** (57:13); **שֹׁכְבִים** (56:10) — **מִשְׁכְּבוֹתָם** (57:2), **משכבך** (57:7, 8); **לא ידעו הָבִין** (56:11) — **בְּאֵין מֵבִין** (57:1); **כֻּלָּם לדרכם פנו איש לְבִצְעוֹ** (56:11) — **בַּעֲוֹן בִּצְעוֹ . . . בדרך לבו** (57:17).

[1-2] The short pericope opening the chapter is best understood as an addendum to the previous chapter describing the death of the righteous and the indifference of the nation's leaders, who are immersed in their sybaritic lifestyle.

[1] The verse is chiastically framed by references to the "righteous man" (**הצדיק**) and the verb (**נאספ(ים**) ("perish[es]"), and also begins and concludes with the noun **הצדיק**, creating a literary *inclusio.*

The righteous man perishes — Cf. Mic 7:2: "The pious man (**חסיד**) has perished (**אבד**) from the earth. None upright are left among men."

And no one takes it to heart — and no one pays any heed to his demise. For the identical phraseology, see Jer 12:11. For the expression **שים על לב**, see v. 11; 42:25; 47:7; for the Akkadian equivalent, see 41:22.

Pious men are swept away — The dutiful and law-abiding people are rapidly dying out; cf. Mic 7:2 cited above; Ps 12:2: "Help, O Lord! For the faithful are no more." For the verb **אסף** (here in the *niphʿal*) as a euphemism for dying, see Isa 49:5; Gen 25:8: "And he was gathered (**וַיֵּאָסֶף**) to his kin"; 2 Kgs 22:20: "Assuredly, I will gather you (**אֹסִפְךָ**) to your fathers, and you will be gathered (**ונאספת**) to your tomb in peace." For the expression **אנשי חסד** ("pious men"), see Prov 11:17; Sir 1:13; 44:1; 4Q394 *(Miqṣat Maʿaśe Ha-Torah)*: "Remember David who was a man of piety (**איש חסדים**)" (E. Qimron and J. Strugnell, *Qumran Cave 4.V: Miqṣat Maʿaśe Ha-Torah,* DJD 10 [Oxford, 1994], 62, line 25, and note 3.5.2.9 on p. 91).

And no one gives a thought — There is not one who pays any attention to the tragedy occurring before their very eyes; cf. 56:11: "They are the shepherds who give no heed (**לא ידעו הָבִין**)." **בְּאֵין** is synonymous with **ואין** in the first stich. (In every other occurrence **באין** precedes a substantive, e.g., Prov 29:18: "For lack of vision (**באין חזון**) a people lose restraint.") This clause is syntactically connected to the next hemistich.

That because of evil the righteous are swept away — Because of the wickedness of the leaders, the righteous are perishing.

[2] *Yet he shall come to peace* — Yet the righteous man shall die in peace; cf. Gen 15:15: "You shall go to your fathers in peace (**תבוא בשלום**)"; Jer 34:5: "You will die a peaceful (**בשלום**) death." **שלום** fills an adverbial function here, as in Isa 41:3.

They shall have rest on their couches — The aforementioned pious men shall lie soundly in their graves; cf. Job 3:17: "There rest (**ינוחו**) those whose strength is spent"; Dan 12:13: "You shall rest (**תנוח**) and rise for your destiny." For **משכב** (lit. "bed, resting place") as a euphemism for the grave, see Ezek 32:25: "They made a bed (**משכב**) for her among the slain, with all her masses; their graves are round about her"; 2 Chr 16:14: "He was laid in his resting place (**במשכב**), which was filled with spices of all kinds." This too is its meaning in Phoenician. See Eshmunazor's curse: "They shall not have a resting place (**משכב**) with the Rephaim, and they shall not be buried in a grave" (*KAI* 14:8; cf. also lines 4, 5, 6, 7, 21); Shipitbaal's burial inscription: "I have made myself this grave (**המשכב**)" (*KAI* 9A:1); and an anonymous burial inscription: "In their peaceful graves (**משכב**) for eternity" (*KAI* 34:5; and see also 35:2). Compare also the Balaam inscription from Deir ʿAlla, second combination, line 11: "You shall lie down (**תשכב**) on your eternal bed (**משכבי**)" (Aḥituv, *Ha-Ketav veha-Miktav,* 400). The same phraseology appears in the *Copper Scroll* from Qumran (3Q15), 11:16: **בית המשכב** ("mausoleum") (M. Baillet et al., *'Les Petites Grottes' de Qumrân,* DJD 3 [Oxford, 1962], 297). For the verb **שכב** ("to lie down") as a euphemism for death, see Isa 14:18: "All the kings of the nations, every one, lay (**שכבו**) in honor, each in his tomb"; Job 14:12: "So man lies down (**שכב**), never to rise"; cf. also Isa 14:8; Job 3:13. For the Akkadian semantic cognate *nâlu* ("to lie down, lay in a grave, bury"), see, e.g., the Gilgamesh Epic X:74-75: "Will I not lie down as he did? Will I not rise again forevermore?"; for further examples, see *CAD* N/1:205-6. In Akkadian the substantive *majālu* ("bed," derived from *nâlu*) also denotes a burial place (*CAD* M/1:118-20).

Who walk straightforward — people who conduct themselves in a true and honest fashion. The word נְכֹחוֹ is derived from the abstract substantive נָכֹחַ, "straight, right"; cf. Amos 3:10: עֲשׂוֹת נְכֹחָה ("doing right"); Prov 8:9: "All is straightforward (נְכֹחִים) to him who understands." Compare 1QIsa[b] נכחה, corroborated by one medieval Hebrew manuscript. Saadyah Gaon (125), however, maintains that the correct vocalization should be נִכְחוֹ, from the substantive נֹכַח, meaning "in front of, facing," e.g., Exod 14:2: "You shall encamp facing it (נִכְחוֹ), by the sea." Compare also Luzzatto: "[The term] is analogous with Prov 4:25: ("Let your eyes look forward [לְנֹכַח]; your gaze be straight ahead") (and cf. also Ibn Ezra and Kimchi). The meaning remains the same, "straightforward."

[3-13] The prophet chastises the nation regarding their foreign cults, steeped in debauchery, which causes them to lose sight of the Lord. The pericope documents the legal proceedings against the people: v. 3: the nation is subpoenaed and brought to trial; vv. 4-11: the indictment, followed by a lurid account of lecherous cults and child sacrifice; vv. 12-13: the divine verdict is served. This trial scene is reminiscent of earlier prophecies, such as 41:1-4; 45:20-21. In these, however, the nations are summoned, whereas here the accused are Israel. This literary unit and vv. 1-2 share common phraseology: v. 1: ואין איש שם על לב — v. 11: לא שמת על לבך; v. 2: מִשְׁכּבותם — vv. 7, 8: מִשְׁכּבך. There are also a number of phrases and similes that are reminiscent of Jeremiah's chastisement in Jer 2:20-28:

Jeremiah 2	**Isaiah 57**
v. 20: כי על כל גבעה גְּבֹהָה	v. 7: על הר גָּבֹהַּ וְנִשָּׂא
v. 20: ותחת כל עץ רענן	v. 5: תחת כל עץ רענן
v. 20: זֹנָה	v. 3: ותזנה
v. 21: זֶרַע אמת	v. 3: זֶרַע מנאף
	v. 4: זֶרַע שקר
v. 23: דרכך . . . דרכיה	v. 10: דרכך
v. 24: ימצאונְהָ	v. 10: מצאת
v. 25: ותאמרי נואש	v. 10: לא אמרת נואש
vv. 27-28: ובעת רעתם יאמרו קומה והושיענו . . . יקומו אם יושיעוך	v. 13: בזעקך יצילך קִבוציך

(See the introduction, §15.)

[3] The prophet heaps vitriol on the nation and refers to them as the offspring of base lechery. For the connection between sorcery and harlotry, see

2 Kgs 9:22: "How can all be well as long as your mother Jezebel carries on her countless harlotries and sorceries?"; Nah 3:4: "Because of the countless harlotries of the harlot, the winsome mistress of sorceries"; Mal 3:5: "But I will step forward to contend against you . . . against those who practice sorceries, who commit adultery."

But as for you, come forward — a summons to trial; cf. Isa 41:1: "Let us come forward (נקרבה) together for trial."

You sons of a soothsayer — For the hapax legomenon עֹנְנָה ("soothsayer"), cf. the masculine מְעוֹנֵן in Deut 18:10, 14; 2 Kgs 21:6; Isa 2:6; Jer 27:9; Mic 5:11. There is no consensus regarding the exact derivation of the root ענן in this context.

You offspring of an adulterer and a harlot! — the offspring of the sinful union between an adulterer (מְנָאֵף — a *pi'el* stem indicating intensity and constancy) and a whore. For the verbal pair זני/נאף, see Hos 4:13: "That is why their daughters fornicate (תִּזְנֶינָה) and their daughters-in-law commit adultery (תְּנָאַפְנָה)." For other examples of the parallel synonyms זרע/בנים ("sons" in the prior stich, and "offspring"), see Isa 1:4; and in reverse, Ps 105:6. The parallelism also appears in Eshmunazor's Phoenician inscription: "Let him have no son or offspring" (*KAI* 14:8). Symmachus, LXX, Vulgate, and Peshitta all translate וְזֹנָה as a noun, rather than as a verb, as in MT ותזנה or 1QIsa[a] ותזנו.

[4] The prophet begins his accusation with an emphatic triad of queries, deriding the nation's lascivious behavior. Other trial scenes in his earlier prophecies also begin with an accusation phrased in the interrogative.

Of whom do you make sport? — Who is the object of your derision? The *hithpa'el* תתענגו denotes "laughing at the expense of another, who is the object of ridicule" (Ehrlich, *Mikrâ Ki-Pheshuṭô,* 3:134). For the expression התענג על in a positive sense, see Isa 58:14; Ps 37:4, 11.

At whom do you gloat — For the expression רחב פה, lit. "to open one's mouth," see 1 Sam 2:1: "I gloat (רחב פי) over my enemies"; Ps 35:21: "They gloat (וירחיבו פיהם) over me, saying, 'Aha, aha, we have seen it!'" The expression על מי is repeated here for emphasis.

And stick out your tongue? — Whom do you deride and insult? For the synonymous pair פה/לשון ("mouth/tongue"), see Exod 4:10; and for the analogous Ugaritic parallel *p/lšn,* see *CAT* 1.93:2.

You are indeed children of iniquity — הלוא serves to emphasize the denunciation: in truth you are children of sin. For the anomalous form יִלְדֵי, caused by attenuation, instead of the regular construct form, יַלְדֵי (Hos 1:2), see GKC §93m.

Offspring of treachery — "Children who mistakenly assume that their mother's husband sired them" (Luzzatto); note the opposite expression in Jer 2:21: "true offspring (זרע אמת)."

[5] *Inflaming yourselves among the terebinths, under every verdant tree* — Some commentators interpret the verb נֵחָמִים as a derivative of the root יחם, "breeding-heat" (a *niph'al* with an elided initial *yod*) (Yehudah ibn David Ḥayyuj, *Three Grammar Books* [Jerusalem 1968], 24, s.v. חם [Heb.]; Menaḥem Ben Saruq, *Sefer ha-Maḥberet,* 90, s.v. חם; Ibn Ganaḥ, *Sefer ha-Riqmah* [ed. Walensky, 188]; Ibn Ezra; Kimchi; Luzzatto), as in Gen 30:39: "The goats were in heat (וַיֵּחֱמוּ)"; Ps 51:7: "In sin my mother conceived me (יֶחֱמַתְנִי)." However, it is preferable to derive it from חמם, "to become warm, heated" (Ibn Ganaḥ, *Sefer ha-Shorashim,* 158), as in Hos 7:7: "They all get heated (יֵחַמּוּ) like an oven." (Cf. the Ugaritic etymological and semantic equivalent *ḥmm,* "to heat up": "As he kisses, there is conception. As he embraces, there is passion [*ḥmḥmt*]" [*CAT* 1.23:51, 56].) The prophet accuses the nation of excessive prurient behavior, of fornicating at every opportunity and in every place. For similar descriptions of all-pervasive venery, see Hos 4:13-14: "Under oaks, poplars, and terebinths whose shade is so pleasant. . . . That is why your daughters fornicate and your daughters-in-law commit adultery. . . . For they themselves turn aside with whores and sacrifice with prostitutes." For intercourse under verdant trees, see Jer 2:20: "Under every verdant tree you recline, whore"; cf. also Deut 12:2; Jer 3:6, 13. For the terebinth and other verdant trees in foreign rituals, see Ezek 6:13: "And you shall know that I am the Lord, when your slain lie among the fetishes round about their altars, on every high hill, on all the mountaintops, under every green tree, and under every leafy oak — wherever they presented pleasing odors to all their fetishes." Some, however, suggest that אֵלִים is the plural of אל ("god"), and interpret the verse as an admonishment against the nation's idolatry. For the worship of foreign cults "under verdant trees," see 1 Kgs 14:23; 2 Kgs 17:10; Jer 17:2. The grammatical construction ב . . . תחת ("among . . . under") is repeated in the following hemistich as well. In contrast with the above-quoted verses, which combine תחת כל עץ רענן with the expression על כל גבעה גְבֹהָה/רמה ("on all mountaintops"), the prophet divides the two here, with על הר גָּבֹהַּ ("on a lofty hill") appearing only in v. 7. One should note that the expression תחת כל עץ רענן ("under every verdant tree") in this context is a sign of Deuteronomistic influence. (See the introduction, §13.)

Slaughtering children in the wadis, among the clefts of the rocks — For the sacrifice of children, see Ezek 16:21 as well as 23:39: "By slaughtering (וּבְשַׁחֲטָם) their children to their fetishes." For ritualized child sacrifice in the valley of Ben-hinnom, see 2 Kgs 23:10; Jer 7:31; 32:35; and for the juxtaposition of lechery and the slaughter of offspring, see Ezek 16:20-22; 20:30-31; 23:37, 39ff.; Ps 106:37-39. This bloody ritual is performed in secret, "among the clefts of the rocks"; cf. Isa 2:21: "And they shall enter the clefts in the rocks (וּבִסְעִפֵי הסלעים) and the crevices in the cliffs, before the terror of the Lord and His dread majesty, when He comes forth to overawe the earth."

[6] The prophet delivers the rest of his rebuke against idolatry and foreign cult using second-person feminine forms.

With the smooth stones of the stream is your portion — a difficult clause. The expression חַלְּקֵי נחל refers to the smooth stones found in the environs of streams and rivers; see 1 Sam 17:40: "He picked a few smooth stones (חַלֻּקֵי) from the wadi." Thus the meaning would be: "There among the stones of the stream is your allotment and portion (חלקך)." (Note the wordplay on the homonymous [ה]נחל and חלק, as in Gen 31:14; Deut 12:12; 1 Kgs 12:16. Note also the repetition of the letters *ḥet* and *lamed* in the first three words: בְּחַלְּקֵי נַחַל חֶלְקֵךְ.) One should note the double entendre evident in the expression חלקך . . . ב, which, similar to its equivalent עם חלקך, denotes "making a common cause"; cf. Ps 50:18: "And throw in your lot (ועם . . . חלקך) with adulterers." Some commentators, on the other hand, derive the term חלק from the homonymous cognates Akk. *ḫalāqu* (*CAD* Ḫ:37) and Ugar. *ḫlq* (*HdO* 1:393-94), "to perish," and explain, "among the stones of the stream you shall perish." (See W. H. Irwin, "'The Smooth Stones of the Wady'? Isaiah 57, 6," *CBQ* 29 [1967]: 31-40; T. J. Lewis, *Cults of the Dead in Ancient Israel and Ugarit,* HSM 39 [Atlanta, 1989], 147-49.)

They, they are your allotment — The clause begins with an emphatic repetition of the pronoun הם. For the nominal pair גורל/חֵלֶק, see Isa 17:14: "Such is the lot (חלק) of our despoilers, the portion (וגורל) of them that plunder us"; Ps 16:5: "The Lord is my allotted portion (חלקי). You control my fate (גורלי)." Moreover, since גורל refers to "stones" that are cast to determine the fate of individuals or to make portentous decisions, as in Jonah 1:7: "They cast lots (גורלות) and the lot (הגורל) fell on Jonah," the word then would create yet another association with the polysemous expression בחלקי נחל in the preceding clause. Instead of the repetition of הם in the MT, 1QIsa[a] reads שמה המה, a variant also found in the Targum (אַף תַּמָּן), "there they are your lot."

Even to them you have poured out libations — You have even (גם) poured out to them your liquid offerings as part of their worship. For the pouring of libations to foreign idols, see Jer 7:18; 32:29. The expression שפך נֶסֶךְ is sui generis since the verb שפך usually appears in nonritual contexts. For similar usages of the adverb גם, see v. 7; Gen 20:4; Prov 17:26; Job 13:16.

Presented offerings — Compare also 66:3: "Who present an offering (מַעֲלֵה מִנְחָה) of the blood of swine." For the pair מנחה/נֶסֶך, see Joel 1:9: "Offering and libation have ceased from the house of the Lord"; cf. also Exod 29:40-41; Lev 23:13; Num 6:15; Joel 1:13.

Should I relent in the face of this? — Is it reasonable that in the face of such cultic iniquity I should yield and not pour out My wrath upon you? For the phrase העל אלה, see also Isa 64:11; Jer 9:8. Note the assonance created between the phrases אֶנָּחֵם . . . העל and the previous הֶעֱלִית מנחה and הַנֵּחָמִים בּאֵלִים.

Note also the repetition of the letters על, here and in vv. 4, 7, 8 (על, עלית, תעלי). For the expression נחם על, see Amos 7:3, 6.

[7-8] A description of the sexual rites (some of them difficult to comprehend) that are performed both in the public domain ("on a high and lofty hill") and behind closed doors ("behind the door and doorpost").

[7] *On a high and lofty hill you have set your couch* — These rites and rituals were performed not only under "verdant trees" but also on mountaintops, as in Jer 3:6: "Going to every high mountain and under every leafy tree, and whoring there." For hilltops and trees in a similar context, see Hos 4:13. For the parallel synonyms נִשָּׂא/גָּבֹהַּ ("high/lofty"), see Isa 30:25. The verb שַׂמְתְּ is repeated again in vv. 8 and 11, and the substantive משכב ("couch"), which is repeated twice more in v. 8, alludes to the lecherous acts taking place on these beds and contrasts with the couches of the righteous in v. 2. The Akkadian semantic equivalent of the Hebrew expression שים משכב is *majālam šakānu* (*CAD* M/1:118).

There too you have gone up to perform sacrifices — Even there on the high mountains you have offered your sacrifices. Hebrew גם שם denotes "in addition to," i.e., in addition to the oblations offered in the streambeds.

[8] *Behind the door and doorpost you have stationed your phallic images* — Your commitment to these rituals is public as well as private. Not only do you perform your sacrifices and lecherous rites on the high mountains and in the low wadis, but also behind closed doors. There are those who explain the term זִכְרוֹנֵךְ as a derivative of זֵכֶר or, in Luzzatto's words, "idols one crafts for commemorative purposes" (cf. also Kimchi). A more likely explanation, however, is that it is a sexual allusion, as in v. 7: "You have set your couch," referring to phallic symbols: "You have set your idols of the phallus [which, according to him, is] a reference to homosexual intercourse" (Saadyah, 126); cf. Ezek 16:17: צלמי זכר ("phallic images"). Compare also the Akkadian etymological and semantic cognates *zikartu,* "masculinity," and *zikūrtu,* "sexual potency" (*CAD* Z:110, 117). Rabbinic Hebrew and Aramaic refer to the phallus in similar terms, זַכְרוּת, e.g., *b. ʿAbod. Zar.* 44a, and זַכְרוּתָא, e.g., *y. ʿAbod. Zar.* II, 40d.

Abandoning Me, you have gone up/you have stripped and lain down — a puzzling clause. Both verbs, גלית and תעלי, may be understood in a number of different ways. According to the Masoretic vocalization, גִּלִּית (a *piʿel* stem) has a sexual meaning and denotes the "uncovering of nakedness" (see Lev 18:6, 17, 18, 19). Alternatively, one may vocalize the verb as a *qal,* גָּלִית, which would then indicate desertion, abandonment (cf. 1 Sam 4:21, 22: "The glory has departed [גלה] from Israel"). This vocalization is corroborated by Aquila, Symmachus, and Theodotion, and is found in some medieval MT manuscripts. The latter interpretation would conform with one of the meanings of the expression עלה מ-, "to leave, to depart" (Rashi; Luzzatto; Ehrlich, *Mikrâ ki-*

Pheshuṭo, 3:137), e.g., Gen 17:22: "God departed from (ויעל מ-) Abraham"; Num 16:24: "Depart from (הֵעָלוּ מ-) the abodes of Korah, Dathan, and Abiram." Others maintain that the second verb, וַתַּעֲלִי, should be appended to the next clause, הרחבת מִשכבך ("You have gone up on the couch you have made so wide"), and should be understood as an allusion to the sexual act, as in Gen 49:4: "You have mounted (עלית) your father's bed." For the sexual connotations of the verb עלי, cf. also Gen 31:10, 12, and its etymological and semantic cognates Akk. *elû* (*CAD* E:119) and Ugar. *'ly* (*CAT* 1.5.V:21). (See Paul, *Divrei Shalom,* 125-26.) In contrast with the above suggestions, H. L. Ginsberg (oral communication) suggested emending the MT to כי אִתָּם גַּלְתְּ ותעלזי ("You have delighted and rejoiced with them").

On the couch you made so wide — You have broadened your bed so as to accommodate your many partners in sin. According to an alternative interpretation: "This so-called bed is not the bed itself, but rather it is a reference to sexual desire. . . . After you abandoned me, you were delighted and eager to welcome your lovers, because you wished to engage with them in sexual intercourse" (Ehrlich, *Mikrâ ki-Pheshuṭo,* 3:137); cf. v. 8: "You have loved bedding with them." For משכב as a reference to the act of intercourse, cf. also Lev 18:22; 20:13; Ezek 23:17. So too its Akkadian semantic equivalent, *majālu* (*CAD* M/1:119).

You have made a covenant with them — an indecipherable clause usually understood to mean, "You have made a covenant with some of them." For the verb כרת without its usual object ברית ("covenant"), cf. 1 Sam 11:2; 1 Kgs 8:9. The verb should be vocalized וַתִּכְרְתִּ (feminine), following the Vulgate, Peshitta, and Targum (וּגְזַרְתְּ), instead of the masculine form וַתִּכְרָת in the MT (see also 1QIsa[a] ותכרותי; but it is possible that this should be read ותכרותו). Since there is no other example of כרת מ-, however, some suggest reading ותכרי (from the root כרי), which denotes purchase or procurement, as in Deut 2:6: "Even the water you drink you shall procure from them (תִכרו מ-) for money." According to this suggestion, one would interpret the clause to mean "You have purchased (sexual favors) from among them."

You have loved bedding with them — Whether vocalized according to the MT, אָהַבְתְּ מִשְׁכָּבָם, or according to an alternate suggestion, אַהֲבַת מִשְׁכָּבִים, the intent is the same: You enjoy making love with them; cf. Ezek 23:17: למשכב דודים ("for lovemaking"). The substantive משכב appears here for the third time.

You have seen their genitalia/chosen lust — Some interpret יד as a euphemism for the phallus; see v. 10; Cant 5:4; 1QS 7:13-14 *(Rule of the Community)*: "And whoever takes his 'hand' (ידו) from under his clothes . . . causing his nakedness to be revealed" (*DSSSE* 1:86-87); and Ugaritic: "El's penis *(yd)* lengthens like the sea. Indeed, El's penis *(yd)* like the flood" (*CAT* 1.23:33-34). (See Paul, *Divrei Shalom,* 247-48 n. 32, 302-4.) Its Akkadian semantic cognate, *qātu* ("hand"), also denotes the male member, e.g., in the Gilgamesh Epic: "O my Ishullanu, let us taste your virility. Put forth your 'hand' and touch our [Ishtar] vulva!" (VI:68-69). According to this interpretation the phrase means: "You have seen/chosen their male members" (for the root חזי, "to choose," see Exod 18:21). Others suggest that יד should be understood as a derivative of ידד, which denotes "love," e.g., Isa 5:1: "Let me sing for my beloved (ידידי) a song of my lover about his vineyard." According to this explanation, אהבה and יד are parallel synonyms as in the Ugaritic Baal epic: "Perhaps the love *(yd)* of El, the king, has excited you, the love *(ahbt)* of the Bull has aroused you?" (*CAT* 1.4.IV:38-39). If so, the stich would mean: "You have chosen lust."

[9] The prophet goes on to describe in mocking terms the diplomatic activities of the nation.

You have traveled to the king with oil — a very difficult clause. The verb וַתָּשֻׁרִי has been interpreted in a variety of ways: (1) as a derivative of the root שׁוּר, which in Arabic *(sāra)* and in Rabbinic Hebrew can indicate travel (e.g., שַׁיָּרָה, "procession, convoy"), meaning: "You travel to the king with oils"; cf. Cant 4:8: "Trip down (תשורי) from Amana's peak" (Amana is a mountain in Lebanon) (Luzzatto); (2) as a denominative verb from the substantive תשורה (from the root שׁוּר, "to see"; see Num 23:9: "As I see them from the rocky heights, gaze on them [אֲשׁוּרֶנּוּ] from the hills"), which denotes a gift one gives to an illustrious personage as a prelude to an audience (see 1 Sam 9:7: "There is nothing we can bring to the man of God as a present, to gain an interview [תשורה]"), and the meaning would then be: "You sent the king oil in order to gain an audience with him" (Saadyah, 126; Ibn Ganaḥ, *Sefer ha-Shorashim,* 504; Rashi; Ibn Ezra). The verb, moreover, may be polysemous, indicating both travel and gift giving; cf. Hos 12:2: "They make a covenant with Assyria, and oil is carried to Egypt" (for a gift of oil [*šamnu*] to the Assyrian monarch as tribute, see *CAD* Š/1:328); (3) on the other hand, Symmachus and the Vulgate translate the clause: "You have adorned yourself to meet the king"; (4) and the LXX renders: "You have multiplied fine oils in order to greet the king." The last translation of the verb may be related to Akk. *šurrû,* "to provide plentifully" (*CAD* Š/2:131-32) and to Arab. *ṯarā(u);* (5) finally, some interpret the verb as being connected to Rabbinic Hebrew שרי and Aram. תרי, "to soak the body or the hair (vocalizing MT מֶלֶךְ as מַלֶּךְ/מִלֶּךְ, comparing Akk. *malû,* "unkempt hair" [*CAD* M/1:173-74]; see Cant 7:6), which may have been done in expensive oils. These explanations (all of which remain inconclusive) are also consistent with those who vocalize מֹלֶךְ ("Molech"), the name of a foreign deity, instead of מֶלֶךְ. (See G. C. Heider, *The Cult of Molek: A Reassessment,* JSOTSup 43 [Sheffield, 1985]; J. Day, *Molech: A God of Human Sacrifice in the Old Testament* [Cambridge, 1989].)

You have multiplied your perfumes — in order to stimulate desire (like a harlot and adulteress), or, alternatively, to send to the king as tribute (Kimchi). For "aromatics" *(riqqu)* dispatched to Assyrian and Babylonian monarchs as part of a tribute, see *CAD* R:370. For carefully prepared perfumes, cf. 1 Chr 9:30: "Some of the priests blended the compound of spices"; 2 Chr 16:14: "Spices of all kinds, expertly blended." For the connection between שמן ("oil") and רִקֻּחִים ("perfumes"), see Exod 30:25: "Make of this a sacred anointing oil (שמן), a perfume (רקח) compounded by the perfumer (רֹקֵחַ)." Compare also the Ugaritic expression *šmn rqḥ*, "perfumer's oil" (*CAT* 1.148:21; 4.91:5). For the combination of *šamnu* ("oil") and *riqqu* ("perfumes") in Akkadian, see *CAD* R:368-71; Š/1:325. The substantive רִקֻּחִים is a hapax legomenon.

And you have sent your envoys afar — וַתְּשַׁלְּחִי (*pi'el* imperfect) indicates the frequency of the said activity: You have habitually sent your envoys (your pimps or panderers) to faraway places with the sole purpose of finding more lovers for your lascivious appetite. For the dispatch of "envoys" (ציר is an Akkadian loanword, *ṣīru*, denoting senior officials and dignitaries dispatched by vassal states in order to pay the tribute owed to their overlord [*CAD* Ṣ:213; J. N. Postgate, *Taxation and Conscription in the Assyrian Empire*, SP 3 [Rome, 1974], 123-25), see Isa 18:2 and Jer 49:14, both of which also employ the verb שלח, as here. The same biblical expression appears in line 4 of the Amherst Papyrus 63, an Aramaic prayer to Horus written in the Demotic script: שלח צירך. (See Z. Zevit, "The Common Origin of the Aramaicized Prayer to Horus and of Psalm 20," *JAOS* 110 [1990]: 213-18.) For a similar depiction of Judean "diplomacy," where Heb. מלאך replaces ציר, see Ezek 23:40-41: "Moreover, they sent for men to come from afar, to whom a messenger (מלאך) was sent, and they came," which is followed by: "You bathed yourself for these men, painted your eyes, decked yourself in finery, and sat on a stately bed, with a set table in front of it — and it was My incense and My oil you laid on it."

Even down to the netherworld — You have sent your emissaries not only to all the earthly kings but even down to the pit of Sheol. For this exaggerated image, see also Amos 9:2; Ps 139:8. For the verb שפל ("go down") in the context of the netherworld, cf. Isa 29:4: "And you shall speak from lower (ושפלת) than the netherworld." One may also interpret this verse as an expression of subject abasement: "You have lowered yourself even down to Sheol" (Ibn Ezra, Kimchi). Compare also Ugar. *špl 'pr*, "Bend down into the dust," parallel to *rd arṣ*, "Go down to the earth [= netherworld]" (*CAT* 1.161:21-22). For the root שפל in the *hiph'il*, with a reflexive connotation, see Jer 13:18; Ps 113:6.

[10] For the linguistic and thematic affinity between this verse and Jer 2:23-25, which castigates the nation for their idolatrous pursuits, see the introduction to the unit.

Though wearied by much travel — to the farthest reaches of the world. For the preposition *beth* with the meaning "though," "despite," see Isa 47:9, 13; Num

14:11: "How long will this people spurn Me, and how long will they have no faith in Me despite all (בכל) the signs that I have performed in their midst?"; Deut 1:32: "Yet despite all that (ובדבר), you have no faith in the Lord your God." Hebrew דרך, similar to its Akkadian semantic analogue, *ḫarranu* (*CAD* Ḫ:110), can also refer to business trips; cf. also Isa 58:13. Moreover, in this context it may be polysemous, serving as a euphemism for the act of intercourse (see Luzzatto); cf. Jer 3:13: "You scattered your 'favors' (דרכיך) among strangers under every leafy tree"; Prov 30:20: "Such is the 'way' (דרך) of an adulteress: She eats, wipes her mouth, and says, 'I have done no wrong'"; Prov 31:3, where דרך is parallel to חַיִל, denoting manly vigor expended on a woman. This euphemism for sexual relations is also present in Rabbinic Hebrew: דרך ארץ (*b. Git.* 70a), and כדרכה and שלא כדרכה (which denote natural and unnatural intercourse) (*Gen. Rab.* 18, end). For the expression יגע ב- ("to be wearied by"), see Isa 43:22, and cf. the similar image in Jer 2:23-24.

You never said, "I give up!" — Despite being worn out by your excessive behavior, you have never given up or stopped hoping; cf. Jer 2:25: "You said, 'It is no use (נואש). No, I love the strangers, and after them I must go'"; Jer 18:12: "But they will say, 'It is no use (נואש). We will keep on following our own plans.'"

You found gratification for your lust — a difficult hemistich, possibly referring to lustful desires. For the noun חיה, here as a synonym of נפש ("appetite"), see Job 38:39: "Can you hunt prey for the lion and satisfy the appetite (חית) of the king of beasts?" (For these two nouns, חיה and נפש, as parallels in another context, see Ps 143:3.) For the term יד indicating love, lust, or virility, see v. 8 and its Ugaritic and Akkadian cognates cited there. Others interpret this obscure expression to mean: "You have found your vigor renewed."

And so you never cared — It thus never concerned you. For the semantic development of the verb חלי from its primary meaning "to be sick" to "to be concerned," cf. 1 Sam 22:8: "No one is concerned (חֹלֶה) for me"; Amos 6:6: "But they are not concerned (נֶחֱלוּ) about the ruin of Joseph." For the same development in Akkadian, cf. its semantic equivalent, *marāṣu* (*CAD* M/1:269ff.).

[11] Although the nation is not God-fearing and gives Him no thought, He nevertheless has withheld punishment for a protracted period. Note the partial literary *inclusio* framing the verse by means of the verb תיראי.

Whom do you dread and fear that you should be false? — In light of the rest of the verse, however, and especially its ending: "That you have no fear of Me," H. L. Ginsberg (oral communication) has suggested to emend the MT ואת מי to ואותם, i.e., "Them you dreaded and feared." For the verb כזב meaning "to be false," see Isa 58:11.

But you gave no thought to Me — The initial *waw* indicates contrast: But you did not pay any heed to Me. The object ואותי ("Me") is emphasized by its position at the beginning of the sentence.

You paid no heed — For the parallel pair שׂים על לב/זכר, see 47:7. The Targum, LXX, and Peshitta all reflect the addition of the word "Me," similar to the previous stich. 1QIsa[a] adds אלה after the verb, as in the parallel clause in 47:7: "You never gave these things a thought."

It is because I have stood idly by so long and heedless — The initial הֲלֹא is emphatic: Indeed, the reason for your apathy is My forbearance. Compare likewise 42:14: החשיתי מעולם; and see there for the meaning of the verb חשי ("to be inactive"). In light of the LXX and Vulgate, however, it may be preferable to vocalize וּמַעְלִם, "and I have disregarded (your conduct)." For the verb עלם in the *hiph'il* stem without an object, see Ps 10:1.

That you have no fear of Me — The object ואותי ("Me") is emphasized, as in the beginning of the verse: It is because I have held My peace that you are not fearful; cf. Jer 5:22: "Should you not fear Me?"

[12-13] The verdict.

[12] *I hereby pronounce your punishment* — Now, after my prolonged inactivity, I have reached a decision regarding your nefarious misconduct. For this meaning of הצדקה, see Isa 1:27; 5:16; 10:22; 28:17.

Your deeds shall not avail you — Some divide the colon differently and attach the first two words of the clause to the former hemistich: "I shall announce the verdict against you regarding your deeds (ואת מעשיך)." According to this division, the remainder of the clause, ולא יועילוך, should be read with the next verse.

[13] Your idols shall provide no succor on the day of judgment. Only he who trusts in the Lord will inherit the land.

When you cry out, let your assembly of idols save you! — A mockery of the people's plight: "When you cry out in fright, let the idols that you have gathered to yourself save you"; cf. Jer 2:27: "But in their hour of calamity they cry [to their fetishes], 'Arise and save us!'"; Jer 11:12: "They will go and cry to the gods to which they sacrifice. But they will not be able to rescue them in their time of disaster." If, however, one accepts the alternative division of v. 12, and attaches the final words there (לא יועילוך) to this verse, then: "When you cry out, it shall be to no avail, your idols shall not save you." (The negative לא is implied here based on the preceding clause, לא יועילוך.) For the same two verbs in a similar context, cf. 1 Sam 12:21: "Do not turn away to follow worthless things, which can neither profit (לא יועילו) nor save (ולא יצילו) but are worthless."

Your assembly of idols — קִבּוּצַיִךְ is a hapax legomenon referring to their idols and images. This term, from the root קבץ ("to gather"), is similar to its cognates Akk. *puḫru* (*CAD* P:485-86), and Ugar. *pḫr* (*HdO* 2:469), which denote an assembly. The Masoretic vocalization is cacophonic, based on the pointing of שִׁקּוּצַיִךְ ("detested objects"), a derogatory term for idols; see Jer 13:27; Ezek 5:11.

They shall all be borne off by the wind — Cf. Isa 41:16: "And the wind shall carry them away." Compare similarly the cognate Akkadian expression: "The wind will carry away their remains" (*BWL*, 114–15, line 50).

Snatched away by a puff of air — an emphatic parallel repetition of the previous hemistich. For הֶבֶל, cf. Prov 21:6: "A vapor driven away." For the parallel pair הֶבֶל/רוח, see Eccl 1:14; 2:11, 17, 26.

But those who seek refuge in Me — The initial *waw* indicates contrast. Cf. Ps 7:2: "O Lord, my God, in You I seek refuge (חסיתי)"; 34:9, 23; 37:40.

Shall inherit the land — For this theme, see Isa 60:21; Exod 23:30; 32:13. The same expression appears also in Ugaritic, *arṣ nḥlth*, "the land of his inheritance" (*CAT* 1.3.VI:16; 1.4.VIII:13-14).

And possess My sacred mount — Jerusalem. For הר קדשי, see Isa 56:7; 65:11; 66:20; and for הר קדשי and ירושלם in tandem, see 27:13: "They shall come to worship the Lord on the sacred mount, in Jerusalem"; Dan 9:16: "From Your city Jerusalem, Your sacred mountain." For the synonymous pair ירש/נחל ("to inherit/to possess"), see Lev 25:46; Num 27:11.

[14-21] The second pericope begins with a call to construct a highway for the Judean expatriates and continues with a message of divine consolation to the downtrodden and broken in spirit. Although the nation has been severely punished, the Lord shall grant them a reprieve and shall heal them, for the time for amends has finally arrived. The wicked, however, will never be safe from the divine wrath. This unit has quite a number of phrases and terms in common with the preceding one as well as with the beginning of the chapter: v. 2: שלום — v. 19: שלום שלום, v. 21: אין שלום; vv. 7, 15: וְנִשָּׂא; v. 9: מֵרָחֹק — v. 19: לָרָחוֹק; v. 9: ותשפילי — v. 15: רוח שפלים,וּשְׁפַל רוח; v. 10: דרכך — various derivatives of the root דרך appear in vv. 14 (twice), 17, 18; v. 10: חַיַּת — v. 15 (twice): להחיות; v. 13: רוח — v. 15: רוח (twice); v. 13: (הר) קדשי — v. 15: וקדוש (שמו); וקדוש (אשכון); and possibly the play on words between v. 5, הַנֵּחָמִים, and v. 18, נִחֻמִים.

[14] *[The Lord] says: "Build up, build up a highway!"* — An emphatic repetition of the verb סֹלּוּ. (See the introduction, §10.A.1.) For a call addressed to the heavenly court without a specific subject, cf. 40:3, 6. According to the reading of 1QIsa[a], ויואמר, the subject is the Lord. The Vulgate has here a first-person singular (ואֹמַר), the subject of which is the prophet; and in the LXX there is a third-person plural verb (ויאמרו). The verb סֹלּוּ is a *qal* imperative of the root סלל (cf. the morphological equivalent סֹבּוּ [Ps 48:13], from סבב), which is employed to denote the erection of a highway (מְסִלָּה, 62:10), a road (דרך, Jer 18:15), or a path (אֹרַח, Prov 15:19); cf. Isa 49:11 (with a different verb): "And My highways shall be built up." The substantive המסלה is added here in 1QIsa[a], harmonizing with the parallel clause in 62:10. For the erection of thoroughfares in Babylon, see *CAD* M/1:185, 363.

"Clear a road!" — Remove all impediments from the route; cf. 40:3: "Clear

in the desert a road (פַּנּוּ דרך) for the Lord! Level in the wilderness a highway (מְסִלָּה) for our God!" The term דרך is a key word occurring here twice, and again in vv. 17 and 18.

"Remove all obstacles from the road of My people!" — Clear away all obstructions from My nation's pathway as they return from Babylon. The root רום appears here (הרימו) and twice more in the next verse (מרום, רם). Compare its employment with the same noun in 49:11. Note the assonance of the letter *mem* in all four words of this clause.

[15] The introductory formula כי כה אמר ("For thus said") appears here without "the Lord" as the subject. In lieu of the Tetragrammaton, several divine attributes are listed. For a similar description of the Lord's sublime grandeur, on the one hand, and His concern for the lowly and contrite, on the other, see 66:1-2; Ps 113:4ff.; 138:6. For a similar blend of motifs in Akkadian literature, cf. the "Great Prayer to Ishtar," where the poet switches from a description of the goddess's grandeur (lines 1-23) to her concern for the welfare of the oppressed and downtrodden (lines 24-26). (See B. R. Foster, *Before the Muses: An Anthology of Akkadian Literature,* 3rd ed. [Bethesda Md., 2005], 602.) An echo of the famous Isaianic prophecy in Isa 6 may most likely be overheard here: The two prophecies contain the expression רם וְנִשָּׂא (in 6:1 it is a reference to the divine throne, and here a reference to God Himself; see the commentary below); and instead of the threefold repetition קדוש קדוש קדוש in 6:3, the term here is doubled. (See the introduction, §14.) There is also a double chiastic parallelism in this verse: שֹׁכֵן . . . וקדוש . . . וקדוש אשכון; and . . . ואת דכא ושפל רוח . . . רוח שפלים . . . נדכאים.

For thus said the High and Exalted One — the Lord who dwells in lofty grandeur. For the synonymous pair נשא/רם, see Isa 2:12, 13, 14; and especially 6:1: "I beheld my Lord seated on a high and exalted throne (רם ונִשָּׂא)." According to the straightforward reading of 6:1, רם ונשא refers to the divine throne. The Masoretic vocalizers, however, placed a pausal accent under כסא, since according to the Masoretes only the Lord himself is "high and lofty." (See S. Kogut, *The Bible: Punctuation and Exegesis* [Jerusalem, 1994], 139, 216-17, 238 [Heb.].) For the verbal pair, see 33:10: "'Now I will arise,' says the Lord. 'Now I will exalt Myself (אֵרוֹמָם), now raise Myself high (אֶנָּשֵׂא)'"; Prov 30:13; Dan 11:12. In the LXX, Peshitta, and a number of medieval MT manuscripts the Tetragrammaton was appended here to the end of the clause.

Who forever dwells — Cf. Ps 68:17: "The Lord shall abide (יִשְׁכֹּן) there forever." For עד denoting infinity, see Isa 9:5: "The Eternal (עד) Father." According to the Targum, however, עד indicates the heavenly abode: דְּשָׁרֵי בִּשְׁמַיָּא ("He who inhabits the sky"), thus paralleling "I dwell on high." Compare also 66:1: "Thus said the Lord: 'Heaven is My throne.'"

Whose name is "Holy" — The attribute "Holy" also serves as a divine name; cf. 6:3; and for ancient Near Eastern parallels see the commentary to 40:25.

"I dwell on high, in holiness" — Following the introductory titles, the Lord delivers His message. (1QIsa[a] adds the prepositional particle and transposes the *waw* and *dalet* of קדוש: במרום ובקודש אשכון: "I dwell in a high and holy place"; cf. also the Targum, בִּרוּמָא.). For similar descriptions of the heavenly abode, see Isa 33:5: "He dwells on high (שֹׁכֵן מרום)"; Ps 102:20: "For He looks down from His holy height (ממרום קדשו)." For the root רמם, which is also used to describe the heavens in Ugaritic literature, cf. Anat's sobriquet: *b'lt šmm rmm,* "Lady of the sublime heavens" (*CAT* 1.108:7). The same expression appears in Phoenician as well, in the temple inscription of King Bodashtart of Sidon from the fifth century BCE: שמם רמם (*KAI* 15:1). This clause repeats three words from the two previous clauses (in a loose chiasm): רם . . . שֹׁכֵן . . . וקדוש — מרום וקדוש אשכון. In lieu of the verb in the first person in the MT, 1QIsa[a] and 4QIsa[d] have the third-person, ישכן, thus interpreting this clause as another divine attribute. The Targum renders by a participle.

"Yet with the broken and the lowly in spirit" — The *waw* indicates contrast: "Even though I dwell in the heavens, nevertheless I am with those who are crushed and lowly." For similar juxtapositions, see 66:1-2: "The heaven is My throne. . . . Yet to such a one I look: to the poor and brokenhearted"; Ps 102:20-21: "For He looks down from His holy height. The Lord beholds the earth from heaven to hear the groans of the prisoner, to release those condemned to death"; Ps 113:5-7: "Who is like the Lord our God, who, enthroned on high, sees what is below, in heaven and on earth? He raises the poor from the dust, lifts up the needy from the refuse heaps"; Ps 138:6: "High though the Lord is, He sees the lowly." The noun דַּכָּא denotes a broken and crushed individual; cf. Ps 34:19: "The Lord is close to the brokenhearted; those crushed (דַּכְּאֵי) in spirit He delivers." For שְׁפַל רוח, a person low in spirit, see Prov 16:19; 29:23.

"Reviving the spirits of the lowly" — I, the Lord, am He who uplifts the flagging spirits of the downtrodden; cf. Gen 45:27: "The spirit of their father Jacob revived (וַתְּחִי רוח)."

"Reviving the hearts of the crushed" — Cf. Ps 51:19: "God, You will not despise a contrite and crushed heart (לב . . . ונִדְכֶּה)." The final clauses of the verse form a chiasm with the immediately preceding clause: דכא ושפל רוח — רוח שפלים . . . נדכאים. For the parallel pair לב/רוח, see Deut 2:30; Prov 11:29; and for the same pair in the opposite order, רוח/לב, see Ezek 36:26; Ps 34:19. The infinitive להחיות appears here for the second time.

[16] *"For I will not always contend"* — כי emphasizes the declaration: I will not always accuse you. For ריב, see Isa 45:9; 50:8.

"I will not be angry forever" — Cf. Ps 103:9: "He will not contend forever or nurse His anger for all time"; cf. also Jer 3:5. The verb קצף is repeated twice in

the following verse, thus forming an emphatic triad. This verse addresses the nation's anguished complaint: "How long, O Lord, will You be angry forever, will Your indignation blaze like fire?" (Ps 79:5).

"Nay, I who make spirits flag" — a very difficult clause. Some explain the verb עטף as "to envelop, cover" (cf. Ps 65:14: "The meadows are clothed with flocks, the valleys covered [יעטפו] with grain"), and interpret the verse thus: "The spirit that covers them, wrapping around them as clothing — I am its source." Others derive the meaning of the verb from its homonym, "to be weak, faint" (cf. Ps 61:3: "I call to You when my heart is faint [בַּעֲטֹף]"; 142:4: "When my spirit is faint [בהתעטף] within me"; see also 143:4, and its Ugaritic cognate, *ʿṭp,* "to be weak" [*CAT* 1.103 + 1.145:2]) and explicate thus: "When a person's spirit flags, it is because I decided it should be so . . . the spirit of man is dependent on My will, and it is My will that he should weaken and perish" (Ehrlich, *Mikrâ ki-Pheshuṭo,* 3:140). According to the first interpretation the initial כי is emphatic; in the second it is temporal.

"Also create the breath of life" — It is I who formed man and breathed life into him (see Gen 2:7); cf. Isa 42:5: "Who gave breath to the people on it." For the synonymous pair נשמה/רוח ("spirit/breath"), see 42:5.

[17-21] Jeremiah's prophecies (Jer 6:13-14 = 8:10-11) left their strong imprint on this passage: "They are all out for unjust gain (בוצע בָּצַע). . . . They offer healing offhand for the wounds (וירפאו שֶׁבֶר) of My people, saying, 'All is well, all is well,' when nothing is well (שלום שלום ואין שלום)"; בַּעֲוֹן בִּצְעוֹ — בוצע בצע (v. 17); וירפאו — וארפאֵהו and ורפאתיו (vv. 18-19; the reference is to the Lord rather than to the false prophets); שלום שלום ואין שלום — שלום שלום (v. 19) and אין שלום (v. 21). If H. L. Ginsberg's emendation (oral communication) to read שבור ("broken"), instead of שובב (v. 17), is accepted, then yet another common linguistic denominator may be added: וירפאו שֶׁבֶר עמי — וילך שבור . . . וארפאֵהו, since one "heals" (רפא) that which is "broken" (שבר); cf. Ps 147:3: "He heals their broken hearts." For a similar motif, cf. Jer 33:5-6: "I struck down [= 'I struck him'] in My anger and rage [= 'I was angry . . . in My wrath'], hiding My face [= 'hiding' (My face)] . . . I am going to bring her relief and healing. I will heal them [= 'I will heal him . . . and I will heal him'] and reveal to them abundance of true favor [= 'It shall be well, well']." (See the introduction, §15.)

[17] *"For his sinful greed I was angry"* — as retribution for Israel's insatiable appetite for unjust gain; cf. Isa 56:11: "Everyone has turned his own way, every last one seeks his own personal gain (לבִצעו)." The verb קצפתי ("I was angry") is added to this clause contrary to the Masoretic trope division.

"I struck him" — The verb ואכהו should be vocalized וָאַכֵּהוּ as a past tense.

"And in My wrath I stayed hidden" — As was the case with ואכהו above,

ואקצף should be vocalized in the past tense, וָאֶקְצֹף. For this motif, see 54:8: "In an outpouring of anger (קצף), for a moment, I hid My face (הסתרתי פני) from you"; 64:6: "For You have hidden Your face (הסתרת פניך) from us." (Both LXX and Vulgate add "My face" to this clause, and cf. Targum, שְׁכִינְתִי ["My Presence"], following the verb הַסְתֵּר.) Instead of MT הַסְתֵּר, an infinitive absolute, both 1QIsa[a] and 1QIsa[d] have the first-person singular, which is consistent with ואקצף. There are those who suggest that the MT should be emended to וְקָצֹף, thus forming a sequence of two infinitives absolute (see Ibn Balaam [ed. Goshen-Gottstein, 224]; Ibn Ganaḥ, *Sefer ha-Riqmah* [ed. Walensky, 326]).

"But he waywardly follows the way of his heart" — In spite of the divine wrath, the nation stubbornly persisted in its willful ways. For שובב, see Jer 3:14, 22: "Turn back, apostate (שובבים) children"; Jer 8:5: "Why is this wayward people, Jerusalem, so persistently wayward (שובבה . . . מְשֻׁבָה)?"; and cf. Deut 29:18: "Though I follow My own willful heart (כי בשרירות לבי אלך)." (For the proposed emendation שבור ["broken"] instead of שובב, see above.) According to Rashi, one should transpose the words and read: "In their sinful greed, they willfully followed the way of their hearts, angering Me, and in My anger I struck them."

[18] The promise of healing contrasts starkly with the previous verse's statement of God's punishment. God notes the people's ways, but rather than turning His face away and continuing to strike them, He decides to heal them. Note also the mention of דרך in both verses.

"Then I noted his ways and I healed him" — Some commentators interpret דרכיו as referring to the people's upright ways, i.e., I saw that the people returned to a more virtuous path, and so I healed them (note once again the correct vocalization should be in the past tense: וָארפאֵהו). Alternatively, one may interpret דרכיו as a reference to the people's iniquities in the previous verse, i.e., in spite of their wayward conduct, I showed them mercy. (H. L. Ginzberg [oral communication] and Kaufmann [*Babylonian Captivity and Deutero-Isaiah,* 233 n. 126) suggest emending the text to דַּכָּיו/דָּכְיוֹ, in lieu of MT דרכיו: "When I saw that he was crushed, I healed him.")

"And I guided/granted him relief" — This verb, which also should be vocalized in the past tense, וָאַנְחֵהוּ, can be interpreted in two ways. According to the MT vocalization, it is derived from the root נחי (in the *hiph'il*) and denotes guidance, i.e., "I guided him." (For the expression הנחה דרך, see, e.g., Exod 13:21; Ps 139:24.) If, however, it is vocalized וָאֲנִחֵהוּ (a *hiph'il* derivative from the verb נוח, "to provide respite"), it would mean "I granted him rest and relief" (cf. Isa 14:3: "And when the Lord has given you rest [הָנִיחַ] from your sorrow"). According to this reading (cf. also LXX and Targum), the meaning would be similar to the solace mentioned in the following hemistich. Both these alternatives are offered by Rashi in his commentary. For another example of a Janus paral-

lelism with this verb, based on variant vocalizations, see 63:14. (See Paul, *Divrei Shalom,* 468-69.)

"And meted out solace to him" — read וָאשלם, in the past tense. The expression שלם נִחֻמִים is a hapax legomenon: I "compensated" him with the coin of consolation. (וְלַאֲבֵלָיו — "And to his mourners," correctly belongs with the next verse.)

[19-21] These last verses, as noted in the introduction to vv. 17-21, bear the stamp of Jeremiah. (Cf. also Ezek 13:10: "Inasmuch as they have misled My people, saying, 'It is well [שלום],' when nothing is well [ואין שלום]." (See Paul, *Divrei Shalom,* 409-10.)

[19] *"And to his mourners, creating fruit of the lips/heartening words"* — The word ולאבליו (see Isa 61:2, 3; 66:10), at the end of the previous verse, has been appended here. But the hemistich itself is very difficult to understand. The root נוב means "to bear fruit" (cf. Ps 92:15: עוד יְנוּבוּן בשֵׂיבָה, "In old age they still produce fruit"), and the substantive (either ניב, according to the Qere and 1QIsa[a], or נוב, according to the Ketib and 4QIsa[d]) denotes "fruit," thus "creating fruit of the lips," i.e., thanksgiving, "to his mourners." According to H. L. Ginsberg, however (oral communication), one should interpret בורא not as a verbal form but as a substantive denoting "hale and healthy," as in Eccl 12:1 and in Rabbinic Hebrew, e.g., "He became mute when he was yet hale (בּוֹרְיוֹ)" (*y. Git.* 7:1, 48c); "He was weaned when he was healthy (בוריו)" (*y. Ketub.* 5:6, 30a). According to this explanation (based on his commentary, *Qohelet Interpreted* [Tel Aviv, 1961], 129 [Heb.]), the Lord grants the mourners heartening words of thanksgiving, the content of which immediately follows.

"It shall be well, well, with the far and the near" — an emphatic doubling (שלום שלום); see also v. 14. "With the far and the near" are polar opposites (1 Kgs 8:46; Jer 25:26), encompassing a message of well-being to everyone. (See the introduction, §10.A.)

Said the Lord, "and I will heal them" — a repetition of v. 18. For אמר ה׳ not at the end of the verse, see, e.g., 59:21; 65:7.

[20] *"But the wicked are like the troubled sea"* — But (the initial *waw* denotes contrast) the wicked are like a stormy ocean. The verb גרש (a homonym of the more common גרש, "to expel") denotes "storming, raging" (Saadyah, 127; Ibn Ganaḥ, *Sefer ha-Shorashim,* 101); cf. Amos 8:8: "Shall it not all rise like the Nile and surge (ונגרשה) and subside like the Nile of Egypt?" Compare also the substantive מְגָרְשׁוֹת ("waves") in Ezek 27:28: "At the outcry of your pilots the waves shall heave." Note too the appearance of this verb in the *Hodayot Scroll* from Qumran: "Against me the assembly of the wicked rages, and they roar like the stormy seas, when their waves crash, heaving up (יגרושו) slime and mud" (1QH 10:14-15); cf. also 1QH 11:33: "heaving up (גורשי) mud"; 1QH 16:16: "They spewed up (גרשו) their mire over me" (Stegemann et al., DJD 40,

132, 144, 216). The verb is also found in Rabbinic Hebrew, מים גורשים/ן (*Sifre Deuteronomy* 39; *Yalqut Shimoni, 'Ekev,* §859; cf. also Rabbi Akiba's *Midrash Alpha-Beta,* in A. Yellinek, *Beit ha-Midrash* [Jerusalem, 1938], 3:13); and in Samaritan, גרושה ("waves") (A. E. Cowley, *The Samaritan Liturgy* [Oxford, 1909], 262, 263). The LXX, Peshitta, 1QIsa[a], and one medieval Hebrew manuscript read נגרשו, in agreement with the plural substantive רשעים, and 1QIsa[b] has בים, instead of MT כים. (For a wordplay based on this verb in Jonah 2:5 and its Ugaritic cognate *grš,* see Paul, *Divrei Shalom,* 485-87.)

"That cannot rest" — הַשְׁקֵט is a *hiph'il* infinitive absolute, denoting the calming of the ocean's waves; cf. Jer 49:23: "They shake with anxiety, like the sea that cannot rest (השקט)." The synonymous root שתק can also indicate the resting of a stormy sea, as in Jonah 1:11: "They said to him, 'What must we do to you to make the sea calm (וְיִשְׁתֹּק) around us?'"; cf. also Ps 107:30. As in the above clause, the LXX, Peshitta, and 1QIsa[a] have a plural form (יוכלו instead of יוכל).

"Whose waters toss up mire and mud" — In the tossing and surging of the waves they bring up contaminants and detritus, an image that serves as a metaphor depicting the wicked "mudslingers." The hapax legomenon רֶפֶשׁ also appears in all the above-quoted verses from the *Hodayot Scroll.* Compare also its Akkadian etymological cognate, *rupuštu,* "spittle, saliva, phlegm, froth" (*CAD* R:414-15).

[21] *"But it shall not be well" — said my God — "for the wicked"* — There is no reprieve, however, for the wicked. This divine threat contrasts with his message of solace for the mourners of Zion. This formula was editorially inserted as a conclusion to the first section of the book, ending in 48:22 (see there).

Chapter 58

The greater part of this chapter (vv. 1-12) is dedicated to a sociomoral admonishment against the nation's conduct, specifically their lack of abstinence from commerce on communal fast days (the reference is most likely to the Day of Atonement; see below). The nation accuses God of being inattentive to their pleas, despite, according to them, their genuine attempt to seek Him. They claim that they fulfill all their cultic obligations, yet the Lord remains unresponsive. In reply to their bitter complaint, however, the Deity Himself accuses the nation of hypocrisy and asserts that a true fast, i.e., "a fast acceptable to Him," is not solely a series of prescribed perfunctory rituals, but must be accompanied by a true moral reversal and by addressing social injustice. How can they be "eager to learn My ways" (v. 2), when on these very fast days "they see to their business and oppress all laborers" (v. 3)? The fast God desires is to provide food to the destitute, who have no choice but to fast. There is no intrinsic value to their mortification if it is not accompanied by aid and succor to the oppressed and by "unlocking the fetters of wickedness" (v. 6). The Lord will answer His supplicants only when they respond, in turn, to the calls of the needy. God desires right, not rites.

This prophecy was deeply influenced by the injunctions regarding the observation of the Day of Atonement found in Lev 16; 23:24-32; 25:9-10. On this, the most holy of days, one of the customs was the blowing of a ram's horn. Compare Lev 25:9: "On the Day of Atonement you shall have the ram's horn sounded throughout your land," to Isa 58:1: "Cry with a full throat, without restraint, raise your voice like a ram's horn." This day is also consecrated by the starving of one's body: compare Lev 16:31: "You shall mortify yourselves" (see also Lev 16:29; 23:29, 31), to Isa 58:3: "Why when we fasted . . . when we mortify ourselves . . . ?"; 58:5: "Is such the fast I desire, a day for one to mortify himself?" According to Leviticus, this should be accompanied by a cessation of labor: Lev

16:29: "You shall do no manner of work" (cf. also Lev 23:28, 31), as opposed to Isa 58:3: "You see to your business"; 58:13: "And do not engage in your business, nor look to your affairs." (For these idioms denoting commercial activity, see the commentary below.) It should be a day of acknowledgment of wrongdoing: Lev 16:21: "[Aaron] . . . shall confess over it all their iniquities and transgressions"; cf. Isa 58:1: "Declare to My people their transgression, to the House of Jacob their sin." And it is a time of pardon and emancipation (on the Day of Atonement of the Jubilee Year): Lev 25:10: "You shall proclaim release throughout the land for all its inhabitants" — Isa 58:6: "To let the oppressed go free"; cf. 61:1-2.

The prophet, however, reinterprets these edicts and concentrates on their social ramifications. He is thus very much akin to his prophetic predecessors who denounced animal offerings, observation of holidays, and even prayer, if they were not accompanied by moral uprightness (see Isa 1:1-17; Jer 7:21-23; Hos 6:6; Amos 5:21-24). All ritual is secondary and dependent on morality. Moreover, the nation's ultimate mission and raison d'être is based on righteous conduct, i.e., the eradication of injustice and bettering the lot of the indigent. In order to bring this to pass, the kings of Mesopotamia would initiate periodic reforms, which were referred to as *kittum u mīšarum,* "truth and justice" (*CAD* K:470), or *andurārum,* "remission of debts, manumission of slaves" (*CAD* A/2:115-17), the goal of which was righting social wrongs, aiding the needy, freeing slaves and prisoners and individuals who were sold in order to pay their families' debts, including the return of ancestral plots to the dispossessed. In contrast to the prevailing custom in the ancient Near East, where these edicts were issued only occasionally by the rulers, Deutero-Isaiah commands the nation in its entirety to conduct themselves in a socially responsible manner. (See M. Weinfeld, *Social Justice in Ancient Israel and in the Ancient Near East* [Minneapolis, 1995].) Regarding the second short unit (vv. 13-14), see below.

This chapter is characterized by repetitive terminology for emphatic purposes: **צום** — seven times (vv. 3 [twice], 4 [twice, and note the wordplay **מַצָּה**], 5 [twice], 6); **קרא** (vv. 1, 5, 9, 12, 13); **יום** — seven times (vv. 2 [twice], 3, 4, 5 [twice], 13); **עינוי נפש** (vv. 3, 5, 10), **עֲנִיִּים** (v. 7); (the homonymic root **ענ׳** appears yet again in v. 9 where it denotes response); **חפץ** (vv. 2, 3 [twice], 13 [twice]); **הן** (vv. 3, 4); **נפש** (vv. 3, 5, 10 [twice, with different meanings], 11); **ראי׳** (vv. 3, 7); **רֶשַׁע** (vv. 4, 6); **הלוא** (vv. 6, 7); **אז** (vv. 8, 9, 14); **ענג** (vv. 13, 14); **דבר** (vv. 13 [twice, with different meanings], 14); (vv. 1, 4) **רום**. The chapter as a whole is also bound by a literary frame: vv. 1-3: "Cry (**קְרָא**) . . . to the house of Jacob (**ולבית יעקב**) . . . eager to learn my ways (**דרכי**) . . . you see to your business" (**תמצאו חֵפֶץ**) — vv. 13-14: "From pursuing your affairs (**חֲפָצֶךָ**) . . . if you call (**וקראת**) . . . and go not your ways (**דרכיך**), nor look to your affairs (**ממצוא חֶפְצְךָ**) . . . the heritage of your father Jacob (**יעקב אביך**)."

There are also a number of phrases and expressions connecting this chapter with chap. 57: 57:4: על מי תתענגו — 58:14: אז תתענג על ה׳; 57:13: "But those who trust in Me shall inherit the land (ינחל ארץ) and possess My holy (קדשי) mount" — 58:13-14: ". . . on My holy (קדשי) day . . . I will set you astride the heights of the earth (ארץ) and let you enjoy the heritage (נחלת) of your father Jacob"; 57:14: פַּנּוּ דרך . . . מִדרך עמי, v. 18: דרכיו — 58:2: דרכי, v. 13: דרכיך (note the different connotation in v. 13); 57:14: הָרִימוּ — 58:1: הָרֵם; 57:20, 21: רשעים — 58:4, 6: רֶשַׁע; 57:15: מרום — 58:4: במרום. The motif of healing also appears in both chapters: 57:18, 19: "And I will heal them" — 58:8: "And your healing will spring up quickly."

[1-2] The opening verses of this prophecy may have been influenced by Hos 8:1-2: "Put a ram's horn to your mouth!" (Hos 8:1) — "Cry with a full throat, without restraint, raise your voice like a ram's horn!" (v. 1); "Because they have transgressed My covenant and rebelled against My teaching" (Hos 8:1) — "Declare to My people their transgression, to the house of Jacob their sins!" (v. 1); "Israel cries out to Me, 'O my God, we are devoted to You'" (Hos 8:2) — "To be sure, they seek Me daily, eager to learn My ways" (v. 2). (See the introduction, §16.)

[1] The Lord appoints the prophet to be His herald; cf. Mic 3:8: "But I am filled with strength by the spirit of the Lord, and with judgment and courage to declare to Jacob his transgression and to Israel his sin." For another portrayal of a prophet as a watchman who blows a horn to warn the nation of impending danger, see Ezek 33:1-6.

Call with a full throat! — This unique expression, which denotes shouting with all one's strength, appears in Ugaritic as well: "So that he may call Mot with his throat (*yqra bnpšh; CAT* 1.4.VII:47); cf. also Dan 3:4: "The herald loudly proclaimed (קָרֵא בְחָיִל)"; 4:11; 5:7. And in Akkadian: "The heralds shall make their proclamations. They let their voice resound in the land" (*CAD* Š/1:489).

Without restraint! — Cry out with the full strength of your vocal cords; hold nothing back, as in Isa 40:9: "Raise your voice with power . . . have no fear."

Raise your voice like a ram's horn! — Let your voice belt out its message like the blast of the ram's horn (as Israel approached Mount Sinai [Exod 19:19]). This image was likely employed because of the ram's horn (שופר) that was sounded on the Day of Atonement (see the introduction to this chapter) and on days of mourning; see Joel 2:15: "Blow a ram's horn in Zion; solemnize a fast."

Declare to My people their transgression — listed below. The LXX, Vulgate, Targum (מַרְדֵּיהוֹן), as well as 1QIsa[a] (פשעיהמה) all read "transgressions," instead of the MT singular; see immediately below.

To the house of Jacob — their sins! — Declare (the verb in the preceding hemistich is implied here as well) to "the house of Jacob" (one of Israel's appellations; see 46:3; 48:1) their offenses.

[2] The divine castigation (in the first-person) of the nation's hypocritical self-acclamation. There is a linguistic affinity between this verse and Deut 4:7-8: "For what great nation (גוי) is there that has a god so close at hand (אלהים קרבים) as is the Lord our God whenever we call upon Him? Or what great nation (גוי) has laws and rules as just (ומשפטים צדיקים) as all this teaching?"

Me they seek daily — They avidly search for My Presence (אותי is placed at the beginning of the hemistich for emphasis) day in and day out. They seek me on a regular basis for instruction regarding proper behavior; cf. Isa 55:6: "Seek (דִּרשׁו) the Lord while He can be found." The nation's conduct, however, is not genuine, and they only "make it seem as if they are desirous of knowing My way" (Yellin, *Ḥiqrei Miqra*, 79). The imperfect ידרשון ("seek") (with the archaic *nun* suffix) denotes frequency, as is further implied by יום יום ("daily"). (For this doubling, see Gen 39:10; Exod 16:5; Ps 61:9.) For an example of the nation's elders seeking God through the agency of the prophet Ezekiel, see Ezek 14:1-3; 20:1. For the expression לדרוש את ה׳, see Gen 25:22.

Eager to learn My ways — "They disguise their intentions and make it seem as if they truly wish to learn My true ways, so as to conduct themselves according to them" (Luzzatto). In contrast, cf. Job 21:14: "They say to God, 'Leave us alone, we do not want to learn Your ways'"; cf. also Jer 5:4: "For they do not know the way of the Lord, the rules of their God." For the parallel synonyms חפץ/דרש, see Isa 62:4, 12: "But you shall be called, 'I Delight (חפצי) in Her' . . . and you shall be called 'Sought Out' (דרושה)." The final word of this hemistich, יחפצוּן, rhymes with ידרשון, the last word in the first hemistich.

Like a nation that does what is right — As a people whose conduct is genuinely just, and not feigned.

That has not abandoned the law of its God — They appear to be like a nation that has continually abided by a righteous code and heeded the Lord's commands. For the paradigm of negative parallelism in which the first element — a positively couched statement (עשׂה) — is followed by a negative parallel (לא עזב), cf. 42:16: "These are the promises — I will keep them (עשיתִם) and not abandon them (ולא עזבתים)." For the parallel between משפט and צדקה, see 56:1: "Thus said the Lord: 'Observe what is right (משפט) and do what is just (צדקה).'"

They ask Me for righteous laws — They ask Me to delineate a mode of observance anchored in justice; cf. Ps 119:7: "As I learn Your righteous laws (משפטי צדקך)." The expression משפטי צדק forms a chiastic parallelism with צדקה and משפט in the preceding clause. For the coupling of משפט and צדק, see Ps 89:15: "Righteousness and justice (צדק ומשפט) are the base of Your throne."

They are eager for the nearness of God — They seek my company, but as the Psalter proclaims: "The Lord is near to all who call on Him, to all who call on Him with sincerity" (Ps 145:18); cf. 73:28: "As for me, nearness to God (קִרבת אלהים) is good."

[3-7] The nation's complaint concerning God's disregard of their appeal on fast days is delineated. The people claim that they observe the ritual requirements, but God does not fulfill His part of the proverbial bargain and does not heed their call. (For a similar grievance cf. Mal 3:14: "You have said, 'It is useless to serve God. What have we gained by keeping His charge and walking abjectly in the presence of the Lord of Hosts?'") The prophet warns the people that in order to be near to God and to know His ways it is not sufficient to fast and offer sacrifices, since ritual has no value in and of itself if not accompanied by morally and socially responsible conduct. It is not enough to humble one's heart and deprive one's body, because "He has told you, O man, what is good, and what the Lord requires of you: Only to do justice, and to love loyalty, and to walk wisely with your God" (Mic 6:8). If they conduct themselves in this manner, they shall be saved.

[3] Two parallel queries and the divine response.

"Why, when we fasted, do You not see?" — What benefit is there to our fast, if You do not chalk it up in our favor? For the query למה ("why") as an expression of futility, cf. 2 Sam 12:23: "But now that he [the child] is dead, why should I fast?" For fasting as a vehicle to gain the Lord's attention, cf. Joel 2:12: "Turn back to Me with all your hearts, and with fasting, weeping, and lamenting." The LXX and Targum (אָמְרִין) add the verb "They say" at the beginning of the clause.

"When we mortify ourselves, do You pay no heed?" — Why do you not take heed of our abstinence and our fulfillment of the precept: "You shall mortify yourselves"? (Lev 23:27). In the words of Ibn Ezra on Lev 16:29: "The rule is that every time 'abstinence' (עינוי) is mentioned in Scripture together with 'self' (נפש), it denotes fasting"; cf. Ps 35:13: "I mortified myself with fasting"; and cf. here, v. 5: "A day for men to mortify themselves." In 1QIsa[a] (נפשותינו), as well as in LXX, Vulgate, and Targum (נַפְשָׁתַנָא), the noun is in the plural instead of the singular (נַפְשֵׁנוּ) in the MT. The term נפש (with some variance in meaning) is a key word in this chapter; see vv. 5, 10 (twice), 11.

Because on your fast day you attend to your business — God's response is preceded by the emphatic interjection הֵן (for other instances of הֵן preceding such clauses, see Gen 15:3; Jer 2:10). Though you fast on these days of self-denial, nevertheless, at the same time, you do not refrain from engaging in commerce. The unique expression מצא חפץ (see v. 13) denotes commercial activity, as does its Akkadian semantic cognate, *ṣibûtam kašādu* (*CAD* Ṣ:169-70). The LXX and Targum (צוּרְכֵיכוֹן) render the noun in the plural and add a pronominal suffix, "your," in accord with the plural of the following clause, עַצְּבֵיכֶם. Ridicule is inherent in the structure of this verse: If they "eagerly desire" the "nearness of God" (v. 2), how can they eagerly (חפץ) continue to do business on a fast day?! Note the assonance of the last three consecutive words containing the letter *ṣade.*

And oppress all your laborers — Though there is some disagreement regarding the exact meaning of the term עַצְּבֵיכֶם (עָצֵב or עָצָב in the singular, from the root עצב, "to pain, hurt, toil"), it most likely refers to hardworking people, browbeaten and downtrodden by excessive labor. For the substantive עֶצֶב with the meaning "toil," see Ps 127:2; Prov 5:10. For the root נגשׂ denoting cruel oppression, see Isa 53:7; 60:17.

[4] *You fast in strife and contention* — The emphatic interjection הן is repeated and further grievances against the nation are listed: Your fast day is not a day on which your spirit is elevated, rather it is a day of conflict and dispute. For the substantive מַצָּה ("contention"; note the similar sounding תצומו and תמצאו in v. 3), derived from the root נצי (see Exod 2:13), see Prov 17:19: "He who loves transgression loves contention (מצה)." The pair ריב ומצה is similar to ריב ומדון in Hab 1:3 (and cf. Jer 15:10). Instead of MT ומצה, 1QIsa[a] has ולמצא and 1QIsa[b] ולמצה, both with the prepositional particle harmonizing with לריב. The *lamed* in לריב of the MT, however, serves double-duty and applies to מצה as well.

And you strike with a wicked fist — On this day you clench your hand into a fist and deliver a wicked punch; cf. Exod 21:18: "One strikes the other with a stone or fist (אֶגְרֹף)."

Your fasting now is not such as to make your voice heard on high — Your self-denial is not instrumental to your goal of achieving nearness to the Deity. For כיום meaning "at this moment, now," see Gen 25:31: "Jacob said, 'Then sell me your birthright now (כיום)'"; 1 Kgs 1:51: "It was reported to Solomon . . . [Adonijah] has grasped the horns of the altar, saying, 'Let King Solomon first swear to me now (כיום) that he will not put his servant to the sword.'" The word מרום ("on high") is a poetic reference to the heavens, as in Isa 57:15: "I dwell in a high (מרום) and holy place"; 33:5: "The Lord is exalted, he dwells on high (מרום)." Note the ironic wordplay with the first verse. Here the nation lifts its voice on high (במרום קולכם), whereas in v. 1 it is the prophet who is commanded to raise his voice on high (הָרֵם קולך).

[5] For some of the same fast-day customs mentioned here, cf. 1 Kgs 21:27: "He [Ahab] rent his clothes and put sackcloth on his body. He fasted and lay in sackcloth;" Ps 35:13-14: "My dress was sackcloth. I mortified myself with fasting. I was bowed with gloom"; Esth 4:1: "And he [Mordecai] put on sackcloth and ashes"; Dan 9:3: "I turned my face to the Lord God, devoting myself to prayer and supplication, in fasting, in sackcloth and ashes." Compare Baal's mourning in the Ugaritic epic bearing his name: "He poured ashes of grief on his head, the dust of humiliation on his forehead" (*CAT* 1.5.VI:14-15). In an As-

syrian inscription King Esarhaddon is portrayed as "stripping himself from his royal garb, and wrapping his body in sackcloth, as befits a penitent sinner" (*CAD* B:137). The Lord quotes the nation's grievances concerning His unresponsiveness and emphasizes by means of a triad of rhetorical questions, all beginning with the interrogative particle הֲ, that empty rituals are not the proper conduit to reach Him. See also v. 3.

Is such the fast I desire — Is "this" (הֲכזה — a pronoun with a referent below) the type of fast day I crave?

A day for humans to mortify themselves? — Is this the type of abstinence that I truly desire?

Is it bowing the head like a bulrush — Does the day of "self-denial" I chose necessarily consist of the abject lowering of your heads like a hook-shaped bulrush (אַגְמֹן)? See Isa 9:13; 19:15. The infinitive לָכֹף, from the root כפף, similar to its Akkadian cognate *kapāpu* (*CAD* K:175-76), denotes "bowing down, bending"; cf. Mic 6:6: "With what shall I approach the Lord, bend (אִכַּף) to God on high?"; Ps 145:14: "And [God] makes all who bend (הכפופים) stand straight." The LXX and 1QIsa[b] have the variant ראשך, second-person singular, instead of MT ראשו, third-person singular.

And lying in sackcloth and ashes? — Do you think that I sincerely desire that you prostrate yourselves and lie in sackcloth and ashes? Cf. Esth 4:3: "Sackcloth and ashes were spread out (יֻצַּע) for the masses." For the root יצע denoting "laying, spreading out," see also Isa 14:11; Ps 139:8. For sackcloth as the garb of fast days, see 1 Kgs 21:27; Joel 1:8; Jonah 3:5-7.

Do you call that a fast — Do you really think that these external accouterments are the essence of such a day? The LXX, Peshitta, Targum (אַתּוּן קָרַן), and IQIsa[d] all read תקראו in the second-person plural, instead of MT תקרא (singular).

A favorable day to the Lord? — Is this a time when you think that the Lord is more inclined to hear your prayers? יום רצון ("a favorable day") is a unique expression, similar to עת רצון ("a favorable time"; Isa 49:8), and שנת רצון לה׳ ("a year of the Lord's favor"; 61:2). The term צום ("fast day") in the previous hemistich and the expression יום רצון create an alliterative sequence.

[6] In lieu of the superficiality of the above rituals, the prophet demands that a fast day be a day of true reformation, a day on which social wrongs (four of which are listed below) are righted.

Is this not the fast I desire — Note the similar expressions at the beginning of this verse, הלוא זה, and in v. 5, הֲכָזֶה. 1QIsa[a] adds אשר after the first two words.

To unlock fetters of wickedness — The type of fast day the Lord desires is one on which the manacles of iniquity are broken and all the unjustly bound are freed. For חַרְצֻבּוֹת (a quadriliteral root also found in Arabic, *ḥaḍrama* [note the metathesis]), "fetters," see the Damascus Covenant (CD-A XIII:10; *DSSSE,* 1:572). The secondary meaning of this term is "pain and suffering," as in Ps 73:4: "They suffer no pain (חרצֻבות). They are whole; their strength is healthy [reading לָמוֹ תָּם, instead of MT לְמוֹתָם]." For פַּתֵּחַ, a *pi'el* infinitive absolute (cf. also the following הַתֵּר and שַׁלַּח), meaning "to unfetter, release," see Ps 105:20: "The king sent to have him freed. The ruler of nations released him (וַיְפַתְּחֵהוּ)"; Ps 116:16: "You have undone (פִּתַּחְתָּ) the cords that have bound me."

And untie the cords of the yoke — הַתֵּר is an infinitive absolute from the root נתר, "to unfasten," parallel to פַּתֵּחַ above (see Ps 105:20; and cf. 146:7). מוֹטָה is a bar of the yoke placed on the neck of a beast or a slave (see Lev 26:13: "[I am the Lord] who broke the bars of your yoke"; Jer 28:13), which is attached to the animal or person by "cords" (אֲגֻדּוֹת). If one vocalizes the word מוּטֶּה (a derivative of נטי), however, it denotes that which is "perverted, perverted justice," as in Ezek 9:9: "The land is full of crime, and the city is full of corruption (מֻטֶּה)." The term thus functions as the pivot of a Janus parallelism (a simultaneously two-directional parallelism): In reference to the preceding hemistich, it is equivalent to רֶשַׁע ("wickedness"); and in reference to the final clause in the verse, it denotes a burden. For further examples of such parallelism based on alternate vocalizations, see Isa 49:7, 17; 57:18; 60:5. (See Paul, *Divrei Shalom,* 457-76, 477-83.)

To let the oppressed go free — To set free those who have been crushed (for רצוץ as synonymous with עשוק ["oppressed"], see Deut 28:33). The verb שַׁלַּח (also a *pi'el* infinitive absolute) means "to release"; see Jer 34:16: "But now you have turned back and have profaned My name. Each of you has taken back the men and women whom you have set free (שִׁלַּחְתֶּם) and forced them to be your slaves again"; Job 39:5: "Who sets the wild ass free (שִׁלַּח)? Who loosens (פִּתֵּחַ) the bonds of the onager?" (note the parallelism here, as in the present verse, between the verbs שלח and פתח); cf. Exod 21:26-27; Deut 15:12, 13, 18.

And snap every yoke? — thereby releasing them from all constraints; cf. Nah 1:13: "And now I will break off his yoke bar from you and snap (אֲנַתֵּק) your cords apart." Note the chiasm with the previous hemistich and the repetition of the substantive מוֹטָה.

[7] This verse lists four additional acts of social justice connected with "the fast day favorable to God": (1) providing food for the hungry; (2) housing of indigents; (3) clothing them; and (4) paying heed to destitute kin. For the connection between feeding the hungry and clothing the needy, see Ezek 18:7: "He has given bread to the hungry and clothed the naked" (see also Ezek 18:16).

It is to share your bread with the hungry — This verse opens, as does v. 6, with הלוא, emphasizing the prophet's words. The first requisite is to share your bread with the hungry, i.e., with those who fast because they have no choice. For the use of the verb פרס in the context of "breaking bread," see Jer 16:7:

"They shall not break bread [יפרסו, and read לחם instead of MT להם] for a mourner to console him for a bereavement"; Lam 4:4: "Little children beg for bread. None gives them a morsel (פֹּרֵשׂ)."

And to take the homeless poor into your home — The second item on the list is to open your home (the pronominal suffix above in לחמך is implied here as well) to the homeless, i.e., "the needy who have no abode in which to dwell and who wander about seeking a place of rest" (Ehrlich, *Mikrâ Ki-Pheshuṭo,* 3:144). For מְרוּדִים, derived from the root רוד, "to wander restlessly, roam" (cf. Targum מְטַלְטְלִין), see Lam 3:19: "To recall my distress and wandering (ומרודִי)"; Lam 1:7: "Her days of woe and wandering (ומרודיה)"; and cf. the Arabic cognate, *rāda (rwd),* which also denotes "to go to and fro."

When you see the naked, to clothe him — 1QIsa[a] adds the word בגד ("clothing"), וְכִסִּיתוֹ בגד, as in Ezek 18:7: "And clothed the naked (ועֵירֹם יְכסה בגד)" (cf. also Ezek 18:16). One may compare this to one of the reforms *(mīšarum)* initiated by Esarhaddon, king of Assyria, in which he declared: *mīrânūte lubuštu ulabbīšma,* "I provided the naked with clothing" (*CAD* M/2:22).

And not to ignore your own kin — If your kith and kin are in need, you are obliged to lend them a helping hand as well. For בָּשָׂר ("kindred blood relations"), see Gen 29:14: "You are truly my bone and flesh (בשרי)"; Lev 18:6. For the verbal expression להתעלם מ-, denoting disregard or evasion, see Deut 22:1: "If you see your fellow's ox or sheep gone astray, do not ignore it (והתעלמת מהם). You must take it back to your fellow."

[8] The long-awaited salvation is imminent and the Lord shall protect His people every step of the way. The first two and final two hemistichs of the verse form chiasms. For the same sequence of motifs, the dawning of light/the sun (representing salvation) accompanied by healing, see Mal 3:20: "But for you who revere My name, a sun of victory shall rise with healing in its wings."

Then shall your light burst through like the dawn — a unique metaphor: Your light, i.e., your salvation and success, shall penetrate the darkness like the first rays of dawn lighting up the night sky. For "light" (אור) representing deliverance, see Isa 51:4: 60:1. For שחר ("dawn") denoting the first rays of the sun, see Neh 4:15: "From the break of day (שחר) until the stars appeared"; cf. also Akk. *šēru* (*CAD* Š/2:331-32) and Ugar. *šḥr* (*HdO* 2:812-13), etymological and semantic cognates referring to both "dawn" and the god of daybreak.

And your healing spring up quickly — For the term אֲרֻכָה, which denotes the healing of a wound, see Jer 8:22: "Why has healing not yet come to my poor people?"; Jer 30:17: "But I will bring healing to you and cure you of your wounds." The words אורך and אֲרֻכתך have the letters א, ר, and כ in common.

Your Vindicator shall be your vanguard — Some translate צדקך in accordance with the Targum זָכְוָתָךְ ("your righteousness"). It is preferable, however, in light of the following clause, to interpret it as elliptical for אלהי צדקך ("your God, your Vindicator"); see Jer 23:6: "And this is the name by which He shall be called: 'The Lord is our Vindicator' (ה׳ צִדְקֵנוּ)." Cf. Ps 4:2: אלהי צדקי. The Lord shall march before you as your vanguard to ensure your safety. For this image, see Ps 85:14: "Justice goes before Him," i.e., is His vanguard.

The Presence of the Lord shall be your rear guard — Behind you, as your rear guard, you shall have the protection of the divine Presence. For אסף meaning "rear guard" cf. Josh 6:9: "The rear guard (והמאסף) marched behind the ark." The final two hemistichs of this verse are almost a literal repetition of Isa 52:12 (albeit with a different intention): "For the Lord is marching before you. The God of Israel is your rear guard (מְאַסִּפְכֶם)," which promises that the Lord will preserve them on their return journey from their Babylonian exile. Here, however, since they have already returned, the image refers to their rehabilitation. The expression כבוד ה׳ ("the Presence of the Lord"), which replaces אלהי ישראל ("the God of Israel") in 52:12, accentuates the transcendental aspect of the Divine. (The *hiphʿil* יַאַסְפֶךָ functions in much the same way as the *piʿel* in the other verses cited above; perhaps the correct vocalization is indeed יְאַסְּפֶךָ.) For the two substantives כבוד and צדק, see 62:2: "Nations shall see your vindication (צדקך), and every king your presence (כבודך)."

[9] *Then, when you call, the Lord will answer* — The conjunction אז ("then") at the opening of the verse is emphatic (as in v. 8): Assuredly, when you call the Lord, under the circumstances mentioned above, He shall answer you, as opposed to His lack of attention on your present days of fasting (v. 3); cf. 65:24: "Before they pray, I will answer"; or, in contrast, see 65:12; 66:4: "Because when I called, you did not answer." Note the assonant terms and phrases יענה (here), עִנִּינוּ נפשינו (v. 3); יום עַנּוֹת (v. 5); and עֲנִיִּים (v. 7); cf. also v. 10: ונפש נַעֲנָה.

When you cry out, He will say: "Here I am" — If you fulfill the above conditions, when you cry out in your hour of need, the Lord shall respond and be present. For the parallel synonyms שוע/קרא ("to call/to cry"), cf. Ps 145:18-19: "The Lord is near to all who call Him (יקראֻהו), to all who call Him with sincerity. . . . He hears their cry (שַׁוְעָתָם) and delivers them." For the presence of the Lord, which is expressed by the term הנני ("Here I am"), see Isa 52:6; 65:1. In all the other occurrences of this expression, a human being is the subject rather than God.

If you banish perversion from your midst — If you do away with the subversion of justice and release the oppressed from their yokes, you too shall be answered when you plead for divine intercession. For the double entendre of מוטה ("yoke" and "perversion"), see v. 6.

The pointing finger — if you banish from your midst one who makes a gesture with his finger in derision or accusation; cf. Prov 6:12-13: "A scoundrel, an evil man . . . pointing his finger (מֹרֶה באצבעֹתיו)." The parallel expression in Akkadian, *ubānam tarāṣu* ("to point one's finger"), denotes the act of accusing or spreading malicious gossip (*CAD* T:211; U/W: 6).

And evil speech — If you remove the scourge of evil and dishonest speech, the Lord will be inclined to hear your prayer. In a bilingual hymn (Sumerian-Akkadian) to the Mesopotamian god Ninurta, which also includes moral injunctions, a similar sequence of injustices appears: "He who says malicious things, spreads calumny, and points his finger behind the back of a person of equal rank" (cf. *BWL*, 119, lines 5-9).

[10] *And you offer your sustenance to the hungry* — and if you provide provisions for those who are without food. The term **נפש**, whose homonym appears in the following hemistich, is the etymological and semantic cognate of Akk. *napištu*, "livelihood, provisions, sustenance" (*CAD* N/1:302-3; see V. A. Hurowitz, "A Forgotten Meaning of *nepeš* in Isaiah LVIII 10," *VT* 47 [1997]: 43-52). Interestingly enough, it is translated as "bread" in the LXX (the Greek version actually has a doublet: **לחמך/נפשך**) and Peshitta, and appears in many medieval MT manuscripts; cf. also *Yalqut Shimoni, Vayikra,* §§665, 796, line 32; *Yalqut Shimoni, Isaiah,* §491 (Jerusalem 1960), 805. The verb **תָּפֵק**, from the root **פוק**, which is a synonym of **מצא** ("to find"; cf. Prov 3:13: "Happy is the man who finds [**מצא**] wisdom, the man who attains [**יפיק**] understanding"; Prov 18:22: "He who finds [**מצא**] a wife has found happiness and has won [**וַיָּפֶק**] the favor of the Lord"), appears also in Ugaritic in the epic of Kirta: "He did not find *(ypq)* a lawful wife" (*CAT* 1.14.I:12), as well as on the sarcophagus inscription of Tabnit, king of Sidon, dated to the end of the sixth century BCE: "Whoever you are, any man who finds (**תפק**) this coffin" (*KAI* 13:3). This hemistich is a thematic repetition of v. 7: "It is to share your bread with the hungry."

And satisfy the famished creature — This hemistich mirrors the previous clause: Instead of gorging your bodies, provide for the starving. For the expression **השׂביע נפש**, cf. v. 11: "He will slake your thirst (**והשׂביע נפשך**) in parched places"; Ps 107:9: "For He has satisfied (**השׂביע נפש**) the thirsty." **נַעֲנָה** is the *niph'al* participle from the root **ענ**י; see also vv. 3, 5.

Then shall your light shine in darkness — Then the darkness shall be pierced by luminescence, i.e., success and salvation — you shall be vindicated; cf. v. 8. See Ps 112:4: "A light shines for the upright in the darkness"; cf. Isa 42:16; 9:1: "On those who dwelt in a land of gloom, light has dawned." For the contrasting image, see 59:9: "We hope for light, and lo! There is darkness." For darkness representing plight, see Mic 7:8: "Though I sit in darkness, the Lord is my light."

And your gloom shall be like noonday — Your darkness shall be lit up as bright as the noonday sun. For another instance of **אֲפֵלָה** ("darkness") and **צהרים** ("noonday") as antonyms, see Deut 28:29: "You shall grope at noon (**בצהרים**) as a blind man gropes in the dark (**באפלה**)." For **אפלה** in conjunction with the synonymous חֹשֶׁךְ, see Joel 2:2. For a contrasting image, see Isa 59:9: "We hope . . . for a gleam, but we must walk in gloom." For the parallel אור/צהרים ("light/noonday"), see Ps 37:6: "He will cause your vindication to shine forth like the light, the justice of your case like the noonday."

[11] In the initial prophecies of Deutero-Isaiah, the provision of potable water in the desert for the returning expatriates was a recurring motif (e.g., Isa 43:20; 44:3). Now that they have already arrived home, the image shifts, and they themselves shall be "like a watered garden, like a spring whose waters do not fail."

The Lord will guide you always — Cf. Deut 32:12: "The Lord alone did guide him (יַנְחֶנּוּ)." Note the recurrent motif of divine vigilance; see v. 8.

He will slake your thirst in withering heat/in parched places — צחצָחות is a hapax legomenon derived from the root צחח (the doubling of the initial consonants is emphatic) and denotes withering heat and dryness (as do the Arabic and Syriac cognates). Some interpret this to be a promise to provide water in times of drought (Targum; Saadyah, 129; Menaḥem ben Saruq, *Sefer ha-Maḥberet,* 149, s.v. צח; Ibn Ganaḥ, *Sefer ha-Shorashim,* 427, s.v. צחח; Rashi; Kimchi). Others explain that the Lord will slake your thirst even in the driest and hottest of locales; cf. Ps 68:7: "While the rebellious must live in a parched land (צחיחה)." This divine blessing conforms to what was previously mentioned: If you shall "satisfy the famished creature" (v. 10, and see also vv. 3 and 5), then the Lord, in turn, shall satisfy your needs in arid environments. The word נפש appears here for the fifth time (see vv. 3, 5, 10 [twice, with different meanings]).

And invigorate/strengthen your bones — Most commentators interpret the verb from the root meaning "to fortify"; see Num 31:5 and cf. Syr. *ḥlyṣwt',* which also signifies strength. On the basis of this interpretation, later Rabbinic Hebrew coined the expression חילוץ עֲצָמוֹת, "the fortifying of the bones" (see *b. Ber.* 16b). According to a variant exegetical tradition found in the writings of some medieval Spanish commentators, however, it denotes "to saturate, to wet," i.e., "to invigorate," and thus is similar to the end of the verse: "You shall be like a watered garden" (Ibn Ganaḥ, *Sefer ha-Shorashim,* 157, s.v. חלץ; Ibn Balaam [ed. Goshen-Gottstein, 228]). For similar images, cf. Prov 15:30: "Good news puts fat on the bones"; Job 21:24: "The marrow of his bones is juicy"; Sir 26:13: "The wife's charm is the delight of her husband, and her wit fattens his bones." Instead of MT יחליץ, 1QIsa[a] reads יחליצו and 1QIsa[b] יחלצו (both plural forms), i.e., they, your bones, shall be invigorated/strengthened.

You shall be like a well-watered garden — Cf. Jer 31:12: "They shall become like a watered garden (כגן רָוֶה)."

Like a spring whose waters do not fail — You shall fare like a water source that never runs dry, but springs eternal. This phrase is the opposite of Jeremiah's description of a dry watercourse: "You have been to me like a spring that fails, like waters that cannot be relied on" (Jer 15:18). For a similar representation of an unfailing source whose "waters are reliable" (Isa 33:16), cf. the Akkadian "Hymn to Shamash": "Like the water of a never failing spring [his] descendants shall never fail" (*BWL* 132–33, line 121). For the expression מוֹצָא מים ("spring"), see 2 Kgs 2:21; 2 Chr 32:30; and for the plural, see Isa 41:18; Ps 107:33, 35. The term מוצא also appears in the seventh-century BCE Siloam Tunnel Inscription: "The water flowed from the spring (מוצא) to the pool" (*KAI* 189:4-5).

[12] Despite the return of the expatriates, the land is yet to be rebuilt and ruins are still all-pervasive.

Men from your midst shall rebuild the ancient ruins — The newly returned Judeans shall rebuild the ruins of yesteryear; cf. Isa 61:4: "And they shall rebuild the ancient ruins (חָרְבוֹת עולם), raise up the desolations of old, and renew the ruined cities, the desolations of many ages." This promise contrasts with the already-fulfilled Jeremian prophecy: "I am going to send for all the peoples of the north — declares the Lord — and for My servant, King Nebuchadrezzar of Babylon, and bring them against this land . . . and make them a desolation, an object of hissing — ruins for all time" (Jer 25:9). For חרבות עולם ("ancient ruins"), see also Jer 49:13, regarding the prophecy against Edom.

You shall restore foundations laid long ago — You shall raise and rehabilitate the buildings that for generations have stood razed, with nothing left but their foundations. For the verbal pair קומם/בני in similar contexts, see Isa 44:26: "It is I who say . . . of the towns of Judah, 'They shall be rebuilt (תִּבָּנֶינָה)'; and I will restore (אקומם) their ruined places"; 61:4: "And they shall build (ובנו) the ancient ruins, raise up (יקוממו) the desolations of old . . . the desolations of many ages." The noun מוסד in Biblical Hebrew denotes the foundation or basis of a structure; see 24:18: "And the earth's foundations tremble"; Ps 18:8: "The foundations of mountains shook." The parallel synonyms עולם/דור דור (see Isa 60:15; 61:4) also appear in Ugaritic: "You shall take possession of your kingship forever *('lmk)*, your rule for all generations untold *(drdrk)*" (*CAT* 1.2.IV.10). The emphatic doubling of דור is also common in Akkadian: *dār dūr, dūr dār* (*CAD* D:108).

And you shall be called: "Repairer of breached walls" — The form קֹרָא is an archaic *qal* passive (see also 48:8; 61:3; 62:2). For the expression גֹּדֵר פֶּרֶץ, see also Ezek 13:5: "You have not gone up into the breaches to repair the walls"; Amos 9:11: "I will mend its breaches and set up its ruins anew" (and cf. the contrasting image in Ps 80:13: "Why did You breach its wall?"). The noun פרץ denotes a breach in a wall or battlement; see Isa 30:13: "Like a spreading breach (פרץ) that occurs in a lofty wall." When the exiled Judeans returned to Jerusalem such indeed was the situation (see Neh 1:3; 2:13; 3:35; 4:1; 6:1).

"Restorer of lanes for habitation" — The expression וקֹרָא לך in the first

hemistich does double-duty. You shall be called the renovator of roads, which were ruined in the disaster of 586 BCE and thus remained uninhabited; see Lam 1:4: "Zion's roads are mourning"; and her cities were "without inhabitants" (Jer 9:10; 33:10); Jer 44:2: "No one inhabits them." Note the play on words: משובב . . . לשבת. For משובב ("restorer"), a *polel* stem derived from the root שוב, cf. Isa 49:5: "That Israel may be restored (לשובב) to Him"; Jer 50:19: "And I will restore (וְשֹׁבַבְתִּי) Israel back to his pasture." (Instead of MT משובב, 1QIsa[b] has the semantic equivalent משיב.) Compare also Isa 44:26, cited above, where the synonymous pair קומם/בני ("to rebuild/to restore") appears in conjunction with a third verb, תּוּשָׁב ("shall be inhabited"), and here with משובב. Instead of MT נתיבות ("lanes"), some exegetes suggest reading נתיצות, "ruined dwellings," parallel to "the ancient ruins" in the initial clause.

[13-14] In the final verses of the chapter, the prophet emphasizes Sabbath observance. This connection, following the description of a "favorable" fast, is not coincidental since both the Sabbath and the Day of Atonement (the biblical fast par excellence) are called שבת שבתון, "a Sabbath of complete rest" (the Sabbath in Exod 31:15; Lev 23:3; the Day of Atonement in Exod 35:2; Lev 16:31); and מִקרא קֹדֶשׁ, "sacred occasion" (the Sabbath in Lev 23:3; the Day of Atonement in Lev 23:27). Moreover, the observance of the Sabbath was especially emphasized during the period of the exile and the return (see Isa 56:2, 4, 6; 66:23), since the desecration of the Sabbath was considered one of the reasons for the national disaster (see Jer 17:24, 27; Ezek 20:12, 13, 15, 20, 21, 24; 22:8, 26; Neh 13:15-18). The prophet therefore promises that if they observe the Sabbath properly, they shall be rewarded with the repossession of the land. This short pericope is associatively connected to the previous one by means of the following phrases: v. 13: תשיב מִשַּׁבָּת . . . לַשַּׁבָּת — v. 12: משובב . . . לָשֶׁבֶת; as well as by the idiomatic expression that appears only here: מִמְּצוֹא חפצך (v. 13) and תמצאו חפץ (v. 3). Both the opening of the chapter and its conclusion employ a common appellation: בית יעקב (v. 1) and נחלת יעקב (v. 14). And both the first and second units conclude with the theme of resettlement. Compare also: דרכי (v. 2) — דרכיך (v. 13); דַּבֵּר אָוֶן (v. 9) — דַּבֵּר דָּבָר (v. 13); יום (vv. 2, 3, 4, 5, 13); and the conditional phrases: אם . . . אז, (vv. 9, 13-14). For prophetic (and general) displeasure against the conducting of business on the Sabbath, see Jer 17:27: "But if you do not obey My command to hallow the Sabbath day and to carry in no burdens through the gates of Jerusalem on the Sabbath day, then I will set fire to its gates. It shall consume the fortresses of Jerusalem, and it shall not be extinguished"; Neh 10:32: "The peoples of the land who bring their wares and all sorts of foodstuffs for sale on the Sabbath day — we will not buy from them on the Sabbath or on a holy day." The rabbis of the Talmud learned many of the Sabbath laws from these verses in Deutero-Isaiah.

[13] In the preceding verses, divine favor was made conditional upon

social reform (conduct relative to one's fellow), while here it is conditional upon Sabbath observance (conduct relative to God). The terms שבת, עשות, חפצך, and the roots כבד, קדש, and דבר all appear twice in this verse.

If you refrain from trampling the Sabbath underfoot — אם opens the protasis of the conditional phrase that concludes in the next verse. The unique expression השיב רגל מ- ("turn back your foot from") is similar to מנע רגל מ- (Prov 1:15); כלא רגל מ- (Ps 119:101); and הסיר רגל מ- (Prov 4:27). Its meaning is spelled out in the following clauses.

From pursuing your affairs on My holy day — If you forgo your business activities on the seventh day (then you will enjoy the heritage of Jacob [v. 14]). The *mem* prefix in משבת also applies to the infinitive construct עֲשׂוֹת (so too 1QIsa[a] and LXX; and cf. below, מֵעֲשׂוֹת דרכיך). For the Sabbath as the Lord's holy day, see Exod 31:15: "But on the seventh day there shall be a Sabbath of complete rest, holy to the Lord (קֹדֶשׁ לה׳)." The expression עֲשׂוֹת חפץ is identical to its Akkadian semantic equivalent *ṣibûtam epēšu,* "to pursue one's affairs" (see *CAD* E:218; Ṣ:170). (Cf. also the expression מצא חפץ below and in v. 3.) The Vulgate, Peshitta, Targum (צָרְכָךְ), 1QIsa[b], and some medieval MT manuscripts read the singular חֶפְצְךָ (as below) instead of the plural חֲפָצֶךָ in the majority of MT manuscripts. For the infinitive absolute עֲשׂוֹת, see Gen 2:4: "Such is the story of heaven and earth when they were created (עֲשׂוֹת) by the Lord God."

If you call the Sabbath "Delight" — The prophet now switches from prohibitions to positive commandments: If you shall treat the Sabbath as a day of joy and delight (cf. Saadyah Gaon: "If you shall celebrate the Sabbath with pleasures"). The substantive עֹנֶג appears again only in Isa 13:22: "In the palaces of pleasure (ענג)." The expression קרא ל- denotes naming or designating; cf. Esth 9:26: "For that reason these days were named (קראו ל-) Purim."

The Lord's holy day "Honored" — if you shall call the Sabbath, which is dedicated to the Lord, "Honored," i.e., a day on which the Lord is to be honored (see the following for the way in which this honor is expressed). In lieu of the expression לקדוש ה׳ ("the Lord's holy [day]"), *b. Shabb.* 103b and two medieval MT manuscripts read לקדוש ישראל ("for the Holy One of Israel"), an appellation of the Deity common in Deutero-Isaiah (see 41:14, 16, 20; 43:3, 14; 45:11; 47:4; 48:17; 49:7; 54:5; 55:5; 60:9, 14).

And if you honor it by not engaging in your business — if you shall give the Sabbath precedence over your commercial activities. The expression עֲשׂוֹת דרכיך is unique and can be clarified by its semantic equivalent in Akkadian, *ḫarrānam epēšu* (lit. "to make one's way"), which denotes a business trip (*CAD* E:208). For שבת as a masculine noun (reflected in וְכִבַּדְתּוֹ), see 56:2, 6.

Nor looking to your affairs — if you honor the Sabbath by not engaging in business. For this idiom, also found in Akkadian, see v. 3.

Nor striking bargains — if you honor the Sabbath by forgoing business deals. Hebrew דַּבֵּר דָּבָר, similar to its Akkadian semantic equivalent *dibbātu dabābu* (*CAD* D:131), denotes negotiation and the striking of a deal; cf. Gen 24:33: "I will not eat until I have concluded my negotiations (דברתי דברי)"; Isa 8:10: "Make plans (דַּבְּרוּ דבר), but they will be foiled"; Hos 10:4: "So they conclude agreements (דִּבְּרוּ דברים) and make covenants with false oaths"; cf. also 1 Sam 20:21.

[14] The prophet describes the spiritual and material rewards of observing the Sabbath, specifically divine favor and the inheritance of their ancestral heritage. The Song of Moses left its linguistic and thematic imprint on this verse: "For the Lord's portion is His people, Jacob His own allotment. . . . He set him atop heights of the earth to enjoy the yield of the fields" (Deut 32:9, 13). Thematically, the Mosaic promise in the song will be fulfilled, provided that the Israelites observe the Sabbath, as delineated in v. 13. Linguistically, the very distinctive idiom הרכיב על במתי ארץ ("to set astride the heights of the earth") appears only here and in Deuteronomy, and both are accompanied by a similar image: "He [Israel] shall enjoy (ויאכל) the yield of the fields" (Deut 32:13); and here: "I shall let you enjoy (והאכלתיך) the heritage of your father Jacob." (One should note that both LXX and Targum [וְאוֹכָלְנּוּן] translate the verb in the Deuteronomic verse as a causative *hiphʿil* [like והאכלתיך here] instead of the MT *qal*, ויאכל.) Moreover, both connect the terms נחלה ("heritage, allotment") and יעקב ("Jacob"). (Perhaps one should add another linguistic item to this comparison: Both Deut 32:12 and v. 11 here feature the verb נחי ["the Lord alone did guide him (יַנְחֶנּוּ)," and "The Lord will guide you (וְנָחֲךָ) always"].) In spite of these common images, there is an important difference between Deuteronomy and Deutero-Isaiah: In the former Israel is the Lord's allotment or heritage, while in the latter the land of Israel is the nation's heritage or reward, which accords with the usual emphasis on return and inheritance in Deutero-Isaiah's prophecy. (See the introduction, §13.)

Then you shall find your delight in the Lord — The reward of one who "calls the Sabbath 'Delight' (ענג)" will be that he shall find his "delight" (תתענג) in the Lord. For the *hithpaʿel* of ענג, see also Ps 37:4; Job 22:26; 27:10.

I will set you astride the heights of the earth — For the expression הרכיב על במתי/במותי ארץ, see Deut 32:12 and the introduction to the verse. For בָּמֳתֵי ארץ alone, see Amos 4:13; Mic 1:3; and cf. its Ugaritic cognate *bmt*, which is used as a poetic description for heights and hills (*HdO* 1:224). The Lord promises His nation that they shall repossess their mountainous heritage. Instead of MT והרכבתיך (first-person singular with a pronominal suffix), the LXX, Targum, and 1QIsa[a] have והרכיבכה (third-person masculine singular with a pronominal suffix: "He shall set you astride"; and cf. similarly 1QIsa[b]: והרכיבך), corresponding to the beginning of the verse that speaks of God in the third person.

And I will let you enjoy the heritage of your father Jacob — I shall grant you the fruits of your father Jacob's heritage, i.e., the land of Israel; cf. Ps 105:11: "To you I will give the land of Canaan as your allotted heritage (נחלתכם)." As in the prior hemistich, the LXX, Targum (וְיוֹכֵילְנָךְ), and 1QIsa[a] (והאכילכה) decline the verb as a third-person masculine singular instead of the first-person singular, והאכלתיך, in the MT. There may be a hidden wordplay here, since the chapter begins with the theme of fasting and ends with "eating" (והאכלתיך), at least in the metaphorical sense. Moreover, the reward of the nation that provides for the hungry (vv. 7, 10) is that they themselves shall have the enjoyment of "eating" (והאכלתיך).

The mouth of the Lord has truly spoken — The prophecy ends with a signature confirming the authenticity of the message (the initial כי is emphatic). Compare likewise 40:5 and 1:19-20.

Chapter 59

The chapter consists of a single literary unit that may be subdivided into three separate scenes: vv. 1-8: the accusation; vv. 9-15a: the confessional lament; vv. 15b-21: divine intercession and redemption of repentant sinners. Since the people did not heed the prophet's call: "Observe what is right and do what is just" (56:1), but rather persisted in their iniquitous conduct and offensive crimes as listed in this chapter, a barrier between the nation and God obfuscates the divine countenance and distances the long-awaited redemption. The prophet insists that God is not the one to blame for this obstacle; rather it is the nation's transgressions. When the Lord, in His warrior garb, sees that there is no one willing to take responsibility for this sorry state of affairs, He girds Himself for a solitary battle against His enemies, so that the whole world will see His splendor and glory. He alone will redeem those of His nation who repent and shall make an eternal covenant with them.

The chapter is rich in metaphor: the conception and birth of falsehood and evil (v. 4), spiders and poisonous snakes (vv. 5-6), darkness and gloom (v. 9), blindness (v. 10), the growling of bears and the moaning of doves (v. 11), God's warrior garb (v. 17). Note also the abundance of words and terms that appear twice or more in this pericope: אין, eight times (vv. 4 [twice], 8, 10, 11, 15, 16 [twice]); שפט, six times (vv. 4, 8, 9, 11, 14, 15); צדק, five times (vv. 4, 9, 14, 16, 17); ישע, four times (vv. 1, 11, 16, 17); פשע, four times (vv. 12 [twice], 13, 20); אָוֶן, thrice (vv. 4, 6, 7); רחק, thrice (vv. 9, 11, 14); כפיהם, twice (vv. 3, 6); דם, twice (vv. 3, 7); הרו, twice (vv. 4, 13); כשל, twice (vv. 10, 14); the expression סוג מֵאַחַר/אחור, twice (vv. 13, 14); אמת, twice (vv. 14, 15); וַיַּרְא, twice (vv. 15, 16); רוח, twice (vv. 19, 21). Moreover, there are words that are repeated twice, thrice, and even four times in the same verse: אין (vv. 4, 16, twice each), ביצים (v. 5, twice), בקע (v. 5, twice), מחשבות (v. 7, twice), שלום (v. 8, twice), פשעינו (v. 12, twice), ישלם (v. 18, twice), כעל (v. 18, twice), מעשים (v. 6, three times),

לבש (v. 17, three times), גמול (v. 18, three times), זרע (v. 21, three times), פֶּה (v. 21, four times).

This chapter is linked to chap. 58 by many common words and phrases: 58:1: "Declare to My people their transgression (פִּשְׁעָם), to the house of Jacob their sin (חטאתם)" — 59:12: "We are aware of our sins (פשעינו), and we know well our iniquities (חטאתינו)," 59:20: "To those in Jacob who turn back from sin (פשע)" (cf. also v. 13); 58:2: "Right (צדקה) . . . law (ומשפט) . . . right way (ומשפטי צדק)" — 59:14: "Redress (משפט) . . . vindication (צדקה)" (for other examples see the list above of terms appearing more than once); 58:7: "and clothe him (וכסיתו)" — 59:6: "serve as clothing (יתכַּסו)"; 58:8: "Burst through (יִבָּקַע)" — 59:5: "Hatch . . . hatches (בִּקֵּעוּ . . . תִּבָּקַע)"; 58:8: "Then shall your light (אורך) burst forth (יבקע) like the dawn," v. 10: "Then shall your light (אורך) shine in darkness (בחשך), and your gloom (אפֵלתך) shall be like noonday (כצהרים)" — 59:9: "We hope for light (לאור), but lo! There is darkness (חשך). For a gleam, and we must walk in gloom (באפֵלות)," v. 10: "We stumble at noon (צהרים), as if in darkness (כנֶשף)"; 58:8: "the Presence of the Lord (כבוד ה׳)" — 59:19: "His Presence (כבודו)"; 58:9: "evil speech (ודַבֶּר אָוֶן)" — 59:4: "and speak (וְדַבֵּר) falsehood . . . and begetting evil (אָוֶן)," v. 6: "deeds of mischief (אָוֶן)," v. 7: "plans of mischief (אָוֶן)."

[1-3] The chapter begins with an admonition addressed to the nation in the second-person masculine plural. The reason the Lord does not save His nation and does not answer their prayers is not because of His inability to do so, but rather because of the barrier of sinful conduct the nation has erected. The first three verses of the chapter bear the thematic and linguistic imprint of Isa 1:15: "And when you lift up your hands, I will hide My eyes from you. Though you pray at length, I will not listen. Your hands are stained with blood." (See the introduction, §14.)

[1] *Indeed, the Lord's arm is not too short to save* — הן is an emphatic interjection that introduces the prophet's response to the people's claims against God (see, e.g., 58:3). For the expression קצרה יד, which denotes weakness and inability, see 50:2: "Is My arm, then, too short to rescue (הֲקָצוֹר קצרה ידי)? Have I not the power to save?"; Num 11:23: "Is there a limit to the Lord's power (היד ה׳ תקצר)?" There is, in fact, no limit to the divine power, as is indicated in v. 16 here: "Then His own arm won Him triumph." The equivalent expression in Arabic, *qaṣurat yaduhu ʿan*, also signifies lack of power.

Nor His ear too dull to hear — His hearing is not impaired or malfunctioning; He is not deaf or unable to hear your prayers. For the expression כבד אֹזֶן, see Isa 6:10: "Deafen his ears"; Zech 7:11: "But they refused to pay heed . . . and turned a deaf ear." This expression comes from the medical jargon, as one learns from the Akkadian cognates *uznā kabta* (*CAD* K:15), and the variant *nešmû kabit* ("heavy or hard of hearing") (*CAD* N/2:192); and cf. the contrasting idiom *nešmû qalālu* ("unimpeded hearing"; *CAD* Q:55). For other handicaps described in similar terms, see Gen 48:10: "Now Israel's eyes were dim (כבדו) with age"; Exod 4:10: "Slow of (כבד) speech and slow of (כבד) tongue."

[2] *But it is your iniquities that have been a barrier between you and your God* — It is not that your prayer is unheard, but rather that your iniquitous behavior has hindered the divine response. For the verb הבדיל, see 56:3: "The Lord will keep me apart (יבדילַני) from His people." The expression כי אם ("but") signifies contrast, as in Exod 12:9: "Do not eat any of it raw, or cooked in any way with water, but (כי אם) roasted."

Your sins have made Him turn His face away and refuse to hear you — It is not the inefficacy of your prayer, but rather your sinful conduct, that has caused the Lord to turn away from you. Read פניו ("His face," as in LXX, Vulgate, and Peshitta, instead of MT פנים). The scribal error was the result of dittography (the *mem* of the adjacent word מכם was mistakenly written twice). For the expression הסתיר פנים ("hide one's face"), see 54:8: "For a moment I hid My face from you"; 64:6: "For You have hidden Your face from us." For the same sequence of ineffective prayer and concealment of the divine countenance because of sins, see Mic 3:4: "Then they shall cry out to the Lord, but He will not answer them. At that time He will hide His face from them, because their deeds are so wicked." For the parallel synonyms חטא/עון ("iniquity/sin"), see Isa 43:24. The verse ends like v. 1, with the infinitive construct מִשְּׁמוֹעַ ("to hear"), and, as in v. 1, the Targum adds here צְלוֹתְכוֹן ("your prayers").

[3-8] A list of the nation's sins; cf. 58:3b-4.

[3] The prophet accuses the people of sinning in their conduct (with their hands and fingers) and in their speech (with their lips and tongues). These sins contrast, then, with the Lord's hand and ear(s) in v. 1.

For your hands are defiled with blood — Your hands are soiled with the blood of innocent victims; cf. 1:15: "And when you lift up your hands, I will hide My eyes away from you. . . . Your hands are stained with blood." The verb נְגֹאֲלוּ (from the root גאל, a by-form of געל, appearing only in late books [Zephaniah, Malachi, Lamentations, Nehemiah, Daniel]) is a hybrid conflation blending the *niphʿal* נִגְאֲלוּ and the archaic *qal* passive נֻגְאֲלוּ; cf. Lam 4:14: "They wandered blindly through the streets, defiled (נְגֹאֲלוּ) with blood." For another conflation from this root, see Isa 63:3: "And all My clothing was stained (אֶגְאָלְתִּי)," which is a blend of the *qal* past tense (גאלתי) and the *niphʿal* future (אֶגָּאֵל).

And your fingers with iniquity — The frequent parallel ידים/אצבעות (e.g., Ps 144:1: "Who trains my hands [ידי] for battle, my fingers [אצבעותי] for warfare"), which also appears in Ugaritic (*yd/uṣbʿt,* e.g., *CAT* 1.19.I:78), is substituted here by a semantically identical but unique pair, אצבעות/כפים. The variant בעולה, in 1QIsa[a], of MT בֶּעָוֹן was influenced by the appearance of this word toward the end of the verse. It is interesting to note that 1QIsa[a]'s version of

Isa 1:15 (see above), following ידיכם דמים מלאו ("Your hands are stained with crime"), has the additional phrase אצבעותיכם בעאון, which clearly was influenced by the clause here.

Your lips speak lies — Cf. Ps 120:2: "O Lord, save me from lying lips (מִשְּׂפַת שקר), from a deceitful tongue!" For the plural form שפתותיכם, see also Cant 4:3.

Your tongue utters treachery — Cf. below, v. 13: "Planning fraud and treachery"; Job 27:4: "My lips will speak no wrong, nor my tongue utter deceit." The parallel synonyms לשון/שׂפה ("lips/tongue"; see Ezek 3:5, 6) also appear in the Ugaritic Baal epic *(špt/lšn)* describing (the god) Mot's insatiable appetite (*CAT* 1.5.II:2-3). The verb הגה ("to utter") is parallel here to דבר ("to speak"), as in Ps 37:30: "The mouth of the righteous utters (יֶהְגֶּה) wisdom, and his tongue speaks (תדבר) what is right"; see also Prov 24:2; Job 27:4.

[4-8] The admonition continues in the third-person.

[4] *No one sues justly* — "No plaintiff makes just claims" (Saadyah, 130; and cf. Ehrlich, *Mikrâ Ki-Pheshuṭo,* 3:145). The word בצדק (like its Akkadian semantic equivalent, *kīniš* [*CAD* K:386]) means "truthfully." For the verb קרא in its legal sense, see Job 9:16: "If I summoned (קראתי) Him and He responded"; Job 13:22: "Then summon (וּקְרָא) me and I will respond; or I will speak and You reply to me." (For the legal connotations of its Akkadian cognate *šasû,* "to call, to summon," see *CAD* Š/2:15.)

Or pleads honestly — And none of those summoned to trial testifies honestly. For other examples of the verb שפט in the *niphʿal* ("to contend, plead"), see Isa 43:26; 66:16; Jer 2:35. For the synonymous pair אמונה/צדק ("justice/honesty"), see Isa 11:5: "Justice (צדק) shall be the girdle of his loins, and honesty (והאמונה) the girdle of his waist"; Ps 96:13: "He will rule the world justly (בצדק) and the peoples in honesty (באמונה)."

They rely on emptiness — They put their trust in nothingness; cf. Isa 49:4: "I have spent my strength for nothing (לְתֹהוּ), to no purpose." The word בָּטוֹחַ is the first of four infinitives absolute, indicating a constant and continual manner of behavior.

And speak falsehood — They utter untruths and speak deceitfully; cf. Ezek 13:8: "Because you speak falsehood (שָׁוְא) and prophesy lies"; Ps 12:3: "Men speak falsehood (שָׁוְא) to one another." The expression דַּבֵּר שָׁוְא ("to speak falsehood") is parallel to דִּבְּרוּ שקר ("they utter treachery") in v. 3; and cf. below, v. 13: דַּבֵּר עֹשֶׁק ("planning fraud").

Conceiving wrong — They plan treachery (and carry it out); cf. Ps 7:15: "See, he hatches evil, conceives mischief (הָרוֹ עמל), and gives birth to fraud"; Job 15:35: "For they have conceived mischief (הָרֹה עמל), given birth to evil." In all these verses the root הרי ("to conceive") is used metaphorically for "hatching a plot."

And begetting mischief — For the same image, see the verses quoted in the commentary to the previous hemistich. For the synonymous pair אָוֶן/עמל ("wrong/evil"), see Isa 10:1; Ps 10:7: Ps 7:15.

[5-6] Note the threefold expanded parallel construction of these two verses: בֵּיצֵי צִפְעוֹנִי ... מִבֵּיצֵיהֶם;וְקוּרֵי עַכָּבִישׁ ... קוּרֵיהֶם;מַעֲשֵׂיהֶם מַעֲשֵׂי אָוֶן. In vv. 5-8 the admonishment switches from a second-person to a third-person address.

[5] The prophet compares the misdeeds of the evildoers to the eggs that poisonous snakes hatch. (For another image of poisonous snakes, see Ps 58:5: "Their venom is like that of a snake.") This image is then followed by an image of a spider who weaves its diaphanous and nefarious plans. The first image continues in the verse's second stich, while the second is elaborated on in v. 6. (It is possible that the same two images exist side by side in Ps 140:4 as well: "They sharpen their tongues like serpents [נחש]; spider's [עכשוב] poison is on their lips," if the hapax legomenon עַכְשׁוּב is understood as a by-form of עכביש ["spider"], which is the version in the *Psalms Scroll* from Qumran. See J. A. Sanders, *The Psalms Scroll of Qumrân Cave 11,* DJD 4 [Oxford, 1965], 48, line 14.)

They hatch adder's eggs — a metaphor for conceiving evil plans. For the poisonous צִפְעוֹנִי snake, see also Isa 11:8; 14:29; Jer 8:17; Prov 23:32. For another occurrence of the verb בקע, referring to the hatching of snake eggs, see Isa 34:15.

And weave spiderwebs — a further image: They, the spiders, weave silken threads, forming their salivary excretions into a web so as to capture unwary prey who wander into the invisible strands. Note the wordplay: קוּרֵי and קֹרֵא (v. 4).

He who eats of their eggs will die — Whoever consumes these eggs will die of their poison. "Just as any who joins them or their plans will perish" (Kimchi).

And if one is crushed it hatches out a viper — Some explain the form וְהַזּוּרֶה (which should be vocalized with a *qameṣ* under the *resh,* since the governing substantive ביצה ["egg"] is feminine; see Ibn Ezra, Kimchi) as an archaic *qal* passive from the root זור, which denotes "trampling, crushing" (see Job 39:14-15: "She leaves her eggs on the ground, letting them warm in the dirt, forgetting they may be crushed [תְּזוּרֶהָ] underfoot, or trampled by a wild beast"). Even though the egg is crushed, it nevertheless still hatches out a poisonous viper (אֶפְעֶה) (for this snake see, e.g., Isa 30:6; Job 20:16). Others interpret והזורה as an adjective describing the eggs, as in *m. Ḥul.* 12:3: ביצים מוזרות ("rotten eggs"), i.e., despite their putrefaction, the eggs will still hatch a venomous viper. For another example of זור ("to be rotten"), see Job 19:17: "My odor is repulsive (זרה) to my wife." It is interesting to note that the image of the hatching (בקע) of אפעה appears in the *Hodayot* scroll from Qumran (1QH[a] 10:29-30), where, however, אפעה has the meaning "deception" (most likely based on its appearance in Isa 41:24) and is parallel to שָׁוְא, "vanity" (Stegemann et al., DJD 40, 133; for other examples of the noun with this meaning, see 1QH[a] 11:13, 18, 19; DJD 40, 144-45).

[6] The prophet further develops the second metaphor, that of the cobweb. For a similar image, cf. Job 8:14-15: "Whose trust is a spider's web. He leans on its house, but it will not stand. He seizes hold of it, but it will not hold firm."

Their webs will not serve as a garment — The gossamer threads of a spider's weave cannot be used for clothing.

What they make cannot serve as clothing — Their web is not something you can use as a covering. מעשיהם signifies the product produced, as in Exod 23:16: "When you gather in the results of your work (מעשיך) from the field"; Hab 3:17: "Though the olive crop (מעשה) has failed." For the root כסי ("to cover") in the context of wearing a garment, see 1 Kgs 11:29: "He had put on (מתכסה) a new robe"; so too in the Ugaritic Baal epic: "For clothing, he covered himself *(yks)* with a ritual tunic" (*CAT* 1.5.VI:16).

Their deeds are deeds of mischief — The conduct of evildoers is iniquitous (see v. 4). Note the conjunction of the twice-repeated מעשיהם, one after another, each with a different nuance.

Their hands commit lawless acts — The term פֹּעַל, similar to מעשיהם in the previous stich, is polysemous. On the one hand, it refers to the lawless acts of evil men; on the other, it denotes the fruit of their immoral and iniquitous actions, or as Luzzatto comments: "the wealth and money in their hands." Cf. Job 7:2: "Like a hireling who waits for his wage (פָּעֳלוֹ)." For the parallel pair פֹּעַל/מעשה, see Isa 5:12. For the connection between "lawlessness" (חמס) and "hands" (כפים), cf. Jonah 3:8; Job 16:17; 1 Chr 12:18.

[7] Both hands and feet take part in their pursuit of depravity. The first two hemistichs are quoted almost verbatim from Prov 1:16 (with only one additional word): "For their feet run to evil. They hurry to shed blood." Compare also Prov 6:16-18: "Six things the Lord hates . . . a lying tongue, hands that shed innocent blood, a mind that hatches evil plots, feet quick to run to evil." (Note the parallel to v. 3 here: "Your lips speak falsehood, your tongue utters treachery"; and v. 4: "begetting mischief [אָוֶן]." The first and last two lines are chiastically parallel.)

Their feet run after evil — They are fleet-footed in their pursuit of wickedness. Note the alliteration of the letter *resh* in this hemistich: רגליהם לרע יָרֻצוּ (and see also the first word of the following hemistich, וימהרו).

They hasten to shed the blood of the innocent — See v. 3, and cf. Deut 19:10: "So that the blood of the innocent will not be shed"; cf. Jer 7:6; 22:3. For the synonymous pair מהר/רוץ ("to hasten/to run"), see the verses from the book of Proverbs quoted in the introduction to the verse.

Their schemes are schemes of mischief — The term אָוֶן is repeated here for the third time; see vv. 4, 6.

Destructiveness and injury are on their roads — Wherever they go, they sow ruin and devastation. For the nominal pair שֶׁבֶר/שֹׁד, see 51:19; 60:18; Jer 48:3. 1QIsa[a] adds חמס to this pair because of the frequent joint appearance of חמס and שֹׁד (e.g., Jer 6:7; Hab 1:3). מסילותם ("their roads") (see also מְמסלותם in Judg 5:20) is a variant form of מסילותיהם; cf. 1QIsa[a] במסלותיהמה.

[8] This verse, which is framed by a chiastic *inclusio*: דרך שלום לא ידעו . . . כל דֹּרֵךְ בה לא ידע שלום ("They do not care for the way of integrity. . . . No one who walks in it cares for integrity"), is an elaboration of the image in v. 7 and describes the nation's wanton ways, expressed by synonymous parallels (נתיב, מעגל, דרך).

They do not care for the way of integrity — For שלום with the meaning "truthfulness, sincerity," cf. Ps 37:37: "Mark the blameless, note the upright, for there is a future for the man of integrity (שלום)." This is also one of the meanings of its Akkadian etymological cognates, *šalimtu* and *šalmu* (*CAD* Š/1:245, 258-59).

There is no justice on their paths — For the parallel synonyms מעגל/דרך, see Prov 4:26: "Survey the path (מעגל) you take, and all your ways (דרכיך) will be secure." Note the chiasm formed by the first two hemistichs.

They make their courses crooked for themselves — They devise devious paths for themselves; cf. Prov 2:15: "Men whose paths are crooked (עִקְּשִׁים) and who are devious in their course"; 10:9: "But he who walks a crooked (וּמְעַקֵּשׁ) path will be found out"; see also 4:11; 5:21.

No one who walks in it cares for integrity — For the synonymous pair דרך/נתיבות (here דֹּרֵךְ appears as a finite verb), see Isa 42:16: "I will lead the blind by a road (בדרך) they did not know, and I will make them walk by paths (בנתיבות) they never knew"; 43:16: "Who made a road (דרך) through the sea and a path (נתיבה) through mighty waters." Instead of the MT's singular בה ("in it"), the LXX, Vulgate, Peshitta, and Targum (בְּהוֹן) all have a plural, which agrees with נתיבותיהם ("their courses") above.

[9-15a] Since the nation was found guilty of so many interpersonal sins, they were punished. The following verses list (in the first-person) the nation's misadventures, their confession, and their admission that their punishment is indeed just. This is followed by a general list of iniquities in vv. 14-15a, which are described by the infinitive absolute.

[9] *"That is why redress is far from us"* — Measure for measure: Since "there is no justice (משפט) on their paths" (v. 8), they are not deserving of "redress" (משפט). The leitmotif משפט ("justice, redress") appears below in vv. 11, 14, 15.

"And vindication does not reach us" — For the parallel pair צדקה/משפט, see 56:1.

"We hope for light, but lo! There is darkness" — We yearn for light, i.e., salvation and deliverance (cf. 60:1). In contrast, darkness represents adversity. See Jer 13:16: "You hope for light, but it is turned to darkness and becomes deep gloom." Compare also the people's hopes and fears regarding the "day of the Lord" in Amos 5:18: "Why should you want the day of the Lord? It shall be darkness, not light!" For a similarly worded contrast, cf. Isa 5:7: "He hoped for justice, but behold, injustice; for equity, but behold, iniquity!"

"For a gleam, but we must walk in gloom" — We seek a gleam of light (= deliverance), but instead we walk in deep gloom (= grave peril). For the substantive parallel pair **נֹגַהּ/אור** ("light/gleam"), see 60:3, 19; and for the antonymous pair **אֲפֵלָה/נֹגַהּ** ("gleam/gloom"), see Amos 5:20: "Blackest gloom (**וְאָפֵל**) without a gleam (**נֹגַהּ**)"; cf. Isa 50:10: "Though he walk in darkness (**חֲשֵׁכִים**) and have no light (**נֹגַהּ**)." A further example of this negative parallelism appears in the Balaam text from Deir ʿAlla (dated to the second quarter of the eighth century BCE): "For there was darkness (**חשך**) there and no gleam (**נגה**)" (see Aḥituv, *Ha-Ketav veha-Miḵtav*, 386, lines 6-7). The plural forms of the abstract nouns **נְגֹהוֹת** ("gleam") and **אֲפֵלוֹת** ("gloom") are sui generis (see the introduction, §11), and together with the immediately preceding **אור** and **חשך** create an alliteration of the *o* vowel. The *piʿel* finite form of the verb **נְהַלֵּךְ** indicates frequency of action. Most of the occurrences of this verbal form are found in the later books; see, e.g., Ezek 18:9; Hab 3:11; Eccl 4:15.

[10-11] It is likely that the curses found in Deut 28:28-29 left their thematic and linguistic imprint on these verses: "The Lord will strike you . . . with blindness. . . . You shall grope at noon as a blind man gropes in the dark. You shall not prosper in your ventures . . . with no one to save you." (See the introduction, §13.)

[10] The metaphor of darkness (representing peril) continues. Since the nation is guilty of abrogating the covenant, the Deuteronomic curses (Deut 28:28-29) have come to pass. The curse of blindness when justice is not present (see vv. 9, 13) is also found in King Esarhaddon's vassal treaty with subservient nations: "May Shamash [the sun god, in charge of maintaining justice] . . . not render you a just judgment. May he deprive you of the light of your eyes so that you will wander in darkness" (D. J. Wiseman, *The Vassal Treaties of Esarhaddon* [London, 1958], 59-60, lines 422-24). For the motif of blindness, see also Isa 42:7, 16, 18, 19; 43:8; 56:10. Compare also the image of groping through darkness, e.g., "May he [Zû, a mythological bird] grope through the darkness. May his eyesight fail" (*CAD* I-J:60).

"We grope like blind men along a wall" — We fumble our way along by feeling the walls at our sides, so as not to stumble or fall. The hapax legomenon verb **גשש** is a borrowing from Aramaic, and appears in Targum Onqelos as the translation of the Hebrew root **מוש/משש** in Gen 27:12, 22. (See the introduc-

tion, §11.) For similar images, cf. Zeph 1:17: "And they shall walk like blind men, because they sinned against the Lord"; Lam 4:14: "They wandered blindly through the streets." נְגַשְׁשָׁה is a first-personal plural cohortative.

"Like those without eyes we grope" — This clause creates a negative chiastic parallel with the preceding hemistich: "like blind men — like those without eyes." Compare the contrasting image in Isa 43:8: "Blind, though he has eyes."

"We stumble at noon as if at twilight" — We encounter obstacles even at the height of day. But since we are unable to see them, we stagger blindly as if it were night. For נֶשֶׁף, see Prov 7:9. For similar images, cf. Deut 28:29: "You shall grope at noon as a blind man gropes in the dark"; Job 5:14: "By day they encounter darkness; at noon they grope as in the night."

"At daytime we are like the dead" — a difficult clause to interpret. Ibn Ezra lists several possible meanings for the hapax legomenon אַשְׁמַנִּים: "There are those who understand it as graves (Targum [קִבְרַיָּא]; Saadyah Gaon)" (and, in the same vein, the Vulgate, Menaḥem ben Saruq, *Sefer ha-Maḥberet,* 35, s.v. אשמן: "It should be understood according to its context: 'in gloom'"; Ibn Ganaḥ, *Sefer ha-Shorashim,* 522, s.v. שמן: "It should be understood according to its context: 'in darkness,' or, more specifically, 'in the darkness of peril,' as if they were in the gloom of the dead, in other words, 'in the graves'; and it [the image] is equivalent to: 'He made me dwell in darkness like those long dead [Ps 143:3]"). Ibn Ezra continues: "The correct understanding, however, is 'like noon' or 'like the living,' i.e., 'among the living.' It is possible that the *aleph* is prosthetic [as in אַרבע or אֶצבע], and one can interpret the clause as: 'among the sturdy' [= the strong, the healthy], i.e., the nations." It is also possible, however, that בָּאַשְׁמַנִּים should be divided, with metathesis, into two separate words: בְּאֶשֶׁן יֹם, "at daytime." For אִישׁוֹן/אֶשׁוֹן with the meaning "time," see Prov 7:9: "In the dusk of evening, at the time of (בְּאִישׁוֹן) the night's darkness" (where it also appears alongside נֶשֶׁף); Prov 20:20: "One who reviles his father or mother, light will fail him at nighttime (בֶּאֱשׁוּן)." It also appears in Targum Jonathan as the translation for "dawn" (שחר) (Gen 19:15), "time" (עת) (Lev 15:25), and "appointed time" (מועד) (Deut 31:10).

[11] The people's desperation is described in further detail as they groan and moan like bears and doves.

"We all growl like bears" — We all snarl and yowl like bears in dire straits. For the verb המי in the context of similar laments, see Jer 48:36: Ezek 7:16.

"And moan like doves" — Dirgelike sounds escape our throats akin to the moaning of doves; see Isa 38:14; Ezek 7:16; Nah 2:8. The expression הָגֹה נֶהְגֶּה, an infinitive absolute followed by a finite verb, is emphatic. For the verb הגי, see vv. 3, 13. In Akkadian literature as well, the sighing sounds doves make resemble the cries of mourners (*CAD* D:60; S:379-80). The first two hemistichs of the verse form a chiasm.

"We hope for redress, but there is none" — We seek vindication (see v. 9), but none is forthcoming. For this formulation, cf. Ps 69:21: "I hope for consolation, but there is none; for comforters, but find none."

"For deliverance, but it is far from us" — We yearn for deliverance, yet it remains elusive and beyond our reach (see vv. 9, 14). For the contrasting image, see Isa 46:13.

[12-13] Regret accompanied by a detailed admission of wrongdoing.

[12] Their communal confession resembles in many ways the similar admission of guilt in Jer 14:7: "Though our iniquities testify against us, act, O Lord, for the sake of Your name. Our disloyalties are many, and we have sinned against You." The nation offers their explanation of God's unresponsive attitude by admitting their guilt in three types of offenses: **פשע**, **חטאה**, and **עָוֹן** (for the three see Exod 34:7). Ultimately, as opposed to the confession in Jeremiah, which ends with God's refusal to deliver Israel (Jer 14:8-9), God does acknowledge Israel's repentance and battles with their enemies in order to expedite their deliverance (vv. 16ff.).

"For our many transgressions are before You" — This verse offers a reason for the national plight and lack of divine response described above: The nation's acts of rebellion (cf. Jer 5:6) are ever-present in God's eyes; cf. Ps 90:8: "You have set our iniquities before You (**לנגדך**)." This is the only place in the entire chapter where God is addressed directly.

"Our guilt testifies against us" — For the verbal expression **ענה ב-**, see Isa 3:9: "Their partiality in judgment testifies against them (**ענתה בם**)"; Jer 14:7: "Though our iniquities testify against us (**ענו בנו**)." The verb **עָנְתָה** is an archaic third-person feminine plural (1QIsa[a] simplifies by writing the third-person masculine plural, **ענו**); cf. Gen 49:22: **בנות צעדה עלי שור**; Deut 21:7: **ידינו לא שפכה [Qere: שפכו] את הדם הזה**; 1 Sam 4:15: **ועיניו קמה**.

"We are well aware of our sins" — The **כי** particle expresses emphasis: We are well and truly aware of our transgressions. For the preposition **את**, here (similar to **עם**) signifying cognizance, see Job 12:3: "Who does not know (**את**) such things?"; Job 15:9: "What do you know that we do not know, or understand that we are not cognizant of (**עִמנו**)?"

"And we know well our iniquities" — We are fully cognizant of our wayward manner; cf. 2 Sam 19:21: "For your servant knows that he has sinned"; Ps 51:5: "For I recognize my transgressions, and am ever conscious of my sin."

[13] In a series of six infinitive absolutes expressing continuity and regularity, the nation enumerates the sins to which they confess. Compare also vv. 6-8.

"Rebellion, faithlessness to the Lord" — We have rebelled and broken faith with the Lord. For the verbal expression **כחש ב-** ("to break faith, act deceptively against"), see Josh 24:27: "Lest you break faith with your God (**פן**

תִּכַחֲשׁוּן באלהיכם)"; Jer 5:12: "They have broken faith with the Lord (כִּחֲשׁוּ בה׳) and said: 'It is not so!'" The verb פשע, which appears here again (twice in the preceding verse), means "to rebel"; see 2 Kgs 3:7: "The king of Moab has rebelled (פשע) against me." Compare also v. 20 below. "To those in Jacob who turn back from sin (פֶּשַׁע)."

"And turning away from our God" — We have deviated from the Lord's path. For this expression, see Zeph 1:6: "And those who have turned away from the Lord (הנסוגים מאחרי ה׳)." נָסוֹג is a *niph'al* infinitive absolute from the root סוג; cf. Isa 14:31: נָמוֹג, from the root מוג.

"Planning fraud and treachery" — We have schemed deviously and planned evil acts. For the expression דַּבֶּר עֹשֶׁק, see Ps 73:8; and for דַּבֶּר סרה see Jer 29:32. For the Akkadian cognates of the latter expression, *sarrātam/ sarrūtam/sartam/surrātam dabābu,* see *CAD* S:179, 185, 186-87, 409-10.

"Conceiving lies and uttering them with the throat" — Both הֹרוֹ, "to conceive" (vocalize as in v. 4, הָרוֹ), and הֹגוֹ, "to utter" (vocalize הָגוֹ; see vv. 3, 11 — and note the assonance created by the two), are rare infinitive absolutes of the archaic *qal* passive. For לב (lit. "heart") as referring to the throat, see Isa 33:18; Ps 19:15.

[14] A reiteration of the motifs (משפט ["redress"] and צדקה ["vindication"]) appearing in vv. 9-10, which are here anthropomorphized. Cf. v. 9: "that is why redress is far from us" — "and so redress is turned back"; v. 9: "and vindication does not reach us" — "and vindication stays afar"; v. 10: "we stumble" — "because honesty stumbles in the public square."

"And so redress is turned back" — Note the recurring wordplay on the root ס/שוג. According to their own confession, the nation has "turned away" (נָסוֹג — *niph'al*) from the Lord (v. 13), and thus vindication "does not reach us" (תַּשִּׂיגֵנוּ — *hiph'il;* v. 9) and justice is "turned back" (הֻסַּג — *huph'al*).

"And vindication stands afar" — from us; cf. v. 11: "We hope . . . for deliverance, but it is far from us." This hemistich forms a chiasm with the preceding one.

"Indeed, honesty stumbles in the public square" — The כי particle is emphatic. For the verb כשל employed with an abstract noun, cf. Jer 50:32: "Insolence shall stumble (כשל) and fall, with none to raise her up." For the parallel pair צדקה/אמת, see Isa 48:1; and for משפט/אמת, see Ps 111:7; and for all three in tandem, see Ps 119:160.

"And uprightness cannot enter" — cannot gain entry into "the public square" (this term is implied from the previous clause). For נְכֹחָה, see Amos 3:10: "They are incapable of doing right."

[15a] The nation's confession concludes.

"Honesty has been lacking" — Honesty is nowhere to be found. For the *niph'al* of the root עדר, see Isa 40:26: "No one fails (נעדר) to appear"; Zeph 3:5: "He issues judgment every morning, as unfailing (נעדר) as the light."

"He who turns away from evil is thought a fool/madman/is despoiled" — There is disagreement among the commentators regarding the meaning of the participle משתולל (the *hithpolel* of שלל). According to Rashi, it means "he is regarded as a fool" (cf. also Ibn Ezra's first commentary; Isaiah of Tirani). In other words, he who does turn away from evil is considered to have lost his mental faculties, i.e., has gone mad. Cf. Job 12:17: "He makes counselors behave like fools/madmen (שׁוֹלָל) and drives judges mad." According to others, it is derived from שׁלל ("spoil"), i.e., whoever turns away from evil is despoiled from his riches; cf. Targum מִתְבָּזְזִין; Ibn Ezra (second commentary). Exegetes are divided along the same lines regarding the second appearance of this verb in Ps 76:6: אֶשתוללו אבירי לב. Some explain it as despoilment ("the stout-hearted were despoiled"), others as madness ("the stout-hearted went mad"). For the expression סור מֵרָע, see Ps 34:15; 37:27; Prov 3:7.

[15b-19] Since the nation exists in a moral vacuum, there is no one to turn to for intercession. Thus the Lord, in His warrior persona, decides to take matters into His own hands and to deliver the nation from its enemies (cf. Isa 42:13; 63:1-6).

[15b] *The Lord saw and was displeased that there was no redress* — The Lord was distraught with the moral turpitude of His nation. The expression אין משפט ("no redress") is repeated here for the third time; see vv. 8, 11.

[16] This verse, with slight variations, is repeated in 63:5: "Then I looked, but there was none to help. I was appalled, but there was none to aid. So My own arm wrought the triumph, and My own rage was My aid"; and both bear the imprint of Ps 98:1-2: "His right hand, His holy arm (זרוע), has won Him victory (ישועתו). The Lord has manifested His victory, has displayed His triumph (צדקתו) in the sight of the nations." For the Deity going out to wage battle by Himself, see Isa 63:3.

He saw that there was no one — The Lord looked around and saw that there was no one on whom He could rely. For this expression in another context, see 41:28.

He was appalled that no one interceded — וישתומם is a *hithpolel* stem from the root שׁמם and denotes "shocked into silence" (Rashi); see also Ps 143:4; Dan 8:27. For the root פגע with the meaning "to intercede," see Isa 47:3; 53:12; Jer 7:16. This is the third occurrence of אין in two verses, twice here and once in v. 15.

Then His own arm won Him triumph — In the absence of others, the Lord Himself goes out to battle and wins the day with His own arm; cf. Isa 52:10: "The Lord will bare His holy arm in the sight of all the nations, and the very ends of earth shall see the victory of our God"; 63:5: "My own arm wrought the triumph." For the "Lord's arm," see 51:5, 9; 52:10; 53:1; 62:8; 63:5, 12.

His victorious right hand supported Him — וצִדקתו ("His victory") is elliptical for "His victorious right hand," with which God wages war. For the pair of synonyms ישועה/צדקה ("victory/triumph"), see 51:8; and cf. 45:21: "No God exists besides Me, victorious and triumphant (צדיק ומושיע);" 51:5: "The victory I grant (צדקי) is near; the triumph I give (ישעי) has gone forth." The verbal pair סמך/עזר ("to aid/to support") appears instead of סמך/ישע ("to win triumph/to support") in 63:5.

[17] A bold anthropomorphic metaphor of God as a war hero dressed in battle garb, preparing to avenge Himself on His enemies. For similar descriptions in Mesopotamian literature, cf. Marduk's preparations on the eve of his battle against the vengeful Tiamat: "For a cloak he was wrapped in an armor of terror. With his fearsome halo his head was turbaned" (*Enuma Elish* IV:57-58; *ANET*, 66). In order to protect their bodies from the enemies' weapons, the soldiers of the ancient Near East girded themselves in a coat of mail and donned a helmet. Compare, for example, Sennacherib's war paraphernalia: "I put on a leather coat and covered my head with the helmet fit for battle" (*CAD* S:313). For depictions of these articles, see E. Sukenik, ed., *Encyclopaedia Biblica*, 5 (Jerusalem, 1968), 959-60, 963-64 (Heb.). For further descriptions of God preparing to wage war, see 42:13.

He donned victory like a coat of mail — As His armor the Lord garbed Himself in "victory" (צדקה). The noun שִׁרְיָן (see also 1 Kgs 22:34 = 2 Chr 18:33) is an Aramaic variant of Heb. שריון (see 1 Sam 17:5, 38; the Canaanite shift of accented *ā* vowels into *ō* vowels did not occur in Aramaic) and denotes a body armor of interlocking scales. It is a Hurrian loanword, *šarian(ni)*, which entered Akkadian (*siriam/širiam; CAD* S:313-15), as well as Egyptian *(ṯrjn)*.

With a helmet of triumph on His head — כובע (or קובע [1 Sam 17:38; Ezek 23:24]) is a loanword from Hittite *kupaḫ(ḫ)i*. For the parallel pair ישע/צדק see the chiasm in the previous verse.

He clothed Himself with garments of vengeance — Compare the image in 61:10: "He has clothed me with garments of triumph." The cognate accusative וילבש תִּלְבֹּשֶׁת accentuates the image; cf. וַיָּצָם (דוד) צום (2 Sam 12:16); (למען) טְבֹחַ טֶבַח (Lev 5:21); וּמָעֲלָה מַעַל (Zech 1:2); קָצַף (ה׳ על אבותיכם) קֶצֶף (Ezek 21:15). But since the MT here contains two words for "clothing" (both בגדי and תלבשת), the clause may be a conflation of two variant constructions: וילבש בגדי נקם and בגדי נקם תלבשתו (the *waw* suffix may have been omitted in the latter due to a haplography caused by the repetition of the *waw* in the first letter of the following word, ויעט). The noun תִּלְבֹּשֶׁת, a hapax legomenon in the Bible, is cognate to Akk. *talbuš/ltu* (*CAD* T:93).

And wrapped Himself in zeal as in a robe — He covered Himself in battle fervor as a person wraps up in a coat. For a similar image, see Isa 61:10: "For He has clothed me (יְעָטָנִי) in the garments of triumph." The verb וַיַּעַט, a *qal* stem from the root עטי, is an apocopated form of ויעטה; cf. similarly ותעשׂ (Gen

27:14) and ותעשׂה (1 Kgs 17:15). For the term קנאה in contexts of battle zeal, see 42:13. For the parallel verbal synonyms עטי/לבש ("to clothe/to wrap"), see Ps 109:29: "My accusers shall be clothed (ילבשו) in shame, wrapped (ויעטו) in their disgrace as in a robe"; and for the parallel מעיל/בגד ("garment/robe"), see Isa 61:10; Ezek 26:16.

[18] The theme of this verse is retribution. The term גמול appears three times and also creates a literary *inclusio*: the verse opens with the expression גמֻלות . . . ישלם and ends with גמול ישלם. First the prophet threatens a general requital, and then he specifies the objects of divine wrath.

According to their deserts, so shall He repay/The Lord of retribution shall deal out retribution — The repetition of the word כְּעַל ("according to, as is befitting"; see 63:7) in this colon is anomalous. Some have interpreted the doubling for emphasis. However, the Aramaic Targum has a variant reading: מָרֵי גְמְלַיָא הוּא גְמְלָא יְשַׁלֵים, "The Master of retribution shall deal out retribution" (reading בעל for the first כעל), which is similar to Jer 51:56: "For the Lord is a God of retribution. He shall repay in full (כי אל גמֻלות ה׳ שלם ישלם)," and it is likely that the resemblance of the letters *beth* and *kaph* in the Hebrew script is what led to this reading; cf. 1 Kgs 22:20: ויאמר זה בכה וזה אמר בכה, to its equivalent verse in 2 Chr 18:19: ויאמר זה כָּכָה וזה אמר כָּכָה; see also 2 Kgs 3:24: ויבו [Qere: וַיַּכּוּ] בה וְהַכּוֹת את מואב. For the second כעל, the Targum reads גמול. For the terms גמול ("retribution") and נקם ("vengeance," appearing in the preceding verse), see Isa 35:4.

Fury to His foes, retribution to His enemies — The Lord shall repay his enemies, and the coin shall be "fury" (חֵמָה) and "retribution" (גְּמוּל). For the parallel pair אויבים/צרים ("foes/enemies"), see Isa 1:24; Mic 5:8. The parallelism also appears in Ugaritic: "Now Baal, now you must crush your enemy *(ibk);* you must destroy your foe *(ṣrtk)*" (*CAT* 1.2.IV:8-9). For the Lord furiously avenging Himself on His enemies, see Isa 63:3, 5, 6; 66:6, 15.

He deals retribution to the coastlands — Divine reprisal shall reach the coastal regions of the Mediterranean.

[19] Following the Lord's retribution, all the world shall revere His name and fear Him; cf. Ps 102:16: "The nations will fear the name of the Lord, all the kings of the earth, Your glory"; Ps 113:3-4. The prophet begins the geographical polar merism with the western direction rather than the eastern, which is unique in biblical literature (for other examples of the standard pair see, e.g., Mal 1:11; Ps 50:1). The reason for this is the associative relationship with the preceding clause, where mention of the distant islands refers to the western regions (see Abravanel). (For the prophet's universalism, see the introduction, §6; and for geographical merisms encompassing the entire world, see Isa 43:5; 45:8 [where examples from cognate languages are listed].)

From the west they shall revere/behold the name of the Lord — There are two traditions regarding the interpretation of the verb ויראו. According to Ibn Ezra, the verb should be understood as deriving from ירא ("to revere"), despite the missing *yod* (i.e., ויראו = וייראו; cf. the Targum [וְיִדְחֲלוּן]; Saadyah Gaon, 132; Kimchi; and Minḥat Shay, who maintains that according to tradition it should be written *plene*, with two *yods*). Others derive the verb from the root ראי ("to behold"). Compare also 60:5. For the expression ירא שֵׁם, see Deut 28:58: "To revere this honored and awesome Name, the Lord your God"; Mal 3:20: "But for you who revere My name a sun of victory shall rise"; cf. also Ps 86:11; 102:16. "Revering the name of the Lord" denotes fully committing oneself to His worship. And for the expression ראה שֵׁם, see Deut 28:10: "And all the people of the earth shall see that the Lord's name is proclaimed over you, and they shall stand in fear of you." For the expression שם ה׳ ("the name of the Lord"), see also Isa 56:6; 60:9.

And from the east, His Presence — "from the east," lit. "from the rising of the sun." The geographical merism "from the west and from the east" is all-inclusive, as in 45:6: "So that they may know, from east to west, that there is none but Me." For "beholding the Lord's Presence," see 66:18: "They shall come and behold My Presence"; and for "revering the Lord's Presence," see Ps 102:16: "The nations will revere the name of the Lord, all the kings of the earth, Your Presence." In this verse, as in Ps 113:3-4: "From east to west the name of the Lord is praised . . . His Presence is above the heavens," the expressions שֵׁם ה׳ ("the name of the Lord") and כבודו/כבודך ("Your Presence/His Presence") appear in parallel; see also Ps 102:16, quoted above.

For He shall come like a hemmed-in stream — According to the Masoretic punctuation, כַּנָּהָר ("like a stream") describes the subject of the verse, צר: "The enemy (צר) shall come like a stream" (Saadyah Gaon, 132; Ibn Ezra; Kimchi). In light of the above context, however, in which the Lord is described as seeking retribution (vv. 17-18), it is more likely that the subject of the verse is the Lord Himself, who "shall come like a hemmed-in stream," vocalizing כְּנָהָר. The word צר is thus an attribute of the river (Abravanel), described as having a devastatingly strong current (so too LXX and Vulgate). Compare the Akkadian etymological and semantic cognate *ṣarāru* ("to flow"), *mê ṣarrūti* ("flowing water") (*CAD* Ṣ:105-6, 114). For a similar image, cf. Isa 66:12.

Which the wind of the Lord drives on — Divinely propelled wind strengthens the current and increases the speed of the flowing water; cf. Abravanel: "With the Lord's wind, His strong wind driving it, the storm becomes all the more awesome." The *polel* stem נֹסְסָה, from the root נוס, similar to its *hiph'il* equivalent הניס (Deut 32:30), means "to drive on, to put to flight."

[20-21] The deliverance.

[20] Isa 1:27: "Zion (ציון) shall be saved in the judgment; her repentant ones (וְשָׁבֵי פשע), in the retribution," left its linguistic imprint on this verse. (See the introduction, §14.)

He shall come as redeemer to Zion — Following the requital, the Lord shall arrive in Zion as a deliverer. Depictions of the Lord as the deliverer (גואל) of His nation are very common in Deutero-Isaiah; e.g., 41:14; 44:6; 47:4; 48:20. (See the introduction, §9.)

To those in Jacob who turn back from sin — a division of the populace into those who repent and those who rebel against divine authority (see below, chaps. 65–66). The Lord's redemption of "Jacob" (see, e.g., 40:27; 41:8; 42:24) shall be restricted to the former. For the idea of repentance and return to God, see 44:22; 55:7. This concept is especially common in Deuteronomy, e.g., Deut 4:30; 30:2, 3.

Declares the Lord — Divine authentication of the prophecy.

[21] The chapter ends with a prosaic verse in which the Lord, for the first and only time in the chapter, addresses the nation personally, proclaiming the eternity of His covenant, guaranteeing prophetic inspiration (the Lord's spirit) to be shared by the entire nation. For the Lord's covenant never again to be annulled, see Isa 54:10: "For though the mountains may move and the hills be shaken, My loyalty shall never move from you, nor My covenant of friendship be shaken — said the Lord, who takes you back in love"; 55:3: "And I will make with you an everlasting covenant"; 61:8: "And I will make a covenant with them for all time." (See also Jer 31:33: The new divine covenant will be written on the heart, as opposed to the covenant at Sinai, which was written in stone.) The Lord's promise that the entire nation will be prophetically inspired is the fulfillment of Moses' wistful hope of Num 11:29: "Would that all the Lord's people were prophets, that the Lord put His spirit upon them!" For the idea that Israel is destined to be a nation of prophets, see Isa 44:3: "So will I pour My spirit on your offspring," and the commentary to 42:6; 49:8. Compare also 32:15; Joel 3:1-2. Here, as in Isa 55:3, an eternal covenant is established between the nation and God, as opposed to the prior exclusive covenant between David and the Deity (e.g., Ps 89:4-5: "I have made a covenant with My chosen one. I have sworn to My servant David: I will establish your offspring forever"). This is one of the few places in Deutero-Isaiah where God addresses the prophet in the first person; cf., e.g., Isa 40:6; 48:16; and the Servant Songs in chaps. 52 and 53.

And this shall be My covenant with them, said the Lord — The initial anacoluthic ואני refers to the principal subject by means of a pronoun; cf. Gen 9:9; 17:4; 37:30. (See GKC §143a.) This, indeed, is the covenant I will establish with them (אותם), i.e., with those who repent and return. The rarity of the expression ברית + אות (found again only in Ezek 16:8; 37:26), instead of the more common ברית + את, is the reason for the variant אתם in 1QIsa[a].

"My spirit that is upon you" — the prophetic spirit; cf. Isa 42:1: "I have put My spirit upon Him"; 61:1: "The spirit of the Lord God is upon me." Note once more that the entire nation shall be inspired by this prophetic spirit, which will

no longer be restricted to the Davidic scion, e.g., "The spirit of the Lord shall alight upon him" (11:2).

"And the words that I have placed in your mouth" — The words of prophecy, as in 51:16: "I have put My words in your mouth." This prophetic motif is taken from Deut 18:18: "I will raise up a prophet for them like you [Moses], one of their own people, and I will put My words in his mouth." Compare also Jer 1:9: "And the Lord said to me: 'Herewith I put My words into your mouth.'"

"Shall never depart from your mouth, nor from the mouth of your children, nor from the mouth of your children's children" — said the Lord — This gift of prophecy shall never leave you or your descendants, as in Isa 54:10: "But My loyalty shall never depart (יָמוּשׁ) from you, nor My covenant of friendship be shaken"; Josh 1:8: "Let not this book of the teaching cease (יָמוּשׁ) from your lips." For the repetitive expression זרע זרעך (unique in biblical literature), cf. the etymological and semantic cognate in Akkadian: "Bless the king, his progeny *(zērišu),* and the progeny of his progeny *(zēr zērišu)*" (*CAD* Z:94).

"From now on, for all time" — for all of eternity; see also Isa 9:6; Mic 4:7.

Chapter 60

Chapter 60 is composed of one uninterrupted eschatological prophecy delineating a plan for the rehabilitation, reconstruction, and all-pervasive glory of future Jerusalem. In this prophecy of salvation, Deutero-Isaiah describes the radiant light that will cover Jerusalem, a beacon all nations shall follow. On their journey, the nations shall bring with them the scattered remnant of Israel and shall bear rich gifts — gold, frankincense, and choice flocks — all for the glory of the Temple. They and their kings, who shall bring with them all types of trees for the reconstruction and adornment of the Temple, shall rebuild the walls, serve in the sanctuary, and praise the God of Israel. The gates of Jerusalem shall never be shut and none shall be molested within its walls. In this new era, all of Israel will be righteous and will continue to enjoy the wealth of the nations and possess the land forever. The formulation of many of the verses in this chapter, as well as many of its motifs therein, was influenced by the oracles of Isaiah ben Amoz, by Deutero-Isaiah's own earlier prophecies, by the Psalter, and by Mesopotamian royal inscriptions.

As for Isaiah, cf. chap. 2, which begins with a multinational pilgrimage to Jerusalem (there the foreigners come to seek guidance in legal issues, whereas here they come to donate riches to the Temple and to serve therein). Compare the similar phrases: "And all nations shall gaze on it with joy (**ונהרו**) and many peoples shall go (**והלכו עמים רבים**)" (2:2-3), and: "O House of Jacob! Come, let us walk by the light of the Lord" (**בית יעקב לכו ונלכה באור ה׳**; 2:5) — "And nations shall walk by your light" (**והלכו גוים לאורך**; 60:3), and: "Then you will see and shine with joy" (**אז ראית ונהרת**; 60:5). Deutero-Isaiah, moreover, takes First Isaiah's rebuke of chastisement regarding Israel's silver, gold, and cedars out of context, along with his pronouncement: "Then man's haughtiness shall be humbled (**ושַׁח**)" (2:11), and reapplies it to the nations that will arrive by the ships of Tarshish with their silver and gold (60:9), bearing with them "Lebanon's majesty," i.e., the cedars (60:13); "bowing before you . . . and prostrating (והשתחוו) at the soles of your feet" (60:14). Compare also 2:19: "Before the terror (פחד) of the Lord and the splendor of His majesty (גאונו)," to 60:5: "Your heart will throb and thrill (ופחד)," and 60:15: "I will make you a pride (לגאון) everlasting." (See the introduction, §14.)

Another pericope that left its impression on Isa 60 is 49:14-26. Compare 49:14: "But Zion says, 'The Lord has forsaken me (עזבני)'" — 60:15: "Whereas you have been forsaken (עזובה)"; 49:18: "Look up all around you and see: They are all assembled, are come to you!" — 60:4 (note the word-for-word repetition): "Look up all around you and see: They are all assembled, are come to you!"; 49:21: "Who bore these for me (מי . . . אלה)?" — 60:8: "Who are these (מי אלה)?"; 49:22: "And they shall bring your sons in their bosoms and carry your daughters on their shoulders" — 60:4: "Your sons shall be brought from afar, your daughters like babes on shoulders"; 49:23: "Kings shall tend your children, their queens shall serve you as nurses" — 60:16: " You shall suck the milk of the nations, suckle at royal breasts"; 49:23: "They shall bow to you, face to the ground, and lick the dust of your feet" — 60:14: "Bowing before you shall come the children of those who tormented you. Prostrate at the soles of your feet shall be all those who reviled you."

Note also the connections between this chapter and Ps 72. An important difference that must be emphasized, however, is that the addressee of the psalmic praises is a Davidic scion, specifically Solomon, whereas in this chapter (and in Deutero-Isaianic eschatology in general) there is no allusion to David or his lineage (cf. also Isa 55:3-5).

Isaiah 60	**Ps 72**
14: The sons of all those who tormented you shall come to you bending low; and all those who reviled you shall prostrate at the soles of your feet	9: Let desert dwellers kneel before him, and his enemies lick the dust; 11: Let all kings bow to him, and all nations serve him
9: With ships of Tarshish in the lead 6: They all shall come from Sheba; they shall bear gold and frankincense	10: Let kings of Tarshish and the islands pay tribute, kings of Sheba and Seba offer gifts 15: And receive gold of Sheba
21: צדיקים	1: וצדקתך; 72:2: בצדק; 72:3: בצדקה; 72:7: צדיק
17: שלום	3, 7: שלום
19: הַיָּרֵחַ; 60:20: וִירֵחֵךְ	5, 7: יָרֵחַ

Isaiah 60	**Ps 72**
19 השמש; 60:20: שמשך	5, 17: שמש
3: ומלכים; 60:11: ומלכיהם	10: מלכי תרשיש . . . מלכי שבא וסבא
13: הלבנון	16: כלבנון
1: וכבוד ה׳; 60:2: וכבודו (cf. 60:13: כבוד [הלבנון])	19 (twice): כבודו

(See the introduction, §17.)

Many of the motifs in this prophecy also appear in Mesopotamian inscriptions (from the end of the third millennium BCE up until the time of Nebuchadnezzar, king of Babylon, and Darius, king of Persia, both from the sixth century BCE), which describe the central sanctuary as an international locus, and the nations who will make donations of Lebanese cedars and other precious woods, and will offer praise to the god of the respective temple. The city in which the temple resides is described as resplendent with the divine presence and filled with righteousness. Compare, for example, the Sumerian hymn to Enlil, god of Nippur: "The city [Nippur] is filled with reverence and glory . . . exploitation and misdeeds . . . shall have no place in it . . . righteousness and justice shall reside within. . . . Its bricks are of red metal, its foundation lapis lazuli. . . . All lands are prostrate before it. . . . The Ekur [the name of the temple], house of lapis lazuli. . . . Its veneration and glory reach unto the sky. . . . All lords and princes bring their pure tributes. They offer sacrifices and prayer before you. . . . You subjugate the most foreign and distant lands. . . . They bring tribute and heavy taxes to his treasury . . . into Ekur they bring this in proper servility." Compare also the hymn to Ishmedagan, king of Isin, from the nineteenth century BCE: "They [the foreigners] bring unsolicited . . . tribute . . . precious stones . . . gold. . . . The Amorite wanderers . . . bring me sheep; they bring cedars and cypress trees from the mountainous land. . . . [The god] Enlil, my king, defeated all foreigners who came against me." And Nebuchadnezzar boasts: "Many nations which the lord Marduk left under my care . . . from the high sea until the low sea, which Marduk put in my hands to pull his burden . . . bring mighty cedars from Lebanon to the cities of Babylon. . . . All the people labored . . . in the construction of the temple." (For these and other examples see Weinfeld, *From Joshua to Josiah*, 114-33; V. A. Hurowitz, *I Have Built You an Exalted House*, JSOTSup 115 [Sheffield, 1992], 204-23.) See also the introduction, §19.B. For other themes in common, see the commentary.

This chapter is also intimately connected to the previous one (Isa 59), and one gets the impression that it serves to counter it.

Chapter 59	Chapter 60
4: No one sues justly (בצדק) 14: And vindication (וצדקה) stays afar	21: And your people, all of them righteous (צדיקים)
6: Their hands commit lawless acts (חמס)	18: The cry, "Violence (חמס)!" shall no more be heard
8: They do not care for the way of integrity (שלום)	17: I will appoint well-being (שלום) as your government
9: And vindication (צדקה) does not reach us	17: Prosperity (צדקה) as your officials
9: We hope for light (לאור), and lo! There is darkness (חשך)	1-2: Arise! Shine (אורי)! For your light (אורך) has dawned. . . . For though darkness (חשך) shall cover the earth
9: We hope for light (לאור) . . . for a gleam (לנגהות); but we must walk in deep gloom	3: And nations shall walk by your light (לאורך), kings by your shining (לנֹגַהּ) radiance; 19: The sun shall no longer be your light (לאור) by day, nor the shining of the moon for radiance (לנֹגַהּ) [by night]
11: And moan like doves (כיונים)	8: Like doves (כיונים) flying to their cotes
11: We hope . . . for salvation (לישועה); but it is far from us	18: You shall name your walls "Salvation" (ישועה)
18: Requital to the coastlands (לאיים)	9: Behold, the vessels of the coastlands (איים) assemble
19: They shall revere/behold . . . His presence (כבודו)	1: The presence (וכבוד) of the Lord; 2: And His presence (וכבודו) shall be seen over you

Also note the abundance of words and expressions appearing more than once in this chapter: זרח (vv. 1, 2, 3), פאר (vv. 7 [twice], 9, 13, 19, 21), בוא (vv. 4, 5, 6, 9, 11, 13, 17), נֹגַהּ (vv. 3, 19), מלכים/ממלכה (vv. 3, 10, 11, 12, 16), גוי/גוים (vv. 3, 5, 11, 12 [twice], 16), אור (vv. 1 [twice], 3, 19 [three times], 20), חומותיך (vv. 10, 18), שעריך (vv. 11, 18), כבוד (vv. 1, 2, 13), קדוש ישראל (vv. 9, 14), זרח (vv. 1, 2, 3), רצון (vv. 7, 10), עליך (vv. 1, 2 [twice], 5), תהִלת/תהִלה (vv. 6, 18), חֵיל גוים (vv. 5, 11), תחת (vv. 15, 17 [four times]), צדקה/צדיקים (vv. 17, 21), שמש/ירח (vv. 19, 20), (ל)עולם (vv. 15, 20, 21).

[1-2] The fulfillment of Isaiah's promise is imminent: "The people who walked in darkness have seen a brilliant light. On those who dwelt in a land of gloom, light has dawned" (9:1).

[1] A future full of divine light dawns on Jerusalem. "As we have already explained (Isa 59:9-10), light symbolizes joy and goodness, and darkness, the opposite, dire circumstances and evil" (Kimchi). For light as equivalent to joy: "Light is sown for the righteous, joy for the upright" (Ps 97:11).

Arise! Shine! — Rise and shine, be joyful, *Jerusalem*! (the last word is added by Targum, LXX, Peshitta, and some Vulgate manuscripts). The double imperative beginning with the verbal root קום prefaces a specific action (e.g., 52:2: קומי שבי; Judg 5:12: קום . . . וּשֲׁבֵה) and is reminiscent of other double addresses (e.g., Isa 51:9; 52:1: עורי עורי), which prompted the LXX to translate: "Shine, shine, O Jerusalem!" For the verb אור (the imperative form appears only here), see Prov 4:18: "The path of the righteous is like radiant sunlight, ever-brightening (ואור) until broad day."

For your light has dawned — As the Targum renders, "The time of your redemption is nigh." Compare similarly 58:8: "Then shall your light burst through like the dawn"; 58:10: "Then shall your light shine in darkness." For the key root אור, see also vv. 3, 19 (three times), 20. The expression בא אור, with the meaning "your light has dawned," is unique since the verb in the corresponding expression, בא השמש, indicates the opposite — "sunset" (see v. 20; Exod 17:12; Josh 10:27). For the pair of verbs בא/זרח in a revelatory context, see Deut 33:2: "The Lord came (בא) from Sinai. He shone (זרח) on them from Seir."

The Presence of the Lord has shone on you — The Lord's Presence, i.e., His glowing halo, shines on you, as in Deut 33:2, quoted above. For a revelatory experience described in terms of light and luminosity, see Exod 13:21: "The Lord went before them . . . in a pillar of fire by night, to give them light, that they might travel day and night"; Ezek 43:2: "And there, coming from the east, was the Presence of the God of Israel . . . and the earth was lit up by His Presence"; Ps 104:2: "Wrapped in a robe of light"; Dan 2:22: "And light dwells with Him." Mesopotamian literature also furnishes ample examples of divine luminescence (note especially the verb *namāru,* "to shine," and the derivative *namrirrū* [*CAD* N/1:237-38]) shining on kings, crowns, weapons, temples, and edifices. There is, but for one possible exception, no example of an entire nation bathed in divine light. For synonyms of this supernatural light, cf. *melammu* (*CAD* M/2:9-12), *puluḫtu* (*CAD* P:505-9), *rašubbatu* (*CAD* R:212-13), and *šalummatu* (*CAD* Š/1:283-85). Note the threefold emphasis on עליך ("on you") in vv. 1-2.

[2] The verse juxtaposes Jerusalem, which shall be infused by divine light, with the rest of the world, which shall be shrouded over in dense clouds. Note the affinity with the plague of darkness against the Egyptians: "And thick darkness descended on all the land of Egypt for three days . . . ; but all the Israel-

ites enjoyed light in their dwellings" (Exod 10:22-23). The Lord's Presence, which abandoned Jerusalem at the time of the city's destruction (Ezek 9:3; 10:18-20; 11:22-23), is now returning in full glory (see also Ezek 43:2, 4-5; 44:4).

For though darkness shall cover the earth — whereas an impenetrable gloom shall descend on the rest of the earth. For another instance of the expression חֹשֶׁךְ כסה, see Eccl 6:4: "And its very name is covered in darkness" (ובחֹשֶׁךְ שמו יְכֻסֶּה).

And thick clouds, the peoples — עֲרָפֶל denotes heavy, thick clouds; see Deut 4:11; Joel 2:2 (= Zeph 1:15). For its cognates, cf. Ugar. *ʿrp, ʿrpt, ǵrpl* (*HdO* 1:184, 326) and Akk. *ereptu* (*CAD* E:302-4), *urpatu*, and *urpu* (*AHw* 3:1432). (For a cloud "covering" in Akkadian, see *CAD* A/2:229; K:300; S:32.)

Yet on you the Lord will shine — The initial *waw* indicates contrast: You, however, shall be graced by the Lord's light, as in 58:10: "Then shall your light shine in darkness."

And His Presence be seen over you — For the revelation of the Lord's Presence (כבוד) seen by all, see Isa 40:5: "The Presence of the Lord shall be revealed, and all humanity, as one, shall see it"; 59:19: "They shall revere/behold . . . His Presence." The final two hemistichs of this verse form a chiasm with the end of v. 1: וכבוד ה׳ עליך זרח . . . ועליך יזרח ה׳ וכבודו עליך יֵרָאֶה.

[3] The Lord's light, which now shines over Jerusalem, shall be a light to the nations. This verse is an amplification of earlier expressions of this idea in 42:6 and 49:6, where Israel is described as a light to the nations.

And nations shall walk by your light — This light, which symbolizes success and divine munificence, shall be a beacon by which the nations shall walk; cf. 2:5: "O House of Jacob! Come, let us walk by the light of the Lord." For the expression ללכת לאור, see Hab 3:11; Job 29:3. Compare also the phrase in Rabbinic Hebrew: לא הלכו אלא לאורו, "They did not walk, but by His light" (*b. Shabb.* 22b).

Kings, by your shining radiance — Kings shall walk in the light of Jerusalem's radiance. (Note 1QIsa[a] לנגד, attested also in the Targum, לְקֳבֵל, "in the presence of," instead of MT לְנֹגַהּ.) For נֹגַהּ, "radiance," see v. 19 (and note the parallelism to אור, "light," as here); 62:1 (parallel to לפיד, "torch"); and 50:10 (opposite of חֲשֵׁכִים, "darkness"). The term also appears in the first combination of the Balaam text from Deir ʿAlla in the Sukkot Valley (east of the Jordan River), dated to the eighth century BCE: "There is darkness (חשך) there and no light (נגה)" (see Aḥituv, *Ha-Ketav veha-Miḵtav*, 386, lines 6-7). Compare also its Ugaritic etymological and semantic equivalent, which appears as a verb *(tgh)* in the Kirta epic (*CAT* 1.16.I:37). For the parallelism of מלכים/גוים, see 45:1; 52:15; 62:2.

[4] For the image of maternal Jerusalem, see 49:17, 20-22; 51:18, 20; 54:1, 13. The first two clauses are a word-for-word quote from 49:18.

Raise your eyes and look about! — Behold your surroundings. Note the assonance: שְׂאִי סביב. The expression "to raise one's eyes and see" is a familiar one in Hebrew borrowed from Ugaritic, e.g., *wtšu ʿnh wtʿn,* "She raised her eyes and saw" (*CAT* 1.10.II:27), which indicates beholding a new sight. See also 51:6: "Raise your eyes to the heavens, and look on the earth beneath."

All of them have gathered together and come to you — Some commentators explain that כֻּלָּם ("all of them") refers to the sons and daughters, immediately following, i.e., it is a reference to the returnees (thus Targum: "all the children of your diaspora"; Ibn Ezra; Kimchi). Others interpret it as being connected with the nations and kings mentioned in the preceding verse (Eliezer of Beaugency, Joseph Kaspi, Luzzatto). However, it is also possible that it refers to both the expatriates and the far-off kings coming to pay their respects to Jerusalem. (For the verb קבץ, "to gather," in contexts of return and repatriation, see 40:11; 43:5; 49:18; 54:7; 56:8; 62:9.)

Your sons shall come from afar — and resettle in Jerusalem; cf. 49:12: "Look! These are coming from afar." In light of the following hemistich here and the parallel to v. 9: "to bring your sons from afar," however, many have suggested emending the active MT form יָבֹאוּ to the passive יֻבָאוּ ("shall be brought"), i.e., the kings and nations shall convey your sons to Jerusalem (e.g., Tur-Sinai, *Peshuṭo shel Miqra,* III/1:142). For the verbal pair בוא/הביא–קבץ ("to gather–to come/to bring") in contexts of the nation's returning to Jerusalem, see 43:5; 49:18; Zeph 3:20. For the transportation of Israel back to Jerusalem by foreigners, see also Isa 66:20.

And your daughters shall be carried on hips — Your daughters shall be carried on "hips" (צד, lit. "side"), as infants are carried. Hebrew תֵּאָמַנָה is a denominative verb derived from the substantive אֹמֵן/אֹמֶנֶת ("foster mother"/"foster father," Num 11:12; Ruth 4:16); cf. Isa 49:23: "Kings shall tend your children (אֹמְנַיִךְ)"; Esth 2:7: "He was a foster father (אֹמֵן) to Hadassah." (Kimchi: "The *nun* in the verb should have been doubled to indicate the absence of the third radical [תאמנּה] instead of תאמנה].") For similar descriptions of such preferential treatment, see Isa 49:22: "And your daughters shall be carried (תִּנָּשֶׂאנָה) on their shoulders" (on the basis of this verse, the LXX, 1QIsa[b] [תנשינה — note the elision of the *aleph*], as well as one medieval Hebrew manuscript have תנשאנה instead of the hapax legomenon תֵּאָמַנָה in the MT); and cf. 66:12: "You shall be carried (תִּנָּשֵׂאוּ) on hips." For a Mesopotamian parallel, cf. the prophetic text from Assyria in which the prophetess promises King Ashurbanipal in the name of the goddess Mullissu (= Ishtar): "I shall carry you upon my hip like a nursemaid" (Parpola, *Assyrian Prophecies,* 39, line 7). For illustrations of parents carrying their children on their shoulders and hips, see M. Haran, ed., *Encyclopedia of the Biblical World: Ezekiel,* XII (Ramat Gan, 1984), 85 (Heb.); O. Keel, "Kanaanäische Sühneriten auf ägyptischen Templereliefs," *VT* 25 (1975): 448ff., nos. 16, 17.

[**5-22**] The source of this image of treasure and wealth flowing into Jerusalem, envisioned as the center of the world, and the subsequent subjugation of peoples are also part of the Mesopotamian temple city/royal sanctuary ideology; cf. also 45:14; 49:23; 66:19-20. (See Weinfeld, *From Joshua to Josiah,* 114-16, 124-31.)

[**5**] *Then, as you behold, you will glow* — As Jerusalem witnesses the return of her children, along with the tide of wealth (described in the adjacent clauses), she will shine with joy. For the verb **נהר**, "to light up," see Isa 2:2 (= Mic 4:1); Jer 31:12; Ps 34:6 (cf. also Jer 51:44). There are two traditions for the vocalization of the first verb, **תִּרְאִי**: (1) as in the MT, as a derivative of **ראי** (thus Targum; LXX; Vulgate; Saadyah Gaon, 133; Rashi; Kimchi); see the beginning of v. 4: "Raise your eyes and look about"; or (2) as in some medieval Hebrew manuscripts, where **תראי** is written with a *metheg* before the *tav* or a *ḥataf* under the *resh* (**תִּרֲאִי**), or with an additional *yod* after the *tav* (see Minḥat Shai, and cf. *Mekilta de-Rabbi Ishmael,* be-Shalaḥ, Shirah, A [ed. H. S. Horovitz and Y. A. Rabin; Jerusalem, 1931], 116, line 4), deriving the verb from the root **ירא**, "to be in awe" (cf. Ibn Ezra: "As a person who is in awe at the arrival of his salvation"). According to the latter, the verb would be parallel to **פחד**, the third verb in the verse. For these two verbs together, see Mic 7:17.

Your heart will throb and thrill — The verb **פחד** is polysemous and creates a Janus (two-directional) parallelism: When it corresponds with the preceding verb, **תראי** (according to the latter derivation from **ירא**, "to fear"), it denotes dread or alarm. And when it relates to the adjacent expression, **ורחב לבבך**, it denotes excitement and thrill, as in Jer 33:9: "They will thrill (**ופחדו**) and quiver because of all the good fortune and all the prosperity that I provide for her"; Hos 3:5: "And they will thrill (**ופחדו**) over the Lord and over His bounty in the days to come." According to the latter interpretation, your heart will exult as you witness the triumphant return of your sons and daughters and the wealth that shall flow into Jerusalem. For the expression **רחב לב** (lit. "widening of the heart"), which refers to rejoicing — "Just as the heart constricts in times of distress, anguish, and mourning, so, conversely, it widens in times of goodness and joy" (Kimchi, and see also Ibn Ezra) — see Ps 119:32: "I eagerly pursue Your commandments, for You make my heart rejoice [lit. widen my heart]." It is semantically similar to the expression **עלץ/עלז לב**, "the heart exults" (see 1 Sam 2:1; Ps 28:7), which is the etymological and semantic cognate of Akk. *libbu elēṣu* ("an exulting heart"), which literally denotes the "expansion of the heart" (*CAD* E:88). Note the variant **ורהב**, instead of **ורחב** in the MT (see Minḥat Shai), which, on the basis of Arab. *rahiba* and Akk. *ra'ābu* ("to fear," "to tremble"; *CAD* R:2-3), is parallel to **פחד** (Yellin, *Ḥiqrei Miqra,* 82).

For the wealth of the sea shall pass on to you — You shall be ecstatic as you witness the "riches of the sea" (cf. Deut 33:19) arriving at your doorstep. For

המון denoting "wealth," see Ezek 29:19: "Assuredly, thus said the Lord God: I will give the land of Egypt to Nebuchadrezzar, king of Babylon. He shall carry off her wealth (הֲמֹנָהּ) and take her spoil and seize her booty; and she shall be the recompense of his army"; 1 Chr 29:16: "O Lord our God, all this great wealth (ההמון) that we have laid aside to build You a house for Your holy name." For the expression המון ים (a wordplay reminiscent of the "crashing of waves"; see Isa 17:12), cf. the equivalent phrases in Akkadian inscriptions, specifically in contexts of the wealth and booty brought as tribute to Assyrian kings: *bilat tâmti* (*CAD* B:232-35), *ḫegal apsi* (*CAD* Ḫ:167), *ḫiṣib tâmti* (*CAD* Ḫ:203), *nuḫuš tâmāti* (*CAD* N/2:321), all of which denote the fruit/treasure/bounty of the sea. For the expression נהפך על, which denotes a sudden reversal in situation, see 1 Sam 4:19: "She was suddenly seized (נהפכו עליה) by labor pains."

The riches of nations shall come/be brought to you — This hemistich creates a chiastic parallelism with the previous one. In addition to the bounty of the sea, the wealth of the nations shall also be yours. For חַיִל ("wealth"), see v. 11; Isa 10:14; 61:6; Jer 17:3; Zech 14:14. Though the subject of the clause is in the singular (חיל), the plural form of the verb (יבאו) is due to its attraction to the adjacent plural noun (גוים); but cf. the singular (יבוא) in 1QIsa[a]. Some commentators suggest, however, to vocalize the verb in the *hiphʿil,* יָבִאוּ, "they shall bring" (e.g., Tur-Sinai, *Peshuṭo shel Miqra,* III/1:143).

[6-7] For the motif of far-flung nations bringing tribute and sacrifice to the central temple, see the introduction to v. 5; cf. also Zeph 3:10; Hag 2:7; Ps 96:8. Here the prophet reverses the chastisement of Jer 6:20, 22: "What need have I of frankincense that comes from Sheba, or fragrant cane from a distant land? Your burnt offerings are not acceptable and your sacrifices are not pleasing to Me. . . . Thus said the Lord: 'See, a people comes from the northland, a great nation is roused from the remotest parts of the earth,'" and applies it in a positive way to the nations who will flock to Jerusalem in the future. These nations will not come in order to wage war, but rather will come as supplicants and their sacrifices will be welcome before the Lord.

[6] *Dust clouds of camels shall cover you* — For שִׁפְעָה ("dust clouds") relating to horses, see 2 Kgs 9:17, "And he saw the dust cloud (שפעת) of Jehu as he approached. He called out, 'I see a dust cloud (שפעת)!'"; Ezek 26:10: "From the clouds (מִשִּׁפְעַת) raised by his horses, dust shall cover you." For this term in an aquatic context, see Job 22:11; 38:34: "A cloud (ושפעת) of waters shall cover you," which according to Tur-Sinai denotes a rain cloud, dark with water (Tur-Sinai, *Book of Job,* rev. ed. [Jerusalem, 1967], 341). In all these verses, except for 2 Kgs 9:17, the substantive appears together with the verb כסה. (Note also the possible connection with the Akkadian verb *šapû,* "to billow, roll in [said of darkness and clouds]" [*CAD* Š/1:489].) For an additional image of the "covering" of the land due to an abundance of flocks (belonging to the Mesopotamian god Nabû), see *CAD* K:300. For tribute transported to Jerusalem on the backs of camels, see Isa 66:20.

Dromedaries of Midian and Ephah — בְּכָרִים (Ezek 27:21) and בִּכְרָה (Jer 2:23) are young male and female camels, cognate to Akk. *bukru,* which appears in a list of tribute to the Assyrian king Tiglath-pileser III (*CAD* B:35). According to the genealogical lists of Genesis and 1 Chronicles, Ephah was the eldest son of Midian (Gen 25:4 = 1 Chr 1:33), and it is clear from the LXX transcription, Ghaiphah, the initial *ayin* is palatal. This group is identified with the people of Ḫayapa, who appear in Assyrian inscriptions of the eighth century BCE together with other nomadic tribes that surrendered to Tiglath-pileser III in battles that took place in Israel. They were defeated (again) by Sargon, and some of them were exiled to Samaria in 716 BCE. (See I. Ephʿal, *The Ancient Arabs* [Jerusalem, 1982], 87-90, 216-17.) The Midianites, similar to the tribes of Ephah, also wandered the vast expanses of the Syrian Desert and were seminomadic camel travelers; see Judg 6:5.

They all shall come from Sheba — Caravans of camels and convoys of dromedaries shall come with treasure (immediately below) from the land of Sheba, a kingdom in the southwestern Arabian Peninsula that was famous throughout the ancient Near East and Mediterranean countries for its expensive exports. See 1 Kgs 10:2: "She [the queen of Sheba] arrived in Jerusalem with a very large retinue, with camels bearing spices, a great quantity of gold, and precious stones"; cf. also 1 Kgs 10:10. They, the Sabaeans *(Sa-ba-'a-a),* are mentioned in the Assyrian annals of Sargon and Sennacherib from the last quarter of the eighth century BCE as tributary vassals. Their tax included gold, precious stones, spices, horses, and camels (see Ephʿal, *Ancient Arabs,* 227-29).

They shall bear gold and frankincense — The camels shall bear tributes of gold and spices from Sheba; cf. Jer 6:20: "What need have I of frankincense that comes from Sheba?"; Ps 72:15: "May he [the king] receive gold of Sheba"; for other references to the gold of Sheba, see Ezek 27:22; 38:13. Note the technical use of the verb נשׂא, which indicates here the "bearing" of tribute, as in 2 Sam 8:2, 6; Hos 8:10; 2 Chr 17:11. The etymological and semantic Akkadian cognate *našû* bears the same meaning (*CAD* N/2:92-93).

And shall herald the praises of the Lord — They shall sing God's praises (תְּהִלּוֹת) at the top of their lungs; cf. Isa 63:7: "I will recount the praises (תְּהִלּוֹת) of the Lord." The verb בשׂר, like its Akkadian cognate *bussuru,* means (in addition "to bring news pleasant to the listener"; cf. Ugar. *bsr,* "to impart good news" [*HdO* 1:243]), "to praise, extol" (*CAD* B:347-48). For a similar motif, cf. Ps 102:16, 22: "The nations will fear the name of the Lord. All the kings of the earth, Your glory . . . that the fame of the Lord may be recounted in Zion, His praises (תְּהִלָּתוֹ) in Jerusalem."

[7] In this new era the Temple cult shall be resumed, after being cur-

tailed during the time of the exile (cf. v. 13; 62:9; 66:20, 23). For the revolutionary universalism apparent in Deutero-Isaiah's allowance of foreigners to bring sacrifices and serve in the Temple, see the comments to 56:7.

All the flocks of Kedar shall be assembled for you — Kedar, which according to the genealogy in Gen 25:13 was Ishmael's second-born son, wandered the Syrian Desert in a coalition of tribes and dealt in sheep and camels; see Jer 49:28-29: "Concerning Kedar . . . they [the Babylonians] will take away their tents and their flocks. . . . They shall carry off their camels"; Ezek 27:21: "Arabia and all Kedar's chiefs were traders under your rule. They traded with you in camels, rams, and he-goats" (vv. 22-23 also mention the "merchants of Sheba"). Documentation of the "sons of Kedar" *(Qidri/Qadari)* is found in the inscriptions of Tiglath-pileser III, Sargon, and Ashurbanipal in connection with conquest and tribute (Ephʿal, *Ancient Arabs,* 223-27).

The rams of Nebaioth shall serve your needs — The male sheep (אֵילִים — so too Akk. *alu* [*CAD* A/1:374-75] and Ugar. *al* [*HdO* 1:47-48]) of Nebaioth shall "serve you" (יְשָׁרְתוּנֶךָ) as sacrifices to be offered upon the altar (see, e.g., Lev 5:15; Num 7:15). The tribes of Nebaioth *(Na-ba-a-a-ti)* wandered in the northwestern Arabian Peninsula and are mentioned (as are the other tribes) in the inscriptions of Ashurbanipal. In light of these Assyrian and other South Arabic sources, it is clear that they, the tribes of Nebaioth, are not to be identified with the Nabateans (Ephʿal, *Ancient Arabs,* 221-23). The verb ישרתונך, repeated in v. 10, is anomalous in this (sacrificial) context, and the appended *nun* is a relic of the ancient archaic third-person masculine plural suffix.

They shall be welcome offerings on My altar — Transpose and read: יעלו לרצון על מזבחי (thus 1QIsa[a]), as in 56:7: "I will bring them to My sacred mount and let them rejoice in My house of prayer. Their burnt offerings and sacrifices shall be welcome on My altar (לרצון על מזבחי). For My House shall be called a House of prayer for all peoples." Some parse the verb יַעֲלוּ as a *qal,* and thus understand the clause as indicating that these rams shall willingly be led to the altar; cf. Lev 6:2: "This is the ritual for the burnt offering: the burnt offering that is offered (הָעֹלָה) on the hearth on the altar all night until morning." Others interpret it as a *hiphʿil:* They, the tribes of Nebaioth, shall willingly offer these rams on my altar; cf. Jer 14:12: "When they present (יעלו) the burnt offering and the meal offering." Note the equivalent terminology in cognate languages: Akk. *šūlû* (the *shaphʿel* of *elû; CAD* E:130) and Ugar. *šʿly* (the *shaphʿel* of the verb *ʿly, HdO* 1:160-61) — also in connection with sacrifices offered to the gods.

And I will add glory to My glorious House — This abundance of willing sacrifices shall add glory to God's already glorious House (בית תפארת, a unique appellation); cf. v. 13: "To adorn (לְפָאֵר) the site of My sanctuary"; 63:15: "Look down from heaven and see from Your holy and glorious (ותפארתך)

height!" Note the LXX variant, בית תפלתי ("My House of prayer"), which was influenced by 56:7, which also refers to the Temple as a house of prayer and a locus for foreign sacrifice on God's altar.

[8-9] The prophet now turns his attention toward the sea and sees in his mind's eye a mighty fleet of ships returning Israel to their homeland. This ingathering is compared to the flitting of clouds moving rapidly across the sky and to doves returning to their cotes, two similes based on the appearance of the ships' sails. For depictions of such ships, see E. Sukenik, ed., *Encyclopaedia Biblica,* 5 (Jerusalem, 1968), 1075-78 (Heb.).

[8] *Who are these that float like a cloud* — Note the assonance of the noun עב (see also 44:22) and the verb תעופֶינה. For similarly worded questions, see 63:1: "Who is this coming from Edom?"; Cant 3:6; 8:5: "Who is this coming up from the desert?" תעופינה is a *qal* stem (third-person feminine plural) from the root עוף ("to fly") and is a variant form of תָּעֹפְנָה (thus according to some rabbinic midrashim). For these two alternate forms, cf. תְּסֻבֶּינָה (Gen 37:7); תָּסֹבּוּ (Josh 6:4).

Like doves to their cotes? — The introductory question in the preceding clause is implied here as well. Hebrew אֲרֻבָּה, "window" (see Gen 7:11; 2 Kgs 7:19, also attested in Ugaritic, *arbt* [*HdO* 1:99-100]), denotes here a dovecote. (Cf. its Akkadian semantic equivalent *aptu,* which also refers to both a window and a dovecote [*CAD* A/2:197-99].) For another depiction of the return of the Diaspora in avian terms, see Hos 11:11: "They shall flutter from Egypt like birds, from the land of Assyria like doves. And I will settle them in their homes, declares the Lord."

[9] The image is now explicated. There is a distinct possibility that Jeremiah's prophecy regarding the assembly of nations (Jer 3:17) left its mark on these verses. Compare: "At that time, they shall call Jerusalem 'Throne of the Lord' (יקראו לירושלם כסא ה׳), and all nations shall assemble (וְנִקְווּ) there, in the name of the Lord (לְשֵׁם ה׳), at Jerusalem," to here: "The vessels (כלי) of the coastlands shall assemble (יְקַוּוּ) . . . for the name of the Lord (לְשֵׁם ה׳) your God"; and v. 14: "And you shall be called 'City of the Lord, Zion, Holy One of Israel.'" (See the introduction, §15.)

The vessels of the coastlands shall assemble — One should combine the first two words (כי לי) and read כְּלֵי ("the vessels") of the coastal nations (see the adjacent "ships of Tarshish"), and instead of יְקַוּוּ, from the root קוי, as vocalized in the MT, read יִקָּווּ, from the homonymous root קוי ("to gather"), as in Gen 1:9: "Let the water . . . be gathered (יִקָּווּ)" (thus Metzudot; Luzzatto; Tur-Sinai, *Peshuto shel Miqra* III/1:143). For כלי ("fleet of ships"), see Isa 18:2: "In papyrus vessels (כלי) upon the water." (For a similar semantic development, cf. Akk. *unūtu,* which refers to a vessel in general [not a sailing vessel], and Heb. אֳנִי [plural אניות] and Ugar. *any* [plural *anyt; HdO* 1:85-86], which denote "vessel[s], ship[s]." This development can also be charted in other languages. Thus Greek *skáphē/skáphion* [Latin *scapha*], refers both to a bowl and to a ship; and cf. English "vessel" [French *vaisseau*], the origin of which is the Latin *vascallum* [a diminutive of *vas*], which can denote either a small bowl, a vase, or a ship.) The (erroneous) Masoretic vocalization was in all likelihood influenced by Isa 51:5: אֵלַי איים יְקַוּוּ.

With ships of Tarshish in the lead — These strong and sturdy ships, referred to as "Tarshish," based on the name of a coastal city on the Mediterranean, navigated the Reed Sea (1 Kgs 10:22 = 2 Chr 9:21; 1 Kgs 22:49) and the Mediterranean, west of Israel (Isa 23:1, 14; Ezek 27:25; Ps 48:8). For other occurrences of the coastlands (איים) and Tarshish (תרשיש) in tandem, see Isa 66:19; Ps 72:10: "Let kings of Tarshish and the islands pay tribute." In this same verse in Psalms the Sabeans are also mentioned, as in v. 6 of this chapter. For Heb. בָּרִאשֹׁנָה, see also Isa 52:4.

To bring your sons from afar — to their dwelling place in Zion, as in v. 4: "Your sons shall be brought from afar"; 49:12: "Look! These are coming from afar." The wording of 43:6: "Bring my sons (בני) from afar!" may perhaps have influenced the variant in 1QIsa[a], בני, instead of MT בניך.

Their silver and gold with them — The nations shall bring their precious metals with them when they congregate in Jerusalem.

For the name of the Lord your God — All these gifts are a tribute in honor of the Lord. This clause, as well as the following, was taken directly from an earlier prophecy in 55:5: "For the Lord your God, for the Holy One of Israel, who has glorified you." Here, however, the substantive שֵׁם is added before the Tetragrammaton.

For the Holy One of Israel, who has glorified you — for the "Holy One of Israel" (one of the many divine epithets; see v. 14; and, e.g., 41:14, 16, 20; 47:4), who has heaped glory upon you, Zion. (See the introduction, §9.)

[10] Just as the prophet includes foreigners in the future Temple service (see vv. 6-7), in stark contrast to the prevalent isolationist policies (see Ezra 4:1-5; Neh 2:17-20; 3:33-38; 4:1-5), so too does he envisage them participating in the reconstruction of the walls of the city.

Foreigners shall rebuild your walls — Just as foreigners destroyed the walls of Jerusalem and brought about the destruction of the Temple, so now they shall participate in their rebuilding. For בני נֵכָר, see Isa 56:6; 61:5; 62:8.

Their kings shall wait on you — The foreign kings, who will assemble at Jerusalem's gates, shall attend upon you as servants. Although the verb שׁרת may occasionally denote everyday labor (e.g., 1 Kgs 19:21), it refers primarily to service in the Temple, and since the prophet envisages cultic participation of the foreigners (see Isa 56:6; 66:21), here too it may have a similar meaning.

For though in My anger I struck you down — cf. 54:8.

In favor I take you back in love — Compare the continuation of 54:8, quoted above: "But with kindness everlasting I will take you back in love (רִחַמְתִּיךְ)." For רצון ("favor") as the opposite of אַף ("anger"), see Ps 30:6.

[11] When there are no enemies threatening the city, there is no reason to close the gates, even at night (Josh 2:5, 7; Neh 7:3). Indeed, they will always remain open to welcome the kings and their treasures.

Your gates shall always stay open — The gates of Jerusalem shall never be shut. The verb וּפִתְּחוּ is an intransitive *piʿel;* see also Isa 48:8: "Your ears were not opened (פִּתְּחָה)"; Cant 7:13: "(If) its blossoms have opened (פִּתַּח)" (see Ibn Ganaḥ, *Sefer ha-Riqmah* [ed. Walensky, 117, 164, 327]). For the combination of "walls" (v. 10) and "gates" (here), see Jer 51:58; Ezek 26:10; and cf. the Ugaritic prayer to Baal: "When a strong one attacks your gates *(ṯġrkm),* a powerful one your walls *(ḥmytkm)*" (*CAT* 119:9).

Day and night they shall never be shut — A repetition of the above, but in a negative formulation: "stay open"/"never be shut" (לא יִסָּגֵרוּ/פתחו); cf. Isa 45:1: "To open (לפתח) doors before him and letting no gate stay shut (לא יִסָּגֵרוּ)"; 22:22: "And what he opens, none shall shut, and what he shuts, none shall open."

To bring to you the riches of the nations — Cf. v. 5: "The riches (חֵיל) of the nations shall come/be brought to you."

With their kings in procession — The kings "shall come one after another, orderly as a shepherded flock" (Luzzatto). For the depiction of kings/emissaries, among them Jehu, king of Israel, standing in line to pay their tribute to the king of Assyria, see Shalmaneser's Black Obelisk (*ANEP,* no. 355). For the parallelism "nations/kings," see vv. 3, 16. Some scholars suggest transposing the *heh* and the *waw* of the passive נְהוּגִים in the MT, to read the active, נוהגים, i.e., "leading" (the tributary procession).

[12] This verse, which is connected to the previous one by the nominal pair "nation(s)/kingdoms/kings," but which interrupts the depiction of the tribute (see v. 13), may very well have been added here on the basis of an inaccurate understanding of the ending of v. 11, namely, the procession of kings was understood as referring to captured kings being led; cf. Targum זְקִיקִין ("in chains").

For the nation or the kingdom that does not serve you shall perish — The כי particle accentuates the clause: Indeed, the nation that shall not serve you shall be annihilated. For a similar wordplay (יעבדוך/יאבדו) in Aramaic, but in a different context, see Jer 10:11: "Let the gods, who did not make (עֲבַדוּ) heaven and earth, perish (יֵאבַדוּ)."

Such nations shall be utterly destroyed — The infinitive construct followed by a finite verb (חָרֹב יֶחֱרָבוּ) denotes emphasis: those nations shall surely be wiped out. For the verb חרב ("to destroy") in the context of obliteration of peoples, see 2 Kgs 19:17: "True, O Lord, the kings of Assyria have annihilated (הֶחֱרִיבוּ) the nations and their lands."

[13] The Temple's magnificence shall be enhanced by trees brought by the nations from distant lands. For cedars in the construction of biblical and ancient Near Eastern temples (cf. Isa 41:19), see Paul, *Divrei Shalom,* 14-17. This verse is framed as an *inclusio* by the root כבד, which appears both in the beginning (as a noun) and at the end (as a verb).

The majesty of Lebanon shall come to you — The trees of Lebanon, which are the pride of its woods, shall be brought to you by subservient nations. Mesopotamian sources consistently laud these cedars, e.g., "Mighty, high, cedars whose beauty is in high esteem, whose dignified stature is gigantic, the abundant riches of the Lebanon" (*CAD* E:274). 1QIsa[a] adds נתן לך, "is given to you" (before "shall come to you"), which is a word-by-word repetition of 35:2.

Junipers, box trees, and cypresses all together — For the identification of these trees, see 41:19, where they appear as part of God's plan to give shade to the returning expatriates on their journey through the Syrian Desert. Here, however, their function is the adornment of the Temple. (See Paul, *Divrei Shalom,* 15-17.) For יַחְדָּו following a series of substantives or verbs, see, e.g., 41:19, 20, 23; 45:21.

To bring glory to the site of My sanctuary — Cf. v. 7: "And I will add glory to My glorious house"; Ezra 7:27: "To glorify the House of the Lord in Jerusalem." For the expression מקום מקדשי, see Jer 17:12.

I will honor the place where My feet rest — Note the chiasm formed by this hemistich and the previous one. For מקום רגלי as a reference to the Temple, see Ezek 43:7: "It said to me: 'O mortal, this is the place of My throne and the place for the soles of My feet (מקום . . . רגלי), where I will dwell in the midst of the people Israel forever.'" The Temple is also referred to as הדום רגליו ("footstool"); see Ps 132:7: "Let us enter His abode, bow at His footstool"; Lam 2:1: "He has cast down from heaven to earth the majesty of Israel. He did not remember His footstool on His day of wrath"; see also 1 Chr 28:2. For the synonymous pair תפארת/כבוד, see Exod 28:2, 40; Isa 4:2.

[14] This verse marks the fulfillment of Isaac's blessing to Jacob in Gen 27:29: "Let peoples serve you and nations bow to you." For the connection between the tribute of nations and kings and their subservience, which is expressed by prostration in the dust, see Ps 72:9-11. A new dimension is added here, that of the renaming of Jerusalem in light of her reconstituted state. For the symbolic renaming of sites and people, see v. 18 (the walls and gates); 58:12; 61:3 (the nation); 62:4 (the land of Israel). Compare also 1:26: "After that you shall be called 'City of Righteousness, Faithful City.'" The key term, "feet," links this verse with the preceding one. What is described in 51:23, where the tormentors of Israel commanded Israel: "Bend down (שְׁחִי) that we may walk over you"; is now reversed: "The sons of those who tormented you shall come to you bending low, and all who reviled you shall prostrate at the soles of your feet."

The sons of all those who tormented you shall come to you bending low — The foreigners who oppressed you shall now come as humble supplicants. The infinitive construct שְׁחוֹחַ ("bowing"), used adverbially, is a hapax legomenon. 1QIsa[a] adds כול, "all," before "the sons of those who tormented you." In the MT the word כל in the following hemistich does double duty and applies to the first clause as well.

And all who reviled you shall prostrate at the soles of your feet — as evidence of their total submission; cf. 49:23: "Kings shall tend your children, their queens shall serve you as nurses. They shall bow to you, face to the ground, and lick the dust of your feet." Compare also similar formulae of servility in royal Mesopotamian inscriptions: *qaqqara ina pān šarri našāqu,* "to kiss the earth before the king"; *šēp šarri našāqu,* "to kiss the feet of the king" (*CAD* N/2:58). Here, in contrast, the subservient nations bow before the city, not before the monarch. For the etymological and semantic equivalents of the verb נאץ, "to revile" (also in 52:5), see Akk. *nâṣu* (*CAD* N/2:53) and Ugar. *n'ṣ* (*HdO* 2:612).

And they shall call you, "City of the Lord" — Cf. Ps 101:8: "To rid the city of the Lord (עיר ה׳) of all evildoers." Naming a city for its god is documented in Mesopotamian literature as well, e.g., the city Nippur is sometimes referred to as "the city of [the god] Enlil" (*CAD* A/1:385). In light of the previously noted absence of the Davidic line from Deutero-Isaiah's eschatology (see 55:3), it is possible that the sobriquet "City of the Lord" comes to replace "City of David" (עיר דוד, as in 2 Sam 5:7; 1 Chr 15:1).

"Zion of the Holy One of Israel" — Some explicate this epithet as a construct form (as translated here). The appellation קדוש ישראל ("the Holy One of Israel") is common; see, e.g., v. 9; 41:14, 16, 20; 43:3, 14; 45:11. Others suggest that עיר ("city") in the previous clause is to be understood here as well: "Zion, the city of the Holy One of Israel." The order of the terms here may have been influenced by 12:6: "O, shout for joy, you who dwell in Zion (ציון)! For great in your midst is the Holy One of Israel (קדוש ישראל)." For a parallelism between עיר ה׳/אלהים ("city of the Lord/of God") and קד(ו)ש ("Holy"), see Ps 46:5: "There is a river whose streams gladden God's city (עיר אלהים), the holy (קְדֹשׁ) dwelling place of the Most High."

[15] *Whereas you have been forsaken, rejected, with none passing through* — For עזובה ("forsaken"), the first of the three substantives describing Zion's forlorn and desperate straits at the time of the Temple's destruction, cf. Isa 49:14: "The Lord has forsaken me"; 54:6-7: "The Lord has called you back as a wife forlorn and forsaken. . . . For a little while I forsook you"; 62:4: "Nevermore shall you be called 'Forsaken'"; 62:12: "A city not forsaken." The second description, שׂנואה, denotes "repudiated, rejected," as in Gen 29:31: "The Lord saw that Leah was repudiated (שׂנואה)"; Judg 14:16: "Then Samson's wife harassed him with tears, and she said, 'You really reject me (שְׂנֵאתַנִי). You do not love me.'"

Compare also Deut 21:15: "If a man has two wives, one loved and the other rejected (שְׂנוּאָה)." And for Aramaic, see Porten and Yardeni, *Textbook of Aramaic Documents,* 2:60, B3.3:7: שְׂנֵאת, "I repudiate you"; line 8: כסף שְׂנאה, "payment for repudiation." The third description of Zion, ואין עובר ("none passing through"), also characterized Jerusalem and its environs following the destruction of the Temple; cf. Jer 9:9: "They [the desert oases] are laid waste. No man passes through (מִבלי עֹבֵר)"; Ezek 33:28: "I will make the land a desolate waste, and her proud glory shall cease. And the mountains of Israel shall be desolate, with none passing through (מֵאֵין עובר)." The LXX's variant, ואין עוזר ("and none would help her"), was influenced by other depictions of Jerusalem and Israel's isolation; see 2 Kgs 14:26; Ps 22:12; 107:12. For תחת ("instead of, whereas") indicating the reversal of the nation's fortunes, see v. 17.

I will make you a pride everlasting — גאון denotes exaltation, majesty, pride. For its employment with negative connotations, see Jer 48:29: "We have heard of Moab's pride (גאון), most haughty is he — of his arrogance and pride (וגאונו), his haughtiness and self-exaltation"; Prov 16:18: "Pride (גאון) goes before ruin."

A joy for age after age — You shall be brimming with happiness (משׂוש) forevermore. For similar descriptions of Jerusalem's bliss, see Jer 49:25: "The citadel of My joy (מְשׂוֹשִׂי)"; Ps 48:3: "Fair crested, joy (משׂוש) of all the earth." For the parallel synonyms דור (ו)דור(ים)/עולם ("everlasting/age after age"), see Isa 51:8; 58:12; 61:4. Compare also Ugar. *ʿlm* and *drdr* (*CAT* 1.2.IV:10).

[16] Suckling at the divine breast is a common motif in descriptions of the rearing of gods and kings in ancient Near Eastern literature. Compare, for example, the Ugaritic Kirta epic: "She shall bear you the lad Yaṣṣib [the name of King Kirta's firstborn], who shall suck *(ynq)* the milk of Astarte, shall suckle *(mṣṣ)* at the breasts of Maiden [Anat]" (*CAT* 1.15.II:25-28). According to *Enuma Elish* (I:85), Marduk "suckled at the breasts of goddesses" (*ANET,* 62). And of the Assyrian king Ashurbanipal it is said: "Her [Ishtar's] four teats are in your mouth. You suck *(enēqu)* at two, and two you milk yourself" (*CAD* E:165). Suckling at the breasts of goddesses confers certain divine attributes. Here this poetic image is picturesquely applied to Zion, who sucks the milk (= the wealth) of the nations (for similar imagery, see 49:23; 66:11).

You shall suck the milk of the nations — You shall gain your sustenance from the milk of the nations, a reference to their wealth (vv. 5, 11); and cf. the Targum, נִכְסֵי עַמְמַיָּא ("the property of the nations").

Suckle at royal breasts — the same idea as above, chiastically expressed in different terms. "Since the metaphor is a type of allegory, [the prophet] speaks of kings rather than queens, and it means that they too shall bring you treasures" (Luzzatto). The vocalization שֹׁד (a variant of שַׁד, "breast") was influenced by its homonym, שֹׁד, "violence, devastation, ruin," in v. 18. According to the Targum, the milk from these royal breasts is interpreted as delighting oneself on the royal spoils. For the parallel terms מלכים/גוים ("nations/kings"), see v. 12. For the Ugaritic and Akkadian etymological and semantic equivalents of ינק, see the quotes in the introduction to this verse.

And you shall know that I the Lord am your Savior — This hemistich and the following one are direct quotes from an earlier prophecy in 49:26. When you "milk" these nations of their wealth, you shall know that the Lord has redeemed you.

I, the Mighty One of Jacob, am your Redeemer — For this divine epithet, see 49:26. Note the chiasm between this hemistich and the preceding one. (See the introduction, §9.)

[17] A quartet of images serves to accentuate the majesty of future Jerusalem. The city life shall change materially and outwardly, and the metropolis shall enjoy Solomonic prosperity; cf. 1 Kgs 10:14, 27: "The weight of the gold that Solomon received every year was six hundred and sixty-six talents of gold. . . . The king made silver as plentiful in Jerusalem as [precious] stones, and cedars as plentiful as sycamores in the Shephelah." (For the same sequence of metals: gold, silver, copper, and iron, see the depiction of the idol in Dan 2:31ff., as well as the metals that David stockpiled in preparation for the Temple's construction in 1 Chr 29:2.)

Instead of copper I will bring gold, instead of iron I will bring silver, instead of wood, copper, and instead of stone, iron — According to Rashi and Kimchi, this gold is recompense for the treasures of the sanctuary stolen by the conquering Babylonians. For תחת, "instead of," see v. 15.

And I will appoint well-being as your government — פְּקֻדָּתֵךְ is an abstract noun, referring to the officials in charge of governance (Rashi, Ibn Ezra; cf. 2 Chr 23:18). (For the Akkadian etymological and semantic cognate *piqittu* ["charge, assignment, post"], referring to administrative responsibilities, see *CAD* P:391-92.)

Prosperity as your rulers — For נֹגְשַׂיִךְ, "rulers," see Isa 3:12: "My people's rulers (נֹגְשָׂיו) are babes." For the parallel pair צדקה/שלום ("well-being/prosperity"), see 48:18: "Then your well-being (שלומך) would be like a river, your prosperity (וצדקתך) like the waves of the sea"; Ps 72:3: "Let the mountains produce well-being (שלום) for the people, the hills, prosperity (צדקה)"; cf. Isa 54:13-14.

[18-20] Three sequential verses reiterate the syntax of promise: לא . . . עוד ("no . . . more"), emphasizing that the newly restored Jerusalem shall herald a time of peace, prosperity, joy, and success. This syntactical paradigm appears also in 51:22; 52:1; 54:4; 62:4; 65:19.

[18] *The cry, "Violence!" shall no more be heard in your land* — Cf. Job 19:7: "I cry, 'Violence' (חמס)!" For the parallel synonyms חמס/שד, see Amos 3:10; Jer 20:8; Ezek 45:9; Hab 1:3.

Nor "Wrack and Ruin!" within your borders — No cries of woe shall be heard ever again in Israel. For the pair שֹׁד וָשֶׁבֶר ("ruin and devastation"), see Isa 51:19; 59:7. For the parallel pair גבול/ארץ ("land/borders"), see Mic 5:5: "He will deliver us from Assyria, when it invades our land (בארצנו) and when it tramples our borders (בגבולנו)."

But you shall name your walls "Salvation" — since the enemy shall never again breach them (the initial *waw* denotes contrast). (For the names given to city walls in royal Mesopotamian inscriptions, see *CAD* D:195; Š/1:243-44; A. R. George, *Babylonian Topographical Texts* [Leuven, 1992]; idem, *House Most High* [Winona Lake, Ind., 1993]; idem, "Studies in Cultic Topography and Ideology," *Bibliotheca Orientalis* 53 [1996]: 363-95.)

And your gates "Praise" — You shall call your gates, which shall never again be closed (v. 11), "Praise," since all who enter shall sing the Lord's praises (v. 6) and since the Lord shall cause Jerusalem's praise to spread throughout the land (62:7). Note the polyvalency of תְּהִלָּה, which denotes both "praise/glory" and "radiance" (61:3) and thus also serves as a precursor to the wondrous light that shall shine on Israel in the following two verses. For this meaning, see also Hab 3:3: "His majesty covers the skies. His radiance (תְּהִלָּתוֹ) fills the earth"; cf. also Isa 13:10: "The stars and constellations of heaven shall not give off their light (יָהֵלּוּ)"; Job 31:26: "If I ever saw the light shining in radiance (יָהֵל)." For the same sequence, שעריך/חֹמֹתיך ("your walls/your gates"), cf. vv. 10-11. For the names conferred upon the gates of Jerusalem see Neh 2:13ff. (For the names given city gates in royal Mesopotamian inscriptions, see *CAD* B:19, and the above-quoted literature pertaining to city walls.)

[19-20] The chapter ends as it began, with divine luminescence shining brightly in Jerusalem. In Deutero-Isaiah's eschatology the Lord Himself shall be Israel's source of light. Note the fourfold repetition of אור ("light") in vv. 19-20, as well as the twofold repetition of שמש ("sun") and ירח ("moon"). For other descriptions of supernatural light, see Isa 30:26: "And the light of the moon shall become like the light of the sun, and the light of the sun shall become sevenfold." The images are all metaphorical, denoting success and joy. For the syntactical construction: לא . . . עוד ("no . . . more"), which is repeated here twice and accentuates the future reversal, see above on vv. 18-20.

[19] *The sun shall no longer be your light by day* — Cf. Jer 31:35: "The Lord who established the sun for light by day (לאור יומם)."

Nor the shining of the moon for radiance [*by night*] — The final bracketed words "by night" (בלילה) are missing from the MT but are found in the LXX, Targum (בְּלֵילְיָא), and 1QIsa[a] following הַיָּרֵחַ. Compare also Jer 31:35: "The laws of moon and stars for light by night (לאור לילה)"; Ps 121:6: "Nor the moon by night (וירח בלילה)." The pair ירח/שמש ("sun/moon") appears also in Ugaritic: "For the days of the sun *(špš)* and moon *(yrḫ)*" (*CAT* 1.108:26); and in the Phoenician Azatiwada inscription: "Only may the name of Azatiwada be forevermore, like the name of the sun (שמש) and the moon (ירח)" (*KAI* 26 V:5-7; see Paul, *Divrei Shalom*, 51-58).

For the Lord shall be your light everlasting Cf. Isa 58:8, 10. Also in Akkadian inscriptions *nūru* ("light") is one of the most common characteristics of the Mesopotamian gods (*CAD* N/2:347-49). For a similar expression to אור עולם, see the first combination of the Balaam inscription from Deir ʿAlla in the Sukkot Valley east of the Jordan, from the second quarter of the eighth century BCE: "There shall be no everlasting light (נגה עלם)." (See Aḥituv, *Ha-Ketav veha-Mik̲tav*, 386, lines 6-7.)

And your God shall be your glory — This is the fifth occurrence of the key root פאר in this chapter, and see v. 21 for yet another example.

[20] The third iteration of the syntactical construction לא . . . עוד ("no . . . more"), accentuating the supernatural reversal in Deutero-Isaiah's eschatological prophecy.

Your sun shall set no more — Compare the beginning of the chapter (v. 1), where the same expression (בא אור) is employed to denote the dawning of Zion's light. For another example of שמש as a masculine noun, see 2 Sam 23:4. The word עוד ("more") is missing from both the LXX and 1QIsa[a].

Your moon no more withdraw — Note the chiasm with the preceding hemistich. For the root אסף denoting withdrawal, see Isa 16:10; Joel 2:10.

For the Lord shall be a light to you forever — a reiteration of the last part of v. 19: "a light forever," i.e., everlasting joy.

And the days of your mourning shall be ended — The verb שלם *(qal)* denotes a temporal conclusion and appears in the Dead Sea Scrolls, both in Hebrew (in a fragment of the book of Tobit: "When the fourteen days of [the wedding celebration] which Reuel promised to make for his daughter came to a close [שלמו]" [M. Broshi et al., *Qumran Cave 4.XIV: Parabiblical Texts,* Part II, DJD 19 (Oxford, 1995), 67]); and in Aramaic (in a fragment of the *Genesis Apocryphon* 6:9: "And in my days, when according to the calculations I had made . . . ten jubilees had elapsed [שלמו]" [M. Morgenstern, E. Qimron, and D. Sivan, "The Hitherto Unpublished Columns of the Genesis Apocryphon," *Abr-Nahrain* 32 (1995): 40]). Compare also Targum Onqelos and Targum Jonathan to Lev 25:30, which translate Heb. מְלֹאת ("to come to an end") by Aram. מִשְׁלַם. The Akkadian verb *šalāmu,* like its Hebrew and Aramaic cognates, also denotes the end of a time period or era (*CAD* Š/1:218).

[21] The formulation of this verse, which declares that the entire nation will be righteous (צדיקים) and that they will repossess the land (ארץ יִירשו), was influenced by Ps 37:29: "The righteous shall inherit the land (ארץ צדיקים יִירשו) and abide forever in it." Only here and in Psalms do the motifs of righteousness and repossession of the land appear side by side. Since all the people

shall be righteous, it follows that they shall never again be punished and their possession of the land shall be absolute and eternal. Moreover, they are further likened to the Davidic scion in Isa 11:1 who shall shoot forth from the stock of Jesse. But here the former Davidic blessings are no longer restricted to his progeny, but rather apply to the people as a whole, as already seen in Isa 55:3. The shoot (נֵצֶר), which Isaiah declared would sprout from the stock of Jesse (11:1), is now reapplied to Israel, who becomes the shoot of God's own planting. (See the introduction, §17.)

And your people, all of them righteous — Whereas צדק was a hallmark of the Davidic scion (Isa 11:4-5), here all of Israel shall be צדיקים.

Shall possess the land for all time — Cf. 57:13: "But those who trust in Me shall inherit the land and possess My sacred Mount"; 65:9: "I will bring forth offspring from Jacob, from Judah heirs to My mountains. My chosen ones shall take possession, My servants shall dwell thereon." The word עולם appears here for the third time in three verses (see vv. 19, 20).

A shoot of My own planting — The people as a whole (not merely the Davidic scion) will be a divinely tended shoot. For another example of God's "planting" (מטע), see 61:3: "'Terebinths of Victory,' planted by the Lord for His glory." For the image of the nation firmly planted by the Lord on their land, see Exod 15:17: "You will bring them and plant them in the mountain that is Your possession"; Isa 5:7: "For the vineyard of the Lord of Hosts is the house of Israel, and the seedlings He lovingly planted are the men of Judah"; Amos 9:15: "And I will plant them on their soil"; Ps 80:9: "You plucked up a vine from Egypt. You expelled nations and planted it." The majority of the ancient translations, including 1QIsa[a], which also adds the divine name (מטעי ה׳) (cf. 61:3: מטע ה׳, "planted by the Lord"), agree with the Masoretic Qere, מטעי, which in turn accords with מעשה ידי ("My handiwork") immediately following. 1QIsa[b], however, has מטעיו ("His plantings") following the Ketib, as well as ידיו instead of ידי. This horticultural image of a "shoot" appears also in royal Assyrian inscriptions referring to the kings Tiglath-pileser III and Esarhaddon as the "precious shoot" of the god Assur. (See Seux, *Épithètes royales,* 144, 225-26; *CAD* P:416-18.)

My handiwork in which I glory — the nation that I crafted and take pride in; cf. 44:23: "He has glorified Himself through Israel"; 46:13: "I will grant . . . to Israel, in whom I glory"; 49:3: "Israel, in whom I glory"; 61:3: "Planted by the Lord for His glory." This is the sixth occurrence in this chapter of the key root פאר. The expression מעשה ידי ("My handiwork"), akin to 45:11: פֹּעַל ידי, recurs again in 64:7. Compare also the cognate expressions in Akkadian: *binût qātē* (*CAD* B:244); *šipir qātē/idī* (*CAD* Š/3:82); *dullu qātē* (*CAD* D:176-77). The last-cited Akkadian expression appears as an Aramaic Akkadianism in the *Genesis Apocryphon* 20:7: דל ידיהא ("her handiwork"). (See Fitzmyer, *Genesis Apocryphon,* 62.) The LXX and the Isaiah scrolls (1QIsa[a] and 1QIsa[b]) have מעשה ידיו ("His handiwork") instead of MT מעשי ידי ("My handiwork"), in accordance with the Ketib of the previous clause, נצר מטעו.

[22] For numerous progeny in the eschatological era, see 44:4; 49:19-20; 54:1; and cf. 51:2.

The smallest shall become a clan — The smallest family unit shall expand and become a clan. For other examples of this meaning of אלף, see Judg 6:15: "My clan (אַלְפִּי) is the humblest in Manasseh"; 1 Sam 10:19: "By your tribes and clans (ולאלפיכם)."

The least, a mighty nation — The most insignificant tribe shall become a mighty people, as in Mic 5:1: "Least (צעיר) among the clans (אלפי) of Judah." For the Lord's blessing to Abraham regarding the future greatness of Abraham's progeny, see Gen 18:18; and cf. Deut 9:14; 26:5. For the synonymous pair קטן/צעיר ("smallest/least"), see 1 Sam 9:21: "Saul replied, 'But I am only a Benjaminite, from the smallest (מִקְטַנֵּי) of the tribes of Israel, and my clan is the least important (צעיר) of all the clans of the tribe of Benjamin!'"; Qumran Psalm 151 (11QPs[a]151): "I was the smallest (קטן) of my brothers and the least (צעיר) of my father's sons" (Sanders, *Psalms Scroll of Qumrân Cave 11,* DJD 4, 55). For גוי as a tribal unit, here parallel to אלף ("clan"), cf. Akk. *gā'um/gāyum* in the Mari letters (A. Malamat, *Mari and Early Israelite Experience* [Oxford, 1989], 38-39).

I, the Lord, will speed it in due time — When the time I appointed shall arrive to expedite this, I shall bring it about without delay. For a similar prophetic promise, see Hab 2:3: "For the prophecy is a witness [read עֵד instead of עוֹד] for a set term, an attester for a time that will come. Even if it tarries, wait for it still; for it will surely come, without delay." For the verb אֲחִישֶׁנָּה ("I will speed it"), a *hiph'il* stem of the root חוש, see Ps 55:9. It is possible that this verse also contains a polemical element addressed to those who demand: "Let Him speed, let Him hasten (יָחִישָׁה) His purpose, so that we will see it" (Isa 5:19). The Deutero-Isaianic verse prompted the following rabbinic midrash: "If they are worthy — I shall hasten it (אחישנה). If they are unworthy — I will bring it in due time (בְּעִתָּהּ)" (*b. Sanh.* 98a).

Chapter 61

This chapter consists of two distinct literary units: vv. 1-9 and 10-11, and has a literary *inclusio* (vv. 1, 11) framed by two clauses with the expression **אדני ה׳** ("Lord God"). In the first three verses of the first pericope, Deutero-Isaiah's appointment to prophecy is described (in the first-person) and his mission delineated: God has anointed him to deliver a message of consolation to give hope to the disheartened, to expedite the release of captives, and to console the bereaved since their grief and mourning is about to be transformed into festive joy. Verses 4-9 describe the rehabilitation of the land, the rebuilding of the ruins, and foreigners extending aid to Israel in the field, as well as providing priestly donations to the nation. The people, who are called "Priests of the Lord" and "Ministers of God" (v. 6), shall have a "double share" of consolation in compensation for their "double share of disgrace," and the Lord shall make a new and everlasting covenant with them. Regarding the second unit, see below.

This chapter is connected to chap. 60 both linguistically and thematically, as the following chart illustrates:

Chapter 60	**Chapter 61**
v. 5 — the wealth of nations (**חֵיל גוים**) shall flow to you; v. 11 — To bring in the wealth of the nations (**חֵיל גוים**)	v. 6 — You shall enjoy the wealth of nations (**חֵיל גוים**)
v. 6 — and they shall herald (**יְבַשֵּׂרוּ**) the praises (**תְּהִלּוֹת**) of the Lord; v. 18 — and your gates "Praise" (**תְּהִלָּה**)	v. 1 — He has sent me as a herald (**לְבַשֵּׂר**) of joy to the humble; v. 3 — a garment of splendor (**תְּהִלָּה**); v. 11 — and shall make praise (**תְּהִלָּה**) blossom before all the nations

Chapter 60	Chapter 61
v. 7 — they shall be welcome (רצון) offerings on My altar; v. 10 — but in favor (ברצוני) I take you back	v. 2 — to proclaim a year of the Lord's favor (רצון)
v. 7 — and I will add glory (אפאר) to My glorious house (בית תפארתי); v. 9 — who has glorified you (פארך); v. 13 — to adorn (לפאר) the site of My sanctuary; v. 19 — shall be your glory (לתפארתך); v. 21 — in which I glory (להתפאר)	v. 3 — turban (פְּאֵר) . . . for His glory (להתפאר); v. 10 — like a bridegroom adorned with a turban (פאר) (פְּאֵר in these two verses is derived from a different root [Egyptian] but serves as a homonym of Heb. פאר)
vv. 7, 10 — they shall serve your needs (ישרתונֶךָ)	v. 6 — Ministers (משרתי) of our God
v. 10 — aliens (בני נכר)	v. 5 — aliens (בני נכר)
v. 12 — such nations shall be destroyed (חָרֹב יֶחֱרָבוּ)	v. 4 — and they shall build the ancient ruins (חָרְבוֹת) . . . and renew the ruined (חֹרֶב) cities
v. 15 — I will make you a pride everlasting (גאון עולם), a joy (מְשׂוֹשׂ) for age after age	v. 7 — joy shall be theirs (שִׂמחת עולם) for all time; v. 10 — I greatly rejoice (שׂוֹשׂ אשׂישׂ) in the Lord
v. 17 (4 times) — instead (תחת)	vv. 3 (3 times), 7 — instead (תחת)
v. 17 — and righteousness (צדקה) as your officials; v. 21 — and your people, all of them righteous (צדיקים)	v. 10 — robe of victory (צדקה); v. 3 — terebinths of victory (הצדק); v. 11 — will make victory (צדקה) . . . blossom
(v. 18) — salvation (ישועה)	v. 10 — salvation (ישע)
vv. 19, 20 — your light everlasting (לאור עולם)	v. 7 — joy . . . for all time (שִׂמחת עולם); v. 8 — a covenant . . . for all time (וברית עולם)
v. 20 — and the days of your mourning (אֶבְלֵךְ) shall be ended	v. 2 — to comfort all who mourn (אֲבֵלִים); v. 3 — to provide the mourners (לַאֲבֵלֵי) in Zion
v. 21 — They shall possess (יִירְשׁוּ) the land (ארץ) for all time	v. 7 — they shall possess (יִירָשׁוּ) a double share in their land (ארצם)
v. 21 — a shoot of My own planting (מטָעַי) in which I glory (להתפאר)	v. 3 — planted by (מטע) the Lord for His glory (להתפאר)

Both chapters are also characterized by a bestowal of new names: 60:14: "And you shall be called 'City of the Lord, Zion of the Holy One of Israel,'" 60:18: "And you shall name your walls 'Victory' and your gates 'Praise'" — 61:3: "They shall be called 'Terebinths of Victory' planted by the Lord for His glory," 61:6: "And you shall be called 'Priests of the Lord' and termed 'Ministers of our God.'"

[1] The verse begins with a first-person address by the prophet (a rare phenomenon; cf. 40:6 [according to the LXX, 1QIsa^a, and one medieval Hebrew manuscript the verse is introduced by וא(ו)מר(ה), "And I said"]); 48:16; 49:1-6, 8), who declares that the spirit of the Lord was conferred on him. The expression לקרא דרור, which appears also in Lev 25:10 (there in reference to the Jubilee Year) and in Jer 34:8, 15, 17 (twice) (cf. Ezek 46:17: שנת דרור), is a reflection of a well-documented practice from the last years of the third millennium BCE in Sumer up until the Neo-Babylonian period (sixth century BCE), namely, the proclamation of *andurāru* ("reformation") by the king, which included acts of social justice, such as reembracing the disenfranchised, remission of (commercial) debts, manumission (of private slaves), return of the banished, tax reform, the return of ancestral plots to their owners and the granting of pardons. (See M. Weinfeld, *Social Justice in Ancient Israel and the Ancient Near East* [Minneapolis, 1995], 75-96; *CAD* A/2:115-17.) The announcement of *andurāru* in Mesopotamia was preceded by the lifting of torches throughout the land so as to promulgate the news (in the Bible the ram's horn was used to spread the word; see Lev 25:9). Here the prophet himself serves as the harbinger and herald of social justice. For the Lord's concern for the indigents of society, see 57:15; 66:2.

The spirit of the Lord God is upon me — See 42:1: "I have put My spirit upon him [the servant]"; 44:3: "So I will pour My spirit on your offspring"; 48:16: "And now the Lord God has sent me, endowed with His spirit"; 59:21: "My spirit that is upon you." Compare also 11:2: "The spirit of the Lord shall alight upon him." However, in contrast to the last quotation, where the bestowal of the spirit is upon the Davidic scion, all of the references in Deutero-Isaiah are to the spirit of the Lord alighting upon the servant of the Lord, the nation, or upon the prophet himself. The Davidic line has no part or portion in the prophet's eschatology (see 55:3). For the appellation אדני ה׳ ("the Lord God") (אדני is absent from the LXX, 1QIsa^a, and several medieval Hebrew manuscripts), see v. 11; 48:16; 50:4, 5, 7.

Because the Lord has anointed me — The Lord's spirit has alighted upon me since I was appointed by Him to deliver messages of consolation to the disillusioned and disenfranchised. The verbal expression משח ל-, indicating an elevated appointment, appears only once more in a prophetic context: "And anoint (תמשח ל-) Elisha son of Shaphat of Abel-meholah to succeed you as prophet" (1 Kgs 19:16). Compare in a royal context 2 Chr 22:7: "During his visit he went out with Jehoram to Jehu son of Nimshi, whom the Lord had anointed (ל-

משחו) to cut off the house of Ahab." For the "spirit of the Lord," which alights upon the divinely anointed, see 1 Sam 16:13: "And he [Samuel] anointed him in the presence of his brothers; and the spirit of the Lord possessed David." For the mention of the anointing of prophets in the literature of Qumran, see the *War Scroll* (1QM): "By the hand of Your anointed ones, the seers of decrees" (11:7-8; see Yadin, *War,* 310-11); and the *Damascus Document* (4Q266): "And he taught them by the hand of the anointed ones with His holy spirit and the seers of the truth" (J. M. Baumgarten, *Qumran Cave 4.XIII: The Damascus Document (4Q266-273),* DJD 18 [Oxford, 1996], 37, 38, frag. 2 ii 12-13); "By the holy anointed ones, who prophesied deceit" (ibid., 41, 42, frag. 3 ii 9). Compare also 11Q13 *(Melchizedek)*: "And the herald is the anointed of the spirit" (F. García Martínez, E. J. C. Tigchelaar, and A. S. van der Woude, *Qumran Cave 11.II: 11Q2-18, 11Q20-30,* DJD 23 [Oxford, 1998], 225-26).

He has sent me as a herald to the humble — For the heraldic motif in Deutero-Isaiah's prophecies, see 40:9: "O herald of joy to Zion . . . O herald of joy to Jerusalem"; 41:27: "And again I send a herald to Jerusalem"; 52:7: "How welcome on the mountain are the footsteps of the herald announcing happiness, heralding good fortune, announcing victory."

To bind up the brokenhearted — The Lord sent me on a prophetic mission to heal the wounded of heart and thus to fulfill a duty that is usually performed by the Deity Himself, e.g., in Ps 147:3: "He heals their broken hearts and binds up their wounds"; Ps 51:19: "O God, You will not despise a crushed and contrite heart," since "the Lord is close to the brokenhearted. Those crushed in spirit He delivers" (Ps 34:19). For the verb חבשׁ (lit. the binding of wounds) in a metaphorical context, see Isa 30:26: "On the day when the Lord binds up His people's wounds and heals the injuries it has suffered."

To proclaim release to the captives — The Lord has sent me to announce to the prisoners that their release is nigh. For the same motif, cf. 42:7; 49:9; 58:6; and see the introduction to the unit. The verb קרא ("to proclaim") is repeated three more times in vv. 2, 3, 6.

Liberation to the imprisoned — Parallel to the previous stich: I was sent to herald the "liberation," פְּקַח-קוֹחַ (a hapax legomenon, which in 1QIsa[a] and a number of medieval Hebrew manuscripts is written as one word, פקחקוח), of captives. This term (similar in form to יְפֵה-פִיָּה in Jer 46:20, in which both the second and third radicals are duplicated) denotes the opening of eyes so as to let in the light and serves as a metaphor (as in Akkadian) for the release of captives; cf. Isa 42:7: "To open eyes that are blind, to rescue prisoners from confinement." (See Paul, *Divrei Shalom,* 14.)

[2] *To proclaim a year of the Lord's favor* — Cf. 49:8: "In an hour of favor (בעת רצון) I answered you"; 58:5: "A day favorable (יום רצון) to the Lord"; 60:10: "But in favor (וברצוני) I take you back in love."

And a day of vengeance for our God — It shall be a year of the Lord's favor for the nation, but the very opposite for the Lord's enemies, as in 63:4: "For I had planned a day of vengeance, and My year of redemption arrived"; cf. also 34:8: "For it is the Lord's day of vengeance, the year of vindication for Zion's cause"; 35:4; 59:17. For the nominal pair שנה/יום ("day/year"), see Deut 32:7; Ps 61:7; 77:6; Prov 3:2; 10:27; Job 32:7. It is also attested in an Ugaritic hymn to the god El (the head of the pantheon): "For the days *(lymt)* of the sun and the moon, and the pleasant years *(šnt)* of El" (*CAT* 1.108:26-27); in Phoenician, in the Azitawada inscription: "Long days (ימם) and an abundance of years (שנת)" (*KAI* 26A III:5-6); in Aramaic: "In his days (ביומוהי) his nation shall be salvaged, and in his years (ובשנוהי) they shall rest easy as one of the tribes of Israel" (Targum Onqelos to Gen 49:16); in an Ammonite inscription on a vial, discovered in Tel Siran in Rabbat-Ammon and dated ca. 600 BCE: "In many days (ביומת) and in far-off years (ושנת)" (Aḥituv, *Ha-Ketav veha-Miḵtav,* 334, lines 7-8); and in Akkadian: "They lived many days *(ūmī);* they added many years *(šanāti)* [to their span]" (*Enuma Elish* I:13; P. Talon, *Enūma Eliš* [Brussels, 2005], 33).

To comfort all who mourn — The Lord appointed me His herald to deliver a message of comfort to all those who mourn (see also Isa 57:18; 66:10; these are the mourners of Zion mentioned in the following verse), since the time of mourning has been terminated (see 60:20: "And your days of mourning shall be ended"). This motif of consolation reverberates throughout his prophecies; cf., e.g., 40:1; 49:13; 51:3, 12; 52:9.

[3] Ceremonies marking bereavement shall be transformed into happy times and joyous occasions. They, the mourners, shall be called by a new name, by which their ties with God will be renewed and strengthened. The description below may have been influenced by the prophecy of salvation in Jer 33:9, where one finds a similar triad: לְשֵׁם שָׂשׂוֹן (= שֶׁמֶן שָׂשׂוֹן), לתהִלה (= מַעֲטֵה תהִלה), ולתפארת (= להתפאר). Compare also Jer 13:11: "That they might be My people, for fame, and praise, and splendor." Both these verses are themselves influenced by Deut 26:19: "And that He will set you in fame and renown and glory, high above all the nations that He has made." (See the introduction, §§13, 15.)

To provide for the mourners in Zion — This clause is incomplete, since the object of the verb לשׂום ("to provide") is not stated. This verb may very well be a doublet of the following verb, לתת, which delineates the changes that will take place in the people's situation (for שׂום and נתן as synonyms, see 43:19-20). Support for this hypothesis may be provided by the LXX and Peshitta, both of which translate only one of these verbs. Others (e.g., Ehrlich, *Mikrâ Ki-Pheshuṭo,* 3:149) suggest emending the text to לשלם, as in 57:18: "And I shall mete out (ואשלם) solace to them and to the mourners among them."

To give them a turban instead of ashes — A transposition of the letters

אפר-פאר accentuates their reversal of fortune. Instead of the "ashes" (אֵפֶר) of mourning, the Lord shall place a turban (פְּאֵר) on their heads, as in Ezek 24:17: "Observe no mourning for the dead, put on your turban (פארך)"; Ezek 24:23: "And your turbans (ופארכם) shall remain on your heads and your sandals upon your feet. You shall not lament or weep." פאר, an Egyptian loanword, repeated once again in v. 10 (see also Isa 3:20), serves as wordplay with Heb. פאר, which appears at the end of this verse (להתפאר). For the custom of pouring ashes or dust on one's head in times of bereavement, see Josh 7:6: "And they strewed dust (עפר) on their heads"; Job 2:12: "And they threw dust (עפר) into the air on to their heads"; cf. also 2 Sam 13:19; Ezek 27:30. For covering oneself in ashes see Jer 6:26: "And sprinkle ashes (אפר) on yourselves! Mourn as for an only child!" Other similar mourning practices are to sit on/in ashes/dust (Isa 47:1; Jonah 3:6; Job 2:8), to make one's bed on ashes (Isa 58:5; Esth 4:3), and to don ashes (Esth 4:1). Strewing ashes on the head appears also in the Ugaritic Baal epic: "He [the god El] pours ashes *(ʿmr)* of grief on his head, dust *(ʿpr)* of humiliation on his brow" (*CAT* 1.5.VI:14-16); and in Akkadian literature (*CAD* E:187).

Oil of gladness instead of mourning — As consolation for the grief they experienced during their exile, they shall anoint themselves in fine aromatic oils, a sign of their newly found happiness. Cf. Ps 23:5: "You have anointed my head with oil"; Ps 133:2: "It is like fragrant oil on the head running down onto the beard." For the self-denial of anointing one's body in oils during the period of mourning, see 2 Sam 14:2: "Pretend you are in mourning. Put on mourning clothes and do not anoint yourself with oil"; Dan 10:2-3: "At that time, I, Daniel, kept three full weeks of mourning . . . I did not anoint myself." The Jews of Elephantine followed a similar custom, as is apparent from their letter (written in Aramaic) to the Persian governor of Yehud, following the destruction of their temple in the fifth century BCE: משח לא משחן ("We do not anoint ourselves in oil"). (See B. Porten and A. Yardeni, *A Textbook of Aramaic Documents from Ancient Egypt,* 1 [Jerusalem, 1986], 72, 75, no. 4.8, line 20.) And, conversely, in times of joy and festivity, anointing was a common practice; see Amos 6:6: "And they anoint themselves with the choicest oils"; Eccl 9:8: "And let your head never lack ointment"; cf. Prov 27:9: "Oil and incense gladden the heart." For the expression שמן ששון ("oil of gladness"), see Ps 45:8.

A robe of splendor/radiance instead of a faint spirit — The prophet describes the nation's joy as a splendid mantle (מַעֲטֵה, a hapax legomenon derived from the root עטי, "to wrap oneself"), which it shall don instead of remaining morose. תהלה (from the root הלל) is a polysemous term meaning both "glory, splendor," and "luminescence"; for the latter, see Hab 3:3; for the verb, see Isa 13:10: "The stars of heaven shall not give off their light (יָהֵלּוּ)"; and this, in turn, creates a fitting contrast to the adjacent "faint (כֵּהָה) of spirit," for which see 42:3: "Or snuff out even a smoldering (כֵהָה) wick." (See Yellin,

Ḥiqrei Miqra, 83; Eitan, "Contribution," 85-86.) For the metaphor of God being "wrapped in a robe of light," see Ps 104:2. This image is also found in Akkadian in praising Ṣarpanitu, Marduk's consort: "Ṣarpanitu, whose clothing is light" (*CAD* N/2:349).

They shall be called "Terebinths of Victory" — Instead of referring to them as "the mourners (אֲבֵלֵי) of Zion," they, the redeemed, shall now be called "Terebinths (אֵילֵי) of Victory" (note the similar sound of the two words). For צדק meaning "victory," see, e.g., Isa 41:10; 45:8; 51:5. For terebinths (אֵילִים), see 57:5; 1:29. For the archaic *qal* passive, קֹרָא (third-person masculine singular), see 48:8, 12; 58:12; 62:2; 65:1. This form was replaced and simplified by 1QIsa[a], as usual, with the plural form, וקראו.

Planted by the Lord for His glory — They shall be called the Lord's shoots, which He has planted and in whom He glories. See too 60:21: they are "a shoot of My own planting, My handiwork in which I glory"; cf. also 44:23; 46:13; 49:3, for God's glory in His nation. Note the possible double entendre of the verb להתפאר, which may also be interpreted as a denominative verb derived from the substantive פֹּארָה/פֻּאָרָה ("branches"), alluding to the "branching out" of the Lord's planting. For פֹּארָה, see Ezek 31:5, 8.

[4] The prophet links the national renewal to the rehabilitation of Israel's ruins. The first two hemistichs: "ancient ruins (חָרְבוֹת עולם) . . . desolations (שֹׁמְמוֹת)," are parallel to the final two: "Ruined cities (ערי חֹרֶב) . . . desolations (שֹׁמְמוֹת)." The prophet's consolation reverses the fulfilled prophecy of Jeremiah: "I will exterminate them and make them a desolation (לְשַׁמָּה) . . . ancient ruins (חרבות עולם)" (Jer 25:9; see also Jer 49:13 regarding the Ammonite disaster). Note also that the expression חרבות עולם appears only in the prophecies of Deutero-Isaiah and Jeremiah.

And they shall build the ancient ruins — Israel shall restore cities that have been desolate since the time of Jerusalem's destruction and the exile of 586 BCE; cf. Isa 58:12: "Men from your midst shall rebuild ancient ruins"; see also 51:3; 52:9. Compare the etymological and semantic Akkadian cognates *ḫarbu, ḫarbūtu* ("ruins," "desolations") (*CAD* Ḫ:97-98, 99), and the verb *ḫarābu* ("to destroy, ruin") (*CAD* Ḫ:87-88).

Raise up the desolations of old — They shall rebuild cities that have remained uninhabited and desolate (שֹׁמְמוֹת) for years untold (for the singular שֹׁמֵמָה, see 54:1; and cf. the alternative form in Jer 51:26, 62: שִׁמְמוֹת עולם תהיה, "You shall be a desolation for all time"). For the desolation of the land and Jerusalem in particular, see Isa 62:4; 64:9; and for the synonymous pair חרבות/שממות, cf. 49:19. The term רִאשֹׁנִים is a temporal reference and denotes antiquity, as in Lev 26:45: בְּרִית רִאשֹׁנִים, "The covenant with the generations long past"; Deut 4:32: לְיָמִים רִאשֹׁנִים, "bygone ages." For the verbal synonyms בני/קומם ("to build/to raise up"), see Isa 44:26; 58:12.

And renew the ruined cities — They shall rehabilitate destroyed cities. The verb חדשׁ *(pi'el),* indicating renewal and rebuilding, is also found in contexts describing the rebuilding of the house of God (2 Chr 24:4, 12) and the altar (2 Chr 15:8), and is identical in meaning to its etymological and semantic Akkadian cognate *edēšu/uddušu,* both of which refer to the refurbishing of temples, fortifications, palaces, cities, and houses (*CAD* E:30-32). For חָרֵב ("ruins"), see Jer 49:13; Ezek 29:10. Note the chiasm this hemistich forms with the preceding one.

The desolations of many ages — They shall renew and restore the desolations of old (1QIsa[a] adds יקוממו at the end of this hemistich, repeating the verb found at the end of the second clause). For the parallel pair דור ודור/עולם, see Isa 51:8; 60:15; and note its appearance in Ugaritic: "Assume your eternal *('lmk)* kingship, your perpetual *(drdrk)* dominion" (*CAT* 1.2.IV:10).

[5] For the prophet's anti-isolationist attitude vis-à-vis foreigners (here they function as the nation's shepherds and vine trimmers, thus serving Israel who shall become a nation of priests), cf. also 56:6-8, which describes their joining the Israelite religious community through the observance of the Sabbath and their participation in the cult; 60:10, where they help construct the walls of Jerusalem; and 66:21, their service in the Temple as priests and Levites.

Strangers shall be ready to pasture your flocks — The verb עמד, followed by a second finite verb, indicates readiness to engage in the action described by the following verb. This grammatical construction is fairly common in Rabbinic Hebrew. See *m. B. Bat.* 1:3; *b. Yoma* 38b. Compare also the expression עמד ל-, which also denotes readiness to perform a set task, e.g., *b. Pesaḥ.* 13b: "Whatever is ready to be (העומד ל-) sprinkled"; *m. B. Qam.* 9:1: "A cow who is ready to (העומדת ל-) give birth . . . a sheep ready to (העומד ל-) be sheared."

Foreigners shall be your plowmen and vine trimmers — For these two occupations, see Joel 1:11; 2 Chr 26:10. The word אִכָּר, an Akkadian loanword, *ikkaru,* which itself is a loanword from Sumerian *engar,* refers to a plowman or farmer (*CAD* I-J:49-54). Hebrew כֹּרֵם is a denominative participle from כֶּרֶם ("vineyard").

[6] The prophet puts forth a revolutionary idea: The status of the nation of Israel as a whole vis-à-vis the foreigners will be similar to the status of the priestly class within Israel, as promised at Sinai: "You shall be a kingdom of priests and a holy nation" (Exod 19:6). (Note that the promise at Sinai is conditional upon obedience [Exod: 19:5: "Now, then, if you will obey Me faithfully and keep My covenant . . .], whereas here it is absolute and irrevocable.) Israel shall be the priests and the nations shall be the donors who shall bring them the prescribed gifts (cf. Num 18:8-19). "Thus Israel shall be to the nations as the priests, the sons of Aaron, are to Israel; and the wealth of the nations shall be in lieu of the sacred donations" (Ibn Ezra). The motif of a nation of priests (cf. Isa 52:11) complements another innovative conception, that of a "nation of prophets"; see Isa 42:6.

While you shall be called "Priests of the Lord" — You, the entire nation of Israel, shall be elevated to a priestly status.

And termed "Ministers of our God" — a synonymous sobriquet; see too Joel 1:9: "Ministers of the Lord (משרתי ה')"; Joel 1:13: "Come, spend the night in sackcloth, O Ministers of my God (משרתי אלהי)." For the verbal parallel יאמר ל-/קרא, see Isa 44:5; 62:4.

You shall enjoy the riches of nations — Cf. 60:5: "The riches of nations (חֵיל גוים) shall come/be brought to you"; 60:11: "To bring in the riches of the nations (חֵיל גוים)." The Akkadian semantic and etymological cognate of אכל, *akālu,* also has the meaning "to enjoy (the use of something)"; *CAD* A/1:252.

And revel in/be provided abundantly with their wealth — For כבוד ("wealth") see 66:12: "For thus said the Lord: 'I will extend to her prosperity like a stream, the wealth (כבוד) of nations like a wadi in flood'"; Gen 31:1: "And from that which was our father's he has built up all this wealth (כבוד)." In Akkadian as well, the cognate substantives *kubtu* and *kubuttû* (*CAD* K:487, 490) also denote presents or precious gifts.

The exact meaning of the hapax legomenon verb תִּתְיַמָּרוּ, however, is unclear. Some suggest that the *yod* comes in place of an expected *aleph* and that this form is a variant of תתאמרו (note 1QIsa[a] תתיאמרו. The *aleph* in the scroll's version, however, may serve as a *mater lectionis;* cf., e.g., יאכה, instead of the Masoretic יכה [Isa 30:31]), which denotes acting proudly, boasting; see Ps 94:4: "All evildoers vaunt (יתאמרו) themselves" (Theodotion, Ibn Ezra, Kimchi, Abravanel). Others suggest that the verb is a derivative of the root מור, "to change, exchange" (see Lev 27:10; Mic 2:4), which then would denote remuneration for the riches that were stolen from the Israelites (Saadyah Gaon, 135; Rashi). Another possibility is that it derives from מרא (cf. מריא, 1 Kgs 1:9; Amos 5:22), and thus should be read by metathesis, תתמָרָיו/תתמָרָאו. The root appears in 1QIsa[a] 11:6, יִמְרוּ ("they shall be fattened"), instead of MT ומריא, and is also found in Rabbinic Hebrew, in Ugar. *mru* (*HdO* 2:571), and in Akk. *marû* (*CAD* M/1:307-8), all referring, however, to the fattening of animals. According to this explanation, the verb would be synonymous with and parallel to תאכלו in the preceding hemistich: "You shall be fattened by the riches of other nations" (thus Luzzatto, and cf. the Targum, תִּתְפַּנְקוּן). It is of interest to note that in Akkadian the *št* form of *marû, šutamrû* means "to provide abundantly" (*CAD* M/1:308), which would fit well into the context here.

[7] The "double trouble" motif occurs here once again; see 40:2: "For she has received at the hand of the Lord double for all her sins," which confirms the fulfillment of the Jeremiah's prophecy (16:18): "I will pay them in full — nay,

doubly (מִשְׁנֶה) for their iniquity and their sins" (see the discussion on 40:2). Since Israel's shame was double, their consolation and reward will now also be doubled. Another theme that exists both in Jeremiah and here is the connection to the land. In Jeremiah the reason for the punishment is the defilement of the land, and here their share in the land will be doubled. According to the MT, the verse begins with an address in the second-person masculine plural and thus is an extension of vv. 5-6, and then switches to the third-person masculine plural until the end of the unit in v. 9. The address in 1QIsa[a], however, does not make this switch and continues in the second-person masculine.

Instead of your shame that was double — For משנה ("double"), see Gen 43:12: "And take with you double (מִשְׁנֶה) the money"; Jer 17:18: "And shatter them with double (וּמִשְׁנֶה) destruction." For תחת indicating replacement or substitution, see v. 3; 60:15, 17.

And instead of the disgrace that they inherited as their portion/they will exult in their portion — a difficult clause, usually explained in two opposite ways, both of which assume that the word תחת in the preceding clause applies here as well: Disgrace shall be the portion of the nations because they reveled (יָרֹנּוּ) in Your disgrace. Or, because of the disgrace they suffered during their exile, they (Israel) shall revel (יָרֹנּוּ) in the portion I shall grant them (Kimchi, Eliezer of Beaugency). Others have suggested emending ירנו to יָרְשׁוּ ("they have inherited"), i.e., because of the disgrace they inherited as their portion. For the synonymous pair כלמה/בֹּשֶׁת, see Jer 3:25: "Let us lie down in our shame (בבשתנו). Let our disgrace (כלמתנו) cover us"; Ps 35:26: "Be clad in shame (בֹּשֶׁת) and disgrace (וכלמה)." 1QIsa[a], חלקכמה ("your portion"), and תירשו (in the following clause), both in the second-person masculine, correspond with the preceding בשתכם ("your shame").

Assuredly, they shall have a double share in their land — לכן is an emphatic conjunction implying assurance and promise. For receiving a double share in a different context, see Job 42:10: "So the Lord restored Job's fortunes . . . and doubled (למשנה) all his possessions."

Joy shall be theirs evermore — Furthermore they shall enjoy everlasting happiness (שמחת עולם); see Isa 51:11; 35:10.

[8] The Lord, who loves justice and abhors unethical behavior, shall now make an everlasting covenant with His nation. Both here and in v. 9 God addresses the nation in the first-person.

For I the Lord love justice — For the expression אֹהֵב משפט, see also Ps 37:28; cf. 33:5; 99:4; and cf. also its Akkadian semantic cognate *mīšara irammu*, e.g., "(The goddess) who loves justice" (*CAD* M/2:117).

I hate robbery and/with injustice — yet another clause that is difficult to fathom. Some interpret it to mean that the Lord hates a burnt offering (עוֹלָה) donated from property that has been stolen (MT גָּזֵל; 1QIsa[a] גזול). Others suggest vocalizing וְעַוְלָה ("and injustice"), instead of MT בְּעוֹלָה, "with a burnt offering" (cf. Targum [וְאָנְסָא], LXX, and Peshitta). It is also possible that עוֹלָה is a variant form of עַוְלָה, as in Job 5:16: "And the mouth of wrongdoing (עֹלָתָה) is stopped;" cf. also Ps 58:3; 64:7: עוֹלֹת. According to this explanation, God hates robbery and wrongdoing. Yet other commentators submit that בעולה is an alternative form of פעולה, "payment" (see the adjacent clause), i.e., the Lord hates the robbery of wages. Saadyah Gaon (136) suggests that the *beth* prefix appended to עולה denotes "with," i.e., "I hate robbery with wickedness." For this preposition denoting "with," see Ibn Ganaḥ, *Sefer ha-Riqmah,* 63, lines 13-16.

I will pay them their wages faithfully — For פְּעֻלָּה ("remuneration"), see Isa 40:10 (= 62:11); 49:4; 62:11; 65:7; Ezek 29:20. For the verb נתן meaning "to pay," see Gen 23:13: "Let me pay (נתתי) the price of the land"; Ps 49:8: "Nor pay (ותן) his ransom to God"; so too Akk. *nadānu* (*CAD* N/2:45-46). 1QIsa[a] continues in the second-person plural.

And make an everlasting covenant with them — I shall make an immutable and eternal covenant with My nation; see Isa 55:3: "And I will make with you an everlasting covenant (ברית עולם)." For other references to covenants in Deutero-Isaiah, see 54:10; 59:21. For an absolute and eternal covenant promised by God following the devastation and exile, independent of Israel's conduct or misconduct, see Jer 32:40; 50:5; Ezek 16:60; 37:26.

[9] Note the literary frame partially beginning and ending with the noun זרע.

Their offspring shall be known among the nations — Following God's beneficence and munificence, the renown of Israel's offspring shall spread throughout the world. Note 1QIsa[a]'s continuation of the second-person plural in this and the next hemistich.

Their descendants in the midst of the peoples — parallel to the above. For the synonymous parallelism צֶאֱצאים/זרע ("offspring/descendants"), see 44:3; 48:19; 65:23.

All who see them shall acknowledge that they are a stock the Lord has blessed — All who take stock of Israel shall quickly identify them as the group singled out by God for blessing, as in 65:23: "For they are the offspring blessed by the Lord." The *mem* appended to יכירום may be enclitic, which is well documented both in Akkadian and in Ugaritic and is also found in Biblical Hebrew as a fossilized suffix attached to both substantives and verbs. If so, contrary to the Masoretic vocalization, the *mem* here does not indicate a pronominal suffix.

[10-11] The joy experienced in divine salvation is described in terms derived from a bridal ceremony. This unit is connected to the preceding one by צדקה, יְעָטָנִי, פאר (v. 10), which form a chiasm with פאר, מַעֲטֵה, צדק (v. 3). Compare too זֵרוּעֶיהָ and תהלה (v. 11) with תְהִלָּה (v. 3) and זרעם and זרע (v. 9).

Note also the agricultural imagery in both units: v. 3: "'Terebinths of Victory,' planted by the Lord for His glory"; and v. 11: "For as the earth sprouts forth its growth and as a garden makes its seeds shoot up"; as well as the references to various wearing apparel (vv. 3, 10).

For the symbolic connection between "salvation/victory" and the donning of a crown/headdress, see 59:17; 62:1, 3. Compare also Ps 132:16-18: "I will clothe her priests in victory . . . while on him his crown shall sparkle." The final two verses of the chapter form a literary frame with v. 3: "To give them a turban (פאר) instead of ashes, oil of gladness (שׂשׂון) instead of mourning, a robe of splendor (מַעֲטֵה תהִלה) instead of a faint spirit. They shall be called 'terebinths of victory' (צדק), planted by the Lord for His glory (להתפאר)" — vv. 10, 11: "I greatly rejoice (שׂוֹשׂ אשׂישׂ) in the Lord . . . For He has clothed me with garments of triumph, wrapped me (יְעָטָנִי) in a robe of victory (צדק), like a bridegroom adorned with a turban (פאר). . . . So the Lord God will make victory (צדקה) and glory (תהִלה) shoot up in the presence of all the nations."

[10] *I greatly rejoice in the Lord* — Jerusalem (cf. Targum, Kimchi, and Luzzatto) or the entire nation (Ibn Ezra, Kimchi, second commentary) announces its exultation vis-à-vis God. The infinitive absolute (שׂוֹשׂ) followed by the finite form of the same verb (אשׂישׂ) serves to emphasize abundant happiness. For the expression -שׂישׂ ב ("to rejoice in"), see 65:19.

Let my whole being exult in my God — Let my entire being be immersed in the delight of my God; cf. Ps 35:9: "Then shall I exult in the Lord (תגיל בה׳), rejoice (אשׂישׂ) in His deliverance." For the synonymous pair שׂישׂ/גיל, see also 65:18; 66:10. The imperfect תָּגֵל is an apocapated second-person feminine singular from the root גיל; cf. the morphologically equivalent תָּשֶׂם, from the root שׂים (1 Sam 9:20).

For He has clothed me with garments of triumph — My joy is overwhelming because the Lord has garbed me in the clothes of the victorious, as a person who has triumphed over his enemies. For similar metaphoric language, see Ps 132:16: "I shall clothe its priests in triumph"; Ps 132:9: "Your priests are clothed in triumph." Compare also Isa 52:1: "Awake, awake, O Zion! Clothe yourself in splendor! Put on your robes of majesty, Jerusalem, holy city!" For the parallel synonyms צדק/ישע ("triumph/victory") in the following clause, see 51:5.

Wrapped me in a robe of victory — parallel to the previous colon: The Lord has dressed me in a coat resplendent in salvation and triumph; cf. 59:17. The Masoretic vocalization יְעָטָנִי (third-person masculine) reflects the *qal* stem of the hapax legomenon root יעט, similar morphologically to יְעָצָנִי, from יעץ (Ps 16:7). However, it is preferable to explain יְעָטָנִי as a conflated form of the *qal* perfect עָטָנִי and the *hiph'il* imperfect יַעֲטֵנִי, from the root עטי ("to wrap"), which also appears in Arab. *ġṭw;* see v. 3: מַעֲטֵה. For the verbal pair עטה/לבש ("to clothe/to wrap"), see Ps 109:29: "My accusers shall be clothed

(ילבשו) in shame, wrapped (וְיַעֲטוּ) in their disgrace as in a robe"; and for the substantive pair מעיל/בגדי ("garments/robe"), see Isa 59:17; Ezek 26:16.

Like a bridegroom adorned with a priestly turban — For פְּאֵר ("turban"; an Egyptian loanword, see v. 3), worn by a priest, see Ezek 44:18: "They shall have linen turbans (פַּאֲרֵי) on their heads"; Exod 39:28. For the custom of crowning the bridegroom on his wedding day, see Cant 3:11: "O maidens of Zion, go forth and gaze upon King Solomon wearing the crown with which his mother crowned him on his wedding day, on his day of bliss." Similar practices were also prevalent during the Second Temple period, as one finds in *m. Soṭah* 9:14: "In the time of the war of [the Roman emperor] Vespasian [which predates the destruction of the Second Temple by three years], they [the sages] decreed against the crowning of grooms," i.e., they decreed that bridegrooms were forbidden to don royal headdresses on their wedding day. For יְכַהֵן, a denominative verb from the substantive כֹּהֵן, see, e.g., Exod 29:1. For the variant in 1QIsa[a], כחתן ככוהן פאר, see Kutscher, *Language and Linguistic Background*, 322.

Like a bride bedecked with her jewelry — For the denominative verb תַּעְדֶּה, derived from the substantive עֲדִי, a piece of jewelry, see Jer 4:30: "By decking yourself in jewels (תעדי עדי) of gold"; Hos 2:15: "When she decked herself (וַתַּעַד) with earrings and jewels"; Ezek 23:40. For Zion as a bride metaphorically bedecked in her progeny, see Isa 49:18. For כלי ("ornaments, jewelry"), see Gen 24:53; Exod 3:22; 11:2; Ezek 16:39: "They shall strip you of your clothing and take away your dazzling jewels (כלי)." Some suggest reading here כְּלִילָהּ ("her crown"), which would then parallel פאר in the previous hemistich (Ehrlich, *Randglossen*, 4:220; Tur-Sinai, *Peshuto shel Miqra*, III/1:144). For כליל in Rabbinic Hebrew (a loanword from Akk. *kilīlu/kulūlu*, a "headband/headdress," worn by kings, queens, and gods [*CAD* K:358, 522-28]), see *b. Git.* 7a: "A bridal crown (כלילא) for his daughter." In the same Mishnah passage quoted above (*Soṭah* 9:14) regarding the rabbinical injunction against bridegrooms wearing crowns, another decree is found regarding brides: "During the war of Titus [the war in which the Second Temple was destroyed], they [the rabbis] decreed against the bridal diadem." (For such a crown called "Jerusalem of Gold," see Paul, *Divrei Shalom*, 333-42.) Note the accumulation of the letter *kaf* in the final hemistichs of this verse: כחתן יכהן פאר וככלה תעדה כליה, as well as the wordplay כַּכַּלָּה . . . כֵּלֶיהָ (or perhaps כַּכַּלָּה . . . כְּלִילָהּ). For the complementary pair כלה/חתן ("bridegroom/bride"), see Isa 62:5; Jer 7:34; 16:9; 25:10; 33:11; Joel 2:16.

[11] The prophet describes Jerusalem's salvation in agricultural terms, as springing forth from the earth. Note the accumulation of the letter *ṣade*: כארץ תוציא צמחה... זרועיה תצמיח... יצמיח צדקה. For the syntactical construction כי . . . כן ("for . . . so"), see Isa 55:10-11; 66:22. The root צמח appears three times in this verse.

For as the earth sprouts forth its growth — צמח is a general reference to sprouting and growth; see Gen 19:25. For the verb יצא, "to bring forth, to sprout," see Gen 1:12. Note the similar meaning of its semantic and etymological cognate in Akkadian: *uṣû* ("to go forth") and *šūṣû* ("to bring forth"), which also refer to sprouting (*CAD* A/2:365ff., 377ff.).

And as a garden makes its seeds shoot up — For גַּנָּה ("garden"), see Isa 1:30; and for זֵרוּעַ ("seed"), see Lev 11:37. For the verbal pair הוציא/הצמיח, see Ps 104:14: "You make the grass grow (מצמיח) for the cattle . . . that he [man] may get food out (להוציא) of the earth." The first two hemistichs form a partial chiasm.

So the Lord God will make victory and glory shoot up in the presence of all the nations — The Lord shall expedite the nation's/thc city's triumph and their victory (צדקה) and glory (תהִלה; note the possible double entendre, as in v. 3: "glory" and "resplendence"). For the image of victory shooting forth, see the comments to 45:8. For the verbal pair הלל/צדק, see 45:25; Ps 35:28; 48:11; 119:164. For Jerusalem's renown, see Isa 62:7: "Until He establishes Jerusalem and makes her renowned on earth." And for the nation's fame and fortune, see Deut 26:19: "And that He will set you, in fame and renown and glory, high above all the nations that He has made, and you shall be, as He promised, a holy people to the Lord your God."

Chapter 62

The chapter is composed of two distinct pericopes: vv. 1-9 and 10-12, and the subject of both is the nation's salvation. The first unit speaks of the nation's revival and reoccupation of the land, and the second is a call to the nation to return from their exile. Another theme that connects both units is renaming: in both, the people, the land, and Jerusalem are given new names that reflect their newly born state (see vv. 2, 4, 12).

This chapter and the previous one have many terms and images in common: 62:11 and 61:3: **ציון**; 62:1: **צדקהּ וישועתהּ** (also v. 2: **צדקך**, v. 11: **יִשְׁעֵךְ**) — 61:10: **ישע . . . צדק** (also v. 3: **הצדק**, v. 11: **צדקה**); 62:1: **יֵצֵא** — 61:11: **להוציא**; 62:2: **גוים** — 61:9: **בגוים**; 62:2: **וקֹרָא לך**, vv. 4, 12: **ולך יִקָּרֵא** — 61:3: **וקֹרָא להם**; 62:3: **תפארת** — 61:3, 10: **פאר**, v. 3: **להתפאר**; 62:4: **יֵאָמֵר לך . . . כי לך יִקָּרֵא** — 61:6: **תִּקָּרֵאו . . . יֵאָמֵר לכם**; 62:4: **שממה** — 61:4: **שֹׁמְמוֹת . . . שֹׁמְמוֹת**; 62:5: **ומשׂוֹשׂ חתן על כַּלָּה ישׂישׂ עליך אלהיך** — 61:10: **שׂוֹשׂ אשׂישׂ בה׳ . . . כחתן . . . וְכַכַּלָּה**; 62:7: **תהִלה** (v. 9: **והללו את ה׳**) — 61:3: **תהִלה**; 62:11: **ופעֻלתו** — 61:8: **פעֻלתם**.

The following terms are repeated in this chapter: **ציון** (vv. 1, 11), **למען** (v. 1, twice), **ישע** (vv. 1, 11), **קרא ל-** (vv. 2, 4, 12), **עזב** (vv. 4, 12).

[1] The Lord shall show no restraint until Zion's salvation shall emerge resplendent.

For the sake of Zion I will not remain silent — The Lord solemnly vows never to rest in Zion's cause. The verb **חשי** does not denote silence per se, but rather refraining from action, inactivity, as in 65:6: "I will not stand idly by (**אֶחֱשֶׁה**) but will repay, repay into their bosom" (see Luzzatto); cf. v. 6; 42:14; 57:11. The variant in 1QIsa[a], **לא אחריש**, has the same meaning as this verb and is parallel to it in 42:14. It may also have been influenced by Ps 83:2, where it parallels **שקט**, as here, in the next colon.

And for the sake of Jerusalem I will not be still — The verb **שקט** can also denote lack of activity, in addition to silence; cf. Ruth 3:18: "For the man will not remain idle (ישקט), but will settle the matter today." For the frequent parallel "Zion/Jerusalem," see Isa 40:9; 41:27; 52:1; 64:9.

Till her victory shines forth resplendent — The Lord shall not rest until Jerusalem emerges triumphant. For נֹגַהּ ("brightness, radiance"), see 60:3: "And nations shall walk by your light, kings, by your shining radiance (לְנֹגַהּ)." The noun *ngh* is also present in Ugaritic (*HdO* 2:622) and in the first combination of the Balaam inscription from Deir ʿAlla in the Sukkot Valley, east of the Jordan, from the mid-eighth century BCE: "Let there be darkness there and forever no light (נגה)" (Aḥituv, *Ha-Ketav veha-Miḵtav*, 386, lines 6-7). For the verb יצא indicating the emergence of light, see Ps 37:6: "He will cause your vindication to shine forth (והוציא) like the light." For the nuance of עד ("till"), see Isa 42:4.

And her triumph burns like a flaming torch — Until her "victory and vindication shall be seen by far-away nations, like a flaming torch that is seen in the distance" (Kimchi). The feminine verb תבער in 1QIsa[a] relates to the feminine noun ישועתה, whereas the masculine verb in the MT refers to the masculine noun לפיד. For another example of this verb with לפיד, see Judg 15:5: "He set the torches aflight (וַיַּבְעֶר)." For the synonyms צדק(ה)/ישועה, see Isa 51:5, 6, 8; 59:17; 63:1. For the pair of verbs יצא/בער, see Jer 4:4; 21:12. This hemistich and the preceding one form a chiasm.

[2] When Jerusalem's triumph shall shine forth, all the world shall see her splendor, and she shall be called by a new name symbolizing her rebirth and elevated state. For the new names of the resplendent capital, see vv. 4, 12; 60:14: "And they shall call you 'City of the Lord, Zion of the Holy One of Israel'"; 1:26: "After that you shall be called 'City of Righteousness, Faithful City'"; Jer 3:17: "At that time they shall call Jerusalem 'Throne of the Lord'"; Jer 33:16: "And this is what she shall be called: 'The Lord is our Vindicator'"; Ezek 48:35: "And the name of the city from that day on shall be, 'The Lord Is There.'" Cities are given new names in commemoration of noteworthy occasions in their history, such as Luz's change of name following Jacob's sojourn in the city and his experience of a divine revelation, which was the catalyst for the new name, Bethel (Gen 28:19; 35:6-7); cf. also Jer 7:32: "And it shall no longer be called 'Topheth' or 'the Valley of Ben-Hinnom,' but 'the Valley of Slaughter.'" Another occasion for a name change is the rebuilding of a city or its conquest (Num 32:38, 41, 42). (Such a custom is also known from Mesopotamian and Egyptian literature.) This is very similar to the renaming of individuals in light of a change in their life situation, e.g., Abram-Abraham; Sarai-Sarah (Gen 17:5, 15); Joseph–Zaphenath-paneah (Gen 41:45); Hadassah-Esther (Esth 2:7): Daniel-Belteshazzar, Hananyah-Shadrach, Mishael-Meshach, Azariah-Abednego (Dan 1:7); or upon their ascension to the throne: Mattaniah-Zedekiah (2 Kgs 24:17). (See A. Demsky, "Double Names in the Babylonian Exile and the Identity of Sheshbazzar," in idem, ed., *These Are the Names*, vol. 2: *Studies in Jewish Onomastics* [Ramat Gan, 1999], 22-40.)

Nations shall see your victory — For the importance of the nations as witnesses of the divine salvation, see Isa 40:5.

And all the kings your glory — Every monarch shall see your luminescence (כבוד), as in 40:5: "The glory of the Lord shall appear, and all flesh, as one, shall behold"; 59:19: "From the west they shall see the name of the Lord, and from the east His glory"; 60:1: "Arise! Shine! For your light has dawned. The glory of the Lord has shone upon you"; Ps 97:6: "The heavens proclaim His righteousness and all peoples see His glory." For the parallel pair מלכים/גוים, see Isa 52:15; 60:3, 16; and for כבוד/צדק(ה), see 58:8; Ps 97:6; Prov 8:18; 21:21.

And you shall be called by a new name that the Lord Himself shall bestow — You shall be given a "new name" (שֵׁם חדש; the expression appears only here) in light of your new and favored status, and this name shall be bestowed on you by the Lord Himself (for the actual names see v. 4). For the expression נקב (ב)שֵׁם ("to bestow a name"), see Num 1:17; Ezra 8:20; cf. also Lev 24:11, 16 (twice). In Ugaritic the verb *nqb* also means "to name" (*HdO* 2:639). For the expression פי ה׳ (lit. "the mouth of the Lord"), see Isa 40:5. In 1QIsa[a] וקראו replaces the rare *qal* passive וְקֹרָא in the MT (see also 48:8; 58:12; 61:3; 65:1).

[3] In the ancient Near East, gods are often described and portrayed as wearing crowns. The motif of a city as a godly diadem appears in Mesopotamian literature as well, e.g., in praise of Marduk it is written: "Babylon is your seat, Borsippa, your crown" (*CAD* A/1:154). Another image is perhaps also alluded to here: The Lord shall place the crown on Jerusalem — a female figure in this passage — and will make her His queen. This is connected, on the one hand, to the new name conferred on Jerusalem as she is elevated to a royal status, and, on the other, may allude to the wedding celebration in v. 5, since (according to *b. Soṭah* 49b) brides were crowned at their weddings with a diadem known as "Jerusalem of Gold" (see the following hemistich). (For the crowning of grooms, see 61:10; Cant 3:11.) The imagery in this verse complements Isa 28:5: "On that day the Lord of Hosts shall become a crown of beauty and a diadem of glory for the remnant of His people."

You shall be a glorious crown in the hand of the Lord — And you, Jerusalem, shall be the Lord's jeweled coronet: "In reverence to God, he did not say: 'On the Lord's head,' rather he said, 'in the hand of' and 'in the palm of,' since because of His affection for you, you shall always be in His hands . . . and the reason for the metaphor of a crown is that the Lord shall find glory in you, as in Prov 12:4: 'A capable wife is the crown of her husband'" (Luzzatto). For Jerusalem's coronation and similar imagery, see Ezek 16:12: "And I [God] put a splendid crown on your head." For the rhyming expression עֲטֶרֶת תִּפְאֶרֶת ("a glorious crown"), see also Ezek 16:12; 23:42; Jer 13:18; Prov 4:9; 16:31; cf. Prov 17:6. The verb לעטר ("to crown") and the substantive עטרת ("a crown") appear in a Phoenician inscription from the first century BCE(?): לעטר . . . עטרת חרץ ("to crown . . . a golden crown") (*KAI* 60:1, 3); and in two Neo-Punic inscriptions: **עטרת** (*KAI* 145:3; 165:6). In Mesopotamia as well, the crowns of gods and kings are described in the same superlative terms (*CAD* A/1:154-55; Š/1:284). Compare also Isa 28.1, 3. **עֲטֶרֶת גֵּאוּת** ("proud crown"). For Jerusalem referred to as a city crown of gold, see Paul, *Divrei Shalom*, 332-42.

And a royal diadem in the palm of your God — parallel to the above clause; see Zech 3:5: "Let a pure diadem (**צניף**) be placed on his head"; and cf. Esth 1:11; 2:17; 6:8: **כֶּתֶר מלכות** ("a royal crown"). For the synonymous pair **כף/יד**, see Ps 18:1: "After the Lord had saved him from the hands (**מכף**) of all his enemies and from the clutches (**מיד**) of Saul"; Prov 31:20: "She stretches out her hand (**כפה**) to the poor and extends her hand (**ידה**) to the needy." For the parallel pair **מִצנפת/עטרה**, see Ezek 21:31: "Thus said the Lord God: 'Remove the turban (**המצנפת**) and lift off the crown (**העטרה**)!'" The Ketib of MT **וצנוף** (corroborated by 1QIsa[a]) creates an alliteration with **מלוכה**.

[4] Jerusalem is now given new names that the Lord bestows on her. A new name implies new stature; cf. also v. 12. For the twice repeated syntactical construction **לא . . . עוד** ("nevermore"), expressing the new state of affairs in which the people are resettled in their land, see 51:22; 52:1; 54:4; 60:18-20; 65:19-20.

Nevermore shall you be called "Forsaken" — You shall never again be referred to as a city that is not cared for, abandoned by its inhabitants; cf. v. 12: "A city not forsaken (**נעזבה**)"; 49:14: "The Lord has forsaken me (**עזבני**)"; 54:6: "As a wife forsaken (**עזובה**) and forlorn"; 54:7: "In a brief outburst of anger I forsook you (**עזבתיך**)"; 60:15: "Whereas you have been forsaken (**ועזובה**), rejected." The verb **עזב** indicates divine abandonment of the city or His "divorce" from it, as does its Akkadian cognate *ezēbu,* which denotes abandonment, and in legal contexts, divorce (*CAD* E:416-17, 422). For the literary construction **לא יֵאָמֵר עוד . . . כי (אם) . . . כי** in a similar context of a name change, and the reason behind it, see Gen 32:29: "He said, 'Your name shall no longer be Jacob, but Israel, for you have striven with beings divine and human and have prevailed.'" (Two women of the Bible bore the personal name **עזובה** [Azubah] — the wife of Caleb son of Hezron [1 Chr 2:18, 19] and Jehoshaphat's mother [2 Chr 20:31].)

Nor shall your land be called "Desolate" — Read **שֹׁמֵמָה** (1QIsa[a] **שוממה**; cf. also Vulgate and Peshitta), the antonym of **בעולה** ("espoused") at the end of the verse, instead of MT **שְׁמָמָה** ("desolation"), as in Isa 54:1: "For the children of the desolate wife (**שוֹמֵמה**) shall outnumber those of the espoused." As long as the land was not "espoused," i.e., in the years of the exile, she remained desolate; cf. 49:8: "desolate (**שֹׁמֵמוֹת**) possessions"; 49:19: "your desolate places" (**וְשֹׁמְמֹתַיִךְ**); 61:4: "The desolations (**שֹׁמְמוֹת**) of old . . . the ruined cities, the desolations (**שֹׁמְמוֹת**) of many ages." For the pair **שממה/עזובה** ("forsaken/desolate"), see

Zeph 2:4: "Indeed, Gaza shall be deserted (עזובה) and Ashkelon desolate (לִשְׁמָמָה)."

But you shall be called "I Delight in Her" (Hephzibah) — For the expression חפץ ב- ("to be desirous of, to be delighted in"), see Gen 34:19: "For he [Shechem] was desirous of (חפץ ב-) Jacob's daughter"; Deut 21:14: "And if you no longer desire her (חפצת בה)"; 1 Kgs 10:9: "Praised be the Lord your God, who delighted in you (חפץ בך)"; Esth 2:14: "She would not go again to the king unless the king desired her (חפץ בה)." Compare also the new name given to Jerusalem in v. 12, דרושה ("Sought Out"). For חפץ and דרש as a synonymous pair, see 58:2. (Hephzibah was also the personal name of King Manasseh's mother, 2 Kgs 21:1.)

And your land "Espoused" (Beulah) — "In the allegorical sense, since an inhabited land is like a woman with a spouse; and when she is 'desolate,' it as is if she has no husband" (Kimchi). See Gen 20:3: "She is a married woman (בעל בְּעֻלַת)"; Deut 22:22: "If a man is found lying with another man's wife (בעל בְּעֻלַת)." For the root בעל, see also vv. 4-5, where it appears four times; 54:1, 5; 62:5.

For the Lord takes delight in you — The etiology of the new name: חֶפְצִי־בָהּ.

And your land shall be espoused — an explanation for the new name, בעולה: "She shall be called 'Espoused' because she shall be inhabited" (Targum, Kimchi). For another example of the *niph'al* stem of this verb, see Prov 30:23: "An unloved woman when she is espoused (תִּבָּעֵל)."

[5] The new and endearing relationship connection between the Lord and Jerusalem is compared to the joyful union of bride and bridegroom. Note the repetition of the letter *beth* in the next five words after the initial כי.

As a youth espouses a young woman — just as a young man takes a young woman as his wife and becomes her husband, as in Deut 24:1: "When a man takes a wife and possesses her (וּבְעָלָהּ)." In biblical poesy בתולה is the feminine counterpart of בחור ("a male youth"); see, e.g., Ps 148:12: "Young men (בחורים) and young women (בתולות) alike;" Lam 1:18: "My young women (בתולתי) and my young men (בחורי) have gone into captivity." Compare likewise Akk. *batultu*, "adolescent, nubile girl" (*CAD* B:173-74); Ugar. *btlt* (the sobriquet of the goddess Anat); and an Aramaic incantation text regarding a "בתולתא, who, though having birth pangs, cannot deliver" (see J. A. Montgomery, *Aramaic Incantation Texts from Nippur* [Philadelphia, 1913], p. 178, 13:9). For כי as a conjunction preceding a comparison, see Isa 44:3; 54:9. 1QIsa[a] has the doublet כיא כבעול instead of MT כי יבעל, with the same meaning.

So shall your sons/builders espouse you — Your sons shall be the possessors of the land (for Jerusalem and her children, see 49:17-21; 51:18, 20; 54:1, 13; 60:4, 9; 66:7, 8). In light of the problem regarding the imagery and the final words of the verse: "Your God shall rejoice over you," some have suggested to read here בֹּנַיִךְ ("your builders shall espouse you"), referring to God Himself, who is the one who "rebuilds (בונה) Jerusalem" (Ps 147:2).

And as a bridegroom rejoices over his bride, so shall your God rejoice over you — The כי conjunction does double-duty and is carried over from the preceding clause. Salvation is envisaged as a joyful wedding ceremony. For the substantive מָשׂוֹשׂ ("rejoicing"), along with the verb שׂישׂ, see Isa 65:18; 66:10; and for the expression שׂישׂ על ("to rejoice over"), see Zeph 3:17. For the verb שׂמח (a synonym of שׂישׂ) defining the intimate relationship between spouses and newlyweds, see Deut 24:5: "To give happiness (וְשִׂמַּח) to the woman he has married"; Prov 5:18: "Find joy (וּשְׂמַח) in the wife of your youth." Compare also the advice of Siduri, the female innkeeper, to Gilgamesh: "Let your spouse rejoice in your bosom" (Gilgamesh Epic X:iii:13; *ANET*, 90).

[6-9] The Lord sets watchmen on the walls of Jerusalem to safeguard the city from potential enemies. He then swears that He shall never again allow foreigners to loot the land and steal the nation's harvests. From here on, Israel shall enjoy the fruits of their labor and shall praise the Lord. The weeping walls of Lam 2:18 ("Their heart cried out to the Lord. O wall of fair Zion, shed tears like a torrent day and night! Give yourself no respite, your eyes no rest!") shall shed tears no longer, for the Lord and His appointed guardians shall preserve Jerusalem from all harm.

[6] *On your walls, O Jerusalem, I have posted watchmen* — For sentinels posted atop the walls of a city, see Jer 51:12: "Raise a standard against the walls of Babylon! . . . Station watchmen!"; Cant 5:7: "The guards of the walls stripped me of my mantle"; cf. also Ps 127:1: "Unless the Lord watches over the city, the watchman keeps vigil in vain." For similar expressions in Akkadian, see *CAD* D:193; M/1:334. For the expression הפקיד על ("to set upon"), see Gen 41:34; 2 Kgs 25:22. Compare also its Akkadian semantic and etymological cognate, *ana . . . paqādu* (*CAD* P:120-22).

Who shall never remain silent by day or by night — These watchmen shall stand their vigil without fail, never resting, and thus they are reminiscent of the Lord Himself, who avows (v. 1): "For the sake of Zion I will not be silent (אֶחֱשֶׁה)"; cf. also Isa 21:8: "And a [1QIsa[a]: watchman] called out: 'On my Lord's lookout I stand all day long, and at my post I watch every night.'" For similar expressions of constancy, cf. 60:11; Jer 52:33; Ps 72:15; Prov 15:15.

You, who invoke the Lord — you, the guardians, who invoke the Lord's name while you stand your vigil. The *heh* prefix appended to the plural participle המזכירים introduces a vocative address, as in Isa 42:18: "Listen, you who are deaf (הַחֵרְשִׁים)"; Cant 8:13: "O you who linger (היושבת) in the garden." For the root זכר in liturgical contexts, see Isa 12:4; 1 Chr 16:4.

Take no rest! — Be constantly on guard. The word דֳּמִי is a substantive from the root דמי; for its morphology, cf. חֳלִי, from the root חלי. Cf. Ps 83:2: "O

God, do not be silent (דֳּמִי)! Do not hold aloof (תֶּחֱרַשׁ)! Do not be quiet (תִּשְׁקֹט), O God!"

[7] *And give no rest to Him!* — Do not let Him cease from acting on your behalf. For another example of prodding the Lord to action, see Num 10:9-10: "When you are at war in your land . . . you shall sound short blasts on the trumpets, that you may be remembered before the Lord your God and be delivered from your enemies. And on your joyous occasions . . . you shall sound the trumpets. They shall be a reminder of you before your God: I, the Lord, am your God." The LXX, Peshitta, and 1QIsa[b] read לכם, "Give yourselves no rest," in lieu of MT לו (referring to God), thus toning down the boldness of the demand.

Until He establishes Jerusalem and makes her renowned on earth — The "establishment (כון/כונן) of a city" consists of building it on strong and permanent foundations; cf. Ps 107:36: "And build a city (וַיְכוֹנְנוּ) to settle in." For the verb כון and its Ugaritic and Akkadian cognates, see Isa 45:18. For the expression לשים תהִלה בארץ ("to make renown on earth"), see Zeph 3:19: "And I will make for them renown (וְשַׂמְתִּים לתהִלה) and fame." Note the doublet in 1QIsa[a]: עד יכין ועד יכונן.

[**8**] The Lord's response to Deutero-Isaiah's bold call. He swears to repudiate the curses of the covenant that have come to pass, e.g., Deut 28:33: "A people you do not know shall eat up the produce of your soil and all your gains"; Deut 28:50-51: "A ruthless nation. . . . It shall devour the offspring of your cattle and the produce of your soil, until you have been wiped out, leaving you nothing of new grain, wine, or oil." Henceforth the nation alone shall enjoy the fruits of their labor; see also Isa 65:21-22.

The Lord has sworn by His right hand, by His mighty arm — The Lord swears by His "hand" and "arm" with which He performs His mighty deeds; see Ps 89:11: "With Your powerful arm You scattered Your enemies"; cf. Ps 89:14: "Yours is an arm endowed with might. Your hand is strong; Your right hand, exalted." For another divine oath, see Isa 45:23; and for the raising of the hand in oath, see Deut 32:40: "Lo, I raise My hand to heaven"; cf. also Dan 12:7: "Then I heard the man dressed in linen, who was above the water of the river, swear by the Ever-Living One as he lifted his right hand and his left hand to heaven." For the parallel pair זרוע/ימין ("right hand/arm"), see Ps 44:4: "But Your right hand, Your arm, and Your goodwill, for You favored them"; as well as 89:14, quoted above; and cf. 98:1. The Lord's arm appears frequently in Deutero-Isaiah's prophecy; see Isa 51:5, 9; 52:10; 53:1; 63:5, 12.

"Nevermore will I give your grain to your enemies for food" — The Lord solemnly swears that He shall never again allow the nation's enemies to derive any benefit from Israel's produce.

"Nor shall foreigners drink the new wine for which you have labored" — For

"grain and new wine" (דגן ותירוש), see Gen 27:28: "May God give you of the dew of heaven and the fat of the earth, abundance of grain and new wine"; Isa 36:17: "A land of grain and new wine." The term תִּירוֹשׁ refers to new wine that has yet to complete the fermentation process. The word appears also in Ugaritic, *trṯ* and *mrṯ* (*HdO* 2:579, 880). Compare the description of the god El's intoxicating imbibing: "El drinks wine until he is sated, new wine *(trṯ)* until he is inebriated" (*CAT* 1.114:15-16). So too: "On this day he poured *ṯmk*-wine, new wine *(mrṯ)*, the wine of princes" (*CAT* 1.22.I:17-18). Note also the Phoenician cognate in the Azitawada inscription from Karatepe, from the end of the fifth century BCE: "May this city be a possessor of grain (שׂבע) and new wine (ותרשׁ)" (*KAI* 26A III:7). For the same expression, שׂבע ותרשׁ, see line 9 of this inscription, as well as Prov 3:10: "And your barns will be filled with grain (שָׂבָע), your vats will burst with new wine (ותירוש)."

[9] *"But those who harvest it shall eat it"* — For only (כי; 1QIsa[a] adds אם) the harvesters of the grain shall eat from it (and not the nation's enemies), as promised in Deut 11:14-15: "You shall gather in your new grain and wine and oil . . . and you shall eat your fill." One should note that in all other passages the act of harvesting is expressed by the *qal* stem of אסף (e.g., Exod 23:10, 16; Lev 23:39; Deut 28:38). The unique use of the *pi'el* here (מְאַסְפָיו) reflects the plurality of the gatherers due to the abundance of the crop.

"And give praise to the Lord" — They, the harvesters, shall give thanks to the Lord (or "to the name of the Lord" [שֵׁם ה׳], as in 1QIsa[a]) for His munificence. For harvesting festivals accomplished by jubilation, see Lev 19:24: "In the fourth year all its fruit shall be sacred, an offering of jubilation (הִלּולים) before the Lord"; Judg 9:27: "They went out into the fields, gathered and trod out the vintage of their vineyards and made a jubilatory festival (הִלּולים)." For the connection between consumption and giving praise to the Lord, see Joel 2:26; Ps 22:27. For the etymological and semantic equivalent of הלל in Akkadian, *alālu*, see *CAD* A/1:331-32.

"And those who gather it shall drink it in My sacred courts" — Those who gather the grapes shall drink the wine in My Temple; cf. Ps 116:19: "In the courts (בחצרות) of the House of the Lord, in the midst of Jerusalem. Hallelujah"; Ps 84:3: "I long, I yearn for the courts (חצרות) of the Lord." For the parallel verbal pair קבץ/אסף ("to harvest/to gather"), see Isa 11:12. 1QIsa[a] appends אמר אלהיך ("says your God") to the end of this verse, as in the MT of 54:6; 66:9.

[10-12] This short pericope, which consists of a call to facilitate the return of the nation, the construction of a road for the benefit of the returnees, and the bestowal of new names on Jerusalem and the nation, is connected both linguistically and thematically to the previous unit: ציון (vv. 1, 11), ישעך/ישועתה (vv. 1, 11), -קרא ל (vv. 2, 4, 12), עזובה/נעזבה (a description of Jerusalem, vv. 4, 12). The main thematic link is the conferral of new names (vv. 2, 4,

12). Moreover, this unit is characterized by a number of phrases and expressions found in previous chapters: v. 10: "Clear the road for the people! Build up, build up the highway! Remove the rocks!" is comparable to 40:3: "Clear in the desert a road for the Lord! Level in the wilderness a highway for our God!"; 57:14: "Build up, build up a highway! Clear a road! Remove all obstacles from the road of My people!"; and the continuation: "Raise an ensign over the peoples!" echoes 49:22: "I will raise My hand to the nations and lift up My ensign to the peoples." For v. 11: "Your Deliverer is coming! See, His reward is with Him, His recompense before Him," see 40:10: "Behold, the Lord God comes in might. . . . See, His reward is with Him, His recompense before Him." For vv. 10-12: "Clear the road for the people! Build up! Build up the highway!. . . . And they will call them 'The Holy People, The Redeemed of the Lord'"; cf. 35:8-10: "And a highway shall appear there . . . the redeemed shall walk it . . . and come with shouting to Zion."

[10] The urgency of the return to Zion is emphasized in a series of seven imperatives.

Pass through! Pass through the gates! — It is difficult to know to whom the double imperative (cf. 40:1; 51:9, 12, 17, and see the introduction, §10.A.1) is addressed — to the nation's leaders, to the nations, or perhaps to divine intercessors (as in 40:3), who are commanded to go from gate to gate and gather all the Jews in the cities of the Diaspora. Compare Exod 32:27: "Go back and forth from gate to gate throughout the camp."

Clear the road for the people! — Remove all obstacles from the path (פַּנּוּ דרך) leading from Babylon to Zion; cf. Mal 3:1: "To clear the way (וּפִנָּה דרך) before Me."

Build up! Build up the highway! Remove the rocks! — Another double imperative for emphasis: Prepare the thoroughfare for the returning expatriates and clear away all "impediments" (1QIsa[a] adds [מאבן] הנגף; Targum [אבן] תַּקְלָא, "stumbling [stone]"), so as to expedite and facilitate the return. Note the assonance of the fivefold repetition of the letter *samekh*: סֹלו סֹלו המסִלה סקלו (and in the following colon: נס). For the synonymous pair (= מסִלה) דרך/מסלול, see Isa 35:8 quoted above; for the motif of return to Israel, see 40:2; 42:16; 43:19; 49:11; 57:14.

Raise an ensign over the peoples! — Raise a standard above all the nations, so as to signal the return. Cf. 49:22, where the similar clause has אל instead of על, as here. Instead of this clause, 1QIsa[a] has אמורו בעמים ("Say among the peoples"), serving as an introduction to the next verse.

[11] Note the rhapsodic threefold repetition of הנה ("Lo/Behold/See") in this verse.

Lo, the Lord has proclaimed to the end of the earth — For קְצֵה הארץ ("the end of the earth") as synonymous with קַצְוֵי הארץ (as in 1QIsa[a]), see 43:6;

48:20; 49:6. 1QIsa[a], השמיעו ("Proclaim"), continues the series of imperatives. For the proclamation formula הַשמיעו ... אִמרו ("Proclaim ... Announce"), see 48:20; Jer 4:5; 31:7; 46:14; 50:2; Amos 3:9.

"Announce to daughter Zion" — Cf. Isa 40:9: "Announce (אמרי) to the cities of Judah: 'Behold your God!'" For the sobriquet "daughter Zion" (בת ציון), see 52:2.

"Behold, your Deliverer is coming!" — Cf. 35:4: "Behold, your God! . . . He Himself is coming to save you." The LXX, Vulgate, Peshitta, and Targum (פָּרְקִיךְ) all translate "your Deliverer," rather than "deliverance" according to the MT.

"See, His reward is with Him" — His reward is His nation, "His treasured possession," which He is bringing back from Babylon. See the comments to 40:10 and the influence of Jer 31:15 on this verse.

"And His recompense before Him" — For "His recompense" (פְּעֻלָּתוֹ) paralleling "His reward" (שְׂכָרוֹ), see Isa 40:10.

[12] New names are bestowed on both Jerusalem and the nation. The prophecy of Jer 30:17: "Though they called you 'Outcast, that Zion whom no one seeks out (דֹּרֵשׁ),'" is now reversed.

And they will call them "The Holy People, The Redeemed of the Lord" — These are the names by which the expatriates shall be called. For the first, see also Isa 63:18; Deut 7:6; and for the second, Ps 107:2. The "Holy People" (עם הַקֹּדֶשׁ) return to Jerusalem, which is the "Holy City" (עִיר הַקֹּדֶשׁ) (Isa 48:2; 52:1).

And you shall be called "Sought Out, A City Not Forsaken" — Concomitantly, Jerusalem shall be called "Sought Out" (דרושה), i.e., a city that is sought after and desirable; and "A City Not Forsaken" (עיר לא נעזבה), a city that shall never again be abandoned and desolate, as in v. 4. The new name, "Sought Out" (דרושה; parallel to חפצי-בה ["I delight in her"] in v. 4), contrasts with her dire state in the years of exile, as in Jer 30:17, cited above.

Chapter 63

The chapter is composed of two units (the second of which continues into chap. 64): 63:1-6; and 63:7–64:11. The first pericope features a dialogue between the prophet and God, who is depicted as a warrior in blood-soaked garments who has just returned from the battlefield in Edom after defeating His enemies. For a similar description of the Lord in His warrior garb, see 59:15b-20. Both describe garments donned by the Divine Warrior: 59:17: "He donned victory like a coat of mail, with a helmet of triumph on His head. He clothed Himself with garments of vengeance and wrapped Himself in zeal as in a robe" — 63:1-3: "Who is this coming . . . in crimsoned garments from Bozrah? Who is this, majestic in attire . . . ? Why is Your clothing so red, Your garments like one who treads grapes? . . . Their lifeblood bespattered My garments and all My clothing was stained." Both passages feature divine retribution and fury: 59:17: "garments of vengeance" — 63:4: "a day of vengeance"; 59:18: "Wreaking anger on His foes" — 63:3: "I trod them down in My anger." Both describe redemption: 59:20: "He shall come as redeemer to Zion" — 63:4: "My year of redemption"; and portray the Lord's solitary march into battle: 59:16 = 63:5; cf. also 42:13. For a noneschatological battle also depicted as grape treading at the winepress, see Judg 8:1-2: "And the men of Ephraim said to him, 'Why did you do that to us . . . when you went to fight the Midianites?' . . . But he answered them . . . 'Are not Ephraim's gleanings better than Abiezer's vintage!'"; Jer 6:9: "Thus said the Lord of Hosts: 'Let them glean over and over as a vine, the remnant of Israel. Pass your hand again, like a vintager, over its branches'"; Jer 49:9: "If vintagers were to come upon you, would they leave no gleanings?" (cf. Obad 5).

It is difficult to set a date to this prophecy against Edom, since this nation was a traditional foe from the outset of the monarchy, and especially in the years of destruction and exile, as well as at the beginning of the return (cf. 2 Kgs 24:2; Jer 49:7-22; Ezek 25:12-14; 35:1-15; Obad 1; Mal 1:2-5; Ps 137:7; Lam 4:21-22).

No specific accusation is leveled at Edom and no reason is given for its destruction. This is apparently the first reference to Edom as the arch-symbol of evil and depravity that left its mark on later literature. (According to rabbinic literature, Edom is synonymous with the Roman Empire. See Y. Hoffman, "Edom as a Symbol of Evil in Prophetic Literature," in B. Uffenheimer, ed., *Bible and Jewish History: Studies in Bible and Jewish History Dedicated to the Memory of Jacob Liver* [Tel Aviv, 1972], 76-89 [Heb.].) The danger from Edom is also cited in Letter 24 from Arad (Aḥituv, *Ha-Ketav veha-Miktav,* 119).

The unit begins with a series of rhetorical questions expressing astonishment and is followed by the answers. For similar rhetorical questions and responses, see Isa 60:8-9; Jer 46:7-8; Job 38:2ff.; Cant 3:6ff.; 8:5.

The beginning of this chapter can be seen as a continuation of the last chapter, which states that salvation is imminent, and in 63:1ff. the process of redemption is described in all its gory glory. Note the words and phrases common to chaps. 62 and 63:

Chapter 62	**Chapter 63**
v. 1: וישועתה — her triumph; v. 11: ישעך — your Deliverer	v. 1: להושיע — to triumph
v. 3: תפארת — glorious	v. 12: תפארתו — His glorious (arm); v. 14: (שם) תפארת — a glorious (name); v. 15: (מִזְּבֻל) ותפארתך — Your . . . glorious (height)
v. 8: ובזרוע עֻזו — by His mighty arm	v. 5: זרֹעי — My own arm
v. 10: על העמים — over the peoples	v. 3: ומעמים — of the peoples
v. 12: עם הַקֹּדֶשׁ — the holy people	v. 18: עם קדשך — Your holy people
v. 12: גאולי ה׳ — the redeemed of the Lord	v. 4: ושנת גאולי באה — and My year of redemption has arrived; v. 9: הוא גאלם — He Himself redeemed them; v. 16: גֹּאלנו — our Redeemer

[1] The prophet, who presents himself in the guise of a watchman on the walls (cf. 21:11-12), sees a rapidly approaching figure and demands that he identify himself. "Edom" and "Bozrah" are both polysemous. On the one hand, they are well-known locales; see 34:6: "For the Lord has a sacrifice in Bozrah, a great slaughter in the land of Edom"; Amos 1:11-12: "For three transgressions of

Edom . . . and it shall devour the fortresses of Bozrah" (from these verses it is apparent that Bozrah was one of the most important cities of Edom). On the other hand, the terms also indicate the ruddy color of God's garb after He "vintaged" (בָּצִיר) the enemy (Luzzatto; Yellin, *Ḥiqrei Miqra,* 84; Tur-Sinai, *Peshuṭo shel Miqra,* III/1:145). For similar wordplays on Edom, see 2 Kgs 3:20-22: "Water flowing from the direction of Edom (אדום) . . . as red as blood (כַּדָּם אֲדֻמִּים)"; Isa 34:5-7: "For My sword shall be drunk in the sky. Lo, it shall come down upon Edom (אדום). . . . The Lord has a sword steeped in blood (דם) . . . and their land shall be drunk with blood (מדם)"; Joel 4:19-21: "And Edom (אדום) shall become a desolate waste . . . in whose land they shed the blood (דם) of the innocent. . . . Thus I will treat as innocent their blood (דמם) which I have not treated as innocent"; cf. also Gen 25:30. (See M. Garsiel, *Biblical Names: A Literary Study of Midrashic Derivations and Puns* [Ramat Gan, 1991], 209-11.) The motif of God's coming from Edom is found in other biblical traditions as well: Deut 33:2: "The Lord came from Sinai and shone on them from Seir [= Edom]. He appeared from Mount Paran"; Judg 5:4: "O Lord, when You came forth from Seir, came marching from the plains of Edom"; Hab 3:3: "God is coming from Teman, the Holy One from Mount Paran."

Who is this coming from Edom — from the land of Edom (אדום); but note the allusion "to the ruddy clothes (אדומים) [stained] by the blood (מדם) of slaughter" (Kimchi). The verb בא is a *qal* participle, as in Isa 62:11.

In crimsoned garments from Bozrah? — Who is this figure arriving from the city of Bozrah (identified as Buseirah in northern Edom; see Jer 49:22) whose stained clothes resemble the garments of one who has returned from the winepress? The unique expression חמוץ בגדים apparently refers to the ruddy color of the clothes. Others interpret it as an allusion to חֹמֶץ יין ("the vinegar of wine"; see Num 6:3), meaning the garments were steeped in a red liquid resembling wine vinegar. Although evidence of the Edomite connection to the wine industry comes only from the later, Roman, period, it should be noted that after the destruction of the First Temple Edomites occupied southern Judah, an area famous for its vineyards and wine industry (cf. Gen 49:11-12). Compare the expression חומץ האדומי, "Edomite vinegar" (*m. Pesaḥ.* 3:1; and the discussion in *y. Pesaḥ.* 3:5, 19b; *b. Pesaḥ.* 42b).

Majestic in attire — The interrogative מי does double-duty from the first stich. The prophet repeats his question: Who is this approaching the city, garbed in such splendid (הדור) attire? Cf. Ps 104:1: "You are clothed in majesty and splendor (והדר)"; Prov 31:25: "She is clothed with strength and splendor (והדר)"; Job 40:10: "Clothe yourself in majesty and splendor (והדר)." Note the appearance of this motif also in Mesopotamian sources, namely, the majestic and awesome clothing *(namurratu/melammu/puluḫtu)* of the gods (*CAD* L:18).

Pressing forward in His great might? — In light of the context, the verb צֹעֶה apparently denotes "marching" (thus Symmachus and Vulgate; but perhaps it should be emended to צֹעֵד; see Judg 5:4): Who is it that strides forward in such a great show of strength? For depiction of the Lord's march to the battlefield, cf. Judg 5:4; Hab 3:12; Ps 68:8. For the expression רב כח, see Ps 33:16: "Warriors are not saved by great strength (בְּרָב כֹּח)." Thus ends the query of the prophet-watchman.

"It is I, proclaiming victory" — the divine response. For the root צדק with the meaning "triumph" and "salvation," see Isa 45:21, 24, 25. Others have explained this clause to mean, "I am He who speaks truly," i.e., always fulfills His word; cf. 45:23: "By Myself have I sworn. From My mouth has issued truth (צדקה), a word that shall not be revoked." Or: "It is I who decrees what is right"; cf. Ps 58:2: "Do you really decree what is just (צדק)?" But the first interpretation is preferable.

"Powerful to give triumph/Who contends in order to save" — It is I whose strength suffices to triumph and save. Or, if vocalized רָב (Symmachus, LXX, and Vulgate, instead of MT רַב): "It is I who contests your cause to save you"; cf. Isa 19:20: "He will send them a savior and a champion (רָב) to deliver them."

[2] The dialogue between God and the prophet-watchman continues with a query regarding the state of God's metaphorical garb, which is stained as red as one who treads grapes in the winepress. Compare this depiction of the deity wallowing in blood to Anat's battle against Baal's enemies in the Ugaritic Baal epic: "Up to her knees she wades in the blood of warriors, up to her neck in the gore of soldiers" (*CAT* 1.3.II:13-14).

"Why is your clothing so red" — It is often assumed that the double *lamed* of ללבושך is the result of dittography (cf. Ibn Ganaḥ, *Sefer ha-Riqmah,* 57, lines 10-13; Ibn Ezra). Others have suggested that the *lamed* denotes the preposition "on" (Saadyah Gaon, 138; for other examples see Ibn Ganaḥ, *Sefer ha-Riqmah,* 61, lines 10ff.). Alternately, it may be a rare example of the emphatic *lamed,* as in Isa 32:1; Eccl 9:4. Note the wordplay of אָדֹם ("red") in this verse and אדום ("Edom") in v. 1.

"Your garments like one who treads grapes in a press?" — This clause is chiastically parallel to the former one. For treading grapes as an image describing God's punishment, see Lam 1:15: "As in a press (גת) the Lord has trodden fair maiden Judah." Note the assonance: ובגדיך . . . בגת. (1QIsa[a] בגד, instead of MT בגת, "may have resulted from the fact that the voiced *dalet* at the end of a word sounded the same as a voiceless *taw.* . . . The preceding ובגדיך may also have been influential" [Kutscher, *Language and Linguistic Background,* 227].) The word for winepress, גת, appears also in Ugaritic, *gt* (*HdO* 1:310-11). The words ללבושך and בגדיך create a chiastic parallelism with בגדים and בלבושו in the previous verse.

[3] The Lord's response to this second query. From an image of grape treading (as in Judg 9:27: "They went out into the fields, picked and trod out the vintage of their vineyards, and held a festival"), the prophet shifts to a description of treading and trampling on enemies whose blood spurts onto God's metaphorical clothing. The question and the answer are phrased in the same terms: כְּדֹרֵךְ (v. 2) — דרכתי . . . וְאֶדְרְכֵם (v. 3).

"I trod out a winepress alone" — Some connect the rare term פורה with an Arabic equivalent from the root *fāra* denoting fermentation, and thereby interpret פורה as a parallel to גת in the previous clause (cf. Targum; Saadyah Gaon, 138; Kimchi), and note the resulting chiastic parallel. Others explain it as a measurement of the wine harvest, as in Hag 2:16: "If one came to a wine vat to skim off fifty measures (פורה), the press would yield only twenty" (Luzzatto; Ehrlich, *Mikrâ ki-Pheshuṭo,* 3:153), i.e., My trampling the grapes yielded a sizable harvest of grape wine.

"No one from the peoples was with Me" — I received no outside aid in My vengeful combat. Tur-Sinai (*Peshuṭo shel Miqra,* III/1:145) suggests that ומעמים ("of the nations") should be read as part of the preceding clause: "I alone trod out a winepress of the peoples, and no one was with me"; cf. v. 6: "I trampled peoples in My anger." The negative parallelism אין איש/לבדי ("alone/no one") emphasizes God's acting alone in the destruction of the adversary. Cf. 44:24: "Who alone stretched out the heavens and unaided spread out the earth." 1QIsa[a] has ומעמי ("and from My people").

"I trod them down in My anger" — vocalize in the past tense, וָאדרכם (also below: וַיֵּז, וָאֶרְמְסֵם; and in vv. 5-6). The root דרך is repeated here for the third time in two verses for emphasis.

"Trampled them in My rage" — parallel to the previous colon. For the synonymous terms חמה/אף ("anger/rage"), see v. 6; 42:25; 66:15; and for רמס/דרך ("to tread/to trample"), see Ps 91:13.

"Their lifeblood bespattered My garments" — נִצְחָם, only in this context and in v. 6, denotes lifeblood (most likely related to the Arabic root *naḍaḥ/ḫa,* "to sprinkle"). As a result of My treading and trampling, the lifeblood of My enemies has spattered over My clothing. ויז (read: וַיִּז) is an apocopated *niph'al* from the root נזי; cf. 2 Kgs 9:33: "And her blood spattered (וַיִּז) on the wall."

"And all My clothing was stained" — The root גאל is a late secondary form of געל, denoting "defilement," "pollution." For other examples, see Mal 1:7; Dan 1:8. The form אֶגְאָלְתִּי is a conflation of the *qal* past tense גָּאַלְתִּי (thus in 1QIsa[a] and 1QIsa[b]) and the imperfect *niph'al* אֶגָּאֵל (see Ibn Ezra). For other hybrid forms of this verb, see Isa 59:3 and Lam 4:14: נְגֹאֲלוּ בדם. Its employment here creates a paronomasia with the expression (ושנת) גְּאוּלַי in the following verse. For the term מלבושים, which is common in later Hebrew, see 2 Kgs 10:22; Zeph 1:8; Job 27:16; 2 Chr 9:4 (twice). (See the introduction, §11).

[**4**] The reason for this graphic vengeance is now explicated: The Lord spends His wrath upon His enemies in order to expedite Israel's redemption; cf. Isa 61:2: "To proclaim a year of the Lord's favor and a day of vengeance of our God"; 34:8: "For it is the Lord's day of vengeance, the year of vindication for Zion's cause." God's enemies are Edomites, both in 34:8 and here.

"For I had planned a day of vengeance" — I set this day aside, out of My own volition, as a day of vengeance. For לבי (lit. "my heart") indicating self-intention/determination, see Num 16:28: "And Moses said, 'By this you shall know that it was the Lord who sent me . . . and it was not of my own devising (מלבי)'"; Num 24:13: "I could not of my own volition (מלבי) do anything good or bad contrary to the Lord's command." In Akkadian as well, the etymological and semantic cognate *libbu* has this same meaning; *CAD* L:169-70. For יום נקם ("a day of vengeance"), see Isa 61:2.

"And My year of redemption has arrived" — The time I had resolved upon for the redemption of My people (and vengeance on the nations) has now come. Note the play on words here between the hapax legomenon גאולי and אגאלתי (v. 3). For other descriptions of the Lord in His redemptive role, see, e.g., Isa 43:14; 44:6; 47:4. The parallel pair שנה/יום ("day/year") is very common (e.g., Job 10:5) and appears in many cognate languages: Phoenician (the Azitawada inscription): "Long days (ימם) and many years (שנת)" (*KAI* 26A III:5-6); Ugaritic: "For the days *(ymt)* of the sun and the moon and the delights of the years *(šnt)* of El" (*CAT* 108:26-27); Aramaic: "In his days (בְּיוֹמוֹהִי) his nation shall be redeemed, and in his years (וּבִשְׁנוֹהִי) they shall reside peacefully as one of the tribes of Israel" (Targum Onqelos to Gen 49:16, with no connection to the original Hebrew); in Akkadian: "They lengthen the days *(ūmī)*, increased the number of years *(šanāti)*" (*Enuma Elish* I:13); and Ammonite: "In many days (ביומת) and in distant years (שנת)" (Ammonite bottle inscription from Tell Siran in Rabbath-Ammon). (See Aḥituv, *Ha-Ketav veha-Miḵtav*, 334, lines 7-8; Paul, *Divrei Shalom*, 51-58.)

[**5-6**] The motif of self-reliance is highlighted in these verses (cf. v. 3). In the absence of anybody else, the Lord wages a solitary war against His enemies and annihilates them. Note that all the verbs in these two verses should be read with a *waw* + *qameṣ* (past tense), instead of a *waw* + *shewa* as in the MT.

[**5**] This verse is a variation on 59:16: "He saw that there was no one. He was appalled that no one interceded. Then His own arm won Him triumph, His victorious right hand supported Him."

"Then I looked, but there was none to help" — Me, on My quest for revenge. 1QIsa[b] has איש instead of MT עֹזֵר, most likely on the basis of 59:16; cf. also 41:28: "But I looked and there is no one (איש)." For the motif of the failure to aid the Lord in His battle against His enemies, see Judg 5:23: "Bitterly curse

its [Meroz's] inhabitants, because they came not to the aid of the Lord, to the aid of the Lord among the warriors."

"I was appalled, but there was none to aid" — parallel to the previous stich. For the synonyms סמך/עזר, see Ps 54:6: "See, God is my helper (עֹזֵר); the Lord is my support (בְּסֹמְכֵי נפשי)." For another example of the *hithpolel* of the verb שמם, see Isa 59:16. 1QIsa[a] has the variant תומך instead of MT סומך. For the synonymous pair תמך/עזר, see 41:10: "I help you (עזרתיך). I uphold you (תמכתיך)."

"So My own arm brought Me victory" — Despite this lack of outside support I achieved triumph with My very own arm (= strength); cf. 52:10: "The Lord will bare His holy arm in the sight of all the nations, and the very ends of earth shall see the deliverance of our God"; Ps 98:1: "His right hand, His holy arm, has won Him victory." For the Lord's mighty arm, see v. 12; 40:10; 51:5, 9; 53:1; 62:8.

"And My own rage was My aid" — In the absence of any external aid, it was My own anger that won the day against My adversaries. The text of many medieval Hebrew manuscripts has צדקתי instead of וחמתי, likely influenced by 59:16. For the connection between the Lord's arm and His rage or fury, see Jer 21:5: "And I Myself will battle against you with an outstretched mighty arm, with anger and rage and great wrath"; Ezek 20:33: "I will reign over you with a strong hand, and with an outstretched arm, and with overflowing fury." For the expression סמך חֵמָה, see also Ps 88:8.

[6] For another description of the massacre of God's adversaries, see Isa 66:16: "For with fire will the Lord contend, with His sword against all humanity; and many shall be the slain of the Lord." For another example of a prophecy against Edom coupled with the nations in general, see 34:2: "For the Lord is angry at all nations"; v. 5: "For My sword shall be drunk in the sky. Lo, it shall come down upon Edom." Point the verbs in the past tense.

"I trampled peoples in My anger" — For the verb בוס ("to trample"), see 41:25; 14:25. This extends the image of the treading on grapes found here in vv. 2-3.

"I made them drunk with My rage/poison" — Note the bivalency of בחמתי, which can either parallel אפי, "My anger" (here and in v. 3), or denote "poison," as in Deut 32:33: "Their wine is the venom (חמת) of asps." The Lord caused the nations to imbibe His wrath, similar to the cup of anger/poison that Israel had drunk from so fully in the past (51:17), and thereby became intoxicated, but not from wine (51:21) — thus fulfilling the divine promise to take the cup of wrath from Israel's hands and deliver it instead to the nation's oppressors (51:22-23). (Instead of MT *pi'el* וַאֲשַׁכְּרֵם, which indicates intensification and plurality [cf. also 2 Sam 11:13; Jer 51:7; Hab 2:15], both 1QIsa[a] and 1QIsa[b] have the *hiph'il* form of the verb.) This image of inebriation is connected to that of treading on grapes, elaborated on above. For a further instance of intoxicating wrath,

see Hab 2:15: "Ah, you who make your companions drink to intoxication as from your cup of wrath" (read מְסַף חמתך instead of מְסַפֵּחַ חמתך, an error due to dittography). Many medieval Hebrew manuscripts have וָאֲשַׁבְּרֵם ("I smashed them") instead of MT וָאֲשַׁכְּרֵם ("I made them drunk"). Note, then, the resultant parallelism between בוס ("to trample") and שבר ("to break"), as in Isa 14:25, quoted above.

"I shall cause their lifeblood to flow to the ground/netherworld" — Commentators disagree regarding the meaning of the term נִצְחָם in this context. Rashi interprets: "the might of their victory (נצחון)"; and in a similar vein Kimchi and Abravanel explain: "their prowess and their mighty bearing"; or perhaps "their splendor," as in 1 Chr 29:11: "Yours, Lord, are greatness, might, glory, splendor (והנצח), and majesty." In light of v. 3, however, Ibn Ezra's comment is more plausible: "I shall cause their lifeblood to flow to the ground." In support of this interpretation one should note that descent to the netherworld is expressed by the root ירד in Hebrew (as here; Isa 14:11, 15; Ezek 32:18; Ps 55:24), *warādu* in Akkadian (*CAD* A/2:219), and *yrd* in Ugaritic (*HdO* 2:977-78). Hebrew ארץ may also be purposely ambivalent. On the one hand, the image depicts blood flowing down to the "ground" (cf. Ezek 21:37: "You shall become fuel for the fire; your blood shall sink into the ground. You shall not be remembered, for I the Lord have spoken"). On the other hand, ארץ may be a reference to the "netherworld," as in 1 Sam 28:13: "And the woman said to Saul, 'I see a divine being coming up from the netherworld' (הארץ)." (The etymological and semantic cognates, Akk. *erṣetu* [*CAD* E:310], and Ugar. *arṣ* [*CAT* 1.5.V:6], also have the same dual meaning.) (See Paul, *Divrei Shalom*, 263-70.)

[63:7–64:11] This lengthy pericope is a national supplication reflecting the dire circumstances and bitter despair in the face of God's ostensible neglect of His people (cf. 59:9-13, and see Ps 44, 60, 74, 79, 80, 83, 85, 89, 90, 94, 106). The prophet's plea harps on the disparity between God's miracles in days of yore (in Egypt at the Reed Sea and subsequently in the desert) and His present-day abandonment of Israel (the destruction of the Temple and the cities of Judah) that has caused the people to despair and to stray from His path. Following the introduction, in which the Lord's prowess is proclaimed in a general statement (v. 7), the prophet reminisces regarding His past kindnesses (vv. 8-9). Contrary to expectations, however, the nation rebelled against the Lord, and thus He became their enemy and waged war against them (v. 10). In their hour of need, the nation remembers God's past compassion, specifically the miracles at the sea and in the desert (vv. 11-14). Note the thematic and linguistic connections between this section and Ps 106:4-10:

> Be mindful of me (זָכרני), O Lord, when You favor Your people. Take note of me when You deliver them (בישועתך). . . . Our forefathers in Egypt did

not perceive Your wonders. They did not remember Your abundant love (רב חסדך) but rebelled (וַיַּמְרוּ) at the sea, at the Sea (בים) of Reeds. Yet He saved them (ויושיעֵם) for His name's sake (שמו), to make known His might. . . . He led them through the depths as through the wilderness (ויוליכֵם בתהֹמות כמדבר). He delivered them (ויושיעֵם) from the foe, redeemed them (ויגאלֵם) from the enemy (אויב).

(See the introduction, §17.) There then follows a desperate cry to God, their Father and Savior, to act again on behalf of their cause, as He did in those long-gone days (vv. 15-16). The nation (or their spokesman, the prophet) laments the destruction of the Temple and accuses God of being culpable for the nation's disregard of the divine precepts (vv. 17-19a). The prophet then suddenly addresses God directly and calls on Him to reveal himself in His full glory in order to redeem His nation (63:19b–64:3). The following verses claim, once again, that God's aloofness is the ultimate cause of their sins, to which they confess (64:4-6). Finally, the nation begs God's consideration and asks that He not be forever angry at them since He is their Father and Maker (64:7-11). Note a modicum of symmetry between 63:19b and 64:1b: a call for divine intercession; 63:16 and 64:7: the nation's plea relies on God's paternity; 63:17 and 64:4b-7: a confession of sin; 63:18-19a and 64:10: the reason for the plea, including the destruction of the Temple; 63:15 and 64:4b-7: desperate rumination regarding God's inactivity.

The unit also shares a number of characteristics with the book of Lamentations, which also deals with the people's consternation regarding divine acts. In both texts the Lord is referred to as an enemy of His people (63:1; Lam 2:4) since He brought the enemy (צר) to destroy Jerusalem and the Temple (Isa 63:18; 64:1; Lam 1:5 [twice], 7 [twice], 10, 17; 2:17; 4:12); and in both there is an allusion to treasures and precious vessels, מחמדיהם (Isa 64:10; Lam 1:7, 10, 11; 2:4). Since the Lord was extremely (עד מאד) angry with Israel (Isa 64:8, 11; Lam 5:22), they pray that He have mercy (ירחם) as His compassion is like a vast bounty, כרב חסדיו (Isa 63:7; Lam 3:32). (For other literary connections see the introduction, §18.) This unit is usually dated to the very beginning of the exilic period, immediately following the destruction of the Temple.

[7] For a similar introduction to an account of God's miracles, see Ps 77:12: "I recall (אזכיר) the deeds of the Lord. Yes, I recall (אֶזכרה) Your wonders of old"; 89:2: "I will sing of the Lord's love (חסד) forever." (Note that the latter psalm also concludes with the query: "O Lord, where are Your former acts of love (חסדיך)?" [v. 50], and cf. Isa 64:15: "Where is Your zeal, Your power?") The Lord's name is mentioned three times in this verse for emphasis. Note the literary frame, in which the verse begins and ends with the word חסד (חסדי . . . חסדיו), and the verb גמל, along with חסד, appears in chiastic parallelism.

I will recount the Lord's acts of love — The verb זכר, like its Akkadian etymological and semantic cognate *zakāru* (*CAD* Z:19), can also denote "to praise"; cf. Isa 26:13; Ps 71:16. For the expression חסדי ה׳ ("the Lord's acts of love"), see Ps 89:2 (quoted above); 107:43; Lam 3.22.

The praises of the Lord — The verb אזכיר is implied here as well. For the same idea cf. Ps 9:15: "I might recount all Your praise (תְּהִלָּתֶךָ)"; 78:4: "Tell the coming generation the praises (תְּהִלּוֹת) of the Lord."

For all that the Lord has done for us — Similarly, Ps 13:6: "I will sing to the Lord, for He has been good (גמל) to me." The verb גמל, like its Akkadian etymological cognate *gamālu,* denotes the performance of benevolent acts (*CAD* G:21-22).

His bountiful goodness to the house of Israel — Cf. Ps 145:7: "They shall celebrate Your abundant goodness (רב טובך)." This is also the meaning of its Akkadian cognate, *ṭūbu* (*CAD* Ṭ:116-17).

That He bestowed on them/us, according to His mercy and His great love — The LXX version, presupposing גמלנו ("bestowed on us"), is preferable to MT גמלם ("bestowed on them"). It is likely that the MT resulted from a combination of the *nun* and the *waw,* which were read as a final *mem.* For the same phenomenon, see v. 19a: בם, instead of the correct בנו. (For other examples of this graphic phenomenon of ligature, see R. Weiss, "On Ligatures in the Bible," in *Studies in the Text and Language of the Bible* [Jerusalem, 1981], 3-19 [Heb.].) Compare also v. 14: תניחנו should be read תניחם, an example of the opposite phenomenon, a final *mem* read erroneously as a *nun* and a *waw.* For the connection between God and His munificence, for He is "a compassionate (רחום) God . . . abounding in love (ורב חסד)" (Exod 34:6), see Ps 25:6: "O Lord, remember Your compassion (רחמיך) and Your love (חסדיך). They are old as time"; 51:3: "Have mercy on me, O God, as befits Your love (חסדך), in keeping with Your abundant compassion (כרֹב רחמיך)"; 106:45: "And in His great love (כרֹב חסדו) relented"; and see also Isa 54:8: "But with love (בחסד) everlasting I will take you back in compassion (רִחַמְתִּיךְ)." For the expression ב/כרב חסדך ("according to Your great love"), see also Ps 5:8; 69:14; Neh 13:22. It is likely that the initial *kaf* of the words כרחמיו and כחסדיו is emphatic, thus accentuating the greatness of God's mercy and kindness.

[8-9] The final hemistich of v. 8 should be appended to the beginning of v. 9, as it correctly appears in the LXX: "So He was their deliverer in all their trouble. It was not [read לא, with the Ketib] an emissary (צִר) or an angel but His presence that delivered them." A scathing polemic against the belief in angels as emissaries between the Lord and His people is reflected in these verses. The roots of this polemic are already apparent in the earliest layers of tradition regarding the exodus. On the one hand, the Elohistic source (E) emphasizes in Exod 14:19: "The angel of God, who had been going ahead of the Israelite army, now moved and followed behind them"; 23:20: "I am sending an angel before you to guard you on the way"; 32:34: "See, My angel shall go before you"; Num 20:16: "We cried to the Lord and He heard our plea, and He sent a messenger who freed us from Egypt." On the other hand, other traditions negate any type of angelic intercession and emphasize God's sole responsibility for the redemption of His people. Thus according to this tradition God, following the sin of the golden calf, punished Israel by informing them that He shall no longer guide them, and instead appoints an angelic emissary (Exod 32:34; 33:2-3). Upon Moses' intervention (33:12-13), however, God relents; 33:14-15: "And He said, 'I will go (פָּנַי) in the lead.' . . . And he said to Him, 'Unless You (פניך) go in the lead, do not send us up from here.'" The same motif of the Lord's presence, i.e., the Lord Himself leading the nation, appears also in Deut 4:37: "And because He loved your fathers, He chose their children after them. He Himself (בפניו), in His great might, led you out of Egypt." This anti-angelic ideology reverberates in the Passover haggadah (based on *Mekilta de-Rabbi Ishmael, Bo, Pisḥa*, 7 [ed. Horovitz-Rabin, 23]). Compare also *y. Sanh.* 2:1, 20a; *Hor.* 3:1, 47a: "The Lord took us out of Egypt, not by means of an angel, nor through an emissary, nor through a messenger, but it was the Holy One blessed be He by Himself." Compare also *Sifre Deuteronomy* 42 (ed. Finkelstein, 88): "'I will grant the rain for your land in season' (Deut 11:14). I will grant it, not by an angel, nor by an emissary, nor through a messenger"; *Sifre Deuteronomy* 325 (ed. Finkelstein, 376): "'To be My vengeance and recompense' (Deut 32:35). I shall avenge Myself upon them on My own, not through an angel nor through a messenger." Although the accepted reading of the verse is based on the Ketib, לא, the rabbis of the Talmud usually availed themselves of the Qere variant, לו ("to Him"), and understood the verse as divine commiseration, i.e., the Lord was with them in all their troubles. See *b. Taʿan.* 16a: "Why does one put wood ashes on the ark? Resh Lakish said: 'Since He was with them in all their troubles' (בכל צרתם לו צר)." For the idea that God Himself will guide the nation, see also Isa 52:12.

[8] The beginning of the verse bears the imprint of Jer 3:19: "I had resolved to adopt you as a son . . . and I thought you would surely call Me 'Father' and never cease to be loyal to Me." Here, as in Jeremiah, we are privy to God's expectations: "I thought" (אמרתי) — "He thought" (ויאמר); "as a child" (בבנים) — "children" (בנים); cf. also "my Father" (אבי) and "our Father" (אבינו) (v. 16). But God's expectations were disappointed, for although He heaped multiple benefits on them, they rebelled against Him: Jer 3:20: "Instead, you have broken faith with me" — v. 10: "but they rebelled." (See the introduction, §15.) The linguistic background of this verse reflects the Israelite covenant paradigm: First the covenant formula is stated — it appears here only in part (cf. Lev 26:12; Deut 29:13; Jer 7:23) — followed by the protection offered by the overlord (God) vis-à-vis His vassal (Israel), the breaking of faith (the verb שקר, "to play false, deceive"), and the punishment of the reneging vassal.

[8a-b] *He thought, "Surely they are My people"* — I was absolutely sure they were My nation; cf. Isa 51:16: "Say to Zion. 'You are My people'"; Zech 13:9: "I will declare: 'You are My people.'" The adverb אך is emphatic, as in Gen 29:14: "You are truly (אך) my bone and flesh"; Gen 44:28: "He [Joseph] surely (אך) was torn by a beast"; see also Isa 43:24; 45:14, 24.

"Children who will not play false" — I was under the impression that they would not break faith or deal falsely with me. For the verb שקר as reneging on the commitments of a covenant, see Gen 21:23: "Therefore swear to me here by God that you will not deal falsely (תשקר) with me or with my kith and kin, but will deal with me . . . as loyally as I have dealt with you"; Ps 44:18: "We have not betrayed (שִׁקַּרְנוּ) Your covenant"; Ps 89:34: "But I will not take away My steadfast love from him. I will not betray (אֲשַׁקֵּר) My faithfulness." It is found also in an Aramaic inscription from Sefire from the mid-eighth century BCE: "You will be false (שקרת) to this treaty" (III:9; Fitzmyer, *Aramaic Inscriptions of Sefîre,* 96; cf. also I.B:38, p. 18). For the substantive parallel בנים/עם, see Isa 1:3-4; Jer 4:22.

[8c-9] *So He was their deliverer in all their troubles* — God thus fulfilled His part of the covenant. The *waw* appended to ויהי indicates purpose. For the motif of the Lord as redeemer of His nation, see, e.g., v. 1; 60:16.

No emissary or angel — He Himself delivered them — Read צִר ("emissary") with the LXX instead of MT צָר ("He was troubled"): God Himself delivered Israel in their times of trouble. No emissary or angel was in any way involved or responsible. For ציר (a loanword from Akk. *ṣīru;* see J. N. Postgate, *Taxation and Conscription in the Assyrian Empire,* SP 3 [Rome, 1974], 123-25), see 57:9: "And you have sent your envoys (צִרַיִךְ) afar"; cf. also Jer 49:14; Obad 1; Prov 25:13. For the parallel synonyms ציר/מלאך ("messenger/emissary"), see Isa 18:2: ". . . which sends out envoys (צירים) by sea. . . . Go, swift messengers (מלאכים)"; Prov 13:17: "Harm befalls a wicked messenger (מלאך). But a faithful courier (ציר) brings healing." For פניו (lit. "His presence, His face") as a reference to the Lord Himself in the context of the delivery from Egypt, see Deut 4:37: "He Himself (בפניו), in His great might, led you out of Egypt." Compare also 2 Sam 17:11: "You yourself (ופניך) shall march into battle." There is no need to vocalize the verb in the plural, הושִׁיעֻם, agreeing with פניו, as is shown by Lam 4:16, where פני ה׳ also takes a singular verb, חִלְּקָם.

In His love and compassion He Himself redeemed them — God, in His infinite compassion, delivered the nation from Egypt; cf. v. 7.

Raised them and sustained them all the days of old — The Lord sustained and delivered them in those days of yore; cf. Ps 28:9: "Deliver (הושיעה) and bless Your very own people. Tend them and sustain them (וְנַשְּׂאֵם) forever

(העולם)." The expression ימי עולם ("the days of old") refers to ancient epochs in the nation's history, as in v. 11: "Then they remembered the days of old"; Amos 9:11: "I will build it firm as in the days of old"; Mal 3:4: "As in the days of old and in years long past." The verb נטל is borrowed from Aramaic and denotes "lifting, raising," as in Dan 4:31: "I lifted (נִטְלֵת) my eyes to heaven"; and often serves as a translation of Heb. נשׂא, e.g., Targum Onqelos to Exod 10:13 (נְטַל = נָשָׂא) and Targum Jonathan to Ps 134:2 (טולו = שְׂאוּ). (For additional Aramaisms in Deutero-Isaiah's prophecy, see the introduction, §11.) The verb נשׂא, moreover (and by attraction, נטל), also means "to support, sustain." See Isa 46:3, 4 and the biblical and extrabiblical parallels quoted there.

[10] Despite their preferential treatment, the people showed no gratitude but instead rebelled against God.

But they rebelled and grieved His holy spirit — Here "they," המה, emphasizes negative responses, as opposed to v. 8, where the term emphasized an expression of fondness: "He thought surely they (המה) are My people." They, however (the *waw* indicates contrast), rebelled and harried God's holy spirit. The root מרי denotes "rebelliousness," as in 50:5, "And I did not rebel (מריתי)"; and in the context of God's spirit, see Ps 106:33: "Because they rebelled (הִמְרוּ) against His spirit." The verb עצב ("to pain, grieve") is also connected to רוח in the expression ועצובת רוח, "grieved in spirit" (Isa 54:6). The two verbs (עצב and מרה) appear in tandem in Ps 78:40: "How often they rebelled against (יַמרוהו) Him in the wilderness, grieved Him (יַעֲצִיבוהו) in the desert." The expression רוח קדשו ("His holy spirit"), repeated in the following verse (cf. רוח ה׳, "the spirit of the Lord," in v. 14), appears only once more in the Bible, in Ps 51:13: "Do not take Your holy spirit away from me." 1QIsa[a] has the plural קדושיו, which does not fit the present passage.

Then He changed into their enemy — In reaction to their rebellion, the Lord was transformed from a compassionate God to a foe (cf. Job 30:21). For the antonymous pair אויב/אוהב, "lover/enemy," see Judg 5:31; Lam 1:2.

And He Himself made war against them — The Lord, who in the past redeemed them (v. 9), then fought against them. 1QIsa[a], והוא, with the additional *waw,* is corroborated by the LXX, Vulgate, some Targum manuscripts, several midrashim (including *Mekilta de-Rabbi Ishmael, be-Shalaḥ, Shirah,* 5 [ed. Horovitz-Rabin, 34]; *Sifre Numbers* 157 [ed. Horovitz, 211]), and many medieval Hebrew manuscripts.

[11-14] The prophecy in Jer 2:6-8 left a decisive impression on the language and the content of these verses. Jeremiah complains that the nation had alienated itself from God: "They never asked themselves, 'Where is the Lord, who brought us up (אַיֵּה ה׳ המעלה) from the land of Egypt, and led us through (המוליך) the desert (במדבר)? . . . Where is (אַיֵּה) the Lord?' . . . The shepherds (הרועים) rebelled against Me." Employing the same expressions,

Deutero-Isaiah maintains that after their rebellion against God and His transformation into their enemy, they asked the very same questions: "Where is He who brought them up (אַיֵּה המעלה) from the sea along with the shepherd (רֹעֵה) of His flock? Where is (אַיֵּה) He . . . who led them . . . in a desert (מוֹלִיכָם . . . במדבר)?" The two sections feature two identical איה queries and the image of a shepherd (רֹעֵה) (albeit in different contexts): Jer 2:8: "The shepherds [= rulers] rebelled against Me" — v. 11: "along with the shepherd of His flock." (See the introduction, §15.) For another example of Moses in his capacity as a shepherd at the time of the nation's delivery from Egypt, see Ps 77:16-21, and especially the final verse: "You led Your people like a flock of sheep in the care of Moses and Aaron."

[11] *Then they remembered the days of old* — According to the Masoretic vocalization, וַיִּזְכֹּר ("He remembered") refers to God's remembrance: Even as He was transformed into the nation's adversary, He remembered the days long past when He had had a loving relationship with the people (vv. 8b-9). On the basis of the rest of the verse, however, it seems more probable that the subject of the verb is the nation (cf. Kimchi: "Israel in their exile in desperate times remembered the days of old"; see also Ehrlich, *Mikrâ ki-Pheshuṭo,* 3:153), and the Masoretic vocalization should be emended to the plural, וַיִּזְכְּרוּ ("they remembered"). For the same expression with the nation as the addressee, see Deut 32:7: "Remember the days of old"; see also Amos 9:11; Mic 5:1; 7:14; Mal 3:4. Compare, too, the Akkadian interdialectal etymological and semantic cognate *ūmū dārûtu* (*CAD* D:117). The motif of remembrance in connection with the nation's sojourn in Egypt and journey across the desert is taken from the book of Deuteronomy. See Deut 5:15; 7:18; 8:2; 9:7, and the introduction, §13.

Him, who drew out His people — The verb מֹשֶׁה (a *qal* participle from the root משי) denotes retrieval or pulling out from water, and in this context indicates deliverance; cf. 2 Sam 22:17 = Ps 18:17: "He drew me out (יַמְשֵׁנִי) of mighty waters." This verb serves, moreover, as an allusion to the popular etymology of the name "Moses"; cf. Exod 2:10: "She named him Moses (משה), explaining, 'I drew him (מְשִׁיתִהוּ) out of the water.'" If one understands the form as a verb, the clause refers to God drawing Israel from the depths of the sea. According to the Peshitta, however, which reads עבדו ("His servant") instead of MT עמו ("His people"), a variant reading reflected also in some midrashim (see *Tanḥuma, va-Yigash,* 1 [ed. Buber, 1964, 204]; *Yalqut Shimoni, 'Eqev,* 862), משה here is a proper name — Moses (see also v. 12), comparable to Exod 14:31: "They had faith in the Lord and in His servant Moses (משה עבדו)." One would then interpret the verse as the nation's memory of Moses, who was the agent of God's deliverance.

"Where is He who brought them up from the sea" — Similar to the previous stich: Where is God who led Israel through the sea? According to Theodotion,

LXX, Peshitta, and 1QIsa[a], no pronominal suffix is attached to the verb (המעלה, rather than הַמַּעֲלֵם in the MT, which may have resulted from dittography of the following *mem*). According to this reading, the adjacent clause is the direct object of the verb: "Where is He who brought up the shepherd(s) of His flock from the sea?"

"Along with the shepherd of His flock?" — "Regarding this word [shepherd], there is a major disagreement among commentaries and commentators. Some texts write רעה with a *heh* (in the singular), whereas others write it with a *yod* (in the plural), and none of them is able to mount a convincing argument regarding this variance" (Minḥat Shay). For the singular, see, e.g., LXX, Targum, Rashi, Ibn Ezra, Isaiah of Tirani, Joseph Kara, Metzudat David, Luzzatto; cf. too the following midrashim: *Sifre Deuteronomy* 41 (ed. Finkelstein, 86); *Yalqut Shimoni, 'Eqev,* 862; *y. Soṭah* 5:4, 20a; and many medieval Hebrew manuscripts. If read in the singular, the verse should be understood to mean: Where is He who brought them up from the sea, along with Moses, the shepherd of His flock? If, however, one reads the above מעלה without the pronominal suffix, then this second clause should be understood (as just mentioned above) as the direct object: "Where is He who brought up from the sea the shepherd(s) of His flock?" Some interpret "shepherds" as referring to Moses and Aaron (e.g., Kimchi), and others (e.g., Abravanel) as referring to the prophets. On the other hand, there are those who explain את as introducing the subject rather than the object: "the shepherd of His flock" refers to God, who elsewhere is named "Israel's Shepherd" (רֹעֵה ישראל) (Ps 80:2). For this rare syntactical phenomenon of את serving to emphasize the subject, see Neh 9:34 (see GKC §117m).

"Where is He who put within him His holy spirit" — Where is God who conferred His holy spirit (see also v. 10) upon Moses (Ibn Ezra, first commentary; Isaiah of Tirani; Luzzatto)? Or, according to other commentators (Targum; Saadyah Gaon, 139; Rashi; Ibn Ezra's second commentary; Joseph Kaspi), in the midst of His people.

[12] *"Who made His mighty arm march at the right hand of Moses"* — a follow-up on the above query: Where is the Lord, whose mighty arm supported Moses on His journey with Israel? For תפארת ("might"), see 46:13 and the additional references there.

"Who divided the waters before them" — Where is the Lord who divided the Sea of Reeds before the Israelites as they left Egypt? For the splitting (בקע) of the sea, see Exod 14:16, 21; Ps 78:13; Neh 9:11.

"To make for Himself a name everlasting" — to ensure His fame forevermore, as in v. 14: "To make for Yourself a glorious name." For the same idea of "ensuring one's fame" in the context of the splitting of the sea, see Neh 9:10-11: "You made a name for Yourself that endures to this day. You split the sea before them." For the expression שֵׁם עולם ("an everlasting name"), see Isa 56:5; and cf.

the cognate expression in Akkadian: *šumam dāriam/ana dārâti šakānu* ("to establish an everlasting name [= fame]") (*CAD* Š/1:144; Š/3:293).

[13-14] Two similes describing Israel's smooth journey as they passed through the Sea of Reeds and traversed the desert. Compare similarly Jer 31:9: "I will guide them. I will lead them to streams of water, by a level road where they will not stumble."

[13] *"Who led them through the watery depths"* — The prophet's rhetorical query continues: "Where is God who guided Israel through the unfathomable depths (תהֹמות) of the Sea of Reeds?" Compare in this same context of the splitting of the sea, Ps 106:9: "He led them through the depths (תהֹמות) as through a wilderness." In light of this common image, perhaps the division of this verse according to the MT should be reconsidered and the pausal accent moved from תהֹמות ("depths") to במדבר ("in a desert"): "Who led them through the depths like a horse in the desert."

"Like a horse in a desert without stumbling" — Where is God, who guided Israel as smoothly as a horse on the flat plain of the desert? If the first words of this clause are read as part of the previous clause, as just suggested, then the final words of this verse, לא יִכָּשֵׁלוּ ("so they did not stumble"), should be read with the beginning of v. 14.

[14] *"Like cattle descending into the plain?"* — Where is the Lord who guided the nation "carefully and slowly" (Ibn Ezra), like an animal descending to a valley, "a flat land with no obstacles" (Rashi)? For the expression ירד ב- ("to descend"), see 1 Sam 9:27; Ps 104:8. The simile, which begins with the *kaph* of comparison (v. 13), concludes with: "Thus (כן) did you shepherd. . . ." If one accepts the suggestion above concerning the redivision of the verses, then here the translation would be: "like cattle descending into the plain without stumbling."

The spirit of the Lord gave them rest/guided them — According to the Masoretic vocalization of the verb, תְּנִיחֶנּוּ, *hiph'il* from the root נוח ("to rest"), God gave the nation respite from their enemies (Kimchi); or, alternatively, God brought them to a place of rest, מנוחה (see Deut 12:9; Ps 95:11). In this context, however, some prefer the vocalization תַּנְחֶנּוּ, *hiph'il* from the root נחי ("to lead, guide"), which would be parallel to the other verbs in this and the two preceding verses: נהגת (immediately below), מוליך, and מוליכָם (vv. 12, 13), i.e., the spirit of the Lord guided the nation (cf. LXX, Vulgate, and Targum, דַּבְּרִינוּן ["He guided them"]; Rashi; Ibn Ezra; Kimchi [second commentary]; Tur-Sinai, *Peshuṭo shel Miqra*, III/1:149). For the employment of this verb in similar contexts, see Exod 15:13; 32:34. (For another example of the confusion between these two roots [נחי and נוח], see Isa 57:18.) The preferable reading here, however, is תַּנְחֵם, "[The spirit of the Lord] guided them"; see Ps 67:5: "You guide [תנחם] the nations of the earth.") Compare also Ibn Ezra's bold suggestion:

"תניחנו is used instead of תנחם," but he quickly tempers it by adding: "And the correct way of understanding the term is that תניחנו alludes to Moses" (v. 11). (For this graphic phenomenon [the division of the *mem* into a *nun* and a *waw*], cf. v. 7, and R. Weiss, "On Ligatures in the Bible.") For the verb נחי, along with the description of the exodus from Egypt as shepherding, see Ps 77:21: "You led (נחית) Your people like a flock in the care of Moses and Aaron"; cf. also Exod 13:14, 21; 15:13; Ps 143:10: Neh 9:12, 19. The expression רוח ה׳ replaces רוח קדשו, which appears twice in vv. 10, 11.

Thus did You shepherd Your people — From this point forth, up to the end of the chapter, the prophet addresses God in the second-person. The term כן ("thus") concludes the simile that began in v. 14. For the correlates כ . . . כן, see 1 Sam 25:25; Ps 48:11. The verb נהג alludes to the guiding of sheep, as in Ps 78:52: "He led out His people like sheep, drove them (וַיְנַהֲגֵם) like a flock in the wilderness." (In this psalm as well the verb נחה appears in the following v. 53.)

To win for Yourself a glorious name — And thus you established for Yourself a glorious name; cf. v. 12. For the expression שם תפארת, see 1 Chr 29:13.

[15-16] The prophet's plea with God to hasten to the nation's aid is based on Jer 31:20: "Truly, Ephraim is a dear son to Me. . . . That is why My heart yearns (המו מֵעַי) for him. I will receive him back in love (רַחֵם אֲרַחֲמֶנּוּ), declares the Lord." The prophet transforms God's message from a verbal statement to a nominal one: המון מֵעֶיךָ ורחמיך, and instead of "son" in Jeremiah, the prophet here addresses God as "our Father" (v. 16). (See the introduction, §15; Paul, *Divrei Shalom*, 399-416.)

[15] *Look down from heaven! And see* — For the exact same plea, see Ps 80:15. For heaven as the abode of the Divine, see Isa 57:15; 66:1. For other instances of these two imperatives in tandem, see, e.g., Ps 80:15; Lam 1:12; and in the opposite order, Lam 1:11; 2:20. All the above-quoted verses are desperate calls of the oppressed for divine intervention.

From Your holy and glorious height! — Observe the desperate state of Your people from Your majestic heights. זְבֻל, which denotes loftiness, is a loanword from Ugar. *zbl* ("prince"), which is employed as an appellative of the gods, including Baal (*CAT* 1.6.III:9), Yam (*CAT* 1.2.IV:14), Yarikh (*CAT* 1.19.IV:2), and Resheph (*CAT* 1.15.II:6). As opposed to Solomon who, when referring to the Temple, declared: "I have now built for You a stately (זְבֻל) house" (1 Kgs 8:13 = 2 Chr 6:2), the prophet states that God's זְבֻל is in the heavens, as in Deut 26:15: "Look down from Your holy abode, from heaven"; Ps 102:20: "For He looks down from His holy height. The Lord beholds the earth from heaven." The same idea is also expressed in Isa 66:1. God's תפארת is referred to for the third time in this unit, see vv. 12, 14.

Where is Your zeal, Your power — to wage battle against our enemies, as in 42:13, where both קנאה, zeal in battle, and the root גבר also appear together.

For גבורה in the plural, see, e.g., Ps 106:2. The query אַיֵּה ("where") is repeated here for the third time; see v. 11 (twice).

Your yearning, and Your love? — which were conferred on us in the past; cf. v. 7: "For all that the Lord has done for us . . . that He bestowed on us/them according to His mercy and His great love." For המו מֵעַיִם, an expression of deep yearning and intense excitement, see Isa 16:11; Cant 5:4. For the influence of Jeremiah on this clause, see the introduction to vv. 15-16.

Let (them) not be restrained/Do not restrain Yourself! — Your zeal, power, yearning, and love are all being held back and You remain remote. One should read, however, אל יתאפקו, "Let (them) not be held back!"; or אל תתאפק, "Do not hold back!" = "Do not restrain Yourself!" For the verb אפק, see 42:14; 64:11. Instead of אלי ("from me") in the MT, the LXX and Targum render עֲלָנָא ("on us"), a version reflected in *Midrash Sekel Tov* to Gen 43:31 (ed. Buber [Tel Aviv, 1980], 271): אלינו (see also Eliezer of Beaugency).

[16] The nation/prophet attempts to rouse God's compassion by twice addressing Him as "our Father" (אבינו) toward the beginning and end of the verse, forming an enveloping poetic frame.

Surely You are our Father — The verse begins with an emphatic כי: Surely You alone are "our Father" (so too 64:7), and we are "Your children" (see v. 8). Compare Kimchi's comment: "The father will not restrain himself, when it comes to his son, but will immediately show him mercy"; and see Ps 103:13: "As a father has compassion for his children, so the Lord has compassion for those who fear Him." This image was influenced by Jeremiah's prophecy quoted in the introduction to v. 8. For the image of God as Israel's father, see Deut 32:6; Jer 31:9.

Though Abraham does not know us — Abraham, the founder of the nation, is far removed from our present predicament, since he is no longer among the living. Abraham is also mentioned in Isa 41:8; 51:2.

And Israel does not recognize us — Israel, the third of the three patriarchs, is no longer among us and is not here to intercede on our behalf. For the mention of the two patriarchs in tandem, see also Mic 7:20: "You will keep faith with Jacob, love to Abraham." For the MT vocalization יַכִּירָנוּ, with a *qameṣ* instead of a *segol* (Job 7:10), cf. also Isa 66:3; Ps 115:12. (See GKC §60d.) 1QIsa[a] הכירנו (perfect), instead of MT יכירנו (imperfect), which is corroborated by *Yalqut Shimoni, Toldot,* 116, was likely influenced by יְדָעָנוּ in the preceding clause.

You, O Lord, are our Father — The prophet repeats this pronouncement for emphasis.

From of old, Your name is "Our Redeemer" — According to the Masoretic accentuation, the translation would be: "Our Redeemer from of old is Your name." An alternate reading of this clause would be to place the pausal punctuation mark on "Our Redeemer" and connect "from of old" with "Your name" (see the remarks of Luzzatto, who found a manuscript with such a division). For other examples of the Lord as "redeemer" (similar to the familial obligation to redeem relatives), see, e.g., Isa 41:4; 43:14; and many other passages. (See the introduction, §9.) The word עולם ("of old") appears in vv. 9, 12, 19; 64:3, 4; and שֵׁם ("name") is found in vv. 12, 14; 64:1, 6; both terms resonate throughout the unit.

[17-19a] After attributing the people's woes and the destruction of the Temple to God, the prophet offers a supplication on behalf of the nation, God's servants.

[17] *Why, Lord, do You make us stray from Your ways* — Why do You cause us to wander away from you? This grievance is contrasted to God's past guarding and shepherding the people (vv. 12-14), while the verb תעי alludes once more to the image of a flock, as in Jer 50:6: "My people were lost sheep. Their shepherds led them astray (הִתְעוּם)." For a similar complaint against God, see Isa 64:4: "It is because You were angry that we have sinned."

And turn our hearts away from revering You? — Although it is customary to explain the verb קשח (found again only in Job 39:16) as referring to obduracy, some commentators correctly interpreted it as being parallel to the verb in the previous colon, with the meaning "to remove," "to turn away from" (Ibn Ezra; Eliezer of Beaugency; Tur-Sinai, *Job,* 546).

Relent for the sake of Your servants — Cf. Exod 32:12-13: "Turn from Your blazing anger and renounce the plan to punish Your people. Remember Your servants, Abraham, Isaac, and Jacob." For the repetitive use of the plural עבדים ("servants") in the second half of the book (as opposed to the singular עבד in the first half of the book [with the notable exception of 54:17]), see 56:6; 65:8, 9, 13 (three times), 14, 15; 66:14.

The tribes that are Your very own possession! — The sobriquet שבטי נחלתך defines God's special relationship with His nation from their tribal days. For Israel as God's נחלה, see, e.g., Deut 9:26, 29; 1 Kgs 8:51, 53; Mic 7:14, 18; and for the reading in 1QIsa[a], שבט נחלתך (in the singular), see also Jer 10:16; Ps 74:2. Compare a similar plea and supplication in Ps 74:1-2: "Why, O God, do You forever reject us, do You fume in anger at the flock that You tend? Remember the community You made Yours long ago, the very own tribe of Your possession."

[18] For the motif of the destruction of the Sanctuary, see also Isa 64:10.

Why have evildoers afflicted Your holy people — Hebrew לַמִּצְעָר is usually understood to mean a short span of time (Saadyah Gaon, 139; Rashi; Ibn Ezra; Kimchi), i.e., Israel's possession of their sanctuary (mentioned in the following colon) was short-lived, and then they were exiled. Luzzatto and Ehrlich (*Randglossen,* 4:154), however, interpreted the clause to mean: "Our foes controlled Your nation for but a little while." Those who accept the LXX variant,

"Your holy mount" (הר קדשך) (see 57:13; 65:11), instead of MT עם קדשך, explain that Israel's holy mount was possessed by the nation for but a short period of time. In light of the other occurrences of מצער, however, which never have a temporal meaning (see Gen 19:20; Ps 42:7; Job 8:7; 2 Chr 24:24), the following emended reading is preferable: למ(ה) צער(ו) רשעים עם קדשך, "Why have evildoers afflicted Your holy people?" The verb צער is found in Aramaic and Rabbinic Hebrew and means "to afflict, inflict pain." Cf. Targum Yerushalmi to Deut 26:6: וַיְעַנּוּנוּ ("They have oppressed us"), translated as וְצַעֲרוּ יָתְנָא. (See the introduction, §11.)

Our foes trampled Your sanctuary? — For Heb. בסס ("to trample"), see Jer 12:10: "They have destroyed My vineyard, trampled (בֹּססו) My field"; cf. Isa 41:25. The root קדש, which appears in this verse twice, also recurs in vv. 10, 11, 15, and in the continuation of the pericope in 64:9, 10, making it a key term.

[19a] A complaint lodged against God for His ostensible abandonment of the nation.

We have become as though You never ruled us — Read בנו (first-person plural) with the LXX, instead of the MT בם (third-person plural) (Ibn Ganaḥ, *Sefer ha-Riqmah*, 328, lines 21-22). For this type of ligature (the conflation of the *waw* and the *nun* to form a final *mem*), cf. also v. 7: גמלם instead of גמלנו, and, conversely, v. 14: תניחנו for תנחם.

As though Your name was never attached to us — We have become like a nation, totally alien to you, as though we were never Your people. Read עלינו ("on us") instead of עליהם ("on them") with the LXX (and see Ibn Ganaḥ, *Sefer ha-Riqmah*, 328, lines 21-22). For the expression נקרא שֵׁם על, which indicates ownership and possession, see 2 Sam 12:28; Isa 4:1; Amos 9:12.

[63:19b-64:3] A bold and desperate cry to God to reveal Himself and to wage a battle of salvation as in bygone days. For depictions of divine revelation accompanied by momentous occurrences in nature in the Bible and the ancient Near East, see S. E. Loewenstamm, "The Trembling of Nature during the Theophany," in *Comparative Studies in Biblical and Ancient Oriental Literatures*, AOAT 204 (Neukirchen-Vluyn, 1980), 173-89; M. Weinfeld, "From the Heavens They Fought," *ErIsr* 14 = *H. L. Ginsberg Jubilee Volume* (1978): 23-30 (Heb.).

[19b] *If You would but rend the heavens and come down* — to aid Your nation. For similar depictions of the Lord's "coming down" from the heavens, see 2 Sam 22:10 = Ps 18:10: "He bent the heavens and came down"; Mic 1:3: "For lo! The Lord is coming forth from His dwelling place. He will come down and stride upon the heights of the earth"; Ps 144:5: "O Lord, bend Your heavens and come down!" For the conjunction לוּא (also with a final *aleph*) meaning "if only!" or "would that!", see also 48:18: "If only (לוּא) you would heed My commandments." Some of the ancient translations, as well as some commentators (e.g., Saadyah Gaon, 140; Luzzatto), interpreted לוא here as a simple negation, which continues the previous two occurrences of לא in this verse. However, the first explanation, an expression of wishful thinking, is preferable.

So that mountains would quake before You — as they did in Your portentous revelations of old. For other instances of mountains quaking at times of revelation, see Exod 19:18: "And the whole mountain trembled violently"; Nah 1:5: "The mountains quaked because of Him"; Hab 3:10: "The mountains see You and writhe"; Ps 18:8: "The foundations of the mountains shook." For similar examples in Mesopotamian sources, specifically of revelations involving Enlil, who is termed "the shaker of mountains" (*CAD* Ḫ:254), see Loewenstamm, "Trembling of Nature." The verb נָזֹלּוּ (a pausal form; cf. 2 Kgs 3:26: יָכֹלּוּ; Isa 34:4: נָגֹלּוּ) is the *niph'al* of זלל, which appears again in 64:2 and in Judg 5:5: "The mountains quaked [read נָזֹלּוּ] before the Lord." Its basic meaning is "to quake and shake" (cf. Arab. *zalzala,* with the same meaning).

Chapter 64

The Masoretic division into chapters is in error here, since 64:1ff. is actually the continuation of 63:7ff. (The correct division exists in the LXX, Vulgate, and Peshitta.) Note the large number of expressions and terms that make up this pericope: 63:7: אזכיר — 64:4: יִזְכְּרוּךָ; 63:12: שֵׁם עולם, 63:14: שֵׁם תפארת, 63:16: מעולם שמך, 63:19: לא נקרא שמך עליהם — 64:1: להודיע שמך, 64:6: קורא שמך; 63:15: הַבֵּט משמים — 64:8: הַבֶּט נא; 63:8: אך עמי המה — 64:8: עמך כֻלָּנוּ; 63:12: זרוע תפארתו, 63:14: תפארת, 63:15: ותפארתך — 64:10: ותפארתנו; 63:10, 11: רוח קדשו, 63:15: מִזְּבֻל קדשך, 63:18: עַם קדשך . . . מקדשך — 64:9: ערי קדשך, 64:10: בית קדשנו; 63:15: מִזְּבֻל קדשך ותפארתך — 64:10: בית קדשנו ותפארתנו; 63:9, 11: ימי עולם, 63:12: שֵׁם עולם, 63:16: מעולם, 63:19: מעולם — 64:3: ומעולם; 63:17: מיראתך — 64:2: נוראות; 63:18: צרינו — 64:1: לצריך; 63:15: התאפקו — 64:11: אֵלֶּה אתאפק; 63:16: כי אתה ה׳ אבינו — 64:7 ועתה ה׳ אבינו אתה; 63:8: עמי — 64:8: עמך; 63:17: מדרכיך — 64:4: בדרכיך; 63:19: ירדת מפניך הרים נָזֹלּוּ — 64:1: מפניך גוים ירגזו, 64:2: ירדת מפניך הרים נָזֹלּוּ. Another point in common is the audacious accusation fingering God as the party responsible for the nation's sins: 63:17: "Why, Lord, do You make us stray from Your ways and turn our hearts away from revering You?" — 64:4: "It is because You are angry that we have sinned."

[1] The direct continuation of the preceding chapter along with the comparison of the Lord's presence to an all-consuming and boiling fire.

As when fire kindles brushwood — The quaking of the mountains when the Lord reveals Himself is compared to the setting of brushwood on fire. The hapax legomenon הֲמָסִים is understood contextually as straw and dry tree branches (Saadyah, 140; Ibn Ganaḥ, *Sefer ha-Shorashim,* 121; Luzzatto; cf. the possible cognate in Arabic, *hašīm(at)* [note the metathesis], denoting "dry branches"). The variant in 1QIsa[a], עמוסים, is either evidence of the general weakening of gutturals (from *ayin* to *heh*), or is related to Arab. *ġamīs,* which denotes thick and tangled undergrowth. For the verb קדח, see 50:11.

And as fire makes water boil — A further simile depicting God's rage as searing flames that cause water to bubble and boil. The *kaph* of comparison from the first hemistich applies here as well. The verb תִּבְעֶה, from the root בעי, denotes here boiling and raising bubbles (in 30:13 it pertains to the swelling of a decayed wall) (Ibn Ganaḥ, *Sefer ha-Shorashim,* 69; Kimchi, *Sefer ha-Shorashim,* 44; Yellin, *Ḥiqrei Miqra,* 85; Luzzatto suggests vocalizing in the *hiphʿil,* תַּבְעֶה, rather than MT *qal,* תִּבְעֶה). The verb also appears in an Aramaic inscription: "Who causes the breath of his nostrils to boil (יבעה)" (Fitzmyer, *Aramaic Inscriptions of Sefîre,* 96, III:2). 1QIsa[a] adds the word לצריכה to this clause after אש, an error caused by the appearance of this term at the end of the following clause.

To make Your name known to Your adversaries — Cf. 2 Chr 6:33: "Thus all the peoples of the earth will know Your name and revere You." The revelation of God to the entire world is a prominent theme in Deutero-Isaiah's prophecy; see, e.g., 45:6: "So that they may know, from east to west, that there is none but Me. I am the Lord and there is none else." Especially important to the prophet is the Lord's famed prowess vis-à-vis His enemies, who malign and blame Him for all of Israel's trials and travails (beginning with their desert journeys and culminating in the destruction of the Temple and their exile), and His supposed inability to save His people in their time of need, as is echoed by Moses himself: Deut 9:28: "Else the land from which You freed us will say, 'It was because the Lord was powerless to bring them into the land that He had promised them, and because He rejected them, that He brought them out to have them die in the wilderness'"; Ezek 20:22: "But I acted for the sake of My name, that it might not be profaned in the sight of the nations among whom they were"; see also Ezek 20:14. For the "Lord's adversaries," see Isa 59:18; 63:18.

So that nations will tremble before You — so that all the nations of the world will quake as You reveal Yourself to them; cf. Exod 15:14: "The people hear; they tremble (ירגזון)"; Joel 2:1: "Let all dwellers of the earth tremble (ירגזו)"; Ps 99:1: "The Lord . . . is king; peoples tremble (ירגזו)." At the sudden appearance of the Lord, mountains quake and people tremble.

[2] Further wonders in the past.

When You did awesome deeds we dared not hope for — Cf. Deut 10:21: "He is your God, who has done for you these marvelous, awesome deeds (הַנּוֹרָאֹת) that you saw with your own eyes"; Ps 106:21-22: "Who performed . . . wondrous deeds in the land of Ham, awesome deeds (נוֹרָאוֹת) at the Sea of Reeds"; see also 2 Sam 7:23; Ps 139:14; 145:6. The verb עשׂי is a key word appearing in three sequential verses beginning here (vv. 2, 3, 4). The negative לא is absent from 1QIsa[a].

You came down and mountains quaked before You — a word-for-word repetition of Isa 63:19. The term מפניך occurs here for the third time and serves as the introduction to the threefold refrain: 63:19: "And mountains quaked before You"; 64:1: "So that nations will tremble before You;" 64:2: "And mountains quaked before You."

[3] The miracles that God performs for those who trust in Him have no precedent. Note the threefold repetition of the negative לא.

Such things had never been heard or noted — Since the dawn of time (מעולם), nothing of this nature has ever been witnessed. For the synonymous pair האזין/שמע, see Isa 1:2; 28:23. There are those who read here לא שמענו, "We have not heard" (as in the LXX), and לא הֶאֱזִינֵנוּ ("We have not noted"). The MT has "They have never heard or heeded."

No eye has seen any god but You, who acts for those who trust in Him — The syntax of this clause is a little tricky, but the basic meaning is quite clear: No mortal eye has ever seen the miracles You have performed for those who await Your salvation. The verb מְחַכֵּה (from the root חכי) is a construct form of the *pi'el* participle; cf. likewise the *qal* participle in Isa 30:18: אשרי כל חוֹכֵי לו ("Happy are all who wait for Him"). The LXX translates: "Our eyes have not seen," which agrees with their version above: "We have not heard."

[4-6] The nation complains that it was the Lord Himself who caused them to sin, since He was angry with them. In other words, in their eyes there is a logical connection between divine anger and human sin.

[4] *Yet you have struck him who would gladly do justice* — a difficult clause that has been interpreted in two different ways: "You have singled out the righteous man and have struck him down." (For the root פגע indicating a fatal blow, see 2 Sam 1:15: "Come over and strike [פְּגַע] him! He struck him down and he died.") Or: "You meet him who rejoices to do what is right."

Who remembers You in Your ways — You have struck down (or, as the alternative translation from the previous clause, "You meet") those who revere You and follow Your path. Perhaps one should understand דרכיך ("Your ways") as a reference to the so-called thirteen divine attributes (Exod 34:6-7; cf. also Num 14:18-19). Note too Moses' similar request to God: "Now, if I have truly gained Your favor, pray let me know Your ways (דְּרָכֶךָ)" (Exod 33:13; see Ibn Balaam [ed. Goshen-Gottstein, 245]; Kimchi; Ehrlich, *Mikrâ ki-Pheshuṭo,* 3:156). Instead of בדרכיך יִזְכְּרוּךָ, the LXX renders: "They remember Your ways." A number of medieval Hebrew manuscripts read יַזְכִּירוּךָ *(hiph'il),* "They would remind You of Your ways" (cf. Tur-Sinai, *Peshuṭo shel Miqra,* III/1:148); or perhaps יזכירוך refers to acclaiming God's praise and glory (Ehrlich, *Mikrâ ki-Pheshuṭo;* idem, *Randglossen,* 4:225), as in Isa 63:7: "I will recount (אזכיר) the kind acts of the Lord, the praises of the Lord."

It is because You are angry that we have sinned — There is a logical and direct connection between the Lord's wrath and the people's sin. Though traditionally this has been interpreted as meaning, "You are wroth at us because we have sinned," Luzzatto's understanding of this clause is preferable: "When You were angry and hid Your face from us, we persisted [in our course] and sinned even more." Thus the destructive circle: The nation's sins bring about God's anger, which, in turn, causes the nation to stubbornly persist in their wayward course. For divine wrath at the time of the destruction and exile, see 47:6; 54:8, 9; 57:16, 17.

Because when You have hidden Yourself, we have acted wickedly/rebelled — another difficult clause to interpret. Some commentators suggest that בהם ("in them") refers to "Your ways" (דרכיך) and explain: If we had remembered or deferred to Your ways, we would have been saved long ago (read מעולם instead of MT עולם, the original *mem* being omitted by haplography — בהם מעולם). Others connect it to the enduring virtue of the righteous that we were saved (thus Targum, Rashi, Ibn Ezra, and Kimchi). However, in light of the first clause, "It is because You are angry that we have sinned," one could also suggest emending the text to בְּהֵעָלֶמְךָ ונרשע/ונפשע ("When You have hidden Yourself, we have acted wickedly/rebelled"). The theme of divine absence reverberates throughout Deutero-Isaiah (e.g., 54:8; 57:17; 59:2) and the Psalter (e.g., Ps 10:1; 13:2; 27:9; 30:8). Only here, however, is there a direct connection between God's hiding His face and the people's sin.

[5] In their confession the nation draws an analogy between their sin and filth, since in biblical thought sin and uncleanness are intertwined, and the sinner is de facto unclean, e.g., Lev 16:16: "Thus he shall purge the shrine of the uncleanness and transgression of the Israelites, whatever their sins"; Ezek 36:17: "O mortal, when the house of Israel dwelt on their own soil, they defiled it with their ways and their deeds. Their ways were in My sight like the uncleanness of a menstruant woman"; Ps 51:4: "Wash me thoroughly of my iniquity, and purify me of my sin"; Lam 1:8-9: "Jerusalem has sinned greatly, therefore she is become as a menstruant woman. . . . Her uncleanness clings to her skirts." Note the repetition of the term כֻּלָּנוּ in this verse and twice more in vv. 7, 8, emphasizing the culpability of the nation as a whole.

We have all become like an unclean thing — because of our sins.

And all our virtues like a soiled rag — The prophet depicts the nation's sin in bold colors: All our good qualities (צִדְקֹתֵינוּ) are like a rag used by women to clean themselves of their menstrual blood. For בגד עִדִּים, see *m. Nid.* 1:1, 7; 2:1; 8:4. Compare also עידון and related terms referring to the menstrual state, e.g., *Gen. Rab.* 48:17 (ed. Theodor-Albeck, 494): "As long as she is young she has her periods, and I, 'I am withered, am I to have enjoyment (עֶדְנָה)?' (Gen 18:12) — (meaning) menstrual cycle (עידונין)." Compare, similarly, Akk. *ulāp lupputi* ("a soiled or stained bandage") and *ulāp dāmi* ("a bloody bandage [covering the genitals]"), i.e., a menstrual bandage (*CAD*, U/W: 71). For similar imagery cf. Ezek 36:17: "Their ways were in my sight like the uncleanness of a menstruant woman."

We are all withering like leaves — Vocalize: וַנִּבֹּל, a *qal* stem from the root נבל, "to wither, wilt" (1QIsa[a] ונבולה); cf. 1:30: "For you shall be like a terebinth withered (נֹבֶלֶת) of leaf"; 34:4: "Like a leaf withering (יִבּוֹל כִּנְבוֹל) on the vine"; 40:7, 8: "Grass withers, flowers fade (נָבֵל)" (rather than the MT vocalization וַנָּבֶל, a *hiph'il* stem from the root בלל, "to confuse"). Alternatively, Yalon (*Ḥiqrei Lashon*, 48) proposes that the verb is a *qal* stem from the root אבל, which is a synonym of the more common נבל (cf. 24:4: "The earth is withered [אבלה] and wilts [נבלה]; the world languishes and wilts [נבלה]"), with the elision of the initial *aleph*, similar to וַיָּרֶב (= ויארב) בנחל in 1 Sam 15:5. Compare its Akkadian etymological and semantic cognate, *abālu*, "to dry up, dry out" (*CAD* A/1:29-31).

And our iniquities, like a wind, carry us off — Our sins sweep us away as a driven leaf — an allusion to the widespread Israelite Diaspora. Read here the plural עֲוֹנֵינוּ (cf. LXX and 1QIsa[a] ועוונותינו), instead of the singular עֲוֹנֵנוּ in the MT; cf. Minḥat Shay and Kimchi: "The *yod* is missing from the text."

[6] The people despair as they blame God for their ignominy.

Yet no one invokes Your name — In spite of all this, no one beseeches You in prayer. For the expression קרא בשם referring to worship, see, e.g., Gen 12:8; 13:4. Compare also the cognate expression in Akkadian, *šumam nabû* ("to call one's name"), i.e., "to invoke a deity" (*CAD* N/1:35).

Or rouses himself to cling to You — Nor does anyone awake from a stupor to hold fast to You. For the expression החזיק ב- ("to cling to"), see Isa 56:2: "The man who holds fast to it (יחזיק בה)"; Job 27:6: "I will hold fast to my righteousness (בצדקתי החזקתי)."

For You have hidden Your face from us — See Isa 54:8: "For a moment, I hid My face from you"; 59:2: "Your sins have made Him turn His face away"; cf. 57:17. This punishment of concealment, which indicates God's reticence in coming to the nation's aid in times of trouble, is common throughout the Bible, e.g., Deut 32:20; Isa 8:17; Ezek 39:23; Ps 102:3. The Lord's present concealment contrasts with His miracles of yesteryear, as in Isa 63:9: "His presence delivered them (פניו הושיעם)."

And delivered us (to our enemies) *because of our iniquities* — Instead of וַתְּמוּגֵנוּ, from the root מוג, "to melt" (see Job 30:22), i.e., "You make us melt away," one should read וַתְּמַגְּנֵנוּ, from the root מגן, "to deliver" (cf. Targum וּמְסַרְתַּנָא, "You handed us over"; LXX; Peshitta; and Saadyah Gaon, 140). See Gen 14:20: "Who has delivered (מִגֵּן) your foes into your hands"; Hos 11:8: "How can I give you up, O Ephraim? How surrender you (אֲמַגֶּנְךָ), O Israel?" According to Kutscher, the reading in 1QIsa[a], ותמגדנו, from the root מגד (the etymological and semantic equivalent of *mgd* in Arabic and Palmyrene Aramaic, denoting the giving of a gift or giving generously; cf. מֶגֶד, Deut 33:13-16; Cant 4:13, 16; 7:14; and מִגְדָּנֹת, Gen 24:53; Ezra 1:6; 2 Chr 21:3; 32:23; as well as Aram. מגדנין and Syr. *mgda/mgdwna,* which also signify precious presents), is to be preferred over the MT (*Language and Linguistic Background,* 252). The two variants, however, ultimately have the same meaning in the present context. For a similar idea, see Isa 50:1: "You were sold for your sins." For ביד as an indication of "cause," see Job 8:4: "He dispatched them for (ביד) their transgressions." Likewise, cf. the Akkadian cognate equivalent *ina qāti* ("as a result of, because") (*CAD* Q:193).

[7-11] From here until the end of the chapter the prophet voices the people's complaints and pleads for mercy on their behalf, all the while expressing his belief in God's munificence. This same connection, which conceives of God as both Creator and Father, is found in Deut 32:6: "Is not He the Father who created you, fashioned you, and made you endure?" (See the introduction, §9.)

[7] *But now, O Lord, You are our Father* — Nonetheless (the initial *waw* is adversative), we turn to You because You are our progenitor (see Isa 63:16; and cf. 45:10); "and thus it is fitting that you pity us and show us clemency" (Luzzatto), "since a father does not forsake his child" (Kimchi). 1QIsa[a] has ואתה instead of MT ועתה.

We are the clay, and You are the Potter — We were formed from wet clay, and You are the craftsman who shaped us; cf. 45:9: "Shall the clay say to the potter, 'What are you doing'?"; Jer 18:6: "Just like clay in the hands of the potter, so are you in My hands, O House of Israel!" For the term יצר ("potter") in cognate languages, see Isa 45:9.

We are all the work of Your hands — We are all Your handiwork (cf. 45:11; 60:21), and You should thus show us pity and protect us, as a potter cares for his handiwork; cf. Job 10:9: "Remember that You fashioned me like clay. Will You then turn me back into dust?" 1QIsa[a] ידיכה (plural) is corroborated by the LXX, Vulgate, and Peshitta, instead of the singular ידך in the MT. For the semantic and etymological equivalents in Akkadian, see *binût qātī* (*CAD* B:244); *epšet qātī* (*CAD* E:241).

[8] *Be not implacably angry, O Lord* — Do not be overly angry with us. The same phrase and wording appears in Lam 5:22. The emphatic עד מאד recurs also at the conclusion of the chapter; see Gen 27:33, 34; Ps 38:9. Both the LXX and Targum add בָּנָא ("at us") following the verb.

Do not remember iniquity forever — The prophet continues his supplication and beseeches God not to recall the nation's sins. (The LXX, one manuscript of the Vulgate, and the Peshitta read עֲוֹנֵינוּ, "our sins"; see vv. 5, 6.) For the expression זכר עָוֹן, see Jer 14:10; Hos 8:13; 9:9. The first two hemistichs of this verse form a chiasm.

Look, we are Your people, all of us! — Cf. Isa 63:8: "Surely they are My people." This is the fourth (and final) occurrence of כֻּלָּנוּ ("us all"), which also appeared at the conclusion of v. 7 (and see v. 5, twice). The word הן at the beginning of the clause is emphatic.

[9] In order to waken God's mercy, the prophet describes the desolate state the land is in following the exile and destruction. Note the similarity to Jeremiah's warnings, 4:27: "The whole land shall be desolate"; 9:10: "And I will make the towns of Judah a desolation." Compare also the sullen picture painted by Neh 2:17: "Jerusalem lies in ruins and its gates are destroyed by fire."

Your holy cities have become a desert — "Your holy cities" (ערי קדשך, only here in the plural) are desolate like the wilderness.

Zion has become a desert — The LXX and 1QIsa[a] read כמדבר ("like a desert").

Jerusalem, a desolation — Jerusalem has become a deserted and ruined city (see Isa 62:4). For the synonymous pair שממה/מדבר, see Jer 12:10: "They have made My delightful field a desolate wilderness (לְמִדבר שממה)." Instead of MT שממה, 1QIs[a] has שוממה (cf. Isa 49:8, 19; 54:1). For the parallel triad ירושלם/ציון/ערי (יהודה) ("cities [of Judah]/Zion/Jerusalem") in reverse order, see 40:9.

[10] Following a description of Zion's devastation, the prophet depicts the state of the ruined Temple (cf. 63:18; Jer 22:5).

Our holy Temple, our glory — our sanctuary, which was our pride and joy; cf. Isa 60:7: "And I will add glory to My glorious (תפארתי) House." For תפארת ("glory") as a reference to the Temple, see also Lam 2:1: "He cast down from heaven to earth the glory of Israel."

Where our fathers praised You — In which our ancestors sung Your praises. For אשר meaning "where, in which," see Gen 39:20: "The place where (אשר) the king's prisoners were confined."

Has been consumed by fire — Cf. Isa 9:4: "Have been fed to the flames, devoured by fire." For the Aramaic cognate equivalent to Hebrew לשׂרפת אש, see Dan 7:11: לִיקֵדַת אֶשָּׁא.

And all that was dear to us is ruined — All that was precious to us (מַחֲמַדֵּינוּ) is destroyed and lies in rubble; cf. Lam 1:10: "The foe has laid hands on everything dear to her (מַחֲמַדֶּיהָ)"; cf. also 1:7. The term מחמד also serves as a reference to the Temple (cf. Ezek 24:21: "I am going to desecrate My sanctuary . . . the delight [מחמד] of your eyes") and may refer to the Temple treasures; cf. Joel 4:5: "And you have carried off My precious treasures (מחמדי) to your palaces" (see also 2 Chr 36:19). Instead of MT לְחָרְבָּה, Symmachus reads לחרפה ("for mockery"); cf. Jer 24:9; 49:13. Some medieval Hebrew manuscripts read מחמדנו in the singular, instead of the MT plural, agreeing with the verb היה in the singular.

[11] At the end of this heartrending soliloquy, the prophet concludes with a bold but forlorn cry for divine salvation.

At such things will You restrain Yourself, O Lord — After such calamities, will You continue to hold back and not come to our aid? See Isa 63:15.

Will You stand idly by and torment us implacably? — At the sight of such misfortune, will You remain aloof and leave us in such agony? For the meaning of the verb **חשי**, see 42:14; 57:11; 62:1; 65:6. For the *pi'el* of **עני** ("to afflict, torment"), see 60:14; and for the expression **עד מאד**, see v. 8 above.

Chapter 65

This chapter functions as a response to the dirge-confession of the previous unit (63:7–64:11). The prophet castigates the nation and declares that the delay in deliverance is not a sign of divine impotence, but rather the result of the nation's refusal to heed God's call and the foul cultic practices in which they choose to engage (vv. 1-7; cf. 59:1ff.). The national schism between those who have abandoned the Lord, who are threatened with dire consequences and potent curses, and those who serve Him, who shall possess the bounty of the land in a time of unimagined divine munificence, is emphasized here. The chapter is connected to the previous unit by multiple terms and expressions:

Chapter 63:7–64:11	**Chapter 65**
63:19: לא נקרא שמך עליהם; 64:6: ואין קורא בשמך	65:1: אל גוי לא קֹרָא בשמי; 65:12: קראתי; 65:15: יקרא
63:14; 64:8: עמך	65:2: עם; 65:3: העם; 65:10: לעמי; 65:18: עמה; 65:19: בעמי; 65:22: עמי
63:10, 11: רוח קדשו; 64:9: ערי קדשך; 64:10: בית קדשנו	65:5: כי קדשתיך; 65:11, 25: הר קדשי
64:10: לשׂרפת אש	65:5: אש יֹקֶדֶת
64:11: תֶּחֱשֶׁה	65:6: לא אֶחֱשֶׁה
64:5: וַעֲוֹנֵנוּ; 64:6: עֲוֹנֵינוּ; 64:8: עָוֹן; 64:10: אֲבֹתֵינוּ	65:7: עֲוֹנֹתֵיכֶם וַעֲוֹנֹת אבותיכם
63:18: יָרְשׁוּ	65:9: יורש . . . וִירֵשׁוּהָ

Chapter 63:7–64:11	Chapter 65
64:6: כי הִסתרת פניך ממנו	65:16: וכי נִסתרו מעיני
63:7: אזכיר; 64:4: יִזְכרוך	65:17: ולא תִזָּכרנה הרִאשֹׁנות
64:4: שָׂשׂ	65:18: שׂישׂו . . . משׂושׂ; 65:19: שׂשׂתי
64:8: עד מאד . . . לעד; 64:11: עד מאד	65:18: עדי עד
64:7: ומעשה ידך	65:22: ומעשה ידיהם

The chapter is replete with key terms that reverberate throughout: דרשׁ (vv. 1, 10); קטר (vv. 3, 7); אכל (vv. 4, 13, 21, 22, 25); חיקם (vv. 6, 7); רִאשֹׁנה (v. 7), רִאשֹׁנות (vv. 16, 17); עבדַי (vv. 8, 9, 13 [three times], 14), עבדיו (v. 15); השחית (vv. 8, 25); הָרָי (v. 9), הר קדשׁי (vv. 11, 25); בחירי (plural, vv. 9, 22); בָּקָר (vv. 10, 25); הָרַע (v. 12), יָרֵעוּ (v. 25); שׂבע (vv. 15, 16 [twice]); בורא (vv, 17, 18); גיל (vv. 18 [twice], 19); שׂישׂ (vv. 18, 19); זֶרַע (vv. 9, 23). Also characterizing this chapter are many words and expressions repeated in the very same verse: שִׁלמתי (v. 6), עֲוֹנות (v. 7), ירשׁ (v. 9), שֵׁם (v. 15), שׂבע (v. 16), גיל (v. 18), בורא (v. 18), בן מאה שנה (v. 20), ימים . . . ימיו (v. 20); cf. also v. 12: יען קראתי ולא עניתם דברתי ולא שמעתם — v. 24: והיה טרם יקראו ואני אֶעֱנֶה עוד הם מדברים ואני אשמע.

Note, moreover, the relative abundance of terminology this chapter has in common with chap. 1, which, together with chap. 66, envelop the entire book of Isaiah with a literary frame:

Chapter 1	Chapter 65
v. 17: דִּרְשׁוּ	v. 1: נדרשׁתי; v. 10: דְרָשׁוני
v. 12: בִקֵּשׁ	v. 1: בִקְשֻׁנִי
v. 15: ובפָרִשְׂכֶם כפיכם	v. 2: פֵּרַשְׂתִּי יָדַי
v. 4: עם; v. 10: עם עֲמֹרָה	v. 2: עם; v. 3: העם; v. 10: לעמי; v. 19: בעמי; v. 22: עמי
v. 5: סָרָה; v. 23: סוררים	v. 2: סורר
v. 11: זבחיכם; v. 29: מהגַּנות; v. 30: וּכְגַנָּה	v. 3: זבחים בַּגַּנות
v. 13: קְטֹרֶת	v. 3: מְקטרים; v. 7: קִטרו
v. 8: נצורה	v. 4: ובנצורים

Chapter 1	**Chapter 65**
v. 7: אֹכְלִים; v. 19: תאכלו; v. 20: תְּאֻכְּלוּ	v. 4: האֹכלים; v. 13: יאכלו; v. 21: ואכלו; v. 22: יאכל; v. 25: יאכל
v. 4: עָוֹן	v. 7: עֲוֹנֹתֵיכֶם וַעֲוֹנֹת
v. 9: לולי ה׳ צבאות הותיר לנו שׂריד	v. 8: לבלתי השחית הכל
v. 4: זֶרַע	v. 9: זֶרַע; v. 23: זֶרַע
v. 4: עזבו את ה׳; v. 28: ועֹזבי ה׳	v. 11: עֹזבי ה׳
v. 20: חֶרֶב; v. 15: אינני שמע; v. 19: ושמעתם	v. 12: לחֶרֶב . . . ולא שמעתם; v. 19: ולא ישמע; v. 24: ואני אשמע
v. 11: לא חפצתי; v. 29: אשר בחרתם	v. 12: ובאשר לא חפצתי בחרתם
v. 29: כי יֵבֹשׁוּ	v. 13: ואתם תֵּבֹשׁוּ
v. 19: טוּב (הארץ)	v. 14: מטוּב (לב)
v. 4: חטא; v. 18: חטאיכם	v. 20: והחוטא

(See J. L. Liebreich, "The Completion of the Book of Isaiah," *JQR* 46 [1955-56]: 259-77; 47 [1956-57]: 114-38; M. A. Sweeney, "Prophetic Exegesis in Isaiah 65–66," in C. C. Broyles and C. A. Evans, eds., *Writing and Reading the Scroll of Isaiah: Studies of an Interpretive Tradition,* 2 vols., VTSup 70 [Leiden, 1997], 1:455-74.)

[1-7] The Lord severely castigates the nation for their refusal to seek Him and for their zealous pursuit of foreign cults and threatens to respond in kind by wreaking revenge upon His disloyal people. For additional accusations, see v. 12; 58:9; 64:6.

[1-3] God vents His frustration in a first-person soliloquy and accuses the nation of extreme provocation. Cf. 50:2: "Why, when I came, was there no one there? Why when I called did no one respond?" The terminology of these first verses contrasts directly with 1:12, 15: "That you come to appear before Me (פָּנָי) — Who asked that of you (בקשׁ . . . מִיֶּדכם)? . . . And when you lift up your hands (וּבְפָרִשְׂכֶם כפיכם), I will turn My eyes away from you. Though you pray at length, I will not listen." Note the threefold repetition of לא(לְ) in vv. 1-2. (See the introduction, §14.)

[1] *I was there to be sought by those who did not ask Me* — In the normal run of days the people would go to the prophet to seek instruction regarding God's will (see, e.g., Exod 18:15; Ezek 20:1). Here, however, matters are reversed:

Although I have been ready and willing to respond to the nation, they have not sought Me. The verb נדרשתי is a "tolerative" *niph'al* (GKC §51c), see Ezek 14:3. 1QIsa[a] ללוא שאלוני (corroborated by Targum לְדְלָא שְׁאִילוּ מִן קֳדָמַי; cf. also the LXX and Peshitta), provides further emphasis to the MT: "to those who did not ask Me." As is common in biblical poesy, however, the implied pronominal suffix is based on its subsequent appearance in the adjacent hemistich, בִקְשֻׁנִי ("seek Me").

I was to be found by those who did not seek Me — Although I was present and would have responded had they beckoned Me, they did not seek Me; cf. Ps 37:36. For the sequence of verbs, דרש . . . מצא . . . בקש, see also Jer 29:13; Zeph 1:6. The verb נמצאתי is another example of a "tolerative" *niph'al*.

I said, "Here I am, here I am" — God's presence is emphasized by the repetitive doubling of הנני. (See the introduction, §10.A.1.) For this divine response, see also Isa 52:6; 58:9.

To a nation that did not invoke My name — that does not adhere by My precepts. The archaic *qal* passive form of the verb קֹרָא (see also 48:8, 12; 58:12; 61:3; 62:2), which is parallel to the *niph'al* נקרא (see 63:19), does not fit the present context and should be vocalized as either a *qal* participle (קֹרֵא) (64:6) or a *qal* perfect (קָרָא); cf. the active forms in the ancient translations (Targum, LXX, Vulgate, Peshitta) and many of the medieval Hebrew manuscripts.

[2] *I constantly spread out My hands* — I begged for your audience incessantly. For the expression פרשׂ ידים, see Ps 143:6; Lam 1:17. However, in marked contrast with the other verses, which speak of human supplication vis-à-vis the Deity, here, paradoxically, the Deity is begging for the attention of inattentive humans. For the synonymous expression פרשׂ כַּפַּיִם, see Exod 9:29 and Isa 1:15, which refer similarly to human supplication of the divine. Compare also the semantic cognate in Akkadian with the same meaning: *qātam tarāṣu,* "to stretch out one's hands" (*CAD* T:211), and its parallel in Ps 88:10: שִׁטַּחְתִּי אליך כפי. The *pi'el* of the verb פרשׂ indicates frequency and is further reinforced by the addition of כל היום ("all day"), which is parallel to תמיד ("continually") in the following verse. For the combination of כל היום and תמיד, see Isa 51:13; 62:6.

To a disloyal people — who rebel against Me. For סורר, see Deut 21:18, 20; Jer 5:23; Ps 78:8. 1QIsa[a] סורה was most likely influenced by the vocalization of the second component of the common hendiadys סורֵר ומורֶה (appearing in the verses cited above); note that in the LXX the second component, מורה, was added to the translation. Compare the Akkadian cognates *sarru,* "criminally fraudulent" (*CAD* S:180-84); *sarrūtu,* "falseness, treachery" (*CAD* S:185), and *sartu* "fraud, misdeed, criminal act" (*CAD* S:186-88).

Who walk the way that is not good, following their own designs — They carry through their own nefarious plans, as opposed to Isa 48:17: "I the Lord am your God . . . guiding you in the way you should go." For the expression

הלך דרך ("to walk on a path") without the prepositional particle ב, see 35:8; and for הלך אחר ("to follow/walk after"), see Deut 13:3, 5.

[3-4] A sequence of four participles, followed by a finite verb and a nominal phrase delineating the forbidden cults practiced routinely by the nation, which in turn provoke God's wrath. The motif of divine provocation is another sign of the Deuteronomic/Deuteronomistic influence on our prophet; cf. Deut 4:25; 9:18; 31:29; 32:16; 1 Kgs 16:13, 26, 33; 2 Kgs 17:11. (See the introduction, §13.)

[3] *The people who provoke My anger continually to My very face* — For the expression על פני indicating opposition and hostility, see Jer 6:7; Job 1:11.

Offering sacrifices in gardens — They (in the MT the pronoun is implied in the verb, whereas the LXX and 1QIsa[a] add המה) make sacrificial offerings in their sacred gardens. For גַּנּוֹת ("gardens/groves") as a locus of the popular cult, see Isa 66:17: "Those who sanctify and purify themselves to enter the gardens"; 1:29: "And you shall be confounded because of the gardens you coveted." It should be noted that in Mesopotamia sacrifices were offered in gardens and orchards (*CAD* K:414-15). For the cultic significance of these gardens, see I. Cornelius, "The Garden in the Iconography of the Ancient Near East: A Study of Related Material from Egypt," *Journal of Semitics* 1 (1989): 204-28, esp. 206-12; D. J. Wiseman, "Mesopotamian Gardens," *Anatolian Studies* 33 (1983): 137-44; J.-J. Glassner, "À propos des jardins mésopotamiens," in R. Gyselen, ed., *Jardins d'Orient,* Res Orientales 3 (Paris, 1991), 9-17, esp. 11, 15-16.

Some commentators suggest reading here גַּגּוֹת ("rooftops") instead of MT גַּנּוֹת ("gardens"), as in Jer 19:13: "On the roofs of which burnt offerings were made"; Jer 32:29: "With the houses on whose roofs burnt sacrifices have been made"; Zeph 1:5: "And those who bow down on the roofs to the host of heaven." Ritual sacrifice on rooftops was also common in Mesopotamia (*AHw* 3:1434-35, 4b). Compare, e.g., the Gilgamesh Epic III.ii:7-8: "[The goddess Ninsun] c[limbed the stairs], mounted to the parapet, ascended the [*roof*], to Shamash offered incense. The smoke-offering set up, to Shamash she raised her hands" (*ANET,* 81). If, however, the prophet had in mind sacrifices on the rooftops, and not in gardens or orchards, the governing preposition would have been על ("on") rather than ב ("in").

Burning incense on brick altars — They offer incense on altars constructed of bricks (Akk. *libittu,* "brick," can also refer to the table used in this ritual; see *CAD* L:177-78; and for the ritual of burning of incense to the Mesopotamian gods, see *CAD* Q:324-25). Rabbinic literature may allude to this foreign ritual: "An Israelite who props up a brick (לבנה) in order to prostrate himself before the Lord" (*b. ʿAbod. Zar.* 46a). For the verb pair קטר/זבח ("to sacrifice/to burn incense"), see 1 Kgs 22:44; Hos 4:13; 11:2. The variant version in 1QIsa[a], וינקו ידים על האבנים, is contextually obscure. Perhaps the reference here is to sexually explicit acts. For יד ("penis"), see Isa 57:8 and the references there; for אבנים in a sexual context, cf. Eccl 3:5.

[4] *Sitting inside tombs* — They sit for vigils at burial sites so that they may inquire of the dead, a practice explicitly forbidden in Deut 18:11. Residing in tombs may also be connected to the practice of incubation, which, according to popular belief, would induce divine revelation. Note too the addendum in the LXX, "for dreams," which also alludes to this practice.

And passing the night in between the rocks — a similar ritual described in different terms. They spend the night in hidden nooks and crannies in order to communicate with the dead or with the Deity. There is some disagreement among commentators regarding the exact meaning of נְצוּרִים. It is usually understood to mean "secret places" (cf. its Akkadian cognate *niṣirtu* [*CAD* N/2:276]), where the dead are interred. According to Ibn Ganaḥ (*Sefer ha-Shorashim,* 316), Kimchi, and Luzzatto, however, the reference is to abandoned or ruined places. More likely is the proposed division of ובנצורים into two separate words: ובין צורים ("and between rocks"). For a burial chamber carved in the bed of a rock, cf. the eighth-century BCE Hebrew inscription from the Siloam village in Jerusalem: חדר בכתף הצר(ח), "a (burial) chamber at the side of the grave" (see Aḥituv, *Ha-Ketav veha-Miktav,* 48). 1QIsa[a] ובנצירים may be interpreted as the plural of נֵצֶר, which, according to Isa 14:19, refers to a cadaver, and this, in turn, would explain the Targum's translation: "They reside with human cadavers." Note the literary chiasm formed by the two initial hemistichs.

Eating the flesh of swine — a practice explicitly forbidden by pentateuchal laws (Lev 11:7; Deut 14:8) and also mentioned in Isa 66:3, 17. For the connection between the sacrifice of pigs (which were considered abhorrent animals in the Semitic, Hittite, and Egyptian milieux) and the ritual worship of netherworld gods, see J. Milgrom, *Leviticus 1–16,* AB 3 (New York, 1991), 650-52; J. C. Moyer, "Hittite and Israelite Cultic Practices: A Selected Comparison," in W. W. Hallo et al., eds., *Scripture in Context,* 2: *More Essays on the Comparative Method* (Winona Lake, Ind., 1983), 19-38, esp. 31-33; R. de Vaux, "The Sacrifice of Pigs in Palestine and in the Ancient East," in *The Bible and the Ancient Near East* (Garden City, N.Y., 1971), 252-69.

With broth of unclean things in their bowls — The Qere ומרק ("broth"), rather than the Ketib ופרק ("piece [of meat]"), is also the reading of the Targum, LXX, Vulgate, and 1QIsa[a]. The noun פִּגֻּלִים refers to unclean or ritually forbidden animals (Ezek 4:14) and to sacrifices eaten after the three prescribed days, a sin for which there is decreed divine punishment (see Lev 7:18; 19:7). The Targum (בְּמָנֵיהוֹן), Vulgate, and 1QIsa[a] (בכליהמה) add the preposition *beth* to the MT.

[5] Until this point the cultic sins of the nation were described. The

prophet now turns to other manifestations of the national schism. The meaning of this verse, replete with ritual terminology (קרב [Exod 40:14; Lev 9:7], נגשׁ, and קדשׁ), is not entirely clear.

Who say, "Keep your distance!" — Stay where you are! Keep your distance from us! Cf. Targum רְחַק לְהָלְאָה.

"Don't come close to me!" — Instead of the MT, אַל תִּגַּשׁ בִּי, which denotes forbidden approach (for the expression: נגשׁ ב- in the *qal*, see Job 41:8; and in the *niph'al*, Amos 9:13), 1QIsa[a] has אל תגע בי ("Don't touch me") — a variant reading that appears in later rabbinic sources (e.g., *y. Hor.* 2:5, 46d; *Yalqut Shimoni, Metzora'*, §568), in medieval Hebrew manuscripts, and in the commentaries of Rashi, Joseph Kara, and Eliezer of Beaugency. The verb נגשׁ, however, may also denote "touch"; see Yalon, *Ḥiqrei Lashon*, 24-26.

"For I am too sacred for you" — Many commentators interpret קְדַשְׁתִּיךָ as an intransitive verb expressing a "holier than thou" idea (cf. Targum אֲרֵי אֲנָא דְכֵינָא מִנָךְ, "for I am purer than you"; Saadyah, 141; Rashi; Ibn Ezra; Kimchi). For an intransitive verb with a pronominal suffix, see GKC §117c. For other occurrences of the verb קדשׁ in the *qal*, cf. Exod 29:21, 37; Hag 2:12. If revocalized in the *pi'el*, קִדַּשְׁתִּיךָ, however, it would mean, "I would render you consecrated." According to this suggestion, the nation believed in the transference of holiness from one individual to another, and thus the warning not to come close or touch.

Such things make My anger smoke — an elliptical phrase in which the verbal element is missing. "Smoking nostrils" (עשׁן באף) is an idiom expressing the full venting of God's anger; see 2 Sam 22:9 (= Ps 18:9): "Smoke went up from His nostrils, from His mouth came devouring fire"; cf. Ps 74:1. According to A. Geiger, אלה ("such things") is likely a scribal emendation substituted for עלה ("to go up, ascend"), which may have been seen as too anthropomorphic (*The Bible and Its Translations* [Jerusalem, 1949], 211 [Heb.]).

A fire blazing all day long — The fire of ire blazes within Me constantly; cf. Deut 32:22: "For a fire has flared in My wrath and burned to the bottom of Sheol." The expression "all day long" appears also in v. 2; and for אשׁ יֹקֶדֶת ("a blazing fire"), cf. Lev 6:6. See also the comments to Isa 64:10.

[6-7] God decides to restrain Himself no longer, and finally to punish the people for their sins and for their fathers' sins. The castigation in Jer 16:18, which threatened the people with "double trouble," a twofold punishment for their sins: "I will pay them in full — nay, doubly for their iniquity and their sins," left its indelible mark on the present verses. (See the introduction, §15.) Deutero-Isaiah, however, split the pertinent phrase borrowed from Jeremiah into two component parts: the first, וְשִׁלַּמְתִּי ("I will pay"), appears in v. 6; and the second, רִאשֹׁנָה ("in full"), in v. 7. (For another example of an expression from Jeremiah divided in two, see 40:10.) Note that the expression שלם אל/על חיק ("to repay sins into one's bosom") appears again only in Jer 32:18.

[6] *See, this is recorded before Me* — All sins are recorded in the divine ledger. For such divine bookkeeping, see Paul, *Divrei Shalom*, 59-70.

I will not stand idly by — I shall no longer restrain Myself. For the meaning of the verb חשי, see Isa 42:14; 57:11; 62:1, 6; 64:11.

But will repay — I shall exact My price from them and repay them their just deserts. The perfect tense (שִׁלַּמְתִּי) expresses the immediacy of God's intention as though it has already been executed; cf. Gen 23:13.

Repay into their bosom — The repetition of the verb שלמתי, "I shall repay" (there are those who claim that this is an error in dittography, and indeed the second occurrence of the verb is not found in the LXX), serves to emphasize God's resolution. According to Luzzatto, the expression שלם על חֵיק is to be understood as: "He repays their sins into their very bosoms; fittingly, since it is there that their money would be placed" (see Prov 17:23; 21:14). Compare similarly Jer 32:18; Ps 79:12. This idiom is also documented in Akkadian; cf. *ana sūni nadānu* ("to pay to"; lit. "to the lap of"; see *CAD* S:388). (According to Minḥat Shay, some manuscripts have אל here [as in the verses just cited] instead of על.) For the literary style of doubling in adjacent clauses, cf. Ps 98:5: "Sing praise to the Lord with the lyre, with the lyre and melodious song." Some commentators attach the first word in the following verse to the end of this one and read, with the LXX and Peshitta, "their sins," third-person plural instead of the Masoretic second-person plural.

[7] An account of the fathers' sins follows the list of the children's sins; for both, the children shall pay.

Your sins and the sins of your fathers as well — said the Lord — This colon is connected to the preceding verse: I shall repay them in full for their sins and for their fathers' sins as well. Both the LXX and Peshitta translate here "their fathers," instead of MT "your fathers," similar to their reading at the end of the previous verse; see above. For an unbroken sequence of sins spanning the generations, see Jer 3:25: "For we have sinned against the Lord our God, we and our fathers from our youth to this day"; Ps 106:6: "We have sinned like our forefathers. We have gone astray, done evil"; Neh 9:2: "And they stood and confessed their sins and the iniquities of their fathers." See also Exod 20:5; 34:7; Num 14:18; Deut 5:9: "Visiting the guilt of the parents upon the children"; cf. also Jer 32:18.

For they made burnt sacrifices on the mountains — since they made burnt offerings to foreign gods on the hills and mountains; cf. 2 Kgs 16:4 (= 2 Chr 28:4); Hos 4:13. For the expression קִטֵּר על, see v. 3; Jer 19:13.

And affronted Me on the hills — with their sacrifices to other deities. For this expression חרף אלהים ("to affront God"), see Isa 37:4. For the parallel pair

גבעות/הרים ("mountains/hills"), see 40:4. Note the chiasm formed by this hemistich and the immediately preceding one.

I will pay back their recompense in full, into their bosom — The verse ends like v. 6, except for the substitution of the parallel verb מדד for שלם. This verb, as can be seen from its semantic and etymological cognate in Akk. *madādu*, means not only "to measure out" but also "to pay" and "to pay back" (*CAD* M/1:6-7). For פעולה ("recompense"), see 40:10; 62:11. For the technical term רִאשֹׁנָה, derived here from fiscal contexts, see Jer 16:18: "I will pay them in full (ראשונה) — nay, doubly for their iniquity and their sins." It is similar to the term רֹאשׁ, which denotes the original or principal sum of a transaction, as in Lev 5:24: "He shall repay the principal amount (בְּרֹאשׁוֹ)." (Cf. also the similar semantic field of the Akkadian cognates *rēšu* [*CAD* R:288] and *qaqqadu* ["head"], which can also denote the principal sum and are used in tandem with the verbs *madādu* and *šalāmu* [*CAD* Q:109-11].)

[8-16] In contrast to the first unit, in which the prophet addressed the nation as a whole, the second pericope emphasizes a national schism between God's servants (עבדַי, repeated here seven times in vv. 8, 9, 13 [three times], 14, 15 [עבדיו — but see there]), His chosen ones (בחירַי, vv. 9, 15), and His nation (v. 10), who are promised vindication and manifold blessings, and those who have forsaken the Lord (עֹזְבֵי ה׳, v. 11), who shall suffer an ignoble fate. Up to this chapter the term עבדִי ("My servant") referred to the people as a whole (41:8, 9; 42:19; 43:10; 44:1, 2, 21; 45:4; 48:20; 54:17); the same was true of the verb בחר ("to choose") and the substantive בחירַי ("My chosen ones") (41:8, 9; 43:10, 20; 44:1, 2; 45:4; 49:7), as well as עמי ("My people") (40:1; 43:20; 47:6; 51:4, 16; 52:4, 6; 53:8; 57:14). From here on the terms refer only to the hard core of believers.

[8] This verse begins to describe the great divide between those faithful to God and those who forsake Him. For the simile comparing Israel to the vine and its fruit, see Isa 5:1-7; Jer 2:21; Ps 80:9, 15. For further instances of the syntactical paradigm כאשר . . . כן ("as . . . so"), see Isa 52:14-15; 55:10-11; 66:22.

Thus said the Lord — the introduction to a new prophecy.

"As when the grape/new wine is present in the cluster" — Though the accepted translation of תירוש as "new wine" is found in all the commentaries, there is a possibility that in the present context it may refer to a "grape" per se, with the meaning that in the same way that there is often but a single good grape in a cluster of rotten ones, so there is one small group of faithful among the many who have not forsaken the righteous path. The noun תירוש may also have this meaning in Deut 11:14; Hos 2:10. Interestingly enough, in *Gen. Rab.* 29 (ed. Theodor-Albeck, 268) תירוש refers to one branch of the vine. (For this meaning see S. Naeh and M. P. Weitzman, "*Tiroš* — Wine or Grape? A Case of Metonymy," *VT* 44 [1994]: 115-20.) The word אֶשְׁכּוֹל ("cluster") is quite com-

mon in Semitic languages, appearing in Akkadian, Ugaritic, Aramaic, and Syriac.

"One says, 'Don't destroy it'" — the entire cluster. For the verb שחת ("to destroy") in similar agricultural contexts, see Nah 2:3; Mal 3:11.

"'There is a blessing in it'" — i.e., the sole good grape in the cluster.

"So will I do for the sake of My servants and not destroy everything" — So will I do for those who have remained faithful to Me. I will not destroy them along with the rest of the vine.

[9] The Lord's faithful are blessed. For the joint blessing of progeny and possession of land, see 60:20-22; Gen 15:3-4. For the occupation motif alone, see Isa 49:8; 54:3; 57:13; 60:21. Note the influence of both imagery and vocabulary of Ps 69:36-37 on this verse: "For God will deliver Zion and rebuild the cities of Judah (יהודה). They shall live there and inherit it (וִירֵשׁוּהָ). The offspring of His servants (וזרע עבדיו) shall possess it. Those who cherish His name shall dwell there (ישכנו)." (See the introduction, §17.)

"I will bring forth offspring from Jacob" — The unique expression והוצאתי זרע, drawn from the plant world (the *hiph'il* of יצא can denote "growth," and זרע, "seed"; cf. Isa 61:11), refers here to the growth of human offspring; cf. v. 23: כִּי זֶרַע בְּרוּכֵי ה׳ המה וצאצאיהם אִתָּם. For the expression זרע יעקב, see 45:19; and for זרע ישראל, see 44:3-4; 48:19; 54:3.

"And from Judah heirs to My mountains" — The verb from the previous stich applies here as well: "I will bring forth heirs from Judah to possess My mountains"; cf. 57:13: "But those who trust in Me shall inherit the land and possess My sacred mount." In light of the common expression הר קדשי ("My holy mount"; see v. 25; 57:13; 66:20), some commentators have suggested vocalizing the noun in the singular rather than the plural, which is unique (so too LXX). Note the wordplay: תירוש (v. 8), יורש, וִירֵשׁוּהָ.

"My chosen ones shall possess it" — My chosen ones, the faithful, shall inherit this land, i.e., the land of Israel. It is very likely that the feminine singular pronominal suffix appended to the verb (וִירֵשׁוּהָ), which does not accord with the masculine plural, "My mountains" (or singular, "My mountain") in the preceding clause, was influenced by Ps 69:36, quoted above in the introduction to the verse.

"My servants shall dwell there" — My servants shall occupy this land forevermore. For the parallelism between the verbs שכן/ירש ("to take possession/to dwell"), see Isa 34:11; Ps 37:29; 69:36-37. For the pair עבדי/בחירי, see Isa 45:1, 4.

[10] The land shall benefit from divine munificence and shall become a grazing ground for flocks.

"Sharon shall become a pasture for flocks" — The Sharon area, the northern flatlands on the coast between the Yarkon River and Mount Carmel, was excessively verdant until the destruction and exile, when it became desolate and

uninhabited (see Isa 33:9: "Sharon is become like a desert"); it shall once again be lush and shall become the grazing land of flocks; cf. 1 Chr 27:29: "The cattle pasturing in the Sharon"; cf. also Isa 35:2; Hos 2:17. The fertility of the Sharon is also documented in the Phoenician inscription of King Eshmunazor, from the second half of the fifth century BCE: "Moreover, the lord of kings gave us Dor and Joppa, the majestic corn lands that are in the plain of Sharon" (*KAI* 14:18-19). For the unique expression נְוֵה צאן, cf. 2 Sam 7:8: "I took you from the pasture (הַנָּוֶה), from following the flock (הצאן)." For the Akkadian etymological and semantic equivalent of Heb. נָוֶה, *namû,* see *CAD* N/1:249-51.

"And the Valley of Achor a place for cattle to lie down" — The Valley of Achor in the vicinity of Jericho was given its name following Joshua's curse of Achan, who secreted away some of the plunder captured in the war against Ai: "What calamity you have brought upon us (עֲכַרְתָּנוּ)! The Lord will bring calamity upon you this day (יַעְכָּרְךָ)" (Josh 7:25). This cursed site shall now become a resting place for cattle. Instead of רֵבֶץ, 1QIsa[a] has the variant מרבץ; cf. Ezek 25:5: לְמִרְבַּץ צאן; Zeph 2:15: מַרְבֵּץ לַחַיָּה. רבץ/מרבץ are the etymological and semantic equivalents of Akk. *narbaṣu* (*CAD* N/1:349) and *tarbaṣu* (*CAD* T:217-20), which also refer to a resting place for animals. For the same motif of the transformation of this valley into a fertile and blessed place in the latter days, see Hos 2:17. For the parallel substantive pair נָוֶה/רבץ ("a place to lie down/a pasture"), see Prov 24:15; cf. also Isa 35:7.

"For My people who seek Me" — These blessings are reserved for the faithful among My nation, to those who seek Me, as opposed to v. 1: "I was there to be sought by those who did not ask."

[11-12] In contrast to the blessings promised to the Lord's servants, who are His chosen ones, the dire fate of those who forsake the Lord and worship other gods by preparing cultic meals is now described. The expression עֹזְבֵי ה' ("[You] who forsake the Lord"), which appears again only in Isa 1:28 and refers to followers of foreign cults, is one of the links between this chapter and chap. 1 (see the introduction to this chapter).

[11] *"But as for you who forsake the Lord"* — The *waw* at the beginning of the verse indicates contrast. For forsaking the Lord as the opposite of seeking the Lord (the end of the previous verse), see 58:2; 1 Chr 28:9.

"Who ignore My holy mountain" — as opposed to the faithful who will inherit My holy mountain(s) (v. 9); see also 56:7: "I will bring them to My sacred mount"; 57:13: "And possess My sacred mount" (see also v. 25; 66:20). The word הַשְּׁכֵחִים is a stative participle.

"Who set a table for Gad" — who prepare a repast for Gad, the deity of good fortune whose name is known from inscriptions, seals, and proper names in Ugaritic, Amorite, Punic, Aramaic, Phoenician, Nabatean, Arabic, and Hebrew. (See J. H. Tigay, *You Shall Have No Other Gods: Israelite Religion in the*

Light of Hebrew Inscriptions, Harvard Semitic Studies 31 [Atlanta, 1986], 13, 66, 69-70; F. Grondähl, *Die Personennamen der Texte aus Ugarit,* SP 3 [Rome, 1967], 126-27; F. L. Benz, *Personal Names in the Phoenician and Punic Inscriptions,* SP 8 [Rome, 1972], 294-95; H. B. Huffmon, *Amorite Personal Names in the Mari Texts* [Baltimore, 1965], 179; J. Teixidor, *The Pantheon of Palmyra* [Leiden, 1979], 88-100; S. Ribichini, "Gad," in K. van der Toorn et al., eds., *Dictionary of Deities and Demons in the Bible,* 2nd ed. [Grand Rapids, 1999], 339-41.) Compare also the biblical appellations Gad (Gen 30:11, one of Jacob's twelve sons), Gaddiel (Num 13:10), Gaddi (Num 13:11; 2 Kgs 15:14, 17), Azgad (Ezra 2:12 = Neh 7:17; Ezra 8:12; Neh 10:16), and the place names Baal-gad (Josh 11:17; 12:7; 13:5) and Migdal-gad (Josh 15:37). The name of this deity is also mentioned in rabbinic sources: **לגדא דהר**, "To the god of fortune of the mountain"; *b. Ḥul.* 40a; **גדא דעבודה זרה**, "By the genius of your idolatry," which is used in oath formulae (*Gen. Rab.* 66 [ed. Theodor-Albeck, 731]). For the "setting of a table" in preparation for a meal, see Ps 23:5; Prov 9:2. (Note the possible wordplay between the terms **עֹרכים** and **עכור** in the previous verse.)

"And fill a mixing bowl for Meni" — They fill a basin with spiced wine for the god Meni, the god of destiny. For **מִמְסָךְ** ("mixing bowl"), see Prov 23:30: "Those who linger late over wine, who gather to drain bowls (**ממסך**)." Compare the Ugaritic interdialectal etymological and semantic cognate *msk,* which refers to "mixture, mixed wine, mixed drink" (*CAT* 1.19.IV:61), and *mmskn* (= **ממסך**), "an earthenware bowl" (*CAT* 4.123:18). **מְנִי** is usually identified as the god Manūtu/Manāt, who was worshiped by the Nabateans and early Arabs. (See S. D. Sperling, "Meni," in van der Toorn et al., eds., *Dictionary of Deities and Demons,* 566-68; and for Israelite names with **מני** as a theophoric element, see Tigay, *You Shall Have No Other Gods,* 13, 67.) For Hebrew **מנת**, denoting one's "portion" in life, hence destiny, see Jer 13:25; Ps 11:6. Note the assonance of the fivefold *mem* in the three consecutive words in this stich and two more in the first colon of the next verse.

[12] There follows the destiny of these worshipers, introduced by a wordplay on the name of the god Meni. (For other wordplays cf., e.g., v. 25: **יִרְעוּ . . . יָרֵעוּ**; 61:3: **פאר תחת אפר . . . מעטה . . . מטע**.) The second half of the verse is almost identical to 66:4. For the same sequence of four verbs: **קרא . . . ענה . . . דבר . . . שמע**, see v. 24; 66:4; and cf. a similar sequence in Jer 7:13.

"I will destine you for the sword" — In retaliation for your worship of the god of destiny (**מני**), I will destine you (**מניתי**) for death by the sword. For the expression **מני ל-**, see Job 7:3; Dan 1:5. Note the Akkadian semantic cognate *manû . . . ana,* "to hand over, deliver" (*CAD* M/1:223-24). Compare similarly in the Gilgamesh Epic, XI:169: "And assigned my people *(imnû ana)* to annihilation." For punishment by sword, see Isa 66:16.

"You will all kneel down to be slaughtered" — All of you shall be made to

prostrate yourselves and shall be butchered like cattle; cf. 53:7; Jer 11:19; Prov 7:22.

"Because I called, but you did not answer" — Since when I addressed you, you did not respond; cf. Isa 50:2; 58:9; 66:4.

"I spoke, but you did not listen" — This cruel fate has befallen you since you did not hearken to me when I called.

"You did what was wrong in My eyes" — You sinned before Me.

"And chose what I do not want" — and chose to conduct yourselves in an unfitting fashion; cf. 66:4.

[13-17] The fate of the faithful and the just deserts of the deserters.

[13] A triad of blessings that God confers on His faithful servants, juxtaposed by an opposing triad of curses (each beginning with ואתם, "but you"), which the wicked and unfaithful shall suffer. Those who prepared a ritual meal for the gods of luck and destiny shall appropriately suffer in kind from hunger and thirst.

"Assuredly," thus said the Lord God — the opening formula of the verdict in favor of the faithful and the indictment against the wicked.

"My servants shall eat, but you shall starve" — The faithful shall eat while the wicked shall hunger.

"My servants shall drink, but you shall thirst" — My servants shall drink to satiety, while you, the wicked, shall thirst for drink.

"My servants shall rejoice, but you shall be shamed" — The faithful shall be perpetually happy; but you, who forsook Me, shall be shamed and frustrated. For the verb בוֹשׁ in similar contexts, see 44:9; 49:23; 50:7; 54:4. For the antonymous pair שׂמח and בוֹשׁ, see 66:5; Ps 109:28. The faithful shall rejoice for God has redeemed them and fulfilled their dearest hopes, as opposed to the desperation of the unfaithful; cf. Prov 10:28: "The expectation of the righteous is joy; but the hope of the wicked is doomed."

[14] A continuation of the blessings of the faithful and curses of the unfaithful.

"My servants shall exalt in the gladness of their hearts" — Cf. Deut 28:47, where the expression טוּב לבב is also parallel to שמחה (as in the end of the previous verse here). Note the Akkadian etymological and semantic cognate *ṭūb libbi*, "gladness of heart, happiness" (*CAD* Ṭ:118-20). 1QIsa[a] and the LXX read בטוב לב instead of MT מטוב לב; but the meaning is the same.

"But you shall cry out in the anguish of your heart" — You, the unfaithful, shall scream in sorrow (note the variant תזעקו in 1QIsa[a] and one medieval Hebrew manuscript, instead of MT תצעקו). The expression כְּאֵב לב ("anguish"), like its semantic cognate in Akkadian, *muruṣ libbi*, "worry" (*CAD* M/2:227), is diametrically opposed to טוּב לב ("gladness"). The nominal form is a hapax legomenon; for the verbal expression, see Prov 14:13.

"Howling with a broken spirit" — Those who forsake God shall wail and whine, heartbroken. The expression שֵׁבֶר רוּחַ (1QIsa[a] variant: שברון רוח) is unique. Note the chiasm with the preceding hemistich. The form תְּיֵלִילוּ is a contracted *hiphi'l* (instead of the longer form, תְּהֵילִילוּ) from the root ילל; cf. 52:5: יהלילו. (See GKC §70c, Rem. 2.)

[15] *"You shall leave behind your name by which My chosen ones shall curse"* — Your memory shall be as a curse in the mouths of My chosen ones. For שבועה ("curse"), see Num 5:21: "Here the priest shall administer the curse (שְׁבֻעַת) of adjuration to the woman, as the priest goes on to say to the woman: 'May the Lord make you a curse (שְׁבֻעָה) and an imprecation among your people.'" For a similar curse based on the names of individuals, cf. Jer 29:21-23.

"'So may the Lord God slay you!'" — a formulaic curse: The Lord shall cause you to expire, just as those who forsook Him in the past. 1QIsa[a] adds the adverb תמיד ("always") to the end of this clause. However, note that the next clause and the first clause of v. 16 are missing from the scroll.

"But My servants shall be called by another name" — In contrast to those who abandon the true God and whose name shall be accursed, those who remain faithful to the Lord "shall be called" (vocalize in the *niph'al,* יִקָּרֵא, with the LXX and many medieval Hebrew manuscripts, instead of the *qal,* יִקְרָא, in the MT) by a different name. They shall be remembered forevermore as blessed. For the verb קרא in the *niph'al* with שֵׁם ("name") as the object, see Gen 17:5; 35:10. In light of the fourfold repetition of עבדי ("My servants") in the two previous verses, and the term בחירי ("My chosen ones") in this verse, it is very likely that עבדיו ("His servants") in the MT is in error and that it should read עבדי, as in the previous verses (the MT is likely the result of dittography — the *yod* of the following word was read, as is very often the case, as a *waw* and was appended to עבדי). For this motif of renaming, see Isa 60:14; 62:2, 4, 12.

[16] *"For whoever blesses himself in the land shall bless himself by the true God"* — Whoever utters a blessing on himself shall do so by employing the name of the true God. This translation, however, obfuscates the difficulty of the clause, which is variously understood by the commentators. According to Rashi: "Whosoever praises and glorifies himself throughout the land . . . shall boast that he is the servant of the one true God." In contrast, Kimchi explains the clause thus: "He who blesses himself shall say: 'The true God shall bless me as he has blessed so and so the righteous.'" The unique expression אֱלֹהֵי אָמֵן indicates that God is true and truthful. Compare likewise האל הנאמן ("the steadfast God"; Deut 7:9) and אל אמונה ("a faithful God"; Deut 32:4). Note the possible allusion of appending אמן to the blessing implied in the colon. For the variant reading in 1QIsa[a], והיה הנשבע באלוהי אמן, see Kutscher, *Language and Linguistic Background,* 289. For the reflexive *hithpa'el* expression התברך ב-, see Gen 22:18 (= 26:4); Deut 29:18; Jer 4:2.

"And whoever swears in the land shall swear by the true God" — as above.

"The former troubles are forgotten" — The כִּי is emphatic: the troubles of the past are now forgotten. For רִאשֹׁנוֹת, see Isa 43:18. The following verse there (43:19) is also very similar to v. 17 here, since both reiterate the theme of renewed creation.

"And are hidden from My sight" — They no longer exist.

[17-25] A new world order is promised to the faithful, wherein the latter days shall be similar to the antediluvian era. All shall enjoy longevity, fecundity, and prosperity; and all members of the animal kingdom shall coexist in harmony. This unit is connected to the above pericope through the following links: הָרִאשֹׁנוֹת (vv. 16, 17); הָרַע (v. 12) — יִרְעוּ (v. 25); תצעקו (v. 14) — זְעָקָה (v. 19); לב (vv. 14, 17); אכל (vv. 13, 21, 22, 25); and the theme of cursing (vv. 15, 20). Compare also vv. 12 and 24; vv. 15-16 and 22-23. In this section the negative לא appears eleven times.

[17] *"For behold! I am creating new heavens and a new earth"* — The Lord, the creator of heaven and earth (42:5; 45:18), makes a festive proclamation: "I am preparing to re-create the heavens and the earth," i.e., the world in its entirety; cf. similarly 66:22.

"The former things shall not be remembered" — Cf. v. 16; 43:18.

"And they shall never come to mind" — For the same parallel construction of this and the previous stich, see Jer 3:16.

[18] Just as the Lord is about to create new heavens and a new earth, so too shall He create a new Jerusalem, which shall be brimming in joy and happiness. For this future gladness, cf. Isa 51:3, 11; 60:15. Note the internal chiastic word order of this verse: שִׂישׂוּ וגילו . . . אשר אני בורא כי הנני בורא . . . גילה . . . משׂושׂ.

"But rather be glad and rejoice forever" — for the troubles of yesteryear are no more. For the expression עֲדֵי עד ("forever"), see Isa 26:4; Ps 132:12; and for the synonymous pair גיל/שׂישׂ ("to be glad [or delight]/to rejoice"), see Isa 61:10; 66:10. The root גיל, which appears again as the substantive גילה ("delight") at the end of the verse, is repeated for a third time in v. 19 (וְגַלְתִּי, "And I will rejoice"). 1QIsa[a] שׂישׂ וגיל (singular), instead of the plural in the MT, accords with the singular forms in v. 16.

"In what I am creating!" — God's creations are described in detail in the following clauses.

"For I shall create Jerusalem as a delight" — Jerusalem shall epitomize joy. Note here the third appearance of the verb בורא (also in the previous clause and in v. 17).

"And her people as a joy" — And Jerusalem's citizenry shall epitomize delight. For מָשׂוֹשׂ, see 62:5; 66:10.

[19] Note the Jeremian influence on this verse: Both Jeremiah's promise to Rachel in 31:15-16: "A cry (קול) is heard in Ramah — wailing, bitter weeping (בְּכִי) — Rachel weeping (מְבַכָּה) for her children. . . . Restrain your voice from weeping (בֶּכִי)"; and the reversal of his gloomy doomsday prophecies: "And I will silence the sound (קול) of mirth (שָׂשׂוֹן) and gladness" (Jer 7:34; 16:9; 25:10; cf. also 33:10), reverberate in Deutero-Isaiah: "And I will rejoice in Jerusalem and delight (שָׂשְׂתִּי) in her people. Never again shall be heard there the cries of weeping (קול בְּכִי) and cries for help." (See the introduction, §15.) For the expression לא . . . עוד ("never again"), which indicates the impossibility of returning to a former state, see v. 20; 51:22; 52:1; 54:4; 60:18-20; 62:4. In the first clause, the motif of national joyfulness and the delight of Jerusalem are repeated from the previous verse, and note also the third reiteration of the synonymous pair גיל/שׂישׂ ("to delight [or be glad]/to rejoice").

"And I will rejoice in Jerusalem and delight in My people" — And I shall have much happiness in My joyous creation of Jerusalem and My people, Israel.

"Never again shall be heard in her cries of weeping and cries for help" — There shall be no distress ever again in Jerusalem; cf. 60:18: "The cry 'Violence!' shall no more be heard in your land, nor 'Wrack and Ruin!' within your borders." For the synonymous pair זְעקה/בכי, see Isa 15:4.

[**20**] A blessing of longevity for those loyal to the Lord. For a blessing in a similar vein, cf. Zech 8:4: "There shall yet be old men and women in the squares of Jerusalem, each with staff in hand because of their great age."

"No more shall there be there an infant or old man" — Hebrew עול ימים is a unique expression denoting a child of tender age (note the synonymous term עויל ימים in 1QIsa[a]; for עֲוִיל, see Job 16:11; 19:18; 21:11; and cf. likewise עוֹלֵל, 1 Sam 22:19; Jer 44:7; עוֹלָל, Joel 2:16; Lam 4:4). For עול, which in Syriac denotes a suckling, see Isa 49:15. Along with its polar opposite, זקן, the expression indicates inclusion of the total population (a merism). According to Saadyah, 143, and Ibn Ganaḥ (*Sefer ha-Riqmah,* 74, line 2): "The [initial] *mem* of משם [lit. 'from there,' i.e., Jerusalem] is superfluous." For the syntactic construction עוד . . . לא ("no more"), see the final clause of the preceding verse.

"Who does not live out his days" — Each will live out the years allotted to him. For the expression מלא ימים, see Exod 23:26. Compare also the Akkadian etymological and semantic equivalent *ūmū/ūmē malû/mullû* (*CAD* M/2:180-81, 186; see Paul, *Divrei Shalom,* 223 n. 11).

"He who dies at the age of one hundred shall be considered a youth" — For he who dies a centenarian will be considered as though he passed away in his youth (Kimchi, Isaiah of Tirani, Joseph Kaspi).

"And he who falls short of a hundred shall be reckoned accursed" — For the root חטא in the *qal* indicating "to be short, missing," see Job 5:24: "When you look round your home you will find nothing amiss (תֶחֱטָא)"; cf. Prov 8:36. The

vocalization of חוֹטֶא with a *segol* (instead of a *ṣere;* cf. Prov 19:2) reflects a *yod* radical in the last letter rather than an *aleph;* see also Eccl 2:26; 9:2, 18.

[21] For other instances of blessings and curses pertaining to both house and vineyard, see Deut 20:5-6; 28:30; Isa 5:9-10; Jer 35:7; Ezek 28:26; Amos 5:11; 9:14; Zeph 1:13; Eccl 2:4. Note the almost identical blessing in Jer 29:5: "Build houses and live in them, plant gardens and eat their fruit," which is further connected to these verses by the adjacent promise of progeny (29:6): "Beget sons and daughters . . . that they may bear sons and daughters"; cf. here v. 23: "They shall not bear children in vain, but they are an offspring blessed by the Lord, and their descendants in common with them." There is, however, a noticeable difference between the two prophecies: Jeremiah's message was delivered to the Babylonian Diaspora (Jer 29:4), whereas Deutero-Isaiah's prophecy is addressed to the newly arrived returnees to Jerusalem. (See the introduction, §15.)

"They shall build houses and dwell in them" — Deuteronomy's curse (28:30): "You will build a house but not live in it," is thus abrogated.

"They shall plant vineyards and eat their fruit" — A second Deuteronomic curse (28:30) is also annulled: "You will plant a vineyard but not harvest it."

[22] This verse is an emphatic reiteration of the previous two verses. For similar blessings, see 62:8-9.

"They shall not build for others to dwell in" — Cf. Deut 20:5: "Anyone who has built a new house but has not dedicated it, let him go back to his home, lest he die in battle and another dedicate it."

"Nor plant for others to enjoy" — Cf. Deut 20:6: "Anyone who has planted a vineyard but has never harvested it, let him go back to his home, lest he die in battle and another harvest it."

"For the days of My people shall be as long as the days of a tree" — which survives for untold generations. For an image of the righteous as a tree, see Ps 92:13-15: "The righteous bloom like a date palm. They thrive like a cedar in Lebanon. Planted in the house of the Lord, they flourish in the courts of our God. In old age they still produce fruit; they are full of sap and freshness."

"My chosen ones shall enjoy the work of their hands" — According to the MT the verse means: "My chosen ones shall outlive [יְבַלּוּ, lit. 'wear out'; *pi'el* from the root בלי] the work of their hands." The preferred reading, however, as in the Peshitta *(n'klwn),* is יאכלו: "They shall enjoy the fruit of their labor." For a similar image, see Ps 128:2: "You shall enjoy (תאכל) the fruit of your labors." Compare also the Akkadian etymological and semantic equivalents of the expression מעשה ידיהם: *šipir qātē (idī)* and *dullu qātē* (*CAD* Š/3:82; D:176-77). The latter expression, *dullu qātē,* appears also in the Aramaic *Genesis Apocryphon* 20:7: ודל ידיהא. (See Fitzmyer, *Genesis Apocryphon,* 62, 123-24; and cf. *b. Pesaḥ.* 28a: דויל ידיה.) For the Akkadian cognate to Heb. אכל, *akālu,* with the meaning "to enjoy," see *CAD* A/1:252.

[23] *"They shall not toil to no purpose"* — Since, as the last verse stated, God's chosen ones shall enjoy the fruit of their toil, their labor shall not be in vain. Their complaint in 49:4, "I have labored in vain (לְרִיק). I have spent my strength for empty breath," will no longer be justified. For לָרִיק ("in vain, to no purpose"), see Lev 26:20; Isa 30:7.

"They shall not bear children in vain" — a probable allusion to miscarriage. For this meaning of בֶּהָלָה, see Ps 78:33: "He made their days end in futility, their years in vain (בבהלה)." Other commentators suggest transposing the letters and read לַהֶבֶל, which is synonymous to ריק in Isa 30:7.

"For they are an offspring blessed by the Lord" — The descendants of Jacob's stock (זרע, v. 9) shall lead a charmed existence. See similarly 61:9: "They are the stock the Lord has blessed."

"And their descendants with them" — Their descendants shall be blessed as they are; cf. the above-quoted 61:9; and 44:3; 48:19. For the term את, meaning "in common with," see Jer 23:28b.

[24] This verse is the polar opposite of vv. 1, 12. For the same sequence of verbs: קרא, ענה, דבר, and שמע, see v. 12; 66:4; and cf. the similar sequence in Jer 7:13.

"Before they call, I will answer" — Even before they pray to Me, I shall respond. Cf. Isa 58:9: "Then, when you call, the Lord will answer. When you cry, He will say: 'Here I am.'"

While they are still speaking, I will hearken — I shall hear them in the midst of their prayer. For the immediate concurrence implied in this expression, cf. Job 1:16, 17, 18: "While (עוד) this one was still speaking, another arrived."

[25] The eschatology in this verse (reminiscent of the primordial garden) bears the strong imprint of Isa 11:6-9.

11:6-9	**65:25**
v. 6: The wolf shall dwell with the lamb, the leopard lie down with the kid.	
	The wolf and the lamb shall graze together.
v. 7: The cow and the bear shall graze, their young shall lie down together.	
v. 7: And the lion, like cattle, shall eat straw.	And the lion, like cattle, shall eat straw.

11:6-9	**65:25**
v. 8: A babe shall play over a viper's hole, and an infant shall sport over an adder's den.	And the serpent's food shall be dirt.
v. 9: They shall not hurt or destroy in all My holy mountain.	They shall not hurt or destroy in all My holy mountain.

The main point of chap. 11, however, is missing. The prophet omits the introduction, which lauds the future Davidic scion: "A shoot shall grow from the stock of Jesse, and a branch shall spring from his roots" (11:1), since the house of David plays no role in the future according to Deutero-Isaiah (see 55:3). (See the introduction, §14.) For the idea of national redemption and peace in the animal kingdom, see also Hos 2:18-22. This irenic motif appears already in the Enki and Ninhursag epic, which describes the Sumerian garden of Eden — Dilmun — where there are no predators: "The lion kills not; the wolf snatches not the lamb. Unknown is the kid-devouring wild dog" (*ANET*, 38).

"The wolf and the lamb shall graze together" — in the same grazing area. The term כְּאֶחָד, which replaces יַחְדָּו in Isa 11:7, appears seven times in the later books of the Bible (e.g., Eccl 11:6; Ezra 2:64; 2 Chr 5:13) and is a loanword from Aramaic, כַּחֲדָה. (See the introduction, §11.) Compare also the etymological and semantic cognate in Akkadian, *kīma ištēn* (*CAD* I-J:277).

"And the lion shall eat straw like the ox" — a revolutionary change in the lion's culinary diet!

"And the serpent's food shall be earth" — The serpent shall eat only from the dirt of the earth, as stated in his curse in Gen 3:14: "And dirt you shall eat all the days of your life." Compare the flowery imagery in Mic 7:17: "Let them lick the earth like snakes, like crawling things on the ground!"

"They shall not hurt or destroy in all My holy mountain" — This irenic scenario of predator and prey in peaceful coexistence shall prevail throughout Mount Zion (for הר קדשי, see v. 11; 56:7; 57:13; 66:20); or perhaps the prophet's intention is for this term to be understood more generally and refer to Jerusalem and the entire land of Israel (Ibn Ezra, Kimchi, Luzzatto; cf. Exod 15:17; Ps 78:54). Note the wordplay: here יָרֵעוּ, and at the beginning of the verse: יִרְעוּ.

Said the Lord — the concluding formula of the prophecy.

Chapter 66

The final chapter of the book begins with a scathing theological polemic against those who wish to build an earthly sanctuary for God who dwells on high, and then continues with a denunciation of the foreign cults practiced by Jerusalem's priesthood, for which they shall be severely punished (vv. 1-4). The national schism is revealed anew, between those who "are concerned for God's word," to whom redemption is promised in the form of a painless birth, and "your brothers who revile you," upon whom God shall pour out His vengeful wrath (vv. 5-9). The redemption of "those who love God" and who partake in Jerusalem's joy is compared to the contented suckling of a babe and the dandling of a child on his parents' knees. Israel shall enjoy the bounty of nations, and their very limbs shall be rejuvenated. Conversely, God shall avenge Himself on His enemies within Israel in a mighty battle (vv. 10-16). Following a second description of the despicable foreign rituals, the prophet declares that God shall spare a remnant from among the foreign nations, who shall be sent as emissaries to deliver the message of God's majesty to far-flung countries. As a result, many nations shall congregate in Jerusalem, bringing back with them the scattered Israelite Diaspora. God will then select from these foreign nations those who will serve as Levitical priests (an unprecedented theological innovation). The chapter concludes with a vision of a new era — the re-creation of heaven and earth and massive pilgrimages to Jerusalem on the new moons and Sabbaths. In contrast, the sinners who forsook God shall expire, and their unburied bodies shall be left to rot (vv. 17-24).

Note the aggregate of terms that are reiterated two or more times in this chapter: השמים והארץ (vv. 1, 22), חָרֵד(ים) (vv. 2, 5), בחר (vv. 3, 4), שׂמח (vv. 5, 10), אֹיביו (vv. 6, 14), חיל (vv. 7, 8 [twice]), ילד (vv. 7, 8 [twice], 9 [twice]), שׂישׂ (vv. 10 [twice], 14), ינק (vv. 11, 12), אש (vv. 15 [twice], 16, 24), כל בשׂר (vv. 16, 24), כבודי (vv. 18, 19 [twice]), הגוים (vv. 18, 19). There are also two words that appear three times in the same verse: קול (v. 6) and נחם (v. 13).

The associative links between this chapter and chap. 65 are many, and the connection manifests itself in the large number of phrases and terms common to both:

Chapter 65	**Chapter 66**
v. 3: Sacrifice in gardens	v. 3: Sacrifice sheep
v. 4: Who eat the flesh of swine	v. 3: Who offer oblations of the blood of swine; v. 17: Who eat the flesh of swine
v. 12: Because I called, but you did not answer. I spoke, but you did not listen. You did what was wrong in my eyes and chose what I do not want.	v. 4: For I called and none responded. I spoke and none paid heed. v. 3: Just as they have chosen their ways and take pleasure in their abominations.
v. 13: My servants shall rejoice, but you shall be shamed.	v. 5: So that we may look upon your joy. But they shall be shamed.
v. 6: But I will repay, repay into their bosom.	v. 6: He will repay retribution to His foes.
v. 23: They shall not bear children in vain.	vv. 7-9: Before she went into labor, she bore a child . . . or is a nation born all at once? . . . Shall I who bring on labor not bring about birth?
vv. 18-19: Be glad and rejoice forever in what I am creating! For I shall create Jerusalem as a delight, and her people, a joy. And I will rejoice in Jerusalem and delight in her people.	v. 10: Rejoice with Jerusalem and be glad for her, all who love her! Join in her jubilation.
v. 5: Such things make My anger smoke, like a fire blazing all day long.	vv. 15-16: See, the Lord is coming with fire . . . to vent His anger in fury . . . His rebuke in flaming fire. For with fire will the Lord contend. v. 24: Nor will their fire be quenched.
v. 12: I will destine you for the sword.	v. 16: And with His sword against all humanity.
v. 3: Sacrifice in gardens.	v. 17: Those who sanctify and purify themselves to enter the gardens.
v. 2: Following their own designs.	v. 18: For I know their deeds and designs.

Chapter 65	Chapter 66
vv. 11, 25: My holy mountain	v. 20: My holy mountain
v. 17: For behold! I am creating a new heaven and a new earth.	v. 22: For as the new heaven and the new earth that I will create.
v. 9: I will bring forth offspring from Jacob. v. 15: But My servants shall be given a different name. v. 23: But they shall be a people blessed by the Lord, and their offspring shall remain with them.	v. 22: So shall your seed and your name endure.

This chapter, like chap. 65, is connected redactionally to the first chapter of the larger book of Isaiah, thus creating a literary frame for the book as a whole:

Chapter 1	Chapter 66
v. 11: I have no desire; v. 29: You have chosen.	v. 4: And chose what I do not desire
v. 10: Hear the word of the Lord.	v. 5: Hear the word of the Lord.
v. 29: They shall be shamed.	v. 5: But they shall be put to shame.
v. 20: Sword	v. 16: With His sword
v. 29: The gardens	v. 17: The gardens
v. 28: But rebels and sinners shall all be crushed.	v. 17: They shall one and all come to an end.
v. 13: new moon and Sabbath	v. 23: And new moon after new moon, and Sabbath after Sabbath
v. 2: And they have rebelled against Me; v. 28: rebels	v. 24: Who rebelled against Me
v. 31: Shall burn . . . with none to quench	v. 24: Nor their fire quenched

Compare also the pilgrimages to Jerusalem described at the beginning of chap. 2 and at the end of chap. 66: "[The time] has come to gather all the nations and tongues; and they shall come . . . to Jerusalem, My holy mountain"

(66:18-20) — "All the nations shall gaze on it [the mount of the Lord's House] and many peoples shall go and say: 'Let us go up to the mount of the Lord, to the House of the God of Jacob'" (2:2-3). (See L. J. Liebreich, "Compilation of the Book of Isaiah," *JQR* 46 [1955-56]: 259-77; 47 [1956-57]: 114-38; W. A. M. Beuken, "Isaiah Chapters LXV-LXVI: Trito-Isaiah and the Closure of the Book of Isaiah," in J. A. Emerton, ed., *Congress Volume: Leuven, 1989,* VTSup 43 [Leiden, 1989], 218-19; D. M. Carr, "Reading Isaiah from Beginning [Isaiah 1] to End [Isaiah 65–66]): Multiple Modern Possibilities," in R. F. Melugin and M. A. Sweeney, eds., *New Visions of Isaiah,* JSOTSup 214 [Sheffield, 1996], 188-218).

[1] A polemic against the popular view that the Temple on earth serves as the divine abode (as in Solomon's prayer in 1 Kgs 8:13: "I have now built for You a lofty House, a place where You may dwell forever"), and that the cherubim and the ark are God's seat and footrest. This belief, that the Temple was God's sanctuary and resting place, is reflected in other biblical verses as well, e.g., Ps 132:7-8: "Let us enter His abode, bow at His footstool. Arise, O Lord, to Your resting place, You and Your mighty ark!"; v. 14: "This is my resting place for all time. Here I will dwell, for I desire it." The motif of a temple as the earthly divine residence is prevalent also in Mesopotamian sources. Compare, for example, the Babylonian epic of creation, *Enuma Elish,* in which Marduk declares: "Below the firmament, whose grounding I made firm, I shall build a house. Let it be the abode of my pleasure. Within it I shall establish its holy place . . . I shall establish my kingship" (V:122-24); and the gods respond: "Your chamber shall be our stopping place. . . . We shall find rest therein" (VI:52; see B. R. Foster, *COS* 1:400, 401.)

In stark contrast with this belief, the prophet states that the Temple is not God's resting place, but rather: "The heaven is My throne and the earth is My footstool" (v. 1). This theological viewpoint appears already in the Deuteronomistic revision of Solomon's prayer quoted above; and see 1 Kgs 8:27: "But will God really dwell on earth? Even the heavens to their uttermost reaches cannot contain You, how much less this house that I have built!" For further accentuation of this idea, the Deuteronomistic redactor adds the word **השמים** ("the heavens") each time there is a reference to God's "resting place" (מְכוֹן שִׁבְתּוֹ); see 1 Kgs 8:30, 39, 43, 49; and cf. Deut 26:15: "Look down from Your holy abode, from heaven." As opposed to the lofty house (בֵּית זְבֻל, 1 Kgs 8:13) in Solomon's prayer, Deutero-Isaiah pleads in 63:15: "Look down from heaven and see, from Your holy and glorious height (זְבֻל)!" According to this revolutionary concept, the Temple is not God's residence, but only serves as the locus and focus of prayers, both Israelite and otherwise (cf. 1 Kgs 8:28ff.); cf. 56:7: "I will bring them to My sacred mount and give them joy in My House of prayer. Their burnt offerings and sacrifices shall be acceptable on My altar. For My House shall be called a House of prayer for all peoples" (see, however, 60:13;

62:8-9; 66:20, 23). (See the introduction, §13.) Similar images of deities sitting on high on heavenly thrones appear in Mesopotamian literature. (See *kussû, CAD* K:490-91; *šubtu, CAD* Š/3:173.) Compare also the Assyrian inscription that records King Esarhaddon's boast: "I have refurbished the [goddess Tashmetu's] royal throne . . . and the footstool overlaid with red gold" (see *CAD* Š/3:173). For illustrations of gods and goddesses as well as earthly kings seated on thrones with their feet resting on footstools, see *ANEP,* no. 458 (Ahiram, king of Phoenicia); no. 460 (Bar-Rakib, king of Aram); no. 459 (Darius, king of Persia); no. 493 (El, the Ugaritic father of the gods); nos. 507-8 (Sumerian goddesses); no. 515 (Shamash, the Babylonian sun god); no. 525 (Ishtar, a Mesopotamian goddess).

Thus said the Lord: "The heaven is My throne and the earth is My footstool" — Cf. 63:15: "Look down from heaven and see, from Your holy and glorious height!"; Ps 103:19: "The Lord has established His throne in heaven." The expression הֲדֹם רגלים ("footstool"), which is often employed as a reference to the Temple (e.g., Ps 99:5; 132:7: "Bow down to His footstool"; Lam 2:1: "He did not remember His footstool on His day of wrath"; cf. Isa 60:13: "To adorn the site of My sanctuary, to glorify the place where My feet rest"), designates here the earth in its entirety. The term appears also in Ugaritic in a description of the god Athtar: "(Who) sits on the throne of mightiest Baal, (but) his feet do not reach the footstool *(hdm)*" (*CAT* 1.6.I:59-60). Note also the Hittite description of the god Teshub, who sits on a throne and whose gigantic feet reach the footstool (*Keilschrifttexte aus Boghazköi* 32:13 [obv. II:5-8 // obv. I:4-6]). For Egyptian *(hdmw)* and Hurrian *(atmi)* cognates, see V. Haas, "Hurritologische Miszellen," *Altorientalische Forschungen* 20/2 (1993): 261-68.

"Where will you build a House for Me?" — Since the Lord fills the entire universe, where could one possibly build a House to contain His presence? The query אי זה ("where") is always written in Biblical Hebrew as two separate words (see, e.g., 50:1; often hyphenated, e.g., 1 Sam 9:18; 1 Kgs 13:12), whereas in Rabbinic Hebrew it appears as one. For the first of the two components of this word, אֵי ("where"), see Gen 4:9: "Where (אֵי) is your brother Abel?"; Deut 32:37: "He will say: 'Where (אֵי) are their gods?'" (cf. Akk. *aj* [*CAD* A/1:220] and Ugar. *iy* (*HdO* 1:133); and זה supplies an emphatic tone; cf. Gen 25:32; Exod 2:20.

"Where will My resting place be?" — According to the Masoretic vocalization, מָקוֹם is in the absolute state and thus the clause should be translated: "Where is the place that would serve as My resting place?" and is thus syntactically equivalent to the preceding clause. If, however, it is vocalized as a construct, מְקוֹם (thus Targum, LXX, and Vulgate), it should be rendered: "Where will My resting place be?" The basic meaning is the same in either case. For the Lord's Temple as His "resting place" (מנוחה), see Ps 132:14: "This is My resting place for all time"; 1 Chr 28:2: "I wanted to build a resting place for the Ark of

the Covenant of the Lord." In Akkadian as well, temples and sanctuaries are also referred to as *ašar tapšuḫti,* "resting place," and *bīt tapšuḫti,* "house of repose" (*CAD* T:195).

[2] The transcendental God has an immanent side as well. He may dwell on high, but He notices each and every individual who is concerned about His word; cf. Isa 57:15: "For thus said the High and Exalted One, who forever dwells, whose name is 'Holy': 'I dwell on high, in holiness [or: in a high and holy place], yet with the broken and the lowly in spirit — reviving the spirits of the lowly, reviving the hearts of the crushed.'" The Lord's faithful, who are referred to here as "oppressed," "brokenhearted," and "concerned about My word," are also called: "the righteous man . . . pious men" (57:1); "those who trust in Me" (57:13); "the mourners among them" (57:18); "humble . . . the broken of heart" (61:1); "those who mourn" (61:2); "the mourners in Zion" (61:3); "My chosen ones" (65:9, 15); and "My/His servants" (65:8, 9, 13, 15; 66:14). The beginning of this verse is a direct continuation of v. 1.

"All these were made by My hand" — "All these" refers to the earth and the sky, as in 41:20: "The Lord's hand has made this"; 45:12: "It was I who made the earth . . . My own hands stretched out the heavens." The Akkadian semantic cognate of Heb. **עשׂי** in these verses, *epēšu* ("to do, to make"), also refers to the creative process (*CAD* E:107).

"And thus they all came into being" — declares the Lord — The clause is syntactically part of the previous hemistich. All this came into being through My own handiwork, and I, therefore, have no need for any house you would build for Me. The LXX adds here **לי**: "All these are mine." The concluding formula of this saying, **נאם ה׳**, which is occasionally found in the middle of verses (as here), highlights the message of the first two clauses; see also v. 22.

"Yet to such a one I look" — The initial *waw* is adversative: In spite of My grandeur and transcendental qualities, I take special notice of the following individuals. The "future" form of the verb **אביט** indicates constancy of action.

"To the oppressed and brokenhearted" — To the oppressed (for **עָנִי** as a victim of oppression, see 49:13; 51:21; 54:11; 58:7) and brokenhearted (**וּנְכֵה רוח**). For the latter and similar terms, see 57:15; Ps 34:19; Prov 15:13; 17:22; 18:14.

"And he who trembles at My word" — See v. 5. The faithful followers of God are also mentioned in the book of Ezra, in the context of the isolationists who would not take foreign wives: "Around me gathered all who tremble (**חרד**) at the words of the God of Israel" (Ezra 9:4); "And all who tremble (**החרדים**) at the commandment of God" (Ezra 10:3).

[3] A sharp condemnation of the Jerusalem priests who present the proper oblations to God but, at the same time, persist in their immoral and foreign cultic practices; cf. also v. 17; 65:3-4, 11. The most common interpretation of the four participial pairs is to assume an implied *kaph* of comparison between

the two elements in each of the four pairs (thus all the ancient translations: Targum, LXX, Vulgate, Peshitta, and partially 1QIsa[a], only the first pair). In other words, one who slaughters an ox is equivalent to one who slays a human, and so on. If the verse is interpreted in this way, however, it would then include an explicit condemnation of ostensibly legitimate cultic practices, and it is hardly likely that this was the prophet's intention, as one gathers from a number of previous texts (e.g., vv. 20-21, 23; see also 56:7; 60:6-7, 13; 62:9). A preferred understanding of the four pairs in the verse is to interpret them appositionally. Thus the priests who sacrifice oxen also slay humans; the priests who sacrifice sheep also immolate dogs. For prophetic objections to the priestly cult of the period, cf. Hag 1:6-14; 2:1-9. (See A. Rofé, "Isaiah 66:1-4: Judean Sects in the Persian Period as Viewed by Trito-Isaiah," in A. Kort and S. Morschauer, eds., *Biblical and Related Studies Presented to Samuel Iwry* [Winona Lake, Ind., 1985], 205-17.)

"He who slaughters an ox, slays a man" — The priest who slaughters (שחט) oxen as an offering to God (cf. 2 Chr 29:22) is also the one who slays human beings (cf. Luzzatto). For the verb מכה (lit. "to strike") denoting murder, see Gen 4:15; Exod 2:12. Perhaps, however, in light of the other predicates in this verse, which are all connected to the cult, the implication here is to human sacrifice; cf. Isa 57:5: "Who slaughter children in the wadis."

"He who sacrifices sheep, breaks the neck of a dog" — The priest who sacrifices (זבח) sheep on the altar also participates in the ritual of breaking the neck of a dog. עורף is a denominative verb from the substantive עֹרֶף, "the back of the neck"; see Exod 13:13; 34:20: "If you do not redeem it, you must break its neck (וַעֲרַפְתּוֹ)." (For Hittite rituals involving the sacrifice of dogs and pigs [see immediately below] to the god of the netherworld, see J. Sasson, "Isaiah LXVI 3-4a," *VT* 26 [1976]: 199-207; J. Milgrom, *Leviticus 1–16,* AB [New York, 1991], 653; W. Houston, *Purity and Monotheism: Clean and Unclean Animals in Biblical Law,* JSOTSup 140 [Sheffield, 1990], 188-93; B. J. Collins, "The Puppy in Hittite Rituals," *JCS* 42 [1990]: 211-26.) For the interchangeability of the verbs שחט and זבח, cf. Exod 23:18 with 34:25.

"He who makes a grain offering, offers the blood of swine" — The participle מַעֲלֵה, vocalized as a construct, is a reference to the priest who brings a grain offering (מִנחה) to God; see Isa 57:6; Lev 2:1-2. However, since the second half of this pair does not contain a participle followed by a substantive, but rather consists of two substantives, דם חזיר ("the blood of swine"), some commentators interpret מעלה as governing both מנחה and דם חזיר, i.e., he who presents the legitimate grain offering also offers the blood of swine as an oblation. (For the sacrifice of pigs and their subsequent consumption, see the references in v. 17 and 65:4.) But since the verb עלי never refers to offering the blood of a sacrifice, it has been suggested to read הֹדֵם חזיר, "tears pigs apart limb by limb," the missing *heh* having been deleted as a result of haplography: מנחה הדם. Com-

pare Dan 2:5: הַדָּמִין תִּתְעַבְדוּן ("You shall be torn limb from limb"), and similarly 3:29. This verb is a Persian loanword (from *[h]andāma*) and appears also in rabbinic literature, e.g., *b. ʿAbod. Zar.* 38b; *ʿErub.* 30a.

"He who makes a memorial offering with frankincense, blesses idols" — The priest who offers an אַזְכָּרָה (מזכיר is a denominative verb derived from אַזְכָּרָה — the portion of the meal offering including frankincense that is burnt before the Lord; see Lev 2:1-2, 9, 16; 5:12; 6:8; 24:7) is also the one who blesses, i.e., worships, idols. For אָוֶן (lit. "iniquity, wickedness") as a derogatory reference to graven images, see 1 Sam 15:23; Hos 10:8.

"Just as they have chosen their ways" — This hemistich initiates a comparison that is concluded in the next verse. For the expression בחר בדרך, see Ps 25:12; Prov 3:31.

"And take pleasure in their abominations" — שִׁקּוּצִים is another cacophonous term for idols; see 1 Kgs 11:7: "At that time, Solomon built a shrine for Chemosh, the abomination (שִׁקֻּץ) of Moab on the hill near Jerusalem, and one for Molech, the abomination (שִׁקֻּץ) of the Ammonites." For the expression נֶפֶשׁ חפצה ("to take pleasure"), see 1 Chr 28:9. This clause forms a chiasm with the immediately preceding one, and both form a chiasm with the next verse: גם המה בחרו בדרכיהם ובשִׁקוציהם נפשם חפצה — ובאשר לא חפצתי בחרו. Compare also Isa 56:4; 65:12 for the same expressions.

[4] The Lord shall retaliate in kind. The end of this verse is almost identical to the final clause of 65:12. For the same order of verbs, see 65:12, 24, and for a similar sequence cf. Jer 7:13.

"So will I, for My part, choose to mock them" — I shall "choose," just as they "chose": They chose wanton rites, so I (emphatic in the Hebrew, גם אני) shall choose to heap derision on them. For this meaning of the root עלל, see Metzudat Zion, and cf. Exod 10:2; Num 22:29. The substantive תעלולים is a hapax legomenon (in Isa 3:4 it denotes "toddlers"). The verb בחר appears here for the third time; see v. 3.

"And I will bring on them the very thing they dread" — My requital shall include the most dreadful punishment that the unfaithful fear. The substantive מְגוּרָה (Ps 34:5; Prov 10:24) denotes "fear, terror"; for the verb יגר along with the verb "to bring," see Job 3:25.

"For I called but none responded" — See Isa 50:2.

"I spoke but none paid heed" — And when I spoke to them, they did not heed My call.

"They did what was evil in My sight" — They persisted in doing what I consider depraved; see Deut 4:25.

"And chose what I do not want" — And the unfaithful invariably chose the wrong path. The two verbs appear in chiastic order with those of the previous verse.

[**5-9**] This unit once again highlights the stark schism within Israel and is associatively linked to v. 2 by the key expression חרד[ים] על דברי. The redemption of this group is powerfully portrayed as a miraculous birth with no pain to the delivering mother.

[**5**] God addresses the faithful concerning those who spurn and revile them.

"Hear the word of the Lord, you who tremble at His word!" — In contrast to the unfaithful who "paid no heed" to the divine message (v. 4), those who revere God are bidden to pay attention to His word. 1QIsa[a] has דבריו, plural, instead of the singular in the MT.

"Your kinsmen who hate you, who spurn you because of My name, are saying" — your brothers who revile you and distance themselves from any contact with you (cf. 65:5). For the verb נדי (the only other occurrence is in Amos 6:3: הַמְנַדִּים ליום רע, "You who thrust aside the evil day"), cf. its Ugaritic semantic equivalent *ydy* (parallel to the verb *grš*): "Who among the gods can expel *(ydy)* the illness, can drive out *(grš)* the sickness?" (*CAT* 1.16.V:20-21). Compare also in a prayer to Baal: "O Baal, expel *(tdy)* the strong one from our gates" (*CAT* 1.119:rev. 28). The postbiblical term נידוי ("excommunication") derives from this root. For a different division of the first two hemistichs, see the next comment.

"'Let the Lord manifest His Presence'" — These words of excoriation leveled at the faithful are difficult to interpret: lit. "Let the Lord reveal His glory for the sake of My name" (attaching here the last two words of the previous hemistich). "'For the sake of His name' (למען שמו) would have been more appropriate here, but God, as He alludes to their words, refers to Himself [in the first-person] (למען שמי)" (Luzzatto; Yellin, *Ḥiqrei Miqra,* 86). Others divide the verse differently and read: "Your kinsmen, who hate you, who spurn you, say: 'Let the Lord's name be honored'" (pointing the verb as a *niph'al,* יִכָּבֵד, rather than in the *qal* of the MT, following LXX, Vulgate, and Peshitta; cf. Lev 10:3). For the "name" of God, see Isa 48:9; 52:5; 56:6; 59:19; 60:9. The belief in God's "name" is a concept deeply entrenched in Deuteronomy and Deuteronomistic literature, e.g., Deut 28:10; 32:3; 1 Kgs 5:17, 19. (See the introduction, §13.)

"'So that we may look upon your joy!'" — a derisive and taunting comment. 1QIsa[a] has יראה (יֵרָאֶה), "it shall be seen," instead of MT נִרְאֶה.

"But they shall be put to shame" — The Lord's response to this ridicule is a promise that the deriders themselves shall suffer ignominy; cf. 65:13: "My servants shall rejoice, and you shall be ashamed (תֵּבֹשׁוּ)." According to Luzzatto: "The proper form should have been 'and we shall be ashamed,' but since God is quoting the wicked, He substitutes the third-person and says 'but they shall be ashamed'" (cf. also Ibn Ezra; Ehrlich, *Randglossen,* 4:230-31; Yellin, *Ḥiqrei Miqra,* 86).

[**6**] The Lord utters a battle cry and proceeds to avenge himself upon

His adversaries. For the motif of the Lord's voice, which characterizes divine warfare, see Ps 29, and cf. Isa 42:13: "The Lord goes forth like a warrior, like a fighter He whips up His rage. He yells, He roars aloud, He charges on His enemies." For similar depictions in Mesopotamian and Ugaritic literature, see M. Weinfeld, "Divine Intervention in War in Ancient Israel and in the Ancient Near East," in H. Tadmor and M. Weinfeld, eds., *History, Historiography and Interpretation: Studies in Biblical and Cuneiform Literatures* (Jerusalem, 1983), 121-47. For additional battle imagery, see v. 15. The term קול is repeated here three times for added emphasis: First it resounds from the city, then from the Temple, and finally it is identified as God's voice.

Hark, tumult from the city! — An uproar emerges from the direction of Jerusalem. For קול together with שָׁאוֹן, see also 13:4; Jer 51:55. The tumult and pandemonium, din and clamor of battle onslaught are all inherent in the word שָׁאוֹן. For the term עִיר as a reference in rabbinic literature to the capital city Jerusalem, see S. Lieberman, *Tosefta ki-Pheshuṭah,* 3: *Seder Moed* (New York, 1962), 62. For the sound of God's voice as it emerges from Jerusalem, see Amos 1:2; Joel 4:16.

Thunder from the Temple! — A tumultuous roar coming from the Temple. For היכל as a reference to the Jerusalem Temple, see Isa 44:28.

It is the thunder of the Lord as He deals retribution to His foes — The unknown pandemonium is now identified as the sound of the Lord as He comes to exact His revenge on His adversaries; cf. 59:18.

[7-9] A miraculous birth is depicted: Zion, in her maternal role, shall have a painless delivery, i.e., redemption. This short section is replete with technical terminology related to birth: חיל, ילד, חֶבֶל, מלט, שׂבר, עצר ("to labor," "to deliver," "pangs," "to bear children," "to bring on labor," "to shut the womb"). For other birth descriptions, see 13:8; Jer 22:23. Here, however, the imagery is unique, for there is no pain or travail involved (reversing Gen 3:16: "In pain shall you bear children") and there are no terms associated with disaster, as in all the other biblical depictions of birth cited above. For the two motifs, God's battle engagement and female labor, see Isa 42:13-14. For the "thunder of the Lord" as a catalyst for birth, see Ps 29:9: "The voice of the Lord causes hinds to calve." (See J. Tigay, "'The Voice of YHWH Causes Hinds to Calve' [Ps 29:9]," in C. Cohen et al., eds., *Birkat Shalom: Studies in the Bible, Ancient Near Eastern Literature, and Postbiblical Judaism Presented to Shalom M. Paul on the Occasion of His Seventieth Birthday,* 2 vols. [Winona Lake, Ind., 2008], 1:399-411.)

[7] *Before she labored, she gave birth* — Before Zion is beset by contractions and labor pains, she shall give birth, a metaphor for imminent redemption. Some commentators interpret this hemistich as a query, as in v. 8: "Is it conceivable that a woman gives birth without labor pains?" For the syn-

onymous pair ילד/חיל ("to labor/to deliver"), see Isa 45:10; 54:1; and note its appearance in Akkadian: "On the day of my labor *(ḫīlūja),* did my face become dark? On the day of my giving birth *(ulādīja)* did my eyes shut?" (*CAD* A/1:289); in Ugaritic: *ḫl ld,* "Writhe (and) give birth!" (*CAT* 1.12.I:25); and in a Phoenician oath from Arslan Tash (seventh century BCE): חל ולד, "Labor and deliver!" (*KAI* 27:27). For Zion as a mother of children (Israel), see, e.g., 49:14-21; 54:1; 60:4, 9; 62:5.

Before her birth pangs came, she bore a son — parallel to the above: Before her labor pains (חֵבֶל) begin, she will have delivered, i.e., her redemption shall occur instantaneously. Other commentators interpret this clause as a query, similar to their understanding of the previous colon. For the root מלט ("to bear") in the *piʿel* (here it is in the *hiphʿil*), see Isa 34:15. The word חבל (in the plural), "contractions," appears also in 13:8; 26:17; Hos 13:13; Jer 13:21; 22:23; 49:24; Job 39:3.

[8] The prophet expands on the image of a painless delivery as a symbol of the redemption that awaits Zion. The astonishment at this sudden turn of events is accentuated in a series of three rhetorical queries: הֲ . . . אם . . . כי. For this formulation, see also Num 11:12; Amos 6:12.

Who ever heard the likes of this? — This verse refers to the events of both this verse and the previous one.

Who ever witnessed such things? — parallel to the first question. For the verbal sequence ראה/שמע, see, e.g., Isa 64:3.

Can a land pass through travail in a single day? — A metaphor based on childbirth and applied to the imminent redemption: Can a country be born after one day's labor? 1QIsa[a] substitutes התחיל (*qal,* identical with the verbal form in the first stich of the previous verse) for the unique *hophʿal,* הֲיוּחַל, of the MT, thus agreeing with the feminine ארץ. For the expression יום אחד ("in a single day") referring to an event that occurs suddenly, see 47:9, portraying the sudden disaster that befell Babylon "in a single day."

Or is a nation born all at once? — For the synonymous pair ילד/חיל, see the previous verse; 54:1; Ps 90:2.

Yet Zion travailed and at once bore her children! — painlessly and immediately.

[9] As above, repeated rhetorical questions are employed as a literary device: הֲ . . . אם: Shall I bring to the point of birth and not deliver, i.e., shall I begin something without seeing it to its conclusion (Rashi, Kimchi)?

"Shall I who bring to the point of birth not deliver?" — says the Lord — אשביר is a denominative verb from the substantive מַשְׁבֵּר, which denotes the opening of the birth canal from which the newborn emerges; see 2 Kgs 19:3 (= Isa 37:3): "The babes have reached the birth canal (משבר), but the strength to give birth is lacking"; Hos 13:13: "Pangs of childbirth assail him . . . for this is no

time to survive at the mouth of the womb (משבר)." In Rabbinic Hebrew the noun signifies a birth stool; see *m. ʿArak.* 1:4: "If she sat down on the birth stool, one waits until she gives birth." For the verb ילד in the *hiphʿil,* with the father as the subject, see Judg 11:1.

"Shall I who cause birth shut the womb?" — said your God — The same as above: Shall I impede the birth? For the root עצר in this context, see Gen 16:2: "Look, the Lord has kept me from bearing (עֲצָרַנִי)."

[10-11] All who love Jerusalem and mourn over her are bidden to rejoice with her. Then, in an extension of the metaphor, redemption is compared to a nursing mother whose breasts are full with milk on which the newborns (the newly redeemed Israelites) shall suckle until satiety. (For the image of breastfeeding in another context see Isa 60:16.) This maternal relationship between Jerusalem and its inhabitants was borrowed from the poetic literature of the ancient Near East, where gods and kings are said to suck at the breasts of goddesses, an image meant to confirm legitimacy and lofty origin. Compare, for example, in Ugaritic, El's blessing of Kirta that his son to be born "will suck *(ynq)* the milk of Astarte, will suckle *(mṣṣ)* the breasts of the maiden Anat" (*CAT* 1.15.II:26-27). The Akkadian creation epic *Enuma Elish* states: "He [Marduk] suckled *(enēqu)* at the breasts of goddesses" (I:85; Foster, *COS* 1:392). It also appears in a prophetic text addressed to the Assyrian monarch Ashurbanipal: "(O Ashurbanipal), whose wet nurse is the Lady of Arbela [= Ishtar]. Fear not! I shall carry you on my hip like a nurse. I shall place you between my breasts (like) a pomegranate. . . . In the daytime I shall give you milk" (Parpola, *Assyrian Prophecies,* 39, text 7, rev. 6-9). In a dialogue between the god Nabu and King Ashurbanipal it is stated: "You were but a babe when you sat on the lap of the Queen of Nineveh [= Ishtar]. Her four teats *(zīzēša)* were put in your mouth; two you suckled *(enēqu)* and two you milked for yourself" (note Ishtar's resemblance to a cow; see A. Livingston, *Court Poetry and Literary Miscellanea,* SAA 3 [Helsinki, 1989], 34, text 13, rev. 6-8). For further such images, see Parpola, *Assyrian Prophecies,* XXVI-XL.

[10] The prophet addresses Jerusalem's well-wishers in an emphatic triad of imperatives: "Rejoice! Be glad! Join in her jubilation!" The reason for this jubilation is that the period of mourning has ended (see 60:20); cf. also 65:18-19.

Rejoice with Jerusalem and be glad for her, all you who love her! — Share Jerusalem's joy with (את) her (the expression שָׂמַח את, "rejoicing with," is unique). The synonymous parallel verbs גיל/שׂמח (cf. Cant 1:4) appear also in the Ugaritic Kirta epic: "We rejoice *(nšmḫ)* in your life, O father. We are glad *(ngln)* in your not dying" (*CAT* 1.16.I:14-15).

Join in her jubilation, all you who mourn for her! — A further command to rejoice directed to those who previously mourned Jerusalem's ignominious fate.

For the synonymous pair גיל/שׂישׂ, see Isa 61:10; 65:18, 19; Ps 35:9. It is also found in line 6 of an Ammonite inscription from Tel Siran dating ca. 600 BCE: יגל וישמח (see Aḥituv, *Ha-Ketav veha-Mik̲tav,* 334). For מָשׂוֹשׂ see Isa 60:15; 62:5. For "Zion's mourners" (אבלים/אבלי ציון), see 57:18; 61:2, 3; and cf. 60:20.

[11] Just as the babe is satiated as he suckles at the breast, so too will Jerusalem's well-wishers enjoy the future abundance.

So that you may suckle from her breast consolation to the full — a metaphor indicating satiety and satisfaction. Zion, the mother, provides her children with total solace. The verb שׂבע signifies satiety not only from eating but also from drinking one's fill; see Jer 46:10; Amos 4:8. This is also the meaning of its etymological and semantic equivalent in Ugaritic, *šbʿ*: "He [El] drinks [wine] to satiety *(šbʿ),* new wine to intoxication" (*CAT* 1.114:16). Compare likewise in Akkadian: "If a baby sucks at the breast but does not become satiated *(šebû)*" (*CAD* Š/2:252); and in Aramaic: "Seven wet nurses shall anoint their breasts, but the baby shall not be satiated (ישׂבע)" (Fitzmyer, *Aramaic Inscriptions of Sefîre,* 14, I.A.21-22). For שׂד ("breast"), a by-form of שַׁד, see Isa 60:16.

So that you may suck from her overflowing bosom to your delight — The unique root מצץ is a by-form of מצי (see 51:17), and for the parallel verbal couplet מצץ/ינק in Ugaritic, *ynq . . . mṣṣ,* see the introduction to vv. 10-11. For the verb התענג ("to take delight"), see also 55:2; 58:14. For the hapax legomenon זיז, which was borrowed from Akk. *zīzu,* "teat" (*CAD* Z:149), see the excerpt from the dialogue between Ashurbanipal and the god Nabu quoted in the introduction to the verse. For כבוד denoting an abundance of wealth (cf. Gen 31:1), see the following verse and the allusions there to breastfeeding. Compare likewise the etymological and semantic Akkadian parallels *kubtu* and *kubuttû* (*CAD* K:487, 490-91).

[12-14] The suckling image is further elaborated, and the contented babe is pictured as being carried on the hip and dandled on the knees. Note the verbal connection between these three verses and the previous section: וִינַקְתֶּם . . . כבוד (v. 12) — תִּינְקוּ . . . כבודה (v. 11) (chiastic parallelism); . . . תְּנַחֲמֶנּוּ אֲנַחֶמְכֶם . . . תְּנֻחָמוּ (v. 13) — תַּנְחֻמֶיהָ (v. 11); ששׂ (v. 14) — שִׂישׂוּ . . . משׂושׂ (v. 10).

[12] *For thus said the Lord* — The imagery in this verse was influenced by Isa 8:6-8, which described a scene from the Assyrian invasion of Judah and completely revised it in the new context of future blessing. (See the introduction, §14.)

"I will extend to her prosperity like a stream" — I will send Jerusalem a gift of munificence and prosperity (שלום) that shall sweep over her like a strong river current. For the same simile, see 48:18: "Then your prosperity (שלומך) shall be like a stream." For the expression נטי אל ("to extend to"), see Gen 38:16; 39:21; Josh 8:18 (twice); Ps 40:2.

"The wealth of nations like a wadi in flood" — parallel to the above: You shall be overwhelmed by material wealth like a stream in flood. For similar images, though in an ominous context, see Isa 30:28; Jer 47:2; 2 Chr 32:4. For כבוד as material "wealth" in a similar context, see v. 11 and the Akkadian cognates. Compare the Babylonian inscription of Nabonidus, where the monarch proclaims: "I offered gifts to the gods . . . the precious gifts *(kubuttû)* of the kings" (*CAD* K:491). For the synonymous pair נחל/נהר ("stream/flood"), see Ps 74:15.

"You shall suck" — an extension of the breastfeeding metaphor above: You shall suck from the riches the nations shall bestow upon you; cf. Isa 60:16: "You shall suck the milk of the nations, and suckle at royal breasts." For the motif of the bestowal of gifts upon Jerusalem by the nations, see 60:5-7, 11; 61:5. The LXX understood the word as a substantive, וְיֹנַקְתָּם ("their infants"; cf. 1QIsa[a], תיהמה[]), and thus attached it to the next clause.

"And you shall be carried on hips" — Back to Jerusalem like babies; cf. 49:22: "I will raise My hand to nations and lift up My ensign to peoples. And they shall bring your sons in their bosoms, and carry your daughters on their backs" (and note the motif of nursing that appears there in the next verse: "Their queens shall serve you as nurses"); 60:4: "Your daughters shall be brought like babes on hips." For illustrations of exiled parents carrying their children on their shoulders and hips, see the references cited in 60:4. If the LXX's version (and that of 1QIsa[a]) of the previous clause is followed, then this hemistich would begin with the words "their children."

"And dandled on knees" — And you shall be bounced, petted, and pampered as a child on his parents' knees. This is reminiscent of the image in 49:23 of royal nursemaids and guardians. The *pulpal* stem of the verb שׁעשׁע, תְּשָׁעֳשָׁעוּ, found only here, was replaced in 1QIsa[a] by the more common *hithpalpel*, תשתעשעו (see Isa 29:9; Ps 119:16, 47; for other paradigm shifts between the scroll and the MT see immediately below). For similar images in Akkadian literature, see the references listed under *birku* ("knee") in *CAD* B:256. For the same combination of motifs in a Mesopotamian composition describing King Ashurbanipal as a child sitting on the goddess Ishtar's lap and sucking at her breast, see Livingstone, *Court Poetry*, 34, text 13, rev. 7-8.

[13] The Lord consoles the mourners of Zion following their exile as a mother would console her child. For further instances of God in feminine roles, see Isa 42:14; 45:10; 46:3-4; 49:15. (See M. I. Gruber, "The Motherhood of God in Second Isaiah," in *The Motherhood of God and Other Studies*, SFSHJ 57 [Atlanta, 1992], 3-15.) The root נחם, a frequently recurring term throughout the book and part of the overall leitmotif of consolation from the very first verse of the book (40:1), is repeated here three times for added emphasis and contrasts with the description of uncomforted Zion prior to her redemption; cf. 54:11; Lam 1:9, 17. For the syntactical paradigm כ(י) . . . כן, see 54:9; 55:10-11; and cf. 1 Sam 25:25; Ps 48:11.

"As a mother comforts her son" — For איש denoting a young child, see Gen 4:1: "I have created a male child (איש) with the help of the Lord"; cf. 1 Sam 1:11.

"So I will comfort you" — Note the positioning of the pronoun "I" (אנכי) first for emphasis. Compare 51:12: "I, I am He who comforts you."

"And you shall find comfort in Jerusalem" — 1QIsa[a] substitutes the more common *hithpa'el* form, תתנחמו, for the relatively rare *pu'al,* תְּנֻחָמוּ (elsewhere only in 54:11) in the MT; cf. the similar paradigm substitution in the previous verse.

[14] The redemption of the Lord's servants shall rejuvenate the desiccated nation and their languishing bones shall flourish, in contrast to their forlorn condition in exile, as described in Ezek 37:11: "Our bones are dried up. Our hope is gone. We are doomed." For heartfelt joy as a balm for sickness, as opposed to sickness that withers the bones, see Prov 17:22: "A joyful heart makes for good health; despondency dries up the bones." The first two hemistichs of this verse were found (with one partial variant, עצמותם ["their bones"] instead of עצמותיכם ["your bones"] as in the MT) inscribed on a stone on the wall surrounding the Temple Mount (the inscription dates to the Byzantine period; see M. Ben-Dov, *In the Shadow of the Temple: The Discovery of Ancient Jerusalem* [Jerusalem, 1985], 219, 222-23). At the end of this verse there is a shift from redemption to divine requital.

"You shall see and your heart shall rejoice" — You shall witness this miraculous occurrence and shall be overjoyed. For the verb שׂישׂ, see v. 10; 61:10; 62:5; 64:4; 65:18, 19.

"Your limbs shall flourish like spring grass" — A simile for rejuvenation compared to the sprouting of spring grass (Heb. דֶּשֶׁא = Akk. *dīšu; CAD* D:163-64). For עֲצָמוֹת ("limbs"), see Judg 19:29; Ezek 6:5.

"The power of the Lord shall be revealed for His servants" — The Lord shall reveal His might in the service of His faithful. For נודע(ה) in a revelatory context, see Ps 76:2: "God has made Himself known (נודע) in Judah." For יד ה׳ (lit. "the Lord's hand"), see 40:2; 41:20; 51:17; 59:1; 62:3; for the Lord's "servants" see 65:13-14.

"But He shall rage/His rage against His foes" — The verb נודעה in the previous stich may apply here as well: The Lord's anger shall be made known to His adversaries; cf. Ps 7:12: "God rages (זֹעֵם) each day"; Hab 3:12: "You tread the earth in rage (בזעם), You trample nations in fury." The translation "His rage," a substantive rather than a verb, "He rages," as pointed in the MT, presupposes that a *waw* was deleted from the text, and should be read: זַעְמוֹ. The term זעם is reserved primarily for divine anger.

[15-16] A detailed description of God's rampage. The Lord dons His warrior garb and arms Himself with weapons: fire (thrice mentioned), whirlwind, and sword. For similar descriptions of the Deity's arsenal and His tools of destruction, cf. Isa 29:6: "She shall be punished by the Lord of Hosts with thunder, and earthquake, and deafening noise, storm, and tempest, and flame of consuming fire"; Ps 7:13-14: "He sharpens His sword, bends His bow and aims it . . . and tips His arrows with fire"; Ps 50:3: "Devouring fire precedes Him and storms around Him fiercely"; Ps 83:15-16: "As a fire burns a forest, as flames scorch the hills, pursue them with Your tempest and terrify them with Your storm." For the divine chariot, see Hab 3:8: "You mount Your steeds, Your victorious chariot." These depictions are a manifestation of a literary tradition spanning the ancient Near East. For the motif of a god's chariot, which appears on seals as far back as the third millennium, see *ANEP*, no. 689, and especially no. 536 (the seal of the Assyrian monarch Tukulti-Ninurta II from the ninth century BCE). In one inscription, King Sennacherib of Assyria reports: "I made a representation of the god Ashur holding a bow and riding in a chariot, with the god Amurru riding with him as charioteer" (*CAD* A/2:182). These images have numerous parallels in epic literature; cf., e.g., the description of Marduk in *Enuma Elish*: "He mounted the terrible chariot, the unopposable Storm Demon, he hitched it to the four-steed team, he tied them at his side" (IV:50-51; Foster, *COS* 1:397); and Adad in the flood epic *Atrahasis*: "The god Adad rode on the four winds . . . the chariot of the gods" (rev. lines 5, 12; W. Lambert and A. R. Millard, *Atraḫasīs: The Babylonian Story of the Flood* [Oxford, 1969], 122, 124).

[15] The substantive "fire" (**אש**) appears at both the beginning and end of the verse, creating a literary *inclusio*. Compare also v. 16: "For with fire will the Lord contend." For other occurrences of fire and storm connected with divine warfare, see Isa 29:6; Ps 83:15-16.

"Lo, the Lord is coming with fire" — The initial **כי** is for emphasis: Behold, fire shall portend the Lord's arrival, and He shall deal severely with His foes; cf. Ps 97:3: "Fire goes before Him, burning His foes on every side." For fire associated with the Deity, see Deut 4:24: "For the Lord your God is a consuming fire, an impassioned God." For similar references in Akkadian, see *CAD* I-J:229. Instead of **באש** ("with fire"), as in the MT, the LXX and some medieval Hebrew manuscripts have **כאש** ("like fire"), which accords with the adjacent clause, **וכסופה** ("like a whirlwind").

"His chariots are like a whirlwind" — Cf. Nah 1:3: "He travels in whirlwind and storm." The Lord's chariot is alluded to in other biblical verses, e.g., Hab 3:8; Ps 77:19. For a similar image connected to an enemy invasion of Judah, see Isa 5:28: "Their horses' hooves are like flint; their chariot wheels like the whirlwind"; see also Jer 4:13. 1QIsa[a] **ובסופה**, instead of **וכסופה**, corresponds with the preceding **באש**.

"To vent His anger in fury" — The Lord contends with fire and gale in or-

der to pour out His wrath on His adversaries. For the verb שוב in the *hiph'il* with this meaning, see Job 15:13: "You vent (תָּשִׁיב) your anger on God"; cf. Deut 32:41: "Vengeance will I vent (אָשִׁיב) on My foes." Luzzatto, however, suggests vocalizing לְהַשִּׁיב, from the root נשב ("to blow"), and translates, "His furious breath blows hotly". For the anomalous חֵמָה אפו, instead of חֲמַת אפו, see Isa 42:25 and the comments there; cf. Ps 18:16.

"His rebuke in blazing fire" — His fury shall be vented in flaming fire (לַהֲבֵי אֵשׁ); the verb in the previous colon applies here as well. For similar expressions, cf. the attack of the locusts in the days of Joel: "With a noise like a blazing fire (להב אשׁ)" (Joel 2:5); and see also Ps 29:7: "The voice of the Lord kindles flames of fire (להבות אשׁ)." For the synonymous pair גערה/חֵמָה ("His anger/His rebuke"), see Isa 51:20.

[16] Compare this verse to Jer 25:31-33: "For the Lord has a case (נשפט) against the nations. He contends with all flesh (לכל בשׂר). He delivers the wicked to the sword (לחרב) — declares the Lord. . . . In that day the earth shall be strewn with the slain of the Lord (חללי ה׳) from one end to the other." (See the introduction, §15.)

"With fire will the Lord surely contend" — The particle כי is for emphasis. For the expression נשפט ב- as legal contention or punishment, see Ezek 38:22. For the variant in 1QIsa[a], כי באש ה׳ יבוא לשפוט ("For with fire the Lord shall come to judge"), cf. v. 15: כי הנה ה׳ באש יבוא ("See, the Lord is coming with fire"); and cf. 65:5; Ps 96:13; 98:9; 1 Chr 16:33. For the divine "trial by fire," see also Amos 7:4: "Lo, my Lord God was summoning to contend by fire." The LXX adds the expression "all the earth"; cf. Ps 96:13 = 98:9; 1 Chr 16:33.

"And with His sword against all humanity" — The Lord shall judge the nations of the world by the sword (the verb נשפט in the previous colon is implied here). For the sword as one of God's chosen weapons, see Isa 65:12; cf. 27:1: "In that day the Lord will punish with His great, cruel, and mighty sword Leviathan, the elusive serpent — Leviathan, the twisting serpent. He will slay the Dragon of the sea"; cf. 34:5-6. For the expression כל בשׂר ("all flesh"), a reference to all humankind, see 66:23, 24; 40:5, 6; 49:26. For the joint appearance of the terms אשׁ and חרב in Ugaritic literature, cf. *išt ištm . . . ḥrb lṭšt,* "Fire of two flames . . . a sharpened sword" (*CAT* 1.2.I:32); and in the reverse order: *ḥrb . . . išt* (*CAT* 1.6.V:13-14).

"And many shall be the slain of the Lord" — Compare also Zeph 2:12: "You Cushites too — they shall be slain by My sword (חללי חרבי)." Instead of MT חללי ה׳ (as in Jer 25:33), 1QIsa[a] has חלליו ("His slain").

[17-18a] The prophet excoriates the nation for their illegitimate ritual practices; see also v. 3; 65:3-4.

[17] *"Those who sanctify and purify themselves (to enter) the gardens"* — They prepare themselves by a ceremony of sanctification and purification (both verbs are in the *hithpa'el*) in order to enter (the verb is supplied) the gardens where they participate in their unorthodox rituals. (Note the assimilation of the **ת** into the **ט** in the *hithpa'el,* הַמִּטַּהֲרִים.) For gardens as the loci of foreign cults, see also 65:3 (and the references there); 1:29: "And you shall be frustrated with the gardens you coveted." For worship in gardens in Mesopotamian literature, see *CAD* K:414-15.

One after another into the center — Neither the Ketib (**אחד**, "one," masculine) nor the Qere (**אחת**, "one," feminine — as corroborated by the Vulgate, 1QIsa[a], and partially by 1QIsa[b]) sheds any light on the meaning of this difficult clause. The Targum (**סִיעָא בָּתַר סִיעָא**, "one group after another"), Symmachus, Theodotion, and Peshitta (*ḥd btr ḥd,* "one after another"), either read or interpret this clause as a procession into the garden. Luzzatto, Ehrlich (*Miqra ki-Pheshuṭo,* 3:162), and Tur-Sinai (*Peshuṭo shel Miqra,* III/1:152) emend the text to **אחד אחד** ("one by one"). According to Ibn Ezra, **אחת** is a reference to the Asherah: "The tree . . . that they walked around from all sides and that is in the center of the garden."

"Eating the flesh of the swine, detestable things/the reptile, and the mouse" — A component of these garden rituals is the consumption of unclean animals — the pig (see also v. 3; 65:4) and the mouse, both of which are categorically prohibited: "The following, however . . . you shall not eat . . . and the swine" (Lev 11:4, 7); "The following shall be unclean for you from among the things that swarm on the earth . . . the mouse" (11:29). The middle term, הַשֶּׁקֶץ (note the variant in 1QIsa[a], **והשקוץ**, a form that was likely influenced by v. 3, **ובשקוציהם** ["and in their abominations"]), denotes something unclean, an abomination (Lev 11:10: "Among all the swarming things of the water and among all the other living creatures that are in the water — they are an abomination [שֶׁקֶץ] for you"; cf., e.g., 11:12, 13, 20, 23). The term here refers to an unclean animal, as in Rabbinic Hebrew; cf., e.g., *m. Nid.* 3:2; *Sanh.* 8:2: **שקצים ורמשים** ("forbidden animals and reptiles"). Some commentators emend **שקץ** to שֶׁרֶץ (see Peshitta *wšrṣ'*), which denotes small reptiles and quadrupeds, and cf. the Samaritan text as well as Targum Onqelos and Saadyah Gaon to Lev 7:21: (**בכל**) שֶׁרֶץ (**טמא**), instead of MT **שקץ**. See Lev 11:10, 29 for this prohibition.

"Shall one and all come to an end" — declares the Lord — For the verb **סוף** ("to perish"), see Esth 9:28: "And the memory of them shall never perish (יָסוּף) among their descendants."

[18a] *"For I [know] their deeds and designs"* — The clause is missing a verb, and many, following the LXX and Peshitta, add the verb **ידעתי** ("I know") (see also Saadyah, 147; Metzudat David). Compare also the Targum: "All their deeds and thoughts are revealed (גְּלַן) before me." For the sequence of evil deeds and designs in tandem, see Isa 59:6-7.

[18b-24] In marked contrast to the derisive comment: "Let the Lord manifest His Presence" (v. 5), the Lord announces that the time has come to gather all the nations to Jerusalem in order to gaze on His revealed Presence (vv. 18, 19). They shall reunite the Israelite Diaspora, and some shall even serve in God's Temple. The nation shall gain immortality, and all humanity shall come to Jerusalem to worship God on Sabbaths and new moons. While there they shall see with their very own eyes the horrendous punishment of the wicked. For the idea of foreigners becoming worshipers of the God of Israel, see 45:14-15, 23-24; 56:7; 60:10.

[18b] *"[The time] has come/I am coming"* — An elliptical clause in which one should perhaps insert **העת** ("the time") as per the context (cf. Ibn Ezra, Kimchi, and Metzudat David). The plural form **באו** in 1QIsa[a], instead of **באה** in the MT, corresponds with the adjacent plurals, **מעשיהם ומחשְׁבֹתיהם** ("their deeds and designs"), but does not help clarify the text. In contrast, the LXX and Vulgate (cf. also Peshitta and Targum) read **בא**, which is attached to the following clause: "I am coming to gather all the nations and tongues."

"To gather all the nations and peoples" — "The time has come," or "I am coming" (whichever reading above is accepted) to assemble all the nations as one. The substantive **לְשֹׁנוֹת** with the meaning "foreign peoples," a semantic extension of **לשון**, "tongue" (as in Zech 8:23: **מכל לְשֹׁנות הגוים**, "from nations of every tongue"), is a Late Biblical Hebrew term that does not appear in earlier strata of the language. Note, moreover, its sevenfold appearance in the Aramaic of Daniel (3:4, 7, 29, 31; 5:19; 6:26; 7:14). The etymological and semantic cognate in Akkadian, *lišānu*, also has this same extended meaning (*CAD* L:214). (See the introduction, §11.) For the verb **קבץ**, which usually refers to the reassembling of the Israelite Diaspora, see, e.g., Isa 43:5; 56:8.

"They shall come and behold My Presence" — They shall assemble in Jerusalem and experience My Presence; cf. 40:5: "The Presence of the Lord shall appear, and all flesh, as one, shall behold." For the meaning of the term **כבוד**, see 40:5.

[19] The Lord shall leave a remnant from the foreign nations, that they may declare God's glory to the nations to Israel's west and north.

I will set a sign among them — Although in every other instance the expression **שׂים אות ב-** has negative connotations (e.g., Exod 10:2; Jer 32:20; Ps 78:43), such is not the case here. In light of the semantic parallel in Akk. *šimtam šakānu* ("to set a sign"), which can denote ownership (*CAD* Š/3:10), the "setting of a sign" may refer to a mark placed on those who are faithful to and protected by the Lord; see Gen 4:15: "And the Lord put a mark on Cain"; and cf. the mark on the forehead of the individuals safeguarded by the Lord in Ezek 9:4, 6. Both 1QIsa[a] and the LXX read **אותות** ("signs"), in the plural, instead of the singular **אות** in the MT, and were perhaps influenced by the verse from Exod 10:2 cited above or the plural **פְּלֵיטים** ("survivors") in the next hemistich.

"And send from them survivors to the nations" — And I shall preserve from among them a remnant to proclaim My name among the following nations. Hebrew פליט designates a fugitive survivor from the battlefield who sometimes functions as a source of information regarding developments in the war; cf. Gen 14:13: "A fugitive brought the news to Abram the Hebrew"; Ezek 33:21: "A fugitive came to me from Jerusalem and reported, 'The city has fallen.'" Compare also the expression in Isa 45:20, פְּלִיטֵי הגוים ("You survivors of the nations").

"To Tarshish" — Tarshish is generally identified with Tarsus on the western coast of Asia Minor, or with Tartesus on the Iberian Peninsula, west of Gibraltar. The prophet Jonah attempted to escape his prophetic mission to Nineveh (the capital of Assyria in the east) by embarking on a ship bound for western Tarshish (Jonah 1:3). Compare also the two geographical poles in the Assyrian king Esarhaddon's inscription, in which he boasts: "All the kings who live in the middle of the (islands of the) sea, from Cyprus (and) Javan to Tarshish, prostrated themselves to my feet. I received from them their heavy tribute" (57:10-11; see R. Borger, *Die Inschriften Asarhaddons, Königs von Assyrien* [Graz, 1956], 86).

"Pul" — Since there is no land or people known by this name (the name refers in the Bible to the Assyrian monarch, Tiglath-pileser III [2 Kgs 15:19; 1 Chr 5:26], which is a transliteration of his Akkadian name, *Pūlu* [see J. A. Brinkman, *A Political History of Post-Kassite Babylonia,* AnOr 43 (Rome, 1968), 61-62, 240-43, 359-60]), most commentators prefer reading (along with the LXX), פוט (identified with Libya, west of Egypt), a nation mentioned together with Lud (as here) in Jer 46:9; Ezek 27:10; 30:5; 38:5.

"And Lud" — identified with Lydia, a nation on the coast of Asia Minor, appearing together with Put (see the above references).

"That draw the bow/Meshech" — archers; cf. Jer 46:9: "And the Ludim who grasp and draw the bow (דֹּרְכֵי קשת)." Since the other nations listed here have no descriptive features attached to their names, and since it is possible that the scribe was influenced here by the verse in Jeremiah (just quoted), some have suggested to read: משך, "Meshech" (corroborated by LXX) instead of MT מֹשְׁכֵי קשת. Meshech is listed among the nations of Asia Minor in Gen 10:2, following Javan and Tubal, as Japheth's sixth son. The three are also mentioned together as slave traders and metal merchants in Ezek 27:13. Meshech, marking the western border of the Assyrian Empire ("From the land of Egypt until the land of Mushki"), is identified with the *Muški* in Assyrian sources and is first mentioned in the inaugural year of Tiglath-pileser I's reign (1116 BCE) and in a number of inscriptions dating to the reign of Sargon. In the Babylonian and Persian periods, Meshech and Tubal (see immediately below) serve as an ethnogeographic marker for the nations of central Anatolia (Ezek

32:26; cf. also 38:2-3; 39:1). If this reading is correct, then the expression "that draw the bow" was incorrectly added under the influence of Jer 46:9 cited above.

"To Tubal" — a kingdom of Asia Minor, which is listed as Japheth's fifth son in Gen 10:2. Usually mentioned together with Meshech (Ezek 27:13; 32:26; 38:2, 3; 39:1), it is identified with the kingdom of Tabal in Assyrian sources beginning with the reign of Shalmaneser III (837 BCE).

"Javan" — listed alongside Tubal and Meshech, according to the list of nations in Gen 10:2, and usually identified with the Ionians, a nation that dwelled on the western coast of Asia Minor, the inhabitants of which are referred to as *Iamanî* in Assyrian sources from the eighth and seventh centuries BCE.

"The distant coasts" — a reference to the Greek and Aegean islands. For the joint appearance of Tarshish and the coastlands, see Isa 60:9; Ps 72:10: "The kings of Tarshish and the islands shall pay tribute."

"That have never heard My fame" — Compare Num 14:15: "The nations who have heard Your fame (שִׁמְעֲךָ)"; Hab 3:2: "I have learned of Your renown (שִׁמְעֲךָ); I am awed."

"Nor beheld My Presence" — Compare v. 18: "They shall . . . behold My Presence."

"They shall declare My Presence among these nations" — Note the third appearance of כבודי, and see v. 18.

[20] The nations shall bring the expatriates to Jerusalem and present them before the Lord, in the same manner that Israel used to offer sacrifices to the Lord in the Temple. This description of offering tribute was most likely influenced by the Mesopotamian royal inscriptions, where the very same animals and vehicles are mentioned in the exact same order as here: *narkabātu* ("chariots"), *ṣumbāti* ("drays, carts, wagons"), *sīsû* ("horses"), *parê* ("mules"), *gammali* ("dromedaries"). (See Paul, *Divrei Shalom,* 17-18.) A further tradition reflected here and well documented in Sumerian hymns and Akkadian royal inscriptions is that of the capital city together with its sanctuary serving as an international center of pilgrimage. Compare, for example, the Sumerian hymn to Enlil, god of Nippur: "All lands bow before it [Nippur]. . . . All the lords and princes bring here pure oblations, and offer you sacrifice and prayer"; and the hymn to Ningursu of Lagash: "At its name [Lagash] foreigners gather from all corners of the sky. The people of Magan and Meluhha come there from their distant lands, bringing trees for the building of the temple of Ningursu." (See Weinfeld, *From Joshua to Josiah,* 124-29.) Compare also 56:7; 60:5, 9. The terms אֲחֵיכם ("your brothers") and מִנחה ("offering") in this verse contrast with the mention of the same terms in vv. 3, 5 in a decidedly negative context.

"And they shall bring all your brothers from all the nations as an offering-tribute to the Lord" — The nations of the world shall transport your kin from

their diaspora as an offering to the Lord. For מִנחה ("offering, tribute"), see 1 Kgs 5:1: "They brought Solomon tribute (מנחה) and were subject to him all his life"; 2 Chr 26:8: "The Ammonites paid tribute (מנחה) to Uzziah." Compare also the Ugaritic etymological and semantic cognate in *CAT* 1.2.I:37-38: "He will bring you [Yam] an offering *(mnḥyk)*"; and Akk. *mānaḫtu* (*CAD* M/1:206). For the nations who will transport Israel back to their ancestral homeland, see also v. 12; 49:22; 60:9.

"On horses, in chariots" — as in 43:17; 2 Kgs 6:14. 1QIsa[a] substitutes the collective רֶכֶב ("chariots") with the plural רכבים, in order to accord with the other substantives, all appearing in the masculine plural.

"And wagons" — Hebrew צַבִּים is an Akkadian loanword, *ṣubbu* > *ṣumbu* (*CAD* Ṣ:244). The term appears only once more in the Bible, in the singular, in Num 7:3.

"On mules" — The mule is the offspring of a female horse and a male donkey. For mules (along with horses) serving as tribute, see 1 Kgs 10:25.

"And dromedaries" — The Hebrew hapax legomenon כִּרְכָּרוֹת represents a type of camel (Ibn Ezra, Kimchi, Abravanel) and is the semantic equivalent of "camels" in the Mesopotamian tribute lists quoted above. Compare a similar image in Isa 60:6: "Dust clouds of camels shall cover you, dromedaries of Midian and Ephah."

"To Jerusalem, My holy mountain" — This clause is connected to the beginning of the verse: Jerusalem is the locus and focus of all this human tribute. Note the variant אל, "to" (1QIsa[a], and cf. also Vulgate and Peshitta), instead of MT על, "on." For the expression הר קדשי ("My holy mountain"), see 56:7; 57:13; 65:11, 25.

Said the Lord — in the middle of a verse, just as in v. 2.

"Just as the Israelites bring an offering in a pure vessel to the House of the Lord" — This tribute that the nations shall bring follows the same pattern of the sacrificial offerings brought by Israel to the Temple. The term מנחה here is a reference to an actual sacrifice rather than a tribute, as at the beginning of the verse.

[21] A cultic innovation, the likes of which is unprecedented in biblical literature: The Lord shall appoint Levitical priests from among the nations to serve Him. For foreign participation in the Israelite cult, see 45:14-15, 23-24; 56:6-7; 60:7, 10.

"And from them likewise I will take some to be Levitical priests" — said the Lord — According to the Masoretic vocalization לַכֹּהנים לַלוים (the LXX and 1QIsa[a] add לי, "for Me"; note the similarity to Num 8:14, 16-18, which may have influenced this addition), the Lord shall appoint assistants to the Levitical priests from among the nations. According to Ehrlich (*Miqra ki-Pheshuto,* 3:162-63), however, the Masoretes had difficulty with the idea that the Lord

would appoint uncircumcised heathens as priests and thus vocalized the *lamed* prefixes with a *pataḥ* (an elision of the definite particle), thereby implying that these new appointees would act in the service of the priests but not actually engage in cultic activities. This is a tendentious vocalization, however, and the first *lamed* should be vocalized with a *shewa,* and the second with a *ḥiriq* (without the elided definite article) (לְכֹהֲנִים לִלְוִיִּם), and be translated: "And from them [the foreigners] likewise I will take some to be Levitical priests." Compare also Rashi and Kimchi, who allude to this correct interpretation. The ancient translations, as well as Rashi, Eliezer of Beaugency, Joseph Kara, and many Hebrew medieval manuscripts, add a *waw* here: לכהנים וללוים. This prophecy terminates the Levitical exclusivity in the Temple ritual, a hereditary responsibility never before brought into doubt.

[22] A new day shall dawn: Israel shall endure forever as do the heaven and earth. For the syntactical construction (כי) כאשר . . . כן, see Isa 52:14-15; 55:10-11; 65:8; and cf. 54:9.

"For as the new heaven and the new earth that I will create shall endure by My will" — declares the Lord — for just as the heaven and the earth, which I am creating anew, shall forever endure "before Me," לפני (= "by My will"; Luzzatto); cf. 65:17: "For behold! I am creating a new heaven and a new earth." For the term לְפָנַי denoting "will," cf. Gen 17:18: "And Abraham said to God, 'O, that Ishmael might live by Your will (לפניך)!'"; Gen 27:7: "That I may bless you with the Lord's approval (לפני), before I die"; see also Num 32:20, 21, 22. (See E. A. Speiser, *Genesis,* AB [Garden City, N.Y., 1964], 51.) For the verb עשי indicating the creative process, see Isa 66:2; 45:7; and for the verb עמד signifying everlasting endurance, see Jer 32:14. "So that they may be preserved (יעמדו) a long time"; Ps 102:27: "They shall perish but you shall endure (תעמֹד)"; Ps 111:3 (= 112:9): "His beneficence endures (עֹמדת) forever." The pair "heaven and earth" are also employed in Mesopotamian literature to indicate eternal durability (*CAD* Š/1:347); and cf. Deut 11:21: "To the end that you and your children may endure . . . as long as there is a heaven over the earth." (For blessings of long life to a king and his dynasty based on the durability of the planetary bodies, see Paul, *Divrei Shalom,* 51-58.)

"So shall your seed and your name endure" — So too shall your stock endure forevermore. The word שֵׁם (lit. "name") refers to "progeny" in this context; see also Isa 48:19; 56:5; 2 Sam 14:7; Isa 14:22. Note the semantic and etymological cognate in Akk. *šumu* (*CAD* Š/3:295-96), which often appears together with *zēru,* "seed" (*CAD* Z:94), in the same context as in this verse.

[23] A pilgrimage of all the nations to Jerusalem to worship the Lord on every Sabbath and every new moon. For similar latter-day prophecies cf. Jer 3:17: "At that time they shall call Jerusalem 'Throne of the Lord,' and all nations shall assemble there in the name of the Lord, at Jerusalem"; Zech 14:16: "All who survive of all those nations that attacked Jerusalem shall make a pilgrimage year by year to bow low to the King, the Lord of Hosts, and to observe the Feast of Booths." The expression כל (ה)בשׂר ("all humanity," lit. "all flesh") appears again in vv. 16, 24; 40:5, 6; 49:26. For Sabbath observance in Deutero-Isaiah's prophecies, see 56:2, 4, 6, 58:13; 66:23. On the basis of this verse, this chapter was chosen as the prophetic reading in synagogues on days when the new moon and Sabbath coincide.

"And new moon after new moon, and Sabbath after Sabbath" — On every new moon and on every Sabbath. For the appearance of these two festivals in tandem, see also Num 28:9-15; 2 Kgs 4:23; Isa 1:13; Hos 2:13; Amos 8:5; cf. also Ezek 46:3: "The common people shall worship before the Lord on Sabbaths and new moons at the entrance of the same gate." The term מִדֵּי, derived from the substantive דַּי ("sufficiency, enough"), meaning "as often as," indicates a cycle (see 1 Sam 7:16: מדי שנה בשנה ["each year"]; cf. also Zech 14:16 [quoted above]; 2 Chr 24:5), and note its appearance in Phoenician: "Day by (מד) day, month by (מד) month, forevermore") (*KAI* 43:11-12). Since שבת is predominately feminine in Mishnaic Hebrew (as opposed to the Bible, where it can also occur in the masculine, e.g., Isa 56:2, 6), 4QIsa[c] renders in the feminine, שבת בשבתה, instead of MT שבת בְּשַׁבַּתּוֹ.

"All humankind shall come to bow down before Me" — said the Lord — in My Temple in Jerusalem. For this motif, see 56:7 and the references to Mesopotamian literature in the introduction to this verse. The expression כל בשׂר appears in the first chapter of Deutero-Isaiah's prophecies (40:5) and thus is part of a literary frame for Deutero-Isaiah's entire collection of prophecies. The LXX adds here "in Jerusalem," likely influenced by a similar verse in Isa 27:13: "And in that day . . . they shall come . . . and worship the Lord on the holy mount, in Jerusalem" (there, however, the context refers to the Israelites alone).

[24] The dire fate of Israel's enemies will be to lie as decaying carcasses with no hope of burial. This severe punishment, alluded to in Isa 14:19 (regarding the Assyrian king Sargon) and Jer 22:19 (regarding Jehoiachim, king of Judah), is well documented in Mesopotamian royal inscriptions, which report on the curse of nonburial and the removal of bones from the grave (*CAD* E:342; Q:202). The expression לא תִכְבֶּה ("shall not be quenched") is part of a series of terms and expressions appearing in both chaps. 65–66 and chap. 1 (v. 31), thus creating a literary frame binding the entire book into one. On the basis of vv. 23-24, *m. 'Ed.* 2:10 states: "The term of evildoers in hell is twelve months, as it is written: 'New moon after new moon'" (this is interpreted as a full twelve-month cycle). Rabbi Yoḥanan ben Nuri maintains: "(Their term is) from Passover until Pentecost, as it is written: 'Sabbath after Sabbath.'" ("Sabbath" is understood here to mean "festival," as in Lev 23:15, and thus means from one "Sabbath" — Passover, to the next "Sabbath" — Pentecost.) This final verse echoes the thematically related conclusion of the first two major sections: Isa 48:22 and 57:21. "There is no safety — said my God — for the wicked."

"They shall go out and gaze on the corpses of the men who rebelled against Me" — When they depart from the Temple, they shall behold the dead bodies of the unfaithful. These are "the slain of the Lord" (v. 16) who did not receive proper burial and were left exposed on the ground. The expression פשׂע ב-, "to rebel against" (e.g., 2 Kgs 1:1; Ezek 20:38), contributes to the macroliterary frame, as it also appears in Isa 1:2. The expression ראי ב- ("to gaze upon") at times has negative connotations, e.g., "to gloat"; see, for example, Ps 22:18; 54:9; 118:7.

"Their worms shall not die" — The כי particle is emphatic: Their rotting bodies shall be consumed by worms and maggots forevermore. For the connection between a corpse and worms, cf. Gilgamesh's sorrowful pronouncement to Siduri at the death of his companion Enkidu: "Enkidu, whom I loved dearly . . . has now gone to the fate of mankind . . . I would not give him up for burial . . . until a worm fell out of his nose" (X.ii:2-9; *ANET*, 89-90). Akkadian *tūltu* ("worm") is the etymological and semantic equivalent of Heb. תולעת in this verse.

"Nor their fire quenched" — It was customary to burn dead bodies to prevent putrefaction; but in the case of the unfaithful, this fire will never cease consuming their maggot-infested flesh. This punishment by fire is connected to the pronouncement in v. 15 regarding the divine revelation: "See, the Lord is coming with fire"; and v. 16: "For with fire will the Lord contend." This horrific image was often used to describe the punishment of evildoers in the world to come in postbiblical literature.

"They shall be a horror to all humankind" — Their rotting carcasses shall emit an offensive odor and will elicit revulsion and disgust in all who behold them. The term דֵּרָאוֹן appears again only in Dan 12:2: "Many of those that sleep in the dust of the earth will awake; some to everlasting life, and others to reproaches of everlasting abhorrence (דראון)." Some commentators connect the term to the similar sounding and basically synonymous זרא in Num 11:20: "Until it comes out of your nostrils and becomes loathsome (זרא) to you" (cf. Luzzatto). The expression כל (ה)בשׂר, which appears here for the third time in this chapter (see vv. 16, 23), occurs also in 40:5, 6, creating another link in the literary *inclusio* of the entire book.

Since there is a tradition in Judaism of concluding every book of the Bible on a positive note, it is customary to repeat the next-to-last verse when the final verse is negative. In addition to Isaiah, this occurs in the conclusion of Malachi, Lamentations, and Ecclesiastes. The mnemonic acronym for these four books is י׳ ת׳ ק׳ ק׳ (ישעיה, תרי עשר, קינות, קהלת) or, alternatively, י׳ ת׳ ק׳ א׳ (ישעיה, תרי עשר, קהלת, איכה). In accordance with this custom, v. 23 is recited once again after v. 24, when the chapter is read in synagogue as the prophetic haftarah portion when the Sabbath and the new moon coincide.

Selected Bibliography

These works are supplementary to the references cited in full in the text. Multiple entries by the same author are arranged chronologically.

Classical Hebrew and Arabic Commentaries and Commentators

Menaḥem ben Saruq. *Sefer ha-Maḥberet.* Wadenburg, 1854. Hebrew.

Kimchi, David. *The Commentary of David Kimchi on Isaiah.* Ed. L. Finkelstein. New York, 1926.

———. *Sefer ha-Shorashim.* Ed. J. H. R. Biesenthal and F. Lebrecht. 1847. Repr. Jerusalem, 1967. Hebrew.

Abravanel, Isaac. *Commentary on the Prophets and Writings.* Tel Aviv, 1960. Hebrew.

Jonah Ibn Ganaḥ, *Sefer ha-Riqmah.* Ed. M. Wilensky. 1928-30. Repr. Jerusalem, 1964. Hebrew.

———. *Sefer ha-Shorashim.* Ed. W. Bacher. 1896. Repr. Jerusalem, 1966. Hebrew.

Saadyah Gaon, Judah ibn Ḥiuj, Jonah ibn Ganaḥ, Maimonides, Solomon Parḥon, Menaḥem ben Solomon, Moses ibn Chiqutilla. In I. Bar-Rav and N. Adar, eds. *Commentaries on the Book of Isaiah.* Vol. 1. Jerusalem, 5731 (1971). Hebrew and Arabic.

Judah ibn Balam, Samuel ben Meir, Joseph Kara, Menaḥem ben Ḥelbo, Eleazar ben Judah, Meir Arama, Solomon ibn Meleh. In I. Bar-Rav and N. Adar, eds. *Commentaries on the Book of Isaiah.* Vol. 2. Jerusalem, 5731 (1971). Hebrew and Arabic.

R. Judah Ibn Balaam's Commentary on Isaiah. Ed. M. Goshen-Gottstein. Ramat Gan, 1992. Hebrew.

Saadyah Gaon. *Saadyah's Translation and Commentary on Isaiah.* Ed. Y. Ratzhabi. Kiryat Ono, 1993. Hebrew.

Rashi, Abraham ibn Ezra, David Kimchi, Joseph Kara, Eliezer of Beaugency, and Joseph Kaspi. In M. Cohen, ed. *Miqraot Gedolot "Haketer."* Jerusalem, 1996. Hebrew.

Selected Bibliography

Modern Commentaries

Baltzer, K. *Deutero-Isaiah*. Trans. M. Kohl. Hermeneia. Minneapolis, 2001.

Beuken, W. A. M. *Jesaja II-III*. 4 vols. Nijkerk, 1979-89.

Blenkinsopp, J. *Isaiah 40–55*. AB 19A. New York, 2002.

———. *Isaiah 56–66*. AB 19B. New York, 2003.

Bonnard, P. E. *Le Second Isaïe: Son disciple et leurs éditeurs: Isaïe 40–66*. Paris, 1972.

Brueggemann, W. *Isaiah 40–66*. Westminster Biblical Companion. Louisville, 1998.

Budde, K. *Das Buch Jesaja, Kap. 40–66*. Heilige Schrift des Altes Testamentes 11. Tübingen, 1922.

Cheyne, T. K. *The Prophecies of Isaiah*. Vol. 2. 2nd ed. London, 1882.

Childs, B. S. *Isaiah*. OTL. Louisville, 2001.

Delitzsch, F. *Biblical Commentary on the Prophecies of Isaiah*. Vol. 2. Trans. J. Martin. Repr. Grand Rapids, 1954.

Duhm, B. *Das Buch Jesaja übersetzt und erklärt*. 4th ed. HKAT 3/1. Göttingen, 1922.

Ehrlich, A. B. *Randglossen zur hebräischen Bibel*. Vol. 4: *Jesaia, Jeremia*. Leipzig, 1912.

———. *Mikrâ ki-Pheshutô*. Vol. 3: *Die Propheten*. New York, 1969. Hebrew.

Elliger, K. *Deuterojesaja 40, 1–45, 7*. BKAT 11/1. Neukirchen-Vluyn, 1978.

Fohrer, G. *Das Buch Jesaja*. Vol. 3: *Kapitel 40–66*. Zürcher Bibelkommentare 10/3. Zurich, 1964.

Gesenius, W. *Philologisch-kritischer und historiker Commentar über Jesaja*. Leipzig, 1821.

Goldingay, J., and D. Payne. *The Message of Isaiah 40–55: A Critical and Exegetical Commentary*. 2 vols. ICC. London, 2007.

Hacham, A. *Isaiah*. II, Daat Miqra. Jerusalem, 1985. Hebrew.

Hanson, P. D. *Isaiah 40–66*. Interpretation. Louisville, 1995.

Herbert, A. S. *The Book of the Prophet Isaiah, Chapters 40–66*. CBC. Cambridge, 1975.

Hermisson, H.-J. *Deuterojesaja*. BKAT 11/9. Neukirchen-Vluyn, 1987.

Hoffman, Y., ed. *Isaiah*. Olam ha-Tanak 10. Ramat Gan, 1986. Hebrew.

Kissane, E. J. *The Book of Isaiah*. Vol. 2. 2nd ed. Dublin, 1960.

Köhler, L. *Deuterojesaja (Jesaja XL-LV) stilkritisch untersucht*. BZAW 37. Giessen, 1923.

König, E. *Das Buch Jesaja: Eingeleitet, übersetzt und erklärt*. Gütersloh, 1926.

Koole, J. L. *Isaiah*. Part 3, vol. 1: *Isaiah 40–48*. Trans. A. P. Runia. HCOT. Kampen, 1997.

———. *Isaiah*. Part 3, vol. 2: *Isaiah 49–55*. Trans. A. P. Runia. HCOT. Leuven, 1998.

———. *Isaiah*. Part 3, vol. 3: *Isaiah 56–66*. Trans. A. P. Runia. HCOT. Leuven, 2001.

Kraus, S. *Isaiah*. Tel Aviv, 1969. Hebrew.

Leslie, E. A. *Isaiah*. New York, 1963.

Luzzatto, S. D. *Isaiah*. Jerusalem, 1967. Hebrew.

Marti, K. *Das Buch Jesaja erklärt*. Kurzer Hand-Commentar zum Alten Testament 10. Tübingen, 1900.

McKenzie, J. L. *Second Isaiah: Introduction, Translation, and Notes*. AB 20. Garden City, N.Y., 1968.

Muilenburg, J. "The Book of Isaiah: Chapters 40–66: Introduction and Exegesis." In *The Interpreter's Bible*. Ed. G. A. Buttrick. New York, 1956. 5:381-773.

North, C. R. *The Second Isaiah: Introduction, Translation and Commentary to Chapters XL–LV*. Oxford, 1964.

———. *Isaiah 40–55: The Suffering Servant of God.* 5th ed. London, 1965.
Orelli, C. von. *Der Prophet Jesaja.* Kurzgefasster Kommentar zu den Heiligen Schriften Alten und Neuen Testamentes sowie zu den Apokryphen 4/1. Munich, 1904.
Oswalt, J. N. *The Book of Isaiah: Chapters 40–66.* New International Commentary on the Old Testament. Grand Rapids, 1998.
Schneider, D. *Der Prophet Jesaja.* Vol. 2: *Kapitel 40 bis 66.* Brockhaus, 1990.
Schoors, A. *Jesaja II.* Boeken van het Oude Testament 9B. Roermond, 1973.
Skinner, J. *The Book of the Prophet Isaiah.* Vol. 2: *Chapters XL–LXVI.* Cambridge Bible for Schools and Colleges. Cambridge, 1898.
Smart, J. D. *History and Theology in Second Isaiah: A Commentary on Isaiah 35, 40–66.* Philadelphia, 1965.
Torrey, C. C. *The Second Isaiah: A New Interpretation.* Edinburgh, 1928.
Tur-Sinai, N. H. *Peshuṭo shel Miqra.* III/1. Jerusalem, 1967. Hebrew.
Volz, P. *Jesaja Zweite Hälfte: Kapitel 40–66 übersetzt und erklärt.* KAT 9. 1932. Repr. Hildesheim, 1974.
Watts, J. D. W. *Isaiah 34–66.* Word Biblical Commentary. Waco, Tex., 1987.
Westermann, C. *Isaiah 40–66: A Commentary.* Trans. D. M. G. Stalker. OTL. Philadelphia, 1967.
Whybray, R. N. *Isaiah 40–66.* New Century Bible Commentary. 1975. Repr. Grand Rapids, 1981.
Wildberger, H. *Isaiah: A Commentary.* Trans. T. H. Trapp. 3 vols. Continental Commentary. Minneapolis, 1991-2002.
Yellin, D. *Ḥiqrei Miqra.* Vol. 2: *Isaiah.* Jerusalem, 1945. Hebrew.
Young, E. J. *The Book of Isaiah.* Vol. 3: *Chapters 40 through 66.* Grand Rapids, 1972.

Studies: General

Ackerman, S. *Under Every Green Tree: Popular Religion in Sixth-Century Judah.* HSM 46. Atlanta, 1992.
Amir, Y. "The Messianic Element in the Message of Second Isaiah." In B. Z. Luria, ed. *Studies in the Book of Isaiah.* Jerusalem, 1980. 1:301-26. Hebrew.
Andersen, T. D. "Renaming and Wedding Imagery in Isaiah 62." *Bib* 67 (1986): 75-80.
Avishur, I. "Deutero-Isaiah." *EJ* 9:61-66.
———. "Isaiah, Chapters 34–35." *EJ* 9:60-61.
Baltzer, D. *Ezechiel und Deuterojesaja.* BZAW 121. Berlin, 1971.
———. "Jes 40,13-14 — Ein Schlüssel zur Einheit Deutero-Jesajas?" *BN* 37 (1987): 7-10.
Barrick, W. B. "On *BMWTW* in 1QIsa[a] 53:9a, Again: A Response to J. A. Emerton." *Maarav* 15 (2008): 39-55.
Barstad, H. M. "On the So-Called Babylonian Literary Influence in Second Isaiah." *SJOT* 2 (1987): 90-110.
———. *A Way in the Wilderness: The "Second Exodus" in the Message of Second Isaiah.* Journal of Semitic Studies Monograph 12. Manchester, 1989.
———. *The Babylonian Captivity of the Book of Isaiah: "Exilic" Judah and the Provenance of Isaiah 40–55.* Instituttet for sammenlignende kulturforskning B-Skrifter 102. Oslo, 1997.

Beaucamp, E. *Le livre de la consolation d'Israël: Isaïe XL-LV.* Paris, 1991.

Begg, C. T. "Babylon in the Book of Isaiah." In J. Vermeylen, ed. *The Book of Isaiah/Le Livre d'Isaïe.* BETL 81. Leuven, 1989. Pages 121-25.

Begrich, J. *Studien zu Deuterojesaja.* 2nd ed. Theologische Bücherei 20. Munich, 1963. Repr. of BWANT 77. Stuttgart, 1938.

Berges, U. *Das Buch Jesaja: Komposition und Endgestalt.* Herders Biblische Studien 16. Freiburg, 1998.

Beuken, W. A. M. "Isaiah 54: The Multiple Identity of the Person Addressed." *OtSt* 19 (1974): 29-70.

Biddle, M. E. "Lady Zion's Alter Egos: Isaiah 47.1-15 and 57.6-13 as Structural Counterparts." In R. F. Melugin and M. A. Sweeney, eds. *New Visions of Isaiah.* JSOTSup 214. Sheffield, 1996. Pages 124-39.

Blank, S. "Studies in Deutero-Isaiah." *HUCA* 15 (1940): 1-46.

Blenkinsopp, J. "Who Is the *Ṣaddiq* of Isaiah 57:1-2?" In P. W. Flint et al., eds. *Studies in the Hebrew Bible, Qumran, and the Septuagint Presented to Eugene Ulrich.* VTSup 101. Leiden, 2006. Pages 109-20.

Boer, P. A. H. de, *Second-Isaiah's Message.* OtSt 11. Leiden, 1956.

Bright, J. "Faith and Destiny: The Meaning of History in Deutero-Isaiah." *Int* 5 (1951): 3-26.

Broyles, C. C. "The Citations of Yahweh in Isaiah 44:26-28." In C. C. Broyles and C. A. Evans, eds. *Writing and Reading the Scroll of Isaiah: Studies of an Interpretive Tradition.* 2 vols. VTSup 70. Leiden, 1997. 1:399-421.

Broyles, C. C., and C. A. Evans, eds. *Writing and Reading the Scroll of Isaiah: Studies of an Interpretive Tradition.* 2 vols. VTSup 70. Leiden, 1997.

Carroll, R. P. "Second Isaiah and the Failure of Prophecy." *ST* 32 (1978): 119-31.

Clements, R. E. "A Light to the Nations: A Central Theme of the Book of Isaiah." In J. W. Watts and P. R. House, eds. *Forming Prophetic Literature: Essays on Isaiah and the Twelve in Honor of John D. W. Watts.* JSOTSup 235. Sheffield, 1996. Pages 57-69.

Clifford, R. J. "Isaiah 55: Invitation to a Feast." In C. L. Meyers and M. O'Connor, eds. *The Word of the Lord Shall Go Forth: Essays in Honor of David Noel Freedman in Celebration of His Sixtieth Birthday.* Winona Lake, Ind., 1983. Pages 27-35.

———. *Fair Spoken and Persuading: An Interpretation of Second Isaiah.* Theological Inquiries. New York, 1984.

———. "Isaiah, Book of (Second Isaiah)." *ABD* 3:490-501.

Cohen, Ch. "The Idiom קרא בשם in Second Isaiah." *JANES* 1 (1968): 32-34.

———. "The 'Widowed' City." *JANES* 5 (1974): 75-81.

Conrad, D. "Zu Jes 65_{3b}." *ZAW* 80 (1968): 232-34.

Conrad, E. W. "The 'Fear Not' Oracles in Second Isaiah." *VT* 34 (1984): 129-52.

———. *Reading Isaiah.* OBT. Minneapolis, 1991.

Crenshaw, J. L. "YHWH *Ṣ^eba'ôt Š^emô:* A Form-Critical Analysis." *ZAW* 81 (1969): 156-75.

Cross, F. M. "The Council of YHWH in Second Isaiah." *JNES* 12 (1953): 274-77.

Dahood, M. "Isaiah 53, 8-12 and Massoretic Misconstruction." *Bib* 63 (1982): 566-70.

Darr, K. P. "Like Warrior, like Woman: Destruction and Deliverance in Isaiah 42:10-17." *CBQ* 49 (1987): 560-71.

Davies, P. R. "God of Cyrus, God of Israel: Some Religio-historical Reflections on Isaiah 40–55." In J. Davies, G. Harvey, and W. G. E. Watson, eds. *Words Remembered, Texts*

Renewed: Essays in Honour of John F. A. Sawyer. JSOTSup 195. Sheffield, 1995. Pages 207-25.
Dobbs-Allsopp, F. W. *Weep, O Daughter of Zion: A Study of the City-Lament Genre in the Hebrew Bible.* BibOr 44. Rome, 1993.
Driver, G. R. "Linguistic and Textual Problems: Isaiah XL–LXVI." *JTS* 36 (1935): 396-406.
Eaton, J. H. *Festal Drama in Deutero-Isaiah.* London, 1979.
Fitzgerald, A. "*BTWLT* and *BT* as Titles for Capital Cities." *CBQ* 37 (1975): 170-80.
———. "The Technology of Isaiah 40:19-20 + 41:6-7." *CBQ* 51 (1989): 426-46.
Fohrer, G. "Zehn Jahre Literatur zur alttestamentlichen Prophetie (1951-1960), VI, Deuterojesaja (Jes 40–66)." *ThR* n.s. 28 (1962): 235-49.
———. *Neue Studien zu Deuterojesaja.* BWANT 4/25. 1938. Repr. Munich, 1965.
Fokkelman, J. P. "The Cyrus Oracle (Isaiah 44,24–45,7) from the Perspectives of Syntax, Versification and Structure." In J. van Ruiten and M. Vervenne, eds. *Studies in the Book of Isaiah: Festschrift Willem A. M. Beuken.* BETL 132. Leuven, 1997. Pages 303-23.
Franke, C. "The Function of the Satiric Lament over Babylon in Second Isaiah [XLVII]." *VT* 41 (1991): 408-18.
———. *Isaiah 46, 47, and 48: A New Literary-Critical Reading.* Winona Lake, Ind., 1994.
Freedman, D. N. "Isaiah 42:13." *CBQ* 30 (1968): 225-26.
———. "Mistress Forever: A Note on Is 47:7." *Bib* 51 (1970): 538.
———. "The Structure of Isaiah 40:1-11." In E. W. Conrad and E. G. Newing, eds. *Perspectives on Language and Text: Essays and Poems in Honor of Francis I. Andersen's Sixtieth Birthday, July 28, 1985.* Winona Lake, Ind., 1987. Pages 167-93.
Gevaryahu, H. M. I. "And Beside Me There Is No God." In B. Z. Luria, ed. *Studies in the Book of Isaiah.* Jerusalem, 1980. 2:331-51. Hebrew.
Ginsberg, H. L. "Some Emendations in Isaiah." *JBL* 69 (1950): 51-60.
———. "The Arm of YHWH in Isaiah 51–63 and the Text of Isa 53:10-11." *JBL* 77 (1958): 152-56.
Glahn, L., and L. Köhler. *Der Prophet der Heimkehr.* Giessen, 1934.
Greenfield, J. C. "The Prepositions '*B . . . Taḥat . . .*' in Jes 57:5." *ZAW* 73 (1965): 226-28. Repr. in S. M. Paul et al., eds. *'Al Kanfei Yonah: Collected Studies of Jonas C. Greenfield on Semitic Philology.* 2 vols. Leiden, 2001. 2:698-700.
Gressmann, H. "Die literarische Analyse Deuterojesajas." *ZAW* 34 (1914): 264-97.
Grimm, W., and K. Dittert. *Deuterojesaja: Deutung, Wirkung, Gegenwart: Ein Kommentar zu Jesaja 40–55.* Calwer Bibelkommentare. Stuttgart, 1990.
Hamlin, E. J. "The Meaning of 'Mountains and Hills' in Isa 41:14-16." *JNES* 13 (1954): 185-90.
———. *Comfort My People: A Guide to Isaiah 40–66.* Atlanta, 1980.
Haran, M. "The Literary Structure and Chronological Framework of the Prophecies of Is. XL–LXVIII." In *Congress Volume: Bonn, 1962.* VTSup 9. Leiden, 1963. Pages 127-55.
Hermisson, H.-J. "Deuterojesaja-Probleme." *VF* 31 (1986): 53-84.
———. "Einheit und Komplexität Deuterojesajas. Probleme der Redaktionsgeschichte von Jes 40–55." In J. Vermeylen, ed. *The Book of Isaiah/Le Livre d'Isaïe.* BETL 81. Leuven, 1989. Pages 287-312.
Holter, K. "The Wordplay on אֵל ("God") in Isaiah 45, 20-21." *SJOT* 7 (1993): 88-98.

Holtz, E. E. "The Case for Adversarial *yaḥad*," *VT* 5 (2009): 211-21.

Hoop, R. de. "The Interpretation of Isaiah 56:1-9: Comfort or Criticism?" *JBL* 127 (2008): 671-95.

———. "Isaiah 40.13, the Masoretes, Syntax and Literary Structure: A Rejoinder to Reinowd Oosting." *JSOT* 33 (2009): 453-63.

Hurowitz, V. A. "A Forgotten Meaning of *Nepeš* in Isaiah LVIII 10[1]." *VT* 49 (1997): 43-52.

Hutton, J. M. "Isaiah 51:9-11 and the Rhetorical Appropriation and Subversion of Hostile Theologies." *JBL* 126 (2007): 271-303.

Janzen, J. G. "Another Look at *yaḥ^a lipû kōaḥ* in Isaiah XLI 1." *VT* 33 (1983): 428-34.

———. "On the Moral Nature of God's Power: Yahweh and the Sea in Job and Deutero-Isaiah." *CBQ* 56 (1994): 458-78.

Kapelrud, A. S. "The Main Concern of Second Isaiah." *VT* 32 (1982): 50-58.

Kaufmann, Y. *The Biblical Captivity and Deutero-Isaiah.* Trans. C. W. Efroymson. New York, 1970. Pages 61-198.

Koch, K. "Ugaritic Polytheism and Hebrew Monotheism in Isaiah 40–55." In R. P. Gordon, ed. *The God of Israel.* Cambridge, Eng., 2007. Pages 205-88.

Koenen, K. "Sexuelle Zweideutigkeiten und Euphemismen in Jes 57, 8." *BN* 44 (1988): 46-53.

Korpel, M. C. A., and J. C. de Moor. *The Structure of Classical Hebrew Poetry: Isaiah 40–55.* OtSt 41. Leiden, 1998.

Leene, H. "Universalism or Nationalism: Isaiah XLV 9-13 and Its Context." *Bijdr* 35 (1974): 309-34.

Lindars, B. "Good Tidings to Zion: Interpreting Deutero-Isaiah Today." *BJRL* 68 (1986): 473-97.

Lipton, D. "Bezalel in Babylon? Anti-Priestly Polemics in Isaiah 40–55." *JANES* 31 (2008): 63-84.

Liver, J. *Deutero-Isaiah Edited from the Lectures of Dr. J. Liver by R. Yarkoni.* Tel Aviv, 1924. Hebrew.

Loretz, O. "Die Gattung des Prologs zum Buch Deuterojesaja Jes 40:1-11." *ZAW* 96 (1984): 210-20.

Mann, T. W. *Divine Presence and Guidance in Israelite Traditions.* Baltimore, 1977.

McKane, W. "Poison, Trial by Ordeal and the Cup of Wrath." *VT* 30 (1948): 474-92.

Melugin, R. F. *The Formation of Isaiah 40–55.* BZAW 141. Berlin, 1976.

Melugin, R. F., and M. A. Sweeney, eds. *New Visions of Isaiah.* JSOTSup 214. Sheffield, 1996.

Millard, A. R., and I. R. Snook. "Isaiah 40:22, Towards a Solution." *Tyndale House Bulletin* 14 (1964): 1-2.

Morgenstern, J. "Deutero-Isaiah's Terminology for 'Universal God.'" *JBL* 62 (1943): 269-80.

Mowinckel, S. "Neuere Forschung zu Deuterojesaja, Tritojesaja und dem Aebäd-Jahwe-Problem." *AcOr* 16 (1938): 1-4.

Naidoff, B. D. "The Two-Fold Structure of Isaiah XLV 9-13." *VT* 31 (1981): 180-85.

Oosting, R. "Returning (to) Zion: Isaiah 52:8 in Light of Verbal Valency Patterns." In F. Postma et al., eds. *The New Things: Eschatology in Old Testament Prophecy: Festschrift for Henk Leene.* Maastricht, 2002. Pages 159-66.

———. "The Counsellors of the Lord in Isaiah 40–55: A Proposal to Understand Their Role in the Literary Composition." *JSOT* 32 (2008): 353-82.

Paul, S. M. *Divrei Shalom: Collected Studies of Shalom M. Paul on the Bible and the Ancient Near East, 1967-2005*. CHANE 23. Leiden, 2005.

Polliack, M. "Deutero-Isaiah's Typological Use of Jacob in the Portrayal of Israel's National Renewal." In H. G. Reventlow and Y. Hoffman, eds. *Creation in Jewish and Christian Tradition*. JSOTSup 309. London, 2002. Pages 72-110.

Preuss, H. D. *Deuterojesaja: Einführung in seine Botschaft*. Neukirchen-Vluyn, 1976.

Raban, N. *Second Isaiah: The Figure, His Prophecy, and His Name: Studies in Isaiah 40–66*. Jerusalem, 1971. Hebrew.

Rappel, D. "Fasting, Repentance, and the Sabbath in Isaiah." In B. Z. Luria, ed. *Studies in the Book of Isaiah*. Jerusalem, 1980. 2:267-85. Hebrew.

Richter, A. "Hauptlinien der Deuterojesaja-Forschung von 1964-1979." In C. Westermann, *Sprache und Struktur der Prophetie Deuterojesajas*. CTM 11. Stuttgart, 1981. Pages 89-123.

Rignell, L. G. *A Study of Isaiah Chs. 40–55. Lunds universitets årsskrift 1/52/5*. Lund, 1956.

Ringgren, H. "Die Funktion des Schöpfungsmythos in Jes. 51." In K. H. Bernhardt, ed. *Schalom: Studien zu Glaube und Geschichte Israels. Alfred Jepsen zum 70. Geburtstag*. Stuttgart, 1971. Pages 38-40.

Rosenbaum, M. *Word-order Variation in Isaiah 40–55: A Functional Perspective*. Studia Semitica Neerlandica 36. Assen, 1997.

Ruiten, J. van, and M. Vervenne, eds. *Studies in the Book of Isaiah: Festschrift Willem A. M. Beuken*. BETL 132. Leuven, 1997.

Sasson, J. M. "Isaiah lxvi 3-4a." *VT* 26 (1976): 199-207.

Schmitt, H. C. "Prophetie und Schuldtheologie im Deuterojesajabuch: Beobachtungen zur Redaktionsgeschichte von Jes 40–55." *ZAW* 91 (1979): 43-61.

Schmitt, J. J. "The Motherhood of God and Zion as Mother." *RB* 92 (1985): 557-69.

Schoors, A. *I Am God Your Saviour: A Form-Critical Study of the Main Genres in Isa XL–LV*. VTSup 24. Leiden, 1973.

Schwartz, G. "Jesaja 50 4-5a." *ZAW* 85 (1973): 356-57.

Segal, M. H. "Isaiah." In E. L. Sukenik, ed. *Encyclopaedia Biblica*. 8 vols. Jerusalem, 1950-82. 3:926-36. Hebrew.

Seidl, T. "Jahwe der Krieger — Jahwe der Tröster: Kritik und Neuinterpretation der Schöpfungsvorstellungen in Jesaja 51, 9-16." *BN* 21 (1983): 116-34.

Seitz, C. R. "The Book of Isaiah 40–66." In *The New Interpreter's Bible*. Ed. L. E. Keck. Nashville, 2001. 6:309-552.

Singer, O. "Selected Studies in the Public Plea in Isaiah 63:7–64:11." In Y. Hoffman and F. H. Polak, eds. *A Light for Jacob: Studies in the Bible and the Dead Sea Scrolls in Memory of Jacob Shalom Licht*. Jerusalem, 1997. Pages 118-40. Hebrew.

Smith, M. S. "*Berît ʿam/Berît ʿôlām:* A New Proposal for the Crux of Isa 42:6." *JBL* 100 (1981): 241-43.

Smith, S. *Isaiah Chapters XL–LV: Literary Criticism and History*. London, 1944.

Snaith, N. H. "Isaiah 40–66: A Study of the Teaching of the Second Isaiah and Its Consequences." In H. Orlinsky and N. H. Snaith, eds. *Studies on the Second Part of the Book of Isaiah*. VTSup 14. Leiden, 1977. Pages 139-46.

Steck, O. H. *Gottesknecht und Zion: Gesammelte Aufsätze zu Deuterojesaja.* FAT 4. Tübingen, 1992.

———. "Der neue Himmel und die neue Erde: Beobachtungen zur Rezeption von Gen 1–3 in Jes 65,16b-25." In J. van Ruiten and M. Vervenne, eds. *Studies in the Book of Isaiah: Festschrift Willem A. M. Beuken.* BETL 132. Leuven, 1997. Pages 349-65.

Stuhlmueller, C. "The Theology of Creation in Second Isaias." *CBQ* 21 (1959): 429-67.

———. *Creative Redemption in Deutero-Isaiah.* AnBib 43. Rome, 1970.

———. "Deutero-Isaiah (Chaps. 40–55): Major Transitions in the Prophet's Theology and in Contemporary Scholarship." *CBQ* 42 (1980): 1-29.

Tate, M. E. "The Book of Isaiah in Recent Study." In J. W. Willis and P. R. House, eds. *Forming Prophetic Literature: Essays on Isaiah and the Twelve in Honor of John D. W. Watts.* JSOTSup 235. Sheffield, 1996. Pages 22-56.

Uffenheimer, B. "Spiritual Characteristics of Second Isaiah." In B. Z. Luria, ed. *Studies in the Book of Isaiah.* Jerusalem, 1980. 2:287 312. Hebrew.

Unterman, J. "The Social-Legal Origin for the Image of God as Redeemer גואל of Israel." In D. P. Wright, D. N. Freedman, and A. Hurvitz, eds. *Pomegranates and Golden Bells: Studies in Biblical, Jewish, and Near Eastern Ritual, Law, and Literature in Honor of Jacob Milgrom.* Winona Lake, Ind., 1995. Pages 399-405.

Vermeylen, J. "Le motif de la création dans le Deutéro-Isaïe." In P. Beauchamp et al., eds. *La création dans l'Orient ancien.* LD 127. Paris, 1987. Pages 183-240.

Vincent, J. M. *Studien zur literarischen Eigenart und zur geistigen Heimat von Jesaja, Kap. 40–55.* Frankfurt, 1977.

Walsh, J. T. "The Case for Prosecution: Isaiah 41.21–42.17." In E. R. Follis, ed. *Directions in Biblical Hebrew Poetry.* JSOTSup 40. Sheffield, 1987. Pages 101-18.

———. "Summons to Judgement: A Close Reading of Isaiah XLI 1-20." *VT* 43 (1993): 351-71.

Ward, J. M. "Isaiah." In K. Crim et al., eds. *The Interpreter's Dictionary of the Bible, Supplementary Volume.* Nashville, 1976. Pages 459-61.

Whitley, C. H. "Textual Notes on Deutero-Isaiah." *VT* 11 (1961): 457-61.

Whybray, R. N. *The Second Isaiah.* Sheffield, 1983.

van Wieringen, A. L. H. M. *Analogies in Isaiah.* Vol. A: *Computerized Analysis of Parallel Texts between Isaiah 56–66 and Isaiah 40–66;* vol. B: *Computerized Concordance of Analogies between Isaiah 56–66 and Isaiah 40–66.* Amsterdam, 1993.

———. "Parallel Clauses between Third and Second Isaiah: A New Kind of Computer Concordance." *BN* 82 (1996): 21-26.

Williamson, H. G. M. "Word Order in Isaiah XLIII, 12." *JTS* 30 (1979): 499-502.

———. "Isaiah 40, 20: A Case of Not Seeing the Wood for the Trees." *Bib* 67 (1986): 1-20.

———. "Gnats, Glosses and Eternity: Isaiah 51:6 Reconsidered." In P. J. Harland and C. T. R. Hayward, eds. *New Heaven and New Earth Prophecy and the Millennium: Essays in Honour of Anthony Gelston.* VTSup 77. Leiden, 1999. Pages 101-12.

van Winkle, D. W. "The Meaning of *yād vāšēm* in Isaiah LVI 5." *VT* 47 (1997): 378-85.

Zimmerli, W. *I Am Yahweh.* Atlanta, 1982.

"Deutero-Isaiah" and "Trito-Isaiah"

Poznanski, S. *Mose b. Samuel Hakkohen ibn Chiquitilla, nebst den Fragmenten seiner Schriften.* Leipzig, 1895. Pages 29-30.

Simon, U. "Ibn Ezra between Medievalism and Modernism: The Case of Isaiah XL–LXVI." In J. A. Emerton, ed. *Congress Volume, Salamanca 1983.* VTSup 36. Leiden, 1985. Pages 257-71.

Renewed Discovery of the Division of the Book of Isaiah

Döderlein, J. Ch. *Esaias: ex recensione textus hebraei. . . .* Altdorf, 1775. Page 168.

Eichhorn, J. G. *Einleitung ins Alte Testament.* 3 vols. Göttingen, 1783. 3:83-97.

Isaiah 34–35

Avishur, I. "Isaiah, Chapters 34–35." *EJ* 9:60-61.

Graetz, H. "Isaiah XXXIV and XXXV." *JQR* 4 (1891-92): 1-8.

Muilenburg, J. "The Literary Character of Isaiah 34." *JBL* 59 (1940): 339-65.

Olmstead, A. T. "II Isaiah and Isaiah 35." *AJSL* 53 (1936-37): 251-53.

Pope, M. H. "Isaiah 34 in Relation to Isaiah 35, 40-66." *JBL* 71 (1952): 235-43.

Scott, R. B. Y. "The Relation of Isaiah, Chapter 35, to Deutero-Isaiah." *AJSL* 52 (1935): 178-91.

Steck, O. H. *Bereitete Heimkehr: Jesaja 35 als redaktionelle Brücke zwischen dem Ersten und dem Zweiten Jesaja.* Stuttgarter Bibelstudien 121. Stuttgart, 1985.

Williamson, H. G. M. *The Book Called Isaiah: Deutero-Isaiah's Role in Composition and Redaction.* Oxford, 1994. Pages 211-21.

"Trito-Isaiah"

Achtemeier, E. *The Community and Message of Isaiah 56–66: A Theological Commentary.* Minneapolis, 1982.

Bastiaens, J., W. A. M. Beuken, and F. Postma. *Trito-Isaiah — An Exhaustive Concordance of Isa. 56–66, Especially with Reference to Deutero-Isaiah: An Example of Computer-Assisted Research.* Amsterdam, 1984.

Begg, C. T. "Foreigners in Third Isaiah." *Bible Today* 23 (1985): 98-102.

Berges, U. "Who Were the Servants? A Comparative Inquiry in the Book of Isaiah and the Psalms." In J. C. De Moor and H. F. van Rooy, eds. *Past, Present, Future: The Deuteronomistic History and the Prophets.* OtSt 44. Leiden, 2000. Pages 1-18.

Beuken, W. A. M. "Isa. 56:9–57:13 — An Example of the Isaianic Legacy of Trito-Isaiah." In J. W. van Henten et al., eds. *Tradition and Reinterpretation in Jewish and Early Christian Literature: Essays in Honour of J. C. H. Lehram.* Leiden, 1986. Pages 48-64.

———. "Does Trito-Isaiah Reject the Temple? An Intertextual Inquiry into Isa. 66:1-6." In S. Draisma, ed. *Intertextuality in Biblical Writings: Essays in Honour of Bas van Iersel.* Kampen, 1989. Pages 53-66.

———. "The Main Theme of Trito-Isaiah: The 'Servants of YHWH.'" *JSOT* 47 (1990): 67-87.

———. "Isaiah Chapters LXV–LXVI: Trito-Isaiah and the Closure of the Book of Isaiah." In J. A. Emerton, ed. *Congress Volume: Leuven, 1989*. VTSup 43. Leiden, 1991. Pages 204-21.

Donner, H. "Jesaja LVI:1-7: Ein Abrogationsfall innerhalb des Kanons — Implikationen und Consequenzen." In J. A. Emerton, ed. *Congress Volume: Salamanca, 1983*. VTSup 36. Leiden, 1985. Pages 81-95.

Elliger, K. *Die Einheit des Tritojesaja*. Stuttgart, 1928.

———. *Deuterojesaja in seinem Verhältnis zu Tritojesaja*. BWANT 63. Stuttgart, 1933.

Emmerson, G. I. *Isaiah 56–66*. Old Testament Guides. Sheffield, 1992.

Fohrer, G. "Deutero- und Tritojesaja." *ThR* 19 (1951): 298-305.

Halpern, B. "The New Names of Isaiah 62:4: Jeremiah's Reception in the Restoration and the Politics of 'Third Isaiah.'" *JBL* 117 (1998): 623-43.

Hanson, P. D. "Third Isaiah: The Theological Legacy of a Struggling Community." In C. Seitz, ed. *Reading and Preaching the Book of Isaiah*. Philadelphia, 1988. Pages 91-103.

Holladay, W. L. "Was Trito-Isaiah Deutero-Isaiah after All?" In C. C. Broyles and C. A. Evans, eds. *Writing and Reading the Scroll of Isaiah: Studies of an Interpretive Tradition*. 2 vols. VTSup 70. Leiden, 1997. 1:193-217.

Holmgren, F. "Yhwh the Avenger: Isaiah 63:1-6." In J. J. Jackson and M. Kessler, eds. *Rhetorical Criticism: Essays in Honor of James Muilenburg*. Pittsburgh, 1974. Pages 133-48.

Hoop, R. de. "The Interpretation of Isaiah 56:1-9: Comfort or Criticism?" *JBL* 127 (2008): 671-95.

Koenen, K. *Ethik und Eschatologie im Tritojesajabuch: Eine literarkritische und redaktionsgeschichtliche Studie*. WMANT 62. Neukirchen-Vluyn, 1990.

Kraus, H.-J. "Die ausgebliebene Endtheophanie: Eine Studie zu Jes 56–66." *ZAW* 78 (1966): 317-32.

Kuenen, A. *Historische-kritische Einleitung in die Bücher des Alten Testament*. Vol. 2: *Die prophetischen Bücher*. Leipzig, 1892. Pages 128-44.

Lau, W. *Schriftgelehrte Prophetie in Jes 56–66: Eine Untersuchung zu den literarischen Bezügen in den letzten elf Kapiteln des Jesajabuches*. BZAW 225. Berlin, 1994.

Lynch, M. J. "Zion's Warrior and the Nations: Isaiah 59:15b–63:6 in Isaiah's Zion Traditions." *CBQ* 70 (2008): 244-63.

Maass, F. "Tritojesaja?" In F. Maass, ed. *Das ferne und nahe Wort: Festschrift Leonhard Rost*. BZAW 105. Berlin, 1967. Pages 151-63.

Murtonen, A. "Third Isaiah: Yes or No?" *Abr-Naharain* 19 (1980-81): 20-42.

Odeberg, H. *Trito-Isaiah (Isaiah 56–66): A Literary and Linguistic Analysis*. Lund, 1931.

Oswalt, J. N. "Righteousness in Isaiah: A Study of the Function of Chapters 56–66 in the Present Structure of the Book." In C. C. Broyles and C. A. Evans, eds. *Writing and Reading the Scroll of Isaiah: Studies of an Interpretive Tradition*. 2 vols. VTSup 70. Leiden, 1997. 1:177-91.

Pauritsch, K. *Die neue Gemeinde: Gott sammelt Ausgestossene und Arme (Jesaja 56–66). Die Botschaft des Tritojesaia-Buches literar-, form-, gattungskritisch und redaktionsgeschichtlich untersucht*. AnBib 47. Rome, 1971.

Rofé, A. "Isaiah 55:6-11: The Problems of the Fulfillment of Prophecies and Trito-Isaiah." In *Proceedings of the Sixth World Congress of Jewish Studies.* Jerusalem, 1977. 1:213-21. Hebrew.

———. "Isaiah 66:1-4: Judean Sects in the Persian Period as Viewed by Trito-Isaiah." In A. Kort and S. Morschauser, eds. *Biblical and Related Studies Presented to Samuel Iwry.* Winona Lake, Ind., 1985. Pages 205-17.

———. "Nevertheless, Trito-Isaiah! On the Integration of the Conclusions of Biblical Research in High School Teaching." *Al ha-Pereq* 2 (1986): 7-15. Hebrew.

———. "How Is the Word Fulfilled? Isaiah 55:6-11 within the Theological Debate of Its Time." In G. M. Tucker et al., eds. *Canon, Theology and Old Testament: Essays in Honor of Brevard S. Childs.* Philadelphia, 1988. Pages 246-61.

———. "The Onset of Sects in Postexilic Judaism: Neglected Evidence from the Septuagint, Trito-Isaiah, Ben Sira, and Malachi." In J. Neusner et al., eds. *The Social World of Formative Christianity and Judaism: Essays in Tribute to Howard Clark Kee.* Philadelphia, 1988. Pages 39-49.

———. "Isaiah 59:19 and Trito-Isaiah's Vision of Redemption." In J. Vermeylen, ed. *The Book of Isaiah/Le Livre d'Isaïe.* BETL 81. Leuven, 1989. Pages 407-10.

———. "The Extent of Trito-Isaiah according to Kuenen and Elliger: Chaps. 54–66." *Henoch* 26 (2004): 128-35.

Ruszbowski, L. "Der Sabbat bei Trito-Jesaja." In B. Huwyler et al., eds. *Prophetie und Psalmen: Festschrift für Klaus Seybold zum 65. Geburtstag.* AOAT 280. Münster, 2001. Pages 61-74.

Schramm, B. *The Opponents of Third Isaiah.* JSOTSup 193. Sheffield, 1995.

Seitz, C. R. "Isaiah 1–66: Making Sense of the Whole." In C. Seitz, ed. *Reading and Preaching the Book of Isaiah.* Philadelphia, 1988. Pages 105-26.

Sekine, S. *Die Tritojesajanische Sammlung (Jes 56–66) redaktionsgeschichtlich untersucht.* BZAW 175. Berlin, 1989.

Smith, P. A. *Rhetoric and Redaction in Trito-Isaiah: The Structure, Growth and Authorship of Isaiah 56–66.* VTSup 62. Leiden, 1995.

Steck, O. H. "Beobachtungen zu Jesaja 56–59." *BZ* 31 (1987): 228-46.

———. "Tritojesaja im Jesajabuch." In J. Vermeylen, ed. *The Book of Isaiah/Le Livre de Isaïe.* BETL 81. Leuven, 1989. Pages 361-406.

———. *Studien zu Tritojesaja.* BZAW 203. Berlin, 1991.

———. "Autor und/oder Redaktor in Jesaja 56–66." In C. C. Broyles and C. A. Evans, eds. *Writing and Reading the Scroll of Isaiah: Studies of an Interpretive Tradition.* 2 vols. VTSup 70. Leiden, 1997. 1:219-59.

Sweeney, M. "Prophetic Exegesis in Isaiah 65–66." In C. C. Broyles and C. A. Evans, eds. *Writing and Reading the Scroll of Isaiah: Studies of an Interpretive Tradition.* 2 vols. VTSup 70. Leiden, 1997. 1:455-74.

Talmon, S. "The Emergence of Jewish Sectarianism in the Early Second Temple Period." In *King, Cult and Calendar in Ancient Israel: Collected Studies.* Jerusalem, 1986. Pages 165-201.

Tiemeyer, L.-S. "The Haughtiness of the Priesthood (Isa 65,5)." *Bib* 85 (2004): 237-44.

Wells, R. D., Jr. "'Isaiah' as an Exponent of Torah: Isaiah 56.1-8." In R. F. Melugin and M. A. Sweeney, eds. *New Visions of Isaiah.* JSOTSup 214. Sheffield, 1996. Pages 140-55.

Zimmerli, W. "Zur Sprache Tritojesajas." In *Festschrift für Ludwig Köhler.* SThU 20. Bern, 1950. Pages 62-74. Repr. in *Gottes Offenbarung: Gesammelte Aufsätze zum Alten Testament.* Theologische Bücherei 19. Munich, 1963. Pages 217-33.

Isaiah 40–66 as a Unified Literary Composition

Albertz, R. "Die Deuterojesaja-Buch als Fortschreitung der Jesaja-Prophetie." In E. Blum, C. Macholz, and E. W. Stegemann, eds. *Die Hebräische Bibel und ihre zweifache Nachgeschichte: Festschrift für Rolf Rendtorff zum 65. Geburtstag.* Neukirchen-Vluyn, 1990. Pages 241-56.

Beuken, W. A. M. "The Unity of the Book of Isaiah: Another Attempt at Bridging the Gorge between Its Two Main Parts." In J. C. Exum and H. G. M. Williamson, eds. *Reading from Right to Left.* JSOTSup 373. London, 2003. Pages 50-62.

Brueggemann, W. "Unity and Dynamic in the Isaiah Tradition." *JSOT* 29 (1984): 89-107.

Carr, D. M. "Reaching for Unity in Isaiah." *JSOT* 57 (1993): 61-81. Repr. in P. R. Davies, ed. *The Prophets: A Sheffield Reader.* Biblical Seminar 42. Sheffield, 1996. Pages 164-83.

———. "Reading Isaiah from Beginning (Isaiah 1) to End (Isaiah 65–66): Multiple Modern Possibilities." In R. F. Melugin and M. A. Sweeney, eds. *New Visions of Isaiah.* JSOTSup 214. Sheffield, 1996. Pages 188-218.

Clements, R. E. "The Unity of the Book of Isaiah." *Int* 36 (1982): 117-29.

Conrad, E. W. "Prophet, Redactor and Audience: Reforming the Notion of Isaiah's Formation." In R. F. Melugin and M. A. Sweeney, eds. *New Visions of Isaiah.* JSOTSup 214. Sheffield, 1996. Pages 306-26.

Evans, C. A. "On the Unity and Parallel Structure of Isaiah." *VT* 38 (1988): 129-47.

Kaufmann, Y. *The Babylonian Captivity and Deutero-Isaiah.* Trans. C. W. Efroymson. New York, 1970. Pages 66-89.

Lack, R. *La symbolique du livre d'Isaïe: Essai sur l'image littéraire comme élément de structuralisme.* AnBib 59. Rome, 1973.

Liebreich, L. J. "The Compilation of the Book of Isaiah." *JQR* 46 (1955-56): 259-77.

———. "The Compilation of the Book of Isaiah." *JQR* 47 (1956-57): 114-38.

Rendtorff, R. "Zur Komposition des Buches Jesaja." *VT* 34 (1984): 295-320.

———. "The Book of Isaiah: A Complex Unity — Synchronic and Diachronic Reading." In R. F. Melugin and M. A. Sweeney, eds. *New Visions of Isaiah.* JSOTSup 214. Sheffield, 1996. Pages 32-49.

Schmitt, J. J. *Isaiah and His Interpreters.* New York, 1986. Pages 18-36.

Seitz, C. R. "Isaiah 1–66: Making Sense of the Whole." In C. Seitz, ed. *Reading and Preaching the Book of Isaiah.* Philadelphia, 1988. Pages 105-26.

Sommer, B. D. "Allusions and Illusions: The Unity of the Book of Isaiah in Light of Deutero-Isaiah's Use of Prophetic Tradition." In R. Melugin and M. A. Sweeney, eds. *New Visions of Isaiah.* JSOTSup 214. Sheffield, 1996. Pages 156-86.

Sweeney, M. A. "The Book of Isaiah as Prophetic Torah." In R. F. Melugin and M. A. Sweeney, eds. *New Visions of Isaiah.* JSOTSup 214. Sheffield, 1996. Pages 50-67.

Vermeylen, J. "L'unité du livre d'Isaïe." In J. Vermeylen, ed. *The Book of Isaiah/Le Livre d'Isaïe.* BETL 81. Leuven, 1989. Pages 11-53.

Williamson, H. G. M. *The Book Called Isaiah: Deutero-Isaiah's Role in Composition and Redaction.* Oxford, 1994.

Unity of Deutero-Isaiah (Isa 40–66)

Buber, M. *The Prophetic Faith.* Rev. ed. New York, 1960.

Glahn, L. "Die Einheit von Kap. 40–66 des Buches Jesaja." In L. Glahn and L. Köhler. *Der Prophet der Heimkehr.* Giessen, 1934. Pages 25-65.

Haran, M. *Between Ri'shonôt (Former Prophecies) and Ḥadashôt (New Prophecies): A Literary Historical Study in the Group of Prophecies Isaiah XL-XLVIII.* Jerusalem, 1963. Pages 93-102. Hebrew.

Klausner, J. *History of the Second Temple.* 6th ed. Jerusalem, 1963. 1:158-75. Hebrew.

Radday, Y. T. *The Unity of Isaiah in the Light of Statistical Linguistics.* Hildesheim, 1973.

Segal, M. H. *Introduction to the Bible.* 2 vols. Jerusalem, 1967. Hebrew.

Sommer, B. *A Prophet Reads Scripture: Allusions in Isaiah 40–66.* Stanford, 1998. Pages 134-40.

Historical Background

Beaulieu, P. A. *The Reign of Nabonidus, King of Babylon, 556-539 B.C.* New Haven, 1989.

Tadmor, H. "The Historical Background of Cyrus' Declaration." In Y. Kaufmann et al., eds. *Oz Le-David: Dedicated to David Ben Gurion on His Seventy-seventh Birthday.* Jerusalem, 1964. Pages 450-73. Hebrew.

Vanderhooft, D. S. *The Neo-Babylonian Empire and Babylon in the Latter Prophets.* HSM 59. Atlanta, 1999.

Yadin, Y. *The Art of Warfare in Biblical Lands in the Light of Archaeological Study.* Trans. M. Pearlman. 2 vols. New York, 1963.

Cyrus in the Prophecies of Deutero-Isaiah

Derby, J. "Isaiah and Cyrus." *JBQ* 24 (1996): 173-77.

Fried, L. S. "Cyrus the Messiah? The Historical Background to Isaiah 45:1." *HTR* 95 (2002): 373-93.

Haller, M. "Die Kyros-Lieder Deuterojesajas." In H. Schmidt, ed. *Eucharisterion: Studien zur Religion und Literatur des Alten und Neuen Testaments — Festschrift Hermann Gunkel.* Göttingen, 1923. Pages 261-77.

Jenni, E. "Die Rolle des Kyros bei Deuterojesaja." *TZ* 10 (1954): 241-256.

Kittel, R. "Cyrus und Deuterojesaja." *ZAW* 18 (1898): 149-62.

Koch, K. "Die Stellung des Kyros im Geschichtsbild Deuterojesajas und ihre überlieferungsgeschichtliche Verankerung." *ZAW* 84 (1972): 352-356.

Kratz, R. G. *Kyros im Deuterojesaja-Buch: Redaktionsgeschichtliche Untersuchungen zu Entstehung und Theologie von Jes 40–55.* Tübingen, 1991.

Reinwald, G. *Cyrus im zweiten Teil des Buches Isaias: Kap. 40–55.* Bamberg, 1956.

Simcox, C. R. "The Role of Cyrus in Deutero-Isaiah." *JAOS* 57 (1937): 158-71.

Rishonôt and *Ḥadashôt*

Haran, M. *Between Ri'shonôt (Former Prophecies) and Ḥadashôt (New Prophecies): A Literary Historical Study in the Group of Prophecies Isaiah XL–XLVIII.* Jerusalem, 1963. Pages 93-102. Hebrew.

Merendino, R. P. *Der Erste und der Letzte: Eine Untersuchung von Jes 40–48.* VTSup 31. Leiden, 1981.

North, C. R. "The 'Former Things' and the 'New Things' in Deutero-Isaiah." In H. H. Rowley, ed. *Studies in Old Testament Prophecy Presented to Professor Theodore H. Robinson.* New York, 1950. Pages 111-26.

Schoors, A. "Les choses antérieures et les choses nouvelles dans les oracles deutéro-isaïens." *ETL* 40 (1964): 19-47.

Stuhlmueller, C. "'First and Last' and 'Yahweh-Creator' in Deutero-Isaiah." *CBQ* 29 (1967): 495-511.

Williamson, H. G. M. "First and Last in Isaiah." In H. A. McKay and D. J. A. Clines, eds. *Of Prophets' Visions and the Wisdom of Sages: Essays in Honour of R. Norman Whybray on His Seventieth Birthday.* JSOTSup 163. Sheffield, 1993. Pages 95-108.

Servant Songs

Alobaidi, J. *The Messiah in Isaiah 53: The Commentaries of Saadia Gaon, Salmon ben Yeruham and Yefet ben Eli on Is 52:13–53:12. Edition and Translation.* Bern, 1998.

Aytoun, R. "The Servant of the Lord in the Targum." *JTS* 23 (1921/22): 172-80.

Barstad, H. M. "The Future of the 'Servant Songs': Some Reflections on the Relationship of Biblical Scholarship to Its Own Tradition." In S. E. Balentine and J. Barton, eds. *Language, Theology and the Bible: Essays in Honour of James Barr.* Oxford, 1994. Pages 261-70.

Blenkinsopp, J. "The Servant and the Servants in Isaiah and the Formation of the Book." In C. C. Broyles and C. A. Evans, eds. *Writing and Reading the Scroll of Isaiah: Studies of an Interpretive Tradition.* 2 vols. VTSup 70. Leiden, 1997. 1:155-75.

Cazelles, H. "Les poèmes du Serviteur: Leur place, leur structure, leur théologie." *RSR* 43 (1955): 5-55.

Ceresko, A. R. "The Rhetorical Strategy of the Fourth Servant Song (Isaiah 52:13–53:12): Poetry and the Exodus–New Exodus." *CBQ* 56 (1994): 42-55.

Clements, R. E. "Isaiah 53 and the Restoration of Israel." In W. H. Bellinger and W. R. Farmer, eds. *Jesus and the Suffering Servant.* Harrisburg, 1998. Pages 39-54.

Clines, D. J. A. *I, He, We and They: A Literary Approach to Isaiah 53.* JSOTSup 1. Sheffield, 1976.

Dion, P. E. "Les chants du Serviteur de Yahweh et quelques passages apparentés d'Is 40–55. Un essai sur leurs limites précises et sur leur origines respectives." *Bib* 51 (1970): 17-38.

Driver, G. R. "Isaiah 52:13–53:12: The Servant of the Lord." In M. Black and G. Fohrer, eds. *In Memoriam Paul Kahle.* BZAW 103. Berlin, 1968. Pages 90-105.

Driver, S. R., and A. D. Neubauer. *The Fifty-Third Chapter of Isaiah.* Vol. 2: *Translations.* 1876-77. Repr. New York, 1969.

Eissfeldt, O. *Der Gottesknecht bei Deuterojesaja (Jes 40-55) im Lichte der israelitischen Anschauung von Gemeinschaft und Individuum. Beiträge zur Religionsgeschichte des Altertums* 2. Halle, 1933.

Ekblad, E. R., Jr. *Isaiah's Servant Poems According to the Septuagint: An Exegetical and Theological Study.* Contributions to Biblical Exegesis and Theology 23. Leuven, 1999.

Engell, I. "The *'Ebed* Yahweh Songs and the Suffering Messiah in 'Deutero-Isaiah.'" *BJRL* 31 (1948): 54-93.

Fischer, M. "Vom leidenden Gottesknecht nach Jes. 53." In O. Betz et al., eds. *Abraham unser Vater: Juden und Christen im Gesprach über die Bibel. Festschrift für Otto Michel.* Arbeiten zur Geschichte des antiken Judentums und des Urchristentums 5. Leiden, 1963. Pages 116-28.

Gelston, A. "Isaiah 52:13–53:12: An Eclectic Text and a Supplementary Note on the Hebrew Manuscript Kennicott 96." *JSS* 35 (1990): 187-211.

Gerleman, G. "Der Gottesknecht bei Deuterojesaja." In *Studien zur alttestamentlichen Theologie.* Heidelberg, 1980. Pages 38-60.

Ginsberg, H. L. "The Oldest Interpretation of the Suffering Servant." *VT* 3 (1953): 400-404.

Grelot, P. *Les poèmes du Serviteur: De la lecture critique à l'herméneutique.* Paris, 1981.

Haag, H. *Der Gottesknecht bei Deuterojesaja.* Erträge der Forschung 233. Darmstadt, 1985.

Hanson, P. D. "The World of the Servant of the Lord in Isaiah 40–55." In W. H. Bellinger and W. R. Farmer, eds. *Jesus and the Suffering Servant.* Harrisburg, 1998. Pages 9-22.

Hermisson, H.-J. "Israel und der Gottesknecht bei Deuterojesaja." *ZTK* 79 (1982): 1-24.

———. "The Fourth Servant Song in the Context of Second Isaiah." In B. Janowski and P. Stuhlmacher, eds. *The Suffering Servant: Isaiah 53 in Jewish and Christian Sources.* Grand Rapids, 2004. Pages 16-47.

Janowski, B. "He Bore Our Sins: Isaiah 53 and the Drama of Taking Another's Place." In B. Janowski and P. Stuhlmacher, eds. *The Suffering Servant: Isaiah 53 in Jewish and Christian Sources.* Grand Rapids, 2004. Pages 48-74.

Kaiser, O. *Der königliche Knecht: Eine traditionsgeschichtlichexegetische Studie über die Ebed-Jahwe-Lieder bei Deuterojesaja.* FRLANT 70. Göttingen, 1959.

Kapelrud, A. S. "The Identity of the Suffering Servant." In H. Goedicke, ed. *Near Eastern Studies in Honor of William Foxwell Albright.* Baltimore, 1971. Pages 307-14.

———. "Second Isaiah and the Suffering Servant." In A. Caquot and M. Philonenko, eds. *Hommages à A. Dupont-Sommer.* Paris, 1971. Pages 297-303.

Kaufmann, Y. *The Babylonian Captivity and Deutero-Isaiah.* Trans. C. W. Efroymson. New York, 1970. Pages 128-61.

Kruse, C. R. "The Servant Song: Interpretive Trends since C. R. North." *Studia Biblica et Theologica* 8 (1978): 3-27.

Laato, A. *The Servant of YHWH and Cyrus: A Reinterpretation of the Exilic Messianic Programme in Isaiah 40–55.* Coniectanea biblica, Old Testament 35. Stockholm, 1992.

Lindblom, J. *The Servant Songs in Deutero-Isaiah: A New Attempt to Solve an Old Problem.* Lunds universitets årsskrift Mitteilungen der altorientalischen Gesellschaft 47/5. Lund, 1951.

Marcus, R. "The 'Plain Meaning' of Isaiah 42:1-4." *HTR* 30 (1937): 249-59.

Mettinger, T. N. D. *A Farewell to the Servant Songs: A Critical Examination of an Exegetical Axiom.* Scripta Minora 3. Lund, 1983.

Miller, J. W. "Prophetic Conflict in Second Isaiah: The Servant Songs in the Light of Their Context." In E. Jenni, J. J. Stamm, and H. J. Stoebe, eds. *Wort-Gebot-Glaube. Festschrift W. Eichrodt.* Abhandlungen zur Theologie des Alten and Neuen Testaments 59. Zurich, 1970. Pages 77-85.

Neubauer, A. *The Fifty-Third Chapter of Isaiah.* Vol. 1: *Texts.* 1876-77. Repr. New York, 1969. Hebrew and Arabic.

North, C. R. *The Suffering Servant in Deutero-Isaiah: An Historical and Critical Study.* 2nd ed. Oxford, 1956.

Orlinsky, H. M. "'Israel' in Isa. XLIX, 3: A Problem in the Methodology of Textual Criticism." *ErIsr* 8 (1967): 42-45.

———. "The So-Called 'Servant of the Lord' and 'Suffering Servant' in Second Isaiah." In H. M. Orlinsky and N. H. Snaith, *Studies in the Second Part of the Book of Isaiah.* VTSup 14. 1967. Repr. with corrections, 1977. Pages 1-133.

———. "The Servant of the Lord." In E. L. Sukenik, ed. *Encyclopaedia Biblica.* 8 vols. Jerusalem, 1958-82. 6:15-22. Hebrew.

Payne, D. F. "The Servant of the Lord: Language and Interpretation." *EvQ* 42/43 (1970-71): 131-43.

Raabe, P. R. "The Effect of Repetition in the Suffering Servant Song." *JBL* 103 (1984): 77-81.

Ratzhabi, Y. "The Commentary of R. Saadia Gaon on the 'My Servant' Section in Isaiah." *Tarbiz* 57 (1988): 327-47. Hebrew.

Rembaum, J. "The Development of a Jewish Exegetical Tradition Regarding Isaiah 53." *HTR* 75 (1982): 289-310.

Reventlow, H. G. "Basic Issues of Interpretation of Isaiah 53." In W. H. Bellinger and W. R. Farmer, eds. *Jesus and the Suffering Servant.* Harrisburg, 1998. Pages 23-38.

Rignell, L. "Isaiah LII:13–LIII:12." *VT* 3 (1953): 87-92.

Roth, W. M. W. "The Anonymity of the Suffering Servant." *JBL* 83 (1964): 171-79.

Rowley, H. H. *The Servant of the Lord and Other Essays on the Old Testament.* 2nd ed. Oxford, 1965.

———. "The Suffering Servant and the Davidic Messiah." In *The Servant of the Lord and Other Essays on the Old Testament.* 2nd ed. Oxford, 1965. Pages 61-93.

Sauer, G. "Deuterojesaja und die Lieder vom Gottesknecht." In G. Fitzer, ed. *Geschichtsmächtigkeit und Geduld. Festschrift der Evangelisch-theologischen Fakultät der Universität Wien.* Evangelische Theologie-Sonderheft. Munich, 1972. Pages 58-66.

Sawyer, J. F. A. "Daughter of Zion and Servant of the Lord in Isaiah: A Comparison." *JSOT* 44 (1989): 89-107.

Scharbert, J. "Stellverstretendes Sühneleiden in den Ebed-Jahwe-Liedern und in altorientalischen Ritualtexten." *BZ* 2 (1968): 190-213.

Schechter, Y. "The Servant of the Lord." In B. Z. Luria, ed. *Studies in the Book of Isaiah.* Jerusalem, 1980. 2:287-312. Hebrew.

Snaith, N. H. "The Servant of the Lord in Deutero-Isaiah." In H. H. Rowley, ed. *Studies in Old Testament Prophecy: T. H. Robinson Festschrift.* Edinburgh, 1950. Pages 187-200.

Steck, O. H. *Gottesknecht und Zion: Gesammelte Aufsätze zu Deuterojesaja.* FAT 4. Tübingen, 1992.

Stern, P. "The 'Blind Servant' Imagery of Deutero-Isaiah and Its Implications." *Bib* 75 (1994): 224-32.

Trever, M. "Isaiah 53." *VT* 24 (1974): 98-108.

Walton, J. H. "The Imagery of the Substitute King Ritual in Isaiah's Fourth Servant Song." *JBL* 122 (2003): 734-43.

Whybray, R. N. *Thanksgiving for a Liberated Prophet: An Interpretation of Isaiah Chapter 53*. Sheffield, 1978.

Wilcox, P., and D. Paton-Williams. "The Servant Songs in Deutero-Isaiah." *JSOT* 42 (1988): 79-102.

Winton Thomas, D. "A Consideration of Isaiah LIII in the Light of Recent Textual and Philological Study." In H. Cazelles, ed. *De Mari à Qumran: L'Ancien Testament. Son milieu. Ses relectures juives. Festschrift J. Coppens*. Gembloux, 1969. 119-26.

Wolff, H. W. "Wer ist der Gottesknecht in Jes. 53?" *EvT* 22 (1962): 338-42.

Zimmerli, W. "Zur Vorgeschichte von Jes LIII." In *Congress Volume: Rome 1968*. VTSup 17. Leiden, 1969. Pages 236-44.

Zimmerli, W., and J. Jeremias. *The Servant of God*. Rev. ed. SBT 1/20. London, 1965. Pages 25-36.

Attitude toward the Nations and Religious Universalism

Blenkinsopp, J. "Second Isaiah — Prophet of Universalism." *JSOT* 41 (1988): 83-103.

Croatto, J. S. "The 'Nations' in the Salvific Oracles of Isaiah." *VT* 55 (2005): 143-61.

Davies, G. I. "The Destiny of the Nations in the Book of Isaiah." In J. Vermeylen, ed. *The Book of Isaiah/Le Livre d'Isaïe*. BETL 81. Leuven, 1989. Pages 93-120.

Dion, P. E. "L'universalisme religieux dans les différentes couches rédactionnelles d'Isaïe 40–55." *Bib* 51 (1970): 161-82.

Franke, C. "Is DI 'PC'? Does Israel Have Most Favored Nation Status? Another Look at 'the Nations' in Deutero-Isaiah." *Society of Biblical Literature Seminar Papers* 38. Atlanta, 1999. Pages 272-91.

Leene, H. "Universalism or Nationalism? Isaiah XLV 9-13 and Its Context." *Bijdr* 35 (1974): 309-34.

Melugin, R. F. "Israel and the Nations in Isaiah 40–55." In H. T. C. Sun et al., eds. *Problems in Biblical Theology: Essays in Honor of Rolf Knierim*. Grand Rapids, 1997. Pages 246-64.

Odendaal, D. H. *The Eschatological Expectations of Isaiah 40–66 with Special Reference to Israel and the Nations*. Nutley, N.J., 1970.

Watts, R. E. "Echoes from the Past: Israel's Ancient Traditions and the Destiny of the Nations in Isaiah 40–55." *JSOT* 28 (2004): 481-504.

Weinfeld, M. "Universalism and Particularism in the Period of Exile and Restoration." *Tarbiz* 33 (1964): 228-42. Hebrew.

Wilson, A. *The Nations in Deutero-Isaiah: A Study on Composition and Structure*. Lewiston, 1986.

van Winkle, D. W. "The Relationship of the Nations to Yahweh and to Israel in Isaiah xl–lv." *VT* 35 (1985): 446-58.

Deutero-Isaiah the Polemicist

Baltzer, K. "The Polemic against the Gods and Its Relevance for Second Isaiah's Conception of the New Jerusalem." In T. C. Eskenazi and K. H. Richards, eds. *Second Temple Studies.* Vol. 2: *Temple and Community in the Persian Period.* JSOTSup 175. Sheffield, 1994. Pages 52-59.

Clifford, R. J. "The Function of Idol Passages in Second Isaiah." *CBQ* 42 (1980): 450-64.

Dick, M. B. "Prophetic Parodies of Making the Cult Image." In M. B. Dick, ed. *Born in Heaven, Made on Earth: The Making of the Cult Image in the Ancient Near East.* Winona Lake, Ind., 1999. Pages 1-53.

Dijkstra, M. "Lawsuit, Debate and Wisdom Discourse in Second Isaiah." In J. van Ruiten and M. Vervenne, eds. *Studies in the Book of Isaiah: Festschrift Willem A. M. Beuken.* BETL 132. Leuven, 1997. Pages 251-71.

Holter, K. *Second Isaiah's Idol-Fabrication Passages.* Frankfurt am Main, 1995.

Rudman, D. "The Theology of the Idol-Fabrication Passages in Second Isaiah." *Old Testament Essays* 12 (1999): 114-20.

Schoors, A. "The Rîb-Pattern in Isaiah, XL–LV." *Bijdr* 30 (1969): 25-38.

Spykerboer, H. C. *The Structure and Composition of Deutero-Isaiah, with Special Reference to the Polemic against Idolatry.* Meppel, 1976.

Trudinger, P. "'To Whom Then Will You Liken God?' A Note on the Interpretation of Isaiah xl 18-20." *VT* 17 (1967): 220-25.

Weinfeld, M. "God the Creator in Gen 1 and the Prophecy of Deutero-Isaiah." *Tarbiz* 37 (1968): 105-32. Hebrew.

Whybray, R. N. *The Heavenly Counsellor in Isaiah xl 13-14: A Study of the Sources of the Theology of Deutero-Isaiah.* Cambridge, Eng., 1971.

Descriptions of Jerusalem

Weinfeld, M. *From Joshua to Josiah: Turning Points in the History of Israel from the Conquest of the Land until the Fall of Judah.* Jerusalem, 1992. Pages 111-32. Hebrew.

Descriptions of God, His Attributes, and His Relationship with His People

Brettler, M. "Incompatible Metaphors for YHWH in Isaiah 40–66." *JSOT* 78 (1998): 97-120.

Freedman, D. N. "Isaiah 42:13." *CBQ* 30 (1968): 225-26.

Labuschagne, C. J. *The Incomparability of Yahweh in the Old Testament.* Leiden, 1966.

Female Imagery

Dille, S. J. *Mixing Metaphors: God as Father and Mother in Deutero-Isaiah.* London, 2004.

Bronner, L. L. "Gynomorphic Imagery in Exilic Isaiah 40–66." *Dor le Dor* 12 (1983-84): 71-83.

Gruber, M. I. "'Will a Woman Forget Her Infant?' — A Reconstruction." *Tarbiz* 51 (1981-82): 491-92. Hebrew.

———. "Feminine Similes Applied to God in Deutero-Isaiah." *Beer-Sheva* 2 (1985): 75-84. Hebrew.

———. "The Motherhood of God in Second Isaiah." In *The Motherhood of God and Other Studies*. SFSHJ 57. Atlanta, 1992. Pages 3-15. Originally published in *RB* 90 (1983): 351-59.

Schmitt, J. "The Motherhood of God and Zion as Mother." *RB* 92 (1985): 557-69.

Weiss, A. L. "Female Imagery in the Book of Isaiah." *CCAR* 41 (1994): 65-77.

Davidic Covenant

Beuken, W. A. M. "Isa. 55:3-5: The Reinterpretation of David." *Bijdr* 35 (1974): 49-64.

Eissfeldt, O. "The Promises of Grace to David in Isaiah 55,1-5." In B. W. Anderson and W. Harrelson, eds. *Israel's Prophetic Heritage: Essays in Honor of James Muilenburg.* New York, 1962. Pages 196-207.

Sweeney, M. A. "The Reconceptualization of the Davidic Covenant in Isaiah." In J. van Ruiten and M. Vervenne, eds. *Studies in the Book of Isaiah: Festschrift Willem A. M. Beuken.* BETL 132. Leuven, 1997. Pages 41-61.

Style and Arrangement of the Book

Style and Literary Devices

Berlin, A. "Isaiah 40:4: Etymological and Poetic Considerations." *HAR* 3 (1979): 1-6.

Boadt, L. "Isaiah 41:8-13: Notes on Poetic Structure and Style." *CBQ* 35 (1973): 20-34.

———. "Intentional Alliteration in Second Isaiah." *CBQ* 45 (1983): 353-63.

Dion, P. E. "The Structure of Isaiah 42, 10-17 as Approached through Versification and Distribution of Poetic Devices." *JSOT* 49 (1991): 113-24.

Geller, S. A. "A Poetic Analysis of Isaiah 40:1-2." *HTR* 77 (1984): 413-24.

Gitay, Y. "Deutero-Isaiah: Oral or Written?" *JBL* 99 (1980): 185-97.

———. *Prophecy and Persuasion: A Study of Isaiah 40–48.* Forum Theologiae Linguisticae 14. Bonn, 1981.

Holmgren, F. "Chiastic Structure in Isaiah LI 1-11." *VT* 19 (1969): 196-201.

Korpel, M. C. A. "Metaphors in Isaiah LV." *VT* 46 (1996): 43-55.

Kuntz, J. K. "The Contribution of Rhetorical Criticism to Understanding Isaiah 51:1-16." In D. J. A. Clines et al., eds. *Art and Meaning: Rhetoric in Biblical Literature.* JSOTSup 19. Sheffield, 1982. Pages 140-71.

———. "The Form, Location, and Function of Rhetorical Questions in Deutero-Isaiah." In C. C. Broyles and C. A. Evans, eds. *Writing and Reading the Scroll of Isaiah: Studies of an Interpretive Tradition.* 2 vols. VTSup 70. Leiden, 1997. 1:121-41.

Paul, S. M. "Polysensuous Polyvalency in Poetic Parallelism." In *Divrei Shalom: Collected Studies of Shalom M. Paul on the Bible and the Ancient Near East, 1967-2005.* CHANE 23. Leiden, 2005. Pages 457-76.

Payne, D. F. "Characteristic Word-Play in 'Second Isaiah': A Reappraisal." *JSS* 12 (1967): 207-29.

Scott, R. B. Y. "The Literary Structure of Isaiah's Oracles." In H. H. Rowley, ed. *Studies in Old Testament Prophecy: T. H. Robinson Festschrift.* Edinburgh, 1950. Pages 175-86.

Taragan, H. "Rhetoric and Prophecy: Rhetorical, Linguistic, and Stylistic Aspects in Isaiah 40–66." Ph.D. diss., Ben-Gurion University of the Negev, March 2006. Hebrew.

Webster, E. C. "A Rhetorical Study of Isaiah 66." *JSOT* 34 (1986): 93-108.

———. "The Rhetoric of Isaiah 63–65." *JSOT* 47 (1990): 89-102.

Westermann, C. "Sprache und Struktur der Prophetie Deuterojesajas." In *Forschung am Alten Testament: Gesammelte Studien.* Munich, 1964. 92-170. Repr. in *Sprache und Struktur der Prophetie Deuterojesajas.* CTM, Reihe A: Bibelwissenschaft 11. Stuttgart, 1981. Pages 9-87.

Arrangement

Goldingay, J. "The Arrangement of Isaiah XLI–XLV." *VT* 29 (1979): 289-99.

Hermisson, H.-J. "Einheit und Komplexität Deuterojesajas. Probleme der Redaktionsgeschichte von Jes 40–55." In J. Vermeylen, ed. *The Book of Isaiah/Le Livre d'Isaïe.* BETL 81. Leuven, 1989. Pages 287-312.

Lack, R. *La symbolique du livre d'Isaïe: Essai sur l'image littéraire comme élément de structuralisme.* Rome, 1973.

Melugin, R. F. *The Formation of Isaiah 40–55.* BZAW 141. Berlin, 1976.

Mowinckel, S. "Die Komposition des deuterojesajanischen Buches." *ZAW* 49 (1931): 87-112, 242-60.

Rendtorff, R. "Zur Komposition des Buches Jesaja." *VT* 34 (1984): 295-320. Trans. as "The Composition of the Book of Isaiah." In *Canon and Theology: Overtures to an Old Testament Theology.* Trans. and ed. M. Kohl. OBT. Minneapolis, 1993. Pages 146-69.

Ringgren, H. "Zur Komposition von Jesaja 49–55." In H. Donner et al., eds. *Beiträge zur alttestamentlichen Theologie: Festschrift für Walther Zimmerli zum 70. Geburtstag.* Göttingen, 1977. Pages 371-76.

Spykerboer, H. C. *The Structure and Composition of Deutero-Isaiah, with Special Reference to the Polemics against Idolatry.* Meppel, 1976.

Williamson, H. G. M. *The Book Called Isaiah: Deutero-Isaiah's Role in Composition and Redaction.* Oxford, 1994.

Language

Hurvitz, A. *The Transition Period in Biblical Hebrew: A Study in Postexilic Hebrew and Its Implications for the Dating of Psalms.* Jerusalem, 1972. Hebrew.

———. "The History of a Legal Formula." *VT* 32 (1982): 257-67.

Melamed, E. Z. "The Influence of Aramaic on the Language of Isaiah." In E. Eliner et al., eds. *Festschrift in Honor of Dr. Moshe Seidel on the Occasion of His Seventy-fifth Birthday.* Jerusalem, 1962. Pages 142-64. Hebrew.

Morag, S. "On Several Linguistic Characteristics of Deutero-Isaiah on Reflection on the Phrase *L'Or Goyim.*" *Beth Miqra* 14 (1969): 13-16. Hebrew.

Rooker, M. F. "Dating Isaiah 40–66: What Does the Linguistic Evidence Say?" *Westminster Theological Journal* 58 (1996): 303-12.

Saydon, P. P. "The Use of Tenses in Deutero-Isaiah." *Bib* 40 (1959): 290-301.

Early Traditions

Anderson, B. "Exodus Typology in Second Isaiah." In B. W. Anderson and W. Harrelson, eds. *Israel's Prophetic Heritage: Essays in Honor of James Muilenburg.* New York, 1962. Pages 177-95.

———. "Exodus and Covenant in Second Isaiah and Prophetic Tradition." In W. E. Lemke et al., eds. *Magnalia Dei — The Mighty Acts of God: Essays on the Bible and Archaeology in Memory of G. Ernest Wright.* Garden City, N.Y., 1976. Pages 339-60.

Gunn, D. M. "Deutero-Isaiah and the Flood." *JBL* 94 (1975): 493-508.

Hoffman, Y. *The Doctrine of the Exodus in the Bible.* Tel Aviv, 1983. Pages 60-66. Hebrew.

Kiesow, K. *Exodustexte im Jesajabuch: Literarkritische und motivgeschichtliche Analysen.* Fribourg, 1979.

Patrick, D. A. "Epiphanic Imagery in Second Isaiah's Portrayal of a New Exodus." *HAR* 8 (1984): 125-41.

Stuhlmueller, C. "The Theology of Creation in Second Isaiah." *CBQ* 21 (1959): 429-67.

Vermeylen, J. "Le motif de la création dans le Deutéro-Isaïe." In P. Beauchamp et al., eds. *La création dans l'Orient ancien.* LD 127. Paris, 1987. Pages 183-240.

Influences of Other Biblical Books

Brueggemann, W. "Isaiah 55 and Deuteronomic Theology." *ZAW* 80 (1968): 191-203.

Cassuto, U. "On the Formal and Stylistic Relationship between Deutero-Isaiah and Other Biblical Writers." In *Biblical and Oriental Studies.* Vol. 1: *Bible.* Trans. I. Abrahams. Jerusalem, 1973. Pages 141-77.

Clements, R. E. "Beyond Tradition-History: Deutero-Isaianic Development of First Isaiah's Themes." *JSOT* 31 (1985): 95-113.

Paul, S. M. "Literary and Ideological Echoes of Jeremiah in Deutero-Isaiah." In *Proceedings of the Fifth World Congress of Jewish Studies.* Vol. 1: *Ancient Near East, Bible, Archaeology, First Temple Period.* Jerusalem, 1972. Pages 102-20. Repr. in *Divrei Shalom: Collected Studies of Shalom M. Paul on the Bible and the Ancient Near East, 1967-2005.* CHANE 23. Leiden, 2005. Pages 399-416.

Pfeifer, G. "Amos und Deuterojesaja denkformenanalytisch verglichen." *ZAW* 93 (1981): 439-43.

Seidel, M. "Parallels in the Books of Isaiah and Psalms." In S. Assaf et al., eds. *Mincha leDavid: The David Yellin Festschrift.* Jerusalem, 1935. Pages 23-47. Hebrew.

———. "Parallels between the Book of Isaiah and the Book of Psalms." *Sinai* 38 (1956): 149-72, 229-42, 272-80, 333-55. Hebrew.

Sommer, B. D. *A Prophet Reads Scripture: Allusion in Isaiah 40–66.* Stanford, 1998.

Terrien, S. "Quelques remarques sur les affinités de Job avec Deutéro-Isaïe." In *Volume du Congrès: Genève, 1965.* VTSup 15. Leiden, 1966. Pages 295-310.

Willey, P. T. *Remember the Former Things: The Recollection of Previous Texts in Second Isaiah.* SBLDS 161. Atlanta, 1997.

Williamson, H. G. M. "Isaiah 62:4 and the Problem of Inner Biblical Allusions." *JBL* 119 (2000): 734-39.

Legacy of the Ancient Near East

Aḥituv, S. *Ha-Ketav veha-Miḵtav.* (The Script and the Scripture.) 2nd ed. Jerusalem, 2005. Hebrew.

Avishur, Y. "'לא שמת להם רחמים' (Isa 47:6): Biblical Style or Translated Idiom?" *Shnaton* 5-6 (1978-79): 91-99. Hebrew.

———. "'Who Has Measured the Waters in the Hollow of His Hand?' (Isa 40:12)." In B. Uffenheimer, ed. *Bible Studies: Y. M. Grintz in Memoriam.* Teuda 2. Tel Aviv, 1982. Pages 131-37. Hebrew.

———. "'מי בעל משפטי יגש אלי' (Isa 50:8): A Stylistic Feature of Biblical Hebrew or a Translated Akkadian Phrase?" *Leš* 52 (1988): 18-25. Hebrew.

Behr, J. W. *The Writings of Deutero-Isaiah and the Neo-Babylonian Royal Inscriptions.* Pretoria, 1937.

Cassuto, U. "The Relationship between Ugaritic Literature and the Bible." In *The Goddess Anath: Canaanite Epics of the Patriarchal Age.* Trans. I. Abrahams. Jerusalem, 1971. Pages 18-52.

———. "Parallel Words in Hebrew and Ugaritic." In *Biblical and Oriental Studies.* Vol. 2: *Bible and Ancient Oriental Texts.* Trans. I. Abrahams. Jerusalem, 1975. Pages 60-68.

Dion, H. M. "Le genre littéraire sumérien de l'hymne à soi-même et quelques passages du Deutéro-Isaïe." *RB* 74 (1967): 215-34.

Eph'al, I. "On the Linguistic and Cultural Background of Deutero-Isaiah." *Shnaton* 10 (1986-89): 31-35. Hebrew.

Fitzmyer, J. A. *The Aramaic Inscriptions of Sefîre.* BibOr 19. Rome, 1967.

Grelot, P. "Un parallèle babylonien d'Isaïe 60 et du Psaume 72." *VT* 7 (1957): 319-21.

Hallo, W. W., ed. *The Context of Scripture.* 3 vols. Leiden, 1997-2002.

Kittel, R. "Cyrus und Deuterojesaja." *ZAW* 18 (1898): 149-62.

Loretz, O. "Mesopotamische und ugaritisch-kanaanäische Elemente im Prolog des Buches Deuterojesaja (Jes 40:1-11)." *ZAW* 96 (1984): 210-20.

Machinist, P. "Mesopotamian Imperialism and Israelite Religion: A Case Study from the Second Isaiah." In W. G. Dever and S. Gitin, eds. *Symbiosis, Symbolism, and the Power of the Past: Canaan, Ancient Israel, and Their Neighbors from the Late Bronze Age through Roman Palestine.* Winona Lake, Ind., 2003. Pages 237-64.

Paul, S. M. "Deutero-Isaiah and Cuneiform Royal Inscriptions." In W. W. Hallo, ed. *Essays in Memory of E. A. Speiser.* JAOS 88. New Haven, 1968. Pages 180-86. Repr. in *Divrei Shalom: Collected Studies of Shalom M. Paul on the Bible and the Ancient Near East, 1967-2005.* CHANE 23. Leiden, 2005. Pages 11-22.

Roth, M. T. *Law Collections from Mesopotamia and Asia Minor.* SBLWAW 6. Atlanta, 1995.

Saggs, H. W. F. "A Lexical Consideration of the Date of Deutero-Isaiah." *JTS* 10 (1959): 84-87.

Smith, M. "Second Isaiah and the Persians." *JAOS* 83 (1963): 415-21.

Stummer, F. "Einige keilschriftliche Parallelen zu Jes. 40–66." *JBL* 45 (1926): 171-89.

Textual Versions, Isaiah Scrolls from the Judean Desert, Translations

Textual Versions

Goshen-Gottstein, M. H., ed. *The Book of Isaiah.* Hebrew University Bible Project. Jerusalem, 1995.

Isaiah Scrolls from the Judaean Desert

Allegro, J. M. *Qumrân Cave 4.I (4Q158-4Q185).* DJD 5. Oxford, 1968.
Burrows, M., ed. *The Dead Sea Scrolls of St. Mark's Monastery.* Vol. 1: *The Isaiah Manuscript and the Habakkuk Commentary.* New Haven, 1950.
Flint, P. "The Isaiah Scrolls from the Judean Desert." In C. C. Broyles and C. A. Evans, eds. *Writing and Reading the Scroll of Isaiah: Studies of an Interpretive Tradition.* 2 vols. VTSup 70. Leiden, 1997. 2:481-89.
Kutscher, E. Y. *The Language and Linguistic Background of the Isaiah Scroll (1QIsa^{a}).* STDJ 6. Leiden, 1974.
Parry, D. W., and E. Qimron, eds. *The Great Isaiah Scroll (1QIsa^{a}): A New Edition.* Leiden, 1999.
Pulikottil, P. *Transmission of Biblical Texts in Qumran: The Case of the Large Isaiah Scroll 1QIsa^{a}*. Journal for the Study of the Pseudepigrapha Supplement 34. Sheffield, 2001.
Roberts, B. J. "The Second Isaiah Scroll from Qumrân (1QIs^{b})." *BJRL* 42 (1959): 132-44.
Tov, E. "The Text of Isaiah at Qumran." In C. C. Broyles and C. A. Evans, eds. *Writing and Reading the Scroll of Isaiah: Studies of an Interpretive Tradition.* 2 vols. VTSup 70. Leiden, 1997. 2:491-511.
Ulrich, E. "An Index to the Contents of the Isaiah Manuscripts from the Judean Desert." In C. C. Broyles and C. A. Evans, eds. *Writing and Reading the Scroll of Isaiah: Studies of an Interpretive Tradition.* 2 vols. VTSup 70. Leiden, 1997. 2:477-80.

Commentaries (Pesharim) on Deutero-Isaiah

García Martínez, F., and E. J. C. Tigchelaar, eds. *The Dead Sea Scrolls Study Edition.* 2 vols. Grand Rapids, 1997-98. 1:312-29.
Parry, D. W., and E. Tov, eds. *The Dead Sea Scrolls Reader.* Part 2: *Exegetical Texts.* Leiden, 2004. Pages 52-59.

Translations

Septuagint

Ottley, R. R. *The Book of Isaiah According to the Septuagint Codex Alexandrinus.* 2 vols. London, 1904-6.
Seeligmann, I. L. *The Septuagint Version of Isaiah.* 1948. Repr. in *The Septuagint Version of Isaiah and Cognate Studies.* Tübingen, 2004. Pages 119-294.
van der Kooij, A. "'The Servant of the Lord': A Particular Group of Jews in Egypt According to the Old Greek of Isaiah. Some Comments on LXX Isaiah 49,1-6 and Related Passages." In J. van Ruiten and M. Vervenne, eds. *Studies in the Book of Isaiah: Festschrift Willem A. M. Beuken.* BETL 132. Leuven, 1997. Pages 383-96.

Ziegler, J. *Untersuchungen zur Septuaginta des Buches Isaias.* Münster, 1934.
———. "Die Vorlage der Isaias-Septuaginta (LXX) und die erste Isaias-Rolle von Qumran (IQIs[a])." In F. M. Cross and S. Talmon, eds. *Qumran and the History of the Biblical Text.* Cambridge, Mass., 1975. Pages 90-115.

VULGATE

Kedar-Klopfstein, B. "Divergent Hebrew Readings in Jerome's Isaiah." *Textus* 4 (1964): 176-210.

ARAMAIC TARGUM

Chilton, B. D. *The Isaiah Targum: Introduction, Translation, Apparatus and Notes.* Aramaic Bible 11. Wilmington, Del., 1987.
Sperber, A. *The Bible in Aramaic.* Vol. 3: *The Latter Prophets according to Targum Jonathan.* Leiden, 1992.

Index of Authors

Aḥituv, S., 167, 200, 228, 391, 462, 504, 519, 533, 540, 551, 561, 565, 594, 620, 654
Albright, W. F., 154, 390, 647
Allegro, J. M., 66, 133, 426, 429, 450, 655
Anderson, B. W., 172, 435, 651, 653
Asaf, S., 231
Avigad, N., 200
Avishur, Y., 189, 635, 641, 654
Avi-Yonah, M., 381

Baillet, M., 139, 140, 462
Baumgarten, J. M., 306, 365, 384, 539
Beaulieu, P.-A., 159, 645
Bechtel, G., 169
Bechtel, L. M., 290
Ben-Dov, M., 622
Benz, F. L., 600
Berlejung, A., 145, 232
Beuken, W. A. M., 415, 435, 611, 634, 636, 637, 639, 640, 641, 644, 650, 651, 655
Biddle, M. E., 415, 636
Biran, A., 356
Black, J. A., 275
Blau, J., 277, 301
Borger, R., 627
Brinkman, J. A., 627
Brooke, G., 15, 229
Broshi, M., 306, 533
Brueggemann, W., 440, 634, 644, 653
Brunner, H., 323

Cagni, L., 425
Carr, D. M., 611, 644
Cassuto, U., 348, 367, 653, 654
Clines, D. J. A., 397, 416, 646, 651
Cogan, M., 14, 17, 165, 167, 180, 188, 274
Cohen, Ch., 296, 421, 617, 636
Cohen, M. B., 402
Cohen, S., 384
Collins, B. J., 614
Collins, J. J., 15
Cornelius, I., 593
Cowley, A. E., 479
Cross, F. M., 127, 172, 323, 656

Darr, K. P., 195, 636
Davidson, Y., 231
Day, J., 469
De Moor, J. C., 359, 641
De Vaux, R., 594
Delitzsch, F., 261, 634
Demsky, A., 551
Deutsch, R., 190, 358
Dick, M. B., 145, 232, 650
Dobbs-Allsopp, F. W., 153, 288, 289, 296, 416, 637
Döderlein, J. Ch., 3, 641
Driver, G. R., 351, 400, 409, 637, 646
Duhm, B., 5, 18, 634

Eichhorn, J. G., 3
Eissfeldt, O., 435, 647, 651

Eitan, I., 237, 238, 244, 300, 542
Eph'al, I., 147, 523, 524, 654
Eshel, E., 306, 533

Felix, Y., 238
Finnestad, R. B., 232
Fitzgerald, A., 147, 288, 637
Fitzmyer, J. A., 174, 366, 458, 534, 571, 582, 605, 620, 654
Ford, J. N., 343
Foster, B. R., 19, 138, 140, 152, 248, 348, 374, 474, 619, 623
Freedman, D. N., x, 128, 195, 294, 636, 637, 640, 650

Galil, G., 381
García Martínez, F., 539, 655
Garsiel, M., 450, 562
George, A. R., 532
Ginsberg, H. L., 373, 390, 399, 468, 471, 478, 579, 637, 647
Glassner, J.-J., 593
Goshen-Gottstein, M. H., 66, 68, 70, 147, 199, 281, 300, 317, 327, 358, 360, 363, 374, 379, 380, 422, 459, 477, 491, 583, 633, 655
Greenberg, M., 450
Greenfield, J. C., 144, 157, 295, 637
Gröndahl, F., 195, 600
Gruber, M. I., 195, 261, 278, 334, 341, 621, 650
Güterbock, H., 195

Haas, V., 612
Hackett, J. A., 334
Hallo, W. W., xii, 145, 274, 395, 415, 594, 654
Haran, M., 11, 17, 339, 520, 637, 645, 646
Heider, G. C., 469
Held, M., 297, 303
Heltzer, M., 190, 358
Hoffman, Y., 381, 561, 634, 639, 653
Hoftijzer, J., 391
Holter, K., 145, 637, 650
Horowitz, A., 145
Horowitz, W., 149
Houston, W., 614
Huffmon, H. B., 600

Hunger, H., 429
Hurowitz, V. A., 490, 516, 638
Hurvitz, A., 284, 412, 640, 652

Irwin, W. H., 466

Jacobsen, T., 145, 195
Japhet, S., 412, 454
Jeppesen, K., 416
Jeremias, A., 290, 649
Jongeling, K., 391

Kaufman, S., 429
Kaufmann, Y., 11, 201, 398, 477, 638, 644, 645, 647
Keel, O., 188, 339, 520
Kilmer, A. D., 306
Kimelman, R., 435
Kister, M., 139, 217, 454
Kogut, S., 252, 386, 474
Krahmalkov, C. R., 260
Kramer, S. N., 289, 306
Kuenen, A., 51, 642, 643
Kutscher, E. Y., 66, 243, 297, 336, 409, 410, 548, 563, 585, 602, 655

Labuschagne, C. J., 230, 650
Lambert, W., xi, 200, 289, 623
Leibel, D., 388
Leisten-Pongratz, B., 275
Levine, B. A., 297, 355
Lewis, T. J., 466
Lichtheim, M., 261
Lieberman, S., 228, 617
Liebreich, L. J., 591, 611, 644
Lindenberger, J., 152, 160, 260, 279, 280
Livingstone, A., 15, 619, 621
Loewenstamm, S. E., 196, 579, 580

Malamat, A., 157, 297, 381, 390, 535
Mann, T. W., 275, 638
Michalowski, M., 288
Miles, J. C., 351
Milgrom, J., 306, 594, 614, 640
Millard, A. R., 15, 623, 638
Moran, W. L., 136
Morgenstern, M., 533, 638
Moyer, J. C., 594

Naeh, S., 597
Naveh, J., 343, 356
Negbi, O., 145
Neubauer, A. D., 398, 646, 648
Newsom, C., 179, 223, 334, 351, 479, 502
North, C. R., 397, 634, 646, 647, 648

Oppenheim, A. L., 13, 297
Orlinsky, H. M., 398, 648

Pardee, D., 248, 348, 363
Parpola, S. A., 137, 146, 164, 166, 168, 191, 253, 256, 267-268, 301, 307, 341, 376, 395, 520, 619
Parry, D. W., 130, 655
Paul, S. M., 50, 61, 135, 168, 175, 188, 189, 190, 203, 205, 221, 226, 255, 263, 315, 323, 324, 328, 336, 386, 430, 433, 453, 468, 478, 479, 487, 528, 533, 539, 548, 553, 565, 567, 576, 596, 604, 617, 628, 630, 637, 639, 651, 653, 654
Pettinato, G., 260
Pfann, S. J., 139, 217, 306
Porten, B., 208, 228, 279, 332, 530, 541
Postgate, J. N., 470, 571

Qimron, E., 462, 533, 655

Reiner, E., 298, 301
Reviv, H., 381
Ribichini, S., 600
Roeder, G., 145
Rofé, A., 442, 614, 643
Roth, M. T., 138, 141, 290, 306, 654

Sanders, J. A., 193, 439, 501, 535
Sass, B., 200
Sasson, J., 289, 614, 639
Schroer, S., 147
Schuller, E., 179, 334, 351, 479, 502
Seeligmann, I. L., 412, 655
Seidel, M., 390, 652, 653
Seux, M.-J., 165, 185, 189, 249, 314, 534
Shaffer, A., 144, 295
Sivan, D., 533
Southwood, C. H., 254
Speiser, E. A., 630, 654
Sperling, S. D., 600
Spycket, A., 145
Stegemann, H., 179, 334, 351, 479, 502, 644
Stiebel, H., 165
Strugnell, J., 139, 462
Sturtevant, E. H., 169
Sukenik, E. L., 140, 398, 509, 525, 639, 648
Sweeney, M. A., 435, 591, 611, 636, 638, 643, 644, 651

Tadmor, H., 180, 617, 645
Tallqvist, K., 151, 230, 289, 293
Talon, P., 540
Teixidor, J., 600
Tigay, J. H., 50, 599, 600, 617
Tigchelaar, E. J. C., 539, 655
Tov, E., 130, 412, 655

Van der Woude, A. S., 539, 655
Van Winkle, D. W., 454, 640, 649
Veldhuis, N., 395

Walker, C., 145, 232, 306
Wallenstein, M., 231
Watson, W. G. E., 340, 636
Weinfeld, M., 63, 131, 138, 144, 154, 187, 257, 264, 306, 383, 384, 430, 450, 451, 481, 516, 521, 538, 579, 617, 628, 649, 650
Weiss, R., 309, 404, 569, 576
Weitzman, M. P., 597
Willey, P. T., 323, 653
Wilson, A., 146, 649
Winton Thomas, D., 142, 403, 649
Wiseman, D. J., 458, 504, 593

Yadin, Y., 142, 160, 265, 306, 429, 539, 645
Yalon, H., 336, 350, 585
Yardeni, A., 208, 228, 279, 332, 530, 541
Yellin, D., 214, 257, 277, 285, 300, 310, 331, 349, 400, 412, 459, 460, 483, 521, 541, 562, 582, 616, 635, 653
Yoel, Y., 231

Zeidel, M., 133
Zevit, Z., 157, 470

Index of Subjects

Aaron, 21, 184, 395, 399, 449, 481, 543, 573, 574, 576
Abraham, Abram, 45, 72, 164-165, 166, 207, 315, 357, 358, 359, 360, 370, 387, 398, 436, 468, 535, 551, 577, 578, 627, 630
Adad (Hadad), 306, 623
Adad-guppi, 411
Aḥriman, 257
Ahuramazda, 257
Akkad, 16, 17, 138, 180, 274
Ammonite, 66, 224, 242, 366, 408, 449-450, 540, 542, 565, 615, 629
Amorite, 599
Anat, 60-61, 152, 208, 277, 301, 334, 340-341, 367, 368, 475, 530, 554, 563, 619
Asherah, 436
Ashman, 223
Assyria, 4, 166, 168, 181, 208, 234, 245, 254, 264, 274, 287, 291, 293, 294, 324, 383, 388, 395, 407, 469, 488, 520, 525, 527, 532, 623, 627
Assyrian, Assyrians, 178, 189, 191, 249, 256, 263, 267, 274, 288, 290, 290, 307, 323, 324, 325, 341, 342, 351, 376, 388, 395, 432, 458, 469, 470, 522, 523, 524, 530, 534, 612, 619, 620, 623, 627, 628, 631
Astarte, 60, 530, 619

Baal, 60-61, 167, 195, 208, 233, 248, 277, 288, 295, 301, 331, 340, 348, 366, 368, 369, 417, 428, 436, 469, 485, 500, 502, 510, 527, 541, 563, 576, 612, 616
Baal-gad, 600
Babylon, 2, 4, 6, 7, 11, 12, 13, 14, 15, 16, 17, 19, 31, 45, 46, 62, 127, 176, 177, 180, 181, 206, 208, 212, 213, 214, 215, 217, 223, 228, 238, 245, 246, 248, 249, 251, 253, 254, 255, 260, 263, 264, 274, 275, 276, 284, 285, 286, 287, 288, 289, 290, 291, 292, 293, 294, 295, 297, 298, 299, 300, 301, 303, 306, 309, 313, 315, 316, 318, 319, 320, 321, 323, 329, 333, 347, 364, 368, 369, 370, 378, 384, 386, 388, 393, 394, 395, 396, 411, 427, 443, 444, 452, 473, 492, 516, 522, 552, 555, 558, 559, 618
Babylonia, 4, 6, 10, 11, 12, 13, 45, 46, 48, 61, 130, 131, 135, 136, 145, 159, 170, 172, 180, 190, 191, 195, 198, 201, 208, 218, 298, 321, 329, 358, 371, 383, 444
Bel (*see also* Marduk), 2, 13, 16, 17, 88, 180, 275, 276, 278, 302
Belshazzar, 13, 276, 551

Canaan, Canaanite, 60, 154, 265, 331, 358, 360, 460, 496, 509
Consolation prophecies, 1, 3, 4, 5, 10, 12, 22, 31, 59, 60, 127-128, 129, 135, 153, 162, 287, 332, 333, 358, 361, 371, 372, 377, 378, 379, 380, 453, 473, 478, 488, 506, 536, 538, 540, 541, 542, 545, 620, 621
Covenant, 1, 2, 10, 18, 21, 24, 45, 49, 127,

166, 170, 184, 185, 189, 273, 311, 329, 335, 346, 375, 395, 415, 416-417, 420, 424, 425, 426-427, 429, 434-435, 437-438, 439, 440, 453, 456, 468, 469, 482, 487, 495, 497, 504, 512, 513, 536, 537, 542, 543, 545, 546, 556, 570, 571, 613
Creation, 17, 20, 31, 45, 138, 140, 141, 142, 144, 145, 146, 148, 149, 152, 153, 154, 163, 187, 188, 189, 209, 213, 239, 243, 245, 246, 257, 262, 263, 268, 285, 310, 357, 361, 375, 424, 603, 604, 608, 611, 619
Croesus, 14, 180, 255
Cult, 12, 13, 21, 22, 65, 68, 144, 218-219, 220, 244, 275, 383, 385, 394, 435, 448-450, 451, 452, 457, 461, 463, 465, 466, 480, 523, 526, 543, 589, 591, 593, 594, 599, 608, 613, 614, 625, 629, 630
Curses, 224, 379, 462, 504, 556, 565, 589, 599, 601, 602, 605, 607, 631
Cyrus, 2, 3, 7, 11, 12, 14, 15-17, 21, 31, 46, 48, 61, 62, 86, 131, 157-161, 165, 167, 169, 176, 177, 179-180, 181, 188, 189, 190, 204, 205, 206, 208, 213, 214, 245, 248, 249-250, 251, 252, 253, 254, 255, 256, 257, 259, 260, 262, 263, 264, 269, 270, 271, 274, 275, 276, 284, 285, 300, 309, 313, 315, 316, 321, 394, 396, 435, 443, 444

Damascus Covenant, 487
Darius, 14, 381, 516, 612
David, Davidic dynasty, 2, 22, 127, 152, 163, 164, 189, 194, 200, 223, 243, 249, 252, 253, 265, 272, 388, 392, 399, 417, 424, 427, 434-435, 437-438, 439, 445, 454, 462, 512, 513, 515, 529, 531, 534, 538, 539, 607
Day of the Lord, 194, 300, 355, 504
Deutero-Isaiah, 1-4, 19-22, 23, 24, 31, 43, 44-61, 62, 66, 71-72, 127, 128, 129, 132, 135, 143, 144, 147, 148, 152, 153, 157, 159, 162, 164, 167, 170, 172, 174, 176, 178, 189, 191, 192, 195, 198, 205, 206, 210, 212, 213, 215, 217, 218, 219, 225, 226, 228, 229, 232, 238, 239, 241, 245, 249, 250, 253, 260, 269, 271, 274, 279, 283, 306, 307, 311, 312, 315, 316, 318, 322, 323, 329, 332, 333, 337, 344, 361, 369, 371, 374, 375, 383, 390, 391, 393, 397, 401, 411, 416, 417, 420, 433, 434, 435, 440, 441, 444, 447, 448, 449, 457, 481, 491, 493, 494, 495, 512, 514, 524, 529, 532, 533, 536, 538, 539, 542, 546, 556, 572, 573, 582, 584, 595, 604, 605, 607, 611, 631
Deuteronomic, Deuteronomistic, 10, 47-50, 149, 164, 346, 440, 465, 495, 504, 593, 605, 611, 616

Ea, 20, 140, 145
Edom, 4, 58, 117, 376, 445, 454, 492, 525, 560-566
Egypt, Egyptians, 23, 45, 46, 47, 48, 130, 136, 137, 166, 174, 181, 186, 190, 194, 199, 207, 208, 210, 212, 213, 215, 216, 217, 222, 223, 234, 252, 264, 265, 273, 280, 289, 290, 291, 296, 297, 300, 312, 317, 319, 320, 331, 347, 349, 367, 368, 369, 370, 381, 383, 387, 388, 395, 396, 405, 432, 441, 444, 445, 446, 469, 478, 518, 525, 534, 567, 570, 571, 572, 573, 574, 576, 594, 627
Egyptian (language, literature), 67, 174, 232, 260, 290, 323, 377, 383, 509, 541, 548, 551, 612
El (chief Canaanite god), 60, 151, 154, 170, 288, 376, 419, 436, 468, 469, 540, 541, 557, 565, 612, 619, 620
Elam, 14
Elephantine, 208, 228, 279, 331-332, 541
Enki, 607
Esagila, 13, 15, 427
Eschatology, eschatological prophecy, 7, 12, 31, 430, 513, 514, 515, 529, 532, 533, 535, 538, 560, 606
Eunuch, 447, 449, 452, 453-455
Exile, Babylonian, ix, 2, 3, 10, 14, 43, 127, 128, 129, 135, 153, 158, 169, 172, 176, 190, 191, 195, 197, 201, 204, 205, 214, 223, 225, 244, 245, 252, 260, 263, 277, 278, 285, 290-291, 294, 311, 312-313, 322, 330, 337, 339, 359, 360, 361, 370, 378, 384, 386, 387, 388, 389, 393, 403, 417, 418, 420, 421, 422, 424, 428, 435, 444, 447, 461, 489, 493, 524, 541, 542, 545, 546, 550, 553, 559
Exile, Egyptian, 388

Exiles, 2, 12, 15, 17, 182, 208, 249, 260, 264, 269, 291, 338, 387, 394
Exodus (Babylonian), 46, 48, 130, 172, 197, 217, 248, 319, 321, 370, 393; (Egyptian), 17, 45, 46, 48, 130, 136, 156, 174, 215, 248, 319, 320, 367, 368, 369, 370, 395, 432, 445, 569, 576

Fasting, fast day, 26, 71, 128, 168, 423, 480, 482, 484-486, 487, 489, 493, 496
Flood, 45, 215, 317, 415, 423-425, 428, 451, 468, 544, 621, 623
Foreigners (*see also* Nations), 10, 18-19, 31, 49, 63, 447-450, 452, 453, 455, 456, 457, 514, 516, 520, 524, 526, 529, 536, 543, 555, 556, 626, 628, 630

Gad (deity of good fortune), 121, 599-600
Garden of Eden, 45, 357, 360-361, 427, 607
Gudea, 195, 383, 384

Hadad (*see* Adad)
Haftarah, 632
Hammurabi, 138, 141, 278, 306
Hannah, 417
Hittite, 169, 195, 509, 594, 612, 614
Hymns, 31, 45, 46, 59, 63, 149, 152, 187, 191, 192, 193, 194, 195, 245, 262, 266, 268, 361, 367, 384, 392, 430, 490, 492, 516, 540, 628

Idols, idolaters, idolatry, 1, 11, 15, 18, 21, 23, 31, 49-50, 74, 79, 80, 84, 87, 88, 92, 108, 122, 144-145, 146-148, 154, 155, 157, 162-163, 164, 165, 166, 167, 169, 173, 174, 176, 178, 179, 180, 181, 182, 183, 191, 198, 199, 210, 218, 229, 230, 232, 233, 234, 235, 236, 237, 238, 239, 240, 241, 242, 243, 245, 250, 267, 268, 269, 270, 274, 275, 276, 277, 278, 280, 281, 282, 283, 300, 302, 307, 308, 309, 311, 313, 317, 321, 408, 465, 466, 467, 470, 472, 531, 600, 615
Inanna, 395
Inscriptions, 13, 14, 15, 61, 62, 130, 137, 144, 146, 147, 150, 152, 153, 154, 155, 158, 164, 165, 166, 167, 174, 175, 179, 180, 181, 183, 185, 188, 189, 190, 195, 201, 203, 207, 208, 221, 223, 226, 228, 236, 247, 253, 256, 259, 265, 270, 277, 295, 306, 315, 318, 323, 324, 325, 334, 342, 355, 358-359, 366, 373, 383, 402, 403, 411, 432, 462, 464, 475, 486, 490, 492, 514, 516, 522, 523, 524, 529, 532, 533, 534, 540, 551, 552, 553, 557, 565, 571, 582, 594, 599, 612, 620, 621, 622, 623, 627, 628, 631
Irony, 148, 232, 234, 239, 260, 271, 282, 485
Isaac, 164, 166, 398, 528
Ishme-Dagan, 516
Ishtar, 137, 155, 163-164, 166, 168, 191, 196, 228, 230, 234, 253, 254, 267, 293, 307, 341, 395, 469, 474, 520, 530, 612, 619, 621
Israelite, Israelites, 2, 7, 18, 20, 21, 124, 126, 129, 138, 152, 153, 156, 158, 170, 172, 174, 184, 189, 194, 198, 199, 204, 205, 208, 210, 212, 215, 216, 217, 218, 225, 228, 230, 235, 245, 248, 249, 251, 273, 278, 285, 307, 315, 320, 329, 348, 360, 368, 369, 370, 371, 385, 387, 395, 397, 398, 401, 410, 443, 445, 446, 448, 449, 452, 453, 456, 457, 495, 543, 544, 569, 570, 574, 584, 585, 593, 600, 608, 611, 619, 626, 629, 631
Istanu, 195

Jacob, Jacob/Israel, 23, 25, 26, 45, 56, 66, 67, 132, 153, 164, 166, 169, 177, 184, 202, 202, 205, 206, 211, 219, 222, 223, 224, 225, 226, 228, 229, 239, 243, 244, 245, 249, 252, 255, 266, 269, 271, 278, 293, 304, 305, 310, 314, 319, 321-322, 326, 327, 328, 329, 333, 344, 370, 379, 387, 391, 419, 444, 447, 448, 475, 481, 482, 485, 494, 495, 496, 498, 507, 512, 514, 519, 528, 531, 534, 551, 553, 554, 561, 577, 578, 598, 600, 606-607, 611
Jerusalem, 1, 2, 6, 7, 8, 10, 11, 12, 13, 14, 19, 22-24, 26, 57, 58, 59, 62, 67, 127, 129, 131, 135, 136, 153, 158, 172, 175, 179, 182, 187, 214, 229, 245, 247, 248, 249, 250, 263, 264, 268, 276, 285, 288, 289, 306, 312, 321, 322, 329, 333, 335, 336, 337, 338, 340, 359, 361, 376, 377, 378, 379, 380, 382-386, 390, 391, 392, 393-394, 395, 415,

416, 418-419, 420, 421, 423, 424, 427-428, 429, 432, 439, 448, 456, 457, 461, 473, 477, 492, 493, 514, 518-519, 520, 521, 522, 523, 525, 526, 527, 528, 530, 531, 532, 539, 541, 542, 543, 547, 548, 549, 550-559, 568, 584, 587, 594, 603-607, 608, 609, 610, 613, 615, 617, 619, 620, 621, 622, 626, 627, 628, 629, 630-631
Joseph, 137, 223, 268, 330, 411, 421, 436, 471, 551, 571
Judah, Judeans, 1, 2, 8, 10, 12, 14, 26, 65, 136, 158, 179, 185, 190, 194, 217, 245, 247-248, 250, 252, 264, 274, 287, 289, 296, 305, 322, 326, 337, 339, 347, 359, 360, 383, 385, 388, 394, 398, 418, 429, 448, 449, 457, 470, 473, 492, 534, 535, 559, 562, 563, 567, 587, 598, 620, 622, 623, 631

Kush, 207, 265

Lachish, 200, 265, 391, 429
Laments, 153, 172, 215, 288, 289, 293, 408
Levites, 19, 21, 65, 147, 395, 448, 455, 543
Light (un)to the nations, light of nations, 11, 18, 19, 22, 94, 174, 184, 189-190, 323, 327, 362, 363, 514, 517, 519, 551
Lud (Lydia), 14, 627

Marduk (*see also* Bel), 2, 13, 14, 15, 16, 17, 19-20, 138, 139, 140, 152, 158, 165, 179-180, 188, 189, 251, 253, 255, 274-275, 276, 366, 370, 374, 425, 443, 516, 552, 611, 619, 623
Mari, 157, 535
Media, 159, 180, 181, 284
Meni (god of destiny), 600
Merodach-baladan, 2, 275, 452
Messiah, messianic, 18, 397, 435
Migdal-gad, 600
Moabite, 66, 265, 334, 448, 449-450
Mockery, 11, 18, 31, 51, 144, 145, 148, 157, 163, 178, 224, 224, 235, 236, 238, 242, 276, 281, 300, 366, 389, 469, 472, 587, 615
Molech, 469, 615
Monotheism, 1, 138, 225, 255, 447, 456
Moses, 18, 24, 45, 46, 134, 164, 184, 185, 186, 200, 220, 221, 226, 227, 241, 252, 266, 294, 348, 353, 395, 397, 398, 443, 495, 512, 513, 565, 570, 573, 574, 576, 582, 583
Mot, 296, 500
Mount Zion, 426, 607
Mourners, Mourners in Zion, 1, 8, 58, 108, 115, 292, 339, 478, 479, 505, 537, 540, 542, 613, 620, 621

Nabonidus, 13, 14-15, 16, 17, 62, 158, 189, 226, 274, 275, 276, 294, 302, 323, 411, 621
Nabopolassar, 12, 275
Nabû, Nebo, 2, 16, 17, 67, 88, 178, 180, 275, 276, 278, 302, 342, 522-523, 619, 620
Naram-Sin, 381
Nations (*see also* Foreigners), 4, 5, 7, 10, 11, 18-19, 21, 22, 24, 25, 26, 49, 51, 56, 60, 62, 66, 67, 127, 131-132, 142, 143, 146, 157, 158, 159, 160, 161-162, 164-165, 171, 176, 179, 185, 186, 203, 207, 208, 209, 210, 214, 223, 227, 228, 245, 251, 252-253, 264-268, 270-271, 273, 287, 291, 293, 294, 296, 311, 313, 315, 316, 317, 321, 323, 324, 325, 326, 327-328, 331, 333, 339, 340, 341, 344, 356, 362, 363, 364, 371, 380, 383, 386, 388, 389, 390, 393, 397-398, 399, 400, 401, 410, 413, 420, 425, 428, 435, 437, 438, 439, 447-448, 450, 457, 462, 463, 487, 489, 504, 505, 508, 510, 511, 514-517, 519, 520, 522, 523, 525, 526, 527, 528, 529, 530-531, 534, 536-537, 540, 543-544, 545, 546, 547, 549, 551, 552, 558, 564, 565, 566, 575, 582, 583, 608, 610-611, 621, 622, 624, 626, 627, 628-629, 630-631
Nebuchadnezzar, Nebuchadrezzar, 12, 13, 15, 136, 245, 252, 262-263, 274, 275, 369, 492, 383, 516, 522
Nebushazban, 275
Nebuzaradan, 12, 275
Neriglissar, 13
Nineveh, 56, 129, 288, 295, 298, 378, 619, 627
Ningal, 189, 226
Ninhursag, 607
Ninurta, 274, 490

Oaths, 166, 178, 268, 272-273, 306, 308, 335, 337, 415, 424-425, 427, 438, 495, 556, 600, 618
Offerings, 4, 15, 19, 21, 49, 50, 63, 70, 72, 130, 137, 143, 147, 218-220, 220, 221, 246, 270, 301, 360, 373, 398-399, 407, 410, 411, 448, 449, 456, 463, 465, 466, 467, 472, 481, 484, 516, 522, 524-525, 537, 545, 546, 557, 561, 593, 594, 596, 609, 611, 614, 615, 628-629

Persia, 2, 4, 67, 158, 159, 179, 180, 245, 249, 251, 255, 276, 284, 381, 394, 435, 452, 516, 612
Persian (language), 249, 615
Persian Empire, 12, 249, 274
Polemic, satire, parody (*see also* Literary Devices, Rhetorical question), 1, 7, 10, 11, 19-22, 23, 25, 31, 46, 58, 138, 139, 140, 144, 148, 152, 154, 155, 157, 158, 160, 161, 163, 178, 179, 181, 198, 210, 219, 222, 229, 230, 232, 233, 234, 239, 243, 246, 249, 257, 259, 260, 261, 269, 274, 276, 280, 283, 285, 292, 295, 302, 303, 306, 307, 315, 321, 359, 448, 449, 455, 535, 569, 608, 611
Priests, 8, 13, 14, 15, 19, 20, 21, 24, 49, 65, 66, 127, 130, 147, 223, 228, 251, 261, 264, 383, 385, 393, 395, 399, 410, 428, 448, 449-450, 455, 470, 536, 538, 543-544, 548, 602, 608, 613, 614, 615, 629-630
Psalmic literature, 3, 56-57, 264, 515
Pul, 627
Put, 627

Qumran, ix, 1, 14, 63-66, 130, 133, 139, 178, 179, 189, 193, 223, 229, 231, 253, 323, 350, 365, 384, 414, 426, 439, 450, 462, 478, 501, 533, 535, 539

Rachel, 135, 417, 604
Rahab (sea monster), 368, 369
Rebekah, 417
Rebuke, 6, 22, 31, 59, 61, 129, 197, 212, 218, 219, 248, 260, 283, 293, 304, 305, 311, 317, 346, 348, 369, 380, 424, 425, 426, 451, 452, 458, 465, 466, 480, 498, 500, 501, 514, 609, 624
Redeemer, 7, 23, 69, 170, 205, 206, 207, 213, 229, 244, 245, 278, 292, 317, 319, 327, 329, 344, 387, 422, 424, 512, 531, 560, 561, 571, 577-578
Redemption, 4, 5, 7, 12, 17, 23, 46, 48, 127, 132, 134, 135, 137, 138, 170, 204, 205, 206, 208, 213, 215, 217, 229, 243, 244, 245, 248, 307, 319, 329, 332, 342, 344, 348, 364, 367, 370-371, 382, 383, 389, 390, 393, 395, 427, 440, 444, 445, 497, 512, 518, 540, 560, 561, 565, 570, 607, 608, 616, 617, 618, 619, 621, 622
Repentance, 69, 71, 128, 506, 512
Restoration (of Jerusalem), 247, 248, 322, 332, 361
Return to Zion, ix, 12, 17, 309, 370, 371, 392, 420, 423, 558

Sabbath, 49, 71-72, 128, 446, 447, 451, 453, 455, 456, 493-494, 495, 543, 608, 610, 626, 630, 631, 632
Sacrifices (*see* Offerings)
Salvation, 21, 60, 132, 153, 159, 168, 169, 170, 173, 189, 190, 191, 201, 204, 205, 212, 252, 259, 267, 270, 272, 283, 284, 286, 303, 319-320, 327, 328, 340, 353, 357, 363, 364, 365, 366, 382, 390, 392, 393, 412, 433, 435, 447, 450, 451, 488, 490, 504, 514, 517, 521, 532, 537, 540, 546, 547, 548, 550, 552, 555, 561, 563, 579, 583, 588
Sarah, Sarai, 45, 219, 261, 357, 358, 359, 360, 417, 418, 551
Sargon, 2, 148, 263, 523, 524, 627, 631
Ṣarpanitu, 542
Seba, Sabeans, 67, 207, 264, 265, 341, 515, 526
Servant songs, 18, 31, 184, 323, 345, 349, 350, 382, 397-398, 399, 406, 415, 512
Shamash, 230, 272, 492, 504, 593, 612
Sheba, 207, 220, 264, 265, 341, 515, 522, 523, 524
Sin (moon god), 13, 180, 189, 226, 230, 275, 302, 324
Solomon, 48, 141, 315, 360, 399, 439, 485, 531, 548, 576, 611, 615, 629
Sumer, 16, 17, 138, 180, 274, 288, 538

Tarshish, 146, 264, 300, 341, 439, 514, 515, 525, 526, 627, 628
Teima, 13-15, 276
Temple (Jerusalem), 2, 3, 6, 10, 12, 14, 19, 21, 46, 48, 58, 62, 127, 128, 131-132, 175, 198, 218, 220, 223, 245, 248, 249-250, 265-266, 267, 285, 306, 331, 371, 383-386, 392, 395, 422, 439, 447-450, 455, 456-457, 514, 525, 526, 528, 529, 530, 531, 543, 548, 557, 562, 567, 568, 576, 578, 582, 587, 611, 612, 617, 626, 628, 629, 630, 631, 632
Temples (others), 12, 13, 14, 62, 149, 175, 223, 238, 248, 250, 274, 288, 290, 383-384, 427, 475, 516, 518, 521, 522, 523-524, 528, 541, 543, 611, 613, 628
Tiamat, 248, 348, 366, 370, 374, 509
Trees, 46, 50, 62, 134, 143, 147, 150, 155, 172, 174-175, 212, 220, 228, 233, 236, 238, 239, 240, 245, 373-374, 375, 402, 444, 445, 446, 452, 465, 467, 471, 514, 516, 528, 581, 605, 625, 628
Trito-Isaiah, 5-12, 611
Tukulti-Ninurta I, 274
Tukulti-Ninurta II, 623

Ugarit, 288, 366
Universalism, 1, 10, 18-19, 68, 327, 510, 524
Ur, 15, 45, 288, 381

Xenophon, 255

Yam, 60, 248, 348, 366, 368, 369, 374, 576, 629

Zion, ix, 1, 4, 5, 8, 10, 12, 17, 19, 22, 26, 27, 45, 46, 58, 60, 63, 67, 69, 135, 136, 153, 154, 177, 182, 187, 191, 203, 244, 247, 269, 280, 286, 288, 289, 303, 309, 321, 322, 329, 332, 333, 335, 336, 338, 341, 345, 346, 357, 358, 359, 360, 361, 362, 370, 371, 375, 379, 382, 383, 384-385, 386, 387, 390, 392, 393, 415-418, 420, 422, 423, 427, 428, 429, 444, 479, 482, 493, 511, 512, 515, 523, 525, 526, 529-530, 537, 538, 539, 540, 542, 547, 548, 550-551, 555, 558, 559, 560, 565, 571, 587, 598, 613, 617-618, 620, 621
Zoroastrianism, 257

LITERARY DEVICES

Assonance, alliteration, 27, 131, 133, 141, 151, 152, 172, 173, 174, 190, 196, 202, 239, 263, 277, 279, 281, 289, 302, 319, 349, 361, 371, 377, 380, 319, 320, 336, 338, 349, 361, 377, 391, 394, 401, 402, 442, 466, 474, 485, 486, 502, 504, 507, 525, 553, 554, 558, 563, 600

Chiastic parallelism, 128, 138, 146, 150, 153, 155, 172, 186, 193, 197, 199, 202, 210, 217, 218, 221, 222, 224, 229, 234, 236, 241, 245, 246, 247, 257, 269, 276, 277, 281, 286, 296, 300, 305, 308, 317, 318, 320, 326, 327, 337, 342, 343, 346, 347, 365, 366, 384, 386, 387, 393, 400, 402, 404, 411, 419, 428, 429, 430, 442, 453, 461, 474, 475, 483, 487, 488, 502, 503, 505, 507, 509, 519, 522, 528, 530, 531, 533, 543, 546, 549, 551, 563, 564, 568, 586, 594, 597, 602, 603, 615, 620

Double entendre, 183, 235, 242, 269, 276, 285, 328, 400, 430, 453, 466, 489, 542, 549
Doublet (*see also* Repetition), 47, 171, 458, 490, 540, 554, 556

Ellipsis, 459

Gender parallelism, 61, 340, 341
Gloss, 147, 264, 301, 358, 377

Hendiadys, 298, 361, 386, 451, 453, 492

Janus parallelism, 168, 193, 194, 328, 335, 386, 477, 487, 521

Literary *inclusio,* 149, 195, 200, 215, 225, 234, 243, 248, 280, 340, 406, 429, 448, 461, 471, 503, 510, 528, 536, 623, 632

Merism, 161, 178, 187, 206, 208, 246, 257, 314, 364, 372, 395, 419, 510, 511, 604

Mirror clauses, 337, 362, 387, 490

Negative parallelism, 155, 166, 198, 216, 222, 243, 286, 355, 387, 391, 407, 418, 421, 431, 459, 483, 504, 564

Parallel nominal pair, 59-60, 130, 131, 133, 136, 140, 143, 146, 150, 153, 169, 179, 183, 191, 197, 199, 206, 207, 217, 218, 221, 227, 229, 231, 234, 240, 244, 264, 270, 271, 284, 286, 294, 323, 349, 363, 366, 379, 400, 419, 472, 473, 475, 502, 503, 504, 507, 509, 510, 531, 532, 543, 552, 553, 556, 565, 596

Parallel synonyms, 324, 368, 371, 464, 467, 469, 483, 489, 492, 499, 500, 503, 530, 531, 547, 571

Parallel verbal pair, 202, 210, 261, 268, 282, 366, 412, 510, 557, 578, 597, 616, 619, 620

Paronomasia, wordplay, 30, 131, 149, 155, 160, 161, 169, 173, 211, 216, 221, 233, 240, 241, 242, 247, 249, 268, 276, 291, 304, 308, 312, 318, 319, 324, 330, 337, 356, 363, 368, 369, 378, 384, 387, 388, 414, 417, 421, 422, 443, 454, 466, 473, 479, 481, 485, 493, 496, 501, 507, 522, 527, 541, 548, 562, 563, 565, 598, 600, 607

Quotation within verse, 26, 47, 51, 56, 66, 135, 139, 153, 174, 198, 241, 273, 295, 298, 465, 502, 519, 531, 538, 572, 576

Repetition, for emphasis (*see also* Doublet), 24, 30-31, 128, 129, 131, 134, 135, 136, 142, 162, 163, 167, 178, 181, 211-212, 219, 221, 228, 232, 238, 239, 240, 241, 243, 249, 251, 252, 256, 260, 266, 269, 271, 276, 277, 278, 279, 282, 285, 290, 298, 310, 313, 316, 327, 331, 335, 338, 350, 353, 354, 362, 363, 366, 367, 370, 372, 376, 384-385, 387, 389, 390, 393, 394, 406, 407, 412, 413, 420, 432, 444, 451, 452, 456, 464, 466-467, 473, 474, 478, 487, 483, 489, 490, 491, 492, 510, 515, 527, 528, 532, 558, 564, 568, 577, 583, 584, 581, 592, 596, 602

Rhetorical question, 20-21, 25-26, 138, 140, 141, 144, 148, 152, 154, 157, 158, 161, 181, 198, 199, 217, 230, 231, 232, 246, 260, 261, 277, 280, 309, 315, 316, 324, 332, 333, 334, 338, 342-343, 346, 347, 378, 408, 422-423, 486, 561, 575, 618

Triad, 26, 138, 139, 148, 164, 166, 181, 185, 195, 202, 207, 209, 212, 240, 241, 261, 270, 307, 311, 313, 325, 327, 332, 337, 338, 360, 364, 391, 394, 399, 404, 405, 411, 421, 427, 428, 438, 443, 464, 476, 486, 540, 587, 601, 601, 619

SCRIBAL PHENOMENA

Cognate, 1, 17-18, 62, 131, 138, 142, 155, 158, 160, 164, 166, 167, 168, 171, 175, 176, 190, 194, 198, 201, 205, 208, 209, 213, 215, 216, 220, 227, 229, 231, 235, 237, 238, 244, 247, 248, 255, 256, 265, 269, 270, 272, 276, 279, 281, 289, 292, 293, 297, 299, 310, 311, 314, 315, 318, 325, 330, 333, 339, 341, 342, 349, 350, 351, 356, 359, 362, 364, 366, 367, 374, 377, 378, 388, 389, 391, 392, 403, 408, 410, 412, 413, 422, 423, 426, 427, 431, 437, 443, 444, 445, 454, 458, 459, 466, 467, 468, 471, 472, 473, 476, 479, 484, 486, 488, 490, 491, 495, 498, 500, 503, 507, 509, 510, 511, 513, 519, 521, 523, 524, 531, 533, 534, 542, 543, 544, 545, 549, 553, 555, 556, 557, 565, 567, 569, 573, 575, 581, 585, 586, 587, 592, 594, 597, 600, 601, 605, 607, 612, 613, 621, 626, 629, 630

Conflation, hybrid form, 253, 289, 301, 389, 391, 400, 404, 419, 499, 509, 547, 564, 579

Denominative verb, 201, 237, 256, 283, 314, 337, 362, 363, 364, 436, 469, 520, 542, 543, 548, 614, 615, 618

Dittography, 139, 179, 212, 234, 266, 282, 302, 353, 372, 403, 408, 412, 491, 499, 563, 567, 574, 596, 602

Enclitic *mem*, 335, 346, 372

Hapax legomenon, 62, 63, 64, 65, 67, 70, 131, 140, 142, 147, 150, 160, 163, 179, 181, 196, 197, 199, 231, 237, 238, 241, 242, 248, 253, 267, 270, 276, 277, 281, 283, 291, 296, 309, 311, 314, 318, 338, 349, 350, 356, 358, 363, 364, 366, 387, 403, 423, 426, 428, 429, 445, 456, 459, 464, 470, 472, 478, 479, 491, 501, 504, 505, 509, 520, 529, 539, 541, 544, 547, 565, 581, 601, 615, 620, 629

Haplography, 139, 143, 180, 202, 214, 226, 236, 238, 266, 269, 273, 330, 365, 379, 402, 404, 409, 410, 459, 509, 584, 614

Ligature, 404, 569, 576, 579

Metathesis, 147, 201, 237, 258, 292, 300, 409, 421, 487, 505, 544, 581

Index of Sources

OLD TESTAMENT
(excluding Isaiah 40–66)

Genesis

1–2 257
1 72
1:1 187
1:1-2 139
1:2 20, 141, 269
1:3 20, 257
1:9 525
1:12 549
1:26 20, 138, 140, 144, 263, 349
1:26-27 20
1:28 159, 360
1:31 163
2:4 263, 494
2:6 187
2:7 188, 476
2:8 361
2:9 402
2:15 361
2:23 388
3:5 178
3:6 402
3:13 261
3:14 607
3:16 276, 617
3:18 445
3:22 20, 140
4:1 622
4:4 220
4:9 346, 612
4:10 261, 392
4:13 129, 412-413
4:15 614, 626
4:18 170
4:22 236
4:23 405
4:26 180
5:22 170
6:4 339
6:12 132, 425, 441
6:17 425
7:4 425
7:6 425
7:10 425
7:11 369, 525
7:12 425
8:21 424
8:21-22 45
9:8-17 427
9:9 512
9:11 425
9:11-17 45
9:12 44
9:15 424
9:16 437
9:24 376
10 207
10:2 627, 628
10:6 207, 265
10:7 265
11:7 20, 140
11:30 417, 418
12:1 45, 135
12:1-3 358
12:1ff. 72
12:8 187, 263, 331, 419, 585
12:10 387
12:13 437
12:17 405
13:4 387, 585
13:9 419
13:10 361
13:16 139
14:13 627
14:18 263
14:20 585
15:1 166
15:3 484
15:3-4 598
15:4 305, 318
15:5 152
15:7 45
15:11 284
15:15 462
15:16 406
15:17 370
15:18-21 45
16:2 619

17:4 512
17:5 551, 602
17:7 437
17:13 437
17:15 219, 551
17:17 146, 295
17:18 402, 630
17:19 437
17:20 360
17:22 468
18:2 336
18:4 342
18:12 333, 584
18:13 346
18:18 535
18:19 450, 451
18:23 216
18:27 242
19:1 341
19:4 460
19:9 338
19:15 505
19:16 441
19:19 437, 452
19:20 437, 579
19:25 549
20:3 554
20:4 466
20:13 453
21:3 370
21:23 571
21:29 177
21:33 154
22:1 390
22:5 239
22:7 220
22:11 390
22:13 398
22:15-17 360
22:16 272
22:16-17 358
22:17 45, 318, 360
22:18 202, 602
23:11 380
23:13 197, 207, 380, 546, 596
23:16 436
24:3 422
24:20 413
24:21 316
24:33 495
24:40 316
24:42 316
24:52 239
24:53 548, 586
24:56 316
24:60 45, 420
24:63 336
25:4 523
25:8 462
25:13 193, 524
25:16 186
25:21 417
25:22 483
25:23 324
25:24 129
25:30 562
25:31 485
25:32 612
26:4 602
26:5 263
26:24 164
26:29 394
27:3 432
27:7 402, 630
27:12 504
27:14 509-510
27:19 386
27:21 338
27:22 504
27:28 557
27:29 528
27:33 586
27:34 586
27:36 423
28:6 134
28:14 45, 419
28:16 266, 325, 404
28:19 551
28:20 443
29:9 370
29:10 159
29:14 571
29:17 400, 402
29:31 417, 529
29:32 452
29:34 452
30:1 339
30:20 262
30:28 137, 405
30:30 420
30:32 137
30:33 137, 460
30:39 465
31:1 620
31:3 205
31:4 544
31:8 137
31:10 468
31:11 600
31:12 468
31:14 466
31:21 291
31:36 168
32:4 251
32:12 318
32:21 299
32:23 205
32:29 553
32:33 308
33:3 239
33:10 130
33:13 138
33:14 378
34:12 405
34:19 554
34:30 216
35:6-7 551
35:8 341
35:10 602
35:11 328
35:29 412
37:7 525
37:11 200
37:22 302
37:30 512
37:34 349
38:11 296
38:12 407
38:16 620
39:6 400, 402
39:10 483
39:20 587
39:21 620

40:1 405
40:10 402
40:23 421
41:8 163
41:21 187
41:22 402
41:34 555
41:45 243, 551
41:51 411
42:1 436
42:4 159, 378
42:6 268
42:15 312
42:23 223
42:38 159, 339
43:12 545
43:14 338
43:15 387
43:20 436
43:23 254
43:31 577
43:34 454
44:2 436
44:13 277
44:17 425
44:28 571
44:33 207
45:8 219
45:26 401
45:27 475
46:2-4 226
46:3 166
46:34 278
47:2 165
47:14 436
48:4 360
48:5 206
48:10 499
48:14 406
48:19 403
49:3 153
49:4 468
49:9 277
49:11-13 562
49:12 436
49:16 540, 565
49:22 506
49:24 344
49:25 370
50:21 129
50:23 411

Exodus

1:9 297
1:10 378
1:12 420
2:7 341
2:10 573
2:12 614
2:13 168, 485
2:14 134, 266
2:17 159
2:20 612
3:4 390
3:6 241, 352, 404
3:7 200, 403
3:8 213, 302
3:15 43, 306, 366
3:22 548
4:10 499
4:13 411
5:8 139
5:18 139
6:1 136
6:6 45
6:7 127
6:9 405
7:18 45, 300, 349
7:19 197
7:19ff. 349
7:21 45, 348-349
8:1 197
8:13 365
8:14 365
9:29 592
10:2 615, 626
10:4 264
10:13 572
10:21ff. 349
10:22-23 45, 519
10:23 282
11:2 548
11:5 290
12:8-9 240
12:9 276, 499
12:11 46, 395, 444
12:13 432
12:23 432
12:31 395
12:33 444
12:35 48, 395
12:48 385
12:51 210, 215
13:3 210
13:9 45
13:13 398-399, 614
13:14 576
13:21 395, 477, 518, 576
13:21-22 46
14:2 463
14:5 319, 396
14:9 216
14:10 464
14:11 349
14:16 45, 46, 574
14:17 216
14:19 46, 48, 395, 569-570
14:19-20 48
14:20 395
14:21 248, 320, 369, 574
14:21-22 45, 215
14:22 46
14:23 216
14:26 45
14:28 45, 216
14:29 45, 46, 215
14:31 573
15 45, 191, 319
15:1 45, 443
15:3 46, 194
15:4 45
15:6 168, 201, 368
15:10 151, 215
15:11 201
15:12 368
15:13 202, 218, 575, 576
15:14 162, 582
15:16 218, 370
15:17 534, 607
15:18 46
15:19 45, 46, 248
15:21 45, 216
16:5 483

16:7 46
16:10 46
16:18 140
16:21 351
16:29 282
17:1-7 46
17:6 320
17:12 184, 518
17:16 43
18:15 591
18:21 469
19:4 280
19:5 543
19:6 21, 328, 383, 393, 543
19:9 244
19:10 460
19:16 161
19:17 44, 244
19:18 161, 580
19:19 482
20:2 206, 212
20:3 191
20:3-5 21
20:4 147, 258, 364
20:5 398, 596
20:11 154
20:12 411
20:20-23 48
20:26 401
21:11 387
21:18 485
21:23-25 207
21:25 206, 405
21:26-27 487
21:30 207
22:8 354
22:9 298
22:20 343
22:22 185, 282-283
22:28 286
23:5 277
23:10 557
23:11 218
23:16 502, 557
23:18 614
23:20 395, 570
23:20-23 48
23:23 46, 395
23:26 604
23:30 473
24:11 166
24:14 177, 270, 353
25:25 314
26:11 276
26:13 419
26:33 276
27:19 395
28:2 528
28:18 428
28:40 528
29:1 548
29:21 595
29:27 302
29:30 455
29:37 595
29:40-41 466
30:12 207
30:13 318
30:23 189, 220
30:25 400, 470
30:31 400
30:34 220
30:36 142, 171
31:2 255
31:14 455
31:15 493, 494
31:16 437, 451, 453
31:17 21, 154, 446
32:3 387
32:9 308
32:11 45
32:12-13 578
32:13 473
32:20 146, 171
32:27 558
32:32-33 221
32:33 570
32:34 48, 395, 570, 575
33:2 48
33:3 308
33:5 308
33:6 387
33:7 270
33:11 282, 392
33:12-13 570
33:13 142, 583
33:14-15 395, 570
33:20 298
33:22 359
34:6 311, 569
34:6-7 583
34:7 221, 398, 506, 596
34:14 191
34:18 425
34:20 399, 614
34:25 614
35:2 493
35:18 419
39:3 252
39:11 428
39:28 548
39:40 419
40:14 595

Leviticus
1:1ff. 72
2:1 220
2:1ff. 220
2:1-2 614, 615
2:9 615
2:13 189
2:16 615
4:3 251
4:5 251
4:13-21 399
4:16 251
4:26 221
5:1 211, 234
5:4 178
5:6 409
5:7 143, 409
5:12 615
5:15 409, 524
5:19 409
5:21 509
5:24 597
6:2 524
6:6 595
6:8 615
7:1ff. 220
7:18 594
7:21 625
8:33 129

9:7 595
9:14 276
10:3 326, 616
10:10 452
10:19 146
11:4 625
11:7 594, 625
11:10 625
11:29 625
11:37 549
11:47 452
12:4 296
12:8 143
13:45 403, 405
13:47 366
14:41 237
14:42 241
15:25 505
16 480
16:2 385
16:16 584
16:21 481
16:22 399
16:24-32 480
16:29 480, 480-481, 484
16:31 480, 493
18:6 291, 467, 488
18:10 291
18:17 467
18:17-18 291
18:18 467
18:19 467
18:22 468
19:3 453
19:7 594
19:13 136
19:14 372
19:22 410
19:24 557
19:28 237
19:30 451
19:32 279, 328
19:35 140
20:11 291
20:18 413
21:5 237
21:21 449
22:3 318, 493
22:24 455
23:13 466
23:15 631
23:24-32 480
23:27 484, 493
23:28 481
23:29 480
23:30 409
23:31 480, 481
23:39 557
23:40 228, 402, 445
24:7 615
24:11 552
24:16 552
25:9 480, 538
25:9-10 480
25:10 481
25:17 372
25:18 295
25:25 23
25:25ff. 229
25:30 533
25:33-55 170
25:46 473
25:47-55 23
26:2 451
26:4 443
26:12 127, 570
26:13 487
26:19 254
26:20 606
26:29 343
26:32 399
26:41 129
26:45 542
27:10 544

Numbers

1:2 152
1:17 552
1:50 395
2:17 454
3:8 395
3:31 456
3:37 419
4:15 395
4:32 419
5:1-4 385
5:3 187
5:21 602
5:25 130
6:3 562
6:11 207
6:15 466
7:3 629
7:9 282
7:15 524
7:89 389
8:14 629
8:16 189
8:16-18 629
10:2 404
10:9-10 556
10:25 396
10:33 395
10:34 395
11:12 137, 340, 341, 520, 618
11:23 348, 498
11:25 185
11:29 24, 185, 227, 512
12:14 352
13:10 600
13:11 600
13:32 265
13:33 149, 365
14:2 317
14:11 185, 297, 320, 470-471
14:14 46, 392, 395
14:15 628
14:18 347, 398, 596
14:18-19 583
14:33 398
15:16 187
15:25 220
16:9 456
16:24 468
16:26 394
16:28 565
17:4 146
18 21
18:2 449, 455
18:2-3 21
18:3 395
18:5 21

18:6 189
18:7 21
18:8-19 543
18:10 312
18:19 189
18:20 152
20:2-11 46
20:3 317
20:8 218, 320
20:10 320
20:11 320
20:16 48, 570
21:20 131
21:27 430
21:28 206, 409
22:14 202
22:26 419
22:29 615
22:35 431
22:38 375
22:41 409
23:5 375
23:9 469
23:12 375
23:16 375
24:5 391
24:7 142
24:13 565
24:17 246
24:18 277
25:4 398
25:12 427
25:13 413
25:15 186
26:53 413
27:1 354
27:2 353
27:5 176
27:11 473
28:9-15 631
30:3 272
30:5 134
30:16 399
31 342
31:5 491
31:12 342
31:26 342
32:20 630
32:21 630
32:21-23 402
32:22 630
32:38 551
32:41 551
32:42 551
33:52 409
35:12 353
35:27 429
35:28 399
35:31 207
35:32 207

Deuteronomy

1:8 159
1:13 403
1:15 403
1:17 176
1:21 50, 366, 431
1:30 253, 396
1:31 278
1:32 297, 320, 471
1:33 395
2:6 436, 468
2:12 318
2:30 475
2:34 170
3:5 253
4:7 440, 441
4:7-8 483
4:11 519
4:12 47, 256
4:16 49, 237
4:18 349
4:19 50
4:20 47, 312
4:23 49
4:24 623
4:25 49, 593, 615
4:26 49
4:28 234
4:29 440, 441
4:29-31 50, 440
4:30 512
4:31 335
4:32 263, 542
4:34 45, 48
4:35 47, 229, 257
4:37 47, 164, 165, 225, 570, 571
4:39 49, 229
4:40 49
4:41 256
5:8 49
5:9 398, 596
5:15 45, 48, 573
5:16 49
5:33 49
6:2 49
6:5 208
6:13 305
7–8 23
7:1 400
7:5 49
7:6 47, 164, 225, 559
7:6-7 47
7:8 48, 308
7:9 47, 328, 424, 426, 438, 602
7:13 48, 360
7:15 142
7:18 48, 573
7:19 45, 48
7:25 49, 50, 146, 327
7:26 49
8:2 46, 48, 573
8:15 46, 50, 172, 197, 226
9:6 307-308
9:7 48, 243-244, 573
9:14 535
9:16 308
9:18 49, 593
9:26 23, 48, 578
9:28 582
9:29 293, 578
10:8 449, 455
10:12 455
10:15 47
10:17 194
10:20 305
10:21 582
11:2 45, 48
11:9 49
11:13 455
11:13-15 437

11:14 570, 597
11:14-15 557
11:21 630
11:23 420
12:2 50, 465
12:3 49
12:5 48
12:6 220
12:9 575
12:11 48
12:12 466
12:21 48
13:2 50
13:3 593
13:5 265, 354, 593
13:6 48
13:7 269
13:9 202
13:15 183
13:16 324
14:2 47, 48, 164, 225
14:5 379
14:8 594
14:21 47
14:23 48
14:24 48
15:4 48
15:7 401
15:12 487
15:13 487
15:15 48
15:18 487
16:3 46, 48, 395, 396, 444
16:12 48
16:20 48, 358
17:3 50
17:12 449
18:7 449, 455
18:10 464
18:10-11 235
18:11 297, 594
18:14 246, 464
18:18 49, 374, 375, 513
18:21-22 10
19:3 429
19:6 170
19:9 450
19:10 49, 502
19:14 429
19:15 134, 433
20:3 396
20:5 605
20:5-6 605
20:6 605
20:19 373
21:7 49, 506
21:8 48
21:13 422
21:14 413, 554
21:15 530
21:18 592
21:20 592
22:1 488
22:7 49
22:19 346
22:20 211
22:22 554
22:29 346
23:2 449, 455
23:2-9 453
23:4 448
23:6 48, 207
23:7 391
23:22 286
24:1 47, 49, 346, 422, 554
24:3 49, 346
24:5 555
24:6 290
24:9 48
24:11 347
24:16 130
24:18 48
24:22 48
25:1 158, 177, 181, 270, 353, 433
25:9 352
25:13 281
25:15 49
25:17 48
25:18 154
25:19 48
26:1 48
26:5 387, 535
26:6 579
26:8 45, 48, 136
26:15 48, 576, 611
26:19 47, 540, 549
27:12-13 135
27:15 49, 50, 146, 198, 234, 269, 309
27:17 429
28:7 159
28:9 47
28:10 49, 511, 616
28:26 458
28:28-29 504
28:29 49, 316, 490, 505
28:30 605
28:33 437, 439, 487, 556
28:37 389
28:38 557
28:41 278
28:47 413, 601
28:49 284
28:50 294
28:50-51 556
28:53 372-373
28:54 289
28:56 289
28:58 209, 511
29:1-3 198
29:4 46
29:13 570
29:16 49
29:17 259
29:18 477, 602
29:19 194
29:21 410
29:22 372
30:1 49
30:2 512
30:3 392, 512
30:4 457
30:10 50
30:18 49
31:8 50, 253, 366, 431
31:10 505
31:17 424
31:19 374, 375
31:20 437
31:27 308
31:29 49, 593

32:1	202, 314, 319
32:1-4	319
32:2	319, 442
32:3	616
32:4	50, 232, 319, 400, 602
32:6	577, 586
32:7	540, 573
32:9	293, 495
32:9-13	49
32:10	217, 269
32:11	156
32:12	491, 495
32:13	49, 495
32:15	49, 50, 131, 226, 231, 232
32:16	49, 212, 593
32:17	231
32:18	50, 232, 261, 359, 360, 372
32:20	585
32:21	49
32:22	50, 595
32:24	377
32:30	50, 347, 511
32:31	232
32:33	377, 566
32:35	291, 570
32:37	50, 232, 346, 612
32:38	221, 266
32:39	47, 161, 211, 213, 229
32:40	556
32:41	240, 624
32:42	324, 344
32:47	49
33:2	210, 518, 562
33:5	49, 131, 226
33:11	262
33:13-16	586
33:19	521
33:26	49, 131, 226, 258
33:26-29	49
33:27	364
33:28	305
33:29	49, 267, 381
34:5	164, 200
34:7	186

Joshua

1:1	200
1:14	201
1:8	399, 513
1:9	431
2:4	400
2:5	527
2:7	527
2:9	299
3:11	422
3:13	422
3:17	248, 320
4:6	446
4:23	370
5:1	404
5:3	324
6:2	294
6:4	525
6:9	395, 489
6:13	395
6:16	194
6:18	224
6:26	429
7:6	541
7:9	454
7:13	224
7:21	402
7:25	599
8:1	50
8:18	620
9:15	427
10:8	300
10:11	418
10:12	159
10:13	282
10:24	381
10:25	50
10:27	518
10:35	171
11:3	331
11:6	159
11:17	600
12:7	600
13:5	600
13:28	193
15:1	209
15:9	237
15:11	237
15:21	193
15:37	600
17:15	135
18:14	237
18:17	237
22:8	413
23:7	305
24:13	209
24:25	187
24:27	506-507
24:29	200
24:31	49

Judges

1:18	429
1:36	193
2:7	49
2:8	200
2:14	347
3:8	347
3:16	171, 324
3:20	328
3:22	324
4:14	253
4:21	236
5:3	150
5:4	562, 563
5:5	580
5:6	131
5:11	273
5:12	367, 385, 518
5:20	503
5:23	565-566
5:26	163, 314
5:30	334
5:31	572
6:5	523
6:15	535
6:29	347
6:34	175
7:3	161
8:1-2	560
8:16	403
9:7	135
9:27	557, 564
10:16	411
11:1	619
11:18	386

11:36 307
13:2 417, 418
13:3-5 225
13:7 323
13:25 163
14:6 175
14:16 529
15:5 551
15:8 44, 51
15:11 44, 51
15:14 175
16:10 242
16:21 290
17:2 338
17:3 198
17:3-4 50
18:2 165
18:3 388
18:7 295, 407
18:9 196
18:14 50
18:17 50
18:18 261
19:29 622
20:28 194

1 Samuel

1:9 200
1:11 622
1:15 413
2:1 464, 521
2:2 50, 271
2:3 139
2:5 417
2:24 401
2:36 318
3:3 216
3:14 272
4:9 283
4:11 388
4:15 506
4:16-17 135
4:17 390
4:19 522
4:21 467
4:22 467
5:3-5 148
5:8 160
6:7 138
6:10 138
7:9 137
7:16 631
8:5 150
9:5 386
9:7 469
9:9 181
9:16 439
9:18 346, 612
9:20 547
9:27 575
10:19 535
11:2 468
12:2 279
12:3 251
12:5 251
12:7 273
12:21 49, 50, 143, 233
13:13 247
13:14 439
13:17 432
14:15 432
14:24 406
14:40 303
15:3 334
15:5 585
15:11 247
15:23 615
15:33 338
16:13 539
16:18 194
17:5 509
17:38 509
17:40 466
17:47 389
17:52 194
18:4 387
18:5 399
18:14 399
19:5 388
20:21 495
20:40 432
21:5 210
21:9 432
22:8 471
22:19 171, 604
23:16-17 163
24:6 251
24:21 318
25:2 407
25:22 243
25:25 576
25:28 3
25:30 439
25:42 159
26:9 251
26:13-14 135
28:5 161
28:6 262
28:14 400

2 Samuel

1:7 298
1:15 583
1:21 458
1:22 351, 444
3:30 412
5:2 152, 249, 439
5:7 529
5:11 201
5:21 276
5:24 253
6:21 439
7:4-17 3
7:8 439, 599
7:10 375
7:12 148, 305, 318
7:13 48, 268
7:15-16 434
7:16 437
7:23 48, 582
8:2 265, 523
8:3 454
8:6 523
8:10 194
8:13 445
10:4 352
11:12 460
11:13 566
12:3 137
12:16 509
12:23 484
12:24 315, 422
12:28 579
13:13 291

13:19 541
13:20 418
13:23 407
14:2 541
14:7 630
14:19 379
15:2 177, 270
15:6 270
15:10 392
15:19 339
15:31 247
15:33 277
16:2 237
16:11 305, 318
17:11 571
17:14 246
18:18 453-454
18:19 135, 390
18:24 390
18:27 391
19:11 196
19:21 506
19:44 454
20:3 421
20:20 338
22:3 50
22:8 149
22:9 241-242, 595
22:10 579
22:16 149
22:17 573
22:32 50, 232
22:37 276
22:43 246, 412
22:44 438
22:44-45 438
22:47 50
22:48 159
23:3 50
23:4 533
23:5 3, 189, 437
24:4 201
24:22 170
24:24 436

1 Kings
1:6 422
1:9 544
1:35 439
1:40 392
1:42 391
1:51 485
2:3 399
2:4 3, 247
2:19 293
2:20 426
2:43 262
3:2 48
3:6 306
3:8 414
3:14 49
3:25 318
5:1 629
5:15 165
5:17 48, 616
5:19 48, 616
5:22 175
5:24 175
5:31 428
6:15 175
6:21 147
6:23 175
6:32 175
6:33 175
6:34 175
7:9 314
7:26 314
7:30 153
7:36 153
8:9 468
8:10 385
8:13 48, 576, 611
8:16-20 48
8:23 49, 427
8:23-26 3
8:27 611
8:27-53 456
8:28 611
8:29 48
8:29-35 48
8:30 48, 149, 611
8:32 49, 353
8:36 48, 49
8:38-39 48
8:39 48, 149, 611
8:41-43 48, 457
8:42 48
8:43 48, 149
8:44 48
8:44-45 48
8:46 478
8:47 49, 241
8:47-49 48
8:48 48, 50
8:49 48, 149
8:51 47, 312, 578
8:53 452, 578
8:60 47, 268
9:3 48
9:7 389
9:11 175
10:2 523
10:7 401
10:9 48, 554
10:10 523
10:14 531
10:22 526
10:25 629
10:27 531
11:3 341
11:5 49
11:7 49, 615
11:29 502
11:37 238
11:38 3
12:6 141, 182
12:10 294
12:14 294
12:16 466
12:19 223
12:24 431
12:31 165
13:12 612
14:7 438, 439
14:8 265
14:9 328
14:23 50, 465
15:8 193
16:2 438, 439
16:13 593
16:26 593
16:31 326
16:33 593
17:15 510

18:24 268
18:30 338
18:39 268
18:45 349
19:2 410
19:9 388
19:15 251
19:16 538
19:18 272
19:21 526
20:1 216
20:10 139
21:2 436
21:27 349, 485, 486
22:3 196
22:19 50, 127
22:20 228, 510
22:24 352
22:28 315
22:34 509
22:44 593
22:49 526
24:44 50
30:43 611
30:49 611

2 Kings

1:1 283, 311, 632
1:14 207
2:21 174, 492
3:7 223, 311, 507
3:20-22 562
3:24 510
3:26 580
4:1 347
4:23 631
5:17 277
6:1 338
6:14 216, 629
6:26 185
7:6 162
7:19 525
8:3 283
8:9 277
9:17 522
9:22 464
9:30 428
9:33 564
10:1 341
10:5 341
10:13 293
10:22 564
12:5 50
12:10 254, 358
12:13 358
13:6 410
13:7 160
14:7 193
14:26 530
15:1 65, 326
15:5 150
15:8 326
15:13 65
15:14 600
15:17 600
15:19 627
15:30 65
15:32 65
15:34 65
16:4 50, 596
16:10 144
17:4 407
17:10 50, 465
17:11 593
17:14-16 308
17:16 50
17:23 10
17:24 420
17:26 422
17:27 422
18:4 50
18:7 399
18:34 44, 423
19:1 349
19:3 618
19:15 268
19:17 527
19:21 289
19:25 285
20:5 439
20:12 275
20:18 452
20:20 359
21:1 554
21:3 50
21:5 50
21:6 464
21:14 201
21:16 49
22:4 404
22:20 462
23:4-5 50
23:10 465
23:13 49, 242
23:24 49
23:25 50
23:27 48
24:2 10, 247, 560
24:4 49
24:13 395
24:14 339
24:14-16 12
24:17 551
25:8 275
25:8-11 12-13
25:14-15 395
25:22 555
25:27 275
25:27-30 13

Isaiah 1–39

1–39 12
1 590, 610
1:1 2
1:1-17 481
1:2 314, 339, 583, 610
1:4 50, 464, 590, 591
1:5 590
1:7 143, 591
1:8 590
1:9 591
1:10 610
1:11 51, 128, 590, 591, 610
1:11-15 218
1:12 52, 590, 591
1:13 590, 610, 631,
1:15 52, 498, 499, 500, 590, 591, 592
1:17 380, 590
1:18 51, 128
1:19 202, 294, 591
1:19-20 496
1:20 51, 132, 591, 610

1:24 344, 436, 510
1:25 312
1:26 387, 528, 551
1:27 52, 472, 511,
1:28 599, 610
1:29 421, 591, 593, 610, 625
1:30 549, 585
1:31 610, 631
2 610-611
2:1 1
2:2 362
2:2-3 52, 514, 611
2:3 362, 474
2:2-4 51, 52, 264
2:4 362
2:5 356, 514, 519
2:6 464
2:9 381
2:12 399, 474
2:14 474
2:14-15 399
2:19 300
2:21 51, 294, 465
2:22 403
3:3 235
3:4 44, 51, 615
3:9 309
3:12 531
3:17 413
3:20 337, 541
4:1 579
4:2 528
4:6 266
5:1 469
5:1-7 597
5:2 358
5:6 156, 445
5:7 504, 534
5:8 247
5:9-10 605
5:11 460
5:12 294, 502
5:14 294
5:15 381
5:16 51, 472
5:18 230
5:19 50, 247
5:20 258
5:24 50, 302
5:26 340
5:28 623
6 2, 127, 128, 474
6:1 2, 63, 399, 474
6:3 51, 128, 133, 474, 475
6:4 128
6:7 128
6:8 128
6:9 200
6:9-10 51, 241
6:10 198, 237, 406
6:11 198
6:11-12 52, 337
7:1 2
7:3 2
7:4 2
7:5 2
7–8 2
7:9 2
7:10 2
7:11 262
7:12 2
7:15-16 166
7:17 2
7:19 51, 138
7:20 2
7:23-25 445
8:4 2
8:6 2
8:6-7a 52
8:6-8 620
8:7 2
8:7b-8 52
8:10 134, 247
8:12 2
8:16 51, 350, 430
9:1 354-355, 518
9:3 365
9:5 474
9:6 513
9:10 2
9:13 51, 296, 486
9:19 343
10:1 501
10:5 2, 251, 293
10:5-6 245, 287
10:6 214
10:7 294
10:7-15 287, 293
10:13 351
10:14 51, 522
10:17 51, 296
10:20 50
10:22 472
10:33 236, 299
10:34 143
11:1 51, 402, 534, 607
11:1-9 2
11:2 140-141, 412, 538
11:4 270
11:4-5 534
11:6 606
11:6-8 52
11:6-9 51, 606
11:7 606, 607
11:8 201, 255, 501, 607
11:9 52, 607
11:12 51, 339, 457, 557
12:1 128
12:4 555
12:6 50, 52, 529
12:9 457
13 2
13:2 339
13:3-5 285
13:4 392, 617
13:5 285, 432
13:6 389
13:8 162, 196, 261, 267, 617, 618
13:10 532, 541
13:12 254
13:17 404
13:22 451, 494
13ff. 287
14:1 448, 452
14:3 309
14:8 462
14:11 170, 486, 567
14:13 301
14:18 462
14:19 51, 594, 631
14:22 630

14:24 284, 337
14:25 567
14:27 213
14:29 501
14:31 507
15:4 604
16:4 266
16:10 533
16:11 577
16:18 544
17:1 400
18:2 470
19:2 162
19:5 51, 172
19:8 379
19:14 303
19:15 51, 445, 486
19:17 247
20 2
20:3-5 207, 210
20:4 264, 291
21:3 196
21:8 555
21:11-12 561
22:13 200
22:16 358, 388
22:18 277
22:24 51
23:3 265
23:4 261
23:7 368
23:12 289
23:18 265
24:2 190
24:4 585
24:14 193, 319, 392
24:18 492
24:21 152
24:23 421
26:3 403
26:4 603
26:13 569
26:14 216
26:17 261, 618
26:18 261
27:1 369, 624
27:13 388, 473, 631
28:1 133
28:4 134
28:9 141, 401, 458
28:17 472
28:19 351, 401
28:23 202, 323, 583
28:27 170
28:28 171
28:29 300
29:1 297
29:2 215
29:4 288, 470
29:5 142
29:6 623
29:9 237, 460, 621
29:15 16 260
29:16 51
29:19 50
29:22 165
30:1 183
30:5 421
30:6 51, 501
30:7 368
30:9 202
30:11-12 50
30:12 355
30:13 299, 307, 582
30:15 50
30:18 583
30:22 198, 241
30:24 171
30:25 51, 467
30:26 539
30:28 621
30:31 544
31:1 50, 297, 355
31:3 267
31:9 51
32:1 238, 563
32:3 51
32:7 158
32:13 445
32:15 413
33:5 51, 475, 485
33:9 598
33:10 51, 128, 399, 474
33:15 270
33:16 51
33:20 418
34–35 51
34 5
34:1 188, 210
34:1-5 4
34:2 202, 566
34:4 134, 580, 585
34:5 566
34:5-6 624
34:5-7 562
34:6 4, 561
34:6-17 4
34:7 344
34:8 4, 405, 540, 565
34:13 218, 445
34:15 280, 501, 618
34:16 153
35 5
35:1 5, 174
35:1-2 4
35:2 4, 5, 599
35:4 5, 136, 198, 510, 540, 559
35:5 5, 51
35:6-7 2
35:7 43, 44, 226, 330
35:8 5, 217, 383
35:8-10 558
35:9 5
35:10 5, 370, 371, 545
36–39 2, 5
36–37 2
36:1 2
36:6 186
36:17 557
36:19 44, 423
36:21 350
36:21-23 56
37:3 618
37:4 596
37:17 2
37:21 2
37:22 289
37:23 50, 224
37:26 285
37:32 278
37:37 2
37:38 2
38:8 2

38:14 505
38:16 410
38:17 352
39 3
39:1 2, 275
39:6-7 4

Jeremiah

1:5 53, 62, 189, 225, 279, 323, 329, 375, 438
1:8 372
1:9 49, 324, 374, 513
1:9-10 54
1:10 336
1:15 136
1:17 252, 256
2:2 346, 424
2:6 174, 197, 269, 402
2:6-8 572
2:7 293
2:8 50, 233, 459, 573
2:10 401, 431, 484
2:11 50, 233
2:14 347
2:20 50, 412, 463, 465
2:20-28 55, 463
2:21 463, 464, 597
2:23 55, 463, 523
2:23-24 471
2:23-25 470
2:24 350, 463
2:25 55, 212, 463, 471
2:26 198
2:26-27 198
2:27 240, 472
2:27-28 241, 463
2:28 301
2:31 269, 347
2:32 53, 332, 336, 337, 372
2:35 500
2:36 234
3:1 49, 346
3:3 308
3:5 423, 475
3:6 50, 465, 467
3:8 47, 49, 54, 346
3:9 444
3:12 423
3:13 50, 212, 465, 471
3:14 418, 421, 477
3:15 249
3:16 50, 358, 603
3:17 385, 525, 551, 630
3:19 570
3:19-20 325
3:20 134, 570
3:21 372
3:22 477
3:23 243
3:25 300, 420, 421, 545, 596
4:1 49, 50
4:2 306, 602
4:4 203, 551
4:5 319, 559
4:9 286
4:13 623
4:16 136, 248, 285
4:17 351
4:19 194
4:20 54, 299, 307, 363, 418, 419
4:22 571
4:23 269
4:28 134
4:30 337, 428, 548
5:3 352
5:4 483
5:6 506
5:11 311
5:12 507
5:13 183
5:15 285
5:16 325
5:20 319
5:21 199
5:22 374, 472
5:23 592
5:31 295
6:2 289
6:6 387, 431
6:7 503, 593
6:9 560
6:11 334
6:13 55
6:13-14 476
6:14 55, 320
6:16 374
6:17 458
6:20 218, 220, 522, 523
6:22 522
6:25 396
6:26 307, 541
6:29-30 312
7:6 49, 502
7:13 600, 606, 615
7:16 292, 414, 508
7:18 218, 234, 466
7:21-23 481
7:21-31 218
7:23 127, 570
7:24 437
7:26 308
7:30 49
7:31 50, 465
7:32 551
7:34 548, 604
8:2 50
8:4-5 347
8:5 477
8:6 202
8:10-11 476
8:11 320
8:17 501
8:19 347
8:22 347, 488
9:4 242
9:6 53, 312
9:7 324
9:8 466
9:9 530
9:10 55, 493
9:11 55
10:3 50, 145-146, 148, 236, 238
10:4 145, 146, 148, 163
10:5 178, 282
10:9 50, 145, 145, 146, 163
10:11 527
10:12 269

10:14 50, 145, 183, 242, 309
10:16 246, 258, 578
10:19 403, 404
10:20 54, 419
10:20-22 418
10:21 459
10:25 203
11:4 47, 127, 312
11:12 270, 472
11:13 50
11:16 142, 402
11:17 50
11:19 54, 406, 407, 408, 441, 601
11:19-21 373
11:20 177
12:1 154
12:2 150
12:9 55, 457
12:10 55, 457, 579, 587
12:11 457, 458, 461
12:12 320, 457, 458
12:16 305
13:11 540
13:16 504
13:17 137
13:18 288, 293, 322, 323, 470, 552
13:19 322
13:20 322
13:21 322, 618
13:23 334, 350
13:24 151, 171
13:25 600
13:26 63, 291
13:27 49, 472
14:3 444
14:6 196
14:7 506
14:8-9 506
14:9 49
14:10 400, 586
14:12 378, 524
14:13 378
14:15 378
14:16 378
14:17 289
14:18 378
14:19 391
14:22 258, 368
15:3 264
15:4 378
15:10 168, 485
15:11 292
15:14 50
15:15 311, 407
15:16 49
15:18 492
15:21 348
16:4 410
16:5 424
16:7 487-488
16:9 548, 604
16:16 131
16:18 49, 53, 129, 293, 595, 597
16:19 243
17:2 50, 465
17:3 522
17:4 50, 355
17:8 228
17:11 409
17:12 528
17:13 339
17:17 431
17:18 545
17:19-27 447
17:24 493
17:26 220
17:27 493
18:6 260, 586
18:11 257, 285
18:12 471
18:13 289
18:15 217, 473
18:19 65, 343
18:21 296, 339, 405
18:23 221
19:1 260
19:5 50
19:9 343
19:13 50, 593, 596
20:5 264
20:8 531
20:9 300
20:10 291
20:11 343
21:4 289
21:5 48, 136, 566
21:9 431
21:12 203, 551
22:3 49, 502
22:5 272, 337, 587
22:7 432
22:8 400
22:13 400
22:17 49
22:19 631
22:22 459
22:23 617, 618
23:1-4 459
23:3 278
23:3-5 249
23:4 50
23:5-6 3, 434
23:6 489
23:7-8 217
23:14 163
23:18 127
23:20 217, 444
23:22 127
23:28 606
23:29 163
24 8
24:1 12
24:6 336
24:9 389, 587
25:9 252, 492, 542
25:10 548, 604
25:15 380
25:15-16 376, 380
25:16 389
25:26 478
25:27 377
25:30 152
25:31-33 624
25:33 624
25:34 389
27:2 387
27:5 53, 263
27:5-6 262
27:6 245, 252, 263
27:9 464

27:16 395
27:20 12
27:21-22 394
28:4 264
28:6 247
28:13 487
28:26 394
29:2 293
29:4 605
29:5 605
29:10 440
29:10-14 55, 440
29:11 440
29:12 219
29:12-14 440
29:13 592
29:13-14 441
29:20 214
29:21-23 602
29:32 507
30:10 50, 226, 366
30:10-11 166, 205
30:14 405
30:16 201
30:17 488, 559
30:18 419
30:19 358, 361
30:24 444
31:3 204
31:3-10 204
31:4 337
31:7 204, 329, 418, 559
31:7-10 329
31:8 204, 329
31:8-9 130
31:9 55, 329, 444, 575, 577
31:9-10 53
31:10 135, 137, 204, 329
31:11 370
31:11-12 54
31:11-13 370
31:12 362, 491, 521
31:13 361, 370
31:14 437
31:15 559
31:15-16 135
31:16 53
31:19 421
31:20 576
31:22 217
31:31 421
31:32 54, 418
31:33 127, 365, 512
31:34 54, 221-222, 421, 441
31:35 374, 532
32:4 392
32:14 630
32:18 194, 595, 596
32:20 208
32:21 48
32:29 466, 593
32:30 626
32:34 49
32:35 50, 465
32:40 54, 55, 546, 365
33:1 407
33:2 268, 268-269
33:3 53, 309
33:5-6 476
33:8 441
33:9 391, 445, 521, 540
33:10 493, 604
33:11 54, 361, 548
33:14-18 3
33:14-26 434
33:15 259
33:15-16 258
33:16 551
33:18 318
33:19-22 3
33:21-22 447, 455
33:22 50
33:24 48, 166
33:25 164, 165
33:26 3, 269
34:3 392
34:5 462
34:8 538
34:15 538
34:16 487
34:17 538
35:7 605
38:11 364
39:1-10 13
39:3 13
39:9 275
39:13 13, 275
39:15 407
40:1 13, 265
40:4 265
40:7 201
41:8 254
42:12 294
43 208
44:2 493
44:3 50
44:5 50
44:7 138, 334, 604
44:8 50
44:17 307
44:28 270
45:3 219
46 287
46:7-8 561
46:9 627, 628
46:10 620
46:11 289
46:12 193
46:14 319, 559
46:16 343
46:18 337
46:20 539
46:26 368
46:27 50, 366
47:2 621
47:6 436
48:3 503
48:7 274
48:16 451
48:18 288
48:29 530
48:36 505
48:40 284-285
48:45 246
48:46 340, 386, 388
49:2 194
49:3 274
49:7-22 560
49:9 560
49:12 200, 376
49:13 492, 542, 543, 587
49:14 470, 571

49:15 64, 327, 402
49:19 230
49:22 562
49:23 479
49:24 618
49:25 530
49:28-29 193, 524
49:31 295
49:36 171
50:2 275, 276, 319, 559
50:3 180
50:5 55, 437, 452, 546
50:6 131, 298, 578
50:8 318
50:9 180
50:17 371
50:19 326, 412, 493
50:32 507
50:33 388
50:36 246
50:37 255
50:38 191
50:41 180
50:44 230
51:1 180
51:5 296
51:6 319
51:7 376, 380, 566
51:9 258
51:11 180, 325
51:12 555
51:13 255
51:17 50, 242-243
51:19 246
51:23 181
51:26 542
51:28 181
51:30 51, 172
51:31 460
51:34 369
51:43 402
51:44 276, 521
51:45 319, 394
51:48 180
51:51 352
51:55 374, 617
51:56 365, 510
51:57 181
51:58 154, 527
51:62 542
52:4-27 13
52:28 12
52:29-30 13
52:31-34 13
52:33 555

Ezekiel

1:4 172
2:4 286
3:5 500
3:6 500
3:7 286, 308
3:8-9 352
3:17 458
4:1 335
4:4-6 398
4:7 393
4:14 594
5:1 324
5:2 51, 171
5:10 343
5:11 472
5:13 389
5:15 366
6:3 131
6:5 622
6:6 183
6:8 270
6:12 327
6:13 465
7:16 505
7:20 179, 242
7:21-22 293
7:25 320
7:26 299
8:12 298
8:17 326
9:1 432
9:3 519
9:4 228, 626
9:6 626
9:9 298, 487
10:18-19 131
10:18-20 519
11:17 210
11:22-23 519
11:23 131
12:2 210
12:8 351
12:25 134, 308
13:5 300, 492
13:8 500
13:10 241, 320, 478
13:19 139
14:1-3 483
14:3 592
14:21 378
16:5 335
16:8 273, 512
16:11 337
16:12 552
16:17 467
16:20-22 465
16:21 465
16:35-37 291
16:37 291
16:39 237, 548
16:46 420
16:57 291
16:60 437, 546
16:61-63 420
17:2 280
17:3 156
17:6 142
17:10 134
17:22 402
17:23 147
17:24 445
18:5 451
18:7 487, 488
18:9 504
18:16 487, 488
18:18 431
19:12 134
19:13 226, 402
20:1 483, 591
20:5 222
20:6-36 310
20:9 313, 393
20:12 493
20:12-24 447
20:13 493
20:13-14 311
20:14 313, 582

20:15 493
20:19 450-451
20:20 493
20:21 493
20:22 313, 582
20:24 451, 493
20:30-31 465
20:33 566
20:38 632
20:43 420
21:10 132, 344
21:12 186
21:15 509
21:26 246
21:31 553
21:36 431
21:37 567
22:8 447, 493
22:20 432
22:20-21 432
22:22 312
22:26 293, 313, 447, 493
22:30 347
23:6 181
23:10 291
23:13 451
23:16 451
23:17 468
23:24 451, 509
23:26 384
23:29 291
23:32-34 376
23:33 381
23:34 377
23:35 328
23:36 222
23:37 465
23:38 447
23:39 465
23:40 337, 548
23:40-41 470
23:42 552
24:17 292, 541
24:21 587
24:23 541
25 287
25:3 240
25:5 599
25:9 460
25:11 132
25:12-14 560
25:17 132
26:3 400
26:6 132
26:10 522, 527
26:16 288, 399, 510, 548
26:20 231, 244
27:3 364
27:6 175
27:10 429, 627
27:13 627, 628
27:16 429
27:19 220
27:21 523, 524
27:22 523
27:22-23 524
27:25 526
27:28 478
27:30 541
27:34 370
27:35 399
28:2 372
28:8 374
28:13 361, 428
28:13-14 427
28:23 132
28:26 605
29:3 369
29:6-7 186
29:7 186
29:10 67, 265, 331, 543
29:19 522
29:19-20 136
29:20 546
30:4 207
30:5 627
30:6 331
30:9 207
30:12 320
30:14 393
30:22 393
30:24 364
30:41 393
31:3-7 174
31:4 238, 370, 445
31:5 445, 542
31:8 542
31:9 361
31:15 348, 349
32:2 369
32:7-8 349
32:10 399
32:18 567
32:23 409
32:25 462
32:26 628
33:1-6 482
33:4 407
33:6 458
33:7 458
33:21 627
33:22 407
33:23-29 8
33:24 165, 359
33:28 530
33:33 308
34:1-10 459
34:12 137
34:13 137
34:23 249
34:23-24 3, 434
34:25 427, 438
34:26 227, 443
34:31 330
35:1-15 560
35:9 247
35:11 194
36:8 451
36:10-11 358
36:17 584, 585
36:19 171
36:20 223, 389
36:21-23 313
36:22 313, 439
36:26 475
36:31 420
36:33 248, 420
36:33-35 361
36:35 337, 420
36:36 336
37:6 308
37:8 308
37:11 408, 622
37:15-24 434

37:24-25 3
37:26 427, 512, 546
38:2 628
38:2-3 628
38:3 628
38:5 627
38:13 523
38:22 624
38:23 251
39:1 628
39:4 431
39:9 239
39:11 409
39:17 210, 458
39:18 343
39:20 194
39:23 585
39:26 420
39:29 227
40:46 449, 455
43:1-11 420
43:2 132, 518, 519
43:4-5 519
43:7 409, 528
43:10 139
43:11 139, 267
44:4 519
44:6-9 449
44:7-9 385
44:12-14 420
44:17 366
44:18 548
44:24 447
45:9 531
45:17 447
46:1 447
46:3 447, 631,
46:4 447
46:12 447
46:14 160
46:17 538
47:12 302
48:35 213, 551

Hosea

1:1 326
1:2 464
1:6 289, 386, 416
2 56
2:1 318
2:4 346
2:5 174
2:9 346
2:10 597
2:12 291
2:13 631
2:14 218
2:15 548
2:17 423, 599
2:18 417
2:18-22 607
2:19 421
2:20 416, 423
2:21 416, 423
2:21-22 424
2:25 416
3:4 328
3:5 521
4:1 351
4:3 326
4:12 148
4:13 238, 464, 467, 593, 596
4:13-14 465
4:17 234
5:13 406
5:14 47
6:4 244
6:5 61, 368
6:6 218, 481
6:7 311
7:3 328
7:7 465
7:9 203, 299, 458
8:1 482
8:1-2 56, 482
8:2 482
8:4 328
8:6 146
8:10 523
8:13 586
9:7 405
9:9 586
10:4 495
10:5-6 274
10:7 424
10:8 183, 615
10:13 298
11:2 593
11:8 372, 585
11:11 525
12:2 242, 469
12:3-5 222
12:4 310
13:2 146
13:3 171, 244, 618
13:4 256, 271, 371
13:10 328
13:13 618-619
13:15 134, 426
14:9 276

Joel

1:5 344, 376
1:8 486
1:9 466, 544
1:11 543
1:12 445
1:13 466, 544
1:19 445
1:20 218
2:1 582
2:2 349, 491, 519
2:3 361
2:5 624
2:7 194
2:10 349, 533
2:12 484
2:15 482
2:16 138, 210, 548, 604
2:17 293
2:25 214
2:26 267, 557
2:27 267
3:1 227
3:1-2 512
4:2 371
4:5 587
4:9 194
4:15 349
4:16 617
4:17 306, 383, 385
4:18 436
4:19-21 562

Amos

1:2 617
1:11-12 561
1:13 334
3:9 559
3:10 463, 507, 531
4:8 620
4:13 495
5:2 289
5:11 605
5:18 459, 504
5:20 504
5:21-24 481
5:22 544
5:24 451
6:3 616
6:6 471, 541
6:12 618
7:3 467
7:4 624
7:6 467
8:5 436, 631
8:8 478
8:11 436
9:2 470
9:11 492, 572, 573
9:12 579
9:13 595
9:14 605
9:15 534

Obadiah

1 560, 571
2 64, 327
5 560

Jonah

1:3 319, 627
1:7 466
1:10 319
1:11 428, 479
1:13 428
2:5 479
2:6 369
2:7 374
3:2 129
3:5-7 486
3:6 288, 541
3:8 502
3:10 298
4:2 311
4:8 330, 379
4:10 238

Micah

1:2 315
1:3 495, 579
1:8 218
2:1 161
2:4 544
3:4 499
3:8 56, 482
3:11 264
4:1 521
4:3 171
4:4 51
4:7 513
4:12 442
4:14 352
5:1 535, 573
5:5 532
5:6 364, 400
5:8 510
5:11 464
5:14 291
6:5 273
6:6 152, 486
6:8 484
6:11 281
6:12 409
7:2 461, 462
7:14 293, 573, 578
7:17 288, 521, 607
7:20 165, 368
14:18 578

Nahum

1:3 311, 623
1:4 197, 248, 348, 369
1:5 580
1:8 423
1:13 487
1:15 391
2:1 56, 382
2:3 382-383, 598
2:8 505
2:13 340
3:4 347, 464
3:5 291
3:7 378, 379
3:9 267, 297
3:10 147, 265, 379
3:14 181

Habakkuk

1:3 485, 503, 531
1:4 185, 363
1:5 401
1:6 289
1:6-8 285
1:10 150
1:11 232
1:15 379
1:16 379
2:3 535
2:8 255
2:12 430
2:13 154
2:15 566, 567
2:16 376
2:18 50, 233
2:19 148, 198, 241, 292
3:2 628
3:3 151, 232, 532, 541, 562
3:5 159, 396
3:7 419
3:8 348, 623
3:10 580
3:11 504, 519
3:12 171, 563, 622
3:17 502

Zephaniah

1:2 326
1:5 593
1:6 507, 592
1:8 564
1:9 409
1:11 142
1:12 178, 295, 339
1:13 605
1:14 63, 193, 194
1:15 349, 519

1:17 160, 505
2:3 358
2:4 554
2:8 224, 366
2:12 624
2:15 56, 295, 339, 599
3:1 343
3:4 223
3:5 351, 363, 507
3:7 134, 325
3:10 522
3:14 244
3:17 555
3:19 556
3:20 208, 336, 520

Haggai

1:6-14 614
1:13 247
2:1-9 614
2:7 387, 522
2:12 431, 595
2:15 213
2:16 564
2:19 213
2:23 3, 434

Zechariah

1:2 509
1:4 129
1:14 133
1:15 293
1:16 392, 423
1:17 361
2:10 436
2:11 436
2:12 387
2:14 418
2:15 448, 452
2:16 385
3:5 553
3:8 434
4:6-10 434
4:14 422
6:5 422
6:9-15 434
7:11 498
7:12 203, 316
7:14 428
8:3 392
8:4 604
8:8 306
8:17 162
8:23 448, 626
9:5 161
9:9 267
9:15 344
10:2 246
10:9 208
11:9 343
12:1 150
12:2 377
12:3 277
12:10 227
13:9 312, 313, 571
14:4 426
14:9 422
14:14 51, 522
14:16 630, 631
14:21 383

Malachi

1:2-5 560
1:4 336
1:10 355
1:11 256, 510
1:14 400
2:11 422
2:14-16 346
2:16 346
2:17 220
3:1 558
3:2-3 312
3:4 217, 572, 573
3:5 158, 464
3:11 598
3:14 484
3:20 488, 511
3:24 224

Psalms

1:3 444
1:4 171
2:2 150
2:4 149
4:2 489
5:8 265, 569
5:9 254
5:12 456
6:11 363
7:2 473
7:3 201
7:12 622
7:13-14 623
7:15 500, 501
8:2 391
8:5 372, 451
8:10 391
9:6 268
9:9 270
9:11 389
9:15 569
10:1 472, 584
10:3 389
10:7 501
10:11 298
11:16 600
12:2 462
12:3 500
12:6 51
13:2 584
13:6 569
14:4 267
16:5 377, 466
16:7 547
16:10 374
17:1 362
17:6 437
17:8 324, 375
18:1 200, 553
18:2 330, 423
18:8 492, 580
18:9 241-242, 595
18:10 579
18:16 624
18:17 573
18:32 232, 271
18:32-33 255
18:37 276
18:43 160, 246, 412
18:44 438, 439
18:44-45 438
19:5 150
19:15 507

20:7	168
21:5	268
22	271, 351
22:2	333
22:7	64, 169, 402
22:11	279
22:12	530
22:16	260
22:18	632
22:24	269, 271
22:24-32	57
22:26	271
22:27	557
22:28	271
22:30	271
22:32	271
23:2	138, 331, 378
23:4	334
23:5	541, 600
24:2	314, 317
24:8	194, 203, 216
25:2	342
25:4	141, 142
25:5	317
25:6	424, 569
25:7	222
25:9	141, 317
25:12	615
26:7	361
26:9	326
27:2	343
27:9	424, 584
27:13	408, 412
28:1	280
28:4	161
28:5	161
28:7	521
28:9	293, 571-572
29	617
29:2	208
29:7	624
29:9	617
30:6	423, 527
30:8	584
31	351
31:3	240
31:5	65
31:11	155, 371
31:14	407
31:16	240
31:21	433
31:23	266, 325
33:3	192
33:5	545
33:9	263
33:16	563
33:21	355
34:3	172
34:5	615
34:6	362, 521
34:15	258, 358, 508
34:19	475, 539, 613
35	351
35:1	169, 343
35:4	198
35:5	171
35:7	388
35:8	299
35:9	172, 547, 620
35:13	484
35:13-14	485
35:14	349
35:21	240, 464
35:23	195
35:25	240
35:26	198, 267, 545
35:27	201
35:28	549
36:1	200
36:4	409
36:7	369
36:8	375
36:9	295, 437
36:10	412
37:2	133, 134
37:4	464, 495
37:6	185, 363, 491, 551
37:9	155, 342
37:11	430, 464
37:27	508
37:28	545
37:29	533, 598
37:30	500
37:31	365
37:36	592
37:37	503
38:6	405
38:9	586
38:14	407
38:19	309
39:5	403
39:8	364
39:9	240
39:10	407
40:2	620
40:4	161, 192
40:9	365
40:15	198, 421
40:18	172
41:9	216
42:5	319, 361, 413
42:7	579
44	367, 567
44:2	368
44:4	556
44:11	246
44:13	347, 387
44:17	224, 366
44:18	571
44:23	407
44:24	367
44:25	153
44:26	288, 381
45:8	541
45:11	437
46:3	426
46:5	264, 529
47:2	319
47:8	422
47:9	385
48:2	264
48:3	530
48:6	396
48:7	196
48:8	526
48:9	264
48:11	549, 576, 621
48:13	473
49:8	546
50:1	510
50:3	623
50:4	314-315
50:9-10	218
50:10	458

50:10-12 143
50:13 344
50:18 466
50:21 230
51 219
51:3 221
51:3-4 219
51:3-6 57
51:4 584
51:5 506
51:6 221, 222
51:7 221, 465
51:11 221
51:13 572
51:19 475, 539
52:7 299, 408
53:4 267
54:6 566
54:9 632
55:7 156
55:9 535
55:21 427
55:24 567
56:8 159-160, 214
57:2 375
57:5 324
58:2 563
58:3 161, 546
58:4 279, 311
58:5 351, 377, 501
58:6 235, 297
59:4 431
59:5 367
59:12 159-160
60 567
60:5 203, 377
61:3 476
61:7 540
61:9 483
62:12 202
63:3 385, 400
63:6 412, 437
63:8 375
63:9 167
63:10 244
63:12 172
64:4 324
64:6 298
64:7 546
64:10 161
64:11 172
65:3 273
65:5 412
65:7 140
65:11 443
65:12 258, 437
65:14 476
66:2 191, 193
66:3 367
66:10 313
66:12 206
67:5 364, 575
68:3 364
68:7 491
68:8 563
68:12 135
68:17 474
68:27 305
68:32 207
69:3 370
69:8 352
69:14 328, 569
69:15 370
69:21 379, 506
69:29 221
69:36 247, 598
69:36-37 598
69:37 456
70:3 198
71:6 278, 307, 324
71:9 325
71:11 201
71:15 286
71:16 569
71:17-18 278
71:18 187, 278, 279
72 515
72:1 515
72:2 332
72:3 317, 515, 531
72:5 366, 515, 516
72:7 430, 515
72:9 341, 515
72:9-11 528
72:10 207, 265, 341, 515, 516, 526, 628
72:10-11 264
72:11 341
72:15 373, 515, 523, 555
72:16 516
72:17 516
72:19 516
73:4 487
73:7 241
73:8 507
73:14 405
73:28 484
74 367, 567
74:1 595
74:1-2 578
74:2 578
74:10 389
74:11 153, 213
74:15 248, 621
74:18 389
75:9 376, 377
76:2 622
76:6 286, 508
76:7 216
77 367
77:5 163
77:6 368, 540
77:12 568
77:13 367
77:16-21 573
77:17 374
77:19 623
77:20 215
77:21 573, 576
78:2 279
78:4 216
78:8 592
78:13 370, 574
78:14 356, 395
78:15 320, 369
78:15-20 320
78:16 320
78:20 320
78:21 239
78:33 606
78:38 194
78:40 217, 572
78:43 626
78:52 137, 330, 576

78:53 576
78:54 607
78:61 385
78:69 250
78:70-72 249
78:71 138, 320
79 567
79:1 386
79:5 476
79:6 203
79:10 153
79:12 596
79:13 218, 330
80 567
80:2 137, 330, 574
80:6 140
80:9 534, 597
80:13 153, 492
80:15 576, 597
80:16 238
81:9-11 212
81:12 202
81:14 317
82:1 127
82:5 149, 241, 355
82:6 178
83 567
83:2 550, 555
83:14 151, 160
83:15 203
83:15-16 623
84:3 557
85 567
85:9 187
85:11 317, 430
85:12 259
85:14 489
86:1 172
86:11 511
86:15 311
87:1 149
87:4 368
88:4 408, 412
88:6 408
88:8 566
88:10 592
89 416, 417, 434, 567
89:2 424, 569
89:4 164, 417, 435, 438
89:4-5 434, 437, 512
89:7 127, 144, 230
89:9 385
89:10 374
89:11 367, 368, 405, 556
89:13 420
89:14 314, 367, 556
89:15 483
89:18 385
89:21 435
89:22 367
89:25 417, 438, 434
89:25-37 3
89:27 232
89:29 417, 426, 438
89:29-30 434-435
89:34 417, 571
89:34-38 435
89:35 417
89:36 417
89:39 435
89:40 417, 435
89:41 417
89:42 417
89:46 417, 421
89:47 153, 417
89:50 417, 438
89:52 417, 435
90 567
90:2 360, 618
90:5-6 133
90:6 155
90:8 506
90:15 405
91:1 324
91:3 277
91:13 564
91:14 389
91:16 411, 412
92:13-15 605
92:15 478
93 367
93:1 385, 392
93:2 307
93:4 152
94 567
94:4 544
94:7 298
95:1 232, 244
95:11 575
96 191-192
96:1 57, 192
96:6 385
96:7 192
96:7-8 57
96:8 192, 522
96:10 392
96:11 192
96:11-12 57, 245
96:12 192
96:13 500, 624
97:1 392
97:3 203, 623
97:5 422
97:6 131, 552
97:7 198, 273
97:11 518
98 191-192, 390
98:1 57, 192, 566
98:1-2 508
98:1-8 390
98:3 57, 192
98:5 361, 596
98:7 57, 192
98:8 57, 192, 332, 445
98:9 364, 624
99:1 385, 392, 426, 582
99:4 545
99:5 58, 612
101:5 241
101:8 264, 383, 529
102:3 585
102:16 510, 511, 523
102:20 152, 475, 576
102:20-21 475
102:22 312, 523
102:25 366
102:26-27 364
102:27 354, 630
102:28 154
103:5 156
103:7 142
103:8 311
103:8-11 441
103:9 423, 475

103:11 442
103:13 577
103:14 403
103:15 132, 133, 372
103:15-16 134
103:15-17 132
103:15-20 56
103:16 132
103:17 133
103:19 612
103:20 133
104:1 368, 562
104:2 149, 150, 419, 518, 542
104:7 348, 396, 426
104:8 575
104:11 458
104:14 549
104:20 458
104:29-30 188
105:3 172, 358
105:6 164, 464
105:10 437
105:11 496
105:15 251
105:20 487
105:23 387
105:28 349
105:29 349
105:38 299
105:41 197, 320
105:42-43 164
106 567
106:2 577
106:3 451
106:4-10 567-568
106:5 172
106:6 596
106:9 248, 348, 369, 370, 426, 575
106:12 192
106:17 259
106:18 203
106:20 237
106:21-22 582
106:33 572
106:34 425
106:37-39 465
106:47 312
107:2 5, 559
107:3 208, 209, 331
107:7 317
107:9 490
107:10 190
107:12 530
107:14 190
107:16 173, 254
107:23 192
107:25 172
107:29 374
107:30 479
107:33 218, 348, 492
107:35 56, 173, 174, 492
107:36 556
107:39 407
107:42 401
107:43 200, 217, 424, 569
109:2 409
109:3 243
109:11 264-265, 437
109:14 222
109:16 172
109:22 405
109:27 176
109:28 601
109:29 510, 547-548
110:1 58, 187, 381
110:4 263
111:3 630
111:7 507
111:9 348
112:4 490
113:2 456
113:3 256
113:3-4 510, 511
113:4 474
113:5-7 475
113:6 470
114:1 441
114:4 445
114:5 388
114:8 173-174, 320
115:3 284
115:4 276
115:5 234
115:5-6 199
115:6 210
115:7 282
115:12 577
116:6 240
116:16 387, 487
116:19 557
117:1 438, 439
118:7 354, 632
118:15 319
119:7 483
119:16 621
119:24 141
119:32 521
119:35 197
119:47 621
119:71 405
119:90 268
119:101 494
119:116 198
119:131 196
119:132 456
119:160 507
119:164 549
119:165 210, 430
119:176 406
120:2 500
120:5 193
121:4 459
121:6 330, 532
122:9 148
125:1 426
125:4 241
127:1 555
127:2 485
127:5 325
128:2 605
128:6 411
129:5 198
129:7 340
130:4 441
130:5 364
130:7 348
132:2 344
132:2-5 249
132:5 344, 419
132:7 58, 528, 612
132:7-8 611
132:9 547

132:10 3
132:11 272
132:12 603
132:14 612
132:16 547
132:16-18 547
133:2 541
134:2 572
135:6 284
135:10 413
135:16 234
136:5-6 421
136:6 188, 246
136:13-14 370
136:14 370
136:16 197
137:1 248
137:1-2 228
137:6 371
137:7 560
138:2 265-266
138:6 474, 475
139:8 470, 486
139:14 582
139:24 477
140:3 431
140:4 501
140:7 241
141:4 403
141:8 413
141:10 379
142:2 252
142:4 476
142:5 199
142:8 190
143:2 162
143:3 170, 231, 471, 505
143:4 476, 508
143:5 408
143:6 592
143:8 142
143:10 576
144:1 499
144:2 160
144:3 451
144:5 579
145:3 155
145:6 203, 216, 582
145:7 569
145:8 311
145:13 267
145:14 486
145:18 441, 484
145:18-19 489
146:7 487
146:7-8 190
147:2 51, 555
147:3 476, 539
147:4 151
147:4-5 56, 151
147:5 151, 155
147:8 443
147:9 443
147:13-14 429
147:15 443
147:18 134
148:11 150
148:12 554
149 192
149:2 422
149:6 171
149:7 328
149:8 265
151:5 193

Proverbs

1:14 281
1:15 494
1:16 502
1:20 186
1:21 358
2:8 141
2:15 197, 503
3:2 411, 540
3:7 508
3:10 557
3:13 490
3:20 258
3:25 299
3:31 615
4:9 552
4:12 156, 338
4:18 518
4:21 241
4:25 463
4:26 503
4:27 494
5:4 171, 324
5:10 485
5:13 437
5:15 227, 359, 555
5:18 423, 555
6:5 277
6:12 441
6:12-13 489
6:16-18 502
6:23 363
6:28 206
6:35 299, 426
7:9 505
7:10 310
7:22 601
7:26 413
8:4 403
8:9 463
8:15 150
8:15-16 150
8:18 552
8:20 141
8:22 216-217, 271, 284
8:23 146, 149
8:25 140
8:27 149, 316
8:36 604
9:2 600
9:5 434, 436, 437
10:22 276
10:24 615
10:27 540
10:28 601
11:11 331
11:12 141
11:17 462
11:18 137
11:29 475
12:4 552
12:19 363
13:2 437
13:9 216
13:17 571
14:13 601
15:9 358
15:13 422, 613
15:14 242

15:19 473
15:30 491
16:2 139, 141
16:11 140
16:12 430
16:14 299
16:18 530
16:19 413, 475
16:31 552
17:3 312
17:6 552
17:19 485
17:22 613, 622
17:23 596
17:26 466
18:14 613
18:18 177
18:22 490
19:2 605
19:11 311
19:21 284
20:20 505
20:29 155, 279
20:30 405
21:2 139
21:4 241
21:6 473
21:14 596
21:18 207
21:21 552
22:17 437
23:1-2 459
23:2 437
23:20 460
23:30 600
23:32 501
23:33 241
23:35 163
24:2 500
24:3 430
24:11 407
24:12 139
24:15 599
25:5 430
25:13 571
25:23 359
25:26 400
26:18 355
27:1 460
27:3 142
27:9 541
27:17 236
27:21 312
28:5 358
28:9 203
28:14 373
29:1 403
29:3 242
29:18 462
29:23 475
30:4 138
30:7 426
30:7 8 378
30:13 399, 474
30:20 471
30:23 554
30:26 193
31:3 471
31:4 150
31:20 553
31:25 562

Job

1:6 127
1:10 420
1:11 593
1:16 606
1:17 228, 606
1:18 606
1:21 456
2:3 451
2:8 541
2:11 379
2:12 541
2:13 289
3:7 339
3:11 279
3:13 158, 462
3:17 462
3:25 615
4:4 167
5:4 201
5:9 155
5:9-11 238
5:10 381
5:12 246
5:14 505
5:16 401, 546
5:23 218
5:24 604
5:25 51
6:20 273
6:21 161
6:22 423
7:1 129
7:2 502
7:3 600
7:7 412
7:9 244
7:10 577
7:12 369
7:18 302
7:21 356
8:4 586
8:7 579
8:11 436
8:14-15 502
8:20 378
8:22 198
9:2 299
9:4 153
9:5 203
9:8 150
9:10 155
9:12 261
9:13 368
9:16 500
9:20 222
9:24 347
9:32 162
10:5 565
10:7 201
10:9 586
10:15 412
11:6 130
12:3 506
12:9 176
12:13 300
12:17 246, 508
12:18 150
12:24 269
13:13 157
13:16 466
13:17 437

13:18 230
13:18-19 353
13:19 157
13:22 500
13:25 300
13:27 160
13:28 354, 366
14:2 133
14:6 129
14:7 155
14:8 51, 150
14:11 248
14:12 216, 462
14:14 129
15:9 506
15:13 624
15:25 195
15:30 402
15:32 436, 445
15:34 339
15:35 500
16:11 604
16:17 409, 502
16:20 223
18:5 216
18:7 338
18:16 401
18:20 399
19:2 381
19:7 283, 531
19:14 403
19:17 501
19:18 138, 604
20:4 279
20:11 421
20:16 51, 501
20:24 308
20:29 433
21:2 437
21:5 401
21:8 51
21:11 604
21:20 377
21:23 297
21:24 491
22:2 240
22:11 522
22:12 442
22:14 149
22:26 495
23:4 230
23:6 153
24:7 349
24:21 418
25:6 170, 372
26:6 451
26:8 244
26:10 149
26:12 64, 368, 374
26:13 369
27:4 500
27:6 585
27:10 495
27:13 433
27:14 51, 500
27:16 564
27:23 240
28:7 284
28:14 370
28:25 139
29:3 519
29:8 328
29:9 401
29:20 151
30:1 459
30:10 352
30:15 244
30:19 280
30:21 572
30:22 585
30:26 258
30:29 218
31:2 433
31:8 51, 188
31:10 290
31:15 279
31:19 349
31:26 532
31:28 258
31:35 168, 353
32:7 540
32:8 188
32:14 181, 230
33:4 188
33:5 230
33:8 338
33:23 223
33:25 421
33:31 157
33:31-33 158
33:33 157
34:20 363
34:36 441
35:5 199, 442
36:21 312
36:25 301
36:26 154
36:28 208, 258
37:6 443
37:11 244
38:2 561
38:3 158, 256
38:4-6 314
38:5 237
38:5-6 138
38:13 386
38:16 370
38:26-27 443
38:28 443
38:32 152
38:34 522
38:39 471
39:1 360
39:3 618
39:4 410
39:5 387, 487
39:7 406
39:14-15 501
39:16 578
39:17 413
39:25 240
39:26 156
40:8 433
40:10 562
40:18 308
40:22 228
40:26 51
41:8 595
41:12 51
41:22 171
42:10 545
42:11 318, 379
42:14 428
42:16 411

Canticles

1:4 619
1:5 193, 336, 419
1:10 391
2:8 400
2:17 135
3:1 169
3:2 169
3:6 525, 561
3:8 403
3:11 377, 548, 552
4:1 290
4:2 339
4:3 500
4:4 429
4:7 426
4:8 469
4:13 586
4:14 189, 220
4:15 227, 359
4:16 209, 586
5:1 436
5:2 392
5:4 468, 577
5:7 555
6:6 339
7:2 391
7:6 469
7:13 310, 373, 527
7:14 586
8:2 344
8:5 525, 561
8:7 206, 348
8:13 555
8:14 319

Lamentations

1:1 296, 339, 421
1:2 59, 128, 428, 572
1:3 428
1:4 58, 371, 493
1:5 381
1:7 58, 313, 428, 488
1:8 291, 371
1:9 294, 313, 378, 428, 621
1:10 58, 383, 386, 587
1:11 58, 371, 576
1:12 381, 403, 576
1:13 246, 418
1:15 58, 289, 563
1:16 371
1:17 378, 428, 592, 621
1:18 403, 554
1:19 148, 294
1:21 428
1:22 371
1–3 59
2:1 58, 528, 587, 612
2:2 223, 338
2:3 246
2:4 58, 203, 568
2:5 215, 338
2:8 58, 237
2:9 214
2:10 58, 288, 289
2:11 378
2:13 289, 378, 379
2:15 58
2:16 338
2:17 216
2:18 59, 555
2:19 58, 215, 379
2:20 343
2:21 294, 356, 381
2:22 314
3 59, 350
3:1 313
3:2 350, 355
3:6 231
3:9 488
3:15 221
3:17 243
3:19 58, 313
3:21 241
3:22 424
3:23 302, 350
3:25 342
3:26 292
3:30 350, 351, 412
3:31-32 423
3:32 58, 381, 568, 569
3:33 381
3:42 350
3:47 378
3:48 378
3:54 408
3:58 343, 350
3:59 350
3:64 58
4–5 59
4 59, 376
4:1 376, 379, 416
4:2 416
4:4 173, 334, 488, 604
4:5 295
4:6 296, 406
4:7 416
4:9 379
4:10 343, 376, 378
4:11 203, 376, 416
4:12 416
4:13 405
4:14 58, 499, 505, 564
4:15 58, 394
4:16 294, 571
4:18 129
4:21 58, 376, 380
4:21-22 560
4:22 58
5:1 416
5:2 416
5:4 435, 436
5:7 398
5:9 379
5:12 294
5:13 155, 290
5:14 294
5:15 58
5:16 58
5:20 243, 333, 416
5:22 58, 166, 416, 568, 586

Ecclesiastes

1:14 183, 242, 473
1:17 247
10:11 436
11:8 295
11:16 607
12:1 478
12:6 186
2:4 605
2:11 242, 473

2:17	473
2:26	473, 605
3:5	594
3:13	412
4:5	343
4:14	339
4:15	504
5:3	286
6:2	403, 437
6:3	437
6:4	519
7:7	246, 389
8:4	261
9:2	605
9:4	453, 563
9:8	541
9:18	605

Esther

1:11	553
2:7	341, 520, 551
2:14	152, 554
2:17	553
4:1	485, 541
4:3	486, 541
5:9-10	196
6:8	553
7:8	443
8:8	213
9:26	494
9:27	448, 452
9:28	625
10:3	391

Daniel

1:2	395
1:5	600
1:7	551
1:8	564
1:20	454
2:1	163
2:3	163
2:5	615
2:14	285
2:21	150
2:22	327, 518
2:31	531
3:4	136, 482
3:5	239
3:19	327
3:33	366
4:31	154, 572
5:2	395
6:8	285, 453
7:11	587
7:23	171
8:9	460
8:27	508
9:3	485
9:4	427
9:9	441
9:16	473
9:18	437
9:24	306
9:27	453
10:2-3	541
10:7	299
10:8	339
10:13	230
11:7	51
11:8	274
11:12	399, 474
11:15	364
11:22	364
11:31	364
11:33	400
11:34	400, 452
11:35	394
11:35-36	295
11:45	375
12:2	632
12:3	400, 412
12:7	47, 154, 556
12:10	394, 400
12:13	462

Ezra

1:1	158
1:1-2	179
1:1-4	14
1:2	249
1:6	586
1:7	395
1:7-11	394
2:12	600
2:64	607
4	8
4:1	249
4:1-5	526
4:3	448
4:12	283
4:20	265
5:11	183, 327
5:14-15	394
6:1-5	14
6:3	250
6:5	395
6:8	265
6:12	432
6:15	6
6:22	388
7:14	285
7:24	265
7:27	528
8:12	600
8:20	552
8:22	203, 216
8:24	223
8:29	223
9:1-2	448
9:2	181
9:3	352
9:4	613
9:12	448
10:2	10, 409
10:3	613
10:5	223
10:10	10
10:11	448
10:14	10
10:17	10
10:18	10
10:44	10

Nehemiah

1:3	492
2:13	492
2:13ff.	532
2:16	181
2:17	587
2:17-20	526
3:14	253
3:33-38	526
3:35	492

3:37 221
4:1 492
4:1-5 526
4:4 155, 404
4:15 488
5 8
5:4 265
5:5 10
5:13 340, 386
5:15 294
6:1 492
6:19 319
7:3 527
7:17 600
8:8 175
8:15 175
9:2 448, 596
9:5 456
9:10-11 574
9:11 215, 248, 574
9:12 395, 576
9:14 447
9:15 320
9:17 311, 441
9:17-18 308
9:19 576
9:25 295
9:32 194, 427
9:34 574
10:16 600
10:32 493
10:32-34 447
10:40 395
11:1 306, 385
11:18 306, 385
12:35 230
12:41 230
13:3 203, 448
13:15 277
13:15-18 493
13:15-22 447
13:22 569
13:25 351, 352
13:26 10
13:27 10

1 Chronicles
1:33 523
2:18 553
2:19 553
4:9 309
4:38 420
5:26 627
7:5 201
9:29 220
9:30 470
11:23 265
12:18 502
14:1 201, 237
15:1 529
16:4 555
16:10 358
16:13 164
16:32 192
16:33 624
17:20 47
18:3 454
18:10 194
20:6 265
21:8 247
21:17 47
21:23 170
22:12 262
22:19 395
24:5 223
25:8 141
27:29 599
28:2 58, 528, 612
28:3 194
28:4 184
28:9 599, 615
29:1 360
29:2 428, 531
29:11 567
29:13 576
29:16 522

2 Chronicles
4:3 144
5:13 607
6:2 576
6:33 582
6:40 200
6:42 438
7:15 200
9:4 564
9:21 526
13:7 457
15:7 137
15:8 543
15:14 273
16:12 410
16:14 462, 470
17:11 523
18:19 510
18:23 230, 352
18:27 315
18:33 509
20:7 165
20:31 553
20:37 300
21:3 586
22:7 538
23:18 531
23:19 386
24:4 543
24:5 631
24:11 413
24:12 260, 543
24:14 395
24:24 579
26:8 629
26:10 543
28:4 596
29:22 614
32:4 621
32:23 586
32:30 359, 492
32:31 223
34:9 404
36:9-10 12
36:17-21 13
36:19 587
36:22-23 14
36:23 249

TRANSLATIONS

GREEK

Septuagint (LXX)
Leviticus
26:30 409

Numbers
21:28 409
22:41 409
33:52 409

Deuteronomy
32:13 495

Zechariah
9:15 344

Isaiah
40 127
40:1-2 66
40:3 130
40:5 67, 132
40:6 133
40:10 69, 136
40:12 139
40:15 143
40:17 143
40:19 146
40:20 147
41:1 67
41:2 159
41:5 161
41:14 67
41:22 177
42:1 66, 184
42:3 186
42:19 67
42:20 200
42:24 70, 202, 203
42:25 70, 203
43:1 205
43:3 67
43:9 210
43:13 213
43:14 214
43:23 220
43:28 223
44:2 66
44:4 64, 70, 427
44:5 229
44:7 70, 230
44:12 236
44:16 240
44:18 241
44:23 258
44:24 246
44:26 247 (Codex Alexandrinus)
45:2 65, 253
45:4 255
45:8 259
45:9 260, 261
45:13 264
45:14 265
45:16 67, 267
45:18 269
45:24 273
46:1 67
46:6 281
46:7 282
46:11 285
46:12 68, 286
47:4 292 (Codex Alexandrinus)
47:6 293
47:13 301, 302
48:5 309
48:8 311
48:9 67
48:11 313
48:14 315, 316
48:15 316
48:19 318
48:20 319-320
49:5 326
49:7 327
49:8 329 (Codex Vaticanus)
49:9 330
49:11 331
49:12 67
49:15 334
49:16 335
49:17 66, 335, 336
49:24 342
49:25 65, 66, 343
49:26 343
50:2 348, 349
50:4 350
50:6 352
50:10 354
50:11 68, 356
51:3 361
51:5 363, 364
51:6 365
51:9 67
51:11 371
51:12 68, 372
51:13 373
51:15 374
51:16 375
51:18 378
51:19 65, 68, 379
51:23 381
52:2 386
52:6 389
52:8 392
52:12 395
53:1 401
53:8 68, 407, 408
53:9 409
53:10 67
53:10a 410
53:11 64, 67, 412
53:12 414
54:2 419
54:5 422
54:9 425
54:11 65, 68, 428
55:1 436
55:5 439
55:11 443
55:13 445
56:2 452
56:5 455
56:6 68, 450
56:11 68, 70, 459
56:12 65, 68, 70, 460
57:3 464
57:9 469
57:11 472
57:14 473
57:15 474
57:17 477
57:18 477
57:20 479
58:1 482
58:3 484
58:5 486
58:10 490

58:13 494
58:14 495, 496
59:2 68, 499
59:8 503
59:10 67
59:19 511
60:1 518
60:4 520
60:5 521
60:6 523
60:7 525
60:19 64, 67, 69, 532
60:20 533
60:21 534-535
61:1 538
61:3 540
61:8 546
62:7 556
62:11 559
63:1 563
63:7 68, 569
63:8c 571
63:8-9 48, 569
63:9 68
63:10 572
63:11 574
63:14 68, 70, 575
63:15 577
63:18 68, 578
63:19 68
63:19a 579
64 581
64:3 583
64:4 583
64:6 585
64:7 586
64:8 586
64:9 587
65:1 592
65:2 592
65:3 593
65:4 594
65:6 596
65:7 596
65:9 598
65:14 601
65:15 602
66:1 612
66:2 613
66:3 614
66:5 616
66:12 621
66:15 623
66:16 67, 624
66:18a 625
66:18b 626
66:19 626, 627
66:21 629
66:23 631

Aquila
Isaiah
40:12 139
40:15 143
41:14 170
44:24 246
54:9 425
57:8 467

Symmachus
Isaiah
40:15 143
42:20 200
44:5 228
49:5 326
49:17 335
49:21 339
51:18 378
51:19 379
54:9 425
55:13 445
56:10 459
56:11 459
56:12 460
57:3 464
57:8 467
57:9 469
63:1 563
64:10 588
66:17 625

Theodotion
Isaiah
40:15 143
41:14 170
49:5 326
49:17 335
52:14 400
54:9 425
57:8 467
61:6 544
63:11 573-574
66:17 625

ARAMAIC TARGUMS

Onqelos
Genesis
18:23 216
19:13 432
22:5 239
24:52 239
27:12 504
27:22 504
33:3 239
34:30 216
49:16 540, 565

Exodus
10:13 572
16:18 140
39:3 252

Leviticus
7:21 625
19:35 140
25:30 533

Targum Pseudo-Jonathan (Jerusalem Targum I)
Genesis
19:15 505
42:15 312

Exodus
16:18 140

Leviticus
15:25 505
25:30 533

Deuteronomy
18:11 235
26:6 579

31:10 505

Isaiah
40:10 69, 136
40:19 147
41:22 177
41:29 70, 183
42:1 185
42:3 186
42:11 193
42:20 200
42:21 200
42:22 202
42:24 70, 202, 203
42:25 70
43:1 205
43:6 209
43:13 213
43:23 64, 70, 220
44:3 227
44:4 64, 70, 227
44:7 70, 231
44:18 241
44:26 247
45:2 254
45:8 259
45:13 264
45:16 267
45:18 269
46:2 278
46:8 283
46:11 285
46:13 69, 286
47:9 235
47:12 235
47:13 301, 302
48:1 305
48:8 311
48:15 316
49:2 325
49:5 65, 326
49:11 331
49:13 332
49:17 335
49:25 343
50:2 348
50:10 354
51:2 360
51:6 364-365
51:11 371
51:12 372
51:18 378
51:19 65, 68, 379
52:2 386
52:5 389
52:6 389
52:8 392
52:11 394
52:13 69
52:14 400
53:8 407
53:10 67, 70
54:2 419
54:5 422
54:7 423
54:9 425
54:15 431
55:13 445
56:2 452
56:5 455
56:7 456
56:10 459
56:11 68, 70, 459
56:12 68, 70, 460
57:6 466
57:8 468
57:11 472
57:15 474, 475
57:16 69
57:17 477
57:18 69, 477
57:19 69
58:1 482
58:3 484
58:5 486
58:7 488
58:8 488
58:11 69, 491
58:12 69
58:13 494
58:14 495, 496
59:2 68, 499
59:8 503
59:10 505
59:15a 508
59:18 510
59:19 511
60:1 518
60:3 65, 519
60:4 520
60:5 521
60:12 527
60:16 530, 531
60:19 64, 67, 69, 532
60:20 533
61:6 544
61:8 546
61:10 547
62:4 554
62:6 69
62:10 64, 69, 558
62:11 559
63:3 564
63:10 572
63:11 574
63:14 68, 70, 575
63:15 577
64:4 584
64:6 585
64:8 586
65:1 592
65:4 594
65:5 69, 595
66:1 612
66:3 614
66:17 625
66:18a 625
66:18b 626

Zechariah
13:9 312

Psalms
134:2 572

Peshitta
Isaiah
40:3 130
40:10 69
40:12 139
40:15 143
41:22 177
41:28 182
41:29 70

42:3	186
42:11	193
42:20	200
42:25	70, 203
43:1	205
43:13	213
43:14	214
43:23	220
43:28	223
44:2	226
44:7	230
44:12	236
44:16	240
44:23	258
44:24	246
45:8	259
45:9	261
45:11	262
45:14	265
45:16	267
45:24	273
45:25	273
46:2	278
46:6	281
46:11	285
46:13	286
47:13	301, 302
48:5	309
48:14	315
48:15	316
49:5	326
49:8	329
49:9	330
49:11	331
49:13	332
49:16	335
49:17	335
49:24	342
49:25	343
50:6	352
50:10	354
51:4	362
51:10	370
51:11	371
51:13	373
51:18	378
51:19	65, 68, 379
52:2	386
52:6	389
52:11	394
52:14	400
53:1	401
53:3	404
53:8	408
53:9	409
53:10a	410
54:2	419
54:5	422
54:7	423
54:9	425
54:12	429
55:1	436
55:4	438
55:5	439
55:12	444
56:2	452
56:5	455
56:10	459
56:11	68, 459
56:12	65, 68, 70, 460
57:3	464
57:8	468
57:11	472
57:15	474
57:20	479
58:5	486
58:10	490
58:13	494
59:2	499
59:8	503
60:1	518
61:3	540
61:8	546
62:4	553
62:7	556
62:11	559
63:11	573, 574
63:14	68, 70
64	581
64:6	585
64:7	586
64:8	586
65:1	592
65:6	596
65:7	596
65:22	605
66:3	614
66:5	616
66:17	625
66:18a	625
66:18b	626
66:20	629

VULGATE

Isaiah

40:3	130
40:6	133
40:10	69, 136
40:17	143
40:19	146, 147
41:14	170
41:22	177
41:28	182
42:3	186
42:11	193
42:20	200
43:1	205
43:13	213
43:14	214
43:23	220
44:2	226
44:18	241
44:24	246
45:5	70
45:8	259
45:16	267
45:24	273
46:6	281
46:11	285
46:13	286
47:13	301
49:5	326
49:8	329
49:9	330
49:13	332
49:16	335
49:17	335
49:21	339
49:24	342
50:2	348
50:4	350
50:11	68, 356
51:5	70

51:11 371
51:13 373
51:15 374
51:16 375
51:18 378
51:19 65, 68, 379
52:2 386
52:6 389
53:1 401
53:8 407, 408
54:2 419
54:9 425
54:12 429
55:5 439
55:13 445
56:2 452
56:5 455
56:10 459
56:12 65, 68, 70, 460
57:3 464
57:8 468
57:9 469
57:11 472
57:14 473
57:17 477
58:1 482
58:3 484
58:13 494
59:2 68, 499
59:8 503
59:10 505
59:19 511
60:1 518
60:5 521
61:2 70
61:11 70
62:1 70
62:4 553
62:11 559
63:1 563
63:10 70, 572
63:14 68, 70, 575
64 581
64:7 586
64:8 586
65:1 592
65:4 594
66:1 612
66:3 614
66:5 616
66:17 625
66:18b 626
66:20 629

QUMRAN

1QIsa[a]
21:8 555
40:6 133
40:10 69, 136
40:12 139
40:13 141
40:17 143
40:18 144
41:2 159
41:5 161
41:20 175
41:22 178
41:23 178
41:25 180
41:27 182
41:28 182
41:29 70, 183
42:1 185
42:3 186
42:5 187
42:6 189
42:11 193
42:13 194
42:20 200
42:21 201
42:22 202
42:25 70, 203
43:3 206
43:6 209
43:8 210
43:9 210, 211
43:14 214
43:19 217
43:21 218
43:23 70, 220
43:25 222
44:2 226
44:3 227
44:4 70, 227, 228
44:6 229
44:8 231
44:9 234
44:11 234, 235
44:12 237
44:13 237
44:16 240
44:24 246
45:1 253
45:2 253
45:3 254
45:4 255
45:7 257-258
45:8 258, 259
45:9 260, 261
45:11 262
45:18 269
45:20 270
45:24 273
46:1 276
46:2 278
46:5 281
46:6 281
46:7 282
46:10 284
46:11 285
46:13 286
47:1 289
47:2 291
47:5 292
47:7 294
47:8 296
47:9 296, 297
47:10 298
47:11 298
47:12 300
47:13 301, 302
47:14 302
48:1 305
48:4 308
48:6 310
48:10 312
48:11 313
48:12 314
48:13 314
48:14 315
48:21 320
49:2 325

49:4	325	54:10	426	61:1	538, 539
49:5	326	54:11	68, 428	61:3	542
49:6	326-327	54:12	429	61:4	543
49:7	327	54:13	430	61:6	544
49:8	328	54:14	430	61:7	545
49:9	330	54:16	432	61:8	545, 546
49:10	331	55:1	436	61:10	548
49:13	332	55:9	442	62:1	550, 551
49:17	335, 336	55:10	443	62:2	552
49:19	338	55:12	444	62:3	553
49:24	342	55:13	445, 446	62:4	553
49:25	66, 343	56:2	452	62:5	554
50:2	349	56:5	455	62:6	555
50:5	351	56:6	449, 456	62:7	556
50:6	352	56:7	456	62:9	557
50:10	354	56:10	458, 459	62:10	69, 558
51:2	360	56:11	459	62:11	558, 559
51:3	361	56:12	68, 70, 460	63:2	563
51:5	364	57:3	464	63:3	564
51:6	364	57:6	466	63:5	566
51:9	368	57:8	468	63:6	566
51:10	370	57:11	472	63:10	572
51:11	371	57:14	473	63:11	574
51:16	375	57:15	475	63:16	577
51:19	68, 379	57:17	477	63:17	578
51:23	381	57:19	478	64:1	581, 582
52:1	385	57:20	479	64:2	582
52:2	386	58:1	482	64:5	585
52:5	389	58:3	484	64:6	585
52:6	389	58:4	485	64:7	586
52:7	391	58:6	486	64:9	587
52:8	392	58:7	488	65:1	592
52:9	393	58:11	491	65:2	592
52:11	394	58:13	494	65:3	593
52:12	396	58:14	495, 496	65:4	594
53:1	401	59:3	499	65:5	595
53:3	403, 404	59:7	503	65:10	599
53:5	406	59:12	506	65:14	601, 602
53:7	407	59:21	512	65:15	602
53:8	408	60:3	519	65:16	602
53:9	409	60:5	522	65:18	603
53:10a	410	60:7	524	65:20	604
53:11	67, 412	60:9	526	66:3	614
53:12	414	60:13	528	66:5	615, 616
54:2	419	60:14	529	66:8	618
54:3	420	60:19	69, 532	66:12	621
54:5	422	60:20	533	66:13	622
54:9	425	60:21	534	66:15	623

66:16 624
66:17 625
66:18b 626
66:19 626
66:20 629
66:21 629

1QIsa[b]
43:6 209
43:8 210
44:24 246
45:2 253
49:5 326
53:1 401
53:7 407
53:11 64, 67, 412
53:12 414
55:8 442
55:13 445
56:3 452
57:2 463
57:20 479
58:4 485
58:5 486
58:11 491
58:12 493
58:13 494
58:14 495
60:4 520
60:21 534
62:7 556
62:10 64
63:3 564
63:5 565
63:6 566
66:17 625

4QIsa[a] (4Q55)
49:7 327

4QIsa[c] (4Q57)
46:13 286
48:11 313
66:23 631

4QIsa[d] (4Q58)
46:11 285
47:3 292
48:11 313
49:5 326
49:7 327
53:11 64, 67
53:12 414
57:15 475
57:17 478
57:19 478

1QM (1QWar Scroll)
5:6 429
5:9 429
5:14 429
11:7-8 539
12:11-12 429

1QS (1QRule of the Community)
7:13-14 468
8:14 130

3Q15 (3QCopper Scroll)
11:16 462

4Q51 (4QSam[a])
2:3 323

4Q164 (4QpIsa[d])
54:11-12 66
54:12 429

4Q165 (4QpIsa[e])
40:12 66

4Q174 (4QFlor)
1-2, i:3-4 65-66, 450

4Q176 (4QTanḥ)
frag. 8/11:12 426

4Q185 (4QSapiential Work)
9-11 133

4Q242 (4QPrNab ar) 14

4Q246 (4QAramaic Apocalypse)
1:9 229

4Q266 (4QD[a])
frag. 2 ii:12-13 539
frag. 3 ii:9 539

4Q268 (4QD[c])
frag. 1:9 365

4Q270 (4QD[e])
frag. ii 2:19 365

4Q271 (4QD[f])
frag. 5 i:17 306
frag. 5 i:17-18 384

4Q298 (4Qcrypt A)
frag. 3-4 i:6 139
frags. 3-4 ii:9-10 217

4Q394 (4QMMT[a])
62:25 462

4Q401 (4QShirShabb[b])
frag. 6:4 223

4Q418 (4QInstruction[d])
frag. 127:6 139

4Q511 (4QShir[b])
frag. 30:4 139
frag. 30:5 140

11Q5 (11QPs[a])
151:1 535
151:5 193
151:11-12 439

11Q13 (11QMelch) 539

11Q19 (11QT[a])
45:11-14 384
47:3-11 384

APOCRYPHA

Tobit
3:16 427-428

Wisdom of Solomon
13 233

Sirach
1:3 138
1:13 462
24:19-21 434, 436
36:12 229
42:1-4 142
43:9 402
44:1 462
45:11 429
48:24 1
49:12 331
50:9 429
51:24 258

NEW TESTAMENT

Matthew
3:3 130

Mark
1:3 130

Luke
3:4 130

John
21:6 229
22:13 229

Revelation
1:8 229
1:17 229

RABBINIC LITERATURE

Mishnah
Shabbat
1:10 241

Pesaḥim
3:1 562

Sukkah
4:5 211

Yebamot
14:1 200
16:7 182

Soṭah
9:14 548

Giṭṭin
4:5 269

B. Qama
9:1 543

B. Batra
1:3 543

Sanhedrin
5:5 222
8:2 625

Makkot
3:15 296

'Eduyyot
2:10 631

'Abodah Zarah
3:3 267

'Arakhin
1:4 619

Kelim
13:4 236
29:4 261

Niddah
1:1 584
1:7 584
2:1 584
3:2 625
8:4 584

Tosefta
Menaḥot
9:10 454

Kelim, B. Metzia
6:12 139

Ohalot
4:14 182

Jerusalem Talmud
Pesaḥim
3:5, 19b 562

Soṭah
5:4, 20a 574

Ketubbot
5:6, 30a 478

Giṭṭin
7:1, 48c 478

Sanhedrin
2:1, 20a 570

'Abodah Zarah
2, 40d 467

Horayot
2:5, 46d 595
3:1, 47a 570

Babylonian Talmud
Berakhot
11a 258
16b 491
28a 406
60a 222
64a 336, 430

Shabbat
4a 219
22b 519
103b 494

'Erubin
30a 615

Pesaḥim
13b 543
27b 239

28a 605
30b 239
42b 562

Rosh Hashanah
9a 423
23a 175

Yoma
38b 543

Ta'anit
6b 443
9b 227
16a 570

Megillah
12a 252
25b 276
31a 71

Ḥagigah
12a 348

Yebamot
87b 222

Ketubbot
20a 222
67b 406

Soṭah
49b 552

Giṭṭin
7a 548
70a 471

B. Metzia
85b 355

B. Batra
80b 156, 175

Sanhedrin
31b 177
56b 235
63b 276
98a 535

'Abodah Zarah
38b 615
42b 267
44a 467
46a 593

Ḥullin
40a 600

Midrash
Genesis Rabbah
13:13 258
18 (end) 471
29 597
48:17 584
66 600

Exodus Rabbah
1:5 336

Leviticus Rabbah
27:7 196

Numbers Rabbah
16:25 330

Song of Songs Rabbah
2:5 283

Lamentations Rabbah
1:5 235

Abot de R. Nathan, Version A
34 233
36 228

Abot de R. Nathan, Version B
37 234

Mekilta de-Rabbi Ishmael
Be-Shalaḥ, Shirah, A 521
Be-Shalaḥ, Shirah, 5 572
Bo, Pisḥa, 7 570
Bo, Pisḥa, 14 388

Midrash Alpha-Beta 479

Pesiqta Rabbati
31 330

Sekel Tov
Gen 43:31 577

Sifre Numbers
157 572

Sifre Deuteronomy
39 479
41 574
42 570
144 212
325 570

Tanḥuma
Va-Yigash, 1 573

Yalqut Hamachiri
Tehillim
23, 1 362
40, 7 438

Yalqut Shimoni
'Eqev, §859 479
'Eqev, §862 573, 574
Genesis, §8 348
Isaiah, §491 490
Metzora, §568 595
Numbers, §459 330
Toldot, §116 577
Vayikra, §665 490
Vayikra, §796 490

ANCIENT NEAR EASTERN LITERATURE

Ammonite Inscriptions
Tel Siran (Rabbat Ammon), 167, 540, 565, 620

Aramaic
Aḥiqar (proverbs), 152, 160, 260, 279-280

Bar-Hadad (inscription), 166, 306
Bar-Rakib (inscription), 612
Demotic prayer, 470
Elephantine Letters, 228, 279, 332, 541
Panamuwa (inscription), 130, 190
Sefîre, 174, 366, 458, 571
Tel Fekherye (bilingual inscription), 144, 236, 295
Zakkur (inscription), 166

Egyptian
Amenemope (proverbs), 261
Ptaḥḥotep (proverbs), 290
Merneptaḥ (Israel stele), 296

Hebrew
Arad Letters 24, 561
Burial inscriptions, 358, 462
Gezer Calendar, 140, 186, 236
Lachish Letters, 200, 391, 429
Meṣad Ḥashavyahu (ostracon), 140
Siloam (inscription), 358, 359, 492, 594

Sumerian
Eannatum stele, 381
Enmerkar (epic), 384
Enmetena, Entemena (inscription), 165
Hymn to Enlil, 63, 384, 430, 516, 580, 628
Hymn to Ningirsu, 63, 165, 383, 384
Lament over the Destruction of Ur and Sumer, 288
Naram-Sin stele, 381
Ur Standard, 381
Uruinimgina, Urukagina (inscription), 165

Akkadian
Amarna letters, 136, 460
Ashurbanipal (inscriptions), 163, 166, 324, 341, 520, 524, 530, 619, 620, 621
Atrahasis (epic), 623
Cyrus cylinder, 14, 15-17, 165, 167, 179-180, 188, 251, 253, 274, 275
Enuma Elish (epic), 19-20, 138, 140, 152, 248, 348, 370, 374, 509, 530, 540, 565, 611, 619, 623
Esarhaddon (inscriptions), 2, 137, 147, 148, 163, 166, 168, 189, 191, 228, 253, 256, 267, 294, 301, 307, 376, 395, 458, 486, 488, 504, 534, 612, 627
Gilgamesh (epic), 196, 324, 355, 427, 463, 469, 555, 593, 600, 632
Nabonidus (inscriptions), 14-15, 158-159
Prophetic texts, 166, 428-429
Sennacherib (inscriptions), 2, 274, 523, 623
Shalmaneser III (inscriptions), 254, 264, 290, 325, 341, 527, 628
Tel Fekherye (bilingual inscription), 144, 236, 295
Tiglath-pileser I (inscription), 627
Tiglath-pileser III (inscriptions), 523, 524, 534, 627

Moabite
Mesha stele, 334

Phoenician Inscriptions
221, 223, 256, 552
Aḥiram, 181, 612
Arslan-Tash, 618
Azitawada 150, 167, 195, 201, 403, 411, 540, 557, 565
Bodashtart, 152, 475
Eshmunazor, 208, 277, 402, 462, 464, 599
Kilamuwa, 167, 195
Lapethos, 259
Osiris Temple, Abydos, 223
Shipiṭbaal, 462
Tabnit, 490
Yehawmilk, 411

Punic Inscriptions
Neo-Punic, 150, 183, 553
Punic, 256, 260, 599-600

Transjordanian
Balaam ben Beor inscription (from Deir ʿAlla), 334, 355, 462, 504, 519, 533, 551

Ugaritic
Aqhat (epic), 60, 241, 301, 376, 377
Baal (epic), 61, 208, 248, 288, 301, 331, 340, 348, 368, 369, 428, 436, 469, 500, 502, 541, 563
Birth of the Beautiful and Pleasant Gods, 173
Kirta (epic), 60, 351, 436, 490, 519, 530, 619
Lamentation in Memory of Niqmadu III, 288

Phoenician, Aramaic, Punic, and Neo-Punic Inscriptions
KAI
1:2 181
4:6-7 270

9A:1 462
10:8-9 411
13:3 490
14:4 462
14:5 462
14:5-6 277
14:6 462
14:7 462
14:8 208, 462, 464
14:11-12 402
14:16 201
14:17 201, 223
14:18-19 599
14:21 462
15:1 152, 223, 475
16:1 223
18:6 306
24:10 195
24:13 167
26 V:5-7 533
26:3 195
26A I:4-5 256
26A I:15 403
26A II:2-3 256
26A II:3-5 167
26A III:5-6 411, 540, 565
26AIII:7 557
26A III:10 201
26A III:12 150
27:27 359, 618
34:5 462
35:2 462
43:11 259
43:11-12 631
49:17 223
60:1 553
60:3 553
69:14 221
74:10 221
78:5-6 256
122:1 183
145 I:5 150
145:3 553
165:6 553
181:17 334
182 236
182:3 186
182:5 140
189:4 358
189:4-5 492
189:6 358
200:5 140
200:6 140
200:8 140
202 C:2 306
202 II:12-14 167
203:1 181
214:12 130
214:16 306
215:8 190
215:13 256
215:48 190
225:10-11 318
228 A:14, 22 318
309 236

Ugaritic Texts

CAT
1.2.I:7 369
1.2.I:9 369
1.2.I:32 624
1.2.I:37-38 629
1.2.II:17 369
1.2.II:22 369
1.2.II:30 348
1.2.III:16 317
1.2.IV:5 288
1.2.IV:8-9 510
1.2.IV:10 366, 492, 530, 543
1.2.IV:14 576
1.3.II:5-7 60
1.3.II:5-8 368
1.3.II:7-8 208
1.3.II:13-14 563
1.3.II:40-41 301
1.3.III:27 211
1.3.III:38 369
1.3.III:39-40 369
1.3.III:40-41 369
1.3.VI:16 473
1.4.I:40 149
1.4.II:12 336
1.4.IV:30 392
1.4.IV:35-37 436
1.4.IV:38-39 469
1.4.V:6-7 295
1.4.V:19 428
1.4.V:31-32 131
1.4.V:38-39 131
1.4.V:53-54 331
1.4.VI:47-54 61, 340
1.4.VII:35 426
1.4.VII:47 482
1.4.VIII:13-14 473
1.5.I:1-2 369
1.5.I:15 269
1.5.I:20-21 454
1.5.II:2-3 500
1.5.II:6-7 167
1.5.V:6 567
1.5.V:21 468
1.5.VI:12-14 60
1.5.VI:12-15 288
1.5.VI:14-15 485
1.5.VI:14-16 541
1.5.VI:16 502
1.6.I:12 277
1.6.I:14-15 277, 341
1.6.I:36 154
1.6.I:54-56 343
1.6.I:59-60 612
1.6.II:14 334
1.6.II:27 334
1.6.III:9 576
1.6.V:13-14 624
1.10.II:27 520
1.10.III:25 334
1.12.I:25 359, 618
1.14.I:12 490
1.14.I:12-13 270
1.14.I:18-19 326
1.14.III:10 292
1.14.III:45 458
1.15.I:1-2 165
1.15.II:6 576
1.15.II:17-18 314
1.15.II:25-28 530
1.15.II:26-27 60, 619
1.15.III:18-19 419
1.15.IV:27 436
1.15.V:10 436
1.15.V:18-20 256
1.15.VI:4-5 436
1.16.I:14-15 619

1.16.I:37 519
1.16.II:33-34 136
1.16.III:3 192
1.16.V:20-21 616
1.16.VI:30 351
1.16.VI:42 351
1.17.I:27-28 288
1.17.I:30-31 60, 376
1.17.I:32 241
1.17.V:31-33 419
1.19.I:78 499
1.19.IV:2 576
1.19.IV:30-31 301
1.19.IV:34-35 334
1.19.IV:48-49 256
1.19.IV:53-54 377
1.19.IV:61 600
1.22.I:17-18 557
1.23:4 173
1.23:6 436
1.23:8-9 296
1.23:33-34 468
1.23:51 465
1.23.56 465
1.93:2 464
1.96:3-5 343
1.103 476
1.108:7 152, 475
1.108:26 532
108:26-27 540, 565
1.114:15-16 557
1.114:16 620
1.114:16-18 376
1.119:9 527
1.119:rev. 28 616
1.145:2 476
1.148:21 470
1.161:21-22 470
1.169:9-10 297
2.30:20-21 167
4.81:1-2 214
4.91:5 470
4.123:18 600
4.204:1 325
4.204:2 325
4.204:4 325
4.421:2-3 214

Index of Commentaries on Isaiah

MEDIEVAL

Abravanel (Abarbanel)
43:14 214
53:11 412
55:6 441
59:19 510, 511
61:6 544
63:6 567
63:11 574
66:20 629

Dunash ben Labrat
56:10 459

Eliezer of Beaugency
53:11 412
60:4 520
61:7 545
63:15 577
63:17 578
65:5 595
66:21 630

Ibn Balaam
40:19 147
42:19 199
45:2 254
45:16 267
46:6 281
47:12 300
48:16 317
49:7 327, 328
49:17 335
51:1 358
51:2 360
51:4 363
51:15 374
51:19 379
51:20 379
51:21 380
54:5 422
56:10 459
57:17 477
58:11 491
64:4 583

Ibn Chiqutilla 3

Ibn Ezra
39:6-7 4
40:1 3, 4, 127
41:2 3
41:6 3
41:9 166
41:25 3
42:5 188
42:21 200-201
43:14 3, 214
43:16 3
44:8 231
44:25 3
45:1 3
45:2 253
45:19 270
45:23 272
46:8 283
46:11 3
46:13 286
48:1 305
48:9 311, 312
49:7 3
50:11 356
51:1 358
51:15 374
51:17 377
51:19 379
52:1 3
52:2 386
53:3 403
53:11 412
54:15 431
56:8 457
56:10 459
56:12 460
57:2 463
57:5 465
57:9 469, 470
59:5 501
59:10 505
59:15a 508
59:19 511
60:4 520

60:5 521
60:17 531
61:6 544
61:10 547
63:2 563
63:3 564
63:6 567
63:11 574
63:14 575-576
63:17 578
63:18 578
64:4 584
65:5 595
65:25 607
66:5 616
66:17 625
66:18b 626
66:20 629

Ibn Ganaḥ
41:16 172
44:14 238
45:2 254
45:16 267
46:6 281
47:13 301
48:16 317
49:7 327
51:1 358
51:4 363
51:17 377
51:21 380
52:14 400
53:9 409
54:5 422
55:6 441
56:10 459
57:5 465
57:9 469
57:17 477
57:20 478
58:11 491
59:10 505
60:11 527
61:8 546
63:2 563
63:19a 579
64:1 581, 582
65:4 594
65:20 604

Ibn Ḥayyuj
57:5 465

Ibn Kaspi
60:4 520
63:11 574
65:20 604

Ibn Quraysh (Karish)
47:13 301

Ibn Saruq
46:6 281
46:11 285
47:13 301
57:5 465
58:11 491
59:10 505

Isaiah of Tirani
59:15a 508
63:11 574
65:20 604

Joseph Kara
63:11 574
65:5 595
66:21 630

Kimchi
13:8 267
24:22 203
40:1 127
40:31 156
41:9 165
42:21 200-201
43:14 214, 215
44:14 238
45:2 254
45:7 257
45:8 259
46:6 281
47:12 300
47:13 301
48:1 305
48:9 312
48:20 319
49:2 325
51:1 358
51:2 360
51:17 377
52:2 386
52:4 388
52:11 395
53:3 403
53:11 412
53:12 413
54:15 431
56:5 455
56:10 459
57:2 463
57:5 465
57:8 467
57:9 470
58:11 491
59:5 501
59:19 511
60:1 518
60:4 520
60:5 521
61:6 544
61:7 545
61:10 547
62:1 551
62:4 554
63:1 562
63:3 564
63:6 567
63:11 573, 574
63:14 575
63:18 578
64:1 582
64:4 583, 584
64:5 585
64:7 586
65:4 594
65:5 595
65:16 602
65:20 604
65:25 607
66:9 618
66:18b 626
66:20 629

66:21 630

Luzzatto
40:1 127, 129
40:30 155
41:9 165
41:12 168
41:27 182
42:14 196
42:16 197
42:21 200-201
43:1 205
43:13 213
43:14 214, 215
43:19 217
44:4 227
44:21 243
45:2 254
45:9 260
45:14 266
45:16 267
45:17 267
46:1 277
46:6 281
46:7 282
47:1 289
47:10 298
48:6 309
48:13 314
49:7 327
49:11 331
49:22 340
50:2 347
50:8 353
51:6 365
51:13 373
51:17 377
52:4 388
52:14 400
52:15 400
53:2 402
53:3 403
53:9 409
53:10a 410
53:11 411-412
53:12 413
54:1 418
56:8 457
56:9–57:13 457
57:2 463
57:4 464
57:5 465
57:8 467
57:9 469
57:10 471
58:2 483
59:6 502
60:4 520
60:9 525
60:11 527
60:16 530
61:6 544
61:10 547
62:1 550
62:3 552
63:1 562
63:3 564
63:11 574
63:16 578
63:18 578
63:19b 579
64:1 581, 582
64:4 584
64:7 586
65:4 594
65:6 596
65:25 607
66:3 614
66:5 616
66:15 624
66:17 625
66:22 630
66:24 632

Metzudat David
60:9 525
63:11 574
66:18a 625
66:18b 626

Metzudat Zion
42:21 200
43:14 214
60:9 525
66:4 615

Minḥat Shai
51:13 373
59:19 511
60:5 521
63:11 574
64:5 585
65:6 596

Rashbam (on Gen 28:16)
40:7 134
45:15 266
49:4 325
53:4 404

Rashi
40:1 127
41:9 166
42:21 200-201
45:1 252
45:2 254
45:19 269
46:6 281
46:8 283
48:9 312
49:11 331
49:20 338
51:13 373
51:19 378, 379
52:2 386
53:3 403
53:12 413
54:15 431
56:10 459
56:11 460
57:8 467
57:9 469
57:17 477
57:18 577
58:11 491
59:15a 508
59:16 508
60:5 521
60:17 531
61:6 544
63:6 567
63:11 574
63:14 575
63:18 578

64:4 584
65:5 595
65:16 602
66:9 618
66:21 630

Saadyah Gaon
40:31 156
41:19 175
44:8 231
44:14 238
45:7 257
46:6 281
48:16 317
49:7 328
49:17 335
51:1 358
51:2 360
51:17 377
51:19 379
51:21 380
52:2 386
52:4 388
53:3 403
57:2 463
57:8 467
57:9 469
57:20 478
58:11 491
58:13 494
59:4 500
59:10 505
59:19 511
60:5 521
61:6 544
61:8 546
63:2 563
63:3 564
63:11 574
63:18 578
63:19b 579
64:1 581
64:6 585
65:5 595
65:20 604
66:18a 625

Shmuel ben Ḥofni
49:17 335

MODERN

Blau, Joshua
46:1 277
47:13 301

Ehrlich, Arnold B.
4:6 266
16:4 266
41:9 165, 166
41:12 168
42:21 200
43:6 209
43:14 214
43:26 222
44:3 226
45:11 262
45:14 266
46:1 277
46:5 280
46:7 282
46:11 285, 286
47:1 289
48:6 309, 310
51:13 373
52:14 400
53:3 403, 404
53:6 406
53:11 412
54:15 431
56:4 453
56:8 457
56:9–57:13 457
56:11 460
57:4 464
57:8 467, 468
57:16 476
58:7 488
59:4 500
61:3 540
61:10 548
63:3 564
63:11 573
63:18 578
64:4 583
66:5 616
66:17 625
66:21 629

Tur-Sinai, Naphtali H.
44:13 237
45:14 265
46:1 277
47:9 297
47:12 300
48:6 310
49:7 328
53:11 412
60:4 520
60:5 522
60:9 525
61:10 548
63:1 562
63:3 564
63:14 575
64:4 583
66:17 625

Yalon, Hanoch
49:17 336
50:4 350
64:5 585
65:5 595

Yellin, David
43:14 214
45:7 257
46:1 277
46:11 285
47:12 300
48:8 310
49:11 331
50:3 349
52:15 400
53:11 412
56:11 459, 460
58:2 483
60:5 521
61:3 541
63:1 562
64:1 582
66:5 616